Yearbook on International Communist Affairs 1989

Yearbook on International Communist Affairs 1989

Parties and Revolutionary Movements

EDITOR:	Richard F. Staar
ASSISTANT EDITOR:	Margit N. Grigory

AREA EDITORS

Thomas H. Henriksen	•	Africa
William Ratliff	•	The Americas
Ramon H. Myers	•	Asia and the Pacific
Richard F. Staar	•	Eastern Europe and the
Robert Conquest		Soviet Union
James H. Noyes	•	The Middle East and
		North Africa
Dennis L. Bark	•	Western Europe

HOOVER INSTITUTION PRESS
Stanford University, Stanford, California

The text of this work is set in Times Roman;
display headings are in Melior. Typeset by
Harrison Typesetting, Inc., Portland, Oregon.
Printed and bound by Braun-Brumfield, Inc.,
Ann Arbor, Michigan.

Hoover Press Publication 385

First printing, 1989
Manufactured in the United States of America
92 91 90 89   9 8 7 6 5 4 3 2 1

International Standard Book Number 0-8179-8851-3
International Standard Serial Number 0084-4101
Library of Congress Catalog Number 67-31024

Contents

ASIA AND THE PACIFIC

EASTERN EUROPE AND THE SOVIET UNION

THE MIDDLE EAST AND NORTH AFRICA

WESTERN EUROPE

Preface

This edition of the *Yearbook*, the twenty-third consecutive one, includes profiles by 84 contributors, covering 128 parties and revolutionary movements as well as seventeen international communist fronts and two regional organizations (the Council for Mutual Economic Assistance and the Warsaw Pact). In addition, biographic sketches of prominent communist leaders follow individual profiles. The names and affiliations of contributors are given at the end of each essay.

This *Yearbook* offers data on the organization, policies, activities, and international contacts during all of calendar 1988 of communist parties and Marxist-Leninist movements throughout the world. Information has been derived primarily from published sources, including official newspapers and journals, as well as from radio transmissions monitored by the U.S. Foreign Broadcast Information Service. Dates cited in the text without indicating a year are for 1988.

Whether to include a party or a group that espouses a quasi–Marxist-Leninist ideology, yet may not be recognized by Moscow as "communist" always poses a problem. It applies specifically to certain of the so-called national liberation movements and, more significantly, to some ruling parties. In making our decisions, the following criteria have been considered: rhetoric, the organizational model, participation in international communist meetings and fronts, and adherence to the USSR's foreign policy line. It seems realistic to consider the regime of Nicaragua, for example, in the same category as that of Cuba. The ruling parties in the so-called vanguard revolutionary democracies appear to be clearly affiliated with the world communist movement. They also are discussed in the Introduction.

Our thanks go to the librarians and staff at the Hoover Institution for checking information and contributing to the bibliography. The latter was compiled by the *Yearbook* assistant editor, Mrs. Margit N. Grigory, who also provided liaison with contributors.

Richard F. Staar

Hoover Institution

The following abbreviations are used for frequently cited publications and news agencies:

CSM	*Christian Science Monitor*
FBIS	*Foreign Broadcast Information Service*
FEER	*Far Eastern Economic Review*
IB	*Information Bulletin* (of the *WMR*)
JPRS	*Joint Publications Research Service*
LAT	*Los Angeles Times*
ND	*Neues Deutschland*
NYT	*New York Times*
WMR	*World Marxist Review*
WP	*Washington Post*
WSJ	*Wall Street Journal*
YICA	*Yearbook on International Communist Affairs*
ACAN	Agencia Central Americano Noticias
ADN	Allgemeine Deutscher Nachrichtendienst
AFP	Agence France-Presse
ANSA	Agenzia Nazionale Stampa Associata
AP	Associated Press
BBC	British Broadcasting Corporation
BTA	Bulgarska Telegrafna Agentsiia
ČTK	Československá Tisková Kancelář
DPA	Deutsche Presse Agentur
EFE	Agencia EFE, Spanish News Agency
KPL	Khaosan Pathet Lao
MENA	Middle East News Agency
MTI	Magyar Távirati Iroda
NCNA	New China News Agency
PAP	Polska Agencja Prasowa
RFE	Radio Free Europe
RL	Radio Liberty
TASS	Telegrafnoe Agentstvo Sovetskogo Soiuza
UPI	United Press International
VNA	Vietnam News Agency

Party Congresses

Country	Congress or National Conference	Date (1988)
Spain (PCE)	12th	19–21 February
Guadeloupe	9th	12–13 March
Zimbabwe	Extraordinary (3rd)	9 April
Luxembourg	25th	23–24 April
Great Britain (CPB, splinter of CPGB)	Extraordinary	24 April
Grenada	2nd	May
Finland (KTP)	1st	23–24 May
Canada	27th	20–24 May
Belgium	Extraordinary	18 June
Malta	4th	15–17 July
Ecuador	11th	21–23 July
Guyana	23rd	30 July–1 August
Jamaica (WPJ)	4th	11–13 September
Costa Rica (PVP)	16th	15–18 September
Australia (SPA)	6th	3 October
Turkey (UCPT)	1st (founding)	12–13 October
New Zealand (SUP)	8th	22–24 October
Norway (AKP)	5th	December (secret)
Portugal	12th	1–4 December
Uruguay	21st	7–11 December
Colombia	15th	12–15 December
India (CPM)	13th	26–31 December

Register of Communist Parties

Status: *ruling # unrecognized
+ legal 0 proscribed

Country: Party(ies)/Date Founded	Mid-1988 Population (est.) (World Factbook)	Communist Party Membership (claim or est.)	Party Leader (general sec.)	Status	Last Congress	Last Election (percentage of vote; seats in legislature)
AFRICA (12)						
Angola Popular Movement for the Liberation of Angola (MPLA), 1956 (MPLA-PT, 1977)	8,236,461	45,000 cl.	José Eduardo dos Santos	*	Second 9–11 Dec. 1985	(1980); all 203 MPLA approved
Benin People's Revolutionary Party of Benin (PRPB), 1975	4,497,150	fewer than 2,000 est.	Mathieu Kérékou (chairman, CC)	*	Second 18–24 Nov. 1985	(1984); all 196 PRPB approved
Congo Congolese Party of Labor (PCT), 1969	2,153,685	8,679 cl. (WMR, Jul. 1988, p. 87)	Denis Sassou-Ngouesso (chairman)	*	Third 23–30 July 1984	95.0 (1984); all 153 PCT approved
Ethiopia Workers' Party of Ethiopia (WPE), 1984	48,264,570	50,000 cl.	Mengistu Haile Mariam	*	First (Const.) 6–10 Sept. 1984	85.0 (1987); 835 all WPE members
Lesotho Communist Party of Lesotho (CPL), 1962	1,666,012	no data	Jacob M. Kena	0 (tolerated)	Seventh "early 1987"	(1985); n/a

Country / Party (founding year)	Population	Party leader	Membership		Last congress	Last election results
Mozambique Front for the Liberation of Mozambique (FRELIMO), 1962	14,947,554	Joaquim Albert Chissano	130,000 cl. (*WMR*, Apr. 1987, p. 53)	*	Fourth 26–29 Apr. 1983	(1986); incomplete
Nigeria Socialist Working People's Party (SWPP), 1978 (Socialist Workers and Farmers Party, 1963)	100,694,000 (*Political Handbook of the World*, 1988)	Dapo Fatogun	no data (probably defunct)	0	First Nov. 1978	(1983); n/a
Réunion Réunion Communist Party (PCR), 1959	557,441	Paul Vergès	2,000 est.	+	Fifth 12–14 July 1980	35.0 (1988); 13 of 44 left coal., 9 for PCR (local assembly); 2 in Paris
Senegal Independence and Labor Party (PIT), 1957	7,281,022	Amath Dansoko	no data	+	Second 28 Sept.–2 Oct. 1984	0.84 (1988); none
South Africa South African Communist Party (SACP), 1921	35,093,971	Joe Slovo Dan Tloome (chairman)	no data	0	Sixth Dec. 1984 or early 1985, in London	(1986); n/a
Sudan Sudanese Communist Party (SCP), 1946	24,014,495	Muhammad Ibrahim Nugud Mansur	9,000 est.	+	Fourth (legal) 31 Oct. 1967	1.67 (1986); 5 of 301; 2 in territ., 3 in grad. constituencies
Zimbabwe Zimbabwe African National Union–Patriotic Front (ZANU-PF), 1963	9,730,000	Robert G. Mugabe (president)	no data	*	Third 9 Apr. 1988 (extraordinary)	76.0 (1987); 77 of 100 (in by-election for 30 formerly white Parl. seats)
TOTAL	257,136,361		246,679			

THE AMERICAS (29)

Country: Party(ies)/Date Founded	Mid-1988 Population (est.) (World Factbook)	Communist Party Membership (claim or est.)	Party Leader (general sec.)	Status	Last Congress	Last Election (percentage of vote; seats in legislature)
Argentina Communist Party of Argentina (PCA), 1918	31,532,538	80,000 est.	Athos Fava	+	Sixteenth 4–7 Nov. 1986	5.3 (1987); none in Broad Front coal. parliamentary and provincial by-elections 6 Sept. 1987; none
Bolivia Communist Party of Bolivia (PCB), 1950 (split, 1985)	6,448,297	500 cl.	Humberto Ramírez (majority faction) Carlos Soria Galvarro (minority faction)	+	Fifth 9–13 Feb. 1985 Extraordinary 26–29 April 1986	2.21 (1985); 4 of 130 FPU coal.
Brazil Brazilian Communist Party (PCB), 1922	150,685,145	120,000 cl. (S. Malina letter to Hoover Institution)	Salomão Malina (chairman)	+	Eighth (called National Meeting of Communists) 17–20 July 1987	(1986); 3 of 487
Canada Communist Party of Canada (CPC), 1921	26,087,536	3,000 est.	George Hewison (gen. secretary) William Kashtan (chairman)	+	Twenty-seventh 20–24 May 1988	.09 (1988); none

Country / Party (founded)	Population	Membership	Leader		Last Congress	Election results
Chile Communist Party of Chile (CPC), 1922	12,638,046	20,000 est.	Luís Corvalán Lepe (in exile)	0	Fourteenth Nov. 1969 (June 1984, a national conference)	(1973); n/a
Colombia Communist Party of Colombia (PCC), 1930	31,298,803	18,000 est. (incl. youth org.)	Gilberto Vieira White	+	Fifteenth 12–15 Dec. 1988	1.4 (1986); 9 of 199 Patriotic Union
Costa Rica Popular Vanguard Party (PVP), 1931	2,888,277	7,500 est. (for all left parties)	Humberto Vargas Carbonell	+	Sixteenth 15–18 Sept. 1988	0.8 (1986); 1 of 57 Popular Alliance
Costa Rican People's Party (PPC), split from PVP, 1984		no data	Manuel Mora Valverde (to Feb.) Lenín Chacón Vargas	+	Fifteenth 23–24 Aug. 1987	(1986); 1 of 57 United People's Coalition
Cuba Cuban Communist Party (PCC), 1965	10,353,932	500,000 est. (75,000 cand. members est.)	Fidel Castro Ruz	*	Third 4–7 Feb. and 30 Nov.–2 Dec. 1986	(1986); all 499 PCC approved
Dominican Republic Dominican Communist Party (PCD), 1944	7,136,748	750 est.	Narciso Isa Conde	+	Third 15–17 Mar. 1984	0.28 (1986); none
Ecuador Communist Party of Ecuador (PCE), 1928	10,231,630	750 est.	René Mauge Mosquera (member of parliament)	+	Eleventh 21–23 July 1988	3.6 (1988); 2 of 71 Broad Leftist Front, FADI
Marxist-Leninist Communist Party of Ecuador (PCE-ML), 1972		200 est.	Jaime Hurtado Gonzalez (nat'l director, MPD)	+		(1988); 2 of 71 participates as Movimiento Popular Democratico (MPD)
El Salvador Communist Party of El Salvador (PCES), 1930 (one of five in FMLN)	5,388,644	1,000 est.	Jorge Shafik Handal	0	Seventh Apr. 1979	(1988); n/a

Country: Party(ies)/Date Founded	Mid-1988 Population (est.) (World Factbook)	Communist Party Membership (claim or est.)	Party Leader (general sec.)	Status	Last Congress	Last Election (percentage of vote; seats in legislature)
Grenada Maurice Bishop Patriotic Movement (MBPM), 1984	84,455	no data	Kenrick Radix (chairman, to May) Terrence Marryshow	+	Second May 1988	5.0 (1984); none
Guadeloupe Communist Party of Guadeloupe (PCG), 1958	338,730	3,000 est.	Guy Daninthe (to March) Christian Céleste	+	Ninth 12–13 Mar. 1988	no data (1988); 22 of 42 left coal. (PCG: 10 of 22), local assembly; also 1 of 3 in Paris
Guatemala Guatemalan Party of Labor (PGT), 1952	8,831,148	250 est.	Carlos González Orellana ("Camarilla" faction) Daniel Rios/Mario Sanchez (National Leadership Nucleus faction)	0	Fourth Dec. 1969	(1985); n/a
Guyana People's Progressive Party (PPP), 1950	765,796	200 est. (100 leadership)	Cheddi Jagan	+	Twenty-third 30 July–1 Aug. 1988	16.8 (1985); 8 of 53 elected members
Haiti Unified Party of Haitian Communists (PUCH), 1968	6,295,570	350 est.	René Théodore	+	First 1979	(1988) (PUCH boycotted)

Country / Party	Population	Status	Leader	Membership	Last Congress	Last Election; results
Honduras Communist Party of Honduras (PCH), 1954 (one of six in the Honduran Revolutionary Movement, MHR, 1982)	4,972,287	0	Rigoberto Padilla Rush (in exile) Mario Sosa Navarro (leader in Honduras)	100 est.	Fourth Jan. 1986 (clandestine)	(1985); n/a
Jamaica Workers' Party of Jamaica (WPJ), 1978	2,458,102	+	Trevor Munroe	100 est.	Fourth 11–13 Sept. 1988	(1983) (WPJ boycotted)
Jamaican Communist Party (JCP), 1975		+	Christopher Lawrence	no data	no data	
Martinique Martinique Communist Party (PCM), 1957	351,105	+	Armand Nicolas	1,000 est.	Ninth 12–13 Dec. 1987	no data (1988); 2 of 45 (local assembly); none in Paris
Mexico Unified Socialist Party of Mexico (PSUM), 1981	83,527,567			90,000 cl.	(Merger Congress, 23 March 1987)	(1988) (presidential)
Mexican Socialist Party (PMS), 1987		+	Gilberto Rincón Gallardo	no data	First 25–29 Nov. 1987	
Nicaragua Nicaraguan Socialist Party (PSN), 1937	3,407,183	+	Gustavo Tablada	no data	Tenth Oct. 1973	1.3 (1984); 2 of 96
Sandinista Front of National Liberation (FSLN), 1961		*	Daniel Ortega (Coord. of Executive Commission)	1,400 est.	FSLN Assembly Aug. 1985	63.0 (1984); 61 of 96
Panama People's Party (PDP), 1943	2,323,622	+	Rubén Darío Sousa Batista	25,600 cl. (based on signatures)	Eighth 24–26 Jan. 1986	(1984); none
Paraguay Paraguayan Communist Party (PCP), 1928	4,386,024	0	Julio Rojas (acting) Antonio Maidana (arrested in 1980)	4,000 est.	Third 10 Apr. 1971	(1983); n/a

Country: Party(ies)/Date Founded	Mid-1988 Population (est.) (World Factbook)	Communist Party Membership (claim or est.)	Party Leader (general sec.)	Status	Last Congress	Last Election (percentage of vote; seats in legislature)
Peru Peruvian Communist Party (PCP), 1928	21,269,074	4,000 est.	Jorge del Prado Chavez	+	Ninth 27–30 May 1987	26.0 (1985); 48 of 180 United Left Coalition; 6 PCP repr. of 48
Puerto Rico Puerto Rican Communist Party (PCP), 1934	3,358,879	100 est.	Frank Irrizarry	+	unknown	(1988); none (did not contest)
Suriname Revolutionary People's Party (RVP), 1980	394,999	no data	Michael Naarendorp	+	no data	(1987)
United States of America Communist Party USA (CPUSA), 1919	246,043,000	20,000 cl. (4,000–6,000 est.)	Gus Hall	+	Twenty-fourth 13–16 Aug. 1987	0.1 (1988); none
Uruguay Communist Party of Uruguay (PCU), 1920	2,976,138	11,000 cl. (*Pravda*, 14, 22 Dec. 1987)	Jaime Perez Gerschuni (gen. sec.) Rodney Arismendi (chairman)	+	Twenty-first 7–11 Dec. 1988	6.0 (1984); none Frente Amplio coal.
Venezuela Communist Party of Venezuela (PCV), 1931	18,775,780	4,000 est.	Alonso Ojeda Olaechea	+	Seventh 24–27 Oct. 1985	2.0 (1988); 1 of 203
TOTAL	705,249,055	916,800				

ASIA AND THE PACIFIC (20)

Party	Population	Membership	Leader	Status	Last Congress	Elections
Australia						
Communist Party of Australia (CPA), 1920	16,260,436	1,000 est.	Judy Mundey (president)	+	Twenty-ninth 6–8 June 1987	0.3 (1987); none
Socialist Party of Australia (SPA), 1971		500 est.	Peter Dudley Symon	+	Sixth 3 Oct. 1988	negl. (1987); none
Bangladesh						
Communist Party of Bangladesh (CPB), 1948	109,963,551	5,000 est. (9,911 cl.)	Saifuddin Ahmed Manik	0/+ (made legal again in March 1988)	Fourth 7–11 Apr. 1987	(1988) boycotted
Burma						
Burmese Communist Party (BCP), 1939	39,632,183	3,000 cl.	[Thakin] Ba Thein Tin (chairman)	0	Third 9 Sept.–2 Oct. 1985	(1985); n/a
Cambodia						
Khmer People's Revolutionary Party (KPRP), 1951	6,685,592	9,000 est. (8,000–10,000)	Heng Samrin	*	Fifth 13–16 Oct. 1985	99.0 (1981); all 117
Party of Democratic Kampuchea (PDK), or Kampuchean Communist Party (KCP), 1951		no data	Pol Pot (officially until 1981)	0	Third 14 Dec. 1975	(1981); n/a
China						
Chinese Communist Party (CCP), 1921	1,088,169,192	47,000,000 cl. (Xinhua, 22 June; FBIS, 23 June)	Zhao Ziyang	*	Thirteenth 25 Oct.–1 Nov. 1987	(1987); all 3,202 CCP approved
India						
Communist Party of India (CPI), 1928	816,828,360	479,000 cl.	C. Rajeswara Rao	+	Thirteenth 12–17 Mar. 1986	2.71 (1984); 6 of 544
Communist Party of India-Marxist (CPM), 1964		450,000 cl.	E. M. S. Namboodiripad	+	Thirteenth 26–31 Dec. 1988	5.96 (1984); 22 of 544

Country: Party(ies)/Date Founded	Mid-1988 Population (est.) (World Factbook)	Communist Party Membership (claim or est.)	Party Leader (general sec.)	Status	Last Congress	Last Election (percentage of vote; seats in legislature)
Indonesia Indonesian Communist Party (PKI), 1920 (split)	184,015,906	1,500 est. ca. 200 exiles	Jusuf Adjitorop (pro-Beijing faction) Thomas Sinuraya (pro-Moscow faction)	0	Seventh Extraord. Apr. 1962	(1987); n/a
Japan Japan Communist Party (JCP), 1922	122,626,038	470,000 est.	Hiromu Murakami (Presidium chairman) Kenji Miyamoto (CC chairman)	+	Eighteenth 26–28 Nov. 1987	9.47 (1986); 27 of 512
Korea (North) Korean Workers' Party (KWP), 1946 (as united party, 1949)	21,983,795	2,500,000 est.	Kim Il-song	*	Sixth 10–15 Oct. 1980	100 (1986); all 706 KWP approved
Laos Lao People's Revolutionary Party (LPRP), 1955	3,849,762	40,000 cl.	Kaysone Phomvihane	*	Fourth 13–15 Nov. 1986	(Dec. 1975); Supreme People's Assembly (all 46 appointed by LPRP)
Malaysia Communist Party of Malaya (CPM), 1930	16,309,306	1,300 est.	Chin Peng	0	1965 (last known)	(1984); n/a
Communist Party of Malaysia (MCP), 1983		800 est.	Ah Leng	0	unknown	(1984); n/a
Mongolia Mongolian People's Revolutionary Party (MPRP), 1921	2,067,624	88,150 cl.	Jambyn Batmonh (Dzambiin Batmunkh)	*	Nineteenth 28–31 May 1986	93.5 (1986); 346 of 370, MPRP approved

Country / Party (founded)	Population	Party membership	Leadership	Status	Last party congress	Last election; seats
Nepal Nepal Communist Party (NCP), 1949 (factions)	18,252,001	10,000 est. (75% pro-Beijing and neutral)	Man Mohan Adhikary	0	Third 1961 (before split; right wing held its own third in 1968)	(1986); n/a
New Zealand Communist Party of New Zealand (CPNZ), 1921	3,343,339 (N.Z. Dept. of Stat.)	50 est.	Harold Crook	+	Twenty-third 22 Apr. 1984	(1987); none
Socialist Unity Party (SUP), 1966		300 est.	George H. Jackson (pres.) Marilyn Tucker (gen. sec.)	+	Eighth 22–24 Oct. 1988	(1987); none
Pakistan Communist Party of Pakistan (CPP), 1948	107,467,457	under 200 est.	Ali Nazish	0 (since 1954)	First 1976 (clandestine)	(1988); n/a
Philippines Philippine Communist Party (PKP), 1930	63,199,807	5,000 est.	Merlin Magallona (gen. sec.) Felicismo Macapagal (chairman)	+	Ninth Dec. 1986	(1987)
Communist Party of the Philippines (CPP), 1968		32,000 est. (35,000 cl.)	Rafael Baylosis (gen. sec.) Jose Maria Sison (chairman)	0	First (founding) 26. Dec. 1968– 7 Jan. 1969	(1987); n/a
Singapore Communist Party of Malaya, Branch (CPM), 1930	2,645,443	350 est.	Chin Peng	0	unknown	(1984); n/a
Sri Lanka Communist Party of Sri Lanka (CPSL), 1943	16,639,695	5,000 est.	Kattorge P. Silva	+	Thirteenth 22–26 March 1987	1.9 (1977); 1 of 168

Country: Party(ies)/Date Founded	Mid-1988 Population (est.) (World Factbook)	Communist Party Membership (claim or est.)	Party Leader (general sec.)	Status	Last Congress	Last Election (percentage of vote; seats in legislature)
Thailand Communist Party of Thailand (CPT), 1942	54,588,731	250 est.	Thong Jaensri (unconfirmed; pseudonym?)	0	Fourth Mar.–Apr. 1984 (clandestine)	(1986); n/a
Vietnam Vietnamese Communist Party (VCP), 1930	65,185,278	2,120,000 cl. (5th plenum communiqué)	Nguyen Van Linh	*	Sixth 15–18 Dec. 1986	98.8 (1987); 496 of 614; all VCP endorsed
TOTAL	2,759,713,946	53,222,400				

EASTERN EUROPE AND USSR (9)

Country: Party(ies)/Date Founded	Mid-1988 Population (est.) (World Factbook)	Communist Party Membership (claim or est.)	Party Leader (general sec.)	Status	Last Congress	Last Election (percentage of vote; seats in legislature)
Albania Albanian Party of Labor (APL), 1941	3,147,352	147,000 cl.	Ramiz Alia (April 1985)	*	Ninth 3–8 Nov. 1986	100 (1987); all 250 Democratic Front
Bulgaria Bulgarian Communist Party (BCP), 1903	8,966,927	932,055 cl.	Todor Zhivkov	*	Thirteenth 2–5 Apr. 1986	99.9 (1986); all 400 Fatherland Front
Czechoslovakia Communist Party of Czecho-slovakia (KSC), 1921	15,620,722	1,705,490 cl. (*Rudé právo*, 3 Sept. 1987)	Miloš Jakeš	*	Seventeenth 24–28 Mar. 1986	99.94 (1986); all 350 National Front
Germany: German Democratic Republic Socialist Unity Party (SED), 1946	16,596,875	2,324,995 cl. (*Neues Deutsch-land*, 11 Jan. 1989)	Erich Honecker	*	Eleventh 17–21 Apr. 1986	99.94 (1986); all 500 National Front

Country / Party, founded	Population	Party membership		Leader	Party congress	Election % / Front
Hungary Hungarian Socialist Worker's Party (HSWP), 1956	10,588,271	816,622 cl. (*Pártélet*, Nov. 1988)	*	János Kádár (to 19 May 1988) Károly Grósz	Thirteenth 25–28 Mar. 1985	98.9 (1985); all 352 Patriotic People's Front
Poland Polish United Workers' Party (PZPR), 1948	37,958,420	2,200,000 cl.	*	Wojciech Jaruzelski	Tenth 29 June–3 July 1986	78.8 (1985); all 460 Fatherland Front
Romania Romanian Communist Party (PCR), 1921	23,040,883	3,709,735 cl. (*WMR*, June 1988, p. 86)	*	Nicolae Ceaușescu	Thirteenth 19–22 Nov. 1984	97.8 (1985); all 369 Socialist Democracy and Unity Front
USSR Communist Party of the Soviet Union (CPSU), 1898	285,200,000 (TASS, 25 Apr. 1988)	19,468,786 cl. (*Pravda*, 14 Apr. 1988, p. 53)	*	Mikhail S. Gorbachev	Twenty-seventh 25 Feb.–6 Mar. 1986	99.4 (1984); all 1,500 CPSU approved (71.4% are CPSU members)
Yugoslavia League of Communists of Yugoslavia (LCY), 1920	23,580,148	2,079,613 cl.	*	Boško Krunić (to June) Štipe Šuvar (president of Presidium)	Thirteenth 25–28 June 1986	(1986); all 308; all LCY approved Socialist Alliance
TOTAL	424,699,598	33,384,296				

MIDDLE EAST (15)

Country / Party, founded	Population	Party membership		Leader	Party congress	Election % / Front
Afghanistan People's Democratic Party of Afghanistan (PDPA), 1965	14,480,863 est.	40,000 est. (205,000 cl. incl. armed forces)	*	Dr. Mohammed Najibullah	Second nat'l. conference 18–19 Oct. 1987	38.0 (1988); 69 of 184 elected of 234 total (National Front) (22.6% and 42 for PDPA)

Country: Party(ies)/Date Founded	Mid-1988 Population (est.) (World Factbook)	Communist Party Membership (claim or est.)	Party Leader (general sec.)	Status	Last Congress	Last Election (percentage of vote; seats in legislature)
Algeria Socialist Vanguard Party (PAGS), 1920	24,194,177	450 est.	Sadiq Hadjeres (first secretary)	0	Sixth Feb. 1952	(1982); n/a
Bahrain Bahrain National Liberation Front (NLF/B), 1955	480,383	negligible	Saif ben Ali (gen. sec.) al-Ajajai (chairman) (Yusuf al-Hassan not noted since 1983)	0	unknown	(1973); n/a
Egypt Egyptian Communist Party (ECP), 1921	53,347,679	500 est.	Farid Mujahid (apparently)	0	Second 1984 or early 1985	(1984); n/a
Iran Communist Party of Iran (Tudeh Party), 1941 (dissolved May 1983)	51,923,689	1,500 est.	Ali Khavari (first sec. of CC, party leader in exile)	0	National Conference 1986	(1988); n/a
Iraq Iraqi Communist Party (ICP), 1934	17,583,467	no data	Aziz Muhammad (first secretary)	0	Fourth 10–15 Nov. 1985	(1984); n/a
Israel Communist Party of Israel (CPI, "RAKAH"), 1948 (Palestine Communist Party, 1922)	4,297,379 (excl. E. Jerusalem and the West Bank)	2,000 est.	Meir Vilner	+	Twentieth 4–7 Dec. 1985	3.7 (1988); 4 of 120
Jordan Communist Party of Jordan (CPJ), 1951	2,850,482	no data	Dr. Yá'qub Zayadin	0	Second Dec. 1983	(1986); n/a

Country / Party	Population	Party membership	Leader		Last party congress	Last election (legislature)
Lebanon Lebanese Communist Party (LCP), 1924	2,674,385 (0.70% growth)	3,000 est. (14,000–16,000 cl.)	George Hawi	+	Fifth 3–5 Feb. 1987	(1972)
Organization of Communist Action in Lebanon (OCAL), 1970		1,500 est.	Muhsin Ibrahim	+	First 1971	
Morocco Party of Progress and Socialism (PPS), 1974 (Moroccan Communist Party, 1943)	24,976,168	ca. 4,000 est. (10,000 cl.)	'Ali Yata	+	Fourth 17–19 July 1987	2.3 (1984); 2 of 306
Palestine Communist Party (PCP), 1982	4,500,000 est. Palestinians (incl. E. Jerusalem, Gaza, Jordan and the West Bank)	no data	Bashir al-Barghuti (presumably)	0	First 1984	n/a
Saudi Arabia Communist Party of Saudi Arabia (CPSA), 1975	15,452,123	negligible	Mahdi Habib	0	Second Aug. 1984	n/a (absolute monarchy)
Syria Syrian Communist Party (SCP), 1924 (as separate party, 1944)	11,569,659	5,000 est.	Khalid Bakhdash	+	Sixth July 1986	(1986); 8 of 195
Tunisia Tunisian Communist Party (PCT), 1934	7,738,026	2,000 est. (4,000 cl.)	Muhammad Harmel (first secretary)	+	Ninth 12–14 June 1987	(1988); none (by-election)
Yemen (PDRY) Yemen Socialist Party (YSP), 1978	2,425,620	31,000 cl. (incl. cand. members)	'Ali Salim al-Bayd	*	Fourth 20–21 June 1987	(1986); all 111 YSP approved
TOTAL	238,494,100	181,900				

WESTERN EUROPE (23)

Country: Party(ies)/Date Founded	Mid-1988 Population (est.) (World Factbook)	Communist Party Membership (claim or est.)	Party Leader (general sec.)	Status	Last Congress	Last Election (percentage of vote; seats in legislature)
Austria Communist Party of Austria (KPO), 1918	7,577,072	15,000 est.	Franz Muhri (chairman)	+	Twenty-sixth 25–28 Mar. 1987	0.72 (1986); none
Belgium Belgian Communist Party (PCB/KPB), 1921	9,880,522	5,000 est.	Louis van Geyt (president)	+	Extraordinary 18 June 1988 Twenty-fifth 18–20 Apr. 1986	0.8 (1987); none
Cyprus Progressive Party of the Working People (AKEL), 1941 (Communist Party of Cyprus, 1926)	691,966	15,000 cl. (official AKEL cl.)	Ezekias Papaioannou (until 22 Apr.) Dimitris Christofias	+	Sixteenth 26–30 Nov. 1986 Extraordinary Congress 20 Dec. 1987	27.4 (1985); 15 of 56
Denmark Communist Party of Denmark (DKP), 1919	5,125,676	10,000 est.	Poul Emanuel (party sec.) Ole Sohn (chairman)	+	Twenty-eighth 16–19 Apr. 1987	0.8 (1988); none
Finland Finnish Communist Party (SKP), 1918	4,949,716	20,000 cl.	Esko Vainionpää (to 29 May) Heljä Tammisola (gen. sec.) Arvo Aalto (to 29 May) Jorma Wahlström (chairman)	+	Twenty-first 12–15 June 1987	9.4 (1987); 16 of 200 SKDL Front (11 of 16 for SKP)

Party	Population	Membership	Leadership		Congress	Electoral
Finnish Communist Party-Unity (SKP-Y), 1986		15,000 est.	Jouko Kajanoja (to 28 Aug.) Yrjö Häkanan (gen. sec.) Taisto Sinisalo (to 28 Aug.) Jouko Kajanoja (chairman)	+	First 5–7 June, 1987	4.3 (1987); 4 of 200 DEVA Front
Communist Workers' Party (KTP), 1988		200 est.	Heikki Mannikko (gen. sec.) Timo Lahdenmaeki (chairman)	+	First 23–24 May 1988	not yet registered; part of DEVA Front
France French Communist Party (PCF), 1920	55,798,282	604,282 cl. (*L'Humanité*, 3 Dec. 1987)	Georges Marchais	+	Twenty-sixth 2–6 Dec. 1987	11.3 (1988); 25 of 577 (plus 2 from overseas depts., and 1 from Dec. by-election)
Germany: Federal Republic of Germany German Communist Party (DKP), 1968	60,980,200 (excl. W. Berlin)	38,000 est. (*Disinformation*, Fall 1988, p. 3; *FBIS*, 11 July 1988)	Herbert Mies (chairman)	+	Ninth 6–9 Jan. 1989	0.5 (1987); none for Peace List in which DKP participated
Great Britain Communist Party of Great Britain (CPGB), 1920	56,935,845	9,700 est. (*Morning Star*, 6 Jan. 1988; *FBIS*, 27 Apr. 1988)	Gordon McLennan	+	Fortieth 14–18 Nov. 1987 Extraordinary 24 Apr. 1988 (by CPB, splinter of CPGB)	0.01 (1987); none

Country: Party(ies)/Date Founded	Mid-1988 Population (est.) (World Factbook)	Communist Party Membership (claim or est.)	Party Leader (general sec.)	Status	Last Congress	Last Election (percentage of vote; seats in legislature)
Greece	10,015,041					
Communist Party of Greece (KKE), 1921		50,000 est.	Kharilaos Florakis	+	Twelfth 12–16 May 1987	9.9 (1985); 13 of 300
Communist Party of Greece–Interior (KKE-I), 1968; (KKE-I Renovating Left), 1987; and		(split into two factions) no data	Giannis Banias	+	Fourth May 1986	1.8 (1985); none
Greek Left (E.AR), 1987		no data	Leonidas Kyrkos	+	24–26 April 1987	
Iceland	246,526					
People's Alliance (PA), 1968		3,000 est.	Olafur Ragnar Grimsson (chairman)	+	Biennial Congr. 7–10 Nov. 1987	13.2 (1987); 8 of 63
Ireland	3,531,502					
Communist Party of Ireland (CPI), 1933		500 est.	James Stewart	+	Nineteenth 31 Jan.–2 Feb. 1986	(1987); none
Italy	57,455,362					
Italian Communist Party (PCI), 1921		1,462,302 cl. (18th Congress, March 1989)	Alessandro Natta (to June) Achille Ochetto	+	Seventeenth 9–13 April 1986	26.6 (1987); 177 of 630
Luxembourg	366,232					
Communist Party of Luxembourg (CPL), 1921		600 est.	René Urbany (chairman)	+	Twenty-fifth 23–24 Apr. 1988	4.9 (1984); 2 of 64
Malta	346,890 (Malta Office of Statistics)					
Communist Party of Malta (CPM), 1969		300 est.	Anthony Vassallo	+	Fourth 15–17 July 1988	0.08 (1987); none
Netherlands	14,716,100					
Communist Party of the Netherlands (CPN), 1909		6,000 est.	Elli Izeboud (chairman)	+	Thirtieth 29 Nov.–2 Dec. 1986	0.6 (1986); none

Country / Party	Population	Membership	Leaders		Last congress	Electoral results
Norway Norwegian Communist Party (NKP), 1923	4,190,758	ca. 1,750 est.	Kaare Andre Nilsen (chairman)	+	Nineteenth 23–26 Apr. 1987	0.2 (1985); none
Workers' Communist Party (AKP), 1973		ca. 6,000 est.	Kjersti Ericsson (to Dec.) (chairman) Siri Jensen (chairman)	+	Fifth Dec. 1988 (secret)	0.57 (1985); none, Red Electoral Alliance (RV)
Portugal Portuguese Communist Party (PCP), 1921	10,388,421	over 199,275 cl. (*Avante!*, 3 Nov. 1988)	Álvaro Cunhal	+	Twelfth 1–4 Dec. 1988	11.0 (1987); 30 of 250 United People's Alliance Coalition (25 of 30 for PCP)
San Marino Communist Party of San Marino (PCS), 1921	22,986	1,200 cl.	Gilberto Ghiotti	+	Eleventh 27 Jan. 1986	28.71 (1988); 18 of 60
Spain Spanish Communist Party (PCE), 1920	39,209,765	ca. 66,000 cl.	Gerardo Iglesias Arguellas (to Feb.) Julio Anguita Gonzalez	+	Twelfth 19–21 Feb. 1988	4.6 (1986); 7 of 350 United Left Coalition
Communist Party of the Peoples of Spain (PCPE), 1984		25,500 est.	Juan Ramos Carmavera (gen. sec.) Ignacio Gallego (chairman)	+	Second 25–27 Apr. 1987	as above
Spanish Workers' Party–Communist Unity (PTE-UC), 1987		14,000 est.	Adolfo Pinedo (gen. sec.) Santiago Carrillo (chairman)	+	First 8 Feb. 1987	1.12 (1986); none, Board for Communist Unity
Sweden Left Party Communists (VPK), 1921	8,393,071	17,800 cl.	Lars Werner (chairman)	+	Twenty-eighth 23–25 May 1987	5.8 (1988); 21 of 349

Country: Party(ies)/Date Founded	Mid-1988 Population (est.) (World Factbook)	Communist Party Membership (claim or est.)	Party Leader (general sec.)	Status	Last Congress	Last Election (percentage of vote; seats in legislature)
Communist Workers' Party (APK), 1977		5,000 cl.	Rolf Hagel (chairman)	+	Twenty-eighth 7 Nov. 1986	(1988); no data
Switzerland	6,592,558					
Swiss Labor Party (PdAS), 1921 (re-established, 1944)		4,500 est.	Jean Spielman	+	Thirteenth 27 Feb.–1 Mar. 1987	0.8 (1987); 1 of 200
Turkey	54,167,857					
Communist Party of Turkey (TCP), 1920		negligible	Haydar Kutlu (gen. sec. of TCP and UCPT)	0	Fifth Oct. or Nov. 1983	(1987); n/a
United Communist Party of Turkey (UCPT), 1988		negligible	Nihat Sargin (president)	0	First 12–13 Oct. 1988	(1987); n/a
West Berlin	1,869,000					
Socialist Unity Party of West Berlin (SEW), 1949		7,000 cl.	Horst Schmitt (chairman)	+	Eighth 15–27 May 1987	0.6 (1985); none
TOTAL	413,451,348	2,579,766				
GRAND TOTAL	4,789,744,408	90,554,984				

MAJOR INTERNATIONAL FRONT ORGANIZATIONS*

Organization (17)	Year Founded	Headquarters	Claimed Membership	Affiliates	Countries
Afro-Asian Peoples' Solidarity Organization (AAPSO) (Murad Ghalib; Nuri Abd-al Razzaqq Husayn)	1957	Cairo	unknown	87	unknown
Asian Buddhist Conference for Peace (ABCP) (Kharkuu Gaadan; G. Lubsan Tseren)	1970	Ulan Bator	unknown	15	12

Organization (leaders)	Founded	Location	Membership		
Berlin Conference of European Catholics (BCEC) (Franco Leonori[1]; Hubertus Guske[1])	1964	East Berlin	unknown	unknown	unknown
Christian Peace Conference (CPC) (Károly Tóth; Lubomir Mirejovsky)	1958	Prague	unknown	unknown	ca. 80
International Association of Democratic Lawyers (IADL) (Joe Nordmann; Amar Bentoumi)	1946	Brussels	25,000	unknown	ca. 80
International Federation of Resistance Movements (FIR) (Arialdo Banfi; Alix Lhote)	1951	Vienna	5,000,000	68	29
International Institute for Peace	1957	Vienna	unknown	unknown	unknown
International Organization of Journalists (IOJ) (Kaare Nordenstreng; Dušan Ulcak[1])	1946	Prague	ca. 250,000	unknown	120 plus
International Radio and Television Organization (OIRT) (Sakari Kuru; Gennadij Codr)	1946	Prague	unknown	unknown	unknown
International Union of Students (IUS) (Josef Scala; Georgios Michaelides)	1946	Prague	ca. 34,000,000[2]	117[2]	110[2]
Organization of Solidarity of the Peoples of Africa, Asia and Latin America (OSPAAL) (Susumu Osaki; René Anillo Capote)	1966	Havana	unknown	unknown	unknown
Women's International Democratic Federation (WIDF) (Freda Brown; Mirjam Vire-Tuominen)	1945	East Berlin	200,000,000	142[2]	124[2]
World Federation of Democratic Youth (WFDY) (Walid Masri; György Szabó[4])	1945	Budapest	150,000,000	ca. 270	123
World Federation of Scientific Workers (WFSW) (Jean-Marie Legay; Stan Davison)	1946	London	740,000	ca. 46	70 plus
World Federation of Teachers' Unions (FISE) (Lesturuge Ariyawansa; Gérard Montant)	1946	East Berlin	26,000,000	124	79
World Federation of Trade Unions (WFTU) (Sándor Gáspar; Ibrahim Zakariya)	1945	Prague	ca. 214,000,000	92	81
World Peace Council (WPC) (Romesh Chandra; Johannes Pakaslahti)	1950	Helsinki	unknown	unknown	143[3]

*All known or presumed participants in meetings of "closely coordinating" international nongovernmental organizations during 1981–1987.

1. *Neues Deutschland* (East Berlin), 20 June.
2. *World Student News* (Prague), no. 2, p. 22; membership figure includes newly-incorporated secondary school students; number of affiliates apparently for university level only.
3. Prague, ČTK, 18 March; *FBIS*, 21 March.
4. *WFDY News* (Budapest), no. 8–9.

Introduction:
The Communist World, 1988

The changes in the central apparatus of the Communist Party of the Soviet Union (CPSU) Central Committee resulting from the introduction of six new commissions and the elimination of several departments did not appear to adversely affect operations of the International Department. Under a new head (former *Novosti* press agency board chairman Valentin M. Falin), the department has been subordinated since the latter part of 1988 to the International Policies Commission under Aleksandr N. Iakovlev, who is both a full Politburo member and a national secretary.[1] This probably means a reduction in departmental stature (Falin is only a candidate for membership on the Central Committee) and tighter control by the CPSU Political Bureau.

The *World Marxist Review* (*WMR*) continues as the vehicle for organizing conferences of "fraternal communist, workers', and revolutionary democratic parties." The most recent conference, 12–15 April, attracted representatives from 93 such organizations to Prague, Czechoslovakia, where *WMR* is headquartered. Although ostensibly assembled to discuss the work of the journal, the delegates also heard an address by CPSU secretary Anatolii F. Dobrynin, who admitted that communist powers of attraction have waned and put forward reasons for this dismal state of affairs.[2]

Glasnost' in the USSR has also contributed to ferment among foreign communist parties, especially revelations concerning crimes during the Stalinist period, which adversely reflect on some aging leaders. The impact of Soviet reforms (*perestroika*) has created a split especially among ruling movements, with some opposed to emulating Moscow.[3]

The Nineteenth National CPSU Conference (28 June–1 July) dealt, not surprisingly, with domestic affairs. Mikhail Gorbachev's more than three-hour-long speech discussed developments since the Twenty-seventh Party Congress and the forthcoming transformation of the USSR political system. The 4,991 delegates received the report with reservations, applause coming when the speaker touched on traditional party values and ideals.[4] There were no claims made concerning the expansion of world communism.

Apparently, there is little if any expansion. The number of communist parties has remained stationary at approximately one hundred, with total membership at "more than 80 million" worldwide.[5] Even the so-called vanguard Marxist-Leninist movements—ruling organizations that are not yet recognized as having reached the maturity of those in Eastern Europe or Asia—number only seven.

The world revolutionary process, thus, is still alive if no longer well. It includes communist and workers parties in 96 countries, with the "world socialist system" comprised of the sixteen in power. Two (Albania and China) are antagonistic or indifferent toward the Soviet Union, and three (Romania, North Korea, and Yugoslavia) are more or less neutral. An inner core, known as the "socialist commonwealth," has ten full members of the Council for Mutual Economic Assistance (CMEA) plus Laos and Cambodia, which have observer status only. (See Table 1.)

The Register of Communist Parties in this volume includes 107 countries with either one or more communist parties, a vanguard "revolutionary democratic" organization, or a more radical national liberation movement not yet promoted to the vanguard category by Moscow. The CPSU acknowledges that more than one communist party exists in Australia, Cambodia, Costa Rica, Ecuador, Finland, Greece, India, Iran, Ireland, Jamaica, Lebanon, Malaysia, New Zealand, the Philippines, Spain, Suriname, and Sweden. It also recognizes communist movements in such nonsovereign territories as Guadeloupe, Martinique, Palestine, Puerto Rico, Réunion, and West Berlin.

Vanguard revolutionary democratic parties include the following seven: Angola, Afghanistan, Congo-Brazzaville, Ethiopia, Madagascar, Mozambique, and South Yemen. (See Table 2.) Revolutionary democratic movements operate in Bahrain, Grenada, Nicaragua (Sandinistas), Suriname, and Zimbabwe.[6] Finally, several Marxist-Leninist movements not recognized by Moscow also appear in the register. (Population data are estimates as of

**Table 1: World Communist System—
Socialist Commonwealth of Nations**

Country	Joined Council for Mutual Economic Assistance
Bulgaria	1949
Cuba	1972
Czechoslovakia	1949
East Germany	1950
Hungary	1949
Cambodia	Observer status
Laos	Observer status
Mongolia	1962
Poland	1949
Romania	1949
Soviet Union	1949
Vietnam	1978

Other Communist-ruled States

Albania	—
China	—
North Korea	—
Yugoslavia	Associate member

SOURCES: Table 1.2 in Richard F. Staar, *USSR Foreign Policies After Détente*, rev. ed. (Stanford: Hoover Institution Press, 1987), p. 11. Ambassadors from the first twelve countries were briefed by A. N. Iakovlev at CPSU Central Committee headquarters, according to *Pravda*, 3 February 1989, p. 5.

July 1988.[7]) The list also identifies the party leader, dates of the most recent party congress or national conference, legal status of the movement, and percentage of votes and number of seats won in the latest national elections. There were 29 congresses and national conferences held during 1988.

Among the sixteen ruling communist parties, China recorded the largest membership increase (almost one million), followed by the USSR (430,000), Vietnam (210,000), and Romania and Poland (about 70,000 each). The largest losses were noted for Yugoslavia (88,000) and Hungary (53,000). Other notable gains were registered by the nonruling parties of Panama (almost 12,000), the illegal Communist Party of the Philippines (17,000), the Communist Party of Greece (8,000), and the Progressive Party of the Working People on Cyprus (3,000). Losses occurred in Italy (122,000) and the Norwegian Communist Party as well as the Workers' Communist Party (about 4,000 for each).

The register notes fifteen new leaders of communist parties, including two each for separate movements in Finland and the Philippines. Most were replaced at congresses (Grenada, Guadeloupe, Spain, Uruguay), a national conference (Hungary), or unification of two parties (Turkey). Others were replaced because of advanced age (Canada, Cyprus, Indonesia) and factional struggle.

During 1988, parliamentary or presidential elections were held in 21 of the listed countries including Afghanistan, where the ruling People's Democratic Party of Afghanistan had no problem packing its national assembly. Communists boycotted the voting in Haiti, lost one seat each in Ecuador and Martinique, were banned in El Salvador, lost two each in Sweden and Venezuela, and gained three in San Marino. Major developments by region are discussed below.

Africa. Self-proclaimed Marxist governments in Africa below the Sahara spent 1988 coping with economic problems that required practical solutions, not revolutionary rhetoric. These regimes, for the most part, looked for market responses to resolve production shortages instead of relying on the tenets of Marxism-Leninism to increase agricultural and industrial output. Political uncertainty or fighting, especially in Angola, Mozambique, and Ethiopia, preoccupied indigenous Marxists.[8] Progress toward peace, and therefore government security, was achieved in southern Africa, where the Marxist regimes in Angola and Mozambique moved toward reconciliation with their powerful neighbor, the Republic of South Africa (RSA).

The most dramatic turn toward peace came in Angola at year's end with the signing of an agreement involving Namibia (Southwest Africa), Angola, and the RSA. Since independence, the ruling Popular Movement for the Liberation of Angola–Labor Party (MPLA-PT) has faced serious rebellion in the country's southern region from the rival National Union for the Total Independence of Angola (UNITA). Each organization gained support from outside the country. Cuba had dispatched between 35,000 and 50,000 combat and other troops by 1988 to aid the embattled MPLA-PT regime. South Africa supported UNITA with equipment, training, and, on some occasions, military incursions against joint Cuban-MPLA forces that moved south with tanks, aircraft, and artillery to dislodge the lightly armed rebels. A breakthrough came in December when the Angolans, South Africans, and Cubans agreed to a complex 27-month

Table 2: Social Composition of Vanguard Parties

Country	Party	Members and candidates		Workers	Farmers
		End of 1970s	Mid-1980s	(percent)	
Afghanistan	PDPA	18,000	155,000	28.0	n.a.
Angola	MPLA-PT	351,000	35,000	35.0	2.0
Congo/Brazzaville	PCT	7,000	8,700	31.5	14.5
Mozambique	FRELIMO	110,000	130,000	18.9	53.5
Ethiopia	WPE	—	44,000	21.7	3.3
Madagascar	AKFM	60,000	n.a.[a]	8.0	70.0
South Yemen	YSP	—	31,700	15.0	n.a.

SOURCE: A. P. Agafonov and V. F. Khalipov, *Sovremennaia epokha i mirovoi revoliutsionnyi protsess* (Moscow: Vysshaia shkola, 1988), p. 158.

[a] n.a. = not available.

phased withdrawal of Havana's troops in return for Pretoria's grant of independence to Namibia[9] and a suspension of its military assistance to UNITA. Jonas Savimbi, head of the latter, vowed to continue the war against the Luanda regime.

Angola's efforts to restructure its economy also appeared uncertain. President José Eduardo dos Santos had initiated a liberalizing program (*Saneamento Economico e Frananciero*, SEF) that encountered problems in the People's Assembly.[10] Meeting in February, the legislature failed to adopt a law establishing free enterprise areas for the economy. The People's Assembly did approve other SEF-related legislation on foreign investment, state companies, planning, and the monetary system.

The People's Republic of Mozambique continued its shift from a centralized Marxist economy to an implementation of individual incentives to increase production and facilitate market efficiency as announced in the Economic Rehabilitation Program in January 1987. Government spokesmen noted higher levels of productivity during the past year.[11] The war also appeared to moderate, as the Front for the Liberation of Mozambique's (FRELIMO's) army benefited from the deployment of the armed forces of Zimbabwe and Tanzania in important areas of the country. The Soviets and Cubans kept up military deliveries for the hard-pressed FRELIMO party, but the rebel Mozambique National Resistance pressed the government's forces in many regions.

The People's Democratic Republic of Ethiopia was faced with a continuing insurgency against its central government. Its struggle differed from those directed against other Marxist regimes in southern

Africa because it involved mainly secessionist wars throughout Eritrea and Tigre. Unlike the rebellions in Angola and Mozambique, the war took a sharp turn for the worse vis-à-vis the ruling Workers' Party of Ethiopia. The liberation fronts representing Eritrea and Tigre defeated Ethiopian forces, killing or capturing thousands of soldiers.[12] President Mengistu Haile Mariam responded by executing several army generals for failure to halt the rebels, ordering all foreign relief workers out of Tigre and Eritrea, exposing the two territories to starvation as revenge, and negotiating an end of the state of war with Somalia (which allowed Ethiopia to shift some 70,000 troops from its southern border to the rebellious north).

In domestic affairs Mengistu, like other Marxist African leaders, strove to expand output by use of incentive. He increased the price paid to farmers for part of their grain harvest and allowed them to sell the balance. Additionally, he lifted internal controls to permit a free market in food to develop. The government, however, remained committed to the goal of a collectivized agricultural society by the year 2000. The regime also stayed wedded to its relocation policy, which has attracted much international criticism in recent years. Under this program tens of thousands of northern inhabitants have been forcibly uprooted and transported to the south, as a means of denying to rebels a friendly population.[13]

Elsewhere in sub-Saharan Africa, economic problems also plagued other Marxist regimes. For example, the People's Republic of the Congo, which is facing critical negotiations with its foreign creditors, finally decided to undertake major changes in its economic policy. The ruling Congolese Party of

Labor marked for shutdown, sold to foreign interests, or transformed into mixed Congolese-foreign control 76 out of some 100 state-owned companies.[14] The regime also cut public expenditures by freezing employment in public service and limiting salary increases to the rate of inflation. A major political problem in the form of Pierre Anga, whose rebellion in the north began in September 1987, ended with his death at the hands of government troops, thereby removing a dangerous threat to the regime of Denis Sassou-Ngouesso.

The People's Republic of Benin, as in previous years, continued to encounter serious economic difficulties. To secure economic assistance from the International Monetary Fund and the World Bank, the Marxist government moved to implement some austerity measures, including dismantling some state enterprises and privatizing others. Salary cuts for civil servants and senior army officers touched off an attempted coup by a Captain Hountondji and some fifteen fellow officers that resulted in the arrest of about one hundred people. The government of Mathieu Kérékou faced pressure from both leftist and rightist officers who opposed his policies. In foreign affairs, Benin continued strengthening ties with the Soviet Union while gaining aid from the West, especially France. The United States, however, issued "strenuous protests" against Benin's tolerance or encouragement of Libyan terrorist activities in its territories.[15]

The ruling Zimbabwe African National Union (ZANU) entered into a merger with its major opposition party, the Zimbabwe African People's Union (ZAPU). At an extraordinary ZANU-Popular Front (PF) congress held in early April, some three thousand delegates approved the merger, establishing a de facto one-party state. Robert Mugabe is president of the reconstituted ZANU-PF; Joshua Nkomo, his long-standing adversary and former leader of ZAPU, is one of two vice presidents of the united party.[16]

The new party affirmed its adherence to the principles of Marxism-Leninism even though its key leaders endorse mixed-economy policies. The government's announcement of an amnesty elicited the surrender of more than one hundred ZAPU combatants. Mugabe integrated ZANU and ZAPU political organs from the local to national levels to accomplish a reconciliation. Mugabe's economic policies, counter to the continentwide movement toward privatization, are to acquire greater control of local large-scale enterprises.[17] The government

also announced its intention of making large investments in strategic industries like mining and energy.

The nonruling Communist Party of Lesotho (CPL) continues its marginal and ambivalent existence. Although the party is illegal but tolerated, the CPL's trade union activities are legal and accepted. In August the leftist Justice Minister Halaki Sello was dismissed by the government; earlier he had been described as a former CPL member and pro-Soviet.[18] A week later the government signed an economic and technical agreement with the People's Republic of China.

Across the border in the RSA another nonruling party, the South African Communist Party (SACP), although banned and mainly operating from exile, remained committed to the goals of its 1984 program, which, among other aims, seeks to lead the working class to end capitalist exploitation and establish "a socialist republic based on the common ownership of the means of production" and the "destruction of the economic and political power of the racist ruling class."[19] This past year party commentators assessed and drew encouragement from the dramatic growth of campaigns against the apartheid policies of the government. The SACP advocated paying special attention to blacks in "apolitical" organizations such as youth movements, women's clubs, sporting organizations, churches, and trade unions. The party also stressed the "activation of broad sectors of whites in various forms of opposition to the system."[20]

Unlike the RSA the Sudan recognizes a communist party that has become a visible part of the parliamentary opposition. In keeping with its political participation (recorded by winning 5 of the 264 contested seats in the 1985 parliamentary election), the Sudanese Communist Party (SCP) advocates a reformist approach to change. This past year saw the SCP refuse to join a "government of reconciliation" with all other parties; it refused because it was against any formal implementation of Islamic law in the Sudan. By year's end, the reconciliation government was fragmented.[21]

In Senegal the several nonruling Marxist parties fared poorly in the country's presidential and National Assembly elections of 28 February, for none won any seats under Senegal's system of proportional representation. Neither the Independence and Labor Party, which enjoys Moscow's official recognition as Senegal's pre-eminent communist movement, nor the Democratic League/Movement for the Party of Labor (LD/MPT) even fielded presidential candidates. Although both groups' showing has slightly improved since 1983, the LD/MPT came closest to winning a seat in the National Assembly.[22] Some tiny Marxist factions declined to participate in the election, which saw the ruling Socialist Party win a victory, albeit at a reduced level, and the return of its leader, President Abdou Diouf, to office.

The Réunion Communist Party (PCR) played an active role in all four of Réunion's elections in 1988. During the French presidential election, the PCR did not support the candidate of the French Communist Party (PCF). Accusing the PCF of Eurocentrism, the PCR backed the socialist incumbent, François Mitterrand, who won the election. The reelected president of France called for National Assembly elections in May. Twenty-four candidates ran for Réunion's alloted five seats, and the PCR retained control of two. In October the PCR ran candidates in 26 cantons out of the 44 open for election. By the second round, the PCR had increased its representation from seven to nine in the General Council. The final voting took place during a referendum on New Caledonia, and Réunion supported the French government's program.

The Americas. Communist regimes maintained their control over Cuba and Nicaragua, while a plethora of Marxist-Leninist parties and movements throughout the Western Hemisphere hoped for power in the future. Most of these groups participated in the often fragile democratic systems of their countries either independently or, more frequently, in formal and informal alliances with other leftist groups. A total of ten party congresses were held during 1988 (more than ever before in a single year), devoted in large part to electoral strategies. Several guerrilla movements waged wars against governments, though all but the Sendero Luminoso (Shining Path) in Peru proclaimed, with varying degrees of enthusiasm, their support for negotiated settlements to domestic conflicts.

On 1 January 1989, Fidel Castro celebrated his 30th anniversary as Maximum Leader of the Cuban revolution. The Soviet Union was represented by Vitali I. Vorotnikov, CPSU Politburo member and chairman of the Russian Soviet Federated Socialist Republic Supreme Soviet.[23] The fall of Alfredo Stroessner in Paraguay early that same month made Castro the only dictator in the hemisphere to be entrenched in power for decades. Because his brother is the designated successor, Castro presides over the single remaining family dynasty in the Americas and remains the foremost communist in

the Americas, though many Latin leftists regard him as an anachronism. At the end of December an international group of some 170 intellectuals called for a plebiscite in Cuba, to which a Foreign Ministry spokesman retorted: "Absurd and inconceivable. Our people had a referendum 30 years ago on the day of the triumph of the revolution."[24]

Recently several international human rights organizations were allowed to visit the island. Ricardo Bofill, longtime head of the Havana-based Cuban Committee for Human Rights, wrote at year's end that the foreign organizations "have done little more than scratch the surface" of national conditions. Although for much of the year reports suggested that human rights violations were decreasing, the end of 1988 and early 1989 brought contrary evidence.[25] At the same time, Castro supposedly has ordered the millions of members in his Committees for the Defense of the Revolution to stop reporting on the activities of their neighbors.

The Cuban economy, with declining production and foreign reserves, remains in shambles, sustained by an estimated $5.7 billion annually in subsidies from the USSR.[26] Refusing to decentralize the economy and loosen central controls, as Soviet leaders have suggested, Castro has instead increased state and communist party authority. Continuing worker apathy suggests that the people lack enthusiasm for current conditions. Through the communist party Castro has vigorously promoted the "war of all the people," a mass mobilization that has made Cuba one of the most militarized countries in the world. This is supposedly intended to forestall a U.S. invasion but is probably more to tighten control over an increasingly restive population and discourage dissidents within the armed forces from challenging regime authority.

Although scorning the reforms proposed in the Soviet Union and China, Castro has maintained solidarity with many revolutionary groups and governments abroad. For example, he continued substantial support to the Sandinista revolution in Nicaragua and to the Farabundo Martí National Liberation Front (FMLN) guerrillas in El Salvador. He boycotted the Seoul Olympics in solidarity with North Korea. At the end of the year, Cuba signed an agreement providing for Namibian independence and the withdrawal of some 50,000 of its troops from Angola by July 1991. Relations with the People's Republic of China have improved considerably in recent years, as indicated by Foreign Minister Isidoro Malmierca's visit to Beijing in January 1989.[27]

The regime in Nicaragua celebrated the end of the Reagan administration, even as the country continued to collapse. Armed conflict between the Sandinistas and the resistance virtually ceased during 1988, although relative peace brought anything but prosperity. Amid a series of what the Sandinista newspaper *Barricada* called "adjustments," prices soared. To a considerable degree black markets sustained the people, and inflation had rocketed to 36,000 percent by January 1989. At the end of that month, President Daniel Ortega announced a severe austerity plan, which included laying off up to 35,000 government functionaries, including 10,000 from the military and 13,000 from the security police.[28]

Meanwhile repression increased during the year, most graphically with the brutal smashing of a peaceful demonstration at Nandaime in July but evident also in numerous lesser incidents. The weekly newspaper of the Nicaraguan Communist Party, part of the united front of organizations from left to right that condemn the Sandinistas, wrote, "The police and courts are highly efficient in fabricating false proofs and jailing workers, peasants, employees, and managers whose only fault is having independent political views and denouncing the daily abuses suffered by citizens."[29]

Sandinista relations with the Soviet bloc remained strong, while those with the United States deteriorated and then improved. American military aid to the resistance ended in February, and the regime sent troops into Honduras during March in an unsuccessful effort to destroy arms supplies of the resistance. In July, the Sandinistas accused the U.S. embassy in Managua of having plotted the "riots" at Nandaime and expelled the U.S. ambassador and some of his staff. The United States retaliated in kind. Although Sandinista leaders took no position in the U.S. presidential election and said that all U.S. political leaders are imperialists, they clearly favored Michael Dukakis. When Ronald Reagan left office, the Sandinistas lifted their virtual siege of the U.S. embassy and called for a revival of the defunct Arias Plan.[30]

Elsewhere in Central America, communist groups engaged in armed conflict while periodically talking of peace. In El Salvador, the right-wing ARENA party won a substantial victory in legislative elections, throwing the ruling Christian Democrats into confusion and opening the door to FMLN ploys to advance its cause. In February the FMLN had described its strategy as follows: "to annihilate and wear down enemy forces, sabotage the war economy, and destabilize and dismantle local and judicial authority."[31] The guerrillas did this by pushing the campaign of sabotage that the U.S. embassy estimates has caused $2 billion in economic losses over the past seven years, by promoting urban confrontations through such front groups as the National Union of Salvadoran Workers, by launching several major attacks on military bases, by blockading transportation and mining roads, and by assassinating and intimidating local elected government officials. For a while the guerrillas threatened to make U.S. citizens targets of attacks, but this was changed in early 1989.[32]

At the same time, guerrilla leaders traveled throughout the region to promote their positions with noncommunist politicians. This for the first time could be done with some consistency because during the year the FMLN had consolidated its organization under the undisputed leadership of the People's Revolutionary Army and its chief, Joaquín Villalobos. In February 1989 the FMLN said that if the government would postpone the March elections until September, it would participate in the electoral process and abide by the people's will. The guerrillas would support the Democratic Convergence coalition, headed by Guillermo Ungo and Rubén Zamora, who had long been the head of the FMLN's political front. Ungo stated in late 1988 that "an election dynamic is opening up" in El Salvador. As of early February 1989 most reactions to the guerrilla proposal were negative, though many fear the upsurge of warfare almost certain to come if the plan is turned down.[33]

Guerrilla groups in Guatemala, united under the banner of the National Revolutionary Unity of Guatemala (URNG), claim to be "a real force" in the country; they are not. Military engagements took place during the year, although the guerrillas devoted more attention to a publicity campaign in Guatemala and abroad. The URNG claimed that the principal obstacle to peace in the country was the government's military.[34]

Honduras has long been a haven for the Nicaraguan resistance and FMLN sympathizers, though there have been few military encounters in the country. During 1988, particularly after the legally dubious arrest and extradition in April of drug dealer Juan Ramón Matta, attacks increased on U.S. personnel and facilities, as well as on Hondurans who support U.S. policies. Costa Rican communists, who have been divided for some time, participated in elections but find it difficult to cooperate to maximize the leftist vote.

In Panama, the communist People's Party (PDP) supports the increasing anti-U.S. rhetoric of Defense Forces chief Manuel Antonio Noriega and thus almost certainly will support his candidate, Democratic Revolutionary Party (PRD) leader Carlos Duque. The PRD, in effect Noriega's party in Panama's captive legislature, has long been strongly influenced by the Marxist-Leninist left and is becoming more so as the U.S.-Panamanian conflict drags on inconclusively. In September, Karen Brutents (first deputy chief of the CPSU International Department) visited Panama for the third time in four years and met with leaders of the PDP and the PRD. Noriega has continued to rely on personal security forces and advisers from Cuba even as he improves ties with the Sandinistas and other leftist and terrorist regimes.

Colombia has had problems with guerrillas for decades, and in recent years the guerrillas have found common cause with the drug dealers, who have already undermined much of the country's judicial and security systems.[35] More than 3,600 people were killed in political violence during the year, and 544 kidnapped Colombians remained unaccounted for at the end of 1988. Rightist death squads are again active to counter the leftist narco/ terrorists. As in years past, the government tried to negotiate with the guerrillas to end domestic unrest, and periods of optimism were followed by renewed fighting. Even as the government reportedly concluded an initial peace agreement with one group (the M-19), the military announced a major offensive against the Revolutionary Armed Forces of Colombia, the armed branch of the Communist Party of Colombia (PCC). Violence escalated in early 1989, with one terrorist attack taking the lives of twelve members of the judicial system in Santander Department.[36] Local intelligence reported that Cuban advisers are involved with several of the Colombian guerrilla groups; Ambassador Enríque Gómez said that when his brother, former Conservative Party presidential candidate Alvaro Gómez, was kidnapped in May, the first contact in the effort to get him free was Fidel Castro.[37] But there is another angle to Colombian communist activities that links the PCC to many other South American states, particularly the Andean countries to its south. The PCC participates in elections through a leftist coalition, the Patriotic Union. The communist parties of Ecuador, Peru, and Bolivia use this same technique.

Ecuadorian communists participated in the 1988 presidential election through the United Leftist Front, which includes the Frente Amplio de Izquierda coalition (FADI) of the pro-Soviet Communist Party of Ecuador (PCE) and the Movimiento Popular Democrático (MPD), founded years ago by pro-Chinese Marxists. The FADI and MPD won two seats each in the national congress. In the runoff presidential election, the PCE supported the winning social democrat, Rodrigo Borja, and has given cautious support to his government.

Peru boasts what is probably the broadest, but also most inherently unstable, leftist front in Latin America—the United Left (IU). The Peruvian Communist Party works with the more moderate members of the IU, the so-called Socialist Convergence, a group that supports some of American Popular Revolutionary Alliance president Alan Garcia's political, not economic, programs, while openly condemning Sendero Luminoso terrorism. Sendero Luminoso, which held a congress in February, shifted its strategy and tactics somewhat in 1988, moving from protracted rural war to promoting urban revolution. Sendero members and supporters have precipitated showdowns in urban demonstrations of other leftist groups and in May marched through Lima under their own banner. Their activities also include routine selective assassinations of government authorities (including police) and political leaders, as well as economic sabotage. Sendero proposes to disrupt the 1990 elections, if possible.

The Chilean Communist Party—in the late 1960s and early 1970s a model for electoral participation—spent most of the year trying to decide whether to support the October plebiscite on an additional term for President Augusto Pinochet. Ultimately it encouraged its members to vote, though it did not cooperate openly with other parties. The communists continue to support the Manuel Rodríguez Patriotic Front terrorists and to advocate violent as well as nonviolent forms of struggle. A stumbling block to broad leftist participation in the 1989 election is the constitutional ban on the communist party and the government's refusal to talk with groups that seem to be fronts for the party.[38]

South America's two largest countries offer very different prospects for communist groups. In Brazil, with its rapidly deteriorating economy, the formal communist parties have little success on their own. The factionalized Workers' Party, somewhat like the Peruvian IU, wins more votes and elects a significant number of candidates but is too diffuse to function as a unified party. Communists in Argentina have always been upstaged in the workers' and other movements by the Peronistas, and so it was last year when the Peronista party positioned itself to win the 1989 presidential election. Remnants of a Trotskyist guerrilla group of the 1970s attacked a military base in January 1989.

Other South American countries in which Marxist-Leninists focus most of their attention on elections include (1) Bolivia, where the communist party and other groups are uncharacteristically a part of the United Left in anticipation of the May 1989 elections, (2) Uruguay, where the communists expect to participate in 1989 elections through the Broad Front, (3) Venezuela, where the communist party and its ally, the People's Electoral Movement, received less than 1 percent of the vote in 1988, while the more moderate Movement to Socialism (MAS) did significantly better, (4) Guyana, where Cheddi Jagan's People's Progressive Party continues to be outmaneuvered by the perpetually ruling People's National Congress, and (5) perhaps Paraguay, if elections are actually held there following the fall of General Alfredo Stroessner.

Other hemispheric countries that focus on elections include (1) Mexico, where the communists— the dominant force in the Mexican Socialist Party— threw their support behind the dissident presidential candidate, Cuauhtémoc Cárdenas, in the July elections and now exercise some influence on him as advisers, (2) the Dominican Republic, where the communists may throw their support to the 1990 presidential bid of Juan Bosch, (3) Guadeloupe and Martinique, where communists have some legislative representation and where the primary concern is the potential negative consequences of West European integration, (4) Grenada, where a charismatic young leader, Terrence Marryshow, has taken over the Maurice Bishop Patriotic Movement and seeks closer ties to the democratic left, (5) Jamaica, where a recently split and debilitated communist party ponders the 1989 election in which it will have no impact, (6) Haiti, where the communists propose a coalition government to set the stage for elections,[39] and (7) Canada and the United States, where communist parties ran some candidates— mainly in the United States and mostly as independents—but had no significant national impact.

Several international conferences were held in 1988, including the third meeting of communist parties from South America in Montevideo during August and the Anti-Imperialist Organization of Central America and the Caribbean, involving dozens of leftist organizations from the Caribbean basin, held in June in Panama City.

Asia and the Pacific. The communist regimes in this region continue to experience severe economic difficulties as well as challenges from within and from without to revitalize their systems of public ownership and collectivist rule.

It was a particularly bad year for the Chinese Communist Party (CCP). Disillusionment with reform policies deepened as inflation worsened and corruption became more pervasive. One retired party cadre was quoted as saying that, after having fought the Japanese and the Kuomintang and having worked hard to rebuild the country in the 1950s, "What was it all for? For a lousy single roll of rationed toilet paper a month?"[40]

At the third plenary session of the CCP Central Committee that met in late September, General Secretary Zhao Ziyang tried to explain what had gone wrong. Excessive demand and acute supply shortages produced an inflation rate above 20 percent, and the state would have to cut back demand and check inflation by placing price reforms on hold. Government investment in fixed assets would be reduced by 50 billion yuan in 1989, some one-fifth less than 1988 investment outlays.[41] Consumption would also be curtailed and the money supply brought under tight control. But could the party deal with the new economic independence of the provinces, when some reported that Beijing's political center could no longer make the provinces toe the new CCP line?[42] Only time would tell.

Chinese dissidents like Ren Wanding, recently freed from prison, vowed to press for more human rights.[43] The controversial television series "River Elegy" (*Heshang*), shown in June, was warmly praised but then severely condemned by Vice-Minister Wang Zhen in September.[44] As demands for democracy, openness, and reform intensify, the party will find it increasingly difficult to justify its monopoly of power and its failure to build a prosperous socialism. The country fared better in foreign affairs. On 2 December, the Chinese foreign minister, Zian Zichen, met Mikhail S. Gorbachev in Moscow. Both sides agreed[45] there would be a Sino-Soviet summit meeting during 15–18 May 1989.

Vietnam's economy continued to suffer severe shortages. To ease that regime's defense burden, all Vietnamese civilian advisers in Cambodia, along with nearly three-quarters of Hanoi's military forces, were reported to have left that country by mid-December. All Vietnamese troops are supposed to be withdrawn by the end of calendar 1989 and are obligated to leave Cambodia even earlier (i.e., by September 1989)[46] if an agreement is reached for a negotiated settlement that will result in a coalition government.

In July a flurry of exchanges between North and South Korea brought the two regimes closer than ever before to serious discussion. The National Assembly speaker from South Korea sent a letter to his counterpart in the North proposing exchanges. The latter responded by proposing a nonaggression pact. The South eventually agreed to its 299 national legislators meeting with the 655 members of North Korea's Supreme People's Assembly, providing that both sides could agree on a date.[47] One unsolved mystery during the year was the abrupt disappearance of O Kuk-yol, who had been replaced as army chief of staff.[48] It is not clear whether O has retained his membership on the Politburo in North Korea.

In the Philippines recently captured documents of that country's communist party revealed a multimillion-dollar network to finance the purchase of arms.[49] These materials also described how the New People's Army (NPA) intended to increase operations during 1989 and promote a "revolutionary mass movement." The party apparently had been able to double its budget since 1987 as members eagerly sought to buy more weapons.

The NPA already has small guerrilla base areas in Samar, Albay province of southern Luzon; Misamis Oriental, Agusan province of northeastern Mindinao; and the three adjoining northern Luzon provinces of Cagayan, Ilocos Norte, and Kalinga-Aapayao.[50] The NPA is also said to have acquired a few Soviet-manufacutred RPG-7-type self-propelled grenade launchers. It is not known whether the guerrillas have Soviet SAM-7 rockets (alleged to cost between U.S. $45,000 and $50,000 each), which could be used to shell cities like Manila for great propaganda effect.

On 21 December in Tokyo, the foreign ministers of Japan and the Soviet Union ended their first talks in nearly three years.[51] A Japanese spokesman stated that "neither side has shown concessions, so the positions are still far apart" on the issue of the four northern islands of Etorofu, Shikotan, Kunashiri, and Habomai. These islands were taken after World War II and USSR military bases built on two of them. Japan has insisted that no peace treaty will be signed until the four islands are returned.

The Japanese Communist Party (JCP) also has turned against the Soviet Union because the latter has been attempting to woo the socialists in Japan. After talks with the CPSU in Moscow, the JCP sent a letter in July describing Soviet efforts as "an expression of great-power chauvinism."[52]

Also critical of Soviet foreign policies, especially the "new thinking," is the Communist Party of India–Marxist (CPI-M), which charges the USSR with selling out the international class struggle for better relations with the Indian and U.S. governments. Talk about healing the split between the weaker Communist Party of India and the stronger CPI-M ended when the latter clarified that discussions had been held regarding "unity" and not "unification."[53]

Eastern Europe and the USSR. Following the Romanian Communist Party's national conference in mid-December 1987, five other ruling movements held similar meetings: the Bulgarians in January and the East Germans, Hungarians, and Yugoslavs during May—all in advance of the CPSU, which opened its convention on 28 June. Two of the parties (those in Czechoslovakia and Poland) remained out of step and did not hold any national conferences during calendar year 1988.

The year also witnessed leadership changes in the Soviet Union, Hungary, Poland, Czechoslovakia, Romania, and Yugoslavia—the latter two under normal rotation of personnel procedures. The USSR attempted to persuade its client states that they should purchase more machinery from Moscow and reduce an accumulated trade surplus of eighteen billion transferable rubles.[54] Gorbachev's speech at the United Nations on 7 December, which announced unilateral cuts in Soviet armed forces, resulted in similar statements by several other Warsaw Pact governments.[55]

Albania still remains the odd man out, a member neither of the East European military alliance nor of the CMEA. However, it maintains state-to-state relations with several of Moscow's client states in the region. The Albanian economy has been sliding, although a new policy of removing conservative bureaucrats may help reverse the decline. Those cadres who had completed five years at the same post were replaced during the month of June.[56] The rotation affected a minimum of 70,000 senior administrators, most of whom had been appointed by the late Enver Hoxha, not by current party boss Ramiz Alia.

Agriculture has been more affected than other parts of the Albanian economy, with 75 percent of the arable land and 80 percent of the livestock managed by 460 large production centers. More than 40 percent of industrial goods exported are of agricultural origin.[57] "No imports without exports" is the slogan, which signifies that Albania refuses to accept loans or credit from any foreign country.

Tiranë continues to have no party-to-party relations with Moscow or any other ruling communist movement in Eastern Europe, but it did send a Politburo member to attend the Seventh Congress of the Brazilian Communist Party. Raoul Marko, first secretary of the "orthodox" Spanish communist party, as well as Terence Bacon from the Canadian (Marxist) communist party were received in Tiranë. The term *Marxist-Leninist* is no longer used by the Albanians, implying that the splinter movements are the only genuine ones.

Bulgaria started off the New Year with a national conference during 28–29 January. Communist boss Todor Zhivkov, 77, suggested that positions in the government not be occupied by those already holding offices in the party and that the latter be limited to a maximum of three terms. It was announced that action would be postponed until the Fourteenth Congress in 1991.[58] At the July plenum of the Central Committee, reputed heir apparent Chudomir Alexandrov "resigned at his own request." That same month, most of the 30,000 functionaries who were scheduled to be rotated out of their jobs were given other administrative posts in municipalities and enterprises.

Inadequate reforms adopted the previous year, followed by decisions and draft laws, were never implemented, which may have been why a new Soviet ambassador—V. V. Sharapov, a top Committee for State Security (KGB) official—was posted to Sofia during March, presumably to serve as a watchdog. That did not prevent the July (see above) or December purges of all possible contenders for Zhivkov's position. Rumors persisted about mutual dislike between the Soviet and Bulgarian leaders. CPSU Politburo member Lev N. Zaikov spent five days in September in Sofia to sign agreements on cooperation between respective party, trade union, and youth organizations.[59]

Czechoslovakia's economy also deteriorated, with political reforms restricted to several (April, October, November) personnel changes. Party leader Miloš Jakeš, who presided over the purge of about 500,000 supporters of Alexander Dubček after the August 1968 Soviet military occupation, emerged more powerful than ever. Economic reform has involved only four hundred enterprises on

an experimental basis. Heavy machinery continues to be produced, even though the USSR has stopped buying it.[60]

Despite the ban on independent groups, about ten new ones surfaced in Czechoslovakia during 1988. The number of illegal journals also has proliferated. Demonstrations for religious freedom, in protest against the 1968 Soviet invasion, in commemoration of the 1918 independence day, and others were dispersed by police.[61] Ten of the thirteen bishoprics remain vacant because the regime refuses to permit the Vatican to play any role in appointments. Nevertheless pilgrimages during the year involved some 700,000 faithful, and almost that many signatures were collected under a petition demanding religious freedom.

The German Democratic Republic (GDR) also has avoided both economic and political reforms to date. Party boss Erich Honecker at age 76 has compared experiments in other East European countries with anarchy.[62] This hard line could not conceal problems in meeting production targets and shortages of consumer goods due to bad investment policies and poor distribution.

About 5,000,000 East Germans visited West Germany during last year, some 80 percent past retirement age. Legal emigrants tripled from the year before to total almost 30,000. Lowering these barriers has raised expectations that reforms in the USSR may soon be emulated in the GDR and that Honecker's reign (since 1971) may be almost over.[63]

Hungary had already experienced a transition in communist party leadership when 76-year-old János Kádár's rule of more than three decades ended in May 1988. His successor is Károly Grósz (58), who had served as prime minister since the preceding year. Introduction of an economic stabilization program produced a 17 to 18 percent inflation rate, a lower standard of living,[64] and a gross national product growth of less than 1.5 percent. In the political arena, the independent organizations now include a Hungarian Democratic Forum, the New March Front, and three former political parties as well as nonregime youth, student, and trade union groupings. Pressured by these developments, the government has rewritten the law on associations to include political parties and will draft a new constitution by early 1990.[65] These potentially significant developments are well ahead of anything elsewhere in the region.

Poland experienced strikes during April, May, and August, as the second stage of economic reform introduced radical price increases for basic needs (food, coal, rent), which led to a 120 percent inflation rate during 1988. Wage demands were met, although the regime refused to recognize the banned Solidarity trade union. It promised a choice in June elections, but these were controlled by the regime (700 opposition candidates for 108,000 posts). Just over half of those eligible voted, the lowest turnout ever.[66]

General Wojciech Jaruzelski's internal affairs minister met with Solidarity leader Lech Wałęsa to end the August 1988 strikes, with a promise of roundtable discussions. These did not open until 6 February 1989, well after the purge of eight hardliners from the Politburo during the previous December, which also saw establishment of a Citizens' Committee that united moderate opposition forces before the talks. With about 70 percent of the youth wanting to leave Poland,[67] only a genuine compromise between regime and Solidarity will change this situation.

Romania has no such problems because the ruling leader, Nicolae Ceauşescu, has reverted to Stalinism. He has stated that economic reform does not mean privatization, that the communist party will not share its political power, and that there are no "ready-made forms of socialist construction."[68] Thus by the year 2000, half of the 13,000 Romanian villages will have been destroyed and, when the project is completed, the rural population moved into about 5,500 agro-industrial centers. In this way, private plots will be eliminated and communist values propagated at the new centers. Despite these policies, the Soviet Union awarded Ceauşescu the Order of Lenin on his 70th birthday, followed by similar awards from East Germany and Czechoslovakia.

Ceauşescu maintains power by rotating key personnel, with wife Elena in charge. Their son Nicu is being trained as first secretary of Sibiu county to assume his father's position. Three brothers of the leader are deputy defense minister, chief of cadres for the internal affairs ministry, and deputy chairman of the State Planning Committee. At a plenum of the Central Committee, Ceauşescu stated that there would be no diminution of the status of the communist party.[69]

Yugoslavia had more problems than any other country in the region. About one hundred demonstrations involved a total of four to five million people. With a deteriorating economy, ethnic disputes centered on Albanian harrassment of minorities in Kosovo and fears that Serbia might become dominant under its energetic party president, Slobodan Milošević. There were more strikes during 1988 than the 1,570 registered the year before, and inflation hit 300 percent. More than a third of all enterprises run at a loss, while 60 percent of the workers are at or below the minimum income level. A national conference during the end of May showed a loss of control over the party agenda.[70]

The reforms that have introduced an open, united, market-oriented economy may take three or more years to implement. Without elimination of corruption and a thorough purge of incompetent officials as well as a basic reform of the communist party itself, nobody expects a change for the better in living standards, which have declined by some 40 percent since 1982 and are now at the mid-1960s level.[71] Resignation of the entire government on 30 December hardly seemed to bode well for the future, despite the fact that in nearly every republic all of the Tito era leaders had been removed during the past year.

The Soviet Union experienced the most open discussion of issues at the Nineteenth CPSU National Conference (28 June–1 July) since the early 1920s. Gorbachev obtained most of what he wanted,[72] despite a packing of delegates by the opposition. Not until 30 September, however, could he break the Secretariat organization at the top by dispersing power among six new commissions, all headed by national secretaries with carefully defined responsibilities. The following day, Gorbachev replaced Andrei A. Gromyko as titular president of the country.

Having consolidated his own political position, the Soviet party/government chief concentrated on the nationality problems within the USSR. The Nagorno-Karabakh autonomous oblast (75 percent Armenian, although inside Azerbaijan), the scene of riots that triggered martial law, was placed under direct control of Moscow in January 1989.[73] The Baltic states attempted to obtain genuine autonomy without violence but were frustrated when Gorbachev announced that certain resolutions adopted by the Estonian Supreme Soviet were "null and void." The national front movements in all three republics remain active, however.

Throughout the East European region, *glasnost'* and *perestroika* have had a mixed reception, as noted in the foregoing. In the rhetoric directed at the rest of the world, talk about "two camps" and "proletarian internationalism" has disappeared. Such spokesmen as Anatolii F. Dobrynin (former head of the International Department and now an adviser to Gorbachev) and Vadim V. Zagladin (first deputy chief of the International Department) have admitted, respectively, that the USSR misjudged the staying power of capitalism and that the Soviets had erred on Afghanistan. In his own vision, Gorbachev seems to put forward a world that is technologically interdependent and that transcends class differences.[74]

The Middle East. Attempts by the ruling People's Democratic Party of Afghanistan (PDPA) to project authority and legitimacy became steadily more desperate in the wake of Gorbachev's dramatic promise to complete withdrawal of Soviet military forces by mid-February 1989. The discredited PDPA's frantic and chameleon-like attempts to obscure its Marxist coloration with Afghan traditionalism not only failed to attract cooperation from any opposition groups but alienated many of the party's small core of militants. Particularly embarrassing defections included President Najibullah's brother Siddiqullah; a cousin, Brigadier General Mohammed Gul (who said that many other key leaders would leave if they could); and a deputy foreign minister who requested asylum in the United States.[75]

As the hollowness of PDPA reports became obvious, Soviet media began instituting a *glasnost'* policy. Against earlier PDPA claims to control all 45 cities, province capitals, and major districts and 55 percent of the villages,[76] the Soviet press revealed that PDPA organizations function in only 900 out of about 23,000 villages.[77] Najibullah's boast of having 500,000 men under arms provoked comment in Moscow that Afghan government propaganda was "partly marked by indiscriminate optimism."[78]

Severe damage to the PDPA's remaining credibility multiplied as the national assembly elections in April—scheduled with a scant one month's notice—were held in violation of electoral laws. Secret ballots were disallowed, polling booths often remained unmanned, children as young as thirteen were seen voting, and candidate lists were published only after the polls opened.[79] Even so, the final election results showed only 44 percent of the votes for leftist candidates, with the remaining cast for candidates described as "independent."[80]

This political debacle for the PDPA and the obvious Soviet priority attached to military withdrawal, regardless of PDPA prospects, could not have been confidence inspiring for the Marxist leaders of the People's Democratic Republic of Yemen (PDRY), as ever heavily dependent on Moscow for

support. Reports that Soviet military resupply during the year more than compensated for PDRY losses from the 1986 civil war raised the familiar concern about possible Soviet pre-positioning equipment for its own future use.[81]

Equally plausible is the speculation that USSR efforts were designed to reassure its PDRY ally that military withdrawal from Afghanistan and declining support for other Third World military involvements did not imply abandonment of its strategic foothold in Aden. An unusually high level of Soviet-PDRY diplomatic and economic activity strengthened this impression. Also reinforcing in the regional context was the opening of diplomatic relations between the USSR and the Persian Gulf state of Qatar during the summer.[82]

The August cease-fire in the Iran-Iraq war, while generally welcomed throughout the region equally with the Soviet withdrawal from Afghanistan, brought unmitigated disaster for the remaining cadres of the communist parties in Iran and Iraq. Following the cease-fire, the Ayatollah Ruhollah Khomeini regime exacted brutal vengeance against its guerrilla opposition, the Mojahedine-e Khalq, which had conducted full-scale military operations into Iran from Iraqi bases. Leftist political prisoners were particularly targeted in a wave of executions involving hundreds. By the end of the year the "Tudeh Party of Iran [asked] the United Nations, the human rights committee, Amnesty International . . . to take prompt action to save the lives of thousands of people whose only crime [was] having a different ideology."[83]

Highlighting the many ambiguities of the Soviet position in a war in which they were the principal military supplier for Iraq yet bent on improving their position in Iran, Soviet gestures on behalf of the Tudeh remained subdued. Tudeh denunciations of the Khomeini regime's atrocities were carried by the Soviet press, however.[84] In a more vigorous move Moscow radio broadcast an unattributed commentary in Persian to Iran questioning "the policy of moral and physical assassination" by those who "sacrifice the interests of the people for the sake of their own greedy interests" and accusing Teheran of "sacrificing members of the Tudeh Party and the Fedaiyin organization to gain the trust and support of [U.S.] imperialism."[85]

For the Iraqi Communist Party (ICP), the cease-fire brought even worse devastation than that suffered by the already decimated Tudeh. Since the war's onset in 1980 ICP activity has been concentrated almost exclusively on the disaffected Kurdish areas of northern Iraq, finally joining in a formal coalition with Kurdish guerrilla parties to fight Saddam Hussein's regime in Baghdad. With Iraq long on the defensive against Iranian forces to the south, much of the north became Kurdish controlled and, with Iranian support, expanded during March with capture of the district capital at Halabja. Iraq's retribution was the highly publicized poison gas attack on that city, which killed more than five thousand people.[86]

But the real onslaught began with the July ceasefire, when Khomeini's support for the Kurds ended and the full force of redeployed Iraqi forces turned to the north. Tens of thousands of Kurds escaped to Turkey and Iran, and large numbers of those remaining were forcibly moved to the southern plains of Iraq.[87] The ICP's desperation surfaced in October in an appeal on Kurdish resistance radio for fighters to return to Iraq and resume the struggle.[88] The exact fate of the ICP is still unknown, but with the resistance shattered it is difficult to imagine an effective role in postwar Iraq for any surviving communists who had cooperated with Iran.

By contrast, Lebanon's two principal communist parties, the Lebanese Communist Party (LCP) and the smaller Organization of Communist Action in Lebanon (OCAL), continued to play an active role in the confusing melee of competing militias, which are freewheeling in the absence of central government authority. Although subject to multiple attacks during the continuing civil war because of their antireligious and pro-Palestinian orientation, both the LCP and OCAL worked within the powerful but loose confederation of forces that supports Syria. The LCP, which is active in the National Resistance Front opposing de facto Israeli occupation of a "security zone" in the south, achieved a significant propaganda victory in November when a 20-year-old female party member shot and seriously wounded Antoine Lahad, commander of the Israeli-created and -maintained South Lebanon Army.[89] With a publishing capability (a weekly plus booklets and pamphlets), as well as its own radio station that broadcasts eighteen hours daily, the LCP is well positioned to exploit such events.[90]

Western Europe. The fortunes of the communist parties in this region have undergone dramatic change. Representatives met in Dublin during the late fall for discussions of the implications that will result from the Single European Act, which will unify eight members of the European community in 1992. Those assembled called for "a Europe from the Atlantic to the Urals, a common home for all peoples."[91]

The French communists were in disarray in the wake of their worst defeat in 60 years, when they received only 9.8 percent of the vote during 1986 elections to the National Assembly. They fared little better in June 1988, with 11.3 percent (a loss of eight seats) in the parliamentary election after François Mitterrand had been returned to the presidency. Relations with the Socialist Party also deteriorated; thus it may be difficult to preserve leftist unity in the March 1989 municipal elections. Nevertheless, an agreement between the two parties was concluded for a maximum list of common candidates.[92]

Another independent-progressive (formerly Eurocommunist) movement, the Italian Communist Party (PCI) dropped in its share of local votes from 37 down to 22 percent. However, this did not change the uncritical support by the PCI for Soviet reforms, even to the extent of threatening to break with the CPSU if Gorbachev were to be ousted.[93] The Italian communists have also been contacting foreign socialist leaders for possible agreements or even a merger in the European Parliament at Strasbourg.[94] The replacement of Alessandro Natta (70) as general secretary by Achille Occhetto (52) may have had something to do with this move.

The CPSU has relations with both the Spanish Communist Party and the Communist Party of the Peoples of Spain (PCPE), which had split off from the former. There also exists a third movement, the Spanish Workers' Party–Communist Unity. Leaders of the first two agreed to end the split at a congress in mid-January 1989.[95] In the meanwhile, PCPE leader Ignacio Gallego was expelled from his party. The unification congress lasted only two days and resulted in 23 co-opted former PCPE members, including Gallego, being taken into the new Central Committee. The CPSU sent a low-level functionary, namely G. Revenko, first secretary of the Kiev *obkom*, to signify their neutrality.[96]

The neighboring Portuguese Communist Party has been losing popular support over the past three elections—from 18.8 percent in 1983 down to 12.2 percent in 1987.[97] An attempt at internal party reforms remained abortive at the Twelfth Congress in December, when a motion for secret ballots gained only 30 votes from the two thousand delegates. Chief ideologist and Politburo member Vadim A. Medvedev represented the CPSU at this congress.[98]

The German Communist Party (DKP) is subject to the same internal challenges as the Portuguese one. Its Ninth Congress, held 6–7 January 1989, had to be broken off and continued a week later because of the "two lines in the party," according to its chairman. The CPSU sent another heavy hitter to the DKP congress, Aleksandr N. Iakovlev, who is a Politburo member and chairman of the International Policies Commission of the Central Committee.[99] The DKP is known for its subservience to the East German regime and has steadily lost members since 1985.

Another movement that split formally (1986) is in Finland. The progressive Finnish Communist Party and hard-line Finnish Communist Party–Unity were joined on 21 May by a third, even more orthodox splinter group, the Communist Workers' Party. The first two have been discussing reunification, which had not led to an agreement by year's end.[100]

In Greece, the Communist Party of Greece (KKE) urged the KKE-Interior (which split last year) to join the forces of the left. KKE general secretary Kharilaos Florakis has attempted to improve relations with the Greek Left, the more moderate of the smaller factions. Some agreement may be achieved early in 1989. Preparations are also being made to enter a common list in the June 1989 elections to the European Parliament.

In neighboring Turkey, the communist and workers' parties agreed to form the Turkish United Communist Party, which remains illegal. It issued a New Year's message, making standard demands against the government and demanding freedom for imprisoned leaders who had returned from eight years of exile in Western Europe during late 1987. They were arrested in Turkey, and their trial continues.[101]

Richard F. Staar
Hoover Institution

NOTES

1. "CPSU Central Committee Plenum Resolution," *Pravda*, 29 November, pp. 1–2. See also *L'Unità* (Rome), 16 October, p. 11.

2. "Communiqué," Toronto, *WMR*, June, pp. 5–6, lists 91 of the movements and states that 2 had requested not to be identified. Dobrynin's address appeared in *Pravda*, 13 April, p. 4.

3. Kevin Devlin, "The Communist Movement in 1988," RFE *Research*, *RAD Background Report*, no. 249, 30 December, p. 1.

4. Heinz Brahm, "Der 'kleine Parteitag' in Moskau (28. Juni–1 Juli 1988)," *Berichte des Bundesinstituts für ost-*wissenschaftliche und internationale Studien* (Cologne), no. 34, pp. 13–16.

5. V. P. Agafonov and V. F. Khalipov, *Sovremennaia epokha i mirovoi revoliutsionnyi protsess* (Moscow: Vysshaia shkola, 1988), p. 201.

6. For a listing of 24 revolutionary democratic movements and vanguard parties, see Table 1.3 in Richard F. Staar, *USSR Foreign Policies After Détente*, rev. ed. (Stanford: Hoover Institution Press, 1987), p. 14.

7. Most of these data are from U.S. Central Intelligence Agency, *The World Factbook 1988* (Washington, D.C.: U.S. Government Printing Office, 1988), CPAS WF 88-001.

8. See B. M. Zmeev, *Politicheskaia ideologiia v stranakh tropicheskoi Afriki* (Leningrad: Izdatel'stvo Leningradskogo universiteta, 1988), pp. 91–105.

9. For the status of the South-West Africa People's Organization (SWAPO), which will probably end up ruling Namibia, see Viktor Sovetov, *Mesto prestupleniia-Namibiia* (Moscow: Politizdat, 1986), pp. 97–101. The organization of SWAPO is patterned after the CPSU. See also Gorbachev's message to SWAPO in *Vestnik Ministerstva Innostrannykh Del SSSR* 35, no. 1 (15 January 1989):5.

10. Radio Luanda, 31 December 1987; *FBIS-Africa (AFR) (Sub-Sahara)*, 6 January.

11. Maputo, *Notícias*, 2 April.

12. *NYT*, 1 April.

13. Note the four-day visit by former KGB chief V. M. Chebrikov to Ethiopia. *Pravda*, 7, 10 January 1989.

14. Paris, AFP, 4 June; *FBIS-AFR*, 9 June.

15. *NYT*, 20 May.

16. "In Brief Items," *WMR*, June, p. 87.

17. See the entry "Zimbabwe" in A. A. Gromyko et al., eds., *Strany Afriki* (Moscow: Politizdat, 1988), pp. 161–67.

18. Radio Umtata, 2 August; *FBIS-AFR*, 4 August, p. 4.

19. London, *African Communist*, no. 114, pp. 73–74. Note the interview given by CPSA national chairman Dan Tlume over Moscow radio, 18 January; *FBIS-Soviet Union (SOV)*, 19 January 1989.

20. *African Communist*, pp. 73–74.

21. Khartoum, *al-Maydan*, 13 December.

22. London, *West Africa*, 7 March.

23. "Conversations in Havana," *Pravda*, 6 January 1989, p. 5.

24. *NYT*, 2, 11 January 1989.

25. *WSJ*, 16 December; *LAT*, 12 January 1989.

26. Central Intelligence Agency, *Handbook of Economic Statistics 1988* (Washington, D.C.: September 1988), CPAS 88-10001, table 157, p. 181.

27. Havana, Radio Reloj, 16, 18 January; *FBIS-Latin America (LAT)*, 19 January 1989, p. 2.

28. *NYT*, 31 January, 5 February 1989.

29. Managua, *Avance*, 9 November.

30. *NYT*, 8 February 1989.

31. Radio Venceremos, 11 February 1989; *FBIS-LAT*, 19 February 1989, p. 13.

32. Miami, *El Nuevo Herald*, 2 February 1989.

33. Mexico City, *La Unidad*, 20 November; *FBIS-LAT*, 10 January 1989; *NYT*, 7 February 1989; *LAT*, 8 February 1989.

34. Managua, *Barricada Internacional*, 8 September.

35. Ambassador Enríque Gómez, "La Droga: Un Arma Estratégica," paper delivered at a National Defense University conference in Washington, D.C., in October; Rachel Ehrenfeld, "Narco-terrorism and the Cuban Connection," *Strategic Review* (Summer 1988):55–63.

36. Bogotá Inravision Television Cadena, 11 January 1989; Paris, AFP, 12 January; *FBIS-LAT*, 12 January 1989, pp. 25–26; Bogotá Emisoras Caracol Network, 19 January 1989; *FBIS-LAT*, 23 January 1989, p. 42.

37. Information given by former Ambassador Gómez from Colombia to the United States. See note 35, above.

38. *NYT*, 30 January 1989.

39. Port-au-Prince Radio Nationale, 10 January 1989; *FBIS-LAT*, 18 January 1989.

40. Ellen Salem, "Things Fall Apart, the Centre Cannot Hold," Hong Kong, *FEER*, 27 October, p. 37.

41. *FBIS-China (CHI)*, 26 October, p. 13.

42. Salem, "Things Fall Apart," pp. 38–39; Nicholas D. Kristof, "Beijing Authority Being Challenged by Local Powers," *NYT*, 11 December, pp. 1, 14.

43. *NYT*, 27 November, pp. 1, 10.

44. Salem, "Things Fall Apart," p. 37; Geremie Barne, "TM Requiem for the Myths of the Middle Kingdom," *FEER*, 1 September, pp. 40–45.

45. *NYT*, 6 February 1989, p. A-4.

46. *NYT*, 26 January 1989, p. A-4; "Statement of Vietnamese Minister," *Krasnaia zvezda* (Moscow), 22 January 1989, p. 3.

47. *FEER*, 4 August, p. 14.

48. Ibid., 7 April, p. 38.

49. Ibid., 28 July, p. 12.

50. Ibid., p. 13. See also *NYT*, 15 January 1989, p. A-8.

51. Susan Chira, "Tokyo and Moscow Fail to End Dispute," *NYT*, 21 December, p. A-6.

52. Devlin, "Communist Movement in 1988," p. 4.

53. Ibid.; *Pravda*, 6 January 1989, p. 5.

54. V. V. Kusin, "Introduction to Eastern Europe in 1988," RFE *Research*, *RAD Background Report*, no. 251, 30 December, p. 3.

55. Gorbachev's speech appeared in *Vestnik Ministerstva Inostrannykh Del SSSR*, no. 24 (31 December):1–8.

56. Tiranë, *Zeri i popullit*, 12 June.

57. Ibid., 22 November.

58. The four principles adopted at the national party conference in Sofia are given in "Party Conferences—Realistic Renewal," *WMR*, October, pp. 46–47; see also Sofia, *Rabotnichesko delo*, 2 February.

59. *Frankfurter Allgemeine Zeitung*, 22 August; *Rabotnichesko delo*, 15 September.

60. Peter Martin, "Czechoslovakia," RFE *Research*, *RAD Report*, no. 251, 30 December, pp. 15–18.

61. Jiri Rohan, BBC, London, CARIS report no. 106/88, 29 December.

62. Seventh SED plenum in East Berlin, *ND*, 2, 3 December.

63. Barbara Donovan, "German Democratic Republic," RFE *Research*, *RAD Report*, no. 251, 30 December, p. 26.

64. The consumer price index shot up by an average of almost 16 percent. Budapest, *Népszabadság*, 2 November.

65. B. Rodionov, "The MSzMP [Hungarian Socialist Workers' Party] Proposes Coalition," Moscow, *Izvestiia*, 19 January 1989, p. 5; Alfred Reisch, "Hungary," RFE *Research*, *RAD Report*, no. 251, 30 December, pp. 28–29.

66. Louisa Vinton, "Poland," RFE *Research*, *RAD Report*, no. 251, 30 December, pp. 39–42.

67. Warsaw, *Rzeczywistość*, 10 January.

68. Cited by Michael Szafir, "Romania," RFE *Research*, *RAD Report*, no. 251, 30 December, p. 43.

69. Bucharest, *Scînteia*, 29 November.

70. See *Pravda*, 30 May.

71. Milan Andrejevich, "Yugoslavia," RFE *Research*, *RAD Report*, no. 251, 30 December, pp. 47–51.

72. See *Theses of the CPSU Central Committee for the 19th All-Union Party Conference* (Moscow: Novosti, 1988), p. 30.

73. "Decree by Presidium of the USSR Supreme Soviet," *Pravda*, 15 January 1989, p. 1.

74. M. S. Gorbachev, *Perestroika i novoe myshlenie* (Moscow: Politizdat, 1988), pp. 137–65.

75. Paris, AFP, 25 October; *San Francisco Chronicle*, 18 November.

76. *Bakhtar*, 14 January; *FBIS-Near East and South Asia (NES)*, 15 January, p. 47.

77. *JPRS*-UIA-88-018, 23 November.

78. *Pravda*, 26 May; *FBIS-SOV*, 1 June, p. 26.

79. U.S. Department of State, *Afghanistan: Soviet Occupation and Withdrawal* (Washington, D.C.: December 1988), special report no. 179, p. 8.

80. *Kabul Times*, 30 April.

81. *CSM*, 11 March.

82. *NYT*, 1 August.

83. Clandestine Radio of the Iranian Toilers, December; *FBIS-NES*, 2 December.

84. *Pravda*, 7 December; *FBIS-SOV*, 8 December, p. 37.

85. Moscow, Radio Peace and Progress, 5 November; *FBIS-SOV*, 30 November, p. 17.

86. Paris, *Le Monde*, cited in *Manchester Guardian Weekly*, 11 September.

87. Nadim Jaber in *Middle East International*, 9 September, p. 3.

88. Istanbul, *Hurriyet*, 2 October; *FBIS-Western Europe (WEU)*, 13 October.

89. Clandestine Voice of the Mountain, in Arabic, to Lebanon, 8 November; *FBIS-NES*, 8 November, p. 46.

90. Rafic Samhoun, "Resisting Ideological Subversions," *WMR*, August, p. 90.

91. "European CP's discuss 1992," London, *Morning Star*, 11 October, listed the communist parties of Ireland, Great Britain, Denmark, France, West Germany, Greece, Portugal, and "the Peoples of Spain" as taking part. Observers attended from Belgium and the *WMR*.

92. Radio Paris, 12 January 1989; *FBIS-WEU*, 13 January 1989, p. 18.

93. Gianni Cervetti, "Perspectives in Renovation," *WMR*, October 1988, pp. 86–89.

94. Rome, *La Repubblica*, 10 November; *FBIS-WEU*, 5 January 1989, pp. 21–22.

95. Devlin, "Communist Movement in 1988," p. 5.

96. "Work of the Congress Ends," *Pravda*, 16 January 1989, p. 6; Moscow radio, 21 January 1989; *FBIS-SOV*, 24 January 1989.

97. Devlin, "Communist Movement in 1988," p. 3.

98. See his interview in Lisbon, *Diario de Noticias*, 4 December, p. 4; *FBIS-SOV*, 12 December, pp. 36–37.

99. "DKP Congress Will Be Extended," *Pravda*, 9 January 1989, p. 7; *Frankfurter Allgemeine Zeitung*, 16 January 1989, p. 4.

100. Devlin, "Communist Movement in 1988," pp. 4–5; "Efforts Toward Reuniting CP," Helsinki, *Hufvudstadbladet*, in Swedish, 22 November, p. 2; *FBIS-WEU*, 5 January 1989, pp. 25–26.

101. Clandestine Our Radio from Magdeburg, GDR, in Turkish, 1 January; *FBIS-WEU*, 3 January 1989, p. 28. See also article by Clyde Haberman in *NYT*, 14 January 1989, p. 2.

AFRICA

Introduction

Africa's Marxist governments spent 1988 largely coping with economic problems that begged for practical solutions, not revolutionary rhetoric. These governments for the most part looked to market responses to resolve production shortages instead of relying on Marxism-Leninism to increase agricultural and industrial output. Political uncertainty or fighting, especially in Angola, Mozambique, and Ethiopia, preoccupied African Marxists. Progress toward peace, and therefore government security, was achieved in southern Africa, where the Marxist regimes in Angola and Mozambique moved toward reconciliation with their powerful neighbor, South Africa.

The most dramatic turn toward peace came in Angola at year's end with the signing of an agreement involving Namibia (southwest Africa) as well as Luanda and Pretoria. Since independence, Angola's ruling Popular Movement for the Liberation of Angola Labor Party (MPLA-PT) has faced serious rebellion in the country's southern region from a rival party, the National Union for the Total Independence of Angola (UNITA). Each party gained support from outside the country. Cuba dispatched combat and support troops, numbering from between 35,000 to 50,000 by 1988, to aid the embattled MPLA-PT regime. South Africa supported its ally, UNITA, with equipment, training, and, on some occasions, military incursions against joint Cuban-MPLA forces that moved south with armor, aircraft, and artillery to dislodge the lightly armed rebels. The civil war thus became a proxy conflict involving outside powers and complicating settlement prospects. A breakthrough came in December when the Angolans, South Africans, and Cubans agreed to a complex 27-month phased withdrawal of Havana's troops in return for a South African grant of independence to Namibia and a suspension of Pretoria's military assistance to UNITA. Jonas Savimbi, UNITA's head, vowed to continue the war

against the Luanda government. Much uncertainty remained for the implementation and consequences of the Brazzaville Protocol at the beginning of 1989.

Angola's efforts to restructure its economy also appeared uncertain. The past year had not witnessed the dramatic reversals of economic policy that occurred in Mozambique. President José Eduardo dos Santos's liberalizing program (Saneamento Economico e Frananciero; SEF) encountered problems in the People's Assembly. Meeting in February, the People's Assembly failed to adopt legislation establishing free enterprise areas of the economy. It did approve SEF-related legislation on foreign investment, state companies, planning, and the monetary system. Resistance to the SEF programs also came from some party cadres who opposed the movement away from central control on ideological grounds or from concerns about the loss of status and privileges.

The People's Republic of Mozambique also seemed to turn a corner in its relations with South Africa. Like Angola, Mozambique has endured a widening rural insurgency ever since a few years after its independence from Portugal in 1975. The thoroughly Marxist Front for the Liberation of Mozambique (FRELIMO) sought to improve relations with Pretoria, which aided the rebel movement Mozambique National Resistance (RENAMO). The 1984 Nkomati Accords, requiring the withholding of support by Maputo and Pretoria from each other's enemies, failed to bring peace to Mozambique, which hoped that without South African assistance the rebels would wither away. Hoping to improve its international standing, South Africa in 1988 provided economic and military aid to FRELIMO. For its part, the Marxist government emphasized the shift from a Marxist, centralized economy to one in which individual incentives were implemented so as to increase production and facilitate market efficiency as announced in the Economic Rehabilitation Program (PRE) in January 1987. Government spokesmen noted higher levels of productivity during the past year. The war also appeared to moderate as FRELIMO's army benefited from Zimbabwe's and Tanzania's military forces employed in important areas. Soviet and

Cuban forces kept up military support to the hard-pressed FRELIMO party.

The People's Democratic Republic of Ethiopia was another Marxist-Leninist state undergoing a continuing insurgency against the central government. Its struggle—the mainly secessionist wars in Eritrea and Tigre—thus differed from the other Marxist regimes in southern Africa. Unlike the rebellions in Angola and Mozambique, the Ethiopian war took a sharp turn for the worse for the ruling Worker's Party of Ethiopia. The liberation fronts representing Eritrea and Tigre defeated the Ethiopian forces, killing or capturing thousands of soldiers. President Mengistu Haile Mariam responded by executing his army generals for failure to halt the rebels, by ordering all foreign relief workers out of Tigre and Eritrea (exposing the two territories to starvation in retaliation), and by negotiating an end of the state of war with Somalia. Ending the state of hostility with Somalia in an accord and restoring diplomatic relations allowed Mengistu to shift some 70,000 troops from the southern border to the rebellious north.

Domestically Mengistu, like other African Marxist leaders, strove to expand output by use of incentive. He increased the price paid to farmers for part of their grain harvest and allowed them to sell the balance. Additionally, he lifted internal controls, permitting a free market in food to develop. The government, however, remained committed to a goal of collectivized agricultural society by the year 2000. The government also stayed wedded to its relocation policy, which has been the subject of much international criticism in recent years. Under this program tens of thousands of northern inhabitants have been forcibly uprooted and transported to the south as a means to deny the rebels a friendly population.

Elsewhere in sub-Saharan Africa, economic problems plagued Marxist regimes. The People's Republic of the Congo, for example, facing critical negotiations with its foreign creditors, finally decided to undertake major changes in economic policy. The ruling Congolese Party of Labor marked for shutdown, sold to foreign interests, or transformed into mixed Congolese-foreign control 76 of the some 100 state-owned companies. The regime also cut public expenditures by freezing employment in public service and limiting salary increases to the rate of inflation.

A major political problem appeared to be at an end with the death of Pierre Anga, whose rebellion in the north began in September 1987. In July, government troops surrounded Anga in a heavily forested area near the town of Owando and shot him to death, apparently removing a dangerous threat to the regime of Denis Sassou-Nguesso.

The People's Republic of Benin, as in previous years, continued to encounter serious economic difficulties. So as to secure some economic assistance from the International Monetary Fund and the World Bank, the Marxist government moved to implement austerity measures, including the dismantling of some state enterprises and the privatizing of others. Salary cuts of civil servants and senior army officers touched off an attempted coup by a Captain Hountondji and some fifteen fellow officers. In the wake of the failed putsch, the government arrested between 100 and 150 officers, some of whom were reportedly tortured. The unsuccessful military takeover occurred at a time when the government of Mathieu Kérékou faced pressure by leftist officers who opposed austerity, privatization, and pragmatism in foreign countries. Kérékou also experienced opposition on his political right from pro-French officers. In foreign affairs, Benin continued strengthening ties with the Soviet Union while gaining aid from the West, especially France. The United States, however, issued "strenuous protests" against Benin's tolerance or encouragement of Libyan terrorist activities emanating from its territories (*NYT*, 20 May).

In Zimbabwe, the ruling Zimbabwe African National Union–Patriotic Front (ZANU-PF) entered into a merger agreement with its major opposition party, the Zimbabwe African Political Union (ZAPU). At an extraordinary ZANU-PF congress held in early April, three thousand delegates approved the merger, establishing a de facto one-party state. Robert Mugabe is president of the reconstituted ZANU-PF, while Joshua Nkomo, his long-standing adversary and former leader of ZAPU, becomes one of the two vice presidents of the reunited party.

The new party affirmed its adherence to the principles of Marxism-Leninism, even though its key leaders endorse mixed economic policies. The government's announcement of amnesty elicited the surrender of more than one hundred ZAPU combatants. Mugabe integrated ZANU and ZAPU political organs from the local to the national levels to accomplish a reconciliation. He also fostered a countrywide coalition between not just the party cadres but also the ethnic communities that form the basis of the two former rival parties. An improving economy matched the political progress, stemming from good rainfall, but was plagued by labor unrest.

Mugabe's economic policies run counter to the continentwide movement toward privatization by acquiring greater control of local large-scale enterprises. The government, furthermore, announced its intention of making larger investments in "strategic" industries such as mining and energy. In foreign relations, Zimbabwe continued to strengthen economic, cultural, and diplomatic ties with communist countries. The Soviet Union and Romania have agreed to increase support. Relations with the United States warmed after Washington lifted a two-year suspension on most forms of aid. Zimbabwe kept a large military force in neighboring Mozambique to guard its rail and road links to the Indian Ocean port of Beira and to reciprocate the support that FRELIMO gave ZANU during its struggle for independence in the late 1970s.

The nonruling Communist Party of Lesotho (CPL) continues its marginal and ambivalent existence. Although illegal but tolerated, the CPL's trade union activities go forward as legal and accepted. In August the leftist law minister, Halaki Sello, was dismissed by the government; earlier he had been described as a former CPL member and pro-Soviet. A week later the government signed an economic and technical agreement with the People's Republic of China.

Across the border in South Africa, another nonruling party encountered no official tolerance. Banned and mainly operating in exile, the South African Communist Party (SACP) remained committed to the goals of its 1984 Constitution, which, among other aims, stated that the SACP seeks to lead the working class to end capitalist exploitation and to establish "a socialist republic based on the common ownership of the means of production" and to the "destruction of the economic and political power of the racist ruling class." This past year party commentators assessed and drew encouragement from the dramatic growth of campaigns against the apartheid policies of the government occurring in the mid-1980s. The SACP advocated paying special attention to blacks in "apolitical" organizations such as youth bodies, women's clubs, sporting organizations, churches, and trade unions. The party also stressed the "activation of broad sectors of whites in various forms of opposition to the system" (*African Communist*, no. 114). Although heartened by the antiapartheid stand of whites and blacks, the party's Central Committee

welcomed the upsurge of trade unions' critiquing capitalism and discussing socialism.

The recent reports of changes in the Soviet Union by Mikhail Gorbachev presented no apparent problems for the SACP's political line. Staunchly supporting Moscow, a SACP review of the Soviet general secretary's book *Perestroika—New Thinking for Our Country and the World* noted that "the experience of the Soviet Union shows that it is excessive centralization and bureaucracy that produce stagnation and even crisis within the socialist system." Later, the same reviewer stated that "*perestroika* will bring socialism back on course" (*African Communist*, no. 113).

Unlike South Africa, Sudan has a recognized communist party that has become a visible part of the parliamentary opposition. In keeping with its political participation (recorded in its winning 5 of the 264 contested seats in the 1985 parliamentary election), the Sudanese Communist Party (SCP) advocates a reformist, not a revolutionary, approach to change. The SCP stated as its goals to reform "the regime of bourgeois parliamentary democracy" and "to make the state administration system accord with the conditions and specifics of the Sudanese society at the present state of its development" (*WMR*, February). This past year saw the SCP refuse to join a "government of reconciliation" formed by all other parties; its refusal was due to its opposition to any formal implementation of Islamic Law in the Sudan. By year's end the reconciliation government was fragmented, presenting opportunities for the SCP because of the government's raising of food prices, thereby creating unrest in major urban areas where the party's limited strength lies. But the mass appeal of traditional religious affiliations or newer Islamic fundamentalism hampers SCP organizing.

Across the continent in Senegal, the several nonruling Marxist parties fared poorly in the country's presidential and National Assembly elections on 28 February. None of these small parties won any seats under Senegal's system of proportional representation. Neither the Independence and Labor Party (PIT), which enjoys Moscow's official recognition as Senegal's pre-eminent communist party, nor the Democratic League/Movement for the Party of Labor (LD/MPT), the other important Senegalese communist party, even fielded presidential candidates. Although both parties have slightly improved their showing since 1983, the LD/MPT came closest to winning a seat in the National Assembly. Some tiny Marxist factions declined to participate in the election, which saw the ruling Socialist Party win victory, albeit at a reduced level, and the return of its leader, President Abdou Diouf, to office. These several Marxist groups continue to exist at the political margin of Senegalese society.

Located off the coast of Africa in the Indian Ocean, Réunion underwent four elections during 1988 in which the Réunion Communist Party (PCR) played an active role. During the French presidential election, the PCR did not support the candidate of the French Communist Party (PCF). Accusing the PCF of Europocentrism, the PCR backed the socialist incumbent, François Mitterand, who won the election. The re-elected president of France called for National Assembly elections in May. Twenty-four candidates ran for Réunion's allotted five seats, and the PCR retained control of two seats. In October the PCR ran candidates in each of the 26 cantons of 44 open for election. By the second round the PCR increased its representation from seven to nine in the General Council. The final voting took place on a referendum on New Caledonia, the last French overseas territory. The people of Réunion supported the government's program.

Thomas H. Henriksen
Hoover Institution

Angola

Population. 8,236,461
Party. Popular Movement for the Liberation of Angola–Labor Party (Movimento Popular de Libertacao de Angola–Partido do Trabalho; MPLA–PT)
Founded. December 1956 (renamed December 1977)
Membership. 45,000 (Radio Luanda, 8 December; *FBIS*, 9 December 1987)
General Secretary. José Eduardo dos Santos
Politburo. 11 members
Central Committee. 90 members
Status. Ruling party
Last Congress. Second, 9–11 December 1985

Last Election. 1980; all 203 candidates MPLA-PT approved
Auxiliary Organizations. National Union of Angolan Workers (UNTA), Organization of Angolan Women (OMA), MPLA Youth (JMPLA), People's Defense Organization (ODP)
Publications. *O Jornal de Angolan* (official newspaper, daily); ANGOP is the Angolan news agency.

For the first time since the civil war began in 1975, Angola witnessed in 1988 the possibility of a genuine peace agreement. The ruling MPLA-PT along with its patrons, Cuba and the Soviet Union, have finally concluded that the thirteen-year civil war cannot be resolved by military force. Ironically, the National Union for the Total Independence of Angola (UNITA) and its backers, the United States and the Republic of South Africa (RSA), have reached an identical assessment. As the year drew to a close, a major peace agreement had been completed, although implementation had not yet begun. Despite this progress, the MPLA-PT consistently refused to negotiate with UNITA toward a government of national reconciliation.

In 1974, Portugal decided to grant independence to its African colonial possessions. In Angola, the three major liberation movements were all recognized by Portugal as the rightful heirs to political power. The three liberation movements—the MPLA, UNITA, and the National Front for the Liberation of Angola (FNLA)—negotiated the Alvor Agreement. Under the terms of the agreement, the liberation groups would form a tripartite government for the fledgling nation. The liberation groups massed in Luanda, the capital, but personality and ethnic conflicts quickly arose. The MPLA, with Soviet and Cuban assistance, drove FNLA and UNITA from the capital and declared the People's Republic of Angola on 11 November 1975. UNITA with South African, Chinese, and U.S. support and FNLA with U.S., Chinese, and Zairian support launched a brief but bitter civil war. The MPLA, along with 12,000 Cuban troops and $200 million worth of Soviet military equipment, quickly decimated FNLA and drove UNITA back into the bush to continue its low-level guerrilla war. Since 1976, UNITA, with military and logistical support from South Africa and the United States, has grown in strength and now has forced the MPLA-PT to reconsider its tactics.

Angola could be a regional power. It has abundant natural resources, including oil, and much agricultural potential. However, the Angolan economy has been shattered by the thirteen-year civil war. The rail system has been destroyed. Traffic on the Benguela Railroad, the crown jewel of Angola's rail lines, has been cut by 90 percent. The Angolan government estimates that damage to the Benguela has cost $2 billion since 1975 (*CSM*, 27 January). Farms have been lost to the encroaching jungle. Once the number two coffee producer in Africa, Angolan production of coffee is down to 5 percent of prewar levels. The country's diamond mines have been closed or effectively sabotaged by UNITA guerrillas. This destruction of the economic infrastructure means that Angola is years from stabilization and growth.

Party Leadership. President dos Santos maintained effective control of the party and state. In February, seven military intelligence officers were expelled from the armed forces and sentenced to long prison terms. The seven were charged with forcing defendants "to belittle and falsely accuse the supreme leaders of the party, the state, and the armed forces." This disrespectful behavior "was aimed at spreading confusion and distrust among the militants and our people and subsequently replacing our party and state leaders in a seemingly legal way" (Radio Luanda, 3 February; *FBIS*, 8 February). Reportedly, the plotters accused President dos Santos himself of corruption.

In May, Kundi Paiama was appointed minister of state security by President dos Santos (ANGOP, 14 May; *FBIS*, 16 May). He retained his other portfolio as minister of state for inspection and control. Two other ministerial changes were also made. On 21 May, Eduardo Paulo Bonga was appointed secretary of state for housing, urban affairs, and water (Radio Luanda, 21 May; *FBIS*, 23 May). On 11 July, President dos Santos relieved Joaquim Guerreio Dias from his position as minister of internal trade and merged the ministry with the Foreign Trade Ministry. The combined ministries were placed under the direction of Domingos das Chagas Simoes Rangel, who was already serving as minister of foreign trade. The merger of the two ministries comes just over a year after a major personnel shake-up. President dos Santos had accused the two ministries in May 1987 of chronic mismanagement and corruption.

Notwithstanding the attempted low-level coup against his leadership, President dos Santos remained securely in power. Having demoted, transferred, or expelled those who disagree with his policies, dos Santos could project a unified party both internally and externally, to friends and foes alike.

Party Affairs. President dos Santos, in his New Year's address to the nation, formally unveiled the economic and financial restructuring program Saneamento Economico e Financiero (SEF). Dos Santos outlined the three major objectives of SEF: to increase productivity, to raise salaries, and to spur consumption. (Radio Luanda, 31 December 1987; *FBIS*, 6 January.)

This liberalizing of the centrally planned economy encountered immediate problems. The People's Assembly meeting in February failed to adopt legislation establishing free enterprise areas of the economy. In his welcoming address to the delegates, the president emphasized that "this session is decisive for the final adoption of the laws and other measures that will allow the materialization of SEF" (Radio Luanda, 24 February; *FBIS*, 25 February). The People's Assembly did approve SEF-related legislation on foreign investment, state companies, budgetary regulations, planning, and the monetary system.

In March, two of the major architects of SEF were dismissed from the body overseeing implementation of the program, the SEF Technical Secretariat. Jose Cerqueira and Mario Nelson were reassigned to other posts. A centerpiece of SEF was to be the establishment of a reasonable exchange rate for Angola's monetary unit, the kwanza. However, instead of a needed devaluation of the kwanza, the government began to print bills in larger denominations. (*NYT*, 12 June.) Implementation of SEF encountered other problems. Some party cadres resisted economic reform because of ideological concerns, bureaucratic inertia, fear of job losses in the overstaffed civil service, or apprehension about the loss of party status and privileges. Still, SEF was supported by President dos Santos and the planning and production minister, Pedro Castro Van Dunem Loy.

Economic growth would be stimulated if Angola could gain admittance to the International Monetary Fund (IMF) and the World Bank. But the two bodies insist that Angola rehabilitate and revitalize its lagging economy. Also, the United States effectively delayed Angola's admission into the two organizations. Yet, as the possibility of peace looms on the horizon, the United States might withdraw its objections. Consequently, it becomes essential that Angola put its economic house in order.

Angola's external debt in 1988 totaled $4 billion. The cost of the civil war absorbed anywhere from 50 to 80 percent of the national budget. There were more than six hundred thousand people who had been displaced by the civil war. Angola had to import foodstuffs to feed the population, despite the potential of its agricultural base (*Africa Report*, May–June). Successful implementation of SEF would prove to critics and supporters alike that the MPLA-PT was prepared to take the necessary steps to provide an economic climate that fostered expansion, constancy, and growth.

Angola was able to reschedule the debt payment with its two largest creditors, the USSR and Brazil. Similar arrangements were concluded with Italy and France. One economic bright spot was in petroleum production. Although international oil prices remained weak, Angola was able to offset this by expanded production and export. In 1987, Angolan oil production reached 350,000 barrels per day (b/d). By June 1988, that figure had climbed to 453,000 b/d. Extensive exploration resulted in Angola's proven oil reserves rising to 2.1 billion barrels (ANGOP, 11 April; *FBIS*, 12 April).

The MPLA-PT Central Committee met 22–24 June to discuss the progress of SEF and the political and military situation confronting Angola in the region. The Central Committee endorsed a plan for paramilitary education for JMPLA members. The committee also reviewed plans for a nationwide exchange of party cards as well as a system of identifying the social background of party members. (*WMR*, June.)

On 24 August, the People's Assembly convened for the fourth ordinary session. President dos Santos briefed the delegates on the peace talks, reiterated his policy of amnesty toward UNITA members, and urged the assembly to implement SEF fully. (Radio Luanda, 24 August; *FBIS*, 25 August.) The MPLA-PT Political Bureau met 8 October to hammer out a unified party position on the regional peace negotiations before President dos Santos visited the People's Republic of China (PRC), the USSR, and Czechoslovakia.

In an effort to introduce democracy into local government, Lucio Lara, the first secretary of the People's Assembly, announced plans to establish municipal assemblies in parts of the nation where security conditions were favorable. Since 1977 local government has been under the direction of state-appointed officials.

The party was reported to have increased its membership to 45,000: 18.1 percent were indus-trial workers; 4 percent agricultural workers; and 18.1 percent were peasants (Radio Luanda, 8 December 1987; *FBIS*, 9 December 1987).

Mass Organizations. In February, the OMA held a congress to discuss ways to involve more women in the activities of the revolution. The congress studied methods to "qualitatively improve and further reinforce the conscious engagement of Angolan women in production, defense, studies, and development in general of Angolan society and humanity" (Radio Luanda, 24 February; *FBIS*, 25 February). From 22 to 31 March, an Angolan delegation was in the USSR to study "some aspects of the CPSU's [Communist Party of the Soviet Union's] ideological work in conditions of restructuring" (*Pravda*, 2 April; *FBIS*, 7 April). From 23 to 31 July, an MPLA-PT delegation was in the Soviet Union "to familiarize itself with the restructuring of the activity of CPSU control and auditing bodies" (*Pravda*, 2 August; *FBIS*, 3 August).

A JMPLA delegation left 20 August for Eastern Europe and the Soviet Union. The youth delegation met with other youth delegations to exchange experiences and information relating to the rule of youth in socialist countries. The JMPLA also assisted in planning for the Eighteenth World Youth and Students' Festival to be held in summer 1989 in the Democratic People's Republic of Korea (DPRK).

International Affairs. On the diplomatic front, Angola established relations with Colombia and Albania. Also in December, Angola officially recognized the Palestinian state declared by the Palestinian National Council. (ANGOP, 30 April; *FBIS*, 2 May; ANGOP, 18 August; *FBIS*, 19 August; *Dakar Pana*, 7 December; *FBIS*, 8 December.)

Cooperation agreements with a number of communist nations were signed during the year. The USSR and Angola signed another fishing protocol that calls for "strengthening cooperation in fishing . . . training of Angolan cadres, and the establishment of exchange between the fishermen associations of the two countries" (Radio Luanda, 16 February; *FBIS*, 17 February). In August, the two sides met in Moscow to discuss previous years' cooperation between fishermen of the two countries. It was noted that the joint Soviet-Angolan fishing expedition has been fishing off the Angolan coast "for a number of years" (TASS, 22 August; *FBIS*, 24 August). Fishing delegations of the two nations met again in November (*Dakar Pana*, 17 November; *FBIS*, 18 November). Bulgaria signed a fisheries agreement in August calling for cooperating "in the field of fisheries and its commercialization" (ANGOP, 26 August; *FBIS*, 2 September). An agreement was signed with Czechoslovakia under which Czechoslovakia will train Angolans in the fields of "civil construction, footwear, confection, and furniture" (Radio Luanda, 28 April; *FBIS*, 29 April). In 1986, trade between the two nations was valued at $5.5 million (Radio Luanda, 30 October; *FBIS*, 31 October). In May, Cuba signed a foreign trade agreement with Angola. Cuba will export "sugar, drugs, books, toys, while Angola will export timber" (Radio Luanda, 11 May; *FBIS*, 12 May). Cuba and Angola already cooperate in the fields of "science and technology, in services . . . agriculture, trade, industry, petroleum, construction, health, education, and culture" (Radio Luanda, 5 July; *FBIS*, 6 July).

Relations with the PRC also continued to prosper. A Chinese delegation was in Luanda in January. In August, Angolan secretary of state for culture Boaventura Cardoso visited Beijing to finalize several cooperative agreements that President dos Santos signed 22 October during his visit to the PRC. The agreements call for bilateral cooperation in "economics, technology and trade . . . culture, education, science, sanitation, sports, publication, and the press" (Beijing, Xinhua, 22 October; *FBIS*, 24 October).

Western nations, too, signed trade, technical, or cooperative agreements with Angola. Sweden signed a fisheries agreement in June. (Radio Luanda, 15 June; *FBIS*, 16 June.) Ironically, considering U.S. aid to UNITA, the United States increased its exports to Angola in 1987 to $94.6 million, while increasing imports from Angola to $1.4 billion (mostly oil). Italy, Brazil, Portugal, and Britain all had major business transactions with Angola.

But the bulk of Angola's foreign affairs in 1988 concentrated on the ongoing regional peace negotiations conducted by Cuba, the RSA, the United States, and Angola. The negotiators were able to sign an agreement in December, after eight months of intensive discussions. A dozen or so bargaining sessions were held in London, Cairo, New York (three), Cape Verde, Brazzaville (five), and Geneva (two). While the Angolan delegation was discussing regional topics, President dos Santos was involved either in shoring up relations with his communist allies, the Soviet Union and Cuba, or in combating the increasing calls by his fellow African leaders for a government of national reconciliation with UNITA.

The peace initiative took new life in March after the South African–UNITA forces were unable to capture Cuíto Cuanavale in southeastern Angola. South Africa, Cuba, and the Soviet Union realized that the civil war could not be won on the battlefield.

At the same time, UNITA and the MPLA-PT took the first tentative steps toward face-to-face talks. In January, representatives of the two movements first met to discuss possible avenues of reconciliation (KUP, *FBIS*, 10 February). Publicly, MPLA-PT officials derided such pronouncements. Angola's ambassador to Portugal said such discussions would be "the highest treason in the whole history of the Angolan people's resistance" (Radio Luanda, *FBIS*, 20 April). Yet rumors continued to swirl throughout the year of contacts between UNITA and MPLA-PT representatives.

President dos Santos met with Jorge Risquet, Cuba's foreign affairs minister, in March to discuss the conduct of the war and peace negotiations (Radio Luanda, 19 March; *FBIS*, 21 March). Less than two weeks later, dos Santos met with Soviet deputy foreign minister Anatolii Adamishin, who reportedly urged the president to negotiate with UNITA. Publicly, Adamishin reiterated Moscow's "firm solidarity with the just cause of the Angolan people" (Radio Moscow, 1 April; *FBIS*, 4 April). Again, dos Santos met with Cuba's Risquet on 30 April to discuss "the prevailing situation in Southern Africa" (ANGOP, 2 May; *FBIS*, 3 May).

In late May, Angola's defense minister, General Pedro Maria Tonha Pedale, traveled to Cuba to discuss the growing number of insurgent activities in northern Angola (Radio Luanda, 2 May; *FBIS*, 23 May).

The MPLA-PT tried a new tactic to counter Jonas Savimbi's annual pilgrimage to the West. During June and July, Savimbi traveled to the United States where he met with President Reagan and then Vice President George Bush. The MPLA-PT, however, hired its own public relations firm, Fenton Communications, in Washington to present Angola's view of the conflict. Savimbi was met with many organized protests around the United States. Additionally, the MPLA-PT sent the minister of planning and production, Pedro Castro Van Dunem Loy, to Washington the week before Savimbi's visit where his delegation acted as a "truth squad" countering Savimbi's anticipated movements. The MPLA-PT delegation met with Secretary of State George Shultz and National Security adviser Lieutenant General Colin L. Powell (*NYT*, 23, 28 June; *WP*, 1 July; Radio Luanda, *FBIS*, 7 July).

As the peace talks grew more intense, Cuba and the Soviet Union had to reaffirm mutual support not only to one another but to Angola. Cuba's Risquet had to deny reports of rifts between the Cuban and Angolan military concerning Cuba's actions in southern Angola, while the Soviet Union had to strongly urge the Cubans to negotiate in good faith. (*The Economist*, 2 July; Radio Lisbon, 4 July; *FBIS*, 8 July.) For its part, UNITA announced that ten thousand Cuban soldiers had accepted Angolan citizenship and as such would not be withdrawn if a peace agreement came to fruition (Voice of the Resistance of the Black Cockerel, 20 August; *FBIS*, 23 August). Later in November, Savimbi announced that Cuba and UNITA had reached a loose agreement not to attack one another. According to Savimbi, the Cubans had not told the MPLA-PT about the pact concluded in August (*Sunday Star*, 20 November; *FBIS*, 21 November).

President dos Santos displayed his hesitation on the peace process in August when he was quoted as saying he would prefer Michael Dukakis to win the U.S. presidential race against George Bush. The MPLA-PT leader believed that if the Democrats won the election "there would be a readjustment in U.S. policy, particularly concerning southern Africa" (Radio Luanda, 9 August; *FBIS*, 10 August).

Other signs of dos Santos's doubts about the reliability of Cuba and the Soviet Union and the sincerity of South Africa can be found during the year. In April, Juliao Mateus Paulo Dino Matross visited Finland seeking "more aid from the socialist countries in order to fight off South African aggression in the southern part of our country" (Helsinki International Service, 9 April; *FBIS*, 12 April). One month later, in May, Angolan defense minister General Pedro Maria Tonha Pedale visited Brazil on an arms shopping mission (*Insight*, 23 May). Dos Santos himself broached the subject of arms sales with China during his visit there in October (Radio Gaborone, 22 October; *FBIS*, 24 October).

On 8 August, Angola, Cuba, and South Africa agreed to an immediate cease-fire in Angola. South Africa vowed to remove its forces from Angolan soil by 1 September. (*NYT*, 9 August.) Three days later, Adamishin publicly urged the MPLA-PT to negotiate with UNITA. "In the absence of those negotiations between the two Angolan parties, the quadripartite negotiations in Geneva will be placed in jeopardy," he said (*WP*, 12 August). Later in the month, in a speech to the People's Assembly, dos Santos rejected a dialogue with UNITA, instead focusing on the need to end the conflict via the military. "Thus, the neutralization of the puppet gang will require a final and additional sacrifice from our people and our armed forces. By combining political and military action, our objectives may meet with success." (Radio Luanda, 24 August; *FBIS*, 25 August.) Two weeks later, the MPLA-PT launched a nationwide military conscription campaign (Radio Luanda, 13 September; *FBIS*, 21 September). On 26 August, acting Organization of African Unity (OAU) president Moussa Traore, president of Mali, arrived in Luanda, reportedly to urge on behalf of the OAU that dos Santos negotiate with UNITA. At a welcoming banquet dos Santos said, "Angola does not accept pressures, from wherever they may come, which aim at the formation of a coalition government." President Traore departed the next morning. (*NYT*, 9 September.) By 30 August South Africa had completed its troop withdrawal from Angola (*NYT*, 31 August).

On 17 October, dos Santos began a tour of Tanzania, the DPRK, the PRC, the USSR, Czechoslovakia, and Morocco. By visiting China first, and reportedly seeking weapons, dos Santos was demonstrating to Moscow that Angola would not be an unintentional victim of the U.S.-USSR cooperation on regional conflicts. According to *Pravda*, dos Santos and Mikhail Gorbachev had "a substantial exchange of views on the development of the situation in southern Africa and on bilateral Soviet-Angolan relations" (*Pravda*, 29 October; *FBIS*, 31 October). In Morocco, dos Santos tried to persuade King Hassan II to grant political asylum to Savimbi, thus paving the way for negotiations with a leaderless UNITA (*WP*, 6 December).

On 13 December the tortuous negotiation process ended with an agreement that paves the way for Namibian independence and the phased withdrawal of Cuban troops from Angola. The Brazzaville Protocol stipulates that (1) 3,000 Cubans withdraw from Angola by 1 April 1989, (2) by August 1989 all Cuban troops redeploy to a line north of the 15th parallel, that is, through Cuíto Cunavale, 200 miles north of the Angola-Namibia border, (3) by November 1989, 25,000 troops will have departed from Angola; the rest will be stationed north of the 13th parallel, that is, the Benguela Railroad, 350 miles north of Namibia, (4) 33,000 Cubans must be gone by April 1990 with 5,000 more leaving before November 1990, and (5) the remaining 12,000 Cubans must depart by July 1991 (*NYT*, 14 December). Apparently, South Africa will end its aid to UNITA, while Angola will cease assistance to the South

West Africa People's Organization and the African National Congress.

Although implementation had not been undertaken by either side, the possibility of peace, and all that entails, was now a real possibility. President dos Santos faced myriad questions. Could the MPLA-PT survive without its Cuban allies? Could the Popular Armed Forces for the Liberation of Angola militarily defeat UNITA? Could dos Santos trust the South Africans to honor the agreement (keeping in mind the Nkomati Accords)? Could dos Santos effectively negotiate with a Savimbi-led UNITA?

During the year dos Santos explored opportunities to loosen his dependency on the Soviet Union and Cuba, but the fact remains that in 1988 the Soviet Union supplied the MPLA-PT with $1.5 billion worth of weapons (*WP*, 14 December). Additionally, 16–19 December, dos Santos began an official visit to Cuba, possibly to assess the strength of Cuban commitment to the MPLA-PT (Radio Maputo, *FBIS*, 14 December).

As 1988 drew to an end, President dos Santos faced a future of uncertainty. His course of action in 1989 may well decide the fate of Angola for years to come.

W. Martin James III
Henderson State University

Benin

Population. 4,497,150
Party. Revolutionary Party of the People of Benin (Parti Révolutionnaire du Peuple du Bénin; PRPB)
Founded. 1975
Membership. Less than 2,000
Chairman. Mathieu Kérékou (also president of the republic)
Politburo. 11 members, elected November 1985: Kérékou; Martin Dohou Azonhiho; Joseph Deguela; Gado Giriguissou; Roger Imorou Garba; Justin Guidehou; Sanni Mama Gomina; Romain Vilon Guezo; Vincent Guezodje; Idi Abdoulaye Mallam; Simon Ifede Ogouma
Central Committee. 45 members

Status. Sole and ruling party
Last Congress. Second (ordinary), November 1985
Last Election. 1984, all 196 National Assembly members on PRPB list, all elected
Auxiliary Organizations. Organization of the Revolutionary Youth of Benin (OJRB); Organization of the Revolutionary Women of Benin (OFRB); National Federation of Workers' Unions of Benin (UNSTB); Committees for the Defense of the Revolution (CDR)
Publications. *Handoria* (PRPB publication); *Ehuzu* (government-controlled daily); *Bénin-Magazine* (monthly), published by the National Press, Publishing and Printing office (government enterprise)

Party and Domestic Affairs. As in previous years, the main domestic problem was the sore state of the economy. In addition, the year witnessed clear proofs of extensive corruption at the highest levels of the party and government. Thus, according to French journalist Paul Raymond Michaud, the Caisse Nationale de Crédit Agricole, one of Benin's largest banks, was heading toward bankruptcy as a result of large loans to the president's friends, usually without collateral, some up to half a million dollars (*FBIS*, 22 January). At the same time, salary increases for the military resulted in new recruits receiving $100 a month, the equivalent of a doctor's income and twice that of the average bureaucrat; some 10 percent of the national budget expenditures go for military salaries (ibid.) in a practically bankrupt country whose economy is close to collapse.

At the same time, in March the Kérékou regime accepted an agreement with the International Monetary Fund (IMF) and the World Bank involving economic restructuring and, as the PRPB Central Committee meeting of 19 March put it, a large dose of "courage and self denial" (*FBIS*, 21 March). In April, President Kérékou specified some of the measures of economic readjustment to be taken, including "the dismantling of a number of lame ducks—sorry, I mean public enterprises and parastatals—[and] the privatization of some of them.... This shows the authorities' desire to be realistic in pursuing the ongoing negotiations with the IMF and to conduct a rigorous policy of austerity." (Ibid., 7 April.) On 29 July, as another indication of a shift in economic policies, Barnabé Bidouzo, the economics minister, was removed in an otherwise minor cabinet reshuffle (*FBIS-Sub-Saharan Africa* [*SSA*], 1 August).

The austerity measures forced on the regime by economic realities and the IMF soon translated into political threats, particularly as a result of Kérékou's decision to cut the salaries of civil servants (who were not paid between January and April) and senior army officers, while maintaining those of soldiers and noncommissioned officers at previous levels. The immediate and spectacular result was an attempted coup led by a Captain Hountondji, a member of the Presidential Guard, joined by fifteen other officers, on 26 March (ibid., 14 April). Although the attempted putsch was promptly put down, between 100 and 150 officers were arrested, a high proportion of the officer corps, including such highly placed figures as Lieutenant Colonel Francois Kouyami, the head of public security, and Lieutenant Colonel Badjogoudme, both close friends of Kérékou since his own 1972 coup (*FBIS-SSA*, 15 April). By June Amnesty International was accusing the Benin government of torturing alleged coup participants, further damaging the regime's international image (ibid., 27 June). In fact, in July Lieutenant Colonel Hilaire Badjogoudme was found dead in detention. Nevertheless, the same month the government seemed prepared to stage a major political trial in which the putschists were to be accused of collusion with the minuscule, externally based Parti Comuniste Dahomeén, wild rumors in Cotonou had it that the plotters were in fact followers of the late Michel Aikpé, a major leader of the 1972 coup, later killed by Kérékou. The attempted coup came at a time when the president was under the conflicting pressures of leftist officers—led by the pro-Libyan Martin Dohou Azonhiho—who were opposed to austerity, privatization, and pragmatism in foreign policy and pro-French military elements to his "right" (*FBIS-SSA*, 27 June).

Foreign Affairs. Following previous patterns, Benin continued to strengthen ties with both China and the Soviet bloc at ideological as well as economic levels while remaining financially and foreign aid-dependent on the West in general and France in particular. At the same time, economic and political relations with Libya remained close.

Relations with China were strengthened by the March visit to Cotonou of a Chinese Communist Party (CCP) delegation led by Central Committee member Yi Dushu, a professor at the CCP Central School, who lectured on both party building and control and the Chinese economic reforms (*FBIS-SSA*, 14 March). The same Chinese delegation, also including Central Committee member Liang Maocheng, offered advice on building "an independent national economy" (ibid., 16 March).

Relations with Cuba remained close, although the two countries' foreign ministers, Isidoro Malmierca and Guy Landry Hazoume, did admit that certain "deficiencies" existed in bilateral ties during their Havana meeting of 10 March (*FBIS-SSA*, 17 March). Relations with the USSR also continued to be close, as demonstrated by the March trip to Moscow of a PRPB delegation led by Politburo member J. Delga, which "familiarized themselves with the CPSU's social policy under the conditions of restructuring" (*FBIS-Soviet Union*, 24 March). Damaging to the regime were consistent reports that ever since 1984 Benin has allowed the Soviets to dump radioactive waste in the country in exchange for air transport planes (*FBIS-SSA*, 27 April; *Insight*, 30 May).

After a few years of relative warming, U.S.-Benin relations once again turned cold following State Department "strenuous protests" against Benin's tolerance or encouragement of Libyan terrorist activities from its territory (*NYT*, 20 May). Although the Cotonou government denied the accusations, on 9 July Libyan ambassador Mustaffa Aboucetta left the country after ten years in office and without any of the normal farewell ceremonies (*FBIS-SSA*, 11 July).

Michael S. Radu
Foreign Policy Research Institute, Philadelphia

Congo

Population. 2,153,685
Party. Congolese Party of Labor (Parti Congolais du Travail: PCT)
Founded. 1969
Membership. 8,679
Chairman. Denis Sassou-Nguesso
Politburo. 10 Members
Central Committee. 60 members
Status. Sole official party

Last Congress. Third, Brazzaville, July 1984
Last Election. 1984, all 153 PCT candidates approved; the party received 95 percent of the total vote.
Auxiliary Organizations. Congolese Trade Union Confederation (CSC), Revolutionary Union of Congolese Women (URFC), Union of Congolese Socialist Youth (UJSC)
Publications. *Mweti* (daily, under government control); *Etumba* (weekly, organ of the PCT Central Committee); *Elikia* (party quarterly)

Domestic Affairs. The country faced two major domestic problems in 1987—the Anga rebellion in the north and the economic crisis. The government has solved the former and has moved decisively on the latter.

On 4 July former Captain Pierre Anga and two of his relatives were surrounded and shot to death by government troops in a heavily forested area near the northern town of Owando (*FBIS-Sub-Saharan Africa* [SSA], 7 July). The death of Anga ended one of the most dangerous threats to the regime ten months after the rebellion had started in September 1987 (see *YICA*, 1988).

Although there were calls for a purge of "right wingers," none occurred. On the contrary, the month of July witnessed a cabinet reshuffle that brought back into the government, as minister of public works, former Captain Florent Tsiba. Tsiba, a leader of the 1979 palace coup that brought Sassou-Nguesso to power, had been purged in 1984. It seems, however, that the main object of the reshuffle was the replacement of Environment Minister Christophe Mbouramoue. In May he was the victim of a failed deal with a Dutch waste disposal company that was to provide for the disposal of one million metric tons of European chemical waste in the Congo, in exchange for $80 million (*FBIS-SSA*, 9 June). Following negative publicity and protests by West European environmental groups, the Congolese government denied the existence of a deal, despite evidence to the contrary (ibid., 2 June). Ex-Minister Mbouramoue was not the only victim of the scandal, however. Abel Michel Tchicou, the director for external trade, and Dieudonné Antoine Ganga, the influential adviser to the prime minister, as well as two other prominent civil servants were also fired and put under arrest "for privately dishonoring the country" (*FBIS-SSA*, 4 August).

The waste disposal imbroglio underscored the critical situation of the economy. After delays and protracted negotiations with its foreign creditors, the regime finally decided to undertake major changes in its economic policy. Seventy-six of the approximately one hundred state-owned companies, almost all of which were big money losers, were marked for shutdown, sold to foreign interests, or transformed into mixed Congolese-foreign enterprises. At the same time the Congo's extremely liberal foreign investment code was expected to help the country reach a 10.7 percent economic growth rate in 1988 (*FBIS-SSA*, 9 June). Some painful and politically dangerous readjustments had to be made as well: drastic cuts in public expenditures, a freeze in employment in the public service, the limitation of salary increases to the rate of inflation, and a census of public employees intended to weed out "ghost" workers (ibid., 30 June). In September the national budget expenditures were cut by 31 percent, from the planned 252 billion francs to 173 billion (*FBIS-SSA*, 8 September).

Such measures, while made possible by the end of Anga and the consequent boost in the regime's confidence, are dangerous in the long run because they will certainly result in higher unemployment of university and high school graduates, historically the most politically radical, volatile, and dangerous sector of Congolese society.

In ideological terms, the newly found confidence of the regime was clearly expressed by President Sassou-Nguesso in an interview with *Jeune Afrique* in August. He claimed that the country enjoys "a certain measure of political stability" after 25 years of revolution (*Jeune Afrique*, 14–17 August). For him, Marxist-Leninist ideology "is a universal science and as such is perfectly adaptable to all societies. It allows each people to apply it to their socioeconomic realities" (ibid.). As for Mikhail Gorbachev's *perestroika*, "it is a good thing. I find his [Gorbachev's] steps at the same time just, sound, and perfectly in conformity with the scientific spirit of Marxism-Leninism. Thus to me, Gorbachev is not heretical. On the contrary, he is a great revolutionary" (ibid.). Along similar lines, he admitted "that we have made a number of errors by making the state do everything. Can you image [*sic*] . . . that we almost set up a yogurt company? . . . We have understood that the state must not seek to grab everything" (ibid.).

Foreign Affairs. It would be no exaggeration to say that 1988 was the Congo's diplomatic moment in the sun. By hosting three rounds of the important negotiations between Cuba, Angola, and South Africa regarding the future of Namibia and the withdrawal of Cuban troops from Angola—negotiations mediated by the United States and observed by the Soviet Union—Brazzaville has briefly become the focus of high-level diplomacy in Africa. Although the personal role of Sassou-Nguesso was limited and official rhetoric has continued to be strongly anti-South African, it is clear that the political orientation of the country has been modified. Not only did Sassou-Nguesso receive and shake hands with the South African foreign and defense ministers (respectively, Roelof Botha and Magnus Malan), it appears that he has also put some pressure on Luanda to reach some kind of agreement with Jonas Savimbi's National Union for the Total Independence of Angola insurgents. This has occurred despite the April meeting (the fourth) in Brazzaville between the party control commissions of Angola, Mozambique, and the Congo, which focused on stricter central supervision of cadres and party building. (*FBIS-SSA*, 8 April.)

While maintaining its political, ideological, and cultural ties with the Soviet bloc, the Congo has intensified its economic relations with the West. This movement, more than before, has been paralleled by a visible change of political attitudes in Brazzaville. Some key examples of the Congo's recent contacts with both the Soviet bloc and the West help illustrate this new duality.

In February, a Congolese trade union delegation led by PCT Politburo member and CSC general secretary Jean-Michel Boukamba Yangouma visited Bulgaria in what has become a regular exchange of visits (*FBIS-Eastern Europe*, 23 February). That same month, a Soviet antisubmarine warfare ship visited Pointe Noire, and on 15 March a Soviet-Congolese agreement on radio and TV cooperation was signed by Brazzaville, with a provision for the training of Congolese journalists in the Soviet Union (*FBIS-SSA*, 16 March). In September, a Congolese military delegation led by the chief of the National People's Army's Main Political Directorate, Lieutenant Colonel N. Dabira, visited the Soviet Union and was received by Defense Minister Yazov and Dabira's Soviet counterpart, army General A. D. Lizichev, chief of the Soviet Army and Navy Political Directorate (*FBIS-Soviet Union*, 19 September).

During the same time relations with the West continued to improve, particularly in the economic sphere. On 15 July, President Sassou-Nguesso, Prime Minister Poungui, and Foreign Minister Ndinga-Oba received in Brazzaville the British minister of state at the Foreign and Commonwealth Office, Lynda Chalker. After amiably agreeing to disagree on the issue of sanctions against South Africa, the two sides reached agreements on a number of issues regarding British assistance to the Congo. Those included technical assistance, such as the sending of British teachers and technicians, and financial aid for the paving of the Brazzaville-Mayama Road. (Ibid., 20 July.)

As has been the case since the Congo became independent in 1960, France has offered the most economic assistance. During his 25–26 November visit to Brazzaville, French minister of cooperation and development Jacques Pelletier promised an additional adjustment loan of 300 million francs (in addition to the 750 million francs in aid given this year), or more than one-half of the Congo's total foreign assistance (*Le Monde*, 29 November). The precondition, however, was that the Congo sign yet another agreement with the International Monetary Fund. In addition to direct aid and soft loans, France also helps the Congo in fighting AIDS—a serious problem because some 7 percent of the population tested positive. It also provides more than three hundred coopérants, of whom two-thirds are teachers or railroad workers, and offers agricultural assistance. France has fifteen military advisers in the Congo and trains 150 Congolese military personnel in France every year (ibid.).

Michael Radu
Foreign Policy Research Institute, Philadelphia

Ethiopia

Population. 48,264,570
Party. Workers' Party of Ethiopia (WPE)
Founded. September 1984
Membership. 50,000
General Secretary. Mengistu Haile Mariam (47, career soldier)
Politburo. 11 full members: Mengistu Haile Mariam, Fikre-Selassie Wogderess, Fisseha Desta, Tesfaye Gebre Kidan, Berhanu Bayih, Legesse Asfaw, Addis Tedlay, Hailu Yimenu, Amanuel Amde Michael, Alenu Abebe, Shimelis Mazengia; 6 alternate members

Secretariat. 8 members: Fisseha Desta, Legesse Asfaw, Shimelis Mazengia, Fasika Sidelil, Shewandagn Belete, Wubeset Desie, Ashagre Yigletu, Emibel Ayele

Central Committee. 136 full members, 64 alternate members

Status. Ruling party

Last Congress. First, 6–10 September 1984, in Addis Ababa; eighth regular session of WPE Central Committee, 31 March

Last Election. June 1987, to Parliament (National Shengo): 85 percent (13.4 million) elected 835 deputies; all are WPE members.

Auxiliary Organizations. All-Ethiopian Peasants' Association; Kebelles; All-Ethiopia Trade Union; Revolutionary Ethiopia's Women's Association; Revolutionary Ethiopia's Youth Association

Publications. *Serto ader*, *Meskerem*, *Yekatit*, *Addis zemen*, *Ethiopian Herald*, *Negarit gazeta*. All are WPE organs, and all articles must be approved by WPE Censorship Committee.

In 1988 Ethiopia was dealt an enormous military setback in its 26-year war with Eritrean and Tigrean secessionists. President Mengistu Haile Mariam responded by halting famine relief to northern civilians and by negotiating an end to the state of war with Somalia.

Civil War. The Eritrean People's Liberation Front (EPLF) killed four thousand Ethiopian soldiers, captured fourteen thousand others, and took control of millions of dollars in military equipment in a spectacular military offensive in the northern town of Afabet between 17 and 19 March. Three Soviet advisers were captured, and one was killed. Near Asmara, Eritrea's capital, Afabet was the main government military garrison in northern Eritrea. Taking advantage of the havoc created among government troops, the Tigre People's Liberation Front (TPLF) captured the towns of Axum, Korem, Maychew, Kisad, and Alage and killed some five hundred Ethiopian troops. President Mengistu declared that government forces were facing "grim battles" against insurgents and called on Ethiopians to "unite" against the rebels (*NYT*, 1 April). Clearly, the offensive by the rebels came as a shock to the Ethiopian government and, with its army reeling from defeat, put it on the defensive. A number of army generals were executed by the government as a result of the EPLF's success. Certainly, the war's initiative has now passed to the rebels, who control 90 percent of both regions.

Responding to Ethiopia's military devastation, Mengistu ordered all foreign relief workers out of Tigre and Eritrea on 7 April. He also ordered a 10 percent war tax imposed on all Ethiopians to "safeguard the unity of the motherland" (*Insight*, 20 June). In addition the air force was ordered to make bombing runs on northern civilian targets.

International Activities. Confronting a disastrous situation, Mengistu moved toward an improvement of relations with states that Ethiopia has been in confrontation with.

On 4 April, eleven years after Somalia invaded Ethiopia's Ogaden region, both countries agreed to resume diplomatic relations. In a signed accord they also agreed to an exchange of prisoners of war, ending support to all liberation movements, the withdrawal of military forces ten miles from each side of the border, the creation of a demilitarized zone around the border areas, and minor frontier adjustments. The peace agreement allowed Ethiopia to shift its 70,000 troops from the border area to the rebellious north.

At the same time Ethiopia and the Sudan held a series of talks aimed at improving their strained relations. The Sudan has given support to Ethiopia's northern rebels while Ethiopia has supported southern rebels opposed to the Sudanese government. According to Mengistu "we have made efforts . . . in the historical brotherly relations between Ethiopia and the Sudan" (*Addis Ababa Domestic Service*, 4 July). In June Mengistu argued for improving ties with the United States but was flatly rejected.

During the year Mengistu traveled to the USSR, the People's Republic of China, and North Korea and signed agreements toward developing Ethiopia's economy with Cuba, the USSR, the German Democratic Republic, Romania, Hungary, Yugoslavia, and Iran. In sympathy with North Korea, Ethiopia boycotted the summer Olympics in South Korea. In October Ethiopia was elected to the U.N. Security Council.

Political Activities. Seven members of the family of the former Emperor Haile Selassie were released from prison after fourteen years. Included were the late emperor's daughter, Princess Tenegne Work, four of his granddaughters, a daughter-in-law, and the widow of a former prince. In a newly released book, *Red Tears*, the former director of Ethiopia's Relief and Rehabilitation Commission maintained that in 1975 Mengistu had former Emperor Haile Selassie killed by suffocation. The author, Dawit Wolde Giorgis, claimed that Mengistu feared that the emperor could be used by his opponents to rally opposition to the new government. Dawit fled Ethiopia in 1985.

Famine. Although seven million people remain at risk from starvation, fears of a new famine have eased due to the onset of heavy rains in July and August. To aid peasant farmers, Ethiopia increased the price for part of their grain harvest and allowed them to sell the balance. It also lifted internal controls on the movement of food inside the country, allowing a limited free market to develop. Ethiopia still retained its commitment to a collectivized agricultural society by the year 2000 (*CSM*, 14 January). The government continued its relocation of families from the north to the southwest. To date, 800,000 have been resettled; 400,000 more peasants are to be moved in 1989. With the resettlement scheme calling for the movement of 1.2 million, this would conclude the program. In January the EPLF attacked an Ethiopian relief column and destroyed 176 tons of relief food being sent to drought victims in the north.

Party Activities. The WPE was convulsed by the rout of Ethiopian forces in Eritrea and spent much of its time organizing civilians to support government actions there. The ninth regular plenum of the Central Committee, which met in early November, was concerned with economic improvements. To this end, it issued resolutions, the most notable of which were to exhort the government to support agricultural development:

> Hence, in order to promote farmers to this level of awareness and establish strong cooperatives, the government should give adequate support to training the required number of organizers, accountants, auditors, and members of cooperatives, and it should render the required bank loan services to enable them to acquire improved production means and tools to accelerate the growth of producers' cooperatives and transform the small commodities sector to a stage of extensive proliferation. (*Addis Ababa Domestic Service*, 11 November; *FBIS-Africa*, 25 November.)

> In order to expand and strengthen producers' cooperative associations—the foundations for the acceleration of the national economy in development and socialist construction—party members will be sent in turn to rural areas for limited periods to live with the farmers and serve as exemplary supporters of the activities under way to change the farmers' lives.

The main aim of organizing cooperative associations is to accelerate the country's economic development by transforming the small commodity sector into a stage of extensive production. (*Addis Ababa Domestic Service*, 11 November; *FBIS-Africa*, 23 November.)

Peter Schwab
State University of New York at Purchase

Lesotho

Population. 1,666,012
Party. Communist Party of Lesotho (CPL)
Founded. 1962
Membership. No data
Chairman. R. Mataji
Secretariat. Jacob M. Kena (general secretary), John Motloheloa, Khotso Molekane
Status. Illegal (but tolerated)
Last Congress. Seventh, early 1987
Last Election. September 1985
Auxiliary Organizations. Mine Workers' Union, Writers' Association of Lesotho, Union of Lesotho Journalists
Publication. *Mazhammokho* (Communist)

Although political party activity is presently suspended in the country, the CPL is tolerated, as it is not looked on as a major opposition movement. It in turn tends to regard the Lesotho ruling establishment as a spectrum running from the relatively "progressive," (anti–South African) King Moshoeshoe II to the "reactionary" (pro–South African) right-wing faction of the Military Council. The CPL's illegal party activities, assuming that it has followed through on its intention of organizing cells throughout the country (see *YICA*, 1988), are balanced by its legal trade union ones (e.g., CPL general secretary Jacob M. Kena holds the same position in the legal Mine Workers' Union) (see *YICA*, 1988).

In a 28 January interview with Maseru's *Weekly Mail*, Kena stated that though he had originally supported the 1986 military takeover, he was now critical of the government because of its failure to restore democratic liberties or to alleviate the bad economic situation. He attributed the latter in part to the military's "loyalty to South African business." On the positive side, Kena thought that the (failed) 1987 miners' strike was useful because of the large number of people it mobilized against the South African government and was encouraged by the growing cooperation between Lesotho trade unions and the Congress of South African Trade Unions.

The "success" of the 1987 strike was reiterated by CPL spokesman Jeremiah Mosotho (see *YICA*, 1988) in the August issue of *WMR* (London). The point stressed here again, but in a more detailed manner, was that "more than 340,000 black mine-workers" (including "around 120,000 Basotho") "in 52 South African gold mines and colleries" successfully cooperated to conduct a strike that lasted for three weeks. The article exaggerated the political and economic consequences of the action on South Africa as a whole and, most important, failed to mention that not a single demand of the strikers had been met.

The CPL's *WMR* representative in Prague, Sam Moeti, was noted as a participant in a seminar on international economic security held by that magazine some time prior to February and in the conference held on the work of the magazine in April (London, *WMR*, Prague, *Rudé právo*, 13 April). It is assumed that Moeti is also involved in the Union of Lesotho Journalists, admitted as an affiliate of the Soviet-line and Prague-based International Organization of Journalists (IOJ) in April (Prague, *IOJ Newsletter* no. 9, May). Note that the Writers' Association of Lesotho apparently had already been admitted to the IOJ by 1986 (Sofia, *X Congreso de la UIP*, 1986, p. 110).

August saw the dismissal of leftist Law Minister Halaki Sello, earlier characterized as a former CPL member with pro-Soviet and pro-African National Congress (ANC) leanings (see *YICA*, 1988). The dismissal was accompanied by rumors of pro-ANC sympathies on the part of Sello, a linkage denied by the government (Radio Umtata, 2 August; Johannesburg, SAPA, *FBIS*, 4 August). Lesotho signed an economic and technical aid agreement with China a week later.

Wallace Spaulding
McLean, Virginia

Mozambique

Population. 14,947,554
Party. Front for the Liberation of Mozambique (Frente de Libertação de Moçambique; FRELIMO)
Founded. 1962
Membership. 130,000 (*WMR*, April 1987)
President. Joaquim Alberto Chissano
Politburo. 10 members: Joaquim Alberto Chissano, Marcelino dos Santos, Alberto Chipande, Armando Emilio Guebuza, Jorge Rebelo, Mariano de Aráujo Matsinhe, Sebastião Marcos Mabote, Jacinto Soares Veloso, Mário de Graça Machungo, José Óscar Monteiro
Secretariat. Julio Zamith Carriho, Pascoal Mocumbi, Aduardo Aaro, José Luís Cabaço
Central Committee. Approximately 130 members
Status. Ruling party
Last Congress. Fourth, 26–29 April 1983, in Maputo (600 delegates)
Last Election. 1986
Auxiliary Organizations. Organization of Mozambican Women (Organização da Mulher Moçambicana; OMM); Mozambique Youth Organization (OJM); Mozambique Workers' Organization (OTM)
Publications. *Notícias* (daily); *O Tempo* (weekly); *Diário de Moçambique* (daily); *Domingo* (Sunday paper); *Voz de Revolução* (Central Committee organ); *Economia* (Chamber of Commerce magazine)

The People's Republic of Mozambique experienced an improving year in 1988 compared with the last several years. Although still facing a serious challenge from anti-Marxist guerrillas in the countryside, the Mozambican government seemed to turn a corner in obtaining better relations with its powerful neighbor, South Africa; in achieving modest increases in agricultural output; and in making military progress against the rebels. The improvements in the level of production were attributed to the Economic Rehabilitation Program (PRE), implemented the previous year, that permitted a measure of economic freedom and allowed market forces to restore incentives for farmers and manufacturers. The ability to charge unregulated prices resulted in greater output than did the strict Marxist controls followed by the government since independence in 1975. But hunger and destitution still stalked the country.

Widespread fighting continued in the countryside as the antigovernment force, the Mozambique National Resistance (*Resistência Nacional Moçambicana*; RENAMO, formerly MNR) continued to sabotage the country's infrastructure and attack the government's forces. But the struggle at times lacked the neat symmetry of government versus opposition movement and instead created social disorder conducive to criminal elements, individual score-settling, and violent crimes for private gain, not for political motives. Without the strict demarcations of a well-defined civil war, some of Mozambique's rural regions became prey to warlordism and interethnic feuds. Naturally, the rebel and government forces blamed each other for the lootings, robberies, and killings that formed so much of daily life in the southeast African country. (William Claiborne, "West Eyes Arms for Mozambique," *WP*, 24 January.)

The war provided the occasion for Pope John Paul II, who visited Mozambique and other countries in southern Africa in September, to call for the Marxist government to join with the Roman Catholic Church to bring peace to the troubled land. The pope's visit marked a reconciliation between church and state that has developed as the government moderated its policies in recent years. The FRELIMO government has been enmeshed in a rural insurgency since a few years after Mozambique's independence from Portugal (see *YICA*, 1982, 1987).

Organization and Leadership. FRELIMO held its second party conference (the first was held in March 1982) in mid-July to prepare for the Fifth Congress, scheduled for 24–31 July 1989. Party spokesmen noted that discussions at the conference were a continuation of the process begun when the FRELIMO Central Committee held its second extraordinary session in March. Topics included the role of the party, the economy, war, mass organizations, scientific and technical development, the reorganization of the armed forces, and international relations.

The FRELIMO party Central Committee examined the report from the second national party conference to determine the themes for the Fifth Congress. This meeting was also concerned with the election of delegates to the Fifth Congress. On the subject of party membership, the Central Committee decided that, rather than granting blanket admission, a case-by-case decision would be made for polygamous persons, small property holders, and individuals who have acquired Mozambican citizenship. Much discussion took place on the nature of the party, concluding that it was necessary to give power to pertinent party structures to carry out specific tasks such as training cadres, fighting discrimination, and constructing socialism. The Central Committee also reiterated the party's leading role over the state while stressing the simplification of the party apparatus, especially at the local level.

On the question of elections of FRELIMO bodies at various levels, the Central Committee emphasized that "one must be careful not to accept regional, racial, tribal, or sexual representativeness as a criterion. Criteria must rest on the candidates' competence as well as political and moral qualities" (Maputo Domestic Service, 3 August; *FBIS*, 8 August). It also reaffirmed the need for regular payment of membership dues.

The continued fighting of RENAMO received much attention by the Central Committee, which recommended the institutionalization of territorial defense and security councils as well as continued nonpreferential conscription into the military forces.

The Central Committee went on record for incentives and financial assistance to Mozambicans with initiative and management skills, particularly those already in agrarian areas. President Joaquim Chissano noted the widespread discussions involved in the process and added that "we want to continue building socialism so that there may be a just, democratic and free society in the People's Republic of Mozambique" (Maputo Domestic Service, 30 July; *FBIS*, 1 August).

Mass Organizations. The ninth Central Committee ordinary session also took up the subject of "mass democratic organizations." It reported that they "are an undoubted force and reality which contribute to strengthening and developing democracy in the country" (Maputo Domestic Service, 3 August; *FBIS*, 8 August). However, it found that differences continue to exist in their operations and that these differences are reflected in weak support and unbalanced methodological guidelines. The session furthermore found that the mass organizations face "serious organizational and financial difficulties."

The Central Committee meeting concluded that these organizations "must become more dynamic and autonomous." Because much discussion took place on the need to manage financial resources to attain self-sufficiency, the Central Committee recommended that the mass organizations "engage in productive actions as the fundamental economic basis for their financing" (ibid.).

The FRELIMO party at a conference set up the War Veterans' Association in September. President Chissano declared that this new nongovernment organization "must be an instrument that will reactivate the involvement of our fighters in our people's current major tasks—in military planning or in the economic effort" (Maputo Domestic Service, 2 September; *FBIS*, 8 September). This new mass organization joins the OMM, OJM, and OTM.

The People's Forces for the Liberation of Mozambique (*FPLM*). The FPLM, weakened and disorganized by years of rural warfare, received much attention by the ninth session of the Central Committee in August. Among the issues dealt with was the charge by black Mozambicans that the better-educated stratum and the whites escaped military duty. In seeking to emphasize the impartiality of military service, it stressed that there was discrimination or privilege on the basis of race, religion, academic qualifications, or social condition. It reaffirmed the need for military conscription of young Mozambicans into the FPLM.

Following the FPLM, the Mozambique People's Police (PPM) underwent changes allowing for the establishment of ranks to create, it was hoped, more discipline in the state's security apparatus. The police's hierarchy came about in a law passed during the People's Assembly's fourth ordinary session (Maputo Domestic Service, 29 August; *FBIS*, 1 September). In the FPLM's reorganization, the Central Committee recommended that special attention be paid to placing women in defense tasks to promote the emancipation of women in society. Furthermore, it recommended the continuation and emphasis of the training and preparation of local defense forces against what it termed "armed banditry" (Maputo Domestic Service, 3 August; *FBIS*, 8 August).

A number of senior political and military figures were moved aside. The government placed 31 on the reserve list including such well-known figures as Armando Guebuza, Armando Panguene, Marcelino dos Santos, Jacinto Veloso, Jorge Rebelo, Óscar Monteiro, and Sergio Vieira. An official statement described the action as a clearing away for "a higher degree of professionalism and specialisation" (U.K., *Southscan*, 6 July).

The British Military Advisory and Training Team (BMATT) reported the training of a third company of Mozambican soldiers, making a total of 800 men receiving instruction in September. The BMATT cooperated with the Zimbabwe National Army in the training, which sought to improve the quality of Mozambique's soldiers in the war against RENAMO (Zimbabwe, *The Herald*, 14 September).

Despite the government's improving conditions, the FPLM still faced a determined and successful adversary in RENAMO. Commanded by Afonso Dhlakama, this rebel movement survived a decline in support from South Africa and a two-year offensive by not only FRELIMO but also ground forces from Zimbabwe and Tanzania. The guerrilla forces, estimated at between fifteen thousand and twenty thousand troops, continued their attacks on railroads, electricity lines, and government posts. Sabotage accounted for the loss of electrical power in Maputo on at least one occasion (Maputo Domestic Service, 3 March; *FBIS*, 4 March). The government, however, made progress in rehabilitating the railroads and roadways across Mozambique in the critical Beira and Limpopo corridors (Karl Maier, "Rebuilding a Vital Rail in Mozambique," *CSM*, 13 October).

Critics contend that much of the government and most of the leadership positions are held by the Ndau ethnic community, a subgroup of the much larger Shona people. Western journalists visited the rebel headquarters near Gorongosa Game Park in Sofala province, one of whom stated that guerrillas enjoy local civilian support (John D. Battersby, "Pariahs Abroad, Mozambique Rebels Fight On," *NYT*, 31 July). To a South African journalist, Dhlakama stated the aims of RENAMO were "to create a more just society with a multiparty system, private economy, and peaceful relations with neighboring countries" (South Africa, *The Star*, 18 February).

The government's offer of amnesty for surrendering rebels, made in December 1987, secured return of some RENAMO members, according to FRELIMO. The government figures vary, however. One report, by Foreign Minister Pascoal Mocumbi, estimated that two thousand former rebels have taken advantage of the government's amnesty program. (The Netherlands, radio report, cited in *Facts & Reports*, vol. 19, no. Q/K, 19 August).

Externally, RENAMO's efforts were hampered by the murderous feuding among the exile leadership (Paul Musker, "The Splintering of RENAMO," South Africa, *Weekly Mail*, 8 July). One section of the foreign wing had been led by Evo Fernandes, who was murdered near Lisbon in April. About a dozen such deaths left the external wing in difficulty. One former member, Gimo M'Piri, formed his own group, Mozambique National Union (UNAMO), which allegedly opposed the Ndau domination of RENAMO ("Intelligence Briefing," *Insight*, 22 August).

Domestic Affairs. While celebrating the 70th anniversary of the October Revolution in Moscow, Marcelino dos Santos, member of the Political Bureau and chairman of the National Assembly, outlined the PRE. In an interview, dos Santos said that "we succeeded in eliminating shortcomings and charting new steps in areas such as factory management, wages policy, workers' financial and moral incentives, the nation's finances, and price formation." He contended that the "volume of consumer goods increased, and so did the fruit and vegetable crop." (*WMR*, January.)

The PRE, announced in January 1987, implemented many changes already foreshadowed in the preceding years. Briefly, its stated objectives entail economic liberalization toward a free market orientation, allowing farmers to charge higher prices for foodstuffs to encourage greater output ("Experimenting with Capitalism," *Africa News*, 4 November). The change in policies, however, necessitated increases in prices of basic commodities and the removal of subsidies. The rise in the cost of such items as rice, sugar, and corn flour reflected the actual prices for these commodities, but no rise in wages accompanied the price increases. This was part of the PRE, but it was not popular with urban dwellers (*Notícias*, 2 April).

Other economic changes involved cuts in the size of the state bureaucracy and devaluation of the Mozambican currency, the metical. Mozambique's minister of finance, Abdul Magid Osman, stated that the government had reduced the civil service by 10 percent and was planning further cuts ("Industrious Mozambique Puts 'Paternalistic' Past to Shame," (U.K., *Guardian*, 15 January). The government devalued the metical three times in 1988. The third time, in October, resulted in a 7 percent devaluation, leaving U.S. $1 equal to 620 meticals at the official rate (France, *Marchés Tropicaux*, 28 October).

The Ministerial Council's fourteenth session in August reported that the agrarian sector registered a continued growth over last year's output. It held that this increase in agricultural produce stemmed from the implementation of the second year of the PRE. At year end, President Chissano declared at the opening of the fifth session of the People's Assembly that the gross national product increased by 4.6 percent in 1988 (Maputo Domestic Service, 20 December; *FBIS*, 27 December).

Foreign trade again was reported to have increased. At the Maputo International Trade Fair, Mozambique Bank Governor Eneas Comiche stated that exports to Portugal increased more than three times between 1986 and 1987 and that Portuguese imports expanded 27 percent (Maputo Domestic Service, 2 September; *FBIS*, 7 September). Trade Minister Aranda da Silva disclosed that 1987 witnessed overall exports reaching $100 million for the first time in several years. Mozambique expanded its exports to include shoes, clothing, coconut, and mosquito nets.

This past year saw the implementation of the Law of Judicial Organization, which was passed ten years ago, because the minimum conditions now exist in Mozambique, according to the president. It provides for the People's Supreme Court, defined by the Constitution as the country's highest judicial organ. Chissano announced Mario Fumo Bartolomeu M'gaze as the president of the People's Supreme Court. Prior to this proclamation, some of the duties of the new court had been performed by the High Appellate Court (Maputo Domestic Service, 17 October; *FBIS*, 18 October).

The crime rate doubled during the first six months of the year in Maputo when compared with the same period in the previous year, according to Interior Minister Manuel Antonio. In a speech to police and representatives from the mass organizations, Antonio held that murder, theft, and robbery could be reduced only by re-creating the close links between the police and public, which had faded. Some of the participants spoke frankly against the behavior of the police and militia men for causing disturbances in the markets when attempting to suppress "black marketeering" (*Domingo*, 14 August; *FBIS*, 26).

The FRELIMO government announced in May the end of Operation Production, a controversial campaign of shipping unemployed people out of cities such as Maputo to rural areas to work the land. Launched in 1983, this program relied on indiscriminate house-to-house searches and identity checks in public places to arrest thousands who were then transported to the countryside. The arbitrary treatment was, in part, the reason for the removal of then Interior Minister Armando Guebuza. Dissatisfaction with the program resulted in RENAMO's recruitment (London, BBC World Service, 9 May; *FBIS*, 10 May).

Despite some improvements in production and trade, life remained harsh, especially for rural Mozambicans. About one million were refugees in neighboring states and more than 1.6 million were displaced in the country itself. War and drought remained, as in years past, the main factors causing the disparate conditions that have made Mozambique one of the world's poorest and cruelest countries.

International Affairs. FRELIMO continued to gain international respectability during the year (Michael Holman, "Tenacity in Adversity," U.K., *Financial Times*, 15 August). An international conference on emergency aid to Mozambique, for example, was held in Maputo during April attended by representatives of foreign governments, U.N. agencies, and religious organizations. As one sign of improved relations with the United States, the first U.S. warship to visit Mozambique since its independence in 1975 was the USS *Pharris*, a frigate, docked in Maputo for three days in August (Maputo, in English to southern Africa, 15 August; *FBIS*, 16 August).

In its quest for foreign support against RENAMO, the Marxist party received a boost from the U.S. Department of State's report in April that charged the rebels with killing civilians in their war against the FRELIMO government, claiming that up to 100,000 noncombatants died at the hands of RENAMO soldiers. Basing its conclusion on interviews with 196 refugees, the report also contended that RENAMO commonly relied on coercion to gain recruits for its military actions (E. A. Wayne, "Mozambique Rebels Slaughter Fleeing Civilians," *CSM*, 21 April). But the rebels benefited, too, from the early policies of the central government in its zeal to transform Mozambique into a Marxist state and make Mozambicans into "new men."

When pressed by the rural insurgency, the FRELIMO government moderated its policies to permit family farms, limited private enterprise, and religious tolerance. It dropped some of the pervasive Marxist rhetoric and moved to seek foreign investment, international aid, and friends from abroad.

The most dramatic turnaround in the foreign office occurred with Mozambique's powerful neighbor, the Republic of South Africa. In April, the Reserve Bank of South Africa rescheduled the Bank of Mozambique's debt, which totaled about 26 million rands' worth of credit extended since February 1984.

President P. W. Botha crossed the border to meet with Chissano in mid-September. Botha stated that "we stand for cooperation and goodwill amongst our neighbors" in what was seen as the most friendly gesture toward FRELIMO since the 1984 signing of the Nkomati Accords. This nonaggression pact between the two countries was marked by accusations of violations and recriminations by both sides. Two months earlier, the Pretoria government loaned Maputo $16 million for the restoration of the power lines and pylons connecting Mozambique's giant Cabora Bassa Dam's electricity to South Africa (John D. Battersby, "Botha and Mozambique Pledge to Bolster Ties," *NYT*, 13 September). South Africa even dispatched logistical equipment to Mozambique to aid FRELIMO against RENAMO ("Pretoria Sends Aid to Fight MNR," U.K., *Guardian*, 28 November).

Despite the warmer relations between the two countries, FRELIMO officials continued their criticism of South Africa as the sponsor of RENAMO. One such report stated that "South Africa's MNR (RENAMO) bandits destroyed 200 meters of railway line from Nacala to Nampula" (Maputo, in English to southern Africa, 14 November; *FBIS*, 15 November). In another, Pascoal Mocumbi, the foreign minister, stated that a South African soldier had been killed while fighting against FRELIMO forces in Maputo province near the border with the Republic of South Africa in July ("Mozambique Reveals Details of Nkomati Breach," (U.K., *Southscan*, 2 November).

The month of September also witnessed a visit by Pope John Paul II, who urged the Marxist government to work with the Roman Catholic Church, which has called for a policy of reconciliation with RENAMO. Mozambique's bishops have been reluctant to condemn RENAMO for the slaughter of the civilian population in the rural regions. Instead, they have pushed the government to talk with the rebels ("All Condemn RENAMO. Except the Bishops," South Africa, *Weekly Mail*, 15 September).

For its part FRELIMO, although hesitant to enter into talks with the rebels, has moved steadily to mend fences with the church. When FRELIMO came to power, it seized church property, including schools and hospitals, and attempted to suppress religious practices. Along with its economic relaxation from rigid socialism, the FRELIMO party returned some confiscated lands and eased restrictions on religious observances to improve relations with the church.

Earlier in the year, FRELIMO entered into a cooperative agreement with Portugal, the onetime colonizer of Mozambique. Following intense discussions between delegations from the two countries, Prime Minister Mário Machungo signed an agreement in Lisbon in February that provided for rescheduling Maputo's debt to Portugal and increasing the credit insurance to cover Portuguese exports (Maputo Domestic Service, 5 February; FBIS, 8 February).

President Chissano visited several foreign countries during the year. In April, he met with Cuban president Fidel Castro in Havana to discuss southern Africa (NYT, 3 April) and received the Jose Marti Order. Thousands of Mozambicans have received education or training in Cuba. From Cuba, Chissano went to Nicaragua for discussions with President Daniel Ortega (Maputo, in English to southern Africa, 5 April; FBIS, 6 April). Later in the year, Chissano returned to Cuba for several weeks to have a medical operation to remove his prostate gland (Maputo Domestic Service, 22 November; FBIS, 23 November). In May, he traveled to Japan where he met with government and business leaders (Maputo Domestic Service, 25 May; FBIS, 27 May).

A number of countries provided aid to Mozambique during the year including the Soviet Union, Cuba, Italy, and Japan. The USSR, for example, agreed to sponsor the rehabilitation of a large foundry in Maputo, which follows a protocol signed between Mozambique and Moscow in 1987 (Maputo Domestic Service, 13 May; FBIS, 18 May). It also agreed to supply some $28 million worth of refined fuel in 1989 (Maputo, in English to southern Africa, 26 October; FBIS, 27 October).

The Communist Party of the Soviet Union and FRELIMO signed an accord whereby the Soviet Union will grant five million rubles worth of equipment and assistance to improve the FRELIMO party's productive units (Maputo Domestic Service, 15 November; FBIS, 18 November). The Soviet military attaché in Maputo, Eugenie Kavrikov, stated that the USSR will continue to strengthen Mozambique's armed forces in its struggle against South Africa (Maputo, in English to southern Africa, 19 February; FBIS, 26 February).

Japan built a floating fishing wharf in Quelimane at a cost of 1.2 billion yen (Maputo Domestic Service, 22 March; FBIS, 23 March). Italy rescheduled its debt with a reduced interest rate of only 1.5 percent (Maputo Domestic Service, FBIS, 13 January). Sweden and Finland provided an $11 million credit line to purchase containers for use at the port of Beira (Maputo Domestic Service, 31 January; FBIS, 2 February).

A gigantic project covering some 213,000 hectares for the Sabie-Nkomati enterprise was launched in September. This irrigation system in Gaza province is estimated to grow thousands of tons of food products and to generate tens of thousands of jobs. Among the economic partners are Italy, Spain, the Soviet Union, the United States, and Yugoslavia (Notícias, 22 September). A small group of wealthy, conservative businessmen and evangelical Christian missionaries supplied bibles, radios, and other nonlethal military equipment to RENAMO (Robert Pear, "Rightists in U.S. Aid Mozambique Rebels," NYT, 22 May).

Publications. Since independence, FRELIMO has controlled the country's print and broadcast media. The party relies on two publications to convey its message: the daily paper Notícias and the weekly magazine O Tempo. In 1981, the government initiated two more national circulation newspapers: Diário de Moçambique in Beira, the country's second largest city, and a Sunday paper, Domingo. (For additional information, see YICA, 1982.) Another publication, Voz da Revolução, deals with Marxist theory and FRELIMO policies. In 1987, the party launched a paper, Economia, under the direction of the Chamber of Commerce as part of FRELIMO's move toward economic liberalization.

Thomas H. Henriksen
Hoover Institution

Nigeria

Population. 100,694,000 (Political Handbook of the World, 1988)
Party. Socialist Working People's Party (SWPP)
Founded. 1963 (SWPP, 1978)
Membership. No data
General Secretary. Dapo Fatogun

Politburo. 4 members: Chaika Anozie (chairman), Wahab Goodluck (deputy chairman), Hassan Sunmonu, Lasisi A. Osunde
Central Committee. No data
Status. Proscribed
Last Congress. First, November 1978
Last Election. August–September 1983, SWPP ineligible
Auxiliary Organizations. No data
Publication. *New Horizon*

Once again there was little visible evidence of Marxist organization and activity in Nigeria, as the ban on political parties (dating from the 31 December 1983 coup) continued and the country remained preoccupied with its severe economic depression and painful, controversial structural adjustment measures. As in previous years, university students and trade unions (the main sources of radical political sentiment, in the absence of political parties) were in the forefront of social and political protest, clashing repeatedly with the government. The most explosive confrontation came over the government's announcement on 10 April of a reduction in the petroleum subsidy and consequently an increase in the price of gasoline and other petroleum products. Six people were killed and several wounded in Jos in riots protesting the price increases. Violent demonstrations took place in several other cities as well, and some 30 universities and polytechnics were temporarily shut down as a result of student strikes and demonstrations against the price increases.

Although a number of individual unions challenged the government during the year in various strikes and protests, the trade union movement was badly weakened by internal divisions. In February, the third quadrennial delegates' conference of the country's sole trade union confederation, the Nigeria Labor Congress (NLC), resulted in a disastrous fracture when the moderate faction, known as the "democrats," boycotted the formal proceedings and held a separate conference. There it claimed to have elected its candidate for NLC president, Takai Shammang, who is president of the powerful Electricity and Gas Workers' Union. At the formally scheduled NLC meeting the next day, Ali Chiroma, candidate of the (Marxist-leaning) "socialist" faction that has dominated the NLC since its establishment in 1978, was re-elected to the NLC presidency (*West Africa*, 22 February, 7 March).

With 20 of the NLC's 42 trade unions supporting Shammang's claim to the office and most of the remainder (and various international trade union groups) recognizing Chiroma, an opening was created for the government to move against the trade unions. On 29 February, five days after Chiroma's disputed re-election, the federal government ordered the dissolution of the rival NLC Executive Councils and the surrendering of all NLC assets to a government administrator who would investigate NLC finances, manage NLC funds, and organize new elections during a six-month tenure. Fed up with union militancy and infighting and particularly apprehensive over the trade unions' vehement opposition to the reduction in the petroleum subsidy, the government, with deft timing and Machiavellian skill, exercised its muscle to subdue the trade union movement (charges of government payments to and backdoor deals with both sides, particularly the democrats, abounded) (*Newswatch*, 7 March, 14 March).

Although the schism in the NLC may partly have been due to personal rivalries and financial considerations (each side charged the other with serious improprieties), ideology and politics also figured prominently. The socialists or Marxists have always accused the democrats of being proestablishment, while the democrats charged the socialists with being too "dictatorial," "oppressive" and "confrontational," particularly in their propensity to call a strike over any and every issue. Some flavor of the conflict was suggested by the socialists' charges that the democrats were being funded not only by the Nigerian government but by the United States, Britain, and/or Israel. Another bone of contention was the socialists' alleged plan to form a workers' political party, or at least a workers' faction, within one of the two parties that will contest the coming elections for a Third Republic. This was opposed as an unaffordable diversion for the NLC by the democratic faction, whose chairman, Godwin Ulocha (general secretary of the National Union of Postal and Telecommunications Employees), charged that the socialist faction had concluded arrangements with the Soviet-front World Federation of Trade Unions to receive logistical and financial support to establish a workers' party in Nigeria (*Newswatch*, 14 March). Conflict was also generated by the continuing powerful role in the NLC of former President Hassan Sunmonu, now general secretary of the Organization of African Trade Union Unity, whom the democrats accused of continuing to run the NLC through Chiroma. Sunmonu was a key figure behind the SWPP, the last open Marxist party to operate legally in Nigeria.

NLC affairs continued to be run by the government throughout the year, as the term of the NLC administrator, Michael Ogunkoya, was renewed for four months in September, despite strong objections from the press, the Bar Association, and of course many trade unions. Labor's internal divisions persisted, and the trade union movement was further weakened in July when one of the most articulate of the 42 member unions of the NLC, the Academic Staff Union of Universities (ASUU), was proscribed by the government following the refusal of its members to heed the government's ultimatum to call off their strike for improved salaries and allowances (which had plunged in purchasing power over the past two years because of the devaluation of the naira).

At the end of the year, the two labor factions bridged their differences. A compromise agreement provided for the withdrawal of both Shammang and Chiroma from the contested NLC presidency and the division of NLC offices between the two factions. Under the agreement, a twelve-person slate of candidates was elected unopposed at a special delegates' conference called by the government administrator on 12 December. The newly elected president, Paschal Bafyau, is general secretary of the Nigerian Union of Railwaymen and was a member of the seventeen-man political bureau that drafted the government's plan of transition to a Third Republic (*West Africa*, 26 December).

Although economic distress was a volatile political issue with the capacity to mobilize class and ideological cleavages, ethnic and religious cleavages continued to be the country's most explosive source of potential conflict. One student died and more than one hundred were injured at Ahmadu Bello University on 14 June in a dispute between Muslim and Christian student factions over the results of the student union election. The conflict came only 36 days after the university, one of Nigeria's largest and most important, re-opened after being closed down for three months following a student strike (*West Africa*, 27 June). Later in the year, the Constituent Assembly, meeting to draft a constitution for the Third Republic, became bitterly divided again over an issue that had almost derailed the transition to the Second Republic in the late 1970s: whether or not to have an Islamic Sharia court of appeal at the federal level. Alarmed by the escalating sectional tension and covert maneuvering of banned politicians, President Ibrahim Babangida declared on 23 October that the government was determined to exclude ideological and religious extremists from participation in the political transition. Religious fanaticism and intolerance, he warned, seriously threatened not only the transition program but the Third Republic and the country's national life (*FBIS*, 1 November).

Foreign Affairs. Although generally pro-Western, Nigeria continued to develop and sustain vigorous and diverse ties with communist countries while manifesting an independent and assertive foreign policy—within the constraints of an enormous foreign debt and severely inadequate oil revenues, which have sharply limited its international influence and maneuverability. Exchanges of several high-level visits between Nigeria and the Soviet Union during the year appeared to reflect warm relations between the two countries. On 5 November, Lieutenant General Sanni Abacha, chief of staff of the Nigerian army and one of the most powerful members of the Armed Forces Ruling Council, returned to Nigeria from a ten-day visit in the USSR, during which he met with Defense Minister General D.T. Yazov, chief of the Ground Forces General Staff; Colonel General D.A. Grinkevich; and other top Soviet officers (*FBIS*, 9 November). Upon his return, General Abacha emphasized that Nigeria would continue to purchase its arms from both the Eastern and Western blocs, that the Soviet Union was willing to sell any equipment to Nigeria to enhance its military effectiveness, and that his visit had sought to bring the USSR closer to Nigeria, particularly in military areas (*FBIS*, 8 November). In December, Colonel General Grinkevich led a Soviet delegation on a visit to Nigeria, assuring Nigeria of continued Soviet cooperation in the development of the huge (and expensive) Ajaokuta Iron and Steel Complex, which remains uncompleted many years after the initiation of construction. On 1 August, a five-man delegation of heads of Soviet ministries involved in the project paid a visit to Nigeria; later in the month Nigeria received the Soviet deputy foreign minister, Vladimir Petrovskiy. Nigeria's state minister for foreign affairs, Mohammed Anka, characterized that meeting as "very successful," revealing new areas of cooperation, particularly with regard to the new Soviet concept of comprehensive international security. "Relations between Nigeria and the Soviet Union now are excellent and have been cemented," Anka declared (*FBIS*, 31 August).

Ties were also cemented with a number of other Eastern bloc countries. On 28 January Nigeria's Bauchi state signed a $39.2 million barter agreement with Yugoslavia under which Nigeria would receive equipment and machinery for two large agricultural processing industries in exchange for raw cotton. On 17 July Czechoslovakia's deputy minister of defense and commander in chief of the air force, Lieutenant General Josef Remek, ended a one-week visit to Nigeria by pledging cooperation in the training of Nigerian air force pilots and engineers. In September Nigeria's chief of general staff (the second-ranking officer in the military government), Vice-Admiral Augustus Aikhomu, made a week-long trip to Romania and Bulgaria in pursuit of new investment and closer economic, educational and cultural ties. In August, China and Nigeria pledged to intensify their cooperation in the fields of traditional medicine and high-yield rice production. In September, chief of navy staff, Vice-Admiral Patrick Koshoni, represented President Babangida at the celebrations in Pyongyang for the 40th anniversary of the Democratic People's Republic of Korea.

Nigeria also continued to be active, at least rhetorically, on the African front. On 11 February a three-man African National Congress (ANC) delegation led by the general secretary, Alfred Nzo, arrived on a five-day visit to receive an honorary law degree for Nelson Mandela from Bayero University in Kano. Nzo praised Nigeria's continuing support for the ANC struggle against apartheid in South Africa. In November, Nigeria hosted an international conference on strategies for dismantling apartheid. In a meeting with a visiting Cuban delegation in March, President Babangida assured Fidel Castro of Nigeria's "total political support" for Cuba's role in containing South African aggression against Angola and, according to the Lagos Domestic Service, "pledged that Nigeria will do all within its power to ensure that the United States did not succeed in its efforts to get the U.N. Human Rights Commission in Geneva to unjustly condemn the government of President Fidel Castro for human rights violations" (*FBIS*, 7 March).

Larry Diamond
Hoover Institution

Réunion

Population. 557,441
Party. Réunion Communist Party (Parti communiste réunionnais; PCR)
Founded. 1959
Membership. 7,000 claimed; 2,000 estimated
General Secretary. Paul Vergès
Politburo. 12 members: Julien Ramin; remaining members unknown
Secretariat. 6 members: Paul Vergès, Elie Hoarau, Jean-Baptiste Ponama, Lucet Langenier; remaining members unknown
Central Committee. 32 members: Bruny Payet, Roger Hoarau, Daniel Lallemand, Hippolite Piot, Ary Yee Chong Tchi-Kan, Alexis Pota; remaining members unknown
Status. Legal
Last Congress. Fifth, 12–14 July 1980, in Le Port
Last Elections. President of the French Republic, 17 April, 24 April; French National Assembly, 5 May, 12 May, 35 percent (2 of 5); Réunion General Council, 25 September, 2 October, 27.2 percent (9 of 44)
Auxiliary Organizations. Anticolonialist Front for Réunion Autonomy, Réunion Front of Autonomous Youth; Réunion Peace Committee; Réunion General Confederation of Workers (CGTR); Committee for the Rally of Réunionese Unemployed (CORC); Committee for the Rally of Réunionese Youth (CORJ); Réunion Union of Women (UFR); Réunion General Union of Workers in France (UGTRF); Réunion General Confederation of Planters and Cattlemen (CGPER)
Publications. *Témoignages* (daily), Elie Hoarau, chief editor; *Travailleur Réunionnais* (semimonthly), published by CGTR; *Combat Réunionnais*, published by UGTRF

The PCR went into mourning in early October after the death of Laurent Vergès, the son of General Secretary Paul Vergès and deputy to the French National Assembly. The Vergès family, along with the Hoarau family, occupy key positions in the party hierarchy, and the tragic loss of Laurent, a dynamic young man of 33 who had worked with his mother Laurence on the party newspaper *Témoignages*, was regretted far beyond the ranks of the PCR. President François Mitterrand and Laurent Fabius, president of the National Assembly to which Vergès had been elected in the course of the year, sent their condolences. Vergès was succeeded by his alternate, Alexis Pota. Another Vergès son was elected to the General Council, the quasi legislature of this French overseas department. The communist-affiliated labor union CGTR held its Sixth Congress from 6 to 8 March. The five hundred delegates elected Georges-Marie Lepinay their general secretary after the resignation of Bruny Payet.

All citizens were called to the polls four times during 1988. First they elected a president, then a National Assembly, and later a part of the local General Council; lastly they voted in a referendum about the future of New Caledonia, one of the last French overseas territories. In the presidential elections the PCR made no effort to support the candidate of the French Communist Party (PCF) and accused the PCF of Europocentrism. They openly supported the socialist incumbent, Mitterrand, and attacked his main rival, Jacques Chirac, as a man allegedly allied with racists. Mitterrand visited Réunion in early February. Candidate Raymond Barre, a native of Réunion, and Chirac also visited. Mitterrand received the overwhelming support of those who voted. (Abstentions are very high in all overseas departments.) The PCF candidate received only 3.2 percent of the vote, much lower than the usual communist vote, and on 24 April Mitterrand, with PCR support, won 60.3 percent of the vote.

The re-elected president of France called for National Assembly elections on 5 and 12 May. A total of 24 candidates ran for Réunion's five seats. The PCR maintained control of two seats with the victories of Elie Hoarau and Laurent Vergès, who had only six months to live. The PCR won more than 35 percent of the popular vote. However, new tensions between the PCR and the Réunion Socialist Federation weakened the strength of the left. The PCR accused the socialists of supporting right-wing parties in runoff elections. The PCR, which has great respect for President Mitterrand, said it was part of the Union of the Presidential Majority.

The third series of elections was held on 25 September and 2 October for 26 general councillor positions out of a total of 44 in the General Council. The PCR ran a candidate in each canton. In the first round the three PCR incumbents won and added one new member. Among the victors was Pierre Vergès, son of Paul and Laurence and brother of deputy Laurent. By the end of the second round the total PCR representation in the General Council rose to nine (seven before the election). The PCR won 27.2 percent of the popular vote. In the fourth call to the polls (6 November) the people of Réunion supported the government's program for New Caledonia. A representative of the Caledonian nationalist movement spoke to the PCR.

In addition to mobilizing for the elections, the PCR directed its attention to three issues: the 1992 integration of Europe, the effects on the French overseas departments, and equality with metropolitan France. Unlike Guadeloupe and Martinique, the Caribbean island overseas departments, the PCR made no claims for the eventual independence of Réunion.

The fear of 1992, when tariffs will disappear among Common Market countries such as France, drove communist and some socialist parties of the overseas departments to meet 20 February in Cayenne, Guyana, to coordinate efforts to protect their interests. They created the Rally of Progressive Forces of the Antilles, Guyana, and Réunion. The issue of the equality of French citizens on Réunion with French citizens in metropolitan France is an old one—the minimum wage is different as are the family allocations. On 19 March the PCR sponsored a rally for social equality and circulated a petition signed by more than twenty thousand people in support of equality. In July Paul Vergès, general secretary of the PCR and deputy to the European Parliament, met Prime Minister M. Rocard to discuss these questions.

Témoignages, the popular daily PCR newspaper, provided many Réunionnais of all political persuasions with their sports, political, economic, and cultural news. A new publication, *Espace de l'Islam* (Islamic Space), appeared as a result of growing Islamic consciousness on Réunion.

Brian Weinstein
Howard University

Senegal

Population. 7,281,022
Party. Independence and Labor Party (Parti de l'indépendance du travail; PIT)
Founded. 1957
Membership. No data
General Secretary. Amath Dansoko

Politburo. 14 members: Amath Dansoko, Samba Dioulde Thiam, Maguette Thiam, Mady Danfaka, Sadio Camara, Seydou Ndongo, Semou Pathe Gueye, Makhtar Mbaye, Bouma Gaye, Mohamed Laye (names of other 4 not known)

Secretariat. 7 members: Amath Dansoko, Semou Pathe Gueye, Maguette Thiam, Samba Dioulde Thiam, Mady Danfaka, Makhtar Mbaye (replacement of Seydou Cissoko not yet named)

Central Committee. 55 members (secretary: Semou Pathe Gueye)

Status. Legal

Last Congress. Second, 28 September–2 October 1984, in Dakar

Last Election. 1988, 0.84 percent, no seats

Auxiliary Organization. Women's Democratic Union

Publications. *Daan Doole*, *Gestu*

The key political event of 1988 for Marxist and all other parties in Senegal's fragile but spirited semidemocracy was the presidential and National Assembly elections of 28 February. The first national elections since 1983 once again resulted in a huge (albeit somewhat reduced) victory for the ruling Socialist Party (PS) and for President Abdou Diouf's re-election. Following a turbulent and bitter three-week campaign, Diouf won a landslide first-round victory with 73.2 percent of the vote (down from 83.5 percent in 1983), while the PS list won 71.4 percent (down from 79.9 percent), giving it 103 of the 120 National Assembly seats (a decline of 8 seats).

As in 1983, the closest competitor and indeed only serious challenger was the moderate, center-left Senegalese Democratic Party (PDS), whose presidential candidate, Abdoulaye Wade, won 25.8 percent of the vote (almost doubling his 14.8 percent showing in 1983). Wade was supported in the presidential election by the two important communist parties in Senegal—the PIT, led by Amath Dansoko, and the Democratic League/Movement for the Party of Labor (LD/MPT), led by Dr. Abdoulaye Bathily. Both parties are pro-Soviet and close to Moscow, though the PIT continues to enjoy Moscow's official recognition as Senegal's pre-eminent communist party. Two other minor parties including the obscure (Trotskyist) Socialist Workers' Organization (OST) also associate with the PDS in a five-party grouping known as the Senegalese Democratic Alliance (ADS).

Although declining to field presidential candidates, both the PIT and the LD/MPT again ran slates of candidates for the National Assembly and once again failed to obtain even a single seat under Senegal's system of proportional representation. The LD/MPT came closest: its 15,664 votes missed the minimum threshold by less than 3,000 votes. Both parties improved their showings from 1983 but only slightly: the LD/MPT garnered 1.41 percent, compared with 1.12 percent in 1983, and the PIT won 0.84 percent, up from 0.55 percent. The PDS, by contrast, made substantial legislative gains, increasing its vote from 14.0 percent to 24.8 percent and its seats from eight to seventeen. It made a particularly strong showing in the Casamance region, which has been the scene of separatist agitation and violence.

The only other Marxist party to contest the elections was the And Jef (Act Together) Revolutionary Movement for a New Democracy (AJ-MRDN). The longtime And Jef leader, Landing Savane, ran for the presidency, but his party did not contest the National Assembly elections, probably because it lacked the national strength to mount any kind of credible campaign. (Its official reason was its intention to dissolve the National Assembly and create a provisional revolutionary government if it won the presidency.) Although the And Jef had been presumed to have some support in Savane's native Casamance region, the party's pathetic showing in the presidential race, in which it won only 2,849 votes (0.25 percent), indicates a lack of any significant popular base. The results would appear to mark a decline in influence for Savane, who became a convinced follower of Mao Zedong during the turbulent years of student rebellion in France in the late 1960s and then organized his party clandestinely for eight years until all restrictions on political parties were lifted in 1982 (*West Africa*, 22 February).

The fourth candidate in the presidential election was Babacar Niang, leader of the left-populist PLP (Party for the Liberation of the People), who won just 0.75 percent of the vote. A member of the communist African Independence Party (PAI) during the 1950s, Niang became disillusioned with communism during the mid-1960s; his current party now manifests a nondoctrinaire, nationalist orientation (ibid.).

Ten of Senegal's seventeen parties did not take part at all in the election including several tiny Marxist parties: the PAI of Mahjemout Diop, whose humiliating showing in the 1983 election (0.17 percent) might have discouraged the party's participation this year, a splinter group of the PAI known as the PAI-M, the OST, and the Communist League of Workers (LCT).

The official electoral returns cannot be taken as a reliable indicator of the overall level of opposition to the ruling PS, given the numerous, vehement, and in some cases well-documented charges of electoral fraud and institutional biases (control of the media and the electoral machinery, lack of guaranteed secret voting) favoring the ruling party. However, the dismal showing of all of the Marxist parties and candidates relative to the liberal PDS, which did win a quarter of the vote, and the failure or unwillingness of many Marxist parties even to contest the elections, shows that Marxist and communist parties in Senegal continue to enjoy only slight popular support (beyond small coteries of intellectuals, students, and workers) and remain enervated by their numerous sectarian divisions. Popular opposition to the PS is diffuse and nonideological, based primarily on economic and social discontent and a general desire for change. Indeed, the PDS campaign slogan of "*sopi, sopi*" (Wolof for change, change) resonated powerfully in a country of great poverty and inequality that has been hit hard by sweeping economic adjustment measures—resulting in food price hikes and sharp reductions in government employment and services—and that has grown increasingly resentful of the corruption and arrogance of the ruling party after 28 years of unbroken rule.

Wade and his party claimed they had won 56 percent of the presidential vote, and news of the PS victory (broadcast prematurely on the night of the election by state radio, despite an electoral reform providing that the results would only be announced by the Supreme Court five days after the voting) provoked an unprecedented outburst of political violence. Chanting *sopi, sopi*, young opposition supporters took to the streets on election night, overturning and burning cars, looting shops and supermarkets, ransacking houses owned by barons of the PS, and damaging some 80 buses (*FBIS*, 2 March; *West Africa*, 7 March). The riots were fueled by the anger and frustration of Senegalese youth, who face deteriorating school facilities and job opportunities and who were already in the midst of a nationwide strike of high school students.

Stunned by the violence, the government immediately declared a state of emergency over the entire Dakar region, closed all high schools and universities, banned demonstrations, and arrested some thirteen opposition leaders, including Wade, Dansoko, and Bathily. Bathily was released but later re-arrested on 4 April during a demonstration called by eleven opposition parties against the state of emergency; he was tried, fined, and given a suspended prison sentence of one month on 20 April. Wade and Dansoko remained in detention for several weeks. (Dansoko's family expressed concern about his detention because he was said to be suffering from diabetes.) On 15 April, Dansoko was acquitted along with four others. On 11 May, after a tense, controversial public trial that drew international attention, Wade was convicted of encouraging the riots and given a one-year suspended prison term; his deputy was sentenced to two years in prison, and two other PDS militants, to six months.

Seeking to mollify the embittered opposition parties, President Diouf invited them at midyear to a national roundtable meeting to consider major national problems. Delegates from nine parties convened on 4 July to discuss reform of the electoral code and access of political parties to state media. The talks, however, failed to produce agreement on reform, and the PDS, PIT, and LD suspended their participation indefinitely on 16 July. The communist PAI was one of four fringe parties that continued discussions with the PS, but the talks produced nothing of consequence. Questioned on 4 July about what the opposition would do if President Diouf did not agree to their demands for new elections and expanded media access, LD leader Bathily vowed, "we will continue the struggle and bring him down by all means" (*FBIS*, 6 July).

By year's end relations between government and opposition remained stalemated and embittered, with the crucial issue of electoral reform unresolved. The year-long student strike over demands for better educational facilities and more teachers was finally settled at the end of October after the government made a number of major concessions to the students. Although the political situation remained volatile, there appeared to be little opportunity in the near future for Senegal's Marxist parties to build a significant popular following.

Foreign Affairs. The moderate socialist government of Abdou Diouf continued its nonaligned foreign policy in 1988, featuring close economic relations with the West but also cordial ties with communist and radical Arab regimes. In January the PS welcomed a delegation from the Communist Party of China (CPC), headed by Jiang Guanghua, deputy director of the CPC International Liaison Department. This interparty visit was returned in August when Hu Qili, a member of the Standing

Committee of the Political Bureau of the CPC, received in Beijing a PS delegation headed by Djibo Ka, a top party official and also Senegal's minister of planning and cooperation. The visit was the third to China by a PS delegation since the PS established relations with the CPC in 1979 (*FBIS*, 30 August). On 3 July Senegal signed what it called a "landmark" cultural cooperation agreement with the PRC aimed at promoting cultural exchanges between the two countries (*FBIS*, 8 July). In late November President Diouf received members of a delegation of the Presidium of the Supreme Soviet of the Soviet Union, including Presidium deputy chairman Aleksandr Mokanu. Also in November Senegal agreed with Libya to establish diplomatic relations and announced recognition of a Palestinian state. Senegal was the first black African country to upgrade a Palestine Liberation Organization (PLO) mission to the ambassadorial level, and in September Senegalese foreign minister Ibrahima Fall received Faruq al-Qaddumi, head of the political department of the PLO, on an official visit (*FBIS*, 30 September).

Larry Diamond
Hoover Institution

South Africa

Population. 35,093,971
Party. South African Communist Party (SACP)
Founded. 1921
Membership. No data
Chairman. Dan Tloome (69, teacher)
General Secretary. Joe Slovo (62, barrister)
Politburo. Chris Hani, chief of staff of the military wing; Ray Simons (pen name, R. S. Nyameko), labor theoretician; Mac Maharaj, political strategist, directs recruitment inside South Africa; Thabo Mbeki, information chief; John Nkadimeng, general secretary of SACTU, the banned labor union; all elected in 1984 at Moscow congress (*Africa Confidential*, 26 August, vol. 29, no. 17).
Leading Organs. Composition unknown
Status. Proscribed

Last Congress. Sixth, late 1984 or early 1985
Last Election. N/a
Auxiliary Organizations. None
Publications. *African Communist* (quarterly, published abroad); *Umsebenzi* (published clandestinely in South Africa)

In the 35th year since its establishment underground, the SACP continued to operate clandestinely and in exile, maintaining its historically close links with the also banned African National Congress (ANC), the country's most prominent African nationalist organization.

The direct descendant of the Communist Party of South Africa (CPSA, the continent's first Marxist-Leninist party, founded in Cape Town in 1921), the SACP is the reconstituted continuation of its aboveground predecessor. During the CPSA's decades of legal existence, its multiracial membership had been active, sometimes controversial participants in the emerging black trade union movement, the ANC, and white and black electoral politics. Faced with imminent banning under the impending Suppression of Communism Act and unprepared for underground politics, a majority of the Central Committee of the CPSA voted to dissolve the party in June 1950. In 1953 prominent members of the dissolved party reversed the 1950 decision and created the clandestine SACP, whose members were under growing harassment within the trade union movement and expanding black opposition to the apartheid policies of the Afrikaner Nationalist Party government, which was elected in 1948.

In the post-Sharpeville state of emergency in 1960, the underground SACP revealed its existence for the first time. During the same period the Nationalist Party government banned the ANC, forcing it to reassess its deeply rooted commitment to open, legal, and nonviolent protest that had characterized the organization since its founding in 1912. Sharing not only opposition to white minority rule and the antiapartheid campaigns of the 1950s and earlier but also enforced illegality and heightened persecution, the ANC and the SACP drew closer together. Leaders of both bodies (including the subsequently imprisoned Nelson Mandela of the ANC and Joe Slovo, the present general secretary of the SACP) secretly created Umkhonto we Sizwe, the military wing of the ANC, to conduct sabotage and train cadres for eventual armed struggle.

Aided by new legislation and policies in the early 1960s that permitted house arrest, unlimited detention, and widespread use of torture against prisoners, the government successfully decimated the nascent underground structures of Umkhonto, the ANC, and the SACP. Leaders from both organizations escaped into exile, where their alliance deepened on the common foundation of determination to end white minority rule. Buoyed by the recrudescence of black opposition within South Africa in the 1970s and strengthened by an infusion of young recruits fleeing the country in the wake of the Soweto uprising of 1976, all three organizations re-established an organized underground presence within the country that focused on widely publicized Umkhonto sabotage, armed attacks on government installations and economic targets, and clandestine political activity in support of the burgeoning trade union movement and new above-ground mass and grass-roots organizations. The establishment of the United Democratic Front (UDF) in 1983 and the coalescing of black trade unions into the Congress of South African Trade Unions (COSATU) in 1985 reflected a further upsurge of politicization and mass resistance that threatened government control and provoked the imposition of a state of emergency in mid-1985.

Despite the arrest of thousands of activists by the government in the successive states of emergency since 1985 and despite government bans on political activity by 31 antiapartheid organizations (including the UDF and COSATU) in 1988 alone, the SACP remains optimistic about prospects for continuing popular militancy. In the words of an SACP spokesman,

the reign of terror failed to break the will of the people. On the contrary, the people have crossed the psychological threshold of submission, preserved their militant spirit, and are ready to fight on. The political consciousness of the masses has risen to a new high...the current uprising in South Africa differs from all previous struggles in that *its demand is, unambiguously and distinctly, the transfer of power from the racist minority to the democratic majority.* The people have rejected all reformist offers from the apartheid regime: they insist that a government based on the will of a racist minority has no right to rule over a majority. (*WMR*, July.)

Organization and Leadership. Based in exile in Europe and in Africa, the top leadership posts of the SACP remain in the hands of representatives of the older generation of party members who were active in the legal CPSA, participated in the cre-

ation of the clandestine SACP in the 1950s, and then, under party orders in the early 1960s, went into exile where they participated in a variety of party, ANC, and Umkhonto activities. Since a party post reshuffle in early 1987, the more ceremonial and diplomatic post of chairman has been held by Dan Tloome, a 69-year-old African and former teacher and trade union official, whereas the administrative and political post of general secretary has been occupied by Joe Slovo, a 62-year-old Lithuanian-born barrister prominent as a defense lawyer for members of the ANC and allied organizations in South Africa in the 1950s and early 1960s. In exile he has been intimately associated with organizing armed struggle for the ANC and with articulating military-political strategies and tactics. In 1964 he became a member of the Revolutionary Council of the ANC and subsequently chief of staff of Umkhonto we Sizwe; in 1985 he was the first white elected to the National Executive Council of the ANC when non-Africans became eligible for membership on the ANC's directing body.

Slovo's assumption of the post of general secretary came only after the SACP requested from the ANC that he be relieved of his post as chief of staff of Umkhonto we Sizwe. Chairman Tloome asserted that

the tasks and duties which now rest on [Slovo's] shoulders have multiplied immensely. As the leading public officer of our party and its chief spokesman, he is called upon increasingly to devote himself to elaborating and projecting its policies and perspectives and to participate in numerous exchanges with both internal and international groups. (*African Communist*, no. 110.)

The characteristics of the intimate links between the SACP and ANC within the "liberation alliance" remain a salient issue, especially amid continuing charges in the United States and Western Europe that the ANC is dominated by the SACP. Both organizations readily acknowledge their longtime close cooperation, but both organizations are equally explicit that each body maintains a separate status respected by the other and that the association has had mutual benefits for each.

Assessing the alliance from an SACP perspective, Brian Bunting, editor of the *African Communist*, observed that

a process of cross-pollination occurred between the communist party and the national movement. On the one hand that communist party achieved and incorporated in its program a truer understanding of the nature and importance of the national movement than it ever had before. On the other hand the national movement was moved toward an appreciation of the class forces which underlie the national conflict in South Africa and to perceive the relationship between the national struggle of the oppressed people of South Africa and the international movement against imperialism and war. The nationalism of the ANC . . . developed an international dimension; the communist party was indigenized. (*Communist Viewpoint*, March 1987.)

In the complementary view of an ANC commentator, "If there is any kind of influence that the communist party has had on the ANC, in our own experience, it has been to make us stauncher nationalists and democrats. Communists have demonstrated by personal example what is meant by dedication and heroism in the struggle against national oppression." (*Sechaba*, July 1987.)

General Secretary Slovo of the SACP sees a clear differentiation of function between the roles of the ANC and the SACP:

Unlike the ANC, which does not and should not commit itself exclusively to the aspirations of a single class, the SACP owes allegiance solely to the working people. And it is our prime function both as an independent party and part of the alliance to assert and jealously safeguard the dominant role of the class whose aspirations we represent. (*African Communist*, no. 106.)

In the face of the present heightened government repression of the mass opposition within the country, the SACP considers that highest priority must be given by both it and the ANC to consolidating its underground organizational presence:

Our party's leadership has drawn an important conclusion about paying particular attention to properly organizing its forces. The SACP is stepping up its activities where workers are concentrated and where it is easier to mobilize them in our struggle. Relying on worker support, we can block enemy attempts at infiltrating the SACP ranks and weakening the party from within . . . together with the ANC, the party is also conducting extensive explanatory work among the people. We hold that, at the present time, organization also means perfecting underground structures, both at factories and in residential areas. The state of emer-

gency and the recent banning of the UDF and COSATU prove that only this underground level of leadership is capable of keeping the resistance going. Only the underground structures are able to preserve our revolutionary cadres, coordinate the various partial insurrections and combat actions of the people's army towards the buildup of conditions for a general insurrection and the seizure of power by the people. (*WMR*, July.)

Outside the country, party members in Europe and Africa—concentrated in Zambia, Angola, and Tanzania—continue their activities both within party structures and within the ANC. To ensure the security of senior party leaders, major party gatherings continue to be held in exile.

Domestic Activities and Attitudes. The SACP remains committed to its 1962 program in which South Africa was recognized as displaying a "colonialism of a special type," characterized by a party analyst as "a form of bourgeois domination in which the black majority of South Africa is separated, fragmented, and subordinated in a variety of ways (economically, politically, socially, culturally), while at the same time being included within the fabric of a relatively advanced capitalist society" (*African Communist*, no. 114).

Thus, the SACP has set as its immediate goal the establishment of a national democratic republic en route to the achievement of socialism. In its 1984 constitution the party's goals were restated:

The communist party aims . . . to organise, educate, and lead the working class in pursuit of this strategic aim (i.e., ending the system of capitalist exploitation and establishing a socialist republic based on the common ownership of the means of production) and the more immediate aim of winning the objectives of the national democratic revolution which is inseparably linked to it . . . the main content of the national democratic revolution is the national liberation of the African people in particular, and the black people in general, the destruction of the economic and political power of the racist ruling class, and the establishment of one united state of people's power *in which the working class will be the dominant force* and which will move uninterruptedly towards social emancipation and the total abolition of the exploitation of man by man (*African Communist*, no. 113).

In the assessment of party commentators the dramatic growth of the mass movement in the mid-

1980s has opened new possibilities in the search for national democracy.

> Out of concrete struggle—indeed because of achievements in organization and mobilization—the question of reaching out to the widest spectrum of the people stands out in even bolder relief. Various tactics have to be employed to win the multitude of the "unorganized" into the struggle. One of the most important is to find common ground with formations which are broadly speaking or potentially antiapartheid to which many of these forces belong and act jointly with them: *the fundamental aim being to raise the consciousness of the masses and activate them to become staunch participants in the struggle for national democracy.* The campaign for a united broad antiapartheid coalition should seek to achieve this main purpose. (*African Communist*, no. 114.)

Particular attention should be paid to blacks in "apolitical" organizations such as youth bodies, women's clubs, sporting organizations, and churches as well as to blacks in "genuinely patriotic organizations" such as black consciousness–oriented trade unions (the National Council of Trade Unions—NACTU) and other bodies, "which pursue some form of democracy or 'socialism' but are blinded by misconceptions and incomprehension of the actual social relations and their interrelationships" (ibid.). It is also argued that

> to make further decisive advances requires the activation of broad sectors of whites in various forms of opposition to the system. What is absolutely necessary is that the consistently democratic and active forces, representing the most oppressed and exploited sections, have to strengthen themselves as well as their rapport if they are to play their historic role. A front is itself a dynamic organism, undergoing organizational and political changes in the process of development. The principle is that it should serve the desired purpose, involve the masses at all levels, and not lead to weakening of democratic organizations or a coalition of such organizations. The UDF is such a coalition. Five years on, it remains an important historical force in the political arena. Hand in hand with the democratic union movement—on the basis of permanent, local, regional, and national structures—the two organizations can only emerge at the head of the broad antiapartheid coalition. (*African Communist*, no. 114.)

The rapid expansion of the trade union movement (centered in COSATU), its continued militancy and willingness to strike, and the explicit adoption by COSATU of the 1955 Freedom Charter of the ANC and its allies provide convincing evidence to the SACP that the working class is taking the leading role, predicted for it by the party, in efforts to achieve national democracy and subsequently socialism. It is essential that the trade union movement strengthen itself by increasing unionization among colored and Asian workers and seek to organize the migrant workers, the unemployed, and the farm workers (including those in the bantustans). To assure that the "victory of the national democratic revolution will mean an uninterrupted advance of our society to the socialist revolution" the Central Committee of the SACP argues that

> the first condition for this is that the working class never succumb to seeing its task as merely leading itself. As a class we maintain the class independence of the communist party and the trade union movement in order that we "should fight with all the greater energy and enthusiasm for the cause of the whole people, at the head of the whole people" (Lenin). In order to "fight for the cause of the whole people" we have to understand that in the South African context the working class must be seen to be acting not only in its own interests but also in the interests of all the oppressed classes and strata. In practical terms this means that the working class must be fully engaged in all formations—the ANC, the SACP, the trade union movement and other formations of the mass democratic movement and in Umkhonto we Sizwe. (*African Communist*, no. 113.)

The Central Committee welcomes the upsurge of interest in trade unions, the increasingly explicit critiques of capitalism, and discussions about socialism that have infused dialogue along the full spectrum of opinions represented in the labor movement and the antiapartheid resistance within South Africa. In the debate over the nature of, and relationship between, workers' control, freedom, and socialism, a party analyst identifies two tendencies, "workerists" and "populists." The *workerist* tendency is a diverse grouping of those who contend that the working class must act alone through trade unions to achieve socialism and those "ultraleftists" who reject the emphasis on the achievement of democracy and coalition with elements outside the working class and condemn any "two-stage" move to socialism via "bourgeois" or "national" democracy; in the definition of the party analyst the *populist* tendency is also a grouping, but all the groups agree that a broad national movement, not "a pure workers-and-unions-only constituency," is a necessary part of any advance toward socialism that can occur within and beyond the achievement of democracy.

Communists, in the eyes of the party analyst, have developed a complex variant of the populist concept that recognizes that the "national liberation struggle and the Freedom Charter are in the *immediate* interests of *all* classes of oppressed and exploited people in South Afrcia; that they awaken the consciousness of wider masses than is possible for any more narrow class or sectarian movement" (*African Communist*, no. 114). From the perspective of the Central Committee it is essential to

> grasp this rising tide of interest in national liberation and socialism as a unique opportunity to further develop the political consciousness and organizational skill of the workers of our country. We communists are particularly well equipped to engage constructively in this debate. Not because we have a monopoly of truth. Not because we are infallible. But because we believe in the unity of theory and practice, and because we are equipped with the science of Marxism-Leninism. (*African Communist*, No. 113.)

International Views and Activities. An underground appeal circulated in the western Cape and printed in the *African Communist* asserted that

> the SACP is a proud and staunch member of the world communist movement. We stand for proletarian internationalism, without which there can be no socialist revolution. We are vigorously opposed to all efforts to undermine and deny the importance of the world communist movement. This anticommunism and anti-Sovietism is the ideological weapon of both the imperialist bourgeoisie and of the opportunist, ultraleft petite bourgeoisie against the working class. (*African Communist*, no. 112.)

Enthusiastically participating in the celebrations of the 70th anniversary of the Bolshevik revolution in Moscow in November 1987, the SACP delegation endorsed "the excellent and refreshing report" of General Secretary Mikhail Gorbachev (*African Communist*, no. 113). Subsequently his book *Perestroika—New Thinking for Our Country and the World* was favorably reviewed. In the critique of the reviewer,

The experience of the Soviet Union shows that it is excessive centralization and bureaucracy that produces stagnation and even crisis within the socialist system. Such methods undermine mass initiative and have no respect for the individual and no consideration for personal dignity. True socialism means true democracy. Gorbachev insists that *perestroika* takes the Soviet Union to a better socialism rather than away from it. Those who hope that *perestroika* will build a different, nonsocialist society and go over to the capitalist camp will be disappointed. The crisis of the seventies and eighties was a result of insufficient consistency in applying socialism, of a departure from its principles and distortion of them. *Perestroika* will bring socialism back on course. (Ibid.)

Delegations from the SACP participate in meetings of international communist organizations such as a discussion of the work of the *World Marxist Review* held in Prague in April, where the SACP delegation was one of 93 "fraternal communist, workers' and revolutionary democratic parties" in attendance (*WRM*, June). In August General Secretary Slovo visited Bulgaria where he was received by General Secretary Todor Zhivkov of the Bulgarian Communist Party (*FBIS*, 26 August). An SACP delegation visited the Front for the Liberation of Mozambique in 1987, described at the time as "the first bilateral exchange between the two parties. The warm, fraternal welcome accorded to the SACP delegation symbolizes the growing comradeship and cooperation of the two Marxist-Leninist parties." (*African Communist*, no. 111.)

Publications. Since 1959 the SACP has published a quarterly, the *African Communist*, "in the interest of African solidarity and as a forum for Marxist-Leninist thought throughout our continent." Printed in the German Democratic Republic and distributed from London, the journal primarily focuses on analyses of South African developments, primarily by party members writing under noms de plume. It also contains a regular feature, African Notes and Comments, that assesses events elsewhere on the continent. Although less frequently than in the past, articles on Soviet, East European, and Cuban topics also appear. Within South Africa the SACP publishes *Umsebenzi*, an underground quarterly whose title is the Zulu/Xhosa word for *worker* and the name of the legal party newspaper published from 1930 to 1936. The SACP disseminates smuggled Marxist-Leninist classics and other party publications, along with clandestinely produced propaganda aimed at mobilizing worker support for itself, the ANC, and Umkhonto.

Like the SACP, the ANC also publishes in exile and underground within the country; its major publication, the monthly *Sechaba*, is also published with support from the German Democratic Republic. The ANC also transmits Radio Freedom, regularly carried on shortwave by the state radios of Angola, Ethiopia, Madagascar, Tanzania, and Zambia.

Sheridan Johns
Duke University

Sudan

Population. 24,014,495
Party. Sudanese Communist Party (al-Hizb al-Shuyu'i al-Sudani; SCP)
Founded. 1946
Membership. 9,000 (estimated)
General Secretary. Muhammad Ibrahim Nugud Mansur
Secretariat. Muhammad Ibrahim Nugud Mansur, Ali al-Tijani al-Tayyib Babikr, Izz al-Din Ali Amir, Abu al-Qasim (Gassim) Muhammad, Sulayman Hamid, al-Gazuli Said Uthman, Muhammad Ahmad Sulayman (Suleiman)
Central Committee. Sudi Darag, Khidr Nasr, Abd al-Majid Shakak, Hasan Gassim al-Sid, Fatima Ahmad Ibrahim, Ibrahim Zakariya, and the members of the Secretariat
Status. Legal
Last Congress. Fourth, 31 October 1967, in Khartoum
Last Election. 1986; 1.67 percent of the total vote in territorial constituencies; 5 seats out of the contested 264 (2 in territorial constituencies and 3 in special ones for "graduates") (Sudan News Agency [SUNA], 25 May 1986)
Auxiliary Organizations. Democratic Federation of Sudanese Students; Sudanese Youth Union; Sudan Workers' Trade Union Federation; Sudanese Defenders of Peace and Democracy; Union of Sudanese Women

Publications. *Al-Maydan* (official party newspaper); *al-Shuyu'i*

Organized communist activity in the Sudan began in the 1920s, but it was not until 1946 that Sudanese intellectuals and students created a formal party organization. The SCP has been both publicly and clandestinely active in Sudanese politics since then. It was active through the Anti-Imperialist Front in the first era of parliamentary politics (1953–1958) and then was part of the opposition to the first military regime (1958–1964). SCP members played a leading role in the 1964 revolution, which overthrew military rule, and participated in the transitional government. However, despite winning eleven seats in the 1965 parliamentary elections, opposition to the SCP by the new prime minister, Sadiq al-Mahdi, led to the party's exclusion from parliament (see *YICA*, 1968). When the second era of civilian politics was brought to an end by a military coup in 1969, the SCP gave strong support to the coup's leader, Ja'far Numayri.

Communists were influential in the first two years of the Numayri regime, but tensions led to an abortive, communist-supported coup in the summer of 1971 and the subsequent vigorous suppression of the SCP and the execution of many of its leaders. The SCP joined other civilian parties in opposition to Numayri and again in 1985 played a leading role in popular demonstrations that led to the overthrow of military rule. The SCP became an active participant in the restored partisan civilian political arena and won 5 of the 264 contested seats in the 1986 elections. Because of its experienced leadership and ties with other social and political groupings, the SCP is now a visible part of the parliamentary opposition.

Leadership. General Secretary Nugud and others in the party leadership have long been active in civilian politics in the Sudan. Nugud was already on the SCP executive committee in the 1960s, and he and others have participated in important political events like the favorably viewed revolutions of 1964 and 1985. As a result, even though the party is small compared with the traditional parties, its leaders have visibility and are respected by most Sudanese. In turn, the party leadership advocates a reformist rather than a revolutionary program. Nugud believes that the resolution of the political crises in the Sudan lies "in a reform of the regime of bourgeois parliamentary democracy in order to get rid of the 'Westminster model,' with its trappings of popular power, and to make the state administration system accord with the conditions and specifics of the Sudanese society at the present stage of its development" (*WMR*, February). More radically oriented leadership does not seem, at the moment, to have much influence within the party.

Domestic Issues. The year 1988 was one of natural catastrophe and political turmoil in the Sudan. Many parts of the country suffered from famine and epidemics, and great floods in August left more than a million people homeless in the area of Khartoum, the capital, and its sister city, Omdurman. In addition, the civil war in the southern regions of the country continued. In this context, the SCP maintained a relatively low level of political visibility. The party continued to criticize government failures to resolve any of the Sudanese crises but did so within the framework of parliamentary opposition.

The role of the SCP in parliament changed during 1988. At the beginning of the year, it was one of a number of parties opposing a government based on a coalition of the two large traditional parties, the Ummah Party, led by Sadiq al-Mahdi who served as prime minister, and the Democratic Unionist Party (DUP), led by Muhammad Osman al-Mirghani. In April, al-Mahdi created a "government of national reconciliation" in which the old parties were joined by the National Islamic Front (NIF) and the southern parties in parliament. The SCP was the only party not to join the new national coalition, partly because of the SCP's opposition to any formal implementation of Islamic Law in the Sudan.

In December the situation changed again. The NIF had begun to work more closely with Prime Minister al-Mahdi, and the DUP became increasingly alienated. At the end of the month, during large demonstrations against government food pricing policies and calls for new negotiations to bring the civil war to an end, the DUP announced its withdrawal from the government. Whether this represented a long-term change was unclear, but it did provide an opening for the SCP, which had worked in a short-lived alliance with Muhammad Osman al-Mirghani's father in the 1960s.

In general the SCP continued its basic positions on the major issues of Sudanese politics. Continuing to support a settlement to the civil war in the southern part of the country that would provide special autonomy for that region, the SCP pressed for a cease-fire, the abolition of Islamic Law measures, the restoration of secular law, and the con-

vocation of a national constitutional conference (*WMR*, January). These ideas received strong support in November when leaders of the DUP and the Sudan People's Liberation Movement (SPLM) held discussions and signed an agreement calling for a cease-fire, suspending the implementation of Islamic Law, and convening a national convention (*FBIS*, 21 November). Although the SCP could praise this agreement and urge the prime minister to act on it (*al-Maydan*, 13 December), the party had no direct involvement in the negotiations.

These developments at the end of the year provided the SCP with new opportunities. There were popular demonstrations in support of the peace agreement and in opposition to the government's raising basic food prices. Under these conditions, as was the case in 1964 and 1985, SCP organization and concentration in the major urban areas can give it added importance. However, the party remains on the periphery of the politics of the Sudan in the 1980s, where Marxist and socialist ideas have less mass appeal than traditional religious affiliations, new Islamic fundamentalism, or the special radicalism of the SPLM.

International Positions. The SCP is a relatively orthodox, Soviet-oriented communist party whose leaders exchange visits with Soviet bloc party officials on a regular basis. However, Sudanese government leaders also maintained friendly, if formal, contacts with major communist governments as well. The Soviet Union and the Sudanese government signed a special protocol for cultural cooperation (*FBIS-Soviet Union*, 3 March), and there were visits by Soviet leaders to the Sudan. The SCP played no special role in these activities or received any particular recognition. Similarly, late in the year, Prime Minister al-Mahdi engaged in discussions with the Ethiopian government as a result of encouragement from the Soviet Union; again the SCP had no role in these developments.

In regional affairs, the SCP continued to support the idea of a negotiated settlement of the Arab-Israeli conflict in the context of an international conference. It also maintained its opposition to apartheid in South Africa. The year 1988 was not one of dramatic initiatives by the SCP in international positions.

In general, the SCP continues to be a party of intellectuals, students, and organized working groups. Among these groups it faces the competition of the nontraditional Islamic ideological groups like the Muslim Brotherhood. There is no indication that the SCP made any significant progress during 1988 in expanding the base of its support. The changing conditions at the end of the year may have created some new opportunities for increasing its influence through possible new political alliances. However, it remains a small party on the margins of the political scene.

John O. Voll
University of New Hampshire

Zimbabwe

Population. 9,730,000
Party. Zimbabwe African National Union–Patriotic Front (ZANU-PF)
Founded. 1963
Membership. No data
First Secretary and President. Robert G. Mugabe
Politburo. 15 seats. Robert Mugabe, Simon Muzenda (holds 2 seats), Meyor Urimbo, Tapumaneyi Mujuru, Maurice Nyagumbo, Enos Nkala, Emmerson Munangagwa, Nathan Shamuyarira, Didymus Mutasa, Dzingai Mutumbuka, Teurai Nhongo, Sydney Sekeremayi, Josiah Tongamirai, Ernest Kadungura
Central Committee. 90 members
Status. Ruling party
Last Congress. Third (extraordinary session), April 1988
Last Election. October 1987 (for 30 new parliamentary seats)
Auxiliary Organizations. People's Militia, Youth Wing
Publications. *Zimbabwe News*. Nearly all news organs are government owned in whole or in part. The major exception is the privately owned weekly, *The Financial Gazette*, which operates independently of party and government.

Party Organization and Domestic Political Conditions. The real power in Zimbabwe lies with the ZANU Politburo, although ultimate authority rests with Robert Mugabe, who serves as party head. Mugabe's position in both government and party continues to grow as a result of the new party structure established at the Second Congress in 1984, the constitutional amendment of 1987 creating a more powerful presidency, and the stunningly successful absorption of the Zimbabwe African People's Union (ZAPU), the opposition party, by ZANU, the ruling party.

As executive president, Mugabe is simultaneously the head of the party, the government, and the state. Although Mugabe has committed himself to ultimately establishing a Marxist state, his increasingly pragmatic economic policies and purges of radical ideologues from the party leadership have won the collaboration of key white leaders in the capitalist sectors and contributed to the viability of those areas of private enterprise that are considered essential to economic growth.

President Mugabe's standing in the country was enormously boosted in 1988 by his achievement of a merger with ZAPU, the major opposition party. At an extraordinary ZANU-PF congress held in early April, three thousand delegates unanimously approved of the merger (*Pravda*, 10 April), thus establishing a de facto one-party state. Nevertheless, Maurice Nyagumbo, a leading member of the Politburo, announced that a one-party system will evolve naturally and not by legislative fiat (*Zimbabwe News*, 28 December). It is now uncertain whether the provision for a one-party state will be added to the constitution in 1990, as announced earlier (*WMR*, June).

Mugabe is president of the reconstituted ZANU-PF; Joshua Nkomo, his long-standing adversary and former leader of ZAPU, accepted the offer to become one of its two vice presidents. The new party affirmed its adherence to the principles of Marxism-Leninism, even though its key leaders support policies favoring a mixed economy. In a conciliatory gesture, the government offered a general amnesty to dissidents; at least 113 former ZAPU combatants responded by surrendering their arms (*WP*, 2 June). Many of these former dissidents have enrolled in the government's Mapfure College to learn vocational and technical skills for re-entry into the economy (*CSM*, 28 April).

In 1988, peace returned to Matabeleland, the old ZAPU stronghold and the center of most antigovernment terrorist activity (*NYT*, 11 June). Throughout the year, the delicate process of coalition building gained momentum, and considerable progress was made in the integration of all organs of ZANU and ZAPU at all levels: national, provincial, district, branch, and local cell (ZIANA, 14 December). The exercise is expected to be completed in late 1989. Plans were also laid for enlarging the party's Central Committee to accommodate former leaders of ZAPU (Frost & Sullivan, Zimbabwe Country Report, annual [F&S], October).

Nearly all observers were struck by the remarkable smoothness of the transition considering the many years of enmity between the two parties and the ethnic hostility between the Ndebele, who composed ZAPU, and the Shona, who continue to play a major role in ZANU. In a further conciliatory move, the government released most, and possibly all, of its political detainees. The dramatic decline in antigovernment guerrilla activity in Matabeleland has been matched by a decrease in antiinsurgency police and army harassment of the civilian population. Overall, the government's civil and human rights record showed remarkable improvement and the country enjoyed a measure of domestic peace and tranquility not experienced in nearly a decade and a half. Nevertheless, the state of emergency, in force for more than a decade, was renewed to allow the government to deal quickly with turmoil that might arise during the tense transition process (*Economist Intelligence Unit* [*EIU*], no. 2).

Domestic Economic Conditions. Zimbabwe's enviable progress in the area of political and national unification was matched by the improvement in its economy, which by mid-1988 found itself moving out of its recession. The recovery stemmed from a combination of good rainfall, falling prices of imported petroleum, and economic policies that greatly boosted the output of ores and food and cash crops for export and domestic consumption. Commercial and peasant farmers produced bumper crops of tobacco, cotton, corn, and soybeans. The manufacturing sector also rebounded, though less spectacularly (F&S, October). Moreover, an aggressive export promotion program and the quiet devaluation of the local currency gave all foreign earnings a substantial boost in local terms (*Africa Analysis* [*AA*], fortnightly bulletin on financial and political trends, 25 November). The real gross domestic product growth rate moved into the positive range, and the overall balance of payments position improved. The country continued, however, to suffer from a serious foreign exchange crisis that created severe shortages of imported spare parts for industrial machinery and transport vehicles. Moreover, the economic turnaround was set against a disquieting backdrop of rising unemployment and worker agitation for wage scales consistent with the quickening pace of inflation (*Africa Economic Di-*

gest [AED], 15 April). The government responded by partially lifting the freeze on wages and prices (*EIU*, no. 2). Worker discontent was not entirely assuaged, and in 1988 the number of strikes and walkouts grew, particularly in the state-owned enterprises, and was best reflected in the paralyzing work stoppage at the Zimbabwe Banking Corporation. The Zimbabwe Congress of Trade Unions was unsuccessful in influencing any changes in government labor policy and began to draw fire from its own rank and file. Pressure was also building to speed the Africanization of management-level jobs in the private sector and to settle the unemployed on rural lands under absentee white ownership (African Consulting Associates [ACA], *Zimbabwe report*, December).

Public corruption and graft emerged as major political issues in 1988. Criticism was also voiced against the growing "bourgeois" tendencies of public servants. Indeed, many government officials, including Vice-Chairman Nkomo and leading members of the Politburo, had begun to enter the private sector as fledgling capitalist entrepreneurs (*AA*, 1 April). Others in the civil service were accused of breaches in the leadership code. Leftists, particularly university students, intelligentsia, and unemployed or landless former guerrillas, initiated a number of demonstrations. On several campuses students, who traditionally supported Mugabe's socialist policies, clashed with police and ZANU party youth cells loyal to the regime (*Washington Times*, 11 October). President Mugabe labeled the dissident faculty and students as "counterrevolutionary," and one outspoken expatriate Marxist at the University of Zimbabwe was expelled from the country (ZIANA, 29 October). Several leftist academics in Harare also criticized Mikhail Gorbachev's policies of *perestroika*, arguing that the liberation struggle in southern Africa was being sacrificed on the altar of East-West détente. This came on the heels of a lecture by a visiting Soviet official who called for peaceful dialogue with the Botha regime and its allies and for a negotiated settlement to avert a destructive racial holocaust (*WP*, 11 October). At the same time Edgar Tekere, a prominent and popular politician, was expelled from the party's Central Committee after his criticism of the government's moves toward a de jure one-party system.

Although the government tolerates, and in some cases supports, the private sector, it continued to pursue its policy of acquiring equity in key private enterprises and thus ran against the continentwide trend toward privatization of the public sector. In 1988, the state-run Zimbabwe Reinsurance Corporation increased its control over the local insurance sector through its buyout of several large, mainly South African–based private concerns (*AED*, 19 August). By the same token, the National Oil Corporation of Zimbabwe in September acquired a large share of a French-based firm, Total Zimbabwe (*AA*, 14 October). The government also announced its intention of making greater investments in "strategic" industries such as mining and energy (American Embassy, Harare, airgram, 29 January). Many Zimbabweans, especially the whites, believe that the financially pressed government can ill afford to tie up so much capital at a time when existing parastatals are annually losing Zimbabwe more than 4 percent of its gross national product (*Times Herald-Record*, 19 December). Industry Minister C. Ndlovu countered that greater government participation in industry was necessary to create jobs in an economy suffering from chronic and deepening unemployment (*AED*, 26 April).

International Relations. Zimbabwe in 1988 continued to strengthen its trade, cultural, and diplomatic relations with Marxist countries. A policy driven not by a new ideological fervor for communism but consistent with President Mugabe's position as chairman of the Non-Aligned Movement, it may also stem from a need to compensate for shortfalls of aid and investment from Western sources as well as from a desire to lessen Zimbabwe's dependence on South Africa. The latter remains Zimbabwe's largest source of imports and purchases the majority of its exports.

The USSR has pledged $108 million to the frontline states, including Zimbabwe, to resist "colonialism and apartheid" (*EIU*, no. 2). In September, a large parliamentary delegation visited the Soviet Union at the invitation of the USSR's Supreme Soviet. Discussions centered on the need for easing regional tensions and for a negotiated settlement of the conflict in Angola and Namibia. (*FBIS*, 15 September.) In May, the government received a delegation of Soviet trade unionists (*FBIS*, 31 May). However, ZANU vice president Joshua Nkomo cautioned Soviet trade officials that the independence of private business in Zimbabwe had to be taken into account in any trade deals between the two countries (ZIANA, 13 May). In June, a communist party delegation traveled to Harare to sign cooperation protocols with ZANU-PF and to launch a Zimbabwe–Soviet Union Friendship Association (*FBIS*, 17 June).

On the issue of Angola, Zimbabwe continued to give diplomatic support to the José dos Santos government and to the Cubans' agreement in January (ZIANA, 24 January). A similar accord was signed with Cuba a month later, though additional provisions were made for closer cooperation in the area of tourism, a sector that has suffered in recent years with the decline of tourists from South Africa (*FBIS*, 18 February). Romania and Zimbabwe continue to draw closer together, especially in the realms of educational and cultural exchanges. By contrast, there has been a perceptible cooling of relations with the Democratic People's Republic of Korea. Key leaders in the private sector and moderates in government would like to improve trade ties with Pacific rim countries, including South Korea, which is regarded as a country with enormous market potential. Nevertheless, Zimbabwe was gratified by Marxist Vietnam's offer to purchase a portion of its huge tobacco crop (ACA, December).

Relations with the People's Republic of China remain cordial, despite the escalating racial tension between Asian and African students in Chinese universities (*NYT*, 30 December). In June, China entered into a joint venture by agreeing to provide half the funding for a $31 million teacher training college in the rural Zimbabwean town of Chinhoyl (*AED*, 18 March). Two months later, Zimbabwe's foreign minister, Nathan Shamuyarira, paid an official visit to Beijing (*FBIS*, 23 August). Within weeks, a $5 million technical management agreement was concluded between China's International Engineering Consulting Corporation and the Zimbabwe Iron and Steel Corporation, one of the country's largest parastatals. Although still comparatively modest in relation to the West, bilateral trade—much of it countertrade—and capital flows from China, the Soviet Union, and communist bloc countries continue to grow.

Zimbabwe's relationships with the African National Congress and the Pan-Africanist Congress have become warmer. Bowing to pressure from South Africa, Mugabe has steadfastly refused to permit either organization to establish headquarters or any other kind of guerrilla operation within Zimbabwe.

Relations with the United States, its second biggest trading partner, greatly improved in August after the Americans lifted a two-year suspension of nearly all forms of assistance. The U.S. ambassador described Zimbabwe as a "model for prosperity and stability in a strategically important region" and committed his country to a $17 million, three-year aid package for the purchase of U.S.-made agricultural equipment and to help reinvigorate Zimbabwe's private sector (*African Business* [*AB*], November). This will complement an $8.5 million World Bank (WB) line of credit to assist small African businesses (WB, *1988 annual report*).

By contrast, little headway has been made in attracting private U.S. investments, even though bilateral trade is quite substantial. The U.S. multinationals complained that Zimbabwe has not provided sufficient incentives or devised an investment code explicitly forbidding nationalizations of foreign holdings.

The country's relations with fellow members of the Preferential Trade Area (PTA) and the Southern African Development Coordination Conference (SADCC) remain productive, and trade within the region is gradually increasing, generally in Zimbabwe's favor. Zimbabwe plays a major role in the PTA: the governor of its reserve bank is executive secretary of the PTA's clearinghouse, and the secretary general of the entire multination trade organization is a prominent Zimbabwean economist. Nevertheless, Zimbabwe has drawn fire from its preponderant role, and there were several disputes in 1988 between SADCC and PTA over each other's roles and parameters of responsibility (*AB*, May). Relations with neighboring Botswana have improved, and the two nations agreed to renew their 32-year-old preferential trade pact.

In regard to Mozambique, the government is continuing its large military presence along the 196-mile vital transportation corridor to the port of Beira. The undertaking has placed a huge burden on the country's hard-pressed budget, but new support has been forthcoming from the West, particularly Great Britain and the Nordic countries, and to a lesser extent from the Soviet Union and communist bloc countries. By October, there were indications that the Mozambique National Resistance, the guerrilla movement seeking to overthrow the Mozambique government, had been contained. This has enabled Zimbabwe and Mozambique to proceed with the rehabilitation of the 350-mile Limpopo Railway to the port of Maputo (*CSM*, 13 October). Support for this project has come mainly from the Canadians, the Americans, and the British.

In conclusion ZANU-PF, under the astute leadership of President Mugabe and Second Vice President Nkomo, emerged from 1988 larger, politically stronger, and more broadly representative of the country's population. The government succeeded in steering a course between socialism and capitalism, pursuing pragmatic, conciliatory strategies, and avoided falling under the control of any one power bloc in the world community of nations. It has won grudging support from a broad spectrum of Zimbabweans, white and black. Nevertheless, to remain on course, it must face the challenge of turmoil in South Africa and the threat of rising domestic unemployment. It must also complete the delicate and tortuous task of merging the two parties.

Richard W. Hull
New York University

THE AMERICAS

Introduction

In the Americas, the strategies and tactics of Marxist-Leninist organizations fell roughly into three timeworn categories: (1) open or covert participation in the often fledgling democratic systems of their countries, usually through labor and student organizations, on the one hand, and multiparty coalitions on the other; (2) waging war against their governments, while, in every case but that of the Shining Path in Peru, protesting at the same time that they really want a negotiated settlement of substantive differences; and (3) practicing some mix of the two.

But there often was nothing routine about the way these general approaches were molded to fit differing national conditions, or how international actors became involved in the plots. Indeed, Marxist-Leninist activities in the Western Hemisphere during 1988 reflected an extraordinary mix of creativity, realism, opportunism, dogmatism, and foreign intervention that brought about startling (and at least short-term) successes, unprecedented national failures, and sordid alliances that make the Nazi-Soviet Pact of 1939 seem almost benign by comparison.

Increasing Marxist-Leninist participation in legal political affairs was reflected in the number of party congresses held between late 1987 and early 1989—well over a dozen, considerably more than ever before in a comparable time period. In every case except that of the Peruvian Shining Path, held in February 1988, these congresses were devoted mainly to strategies and tactics of electoral participation.

International involvement in the hemisphere took such varied forms as continuing massive Soviet aid to Cuba and Nicaragua, Moscow's role as chief munitions supplier for Peru, and extensive Soviet trade and other connections with Argentina. In addition to the numerous contacts between American communists and Soviet-bloc officials in East Euro-pean countries, there were contacts in the Americas, as when Karen Brutents, deputy chief of the CPSU Central Committee International Department visited Panama in September, for the third time in four years, and met with leaders of the country's communist and ruling parties. Among the international meetings convened were the Third Meeting of Communist Parties of South America, in Montevideo in August, and the session of the Anti-Imperialist Organization of Central America and the Caribbean in June that involved dozens of leftist organizations from the Caribbean Basin.

On 1 January 1989, Fidel Castro celebrated his 30th anniversary as Maximum Leader of the Cuban Revolution. With the fall of Alfredo Stroessner in Paraguay in early 1989, Castro became the only dictator in the hemisphere who has been entrenched in power for decades. Indeed, since Brother Raúl is his designated successor, this sinister Pooh Bah, who is lord-high everything in the country, presides over the only remaining family dynasty in the Americas. Castro remains the foremost communist in the Americas by virtue of his longevity, his reputation as the first Latin to get away with punching Uncle Sam in the nose, and his strength, derived both from his relentless anti-Americanism and the massive support he receives from the Soviet Union. Nonetheless, many Latin leftists increasingly consider Castro an anachronism. At the end of December 1988, an international group of some 170 intellectuals called upon Castro to hold a plebiscite in Cuba, to which the Cuban Foreign Ministry retorted: "Absurd and inconceivable. Our people had a referendum 30 years ago on the day of the triumph of the revolution."

The Cuban economy remains in shambles, with declining production and foreign reserves, sustained by an estimated $5 billion in economic and military aid from the Soviet Union. What is more, Castro has not just refused to decentralize the economy and loosen up central control, as Soviet leaders have suggested, he has instead increased the authority of the state and Communist Party of Cuba. Worker apathy suggests that the Cuban people lack enthusiasm for current conditions and Castro's responses to them. Through the communist party, Castro has vigorously promoted the War of All the

People, a mass mobilization that has made Cuba one of the most heavily militarized countries in the world. The mobilization is supposedly intended to forestall a U.S. invasion, but in fact it is probably intended more to tighten Castro's control over an increasingly restive population and to discourage dissidents within the armed forces from challenging his authority.

Castro allowed several international human rights organizations to visit Cuba in 1988, but Ricardo Bofill, long head of the Havana-based Cuban Committee for Human Rights, wrote in *The Wall Street Journal* in December that these organizations "have done little more than scratch the surface" of national conditions. Although for much of 1988 there were reports that human rights violations were decreasing, the end of the year and early 1989 brought much contrary evidence. At the same time, Castro reportedly has ordered the millions of members of the Committees for the Defense of the Revolution to stop preparing reports on the activities of their neighbors.

Though scorning the reforms proposed in the Soviet Union and China, Castro has maintained his solidarity with many revolutionary groups and governments abroad. For example, he has continued his substantial support for the Sandinista revolution in Nicaragua and for the FMLN guerrillas in El Salvador. He boycotted the Seoul Olympics held in South Korea in solidarity with North Korea. At the end of the year Cuba, South Africa, and Angola signed a peace treaty providing for Namibian independence and the withdrawal of some 50,000 Cuban troops from Angola by July 1991. Cuban relations with the People's Republic of China have inproved considerably in recent years, as indicated by Foreign Minister Isidoro Malmierca's visit to Beijing in January 1989.

The Sandinista government in Nicaragua celebrated the end of the Reagan administration in January 1989 with banners proclaiming: "Reagan is Going, the Revolution Remains." Even as they did so, day by day the country collapsed from within. Armed conflict between the Sandinistas and the Nicaraguan Resistance virtually ceased during 1988, but relative peace brought anything but prosperity. Amidst a series of what the Sandinista paper *Barricada* called "adjustments," prices soared and to a considerable degree informal markets sustained the people. In September, *Barricada* reported a "dizzying rise of the black market in meat" and other products. By January 1989 inflation had rocketed to 36,000 percent. At the end of January 1989,

President Daniel Ortega announced a severe austerity plan that included laying off up to 35,000 government employees, including 10,000 from the military and 13,000 from the security police. The fact that 13,000 members of the security forces could be laid off and a substantial number still remain demonstrated the pervasiveness of Sandinista control in the country.

Repression increased during 1988, as was shown most graphically in the government's smashing of a peaceful demonstration at Nandaime, south of Managua, in July. But it was evident also in numerous lesser incidents throughout the year, including unexplained deaths, beatings, and disappearances of opposition political and labor leaders. In November, *Avance*, the weekly paper of the Nicaraguan Communist Party, a member of the united front of organizations encompassing both left and right that has condemned the Sandinistas, said: "The police and courts are highly efficient in fabricating false proofs and sending workers, peasants, employees, and managers to jail, whose only fault is having independent political views and denouncing the daily abuses suffered by citizens." Even Americas Watch, a New York human rights organization generally more critical of the right than the left, concluded in August that killings "are numerous enough to suggest tolerance or complicity by higher authorities." "The only time the government spends any money on the people these days," one worker in the Managua streets told me in August, "is when it builds more jails."

Sandinista relations with the Soviet bloc remained strong, while those with the United States deteriorated through the end of the Reagan administration in January 1989. U.S. military aid to the resistance ended in February, and the Sandinistas sent troops into Honduras in March in an unsuccessful effort to destroy the resistance's arms supplies. In July, the Sandinistas accused the U.S. embassy in Managua of having plotted the "riots" at Nandaime and expelled the U.S. ambassador and some of his staff. The United States retaliated in kind. Although Daniel Ortega said in September: "We harbor no hopes about the next U.S. president—either Bush or Dukakis—as we know they support the same interests. Both will try to hinder or even eliminate the Nicaraguan Revolution," the Sandinistas clearly favored Michael Dukakis. Still, when George Bush took office in January 1989, the Sandinistas lifted their virtual siege of the U.S. embassy and called for a revival of the defunct Arias Peace Plan.

Elsewhere in Central America, most communist groups engaged in armed conflict while talking periodically of peace. In El Salvador, the right-wing ARENA party won a substantial victory in legislative elections, throwing the ruling Christian Democrats into confusion and opening the door to ploys by the Salvadoran Farabundo Marti National Liberation Front (FMLN) intended to advance its cause. In February, the FMLN described its strategy on its Radio Venceremos: "to annihilate and wear down enemy forces, sabotage the war economy, and destabilize and dismantle local and judicial authority." The guerrillas did this by a campaign of sabotage that the U.S. embassy estimates has caused $2 billion in economic loss in the past seven years, by promoting urban confrontations through such front groups as the National Union of Salvadoran Workers, by launching several major attacks on military installations, by stopping transportation and mining roads, and by assassinating and intimidating local elected government officials. For a while the guerrillas threatened to make U.S. citizens targets of attacks, but this policy was changed in early 1989.

At the same time, guerrilla leaders traveled in the region to promote their positions with noncommunist political leaders. For the first time this could be done with some consistency, for during the year the FMLN consolidated its organization under the undisputed leadership of the People's Revolutionary Army and its chief Joaquín Villalobos. In February 1989, the FMLN made its most daring move ever, proposing that if the government would postpone the March presidential election until September, the guerrillas would participate in the electoral process and abide by the people's decision. The guerrillas would support the Democratic Convergence, a coalition headed by Guillermo Ungo and Rubén Zamora, both longtime spokesmen for the FMLN's political front. As of early February most reactions to the guerrilla proposal were negative, though many fear the upsurge of warfare that is almost certain to come if the plan is turned down.

Guerrilla groups in Guatemala, united under the banner of the National Revolutionary Unity (URNG), claim to be "a real force" in the country, but in 1988 they were not. Though there were military engagements during the year, much attention was devoted to a publicity campaign in Guatemala and abroad. The URNG claimed, in the Sandinista's *Barricada Internacional* in September, that the principal obstacle to peace in the country is the military.

Honduras has long been a haven for both the Nicaraguan Resistance and for FMLN sympathizers, though military conflict in the country was minimal. During 1988, particularly after the legally dubious arrest and extradition in April of drug dealer Juan Ramón Matta, attacks increased on U.S. personnel and facilities, as well as on Hondurans who cooperated with the United States against the Sandinistas.

Costa Rican communists, who split several years ago, have participated in elections for some years but have recently found it difficult to cooperate and thus to maximize the effect of the leftist vote. Nonetheless, the country remains a haven for leftists from many countries in the hemisphere.

In Panama, the communist People's Party (PDP) likes the increasing anti-U.S. rhetoric of Defense Forces (PDF) chief Manuel Antonio Noriega and thus almost certainly will support his candidate, Democratic Revolutionary Party (PRD) leader Carlos Duque, in presidential elections scheduled for 1989. The PRD, which is the PDF's voice in Panama's captive legislature, has long been strongly influenced from within and without by the Marxist-Leninist left, and is becoming more so as the U.S.-Panamanian conflict drags on inconclusively. When Karen Brutents visited Panama in September, he met with leaders of the PDP and PRD. Noriega has continued to rely on personal security forces and advisers from Cuba, even as he strengthens ties to the Sandinistas and other leftist and terrorist nations around the world.

Colombia has had problems with guerrillas for decades, and, in recent years, the guerrillas have made common cause with the drug dealers who have already undermined much of the country's judicial and security systems. More than 3600 people were killed in political violence during the year, and 544 kidnapped Colombians remained unaccounted for at the end of the year. Rightist death squads became more active again to counter the terrorists of the narco-leftist alliance. As in years past, the government tried to negotiate with the guerrillas to end domestic unrest, and periods of optimism were followed by the realities of renewed fighting. Even as the government reportedly concluded an initial peace agreement with one group, the M-19, in January 1989, the military announced a major offensive against the Revolutionary Armed Forces of Colombia (FARC), the armed branch of the Colombian Communist Party. Violence escalated in early 1989, with one terrorist attack in January taking the lives of twelve members of the judicial system in Santander Department. Colombian intelligence reports that Cuban advisers are involved with several of the Colombian guerrilla groups.

But there is another angle to Colombian communist activities, one that links the Colombian Communist Party (PCC) to many other South American countries, particularly the Andean countries to its south: participation in elections through a leftist coalition. In 1988 the PCC ran candidates in mayoral, municipal council, and state assembly elections as the leading force of a leftist coalition called the Patriotic Union; its members seem to have been special targets of death squads.

Ecuadorian communists participated in the 1988 presidential election through the United Leftist Front (FIU), which included the Broad Leftist Front (FADI) of the pro-Soviet Communist Party of Ecuador (PCE) and the Democratic Popular Movement (MPD), founded years ago by pro-Chinese Marxists. The FADI and MPD won two seats each in the national congress. In the runoff presidential election, the PCE supported the winning social democrat, Rodrigo Borja, and has given cautious support to his government.

Peru boasts what is probably the broadest, but also one of the most inherently unstable, leftist fronts in Latin America: the United Left (IU). The Peruvian Communist Party (PCP) works with the more moderate members of the IU, the so-called Socialist Convergence (COSO), a group that has supported some of the political—but not recent economic—programs of President Alan García, of APRA, while openly condemning the terrorism of the Shining Path (Sendero Luminoso). The COSO wing of the IU dominated the first IU congress, which reportedly brought together 3,500 delegates in Lima in January 1989.

The Shining Path guerrillas, who held a congress in February, shifted their strategy and tactics somewhat in 1988, moving from their previous support for protracted rural war to promoting urban revolution. Sendero members and supporters have precipitated violence in urban demonstrations organized by other leftist groups and even, for the first time, marched through Lima under their own banner. Shining Path activities also include their now-routine selective assassinations, which focus on government authorities (including police) and political leaders, a more indiscriminate terrorism, and economic sabotage. They propose to disrupt the 1990 elections, if possible.

The Chilean Communist Party, in the late 1960s and early 1970s the model of electoral participa-

tion, spent most of 1988 trying to decide whether or not to support the October plebiscite on an additional term for President Augusto Pinochet. Ultimately the party encouraged its members to vote "no" in the plebiscite with the rest of the left—and the majority of the people—though it did not cooperate openly with other parties. The communists continued to support the Manuel Rodríguez Patriotic Front terrorists and to advocate violent as well as nonviolent forms of struggle. A stumbling block to broad leftist participation in the 1989 election is the constitutional provision outlawing the Communist Party and the government's refusal to talk with groups that seem to be fronts of the party.

South America's two largest countries offer very different prospects for communist groups. In Brazil, with its rapidly deteriorating economy, the formal communist parties have little success on their own. But the more diffuse and factionalized Worker's Party, somewhat like the Peruvian IU, has for some years won many votes and elected a significant number of candidates. Communists in Argentina have always been totally upstaged in the workers' and other movements by the Peronistas, and so it was in 1988 when the Peronista party, having dominated the congressional elections in 1987, positioned itself to win the 1989 presidential election.

Other South American countries where communists focus most of their attention on elections include: (1) Bolivia, where the communist party and other groups are loosely unified in the United Left (IU), in anticipation of May 1989 elections; (2) Uruguay, where the communists expect to participate in 1989 elections through the Broad Front; (3) Venezuela, where the communist party and its ally, the People's Electoral Movement, got less than one percent of the vote in 1988, while the more moderate Movement To Socialism (MAS), a splinter from the communist party in the early 1970s, did significantly better; (4) Guyana, where Cheddi Jagan's People's Progressive Party continues to be outmaneuvered by the perpetually ruling People's National Congress; (5) and perhaps Paraguay, if elections are actually held there following the January 1989 overthrow of General Stroessner.

Other countries in the hemisphere where the communists focus on elections include: (1) Mexico, where the communists, the dominant force in the Mexican Socialist Party, threw their support behind the dissident presidential candidate, Cuauhtémoc Cárdenas, in the July elections, and now exercise some influence on him as advisers; (2) the Dominican Republic, where the communists may give their support to the 1990 presidential bid of Juan Bosch; (3) Guadeloupe and Martinique, where communists have some legislative representation and their primary concern is the potential negative consequences for themselves of the integration of Western Europe; (4) Grenada, where a charismatic young leader, Terrence Marryshow, has taken over the Maurice Bishop Patriotic Movement and seeks closer ties to the democratic left; (5) Jamaica, where a recently split and debilitated party pondered the 1989 election in which they will have no impact; (6) Haiti, where the communists boycotted a 1988 election; and (7) Canada and the United States, where communist parties ran some candidates—mainly in the United States, and mostly as independents—but had no significant national impact.

William Ratliff
Hoover Institution

Argentina

Population. 31,532,538
Party. Communist Party of Argentina (Partido Comunista de la Argentina; PCA)
Founded. 1918
Membership. 80,000 (claimed; 25,000 militants)
General Secretary. Athos Fava
Politburo. 12 members: Athos Fava, Jorge Pereyra, Patricio Echegaray, Luis Heller, Ernesto Salgado, Fanny Edelman, Guillermo Varone, Miguel Balleto, Eduardo Sigal, Rodolfo Casals, Enrique Dratman, Francisco Alvarez
Central Committee. 100 members, 15 alternates
Status. Legal
Last Congress. Sixteenth, 4–7 November, 1986
Last Election. 1987 (parliamentary and provincial midterm elections), no representation
Auxiliary Organizations. Communist Youth Federation, Union of Argentine Women, Committee in Solidarity with Nicaragua, local branch of the World Peace Council. The party effectively

controls the Argentine Permanent Assembly on Human Rights.
Publications. *¿Qué Pasa?* (weekly); *Aquí y ahora* (monthly). The popular political gossip magazine *El Periodista* (weekly) is generally regarded as controlled by party members.

The year 1988 was President Raúl Alfonsín's last full year in office; elections for a new president and Congress are scheduled for 14 May 1989. This fact dominated the political year, conditioning the activities of all parties, including, of course, the communists.

Although many Argentines found Alfonsín's performance disappointing, particularly in the area of economics—inflation exceeded 300 percent in 1988, and real wages had dropped 35 percent since 1984—from a political point of view his accomplishments, judged against the background of Argentine history, were considerable. When the president hands over the sash and seals of office to his elected successor next year, it will be the first such act accomplished within the framework of the constitution since 1928. Moreover, during his six years, Alfonsín and his ruling Radical Party were forced to confront the tangled moral and political legacies of the war against leftist terrorism and the disappearance of at least 9,000 persons. Since 1983, the Argentine government has brought to trial the principal officers of the junta (1976–1983) for human rights violations; imposed a measure of civilian control over the armed forces; and re-established the full range of political freedoms in a country long accustomed to dictatorship.

This was not done without facing down serious opposition from younger elements of the army officer corps. In 1987, an Easter Week uprising was led by Lt. Col. Aldo Rico, a hero of the 1982 war against Great Britain over the Malvinas (Falkland) Islands (see *YICA*, 1987). In January 1988 and again in December of that year, soldiers loyal to the now-imprisoned Colonel Rico staged abortive uprisings in the Province of Buenos Aires, in one case seizing a local garrison, in another, the infantry school. Though both rebellions were quickly crushed by the authorities, the second was quelled only after several days of negotiations. Though President Alfonsín denied that any concessions had been made to the rebels in exchange for their surrender, a few days afterwards army chief of staff Gen. Jose Dante Caridi—thought by the insurgents and their supporters to be insufficiently zealous in defending military interests vis-à-vis the civilian political establishment—was prematurely retired. Significantly, the same fate befell his predecessor in the wake of the Easter 1987 affair.

The recurrence of military disturbances—three since mid-1987—though not threatening to the life of the regime, underscored continuing divisions within Argentine society. The rebels insisted that their purpose was not to overthrow the government but to vindicate their role in the so-called dirty war (1976–1979) and to obtain freedom for the imprisoned leaders of the junta. The government implicitly acknowledged the seriousness (if not legitimacy) of their claims by sponsoring "due obedience" legislation in Congress, which in effect exempted younger officers from prosecution for human rights offenses. For her part, former President Isabel Perón (1974–1976), who returned from Spain in mid-November after several years of self-imposed exile, publicly expressed support for granting amnesty to the officers who had overthrown her. From the point of view of the Argentine left, these developments—particularly the "due obedience" legislation—were profoundly troubling, all the more so since the Peronist front-runner for the presidency in all the polls, the governor of La Rioja, Carlos Saúl Menem, was known to be close to extreme right-wing elements within his own party.

Current Leadership and Party Organization. The PCA leadership had to absorb and integrate two new developments: the Gorbachev phenomenon in the Soviet Union, and a domestic backlash within party ranks arising out of the purges of the Sixteenth Congress (see *YICA*, 1987). Historically, the Argentine party has been one of the most "orthodox" in Latin America—that is, rigorously faithful to every twist and turn of the Soviet line. This has produced a political culture that is resolutely Stalinist (or perhaps, better put, neo-Stalinist); to what degree it will be able to adjust to changes in Soviet practice at home without upsetting the entire basis of internal party life remains to be seen. In a major review of party policy, General Secretary Athos Fava mentioned *perestroika* but not, significantly, *glasnost'* (*WMR*, March).

At the same time, Fava was forced to confront a rebellion within party ranks arising out of purges effected at the Sixteenth Congress (see *YICA*, 1987). A group of members calling themselves "Trend in Defense of the Sixteenth Congress" petitioned an Argentine electoral court to be recognized as an internal caucus of the party. This recurrence to the organs of the bourgeois state to resolve intra-party differences was virtually unprecedented; in the past, such divisions normally ended in schism. The outcome of the appeal to the civil tribunal was unclear at year's end.

Domestic Party Affairs. Since 1945, the most serious challenge to the Argentine Communist Party has been not the military or the right but the Peronist party, which effectively captured control of the labor movement, as well as those working-class and lower-middle-class elements of society that the PCA claimed to (and to a certain extent did) represent. For two decades, the communists were found in every anti-Peronist alliance, including those led by the most conservative elements in Argentine life. When it became apparent that the working class would remain loyal to Perón even after his departure for Spanish exile in 1955, the communists and other elements of the Argentine left began to regard him in a different and more favorable light—as representative of an inchoate form of "national and popular power." As a result of this new, "revisionist" view of Peronism, the line between it (and particularly between that movement's left wing) and communism—as well as Trotskyism and other forms of leftism—became increasingly indistinct. A Peronist "New Left" arose to incorporate all of these elements in an urban guerrilla movement; it also led most left-wing groups, including the PCA, which joined the electoral coalition that returned Perón to power in 1973. (The PCA also supported Peronist presidential candidate Italo Luder in 1983.)

In 1988 the party once again reverted to its "anti-Peronist" position, complete with a lengthy self-criticism of its conduct in relation to the military dictatorship deposed in 1983. As General Secretary Fava explained, in recent years the party had committed "opportunistic mistakes . . . at one point [it] was effectively turned into a political force not aspiring to power." During the 1970s, it "entertain[ed] illusions about reformism . . . ignor[ing] the other revolutionary and left-wing organizations." Such "sectarianism, dogmatism and opportunism" had isolated it from other revolutionary forces. The order of the day was now to expose *both* the Peronists and the Radicals as essentially under the control of the "monopoly-type big bourgeoisie," avoid pacts with both, and construct a broad alliance of the left (*WMR*, March).

In November, after months of negotiations, the communists announced the creation of the United

Alliance of the Left (FRAL), carried out together with the Intransigent Party, the Movement Toward Socialism (MAS), and more than a half-dozen smaller leftist groups. The purpose of this alliance would be to present a single list of candidates and a common program in the 1989 elections. On December 18, the FRAL held internal elections to select its leadership, allowing militants as young as sixteen years of age to participate. According to leaders of the alliance, they intended to offer an "electoral alternative" to persons of revolutionary Marxist persuasion, but without necessarily "breaking ties with the organization and representatives of the Peronist left" (*La Nueva Provincia*, 24 October; *FBIS*, 22 November). Among other things, the FRAL called for nationalization of the country's banking sector, land reform, and nonpayment of the country's $57 billion foreign debt.

International Views, Positions, and Activities. The PCA re-established ties with the Chinese Communist party, broken off 28 years ago. General Secretary Fava visited that country, as well as Bulgaria.

In September, the Argentine Communist Party participated in a meeting of Southern Cone communist parties in Montevideo presided over by Karen Brutents, deputy chief of the International Department of the CPSU. Though the ostensible purpose of the meeting was to iron out differences between the Uruguayan and Chilean parties on the proper response to the Pinochet dictatorship and its call for a plebiscite (see "Chile"), one press report speculated that Brutents was also in the area to evaluate the PCA's new approach to other leftist groups, which had culminated in the FRAL (TELAM, 4 September; *FBIS*, 6 September).

Relations with the Soviet Union and Other Bloc Members. The close and often cordial relations between the Argentine government and the Soviet Union continued throughout 1988. Senator Antonio Berhongaray, chairman of the Defense Committee of the Upper House, visited the Soviet Union. The USSR Deputy Minister of Foreign Trade visited Argentina, as did a special envoy whose mission was to explain the Soviet view of the US-USSR disarmament agreements.

In June, the authorities in Buenos Aires renewed for two years existing treaties allowing both the Soviet Union and Bulgaria to fish in Argentine jurisdictional waters in the South Atlantic. In July, the Soviets agreed to dredge the port of Bahía Blanca

(with new industrial machinery and equipment that would remain the property of the Argentine state) as a way of partially correcting the negative trade balances arising from the USSR's massive purchase of Argentine cereals (450,000 tons in 1988). In October, the Argentines resumed export of chilled beef to the Soviet Union; it was also announced that in the future the Soviets would invest in the creation of new enterprises to export Argentine meat to the Soviet market and to third countries.

In the same month, the Atomic Energy Commission (CNEA) concluded an agreement with a Soviet firm whereby the latter would enrich Argentine uranium to a concentration of 20 percent, subsequently reshipping it to Argentina to produce fuel for the RA 3 radioisotope-producing reactor of the Ezeiza nuclear plant. In November, the first joint fisheries expedition was concluded—utilizing a Soviet fishery research vessel, but with the participation of Argentine crews.

Vice President Enrique Martínez made a state visit in April to the German Democratic Republic, and in September the Mixed Argentine-GDR Commission met in East Berlin to discuss commercial relations. In August, Susana Ruíz Cerutti, international relations secretary of the Foreign Ministry, toured four East European countries (Czechoslovakia, Hungary, Romania, and the GDR) to discuss bilateral commercial relations.

President Alfonsín made a 70-hour visit to the People's Republic of China in May to sign a series of economic agreements, including one committing the Chinese to purchase Argentine wheat; in June, a Council for Cooperation with the People's Republic of China was created to implement the agreements. A commercial delegation from the PRC visited in September, as did one of the three deputy chiefs of staff of the People's Liberation Army. Foreign Minister Dante Caputo found it necessary to deny persistent reports in the press that Argentina had acquired Silkworm missiles and fighter planes from the Chinese, as well as rockets with a range capable of reaching the Malvinas Islands.

Other Leftist Groups. The Movement Toward Socialism is the only leftist party that has shown significant growth in recent times. According to a recent report in the Argentine press, its membership has increased nearly 400 percent since 1985, 40 percent of which has occurred since the Easter rebellion in 1987 (*Clarín*, 5 May; *FBIS*, 9 May). It is now only three provinces short of the requirements for recognition as a national party. Its adherence to an electoral pact was the *sine qua non* of the FRAL.

There was relatively little illegal activity, in spite of frequent declarations by conservatives that outbreaks of terrorism were imminent. In March, a group calling itself the Ché Guevara Brigade claimed credit for a bomb attack on a Parke-Davis pharmaceutical plant in Buenos Aires; and in October, police uncovered a large arsenal in Bella Vista, a distant suburb of the capital, arresting four persons. The cache included not merely weapons and Marxist literature (authored by the People's Revolutionary Army [ERP], one of the guerrilla groups active in Argentina during the early 1970s), but also instructional material on explosives and booby traps, as well as drugs, including cocaine.

Mark Falcoff
American Enterprise Institute

Bolivia

Population. 6,448,297
Party. Communist Party of Bolivia (Partido Comunista Boliviana; PCB
Founded. 1950 (latest split in 1985)
Membership. 500 (claimed)
General Secretary. Humberto Ramírez (majority faction); Carlos Soría Galvarro (minority faction)
Status. Legal
Last Congress. Fifth, 9–13 February 1985; Extraordinary, 26–29 April 1986
Last Election. July 1985; the United People's Front (FPU), the electoral coalition in which the PCB participated, won only 4 of 130 seats in the Chamber of Deputies. For the elections of 7 May 1989, the PCB is aligned with other parties of the extreme left in the United Left (IU), with Antonio Aranibar of the Free Bolivia Movement its candidate.
Auxiliary Organizations. Communist Youth of Bolivia
Publications. Both factions publish a paper called *Unidad*

In a country where politics is the national pastime, the events that shaped Bolivia in 1988 were the activities devoted to the presidential elections of 7 May 1989. Bolivia's numerous Marxist-Leninist elements have led the criticism of the government and will be participating in the elections uncharacteristically unified. A newly-formed coalition of various Marxist parties, including the Communist Party of Bolivia (PCB), could emerge in third place, giving it possible leverage in determining the final winner. Bolivia's election law has no provision for a runoff election between the two top vote-getters. If no candidate receives a majority—and it is virtually an impossibility in Bolivia's fractious politics for a presidential candidate to gain a majority of the votes—then the president is selected by the newly-elected Congress. The party whose candidate finishes in third place can thus find itself in the "king-making" role by delivering the votes needed to put either the first- or second-place finisher over the top, and gathering for itself some choice IOUs from the new president. The 1989 elections could be one of those times when finishing third is better than finishing first.

Elections are rarely routine in Bolivia, and the "winner," due to the number of competing candidates, comes into office with far more people having voted against him than for him. But in a country that has had more military coups than any other in Latin America in the years since it gained independence, the very act of changing governments via the ballot instead of the bullet is yet another sign that democracy is becoming institutionalized. But in 1989 events could put Bolivia's nascent democracy to its severest test in many years.

The incumbent National Revolutionary Movement (MNR) government of President Víctor Paz Estensorro, smarting under continual criticism of insensitivity to the needs of the working class because of its austerity-based "New Economic Policy," is likely to suffer a stinging defeat at the polls in May, if the results of the December 1987 municipal elections are any guide. In Bolivia's first such elections in 40 years, MNR candidates received less than a third of the votes the party gained in the 1985 presidential elections—138,906 to 456,754. Even more ominous was the decline in percentage of MNR votes of the total votes cast—8 percent in 1987 compared to 24 percent in the 1985 general elections. Left-of-center parties made the most significant gains at the MNR's expense, especially the Movement of the Revolutionary Left (MIR), which is headed by former vice president Jaime Paz

Zamora. The MIR pulled in 31 percent of the total votes cast—308,714, about twice as many as it received in the 1985 elections (*El Diario*, 11 June).

The MIR, which was considered by the military governments of the past a party of the far left—its name, inflammatory rhetoric, and many of its actions certainly suggested this orientation—has modified its position and is thought by the Marxist elements to have deserted the leftist cause. Conservatives are not sure if the MIR's move to the center is genuine, or merely a political maneuver.

The National Democratic Action Party (ADN), led by a former president, Gen. Hugo Banzer, saw its vote total decrease from 493,375 in the 1985 general elections to 336,684 in 1987, but this still represented 35 percent of the total votes cast, more than any other party received (ibid.). Banzer will probably again finish in first place in the general elections. After nudging out Paz Estensorro in 1985, Banzer gracefully accepted the vote of the new Congress, which gave the MNR the victory, and the "Pact for Democracy" was formed by the MNR and the ADN. If the MNR finishes in third place, a similar alliance could be forged, but this time with Banzer moving into the office he occupied for seven years in the 1970s.

Banzer is running on the promise of returning Bolivia to the relative prosperity it enjoyed during his almost unprecedented length of time in office (1971–1978). Only the presidency of Marshal Andres Santa Cruz, who ruled from 1829 to 1839, was longer than that of Banzer. He and his party, although in alliance with the MNR, have been able to escape much of the criticism heaped on the MNR, and the ADN has going for it a reputation for efficiency, as much because of the nostalgia for the "good old days" of the first Banzer presidency as for the competency displayed by ADN mayors in cities and towns around the country.

The wild card in the 1989 elections has been introduced by the parties of the extreme left. They have put aside their differences, at least temporarily, and formed the United Left (IU). If the IU nudges out the MNR for the pivotal third place in the upcoming elections, this coalition could swing the vote in the Congress to Paz Zamora of the MIR. This turn of events could create a political crisis of the first order.

If Banzer finishes in first place once again in the general elections, but the IU and the MIR combine to block what Banzer and his supporters—especially the army—consider his deserved victory, a conservative backlash can be expected. For many

on the right, it is one thing to concede to the MNR and the venerable Víctor Paz Estensorro; it is quite another to have a plurality of votes and see the presidency snatched by a coalition of parties representing an ideology decidedly at odds with that of the ADN, and with what these conservatives believe is in the best interests of Bolivia. They remember the last time that a far-left coalition gained power—the government of Hernán Siles Suazo (1982–1985), whose ecomonic policies contributed directly to Bolivia's current disastrous economic situation. Should the military move to stop an MIR-IU coalition from denying the presidency to first-place finisher Banzer, the generals would rationalize their actions as defending, not subverting, the democratic process.

Had Bolivia amended its election law to permit a runoff election between the top two candidates, as so many nations in Latin America have done, such a crisis could be avoided. The president who would emerge from such an election would have a clear mandate. In Bolivia, calls to change the law have received little support. To his credit, Paz Zamora has suggested that the Congress elected in the 1989 general elections be designated a Constituent Assembly to address changes to the constitution, including the electoral law. Both the MNR and the ADN have voiced agreement with his initiative.

Government Programs. The MNR government has suffered in popularity because of the austerity program it imposed in an effort to bring the runaway inflation under control and stimulate the moribund economy. The inflation rate that had reached astronomical rates during the presidency of Siles Suazo—some estimates put it at 24,000 percent annually—has indeed been brought under control by the Paz Estensorro government, as it is now less than 20 percent. At the outset of his administration, Paz Estensorro took Draconian measures to curb inflation: wages were frozen; the peso devalued; taxes increased. In an act of political courage, the president moved to streamline the bloated and bureaucratic government-controlled mining sector. Thousands of miners were laid off in an effort to make Bolivia more competitive on the world tin market. As a direct consequence of the MNR programs, inflation did fall, but so too did the real incomes of workers, export earnings and the gross domestic product. Unemployment and underemployment increased to the point where over half of the country's labor force has been affected. Although the economy has finally started to show signs of turning around, having grown by 2.4 percent in 1987, with similar growth expected for 1988, the suffering among Bolivia's poor has been intense. Criticism has been directed more toward the government providing the cure than at the one that caused the illness. Paz Estensorro has paid a high price to for his courageous efforts to turn Bolivia around.

In September, MNR Planning Minister Gonzalo Sánchez de Losada, point man for MNR efforts to stabilize the economy, won the party's presidential nomination. Because even Paz Estensorro's critics are reluctant to speak harshly of the octogenarian "father of the Bolivian Revolution," Sánchez de Losada is likely to pay the price in the general elections for the pent-up frustrations of the electorate. The PCB and other elements of the far left are accusing the MNR of selling out to the "imperialists" in Washington. Sánchez de Losada, who speaks Spanish with a strong American accent due to his years of living in the United States, is made to order for leftist propaganda that he is "Washington's candidate."

The Extreme Left, Drugs, and Anti-Americanism.
During the 1980s, Bolivia has had only one growth industry—cocaine. But, spurred by the United States, the MNR has moved vigorously to crack down on the illegal narcotics industry, and to limit coca processing and cultivation. In July, the government arrested Roberto Suarez, Bolivia's top drug dealer (*La Red Pan-americana*, 22 July), and Congress passed the "Law of Special Regulations for Coca and Controlled Substances." It calls for convicted drug traffickers to be jailed for 5 to 25 years, and limits coca production to no more than 12,000 hectares for traditional and medicinal use. Surplus coca crops are to be replaced/eradicated at a rate of 5,000 hectares a year, and this rate is to be increased in the future to 8,000 hectares each year (*La Red Pan-americana*, 6 July).

The extreme left in Congress opposed the law, and the Bolivian Workers Federation (COB), under the control of the PCB, publicly criticized it, claiming that the law is another example of the U.S. domination of Bolivian life. The MNR responded that the COB was acting in a "subversive" manner, and was "antidemocratic," as it was inciting to disobedience of a law approved by the state (*El Diario*, 11 July).

Anti-Americanism took a particularly ugly turn in August, when dynamite was thrown at the caravan of cars bringing U.S. Secretary of State George Shultz from the airport to La Paz during a visit to Bolivia (*NYT*, 5 August). Although an amateurish effort, the attack nevertheless underscored the resentment felt by many in Bolivia because of the hard line Washington has taken toward cocaine production. The U.S. Drug Enforcement Agency (DEA) is working closely with the Bolivian government in efforts to destroy the coca-producing infrastructure of the country, conducting what some DEA agents have described as "guerrilla warfare" (*WP*, 16 January, 1989). In fact, the DEA agents are closer to combat in Bolivia than are U.S. military advisers in El Salvador.

As part of the effort to turn public sentiment against the United States, elements on the left, especially the PCB, are fueling Bolivia's potent rumor mill, claiming that the United States is attempting to corner the cocaine market as a means to generate funds to support the Nicaraguan contras (ibid.). Other equally preposterous rumors include the one claiming that the United States is planning to build a strategic military base in Bolivia so as to wage all-out war on coca production.

The Rise and Decline of the PCB.
The PCB is badly split, and no longer a key actor in national politics in its own right. Its most recent schism occurred in 1985, when, after its Fifth Congress, it split into two factions, the principal one headed by Simón Reyes, and the smaller, dissident, more radical element led by Carlos Soría Galvarro. The main element of the PCB does have influence in the Bolivian labor movement, and Reyes was elected general secretary of the COB in 1987. He then turned over the leadership of the PCB to his long-time ally Humberto Ramírez.

Ironically, the demise of the PCB in the 1980s is a reflection of the very conditions that propelled it into existence in 1950. In that year young radicals became frustrated with the actions of Bolivia's communist standard bearer, the Revolutionary Party of the Left (PIR). These university students felt that the PIR leadership had compromised the revolutionary ideals of the party by collaborating with the conservative elements that dominated Bolivia in the late 1940s. They broke away and created the PCB.

The PIR, along with the MNR, had come into existence in the aftermath of the Chaco War of the 1930s, the seminal event of twentieth-century Bolivia. The two radical parties became the political magnets for young Bolivian intellectuals who felt the country had been betrayed by the conservative parties whose bumbling had caused Bolivia to suffer an ignominious defeat by Paraguay.

The PIR—unified in its populist Marxism—was initially the stronger of the two parties, as the MNR, with competing factions, struggled to find its place in the Bolivian political landscape. The MNR enjoyed a brief period in power as a result of a coalition with the military in the mid-1940s until it was toppled in 1946. Many of its key leaders, such as Paz Estensorro, were driven into exile. The PIR, in contrast, survived as a political party by collaborating with the conservative parties, and in 1950 was surpassed as the dominant voice on the left by the breakaway PCB. The MNR, meanwhile, stormed back from exile in 1952, defeated the Bolivian army in a populist uprising fueled by charges of electoral fraud, and set in motion the reforms of the Bolivian National Revolution, adopting many of the positions long espoused by the PIR, which soon vanished as a political actor.

Just as it supplanted the PIR, so too has the PCB now been moved from the center stage of radicalism in Bolivia. As is the case in so many countries of Latin America where the old-line communist parties are considered discredited remnants of the past, the PCB holds little attraction for the younger generation of Bolivians, who see the other parties of the left as more promising routes to power.

The PCB's Quest for Power Through Coalition. The PCB has attempted to parlay what political strength it has by participating in the recurring coalitions the far left has put together over the years in efforts to maximize its strength. Despite its own internal problems, the PCB continues to preach that unity is the only way the left in Bolivia can achieve power. This theme was emphasized in an article written by PCB General Secretary Humberto Ramírez in August 1988. Ramírez demonstrated that the PCB is cognizant of the problems it faces in Bolivia, and sees unification of anti-right wing forces as essential. He wrote that "the Communist Party of Bolivia is aware of the need to overcome certain obstacles, such as sectarianism and anti-communist attitudes which play into the hands of right wing forces. It is also important to eliminate other factors of disunity among the left, democratic and progressive forces" (*WMR*, August).

The most recent effort of the PCB and other parties of Bolivia's far left to gain political power is the creation of the aforementioned United Left, which was formed on 10 September 1988 (*EFE*, 11 September). The IU's presidential candidate is An-

tonio Aranibar, who formerly headed the far-left faction of the MIR, but then broke away and formed the Free Bolivian Movement (FBL), which gained a surprising 89,000 votes in the municipal elections (*El Diario*, 11 June). In the 1985 general elections, Aranibar had given the support of his faction of the MIR to the PCB, and also supported Reyes in the COB election in 1987. The IU intends to run a populist campaign, criticizing the MNR's "neo-liberal" economic policy, which the left claims has placed the burden of Bolivia's economic recovery on the backs of the poor.

In commenting on the prospects of the IU, one of Bolivia's most astute political columnists, Father José "Pepe" Gramunt, a Spanish Jesuit who has lived in Bolivia for 35 years, wrote that "the IU would bring in even more votes if it were capable of offering the country a convincing alternative economic policy . . . The majority of the voters . . . no longer have any confidence in the various forms of Utopia that the radical left was in the habit of proposing until just a short time ago . . . These and other solutions . . . no longer appear convincing, even to leftist voters in the Western democracies. I fear these proposals will not win over any majorities here either" (*El Mundo*, 14 September).

If the IU follows Father Gramunt's advice, it can play a critical role in the forthcoming elections for three reasons. The first is that a change in the electoral law now makes it impossible for candidates to run for Congress and the presidency at the same time. In years past, small leftist parties would nominate their leader for president as a means of gaining prestige for the party, but this split the left's vote. Under the new law, the leaders of these small leftist parties are likely to eschew the presidential race, and run only for seats in the Congress. If the parties of the far left remain united—and this is not at all certain, given their internal cleavages—then Aranibar will enjoy the bulk of the "protest" vote from the left against the MNR policies of the last four years.

The second factor is the IU's principal rival on the left, the MIR. Although it made an excellent showing in the municipal elections, many observers believe this was as a result of the quality of the candidates and local conditions, not national identification with the party. The main negative baggage that the MIR must carry in the general elections is that its candidate, Jaime Paz Zamora, was vice president in the government of Hernán Siles Suazo, an administration generally considered an economic disaster and the cause of many of Bolivia's current problems. In his efforts to move to the center and attract voters from both the MNR and the ADN, Paz Zamora has taken the position that the economic policy carried out by the MNR government, austere though it is, is the only realistic policy for Bolivia to follow, although he joins the chorus of MNR critics that the government has been "insensitive." His variation of the MNR policy would emphasize growth, not just belt-tightening. But his support for the goals of the MNR policy has caused many of his followers to criticize him and threaten to bolt the party. The IU is the obvious beneficiary of any MIR defections.

A third factor that could work to the advantage of the IU derives from the previously mentioned anomaly of the Bolivian election law, according to which the third-place party may have the "swing votes" in the new Congress to pick the president from the two top candidates. The IU could deliver the presidency to Paz Zamora and thus gain considerable leverage in the new administration. The PCB, because its strength is concentrated in the labor movement, could be expected to exert influence in such a government far out of proportion to its vote-pulling strength.

The PCB and the Labor Movement. Although Bolivia certainly had its normal share of strikes and work stoppages during 1988, the year was a relatively calm one by the standards of the past. The stronghold of the PCB, the Bolivian Mine Workers Federation (FSTMB), long the kingpin of the Bolivian labor movement, has fallen on hard times. At its convention in November, the FSTMB admitted that it now counts only about 13,000 members in its ranks, which numbered 60,000 members a few years ago. At the convention, the divisiveness that has plagued the FSTMB in recent years was evident. The Simón Reyes-Humberto Ramírez element of the PCB was outmaneuvered by the faction that broke away at the Fifth Congress in 1985, and as a result a member of this more radical element, Edgar Ramírez, was elected general secretary of the FSTMB. The FSTMB demonstrated its lack of ideological coherence by then electing a member of the MIR to the post of relations secretary.

In what turned out to be a public-relations blunder for the FSTMB, the radical PCB-Fifth Congress faction was able to get a position paper approved that called for "subversive resistance" and suggested that "force" may be necessary to achieve labor's goals. This led to a series of attacks in the press (*El Diario*, 17 November) that criticized the FSTMB for taking an "anti-democratic line." If the radical element of the PCB was floating a trial balloon to test the country's willingness to use violence in reaction to the hardships brought on by the government's economic programs, it was soon punctured.

The Left's Nemesis: The Bolivian Military. Since Marxism became popular in Bolivia in the 1930s, the principal adversary of the far left has been the Bolivian military. Describing itself as the "Institucíon Tutelar" of the nation, the armed forces have frequently played the role of political party with artillery. The corrupt regime of Gen. Luis García Meza of the early part of the decade ended, at least temporarily, the latest chapter in direct military rule. But the military is suspicious of the extreme left, in particular of the PCB, and is likely to be unwilling to see the IU in an influential position in a MIR government.

During the years of Siles Suazo's presidency (1982–1985), conservative and business elements exerted pressure on the Bolivian army to stage a coup in order to "save the country." The army, not wanting to inherit the economic mess created by Siles Suazo, refused. Moreover, the commander of the Bolivian army during much of this period, Gen. Raúl López Leyton, had a genuine desire to remove the military from the political scene. López and another key officer, Gen. Gary Prado Salmon, famed for capturing "Che" Guevara in 1967, retired in 1988. Both were leaders of an informal clique known as the "Generational Group," consisting of key members of the officer corps who entered the army after the revolution of 1952. They were judged more socially conscious and politically astute than those who went before them. The retirement of López and Prado signals a changing of the guard in the military.

Both have now decided to enter politics. The decision of López to run for senator on the MNR slate rather than that of the ADN is probably a calculated political choice to be the party's principal military voice, an impossibility in the Banzer-dominated ADN. Prado has surprised his colleagues by his decision to run for senator with the MIR. In November, rumors circulated in La Paz and Washington, where Prado was serving at the Inter-American Defense Board, that he would be Paz Zamora's running mate. Long considered the most *presidenciable* member of the military, he was wounded in 1981 and left a paraplegic, but he is intelligent, urbane, and respected in civilian circles.

Despite the presence of López and Prado in the other main parties, the military is naturally inclined toward Banzer. Many of today's key unit commanders were cadets in the military academy whence Banzer launched his coup against the leftist government of Gen. Juan José Torres in 1971. The threat of terrorism and communist-inspired violence is always a concern to the military, and the December murder in La Paz of the Peruvian naval attaché (*NYT*, 7 December) will make the armed forces even more apprehensive of the threat posed by the far left. It is not known whether the murder was carried out by the Peruvian Sendero Luminoso. To date, the military has denied reports that Peruvian terrorists were operating in Bolivia (*Insight Magazine*, 7 November).

Any indication of an alliance between Bolivia's extreme left and the Sendero Luminoso would be viewed with alarm by the military. Much of Bolivia's recent history has been the uneasy relationship between the military and the left, extreme and moderate. The events set in motion in 1988 could provide the setting for still another chapter in this drama.

Col. Lawrence L. Tracy, U.S. Army (Ret.)
Americans for Democracy in Latin America

Brazil

Population. 150,685,145
Parties. Brazilian Communist Party (Partido Comunista Brasileiro; PCB), pro-Soviet; Communist Party of Brazil (Partido Comunista do Brasil; PCdoB), pro-Albanian; Workers' Party (Partido dos Trabalhadores; PT), strong Marxist-Leninist-Trotskyist influence
Founded. PCB: 1922; PCdoB: 1961 split from PCB; PT: 1981
Membership. PCB: 120,000 (Letter to Hoover Institution from PCB President Salomão Malina); PCdoB: 50,000 claimed, 20,000 estimated (*Folha de São Paulo*, 28 June 1987); PT: 450,000 (*O Globo*, 8 May; *JPRS*, 17 June)
Top Official. PCB: Salomão Malina (66), presi-

dent; PCdoB: João Amazonas (76), president; PT: Luis Gushiken, acting president, temporarily replacing Olivio Dutra, mayor-elect of Porto Alegre. Luis Inácio Lula da Silva had previously resigned to campaign for presidency.
Executive Committee. PCB: vice president Roberto Freire, Amaro Valentin, Carlos Alberto Torres, Domingos Tódero, Flávio Araújo, Francisco Inácio Almeida, Geraldo Rodríguez dos Santos, Givaldo Siqueira, Hércules Corrêa, Jarbas de Hollanda, José Paulo Netto, Luiz Carlos Moura, Paulo Elisiário, Regis Fratti, Sergio Morães, Severino Teodoro Melo; alternates: Luiz Carlos Azedo, Paulo Fábio Dantas, Byron Sarinho, Raimundo Jinkings; PCdoB: José Duarte, Dyneas Fernández Aguiar, José Renato Rabelo, Roberto D'Olne Lustosa, Ronaldo Cavalcanti Freitas, Elsa de Lima Monnerat, João Batista de Rocha Lemos, Pericles Santos de Souza, Alanir Cardoso, Maria do Socorro Moraes Vieira; PT: 19 members, including Luis Inácio Lula da Silva, General Secretary José Dirceu, Olivio Dutra, José Genoino, Eduardo Jorge, Eduardo Suplicy, Helio Bicudo, Plinio de Arruda Sampaio
Central Committee. PCB: 63 active members, 23 alternates
Status. All legal
Last Congress. PCB: Eighth, 17–20 July 1987
Last Election. 15 November, municipal. Overall percentages on city councils not available. The PCB and the PCdoB did not elect any mayors. The PT elected mayors in several important cities, including São Paulo and Porto Alegre. In the 487-seat national congress, the PCB has three deputies; the PCdoB has three; and the PT has 16.
Auxiliary Organizations. PCB: dominant in the Agricultural Workers' Confederation (Confederação Nacional dos Trabalhadores na Agricultura; CONTAG), some leadership in General Workers' Central (Central Geral dos Trabalhadores; CGT); PCdoB: previously dominant in National Student Union (União Nacional dos Estudantes; UNE), minor position in CGT; PT: dominant in Single Workers' Central (Central Unica dos Trabalhadores; CUT) and UNE, strong influence in Basic Christian Communities (Comunidades Eclesiais de Base; CEBs) and Landless Movement (Movimento dos Sem Terra)
Publications. PCB: *Voz da Unidade*, Luiz Carlos Azedo, director; PCdoB: *Tribuna da Luta Operária*, Pedro de Oliveira, director

A strong government campaign and some gentle pressure from the military helped persuade the Constituent Assembly to overturn its earlier adoption of parliamentary government and reinstate the presidential system. The new constitution was promulgated in October and President José Sarney's successor will be elected in November 1989. Municipal elections were held as scheduled on 15 November. The relatively strong showing of the left is seen primarily as a protest vote against runaway inflation and official corruption. It has nonetheless created a great deal of nervousness, given the very short period before presidential campaigns begin and the absence of any unifying candidate of the center.

PCB. Since 1985, the PCB has been operating legally as a "party in formation." In December 1985, it received provisional registration and was given one year to meet membership requirements for definitive registration. President Salomão Malina claimed a membership of 120,000 in September, an eightfold increase from mid-1987, and the goal is 300,000 by the end of 1988. The massive recruitment drive has met some resistance from purists who object to the liberalization of admission standards, but the alternative is loss of the right to participate in elections or coalitions. Executive committee member Amaro Valentin feels that the PCB can become a mass party and "must not be allowed to remain small, inward oriented and isolated from the masses" (*WMR*, April).

Another PCB priority, outlined in an August position paper of the executive committee, is the formation of a democratic and progressive political bloc, capable of winning the municipal and presidential elections. Even though it is very small, the PCB believes it has the political weight to advocate such a step, particularly since its image has benefited greatly from the Soviet Union's policy of *glasnost'*. (*Correio Braziliense*, 19 June; *JPRS*, 19 August.) No front materialized for the municipal election, but the PCB joined other slates where possible. For example, it participated in winning coalitions led by the Socialist Party (Partido Socialista Brasileira; PSB) in Manaus and Amapá; with the governing Party of the Brazilian Democratic Movement (Partido do Movimento Democrático Brasileiro; PMDB) in Goiânia; and with the Democratic Labor Party (Partido Democrático dos Trabalhadores; PDT) in São Luis. In several cities, including São Paulo and Porto Alegre, the PCB even supported PT slates, previously considered too

radical. (In São Paulo, the party reportedly would have preferred an alliance with the Brazilian Social Democratic Party [Partido Social Democrático Brasileiro; PSDB], a new, moderate-left breakaway from the PMDB.) The PCB and the PCdoB elected only one councilman each in São Paulo, but here as in other cities where they joined winning tickets, they will be entitled to some administrative posts. The candidacy of Roberto Freire for the presidency in the 1989 election has been announced but may be changed if coalitions are formed. PCB's president Malina argues that, though successes may seem limited, in fact to have moved from illegality five years ago to its present degree of influence is a great achievement for the PCB. Overall, the elections at the end of the year show that the Brazilian people disagree with governmental policies and that "the situation is now ripe for radical changes." (*Népszabadság*, Budapest, 9 December; *FBIS*, 14 December.)

A delegation led by Salomão Malina visited the Soviet Union, Poland, and Bulgaria in July and August. In a conversation with the CPSU central committee secretary, A. F. Dobrynin, the importance of the October visit to the USSR by Brazilian President José Sarney was stressed. (Sarney also visited the People's Republic of China in July.) The Bulgarian and Brazilian leaders emphasized that renewal and restructuring based on new political thinking represent an objective need not only for the ruling parties in the socialist countries, but also for the entire international communist movement (*Sofia BTA*, 12 August; *FBIS*, 24 August). Deputy Augusto Carvalho (Federal District) was a member of the congressional delegation observing the Chilean plebiscite in October, and PCB delegates participated in the third meeting of South American Communist Parties in Montevideo. A document released by the conference stated, among other things, that "*perestroika* in the Soviet Union, the correction of Cuban mistakes, and the process of reorganization and renewal in other socialist countries, all give new strength to the movement throughout the world" (Moscow broadcast, 9 August; *FBIS*, 11 August).

PCdoB. Like the PCB, the PCdoB joined a number of different coalitions in the municipal elections, with equally unremarkable results. Distaste for some of the party's temporary associates was ill-concealed. At a ceremony in São Paulo announcing the formation of the PT-PCB-PCdoB coalition, João Amazonas refused a photographer's request to shake hands with PCB regional director Jarbas de

Hollanda, saying "we both support [PT mayoral candidate Luiza] Erundina, but our other differences continue" (*O Estado de São Paulo*, 4 August). In October, the PCdoB walked out of a University of São Paulo seminar on *perestroika* to protest the presence of Soviet speakers, "the worst kind of people," according to Haroldo Lima, deputy from Bahia (ibid., 8 October).

The PCdoB will promote a popular and leftist front for the 1989 presidential election, and a December meeting of the central committee named a committee of six to make contacts with other parties. Because of its strong showing in the municipal elections, the PT figures largely in these plans, but, according to Amazonas, this does not necessarily mean the PCdoB will support da Silva's candidacy: "Everything depends upon the PT's proposed solutions to national problems" (ibid., 13 December). The PCdoB had earlier accused the PT of fraud when it lost control of the UNE to the PT's presidential candidate, Juliano Coberline, in October elections.

Two members of the PCdoB central committee made separate visits to Albania in 1988. Ramiz Alia, first secretary of the AWP's central committee, received José Renato Rabelo in March and Dyneas Aguiar in October. Aguiar participated in activities connected with the 80th birthday of Enver Hoxha.

PT. Founder Luis Inácio Lula da Silva will launch his presidential campaign in January 1989. With those elections less than a year away, the PT's unexpected victories in three state capitals—São Paulo, Porto Alegre, and Vitória—as well as in many smaller cities, is a disturbing development for many Brazilians. The elusive nature of the PT's brand of socialism contributes to the unease. In an interview after the elections, PT ideologue Francisco Weffort was clear on what the party is not: it is not a "bureaucratic socialism of the Eastern European type," nor is it a social democracy along Spanish or German lines. He finds, however, no example "in the literature that could be designated as a model." (*Jornal da Tarde*, 17 November.) Some analysts, such as Fernando Pedreira, believe a PT in power would soon reveal itself as a near copy of the "statist, corrupt, technobureaucratic governments of the military regimes" (*O Estado de São Paulo*, 27 November). Others hope that the new mayors will discredit themselves, as former PT mayor Maria Luisa Fontenelle did with her disastrous administration in Fortaleza. (She was expelled from the party.)

The mayor-elect who will be watched most closely is Luiza Erundina in São Paulo, who is now drafting emergency plans for the first hundred days to counter serious budget deficits. Her priorities will be child care, transportation, schools, and low-cost housing. Representatives have been dispatched to France and Spain to seek donations from sympathetic socialists that would help her administration meet these needs (ibid., 11 December).

It is proof of the existence of internal democracy in the PT that Erundina was not da Silva's choice for mayor and does not belong to his "Articulation" tendency. She comes from popular base groups with strong ties to the Catholic Church and was active in civil-servant strikes and land invasions. Promising "never to suppress the right to strike," she hopes to avert strikes as well as land invasions by anticipating demands and inviting discussion of them.

Channels of communication with grass-roots organizations will be established through popular councils in each administrative region of the city. Such councils already exist in the Eastern Zone, 80 of them in the health sector. These and additional councils to be created by the mayor will be institutionalized in municipal law. Municipal and regional councils will be organized by the public. According to State Deputy Roberto Gouveia, "Groups such as the Landless Movement could easily be transformed into regional or national councils...This type of mass mobilization will be used by the PT to counteract pressures from land speculators and owners of public transportation, for example." (Ibid., 4 December.)

The growing strength of both the PT and the landowners' organization, the Rural Democratic Union (União Democrática Rural; UDR), foreshadows increased polarization in the countryside. The UDR is organizing politically and succeeded in pushing through a mild agrarian reform in the Constituent Assembly: productive land and small- and medium-sized rural properties cannot be expropriated. The PT plans to increase rural unionization, especially of agro-industrial workers, from the present two or three million to fifteen million within the next five years. (Ibid., 30 August, 18 November.)

A study by the United Nations Economic Commission for Latin America shows that from 1985 to 1987 the buying power of the minimum wage decreased more in Brazil than in any other Latin American or Caribbean country (ibid., 2 October). During the same period, wage policy changed three times and anti-inflation plans lowered or froze cost-of-living adjustments. The result in 1988 was an

endless wave of strikes in the public sector—
ministries, banks, hospitals, petroleum, ports,
steel, electricity, and so on—with occasional violence. (Three strikers were killed when the army
was called in to control a takeover of the Volta
Redonda steel mill a few days before elections.)
Some of the strikes stemmed from demands for
benefits guaranteed by the new constitution, such as
the shorter workweek (reduced from 48 to 44
hours) and time-and-a-half overtime pay. The CUT
was active in a majority of the movements.

The strikes were negotiated on a case-by-case
basis while the government tried at the same time to
control inflation with a social pact, agreed to by
government, management, labor, and later, political
parties. The CUT and the leftist parties refused to
participate. Most analysts agree that the pact staved
off a hyperinflationary spiral. Moderate labor leaders, however, threaten to abandon the pact and call
monthly strikes, with CUT support, if a serious
anti-inflationary policy is not adopted. CUT president Jair Meneguelli predicts increased private-
sector strikes in 1989. Meneguelli denies any direct
connection between the PT and the CUT, but he
helped draft the PT's "alternative emergency economic plan." Its measures include a single index for
correction of wages, taxes, and prices; a redistribu-
tive tax reform; reduction of the trade surplus and
privatization of nonessential industry. One of the
principal points is creation of an Investment and
Social Policy Fund to maintain economic growth
and employment. It would be financed by savings
achieved through application of the plan and from
suspension of foreign debt payments. (Ibid., 20
December.)

Subversive Tendencies Within the PT. *O
Estado de São Paulo* published a document compiled by "two agencies of the intelligence community" describing nine groups with alleged links to a
number of isolated terrorist actions. The two most
worrisome were both from São Paulo: the National
Liberation Front/80 (Frente de Libertação Na-
cional/80; FLN/80), inspired by the Sandinista
revolution, the members of which are ex-volunteers
in Nicaragua; and the Revolutionary Socialist
Vanguard (Vanguarda Revolucionária Socialista;
VRS), which identifies with the Vietnamese Communist Party and is influenced by Libya and Iran.
The other seven appear to have been around for
awhile (see *YICA*, 1985–1987). They are listed as
having left the PT and include four Trotskyist
groups: Struggle and Work (Luta, an offshoot of
Libelu); Labor Cause (Causa Operária; COP);

Socialist Democracy (DS); and Socialist Convergence. The other three are Marxist-Leninist:
Revolutionary Communist Movement (MCR);
Revolutionary Brazilian Communist Party (PCBR);
and the Communist Revolutionary Party (PRC),
represented in congress by José Genoino.

PT leader José Dirceu said that the last seven
continue to exist as open factions within the PT,
although the first is called just Work, not Struggle
and Work, and that the MCR is dissolving itself.
Genoino denied any connection with the PRC, but
said he is "Marxist and a member of a PT tendency
that is not clandestine." (*O Estado de São Paulo*, 15
and 16 December.) In July party leaders were investigating the situation of a PT group that may have
been sent to Libya for guerrilla training rather than
to a political seminar as claimed (ibid., 23 July).

The intelligence dossier is believed to be largely
responsible for Sarney's uncharacteristically pessimistic statements to the effect that "the country is
headed for totalitarianism . . . a socialist revolution . . . The left is made up of determined, organized people with well defined objectives . . . If the
center does not organize itself" power will be
turned over to the left (ibid., 4 December). Hard-
line military officers have said they would prefer a
populist Brizola government to the "ideological
left" of da Silva and some others. Leonel Brizola's
name has been anathema to the armed forces since
his days as a radical governor of Rio Grande do Sul
in the early 1960s. Since his return from exile,
Brizola has been governor of Rio de Janeiro and is
now presidential candidate of his Democratic Workers Party (Partido Democrático dos Trabalhadores;
PDT). The PDT elected the mayor in Rio de
Janeiro, but lost its former stronghold in Porto
Alegre to the PT.

Carole Merten
San Francisco, California

Canada

Population. 26,087,536
Parties. Communist Party of Canada (CPC); Com-
munist Party of Canada (Marxist-Leninist) (CPC-
ML); Revolutionary Workers' League (RWL);
Trotskyist League (TL); International Socialists
(IS)

Founded. CPC: 1921; CPC-ML: 1970; RWL: 1977; TL: 1975

Membership. CPC: 3,000; CPC-ML: 500; RWL: 200 (all estimated)

General Secretary. CPC: George Hewison; CPC-ML: Hardial Bains; RWL: John Riddell

Central Committee. CPC: 65 members

Status. All legal

Last Congress. CPC: Twenty-seventh, 20–24 May 1988, in Toronto; CPC-ML: Fifth, 28–30 December 1987, in Montreal; RWL: Sixth, 28 July–3 August 1986, in Montreal

Last Federal Election. 21 November 1988; CPC: 52 candidates, average vote 126; no representatives; CPC-ML: no official candidates; RWL: no official candidates

Auxiliary Organizations. CPC: Parti communiste du Québec, Canadian Peace Congress, Conseil québecois de la paix, Association of United Ukrainian Canadians, Congress of Canadian Women, Young Communist League, Workers' Benevolent Association of Canada; CPC-ML: Peoples' Front Against Racist and Fascist Violence, Revolutionary Trade Union Opposition, Democratic Women's Union of Canada, Communist Youth Union of Canada (Marxist-Leninist), Canada-Albania Friendship Association; RWL: Young Socialist Organizing Committee, Comité de la jeunesse révolutionnaire (CJR)

Publications. CPC: *Canadian Tribune* (Tom Morris, editor), *Pacific Tribune*, *Combat*, *Communist Viewpoint*, *Le Communiste*, *Rebel Youth*, *Jeunesse militante*; CPC-ML: *Marxist-Leninist*, *Le Marxiste-Leniniste*, *Voice of the Youth*, *Voice of the People*, *Democratic Women*, *Peoples' Front Bulletin*, *Canadian Student*, *BC Worker*; RWL: *Socialist Voice* (Michael Prairie, editor), *Lutte ouvrière*; TL: *Sparticist Canada*; IS: *Socialist Worker*

A number of Marxist-Leninist organizations exist legally in Canada. The oldest, largest, and best organized is the CPC. Founded in 1921, it has adhered faithfully to a pro-Moscow line. The CPC-ML began in 1970 as an ardent follower of the Chinese brand of communism but since then has eschewed Beijing for the Albanian model. In addition, there are several Trotskyist groups functioning, the most active of which is the RWL.

The Canadian political scene at the federal level has proven to be quite volatile over the last eighteen months. From a low point of 23 percent popular support in July 1987, the fortunes of Brian Mulroney and the Conservatives rebounded sufficiently in 1988 to enable the prime minister to prorogue the 33d parliament and call a general election for 21 November. The government's free-trade agreement (Bill C-130) negotiated with the United States quickly emerged as the dominant issue. Both John Turner, leader of the Liberal Party, and Edward Broadbent, head of the New Democratic Party (NDP), waged a vigorous campaign against the free-trade deal, arguing that it would seriously undermine Canada's economic, and ultimately its political sovereignty. These concerns were echoed by a plethora of nationwide organizations, including the Canadian Labor Congress (CLC), the National Action Committee on the Status of Women, and the Council of Canadians. All sought to prevent the Conservatives from obtaining the electoral mandate to proceed with the bill. However, supported broadly by the business community and by eight of ten provincial premiers, Brian Mulroney soundly defeated his free-trade opponents at the polls, securing the parliamentary majority necessary to pass the legislation.

CPC. The CPC operates from its national office in Toronto on a meager budget of approximately $300,000 (Canadian) a year. In the 1988 federal election the party fielded 52 candidates, winning no office and garnering a paltry 6,537 votes (less than one-tenth of 1 percent of all votes cast). It also ran five candidates in the Manitoba provincial election (26 April); all received a negligible vote.

During the year the CPC held its 27th Congress from 20 to 24 May in Toronto. William Kashtan (79 years of age) used the occasion to step down after 23 years as general secretary, making way for a younger leader. George Hewison (43), who had been nominated to succeed Kashtan by a plenary meeting of the Central Committee (CC) was unanimously endorsed by the 146 delegates attending the congress (*Canadian Tribune*, 6 June). Hewison, a former secretary-treasurer and vice president of British Columbia's United Fishermen and Allied Workers' Union, had been a CPC stalwart for over twenty years on the West Coast before moving to Toronto in 1985, when he was elected to the party's Central Executive Committee (CEC) and to the post of Secretary for Trade Union Affairs (*WMR*, August; *International Affairs*, 25 May).

As the new general secretary, Hewison faces an uphill struggle. The membership of the party has been mired for many years at about 3,000; party finances are in a precarious state; and public response to its programs has ranged from apathy, at best, to scorn and repugnance (*The Toronto Globe and Mail*, 28 December 1987). A reflection of the CPC's shrinking base was evident in the congress's decision to reduce the membership of the newly elected CC by 15 percent. The policymaking body was trimmed from 77 to 65 (with 22 alternates). As well, the full-time CEC—the body charged with the day-to-day leadership of the CPC between CC meetings—was downsized to 11 members with no alternates (*Canadian Tribune*, 10 May, 6 June).

Along with these changes in the CPC's top leadership, the congress adopted several "action" resolutions and policy directives. Included was a resolution on aboriginal peoples that instructed the CEC to create a commission on aboriginal affairs to "provide analysis, research and help coordinate political work" to enable the party "to explore links with the growing number of socialist-minded Native Peoples." A "special" resolution on poverty and homelessness called for the minimum wage to be upped to at least $6.50 an hour along with a crash program "to provide shelters, hostels and temporary housing so that not one person is turned away." Finally, a resolution was carried recognizing the need for young people to be involved in the "political struggle" across Canada. In this regard, the CPC plans to expend greater energy and resources in increasing the size and influence of the Young Communist League. (*Canadian Tribune*, 6 June.)

The congress was attended by twenty delegations from communist and "workers parties" from around the world. Among the most prominent was the CPSU delegation led by K. N. Brutents, candidate member of the CPSU Central Committee and deputy chief of the CPSU Central Committee's International Department (*Pravda*, 22 May; *International Affairs*, 1 June). Also in attendance was a contingent of the Czechoslovak Communist Party headed by that country's First Deputy Prime Minister, Bohumil Urban (ibid., 25 May), and Dr. Erich Hahn, CC member of the SED (ibid., 6 June).

Two prominent party members died in 1988: Tom McEwen (97) and Oscar Ryan (84). McEwen, journalist (editor of the *Pacific Tribune* for 25 years) and militant trade unionist, had been an active member of the CC for almost 35 years. In 1931, he (along with CPC leader Tim Buck and five others) was arrested, tried, convicted, and sentenced to a five-year prison term for seditious activity. After his release, McEwen served briefly as the CPC's Comintern representative in Moscow. His autobiography, *The Forge Glows Red*, was published in 1974

(*Canadian Tribune*, 23 May). Oscar Ryan was also a lifelong party member who reported on the world of theater for various communist papers. For over three decades, his columns and reviews surveyed Canadian theatrical productions from a Marxist perspective. In 1975 he published *Tim Buck: A Conscience For Canada*, the official biography of the CPC's longtime general secretary. In the course of his career, Ryan wrote a number of plays and a novel, *Soon To Be Born* (1980), espousing the communist cause (ibid., 15 August).

The problem of new recruitment has continued to have high priority, as has increased circulation of the *Canadian Tribune*. The party has set a goal of 5 percent overall increase in membership and a yearly target of 15 percent growth in the number of the newspaper's subscribers. In both cases, it is difficult to ascertain if these objectives have been achieved, since the party does not publish precise figures. The *Tribune* was not overly successful in a $100,000 sustaining drive (the money needed to operate the newspaper), collecting only $69,000 (ibid., 6 June). Nor has the $30,000 "modernization" campaign—funds necessary to purchase new equipment and upgrade the newspaper's editorial facilities—reached its goal. A carryover from the previous year, this campaign has netted thus far only $15,000 (ibid., 29 February). Given this state of affairs, it appears that the *Tribune's* aim of eventually producing a daily rather than a weekly is still a long way off.

Throughout 1988, the CPC was particularly concerned about Mulroney's free-trade initiative. Editorials in the *Canadian Tribune* repeatedly argued that free trade with the United States was a bad deal that in the long term would result in the loss of Canada's political as well as economic independence (ibid., 22 February, 2 May). In the election campaign the party stridently attacked the trade pact; under the slogan "Canada: Don't Trade It Away," it urged Canadians to "come together" and defeat the Tories (ibid., 26 September, 31 October). Despite the decisive Conservative victory at the polls, the CPC vows to carry on its fight against the trade deal. It points out that, although the Conservatives have a parliamentary majority with 43 percent of the vote, it is not a "people's majority" since 56 percent of Canadians in fact voted against the Mulroney trade deal (ibid., 28 November, 5 December).

The CPC also continues to denounce the so-called Meech Lake Accord, signed on 3 June 1987. This constitutional amendment, which is still to be ratified by all the provincial premiers, ostensibly ends Quebec's constitutional isolation from the rest of Canada. Yet the CPC believes that the document is seriously flawed because it denies the right to self-determination for French Canadians, while subverting the legitimate interests of the aboriginal peoples and other minority groups (*Communist Viewpoint*, Summer; *Canadian Tribune*, 10 October). At the same time, the party maintains, it undermines the ability of the federal government to determine its own policies by giving greater power to the provinces (see *YICA*, 1988).

On the domestic scene generally, the CPC is highly critical of the Tories. It accuses the Mulroney administration of a "neoconservative drive to dismantle the public sector, ravage social services, and shift an ever larger share of the social wealth into the hands of the monopolies and multi-nationals" (*Communist Viewpoint*, Summer). It calls Finance Minister Michael Wilson a "trickster" for bringing down a two-stage tax reform plan "which will put a few pennies in our pockets during election year and then rob us blind as consumers the following year" (*Canadian Tribune*, 11 January). The CPC's tax-reform platform advocates the elimination of income taxes for those earning less than $25,000 a year and an increased corporate tax based on "the recognition that corporations and banks do not carry a fair share of the tax burden" (see *YICA*, 1988).

To combat these and other "disastrous" policies of the Mulroney government, the CPC urges the formation of a "people's majority outside of Parliament." In this regard, the party favors a broad coalition of communists with the NDP, left Liberals, and the trade-union movement (*Canadian Tribune*, 2 May). At the same time it endeavors to press the NDP to advance a "more coherent program against state monopoly capitalism," to oppose deregulation and privatization, and to do battle for Canadian independence. During the election campaign, the CPC gave "critical support" to the NDP, while noting that the NDP leadership is "tied to capitalism and capitalist perspectives and solutions and thus cannot be trusted to represent the true interests of the working class" (ibid., 6 June; *Communist Viewpoint*, Summer).

The CPC follows a similar strategy in its approach to trade unions, particularly to the CLC. The party recognizes that, as the largest organized section of the working class, the CLC "offers the potential to lead the nation into a fundamentally new path for peace, independence, and social progress" (see *YICA*, 1988). In a show of solidarity with organized labor, the *Canadian Tribune* throughout the year has given wide coverage to a number of strikes and lockouts, such as the highly publicized dispute between the Alberta government and the United Nurses Union, in which over 11,000 nurses participated in a protracted illegal walkout (*Canadian Tribune*, 8 February, 15 February).

The CPC has wholeheartedly endorsed the Soviet Union's fifteen-year peace proposals (announced in 1986) and gives full credit to Mikhail Gorbachev for his peace initiatives that resulted in the INF treaty. The treaty is seen as a "historic step... which for the first time actually reduces nuclear weapons and with it the danger of nuclear war" (ibid., 11 January).

The main threat to the achievement of peaceful coexistence and a globe free of nuclear arms, according to the CPC, is still U.S. imperialism (*Communist Viewpoint*, Spring). The party maintains that the U.S. objective is to achieve military superiority in space (via SDI), while wearing down economically the Soviet Union and the socialist countries in order to exact concessions from them.

The CPC accuses the Mulroney government of complicity in these U.S. strategic aims. It points to Ottawa's White Paper on defense, which in part advocates the building of ten to twelve nuclear submarines for use in Arctic waters, as evidence, suggesting that the document is a blueprint to promote Canada's military integration with the United States by further militarizing the North and tying it more directly to the NORAD command structure and SDI planning (*Communist Viewpoint*, Spring; *Canadian Tribune*, 25 April). Numerous articles in the *Canadian Tribune* reiterated CPC demands that Canada halt the testing of cruise missiles on Canadian territory; that the government reject all plans to upgrade NORAD and the DEW system; that it publish all secret U.S.-Canada military agreements; and that, ultimately, Canada pull out of both NORAD and the NATO alliance (ibid., 22 February, 2 May). The above actions are necessary, the party contends, if Canada is to develop an independent foreign policy rather than be reduced to "a U.S. satellite" (see *YICA* 1988).

In international affairs generally, the CPC follows a two-tiered line of stoutly supporting the Soviet position, while condemning that of the United States. Editorials in the *Canadian Tribune* have been particularly critical of U.S. foreign policy in Central America, labeling it a "dismal failure," especially Washington's continued support of the contras in their war against Daniel Ortega's regime in Nicaragua (4 August).

Other Groups. (1) **CPC-ML.** The CPC-ML operates from its national headquarters in Montreal. Since its fifth party congress in December 1987, it has not been very active. Although it continues to produce *Marxist-Leninist*, the publication appears irregularly and is not widely distributed or easily obtained. The CPC-ML remains a doctrinaire organization that believes that the transformation of society from capitalism to socialism can only be ensured through "revolutionary violence." Eighteen years after its founding, the party continues to exist very much on the political fringe with a tiny (albeit hard-core) following.

(2) **RWL.** The RWL is the Canadian section of the Trotskyist Fourth International. The League's aim is "to build the mass revolutionary party needed to lead the entire working class and its allies in the fight to take political power away from the ruling rich and establish a workers' and farmers' government in Ottawa" (*Youth and the Socialist Revolution* [RWL publication], March 1987). In the past several years, however, the RWL has been preoccupied with internal restructuring due to a decrease in membership and financial difficulties (see *YICA*, 1988). Like the CPC-ML, the RWL is very much on the political periphery, with no more than about 200 members throughout the country.

(3) **TL and IS.** The TL and IS are two other Marxist-Leninist groups that appear to operate, at least nominally, in Canada. The TL believes in "permanent revolution," denounces all other Trotskyist organizations and advocates a reforged Fourth International, while the IS is more populist in nature, calling for the building of socialism from below by the establishment of well-organized branches in major cities. On the whole, however, whether through lack of funds and/or personnel, the activities of the TL and IS were minimal in 1988.

J. Petryshyn
Grand Prairie Regional College
Grand Prairie, Alberta, Canada

Chile

Population. 12,638,046 (1988)
Party. Communist Party of Chile (Partido Comunista de Chile; PCC)
Founded. 1922
Membership. 20,000 (estimated active militants); 200,000 claimed in 1973 before military coup and party was declared illegal
General Secretary. Luís Corvalán Lepe
Politburo. 20 members (clandestine and in exile)
Secretariat. 5 members (clandestine and in exile)
Central Committee. More than 100 (clandestine and in exile)
Status. Illegal, but functions underground, issues public statements, and works through front groups
Last Congress. Fourteenth, November 1969; Fifteenth was planned for late 1973, prevented by 1973 coup; a national conference, officially described as "to some extent a congress," was held in 1984. Fifteenth Congress scheduled for 1989.
Last Election. March 1973, 16 percent, 23 of 150 seats in lower house; no congressional representation since 1973 coup
Auxiliary Organizations. Communist Youth (illegal). PCC dominates reorganized (illegal) labor confederation United Workers Central (CUT), although the CUT is headed by a Christian Democrat. Member of the United Left (IU) coalition, and its successor organization, the Broad Party of the Socialist Left (PAIS), created in November 1988. Has links to the Manuel Rodríguez Patriotic Front (FPMR), a terrorist organization with independent lines to Havana and Moscow.
Publications. *El Siglo* (clandestine newspaper that may begin to appear publicly in 1989); *Principios* (clandestine theoretical journal)

The year 1988 was dominated by the October 5th plebiscite on an additional eight-year term for President Augusto Pinochet. Already in late 1987, it was evident that the Communist Party was divided on whether or not to participate in a vote that it had frequently denounced as fraudulent, under a constitution adopted by a snap plebiscite in 1980, the legitimacy of which the party denies. There was never any question that the party would not register under the Political Parties Law, since it had been outlawed by the junta immediately after the 1973 coup, and an earlier front group, the Popular Democratic Movement (MDP), had been declared a totalitarian organization by the courts under the provisions of Article 8 of the constitution. However, when the electoral registry opened, the issue was whether or not to encourage party members to register, and thereafter whether they should vote in the plebiscite.

Party leaders were divided on the issue, but finally decided to encourage registration while reserving until later the decision on whether to boycott the plebiscite itself. Because the party had been committed since 1980 to "all forms of struggle," including violence against the Pinochet dictatorship, the centrist parties led by the Christian Democrats were unwilling to cooperate publicly with the communists, although informal contacts were maintained. On 2 February, when the Command for the No, a coalition of thirteen (later sixteen) centrist and left opposition parties was formed, the communists did not participate. The Command published a program of reforms that included the repeal of Article 8 so that all parties accepting democracy could participate, but no effort was made to secure the affiliation of the communists, since the Pinochet government propaganda continued to accuse the opposition of being Marxist-dominated. The communists did not participate in the Committee for Free Elections, although they had some influence through front groups that joined the Social Accord for the No (ACUSO). When the faction of the Socialist Party led by Ricardo Nuñez formed the Party for Democracy (PPD) as an "instrumental" party to promote a democratic transition, some communists joined as individuals. In March, the PPD complied with the complicated procedures for official recognition, and thus was entitled to appoint pollwatchers in the plebiscite. The government accused its most prominent leader, Ricardo Lagos, of communist sympathies but was unable to make the accusation stick.

The party gradually shifted its position on participation in the plebiscite, and in June the Central Committee formally voted to encourage participation as part of a broader strategy of social mobilization (Radio Moscow, 16 June; *FBIS*, 23 June). As late as April, however, Luís Corvalán, the party's general secretary, speaking from Moscow denounced the vote as "a great fraud stemming from the Constitution, which in its Article 8, establishes the proscription of political parties that are representative of large national sectors" (Radio Moscow, 15 April; *FBIS*, 20 April). By August, communist leaders were giving press conferences in Santiago urging "total and firm participation" in the plebiscite (EFE, 11 August; *FBIS*, 18 August).

One of the reasons for the change may have been the large number of registrants, which far exceeded expectations, as well as a decision of the Constitutional Tribunal mandating access to state television for the opposition. In September, the opposition broadcast 27 fifteen-minute programs supporting a "no" vote. The television campaign was organized by the Christian Democrats and Socialists, but some prominent communist artists and intellectuals provided support and technical assistance. The government's fifteen-minute programs mainly attacked Lagos and argued that a "no" vote would mean a return to the violence and Marxism that had characterized the Allende period (1970–1973).

The Movement of the Revolutionary Left (MIR), which had been a bitter opponent of the communists in the Allende period, also favored participation in the plebiscite, but the Manuel Rodriguez Patriotic Front continued to denounce the vote. The FPMR ceased its attacks on electricity transmission towers and police stations during the period immediately prior to the plebiscite. The governmental Investigative Police also claimed that the Communist Party had created its own military front, composed of FPMR dissidents, and warned against "Operation Tranquility," which it claimed was designed to make terrorist organizations appear democratic (*El Mercurio*, 29 August; *FBIS*, 8 September).

The state of emergency that in various degrees had been in force since the coup of September 1973 was lifted a few days before General Pinochet was formally nominated as a candidate by the junta on 30 August. Exiles returned in considerable numbers including communist Senator Volodia Teitelboim, who announced on 23 September that if the opposition defeated General Pinochet in the plebiscite, it should declare a provisional government (*NYT*, 24 September). The Command for the No was quick to disavow Teitelboim's statement and to reiterate that the communists were not members of the opposition coalition. Informal cooperation did take place however, and it was especially important in assuring that there were no violent demonstrations on the night of the vote that could be used by the government as an excuse to impose martial law—reportedly a plan favored by Pinochet and some of his advisors.

In fact, the vote took place in what was described by both sides as "an atmosphere of absolute tranquillity," and the no vote triumphed with 55 percent to 43 percent. Following the vote, the Command for the No was renamed the Coalition (*Concertación*) of Parties for Democracy, and it proposed a dialogue with the armed forces about changes in the constitution, including the repeal of Article 8 "to guarantee effective pluralism" (Radio Chilena, 14 October; *FBIS*, 17 October). Patricio Aylwin, the spokesman of the *Concertación* emphasized, however, that "we are clear and definite adversaries of the Communist Party . . . because we disagree on principles, objectives, and methods" (*La Vanguardia*, Barcelona, 10 October; *FBIS*, 14 October).

After the vote, Pinochet rejected any negotiation on constitutional amendments, and 14 December 1989 was set as the date for congressional and presidential elections. Pinochet will leave office on 11 March 1990, but he can remain as army commander, member of the military-dominated National Security Council, and a lifetime senator. The transition to democracy has begun, but it will be several years before it is complete. In the meantime, the MIR is now discussing electoral participation (*El Mercurio*, 12 November; *FBIS*, 28 November); and the communists have announced that *El Siglo* will no longer be published underground, and that they plan to hold their first public party congress since 1969. They have also joined the newly organized Broad Party of the Socialist Left (PAIS), which raises for the government the question whether it can outlaw PAIS, a much broader coalition than the communist-dominated Popular Democratic Movement that had been banned earlier. Even though they will not be able to run communist candidates, the December 1989 vote will be an interesting test of the degree to which the communists have been able to maintain their organization and support despite sixteen years of repression.

Paul E. Sigmund
Princeton University

Fifteenth National Congress Planned. On 6 December the PCC held a press conference at the El Libertador Hotel in Santiago to release a long, sometimes rambling Central Committee document entitled "To Restore and Deepen Democracy: the Unity of the People Until Victory." The document is the most important PCC statement released in many years, combining self-criticism, self-aggrandizement, and the latest analyses of some of the most important developments of the past twenty years in

Latin America by what was long the strongest and most influential communist party—and the cornerstone of Soviet policy—in South America. It will "serve as a basis for discussions" at the PCC's Fifteenth National Congress, planned for 1989, and was broadcast by Radio Moscow in twelve segments between 7 and 18 December. (See *FBIS: SOV*, 15, 20, and 21 December.)

The PCC notes that international developments bode well for Chileans in the wake of the "great triumph at the plebiscite." Profound changes are occurring in and are strengthening the Soviet Union even as U.S. power and influence in the hemisphere are declining. The U.S. decline is seen in: the expansion of other "imperialist centers of world power," particularly the European Economic Community and Japan; the consolidation of the Cuban and Nicaraguan governments and the successes of leftist forces from Brazil to El Salvador, including the "advanced Christian movement"; and the successes of the Contadora Group, the Esquipulas Accord, the Group of Eight Presidents, and the "independent stance of Panama."

The PCC proclaims that the Popular Unity government under Salvador Allende was "the greatest historical achievement of the revolutionary forces since independence," and the source of popular domestic and international policies. Even though foreign imperialism and domestic reaction ganged up on the Popular Unity, "our defeat can be attributed to our errors and the inability to solve the power problem, an essential matter in all revolutions." "We should have concentrated harder on the ideological-political struggle within the popular and revolutionary forces." But the PCC was "tangled up with legalisms and excited over the peaceful development of the revolution. We did not take into account the Leninist theory that maintains that in times of revolution, the class struggle often leads rapidly to open civil war." "Leftist deviations" in the early 1970s, the document admits, "reflected to a great extent the true problems that the [PCC] leadership had not tackled or had solved in a poor manner."

After the 1973 coup, the U.S. "national security doctrine" became the official doctrine of the Chilean government, and the country was returned to the foreign imperialists and domestic reactionaries: "The fascist dictatorship has fully implemented a counterrevolution." In the mid-1970s the PCC developed its policy of "popular rebellion of the masses" to bring "in a single process, the overthrow of the dictatorship and the implementation of an advanced democracy." The policy, announced on the eve of the 1980 plebiscite for the "fascist constitution," forced the party to recognize "a need and duty to play a political leadership role, including military aspects, aimed at toppling the fascist dictatorship."

But development of the popular rebellion was hindered by "differences within the PCC leadership over the actual existence of a revolutionary situation and over the formulation of a policy to topple Pinochet in 1986." Differences persisted into 1988, when the party finally decided to support the no vote in the plebiscite, thus using "the regime's own institutional system to fight it," while recognizing that the establishment of "bourgeois" democracy, though a step forward, still "will not meet the demands and fulfill the yearnings of the masses." Thus as the PCC goes into its Fifteenth Congress, it still proclaims its policy of popular rebellion: "the need to use all types of struggle to discontinue the legal system established by the regime . . . to rebel against tyranny."

The PCC "hailed the birth" of the FPMR, "encouraged its development"—not least by having party militants and Communist Youth members join its ranks—and "will continue to encourage the actions and development of any organization that stands for the people's self-defense and contributes to their struggle." Even though the no vote won in the plebiscite, the situation still calls for "relentless struggle until democracy is fully recovered," and indeed "the need for a mass uprising and a national rebellion can at any time come to the fore." By the end of 1988, the PCC seemed to support the minority faction of a splintered FPMR—and a minority faction of the MIR as well—that opposed the "national patriotic war" line of the majority ("Autonomous") group. (*Cauce*, 31 October; *FBIS*, 13 and 27 December; *APSI*, 12–18 December.)

At the same time, supporting all forms of struggle, the party calls also for a "popular, democratic, anti-imperialist and anti-oligarchic" revolution stressing the unity of communists and Socialists and seeking an understanding among the other elements of the left. The PCC maintains that right now the workers will play the main role in the struggle for democracy and change, and that the PCC is their vanguard, but the party professes to hope that "in the future all of us [on the left] may constitute a single vanguard organization." One of the main obstacles to that at the present time is the anti-Sovietism and anti-communism of the bourgeois democratic forces. "Any democrat who is consistent with his beliefs," the party concludes, "is under an obligation to denounce anti-communism without hesitation."

William Ratliff
Hoover Institution

Colombia

Population. 31,298,803 (1987)
Party. Communist Party of Colombia (Partido Comunista de Colombia; PCC)
Founded. 1930
Membership. 18,000 (estimate, including Communist Youth Organization)
General Secretary. Gilberto Vieira
Executive Committee. 14 members
Central Committee. 80 members
Status. Legal
Last Congress. Fifteenth, 12–15 December 1988
Last Elections. 1988: 18 mayors, 364 municipal council members, 13 deputies and 5 alternates to state assemblies. 1986: presidential, 4.5 percent; congressional, 1.4 percent, 5 of 114 senators, 9 of 199 representatives
Auxiliary Organizations. United Workers Confederation (CUT); Federation of Agrarian Syndicates; Communist Youth of Colombia (JUCO), claims 2,000 members
Publications. *Voz* (weekly), 40,000 circulation; *Margen Izquierda*, political journal; Colombian edition of *World Marxist Review*, 2,000 circulation

In 1988 Colombia experienced the highest levels of guerrilla and politically motivated violence it has known since *La Violencia* of the 1940s and 1950s. According to Defense Minister Gen. Rafael Samudio Molina, armed subversion is the greatest threat to public and state security. In his annual report to Congress in July, Samudio said that "peace is being disturbed by the violence of subversion, terrorism, and narcotics-smuggling groups seeking to destabilize the democratic system" (*El Tiempo*, 25 July).

According to Colombian state security statistics,

a total of 3,639 persons died as a direct result of political violence during the year—156 policemen, 563 military men, 2,157 peasants, and 763 guerrillas. The government reported 166 guerrilla "harassments" against military and National Police posts; 74 ambushes against army and National Police forces; 60 attacks on National Police garrisons, stations, and substations; 97 attacks against vehicles; and 37 incursions into small towns, mostly in remote areas. In addition, 544 citizens were kidnapped by guerrillas and are still being held captive at year's end (*El Siglo*, 3 January 1989).

Although not officially abrogated, the four-year-old truce between the Colombian government and the Revolutionary Armed Forces of Colombia (FARC)—the country's largest guerrilla movement—exists in name only. According to the defense ministry, between January and November the FARC killed 180 soldiers and suffered 248 casualties in its own ranks (ibid., 20 November). The government's fragile agreement with the FARC has been further eroded by mounting evidence of cooperation between the guerrillas and Colombia's powerful drug rings.

The threat to peace in Colombia is exacerbated by persistent charges that middle-level army officers may be involved in the paramilitary groups and right-wing death squads that were responsible for the murder of more than 300 leftist political leaders and activists in 1988. Amnesty International reported in April that "human rights violations on a massive scale are not only tolerated within the Colombian armed forces, but are in fact the result of a deliberate policy of political murder" (*Amnesty Action*, May/June).

M-19 guerrillas kidnapped former Conservative presidential candidate Alvaro Gómez Hurtado on 29 May as part of its strategy to force the government to promote peace talks. Although the government did not participate directly in a national dialogue held by various political sectors on 29 July, President Virgilio Barco announced a major peace plan on 1 September consisting of an initial phase of pacification, a transitional phase of demobilization, and a phase of definitive reintegration into civilian life.

Guerrilla movements responded to Barco's peace proposal with their biggest offensive in years, prompting General Samudio to declare an "all-out offensive to destroy the enemy" (*El Tiempo*, 5 November). President Barco called his defense minister's mandate a "simplistic solution" and reiterated the government's resolve to offer "an extended, but firm hand" to subversives (AFP, 5 November). Samudio promptly resigned and was replaced by General Jaime Guerrero Paz, who reasserted the armed forces' respect for civilian government and support for the president's policy (*El Espectador*, 11 November).

In December the FARC's high command, speaking for the Simón Bolívar Guerrilla Coordinating Board (CNG), declared a unilateral cease-fire through Christmas and reaffirmed its support for an alternate peace plan proposed by an opposition politician in mid-November (*La Prensa*, 15 December). Unofficial talks between government representatives and M-19 leaders in December, along with a letter from FARC to President Barco proposing a dialogue between the CNG and the government, offered encouraging signs at year's end that direct contacts would be established early in 1989 to discuss the bases of a new peace agreement.

Although Colombia is in no immediate danger of being taken over by leftist extremists or by a security-conscious military, uncontrolled violence throughout the year continued to undermine the country's democratic institutions.

PCC. The communist movement in Colombia has undergone various transformations in both name and organization since the party's initial formation in December 1926. The PCC was publicly proclaimed on 17 July 1930. In July 1965, a schism within the PCC between pro-Soviet and pro-Chinese factions resulted in the latter's becoming the Communist Party of Colombia, Marxist-Leninist (PCC-ML). Only the PCC has legal status. It has been allowed to participate in elections under its own banner since 1972. In 1988, the PCC participated in mayoral, municipal-council, and state-assembly elections as the leading member of a leftist coalition called the Patriotic Union (Unión Patriótica; UP). The UP was formed in 1985 on the initiative of the FARC as a broad front to achieve political and social reforms. From the day the movement was founded, the PCC has been active in its leadership and work. The UP presented candidates for mayor or council in 395 municipalities in the March elections, approximately one-third of the country's total. It claimed 18 of its own mayoral candidates elected and 111 others whom it supported as coalition candidates. The UP elected 364 partisans to municipal councils, and claimed victory for an additional 37 coalition candidates. The popular vote for UP lists did not exceed 60,000, far below the 250,000 votes its congressional candidates received in 1986. However, this figure does not take into account some 230,000 votes for coalition lists in which the UP took part (*Voz*, 31 March, 7 April).

According to U.S. intelligence sources, the PCC has 18,000 members, including members of the Communist Youth Organization. Although the party contends that its ranks have increased "by more than 5,000" in recent years, the party's growth has been less rapid than its leaders had hoped, especially outside the Federal District of Bogotá. Most of the party's success in establishing new primary party organizations has occurred in Arauca, Urabá, César, Caquetá, Meta, Bolívar, and Santander. (*WMR*, July 1987.) The PCC exercises only marginal influence in national affairs.

The highest party authority is the congress, convened at four-year intervals. A major source of the party's influence is its control of the United Workers Confederation, reportedly Colombia's largest trade-union confederation with 800,000 members. Although the party officially disclaims any control over the CUT, it insists on the right to "occupy and exercise any leadership positions that may be assigned to it" (*Voz*, 30 April 1987). Writing in *Voz*, PCC member Miguel Antonio Caro stated that communists have the obligation to observe "exemplary behavior" in the consolidation of the CUT and the development of its plans. He added that the party must "contribute decisively to the organization of mass movements on May first against the 'dirty war,' the foreign debt, and scarcity, and for the right to life and democracy" (*Voz* supplement, 28 April). The CUT's president, Jorge Carrillo, resigned on 1 November. He accused the PCC and the UP of "violating the principles of unionism" by their efforts to make the CUT "the spearhead of their political purposes" (EFE, 1 November; *FBIS*, 2 November). The CUT's vice president Gustavo Osorio and its general secretary Angelino Garzón are members of the PCC's Central Committee.

The PCC's youth organization, the JUCO, plays an active role in promoting party policy among university and secondary-school students. The JUCO's Central Committee held a plenary in Bogotá on 29–31 January to review its recent accomplishments and to finalize plans for the electoral campaign (*Voz*, 11 February). JUCO organized marches in the principal cities and held special acts in major universities throughout the country. The group also organized festivals and youth meetings in rural areas in support of democratic agrarian reform. According to documents prepared for the Fifteenth Party Congress, the party believes it must pay greater attention to JUCO's political and organizational development. JUCO is described as "weak, vulnerable to cyclical leadership, and with little impact on the principal youth concentrations." The party also criticized JUCO leaders for their lack of initiative, irresponsibility, and formalism (*Voz* supplement, 4 August). Although JUCO plays an active role in student politics at the national level, its middle-level leadership is only marginally involved at the regional and grass-roots levels. The JUCO's political role in support of the PCC's electoral and organizational objectives is carried out through the Union of Patriotic Youth. The JUCO's general secretary is José Anteguera.

Guerrilla Warfare. Although not a serious threat to the government, guerrilla warfare has been a feature of Colombian life since the late 1940s. The current wave began in 1964. The four main guerrilla organizations are the FARC, long controlled by the PCC; the M-19, which began as the armed hand of the National Popular Alliance (ANAPO); the pro-Chinese People's Liberation Army (EPL), which is the guerrilla arm of the PCC-ML; and the Castroite National Liberation Army (ELN), also called the Camilist Union Army of National Liberation (UC-ELN) in memory of Camilo Torres. Other, smaller guerrilla movements that have emerged in recent years include the Trotskyist-oriented Workers Self-Defense Movement (ADO); the Revolutionary Workers Party (PRT); the Free Fatherland (Patria Libre), which some observers believe to be a spinoff of the EPL; and the Quintín Lamé, a pro-Indian group that operates primarily in the Valle del Cauca and Cauca departments. In September 1987, leaders from the six principal subversive movements in the country created the Simón Bolívar National Guerrilla Coordinating Board (CNG). The principal leadership within the CNG is provided by the FARC. Among the guerrilla columns functioning under the umbrella of the CNG's coordinated command is the so-called America Battalion, said by its leaders to consist of leftist rebels from Colombia, members of the Alfaro Lives movement of Ecuador, and guerrillas from the Tupac Amaru II movement of Peru. According to Colombian intelligence sources, Cuban advisers are operating within different FARC and ELN fronts, including those that have attacked oil pipelines and installations (*El Siglo*, 30 January).

In a communiqué issued at a guerrilla summit held on 30 March, the CNG proposed the adoption of a new constitution to reflect "the new social and political forces in the country and their aspirations." The document also denounced the "dirty war" being waged in Colombia, and called for the suspension of the state of siege, the dismantling of paramilitary groups, and the repeal of the antiterrorist statute (*Voz*, 7 April). In October, the CNG proposed that President Barco establish a high-level government commission to prepare the way for direct negotiations with guerrilla leaders (*El Tiempo*, 25 October). According to FARC leader Jacobo Arenas, the CNG "has not operated militarily" (EFE, 5 January; *FBIS*, 5 January). However, military authorities attributed several major attacks during the year to guerrilla units coordinated by the CNG (*El Tiempo*, 9 October). Estimates of guerrilla strength range from 10,000 to 15,000 men and women spread over some 80 different fronts (*NYT*, 15 December).

FARC. According to Colombia's defense minister, the FARC has a total of 4,500 men (other estimates range as high as 12,000) operating on 39 fronts (*YICA*, 1987). According to the movement's principal leader, Manuel Marulanda Vélez, the FARC has expanded its areas of influence in recent years to include portions of the departments of Huila, Caquetá, Tolima, Cauca, Boyacá, Santander, Antioquia, Valle, Meta, Cundinamarca, and the intendance of Arauca. The FARC's general headquarters is located at La Uribe. Jacobo Arenas is Marulanda's second-in-command; other members of the FARC's general staff are Alfonso Cano, Raúl Reyes, and Timoleón Jiménez. Although Marulanda has never confirmed officially that the FARC is the armed wing of the PCC, it is widely believed that the leadership mechanisms and general policy of the FARC are determined by the PCC's bylaws, and political resolutions emitted at party congresses and plenums are presumably transmitted to the fronts through Marulanda's directives.

In an open letter dated 31 January, FARC's high command declared that "Colombia is experiencing a period of profound social and political turmoil, which could lead to a bloody civil war if the people fail to unite." It called for the formation of a nationalist coalition government "capable of restoring democracy and a policy of independent and sovereign development" (*Voz*, 18 February).

FARC increased its actions following the March elections. Clashes were reported in Antioquia, Huila, Boyacá, Santander, Caquetá, Meta, El Vaupés, and Casanare over a four-month period. On 7 July, combined FARC and ELN units killed fifteen soldiers and wounded seven in a skirmish in El Bagre, in northwestern Antioquia, prompting Colombia's defense minister to declare that "as long as soldiers continue to be killed, there cannot be any dialogue with guerrilla groups" (AFP, 12 July; *El Espectador*, 14 July). He later warned that despite the existing partial truce agreement, the FARC "is still the main threat to the country." According to General Samudio, FARC has expanded its military operations to 39 fronts since 1984 and is responsible for organizing several peasant marches in northeastern Colombia (*El Tiempo*, 25 July). On 14 August, FARC released two U.S. students held since October 1987 (ibid., 18 August).

In response to President Barco's peace initiative, the FARC proposed a 60-day general cease-fire to facilitate negotiations aimed at peace. Arenas insisted that the country's foremost need is "to end the dirty war" (ibid., 23 September). In early October FARC guerrillas ambushed a military patrol in the jungles of southern Caquetá, killing fifteen and wounding thirteen (AFP, 2 October). Other FARC units of 300 to 400, reportedly backed by ELN and EPL guerrillas, attacked military and police outposts in Córdoba, Magdalena, Bolívar, and Santander departments over a six-week period. The FARC demonstrated a high level of operational capability in this offensive, leading to speculation that its leadership is seeking to give the foreign press the impression that Colombia is virtually in a state of war. The FARC may also want to make a show of strength before undertaking peace negotiations with the government (*El Tiempo*, 9 October). Military authorities based in Villavicencio reported that two noncommissioned officers and nine soldiers were killed on 1 November when the FARC's 31st Front attacked a convoy of military engineers in Meta department (*El Espectador*, 2 November).

In November the FARC and M-19 agreed to an alternate peace initiative proposed by Senator Alvaro Leyva Durán. Under Leyva's proposal, a five-member commission appointed by the government would have 30 days to determine whether minimum conditions exist for a direct dialogue between the government and the guerrillas. The government would then take twenty days to decide how, when, and where direct talks could be held. A dialogue would then be held within 30 days and lead to the signing of a peace treaty (Emisoras Caracol Network, 29 November; *FBIS*, 30 November). In a note to the Colombian Congress in mid-December, the FARC proposed that the Congress undertake its own appraisal of the Leyva peace plan. The FARC's high command, together with M-19, proclaimed a unilateral cease-fire through Christmas and denounced the fact that their messages and peace actions have received little credence from the government and the military high command (EFE, 13 December; *FBIS*, 13 December). In a letter to President Barco, the FARC's leadership reaffirmed its "willingness, shared by all of the members of CNG, to talk with your government to find a political solution to the country's problems" (*La Prensa*, 15 December).

Domestic Attitudes and Activities. The PCC recognizes the experience of the Communist Party of the Soviet Union (CPSU) as an ideological source, but it also takes "maximum account of the national characteristics and revolutionary and democratic traditions of the Colombian people." This has enabled the party to devise its own tactics, which combine diverse forms of struggle ranging from electoral campaigns to guerrilla warfare.

The documents and declarations approved by the PCC's Fifteenth Congress indicate that the strategy and tactics of the PCC will continue to be a combination of all forms of struggle. According to the party's assessment of the national situation, the country is moving into a new phase where the likelihood of intensified struggle between the forces demanding change and those resisting them is ever greater. The prospect is for increased armed clashes, which will make mass action more difficult. Therefore the party proposes not to limit itself to legal mass actions, many of which have become increasingly restricted. Rather, it must "learn to appreciate the significance of newer forms of struggle that have arisen through the initiative of the popular masses . . . such as the occupation of public establishments, prolonged peasant marches, disruption of traffic, and agrarian strikes" (*Voz* supplement, 4 August). At the opening session of the party congress, Vieira stated that "guerrilla actions are totally justified as a response to institutionalized violence" (Inravision Television Cadena, 12 December; *FBIS*, 14 December).

Much of the PCC's political activity in 1988 directly concerned its participation in the leadership and activities of the Patriotic Union. The UP was established by the PCC, trade-union, and other independent leftist forces in November 1985 to facilitate the transition of FARC guerrillas to legal political life. The official communist view is that the UP has emerged as an alternative to the traditional parties, having a well-defined program of social, economic, and political reforms. According to Vieira, the UP is "an independent movement that grew out of a FARC initiative" (*WMR*, July). The UP's consolidation as a political organization has been impeded by the ceaseless killings of its members by death squads. Twenty-nine of its mayoral candidates and over 100 of its candidates for municipal councils were assassinated in the months leading up to the March elections (*Latin America Update*, March–May).

The PCC's Central Executive Committee (CEC) issued a statement in January condemning the assassination of Attorney General Carlos Mauro Hoyos. It appealed to all Colombians to take part in demonstrations on 27 January to condemn the "dirty war," terrorism, and institutionalized violence (*Voz*, 28 January). The CEC issued a similar statement in February denouncing the resurgence of violence directed against the UP and PCC. It called for a "massive popular mobilization" on 24 February to repudiate the "antiterrorist statute," the government's "plan of extermination," and military violence, and to demonstrate solidarity for the defense of human rights and international supervision of the March elections (ibid., 25 February).

According to Vieira, the most important aspect of the March elections was "the expression of broad coalitions in the election of mayors." UP's share of the popular vote did not match its expectations. However, in regions such as Guaviare and Arauca "institutionalized terrorism prevented many UP partisans from exercising their right to vote" (ibid., 17 March). A report prepared for the Central Committee's plenum on 2–3 April cited the "weakness of leftist currents that in some cities and regions participated without any clear understanding." Positive electoral results were obtained wherever coalitions existed, although there were exaggerated expectations of support in the larger cities. In some cases anticommunist sentiments were expressed and misunderstandings occurred over the extent of coalition unity. The report calls for the party to "maintain its independence, since we are concerned with operating in the political mainstream and not on the margins" (ibid., 7 April).

At a UP plenum for Cundinamarca department in April, Vieira denounced the "dirty war," and charged that "Yankee imperialism has converted Colombia into a laboratory for low-intensity conflict, where assassinations are used to weaken the revolutionary movements." He noted that "not one arrest" has been made for crimes committed against popular leaders. (*Voz*, 28 April.) A PCC delegation consisting of Alvaro Vásquez, Hernando Hurtado, and Manuel Cepeda attended a meeting of the National Dialogue Commission on 27 July. They presented a declaration prepared by the Central Executive Committee that identified the "dirty war" as the highest political priority for discussion. In the party's view, until the government and the traditional parties demonstrate their willingness to "disband the paramilitary groups, do away with gangs of thugs, purge the military ranks, and punish those guilty of crimes," other considerations are worth very little (ibid., 28 July).

The party considers the consolidation of the UP one of its most important achievements in recent class struggles. According to documents prepared by the Central Committee for presentation at the Fifteenth Party Congress, there is a "clear tendency toward increased class struggle in recent years, evident in the development of new political alternatives to the traditional parties." In reviewing political developments since 1984, the party concluded that "conditions have improved for the popular struggle to achieve advanced democracy." The current situation signifies "a deepening of the class struggle and a break with political immobilization." The party calls for renewed efforts to unify leftist forces in Colombia by "forging a broad political and ideological convergence of all revolutionaries in the common struggle for the social and national liberation of the people." An essential element in raising the people's consciousness is the struggle against militarism. This means the party's continued opposition to the state of siege, paramilitary actions, disappearance of popular leaders, persecution of the UP, discrimination against the labor movement, and militarization of the universities and popular barrios. Party leaders believe that the formation of a solid, unified base for popular action "presumes a politics of compromise, negotiation, and participation at all levels." (*Voz* supplement, 4 August.) At the opening session of the party congress, Vieira stressed the democratic opportunity created by the popular election of mayors and the recognition of the UP as a political party (Inravision Television Cadena, 12 December; *FBIS*, 14 December).

In an article written for the Czech newspaper *Rudé Právo*, Manuel Cepeda stated that "it has proven impossible to push through President Barco's peace plan, since it is based on the presumption that the guerrilla movement has been defeated." He reiterated the PCC's support for a political solution to the conflict, and noted that the removal of General Samudio "shows that a political way out of the conflict is possible" (*Rudé Právo*, 28 November).

International Views and Positions. The PCC faithfully follows the Soviet line in its international positions. According to Vieira, the party is engaged primarily in the struggle for the emancipation of the Colombian people. However, the PCC insists that it is impossible to remain neutral in the "great international struggle" between socialism and capitalism. The party therefore works actively for the unity of the international revolutionary movement. It supports the "historic transformations" taking place in the Soviet Union and applauds the leadership role of Gorbachev in the pursuit of arms control and the elimination of intermediate range missiles (*Voz*, 4 August). At the same time, the party claims that it is not dependent on Moscow, Havana, or "any foreign place," nor does it serve as the agent for the international policy of any foreign country. The PCC wants a Colombian international policy that is "independent and autonomous." The PCC believes that its experience in employing all forms of popular action is proving useful in other Latin American countries.

The PCC is consistently internationalist and invariably displays solidarity with the struggles of fraternal parties and peoples. At the Central Committee plenum on 2–3 April, the party proclaimed its unconditional support for the Cuban Revolution and solidarity with the "sister republic of Nicaragua and with the struggle for liberation of the peoples of Central America." It also passed resolutions in support of the World Labor Federation, the "continental struggle" against payment of foreign debt, the New International Economic Order, and Latin American integration (*Voz*, 7 April). According to Vieira, the U.S. "industrial and military complex" gravely threatens world peace, while the world socialist system, headed by the Soviet Union, works to defend it.

The Maoists. The PCC-ML is firmly pro-Chinese, although in recent years the party has looked more toward Albania for political guidance. Its present leadership hierarchy is not clearly known. The PCC-ML has an estimated membership of 1,000. Unlike the PCC, it has not attempted to obtain legal status, and its impact in terms of national life is insignificant. Its official news organ is *Revolución*. The Marxist-Leninist

League of Colombia publishes the monthly *Nueva Democracia*.

The PCC-ML's guerrilla arm, the EPL, was the first to attempt a "people's war" in Latin America. The EPL has conducted only limited operations since 1975, although according to Colombian intelligence, it still has an estimated 750 guerrillas organized over fifteen fronts (*YICA*, 1987). The EPL operates mainly in the departments of Antioquia, Córdoba, and Caldas, with urban support networks in several of the country's larger cities.

The EPL was among the guerrilla movements that concluded a peace agreement with the government in August 1984. However, the murder of several prominent EPL leaders in late 1985 led the movement to disavow the truce. Current members of the EPL's general staff include Francisco Caraballo, Javier Robles, and Tobías Lopera.

According to a report provided by state security agencies, the EPL killed 58 soldiers in ambushes and attacks on military outposts. The EPL, in turn, lost 142 members, with an additional 89 wounded. (*El Siglo*, 7 November.) Almost a quarter of the EPL's casualties were inflicted during intensive counterinsurgency operations in the Alto Sinú mountains of Córdoba department in February, following an EPL ambush in which, for the first time in the history of insurgency in Colombia, an officer having the rank of lieutenant colonel was killed (*El Tiempo*, 19 and 26 February). In April, EPL supporters briefly occupied a television station in Antioquia and trasmitted slogans against the government to protest the killing of peasants in Urabá (Inravision, 23 April; *FBIS*, 25 April). The EPL refused to attend the national dialogue meeting on 29 July, stating that it would not accept the preconditions of disarmament and demobilization proposed by the government while the "war against the people continues" (EFE, 28 July; *FBIS*, 29 July). In October, an EPL unit seized control of the Bogotá installations of the Circuíto Todelar radio network and forced its personnel to broadcast a message in support of the national strike scheduled for 27 October (AFP, 14 October). According to a clandestine radio broadcast, leaders from the EPL, the PCC/ML, and the UC-ELN met in November to review guerrilla strategy in southwestern Colombia (Radio Patria Libre, 9 November; *FBIS*, 15 November).

The Independent Revolutionary Workers' Movement (MOIR) has aspired since 1971 to become the first mass-based Maoist party in Latin America. Its leadership and organization are independent of those of the PCC-ML. The MOIR has no military branch and has been unable to strengthen its political position in recent years. The MOIR's general secretary is Francisco Mosquera.

The M-19. The M-19, which first appeared in January 1974 as the self-proclaimed armed branch of ANAPO, takes its name from the contested presidential election of 19 April 1970. Since 1976, the M-19 has been actively involved in Colombia's guerrilla movement, pursuing "a popular revolution of national liberation toward socialism." The Colombian Defense Ministry's official estimate of the M-19's strength is 450 men operating on two fronts (*YICA*, 1987). Other estimates of the movement's size range up to several thousand.

The M-19 held out for what it considered a "broader peace agreement" from that reached by the government with the FARC. For most M-19 leaders, the peace accord signed with the government on 24 August 1984 constituted an agreement to end hostilities in order to open the way to a "national dialogue." Unlike the FARC, the M-19 has lacked a consistent policy regarding the cease-fire, the national dialogue, or its political future. In addition, the movement's loss of leadership in recent years has created internal dissension. Since resuming guerrilla activities in June 1985, the M-19 has been engaged in continuous warfare with the armed forces. Until this year, the M-19 supplied most of the manpower and leadership for the guerrilla columns operating through the self-styled National Guerrilla Coordinating Board, including the América Battalion. The M-19's principal commander is Carlos Pizarro Leongómez. Other surviving members of the M-19's central staff are Antonio Navarro, Germán Rojas Patiño, Vera Grave, Pedro Pacheco, Rósemberg Pabón, and Libardo Parra.

The M-19 maintained a low profile during much of the year, especially in the months following Pizarro's announcement on 22 January of a unilateral six-month truce (AFP, 22 January). Official statistics on guerrilla violence through November showed the M-19 killing seventeen soldiers, while the movement sustained 80 casualties in operations conducted largely in regions of southeastern Cauca, southern Tolima, and Caquetá (*El Siglo*, 20 November).

The M-19 broke its truce in dramatic fashion with the kidnapping of Alvaro Gómez Hurtado on 29 May. In a communiqué to the government, Pizarro made Gómez's release conditional on a national dialogue with an open agenda, a 60-day cease-fire, and direct talks between military commanders and the CNG. He stated that the M-19 was prepared to "demobilize as guerrillas, but not to demobilize the resistance of the people under a leadership class that has been selfish in the management of national politics" (*El Espectador*, 2 July; ACAN, 6 July). The government confirmed on 6 July its willingness to make concessions in exchange for Gómez's release, but it condemned M-19 terrorism and blackmail in holding him hostage to gain national attention for its political plan (*El Tiempo*, 7 July). Gómez was released on 20 July after a first round of talks took place in Panama, attended by delegates from political parties, industry, the working sector, and the Church, but not the government. The dialogue continued in Bogotá on 29 July. On 3 August, Defense Minister Samudio announced that the armed forces would not participate in the deliberations (ibid., 4 August).

In early December President Barco's peace adviser said that the M-19 is "perhaps the only insurgent group that lately has shown its tacit willingness to hold a dialogue aimed at achieving peace in the country" (Emisoras Caracol, 1 December; *FBIS*, 5 December). Pizarro reaffirmed the M-19's support for the peace initiative proposed by Senator Leyva and declared a cease-fire through Christmas. However, he warned the government on 6 December that the M-19's "patience is running out," and that civil war will be unleashed if it receives "no realistic proposals to negotiate peace" (EFE, 6 December; *FBIS*, 7 December). Despite such threats, M-19 leaders reportedly had plans to hold a top-level summit to discuss strategies for the demobilization of its military fronts and to plan its internal transformation in preparation for becoming a political party (*La Prensa*, 19 December).

ELN. The ELN was formed in Santander in 1964 under the inspiration of the Cuban Revolution. It undertook its first military action in January 1965. Once recognized as the largest and most militant of the guerrilla forces operating in Colombia, the ELN has never recovered from the toll exacted on its leadership and urban network by an army offensive in 1973. The ELN was the only major guerrilla movement that did not sign a cease-fire agreement with the government in 1984. The Simón Bolívar and Antonio Nariño fronts accepted a peace agreement with the National Peace Commission in December 1985. Members of the Gerardo Valencia Cano front, which operates in Cauca, Nariño, and a large sector of the Atlantic Coast, signed a similar agreement in April 1986.

According to Colombian intelligence, the ELN has approximately 950 men distributed over 15 fronts. Its principal leader is Manuel Pérez. Other members of the central staff are Nicolás Rodríguez, Milton Hernández, and Gabriel Borja. The ELN operates in a vast region of northeastern Colombia, North and South Santander, Bolívar, Cauca, and Antioquia, and in the intendance of Arauca. Because of its revenue from kidnappings, extortion, and bank robberies, the movement is believed to be financially self-supporting.

The ELN was the second most active guerrilla movement in 1988. According to official data, the ELN was responsbile for seven attacks on military installations and eleven ambushes, in which a total of 91 soldiers and policemen and 142 guerrillas were killed (*El Siglo*, 20 November). In addition, ELN units carried out over fifty attacks on Colombia's main petroleum pipeline between Caño Limón and Covenas, which links the eastern plains and the Caribbean coast.

During late April and early May, the ELN kidnapped over a dozen diplomats, reporters, and politicians to call world attention to Colombia's human rights situation, to criticize the government's oil policy, and to demand the nationalization of the petroleum industry. In a communiqué announcing arrangements for the release of the hostages, Pérez expressed the ELN's support for Amnesty International's report on Colombia and proposed the creation of an international tribunal to identify those responsible for the "dirty war" (Inravision Television Cadena, 6 May; *FBIS*, 9 May). According to military sources, approximately 60 members of the Armando Cacua Guerrero Front occupied the village of Salazar de las Palmas in North Santander on 5 May (*El Tiempo*, 6 May). Five guerrillas, including leader Isnardo Luna, were killed in a clash with troops in northeastern Santander, following the discovery of an ELN operations center in San Vicente de Chucurí (AFP, 17 June). In a communiqué sent to the news agency EFE on 13 September, the ELN rejected the peace plan announced by President Barco (Inravision Television Cadena, 13 September; *FBIS*, 14 September). Guerrillas belonging to the Efraín Pabón Pabón Front attacked a group of soldiers at Cerrito, Santander, on 10 October, killing six and wounding twelve others (ibid., 10 October; *FBIS*, 11 October). In October the ELN announced that Radio Patria Libre had begun transmitting; it is reportedly the first clandestine guerrilla radio station to operate in Colombia (Radio Progreso Network, Havana, 11 October; *FBIS*, 13 October). Sporadic ELN attacks continued during November and December, the worst of which killed eight policemen in Cesár department (*El Espectador*, 3 December).

Daniel L. Premo
Washington College

Costa Rica

Population. 2,888,227
Party. Popular Vanguard Party (Partido Vanguardia Popular; PVP). A splinter faction is the Costa Rican People's Party (Partido del Pueblo Costarricense; PPC), up to 1988 led by PVP founder and former general secretary Manuel Mora Valverde and his brother Eduardo. Other secondary leftist parties are the Broad Democratic Front (Frente Amplio Democrático; FAD) associated with the PVP and led by Rodrigo Gutiérrez; associated with PPC are the New Republic Movement (Movimiento de la Nueva República; MNR) led by Sergio Erick Ardón; the Socialist Party of Costa Rica (Partido Socialista Costarricense; PSC) led by Alvaro Montero Mejía.
Founded. PVP: 1931; PPC: 1984; MNR: 1970 (as the Revolutionary People's Movement, MRP); PSC: 1972
Membership. 5,000 to 10,000 for all of the above-mentioned parties and groups (est.)
General Secretary. PVP: Humberto Vargas Carbonell; PPC: Lenin Chacón Vargas, (replaced Manuel Mora Valverde, 6 February 1988)
General Undersecretary. PVP: Oscar Madrigal; PPC: Eduardo Mora Valverde
Central Committee. PVP and PCC each has 35 members, 15 alternates
Status. Legal in all cases
Last Congress. PVP: Sixteenth, 15–18 September 1988; PPC: Fifteenth, August 1987.
Last Election. 1986: Popular Alliance (Alianza Popular; AP), including PVP, less than 1 percent of the presidential vote, 1 legislator elected; United People (Pueblo Unido; PU), including

PPC, less than 1 percent of the presidential vote, 1 legislator elected.
Auxiliary Organizations. Unitary Workers' Central (Central Unitaria de Trabajadores; CUT); General Workers' Confederation (Confederación General de Trabajadores; CGT); National Peasants' Federation (Federación Campesina Nacional; FCN); Costa Rican Peace and Solidarity Council (umbrella group of approximately 50 unions and solidarity committees)
Publications. PVP: *Libertad Revolucionaria* became *Adelante* (weekly), Manuel Delgado, director; PPC: *Libertad* (weekly), Rodolfo Ulloa B., director.

The campaigning for the 1990 presidential elections started even earlier than usual. By the fourth quarter of 1988, both major parties, the incumbent Partido Liberación Nacional (PLN) and the opposition Partido Unidad Social Cristiana (PUSC) had selected their presidential candidates. All the polls indicate that PUSC's candidate, Rafael Angel Calderón, has a wide lead over PLN's Castillo Morales. The dramatic decline during 1988 in the popularity of President Oscar Arias and the serious split over candidates within the PLN seem to give the PUSC a significant advantage. The challenge to the left was to unify its forces to better take advantage of the unpopularity of several of the government's programs that kept Costa Rican society agitated during all of 1988. By December 1988, it was not clear that a definitive and effective program of unification was forthcoming from the left.

Domestic Activities. On 8 February 1988, the general secretary of the PPC, Manuel Mora Valverde, aged 78 and a communist militant for 56 years, resigned. His brother, Eduardo, also resigned as director of the party paper *Libertad*. They had been founding members of the Costa Rican Communist Party in 1931, later called the Partido Vanguardia Popular. A split within the PVP in 1983 led the Moras and their followers to found the PPC, an act which debilitated the left, the weakness of which was evidenced in its electoral failure: its representation in the Legislative Assembly declined from four deputies in 1982 to two in 1986.

Manuel Mora continues to hold the positions that had led to the 1983 split: willingness to negotiate with his class and international enemies, and unwillingness to accept the thesis that the "relation of forces" in Costa Rica favors revolution. He favors negotiations between the United States and the Caribbean Basin nations "so the security demanded by the United States and the sovereignty of the Caribbean countries will be guaranteed." (*La Nación*, 9 February); *Libertad*, 12–18 February.) Even as he made his exit as general secretary, his ideas continued to be influential. They were evident in the declaration of the Fifth Plenary Session of the Central Committee of the PPC: the moderate forces of Costa Rica's bourgeoisie "have managed to keep the initiative in the field of peace," while the reactionary forces in Costa Rica have "lost the political initiative" (*Libertad*, 5–11 February). All this seems to warrant Mora's repeated calls for a "realistic minimum program."

Replacing Mora as general secretary of the PPC was Lenin Chacón Vargas, who had joined the PVP's Communist Youth in 1962. In 1986, he was elected Regidor Municipal (alderman) of the Canton of Central San José on the Pueblo Unido ticket. Chacón portrays himself as a renovator, ridding the party of the "corrupting influences that had distanced [it] from Leninist principles" (*Libertad*, 17 March). It is not easy to discern, however, significant shifts in the PPC's public ideological postures. His leadership has led the PPC to join serious discussions on the "unitary process," that is, a possible coalition of left forces in 1990 and beyond. Indeed, in August the PPC, the PVP, and the FAD signed an understanding of collaboration published under the title "Political Principles for the Unity of Left and Democratic Forces." (*WMR*, September.)

While the PVP and its general secretary Humberto Vargas Carbonell appeared the most eager for a merger, the reasons for such an electoral "popular front" with a single presidential candidate were compelling for much (though not all) of the left. In fact, several developments indicate that it could mean their survival as political actors. First, there is a financial angle: because the votes their candidates received in 1986 did not reach the minimum tally established by law, the PVP and other left parties must repay substantial sums of state-provided campaign funds. (The PVP alone owes fourteen million colones.) The situation is rendered all the more precarious by the new mandate of the Electoral Code requiring of a political party, as a precondition for its participation in an election, that it have received a minimum of 1 percent of the votes cast in the immediately preceding election. Based on 1986 results, this means 11,000 votes, substantially more than the 3,718 of the AP presidential candidate, or the PU candidate's 2,624 votes. Vargas protested this new ruling as undemocratic and in violation of the Esquipulas Treaty's requirement of democratization (*Adelante*, 15–21 April). Be that as it may, 1990 appears to present an electoral opportunity for the left that did not exist in 1986: neither PLN's Castillo nor PUSC's Calderón appear to have the appeal to significant sectors of the left that Oscar Arias had. This might tend to reduce the traditionally large number of crossover voters who voted for leftist candidates for the Assembly but for the PLN's candidate for president. In 1986, 41,639 voted for leftist deputies, but only 6,342 for leftist presidential candidates. A unified movement with an attractive presidential candidate could not only keep the movement alive after 1990, but also provide the left with critical leverage in the Assembly, should neither the PLN nor the PUSC emerge from the election with an absolute majority.

What, however, are the prospects of an effective coalition of the left, not just for the 1990 election, but beyond? The sidelining of the major protagonists of the 1983 split (Mora Valverde of the PPC and Arnoldo Ferreto of the PVP) certainly improves those chances, but only slightly. Major differences between the leftist forces remain, including lingering personal rivalries and pettiness. For instance, the PVP's literature pays homage to all the early members of the Costa Rican communist movement except its two founders, the Mora Valverde brothers. Other obstacles remain: (1) smaller parties (PSC and MNR) have so far refused to join the discussions intended to achieve unity; (2) the two major parties (PVP and PPC) continue to have fundamental differences, not only with respect to tactics but also in their theoretical interpretations of domestic and international processes. As distinct from the PPC's "minimum program" and tactical flexibility, the PVP does not seem to have settled on a coherent party doctrine. Nothing made this clearer than the deliberations of the Sixteenth Congress, 15–18 September. At this congress, called the "José Angel Marchena" Congress after the general secretary of the party's youth branch who died fighting with the FLMN in El Salvador, there was much discussion of many other party members who had died fighting in El Salvador and Nicaragua. Their example, said General Secretary Vargas, "is the essence of the kind of man this party has built and wishes to build even more perfectly." (*Adelante*, 5–11 August.) Indeed, article 1 of the new party program describes the PVP as a Marxist-Leninist part of the International Communist Movement that practices "proletarian internationalism." Despite this revolutionary rhetoric, the new program calls for respect for "the best aspects" of Costa Rica's institutional life and for political pluralism, omits any notion that the PVP is *the* vanguard party, and modifies—through more subdued language—the description given in the old program of the Costa Rican economy and of the nature of U.S. imperialism. Seventy years was made the age of mandatory retirement for the general secretary and general subsecretary. Clearly, the party is attempting to bridge the gap between its revolutionary members and the exigencies of the process of achieving unity with other parties. Strong disagreements with this internal "*perestroika*" from party hard-liners such as Arnoldo Ferreto (*Adelante*, 19–25 August) were soon in evidence. Finally, there is no evidence that the dramatic decline in government popularity has redounded to the benefit of the communists. After a six-month-long recruiting campaign, the PVP managed to add 296 "militantes" plus 171 "afiliados" to its roster. They also "reincorporated" 73 members. (*Adelante*, 12–18 August.)

The situation of the left was spelled out by José Merino del Rio of the PPC's Central Committee: internally there was no climate of trust and of dialogue; there was no unified "vanguard"; internationally, communism was in a period of transition and facing "a conservative wave that has hurt everyone." He warned the left to avoid "illusions and sterile voluntarisms." (*Libertad*, 18 August.)

International Views and Positions. With the economic situation still unsettled, all groups on the left kept up their attacks on the regime's "neoliberalism" and its "international masters," the IMF and the World Bank. Government programs, such as the partial privatization of the banking system and wage restraints, became specific targets. It is not evident, however, that the left captured the leadership of the various urban and rural strikes and protest movements that agitated Costa Rican society. As the PVP's general secretary rationalized his party's lack of success in this regard, it must help the masses "gain their own experience of struggle" (*WMR*, February 1988).

Defense of the Sandinista revolution remained the major international objective of all groups on the left. To that end, they strongly supported the Arias Peace Plan, even as Arias himself was targeted for criticism. Especially grating were his positions in relation to Cuba and the USSR. No diplomatic relations with Cuba were possible, said Arias, while those who "resort to continuous violent demonstrations . . . have, if not material sup-

port, at least moral support from Fidel Castro" (*FBIS*, 11 July). Further, in a letter to Gorbachev, Arias asked that he "take his hands off Central America" (*FBIS*, 27 April). He later suggested that Gorbachev apply the Afghanistan model to Nicaragua (*FBIS*, 3 May).

The defense of Nicaragua was joined with the defense of Panamanian sovereignty. The difference in the discussions of the two countries is that while both *Libertad* and *Adelante* invariably praise President Ortega, Panamá's Manuel Antonio Noriega is never mentioned.

The Iran-Contra hearings in Washington and especially the *Tower Report* proved to be a goldmine for the left. Accusations of contra links to drug traffic and that certain American landowners in Costa Rica were connected to both the contras and drug trafficking filled the pages of the left's publications. Serious charges of coverups and even direct involvement by high officials of the present and previous PLN administrations might not have been proven, but they echoed accusations made within the councils of the PLN itself.

The left certainly has targeted the main issues agitating Costa Ricans. The question is whether the parties of the left can patch up their differences long enough to take on their greatest challenge: overcoming the traditional anti-communism of the Costa Rican electorate.

Anthony P. Maingot
Florida International University
Latin American and Caribbean Center

Cuba

Population. 10,353,932
Party. Communist Party of Cuba (Partido Comunista de Cuba; PCC)
Founded. 1965
Membership. 500,000; 75,000 candidates (both estimated)
General Secretary. Fidel Castro Ruz, 62; title: First Secretary
Politburo. 14 members: Fidel Castro Ruz, Raúl Castro Ruz (second secretary), Juan Almeida

Bosque; Julio Camacho Aguilera, Osmany Cienfuegos Gorrián, Abelardo Colomé Ibarra, Vilma Espín Guillois, Armando Hart Dávalos, Esteban Lazo Hernández, José R. Machado Ventura, Pedro Miret Prieto, Jorge Risquet Valdés-Saldaña, Carlos Rafael Rodríguez, Roberto Viega Menéndez; 10 alternate members

Secretariat. 9 members: Fidel Castro Ruz, Raúl Castro Ruz, José R. Machado Ventura, Jorge Risquet Valdés-Saldaña, Julián Rizo Alvarez, José Ramón Balaguer Cabrera, Sixto Batista Santana, Jaime Crombet Hernández-Baquero, Lionel Soto Prieto

Central Committee. 142 members, 77 alternates. Two members died in 1988: Flavio Bravo, an Old Guard communist, and Brigadier General Francisco Cruz Bourzac, a deputy defense minister, in Angola when a Cuban transport plane was mistakenly shot down by a Cuban anti-aircraft missile.

Status. Ruling party

Last Congress. Third, two sessions: 4–7 February, 30 November–2 December 1986.

Last Election. 1986, all 499 members of the National Assembly of People's Power PCC approved. Fidel Castro and Raúl Castro re-elected as president and first vice president of the Council of State for 1987–1992. The council has five vice presidents, a secretary, and 23 members (ministers).

Auxiliary Organizations. Union of Young Communists (Unión de Jovenes Comunistas; UJC), Union of Cuban Pioneers (Unión de Pioneros de Cuba; UPC), Federation of Cuban Women (Federación de Mujeres Cubanas; FMC), Committees for the Defense of the Revolution (Comités de Defensa de la Revolución; CDR), Confederation of Cuban Workers (Confederación de Trabajadores de Cuba; CTC), National Association of Small Farmers (Asociación Nacional de Agricultores Pequeños; ANAP)

Publications. *Granma* (six days a week), official organ of the Central Committee, Enrique Roman, editor; *Juventud Rebelde* (daily), organ of the UJC

On 1 January 1989, Cuba observed the 30th anniversary of Fidel Castro's Revolutionary Rule. Thirty years ago, the then-32-year-old guerrilla leader, having defeated the strong military regime of Gen. Fulgencio Batista, became the undisputed leader of Cuba. He seemed to symbolize the dawn of a new, prosperous era for the civil-war torn and corruption-ridden nation of six million people. The victorious revolutionary promised milk and honey, and millions were captivated by his strong personality and his vision of democracy: humanism, social justice, personal freedoms, and the rule of law.

It was not to be. Soon Castro's dictatorial streak emerged: he saw himself as the only dispenser of truth and the only expert on all issues. Enemies, real and imagined, foreign and domestic, were relentlessly fought and, in the case of domestic adversaries, defeated. For various reasons, either because he had been a closet Marxist, or more likely, because it assured him of open-ended rule, Castro turned communist and became a political ally of the Soviet Union. Cuba became almost totally dependent for survival on Moscow. What began as a symbiotic relationship, even though Castro was not always trusted by Soviet leaders, turned into what some Soviets thought was a parasitic one in which Moscow gave much and received little more than thanks in return. (In 1988, the aid given Cuba by the USSR totaled $5 billion, according to U.S. estimates.)

Even though there were some initial social gains as a result of the Castro revolution, basically in education and health services, the steady economic decline has accelerated in recent years. Cuba became a nation of ten million tired people without hope for the future, nor even for a renewal such as has been attempted in most other communist countries. The only thing that the Castro revolution has really been able to do in the last 30 years has been to survive.

Leadership and Party Organization. With only minor exceptions, the Cuban leadership has remained unchanged since January 1959. Having completed 30 years in power, Fidel Castro has presided over Latin America's longest regime, with only Paraguay's President Alfredo Stroessner, thirteen years his senior, being the ruler of his country longer, by four years. Perhaps except for Castro's brother, Raúl, the party's second secretary and defense minister, not one Cuban party and government leader had a real voice in policymaking. The Politburo has continued to be a group of Castro cronies, most of whom have been his subordinates since prerevolutionary days, and whose stature has not grown over the years. In 1988, as in the years past, only President Castro in his speeches to the country, or in interviews with foreign news media, was the spokesman for this government and party. In that respect, the Cuban leader did not appear to have changed in 30 years. New initiatives of his government are first articulated by him, and then explained repeatedly in his speeches and lectures throughout the country to give the party apparatus the rationale for the current party line.

This certainly was the case in 1988 with the Cuban party's formal rejection of Mikhail Gorbachev's policy of *glasnost'* and *perestroika*. While some foreign observers thought Castro's strongly worded position on the issue surprising, especially in view of Cuba's economic dependence on the Soviet leader's largesse, it could hardly have been otherwise. In the Soviet Union, the changes came as result of a new leadership that has been implementing them by pressure—not always successful—from the Politburo down. In Cuba, not unlike in North Korea, where the top leadership is entrenched and fossilized, any restructuring would have to begin at the lowest level and would obviously stop before affecting the upper echelons of the ruling elite. The same is true of *glasnost'*: in the Soviet Union, the media and ordinary people attack Stalin and Brezhnev for the myriad problems the country faces, and which Gorbachev has inherited and is only marginally responsible for. In Cuba, *glasnost'* would mean blaming Fidel Castro and the rest of the leadership for countless errors committed over the last 30 years in every segment of the country's life, as well as for betrayal of early promises to institute true representative democracy. Castro, who has no capacity for self-criticism, could certainly not allow criticism by others of his policies and actions.

President Castro rejected *perestroika* and *glasnost'* on the basis of: (1) Marxist-Leninist orthodoxy; (2) Cuba's independence to follow its own socialist model; and (3) the country's geopolitical situation, which, he said, did not allow it to weaken its internal cohesion and its one-party rule. "Ours was a creative Revolution. It did not follow stereotypes, and in constructing socialism our Revolution made many contributions while remaining faithful to the principles of Marxism-Leninism," Castro said on 26 July in a major speech on the subject. "We do not want to be more virtuous than anybody, more pure than anybody else, but we are 90 miles from the most powerful empire in the world and 10,000 from the Socialist camp. We are proud of our ideological purity . . . We do not have to rectify anything whatsoever. We are not going to deviate from our path a single inch . . . Our party is aware that it cannot make any mistake that would weaken it ideologically . . . Cuba will never adopt the methods, styles, philosophies, or idiosyncrasies of capitalism." The preservation of one-party rule was essential, he said, and Cuba would not allow

"pocket-sized parties to organize counter-revolutionaries, the pro-Yankees, the bourgeoisie . . . We have no need of capitalist political formulas. They are complete garbage." Lest some Cuban communists be tempted to follow the Gorbachev line, Castro warned: "I have nothing but contempt for the faint-hearted, the feeble-minded, the weak-willed who fail to understand these realities . . ." (*Granma*, 7 August).

Because Gorbachev canceled his scheduled visit to Cuba following the disastrous earthquake in Armenia, one can only speculate what he and Castro would have agreed to say in public about their differences of opinion on the issue of internal changes. Before the cancellation, the visit was described by Havana as a "high point in the years of relations" between the two countries and a "major event in the history of the Western Hemisphere."

Several months earlier Castro had tried to minimize the differences, saying they had been exaggerated by Western news media. "What I can't understand is that whole campaign trying to differentiate the Soviets from the Cubans; even trying to sow division between Soviets and Cubans. I've spoken to Gorbachev about this—I have excellent relations with Gorbachev, and I've had excellent exchanges with him for hours on many subjects, and I have even occasionally said to him, 'They are trying to divide us because we don't do things the same way.' And Gorbachev's reaction was, 'Why must we do things the same way?'

"I want you to know that there aren't any problems between Gorbachev and myself, that Soviet-Cuban relations are good, but we do things in a different way. Because if you make a mistake, it should be your own kind of mistake, not the mistake of others. And then we were constantly accused in the past of being Soviet satellites, and whenever we did something they said it was on account of the Soviets, and now it turns out that we are being accused of not doing what the Soviets are doing. What will it be? How are we going to end up?" (*Granma*, 28 August).

Yet on another occasion, Castro strongly criticized the participation of the Soviet bloc countries in the Olympic Games in Seoul and called the medals the nations won there "made of dirt not of gold." Cuba had boycotted the games because of its solidarity with North Korea and "it is very improper" to have that country "forgotten" by the rest of the Socialist bloc, he said. (*El Nuevo Día*, 25 September.) The Cuban media did not report the beginning or the results of the games in Seoul.

Can Cuba remain impervious to Soviet-inspired winds of change? Havana is doing its utmost to avoid what it regards as contamination of true Marxism-Leninism. Cuban media inform the Cuban public only briefly about the bare facts of the Soviet reforms. The words *glasnost'* and *perestroika* were not mentioned on radio and television and did not appear in print, and the circulation of Soviet publications in Cuba, among them the Spanish-language *Novedades de Moscú* and the Russian *Novoye Vremya*, both read by intellectuals, was curtailed.

That is not to say that the Cuban Communist Party did not have its own version of *perestroika*, if not of *glasnost'*. But its process of "rectification of errors and negative tendencies" was the revival of methods tried unsuccessfully in the middle 1960s and inspired by Ernesto Ché Guevara's idea of creating a "new socialist man" in Cuba through "moral incentives." That much-publicized policy was abandoned after a decade, and Cuba, toward the end of the 1970s, began to attempt a limited economic liberalization. The experiment was halted abruptly by Castro not because it failed, but because it was creating a new wealthy class in Cuba, "kulaks" in the countryside and small entrepreneurs in the cities, which, the president indicated in April 1986, had upset the supposedly egalitarian Cuban society and constituted an "ideological deviation."

The Cuban Communist Party was becoming bureaucratized, Havana conceded. In September, top party leaders called for the "restoration of the Party's authority at the grass-roots level, municipal and provincial. In many places, party members put their effort into improving internal organizational structure, while paying little attention to production . . . Radio and television programs, newspapers and magazines are boring and not very daring." (*Granma*, 18 September.)

The Economy. While the lower party echelons were less than interested in production results, the top party leadership was analyzing them with unmasked concern. The Politburo, the Secretariat, and the Central Committee (to which all Politburo and Secretariat members belong) held its Eighth Plenary Meeting on the subject in December.

In September, the party leaders called upon PCC members to make a "special effort to deal with and overcome organizational deficiencies and the still-prevailing lack of a consistently rational practice in our economy . . . We must produce more with the resources we have and save on energy, raw mate-

rials, and goods . . . In our endeavors to push ahead, austerity must characterize life in our society, particularly the life of our cadres." The meeting also examined "incompetence and flaws in government . . . indolence and negligent attitudes . . . manifestations of labor and social indiscipline," which were described as "persisting" in Cuba, but ended without any meaningful recommendations. (*Granma*, 20 October.)

The December meeting was, if anything, more pessimistic. Commenting on a report by Antonio Rodríguez Maurell, Central Committee member and minister president of the Central Planning Board, Castro said that in 1989 "the nation will face a tougher situation than it did in 1988." Among the new difficulties mentioned at the meeting were shortfalls in the cement production because the conditions of Cuban cement plants "were actually worse than realized"; "unjustified bonuses" paid to workers and officials; and an acute shortage of hard currency, which could lead to "closing more than fifteen embassies and some consulates in countries with which Cuba has relations." (*FBIS*, 16 December.)

Although Castro asserted at the December meeting that in 1988 the Cuban GNP had grown by 2.3 percent, U.S. officials believed that the economic situation in Cuba resembled that of the chaotic period of the 1960s. (*Miami Herald*, 23 September.) In the view of American specialists, Cuba's GNP showed a real growth rate of 0.0 percent. Havana's figures for the 1987–1988 harvest of sugar—the country's principal product that represents 87 percent of its exports—added to the confusion. Prensa Latina, the Cuban news agency, reported late in June that sugar production had fallen by 2.9 percent, which accounted for 13 percent of the drop in the total economy. The agency also said that a drought, enduring for the third straight year, had severely affected other crops and lowered cattle production (*Miami Herald*, 26 June). In December, the government said that the volume of the 1987–1988 sugar harvest was 7,086,623 metric tons, of which 5,085,104 tons were destined for export. Of the quantity to be exported, 4,411,100 tons were earmarked for the Soviet bloc. Sugar deliveries to the Soviet Union totaled 2,796,100 tons, the government said. (*El Nuevo Herald*, 4 December.)

However, five months earlier government sources in Havana quoted by the same Spanish news agency, EFE, had claimed that the sugar crop reached almost eight million tons.

In September, the European community and

Cuba agreed to establish diplomatic relations, as Havana was again renegotiating its $4-billion debt with noncommunist nations, principally Spain, Japan, Canada, France, and West Germany. Cuban debt payments were reduced to a trickle, although Castro, who urged Latin American nations to do so, did not repudiate his foreign debt. To obtain more foreign exchange, Cuba was expanding its tourist industry, establishing for that purpose a mixed Spanish-Cuban enterprise, for the first time in the 30 years of the revolutionary regime. The new entity, Hoteles de Cuba, S.A., will build four hotels in Havana in the next five years at the cost of about $90 million. Cuba wants to multiply ten times the present number of foreign tourists—250,000 a year—and expects many to visit the country for the Panamerican Games in Havana in 1991.

Domestic Affairs. The observance of human rights and political prisoners in Cuba were issues of primary importance for the Castro government's domestic and international image in 1988. Under pressure from the Reagan administration, which had estimated at 15,000 the number of political prisoners held by Castro, and from human rights groups (among them Amnesty International, which in its 1988 report said the number was "at least 600"), the government agreed at a spring meeting of the U.N. Human Rights Commission in Geneva to let the commission's team enter Cuban jails and talk to dissidents in the country. The six-member team, made up of diplomats from Bulgaria, Colombia, Ireland, Nigeria, and the Philippines, visited Cuba from 16 to 25 September. In its preliminary report to the full 43-member commission, the team concluded that "human rights abuses have declined" in Cuba. It also found evidence that "only 121 long-term political prisoners were still being held in Cuban jails." The team said it had received complaints "of human rights violations from 1,700 Cuban citizens, more than half of whom said they could not leave the country, and many others that concerned harassment of small Protestant denominations like the Seventh-Day Adventists." (*NYT*, 18 December.)

Earlier in the year, International Red Cross representatives conducted a series of interviews with prisoners in several Cuban jails, and other human rights groups from the United States and Western Europe did the same. American churchmen who visited Cuba, among them John Cardinal O'Connor, archbishop of New York, and political figures such as Senator Edward Kennedy and Jesse Jackson,

were instrumental in obtaining the release of a number of political prisoners, who subsequently emigrated to the United States. At the year's end, there were hints from Havana that all long-term political prisoners would be released.

Cuba allowed two illegal human rights groups to operate in Havana. The best known human rights leader, Ricardo Bofill, who had spent twelve years in prison, left Cuba, but another, Elizardo Sánchez, continued his activities in Havana. Although frequently harassed, the leaders of these illegal groups met with foreign journalists and delegations from international human rights organizations to denounce the government's repressive measures. After seeing the reports of the human rights groups that had sent delegations to Cuba—including the U.N. Commission on Human Rights and Amnesty International—Bofill concluded that they "have done little more than scratch the surface of the national reality" (*WSJ*, 16 December). During much of the year, international pressures on Havana seemed to force the government to ease up on its repression. But in December, Sánchez and other activists in Cuba reported increased beatings, arrests, and surveillance of human rights workers, and the use of electric shock and psychoactive drugs. (*LAT*, 12 January 1989.)

By midyear, Cuba's neighborhood watchdog committees were ordered to stop preparing routine reports on their neighbors' political loyalty, moral and general conduct. These reports had been one of the most hated features of the Cuban regime. The National Secretariat of the Committees for the Defense of the Revolution (CDR) told its members at the block level that "all information provided by the CDRs must be public in nature," and that individual reports will have to be authorized by higher authorities. (*Miami Herald*, 30 June.)

Until now, many aspects of Cubans' lives were influenced by the CDR reports. A person sometimes handed in a copy of his or her own report when dealing with a government agency, but more often it was provided, without the knowledge of the individual, to an organization seeking more information on the person. The result was that secret, anonymous accusations were often made against many individuals who had no way of knowing what the accusations were and had no chance to respond.

Over the years, the CDR reports prevented an undetermined number of people from entering universities or holding important jobs, and in some cases were believed responsible for firings and even mental breakdowns. The newspaper of the Communist Party of Cuba, *Granma*, reporting the decision to suspend the CDR reports, said the documents "have generated problems and complaints from neighbors, since the information has not been accurate in all cases."

But Cuba did not stop its persecution of persons engaged in private enterprise. People were arrested for manufacturing and selling furniture, as were some carpenters who owned individual shops and some auto mechanics licensed to make minor repairs, apparently because their businesses grew too fast, and other artisans for providing needed services in the construction sector.

The Castro government continued to improve relations with the Roman Catholic Church. It allowed dozens of foreign priests to join various Cuban dioceses and allowed the sale of Christmas trees. Castro was making these concessions apparently in the hope of persuading Pope John Paul to visit Cuba, which could happen in 1989, according to hints from Rome.

Cuba and Africa. After years of patient diplomatic maneuvering that had been initiated by the U.S. State Department, on 22 December at a U.N. ceremony in New York, an agreement was signed by representatives of Cuba, Angola, and South Africa to bring peace to South West Africa. The conflict in that part of Africa began in 1974, when a pro-Soviet regime took over in Angola following the withdrawal of colonial Portuguese authorities. A civil war erupted almost immediately and South African troops stationed in Namibia, a former German colony South Africa has been occupying since 1918, entered Angola. In early 1975, a Cuban military contingent sent by Castro helped to repel the South African invasions. The Cubans stayed on and their expeditionary force grew to some 30,000. Over the years, Cuban soldiers trained and fought alongside the forces of the Luanda government, repelling various smaller South African incursions and attacks by antigovernmental Angolan rebels. Late in 1987, Angola faced a major South African attack on the Angolan town of Cuito Guanavale and requested Cuban reinforcements. Fresh Cuban troops, including squadrons of MiG-23 and MiG-21 fighter airplanes, arrived in Angola in the first weeks of 1988. In January and February, the Cubans, by then 50,000 strong, fought a series of hard battles with the South African forces. These were division-sized engagements involving tank and artillery battles and air raids. Finally, at the end of March, having suffered many casualties, South

Africans withdrew from Angola across the Namibian border. It was then that diplomatic talks aimed at reaching a peaceful solution to the conflict in South West Africa received a new impetus.

Under the U.N. agreement, Namibia was scheduled to begin a transition to independence on 1 April 1989, and the Cuban troops were to leave Angola by 1 July 1991. The timetable for the Cubans' withdrawal was as follows:

- 3,000 Cubans will leave Angola by 1 April 1989, the start-up date for a United Nations independence plan for Namibia.
- By 1 August 1989, all Cuban troops will withdraw north of the 15th parallel, away from Angola's border with Namibia.
- By 1 November 1989, the date set for elections in Namibia, all Cuban troops will withdraw north of the 13th parallel.
- Also by 1 November 1989, 50 percent of the 50,000 Cuban troops will have left Angola.
- By 1 April 1990, two-thirds of the Cuban troops are to have left Angola.
- By 1 October 1990, 76 percent of the Cuban troops will have departed.
- By 1 January 1991, not more than 12,000 Cuban troops will remain in Angola.
- By 1 July 1991, all Cuban troops will have left.

U.S. Secretary of State George Shultz described the agreements calling for Namibian independence from South African rule and the phased withdrawal of Cuban troops as "perhaps miraculous," and Havana described them as the Castro government's military and political triumph. (Texts of agreements in *NYT*, 14 and 23 December.)

Cuban troops were also playing a diminishing role in Ethiopia where a decade ago they also intervened to help the country's pro-Soviet government. Although at one time about 25,000 Cuban military were said to be stationed in Ethiopia, recent reports put the figure at less than 2,000.

Cuba and the United States. Relations between Cuba and the United States remained unchanged as Havana waited for the Bush administration to move toward some kind of accommodation. The Cuban media attached great importance to the postelection visit to Havana of Senator Claiborne Pell, chairman of the Senate Foreign Relations Committee, who at the end of a four-day stay in Cuba in November declared there, and later in

Washington, that the United States should normalize its relations with the Castro government. Under his normalization plan, Cuba would take the first step by releasing its remaining political prisoners, whose number he estimated between 200 and 300. His proposal calls for the United States to reciprocate by partially lifting its 28-year-old trade embargo, permitting shipments of medical supplies to Cuba. Senator Pell also said that the two countries could cooperate in trying to stop the drug trade, and expressed his opposition to the establishment of TV Marti, a U.S.-sponsored and -financed television station that would broadcast to Cuba.

A few days before the talks between Castro and Senator Pell from 24 to 28 November, President-elect George Bush declared: "There is plenty of room for *glasnost'*, there is plenty of room for *perestroika* in Cuba, and I would like to see that regime take a lesson from Mr. Gorbachev and start lightening up." While Mr. Bush pledged that his administration would not change its attitude toward Cuba until the Castro regime changes its internal and external policies, liberal and even conservative groups were calling for a review of American-Cuban relations. The Council for Inter-American Security, a conservative organization that in 1981 had urged the new Reagan administration to overthrow Fidel Castro, recommended in December that the incoming Bush administration consider restoring relations with Cuba.

Despite the strong anti-Castro rhetoric of Ronald Reagan before his 1980 election and during his two terms as president, relations between Washington and Havana were not worse on 20 January 1989 than they had been eight years earlier. Before his first election, candidate Reagan suggested that he might impose a blockade of Cuba to stop Soviet military supplies from reaching the island. After the inauguration, Reagan's first secretary of state, Alexander Haig, made such a proposal, this time to interdict Cuban military supplies destined for Salvadoran guerrillas and Sandinista Nicaragua. But in November 1981, Reagan sent Haig to Mexico City to meet secretly Cuban vice president Carlos Rafael Rodríguez, apparently to try to persuade Cuba to become politically more independent from the Soviet Union.

In March 1982, Haig sent the administration's political troubleshooter Gen. Vernon A. Walters to speak with Castro in Havana, apparently to follow up on Haig's Mexico City meeting. The U.S. invasion of Grenada a year later was principally motivated by that island's internal ultra-leftist upheaval, which Castro did not support and later denounced,

rather than being a strategic anti-Cuban move. While the president called Castro a "roving wolf" attacking U.S. allies in Latin America, his officials were negotiating with Cuba. On 14 December 1984, an agreement was signed under which Cuba agreed to take back 2,746 criminals who had come to the United States in the exodus from Mariel, and the United States agreed to admit 20,000 Cuban immigrants annually. The accord was abrogated by Castro in May 1985 after Radio Martí began broadcasting programs to Cuba. Two years later, the State Department's director of Cuban affairs, Kenneth Skoug, made a secret visit to Cuba and met with Castro; in November, the 1984 accord was restored. Two months earlier, the U.S. government had named John Taylor chief of its Interest Section in Havana, making him in effect an American ambassador without the title. Since November 1987, the bilateral relations have stabilized, and the implementation of the immigration accord has proceeded, albeit at a slower pace than anticipated in the agreement. Restrictions on importing and exporting books, films, photographs, records, and other informational material to and from Cuba were eliminated by a trade bill signed by President Reagan in August.

Cuba and Latin America. Fidel Castro continued to pursue a policy of maintaining and expanding relations with established governments in Latin America. Ecuador re-established ties with Cuba after Castro attended the inauguration of the new Ecuadoran president, Rodrigo Borja, and Argentina expanded economic exchanges with Havana.

Castro paid special attention to his relations with Mexico, the only country in Latin America that refused to break ties with Cuba in the 1960s. In November, outgoing Mexican president Miguel de la Madrid visited Havana, and several weeks later Castro attended the inauguration of Carlos Salinas de Gortari as the new president of Mexico. Castro's visit and his previous congratulatory letter to Salinas strained very considerably his relations with the Mexican left. Salinas's narrow win in the elections held on 6 July has been hotly disputed by the left-of-center coalition, whose presidential candidate was Cuauhtémoc Cárdenas, son of the late President Lázaro Cárdenas, for years Castro's supporter. The Mexican left considered the Cuban leader's endorsement of Salinas, who they say was elected fraudulently, as something resembling Stalin's 1939 pact with Hitler.

George Volsky
University of Miami

Dominican Republic

Population. 7,136,748
Party. Dominican Communist Party (Partido Comunista Dominicano; PCD)
Founded. 1944
Membership. 500–1,000
General Secretary. Narciso Isa Conde, 46
Central Committee. 27 members
Status. Legal
Last Congress. Third, 15–17 March 1984
Last Election. 1986, 0.28 percent, no representation
Auxiliary Organizations. No data
Publications. *Hablan los Comunistas* (weekly); *Impacto Socialista* (theoretical journal, appears every two months)

In 1988 the much-divided extreme left of the Dominican Republic was faced with a politically difficult dilemma: whether to support or to oppose the 1990 presidential bid of Juan Bosch, the leader of the leftist, but not Marxist, Dominican Liberation Party (PDL). It was a Hobson's choice, principally for the Dominican Communist Party, led by Narciso Isa Conde, a 46-year-old lawyer and intellectual. Either course of action would further debilitate the party at the time when it was trying to broaden its base. If it backed Bosch, or if it opposed him, the party would lose a large part of its electoral support.

The emergence of Professor Bosch as a major political figure in the Dominican Republic was an occurrence that was typical of that country, for its population seems to trust older leaders who in other nations would be regarded as well past their retirement age. The 79-year-old Bosch was expected to be the main opponent, in the 1990 presidential election, of President Joaquín Balaguer, who is 81, blind, and reportedly in poor health, but who is expected to be ready to run for his sixth, although not consecutive, term in office.

Called "professor" because, although self-educated, he had lectured in various Latin American and U.S. universities during many years of his exile in the 1930s from the Trujillo dictatorship, Bosch was elected president in 1962, in the first free election after the end of the Trujillo era. Inaugurated in February 1963, he was deposed seven months later by a military coup. When a group of young pro-Bosch officers staged an uprising and were about to defeat the more conservative military, President Johnson sent in U.S. Marines to prevent further bloodshed. At that time, Bosch, who regarded himself as a Third World leader, was called a communist by his opponents.

One of the founders of the center-left Dominican Revolutionary Party (PRD), which was in power for eight years before its defeat in 1986 by President Balaguer, Bosch broke with that party in 1973 and founded the PLD, calling it a classic party of national liberation. He has been an occasional visitor to Havana, having met Fidel Castro during his long exile in Cuba in the 1940s and 1950s, and for years appeared a perennial unsuccessful gadfly and presidential contender. Slowly the political views of PLD began to change as Bosch gave it a moderate, more pragmatic, more nationalistic image without headline-catching anti-American rhetoric. It became the most disciplined political party in the Dominican Republic, attracting young professionals, businessmen, and politically active students, the same groups that the extreme left has been trying to penetrate without much success for years. Polls conducted in late 1988 showed that Bosch was the most popular politician in the country. Bosch, in a number of press interviews, stated that he had never been a Marxist.

As the PLD was surging forward in the public-opinion surveys, the other left-of-center political party, the PRD, was being torn apart by factionalism and weakened by accusations of corruption during its terms of power. There were two apparently unreconcilable PRD factions, one led by Jacobo Majluta and the other by José Francisco Peña Gómez.

The communists were doing no better. Revealing a fundamental problem in the PCD's organization, Isa Conde, in an interview with *Granma* during his visit to Havana in February, said: "Our shortcomings are in the vanguard, our weakness lies in the process of shaping the vanguard." At the same time, the PCD's general secretary said the party was changing its policy toward the Catholic Church: "I can say that particularly during the last year this has made remarkable progress. Liberation theology has caught on among the Christian masses, in the church's grass roots and intermediate levels. It isn't, of course, as strong in the church hierarchy, although they have taken a positive stand on some of the country's problems—poverty, unemployment, salaries, the land. To a certain extent, theirs is a progressive stand.

"The church's grass roots and some intermediate levels are taking active part in the popular movement's struggles in land takeovers, for example. These are priests who openly defend the peasants' right to take over land, call strikes, call into question the established capitalist order..."

Given this reality, the Dominican Communist Party has formulated a different policy concerning the problem of religion. "We even have Christians in the party," Isa Conde declared. "We're against dogmatism and inflexibility. We consider the revolutionary Christians to be as revolutionary as we are and we even maintain that we can learn a lot from them, because the periods when the revolutionary organizations are allowed often numb their spirit of struggle, sacrifice and ability to communicate with the masses. And this is something to be admired in Christians.

"We're in the midst of a process where we say that we must change the Party to change the country; we must change the left to change the country, but we must not do it in a social-democratic way as has happened in other processes where reformist efforts have predominated, but instead making the changes by emphasizing their revolutionary essence." (*Granma*, 20 March.)

In 1988, the PCD endorsed Gorbachev's *perestroika* as its own policy line. Speaking at a discussion on "*Perestroika* in the USSR and the International Communist Movement," sponsored by the World Marxist Review and attended by several party representations, José Riva, member of the Political Commission of the PCD's Central Committee and the committee's secretary for international relations, said: "*Perestroika* is [also] important to the [Marxist] dissidents in our country who opposed the Soviet Union and the policies of the Dominican Communists. Today, even the more extremist groups have run out of ammunition to attack the USSR. True, they continue to criticize our Party, but they are doing that under the banner of 'renewal,' in an attempt to impose a boundless democratization on the PCD and to weaken our party discipline...I think that the most important aspect of *perestroika* is that it seeks to put an end to the schematism and dogmatism which used to dominate the communist movement. It makes it incumbent on us to interpret creatively the Marxist-Leninist

heritage and apply it to today's reality." (*WMR*, September.)

George Volsky
University of Miami

Ecuador

Population. 10,231,630
Party. Communist Party of Ecuador (Partido Comunista Ecuatoriano; PCE), pro-Moscow, participates in elections as part of the Frente Amplio de Izquierda coalition (FADI); Marxist-Leninist Communist Party of Ecuador (PCE-ML), participates in elections as the Movimiento Popular Democrático (MPD); Ecuadorean Socialist Party (Partido Socialista Ecuatoriano; PSE)
Founded. PCE: 1928; PCE-ML: 1972; PSE: 1926
Membership. PCE: 750; PCE-ML: 200 (both estimated)
General Secretary. PCE: René Mauge Mosquera; MPD: Jaime Hurtado González (National Director)
Central Committee. PCE: Milton Jijón Saavedra, José Solís Castro, Efraín Alvarez Fiallo, Bolívar Bolaños Sánchez, Ghandi Burbano Burbano, Xavier Garaycoa Ortíz, Alfredo Castillo, Freddy Almeidau, Luis Emilio Veintimilla, Edgar Ponce
Status. Legal
Last Congress. PCE: Eleventh, 21–23 July 1988, in Quito
Last Election. 31 January 1988 (for president); Frank Vargas Pazzos, coalition including PSE, 10.5 percent; Jaime Hurtado González, coalition including FADI and MPD, 4.2 percent. 31 January 1988 (for Congress), PSE: 4 of 71 seats; FADI: 2 of 71 seats; MPD: 2 of 71 seats.
Auxiliary Organizations. PCE: Ecuadorean Workers' Confederation (Confederación de Trabajadores del Ecuador; CTE), comprises about 20 percent of organized workers; Ecuadorean University Students' Federation (Federación de Estudiantes Universitarios del Ecuador; FEUE); Ecuadorean Indian Federation (Federación Ecuatoriana de Indios; FEI)

Publications. PCE: *El Pueblo*, editor, René Mauge Mosquera; MPD: *Patria Neuva*

Political affairs in 1988 were dominated by national elections and by the transmission of power from the conservative, free-market government of León Febres Cordero to the new center-left administration of Rodrigo Borja Cevallos. They were further colored by the economic hardships produced by falling petroleum revenues and the mounting foreign debt. Given the continuation of the democratic system, however flawed and fragile, it was also a year of intense activity for the parties and movements of the left. Their options, especially regarding elections, were numerous, a fact which further encouraged the continuing divisions and rivalries among Marxist organizations. In addition, they were confronted with decisions about cooperation with, or opposition to the social-democratic government inaugurated in August.

Domestic Affairs. The first round of presidential elections, as well as congressional races, took place on Sunday, 31 January. For Ecuadorean Marxists, this presented but the latest of many opportunities to unite, at least for transitory electoral purposes. While there were a number of parties and movements, three provided the most important focus for the left: the Broad Leftist Front (Frente Amplio de Izquierda; FADI), the Democratic Popular Movement (Movimiento Popular Democrático; MPD), and the Ecuadorean Socialist Party (Partido Socialista Ecuatoriano; PSE). The first constituted the electoral arm of the Ecuadorean Communist Party (PCE), which traces its origin to 1926. Its principal leader was René Mauge Mosquera, president of the FADI and one of the two communist congressmen prior to 1988 elections. The second originated from the 1963 departure of Maoists from the PCE that produced the Marxist-Leninist Communist Party of Ecuador (Partido Comunista Ecuatoriano-Marxista Leninista; PCE-ML). It was headed by Jaime Hurtado González and had a pre-election congressional delegation of four. Like Mauge, Hurtado had stood for the presidency in 1984. Finally, the Ecuadorean Socialist Party had sought an independent role of its own, and had also run a presidential candidate in 1984.

Extensive discussions throughout 1987 sought to produce an accord that would allow a single candidate for the unified left. On 27 January, the FADI, MPD, and PSE first met officially to begin molding a united leftist front. A number of mini-parties also

attended, as did representatives of several labor organizations. A subsequent meeting in Quito adopted a so-called Unitary Program of the Left (Programa Unitario de la Izquierda), which provided a doctrinal basis for electoral collaboration. A National Unity Committee (Comité Nacional de la Unidad) was created, with representatives from a dozen leftist organizations (*Punto de Vista*, 13 April 1987). Its prime responsibility was seen as building a common front based on the existing program, thus permitting the mounting of a unified election effort.

Meanwhile retired General Frank Vargas Pazzos's challenges to President Febres Cordero and his administration had lifted Vargas to the level of national leader, as well as a potential candidate in the eyes of many government critics. Thus propelled into the spotlight in a nimbus of personal integrity and charisma, Vargas was viewed by many Marxists as an ideal vehicle for antisystemic nationalism, as well as for achieving a measure of electoral success. The process was seemingly launched in May of 1987 when the general was incorporated into a small nationalistic party, Ecuadorean Revolutionary Popular Action (Acción Popular Revolucionaria Ecuatoriana; APRE), and soon thereafter was named presidential nominee.

Among the Marxist parties, the FADI in particular was sympathetic at the outset. Under the intelligent leadership of René Mauge Mosquera, it had demonstrated a proclivity to pragmatism and to a realistic assessment of the political landscape. For Mauge, an alliance of "all progressive forces" was a crucial step in the struggle against the local oligarchy and monopolistic imperialism (*WMR*, April). In contrast, the MPD was more rigidly ideological, and expressed doubts about Vargas's political predispositions toward policies consistent with its own vision of Ecuadorean Marxism. The matter was further complicated when Vargas, while espousing broadly nationalistic sentiments, identified several major points in the Unitary Program of the Left with which he disagreed. These included: (1) abrogation of the National Security Law; (2) nonpayment of the foreign debt; (3) nationalization of the banks and foreign trade; (4) democratization of the armed forces; and (5) revision of all military pacts, especially the Rio Treaty of Reciprocal Assistance (*Punto de Vista*, December 1987).

Ultimately, the Ecuadorean left divided into two groupings, each of which presented its own slate of candidates in the 1988 elections. The United Leftist Front (Frente de Izquierda Unida; FIU) was created by ten separate organizations, the most important of which were the FADI and the MPD. On 6 August 1987, the FIU nominated Jaime Hurtado González of the MPD as its candidate, accompanied by Efraín Alvarez of the Communist Party. Hurtado had run fourth in the 1984 race, easily the best showing among candidates of the left. A month later the Partido Socialista, the APRE, and a dissident faction of the FADI came together as the People's Patriotic Union (Unión Patriótica del Pueblo; UPP) to nominate Frank Vargas. The Socialists' Enrique Ayala was named his running mate. When voters went to the polls on 31 January 1988, their choices consequently included two Marxist slates. At stake, in addition to the chief of state, were: 71 deputies (12 national and 59 provincial); 19 provincial prefects and councillors; and, at the municipal level, 126 council presidents and 1,076 regular members.

Rodrigo Borja Cevallos of the Democratic Left (Izquierda Democrática; ID) won the first round with 20.5 percent of the vote, followed by Abdalá Bucaram of the Ecuadorean Roldosista Party (Partido Roldosista Ecuatoriano; PRE) with 14.7 percent. On the left, Frank Vargas finished in fourth place with 10.5 percent; Jaime Hurtado polled 4.2 percent to place seventh in a field of ten. Vargas did somewhat better than expected, easily winning the contest within the left by combining his own popularity, a populist style, and assertive nationalism. He captured his home province of Manabí, while running a close second in Imbabura, where the PSE was strong (*Analysis Semanal*, 5 February). The UPP placed four members of the PSE in congress, while two members from the FADI and two from the MPD were successful in the FIU lists. In the wake of the elections, attention turned to the decisive runoff between Borja and Bucaram, as both coalitions pressed their own policies upon the two contenders as the price for support.

By March the UPP opted for independence, refusing to endorse either Borja or Bucaram. The FIU itself dissolved as a consequence of strategic differences between FADI and the MPD. The former chose to back the ID candidate, arguing that a social-democratic government would be better for Ecuadorean democracy than what it saw as personalistic opportunism on the part of Bucaram and the PRE. The MPD contended that neither the ID nor the PRE had provided acceptable responses to the original FIU inquiry, and thus were unworthy of support. The MPD was joined by the PSE in calling for the casting of a null or blank vote. In the runoff on 8 May 1988, Rodrigo Borja won 53 percent of the valid votes. The FADI was the one Marxist group that had reason to seek reward from the victor, and it was prompt in putting forward its requests. Among these was the vice-chairmanship of the Tribunal of Constitutional Guarantees (Tribunal de Garantías Constitucionales; TGC). In the first legislative session of the new chamber, the FADI generally supported government measures, although Borja himself was sharply criticized for his economic policies. The MPD and PSE were even more selective in this regard. All three maintained their ties with the labor movement and supported the nationwide work stoppage called for 24 November.

As the principal Marxist group to endorse Borja, as well as the dominant force in the FADI, the PCE defined further its current goals and objectives at its Eleventh Party Congress. Convening in Quito on 21 July, the congress adopted a revised set of "Political Theses" that stressed organizational discipline, democratic centralism, and attacked caudillism and personality cults. Unity of anti-imperialist forces was stressed, while collaboration with the coming reformist government was described in cautious generalities (*El Pueblo*, 24–30 June).

Auxiliary Organizations. The Frente Unitario de Trabajadores (FUT) remains the umbrella organization embracing Ecuador's three primary trade union confederations. With the majority of the nation's workers still unorganized, the impact of the FUT and its components remains limited, especially as compared with other South American cases. However, in 1988 it continued to exert pressure through strikes and threats of work stoppages. This was especially true during the final months of the Febres administration, which had adopted and maintained a confrontational stance toward organized labor throughout its time in power. Demonstrations against the government and denunciations of its alleged repression and human rights violations were extensive. For labor, a related tactic was that of applying pressure on behalf of free elections and the maintenance of constitutional succession.

More general preoccupations focused on the dreary economic situation, which contributed to the further deterioration of living conditions for the workers. Rodrigo Borja's austerity program was received with distrust and criticism, although labor leaders recognized the inevitability of initial emergency measures. It was skepticism about the effectiveness of such measures that helped to precipitate the November protests. A characteristic expression of labor demands was that of the communist-dominated Confederation of Ecuadorean Workers (Confederación de Trabajadores de Ecuador; CTE) shortly after Borja's inauguration. Denouncing prices and the government's implementation of price controls, the CTE called on the government to provide protection for consumers, "thus ending the abuse, speculation, and exploitation being suffered" (*FBIS*, 23 August).

Guerrilla Activity. Ecuador experienced limited guerrilla violence and terrorism during 1988, although there is danger that the violence now racking the neighboring states of Colombia and Peru might spill across the borders. The two organizations now operational are both at the extreme left of the political spectrum: Alfaro Vive, Carajo! (Alfaro Lives, Dammit!) and an offshoot known as Montoneras Patria Libre (MPL). Both had been the targets of harsh government treatment under the Febres government, which demonstrated exaggerated concern over their revolutionary potential. Among the last public reports about these organizations was given in mid-April, when Febres's government minister Heinz Moeller told the press that the Alfaro group remained active, and that three of its members had just been arrested (*FBIS*, 19 April; Radio Quito).

Although much of its leadership had been killed in clashes late in 1986, Alfaro managed to maintain its identity in the public's view. In a communiqué issued after the inauguration, it gave conditional support to President Borja's call for national reconciliation. Claiming that its struggle had been directed against Febres's "tyranny," the rebel group called for amnesty as a means of achieving social peace (*FBIS*, 25 August; Reuters). There were indications that there was greater disruptive potential in the hands of the Montoneras Patria Libre. Its four-hour kidnapping of four media employees in late August provided the occasion for its representatives to announce the group's belief that the Borja policies were mere continuations of previous administrations. The MPL called for nonpayment of the foreign debt, nationalization of banks, expulsion of foreign oil companies, and distribution of land among the Indians. It also demanded the release of political prisoners and a trial of security officials active in the Febres campaign against the MPL (*FBIS*, 1 September; AFP).

International Views and Positions. Cordial relations were maintained between the Communist Party of the Soviet Union and the PCE. Messages of cordiality were exchanged on the occasion of the Eleventh Congress of the PCE, while members of the Soviet delegation to Borja's inauguration met with the PCE leadership. That gathering was also notable for the presence of Fidel Castro and Daniel Ortega, both of whom spent time with Ecuadorean Marxists. The former was much in evidence, granting extensive interviews, while mingling with the other chiefs of state in attendance. Ortega was more withdrawn and kept closely to protocol throughout his visit. Both men avoided any appearance of involvement in local politics, although Ecuadorean leftists in general heralded the occasion and encouraged as many meetings and exchanges of views with Castro and Ortega as possible.

John D. Martz
Pennsylvania State University

El Salvador

Population. 5,388,644
Major Marxist-Leninist Groups

• Communist Party of El Salvador (Partido Comunista de El Salvador; PCES)
  Founded. March 1930; destroyed two years later; reorganized during the late 1940s
  Membership. Less than 1,000
  Leadership. Jorge Schafik Handal (since 1970)
  Governing Body. Central Committee
  Status. Illegal
  Last Congress. Seventh, April 1979
  Fronts and Auxiliary Organizations. The Nationalist Democratic Union (UDN) became the PCES front in 1965; illegal since 1980. In July-August 1988 its leaders, including General Secretary Mario Aguinada Carranza, Tirso Canales, and Aronette Díaz de Zamora returned to El Salvador and became openly active again. The Armed Forces of Liberation (Fuerzas Armadas de Liberación; FAL) is the party's military branch. Together with elements of FARN and FPL, the PCES controls the National Union of Salvadoran Workers (Unión Nacional de

Trabajadores Salvadoreños; UNTS), established 8 February 1986 and led by Humberto Centeno and Marco Tulio Lima.

Publications. *Voz Popular* (irregular); *Fundamentos y Perspectivas* (theoretical, irregular)

• Farabundo Martí Popular Liberation Forces (Fuerzas Populares de Liberación Farabundo Martí; FPL)

Founded. April 1, 1970, by dissidents from the PCES

Membership. Ca. 1,200 cadres and fighters, about 20,000 civilian dependents and supporters

Leadership. Leonel González, first secretary of the Central Committee since August 1983, commander of the Popular Liberation Army (EPL, see below); Dimas Rodríguez, second in command of the EPL and of the FPL; Ricardo Gutiérrez, chief of staff of the EPL; Salvador Guerra.

Governing Body. Central Committee (membership unknown, except for above)

Status. Illegal since inception

Last Congress. Seventh Revolutionary Council, August 1983

Front and Auxiliary Organizations. The People's Revolutionary Bloc (BPR), established in July 1975 as an FPL-controlled umbrella including unions and professional groups. The "sub-regional governments of people's power" in the department of Chalatenango were sporadically operative in certain areas until 1985, when the FPL lost permanent control over them; their leader was Evaristo Lopez.

Publications. *El Rebelde* (irregular); *Farabundo Martí Weekly Informative* (external propaganda); the FPL also controls the second most active radio station of the FMLN, the Radio Farabundo Martí. The BPR (see below) publishes irregularly the *Weekly Popular Combat* (abroad) and the *Juan Angel Chacón Bulletin*, since 1981.

• People's Revolutionary Army (Ejército Revolucionario del Pueblo; ERP)

Founded. 1971, as The Group (El Grupo); acquired present name following bloody internal purges in May 1975

Membership. Ca. 2,000 cadres and fighters; as many as 20,000 civilian supporters and dependents

Leadership. Main leader Joaquín Villalobos (alias of René Cruz)

Political Commission. Villalobos; Ana Guadalupe Martínez; Ana Sonia Medina Arriola ("Mariana"); Mercedes del Carmen Letona ("Luisa"); Claudio Rabindranath Armijo ("Francisco"); Juan Ramón Medrano ("Balta"); Jorge Meléndez ("Jonas"). In addition, former army captain Francisco Mena Sandoval ("Manolo"), who defected in 1981, is an increasingly prominent military leader on the northwestern front.

Status. Illegal since inception

Last Congress. July 1981

Front and Auxiliary Organizations. Party of the Salvadoran Revolution (PRS) and the popular front organization of Popular Leagues—28 February (LP-28) were both established in 1977 as largely fictitious expansions of the militaristic ERP. Both are now largely defunct or inoperative.

Publications. Controls (through "Luisa") the FMLN Radio Venceremos

• Armed Forces of National Resistance (Fuerzas Armadas de la Resistencia Nacional; FARN)

Founded. May 1975, as a result of the ERP purges, by a group of dissident youth from the PCES, FPL, and Christian Democratic party

Membership. Fewer than 1,000 cadres and guerrillas; some 10,000 civilian supporters and dependents

Leadership. Fermán Cienfuegos (alias of Eduardo Sancho Castañeda); "Luis Cabral" is second in command.

Governing Body. Seven-member National Leadership (equivalent of a politburo) that selects an "extended leadership" (i.e., central committee)

Status. Illegal since inception

Fronts and Auxiliary Organizations. United People's Action Front (FAPU), established by Marxist Jesuit priests in the early 1970s and transferred to FARN, almost nonexistent since 1981; Party of National Resistance, established in 1975 to control the military branch, remains ineffectual. FARN is by far the most successful FMLN group in terms of infiltrating legal organizations, particularly student groups at both the National and Central American (Catholic) universities, as well as various "human rights" organizations such as COMADRES (Committee of the Mothers of the Disappeared).

Publications. *Pueblo Internacional* (irregular); *Parte de Guerra* (war bulletin)

• The Revolutionary Party of Central American Workers (Partido Revolucionario de los Trabajadores Centro Americanos; PRTC)

Founded. January 26, 1976 in San Jose, Costa Rica, as a regional Trotskyist party with planned branches in Costa Rica and Guatemala, which were never formed; and in El Salvador and Honduras, which were formed and became independent in October 1980

Membership. Fewer than 200 members, mostly urban; some 1,000 sympathizers and dependents

Leadership. Roberto Roca, supreme leader; Jaime Miranda, representative to Mexico; important Central Committee members include Mario Gonzalez ("Mario"), urban terrorist leader Ismael Dimas Aguilar ("Ulysses"), Maria Concepción de Valladares ("Nidia Díaz")

Governing Body. Central Committee (complete membership unknown)

Front and Auxiliary Organizations. Popular Liberation Movement (MLP), established in 1979, largely disappeared in 1981

• The Revolutionary Democratic Front (Frente Democratico Revolucionario; FDR), an umbrella alliance including the guerrilla organizations of the FMLN along with their parties and fronts (including all of the above) and a few minor civilian parties, including the allegedly social-democratic National Revolutionary Movement (MNR), led by Guillermo Ungo, a vice president of the Socialist International; and a smaller splinter from the Christian Democratic Party, the Social Christian Popular Movement (MPSC), led by Rubén Zamora

Founded. 1980

Membership. A few hundred intellectuals and internationally-connected professionals

Leadership. Ungo, Zamora

Politico-Diplomatic Commission. Members include Ungo (MNR), Zamora (MPSC), Mario Aguinada Carranza (UDN), José Rodriguez Ruíz (FAPU), Ana Guadeloupe Martínez (LP-28), Salvador Samayoa (BPR).

Status. Illegal; however, in 1988, Ungo, Zamora, Héctor Oqueli, and Aguinada returned to El Salvador and formed a legal organization called the Democratic Convergence.

For the left in El Salvador, 1988 was characterized by increasing internal polarization and advancing encroachment upon the country, while the Duarte government proved increasingly ineffective and indecisive. Militarily, 1988 continued the general stalemate of 1987, with growing indications that both sides may be preparing for a final showdown during 1989.

Domestic Affairs. The most important events of the year were the legislative and municipal elections of 20 March, the collapse of the ruling Christian Democratic Party (PDCS), and the re-emergence of the pro-guerrilla left as a legal, albeit minor, political actor.

The March elections resulted in the crushing defeat of the Christian Democrats and the emergence of the conservative national Republican Alliance (ARENA) as the largest—indeed dominant—political force in the country. ARENA won 31 of the 60 seats in the National Assembly and 205 mayoralties out of 262, including that of San Salvador, where ARENA candidate Armando Calderon Sol defeated President Duarte's son Alejandro. Among the new ARENA members of the Assembly, the most prominent is retired colonel Sigifredo Ochoa Pérez, now deputy speaker. Formerly El Salvador's best counterinsurgency commander, Ochoa has rapidly become his party's main spokesman on military matters. His growing influence, combined with that of the party's leader and presidential candidate, Alfredo Cristiani, has largely reduced the power of ARENA's founder and most charismatic leader, Roberto D'Aubuisson.

ARENA is a conservative party with strong support from the middle and lower-middle classes and the business community, as well as a regional stronghold in the western parts of the country. It is strongly anticommunist and opposes most of the social and land reforms of the Duarte government, as well as the nationalization of banks and the government monopoly on foreign trade. Furthermore, the party not only has old links to the military (mostly through personalities like Ochoa and D'Aubuisson), which the Christian Democrats have always lacked, but also the technical expertise to influence the army's counterinsurgency strategy. ARENA's ties to the business community could also be expected to result in better communications with, and cooperation from that community.

The Christian Democrats saw their representation in the Assembly shrink from 33 to 23. The other six seats went to the traditional, opportunistic Party of National Conciliation, which previously held 12 seats and was practically eliminated from provincial political power by disastrous losses at the municipal level.

After apparently trying, unsuccessfully, to deny

ARENA a majority in the Assembly (*WP*, 13 April; *NYT*, 13 April), the PDCS became enmeshed in internecine conflicts over the selection of its presidential candidate for the March 1989 election. Since President José Napoleón Duarte is constitutionally banned from seeking re-election, jockeying for his succession started at the beginning of the year (*Latin America Regional Reports [LARR]*, 18 February). The two leading contenders have been party chief Julio Adolfo Rey Prendes and former foreign minister Fidel Chávez Mena, roughly representing the left and right wings of the party respectively. On 29 April, following a raucous and divisive party convention, in which Rey Prendes was elected as the candidate, the Chávez Mena faction rejected the vote and proclaimed its leader to be the legitimate standard bearer (*NYT*, 1 May). In June, however, a new election took place, probably under pressure from the U.S. embassy, long known to favor Chávez Mena. The latter was selected as the Christian Democratic candidate (*NYT*, 29 June). The Rey Prendes faction then officially split with the party and decided to present its candidate as that of a new party. Not surprisingly, the Christian Democrats' split was mockingly "congratulated" by the FMLN, which stated that it reflected "the failure of the anti-insurgency policy of the Duarte dictatorship supported by the U.S. government" (*LARR*, 9 June).

Until June, however, President Duarte's position as the founder of the party, his charisma, and his appeal to the U.S. Congress and prominent Latin American and West European politicians helped to keep intraparty fights relatively discreet and benign. That month, however, it was made public that Duarte was afflicted with terminal cancer. He has since spent most of his time in American or Mexican hospitals, losing both the ability to run the administration and his prestige within the party.

The third, and most ominous, development on the domestic political scene is the return to legality of the FMLN's fronts and allies. They are taking advantage of the paralysis of the government, the provisions of the Esquipulas accords, and the uncertainty produced by the presidential elections in the United States.

The FDR's intention to return to El Salvador was made clear during 1987, when Rubén Zamora made an exploratory trip to that country. On 24 January he returned to stay, and by July had been followed by Guillermo Ungo, Héctor Oqueli, and other prominent FDR leaders. Zamora has been the main negotiatior with other elements of the legal left in El Salvador, particularly the Social Democrats led by Mario Reni Roldan, with whom he established a common electoral front, the Convergencia Democratica (Democratic Convergence; CD). Zamora is the head of the CD, while Ungo is the presidential candidate and Roldan his running mate. According to most polls the CD runs fourth in voters' preference, after "none of the above," ARENA, and the Christian Democrats (*CSM*, 25 January).

The CD did not participate in the March parliamentary and municipal elections, ostensibly for lack of funds and organization, but in fact because it has little support outside the capital. Furthermore, considering the FMLN's violent rejection of those elections, it would have been put in an untenable political position. Until 25 July, when Ungo's candidacy was declared, it was unclear in fact whether or not the CD would participate in the March 1989 presidential elections, in view of the preconditions demanded by Zamora as late as June, which included "freedom of movement . . . respect for the personal safety of all CD members . . . and equal access to the media" (*FBIS-LAM*, 20 June). Indeed, as FMLN murders of ARENA and Christian Democratic politicians—particularly local mayors—demonstrated throughout the year, no party, even the ruling one, enjoys such advantages.

Regarding the U.S. elections, the CD was openly hopeful of a victory by the Democratic candidate because, as Zamora put it, ". . . the alternative of finding a political solution [to the civil war] is gaining support within the U.S. Democratic Party" (ibid.). The major campaign theme of the CD, rather than a socialist program, is peace through a negotiated solution. The most delicate issue, however, is the relationship between the FMLN and the CD in general, and between the guerrillas and the FDR-CD leadership in particular. Officially and publicly, the differences between the FDR-CD leaders and the FMLN are played down by both sides, with Ungo stating that ". . . there will be some similarities between our proposals and the FMLN's positions [on negotiations] . . . There should be basic agreement and understanding between us . . . On the other hand, I suppose there will be differences, which we should mutually respect. The FMLN is a political but also a military organization. Our organization is strictly political." (Ibid., 13 July.)

In fact, however, the only significant difference between the stated goals of the FMLN and those of the FDR-CD, other than the latter's decision to participate in the presidential elections of 1989, is in regard to the murder of civilian mayors by the guerrillas. On 23 December, Ungo specifically stated that civilians, including elected mayors, should not be targeted by the FMLN (ibid., 23 December), while during the same month "Jonas" claimed that "...mayors and other officials are enemies of the people as long as they are part of the counterinsurgency plan" (ibid., 29 December).

It was this ambiguity of the CD's position with respect to the FMLN that produced the sharpest domestic reactions. President Duarte publicly stated that "the FDR's political discourse is one of conspiracy with and support for the FMLN's violent stance" (ibid., 29 April). More dramatically, a newly minted "death-squad," the Revolutionary Anticommunist Extermination Action (ARDE), publicly accused the CD and specific components of it, such as the UDN, of treason. It threatened to "eliminate" their leaders, including Ungo, Aguinada, and Zamora, as well as the leaders of UNTS, particularly Centeno, all described as being in cahoots with the FMLN. (Ibid., 28 December.)

The FMLN violently opposed the elections of March 1988 with both military and terrorist actions, as well as public statements. Politically, FMLN reactions varied from Cienfuegos's statement that the elections resulted in a "vacuum of political alternatives and a power vacuum" (ibid., 4 April) to Leonel Gonzales's claim that the electoral exercise was just "serving the interventionist war carried out by the Reagan Administration" (ibid.), to Handal's argument that the results were a "rebuff of the counterinsurgency plan" (ibid., 15 April). Roca, for his part, repeated Villalobos's claim that the elections, by polarizing the political scene, were a great victory for the FMLN, and that there would be mass defections from the losing Christian Democrats to the guerrillas (ibid., 29 March).

In terms of military action, "Luisa" claimed that "elections are part of the [U.S.] counterinsurgency plan and we won't make them easy" (CSM, 7 March). To follow through on this threat, the FMLN declared a traffic ban throughout the country, attacked the town of Chinameca after the polls were closed, caused yet another power cut in most of the country by blowing up 100 power towers and utility poles (LAT, 21 March), and generally made life miserable for most Salvadorans. Villalobos himself, after mentioning the FMLN's sabotage, terror, and intimidation, claimed that absenteeism in the elections was his organization's biggest success (Granma, 5 June).

Guerrilla Activities. The process of unification within the FMLN advanced during the year. Further progress was made toward the ideological, political, and military homogenization of the five original component groups of the FMLN. It can now be said that intra-FMLN unity is far more advanced than most observers would have predicted only a few years ago, and more complete than that of the Nicaraguan FSLN at the moment of the 1979 victory. Unlike the FSLN, however, the FMLN clearly appears to have an unchallenged leader in Joaquín Villalobos, whose long-standing position as the dominant FMLN leader seems to have taken a new turn with the incipient development of a personality cult. Beyond this, there is an increasingly well-defined public division of roles and tasks among the top guerrilla leaders, with Roca in charge of urban terrorism, Handal as a general political spokesman and liaison with the Soviets (he alone signed the FMLN letter of condolences to Moscow after the Armenian earthquake), Cienfuegos as conductor of most of the diplomatic activities outside the Soviet bloc, and Leonel Gonzales as Villalobos's shadow (also joining Cienfuegos on diplomatic ventures). Most important, however, is the growing public role of ERP leaders like "Jonas," "Luisa," and Ana Guadalupe Martínez, as well as Mena Sandoval. The former three are often more outspoken than the supreme leaders of the other four FMLN groups. Overall, it appears that the FMLN is at the stage where it could practically be defined as a genuine Leninist "vanguard" party, with a politburo (the High or Supreme Command) including a majority (or at least a disproportionate number) of ERP leaders, a de facto chairman in Villalobos, and a hierarchy of deputy leaders topped by Handal and Cienfuegos.

The facts that the Soviet-controlled WMR and Information Bulletin are by now publishing only FMLN (rather than PCES) statements, and that even Handal is now described only as an FMLN leader rather than as the general secretary of the PCES, are indications that the USSR now sees the FMLN as one party—an incipient one, perhaps, but one organization rather than an umbrella (see for instance "El Salvador: the Hour of People's Victory is Near," Information Bulletin, April 1988). The most evident result of such trends is that it has become unrealistic, in fact increasingly irrelevant, to try to find differences between supposed "doves" and "hawks" within the FMLN, since all relevant spokemen are subject to the same party discipline and rules of "democratic centralism." It thus appears that 1988 could be defined as the watershed in the convulsed history of the Salvadoran Marxist-Leninist left, the time when it finally reached a point where ideology, rather than personalities and tactics, dominated its behavior.

FMLN statements and activities during the year demonstrate that the Salvadoran left has rethought its guerrilla strategy. According to Villalobos ". . . the basis of our strategy [is] . . . incorporating people into the revolutionary war in diverse ways, ranging from the direct—such as the integration of permanent forces—to the creation of clandestine forces of all types and the encouragement of popular insurrection and radicalization, which, at this time, has great prospects" (*FBIS-LAM*, 9 June).

Regarding the "incorporation" of the population into the war, Villalobos bluntly stated that "as far as we are concerned, the people only have two alternatives: to fight or die of hunger" (ibid., p. 8). This is as clear an indication as possible that the FMLN's accelerating campaign of economic sabotage and destruction is intended to force an insurrection through epidemic despair. Despair, however, is only one instrument to be used; provocation is the other, and in this respect the FMLN fronts also made great strides during the year. The most active among those fronts was UNTS, which on 21 July staged a "demonstration" in front of the Treasury Police's headquarters in San Salvador, burned ten vehicles, and attacked policemen (*FBIS-LAM*, 22 July). According to the government, these actions were part of a long-term strategic plan, code-named "Plan Fuego," involving the use of FMLN urban "militias" to "wear out the political-military structure" of the government (ibid.). That assessment was indirectly but clearly confirmed by the FMLN, which described the 21 July episode as "genuine revolutionary violence" (*FBIS-LAM*, 22 July). In fact, UNTS leader Centeno's answer to accusations of vandalism was to admit and justify it as the legitimate reaction of people "mad" at military "provocation" (ibid., 25 July). As for "Plan Fuego," Roberto Roca himself implicitly admitted its existence and claimed that it indicates that "the radicalization of the popular struggle is unstoppable" (ibid., 29 March).

In another, prior, indication of the growing paramilitary nature of UNTS, Marco Tulio Lima read an organization statement on 30 April admitting that "compañeros" were "guarding" UNTS headquarters

and "resisted arrest" during a previous clash with the National Guard (ibid., 3 May).

In June 1988, cadres of the old and now defunct FPL, FARN, and ERP fronts (BPR, FAPU, and LP-28 respectively) joined efforts under a new umbrella, the Bread, Land, Work, and Liberty Movement (Movimiento Pan, Tierra, Trabajo y Libertad; MPTL). The new group's leaders included Jorge Villegas, Santiago Flores, and Alejandro Estevez (*FBIS-LAM*, 20 June). It is increasingly clear that the UNTS-MPTL structure is becoming a far more effective version of the guerrillas' "popular organizations" of the late 1970s and early 1980s. Together with various "human rights" groups, like the CDHES (see *YICA*, 1988) and the Committee of the Fired and Unemployed (CODYDES), these fronts, often bolstered by urban terrorist cells, are increasingly able to produce an atmosphere of violence and lawlessness in San Salvador.

Each and every one of these organizations has been clearly proven by the Salvadoran government to be led, controlled, or used by the FMLN. In some cases, such as that of the National University, terrorist labs for producing bombs have been found, and PRTC cadres have been arrested in connection with them. The murder of pro-FMLN CDHES leader Herbert Anaya Sanabria may have been a particularly spectacular example of FMLN provocation tactics. According to the government, (*FBIS-LAM*, 12 January), the FMLN (specifically the ERP) murdered Anaya to portray the Salvadoran regime as a violator of human rights.

The entire strategy of the FMLN during the year was succinctly defined in a statement made public on 10 February that confirmed previous claims made public by the military following the capture of documents. As described by the FMLN, "ours is a well-defined plan to annihilate and wear down enemy forces, sabotage the war economy, and destabilize and dismantle local and judicial authority and the political-economic plans mentioned in the 'United to Reconstruct' operation" (*FBIS-LAM*, 19 February). For all practical purposes, that strategy (which in all likelihood was Villalobos's creation) was pursued literally.

The "wearing down" of the government was clearly pursued and was extended to the society as a whole by the extensive and relentless sabotage of the country's economic and commercial infrastructure, as well as the use of terror against civilians. In a single week in November, the FMLN claimed to have destroyed 77 electrical towers, three telecommunications offices, three town halls, and two civil command posts (*Central American Report* [*CAR*], 9 December). The American embassy estimates that over $2 billion in economic damage has been done by the insurgents in the past seven years (*NYT*, 26 June).

The "destabilization" and "dismantling" of civilian authority took the form of a sustained, year-long campaign of terror and intimidation against elected officials. Radio Venceremos, in a 16 April broadcast, defined FMLN policy regarding civilians, making it clear that all those using army helicopters and vehicles, traveling in army-protected convoys, living in the proximity of military garrisons and installations, serving as guides for military patrols, or simply not "follow(ing) the instructions given by the FMLN . . ." were seen as legitimate targets (*FBIS-LAM*, 19 April).

To the time of this writing in December, eight mayors, from both ARENA and the PDCS, have been murdered by the FMLN (ibid.). Many more have been kidnapped, and still many more so intimidated that they resigned their offices. For instance, Pedro Ventura, the popular mayor of San Isidro in Morazán who was re-elected in March, was shot in front of his family in April because he defied the guerrillas' "order" not to run in the elections (*NYT*, 20 April). On 22 August, Radio Venceremos proudly announced that "our guerrilla forces captured Lolotiquillo Mayor Dolores Molina . . . War criminal Dolores Molina has been executed" (*FBIS-LAM*, 24 August). The murder of Dolores Molina and the FMLN statement admitting it both throw a special light on FMLN's strategy and mentality. The statement claimed that mayors in general "actively participate in the regime's counterinsurgency operations by forming civil defense groups and disinformation networks and by criminally repressing people" (ibid.). Furthermore, "as is true of all Christian Democratic officials, mayors are bloodstained with repression and sullied with the dollars of corruption" (ibid.).

The elimination through murder or intimidation of local elected officials was only part of the FMLN strategy regarding noncombatants. The organization has tried to intimidate U.S. politicians with the specter of Americans' coming home in body bags. In the wake of the U.S. presidential elections, the FMLN repeatedly stated in public—often through Roberto Roca, whose PRTC urban cells are responsible for most U.S. casualties since 1981—that Americans are now seen as legitimate targets. In Roca's words, "for the FMLN, the Americans have always been the real authors of this war . . ." (*FBIS-*

LAM, 24 February). Not only did he claim that ". . .the U.S. military personnel cannot consider themselves immune . . . ," he also stated that "the counterinsurgency war imposed on our people by the Americans . . .is directly financed and directed through U.S. advisers and CIA agents linked to the intelligence services and linked to the legal war against the trade union movement as well as against all forms of popular organization independent of the regime" (ibid.). Such a "definition" of the role of American citizens in El Salvador, including those giving legal, union, intelligence, military, and just about any other form of advice, makes all Americans "legitimate" targets for assassination.

Since FMLN "conditions" for avoiding civilian casualties were virtually impossible to comply with, the number of victims increased drastically. In general, the poor were hardest hit by FMLN-decreed transportation stoppages and the still-growing use of mines throughout the countryside. The result was that the Salvadoran electorate turned right in March elections, and seems inclined to do so again in the presidential elections of March 1989. The FMLN fronts' ability to attract or coerce people to participate in their strikes and violent demonstrations declined dramatically (*NYT*, 26 June), just as their capability for violence has increased, and popular support for the CD, widely seen as an FMLN front, is bound to grow smaller and smaller. In fact, Zamora himself admitted that the FMLN's use of violence during its fronts' demonstrations and strikes, especially those of UNTS, resulted in a situation whereby "they drove away a thousand people who would have listened to our speeches . . . . People do not want violence" (ibid.).

In more strictly military terms, the year has witnessed a general stalemate, with the guerrillas able to sporadically penetrate some western departments, such as Ahuachapan, where they were never active before (*CAR*, 9 December). They were also able to expand their activities in San Salvador. The military, meanwhile, increased its use of small patrols and ambushes, as well as the effectiveness of its airborne operations (*LAT*, January 16).

At the end of the year, the new chief of staff of the armed forces, Col. René Emilio Ponce, claimed that during 1988 the army carried out 72,440 patrols, staged 45,826 ambushes, killed 914 guerrillas, wounded 702 and captured 517 (*FBIS-LAM*, 21 December). Those figures are impossible to verify independently, but they appear at the very least to indicate a dramatic shift in priorities. Small-unit patrols and ambushes finally are replacing the large-scale, largely ineffective operations that were producing high body counts often including many noncombatants. That shift seems to be at least in part due to the drastic restructuring of the Salvadoran military command during the year, in which members of Col. Ponce's own Salvadoran Military Academy class of 1968 (the "tandona") took over practically all field and staff commands.

Among the guerrillas, 1988 saw the ERP continue, perhaps to a decisive degree, to consolidate its dominance over all other groups. Of the four FMLN fronts, only ERP and the FPL (now under ERP influence), are active at all. FARN is restricted to the practically defunct Guazapa operational area of the central front and to the central-eastern and eastern fronts (surprisingly, and despite its capabilities for, and experience in political infiltration, FARN seems to be militarily absent from San Salvador). The PCES is restricted to Guazapa and the metropolitan areas of the central front, apparently an indication that the party's military strength has declined. Finally, the PRTC, while active on the central-eastern and eastern fronts, seems to still concentrate most of its efforts in San Salvador (*CAR*, 9 December).

The ERP's and especially Villalobos's growing strategic and military dominance are also demonstrated by the patterns of military activities carried out by the FMLN during the year. Despite the military's overwhelming superiority in the air—compounded by the apparent refusal of the USSR, Cuba, and Nicaragua to provide the FMLN with antiaircraft missiles—a return to large-scale operations could be detected in the guerrillas' operational behavior. On 17 February, they attacked the Usulután garrison; on 13 September, the Chalatenango headquarters of the Fourth Infantry Brigade; on 1 November, the National Guard's barracks in San Salvador; and also in November, the Air Force's Ilopango base and the San Miguel Third Brigade's headquarters (*CAR*, 9 December). In the absence of effective antiaircraft weapons, these attacks netted the guerrillas short-lived public-relations successes in exchange for high and virtually irreplaceable guerrilla casualties. This all fits Villalobos's view of the war, however. Indeed, in November he described the FMLN's military strategy as one that does not involve ". . . a final offensive, but a process of gradual offensives." (Ibid.)

Despite the triumphant military communiqués claiming the death of Cienfuegos, Mena Sandoval, and Gonzales, no major leader of the FMLN was killed in combat during the year, perhaps because most were outside the country. Nevertheless, in April the National Guard did announce the capture of the FPL's financial, and thus logistical, leader in San Salvador, Vicente Antonio Sibrian Guardado, alias "Israel" or "Jorge." "Israel," a forty-six-year old ex-Catholic priest who joined the FPL in 1980 in Cabañas, was also in charge of transportation of FMLN cadres to Nicaragua and Cuba. He handled amounts between $40,000 and $70,000 a month, most received through "international solidarity"—i.e. Western—sources (*FBIS-LAM*, 19 April).

The previous pattern of FMLN infiltration of the Salvadoran universities also continued, as demonstrated by the statements of captured PRTC cadre Manuel de Jesus Amaya Renderos, a.k.a. "Moris" and "Santos." He was recruited in January 1988 by the same PRTC cell that killed a large number of American, Salvadoran, and Guatemalan citizens in 1985, was paid between 200 and 500 colones per month to pose as an unemployed person, and became a squad leader of the PRTC terrorist network in the capital (*FBIS-LAM*, 22 November). He was trained in the use of weapons and bomb-making on the third floor of the University of El Salvador's School of Chemistry and was actually recruited at the headquarters of CODYDES (ibid.).

Negotiations and International Activities. Throughout the year, the FMLN continued its previous dual strategy of pursuing the war vigorously while simultaneously trying to improve its international image and convey the impression that it is eager to reach a negotiated end to the civil war. The FMLN and its FDR allies have publicly expressed their hope that the Democratic Party will win the U.S. presidential election and implement a new policy toward El Salvador. To a large extent, such hopes were encouraged by the actions and statements of prominent Democratic politicians, including Jesse Jackson, who described the Salvadoran civil war as the result solely of the government's murdering its own people. On 18 June, a delegation of the Salvadoran left led for the FMLN by the ERP's Ana Guadalupe Martínez and the PCES's Mario López, and for the FDR by Ungo and Zamora, went to Mexico City. There, they met with former Massachusetts governor Edward King, special assistant to then-Senate majority–leader Robert Byrd; but no specific conclusions were reached. (*FBIS-LAM*, 16 June.)

The insurgents' political strategy centered around taking maximum advantage of the opportunities provided by the provisions of the Esquipulas II accords, and especially the chance to operate openly in Nicaragua and Costa Rica. Thus, for the first time in years, Villalobos gave interviews in Managua, while Martínez and López were officially received in May by President Oscar Arias of Costa Rica. In all instances, the guerrilla leaders claimed that the Duarte government has lost whatever representativeness, power, and legitimacy it had, particularly after the March elections (later in the year Duarte's illness offered yet another argument for this claim), and thus that direct negotiations with the government are useless. Instead, they proposed talks with the United States, the military, and even ARENA. As the FPL's Salvador Samayoa stated, talks with U.S. congressmen should seek an "alternative" to previous approaches (*FBIS-LAM*, 16 June). Ana Guadalupe Martínez went so far as to claim that "we believe that the solution must be provided by Salvadorans. Naturally, private enterprise and ARENA . . . are Salvadoran" (ibid., 8 June).

Interestingly, and typically, the FMLN's most significant proposal for talks came in May in Costa Rica (*LAT*, May 22). It was further defined the following month, at the very time when the Christian Democrats split, when ARENA was fighting in court government attempts to deny it a majority in the Assembly, and when the president's cancer was discovered. The timing for the proposed cease-fire was thus chosen precisely in order to demonstrate that the government of El Salvador is "unwilling" to engage in serious negotiations. In fact, as Col. Ponce stated at the time, "There is weak government [and] a lack of national objectives . . . This is completely negative and is taking us to a situation of anarchy . . ." (*CAR*, 9 June).

There were two main reasons no serious negotiations took place during the year: the rebels' excessive demands and vague proposals; and the government's growing paralysis. The first point was clearly demonstrated in at least three instances. First, the FMLN's May-June proposal for a cease-fire was made at a time of maximum turmoil in San Salvador. Second, simultaneously with the cease-fire proposal, the FMLN proposed to renounce the use of landmines—perhaps the most unpopular aspect of FMLN tactics—in exchange for the army's promise to give up the use of aircraft and long-range artillery, by far its most important advantages over the FMLN (*LAT*, May 22). Third, the December proposal for a cease-fire over the holidays was conditioned on the army's halting all operations and garrisoning all its troops, while the guerrillas

supposedly would cease all "offensive operations." (*FBIS-LAM*, 20 December.) Such conditions, which would have effectively allowed the FMLN to regroup its forces and replenish its supplies unhindered, were summarily rejected by the armed forces.

The Duarte government's attempts to comply with the amnesty provisions of the Esquipulas accords were largely blocked by the vocal opposition of the United States and the conservative political groups. The attempt to release the PRTC members who had murdered six Americans, a Chilean, a Guatemalan, and five Salvadorans in June 1985 was given up following threats by the U.S. Congress to cut $18 million in aid to El Salvador (*FBIS-LAM*, 12 April). The National Guard members jailed for the killing of four American nuns in 1983 were also denied amnesty in January (ibid., 12 January).

Throughout the year, the official statements from San Salvador continued to link progress on negotiations with the FMLN, regional peace and cooperation, and amnesty, with the activities of the Nicaraguan government. In January, following a Central American summit in San José, Duarte clearly stated that ". . . there will be no peace in Central America if there is no democracy in Nicaragua." More specifically, regarding Nicaragua's impact on the Salvadoran civil war, he also expressed support for Costa Rican president Oscar Arias's demand that "Nicaragua expel from its territory all the [FMLN] rebel leaders . . ." and stated that "basically, the FMLN is supported by Cuba and Nicaragua . . ." (*FBIS-LAM*, 20 January). Similar accusations were made by Defense Minister Eugenio Vides Casanova, who claimed that FMLN terrorists are trained in Nicaragua—including fifteen trained in handling SAM-7 antiaircraft missiles, similar to the American Stinger—and that Managua interferes in Salvadoran affairs by providing logistical support to the FMLN, including weapons, ammunition, training, and treatment for its wounded (ibid., 2 February).

In military and political terms the situation in El Salvador remained in a state of flux throughout the year, but it appears that 1989 will bring about a much clearer picture. The new military leadership will be in a position to implement long-needed tactical and strategic changes, probably with support from the now-dominant ARENA party. If, as is widely expected by everyone, including the FMLN, ARENA succeeds in consolidating its control by winning the presidency in March, the Salvadoran government will finally be able to speak with a unified voice. At the same time, the internal dynamics of the FMLN will also allow it to further consolidate the trend toward a unitary position on both military and political issues.

Michael Radu
Foreign Policy Research Institute, Philadelphia

Grenada

Population. 84,455
Party. Maurice Bishop Patriotic Movement (MBPM)
Founded. 27 May 1984
Membership. No data
Chairman. Terrence Marryshow
Status. Legal
Last Congress. May 1988
Last Election. 3 December 1984; 5 percent, no seats
Auxiliary Organizations. The Maurice Bishop and Martyrs of October 19, 1983, Memorial Foundation; The Grenada Foundation, Inc.; The Maurice Bishop Youth Organization (MBYO)
Publications. *The Indies Times* (weekly), *The Democrat* (biweekly)

The year 1988 marked a turning point for Grenada's four-year-old MBPM. During the party congress in May, Terrence Marryshow was elected MBPM leader, replacing the discredited chairman Kenrick Radix, who insisted he was stepping down for health reasons. Marryshow, a 35-year-old Cuban-trained doctor, brings a charisma and oratorical skill to the leadership role that is reminiscent of the party's slain eponym, Maurice Bishop. Marryshow headed the late Prime Minister Bishop's security detail before going to Cuba for his medical studies. He is also the grandson of Grenada's foremost national hero, Theophilus Alfred Marryshow. Einstein Louison, former chief of staff of the disbanded People's Revolutionary Army (PRA) was elected as the MBPM's deputy leader, while Benny Langaigne (ex-permanent secretary in the office of Prime Minister Bishop) was named party financial secretary. (*Barbados Advocate*, Bridgetown, 2 June).

Marryshow announced a pragmatic approach to rebuilding the MBPM's dwindling support among Grenada's electorate. Admitting that his party's chances of winning the island's 1989 elections were slim, he asserted that by the 1994 elections the party should be in a far better position. The interim, he said, would be spent in mobilizing support among three key groups—workers, youth, and women. Marryshow's strategy also calls for strengthening ties with the democratic left throughout the Caribbean, beginning with Barbados's ruling party, the Democratic Labour Party. Another MBPM spokesman, Tarley Francis (identified as a member of the party's Council of Representatives), told a Soviet reporter that the MBPM entertained no illusions about its present weakness but was working toward restoring the revolutionary consciousness of the people of Grenada (*Izvestiia*, 26 October).

International Contacts. In September, Marryshow embarked upon a six-nation African tour, visiting Angola, Zimbabwe, Libya, Ethiopia, Ghana, and Uganda. He was accompanied by Joseph Carter, a member of the MBPM executive who is based in Sweden. The official purpose for Marryshow's visit was to renew contact with the countries of "our motherland" and to express to the struggling people of Africa solidarity from "our people and our party." (*Cana*, 3 September.) Earlier in the year, Kenrick Radix had visited Panama to attend a solidarity meeting of leftist groups from the Caribbean and Central America (*Indies Times*, St. George's, 11 June).

Representatives from a variety of Marxist-Leninist governments and organizations, reportedly including Cuba and Libya, were invited to attend the MBPM's May convention but were denied entry by the government of Grenada. Those foreign leftists who were allowed into the island for the convention included James M. Warren of the Socialist Workers' Party (SWP) of America, Rena Cacoullous, national secretary of the U.S.-based Young Socialist Alliance, and Themba Ntinga, deputy representative of the African National Congress's (ANC) U.N. observer mission. (*Trans World Radio*, Bonaire, 31 May.)

By year's end, the MBPM had established itself as Grenada's only viable communist political party. The New Jewel Movement (NJM) had disappeared, except for Bernard Coard, ex-deputy prime minister of the People's Revolutionary Government, and his thirteen codefendants who have been sentenced to hang for the murder of Maurice Bishop and others. Coard, Hudson Austin, and their henchmen are appealing their convictions. The MBPM has taken a hard line on its former NJM comrades, supporting the death penalty for them and dismissing the "remnants of the New Jewel Movement" as "condemned to the dustbin of history." (*Barbados Advocate*, Bridgetown, 2 June.)

Under the leadership of Terry Marryshow, the MBPM could well develop into a potent political force in Grenada. Public turnout for MBPM rallies and other events has grown over the past year, and many Grenadians seem disenchanted with the current government and frustrated by the slow pace of economic growth. The "martyred" Maurice Bishop has become almost a cult figure among young Grenadians, and Marryshow is perceived by many as "the new Maurice Bishop."

Timothy Ashby
Washington, D.C.

Guadeloupe

Population. 338,730
Party. Communist Party of Guadeloupe (Parti Communiste Guadeloupéen; PCG)
Founded. 1944 as section of the French Communist Party (PCF), 1958 as independent
Membership. 3,000 (estimated)
General Secretary. Christian Céleste
Politburo. 14 members: Henri Bangou, other members unknown
Central Committee. Christian Céleste (secretary)
Status. Legal
Last Congress. Ninth, 11–13 March 1988
Last Election. 24 April, 8 May 1988, president of France; 5 and 12 June 1988, French National Assembly; 25 September, 2 October 1988, Guadeloupan General Council, 10 (members and allies) of 42 seats
Auxiliary Organizations. Union of Guadeloupan Communist Youth (Union de la Jeunesse Communiste Guadeloupéenne; UJCG; Fred Sablon, general secretary), Union of Guadeloupan Women (Union des Femmes Guadeloupeennes; UFG),

General Confederation of Guadeloupan Labor (CGTG)
Publications. *L'Etincelle* (PCG weekly), *Madras* (UFG monthly)

The Parti Communiste Guadeloupéen celebrated its thirtieth anniversary with a little *perestroika* of its own. At its Ninth Congress, held 11–13 March, Guy Daninthe stepped down after eighteen years as general secretary and the 40-year-old Christian Céleste, who had been secretary of the Central Committee, took his place. Three other older members of the leadership followed Daninthe into retirement. Furthermore, the party changed procedures for electing the general secretary: he or she would henceforth be elected by the Central Committee instead of by the congress and balloting would be secret. The new slogan for the PCG would be "Socialist-oriented national independence, the stage of advancement to which should be democratically decided by the people of Guadeloupe." The new fourteen-member Politburo included Guy Daninthe who, however, faded quickly from public view after the congress.

Céleste, born in 1948, started his PCG career in 1967 as a member of the young people's organization, the Union of Guadeloupan Communist Youth (Union de la Jeunesse Communiste Guadeloupéen). At the age of twenty he was admitted into the PCG. In 1971 he won a seat on a municipal council, and the following year he was made a member of PCG's Central Committee. In 1976 he became a member of the Politburo. In 1983 he was elected to Guadeloupe's Regional Council.

One older member of the party leadership, Dr. Henri Bangou, did not resign. Bangou, who is also a senator and the mayor of Pointe-à-Pitre, spoke frequently. He also continued his writing career with the publication of *Les voies de la souveraineté* (The Roads to Sovereignty). Ernest Moutoussamy, one of the island's deputies to the French National Assembly, wrote two books, *La Guadeloupe et son Indianité* (Guadeloupe and its Indianness) and *Les Dom-Tom: Enjeu géopolitique, économique et stratégique* (The overseas departments and territories: Geopolitical, economic and strategic stakes). The book on the Indian contribution to Guadeloupe and presence there appeared at a time of an increasing sense of identity among the small population in the French West Indies whose ancestors came from South Asia.

All these leaders denounced the anticipated negative consequences of the 1992 integration of

Western Europe. It was even said that Guadeloupe might "disappear," in the sense that its distinctive culture and institutions might be overwhelmed by an influx of Europeans. Thus, on 20 February the PCG joined with communist and socialist parties in Cayenne, French Guiana, to create the Rassemblement des Forces de Progrès des Antilles, de la Réunion et de la Guyane (Assemblage of progressive forces of the Antilles, Réunion, and French Guiana) to protect overseas departments' interests against the consequences of European integration.

All French citizens were called to the polls four times during the year. Presidential elections were held 24 April and 8 May. The French Communist Party sent delegates to Guadeloupe to encourage support for their candidate André Lajoinie, and François Mitterrand visited between the two rounds. The communist candidate received only 4,198 votes in Guadeloupe, or less than the far right candidate J.-M. Le Pen. F. Mitterrand received 42,539. In the second round, incumbent Mitterrand crushed Jacques Chirac with 68.41 percent of the vote in Guadeloupe. Obviously, the communists preferred the socialist candidate over their own communist candidate.

Elections to the French National Assembly were called for 5 and 12 June by the re-elected president, who hoped to secure a socialist majority. The PCG ran four candidates for the four seats of Guadeloupe. E. Moutoussamy, deputy since 1981, won again; two socialists also won, and they were joined by one deputy from the right. Moutoussamy's Indian identity became a matter of discussion during the campaign. This discussion seems to be new in Guadeloupan politics.

On 25 September and 2 October, voters went to the polls for elections to the local legislative body, the General Council. Twenty-one seats out of 42 were open, and the PCG ran fourteen candidates. They won four seats, giving the PCG a total of ten seats in the council, not all of whom are actually party members, some being allied. Unexpectedly, E. Moutoussamy lost his seat to another person of Indian ancestry, who seems to have emphasized his Indian identity more than Moutoussamy was willing to do. After the elections, the socialists counted fourteen members of the General Council, and the unaffiliated or diverse left had two seats, making a total for the left of 26 seats out of 42. Thus a socialist was elected president of the council, and a member of the PCG took the position of second vice president. On 6 November, the people of Guadeloupe went a last time to the polls to vote for a plan to reform the political system of New Caledonia, a French overseas territory in the Pacific.

L'Etincelle, the weekly PCG newspaper, ran several articles on Haiti and on *perestroika* in the Soviet Union. In July, a PCG delegation went to Georgetown, Guyana, to meet with left parties from Puerto Rico, Trinidad and Tobago, Cuba, and Venezuela. The PCG broadcast over its own radio station, GAIAC, and is hoping to set up a television station in cooperation with the socialists.

Brian Weinstein
Howard University

Guatemala

Population. 8,831,148
Major Marxist-Leninist Organizations

• The Guatemalan Party of Labor (Partido Guatemalteco de Trabajo; PGT)
  Founded. September 28, 1949. The first Guatemalan Communist Party was created by the Comintern in 1922, and was destroyed in 1932. In September 1949 an illegal, new party was formed, which became legal three years later under the present name, then became illegal again following the 1954 coup.
  Membership. Unconfirmed estimates of 200–300 for all factions
  Factions and Leadership. "Camarilla" faction: Carlos Gonzales (also general secretary of the Central Committee and head of the Political Commission); National Leadership Nucleus faction: Daniel Rios (Rios seems to have been supplanted in 1988 by Mario Sánchez, who had been "in charge of general political questions"); Military Commission faction: unknown
  Leading Body. The Political Commission. The membership and size of the Political Commission are unknown. The nature of the top structures of the other factions is also unknown.
  Status. All factions illegal
  Last Congress. Fourth, December 1969
  Last Election. N/A
  Auxiliary Organizations. Autonomous Fed-

eration of the Guatemalan Trade Unions (FASGUA); Patriotic Youth of Labor (JPT)

Publications. *Verdad* (irregular, published abroad)

● Rebel Armed Forces (Fuerzas Armadas Rebeldes; FAR)

Founded. 1962; broke with the PGT in 1968; largely inactive 1968–1978

Membership. Probably less than 800

Leadership. Jorge Ismael Soto García (alias Pablo Monsanto)

Status. Illegal

Auxiliary Organizations. National Committee of Trade Union Unity (CNUS), founded in 1976, now practically defunct

Publications. *Guerrillero* (irregular, published abroad)

● Armed People's Revolutionary Organization (Organización Revolucionaria del Pueblo en Armas; ORPA)

Founded. 1971; militarily active after September 18, 1979

Membership. ca. 600

Leadership. Rodrigo Asturias Amado (alias Gaspar Ilom)

Status. Illegal

Auxiliary Organizations. Infiltrated FAR's CNUS and EGP's CUC (see below)

Publications. *Erupción* (irregular)

● Guerrilla Army of the Poor (Ejército Guerrillero de los Pobres; EGP)

Founded. January 1972, in Mexico; militarily active since 1979

Membership. ca. 700

Leader. Ricardo Ramírez de León (alias Rolando Morán)

Auxiliary and Front Organizations. Peasant Unity Committee (CUC); January 31st Popular Front (FP-31); Vicente Menchú Revolutionary Christians; Robin García Revolutionary Student Front (FERG). Most are now inactive or defunct.

Publications. *Compañero* (irregular, published abroad; sometimes translated into English; *Informador Guerrillero* (irregular)

● National Revolutionary Unity of Guatemala (Unidad Nacional Revolucionaria de Guatemala; URNG), an umbrella organization that includes FAR, ORPA, EGP and the National Leadership Nucleus faction of the PGT. The URNG has never succeeded in actually unifying the insurgent organizations, all of which continue to operate autonomously. The guerrillas' respective fronts, allied minor civilian groups of exiles, and other sympathetic groups, such as the Guatemalan Church in Exile, are more or less united under the political umbrella of the Representación Unitaria de la Oposición Guatemalteca (RUOG). RUOG's most prominent figures are Francisco Villagrán Kramer, a former vice president, Rigoberta Menchú, and Rolando Castillo. It operates largely out of Mexico, Nicaragua, and Cuba.

Founded. 7 February 1982

Publications. URNG distributes its propaganda through *Noticias de Guatemala* (in Mexico); the press agency CESGUA; the clandestine radio station La Voz Popular de Guatemala

Domestic Affairs. The year was marked by increased tensions between the government and elements of the military, largely regarding the issue of negotiations with the URNG. Some apparently new fissures have opened in the insurgent movement, and the army has maintained relative control of the military situation.

By far the most significant event of the year was the apparent attempted coup of 11 May, the origins and dimensions of which remain unclear. Immediately after the coup attempt there was much confusion, and many conflicting statements from both the presidential office and the military high command. The army's initial communiqué stated only that "certain acts of indiscipline" occurred in two of the country's 74 military zones: Jutiapa and Retalhuleu (*El Grafico*, 12 May). Defense Minister Héctor Gramajo reiterated that "we have had problems of indiscipline" at the same two bases, but blamed "radical civilians [who have] succeeded in winning over some officers who, out of ignorance, rebelled" (*FBIS-LAM*, 12 May). In contrast to such early attempts to minimize the importance of the episode, it was revealed on 31 May that three colonels—the commanders in Zacapa and Jutiapa, and the chief of the Air Force's Tactical Security Group—had all been dismissed; the director of the National Police was also eased out, and six officers were arrested (ibid., 1 June).

While the top military leadership understandably tried to minimize the role of the officers involved, President Cerezo also decided to put the blame on civilian politicians. Specifically, he publicly accused of complicity—and promised to put on trial—Gustavo Anzueta Vielman, a former presidential candidate of the conservative Nationalist Authentic Central (CAN), TV producer Mario David García, and Mario Castejón, another CAN leader (ibid., 19 May). The prospect of well-publicized political trials of officers and prominent politicians raised considerable fears, in addition to causing embarrassment. These concerns resulted in Decree no. 32-88, issued by the Guatemalan Congress on 23 June, giving amnesty to "all people who have committed any crime against domestic political order, public order, or social peace" through 23 June (*La Prensa Libre*, 24 June).

Foreign Affairs. 1988 has shown some uncertainty in Guatemalan foreign policy. On one hand, the Cerezo government continued making proclamations of friendship with the United States and demanding democratization in Nicaragua. Cerezo has also refused, almost blatantly, to adhere to some key provisions of the Arias Plan, such as substantive talks between the Guatemalan government and the URNG. On the other hand, Guatemala has taken a generally independent approach to a variety of issues and proclaimed its "active neutrality" on Central American issues.

Relations with Mexico have improved further during the year, as demonstrated by President Cerezo's visit to Mexico and by President-elect Carlos Salinas de Gortari's preinauguration trip to Guatemala City. The two problems dominating bilateral discussions were both related to the insurgency: the use of Mexican territory by URNG elements and the situation of some 40,000 Guatemalan refugees in the states of Chiapas, Campeche, and Quintana Roo. This population has been consistently (and to a large extent correctly) accused by Guatemala of serving as a support group for the guerrillas.

Regarding the first issue, Cerezo stated that "in the past Mexico has probably not shown much concern for controlling arms trafficking, but I believe this situation is changing because our country's stability is in Mexico's interests" (*La Prensa Libre*, 21 April). Regarding the second problem, efforts continued throughout the year to return the refugees to Guatemala, but with only limited success. The main difficulty remains the refugees' demand that the areas they would resettle be free of the army—a request clearly unacceptable to the military.

Previous contacts with Soviet and Cuban representatives yielded one concrete result when in March the Soviet news agency TASS and Cuba's Prensa Latina both opened offices in Guatemala City. This was the first form of official Soviet-bloc presence in the country since the fall of the Arbenz regime in 1954. The opening of the press offices seemed to be part of a governmental policy of broader contact with the Soviet bloc. The year also witnessed a trip to Cuba by the president's wife, and athletic and cultural exchanges.

The presence of communist journalists was greeted with considerable uneasiness and unhappiness by conservative political sectors and the military. Rumors were widespread that TASS correspondent Alexandr Trushin was a KGB operative trying to establish direct links with the PGT underground (*Insight*, 14 March). On 18 May, only one week after the attempted coup, the TASS offices as well as Trushin's residence and car were bombed and totally destroyed. No one was injured or killed. Responsibility for the bombing and the concomitant death threats against Prensa Latina's Manuel Guerrero Torres was assumed by the shadowy anticommunist organization ESA (Ejército Secreto Anticomunista). (*CSM*, 23 June.)

Probably acting under pressure from the military, the government promptly declared that it could no longer guarantee the safety of the two journalists; as a result both Trushin and Guerrero left the country (ibid.; also *Insight*, 20 June). Public Affairs Secretary Claudia Arenas declared that the correspondents' departure was only "temporary." The government, however, claimed that their presence "was bringing no benefits to the country," and Foreign Minister Alfonso Cabrera stated: "I always opposed the presence of TASS and Prensa Latina" (*FBIS-LAM*, 1 June). At the same time, a Guatemala City concert by the Moscow Symphony Orchestra was cancelled (*Index on Censorship*, October 1988).

Guerrilla Activities. In political terms, the Guatemalan revolutionary left's activities were dominated by two issues: the question of negotiations with the government, and the level of internal unity. The PGT seems to have moved toward a reconciliation between its two major factions, the "*camarilla*" led by General Secretary Carlos Gonzales and the National Leadership Nucleus led by Mario Sánchez. The best indication of the reconciliation was provided by the document entitled *Guatemala: For a National Dialogue and Genuine Peace with Respect for Human Dignity and Social Justice*, a joint statement of the Central Committee and the National Leadership of the PGT on the occasion of the party's 38th anniversary, published in the Soviet-sponsored *Information Bulletin* (January 1988).

The document has several significant implications. One is that the Soviets themselves have decided to recognize both factions, and probably put pressure on them to show unity. Another is that the *"camarilla"* faction under Gonzales is, in fact, the leadership group in exile, while the National Leadership is in control of the party's underground in Guatemala. The apparent reconciliation also implied *"camarilla"* support for the URNG strategy of negotiations: "We Guatemalan communists wholeheartedly uphold the principled statements and proposals by the National Revolutionary Unity of Guatemala on talks with the government and a national dialogue; we believe it to be the only road leading to peace . . . We are urging all Guatemalan parties . . . to abandon political and ideological sectarian attitudes" (ibid.). Furthermore, an even more important indication of the *"camarilla"* faction's change of mind is the fact that, instead of dismissing the URNG (see *YICA*, 1988), it explicitly accepted it as "the military-political vanguard of the revolutionary movement in our country" (ibid.). Finally, the document—signed by both Gonzales and Sánchez—made the interesting remark: "We have much regard for the activities of the Latin American Contadora Group and the Support Group which together with Nicaragua's courageous and able diplomacy have deterred direct military aggression by the U.S. against that sister country" (ibid.).

Little doubt exists that Soviet (and probably Cuban and Nicaraguan) pressures brought about the reconciliation between the major PGT factions and between the party and the URNG, as well as a consensus on negotiations with the government. At the same time, however, the extreme left was moving in the opposite direction. The radical elements that formerly constituted the IXIM movement (see *YICA*, 1987), and that have plagued the established Marxist-Leninist groups in Guatemala since the late 1970s, have remained intransigent. In October they formed a shadowy new group: The Frente Central de Resistencia-Partido Guatemalteco del Trabajo (FCR-PGT; Central Resistance Front-Guatemalan Party of Labor). The very name of the group suggests that it was formed by the same elements that previously split from the PGT under the name of the Military Commission, in alliance with ex-IXIM members who had previously left the EGP, the ORPA, or the FAR origins.

All that is known about the FCR-PGT comes from a document made public on 3 November,

entitled "Justice for the People is Only Possible with a Weapon in Our Hands." The document described the bombing and arson of public-transportation vehicles as "a warning [to those] who are prepared to negotiate the definition of the people's revolutionary war through conciliatory gestures with our enemies, sponsoring dialogues for a surrender and underestimating the people's hopes for their liberation—which is expressed in the armed struggle" (*El Gráfico*, 4 November). The document also claimed credit for the destruction on 26 October of buses owned by "war criminal" Manuel de Jesús Valiente Tellez (ibid.).

A "Constitutional Declaration" was published at the same time by the "Popular Revolutionary Commandos," apparently a *nom de guerre* of the FCR-PGT. It accused the URNG leadership of pursuing "the road of the bourgeois democracy, [and] executing the plans and policies of imperialism," while claiming that "armed conflict is the only possible way to achieve the revolutionary triumph" (*Central America Report*, 21 October).

In military terms, the PGT remained as marginal as ever. Its most significant action of the year was a brief takeover of Radio Festival by four commandos seeking to make a 5-minute-long pro-PGT broadcast (*FBIS-LAM*, 22 July). The intransigent FCR-PGT was also irrelevant, with the sabotage on 26 October its only action known by the end of the year.

The three major guerrilla groups continued to pursue a low-level, geographically limited strategy of attacks against small military outposts. The targets are generally and increasingly concentrated in the departments of San Marcos, El Petén, Sololá, and Quiché. The first and last are traditional strongholds of the EGP; the second, of FAR; and the third, of ORPA. All but Sololá are Mexican border areas, marginal in military, political, and economic terms. This fact gives credibility to Defense Minister Héctor Gramajo's claim in November that "the guerrillas are really small armed groups that are still sowing terror in the most remote areas of the country, including isolated hamlets" (*FBIS-LAM*, 22 November). The total number of guerrillas remains hard to establish with any precision, but there are clear indications that it does not exceed 3,000. In fact, "Pablo Monsanto" himself put the figure at 3,000 (*FBIS-LAM*, 14 September), and his colleague "Gaspar Ilom" at 3,000–3,500 (*Latin America Regional Reports*, 9 June). The official figure given by the military is 1,000. President Cerezo claims that the number is 700 (*FBIS-LAM*, 26 August), while respected independent sources estimate it at 1,200–1,500 (*LAT*, 29 August).

The declining strength of the guerrillas in general, and of ORPA in particular, was spectacularly demonstrated by the growing number of civilians murdered as reprisals against collaboration with the military. Two tenant farmers were murdered by ORPA in Suchitepequez and 40 kidnapped in Sacatepequez on 2 November (*FBIS-LAM*, 4 November). In the year's most brutal episode, 22 peasants were tortured and strangled by ORPA at El Aguacate, in Sololá, on 24 November (*NYT*, 3 December). The El Aguacate episode was particularly significant since all the victims were friends or relatives of the local military commissioner, who had himself been kidnapped and murdered two days before; their murder clearly suggested growing guerrilla frustration and anger at the hostility of the population.

Despite such realities, the Ixil—the only major Indian group to ever seriously and massively support the guerrillas (especially the EGP)—seem to have retained some loyalty to the left. That is the best explanation of the fact that of all URNG (read EGP) actions in 1988, the largest and most damaging (in terms of army casualties) took place in the Ixcán area. Three soldiers were killed in La Resurección on 17 September. In Cabá and in Amachel on 9 September, a total of twelve military personnel were wounded or killed. Fighting also took place in Tercer Pueblo and El Toro in October. All this action occurred in the Ixcán region (*Central America Report*, 21 October).

While FAR continued its pinprick attacks in El Petén, ORPA was badly weakened in Sololá by the army's 1987 offensive there (see *YICA*, 1988). The latter group has managed to remain marginally active in and around some communities surrounding Lake Atitlán. The army, for its part, continued to combine massive offensives (such as "Fortaleza 88" in March–April) with relentless pressure from armed civilian patrols. The left's hopes that the Cerezo government would neutralize the civilian forces were put to rest when the president emphatically stated, "We are not going to disband the patrols. It would be a mistake not to use such a major organization for positive purposes" (*FBIS-LAM*, 22 April).

The overall strategy of the insurgents seems to have only a limited relationship to their weak military position in relation to the government. It remains centered on public proclamations of the insurgents' intentions to reach a negotiated settlement, while low-level attacks continue in an attempt to recover from the defeats of the last few years. On the extreme right, the military opposition is openly showing itself to be unhappy and uneasy with the idea of negotiations; the conservative civilian opposition is even more vocal. The more liberal elements of the ruling Christian Democratic Party (DCG), along with university and "human rights" groups and some elements of the media, tend to support talks at any cost. The president is caught between these conflicting pressures and has tried to placate both sides. Foreign Minister Cabrera, seeking the DCG presidential nomination for 1990, also has attempted to straddle these diametrically opposed views regarding negotiations. Cabrera, who is the Christian Democrats' party leader, was also forced to admit that the insurgents are recruiting members of his own party "so they can later make this known and compromise our party and the government." (*FBIS-LAM*, 4 November.)

The result of such contrasting considerations was a year-long public-relations, diplomatic, and political minuet that yielded little for any side (although the URNG did make some significant, if temporary, political inroads). Indeed, URNG could point out that its "peace offensive" has resulted in three events that have provided it with a previously unheard-of degree of domestic and international legitimacy.

The first, and potentially the most important in domestic terms, was the government's acceptance of a visit to Guatemala by prominent RUOG leaders, including Rigoberta Menchú and Rolando Castillo, on 18 April. Clearly, at least as far as the URNG-RUOG were concerned, the visit was to be a full-dress rehearsal for an attempt to insert its fronts into the legitimate political system of Guatemala, in the same fashion that the FDR has entered the arena in El Salvador. Significantly, the visit, disguised as an attempt to verify the conditions for the return of refugees, took place at the very moment an Inter-Parliamentary Union delegation was also visiting the country; this increased the pressure on the government to see to it that the visit yielded positive results. The army, however, arrested the visitors for a few hours anyway, ostensibly in order to "verify their status" (*Insight*, 23 May), but in fact to make its disapproval obvious. "Death squad" machinations, political opponents of the government, and pressures from the army soon forced the visitors to depart in haste. There seems to be no chance that members of RUOG fronts will be accepted as legitimate actors in the country's political arena anytime soon.

The URNG leaders, including "Monsanto," "Ilom," and Morán, have managed to take advantage of the Arias Plan to increase their own international exposure, mostly by obtaining access to President Oscar Arias of Costa Rica and—for the first time publicly—Daniel Ortega of Nicaragua. The first meeting with Ortega was a diplomatic coup for the URNG; the second legitimized what was an open secret in Central America for years: that the URNG leaders were frequent residents of Managua, and received political, diplomatic, and other forms of aid from Nicaragua. In the political atmosphere generated by the Arias Plan, Guatemala City found it difficult to complain about such political inroads by URNG-RUOG.

Less important, perhaps, to URNG's strategy— while also much trickier and far less successful— were its attempts to establish a "dialogue" with Guatemala City. In fact, at every turn of those negotiations, military and conservative political opposition forced the Cerezo government to be reluctant, cautious, and noncommittal. Such a stance was further prompted by URNG's attempts to combine purely political questions with military questions under the general rubric of "negotiations."

At the military level, the URNG tried throughout the year to obtain cease-fire agreements that, by easing the government's military pressure, would allow URNG to resume mobilization and recruiting. On 3 January, a military spokesman made it clear that an URNG offer of a "truce" for the 1987 Christmas holidays was unacceptable, "because there cannot be any agreements with armed groups" (*FBIS-LAM*, 4 January). On 28 February, the URNG representative in Hamburg, Francisco Mendizabal, offered another cease-fire and a "humanization" of the war (ibid., 1 March). Similarly, nothing came of this appeal. On 23 March the Guatemalan government rejected URNG's cease-fire proposal for Easter because, as Vinicio Cerezo stated, "we are not at war here." Presidential spokesman Julio Santos further illuminated the government's opinion of the insurgents, saying that they "are represented by small groups that have already been annihilated in battle" (ibid., 25 March). As a rule, URNG attempts to stop the war at its convenience were coldly rebuffed by the Guatemalan military.

As far as other political negotiations were concerned, the URNG tried to engage in discussion Central American organizations like Costa Rica's CEDEP (Center for Political Studies), to which it offered a meeting to describe its views of Guatemalan realities (*FBIS-LAM*, 14 March). The results remain to be seen, but such efforts are highly unlikely to alter the Guatemalan government's position.

Thus, despite URNG's calls for equality in participation, the government seemed resolved to accept only those URNG members or leaders showing "a clear sign of [their] willingness to incorporate and participate in the political life of the country." The government promised that such members or leaders would "not be physically repressed, nor persecuted legally" (*Latin American Regional Reports*, 5 May).

In formal keeping with its promises at Esquipulas, the government announced in April that it was prepared to have the National Reconciliation Commission (CRN) meet the URNG leaders under the conditions set forth above. At the same time, four political parties, including the two largest (DCG and the National Center Union) also offered to talk to the insurgents about "humanizing" the conflict. The first and last direct meeting of the year between the CRN and the URNG took place in Costa Rica on 23 August. The guerrillas were represented by all three of their major leaders (Morán, "Ilom," and "Monsanto"), all of whom insisted on direct negotiations with the government. The communiqué issued at the end of the meeting stated the obvious fact that "the CRN is not a mediator, a negotiator, nor a representative of any of the parties involved and . . . its actions are completely independent" (*FBIS-LAM*, 25 August).

Commenting after the meeting, "Monsanto" reiterated the guerrillas' demand for direct talks as well as for a number of "guarantees," including a 90-day truce in advance of such talks and measures to "humanize" the war (ibid.). Those measures are supposed to include the treatment of captured guerrillas as prisoners of war, "respect for civilians," and access for humanitarian groups to "war victims." Beyond such lofty rhetoric, however, the demands also included: (1) government recognition of the URNG as a legitimate participant in a civil war; (2) legal tolerance of the insurgents' supporters; and (3) access by the insurgents to foreign aid—all unrealistic proposals with no reasonable chance of ever being accepted by the Guatemalan military.

Michael Radu
Foreign Policy Research Institute, Philadelphia

Guyana

Population. 765,796
Party. People's Progressive Party (PPP); Working People's Alliance (WPA)
Founded. PPP: 1950; WPA: organized 1973, became formal party in 1979
Membership. PPP: 100 leaders and several hundred militants above non-Marxist rank and file; WPA: 30 leaders (both estimated)
General Secretary. PPP: Cheddi Jagan
Leadership. PPP, 9-member party secretariat elected August 1988: Cheddi Jagan, general secretary; Janet Jagan, executive secretary; Harry Persaud Nitka, organization secretary; Shree Chand, finance secretary; Clinton Collymore, information and publicity secretary; Feroze Mohamed, education secretary; Donald Ramotar, membership secretary; Clement Rohee, international secretary; Pariag Sukhai, mass organization secretary. WPA, 17-member collective leadership body announced May 1988: Eusi Kwayana, Moses Bhagwan, Andaiye, Rupert Roopnarine, Clive Thomas, Karen De Souza, Wazir Mohamed, Tacuma Ogunseye, Josh Ramsammy, Nigel Westmass, Ameer Mohamed, Stanley Humphrey, Bissoon Rajkumar, Danuta Radzik, Eric La Rose, Kassim Kamaludin, Vanda Radzik
Status. Legal but occasionally harassed
Last Congress. PPP: Twenty-third, 30 July–1 August 1988
Last Election. 9 December 1985. PPP: 45,926 votes, 16.84 percent, 8 of 53 seats in National Assembly. WPA: 4,176 votes, 1 seat in National Assembly
Auxiliary Organizations. PPP: Progressive Youth Organization (PYO), Women's Progressive Organization (WPO), Guyana Agricultural Workers' Union (GAWU)
Publications. PPP: *Mirror* (weekly), *Thunder* (quarterly); WPA: *Dayclean* and *Open Word* (weeklies)

Under the leadership of President Hugh Desmond Hoyte, the ruling People's National Congress (PNC) maintained in 1988 the two-track policy approach initiated in 1986 in both domestic and foreign affairs. New domestic and foreign policy adjustments, chiefly in the economic sphere, brought further improvement in relations with the private sector, Western nations, and the International Monetary Fund (IMF). At the same time, ties with the Eastern bloc and Third World radical states established during the rule of the late Forbes Burnham (1964–1985) were actively maintained.

Economic liberalization, however, continued to be unmatched by domestic political opening. While allowing a controlled relaxation of media restrictions for the benefit of the private sector, the PNC maintained its authoritarian grip on the government and all repressive sectors of the state. But because Moscow, Washington, and their respective allies remained generally sanguine about Hoyte's effort to revive a destitute economy through increased Western engagement, and because the West appeared willing to overlook the absence of domestic democratization, the Moscow-line PPP and the democratic-socialist WPA remained sidelined and with little leverage as the reign of the minority-backed PNC entered its 25th year.

Having declared 1988 the "year of staying resolutely on course," Hoyte finally made public in February that the primary goal of his government's economic adjustment program was to secure a debt-restructuring agreement with the IMF and World Bank (*Caribbean Insight*, February). Formal discussions with the two bodies began in April, based on a draft policy document submitted by the government the previous year. According to financial sources in Guyana, a "shadow IMF program" had actually been in place since 1987 (ibid., June), lending credibility to longstanding charges by the PPP and WPA that the government had been secretly negotiating for a deal.

In May, during meetings with potential investors in London and Brussels, Hoyte expressed confidence that an agreement would be in place by September (ibid.). At the end of the year, however, negotiations continued to drag on, with Hoyte's economic team scrambling to find a point of balance between the IMF's austerity requirements and escalating opposition from the labor sector. And while the PPP and WPA were able to derive some political capital from the government's clash with the unions, Hoyte appeared more concerned with the maneuvering among still powerful PNC hard-liners who signaled increasing skepticism over his ability to deliver an IMF package without undermining the PNC's hold on the country.

Assessing the actual threat of PNC hard-liners to Hoyte's control of the party (and therefore of the government) remained difficult, but Hoyte was sure to be flashing this card at the IMF in order to secure a deal as soon as possible in 1989. Another concern was that the unprecedented October split in the previously PNC-dominated Trade Union Congress (TUC) would add to the IMF's apparent hesitation. Because Hoyte had staked his administration on the IMF strategy, further delay in 1989 would strengthen the position of Hamilton Green, Hoyte's chief rival in the PNC and, as prime minister, the government's second-ranking official.

While Hoyte was busy abroad, Green spent 1988 expanding his base within the PNC party machinery, particularly among the hard-line and Marxist elements that formed the political base of former leader Burnham (*Caribbean Insight*, November). In an interview following Hoyte's trip to Europe, Green rejected the notion that Guyana was replacing socialism as enshrined in the 1980 constitution with private enterprise, stating, "It is our view that at this stage the private sector can play a more dynamic role" (AP, 13 July).

Although Hoyte was concerned by the delay in securing an IMF package, he could point to other foreign-policy achievements in his effort to win Western support. His September meeting with President Reagan in Washington capped an extended diplomatic effort that resulted in Guyana being designated a beneficiary of the U.S. Caribbean Basin Initiative (CBI). Earlier, during a successful May visit to London and Brussels to promote Western interest in a liberalized foreign investment code, Hoyte was received by Prime Ministers Thatcher and Martens. By the end of the year, he had also initiated or expanded joint economic ventures, both public and private, with Canada, Japan, Jamaica, Venezuela, and the European Community (EC).

On the other side of the international relations ledger, Guyana maintained—and in some cases increased—ties with the Eastern bloc and with revolutionary states and movements in the Third World. The second visit in twelve months by a special Soviet economic delegation was reciprocated by a Guyanese delegation to Moscow in mid-1988 to finalize details of expanded Soviet participation in Guyana's state-run bauxite industry (CANA, 24 April; *FBIS-LAT*, 27 April). In April, Hoyte received a delegation of Soviet parliamentarians led by A.A. Mokanu, deputy chairman of the USSR Supreme Soviet Presidium, who "expressed confidence that bilateral ties between the USSR and Guyana will develop on a stable and mutually advantageous basis" (*Izvestiia*, 22 April).

In August, a Guyanese delegation led by Foreign Minister Rashleigh Jackson was received in East Berlin by SED General Secretary Erich Honecker. Meetings were also held with Foreign Minister Oskar Fischer and Chairman of the GDR Council of Ministers Willi Stoph. Honecker and Jackson "welcomed the excellent level achieved in bilateral relations," and noted that "the far-reaching agreement of both states on the basic questions of our time forms a favorable basis for strengthening them even more" (ADN International Service, 31 August; *FBIS-EEU*, 1 September).

In 1988, the PNC government also maintained both economic and political ties with Cuba. Following the thirteenth session of the Joint Cuban-Guyanese Economic, Technical and Cultural Commission held in Havana in January, a series of protocols for increased trade and technical cooperation were signed for 1988. In October, a PNC delegation led by Labor Minister Seerum Prashad was received in Havana by Jorge Risquet Valdés, member of the Politburo of the Communist Party of Cuba. After signing a new cooperation protocol between the two political parties, a joint statement was made noting the "exemplary nature of the ties which the PNC of Guyana and the Communist Party of Cuba have maintained for over fifteen years" (Havana Television Service, 14 October; *FBIS-LAT*, 17 October).

According to diplomatic sources in Guyana, an official invitation was issued during the Havana meeting for Hoyte to visit Cuba, but that Hoyte was hesitant to respond while the United States was still mulling over Guyana's request for designation as a CBI beneficiary (*Stabroek News*, 12 October). Hamilton Green may or may not have been seeking to undermine Hoyte when he lauded Cuban assistance to Guyana in an interview with the Cuban newspaper *Granma* a few weeks later (*Granma*, international edition, 13 November). But in late November, with entry into the CBI guaranteed, Hoyte appeared to seize the opportunity provided by a fire in Havana to shore up his personal ties with Fidel Castro. In a publicized message, he stated, "I assure you, my brother, of my own profound sympathy and concern, as well as that of the Government and people of Guyana, at the loss sustained as a result of this tragedy" (CANA, 25 November; *FBIS-LAT*, 28 November).

In February, during a visit by a Palestine Liberation Organization (PLO) delegation to George-town, PNC sources confirmed that the government would allow the PLO to establish an embassy in Guyana (AFP, 17 February; *FBIS-LAT*, 19 February). The sources stated that the embassy would have a chargé d'affaires and a nonresident ambassador. By the end of the year, however, there had been no official announcement.

PPP Domestic Views and Activities. The PPP held its 23rd Party Congress from 30 July to 1 August. The husband-and-wife team of Cheddi Jagan, who had founded the party in 1950, and Janet Jagan retained the top party leadership, general secretary and executive secretary, respectively. The new party secretariat featured only some minor shuffling of familiar faces.

The preparation of the new party platform revealed that the PPP was far from resolving the contradictions in its confrontation with the Hoyte-led PNC. At its previous congress in August 1985, the PPP had resolved to seek the formation of a "national front government" incorporating the PNC, the WPA, and itself. But after the fraudulent December 1985 elections, the PPP entered into the Patriotic Coalition for Democracy (PCD) with the WPA and three tiny centrist parties—the Democratic Labor Party (DLP), the National Democratic Front (NDF), and the People's Democratic Movement (PDM). The coalition was formed to pressure the PNC for electoral reform and a chance to defeat the PNC at the ballot box. At the 1988 party congress the PPP was still attempting, without success, to juggle the two initiatives.

On the one hand, Cheddi Jagan declared, "Socialism is the thing of the future." His call for a "people's government" to implement it emerged as a rehash of the old national-front proposal. On the other hand, the 1988 party platform called for "the restoration of political democracy," and increased pressure on the government for electoral reform by the PCD. (*Stabroek News*, 6 August.) The Marxist-Leninist PPP therefore remained snarled in the contradictory strategy of threatening the PNC with the stick of representative democracy in order to achieve its long-held objective, a share of the power in a nondemocratic government.

Hoyte continued in 1988 to easily exploit this contradiction as well as the ideological contradictions within the PCD. Each time the PPP emphasized the electoral reform initiative of the coalition, the PNC invited the PPP to take part in separate party-to-party talks. And each time, lured by the

prospect of cutting a deal, Jagan would agree to meet. Inevitably, Jagan would come away with nothing and the inherently unstable PCD, which the government consistently refused to recognize, would be weakened further.

The pattern repeated itself most clearly at the time of the PPP's party congress. News reports emanating from the gathering suggested that the PPP was "favorably inclined" to contesting the next scheduled election in 1990 on a joint PCD platform. Indeed, the PPP had resolved, "The PCD must become the democratic alternative to the PNC minority rule." But when pressed by the media at the end of the congress, Jagan stated that no decision on electoral alliances had been made, announcing in the next breath that the PPP had accepted the PNC's latest invitation for talks in three days. (*Stabroek News*, 6 August.)

Praise for the Soviet Union's *glasnost'* and *perestroika* initiatives in the PPP's party platform added irony to contradiction. When Hoyte in 1985 began leading Guyana away from the rigid "anti-imperialism" of Forbes Burnham and toward increased engagement with the West, the PPP had hoped that Moscow would finally give it full support against the PNC. By 1988, however, it was obvious that the Hoyte project was in essence a Third World version of the Gorbachev project that the PPP was hailing. And as in the Soviet Union, Hoyte's project did not include any plans for deviating from one-party rule. Further, the Soviet Union's support for Hoyte's project meant that, just as in the days of Burnham, Moscow was content to leave its fraternal party squawking on the sidelines.

The official CPSU greeting to the PPP's party congress left little doubt that Moscow was satisfied with the status quo in Guyana. The congratulations were perfunctory, and praise for the PPP was limited to acknowledging the party's "great contribution to the cause of ridding its country of colonial domination," that is, independence from Great Britain, an event that happened over two decades ago (*Pravda*, 30 July). The CPSU also saw fit to send to the congress a low-level delegation that, moreover, kept a low profile during its stay (*Pravda*, 28 July and 9 August).

If the PPP was hoping that it might receive firmer support from the GDR because of friction between Gorbachev and Honecker over *glasnost'/perestroika*, the prospect diminished during the party congress, and evaporated with the SED's warm reception in East Berlin of Guyanese foreign minister Rashleigh Jackson a few weeks later. Honecker's official message to the PPP congress was limited to "fraternal greetings" and "satisfaction" that ties between the two parties remained close (*Neues Deutschland*, 30–31 July). The SED delegation to the congress actually gathered more interest when it met with PNC deputy party chief Ranji Chandisingh for discussions on nuclear disarmament before returning to the GDR (ibid., 5 August).

Despite itself, and despite the lack of allied international support, the PPP was given an opportunity at the end of 1988 to make some headway against the PNC in the labor sector. The PPP's labor arm is the GAWU, the sugar workers union. Despite being one of the largest unions in the country, the GAWU has never been strong enough to take on the PNC government by itself. And because the PNC has effectively controlled the 24-member Trade Union Congress (TUC) to which the GAWU belongs, no GAWU strike has received support from other unions.

In 1988, however, PNC control of the TUC began to break down. For the Guyanese labor force, Hoyte's economic liberalization meant lower real wages because of the 1987 currency devaluation and retrenchment as the PNC sought to scale back public spending. By the end of 1987, many TUC members, including unions traditionally coopted by the PNC, began to balk. The PNC responded in February by unilaterally amending the 1980 constitution to remove the legal right of unions to participate in the government's decisionmaking process (*Latin American Regional Reports: Caribbean*, 31 March). The measure led to the first split in the TUC in twenty years.

At the annual TUC conference in October, seven unions walked out. While constituting a minority of the organizations in the TUC, these unions represented approximately half the Guyanese labor force. And while the GAWU was one of the seven, it was actually the previously docile public-service workers that led the walkout. The seven unions formed an independent federation in November.

The PNC response was intimidation and verbal attack directed at the GAWU, denouncing it as a PPP instrument for sabotaging the TUC and therefore the PNC's IMF negotiations. The strategy seemed to fit the longstanding PNC pattern of seeking Western support, in this case an IMF package, by portraying its chief opposition as Marxist-led. By the end of the year, however, the strategy seemed to be backfiring. The other six unions were less concerned with the IMF than they were with the return of union rights. Their resentment at being attacked for their association with the PPP only diminished the prospect for reconciliation with the TUC, a development not unnoticed by IMF negotiators who appeared more concerned than impressed by the PNC's labor policy.

The question at the beginning of 1989 was whether the PPP would be able to take advantage of the GAWU's membership in a new and potentially powerful labor federation. Its continued failure to formulate a coherent strategy in the political sphere, however, particularly in its relations with the other opposition parties in the PCD, did not bode well.

PPP International Views and Activities. In June, Cheddi Jagan represented the PPP in Panama at the third assembly of the Anti-Imperialist Organization of Central America and the Caribbean. The organization, consisting of dozens of left-wing and Marxist political organizations from around the Caribbean Basin, was founded in Havana in 1984. The assembly was greeted by Gen. Manuel Antonio Noriega, Panamanian military chief, and joined him in condemning the "U.S. doctrine of aggression." Jagan was elected the new chairman of the coordinating committee of the organization at the close of the meeting. (Havana Tele-Rebelde Network, 23 June; *FBIS-LAT*, 23 June.)

Jagan was scheduled to represent the PPP in Montevideo at the third meeting of the Communist Parties of South America (*La Hora*, 9 August; *FBIS-LAT*, 18 August). The PPP had been present at the first two meetings. Jagan canceled his attendance, however, when Hoyte and the PNC offered to meet with the PPP on the same date as the Montevideo meeting, 9 August.

As he has usually done, Jagan traveled to Moscow in the month after the PPP's party congress. He was received by Anatoly Dobrynin, then chief of the CPSU Central Committee's international department. Jagan reportedly informed Dobrynin about the PPP's recent congress, and the "tasks which the party is resolving in its work among Guyana's working people." On the subject of international relations, Jagan "voiced full support for the new thinking" in Soviet foreign policy. It was further reported that Dobrynin briefed Jagan on the progress of *perestroika* in the Soviet Union. (*Pravda*, 11 September.)

In November, Jagan traveled to New York where he was received by the CPUSA. He recited the PPP's standard rejection of the IMF, advocating that indebted countries either suspend payments or, at a minimum, follow the lead of Peru and Zambia by limiting interest payments to less than 10 percent of export earnings. (*People's Daily World*, 16 November.)

WPA Domestic Views and Activities. In 1987, the party began a campaign, led by the WPA's sole member in the National Assembly, Eusi Kwayana, for an inquest into the 1980 bombing death of historian and WPA founder, Walter Rodney. By 1988, the WPA had succeeded in getting a degree of support for its effort from other countries in the English-speaking Caribbean. Rodney's reputation in the region and Hoyte's stated desire to mend ties with the Caribbean Community (Caricom) provided leverage.

The PNC government finally held the inquest in February. After two weeks, however, and after setting aside significant portions of the evidence prepared by the WPA, the coroner announced a verdict of "accident or misadventure." The verdict was rejected by the WPA, which described the hearings as "a demonstration inquest to get it out of the way and for the record." (*Caribbean Insight*, March.)

On the political front, the WPA spent the year unsuccessfully pressing the government on electoral reform and democratization. Although the PNC was not bound to hold elections until December 1990, the WPA feared that Hoyte would hold a fraudulent snap election in order to manufacture a mandate for his IMF policy. At a meeting of the party's collegial leadership in May, the WPA denounced the government's "shortsighted" economic policy that "put the question of democracy in Guyana on the backburner." The party's statement concluded by reiterating its call for negotiations on "democratization" between the government and the five opposition parties of the PCD. (*Stabroek News*, 4 June.)

Within the PCD, the WPA's position in relation to the PPP became more strained. Having been embarrassed in 1987 after its secret talks with the PPP were exposed by the government-controlled press, the WPA distanced itself from the PPP in 1988. It became increasingly critical of the PPP's willingness to accept talks with the government while the government was refusing to acknowledge the PCD. In September, the WPA finally demanded that both the PPP and PNC give a full accounting of their on-and-off discussion (*Stabroek News*, 9 September). When both parties refused, the already high level of distrust within the PCD increased, and slim prospects for forming an electoral alliance from the coalition decreased further.

WPA International Views and Activities. Frustrated on the domestic front, the WPA and the small centrist parties of the PCD tried to solicit external support for their democratization cause.

In July, the PCD issued a statement expressing its disappointment over the lack of support from Caricom leaders for its call for talks with the government on democratization (*Stabroek News*, 9 July). But the democracies of Caricom remained hesitant to pressure the Hoyte government, especially as it appeared that Hoyte remained willing to improve the regional relations disrupted under Burnham.

In November, the PCD sent a public letter to the chairman of the United Nations Commission on Human Rights requesting an extraordinary meeting. It informed the chairman that it was seeking support for free and fair elections, and backing for its proposal to hold an "International Convention on Democracy" in Guyana in 1989 (*Stabroek News*, 30 November). While the commission acknowledged receipt of the letter, no concrete response had been given by the end of the year.

At the end of 1987, Eusi Kwayana had represented the WPA at a meeting in Caracas of the Latin American Committee of the Socialist International. The WPA had been admitted as a "consultive member" of the Socialist International in 1986. At the Caracas meeting, Kwayana successfully solicited support for the PCD's request for multiparty discussions on electoral reform (CANA, 17 December; *FBIS-LAT*, 18 December). The committee met twice in 1988, in Brazil and Santo Domingo, but the WPA did not send a representative to either meeting, probably prevented from doing so by a lack of resources.

Douglas W. Payne
Freedom House, New York

Haiti

Population. 6,295,570
Party. Unified Party of Haitian Communists (Parti Unifié des Communistes Haïtiens; PUCH)
Founded. 1934 (PUCH, 1968)
Membership. 350 (estimated)
General Secretary. René Théodore

Politburo. René Théodore, Max Bourjolly, Gérard Joseph (?)
Status. Legal since 1985; in the open in Haiti with the return of Théodore in March 1986
Last Congress. 1979 (first)
Last Election 29 November 1987, canceled; 17 January 1988, boycotted
Auxiliary Organizations. No data
Publications. Publications in French and Creole: account of first congress in 1978; explanations about PUCH

The PUCH continued to march the long road toward legitimacy in the context of strong anticommunist sentiment carefully nurtured by the Duvalier family from 1957 to 1986. Although René Théodore, the 48-year-old general secretary, ran for president in the elections of 29 November 1987 that were canceled at the last minute, he boycotted the elections of 17 January 1988, along with most other candidates. He then continued to criticize the military, widely believed to have staged and manipulated the elections, until the military coup of 18 September 1988, after which Gen. Prosper Avril replaced Gen. Henri Namphey. Théodore and the number two leader of the party, Max Bourjolly, traveled to Europe and in the Caribbean to promote the party.

No other leaders were presented to the public, and during the author's visit to party headquarters in December 1988, the person in charge of "external relations" said that other party officials' names would not be revealed for the time being. The reason may be simply a matter of personal safety, since PUCH has feared an attack from the military or the barely disguised former Tontons Macoute.

Party headquarters, a prominent building near the center of Port-au-Prince, are better equipped, staffed, and organized than they were in 1986, when the author last visited them. Documents in French and Creole are available; they include the "Manifesto Program" of September 1978, an account of the first party congress, and the statutes of the party in French; and an explanation of the communist cell in Creole. According to party statutes, a prospective member must be introduced by someone who is already a member, but the author saw membership forms in Creole that people merely filled in, it seemed, to become a member. Judging by its headquarters, PUCH is one of the most dynamic among the more than a dozen serious parties in Haiti. Visitors were required to carry a slip of paper indicating whom they were visiting in order to be allowed to enter the offices; the personnel of PUCH headquarters issued a petition calling for the arrest of some notables alleged to be Macoutes; books on Marxism-Leninism were available in a small library; and a receptionist cheerfully welcomed visitors, asking, however, if they belonged to a sister or brother communist party in the United States or elsewhere.

There are no PUCH offices outside Port-au-Prince. Books to be used to set up a library in Cap Haïtien, the country's second largest city, were stolen, but in answer to the question about the existence of a cadre school, the spokesperson said there were regular seminars in the provinces. Plans are also apparently being made for the second party congress, which will permit the party to publish their new plans for a new Haiti.

Thus far, PUCH has adopted a very pragmatic approach to Haiti's problems based on a few doctrinal principles, at the center of which is a strident and consistent anti-Americanism. In addition to the predictable claim that the United States should be blamed for most of the evil afflicting Haiti under the Duvalier family and their immediate successor, Gen. Henri Namphey, the PUCH opposed American efforts to extradite Col. Jean-Claude Paul, alleged international drug dealer, appealing to primary nationalist sentiments.

On 29 November 1988, the first anniversary of the violence that prevented the first presidential and legislative elections from taking place, René Théodore blamed foreigners, mainly the United States, for the violence. In an interview with an East German newspaper, the general secretary said Haiti had never been free of foreign control: After colonialism came neo-colonialism and foreign occupation (*Neues Deutschland*, 19 April). He traveled to Cuba, Hungary, USSR, Bulgaria, Germany, and elsewhere to speak about these and other themes.

After the September 1988 coup by General Avril, the PUCH suddenly seemed to make its peace with the government, as did other parties and foreign embassies. Théodore met with the president for two hours and said he hoped for the best under the new military regime. For this meeting and his statement, he was condemned as an opportunist by the leading labor federation, CATH (Centrale Autonome des Travailleurs Haïtiens: Autonomous Central of Haitian Workers). PUCH has also called for a popular-front government or, specifically, a "People's Democratic Front" or broad alliance that would eventually replace military rule.

Thus, for many observers PUCH is very much in

the mainstream of leftist established parties in Haiti. Other movements are called "extremist" and "radical," but not the communists. These other movements include some consisting of parish priests and their followers who are inspired by liberation theology, some peasant movements, and various ad hoc organizations. The most popular single figure proposing an as yet poorly defined radical change for Haiti is Father Jean Bertrand Aristide, who was expelled from the order of Salesian Fathers in December.

Important intelletuals returning from exile such as Dr. Gérard Pierre-Charles and Dr. Suzy Castor created the Centre de Recherches et Formation Economiques et Sociales pour le Développement (CRESFED), and they have started to publish important political and economic studies that should be useful for PUCH and many other groups and parties as well. Dr. Castor's book on the U.S. occupation of Haiti (1915–1934) has been translated from the Spanish into French and published in Port-au-Prince. The theme of that occupation and the contention that the United States might invade again are growing in importance, as is the symbol of Charlemagne Péralte, leader of a resistance movement against the U.S. forces. Péralte is being used by many movements as a symbol of Haitian pride and resistance to outside control. He now appears on Haitian coins, and his image carved in wood is sold in the market places of Port-au-Prince.

PUCH has not received permission to begin broadcasting over its own radio station despite its request. It has a regular two-hour-long Saturday broadcast over the privately owned Radio-Caraïbe.

Brian Weinstein
Howard University

Honduras

Population. 4,972,287
Major Marxist-Leninist Organizations

• Communist Party of Honduras (Partido Comunista de Honduras; PCH)
  Founded. 1927, dismantled by 1932, re-established 1954

Membership. Probably less than 100 permanent cadres in the country
General Secretary. Rigoberto Padilla Rush
Status. Illegal
Last Congress. Fourth, January 1986
Publications. *Vanguardia Revolucionaria*; *Voz Popular* (both irregular, published abroad)

• Revolutionary Party of Central American Workers (Partido Revolucionario de los Trabajadores de Centro America; PRTC)
  Founded. 1976 in Costa Rica, as Honduran branch of regional party; became independent in 1979
  Membership. Probably less than 100
  Leadership. Wilfredo Gallardo Museli
  Status. Illegal
  Last Congress. No data
  Publications. No data

• Morazanist Front for the Liberation of Honduras (Frente Morazanista para la Liberación de Honduras; FMLH)
  Founded. 1969 claimed, but was inactive until 1980. Reactivated with direct input and leadership from the Salvadoran Popular Liberation Forces
  Membership. Probably less than 100
  Leadership. Octavio Pérez, Fernando López (both aliases)
  Status. Illegal
  Last Congress. No data
  Publications. No data

• Lorenzo Zelaya Popular Revolutionary Forces (Fuerzas Populares Revolucionarias Lorenzo Zelaya; FPR-LZ)
  Founded. 1980
  Membership. 100 (estimated)
  Leadership. No data
  Status. Illegal
  Last Congress. No data
  Publications. *Lorenzo Zelaya* (irregular, published in Mexico)

• "Cinchoneros" Popular Liberation Movement (Movimiento Popular de Liberación Cinchoneros; MPL-Cinchoneros)
  Founded. 1981, as successor to the People's Revolutionary Union; established in 1980 as Honduran front for the Salvadoran People's Revolutionary Army
  Membership. Some 300

Leadership. No data
Status. Illegal
Last Congress. No data
Publications. No data

Umbrella Organization

• Unified National Directorate of the Honduran Revolutionary Movement (Dirección Nacional Unificada del Movimiento Revolucionario Hondureño; DNU-MRH)
  Founded. 1982, though largely ineffective
  Membership. All the above parties, as well as the Socialist Action Party (Partido de Acción Socialista de Honduras; PASOH), led by Virgilio Carias, headquartered in Nicaragua

Domestic Affairs. There were few indications in 1988 that the weak Honduran revolutionary movements under the DNU-MRH have expanded their operations or gained a significant number of recruits. These facts—the country's continuing relative stability and the government's ability to maintain that stability—are of even greater importance than they would be per se, were the country in a less critical geographic and geopolitical position. Honduras, sharing borders with Nicaragua, Guatemala, and El Salvador, can accurately be described as being at the center of Central America's swirling crises.

Indeed, foreign guerrilla forces have posed greater challenges to Honduras than domestic ones. While the border with Nicaragua and the use of Honduran territory by the contras have been sources of well-publicized problems for the country, the border with El Salvador and the use of Honduran territory by the FMLN have received less attention in the mainstream media. FMLN activities on Honduran territory—along the disputed border areas, among the Salvadoran refugees, and in Tegucigalpa itself—have become even more brazen than before.

The FMLN has often been accused of planting bombs and shooting at Honduran security forces (*FBIS-LAM*, 24 May). In fact, the FMLN even proposed a "dialogue" with the Honduran government "to clear up positions and avert the spread of the war in Central America" (ibid.). Tegucigalpa seems to take the FMLN seriously, as in the instance when the military's spokesman, Juan Sierra Fonseca, complained that "the Salvadoran guerrilla forces have *unnecessarily* entered Honduran territory many times" (emphasis added; *FBIS-LAM*,

11 May). The implication is that the Hondurans would prefer to be able to discreetly ignore the FMLN's activities.

That, however, was made far more difficult in the past year as reliable reports have confirmed what the Honduran and Salvadoran militaries both have long claimed: that the large numbers of Salvadoran "refugees" in Honduran camps (particularly, but not only Mesa Verde), are little more than camp followers of the FMLN, mobilized, organized, and controlled by it; and serving as a source of supply, rest, and recreation for the Salvadoran revolutionaries.

Another development is probably even more important and ominous for the future of Honduras's stability. Although no conclusive statement can yet be made, indications are that Honduras may have become yet another Latin American country where drug traffickers and leftist guerrillas have opportunistically joined forces against the government. This, if true, potentially could strengthen the DNU-MRH to a great degree. The first indications of a *narcotraficante*/guerrilla connection became apparent following the most controversial political event of the year in Honduras: the legally dubious capture on 5 April and expulsion to the Dominican Republic (where he was arrested by U.S. marshals and taken to the United States) of Juan Ramón Matta Ballesteros, widely known as the major cocaine-traffic kingpin in Honduras. In the United States, Matta, who is linked to the Colombian Medellín cocaine cartel, is to face charges of drug trafficking and escape from prison.

Matta Ballesteros's fortune, estimated at a minimum of $1 billion (*NYT*, 6 April), was particularly important, for his native province of Olancho, on the Nicaraguan border, is Honduras's largest and least secure province. There Matta built schools and provided employment for many people otherwise neglected (*NYT*, 13 April). Matta's arrest and expulsion, which amounted to his *de facto* extradition to the United States, provoked some dissension within the military, and particularly between the army and the police (*NYT*, 5 April). More important, it became a lightning rod for the small minority of Hondurans engaged in anti-Americanism on both the right and the left. The immediate results were riots directed at the U.S. embassy and its annexes on 6 April (in which five Hondurans were killed) and the burning of an embassy annex.

There were soon indications that the violent left has seized upon the Matta case to stir up anti-U.S. sentiments and take advantage of Matta's local popularity in strategic Olancho. The most openly out-spoken group in this respect was the PRTC-H. In a statement from its headquarters in Managua, the organization asked that President Azcona and armed forces chief Gen. Humberto Regalado Hernandez be "put on trial" for the deaths of five "students," whom it described as "patriots" killed by the U.S. embassy's Marine guards, despite the total lack of evidence to that effect (*FBIS-LAM*, 11 April, p. 21). As for Matta himself, the PRTC-H claimed that his expulsion was "illegal" and detrimental to "national sovereignty and dignity" (ibid.). The PCH also protested the government's action, although it tried to distance itself from Matta by claiming that the demonstrations at the U.S. embassy "were not an expression of solidarity with drug trafficker Juan Ramón Matta Ballesteros . . . it was a real flare-up of anger and protest against the presence of U.S. forces . . . against the gross infringement upon our sovereignty" (statement by Rigoberto Padilla quoted in *IB*, July).

The pro-DNU-MRH left in the United States (see, for example, "Add Honduras to List of Our Former Friends," by Jerry Genesio, National President, "Veterans for Peace," *NYT*, 29 April) also tried to make the Matta affair an international issue on the basis of offended Honduran nationalist sensitivities.

The question of a link between drug traffickers and the left should also be seen in conjunction with a number of well-documented contrasting cases in which prominent Honduran officers, both active and retired, have been linked to the trafficking of cocaine to the United States or associated with Colombian traffickers. Those involved included General Regalado's own brother, who was arrested in the United States, as well as a military attaché in Colombia and a few others. The government and the military have both claimed that the link is between drug trafficking and the subversive left, not between the former and themselves. They have blamed the attacks on the U.S. embassy on this alleged relationship between the left and drug traffickers: "The most recent criminal incidents are part of a broad variety of activities that the hordes of violence are using as a protest. The narco-subversion relationship is one such activity" (*FBIS-LAM*, 11 April). Specifically, the government accused drug traffickers of arming subversive groups in Tegucigalpa and San Pedro Sula in the wake of the Matta affair (ibid.).

Guerrilla Actions. The government has accused the Salvadoran FMLN of "infiltration" and of wanting to "extend its tentacles to our country" (ibid.). A number of facts seem to indicate that the FMLN was indeed behind a number of violent activities in Honduras, sometimes directly but most often through its Honduran front, the "Cinchoneros." The first terrorist action of the year, on 5 January, was indeed claimed by the "Cinchoneros"; it was the murder of Isaias Vilorio, described in the group's statement as "an executioner with the DIN [Department of National Investigation] and prominent death-squad member . . ." (*FBIS-LAM*, 11 January).

Following the disturbances caused by the Matta affair, Molotov cocktails were discovered in the Francisco Morazán Teachers' School in Tegucigalpa (*FBIS-LAM*, 11 April), a known center of recruiting by the "Cinchoneros," hence by the FMLN. On 17 July, five U.S. soldiers were attacked and wounded in San Pedro Sula, the country's second largest city, with the "Cinchoneros" claiming credit. They stated that it was an operation carried out by their "Lempira Command," with the aim of "telling our people that the gringos are not invincible, that bullets do penetrate them, which has already been demonstrated by the heroic people of Vietnam, Cuba and Nicaragua" (ibid., 20 July). To give their actions some national color, the "Cinchoneros" also claimed that "there will be no peace" as long as there are contras and American military personnel on Honduran territory, and the "national puppet army defends the wealthy exploiters of the people" (ibid.).

The issues arising out of the U.S. presence in Honduras have become the rallying cries of the left, and events seem to indicate that they may also provide some common strategy for the perennially fractious Honduran revolutionary groups. The "7 April Martyrs Command" of the "Morazanist Patriotic Front"—probably another version of the FMLH's name—claimed credit for the bombing on 19 December of the U.S. Peace Corps office in Tegucigalpa, stating that it was a "protest against the presence of U.S. troops in the country" (*FBIS-LAM*, 20 December). PCH general secretary Padilla recently provided the outlines of what may constitute strategy for the Honduran left as a whole in the wake of the Arias Plan and the Esquipulas Accords. The basic elements of such strategy are: the consolidation of the Sandinista regime in Nicaragua; the removal of the U.S. military presence in Honduras and the cessation of military collaboration between the two countries; and a united-front approach by the Honduran left, which would force the government into negotiations with it.

With regard to Nicaragua, Padilla reiterated the party's positions, taken at the PCH's Fourth Congress and at the Third Plenum of its Central Committee in 1987, that "The defence of the Sandinista people's revolution is our bounden duty and obligation" (*WMR*, April 1988). The contras, whom Padilla compared with the rebellious peasants of the Vendée during the French Revolution, were consistently described as U.S. puppets and mercenaries protected by the Honduran government and military, while the "policy of doing away with [conflict] conducted by the revolutionary governments not only in Nicaragua but also Afghanistan, Kampuchea and other countries is . . . dictated by their yearning for peace" (ibid.).

On the other hand, Padilla describes Honduras as a "knot of contradictions," which is the result of its being "turned into a regional centre of U.S. militaristic activity. The strategic situation of Honduras and the traitorous attitude of the ruling élite have determined its role in implementing interventionist schemes" (ibid.). Since the party perceives a development of anti-U.S. sentiments in Honduras among "popular organizations," sectors of the Catholic Church, and various political groups, it has sought to spark the formation of a real popular front. As Padilla put it, "That is why *our party has now put forward slogans for a restoration of national sovereignty, the immediate expulsion of the contras, a review of military treaties with Washington, 'legitimising' the presence of U.S. troops on our territory, and scrupulous fulfilment by the Azcona Hoyo government of the Guatemala Accords*" (ibid.; emphasis in text). While probably exaggerated, Padilla's claims that the PCH has successfully used nationalism to reach agreements "with all organizations of the revolutionary left in Honduras, as well as with other patriotic forces, such as the Social Democrats, Christian Democrats, and circles of the Catholic Church" (interview in *Rabotnichesko Delo*; *FBIS-LAM*, 29 August) should be taken very seriously.

Despite this apparent development the Honduran left's still-low levels of strength and membership are indicated by Padilla's basis for demanding a "dialogue" with the government. The only argument Padilla could think of for demanding a "dialogue," other than the legally arguable texts of Esquipulas, was that "only over the past few years more than 150 popular leaders and Communists have been ab-

ducted, have disappeared, or have been subjected to torture and killed; dozens of our compatriots have to live in exile . . ." (*FBIS-LAM*, 11 January).

The left's weakness has made it easier for Tegucigalpa to reject Padilla's complaints that the government refuses to establish a "national reconciliation commission" through which to "negotiate" with the revolutionary left (*WMR*, April 1988). In fact, a communiqué from the Foreign Ministry clearly stated that "Honduras believes that it has no obligation to establish a National Reconciliation Commission. It feels that the provisions outlined for states suffering from civil wars do not apply in its case." Tegucigalpa's earlier establishment for a short time of such a commission, which did not engage in talks with the DNU-MRH, was intended "to refute those who have argued that our nation has not implemented the Guatemala accords" (ibid.).

Claims relating to human rights, arrests, abductions, and murders further illustrate the tiny size of the Honduran left. Both former army-intelligence interrogator Florencio Caballero and ex-FPR-LZ cadre Inés Murillo, the daughter of a former army officer, confirmed that the total number of DNU-MRH captives since 1983 was 100–150 (*NYT Magazine*, 5 June). Even the stoutly pro-left Human Rights Committee claimed, with little or no serious proof, that there were 263 "extra-judicial" murders by government forces in 1987 and 383 since President Azcona took office in January 1986 (*El Tiempo*, San Pedro Sula, 11 January). Any significant level of such an activity as "extra-judicial murder" is, of course, serious, and these claims may well have some legal importance. In light of the committee's prior history of false or excessive claims, however, one has to consider even these relatively low claims wildly exaggerated. They picture a lightweight Honduran left.

Nevertheless, the real and alleged abuses of the left's human rights in Honduras—most of the claims originate with the self-proclaimed Human Rights Commission—were enough to make that country the first one in Latin America to be "tried" for "human rights abuses" by the Inter-American Court on Human Rights, an OAS-affiliated organization headquartered in Costa Rica (*NYT*, 19 January; *CSM*, 29 January). Predictably, Honduras was found to be "guilty."

Relations with Nicaragua. Throughout the year, as during 1987, the main problem facing Honduras in foreign affairs was neighboring Nicaragua. The Esquipulas Accords have in fact dramatically increased, rather than lessened, Honduran anxieties. Perceived from Honduras, the major, interrelated issues relative to Nicaragua are Honduran security (both internal and external) and the Nicaraguan internal situation. Internally, the Honduran authorities are on permanent alert against guerrilla infiltration, terrorist attacks, and spying from Nicaragua. All DNU-MRH groups are headquartered in Managua, where they have unlimited access to government-controlled media and are in a position to recruit and train new members. Sporadic but persistent reports that Honduran insurgents are ready to cross the border abound; the latest, involving an alleged 3,000 guerrillas, was in August (*FBIS-LAM*, 24 August). Most such rumors are exaggerated, and often uncorroborated by the military. But well-documented previous cases give them credibility, as do statements like President Azcona's to the effect that the left in Honduras are "people learning to be guerrillas in Cuba and Nicaragua" (ibid., 30 June).

In July, the assistant secretary general of the Christian Democratic Youth, Juan Ramón Flores Huezo, was arrested and accused of spying for Nicaragua (ibid., 15 July). In addition to Nicaraguan activities directed against the Honduran government, mostly through the FPR-LZ, there are numerous data on Nicaraguan agents operating in the border areas against the camps of the insurgents and among Nicaraguan refugees.

The threat posed by the Nicaraguan military buildup of the past eight years is acutely felt in Honduras, particularly in respect to heavy armaments that could not plausibly be justified by the needs of counterinsurgency warfare. Referring to that question, Azcona stated that "the military aid which Honduras receives from the United States bears no comparison with the aid Nicaragua obtains from the Soviet Union. It certainly makes us concerned about our security, and this forces us to spend resources which we should perhaps earmark for other activities, especially in the social field." (Ibid., 30 June.)

From a Honduran point of view, all these problems are a direct result of the internal situation in Nicaragua. "We are very tired of Nicaraguan problems always ending up affecting Honduras," Azcona said. "We are very tired of the Nicaraguan situations. Let them open their jails, let them hold talks, let them sign agreements, let them do whatever is necessary to leave us alone." (Ibid., 30 March.)

Apart, but not quite separate, from the general issues related to the Esquipulas Accords, Honduras's relations with Managua have been particularly poisoned by Nicaragua's action at the International Court of Justice. There Nicaragua has claimed that Honduras violates international law by allowing the contras on its territory. This action is seen by Honduras as being against both the spirit and the letter of the Esquipulas Accords; the agreement, concluded on 7 August 1987, provides for the postponement of the suit. It is noteworthy that Honduras does not press a similar suit regarding the headquarters in Managua of the DNU-MRH groups.

The issue produced a particularly harsh exchange of letters between the two countries' foreign ministers, with Honduras's Carlos López Contreras accusing his Nicaraguan counterpart of possessing a "vivid imagination," of being "incomprehensibly emotional," and his government of "send[ing] high-ranking government officials to beg for military or economic aid from other countries" (*La Tribuna*, Tegucigalpa, 30 June). Nevertheless, in December the International Court of Justice accepted the Nicaraguan suit, further infuriating the Hondurans and making the tense relations between the two countries more precarious still.

Michael Radu
Foreign Policy Research Institute, Philadelphia

Jamaica

Population. 2,458,102
Party. Workers Party of Jamaica (WPJ)
Founded. 1978
Membership. 100 (est.)
General Secretary. Dr. Trevor Munroe
Status. Legal
Last Congress. Fourth, 11–13 September 1988
Central Committee. Expanded from 16 to 31 members (one-third women; one-third from rural parishes; one-third workers and small farmers)
Last Election. 1986 municipal elections
Auxiliary Organizations. University and Allied Workers' Union (UAWU)
Publications. *Struggle*

Jamaican attention was focused on two processes during 1988: politics and the damages wrought by Hurricane Gilbert. The latter soon became part of the political process as Jamaicans tried to figure out how the destruction and the reconstruction of destroyed or damaged buildings and so forth would affect the time and outcome of the elections. The effect on the time of the elections soon became clear when Prime Minister Edward Seaga was given the three extra months beyond the five-year limit that the Jamaican constitution allows under extraordinary circumstances. They will have to be held before April 1989.

Relief assistance after the hurricane was massive, allowing incumbent Prime Minister Edward Seaga and the Jamaican Labour Party to briefly improve their standing in the polls. Not enough, however, to overcome the commanding lead that the rival People's National Party and its leader, Michael Manley, have enjoyed since 1986. Additionally, the hurricane dealt a serious blow to the economic recovery that had begun to pick up momentum in 1986. Increased world demand for bauxite and alumina and back-to-back successful tourist seasons had sparked this economic turnaround. Both sectors continued to be strong, but infrastructural rebuilding (said to cost over US$1 billion) was starting to redirect government resources from areas of investment that have been traditional sources of patronage and political payoffs.

Jamaica has a solid two-party system, with both parties fully committed to the parliamentary system. The electoral machinery—including an up-to-date voting list—formerly a source of contention, is now in place, and the leaders of the two parties have been holding periodic, and increasingly amiable, meetings. Fear of a repetition of the violence that accompanied the 1980 elections, which claimed an estimated 800 casualties, led Manley and Seaga to sign a peace agreement. Such is the influence of these two leaders that fully 76 percent of Jamaicans polled after the treaty believed the next elections would be peaceful. In such a context, what role does Jamaica's Marxist-Leninist party, the WPJ, play?

Current Leadership and Party Organization. Rumors that there existed a fissure within top party ranks of the WPJ were proven true when Dr. Don Robotham, a professor at the University of the West Indies and a member of the Central Committee of the WPJ, made his resignation public. "Several" other resignations were said to have followed. The cause of the division had a familiar ring: conflict between orthodox Marxist-Leninists (represented by Secretary General Trevor Munroe) and those favoring democratization. Robotham's letter was blunt: the party does not allow diverse interests to flourish "because its ideology of Marxism-Leninism is narrow and dictatorial and its organizational forms require that individual members are subordinated, manipulated and stifled. . ." (*The Jamaican Weekly Gleaner*, 29 August).

Interestingly, this break came two months after the secretary general had led a party delegation to the USSR to observe the "restructuring" taking place in the Communist Party of the USSR. With the dissidents out, Dr. Munroe was re-elected unopposed at the party's Fourth Party Congress, held on 11–13 September. (*FBIS*, 4 November.)

Despite the secrecy surrounding internal party affairs, it is known that the dismal electoral performance of its first try as an independent political force (0.2 percent in the 1986 municipal elections) left the party membership further dispirited. Things had not been going well since the debacle in Grenada in October 1983 revealed that Munroe and the WPJ were key advisors of the hard-line Coard faction that destroyed the Maurice Bishop regime.

But 1988 was not without victories for the WPJ. A major dispute over wages disrupted operations in the sugar industry in January. Workers ignored a ruling from the Industrial Dispute Tribunal that they should return to work. They also ignored the call from their historical union leadership, the JLP-affiliated Bustamante Industrial Trade Union (BITU) and the PNP-affiliated National Workers' Union (NWU), to return to work. The WPJ and its affiliate, the UAWU, had been attempting for years to break the monopoly of the BITU and the NWU; they now had their chance. They were given the legal green light when the British Privy Council (still Jamaica's last court of appeal) sustained rulings of the Jamaican Supreme Court and Court of Appeal allowing a poll to be taken among sugar workers. On 1 November, in a poll conducted by the Ministry of Labour, the UAWU handily won the representational rights for a major sugar estate. (*J. W. Gleaner*, 14 November.) By midyear, the sugar industry was back in full production, and it is not known what, if any, further inroads the UAWU made among sugar workers. The monopoly of the two traditional, and party-related, unions had been broken, however.

Domestic and International Positions. The strongly anti-communist rhetoric of the 1980 electoral campaign has virtually disappeared from the political arena. One reason is surely Jamaica's improved relations with the USSR. In early May, a delegation from the Supreme Soviet was welcomed by Prime Minister Seaga, who thanked them for their interest in buying additional bauxite and alumina (*Insight*, 6 June). The USSR had purchased 850,000 tons of bauxite in 1987 and was now being called "the market of the future" by Jamaican leaders (*J. W. Gleaner*, 13 June). China also bought 50,000 tons of alumina in 1988.

A confusing incident in which a supposed Soviet "intelligence officer" was reported by the government to have defected in Jamaica, was quickly settled by the Soviet Embassy in Kingston. It was, they said, a simple case of a Soviet university professor married to a Jamaican who had decided to stay in Jamaica. Upon the *Gleaner*'s revelation (*J. W. Gleaner*, 13 June) that the Jamaican wife was a member of the WPJ who had encountered severe racism in Russia, it was left to Dr. Munroe to try to salvage what he could from a damaging situation. It had not been racism but rather "bureaucratic delays" and other such "indignities" encountered in getting a ten-day exit visa that had led the couple to opt for Jamaican residence (*FBIS*, 14 June). Whatever the real story, even a suspicion of racism in race-conscious Jamaica could not have benefitted the WPJ, which has intimate ties with Moscow.

The WPJ entered the pre-election period of most intense political activity and debate debilitated in several respects: First, there is the split within the top cadres of the party. Second, the left-wing of the PNP, which in the 1970s had encouraged the "critical support" of the WPJ, has not been in evidence in the party's slate of candidates or its platforms. This last point is directly related to the most important reason for the almost complete invisibility of Dr. Munroe and the WPJ: the ideological metamorphosis of Michael Manley. He now says that he is "wiser" and more "mature," and that he would not "rock the boat" or create any sudden ideological "lurches." Before a Miami audience of bankers and business people, he was adamant: "[W]e do not ever intend again to allow the relationship with Cuba to become internally divisive or a source of trouble with Washington" (*J. W. Gleaner*, 13 June). The propitious circumstances of the 1970s that gave Munroe and the WPJ much greater prominence than the party's size seemed to warrant, have vanished. Jamaican communists are having to make do on their own merits now.

Anthony P. Maingot
Florida International University
Latin American and Caribbean Center

Martinique

Population. 351,105
Party. Martinique Communist Party (Parti Communiste Martiniquais; PCM)
Founded. 1921 (PCM, 1957)
Membership. Less than 1,000
General Secretary. Armand Nicolas (62; French citizen)
Politburo. 3 members
Secretariat. 4 members
Central Committee. 33 members
Status. Legal
Last Congress. Ninth, 12–13 December 1988
Last Elections. 24 April, 8 May, president of France; 5 and 12 June, French National Assembly, no seats; 25 September, 2 October, Martinique General Council, 2 of 45
Auxiliary Organizations. General Confederation of Martiniquan Labor (CGTM); Martiniquan Union of Education Personnel (SMPE-CGTM); Union of Women of Martinique (Union des Femmes de la Martinique); Martiniquan Committee of Solidarity with the Peoples of the Caribbean and of Central America
Publications. *Justice* (weekly newspaper)

The Ninth Congress of the Martinique Communist Party (PCM) took place 12–13 December, and discussions focused on the effects of European integration that will take place at the end of 1992. Armand Nicolas, PCM general secretary, expressed the fear of Martinicans that with the disappearance of barriers among Common Market countries, Martinique's products will lose their protected market in France, while the island itself will be swamped with German, Dutch, Italian, and other countries' goods, investments, and citizens.

The economic situation is already bad enough, as about 31 percent of the active population is unemployed. To try to improve this situation, and to defend Martinique against the possible effects of 1992, the PCM met in Cayenne, in French Guiana, with other communist and socialist parties of the other overseas departments: Guadeloupe, French Guiana, and Réunion. They created the Assemblage of Progressive Forces of the Antilles, French

Guiana, and Réunion (Rassemblement des Forces de Progrès des Antilles, de la Guyane et de la Réunion). From now on there will be increased cooperation in the study of the effects of the planned integration of the Western European countries and in the expected struggle to maintain and improve the economies of the four overseas departments. A delegation from the Spanish-controlled Canary Islands visited Fort-de-France, the capital of Martinique, to discuss their view of the European integration.

As the French presidential elections approached, the PCM and others expressed fears that the National Front of Jean-Marie Le Pen, perceived as antiblack and anti-Semitic, would organize in Martinique. The fears proved to be unwarranted because during the first round of elections Le Pen received a paltry 1,365 votes out of 116,938 cast. Although the PCM said it supported André Lajoinie, the French Communist Party candidate, he did not fare better than Le Pen, winning only 2,319 votes or 1.98 percent of the total number, as compared with 6.76 percent in metropolitan France. During the second round on 8 May, the communists supported incumbent François Mitterrand, who won easily.

Once re-elected, Mitterrand thought he could obtain a socialist majority in the National Assembly, and he therefore called for legislative elections on 5 and 12 June. As usual, the PCM proposed a unified left, and, as usual, the socialists and the Martinique Progressive Party were cool to the idea. Relations with the PPM were good, however, and communist invitees attended the closing session of the Martinique Progressive Party's ninth congress, 18–20 March. There was no general agreement among the three leftist parties about the four deputy positions. The PCM presented one candidate, but he lost. Partial elections for 22 out of 45 seats in the General Council took place on 25 September and 2 October. Out of four PCM candidates, two won. There was a last call to the polls on 6 November as the French were asked to approve a project of reform for New Caledonia, an overseas territory. Martinique approved.

Events in Haiti drew the attention of the PCM. In the former French colony, the communist party, or PUCH (Unified Party of Haitian Communists), was attempting to build a constituency.

Martinique's communist party published brochures during and after its ninth congress to explain party positions, and it printed a special publication, *New Proposals of the Martinique Communist Party to Create Employment and Responsibility*. The

PCM joined other Martinicans in celebrating the bronze medal won for France by a compatriot at the Seoul Olympics.

Brian Weinstein
Howard University

Mexico

Population. 83,527,567
Party. Mexican Socialist Party (Partido Mexicano Socialista; PMS)
Founded. 1919 (PMS, November 1987)
Membership. 90,000 (claimed)
General Secretary. Gilberto Rincón Gallardo
Political Commission. Gilberto Rincón Gallardo, Jorge Alocer Villanueva, Raymundo Cárdenas Hernández, Heberto Castillo Martinez, Eduardo Valle Espinosa, José Luis Hernández, Jesús Ortega Martínez, Graco Ramírez Garrido-Abreu, Miguel Alonso Raya, Carmelo Enrique Rosario, Rodolfo Armenta, Camilo Valenzuela Fierra, José Domínguez, Manuel Terrazas Guerrero (*La Jornada*, 15 November)
Executive Committee. 36 members
National Committee. 159 members
Status. Legal
Last Congress. First, 25–29 November 1987
Last Election. 6 July 1988, presidential
Auxiliary Organizations. Independent Center of Agricultural Workers and Peasants (CIOAC), Sole National Union of University Workers (SUNTU)
Publications. *Asi Es* (weekly, Mexico City; status not clear since November)

The communist left is in an unprecedented state of flux in the aftermath of Mexico's presidential elections on 6 July 1988. Traditionally, the Marxist left operated on the fringes of political life, splintered by dogma, electorally irrelevant, and overshadowed by the single-party rule of the Party of the Institutional Revolution (PRI). However, the 1988 breakaway presidential candidacy of dissident Priista, Cuauhtémoc Cárdenas, has profoundly invigorated the populist forces of Mexican politics, while simultaneously posing dilemmas for the communist left. The meteoric rise of Cárdenas, an ex-PRI noncommunist politician, has placed pressures on the communist left to abandon its traditional orthodoxy.

Cárdenas is the son of former president Lázaro Cárdenas, hero of the PRI left. The name of Cárdenas is associated with the massive land redistribution and nationalization of the oil industry implemented by his father during the 1930s. A fifty-five-year-old engineer, Cuauhtémoc Cárdenas spent his entire career within the PRI, most recently, as governor of the state of Michoacán. Cárdenas views himself as the modern political heir of his father's populist legacy.

The Cárdenas phenomenon is a product of deep ideological divisions within the PRI. His popularity among former PRI supporters reflects the political costs of former president Miguel de la Madrid's (1982–1988) relatively conservative policies of privatization, trade liberalization, debt repayment, and wage austerity. These policies precipitated an ideological crisis of identity within the PRI. Cárdenas's calls for the renationalization of the sugar industry and the preservation of the state telephone monopoly are examples of the traditional statism that was once the PRI's leitmotif.

Cárdenas represents the left wing of the PRI, an indigenous brand of Mexican leftism more aptly described as populist than orthodox Marxist. Cárdenas is inclined toward a variety of Mexican nationalism expressed in anti-Yankee sentiment and a preference for economic autarchy. This includes a wariness of both foreign investment and enhanced trade with the United States. In domestic economic matters, Cárdenas would prove accommodating toward small business, hostile toward large capital, and reluctant to relinquish state ownership of large sectors of the economy. In matters of foreign policy, Cárdenas shares in a Third World fervor for, and identification with, revolutionary movements typical of the era of former PRI president Luís Echeverria (1970–1976).

Cárdenas broke with the PRI and launched his own campaign in 1987. He possesses no political party of his own. He ran at the head of the ideologically disparate, multi-party coalition, the National Democratic Front (FDN), which unified the Mexican left at the national level. The mystique of the Cárdenas name was a powerful inducement to unity, offering an attractive symbol with mass appeal around which most factions of the Mexican left could coalesce. The Cárdenas coalition brings together four parties: the Mexican Socialist Party (PMS); the Popular Socialist Party (PPS); the Socialist Worker's Party (PST); and the Party of the Authentic Mexican Revolution (PARM). Four principal currents can be detected within the Cárdenas movement, including Mexican communist, advocates of European-style socialism, eclectic former satellite parties controlled by the PRI, and Trotskyites.

Mexican communist party elements are represented in the Cárdenas movement under the name of the Mexican Socialist Party (PMS). The chief leaders of the PMS are Arnoldo Martínez Verdugo, Pablo Gómez, Gilberto Rincón Gallardo, and Heberto Castillo. The former three have a long career of holding leadership positions in former permutations of Mexican communism, including the Mexican Communist Party (PCM), which was merged into a new party, the Unified Socialist Party of Mexico (PSUM), in November 1981. Martínez, Gómez, and Rincón are disciples of Eurocommunism, influenced by the Italian-communist example of Enrico Berlinguer. All three were prompted by the Soviet invasion of Czechoslovakia in 1968 to distance the PCM and later the PSUM from the Soviet sphere. All three are also the product of the 1968 student movement in Mexico City. Their experience with the repressive powers of the Mexican state encouraged greater sensitivity to open forms of government.

Heberto Castillo was formerly the head of the Mexican Workers Party (PMT). Castillo has carved out a reputation as an elder statesman of the Mexican left, an intellectual who is both nationalistic and resistant to foreign ties. The PMS is the product of a union in November 1987 of the communist PSUM and Castillo's socialist PMT. Castillo was selected to head the newly created PMS presidential ticket as part of the negotiations that led to the fusion of the PMT and PSUM. However, upon the announcement of the Cárdenas candidacy, pressures mounted for Castillo and the PMS to cede to a unified campaign headed by Cárdenas. Castillo and the PMS threw their support to Cárdenas in the last two weeks of the campaign period, contributing to a last minute electoral surge in favor of Cárdenas.

Although the PMS retains its separate party identity, the gravitational pull of Cárdenas makes it likely that it will dissolve its identity and enter into a new party dominated by Cárdenas. The reluctance of Heberto Castillo to relinquish his candidacy is, however, but one indication of the suspicion with which the PMS views the Cárdenas phenomenon. The PMS must decide whether or not to permanently join forces with Cárdenas. This question severely divides the cadres of the PMS. Older generation communist-party leaders, including labor leaders Valentín Campa and Manuel Terrazas, oppose unification with Cárdenas. They fear their eventual dilution and ultimate expendability within an ideologically moderate Cárdenas movement.

The younger communist-party leaders Martínez and Gómez appear to be more inclined to join forces with Cárdenas. They are acutely aware of the fact that the Cárdenas coalition is far greater than the sum of its individual parts, and that the PMS risks extinction if it fails to make common cause with Cárdenas. Harnessed to the magic of the Cárdenas name, the Mexican left polled 31.06 percent of the vote, in contrast to the 12 percent polled in 1982. However, of the parties that benefitted from the Cárdenas coalition, the PMS was the only party unable to win a plurality victory in a single-member congressional district. Its future survival as an independent party may be at stake. The PMS has offered its party registration as a permanent base of operations for the Cárdenas forces, thereby hoping to retain its party identity and benefit from identification with Cárdenas. Cárdenas has, however, rejected the overtures of the PMS, fearing excessive identification with the communists. This places even more pressure on the PMS to dissolve eventually and to jump on board the new party created by Cárdenas.

The Cárdenas movement also encompasses a small but influential wing inclined toward the perspectives of the Socialist International, especially as they are embodied in the figures of France's François Mitterrand and Spain's Felipe Gonzalez. This faction is headed by PRI defector Porfirio Muñoz Ledo, who formerly served as the president of the PRI and ambassador to the United Nations. Porfirio Muñoz Ledo is widely viewed as a brilliant, if eccentric negotiator and the chief political strategist for Cárdenas. The remainder of the Cárdenas coalition consists of a sprinkling of influential activists from the Movement Toward Socialism (MAS) and former Trotskyites. Additionally, eclectic former satellite parties such as the PARM, under whose registry Cárdenas ran for president, and the PPS united behind the Cárdenas banner. Both are accustomed to receiving patronage from the PRI and are likely to expect similar benefits from their alliance with Cárdenas.

Cárdenas announced his intention to form a new Party of the Democratic Revolution (PRD), on October 21, 1988. His *Call to the People of Mexico*, a declaration published in major Mexican newspapers (among them *La Jornada*), was signed by a long list of individual supporters. The names of Gómez, Martínez, Rincón, and Castillo were among those subscribing to the formation of the new party. Their signatures on the declaration seemed to indicate the beginning of the end of the PMS as an independent party. However, the divisions within the Cárdenas coalition remain formidable. The merger of communist-party cadres within the Cárdenas-led PRD would be the political equivalent of convincing Georges Marchais to join forces with François Mitterrand. A battle will undoubtedly ensue between those who wish to see the new PRD follow the model of European socialism and those who favor traditional brands of communism. Similarly, former Trotskyites, such as Ricardo Pascoe, are influential within the Cárdenas movement, but are uncomfortable with the tug toward the ideological center exerted by Cárdenas and Muñoz Ledo. The PRD will also face the additional difficulty of fulfilling the requirements to obtain legal recognition and formal registration as a political party.

The forces of Mexican communism as expressed in the PMS will find 1989 to be a year of transition. Ideological differences may prevent the PMS from merging into a unified Cárdenas-led movement under the new PRD. In such a case, the Mexican communist left is likely to be even more remote from the possibility of electoral success. In the event of a merger with the PRD, PMS cadres may find opportunities to increase their influence in the Cárdenas movement by virtue of their organizational capacity. They also, however, run the risk that their influence within the new party will remain minimal.

Neither the PRD nor the PMS can expect much in the way of assistance from Cuba, Nicaragua, or the Soviet Union. Rather, the presence of Fidel Castro and Daniel Ortega at the inauguration of PRI President Carlos Salinas de Gortari on 1 December 1988 was a clear affirmation of their support for the PRI. Castro's seal of approval on Salinas's presidency defused Cárdenas's efforts to discredit the PRI's electoral victory and claim the mantle of revolutionary legitimacy. Cárdenas and PMS leaders openly expressed their fury and indignation.

M. Delal Baer

Center for Strategic and International Studies,
Washington, D.C.

Nicaragua

Population. 3,407,183
Marxist-Leninist Parties.

• Sandinista Front of National Liberation (Frente Sandinista de Liberación Nacional; FSLN)
   Founded. 1961
   Membership. Ca. 1,400
   National Directorate. Daniel Ortega Saavedra, Humberto Ortega Saavedra, Victor Tirado López, Tomás Borge Martínez, Bayardo Arce Castaño, Henry Ruíz Hernández, Jaime Wheelock Román, Luís Carrión Cruz, Carlos Nuñez Téllez
   Executive Commission. A 5-member commission is in charge of party affairs: Daniel Ortega Saavedra (coordinator), Bayardo Arce Castaño (deputy coordinator), Humberto Ortega Saavedra, Tomás Borge Martínez, Jaime Wheelock Román.
   Main Party Organs. The Sandinista Assembly (105 members), supposed to convene yearly. Routine party operations are under the control of seven auxiliary departments: general affairs (René Nuñez); organization (Lea Guido); agitation and propaganda (Carlos Fernando Chamorro); political education (Vanessa Castro Cardenal); international affairs (Julio López); finances (Plutarco Cornejo); studies of Sandinismo (Flor de María Monterrey).
   Party-State Relationship. The following top FSLN leaders are also members of important state institutions: Daniel Ortega Saavedra, president of the Republic; Humberto Ortega Saavedra, minister of defense; Tomás Borge Martínez, minister of the interior; Luís Carrión Cruz, responsible for the economy; Henry Ruiz Hernández, minister of planning and external cooperation; Jaime Wheelock Román, minister for agrarian reform; Carlos Nuñez Téllez, president of the National Assembly.
   Status. Ruling party
   Last Congress. August 1985, FSLN Assembly
   Last Elections. 4 November 1984; presidential election 63 percent; Constituent Assembly, 61 of 96 seats

   Fronts and Auxiliary Organizations. Sandinista Defense Committees (Comités de Defense Sandinista; CDS), membership estimated at 150,000, led by former secret-police chief Omar Cabezas; Sandinista Youth-19 of July (Juventud Sandinista-19 de Julio; JS-19), led by Carlos Carrión; "Luisa Amanda Espinosa" Association of Nicaraguan Women (Asociación de Mujeres Nicaragüenses Luisa Amanda Espinosa; AMNLAE), led by Glenda Monterrey; Sandinista Workers' Central (CST); Farmworkers' Association (Asociación de Trabajadores del Campo; ATC)
   Publications. Barricada (party daily, circulation 110,000), El Nuevo Diario (government daily, circulation 60,000), Nicarahuac (ideological journal), Segovia (army journal), Bocay (Interior Ministry monthly); all television stations and the two major radio stations, Radio Sandino and La Voz de Nicaragua, are party-controlled and owned.

• Socialist Party of Nicaragua (Partido Socialista de Nicaragua; PSN), oldest pro-Soviet communist party in the country
   Founded. 1937; first congress, July 3, 1944
   Membership. Unknown
   Leadership. Gustavo Tablada, general secretary
   Political Commission. Gustavo Tablada, Domingo Sánchez Salgado, Luís Sánchez Sancho, Adolfo Evertz, José Luis Medina, Juan Gaitán (elected by the plenums, which also elect the general secretary)
   Status. Legal
   Last Congress. Eighth Plenum, July 1985
   Last Election. November 1984; less than 2 percent, two seats in Constituent Assembly (Sánchez Salgado and Sánchez Sancho)
   Auxiliary Organizations. General Confederation of Workers–Independent (CGI)
   Publication. El Popular (weekly)

• Communist Party of Nicaragua (Partido Comunista de Nicaragua; PCN)
   Founded. 1970, as splinter of PSN
   Membership. Unknown
   General Secretary. Eli Altamirano Pérez
   Politburo. 7 members: Eli Altamirano Pérez, Ariel Bravo Lorio; Allan Zambrana Zalmerón, Angel Hernández Zerda, René Blandón Noguera, Manuel Pérez Estrada, Alejandro Gutiérrez Mayorga
   Status. Legal

Last Congress. Second, June 1986. National Conference, December 1986

Last Election. November 1984; less than 2 percent, two seats in Constituent Assembly (Zambrana and Hernández)

Front and Auxiliary Organizations. Central for Trade Union Action and Unity (CAUS)

Publication. *Avance* (weekly, circulation ca. 20,000)

• Nicaraguan Marxist-Leninist Party (Partido Marxista-Leninista de Nicaragua; PMLN), until 1986 called Popular Action Movement-Marxist-Leninist (Movimiento de Acción Popular-Marxista-Leninista; MAP-ML)

Founded. 1970, as splinter of FSLN; expelled from FSLN in August 1972

Membership. Unknown

General Secretary. Isidro Téllez

Other Party Leaders. Fernando Malespín, Alejandro Gutiérrez, Carlos Cuadra, Carlos Lucas

Governing Body. Central Committee, last meeting in August 1985

Status. Legal

Last Congress. National Conference, September 1985

Last Election. November 1984; less than 2 percent, two seats in Constituent Assembly (Cuadra and Lucas)

Auxiliary Organization. Workers' Front (Frente Obrero; FO)

Publication. *Prensa Proletaria* (bimonthly)

Others: The far-left Workers' Revolutionary Party (Partido Revolucionario de Trabajadores; PRT) and its close ally, the Central American Unification Party (Partido de Unificación Centro Americana; PUCA), are both spin-offs of the PRTC (see profiles of Honduras and El Salvador). Both these tiny parties operate on the margins of legality; neither was allowed to participate in the 1984 elections, but they are still tolerated. Their leaders are Bonifacio Miranda (PRT) and Alejandro Pérez Arévalo (PUCA). The PRT publishes a biweekly newspaper, *El Socialista*, largely preoccupied with ideological attacks on the PCN.

The two major trends dominating the Nicaraguan scene in 1988 were the political and military collapse of the opposition and the complete breakdown of the economy, which is now the worst in the Western Hemisphere.

Party Affairs. There were no significant changes in the structure or ideological direction of the FSLN during the year. The only changes at the leadership level were the shifting of Luís Carrión Cruz from the Ministry of the Interior to the Ministry of the Economy, and the growing outspokenness of Tomás Borge. Borge was finally given the rank of division general in October, a move that formalized the militarization of his ministry. His position was further strengthened when Carrión Cruz, his deputy but (technically) political equal, departed to take over the economy. Borge's strength was clearly demonstrated by his sharp criticism of Humberto Ortega following the defection of Roger Miranda Bengoechea (see *YICA*, 1988). Borge was alleged to have sent a memorandum to Humberto Ortega, stating that "never in my revolutionary history have I experienced the shame of having a traitor within the cadre of the FSLN Directorate," and claimed that Miranda's "desertion" "is the fruit of the feeble discipline and lack of vigilance over subordinates..." (*La Prensa Libre*, Guatemala City, 5 January).

While his strength relative to that of the dominant Ortegas (and their groups) may have grown somewhat, it is unclear to what extent Borge's public statements express anything more than his own opinions. In fact, at least insofar as relations with the Soviets are concerned, it appears that he even disagrees with his former close associates Henry Ruíz and Bayardo Arce. While Borge would prefer the Sandinista government to be as independent from the USSR as possible, Ruíz has praised the Soviets for providing massive aid. Arce, for his part, has at least implied that *perestroika* is something to learn from (see below); and Omar Cabezas, the former secret-police chief now in charge of the CDSs, has claimed that he is engaged in a *perestroika*-type of change in those organizations (*Barricada*, 23 June). Borge, though, appears to remain as much of a dogmatic hard-liner as ever. In a February interview with the Italian newspaper *La Republica*, he not only stated that "for a long time our outlook was orthodox" and defined orthodoxy as "Marxism-Leninism, of course," but he also repeated that "yes, we considered ourselves Marxist-Leninists and had in mind a communist society. We did not like the social-democracies..." (*FBIS-LAM*, 26 February).

Although Borge went on to claim that "now we are convinced that political pluralism is not only possible but necessary in Nicaragua...," and even said that a coalition with other parties "is a possibility that should not be rejected," he was openly skeptical about recent Soviet developments in general, and the attacks on Stalin and Brezhnev in particular. Indeed, he stated, "I do not like this iconoclastic furor toward the Soviet Union as it was until just the other day. It is a great country that has achieved formidable objectives..." When reminded that Gorbachev himself is one of the critics of the Soviet past, Borge bluntly stated, "So allow me to disagree with Mr. Gorbachev" (ibid.).

At the end of the year, in a long interview with *Barricada*, Arce, still the main leader of the party apparatus, examined the FSLN's domestic and internal situation and indicated the direction of change for the coming year. He stated that the FSLN "must stop playing the role of an administered party. The FSLN must be a party of militants, a party that mobilizes and organizes people, and a party that is more oriented to the masses than to political power." (*Barricada*, 28 December.) He also admitted that the civil war and the collapse of the economy have resulted in a situation in which "even within our own ranks there were those who...hesitated and preferred to switch to the opposing camp—and there you have the traitors and the deserters" (ibid.).

Without being specific, Arce declared that "now we have different ideas than those we had when we were fighting the dictatorship," and offered a number of reasons for such change, "after seeing what is happening in the USSR with *perestroika*; the rectification of mistakes and negative attitudes in Cuba; the economic exploration in Hungary and China; the economic development in the FRG and Japan; and the Latin American situation..." (ibid.). In more concrete terms, it appears that the FSLN now dismisses the political opposition, which Arce defined as "poor little things," but may be prepared to reach some agreement on economic matters with representatives of the private sector, including, again according to Arce, such leaders of COSEP (Higher Council of Private Enterprise) as Enrique Bolaños and Ramiro Gurdián. These are the same people the Ortega brothers and Borge have consistently described as traitors and CIA agents.

Similar differences of accent—but never of policy—were detectable in regard to the essential issues of power and democracy. Vice President Ramírez claimed that if the FSLN loses the elections of 1990, "...we will cede power. That is how it is in elections." (*FBIS-LAM*, 31 October.) Daniel Ortega, on the other hand—in a Soviet-controlled publication—made it clear that "when we say that we shall not relinquish power, we say this very

seriously...Even if the people vote for a party which presents a program that appears to be progressive and then this party wants to carry out its counterrevolutionary program on the basis of this hypothetical vote, the people won't allow it to do so. I as a member of the Sandinist Front do not believe that the people would ever vote for any party other than the SNLF." (*IB*, October 1988.)

The only meeting of the Sandinista Assembly, the equivalent of a Central Committee Plenum, took place on 13 March, prior to the first public meeting between the FSLN and the National Resistance leaders at Sapoá, on the Costa Rican border. It approved the National Directorate's decision to go forward with the meeting, while also recommending a "strengthening [of the] military defense." It condemned the "interventionist policy" of the United States toward Panama, and expressed its solidarity with the "struggle of peoples for their liberation in Asia, Africa and Latin America, especially for the heroic resistance of the peoples of South Africa and Palestine." (*FBIS-LAM*, 14 March.)

More interesting than the changed approach to economics taken by some in FSLN's leadership ranks were the dramatic shifts in the general ideological outlook of some of the other parties of the Marxist-Leninist left. While some of them, particularly the PSN and the PCN, have already established a habit of cooperation with "bourgeois" opposition parties (see *YICA*, 1988), it appears that they are now on the brink of actually renouncing Marxism-Leninism completely. The most significant events occurred in August, when a new umbrella group including the PSN and the PCN was established under the name of The Movement of Revolutionary Unity (Movimiento de Unidad Revolucionaria; MUR) (*FBIS-LAM*, 24 August). Considering the old sectarian enmity between the two parties, their collaboration was a surprising development indeed; it can be explained by the fact that the new group was established at a time when both parties were undergoing a significant ideological shift.

On 16 August, Hortensia Rivas Zeledón, a member of the PSN's Political Commission and Central Committee, revealed that in a meeting on the previous day the Central Committee had decided that the party should renounce Leninism "...because Leninist parties are pursuing another ideological current, Stalinism," and by so doing have made Marxism a "thing of the past" (ibid., 17 August). The PSN is now effectively "estranged" from the

Soviet Union. According to Luís Sánchez Sancho, the very changes in Moscow, including *perestroika*, have demonstrated that "it is necessary to redefine the path of the Nicaraguan revolution" (ibid.). Sánchez claimed that the PSN remains a socialist party, but that socialism has to be redefined "as a plan for economic development and prosperity... [that] can function only in a climate of peace, and this means a climate of liberty and real democracy" (ibid.). Furthermore, he directly accused FSLN policies, rather than the civil war, for the catastrophic economic situation. Later in the year Sánchez defined the FSLN's ideology as "an aberrant and degenerate Marxist-Stalinist-Castroite variant, the weaknesses of which have been exposed in various world forums" (*FBIS-LAM*, 20 June).

Only two days later, a document allegedly prepared by a minority faction of the PCN, which included Jamileth Bonilla, Flor Argenal, and Angel Hernández was made public. It accused the party leadership, particularly Eli Altamirano, Allan Zambrana, and Ariel Bravo, of pursuing "dangerous rightist leanings" in the name of a "false policy of alliance." (Ibid., 18 August.) This was probably an allusion to the MUR. Bonilla admitted that purges were on the way, but both she and Hernández refused to repeat publicly the claims included in the document.

In addition to cooperating with each other and moving "rightward," the PSN and PCN strengthened their cooperation with democratic unions and parties, directly as well as through their remaining labor-union groups. On 7 February, what appears to have been the largest anti-Sandinista labor protest ever took place, involving some 10,000–15,000 participants. Largely as a result of the incipient PSN-PCN cooperation, the groups behind the demonstration were united in a loose umbrella organization, the Permanent Workers' Congress (CPT) (*FBIS-LAM*, 12 February). The most prominent constituent groups of the CPT are the PCN's CAUS, the PSN's Independent General Confederation of Labor, the Social Christian People's Party's Central Organization of Autonomous Workers, and the Social-Democrats' CUS (see *YICA*, 1988).

On 4 May, the government cracked down on a demonstration showing solidarity with CPT leaders who were on a hunger strike. Among the politicians briefly arrested were Eli Altamirano, Allan Zambrana, and Ariel Bravo of the PCN, Adolfo Evertz of the PSN, and democratic politicians such as Erick Ramírez and Augusto Jarquín (ibid., 5 May).

In sharp contrast to the FSLN's view, the PSN and PCN consider the unions to be an autonomous force with a legitimate political role. Luís Carrión Cruz clearly stated the FSLN's position when he said that, although "it is very important to have adequate communications... between the administration and the union... this should not be a case of constant claims, because this is bad for the worker; it separates him from his group... I feel the unions' main task is to make the workers aware... of the specific manner in which they should participate in this great national effort to defend the economy." (Ibid., 15 September.)

The ideological differences between the FSLN and the leftist opposition have always been sharp. Since the Sandinistas have begun to repeatedly and publicly associate the left with the rest of the opposition, however, their anti-PSN/PCN/PMLN rhetoric has been intensified. For Daniel Ortega, for instance, "... the so-called Communists, the so-called Marxist-Leninists, the so-called Socialists..." are simply "turncoats belonging to right-wing parties that describe themselves as opposition members..." (*FBIS-LAM*, 19 September). For Víctor Tirado, "... the rainbow of rightist and so-called leftist political organizations are bound by the same interest, which is to destroy the revolution" (*El Nuevo Diario*, 25 July).

While the PSN and PCN remain the largest groups of the Nicaraguan far-left, they are not the only ones, nor is their recent evolution typical of that of the leftist fringes of Nicaragua's political spectrum. The PMLN, through its deputy Carlos Cuadra, blamed the FSLN for the Nandaime and "Melton Plan" affairs, on the grounds that the regime's political opening allowed "foreign powers" and "forces organized by those very foreign powers within the country..." to interfere in Nicaragua (*FBIS-LAM*, 13 July). The PMLN, according to Cuarda, rejects the Esquipulas agreements and agrees with the FSLN's decision to close down opposition media organs, because those have "served... foreign and pro-imperialist interests" (ibid.).

The Economy. By all accounts, including those of the highest-ranking officials of the regime, the Nicaraguan economy approached a state of total collapse. The gravity of the situation was underscored by the appointment of National Directorate member Luís Carrión Cruz as the main economic official. Previously Carrión was deputy interior minister in charge of intelligence and counterintelligence, and he is probably the best-educated member of the nine-member Directorate (a graduate of Phillip Exeter Academy, Andover, and the Rensselaer Polytechnic Institute).

According to economist Francisco Mayorga of Managua's Central American Institute of Business Administration (who is technically independent of, but is sympathetic to the FSLN), the national inflation rate in December 1988 reached 27,000 percent. The figure is also accepted by Fr. Xavier Gorrostiaga, a long-time Jesuit supporter and adviser of the FSLN, and director of the government-controlled Economic and Social Investigation Regional Coordinating Board (CRIES) (ibid.). The value of exports will decrease from $200 million in 1988 to $165 million; that of imports will increase from $800 million to $820 million, resulting in a trade deficit of $655 million. Meanwhile, the country's current $8 billion debt will increase and the national currency will lose value ". . .by more than 306,000 percent [sic!], as it did in 1988" (ibid.). Mayorga, as an economist, also claimed that "inflation has mutilated economic policy, and the government is losing its power to govern," and that "in Nicaragua, inflation controls the economy. It has a life of its own and determines the economic country's destiny." (Ibid.)

Such a gloomy assessment was indeed borne out by the realities of the economy throughout the year. On 14 February, a new economic plan was put into effect that included drastic price increases—gasoline went up 1,000 percent, for instance—and a new cordoba worth 1,000 old cordobas (*WP*, 5 March). Nevertheless, six new devaluations of the cordoba followed during the year, including five by July, each ranging from 25 to 50 percent (*FBIS-LAM*, 5 July). The new cordoba, originally set at a 10/1 exchange rate against the U.S. dollar, reached a rate of 180/1 by July and 320/1 by August (*Central American Report*, 27 October).

The government's unrealistic exchange rates and official prices for staple foods resulted in the disappearance from the market of basic staples, including beans and rice. In response, the regime launched a massive campaign of repression against black-market vendors, further diminishing supplies. By July the situation had reached the point where the regime felt compelled to classify employees in priority categories for the receipt of basic food supplies. Military personnel were to receive 10 lbs. of beans and rice and 5 lbs. of sugar per month. Those with lower wages would pay for these goods with 5 percent of their wages; those on the higher levels would pay 10 percent. (*FBIS-LAM*, 8 July.)

Finally, the previous policy of governmental control of salaries in the private sector was abandoned, and enterprises were allowed a degree of flexibility. President Ortega himself went so far as to state that "we are establishing incentives for production workers. We are operating under the premise that if workers in the production sector receive incentives, they will have the chance to increase their wages as they produce more." (Ibid.)

As it always has since 1979, the regime blamed most of its economic woes on the United States. 1988 briefly provided a new scapegoat: Hurricane Joan, which struck the country on 22 October. According to president Daniel Ortega, Joan inflicted $828 million in direct damages, most of which were concentrated in the infrastructure, including damage of $414 million to the "social" infrastructure (housing, public and health buildings, etc.), damage of $198 million to the "economic infrastructure" (roads, ports, etc.), and lost-production damages of $76 million (*FBIS-LAM*, 16 November).

With the exception of the damages produced by "Joan," however, the Sandinista regime steadfastly refused to accept any responsibility for the state of the economy, insisting that all blame lay with the United States. On 27 April, Daniel Ortega still claimed that "despite the war and aggression, the Nicaraguan economy has not collapsed. We have succeeded in working out an economic policy that takes account of the country's difficult situation. We have not capitulated when faced with economic adversity that is due to the war and the Third World crisis, which has its origins in the unjust international economic order." (*IB*, October 1988.)

Vice President Sergio Ramírez opened the "First Congress on Economic Crimes" at the "Olof Palme" Convention Center in Managua on 28 November by admitting that "embezzlement, fraud, or crimes against state property" are common, and that they are the result of "political and economic instability, low salaries, deficient administrative controls, excessive bureaucracy. . ." (*FBIS-LAM*, 30 November). Ramírez also admitted that the postrevolutionary economic expectations of many Nicaraguans remain unfulfilled, but he rejected the idea that "embezzlement" or corruption should be seen as a solution (ibid.). The same month, Bayardo Arce promised the population that the "plight of the workers" will be understood, but that "we will have to work and produce more" (ibid.).

One of the means seen by the government as

necessary to increase production was the nationalization of the largest remaining privately-owned agro-industrial enterprise in the country, the San Antonio sugar plantation and mill owned by the generally pro-Sandinista Pella family. With the takeover of the San Antonio enterprise, the government is now in complete control of all industrial and agricultural enterprises of significance in the country. The official explanation for the takeover was offered by Jaime Wheelock: "By expropriating the San Antonio sugar mill the revolution has halted the collapse of this work center and prevented thousands of working heads of families from losing their jobs" (*Barricada*, 15 November).

Internal Politics. The dominant event on the domestic political scene was the dramatic collapse of any credible, organized political opposition to the ruling FSLN. Several factors contributed to this: the combination of adroit Sandinista use of classic "salami" tactics to divide and temporarily coopt opposition politicians, the heavy use of repression and intimidation against individual opposition politicians, the opposition's feeling of isolation following the Esquipulas II accords, and the all-pervasive factionalism and personalism of Nicaraguan politicians.

The regime's attempts to separate the legal political opposition from the armed resistance became a clear feature of its policy after January. Indeed, after members of the strongest internal opposition group, the "Ramiro Sacasa Guerrero" Democratic Coordinating Board (CD) met RN leaders Adolfo Calero and Enrique Bermúdez in Guatemala City on 14 January, the Interior Ministry promptly arrested the CD members (see *YICA*, 1988). It accused them of plotting "the creation of a single front" and of trying to "promote conspiracies and terrorist actions." It also proclaimed that the meeting was promoted by the U.S. Central Intelligence Agency. (*FBIS-LAM*, 15 January.)

When the RN demanded that the legal opposition parties, particularly the CD, should be part of the Sapoá meeting, Vice President Ramírez rejected the suggestion out of hand on the basis that those talks involved armed groups only (*FBIS-LAM*, 15 March). More important (and typically), in January a number of opposition parties—including the most important ones like the Independent Liberals (PLI) and Democratic Conservatives (PCD), as well as the minor PSN, PCN, and Popular Social Christian Party (PPSC)—all rejected the idea of the CD's involvement in negotiations (*FBIS-LAM*, 12

January). This stemmed from their fear of being marginalized, despite the fact that some of them are vocally anti-FSLN. As a result, any chance of an effective political-military coalition facing the FSLN at the negotiating table was permanently lost. This took place despite Calero's statement that the legal opposition "is a party to this conflict and should participate with the right to voice and vote in a meeting like the one in Sapoá" (ibid., 15 March).

Each and every legal opposition party of any importance has been further split during the year by personality conflicts, Sandinista infiltrations, enticements, provocations, and repressions, or simple despair. The Independent Liberals split again in August, when a small group led by Eduardo Coronado formed the Liberal Party of National Unity (PLIUN), which claims to be a constructive force in opposition to the FSLN and to be "against those who adhere to reactionary, anti-patriotic positions..." (*FBIS-SOV*, 16 August) and calls for the military surrender of the insurgents (*FBIS-LAM*, 22 September). There are now four splinters of the once-dominant Liberal Party. The other historic party, the Conservatives, are in equally bad shape, particularly as a result of long-time Sandinista penetration. The three largest factions are the Democratic Conservatives and the factions led by Mario Rappaccioli and Fernando Chamorro, but two other factions are also active. (*FBIS-LAM*, 24 August.) There are now three splinters of the Social Christian Party, led by Erick Ramírez, Eduardo Rivas Gasteazoro, and Augustín Jarquín, respectively.

The opposition was further damaged both militarily and politically by the high-level defection from the military effort against the regime of Fernando "El Negro" Chamorro, one of the oldest guerrilla leaders. Chamorro led guerrilla forces against the Somoza regime from the 1950s until the 1979 Sandinista takeover, and against the Sandinistas (from exile in Costa Rica) beginning in 1980. He founded and led the UDN-FARN (see *YICA*, 1988), but upon his return to Nicaragua in 1987 he assumed a place in the leadership of a faction of the Conservative Party. He pledged cooperation with the CD, justifying his decision as a means to "...make an effort to consolidate peace among brothers" (*FBIS-LAM*, 3 February).

While the political parties continued to split inside Nicaragua, outside they tried to form various alliances, sometimes with most unlikely partners. In September, Edén Pastora, probably the most divisive figure of the exile community, met in Costa Rica with Erick Ramírez and decided to form an alliance, a "third force" between the FSLN's Marxism-Leninism and the RN's "extreme Right" (*Latin American Regional Reports*, 1 December, p. 3). Pastora and Ramírez also encouraged the PSN, PCN, and PLI to join them. Previously, Pastora had claimed that he intended to return and "march on Managua" in August and to "try to manipulate" the Sandinistas (*FBIS-LAM*, 2 August), but he never did so.

Paradoxically, the collapse of the political opposition came at the very time its popular support was at its highest, and when popular dissatisfaction with the regime reached the highest levels since 1979.

In January, the regime had decided to repeal some of the most repressive laws against the opposition. On one day, 19 January, the regime issued Decree 296, which dismantled the "People's Anti-Somozist Tribunals," and Decree 297, which ended the state of emergency. Following these actions, the legal opposition, ranging from parties to unions to the media, interpreted the new situation as an opportunity for free activity. This feeling existed despite the fact that before the day was over the two decrees had been repealed and prominent opposition leaders, returning from Costa Rica, had been arrested on the grounds that they were plotting a united front with the insurgents. (*FBIS-LAM*, 20 January.)

The apparent opening of the political scene was soon overshadowed by the regime's reaction to the ensuing massive demonstrations of opposition to its policies. On 8 February, a recruiting team of the EPS (Ejército Popular Sandinista; Sandinist Popular Army) in Masaya was attacked by enraged citizens, mostly mothers of would-be soldiers. Violence took place and was promptly and harshly put down by the Interior Ministry's forces (*NYT*, 28 February). Civilians were preparing to produce bombs, and the center of opposition became Monimbó, the same Indian area of Masaya that had started the insurrection against the Somoza regime a decade before.

Even more important, and far larger in size and political impact, was the popular demonstration in Nandaime on 10 July organized by the CD. Once again, some 15,000 people gathered to protest governmental policies and, more important, to demand a government of national reconciliation. Interior Ministry plainclothesmen and paid gangs from the CDSs attacked the demonstrators and arrested the organizers of the rally, including Augustín Jarquín, Miriam Arguello of the Conservative Party, labor leader Carlos Huembes, and Roger Guevara. Some 38 leaders of the rally were accused of "criminal association, causing injury [to the police and CDS provocateurs], destroying property and...opposing the government" (*NYT*, 8 December). After being kept in jail—and, according to the opposition, mistreated—all were released by mid-December following strong political and economic pressures from West European governments (ibid.).

The Nandaime episode clearly jolted the regime and resulted in a furious assault against the newly-allowed political and civil liberties, as well as against the United States, which was made the scapegoat of the entire episode (see below). Under the pretext that the Nandaime demonstrations were all a CIA operation—a claim based on nothing but knee-jerk propaganda and the unproven statements of U.S. House of Representatives Speaker Jim Wright, and vehemently contradicted by the Reagan administration—the regime cracked down on all forms of political, union, and media expression. In fact, commenting on Wright's statements, *Barricada* claimed that he has "really revealed nothing new in his statements on U.S. Government agents' involvement in anti-government demonstrations in Nicaragua..." (*Barricada*, 21 September). On the other hand, Cardinal Obando y Bravo publicly accused Wright of making statements harmful to Nicaraguan political opposition forces for "...the benefit of his party—the Democrats—in the presidential elections" (*FBIS-LAM*, 26 September).

Embracing the idea that its opposition is entirely CIA-controlled, and "proving" it by quoting Wright's statements, the regime continued in its massive crackdown against all forms of expression by the opposition. In addition to the already-mentioned arrest of the CD leaders following the Nandaime affair, the regime suspended the COSEP's Radio Mundial for "slandering" the government (*FBIS-LAM*, 13 October). The independent Radio Corporacion's "Diez en Punto" broadcast in June was suspended (ibid., 7 June), and *La Prensa* was closed for fifteen days. Finally, after repeated attempts to close the Catholic Church's Radio Católica, the government forced the station to forgo its news bulletin.

The Military Situation. The regime's pattern of military activities followed lines similar to those of its political approach—maximum pressure at the time the opposition was at its weakest; temporary retreat when political conditions required it. In general terms, however, there were few major clashes after April, and an uneasy, often-broken and always-uncertain cease-fire persisted throughout most of the year.

By far the largest Sandinista military operation of the year, and one of the largest of the entire war, took place in March. It was code-named "Operation Danto," and the government described it as a great success. Daniel Ortega even claimed, with little evidence, that "one effect of the defeats that the mercenary forces have been suffering, of the overwhelming impact of the Danto operation this year, was that a historic agreement was reached—the Sapoá Agreement" (*FBIS-LAM*, 3 January 1989).

In fact, the entire operation was a military failure. On 6 March, only a month after the U.S. Congress had cut off all military aid to the resistance, as many as 4,500 EPS and special troops of the Interior Ministry launched a massive attack against the resistance's advanced supply bases on both sides of the border with Honduras. The obvious target was the 250,000 lbs. of ammunition and other military supplies the resistance had concentrated in the area of San Andrés de Bocay; the intention was to capture the stockpile if possible, to destroy it if necessary. (*NYT*, 17 and 22 March.) Either would have been a deadly blow to the resistance, since it had no further source of resupply.

While strategically and politically the operation was well-timed, tactically it was flawed. The operation was launched at the very time when resistance fighters inside Nicaragua were forced to return to their Honduras camps following the aid cutoff; as a result, their numbers in the area probably surpassed those of the attacking EPS force. Moreover, Honduras replied by bombing EPS concentrations on its side of the border, while the United States dispatched troops to Honduras. The final result was that the supply depots were not reached and the resistance retreated into Honduras after inflicting significant casualties. (*WP*, 23 March.)

A lack of ammunition and food, the deterioration of equipment, and the cease-fire agreement of Sapoá prevented the insurgents from engaging in significant operations and forced many of their fighters to retreat into Honduras. At the end of the year, however, they remained active in most of their areas of traditional strength, and retained their popular support (see for instance *CSM*, 1 February). These include the departments of Chontales and Boaco in the center of the country, the Nueva Guinea region in the southeast and particularly the departments of Matagalpa and Jinotega in the north. Most clashes with the EPS during the second half of the year were localized and relatively minor, with few casualties on either side. Most of those casualties occurred during clashes in guerrilla-controlled or -influenced areas, where the EPS and the Interior Ministry troops continued throughout the year to round up insurgent supporters despite the technical cease-fire in place (*The Miami Herald*, 12 December).

Perhaps the most important adumbration of the resistance's potential to hold itself together despite the cutoff of aid lies in the extremely small number of fighters who have accepted the government's amnesty and defected—probably less than 100 out of some 10,000 combatants. This fact is all the more remarkable considering the resistance's own internal political problems: major commanders have left the field as a result of political squabbles with the general command of the National Resistance (Resistencia Nacional; RN). In April four major field commanders under the influence of former RN Director Pedro Joaquín Chamorro—"Rigoberto," "Fernando," "Toño," and "Tigrillo" (the latter two have been among the resistance's most popular)—staged a short-lived, bloodless rebellion against Supreme Commander Enrique Bermúdez and were expelled from Honduras as a result. Although these commanders subsequently made public statements against Bermúdez, the Council of Regional Commanders of the RN in a statement made on 15 May left the door open for their reintegration (*FBIS-LAM*, 25 May).

Less damaging to the insurgent command structure was the 27 July decision by southern-front commanders, led by General Commander Pedro Lara ("Ganso"), who had broken ties with the RN a week before, to reject Bermúdez on the basis that he was "a radical Somozist" (a fact they had discovered after working with him for years), and because their forces had not received ammunition, food, or medicine (*FBIS-LAM*, 29 July). Considering the chronic ineffectiveness of the southern front since 1983 and Costa Rica's cessation of any support for the resistance along its border, the Lara group's decision had no impact whatsoever on the military balance.

The key factor in the stance of the resistance remains the behavior of the rank and file. It appears that the U.S. Congress's cutoff of aid has, if anything, strengthened the resolve of local commanders and their young followers to continue on their own (see, for instance, *The Miami Herald*, 12 December).

Negotiations. Publicly and officially the year was dominated by negotiations with both the internal opposition groups—the "poor things," as everyone from Arce to Ortega to Borge to the CIA has chosen to describe them—and the armed resistance.

The negotiations between the Nicaraguan regime and the insurgents of the RN went through a number of stages, starting with meetings in Guatemala in January and February. There was a major meeting in Sapoá in March, follow-up negotiations in Managua in April and June, and a promise to hold another meeting in January 1989. The most important meeting, and the only one resulting in a formal agreement, was that at Sapoá, on the Nicaraguan side of the border with Costa Rica, on 24 March.

The Sandinista delegation was led by Humberto Ortega and EPS Chief of Staff Cuadra, the RN delegation by Adolfo Calero, Alfredo César, and Aristides Sánchez, as well as by commanders "Toño," "Fernando," "Omar," and "Blas." The negotiators reached a number of agreements related to military matters—a general amnesty, areas of guerrilla concentration, release of prisoners, and a cease fire (*NYT*, 25 March)—but none related to major political issues. The RN saw the accords as a means of involvement in the domestic political situation, while the Sandinistas interpreted the meeting as a form of general capitulation by the RN. Neither side was prepared to accept the other's definition of the problem: the FSLN sees the struggle as a military one; the RN sees it as a political one.

The cease-fire agreed upon at Sapoá was to last for 60 days. It has never been formally renewed, although the government has claimed since the cease-fire's expiration that it has unilaterally extended it. The accords also provided for the release of political prisoners. Half were to be released when the guerrillas entered the cease-fire zones, the remaining half upon the signing of a permanent cease-fire agreement. Compliance with the provisions was to be verified by a commission led jointly by Cardinal Obando y Bravo of Managua and the OAS general secretary, João Clemente Baena Soares.

Further talks took place in April and May in Managua, but brought no solution; there were no public contacts between the government and the RN after June. The main reason for the collapse of talks was the behavior of the government. Not only did it persist in interpreting the negotiations as a formula for the surrender of the insurgents, it also violated most of the provisions of the Sapoá agreements.

Managua committed most of the violations openly. For instance, Daniel Ortega, speaking in December, claimed that there were 1,744 former National Guard members still in jail, compared with a total of 2,072 in August 1987, and 1,398 "contras," compared with 2,404 in 1987 (*FBIS-LAM*, 13 December). According to the Sapoá agreements half of both groups should have been freed by June.

Far more important in regard to the government's attitude toward the Sapoá agreements was its treatment of the opposition and the media, in direct violation of article 5 of those agreements. The most massive wave of repression since the 1979 revolution took place in July, following the Nandaime demonstrations. Not only were 39 opposition and labor leaders arrested, but the next day *La Prensa*, the main voice of the opposition, was closed down for fifteen days, a decision the newspaper protested as "barbaric" (*FBIS-LAM*, 14 July). At the same time, Radio Católica was closed down indefinitely, soon followed by Radio Corporación.

Equally significant was the increasing number of assassinations of prominent opposition members, often by men in military uniforms. Among the victims were prominent Conservative leader Eleazar Herrera, Liberal leader Francisco Aguilera, and three members of CUS (*La Prensa*, 6 October). In none of those cases did the police present a convincing explanation. In some cases, the alleged criminals were themselves killed "trying to escape"; others involved retracted their statements, and so on.

At year's end the stalemate in negotiations and the governmental repression continued, despite a new proposal by the Alfredo César faction of the RN (the Democratic Center Coalition). The proposal, which includes a call for democratization, the repeal of compulsory military service, independent supervision of elections, freedom of expression, and the dismantling of the EPS and its replacement by a nonpartisan national army (*La Prensa*, 31 December) stands very little chance of being seriously considered in Managua.

Foreign Affairs. The foreign policy of Nicaragua during the year was characterized by deteriorating relations with her neighbors, as well as by serious diplomatic conflicts with, and increasingly shrill accusations against the United States.

The House of Representatives' vote on 4 February to deny aid to the RN was very well received in Managua, and much praise was given to House Speaker Jim Wright. Indeed, Nicaragua's ambassador to Washington, Carlos Tünnermann, stated that the vote was "a personal victory for House Speaker Jim Wright, who from the start expressed opposition to counterrevolutionary aid" (FBIS-LAM, 6 February). The most serious episode in the conflict with Washington came on 11 July, in the wake of the Nandaime rally, when Managua expelled U.S. ambassador Richard Melton and seven other American diplomats, accusing them of having incited the demonstrators to violence. Foreign Minister D'Escoto claimed that Melton's presence at the rally was a "totally incredible fact..." and described the expulsions as "indispensable measures to defend and maintain the sovereign rights and independence..." of Nicaragua (FBIS-LAM, 18 July). He also characterized U.S. policy as "state banditry," and declared himself "...profoundly, profoundly saddened and disappointed by the lack of substance, moral substance, and character of many people in the United States Congress" (ibid.).

Washington's reaction was to deny all Sandinista accusations against the U.S. ambassador and other diplomatic staff, and to expel in retaliation Carlos Tünnermann and seven of his staff. The measure brought sharp protests from Managua, mostly on the grounds that since Tünnermann was also ambassador to the OAS, the United States had no right to expel him. Nevertheless, Tünnermann did leave Washington.

Other indications of the tense relations between the two countries came in the wake of Hurricane Joan, when the United States refused to send aid on the basis that "the Sandinista government could not be trusted to use the assistance for disaster relief" (NYT, 25 October). In December, Ortega canceled his trip to the U.N. headquarters in New York after Washington rejected the visa applications of some of his entourage and imposed restrictions on his travel. Ortega called the measure a proof that "the United States has violated international norms and its promises to the United Nations...," while the U.S. ambassador to the United Nations, Vernon Walters, stated that "we guaranteed his right to come to the United Nations.... But we did not guarantee his right to bring unlimited numbers of people with him, nor did we guarantee his right to tourism in the United States" (NYT, 6 December).

Managua took no official position during the presidential campaign in the United States. Daniel Ortega stated that "regardless of whether this administration is Democratic or Republican, it will try to impose its criteria on Nicaragua" (FBIS-LAM, 9 November). When George Bush was elected,

Ortega stated that "we must expect the worst and prepare for the worst, but we must let Mr. Bush know that Nicaragua is willing to participate in a serious and formal dialogue with the United States to normalize our relations" (ibid.). On the other hand, prior to the elections, Vice President Ramírez stated, "I believe it possible that an administration led by Dukakis would pursue a policy characterized by mutual respect...," because "in my opinion, what Dukakis says is correct. He says that the policy of the Reagan administration was illegal and immoral because it violated international law and even U.S. laws." (Ibid., 30 June.)

Anti-U.S. shrillness in Managua reached new heights when Daniel Ortega claimed that "if there is a totalitarian regime disguised by the term democratic, that totalitarian regime is in the United States of America. U.S. democracy is mere fiction. Where is party pluralism in the United States? It does not exist. Where is the mass participation of the people in U.S. elections? Such mass participation does not exist." (FBIS-LAM, 11 October.) Given such statements and the perceptions underlying them, it is difficult to foresee any improvement of relations in the near future.

Nicaragua's relations with all Central American countries deteriorated markedly (see YICA profiles of Honduras, Guatemala, and El Salvador). Among the year's events in this regard were the expulsion of the Costa Rican ambassador and military clashes with regular Honduran forces along the border. Both major presidential candidates in El Salvador, meanwhile, are long-time enemies of Managua's regime. Furthermore, the International Court of Justice suit against Honduras further deepened the enmity of that country's government toward Managua, while the Salvadoran military consistently accused Managua of providing help to the FMLN. Daniel Ortega's meetings with URNG leaders did nothing to improve relations with Guatemala. Managua's efforts in the larger world arena included Daniel Ortega's visit to the Vatican, where he was given a markedly cool reception by the pope (NYT, 30 January).

Relations with communist countries continued to improve, however. Ideological, military, and economic ties were further strengthened. In an interview published in January, Daniel Ortega praised the U.S.-Soviet INF treaty and sharply condemned Washington's "obsession" with strategic defenses (WMR, January 1988). He also hailed perestroika as proof that "...any revolution calls for continuous perfection, readjustment and enrichment of forms..." and praised the October Revolution as offering "an example of flexibility in relations between nations..." (ibid.). The question of just who the Sandinistas' real friends are was partly answered by the travels of Daniel Ortega, Bayardo Arce, and other Sandinista leaders. In July, the FSLN concluded a party-to-party cooperation agreement with South Yemen's (PDRY) ruling Yemen Socialist Party that provided for a "broadening" of interparty contacts. Speaking at the ceremony, Ortega stressed the importance of "...more extensive cooperation between the two friendly countries, and the need for the unification of all the progressive and revolutionary forces in the world in a single front of struggle against imperialism..." (*WMR*, August 1988).

Arce traveled to East Germany and Czechoslovakia, two countries notorious for their reservations about *perestroika* and *glasnost'*. In East Germany, he was received by Erich Honecker; the men agreed upon "strict respect" for human rights norms and support for Soviet arms-control proposals (*Neues Deutschland*, 5/6 March). In Prague, Arce was received by party leader Miloš Jakeš and by Vasil Bil'ák, the main hard-liner in the Czech leadership. After underscoring the "firm solidarity" of Czechoslovakia with Nicaragua, Bil'ák "briefed" Arce on the Czechoslovak party's efforts to restructure the economic mechanisms and improve socialist democracy (*FBIS-Eastern Europe*, 10 March). Finally, during a trip to Bulgaria, Major Adolfo Chamorro Teffel, first deputy chief of the EPS's Central Political Administration, stated that "we witnessed the correct political approach taken during the induction of young soldiers...and...the planning and conduct of party-political and cultural-educational work among soldiers. The party-political work in the Bulgarian People's Army and the Sandinist People's Army is essentially similar regarding both ideological aspects and the end goals pursued." (*Narodna Armiya*, Sofia; quoted in *FBIS-LAM*, 26 September.)

Relations with Cuba remain the mainstay of Nicaragua's foreign policy. This was made apparent during the visit to Havana of Daniel Ortega, Jaime Wheelock and Luís Carrión in June. Ortega stated that "we have particularly fraternal relations with Cuba. We went to Cuba to exchange views on the economic situation and the way the Cuban people face it..." (*FBIS-LAM*, 1 July). That appeared to be a hint that the economic collapse of Nicaragua might be solved through the same ideological and coercive means used by Havana. Cuban assistance to the Sandinistas appears to continue apace. Or-

tega claimed that Cuba has written off Nicaragua's $50 million debt to it and increased its subsidies to Managua by raising what he alleged to be a ratio of $1.70 of Cuban products for each dollar of Nicaraguan goods to an even more preferential ratio of 2 to 1 (ibid.). Ortega also claimed that Cuba will donate 90,000 tons of oil per year for the period 1988–1990, amounting to 270,000 tons, and 15,000 tons of cement each year until 1990 for the reconstruction of the Atlantic Coast communities destroyed by Hurricane Joan (ibid.). Furthermore, Ortega claimed that Cuba rejects the idea of joint investments with Nicaragua in lumber mills in Northern Zelaya (the area claimed as their own by the Indian insurgent groups), and prefers instead to invest only in equipment in the area. Ortega claimed that with the addition of assistance in the cultivation of cattle and tobacco, total Cuban aid amounted to $150 million (ibid.).

All year (though particularly after the devastation caused by Hurricane Joan), the Managua regime publicly acknowledged receiving large amounts of aid from Cuba, the Soviet Union, and the East Europeans. Bulgarian deliveries of 6,000 tons of wheat and Soviet grants of 700 tons of fish were prominently mentioned (*FBIS-LAM*, 15 April), as were COMECON investments for deepening the El Bluff harbor, gifts of 24,000 tons of wheat from the GDR, and a joint Soviet-Dutch project for the development of the Bluefields port (*FBIS-LAM*, 29 March).

The most important information regarding Soviet aid to Nicaragua was disclosed at the beginning of the year by Henry Ruíz, the National Directorate member in charge of administering economic ties with the USSR. Commenting on his January meeting with Soviet economic officials in Moscow and the agreements he signed, Ruíz declared that the new economic arrangements with Moscow are based on increasing the level of Soviet aid each year. Specifically, he stated that "[Soviet] aid to Nicaragua in 1988 cannot be less than the aid in 1987; and the aid in 1987 cannot be less than that of 1986. I thus wish to clear up a series of doubts that arose concerning our relations with the Soviet Union. Soviet aid to Nicaragua has increased in volume and [words indistinct] merchandise. Given the volume of our economic ties, they tend to increase rather than deteriorate" (*FBIS-LAM*, 21 January). In response to Soviet and Western accusations that aid is mismanaged, José Angel Buitrago, deputy minister for foreign cooperation, admitted that the USSR supplies most of Nicaragua's oil needs and sponsors all COMECON-financed projects, and that there are "difficulties" in assimilating modern technology (ibid., 13 January). He promised better efforts to "gradually" develop it.

Michael Radu
Foreign Policy Research Institute, Philadelphia

Panama

Population. 2,323,622
Party. People's Party (Partido del Pueblo; PDP or PdP) or People's Party of Panama (Partido del Pueblo de Panama; PPP)
Founded. 1930 (PDP, 1943)
Membership. Party claims 25,600 members based on number of signatures presented to government electoral commission in October; 500–1,000 militants (estimated)
General Secretary. Rubén Darío Souza Batista (or Sousa)
Politburo. Includes César Agusto De León Espinosa, Miguel Antonio Porcella Peña, Anastacio E. Rodríguez, Cleto Manuel Souza Batista, Luther Thomas (international secretary), Felix Dixon, Darío González Pittí, Carlos Francisco Changmarín
Central Committee. 26 members
Status. Legal; gained registered status in November 1988 after submission of approximately 25,600 signatures to government electoral commission (19,252 required)
Last Congress. Eighth, 24–26 January 1986
Last Election. 1984, less than 3 percent of vote, no representatives in National Assembly
Auxiliary Organizations. Panama Peace Committee, Committee for the Defense of Sovereignty and Peace, People's Party Youth, National Center of Workers of Panama (Central Nacional de Trabajadores de Panamá; CNTP), Union of Journalists of Panama, Federation of Panamanian Students (Federación Estudiantil de Panamá; FEP), National Union of Democratic Women
Publication. *Unidad* (weekly), Carlos Francisco Changmarín, director

The domestic challenge to military rule that began in June 1987 evolved in 1988 into a full-scale confrontation between Washington and Panamanian strongman Gen. Manuel Antonio Noriega. In February, two Federal grand juries in Florida indicted Noriega on drug-trafficking and money-laundering charges. President Eric Arturo Delvalle, installed by Noriega in 1985, dismissed him as commander of the Panamanian Defense Forces (PDF). But within eight hours Delvalle was deposed by the Noriega-controlled National Assembly and replaced by education minister and Noriega loyalist Manuel Solís Palma. The United States continued to recognize Delvalle, who became "president-in-hiding," and applied economic sanctions and political pressure with the stated intention of dislodging Noriega. By mid-March U.S. Assistant Secretary of State Elliott Abrams, anticipating an imminent national uprising, stated that the general was holding on to power "by his fingertips" (*NYT*, 30 May).

At the end of the year, however, Noriega was still in place, having withstood U.S. pressure, the collapse of the economy, and at least two coup attempts from within the PDF. His survival was in part attributable to the failure of the civilian opposition, led by the business-based National Civic Crusade and supported by center-right political parties, to mobilize effectively. But it was his skill in consolidating his domestic and international support base that allowed him to maintain power.

Following the first coup attempt in March, Noriega created a hand-picked, twenty-member Strategic Military Council to monitor the PDF general staff and act as a watchdog within the military. The council was subsequently key in detecting and snuffing out the second coup attempt in the fall.

In domestic politics, Noriega strengthened his position by expanding the role of the Democratic Revolutionary Party (Partido Revolucionario Democrático; PRD) in the government bureaucracy. The PRD was created by the late Omar Torrijos as the political front of the PDF, and since 1984 has been the military's ruling instrument in the National Assembly. The party's leftward turn in 1986 caused some tension between it and Noriega, but it fully supported him against the Civic Crusade in 1987, and against Delvalle in February. In April, during the height of the crisis, Noriega had Solís Palma name a new cabinet that increased the PRD's share of positions from six to nine in the twelve-member body.

The appointment of Orville Goodin, a prominent member of the left-wing *tendencia* of the PRD, as treasury minister, led business and opposition leaders to warn of a radicalization of domestic government policy. The *tendencia* is composed mainly of members of leftist and Marxist organizations that dissolved themselves in 1978 in order to assist in creating the PRD. But the common denominator among Goodin and the other six new cabinet heads was not ideology, but loyalty to Noriega. The general's intentions became clearer when he had Rómulo Escobar Bethancourt, an often erratic politician, replaced by his long-time yes-man and business crony Carlos Duque as president of the PRD in June.

It was in foreign policy, and in particular on the issue of the United States, that Noriega's interests converged with the "anti-imperialism" of the PRD *tendencia*. The increased influence of radicals in the party and in government was in fact a function of the deterioration of relations between Noriega and Washington since the end of 1985. Two examples were the placement of Luis Gómez as chief of the National Assembly Committee on Canal Affairs, and the hold on the position of assistant general secretary in the PRD by the *tendencia* since 1986. The clash with Washington also resulted in the emergence of radical PRD leaders not completely identified with the *tendencia*, but who were staunchly anti-U.S. and willing to defend Noriega before the world community. Prominent in this category were Foreign Minister Jorge Ritter and PRD international secretary Nils Castro.

Noriega's strategy on the international front was to blur the reality of his corrupt military dictatorship by portraying himself as the leading defender of Panamanian sovereignty and the target of a U.S. plot to abrogate the 1977 Canal Treaties. Ritter, advised by Castro, headed the diplomatic effort in the United Nations, the Nonaligned Movement, the Organization of American States (OAS), and the 23-nation Latin American Economic System (SELA). The effort helped to secure nearly universal opposition to U.S. political pressure and economic sanctions. However, it failed to fully secure political legitimacy for Noriega and Solís Palma, his new presidential instrument, except within the Eastern bloc and among Third World radical states and movements.

The failure to achieve political legitimacy was most manifest in the continued suspension of Panama from the Group of Eight. Composed of the eight Contadora countries (Panama was one of the original four), the organization was formally instituted in 1987 as a body of democratic nations

concerned not only with Central America, but also with the overall hemispheric issues of democratization, indebtedness, and drugs. By 1988, the Group of Eight had at least equaled in influence the foundering OAS (of which the United States is a member), previously the most influential regional organization in Latin America. When Noriega dumped Delvalle in favor of Solís Palma, the other seven countries—Argentina, Venezuela, Uruguay, Mexico, Colombia, Brazil, and Peru—agreed to suspend Panama from the group, pending the return of democratic rule there.

By the end of August it was becoming evident that Noriega would outlast the Reagan administration, and that any further U.S. initiative to oust him would be put on hold until a new administration had taken over in 1989. Noriega therefore assigned his diplomatic corps the task of regaining political legitimacy in the hemisphere, a necessary first step in securing international economic aid and neutralizing the damage caused by U.S. sanctions. While Jorge Ritter directly lobbied the governments of the Group of Eight, Nils Castro worked within two regional party organizations: the Latin American Committee of the Socialist International (SI), and the Permanent Conference of Latin American Political Parties (COPPPAL). The PRD is a member of both, and both overlap substantially with the Group of Eight.

The PRD fared better in COPPPAL because (1) it was a founding member; (2) Nils Castro was executive secretary of the organization when the crisis broke out; and (3) a majority of the 36 member parties (from 21 countries) are either nondemocratic (e.g., the Nicaraguan Sandinista Front [FSLN]), or prefer to put their "anti-imperialism" before their professed commitment to democracy in the hemisphere (e.g., the ruling Aprista party [APRA] of Peru). At the September meeting in Nicaragua, COPPPAL, not surprisingly, backed Panama against the United States. It denounced Washington and accepted the PRD's promise that the Noriega/Solís Palma government would subscribe to democratic norms when the United States recognized it and lifted economic sanctions. In a further show of support, it elected Carlos Ozores, PRD vice president, as COPPPAL president.

But at the October meeting of the Group of Eight presidents, Peru's proposal, backed by Mexico, to reconsider Panama's status on the basis of promised democratization was rejected by the other five leaders, and Panama remained suspended. The message to Noriega was that Panama's readmission would depend on the quality of national elections constitutionally scheduled for 7 May 1989. The response from the Socialist International was essentially the same, despite hard PRD lobbying and support from the more radical member parties. The Group of Eight and the Socialist International also rejected the idea, floated by Noriega's diplomats and the government-controlled media, that a plebiscite would redeem political legitimacy in lieu of competitive elections.

With the approach of 1989, Noriega, Solís Palma, and the PRD therefore confronted the task of maneuvering to ensure victory over opposition political parties in May, despite evidence of little popular support. A survey conducted in November by Doxa C.A., an Italian polling company, showed that 87 percent of respondents wanted the country to be governed by an elected president, that less than 1 percent favored Noriega for the post, and that 81 percent said he should leave power (*WP*, 27 December). The results paralleled those of a poll done earlier in the year by an affiliate of the Gallup Organization, and suggested strongly that in Panama, as in the rest of Latin America, Noriega's real support was limited largely to leftist and anti-American elements.

By November, it appeared that Noriega had developed a three-way strategy in order to prevail in May. First, he would maintain conditions so repressive that the opposition would refuse to participate in elections. All independent media, shut down in March, remained so. Political prisoners were still being detained, and opposition leaders physically intimidated and driven into exile. Once the center-right opposition took itself out of the game, a calculated and limited easing of conditions would occur for the benefit of international observers with short attention spans.

Second, he would create an artificial opposition, centered around the Labor Party (PALA) headed by his brother-in-law, to legitimize the election when the real opposition stayed out. And third, he would utilize the PRD to form an electoral front, a "national liberation alliance," from left-wing elements and party factions coopted or salami-cut from independent parties. That front would then provide the electoral vehicle for either his own candidacy, Solís Palma's, or that of another individual controlled by Noriega. Under the electoral law that he had amended in 1988, Noriega had until 7 February—three months before the vote—to resign his military post in order to run.

The entire scenario was remarkably similar to the way the Nicaraguan electoral process was conducted in 1984. Noriega could view this exercise in electoral management as feasible because by the end of 1988 he controlled (like the Sandinistas) the ruling party, the military, the government, and the national electoral commission. The Nicaraguan case also provided evidence that machinations of this sort could, with proper staging, win approval from a majority of the world community. If Noriega were to succeed, Washington's policy of fashioning a democratic government to receive ownership of the canal in the year 2000 would be further isolated. At the beginning of 1989, Washington was still recognizing Delvalle, while most of the world's nations were giving at least de facto recognition to Solís Palma.

Though Noriega seemed to have a step up, he confronted two major problems. First, the PRD leadership was unable to persuade the generally anti-U.S. labor sector to get behind a new promilitary electoral alliance. Labor's rank and file, particularly the public-service workers, were still smarting from the austerity measures imposed during Delvalle's tenure of the presidency, when Noriega was courting deals with international financial institutions. When the unions perceived that the government was unwilling to ease their plight during the 1988 economic collapse, labor support for the regime dropped precipitously.

The second, and possibly more difficult problem arose at the end of the year when the main parties of the political opposition overcame demoralization and internal disagreement and chose to contest the elections despite the repressive conditions. Their potential electoral strength and their ability to decide on a sole presidential candidate remained in question. The backing of the Civic Crusade was expected to help, but Noriega had weakened the business alliance by driving most of its leadership into exile.

The opposition, however, buoyed by the victory of the democratic opposition over General Pinochet in the October Chilean plebiscite, and aware of the failure of the opposition's boycott in Nicaragua in 1984, was nonetheless determined not to play into Noriega's hand. The key would be whether they could secure in a short time a measure of the international support received by the Chilean opposition in 1988.

It was hard to determine if Noriega had been caught off guard by the opposition's decision to compete, but he seemed to have been put on the defensive. When the Christian Democratic Party and the Crusade arranged for Genaro Arriagada, the executive secretary of the victorious Chilean "No" movement, to address a December meeting in Panama, the government refused to give him a visa.

Then, in the first week of January 1989, he scrapped the idea of artificial opposition in favor of marshaling all available political support into an electoral alliance. PRD president Duque announced that the alliance of seven political parties would include the PRD; the People's Party (PDP); the Labor Party (PALA); the Revolutionary Panamenista Party (PPR), a small paramilitary group directed by a Noriega associate; the Democratic Workers Party (PDT), a tiny leftist organization; and the coopted factions of two small rightist parties, the Liberals and the Republicans, that had split earlier in the year. Duque said the alliance's presidential candidate would be announced later.

PDP Domestic Views and Activities. Since the 1986 party congress the PDP has advocated the creation of a "broad, anti-imperialist, democratic front" to be formed by "patriotic military officers loyal to Torrijism" and the PRD, on the one hand, and by the PDP and other leftist parties and popular organizations, on the other (*WMR*, April 1987). Prior to the outbreak of the political crisis in June 1987, Noriega had not been identified by the PDP as one of the officers loyal to Torrijism, although he had been praised as "a fighter for the nation's sovereignty" (ibid.).

PDP support for Noriega subsequently grew as the conflict between the general and the United States increased. When Washington backed the Civic Crusade's demand that the military remove itself from politics in the second half of 1987, the PDP stated, "General Noriega has come from the midst of patriotic officers as the man prepared to carry on the Torrijos legacy...The General is being personally vilified in an effort to deprive the democratic and anti-imperialist movement of its leader" (*WMR*, October 1987).

At the outset of 1988, when there was the suggestion that Noriega, with Delvalle, was considering some kind of deal with Washington, the PDP appeared to hedge its bet. In early February the party stated, "At the new stage General Noriega has come to the fore as a potential leader in the Panamanian people's struggle for liberating the country from colonial dependence...It is necessary just now for General Noriega to understand that the people want a leader capable of taking the country to victory" (*IB*, June).

After Noriega had rid himself of Delvalle, however, and Washington had made clear its intention to oust him, PDP support for him was unqualified. In May, PDP general secretary Souza stated, "Our Party is convinced that General Noriega expresses the will of the Panamanian people to create an independent democratic country with the participation of the masses...He has developed into a strong politician who is able to pull our people together for the defense of national rights in the face of American aggression" (*Rudé právo*, 4 May).

In the fall, when Noriega turned his attention to electoral politics, the PDP sought for the first time to become a political actor exerting significant influence. In 1984 the party had run alone, dwarfed by the contending official and opposition coalitions, and failed to garner the 3 percent of the vote required to maintain its legal status. In 1986 the party set out to gather the 19,252 signatures necessary to register for the 1989 elections. After a September party convention, the PDP applied to the electoral commission with approximately 25,600 signatures, and became officially registered on 7 November at the government ceremony opening the electoral campaign.

In November, the PDP proposed forming an electoral alliance of the government, the PDP, other leftist parties, and the labor unions—essentially the "broad, anti-imperialist front" it had been already advocating (Moscow Radio Peace and Progress, 23 November; *FBIS-SOV*, 28 November). The proposal appeared to match Noriega's own electoral front strategy. In fact, the seven-party electoral alliance announced by PRD president Duque in January 1989 (see above) was nearly identical to the one envisioned by the PDP.

The PDP also strongly suggested that Noriega himself should be the candidate of the electoral front. At the end of November, Cleto Manuel Souza, PDP politburo member and brother of the PDP general secretary, stated that Noriega "fulfills the requirements" to be the next Panamanian president, that he "is the man best suited to lead a strong government capable of taking Panama out of the crisis" (AFP, Panama City, 28 November; *FBIS-LAT*, 30 November).

PDP International Views and Activities. Prior to Noriega's removal of Delvalle at the end of February, the PDP appeared to acknowledge the domestic basis of the political crisis that had begun in 1987, expressing concern that it was "paving the way for steadily mounting U.S. intervention in the affairs of Panama" (*IB*, May). After the United States specifically targeted Noriega, however, the PDP, echoing Noriega, blamed the crisis on the "U.S. militarist policy" behind a plot to overturn the 1977 Canal Treaties and maintain military bases in Panama (CTK, Prague, 15 April; *FBIS-LAT*, 18 April).

In August, the PDP's position was backed by the Third Conference of the Communist Parties of South America held in Uruguay and attended by a PDP delegation. The communiqué issued by the conference condemned U.S. policy in Panama, stating, "The government and people of Panama have been suffering the consequences of a cruel campaign, the single purpose of which is to repudiate the Torrijos-Carter treaty, so the Pentagon can continue to keep in its hands the colonial enclave and military bases used for aggression and hemispheric control" (*La Hora*, Montevideo, 9 August; *FBIS-LAT*, 18 August). Delegations from the communist parties of Cuba and the Soviet Union, and from the Nicaraguan FSLN and the Farabundo Marti National Liberation Front (FMLN) of El Salvador, attended the meeting as observers (ibid.).

The PDP also began to campaign for a strengthening of Panama's relations with the Soviet Union. General Secretary Souza stated in May, "The U.S. would like to create a puppet government in Panama, which would maintain only one kind of foreign relations—with the U.S. It is necessary to break this bilateralism; it is necessary to negotiate with all nations about the Panamanian crisis, namely with the Soviet Union and other Communist nations" (*Rudé právo*, 4 May). In November, PDP international secretary Luther Thomas advocated trade relations between Panama and the Soviet Union, stating, "We have waited for this step and welcome it as a historic and important step that reaffirms Panama's independence . . . We find it hard to understand why Panama, a nonaligned country, has not yet established relations with the Soviet Union" (Telemetro Television, Panama City, 22 November; *FBIS-LAT*, 29 November).

In mid-September, a delegation headed by Karen N. Brutents, deputy chief of the CPSU Central Committee's International Department, visited Panama for the third time in four years at the invitation of the PDP. *Pravda* reported on 20 September that opinions on the international situation were exchanged, and that the CPSU delegation also met with the leadership of the PRD.

A few weeks later, the PDP praised the Soviet Union's decision to sign the Panama Canal neu-

trality protocol. In its statement, the party called for an official Panamanian diplomatic mission to meet with the Soviet government "as soon as possible to discuss the U.S.-Panama Canal situation and the eventual establishment of Panama-USSR relations (*Televisora Nacional*, 6 October; *FBIS-LAT*, 12 October).

Eastern Bloc Relations. The trend toward closer relations between Panama and the Eastern bloc that had begun in 1985 continued in 1988. Throughout 1987 there had been numerous reports in Panama that diplomatic relations between Panama and the Soviet Union would be established. Two concessions sought by Moscow—landing rights for Aeroflot and port rights for the Soviet fishing fleet—had been granted by the beginning of 1988, but the spring crisis appeared to put the issue on hold.

During the crisis, Moscow expressed its support for Noriega primarily through Soviet media coverage and commentary, and by sending delegations from international front organizations to Panama. At the end of April, a World Peace Council delegation visited Panama. It met with Solís Palma at the presidential palace and with Noriega at PDF headquarters, and expressed its "hope that the Panamanian people's moral strength will lead the United States to change its mind" (*La Estrella de Panama*, 26 April).

During the same week, a delegation from the World Federation of Trade Unions participated in the "First International Labor Union Meeting of Solidarity with Panama, for Peace, Nonintervention, and Sovereignty." The resolution issued by the participants declared "Ronald Reagan as the Number One enemy of the peoples of the world," and "permanent solidarity with the Panamanian people and Government until we defeat the imperialist aggression" (Panama City Domestic Service, 2 May; *FBIS-LAT*, 3 May).

In July, a delegation of the Soviet Committee for Solidarity with the Peoples of Latin America visited Panama, meeting with the leadership of the PRD and the PDP (Moscow Domestic Service, 31 July; *FBIS-SOV*, 4 August). In November, at the invitation of the Soviet Committee, the PRD's Nils Castro and Carlos Ozores led a COPPPAL delegation to Moscow (*La Estrella de Panama*, 17 November). The delegation included representatives of the ruling parties in Peru, Mexico, and Nicaragua, as well as the Democratic Workers Party (PDT) of Brazil, the Movement of the Revolutionary Left (MIR) of

Bolivia, and the Movement Toward Socialism (MAS) of Venezuela (ibid.).

In mid-September, when it was clear Noriega had consolidated his position at home, the establishment of formal diplomatic ties with Moscow appeared imminent. Days after the visit of the Brutents delegation, Noriega stated in an interview on Soviet television, "We know the history of the Soviet people. We know that they are a great people. As a result of our present development, we want Panama to come closer to such people as the Soviets" (Moscow Television Service, 28 September; *FBIS-SOV*, 29 September).

Moscow, however, showed more interest in first establishing trade ties, and an agreement was worked out in October. In November, foreign minister Ritter stated that Panama was about to establish diplomatic ties with two communist countries, although he did not name them (DPA, Hamburg, 22 November; *FBIS-LAT*, 25 November). When nothing happened, however, there was speculation in Panama that Moscow had changed its mind because Noriega was only seeking to provoke Washington, or that it was delaying until 1989 because it did not want the issue of its support for Noriega to interfere with the Reagan-Gorbachev summit in New York in early December.

The matter of trade relations was less controversial and hardly caused a ripple in Washington when the October agreement was approved by the Panamanian National Assembly in early December. Observers noted that a trade agreement had actually been in existence since 1977. However, Panamanian officials stressed that the new trade pact was the "first step" toward diplomatic relations, inasmuch as an annex to the agreement granted the Soviet trade mission "all the immunities and privileges" given to foreign diplomats (ACAN-EFE, 2 December; *FBIS-LAT*, 6 December).

Panama was clearly eager to cement ties. And while Moscow appeared hesitant, for whatever reasons, it was still happy to grant prime space in the Soviet media to Panamanian officials for the expression of their desire. In an interview on 10 December with *Izvestiia*, Solís Palma stated, "The Soviet Union's decision to become a signatory to the protocol to the treaty on the permanent neutrality of the Panama Canal is a powerful incentive to recognize the need to establish diplomatic relations between Panama and the Soviet Union, and expand trade, economic, scientific, and cultural cooperation . . . the Panamanian government attaches great importance to developing relations with the Soviet Union and other states in the socialist community."

Relations with Radical Third World States. When Noriega's removal of Delvalle in February led to a direct clash with the United States, Cuba appeared to step in with immediate support. Early reports of major military involvement turned out to be exaggerated, however. Direct assistance appeared to be limited to the presence of top-flight Cuban advisors and possible munitions shipments. Once Noriega had reconsolidated his rule, though, Havana made an effort to lower its profile and defuse the outcry in Washington over its involvement.

Panamanian Air Force major Augusto Villalaz defected to the United States in March. He claimed that he had helped fly munitions from Havana to Panama on three occasions. He added that a total of sixteen flights had been planned to transport 50,000 pounds of weapons to Panama. The shipments were to be stashed outside Panamanian military facilities in the event of a U.S. invasion or for whenever Noriega needed them. In May, U.S. military and diplomatic officials based in Panama said that while Villalaz might have been telling the truth, the alleged weapon shipments had yet to turn up. They did affirm, however, that a group of high-level Cuban advisors had arrived in Panama at the beginning of the crisis. (*Hemisphere*, Fall 1988.)

American intelligence officials asserted that the Cuban team numbered 30 to 50, and were directly involved in helping Noriega manage the crisis. They also said that they accepted the account of Major Villalaz. (*WP*, 3 May.) According to Washington-based, nationally syndicated columnist Georgie Anne Geyer, the Cuban team included seven top Cuban military and intelligence specialists, among them, Ramiro Abreu of the Americas Department of the Communist Party of Cuba (*Washington Times*, 18 April).

It was further reported that following the March coup attempt, Noriega tripled his personal security force to about 75 members, bringing in Cubans and other non-Panamanians to make up the bulk of the unit (*WP*, 29 May). The same report, however, said there was no evidence of an alleged, Cuban-dominated "Marxist brigade" of up to 1,800 troops in Panama.

While weighing in with intense political support for Noriega against "Yankee imperialism," the Castro regime appeared eager to quiet the flap over allegations of direct assistance, allegations which it denied. Cuban fishing vessels that normally change crews in Panama were ordered to transfer the operation to Peru. Vessels that normally utilized Panamanian ports for repairs were also redirected to Peru, as were Cuban sports and political delegations that frequently utilize Panama as a transit point. (*Hemisphere*, Fall 1988.)

For its part, the Sandinista government lent steady and unqualified political support to the Noriega regime. As in 1987, it maintained a higher profile than Cuba in doing so. In May, Solís Palma received at the presidential palace Bayardo Arce, a member of the five-man executive committee of the FSLN National Directorate, who reasserted Nicaragua's full solidarity with Panama (Panama City Domestic Service, 15 May; *FBIS-LAT*, 16 May).

In August, Solís Palma received Nicaraguan president Daniel Ortega during a two-day official visit, Ortega's second official visit since the crisis began in 1987. Ortega was accompanied by Nicaraguan foreign minister Miguel D'Escoto, and both were received as well by General Noriega at PDF headquarters. Ortega and D'Escoto also met with the executive commission of the PRD. In Panama Ortega stated, "We are here to make clear the recognition of the Nicaraguan people for the Panamanian people, now that Panama, too, finds itself under attack from U.S. imperialism" (*El Diario-La Prensa*, New York, 9 August).

Before leaving Nicaragua for Panama, Ortega had declared that "the struggle against imperialist aggression is led by Panama and Nicaragua . . . Our sister governments of Panama and Nicaragua, as well as the Democratic Revolutionary Party and the FSLN, have mutual goals to fight for and mutual problems to face" (*Critica*, Panama City, 2 August; *FBIS-LAT*, 3 August).

As he had in the previous year, Noriega again solicited support from the regime of Moammar Khadafy in Libya. In 1987, Noriega reportedly sought $200 million in emergency economic aid plus a $100 million deposit by Libya in Panamanian banks to alleviate the effects of capital flight (*WP*, 16 December 1987). In 1988, however, there was no evidence that Noriega was receiving anything like the aid he was requesting, and political support seemed diluted in comparison with the year before. Most of the communication between Noriega and Khadafy appeared to be one-way.

In March, Tripoli reported that Noriega had solicited Libyan "support and backing" in a phone call to Khadafy, but it did not report any response (Tripoli Television Service, 10 March; *FBIS-NES*, 11 March). Two months later, Tripoli reported a message from "brother leader" Noriega requesting "solidarity and understanding," again reporting no response (ibid., 3 May; *FBIS-NES*, 4 May).

In August, the Libyan official press agency reported that Noriega stated, upon presenting a medal to the secretary of the Libyan People's Bureau in Panama, "It is my pleasure to present this fine medal to the leader of the revolution, Colonel Moammar Khadafy, and the Libyan Arab people whom we admire and respect for their stand on our side and supporting us in the difficult events we faced" (JANA, 28 August; *FBIS-LAT*, 29 August). In November, Noriega, as he had done in 1987, dispatched a delegation to Libya led by Luis Gaspar Suarez, head of the Revolutionary Panameñista Party, a paramilitary organization allied with the PRD-led ruling coalition. It could not be determined if Suarez was received by Khadafy as he had been the year before.

Douglas W. Payne
Freedom House, New York

Paraguay

Population. 4,386,024
Party. Paraguayan Communist Party (Partido Comunista del Paraguay; PCP)
Founded. 1928
Membership. 4,000 (estimated)
General Secretary. Júlio Rojas (acting); Antonio Maidana (official) is under arrest.
Status. Illegal
Last Congress. Third, 10 April 1971
Last Election. N/a
Auxiliary Organs. No data
Publications. *Adelante* (underground weekly)

The Paraguayan Communist Party (PCP) radiated more optimism in 1988 than at any time in the past four decades. The reason was to be found in the growing confusion that seems to be spreading in the top echelons of the Stroessner government and the increasing boldness of the regime's opponents. Having split his own Colorado Party by using high-handed tactics at its convention last August,

Stroessner appeared to be politically isolated, but that did not prevent him from engineering his seventh election as Paraguay's president in February 1988. Even the U.S. ambassador, Clyde Taylor, was keeping his distance from Stroessner and lending a sympathetic ear to the parties of the National Accord, an opposition front. Hugo Campos, a PCP Politburo member, accused the United States, in an interview held in Budapest in March, of helping to orchestrate Stroessner's re-election, while also keeping the National Accord as an option to fall back on "in case the old general becomes unable to fight" (*FBIS*, 18 March).

Although Campos noted that the PCP still was subject to "continuous persecution" by the government and that its first secretary, Antonio Maidana, was still a political prisoner, the party recently had celebrated its 60th anniversary and was busily preparing to hold its fourth congress in the near future, in order to plan its strategy for the post-Stroessner period. What made Campos and other Paraguayan communists suddenly so optimistic about the future was the emergence of a number of new, left-wing opposition groups outside of the older, more conservative National Accord, which has always rejected the PCP's advances. The new Popular Democratic Movement, the Democratic Liberation Movement, the Paraguayan Peasant Movement, the Workers' Inter-Syndical Movement (MIT), and various independent university student organizations all remain outside of the traditional political parties. Of these, the Popular Democratic Movement (MDP) appears to be the boldest and most publicly active. For example, on 14 August, the day before Stroessner's inauguration, it stopped traffic at a downtown intersection to hold a lightning demonstration and pass out antigovernment leaflets.

It is difficult to predict how far cooperation between the PCP and these new groups will go, but the *New Times* of Moscow (no. 4, January 1988) proclaimed that the MDP "has the support of the Paraguayan Communists." The MDP, founded only in September 1987, claims to shun all parties, but its vocabulary is classist: its aim is to "confront the dominant classes."

To take advantage of this new ferment, the PCP's Central Committee recently decided to put more effort into improving the organization, finances, and propaganda of its youth wing, noting that 70 percent of Paraguay's population is under 30 years of age. In its report, the CC noted with pleasure that communist influence was spreading in Paraguay, but also felt that more needed to be done to link the

PCP with the new movements. The report also hinted at continuing factional problems in the PCP, however. References were made to "honest but misguided comrades," "incorrigible opportunists," and the "infiltration of enemies and CIA agents." One CC member indicated that a major source of factionalism may be a difference in views between the PCP exiles in Buenos Aires and those militants operating inside Paraguay. (*IB*, January.)

Paul H. Lewis
Tulane University

Peru

Population. 21,269,074 (*World Factbook*, July, 1988)

Party. Peruvian Communist Party (Partido Comunista Peruana; PCP)

Founded. 1928

Membership. 4,000

General Secretary. Jorge del Prado Chavez (b. 1910; member of Senate)

Central Committee. 47 members

Status. Legal

Last Congress. Ninth, 27–30 May 1987; Sixteenth Plenary, 29–30 November 1986

Last Election. 1985 presidential and parliamentary. The PCP has six delegates and is part of the United Left coalition that has 26 percent of the delegates in the Chamber of Deputies. The PCP has two senators in the coalition that has 25 percent of the representation in the Senate.

Auxiliary Organizations. General Confederation of Peruvian Workers (Confederacíon General de Trabajadores Peruanos; CGTP), Peruvian Peasant Confederation (Confederacíon Campesino Peruana; CCP)

Publications. *Unidad* (newspaper of the PCP; Carlos Esteves, editor); *El Diario* (pro–Sendero Luminoso newspaper of the Popular Democratic Union, Luís Arce Borja, editor); *Cambio* (magazine that is pro-Revolutionary Movement of Túpac Amaru)

In 1988 the PCP celebrated the 60th anniversary of its founding and its eighth year as the largest constituent party of the United Left (Izquierda Unida; IU). The Peruvian left is the largest in Latin America and, proportionately, one of the largest in the "western" world (*Debate*, Lima, March–April 1988; *JPRS*, 1 June). More important, throughout 1988 public-opinion polls showed the IU and one of its members, Dr. Alfonso Barrantes Lingán, as the party and candidate favored to win the general and presidential elections scheduled for 1990. The current government of the American Popular Revolutionary Alliance (APRA), under the leadership of Alan García, has presided over the most precipitous economic collapse in Peruvian history, and it has made little headway in the eight-year-old internal war with the revolutionary guerrilla movement of Sendero Luminoso (Shining Path). Leaders of the PCP are confident that the time is right for electoral victory, and the popular sectors in Peru have high expectations that the left will deliver on its promises. Thus the IU is preparing for the campaign. The strength of the left and the complete failure of the APRA's nationalist economic policy have stimulated fragments of ex-president Belaúnde Terry's Popular Action Party, the middle-class, Lima-based Popular Christian Party, and independent conservatives to coalesce around the intellectual Mario Vargas Llosa in a Democratic Front (FREDEMO). The 1990 elections could, therefore, be the arena of an historic confrontation between the political right and left, if the democratic system lasts that long.

Leadership and Party Organization. In the eight years since the IU's founding, the public has increasingly perceived it as an entity with more cohesion than it has in fact had. But that perception, the actions of grass-roots partisans, and pressure to maximize the opportunity of a victory in 1990, resulted in greater efforts in 1988 to define the coalition as a party. Of the constituent units, the pro-Soviet PCP is the only one having grass-roots organizations that do not split. The other "parties" are either coalitions that have consolidated and divided several times since 1980—Union of the Revolutionary Left (UNIR) and the Unified Mariateguista Party (PUM)—or are groups with prominent "leaders" but only small numbers of cadres or members—the Revolutionary Socialist Party (PSR), the Revolutionary Communist Party (PCR) and the Trotskyist Worker, Peasant, Student, and Popular Front (FOCEP). In fact, the independents and so-called "non–party members" (*non-partidizadoras*)

are so numerous that they have consolidated within the IU to demand a role as important as the founding, constituent units.

For the IU, 1988 was a "year of definition." Much time and effort went into preparing for the party's First National Congress. Although the meeting was postponed until 1989, the commission to prepare for the congress made significant organizational advances. They created 120 provincial committees and 39 district committees in Lima. Questions about representation continued to cause problems for the organizers, though. By the end of the year they still had not resolved whether "sectors," such as the nonparty Socialists, would be allowed to participate as a "party." It was agreed, however, that districts with fewer than 100 members would be allowed representation because most rural districts fell short of that number. (*Quehacer*, Lima, vol. 53.) And yet membership inscriptions proceeded at a pace almost three times the committee's goal. More than 130,000 people enrolled in the IU in the registration campaign (*Resumen Semanal*, 9–15 September). On December 31, the commission approved the designation of 1,557 national delegates elected by the provinces and 730 for metropolitan Lima (*Resumen Semanal*, 31 December–5 January 1989).

This dramatic growth was not necessarily shared by the individual parties. Jorge del Prado, general secretary of the PCP, indicated concern with party membership and its sphere of influence at the Ninth Party Congress. He lamented having only "1,500 new recruits in the last few years," a number which fell short of the PCP's goal to have communists and party cells in all major proletarian centers. (*WMR*, June.)

The relationship between the parties of the coalition and the members of the IU has been a problem for years. Unity has been achieved by avoiding debate that might be divisive, by alternating leadership, and by allowing the pursuit of individual programs. In order to seriously contest the 1990 elections, the party had to agree on a plan of government, produce documents on strategy and tactics, and lay the groundwork for the revolutionary front. This process of definition was not easy. By the end of the year, two main forces had emerged within the IU—the moderate Socialist Convergence (Convergencia Socialista; COSO) and the radical PUM vanguard—and the First National Congress of the IU was postponed from September 1988 to 19 January 1989.

The division between the Socialist Convergence

and the PUM turns on several interrelated points: their stance toward APRA; their strategic priority; and their position on political violence. The COSO was formed at the First Plenary of the Socialists of the IU in April by members of the PSR, non-Marxist socialists, and independents. The national coordinators are Alfredo Filomeno (PSR), Tomás Montoya, leader of the Non-party Socialists, and an independent, Francisco Guerra García. The 365 delegates affirmed that socialism "ought to be the major political force in Peru," and that the "IU ought to convert itself into the best alternative of government." IU coordinator-in-turn Alfredo Filomeno argued that "construction of socialism in democracy from a national popular perspective [is] the indispensable response to the social and economic crisis and the spiral of violence and drug trafficking that is devastating and bloodying the country" (*Resumen Semanal*, 15–21 April). Enrique Bernales (PSR) emphasized the consensus on electoral strategy as their immediate goal, saying, ". . . we want to attain government through the electoral route . . . , committing ourselves to the mechanisms of the democratic struggle. We would not negotiate this" (*Caretas*, 13 June; *JPRS*, 19 August).

Members of the Socialist Convergence are concerned about the continuation of the democratic system. As the economic crisis deepened, Barrantes was quite vocal in recommending that politicians and economists from all parties work on an emergency platform to overcome the crisis. Such pragmatic concerns were not popular with the more confrontation-oriented components of the IU and led to charges that the COSO was a mere springboard for Alfonso Barrantes's candidacy for president and divisive for the IU. While Barrantes himself maintained it was not a political party, but "a call to diverse sectors of socialists to work together," there was considerable concern that the differences between the members of the moderate socialist group and the radical PUM vanguard were too great for them to agree on any electoral program. (*Resumen Semanal*, 13–19 May.)

Formed by the consolidation of the Mariateguista and Marxist-Leninist groups in 1986, PUM has adopted the strongest line of confrontation in the IU. Its leaders viewed the Socialist Convergence's commitment to the "mechanisms of the democratic struggle," as a "reformist" agenda that undermined the IU. They charged that the IU would be paralyzed by the moderates' "parliamentary orientation that was geared for elections and concerned with a favorable stance toward fascism [APRA]."

(*Resumen Semanal*, 19–25 August.) They rejected any discussion that sought government-opposition conciliation or the *concertación* called for by García. As Carlos Malpica argued, the "IU does not want to manage a crisis as part of any deal, rather it wants power itself to at least lay the groundwork for a socialist Peru" (*Caretas*, 13 June; *JPRS*, 19 August). Along with their refusal to cooperate with APRA came an increased tendency to view violent confrontation as the necessary route to revolutionary change.

At the PUM's Second National Congress in July, the faction espousing the most radical views, the so-called *libios*, took the leadership when Eduardo Caceres Valdivia was elected the new general secretary. A majority of the 550 delegates made "preparation for confrontation" their priority, accepting the principle that "revolution is imminent and the party must develop an armed branch for self-defense and an eventual insurrection" (*Caretas*, 25 July; *JPRS*, 22 September).

This position of the PUM was disavowed by the Socialist Convergence, which then tried to exclude the group from the upcoming congress of the IU. The PCP was in a pivotal position, as del Prado wanted PUM in the IU, but he was still willing to work with Barrantes. In November the minority factions of PUM left it to form yet another group, the National Mariateguista Coordination, which rejected the "vanguard-militarism" of Caceres and Javier Diez Canseco, but is not quite comfortable with the "reformism" of Barrantes. (*Caretas*, 25 July; *JPRS*, 22 September; *Resumen Semanal*, 4–10 November.)

Even though the Socialist Convergence and the PCP have given the electoral strategy priority, they have by no means forsaken the use or denied the necessity of violence. But they distinguish among the violence of Sendero Luminoso against the population, which del Prado calls erroneous, violence in order to provoke a rebellion, which they think is unwarranted at this moment, and violence serving to protect popular gains against encroachment upon them by the government or by Sendero, which they consider necessary. Therefore, the trend on the Peruvian left in 1988, even among the moderates, was a more militant tone in response to perceived threats from both Sendero and the political right, with a growing belief that there may be a need to defend its gains against a military coup.

The PCP and the IU have consistently denounced the "militarization" of the regime's counterinsurgency policies and recommended social and economic development to undermine Sendero's appeal. But the IU's own attempt to use peaceful means of political organizing to compete with Sendero for the support of peasants, miners, laborers, and students became more difficult, as the IU was a prominent target of selective assassination, direct confrontation at political rallies, and infiltration into organized movements. Del Prado contended that the PCP would respond in kind to Sendero's offense. He said he preferred to talk, but "when they choose weapons, we respond with weapons. If they want war, they will get it. We are ready" (*La Republica*, Lima, 13 March; *FBIS*, 22 March).

On the other hand, as the IU's popularity grew, there was fear that an anticommunist front larger than Vargas Llosa's FREDEMO might appear. Specifically, the IU's leaders felt that the APRA government had undermined the political liberties of the left in a move to the right as the administration's program deteriorated. In competing for the loyalties of some of the same people, the IU alleged that the APRA used illegal means to withhold or to deliver goods and services for partisan advantage at the municipal level, and unconstitutional maneuvering in parliament. (*Resumen Semanal*, 8–14 July; 7–13 October.) Government harassment took various forms. IU political leaders were routinely detained after major terrorist attacks; applications to hold political demonstrations were often denied for "security" reasons; human rights officials and workers were the targets of government scrutiny; greater restrictions were placed on travel in the emergency zone; and police repression of union activities grew.

The IU leaders believe that the best bulwark against Sendero is an organized population that will "isolate and marginalize terrorist action" (*Resumen Semanal*, 4–10 March). Similarly, the best defense against a military coup, argued del Prado, is an organized population in the form of the National People's Assembly created in 1987, which "coordinates actions of working people in the everyday struggle and the preservation of gains. If IU wins the elections, the Assembly would be a forum linking all sectors of society. In the event that IU's victory precipitates a coup, the Assembly would be able to declare a national strike and act against the coup" (*Rudé Právo*, Prague, 20 May; *FBIS*, 27 May). Del Prado's concern with increasing the number of PCP cells also reflects his recognition of the need to carry on clandestinely in such a case (*WMR*, June).

The PUM's split meant that the moderates held sway in the IU at the end of the year, but the overall situation was highly charged and armed defense of popular organizations was openly discussed, even by Barrantes, who has not ignored the possibility that the IU's success might be prevented before it happens, or, like Allende's, halted in midterm (Farnsworth, *World Policy Journal*, Fall).

Domestic Affairs. Peruvian democracy barely weathered the storms of 1988. García's "heterodox" economic policies produced the worst economic situation of the century and thereby fueled widespread social and labor unrest. His inability to halt the continued growth of revolutionary violence or to stem the corrupting drug trade enhanced the role of the military in governing the country. The approval rating of the once immensely popular president had plummeted to 15 percent, with calls for his resignation coming from within his own party, as well as from the opposition. Many observers noted that the only reason there was not a coup was that even the military did not want to take power under these circumstances (*Latin American Weekly Review* [*LAWR*], 22 September; EFE, 25 October; *FBIS*, 26 October).

Although the PCP and the IU had supported García's nationalist economic model, which put a ceiling on the foreign debt, emphasized domestic production, and promised nationalization of the financial community, he never pursued these policies to their conclusion. An about-face that negated the bank nationalization and proposed selling profitable state enterprises and austerity plans made to gain approval from the International Monetary Fund ended all hope of the IU's tacit cooperation. (*LAWR*, 13 October.)

Del Prado charged that García's economic policy was merely an extension of the previous international capitalist orientation, with the limit on external debt payment the only innovation. Del Prado maintained this was evident in the attempt to nationalize the banks, when the administration proved too weak in the face of opposition to take that step. Del Prado blamed García's failures on "an alliance with the entrenched right wing, corrupt senior officialdom, and the reactionary military" (*WMR*, June).

The IU's demands to APRA in early 1988 had included: establishing a basic "family basket" of goods with stabilized prices; declaring a unilateral moratorium on Peru's external debt; creating financial and labor communities; progress in the decentralization of administration; and concerted planning with cooperatives, communities, and small and medium businesses to confront the monopolies (*Resumen Semanal*, 29 January–18 February). Throughout the year, the García administration retreated further from the IU position. With each *paquetazo* (new economic plan), the number of subsidized items diminished and the purchasing power of the poor was eroded further.

In March, faced with no foreign reserves, inflation that had been 140 percent for the past twelve months, declining exports, and a deficit equal to 8 percent of the GDP, García introduced a "war economy." The austerity plan, which tried to reorient growth and protect the poorest sectors at the same time, failed miserably, producing higher interest rates, a greater demand for dollars, and hyperinflation. (*Resumen Semanal*, 4–10 March; *LAWR*, 24 March; *Latin American Regional Reports* [*LARR*], 19 March.) Minor adjustments were unsuccessful, so García announced a "shock" program in September. The inti was devalued by 87 percent; prices of basic goods trebled, with gasoline going from $.30 to $1.00 a gallon; and sales and export taxes escalated. To soften the blow to the poor, an emergency social plan for food subsidies went along with the package. Although the intent was to stifle inflation, the expectation of further price increases led to unjustifiable markups and shortages; inflation thus soared to 114 percent for the month. At the same time, the majority of the population had less to spend; demand declined for some products, such as tobacco and beer; and therefore production went down, and workers were laid off. (*NYT*, 30 October; *LAWR*, 22 September, 13 October.)

When the year ended, Peru was close to collapse. Inflation had accumulated to 2,120 percent for twelve months, and García had sought the acceptance of the international banking community by bringing an IMF mission to the country (*Resumen Semanal*, 31 December–5 January 1989). The bank-nationalization law had been negated in practice; decentralization had been postponed for three years; and transnational corporations were being courted to develop natural gas in the Andes.

The deteriorating economic situation fueled ever greater social and labor unrest. After the "shock program" in September, mobs rioted and looted the main markets in Lima. During 1988 there were four general strikes called by the PCP-oriented Confederation of Peruvian Workers (CGTP); in May alone there were 132 walkouts; and in July, one million workers were picketing, which affected five million more (*LAWR*, 23 June, 28 July). The transportation sector, the public sector, and the mining and metal workers were most active in voicing their grievances, but given the economic crisis, all sectors were under stress. National strikes in Peru have generally been disruptive, but nonviolent. This year, however, Sendero Luminoso took advantage of the political tension and incited violence during the labor demonstrations.

On January 28, the CGTP led the second national strike since García took office. It was concerned that national economic priorities be set that would alleviate the desperate situation of workers faced with expensive food, no health care, and inadequate housing and education benefits. Though the strike was successful, with 90 percent participation by union members, confrontations with Sendero detracted from the political goals of the CGTP. In Lima the terrorists attacked an IU rally, and in Huancayo they provoked the police, whose response resulted in the death of a striker. (*Resumen Semanal*, 22–28 January; *LARR*, 3 March.) The second general strike of the year was called for 18–19 July, and this time a faction of the Aprista Confederation of Peruvian Workers (CTP) participated to protest the rapid decline in real wages (*LAWR*, 28 July; *Resumen Semanal*, 15–21 July).

In October, Peru endured its third, and most expensive, general strike. This one had the support of the 70,000-member mining and metallurgical sector, which in a previous strike had won from the government the concession that a single bargaining federation for all miners could be formed. On the appeal of private mine owners, however, the courts overturned that ruling in August. When this sector is not working, the whole nation suffers greatly because foreign exchange is lost. The three mining strikes in 1988 cost Peru $200 million. The October work stoppage was also marked by violence, as Sendero dynamited power stations, destroyed a petrol warehouse, and killed two miners, one Aprista and one communist. (EFE, 17 October; *FBIS*, 20 October; *LAWR*, 10 November.)

The fourth national strike of the year, on 1 December, was not as successful as the others, drawing only 25 percent compliance. This may be attributed to greater fears about losing jobs in a collapsing economy and concern with the increased likelihood of violence at labor demonstrations. (*Resumen Semanal*, 2–15 December.)

Not only was the economy out of control, civilian control over the war against Sendero diminished in 1988, and human rights violations climbed to pre-1985 levels. García's economic and social initiatives stalled and greater reliance was placed on the military's counterinsurgency efforts, which were now being assisted by the United States. In July, IU deputy Agustín Haya de la Torre charged that U.S. helicopter pilots participating in action against drug traffickers were also intervening in the emergency zones. The 52 U.S. military advisers in Peru are, by U.S. law, not allowed to directly participate in antiguerrilla actions, but according to the U.S. embassy, they "counsel Peruvian security forces in ways to improve their fight." (*LARR*, 28 July.) There are continued allegations by the left, however, that the difference between "drug-busting" and antiguerrilla actions by employees of the U.S. Drug Enforcement Agency is negligible. IU leaders are worried about any efforts to create a unified command in the military, or to give it more autonomy of power, as apparently was suggested by U.S. advisers in May (*Andean Newsletter*, 11 July).

The greater importance given to a military response was evident in the increase in the number of military engagements and of deaths of members of the security forces and in the rise of human rights violations. In 1988, the death totals for the armed forces were more than double the 53 in the previous year, reaching 136 as of November. (*Resumen Semanal*, January-December.) The frustration felt by the military in the face of its vulnerability produced yet another massacre and symbol of military repression. On 14 May, the day after an attack on a military convoy, the security forces gathered together the population of Cayara and killed 30 peasants. Although García visited the site and asked for a probe, investigations were hindered by the military. Journalists were kept out until 27 May, and by then the bodies had disappeared. (*Resumen Semanal*, 13–19 May; *LAWR*, 9 June, 23 June.)

Disappearances have continued to be a problem in Peru. The National Association of Families of Disappeared claims that 15,000 persons have disappeared since 1980, but only one-third of them have been reported. U.N. statistics show that 79 were reported in 1987, more than in any other country that year. (EFE, 1 September; *FBIS*, 2 September.) Yet, in 1988 there were 250 reported disappearances, including key witnesses of the Cayara killings. Investigator Juan Mendez complained that for the first time under García, Americas Watch observers were stopped from traveling in the emergency zone. He felt that, "García, in a mood of resignation, is now tolerating abuses and allowing the military to act with impunity." (*NYT*, 3 November.) International human rights organizations,

such as Americas Watch and Amnesty International, have also charged that Sendero Luminoso is responsible for the deaths, torture, and deprivations of a great number of innocent victims (*Resumen Semanal*, 30 September–6 October).

The high and low point for the administration in its confrontation with Sendero Luminoso was the capture on 11 June of Osmán Morote Barrionuevo, the 43-year-old military strategist who was second-in-command of that organization. The capture was said to be due to a combination of an informant's greed (a five million inti reward had been offered) and diligent intelligence work (*Resumen Semanal*, 10–16 June). Morote was charged with seven crimes; he was acquitted on one count in July, but in October he was given a fine and sentenced to fifteen years in jail (*Resumen Semanal*, 8–14 July; Television Peruana, Lima, 20 October; *FBIS*, 20 October).

When Morote was cleared of the first charge because "mere association" with terrorists was not a crime, conservative frustration boiled over. García called it a national scandal and argued for clearer laws to allow the judiciary no loopholes (EFE, 23 July; *FBIS*, 25 July; *Andean Newsletter*, 11 August). In his Independence Day Message, García promised to expand the definition of terrorism to include illicit association and apologies for, or instigation of, terrorism; and to make the illegal possession of arms a criminal offense. His statement emphasized the military aspects of counterinsurgency, with no mention of sociopolitical initiatives or suggestions of human rights concerns, which had been part of his previous messages. (*Andean Newsletter*, 11 August; *Resumen Semanal*, 22 July–4 August.)

A spiral of violent revenge began with the murder of Osmán Morote's lawyer, Manuel Febres Flores, on 28 July. The group that claimed responsibility for the assassination was the "Comando Rodrigo Franco." Franco was an Aprista official killed in Naña in 1987. The Comando announced that it would kill a terrorist for every Aprista killed, and that it was "tired of the incapacity of government, the demagoguery of García, and the indecision of the forces of order." (*Resumen Semanal*, 5–11 August; EFE, 29 July; *FBIS*, 1 August.) *Oiga* claimed that the group had been formed by policemen who had attended antiterrorist classes in the United States from 1986 to 1988, and that it was connected to Deputy Interior Minister Agustín Mantilla. The evidence for these claims was that when a bomb exploded outside offices of *El Diario* in October, the perpetrators who survived were Apristas who were taken to the police hospital and never interviewed or charged (*NYT*, 4 December). The group has sent death threats to politicians and journalists they feel have been critical of APRA, and sympathizers, if not activists, of Sendero.

The crime that shook the nation, however, was the assassination in La Paz, Bolivia, of a Peruvian naval attaché on whose body a note was found declaring the deed a response to the Febres murder. Four days later a member of the PCP-Patria Roja was killed. Many feared Peru had slipped into a pathological spate of violent retribution. (*Resumen Semanal*, 2–15 December.)

There was definitely a lack of confidence in García. From September until the end of the year, calls from prominent politicians for his resignation appeared almost daily. Some wanted early elections or a multiparty cabinet, and there were persistent rumors of the imminence of a military coup. For the IU's Barrantes, this was not the solution; in November he called for a minimum unity of all political forces so that an emergency plan to solve the crisis could be created. Although party leaders have not supported this idea, opinion polls in November showed that an overwhelming majority of the population wanted to solve the nation's problems without a military coup; and 79 percent wanted García to continue to serve until his term ended. (*CSM*, 22 November.)

International Views and Positions. The interests of the PCP and the IU continued to coincide with García's foreign-policy agenda with regard to political affairs, but they clashed dramatically with it in the international economic sphere. The youthful García continued his rhetorical enthusiasm for Third World solidarity, nonalignment, regional debtors' agreements, and strengthening of the Andean Pact and of the Group of Eight. But the reality of the Peruvian economic collapse and the lack of support from other debtor nations undermined his attempt to play by new rules in the international economic community and forced him to reorient his policies to gain its approval.

Del Prado praised García for his solidarity with Nicaragua, and for the struggle in Central and South America against military and fascist dictatorships (*Rudé Právo*, Prague, 20 May; *FBIS*, 27 May). García was steadfast in his support of nonintervention in South America, and he pushed hard for some success with the Contadora peace process. He, along with most of the Peruvian Congress, harshly condemned the U.S. operation in which 3,000 Marines were sent to Honduras. Barrantes called upon the government to "use all its resources to assure the cessation of aggression and respect for nonintervention" (*Resumen Semanal*, 18–24 March). Although García did not break ties with the United States, as requested by Carlos Malpica (PUM), the Apristas' did extend support to Nicaragua by sending the youth brigade "Haya de la Torre," along with doctors, lawyers, and engineers, to contribute their services to peace (ibid.).

García's anti-imperialist platform came apart in 1988, and he sought to improve his relations with the United States and Western Europe in hopes of receiving badly needed economic assistance, including donations of food to make up for dramatic shortages. In January, Chamber of Deputy president Luís Alva Castro went to Europe seeking cooperation with Peruvian socioeconomic development projects intended to combat poverty and illiteracy, which, he argued, were the bases of the continued growth of subversion. Both France and Spain helped through the year by extending credit for food imports. (*Resumen Semanal*, 31 December–7 January.) In August, a French consortium became the first entity to accept Peru's offer to use silver as collateral for a loan (*LAWR*, 11 August).

García's need to increase foreign investment extended to oil and gas exploration. Royal Dutch Shell made a significant gas find in the Camisea region, and contract negotiations were underway with several other transnationals. The protests of the IU and local officials against the Shell contracts had a significant impact even on the Aprista senators, who also challenged it as antinationalist. The question was why transnationals were used for development and not national companies such as PEMEX (Mexico) or PETROBRAS (Brazil). (*LAWR*, 1 September.)

Mending relations with the international financial community went so far as having Minister Salinas attend the annual meetings of the World Bank and the International Monetary Fund in Berlin in October. An IMF mission arrived in Peru late that month to evaluate García's austerity measures. (*LAWR*, 13 October.)

A shift in APRA's orientation was also noted in its increasingly closer ties to the United States. This is in contrast to its position in the past. The attention from the United States came from the part that Peru plays in the international drug trade, over one-half of the world's supply of coca coming from the Upper Huallaga Valley. The interest of the United States in stifling the drug trade at its source and García's concern for halting the operations of both drug traffickers and guerrillas in the area combined to produce an agreement by which the United States will increase arms supplies and training for the Peruvian army. For some time the United States has been involved in coca crop-substitution programs. In the last three years, the U.S. Drug Enforcement Agency's "Operation Snowball" has provided direct support of coca eradication, but U.S. military assistance has been minimal. Although the PCP and the IU fear the "Pentagonization" of the military and the "Vietnamization" of the guerrilla war, it is unlikely that any major change in suppliers will come soon. For twenty years the Peruvian army, which is now the largest on the continent after Argentina's, has been supplied by the Eastern bloc, particularly the Soviet Union. (*Resumen Semanal*, 18–24 March; *West Watch*, October.)

Relations with the USSR continued to be good, with Peru renegotiating its debt so that it could pay with nontraditional products. New agreements were also reached for the purchase of $150 million worth of machinery and equipment, and fishing contracts were extended (Lima Television, 9 October; *FBIS*, 12 October). Continuing his interest in expanding Peru's relations with other Pacific Rim countries, García encouraged new cooperative agreements with the People's Republic of China for $600 million over three years for state mining companies (*LAWR*, 28 July).

Government officials traveled to Czechoslovakia, the German Democratic Republic, Bulgaria, and Yugoslavia in 1988 to renegotiate debts, expand commodity agreements, and to exchange scientific and technical information. Peru became the first Latin American country to which Yugoslavia sent work organizations. They are participating in the third phase of the Chira-Piura irrigation project, which is a $520 million investment. (*Tanjug*, Belgrade, 2 March; *FBIS*, 3 March.)

The international involvement of the Peruvian PCP is extensive. In 1988 important trips by its members included Jorge del Prado's journey to North Korea to celebrate the 40th anniversary of that nation's communist party, Valentín Pacho's participation as an observer in the Chilean plebiscite, and the sending of a large contingent to the South American Communist Parties Meeting in Montevideo in August. (KCNA, Pyongyang, 7 September; *FBIS*, 8 September.)

Terrorist Activities. The U.S. Department of State had ranked Peru third in the world in the number of terrorist incidents for 1987 with 1,413. As of November 1988, there had already been 1,414 terrorist acts resulting in 1,086 deaths (*Resumen Semanal*, January–December). Estimates of the number of people killed in the eight-year-old internal war range from 11,000–15,000, the uncertainty being about the number of deaths in the early years. The downward trend in the number of deaths under García was reversed in 1988. The monthly total in November—292—was the highest since February 1985, with the exception of that for June 1986, which included victims of the prison massacres. The political violence has also accounted for over $5 billion in damages to Peruvian infrastructure and manufacturing enterprises.

This year marked a turning point for Sendero Luminoso, the revolutionary guerrilla group that launched its armed struggle against the government in 1980. The mysterious, virtually impenetrable Maoist group exhibited significant changes in its overall strategy and tactics. Its goal remained the destruction of the state and the creation of a new democracy based on the peasants and urban workers, but it exchanged its strategy of protracted rural war for that of a quicker, urban-based revolution. In the first interview ever given to *Caretas*, *senderista* Isidoro Santigo Nunja García said that Sendero believes in "armed insurgency in the city now," with success to come "in two or three years..." (*Quehacer*, Lima, vol. 53). As a result, the group became more visible in its efforts to attract the urban masses, exacerbate social and economic tensions, and precipitate a military coup. For the first time *senderistas* appeared in public, and interviews were given; for the first time also an important member, Osmán Morote, was captured; and the first sign was given that Sendero's founder and leader, Dr. Abimael Guzmán Reynoso, was alive.

In its efforts to attract the urban masses, Sendero has increased its presence at leftist meetings and demonstrations. The IU and the PCP have called this "infiltration," whereas Sendero considers it the advancement of the revolution. The internal operation of many popular organizations is now marked by debates over representation of, and relations with radicals. Organizations that were once independent are now identified as "fronts" for Sendero. In some, its sympathizers have taken over, but in others, control by Sendero is still a matter of conjecture. Those organizations that operate legally, but are identified with Sendero's cause, include the Association of Democratic Lawyers, whose members have defended individuals charged with terrorist activity; Popular Aid (Socorro Popular), which assists imprisoned guerrillas and since 1982 has provided logistical support by lodging and storing weapons; and the Committee of Families of Prisoners of War and Political Prisoners, which organizes public protests.

The newspaper *El Diario* was taken over two years ago by the Popular Democratic Union (UDP), which made no attempt to hide its support for Sendero Luminoso. Editor Luís Arce Borja has denied being a *senderista*, but the paper has been a public vehicle for Sendero's perspective on society (*Quehacer*, Lima, vol. 51). Although the administration had allowed it to circulate freely, *El Diario* overstepped its bounds when it published an entire issue, 48 pages long, devoted to an interview with Sendero's theretofore invisible leader, Dr. Abimael Guzmán Reynoso. Most issues were confiscated, and *El Diario* was able to print only "emergency" editions after August 1 because no printing company would accept its business. (*Resumen Semanal*, 19–24 August.)

In some cases, Sendero has created new political organizations to compete with those already existing. Thus the Movement of Class Conscious Workers and Laborers (Movimiento Obrero y Trabajadora Clascista; MOTC) and the Neighborhood Movement (Movimiento Barrial) seek to organize union workers and the barrios. While social tensions are right for such organizing, Sendero's brutality has usually worked against them in areas where the IU is strong.

The most audacious moves of Sendero this year were its public marches and participation in national strikes called by the CGTP. The intent, said Nunja in his interview, was for Sendero "to give union and political demonstrations a new aspect, that of class and not the opportunism of del Prado, Breña, and Diez Canseco" (*Quehacer*, Lima, 53). Ski-masked protestors appeared at meetings to shout down speakers and demand support for the armed struggle and incited violence by throwing stones and dynamite during demonstrations. On several occasions they provoked overreactions by the police that resulted in the injury and even death of protestors.

The first time that Sendero Luminoso openly participated in a labor demonstration called by the CGTP was the general strike of 28 January. *El Diario* said the MOTC called for a "combative strike in which the masses express repudiation of the corporativist, fascist, Aprista government and its revisionist accomplice, the IU" (*Resumen Semanal*, 22–28 January). Forty *senderistas* interrupted an IU rally during the strike. They shouted cheers for Comrade Gonzalo as they exploded dynamite, wounding four workers, and directly assaulted people, including PCP leader Jorge del Prado (*Resumen Semanal*, 22–28 January).

The group also pressed for influence within certain unions. The Unitary Peruvian Teachers Union (SUTEP) has 200,000 members spread throughout the nation. Teachers located in remote areas are often the only representatives of authority, so they are under great pressure to cooperate with Sendero. When they struck with other government employees for cost-of-living salary increases, Sendero urged them not to settle at all. (*LAWR*, 23 June.)

In May, Sendero Luminoso, as a group, appeared in public for the first time when 250 activists and sympathizers marched through central Lima. The two-hour event was not stopped by police until seven bombs had been thrown into buildings and flags draped over trees along the avenue. The minister of the interior was criticized for being unable to halt this "affront." *El Diario* noted that "the march without fear" marked a new stage in the popular struggle (*Resumen Semanal*, 22 April–5 May).

As in previous years, Sendero's violence came in waves around particular anniversaries, such as that of the launching of their armed struggle, of national independence, and of the prison massacres, or around events such as the pope's visit and the national strikes. The group's targets remained disturbingly familiar. In addition to selective assassination of governmental authorities, political leaders, and "informers," they attacked the electrical infrastructure, producing lengthy and disruptive blackouts. They also destroyed development projects and public works. Through extortion and intimidation they enforced *paros armados*, armed stoppages that closed down all commerce in highland towns and cut off transportation in order to disrupt the supplying of food to the urban areas.

The war in 1988 struck not only the military, leftist political groups, and government officials, but also international development workers and tourists. The first American killed in a direct attack, a U.S. AID agricultural worker, Constantin Gregory, was ambushed with his Peruvian counterpart in Jauja province on 13 June (*LAT*, 16 June). In April, a Yugoslav businessman was killed, and in December two French engineers working on a social project were singled out for execution. For the second time, the tourist train to Machu Picchu was bombed; this time the victims included the wives of the mayors of Cusco and Jersey City, New Jersey. (*Resumen Semanal*, 2–15 December.)

Sendero's actions were calculated to heighten the possibility of a military coup. The street marches and provocations brought demands for more repression and radical measures from the conservative sectors. In addition, more deadly and systematic attacks on the armed forces created pressure for a military response. The risk for Sendero in moving to the city, however, was that it would have less security but more interaction, circumstances which provided the government with its first real intelligence break in the capture of Osmán Morote, along with documents about Sendero actions and party files. Raúl González speculated in late June that the party's confusion and demoralization after Osmán Morote's capture could only be overcome by months of rebuilding security and spectacular actions, "such as the public appearance of Guzmán, if he is still alive" (*Quehacer*, Lima, vol. 53).

That is exactly what happened. A ten-year-long silence was broken, and much speculation as to his existence was put to rest when leader Abimael Guzmán, "Comrade Gonzalo," gave his interview to *El Diario* on July 24. He said the Sendero Congress had decided he should speak. He quoted Mao extensively, emphasizing "violence is a universal law, without exception." Guzmán also said they would stop the 1990 elections if possible, and he rejected any political dialogue because it "would only undermine the people's war." (EFE, 24 July; *FBIS*, 25 July.)

In the people's war the enemies included the government, the IU, and the other major revolutionary group active in Peru, the Revolutionary Movement of Túpac Amaru (MRTA). At the party's national congress in February, the MRTA was described as "the principal enemy of the revolution . . . that must be confronted because there cannot be the triumph of two revolutions" (*Quehacer*, Lima, vol. 53).

The MRTA also gained strength through 1988. An alternative to Sendero, its ties with the legal left appeared to grow as the overall national situation deteriorated. Armed struggle with a purpose and minimum of bloodshed has distinguished this group, whose motto is "For the cause of the poor; with the masses; up in arms." From its middle-class, urban beginnings, the MRTA expanded into the central highland. Unlike Sendero, it has external links. It cooperates with other groups, especially M-19 in Colombia; it responds to international

events with actions and communiqués; and it focuses on symbols of imperialism as targets, doing so most aggressively against the United States. (cf. James Anderson, *Sendero Luminoso: A New Revolutionary Model?*, London: Institute for the Study of Terrorism, 1987.) Also in contrast to Sendero, the MRTA has a penchant for publicity. It invited a TV film crew to accompany its forces into villages in San Martín, where they compete with Sendero and drug traffickers for territorial control, arguing that they protect the peasants from the brutality of the others. (*LAWR*, 7 January.)

Yet another difference of the MRTA that makes it more attractive to Peruvian youth, is that it generally has connected its actions to its message. Its members tried to attract the attention of the pope by taking over a convent and calling upon him to "bring to heel the merchants of death and corruption in the country" and "to improve prison conditions." As he had on his previous trip, the pope condemned the political violence rampant in Peru. Despite elaborate security precautions, the pontiff's arrival was marked by attacks that left sixteen dead and by a major blackout in Lima. (*LAWR*, 26 May.)

In this year of economic hardship, the MRTA has turned to kidnapping. In July, they captured Gen. Hector Jerí, a retired air-force leader who is now head of a battery factory. After holding him for 108 days, they negotiated a ransom that included distribution of 7,000 bags of food to seven Lima neighborhoods together with, it is rumored, $3 million (EFE, 24 October; *FBIS*, 26 October). It is this action-oriented "Robin Hood" image that appeals to the urban youth. In fact, the youth representatives to the PCP's Ninth Congress were said to be MRTA members (*La Republica*, Lima, 13 March; *FBIS*, 22 March).

In Peru's desperate situation, the appeal of Robin Hood is strong, and the year ended with many groups' claiming to be Peru's only "salvation." Despite the simmering internal war, the interests of both the right and the left are served by maintaining the democratic system; only Sendero's purposes are otherwise. The legal left has participated in the political process long enough to be accepted by the right, and the political right is wary enough of the left's mass support to be respectful of its demands. Since the military is skeptical enough about the economic situation to let someone else deal with it, the "minimum unity" suggested by Barrantes may help Peruvian democracy survive until the end of García's term.

Sandra Woy-Hazleton
Miami University

Puerto Rico

Population. 3,358,879
Parties. Puerto Rican Socialist Party (Partido Socialista Puertorriqueño; PSP); Puerto Rican Communist Party (Partido Comunista Puertorriqueño; PCP)
Founded. PSP, 1971; PCP, 1934
Membership. PSP: 150; PCP: 100 (both estimated)
General Secretary. PSP: Carlos Gallisa; PCP: Franklin Irrizarry
Leading Bodies. No data
Status. Legal
Last Congress. PSP: Second, 1979; PCP: unknown
Last Election. 1988. Neither PSP nor PCP participated with its own slate.
Auxiliary Organizations. No data
Publications. PSP: *Claridad* (weekly)

Puerto Rico's Marxist left was less active in 1988 than in previous years, even though the island chose its governor and Legislative Assembly in November. Puerto Rico continued to enjoy a period of prosperity, now in its fifth year, and Gov. Rafael Hernández-Colón was re-elected for another four-year term. The PSP supported the Puerto Rican Independence Party, which, as usual, finished as distant third, behind the winning left-of-center Popular Democratic Party and the slightly more conservative New Progressive Party.

The PSP also supported the annual appeal of the *independentistas* that the question of Puerto Rico's independence be settled in their favor at the United Nations. This has been the principal task of former PSP general secretary Juan Mari Bras. Mari Bras, who has retired from the party's post because of poor health, traveled to New York and the capitals of several Latin countries to ask for endorsement of a Cuban resolution on Puerto Rico presented to the U.N. Decolonization Committee. The U.N. body discussed the issue in August and, as on previous occasions, the resolution was tabled.

In May, a public opinion poll conducted by the firm of Hamilton, Frederick & Schneider for the San Juan television station Telemundo, showed that 59 percent of Puerto Ricans favored the current status of "free associated state"; 31 percent wanted the island to be the 51st State of the Union; and 3 percent wanted it to be an independent country.

In his address on 2 January 1989 at the start of his second term, Gov. Hernández-Colón called for a plebiscite on Puerto Rico's political status. He gave no date for the vote, which was to be approved by the Legislative Assembly of Puerto Rico. In a similar plebiscite in 1967, residents voted for more autonomy within the Commonwealth, but the United States never granted it.

Puerto Rico's present status was granted in 1952, and until the late 1960s residents consistently elected pro-Commonwealth governors. But since then, the island's top executive office has repeatedly changed hands between supporters of commonwealth status and statehood. Gov. Hernández-Colón said that in the next plebiscite the voters will have the choice between statehood, independence, and more autonomy, to expand the present free-associate commonwealth status.

The illegal, small extreme left wing groupings: Armed Forces for National Liberation (FALN); Volunteers for the Puerto Rican Revolution; Boricua Popular Army, or the Macheteros; and Armed Forces of Popular Resistance, appeared to be inactive in 1988.

George Volsky
University of Miami

Suriname

Population. 394,999
Party. Revolutionary People's Party (Revolutionaire Volkspartij; RVP), Cuban-oriented, an offshoot of the defunct People's Party (Volkspartij; VP; Maoist-oriented); now defunct: the Surinamese Communist Party (Communistische Partij Suriname; CPS; Albanian-oriented); and the Democratic People's Front (Demokratisch Volks Front; DVF), successor to an earlier Surinamese Communist Party (Kommunistische Partij Suriname; KPS; Soviet-oriented).

Founded. RVP: 1980; VP: 1975; CPS: 1980; DVF: app. 1972; KPS: app. 1970

Membership. No data

Leadership. Michael Naarendorp

Status. Restrictions on political parties were lifted in the fall of 1985. To compete in elections, a party must demonstrate that it has the support of 1 percent of the population. None of those named had ever managed to come within even half of this figure in earlier elections.

Last Congress. No data

Last Election. 25 November 1987 (none of the above-named parties participated)

Pulling the deadweight of a powerful and corrupt military, Suriname's civilian leadership went nowhere fast in its first full year (1988) of democratic government following the military coup of 1980. Despite its overwhelming victory in the elections of 25 November 1987, the Front for Democracy and Development (Front voor Democratie en Ontwikkeling; FDO) was unable to end an economically crippling guerrilla war with the Bush Negroes of the interior, to reclaim from the military full control over the country's foreign-exchange earnings, or to convince the Dutch to resume their $1.5 billion aid program that had been suspended in 1982. Army commander Desire (Desi) Bouterse clearly retained a substantial veto over national policy initiatives, and no one in the new government seemed willing to force him into a showdown.

Domestic Affairs. Bouterse had earlier resisted redemocratization, having fifteen prominent civic leaders executed in December 1982 for their political activities. In 1984 he reluctantly assembled a "national assembly" to advise him and begin work on a new constitution. Loading the body in favor of his 25th February Movement (named after the date of the 1980 coup), he was tempted by a handful of radical officers (led by Badrissein Sital and Chas Mijnals) to create either Yugoslav- or Cuban-like legislative bodies (the first providing functional representation for officially recognized interest groups; the latter elected indirectly by lower district assemblies) in order to overcome and transcend the ethnic orientation traditional to Suriname's politics. These ideas didn't "take" among others in the assembly, and the old ethnicity-based political parties (later bundled together in the FDO) pressed for the return of the old democratic system. A substantial assist was offered by the Dutch, who rejected Bouterse's advisory assembly as undemocratic and set strict constitutional and human rights conditions on the resumption of their aid.

Bouterse apparently valued power over ideological objectives and decided that he could secure the former under any form of government. Much to the chagrin of some of his more purist leftist supporters (i.e., the RVP, the Progressive Workers' and Farmers' Union [Progressieve Arbeiders en Landbouwers Unie; PALU], and the Surinamese Labor Party [Surinaamse Partij van de Arbeid; SPA]), Bouterse and his top officers enriched themselves and kept the military well armed, even as the economy was collapsing, by their control over the national rice-marketing board and alleged involvement in the international drug traffic.

Thus, despite leftist control of the popular assembly, Bouterse accepted most of the old political parties' demands and acceded to the restoration of the old structures with very little modification. Radical language consistent with Third World democratic socialism characterized much of the "social program" chapters of the new constitution—the only substantial addition to that document. An article dealing with the military, however, vaunted that body as "the military vanguard of the people" that "labours for the national development and for the liberation of the nation" (Art. 177) and hinted at a permanent political role for the military. Nevertheless, the military's participation in decisionmaking was limited to membership in the advisory Council of State and, in an emergency, to a special National Security Council. The old parties felt that they had probably gotten all they could for the transition. The public clearly agreed. Despite strong reservations expressed by the Committee of Christian Churches regarding the military's still unchecked power, voters overwhelmingly accepted the new constitution in September 1987.

Less than two months later, on 25 November 1987, voters went to the polls again, this time to fill the new National Assembly, which, in turn, would select an accountable executive. With a turnout of over 88 percent, over 83 percent of the votes cast went for the FDO coalition of old parties: the Progressive Reform Party (Verenigde Hervormde Partij; VHP), National Party of Suriname (Nationale Partij Suriname; NPS), and Indonesian Farmers Party (Kaum Tani Persatuan Indonesia; KTPI) (*De West*, Paramaribo, 16 December 1987). Because of the year-old guerrilla war, three districts in the interior had been left depopulated, and it was here that the PALU and Bouterse's new National Democratic Party (Nationale Democratische Partij; NDP), with only a handful of votes, were able to get four and two of their members elected, respectively. In more populated areas, the FDO swept 40 of the 41 available seats, the NDP getting the remaining seat in the capital, Paramaribo. Bouterse and his supporters may have hoped to win at least one-third of the Assembly's seats to assure their say in the selection of the president and any amendments contemplated for the constitution (Art. 83.3). With only seven of the Assembly's total of 51 seats, the NDP and PALU fell far short of the mark.

The National Assembly chose venerable VHP-leader Jaggernath Lachmon as its speaker, and former prime minister and NPS-leader Henck Arron returned to the post from which the 1980 coup had removed him, that of the cabinet's presiding officer (now the vice president under a ceremonial president). For the presidency, the two leaders (together with the KTPI leader Willy Soemita) picked a relatively unknown businessman affiliated with the VHP, Ramsewak Shankar.

Curiously, rather than giving them confidence to press forward with an ambitious agenda, the FDO's landslide left them unusually skittish and conciliatory (*NRC-Handelsblad*, 27 August). The situation was exceedingly delicate. Popular pressures existed to change the constitution and strip the military of its power—actions that could precipitate a disastrous confrontation. Yet continued consultation with the military over decisionmaking began to lose the old parties their widespread support. In October, on his triumphal return from the Olympics, gold medal-winner Anthony Nesty was cheered at a rally in the soccer stadium, while Vice President Arron was booed (*NRC-Handelsblad*, 11 October).

The primary concern about Suriname's political future is directed to the struggle between the new civilian authorities and the outgoing (but not yet gone) military dictatorship. Principal concerns involve (1) the termination of hostilities between the government in Paramaribo and the Bush Negro guerrillas of the interior; and (2) renegotiation of the development-aid package established in 1975 by the Dutch and suspended at the time of the 1982 executions. Bouterse and his military compatriots stand in the way of the achievement of both these goals.

With regard to the insurgency (*NYT*, 18 June 1987), Bouterse has condemned Shankar's efforts, made through the Committee of Christian Churches, to negotiate a ceasefire and amnesty (*NRC-Handelsblad*, 6 and 8 April, 8 June; *Wash-

ington Report on the Hemisphere, 27 April, 6 July). Although the uprising was founded on demands for democratic elections and an end to corruption, Bouterse has persistently called the guerrillas "terrorists" and refuses to participate in a cease-fire (Franszoon; *NRC-Handelsblad*, 21 and 22 July). On several occasions during the year, apparently without governmental authorization, military forays were undertaken against the guerrillas, and in late November a people's militia group made up of Amerindians ambushed a group of Bush Negroes suspected of ties with the guerrillas and killed them (*NRC-Handelsblad*, 25 July, 1 and 5 August, 29 November).

Foreign Affairs. The Bush Negro insurgency strained Suriname's relations with France, as approximately 10,000 Bush Negroes fled the combat area to sanctuary in neighboring French Guiana (*NRC-Handelsblad*, 9 April, 22 July). Fighting was concentrated in the region bordering the Marowijne River, along the upper reaches of which the rebel leader Ronny Brunswijk had his headquarters. Bouterse continued to accuse the French (and Dutch) of abetting the guerrillas in their actions, charges that both countries denied (*NRC-Handelsblad*, 26 February, 3 and 4 August; *Latin American Regional Reports-Caribbean*, 3 November).

Negotiations were on and off throughout the year regarding restoration of the $1.5 billion Dutch development-aid program. The Dutch prime minister, foreign minister, and development cooperation minister, backed by the principal parties in the Dutch parliament, insisted that development aid should not be resumed until peace had been restored. Both the civilian and military leaders in Suriname cried out in protest. But the original aid agreement had stipulated that such funds should benefit "all Surinamers." Under the insurgency, the Dutch argued, Bush Negroes and other peoples of the interior could make no use of the aid. (*NRC-Handelsblad*, 22 July, 8 November.) Protest marches against the corruption of Bouterse's business associates took place in September (*NRC-Handelsblad*, 8 September), and the Dutch negotiators added to their list of conditions on aid that all relief supplies be subject to their oversight to avoid black-marketeering (*NRC-Handelsblad*, 23 July). At year's end, only a modest package of humanitarian aid had been approved (*NRC-Handelsblad*, 5 December).

A new tangle in Suriname's relations with The Netherlands arose in August, when the Dutch minister of justice declared that human rights conditions in Suriname had improved sufficiently for illegal aliens from that country to be repatriated (*NRC-Handelsblad*, 22 February). This brought forth protests from the immigrant community, as well as from the government of Suriname itself, which argued that there was no way to assimilate the immigrants economically. The issue became front-page news in The Netherlands when a returning alien was taken into custody in Suriname by the military police and was subsequently found hanged (*NRC-Handelsblad*, 10 November). Combined with demands by Bush Negroes for impartial investigation of a number of human rights violations by the armed forces (Franszoon; *NRC-Handelsblad*, 14 May, 22 July, 6 and 10 September), events such as this raised doubts about the civilian government's ability to control the military.

Whether Bouterse could be brought to heel by Dutch pressures and Surinamese manipulation was unclear. Control over the rice-marketing board (chaired by the radical military official Badrissein Sital) provided the military with an independent source of foreign exchange. The conviction in Miami in 1986 of Bouterse's second-in-command, Etienne Boerenveen, on drug-related charges suggests another source of funding. In October, the Dutch newspaper *NRC-Handelsblad* reported that "a cartel in the Colombian city of Medellin underwrote the purchase" of twelve Brazilian Vulcano fighters (at $25 million each) for the Surinamese military, together with a number of armored cars (31 October). Equipped with machineguns and bombsights, the Vulcanos might make the difference in the guerrilla war. Delivery was expected by the end of 1988.

As in other South American countries making the painful transition back from military rule, Suriname was walking on a tightrope. Under these circumstances, leftist parties of various stripes waited expectantly for a showdown, assuming that their chance for influence would rise once more if Bouterse came to power. Yet earlier experience should have demonstrated that the military leaders were interested in little except personal aggrandizement. Perhaps that, too, was all the leftists sought. Because of their arrogance and pedantry, the leaders of the small leftist parties—mostly students returning from The Netherlands—faced ostracism at home. Throwing in once more with these groups could not be a very attractive prospect for Bouterse and company. They had only brought international isolation and economic hardship in the preceding

eight years. It thus seems reasonable to predict a bitterly slow retreat before the civilian authorities in 1989.

Edward M. Dew
Fairfield University

United States of America

Population. 246,043,000
Party. Communist Party U.S.A. (CPUSA)
Founded. 1919
Membership. 20,000 (claimed), 4–6,000 (probable)
National Chairman. Gus Hall
National Board. Gus Hall, Evelina Alarcon, Kendra Alexander, John Bachtell, Arnold Becchetti, Barry Cohen, Elsie Dickerson, Louis Diskin, Lee Dlugin, Joelle Fishman, Clyde Grubbs, James Jackson, Maurice Jackson, Judith leBlanc, Robert Lindsay, Carole Marks, Scott Marshall, George Meyers, Charlene Mitchell, Rick Nagin, Daniel Rubin, Betty Smith, James Steele, Sidney Taylor, Jarvis Tyner, Sam Webb, Jim West, Michael Zagarell
Status. Legal
Last Congress. 24th National Convention, Chicago, 13–16 August 1987
Electoral Activity. The party did not run a presidential candidate in 1988, but fielded or supported several local candidates. Its share of the presidential vote in 1984, the last year it had a national candidate, was under 0.1 percent.
Publications. *People's Daily World* (New York), Barry Cohen, editor; *Political Affairs* (theoretical monthly), Michael Zagarell, editor

The CPUSA is the largest Marxist-Leninist organization in the United States. Emerging from the fusion of two groupings founded in 1919, the CPUSA attained considerable influence during the 1930s and 1940s, playing a significant, if controversial role in the labor movement and finding allies and support among liberal, labor, and farm-oriented politicians in a number of states. Beginning in the 1920s, the party also exercised an important influence in the Black community.

The party reached its greatest size, claiming some 80,000 members, during World War II, thanks to the general national warmth toward America's then-ally, the Soviet Union. In addition, at least a million Americans stood on the party's periphery, supporting it without officially joining. With the end of the wartime alliance and the arrival of widespread disillusion with the Stalin regime's postwar policies, liberals and radicals began to distance themselves from the party. This process was accentuated in the union movement, where the strategic and tactical subservience of major CPUSA-controlled unions, such as the United Electrical Workers (UE) and the National Maritime Union (NMU), to the "twists and turns" of the party line cost the party much of its labor support. In addition, CP-dominated unions such as the International Union of Mine, Mill and Smelter Workers and the National Union of Marine Cooks and Stewards were well known for undemocratic and corrupt internal practices. A similar alienation from the party had already taken hold among many Black intellectuals, who were disturbed by the party's failure during World War II to support Black civil-rights efforts.

These characteristics of the party made its increasing isolation after 1945 almost unavoidable. In addition, a major obstacle to the party's growth appeared in the form of a widely-organized anticommunist sentiment, which, until that time, had been largely subdued in the national consciousness. National and state leaders were tried, sentenced, and imprisoned for violation of the Smith Act, which barred political activities aimed at the overthrow of the U.S. government (and which had first been applied, to the glee of the CPUSA, against their Trotskyist critics). During the Truman and Eisenhower presidencies, the party leadership responded both to the crisis of its credibility with the broader liberal community and to the pressure of domestic anticommunism, with its "fascism and war" thesis, predicting the immediate introduction of a Nazi-style dictatorship in the United States, and the commencement of a third world war. One decision taken during the early 1950s directed considerable numbers of party members to leave the organization, while selected cadres built an underground network in preparation for fascist rule.

Thus, by 1956, the party had been reduced to a skeleton of stalwarts, numbering no more than 20,000, and was perilously close to disintegration. In that year the anti-Stalin speech of Nikita S. Khrushchev at the Twentieth Congress of the CPSU, and the bloody repression of the Hungarian Revolution, led first to a convulsive attempt to reform the party from within (a variety of "Eurocommunism" *avant la lettre*) under the leadership of the largest state organization, that in New York. When this short-lived effort, identified with New York party leader John Gates, failed, most of the historic "proletarian core" finally left the party. Symbolic of the period, the party dailies in New York (*Daily Worker*) and San Francisco (*Daily People's World*) were reduced to weekly publication.

From 1956 to the present, the CPUSA has remained a marginal element of American political life. With the departure of the "Gatesites," the party, put under the guidance of the internally-popular but intellectually-limited Gus Hall in 1959, was effectively re-Stalinized. As we shall see, this experience has very much determined the international role of the party today.

During the 1960s the party briefly had some success among young radicals, organizing a new youth wing, the W.E.B. DuBois Clubs of America, which eventually became the current Young Communist League (YCL). But the party never attempted to go beyond organizing its "red diaper babies," the children of old communists, to a campaign to bring in the thousands, if not millions, of students who joined Students for a Democratic Society, or who marched in demonstrations against the war in Vietnam controlled by the Trotskyist Young Socialist Alliance. In addition, it recruited very few leading figures from the new mass movement, and its only intellectual figure of some prestige from the 1960s, Angela Davis, has never made the promotion of the party a central focus of her public activity, in the way that was standard for the party-oriented intellectuals of the 1930s. The combination of inflexibility and passivity made the party unattractive; and so, curiously enough, by 1980 it played less of a role in national left-wing politics than it had in 1960, when it was able to at least stir a basic curiosity in the generation raised on the past decade's anticommunism. It has neither sought to nor succeeded in breaking out of this marginality.

Leadership and Party Organization. The elderly Gus Hall continued as party leader through 1988, with no immediate succession in view. Hall (born Arvo G. Halberg) has led the CPUSA longer than any other individual and is among the longest-tenured communist-party leaders in the world. Other major figures include Jim West, head of the National Review Commission (the control commission of the CPUSA); John Bachtell, head of the YCL; Maurice Jackson, leader of the party in Washington, D.C.; Michael Zagarell, a New York activist; Carl Bloice, Moscow correspondent for the party newspaper *People's Daily World* (published four days per week); and Herbert Aptheker, a semiacademic historian of uneven reputation who is known within the party as an ideological watchdog.

The *People's Daily World* (*PDW*) is the party periodical directed to "the masses." It emerged in 1986 from a fusion of the former *Daily World*, begun in 1967 to replace *The Worker*, then a semiweekly publication, and the then-weekly *People's World*, published first in San Francisco, then in Berkeley, beginning in 1938. The *PDW*, a multicolor daily tabloid of twelve pages with a weekend edition of 24 pages (including a Spanish-language supplement), has a reported daily circulation of 12,000. The *PDW* has followed in the tradition of its predecessor *The Worker* in being one of the least intellectually stimulating periodicals published on the left, being composed in an uninspired, leaden style, and based mostly on gleanings from the major media. The defunct West Coast *People's World*, perhaps reflecting the stronger links between the West Coast party and the general radical culture, was considered a livelier and more open publication. The *PDW* and other party literature is distributed through a network of eighteen bookstores around the country, which also serve as party headquarters.

The CPUSA's 24th national convention, held in 1987, was attended by 400 delegates and some 600 guests. Statistics show that 60 percent of the delegates were under the age of 45; 40 percent had been members of the party for fewer than 10 years; 43 percent were women; 21 percent were Black; 4 percent were Mexican-American; and 2 percent were Puerto Rican. Union members comprised 33 percent and represented 43 labor organizations.

Domestic Party Affairs. Although the party did not nominate a national presidential candidate, the 1988 election was its main concern throughout the year. The party began the year with the exaggerated promise that it would put 100 party members and 25 YCLers on local ballots (*WMR*, January). This pledge was repeated at midyear (*WMR*, July). In the event, however, the party's electoral profile was extremely minor, in consonance with its meager ranks.

Party candidates, nearly all of them identified as independents, included the following, whose names are accompanied by the title of the office sought and final electoral results: Louis Godena, in Massachusetts, for U.S. Congress, 28 percent of total; Evelina Alarcon, for California State Assembly from the 55th district, Los Angeles, on the ticket of the CPUSA-dominated Peace and Freedom Party, ca. 9,000 votes, or 15.5 percent; Frank Lumpkin, for Illinois State Assembly from the 25th district, Chicago, as an Independent Progressive, ca. 5,000 votes, or 16 percent; Rick Nagin, for state representative, 11th district, Cleveland, Ohio, as a Communist candidate, ca. 1,400 votes or 6 percent; Gina Graziano, for San Francisco Board of Supervisors, a nonpartisan office, 13,219 votes, 5.5 percent; Eric Fried, for U.S. Congress, 1st California District (North Coast), Peace and Freedom, ca. 8,000 votes, 9.1 percent; Richard Green, California State Assembly, 58th district, Los Angeles, ca. 1,400 votes; Lorenzo Torrez, Arizona State Legislature, District 10, Tucson, People Before Profits ticket, 1,574 votes, 5.5 percent; John Rummel, U.S. Congress, 14th New Jersey District, 533 votes. Other candidates, most credited with around 5 percent of the vote, included Edie Fishman (county representative), Charlene Mitchell (U.S. Senate), Michael Zagarell (U.S. Congress), and Mark Almberg (U.S. Congress). Lumpkin is a Black steelworker, and Torrez a well-known labor figure in the copper industry; Graziano is a teenaged student and musician. The rest seem to be professional activists or party officers. Organizationally, this showing falls far short of the 100–125 standard-bearers announced in *WMR*. (Statistics from *PDW*, 10, 11, 16, 23 and 29 November; 5 January 1989.)

In addition to its own partisan electoral activity, the party has had a single ongoing success in the creation of an electoral "popular front" in the form of the Berkeley Citizens' Alliance (BCA), which has governed Berkeley, California, for several years. BCA's past mayor, Gus Newport, was a prominent supporter of such party-line causes as the World Peace Council. In the 1988 elections BCA managed to retain its grip on Berkeley, although a BCA candidate who writes frequently for *PDW*, Chuck Idelson, was defeated in his bid for a seat on the city's rent board, receiving 17,000 votes. The BCA experience has been extended with smaller success to other regional communities, including the city of Oakland, but in 1988 in the neighboring working-class city of San Pablo, a "progressive," Leonard MacNeil, became the first such candidate to win a San Pablo city-council seat. Party support also plays a role, if not an important one, in San Francisco's electoral picture. In an interview, published in the *New York Times* of 8 December, Gus Hall stated that in the 1988 voting some communists were elected to office on other parties' slates without publicly identifying themselves as communists. On the same occasion, Hall credited the party with "half a million" supporters, but with only 20,000 dues-paying members. Surprisingly enough, in a year-end message printed in the *PDW*, Hall repeated his assertion that communists, apparently not publicly known as such, had been elected to public office (*PDW*, 5 January 1989).

CPUSA has attempted to launch a national effort in emulation of its success in Berkeley through participation in Jesse Jackson's Rainbow Coalition, a faction of the Democratic Party. However, its support for Jackson and the importance of Black cadre for the party have not prevented the organization from criticizing some controversial actions by Black political figures. One prominent example of such criticism was directed at the Tawana Brawley case, in which a Black teenager from upstate New York gained a considerable amount of attention from the press by claiming she had been raped and otherwise brutalized by white policemen. Three Black advocates from New York City, the lawyers Alton Maddox and C. Vernon Mason and the Rev. Al Sharpton, took control of the campaign in support of Miss Brawley and launched scurrilous attacks on such Democratic New York state officials as Governor Mario Cuomo and Attorney General Robert Abrams. The CP, which had previously crossed swords with Sharpton, seems to have been the only Marxist-Leninist group in the country not to make the Brawley case a cause of its own. Indeed, the party went so far as to label the Brawley case "a media diversion" (*PDW*, 12 and 13 October).

A somewhat similar furor erupted in Chicago, where the mayoral administration of the deceased Harold Washington had been known for its openness to the CPUSA and other Marxist-Leninist groups. Here a Black mayoral aide, Steve Cokely, issued a number of declarations charging that Jewish doctors had invented the AIDS virus in order to kill Blacks. Cokely was fired, but the incident spotlighted rising Black anti-Semitism, which had previously tainted Jesse Jackson. Here again, the party criticized Cokely in a manner far more blunt than

that employed by the rest of the Marxist-Leninist left (see, for example, *PDW*, 16 June).

Although the party itself remains an unimportant element in national politics, it has been frequently noted that openings such as that observed in Berkeley are possible elsewhere. This is taken to reflect the decline of anticommunist attitudes in the country.

Allied Organizations. The party has an affiliated youth section, the Young Communist League, and several foreign-language groupings. In addition, the party maintains a number of active front groups, the most prominent of which is, currently, the National Council of American-Soviet Friendship, headed by the actor John Randolph, who is, aside from Angela Davis, the only well-known public figure aligned with the party. The U.S. Peace Council, affiliated with the World Peace Council, had been very active in protest activities against U.S. involvement in Central America, but has not played a dominant role. Other such groups include the National Alliance Against Racist and Political Repression and Trade Unionists for Action and Democracy. However, these fronts are not very active at the present time.

Activities directed to speakers of foreign languages constitute a feature of the left-wing tradition in the United States that today is little known, but in which the party has maintained an interest. Many American radical groups were strongly represented among immigrant workers. The Socialist Labor Party, founded in the nineteenth century, maintained periodicals in some East European languages until the 1970s, while the anarcho-syndicalist Industrial Workers of the World (founded 1905) published a Finnish-language daily newspaper in Duluth, Minnesota, almost as late. Most of the CPUSA's cadres in this field come from "language federations" in the Socialist Party, a number of which broke from the SP to join the CP at the time of the latter's foundation. Some six foreign language periodicals following the CPUSA line continue to appear: *Työmies-Eteenpäin* (The worker-forward), published in Finnish in Superior, Wisconsin; a women's journal, *Amerikai Magyar Szó* (American Hungarian word), in Hungarian, from New York; *Russky Golos* (The Russian voice); *Ukrainski Vistnik* (The Ukrainian news), also from New York; and *Vilnis* (The surge), published in Lithuanian in Chicago. These periodicals are now mainly reduced to monthly publication, although some of them were published daily until the early 1960s. This year saw the demise of a second Lithuanian paper, *Laisve*. It is perhaps worth noting that these papers have tended to concern themselves as much with the foreign-language tradition of labor and fraternal organization in the United States as with purely propagandistic aims connected with communist regimes in "the old country." (*Russky Golos*, a former Socialist Party organ, had for some time been edited, under the title *Noviy Mir* or *New World*, by Nikolai I. Bukharin and Leon Trotsky.)

A special case was that of *Morgen Freiheit* (Morning freedom), a Yiddish-language paper that also passed out of existence in 1988. *Freiheit*, unlike most of the other CP foreign-language papers, was not inherited from the Socialist Party; rather, it was founded in 1922 in direct competition with the giant Socialist Yiddish daily, presently a weekly, *Forvertz* (Forward). In 1967, still appearing as a daily, *Freiheit* broke with the party over the issue of Soviet support for the Arab powers against the state of Israel. In this incarnation, *Freiheit* became a useful source of information on anti-Stalinist and "Eurocommunist" developments inside the USSR and in the ranks of communist parties around the world. But this also made it almost inevitable that the closing of *Freiheit* would elicit a gleeful declaration from Gus Hall, who argued that the paper had come to an end because of its failure to abide by the party's line (*PDW*, 15 September). This indulgence in political *Schadenfreude* elicited a response from a number of people who pointed out that the end of *Freiheit* was clearly due to a less political phenomenon: the disappearance of a Yiddish readership (*PDW*, 27 September).

In a related area, the West Coast-based International Longshoremen's and Warehousemen's Union applied for affiliation with the AFL-CIO. Dominated by the party or by its sympathizers from its foundation in 1938 at least until the mid-1970s, and still a major arena for Marxist-Leninist labor activities, ILWU had been expelled from the then-separate CIO in the early 1950s. ILWU is the sole bargaining representative for longshoremen on the West Coast of the continental United States and has significant memberships in the West Coast warehouse industry and in agriculture and industry in the Hawaiian Islands. However, ILWU is plagued by a weak leadership and has suffered serious reverses in the past decade. Of the national unions expelled from the CIO because of communist domination, only the United Electrical Workers (UE) will remain an independent union, as ILWU will join AFL-CIO. UE has survived thanks to "sweetheart contracts" with the large employers in the electrical industry of the Northeast.

One area of American life in which CPUSA enjoys a certain attractiveness is the community of academic historians. Many works defending the record of CP activists in the labor and civil rights movements have appeared over the past twenty years in the form of published graduate theses. During 1988, to cite but one area of interest, four different books were published on the radical movement among West Coast maritime workers during the 1930s. The most notable of these was Bruce Nelson's *Workers on the Waterfront*, published by University of Illinois Press. CPUSA has responded to this interest in a variety of ways. When Hosea Hudson, a Black CP activist in the south, died in 1988, material in the *PDW* concentrated on an academic volume on his life published some years ago by Yale University Press. An interesting historical survey of the 1960s, with information on the W.E.B. DuBois Clubs, forerunner of the present YCL, was published in *PDW* (15 December). The CPUSA observed the 25th anniversary of the assassination of President John F. Kennedy, a topic it has tended to avoid, by publishing a statement insisting on CIA involvement in the crime (*PDW*, 22 November).

International Views, Positions, and Activities. The single element of CPUSA activity that makes this small party worthy of note would seem to be its position on *glasnost'* and *perestroika*, the reform movements launched by the Gorbachev leadership in the USSR. CPUSA has followed the rest of the American left in either maintaining silence on, or showing hostility to these reform efforts, save for occasional columns by *PDW*'s Moscow correspondent, Carl Bloice, and a very occasional reprinting of a Gorbachev speech. The publication by *Political Affairs*, the party's ideological journal, of a speech by Nikolai Bukharin, must have been something of a shock for old party members (April 1988).

Indeed, in the international arena CPUSA has emerged as a leading opponent of *glasnost'*-era rethinking of ideology. This posture is especially visible in two interventions by Jim West, a veteran party official and head of the party's control commission, published in *WMR*. In a dialogue between West and Gary Pocock, a leader of the Communist Party of Great Britain, West struck out in classically dogmatic and rigid fashion against the organizational and political flexibility of the "Eurocommunist"

CPGB. West described Eurocommunism as "a departure from Marxism-Leninism," classifying the later development of the Italian and other mass parties as nothing more than "Browderism" *redux*; i.e. as the "revisionist" doctrine of the Popular-Front-era leader of the CPUSA, Earl Browder, expelled in 1946 when the Soviet Union and the world communist movement shifted to a "cold-war" stance of active subversion in the West. West even criticized the connection between "this tendency" and "the revelations about Stalin" in 1956 (*WMR*, July 1988).

Even more remarkable statements by Jim West are to be found in a round-table discussion entitled "Perestroika in the USSR and the International Communist Movement," which included West, Professor Yuri Krasin, rector of the Social Sciences Institute under the Central Committee of the CPSU, and representatives of the Dominican, Israeli, Mexican, and Spanish communist parties. In this discussion, West and the Israel and Dominican delegates lined up against the pro-*glasnost'* representatives, including Krasin and the Mexican and Spanish delegates. The dialogue was quite acerbic. West attacked the identification of *perestroika* with the Czech reform movement of 1968, which West called a "counterrevolutionary attempt"; he admitted, however, that views favorable to the Czech experiment exist within the CPUSA. José Riva of the Dominican CP expressed what most consider a Castroite view in warning that the Soviet Union, in its search for a peaceful accommodation with the West, is threatening to abandon the Third World liberation struggle. But it was West who carried the banner against reform. The CPUSA representative attacked the reformist Soviet press organs, including *Moscow News, New Times*, and even *WMR*. He also attacked the insistence of the Mexican delegate, Pablo Sandoval Ramirez, on a revision of the line on the murder of Trotsky, which, Sandoval noted, profoundly compromised the Mexican communists. Finally, West returned to the attack on Eurocommunism as a symbol of reformist communism in general (*WMR*, September).

Aside from its peculiar closed-mouthedness on *glasnost'* and *perestroika*, the chief international policy trend visible in the pages of *PDW* was a new and considerable interest in the North Korean dictatorship of Kim Il-song (see, for example, *PDW*, 12 October). The possibility cannot be excluded that, with a withdrawal of the Brezhnev-era Soviet funding that seems to have made possible the reestablishment of a daily CPUSA organ, the party is

now searching for a new patron. That the party's financial situation has become difficult is demonstrated by its announcement that *PDW* would cut back to four issues per week (22 December).

Since the loss of its labor base in the 1950s, CPUSA has been notable for its active agitation around a wide range of foreign-policy questions. Its pronounced anti-Israel sentiment, beginning in 1967, drove away significant numbers of Jewish stalwarts. During 1988, however, links between CPUSA and Cuba created a number of curious incidents. In one instance, a disinformational story regarding the supposed kidnapping of infants in Latin America so that their internal organs could be used in transplant operations in the United States, a report which had been more or less officially abandoned and denied by the Soviet press, surfaced in *PDW* via La Habana. This led to rather silly accusations on national U.S. television that the USSR was violating its *glasnost'* pledges, when, in reality, the story had been passed along by a Cuban, not a Soviet source. (*PDW*, 28 May.)

A similarly curious phenomenon has been the attitude of CPUSA toward Gen. Manuel Antonio Noriega, the dictator of Panama. Although *PDW* attacked U.S. President-Elect George Bush as a supposed crony of Noriega, the paper has also published a considerable number of dispatches, of Cuban origin, defending Noriega, who is allied with Castro and with the Sandinistas in Nicaragua (see, for example, *PDW*, 5, 14, and 22 October).

Other Marxist-Leninist Organizations. The American left is replete with small, sectarian groups of Marxist-Leninist as well as other casts. Remnants of the Socialist Labor Party and the Industrial Workers of the World survive, although the death of their veterans and the devolution of responsibility for these organizations on children of the 1960s has transformed them from once distinctive, if not unique political formations into leftist groupings indistinguishable from the CPUSA in their general approach to issues. The same can be said of the Catholic Worker Movement led for so long by Dorothy Day.

Many leftist groups have a cultish character. The passing of the "Marxist-Humanist-Maoist-Africanist-Feminist-Luxemburgist-Trotskyist" Rae Spiegel, who called herself Raya Dunayevskaya, and whose periodical *News and Letters* resembled a religious tract more than any other leftist publication, including *The Catholic Worker*, was the occasion for truly worshipful obsequies, even though

Spiegel's works are known only to a tiny fraction of the world's literates.

There is a fairly serious agglomeration of groups under the banners of the many varieties of Trotskyism. During the 1930s the American Trotskyists, mainly organized in the Socialist Workers Party (SWP; founded 1938), were something of an inspiration for their fellow Trotskyists around the world because of their involvement in the creation of the modern Teamsters Union, which was considerable. The union itself fell into the hands of organized crime after the imprisonment of the Trotskyist activists in 1941 under the Smith Act.

But during that trial, the SWP adopted a position of American constitutionalism that was to contribute to its transformation from a party of extremist communists to a party that, even in the late 1960s, when it partially dominated the protest movement against the Vietnam War and had great prestige among Blacks (because of its past friendship for the Black nationalist leader Malcolm X) was mainly concerned with running socialist candidates in local elections. It was loosely organized and lost people as quickly as it recruited them.

However, the Trotskyist movement had, ironically, an influence among intellectuals in the United States during the 1940s that the CPUSA never attained. Irving Kristol, a leading political analyst, has written brilliantly on the period. An American Trotskyist academic of the 1960s generation, Alan Wald, has published a history of this phenomenon, *The New York Intellectuals* (University of North Carolina Press, 1987), which tries but fails to explain why the great majority of these intellectuals broke with the left and eventually became neoconservatives.

This latter evolution cannot be explained simply by opportunism. In 1940 a large group left the SWP and formed the Workers Party under the leadership of Max Shachtman, a former CPUSA functionary, and James Burnham, a philosophy professor. The basis of the split was a disagreement with Trotsky, who insisted that the USSR under Stalin was still a "workers' state," however degenerated. Shachtman and Burnham could not accept that a workers' state would ally with Hitler in the interest of carving up Poland, as had transpired in 1939. The "Shachtmanite" movement continued on until, in 1962, Shachtman took his group into the remnant of the Socialist Party, by then limited to a stratum of union officials in New York along with some political activists in Wisconsin and elsewhere. Shachtman had arrived at a position of defense of American democracy—recapitulating a trajectory followed twenty years before by another group, now forgotten, the Lovestoneites—and even defended the Vietnam War. Shachtman's group survives today as Social Democrats, USA, who are seriously involved in the Democratic Party and, alongside the ex-Lovestoneites, in AFL-CIO affairs; it is frequently assailed by CPUSA. Another remnant of the Shachtmanites of a more leftist bent, the Solidarity group, has been the main U.S. leftist group to concern itself with *glasnost'*.

The SWP itself fell apart in the 1980s, with most of its veterans leaving to form a group called Socialist Action. Smaller groups of former SWP militants constituted themselves as the North Star Network, the Fourth International Tendency, etc. The remnant of the SWP has become a kind of public relations firm for Castro and the Sandinistas. It controls a publishing house, Pathfinder Press, and a chain of 35 bookstores that also function as SWP headquarters.

On its way, the Trotskyist movement spawned many sectlets. During the 1930s the ultra-Trotskyist movement led by Hugo Oehler, which is today forgotten, drew off many radical workers. The labor writer Sidney Lens is a product of this movement. During the 1960s the SWP spun off a series of new splinter groups, such as the cultlike Spartacist League. Another, formed by former SWPer and Spartacist Lyn Marcus (Lyndon LaRouche, Jr.) as the National Caucus of Labor Committees, has received national publicity since the turn of LaRouche himself to more bizarre forms of extremist behavior, in an apparently fascist direction. A strange group of Black nationalists influenced by psychoanalysis broke off from the LaRouche movement to form the New Alliance Party. Yet another such faction, originally out of the SWP along with the Spartacists, developed into the Workers League, affiliated with the British Healyites (Workers' Revolutionary Party et al.). A number of SWP fragments have become active in feminist politics. The roster of tiny Trotskyist groups seems endless, but their invisibility in American political life renders it superfluous to mention them all.

The third main grouping of Marxist-Leninists in the United States, alongside the CPUSA and the Trotskyists, consists of groups originating in the Maoist movement of the 1960s. Some of these groups, such as the bizarre mixture of Trotskyism and Maoism known as the Workers World Party, or the quasicult known as the League of Revolutionary Struggle (publishing the newspaper *Unity*) have attained some limited success in electoral coalitions with Black politicians in Chicago, the San Francisco Bay Area, and elsewhere. The largest of them seems to be the Line of March grouping.

A case apart seems to be that of the Revolutionary Communist Party (RCP), a group faithful to the memory of Mao and the "gang of four," with a high profile of public propaganda and provocation, and which runs a chain of twelve bookstore/headquarters around the country. RCP claims to serve as an American solidarity network for the Peruvian terrorist movement Sendero Luminoso (Shining Path), but such claims seem clearly exaggerated.

So great is the proliferation of such groups in the broad reaches of the American political landscape, in which, nonetheless, they remain only microscopically evident, that it would require a separate yearbook to describe them all. For each example mentioned above, there seem to be dozens of similar entities, Trotskyist, Maoist, feminist, and Black nationalist. Finally, there are strains influenced by anarchism and the extremist leftism of European Communism during the 1920s. Altogether, Marxism-Leninism in the United States provides a complicated, if fundamentally irrelevant inventory of groups and types.

Stephen Schwartz
San Francisco, California

Uruguay

Population. 2,976,138
Party. Communist Party of Uruguay (PCU)
Founded. 1920
Membership. 30,000 (estimate based on claims; 11,000, *Pravda*, 22 December 1987; and 27,000 increase in last three years according to Report to 1988 Congress)
General Secretary. Rodney Arismendi, until December; Jaime Pérez thereafter
Executive Committee. Pérez, general secretary; Arismendi, president; Daniel Baldassari, Leopoldo Bruera, Thelman Borges, Félix Díaz, Edgar Lanza, León Lev, José Luis Massera, Jorge Mazzarovich, Rafael Sanseviero, Juan Angel

Toledo, Pedro Toledo, Andrés Toriani, Esteban Valenti, Eduardo Viera
Status. Legal
Last Congress. Twenty-first, 7–11 December 1988
Last Election. November 1984; PCU ran with Frente Amplio coalition, 6 percent, no seats
Auxiliary Organization. Union of Communist Youth
Publications. *La Hora*; *El Popular*

1988 was a year that brought several surprises to Uruguay. The petition drive to call a plebiscite on the law granting amnesty to the military proved successful, despite government and military opposition. The Frente Amplio (Broad Front), as the coalition of leftist parties in Uruguay is known, suffered a possibly fatal split between its democratic-socialist and Marxist-Leninist elements. Two major figures of the governing Colorado Party, Senator Jorge Batlle and Vice President Enrique Tarigo, agreed to a primary election to determine who would be the presidential candidate for their wing (Batllista) of the party. Finally, the economy grew less than expected while inflation proved troublesome and labor unrest increased.

The main story within the Frente Amplio was the increasingly bitter split between the democratic-socialist wing consisting of the Christian Democratic Party and, more important, the Party for the Government of the People (PGP) headed by Senator Hugo Batalla, and the more Marxist elements dominated by the Communist Party of Uruguay (PCU). Beginning in April, the more moderate group called for the reorganization of the Frente Amplio's decisionmaking apparatus and a reformulation of the Frente's political strategy. These suggestions reflected the fact that Batalla, who received over 40 percent of the left's vote in the 1984 elections, did not have commensurate voting power within the coalition's governing council. More important, Batalla also pressed the question of whether the Frente would continue to see itself as merely an oppositional group or begin to regard itself as a truly alternative future government for Uruguay. The Marxist-Leninist groups, dominated by the Communist Party, opposed Batalla's suggestions. Several attempts at compromise and reconciliation between the Frente's leader, Liber Seregni, and Senator Batalla, failed, including a solution based on having both men run as presidential candidates for the Frente. Such a solution is possible under Uruguay's election laws, and, in fact, both the Blanco and Colorado Parties are each expected to field two or three presidential candidates in the November elections.

On 17 December, the social-democratic forces walked out of a meeting of the Frente's Plenary Committee when they were denounced as traitors. The committee then proclaimed the single presidential candidacy of General Seregni. As the year ended it was unclear whether Batalla's party would remain in the Frente. The Christian Democrats, led by Héctor Lescano, considered their departure as virtually irreversible. Perhaps if the Communist Party agreed to Batalla's candidacy for *intendente* (mayor) of Montevideo—the second most important elective position in Uruguay—the coalition could hold together. Batalla would be a formidable candidate for *intendente*, a position the Frente lost by less than 30,000 votes in the 1984 election.

President Sanguinetti visited Moscow in March. His principal purpose was the promotion of trade. An expected reciprocal visit by General Secretary Gorbachev has now been postponed until 1989. A flap involving a Soviet diplomat, Embassy First Secretary Atabekov, and Yamandú Fau, a congressman with Senator Batalla's party, erupted late in the year. Fau was angered when the Russian persisted in pressing him concerning his party's position in face of the crisis in the Frente Amplio. Senator Batalla as head of the PGP wrote a strong letter to Soviet Ambassador Igor Laptev complaining of interference in the internal affairs of the country and of his party. This incident highlighted the increasing hostility between the democratic-socialist and communist factions of the Frente Amplio.

A second and less surprising diplomatic incident involved Defense Secretary Hugo Medina, the retired commander of the armed forces, which post he held at the end of the dictatorship, and Cuban ambassador to Uruguay, Joaquin Mas Martínez. During a reception in honor of the queen's birthday at the British Embassy, the two gentlemen exchanged harsh words about the political situation in Uruguay. Cuban Deputy Minister Ricardo Alarcón flew to Montevideo in June in an attempt to smooth over the incident.

This year the major story for Uruguay—and for human rights in Latin America—involved the petition to have a referendum to annul the law that granted amnesty to the military for any crimes they may have committed during more than eleven years of dictatorship. This law had been passed in December 1986 in the face of the military's refusal to have soldiers testify in some three dozen human rights cases that were pending in the courts. Government hostility to the collection of signatures for the referendum during 1987 was followed by the painfully slow verification of these signatures by the Electoral Court. The process took almost one year and was punctuated by the "loss" of electoral registration sheets, the elimination of tens of thousands of signatures, and a general presumption by the court that each signature was questionable, rather than the usual presumption that the signatures were valid unless proved otherwise.

As 1988 grew older, fewer and fewer people, even among the Proreferendum Commission, believed that the requisite 555,701 signatures, representing 25 percent of the electorate, would be validated. Until the very end, the government and the U.S. Embassy gave the impression there were simply not enough valid signatures. Finally, in late November and early December, the Electoral Court verified a total of 522,700 signatures, and declared some 36,000 additional signatures in suspension. The court then set up a three-day period from 17 to 19 December, during which time these 36,000 individuals were asked to present themselves to the court to confirm that they had indeed signed the petition and thus have their signatures validated. The Proreferendum Commission, believing its task almost impossible, debated whether to go along with this final hurdle, or simply refuse and denounce the entire verification process. It was finally decided to try to get the needed 23,000 people to show up and validate their signatures. Using computers and hundreds of volunteers, the tens of thousands of individuals named by the court were contacted. Since many of them live abroad or in the interior of the country, the proreferendum forces had an especially hard task before them. At the end of the first two days, some 21,000 individuals had had their signatures recertified. But the last day was reserved by the court only for those individuals who were registered to vote in one department of Uruguay but had signed for the plebiscite in a different one. Things looked gloomy and matters were complicated when a terrible electrical storm hit Montevideo on that fateful Monday morning. In addition, 19 December was the start of summer hours in all government offices. Therefore people had only until 2:00 P.M. to report. A request to extend the hours was rejected by the court by a vote of six to three. Yet, almost miraculously, enough people showed up in the last two hours so that when it was all over, members of the Electoral Court announced that the referendum petition had carried by about 230 signatures more than the required 555,701.

Within a couple of days the government was conceding that the referendum would have to take place, but it was not happy about it. President Sanguinetti indicated that the country would enter a "long, risky, and dramatic period of confrontation" if the amnesty law were annulled, but was confident that the citizenry "is going to ratify the pacification contained in the amnesty law" (ANSA, 22 December). The first response from the military disparaged those who want to overturn the amnesty law and warned of military solidarity in the face of such action.

The depiction by the political right of the pro-referendum effort as solely the work of the extreme left, including the Tupamaros (the guerrilla movement of the late 1960s and early 1970s), was an act of frustration and distortion. The Tupamaros are a marginal and legal political movement in today's Uruguay with an active membership of several hundred, a biweekly newspaper, and a radio station in Montevideo. The two-year-long struggle to collect over 600,000 signatures (in a country of 2.2 million registered voters) and have them verified in the face of a frightened government and an unrepentant military was the result of the hard work of thousands of Uruguayans of all political persuasions. The outpouring of emotion on the streets of Montevideo when the Electoral Court finally agreed that there were enough signatures was not a Tupamaro victory party. It was a victory for truth, decency, and courage. The fact that the citizens of Uruguay will vote on whether to grant amnesty to the military for its past abuses is a significant human rights story in Latin America this year and a unique chapter in the annals of civil-military relations in the aftermath of a dictatorship. It is a story that deserves close and sustained attention.

1989 will be a highly charged political year in Uruguay. The referendum on the amnesty law will take place in April. The primary election in which Senator Batlle and Vice President Tarigo will be pitted against each other, and that will determine the Batllista presidential candidate of the Colorado Party will likely occur in May or June. Finally, everyone, including the internally feuding and possibly fractured Frente Amplio, will direct his energies toward the nationwide elections in November.

1988 was a year of transition for the PCU. At its 21st Congress in Montevideo in mid-December, Rodney Arismendi retired as general secretary and was replaced by Jaime Pérez. Arismendi was given the new post of president of the Central Committee. Soviet sources reported that more than 3,000 persons attended the congress, including delegates from the PCU, delegations from fraternal communist parties around the world and representatives from other political parties and organizations forming the Frente Amplio. At the congress, Pérez was given the "Friendship of Peoples" award by CPSU Central Committee member and delegation head, S. A. Niyazov. (*Pravda* and TASS, 12 December; *FBIS-SOV*, 13 December.)

The report of the Central Committee to the congress claimed that party membership had increased by 27,000 in the past three years and that the Union of Communist Youth had gained 15,000 new members. The 22nd Congress is planned for 1990 or 1991; the promulgation of the new party program will be at the top of its agenda.

The final declaration of the 21st Congress, dated 11 December, said that the Uruguayan people face a dramatic choice: to use their resources to consolidate democracy, spread justice, promote development, and project the country into the future, or to "continue with the current administration of misery and poverty that legitimizes the privileges of a very small group of 'bad Uruguayans.'" This transformation could come only from the unity of all democratic Uruguayans, particularly members of the Broad Front. The declaration quoted Gen. Liber Seregni's words to the congress, that "Uruguay is uninhabitable without the FA" and proclaimed PCU support for Seregni's candidacy for president in the elections at the end of 1989. (*La Hora*, 15 December; *FBIS*, 30 December.)

Martin Weinstein
William Paterson College of New Jersey

Venezuela

Population. 18,775,780
Parties. Communist Party of Venezuela (Partido Comunista de Venezuela; PCV), pro-Soviet; Movement to Socialism (Movimiento al Socialismo; MAS), democratic socialist
Founded. PCV: 1931; MAS: 1971, PCV splinter

Membership. PCV: 4,000 estimated

Top Leaders. PCV: Alonso Ojeda Olaechea (70), (general secretary); MAS: Pompeyo Márquez (president)

Politburo. PCV: seven members, Alonso Ojeda, President Jesús Faría, Pedro Ortega Díaz, Eduardo Gallegos Mancera, Trino Melean, Silvio Varela, Alí Morales. Three alternates, including Luis Ciano and José Manuel Carrasquel

Executive Committee. MAS: 15 members, including Pompeyo Márquez, General Secretary Freddy Muñoz, Teodoro Petkoff, Victor Hugo de Paola, Mayita Acosta, Rafael Thielen, Leopoldo Puchi, Manuel Molina Peñaloza, and Luis Manuel Esculpi

Central Committee. PCV: 65 members; MAS: National Directorate, 45 members

Status. Both legal

Last Congress. PCV: Seventh, October 1985; MAS: Sixth National Convention, June–July 1985

Last Election. 4 December. PCV: one of 203 federal deputies; MAS: 19 federal deputies, 3 of 46 senators

Auxiliary Organizations. PCV: Unitary Central of Venezuelan Workers (Central Unitária de Trabajadores Venezolanos; CUTV), Communist Youth (Juventud Comunista; JC)

Publications. PCV: *Tribuna Popular*, weekly, Eduardo Gallegos Mancera, director; *CantaClaro*, monthly ideological supplement of Central Committee

As expected, former president Carlos Andrés Pérez (1973–1978; Acción Democrática; AD) was reelected with an impressive 54.5 percent of the vote. The AD lead dropped to 43.7 percent on the congressional ballot, followed by the Social Christian Party (COPEI) with 31.4 percent. MAS was a distant third with 10.2 percent, and the labor-based Radical Cause (Causa R) elected three deputies with its 1.6 percent. The PCV and its ally, the Peoples Electoral Movement (Movimiento Electoral del Pueblo; MEP) returned one and two deputies, respectively, by proportional representation. Each polled less than 1 percent of the total vote, however, and both will have to revalidate their membership lists to qualify for a new national registration.

PCV. The PCV and MEP supported the Moral Movement's independent presidential candidate Edmundo Chirinos. The campaign of the former Central University rector stressed the importance of defeating the entrenched two-party system and the corruption it has engendered. For voters reluctant to "waste" their presidential vote, the PCV and other opposition parties promoted ballot splitting to break the ruling party's monopoly in congress. This occurred to a greater degree than in previous elections, but not to the benefit of the PCV. Unless election results are changed by recounts, the party will lose two of its three federal deputies.

Just a month before the election, the eleventh plenum of the Central Committee predicted an increase in the PCV's share of the vote. The erroneous analysis was based on optimistic reports of effective regional alliances. Although the MAS refused any alliance with the PCV on the presidential slate, the two parties participated jointly in eleven unity slates for state assemblies and four for the national congress. Alonso Ojeda cited this fact as proof that "unity agreements based on a concrete program are possible, despite exclusivist forces at the national level of the MAS" (*Tribuna Popular*, 11–17 November).

The alliances may prove valuable in the April 1989 municipal elections, when state governors will also be elected for the first time. These elections may be postponed if parties decide to run city council candidates nominally rather than by lists, as provided in the election reform law. PCV leadership supported this reform but does not believe it will cure the ills caused by the "Venezuelan state's dependency on local and transnational monopolies" (ibid., 13–19 May).

Venezuelan communists are becoming less cautious and more openly enthusiastic about *perestroika*. Eduardo Gallegos editorialized that "it is not enough to agree with it; we have to understand it well in order to explain it. The revolutionary changes taking place in the USSR are not only internal. They have become the patrimony of all humanity" (ibid., 18–24 March). Gallegos said that Mikhail Gorbachev's book is being read aloud in his PCV cell, as the local version is too expensive for many members to buy.

The PCV walked out of an armed-forces ceremony honoring the heroes of the 1958 revolution when none of the important communist protagonists were mentioned. Two other important anniversaries were celebrated successfully, however. *Tribuna Popular* completed 40 years of continuous publication and was honored at a reception offered by the Committee for International Solidarity, an affiliate of the World Peace Council. CUTV commemorated its 25th birthday at a ceremony attended by labor delegates from Cuba, Panama, El Salvador, Puerto Rico, and Vietnam. Earlier, CUTV president José Manuel Carrasquel and Valentin Makeev of the Central Council of Soviet Unions signed a protocol in Caracas to strengthen relations between the two groups through exchanges and joint seminars that is binding for two years.

Reacting to the massacre on 29 October of fourteen fishermen by Venezuelan security forces in the Colombian border region near El Amparo, PCV deputy Raúl Esté said "the Disip [political police] wanted to establish a precedent of terror as the basis for its presence in this zone" (*El Nacional*, 8 November). The most generally accepted version of the incident is that the boatful of fishermen were mistaken for guerrillas and shot. Trying to cover up, the border patrol—consisting of army, Disip and national guard—moved the unarmed bodies to army headquarters in Táchira and reported that sixteen Colombian guerrillas had been killed in a skirmish. Two had survived, however, and swam back to town.

The army tried to uphold its discredited story, and a military court ordered the arrest of the survivors. The two took refuge in the Mexican embassy and were given asylum in Mexico in early December. On 31 December, the military court finally ordered a trial of the 19 soldiers and police officers involved.

A *Tribuna Popular* columnist, Alvaro Carrera, had written several times earlier in 1988 of the "incipient Vietnam" in the border zone, citing disappearances, persecution, and false arrests of peasants: "nine were absolved [in May] for lack of proof after almost three years in prison" (ibid., 20–26 May). Both Esté and Carrera maintain that landowners in the area are using security forces to harass peasants who are on desirable land (ibid., 11–17 November; *El Nacional*, 8 November). The Amparo killings touched off another wave of violent student protests throughout the country. The UCV rector defended the students, saying "what incites the violence is the government's attempts to deceive the people" (*Tribuna Popular*, 11–17 November).

In February, a congressional delegation led by AD deputy Carlos Canache Mata visited the Soviet Union, an important opportunity, according to PCV delegate Lino Pérez Loyo, for "mainstream political leaders to see the profound changes that are taking place in the USSR" (ibid., 11–17 March). Representatives from the four labor centrals and the journalists' union (SNTP) were invited to celebra-

tions of 1 May in Moscow, and Ugo Cusati of the PCV Central Committee Secretariat led a party delegation to the USSR from 17 to 30 May. Invited by the CPSU Central Committee, the Venezuelan delegates expressed satisfaction at the meeting then under way in Moscow between General Secretary M. Gorbachev and U.S. president R. Reagan. They stressed the tremendous significance of emerging positive changes in Soviet-U.S. relations. (*Pravda*, 1 June; *FBIS*, 9 June.)

The University of the Andes in Mérida hosted an International Encounter for Peace, Disarmament, and Life from 19 to 24 April. The larger conference provided an auspicious ambience for the 21–23 April meeting in Mérida of more than 60 groups of the Colombian and Venezuelan Communist Youth.

MAS. The Revolutionary Left Movement (Movimiento de Izquierda Revolucionária; MIR) presented joint slates for congress with the MAS and supported MAS presidential candidate Teodoro Petkoff. The MIR broke away from the AD in 1960 and is led by General Secretary Moisés Moleiro and President Hector Pérez Marcano. Although Petkoff polled less than 3 percent of the vote, the MAS strategy of playing down revolutionary rhetoric and playing up practical issues paid off. This was particularly true in the states of Lara, Zulia, and Aragua where MAS has strong regional leaders (*Veneconomy Monthly*, November). With nineteen deputies and three senators (10.2 percent of the congressional vote), the MAS-MIR coalition will have some influence as the holder of swing votes.

Petkoff presented the coalition's program in November, emphasizing the need for structural reform at all levels: ". . . current political, social and economic crises cannot be overcome under the existing model of development" (*El Nacional*, 9 November). According to the program, the economy can only be reactivated if it is democratized. The lengthy list of proposals to this end include: just wage and tax systems; real and enforced agrarian reform; rationalized government spending directed to basic industrial and social needs; and drastic reductions in the foreign-debt servicing that is draining funds needed for development.

The MAS candidate wondered if President Jaime Lusinchi's acceptance of the widely questioned army versions of two incidents—the Amparo massacre and the dispatching on October 26 of 30 tanks to surround the presidential palace and the Interior Ministry—had any deeper significance or "reasons of state." (The mobilization of the tanks was reportedly in obedience to a mysterious telephone call made in the name of a high-ranking officer. Investigations are under way.) Petkoff said he preferred to accept the word of MAS deputy Walter Márquez on the Amparo affair. Márquez is a popular human rights defender in his own state of Táchira and all the border region. He demanded the reconstruction of the Amparo incident that definitively discredited the military version. (Ibid., 8, 9, and 10 November.)

Other Leftist Parties. The MEP, led by President Luis Beltrán Prieto Figueroa, General Secretary Adelso González, and Vice President Jesús Paz Galarraga, lost deputies in this election and must reregister as a national party. The MEP was a splinter of the AD that broke away in 1968, and that had its base in the AD-dominated Venezuelan Labor Confederation (Confederación de Trabajadores Venezolanos; CTV). Causa R, however, is a grassroots movement that elected at least three deputies and controls the 17,000 member union of the state steel company Sidor. Causa R leader and presidential candidate, Andrés Velásquez, will become a deputy together, probably, with Pablo Medina and Tello Benítez.

The Socialist League (Liga Socialista; LS) was barely mentioned in the election results. Its presidential candidate, David Nieves, managed for ten years to avoid serving a prison sentence by reason of his election to congress. Sentenced eleven years ago for his part in the kidnapping of an American executive, he was pardoned by President Lusinchi in December. Another LS candidate, Gabriel Puerta, received a pardon in September. Puerta was a leader of the guerrilla group Red Flag (Bandera Roja) and had been in prison for armed rebellion.

Guerrillas. Throughout 1988, security forces reported clashes with narcotics dealers and guerrillas in the border zone and several presumed guerrillas were killed. In August, a military court ordered the trial of 31 persons arrested by the Disip and accused of belonging to the Venceremos Group (*Diário Las Américas*, 29 August). The group is implicated in bank robberies in Caracas and elsewhere and accused of inciting and participating in disturbances during student demonstrations in Caracas, Barquisimeto, and Mérida (*El Universal*, 19 August; *FBIS*, 29 August).

Carole Merten
San Francisco, California

ASIA AND THE PACIFIC

Introduction

The final three years of the 1980s will likely be remembered as a major watershed for communism in Asia as significant as the last few years of the 1950s, when the communist world movement divided into two major ideological camps.

Important reforms and changes have been taking place in the communist-ruled states of the People's Republic of China (PRC), North Korea, Vietnam, Cambodia, and Laos. In early February 1989, the foreign ministers of the Soviet Union and the PRC agreed to convene a summit meeting sometime in the first half of 1989 to be held in Beijing, probably in mid-May. By early 1989, the governments of North and South Korea were inching toward a dialogue that held some promise of reducing tensions on the Korean peninsula for the first time since the Korean War. In early 1989, the Soviet Union was rapidly withdrawing its troops from Afghanistan, and there appeared to be the prospect of a complete withdrawal by mid-February 1989. Throughout 1988, Vietnam had been removing its troops from Cambodia. In 1988 and 1989, the communist parties in Vietnam and Laos were seriously considering limited economic and political reforms to revitalize those societies. With the exception of the Philippines, the communist parties and their supporters elsewhere in Asia and the Pacific were in retreat or on the defensive.

How long this new era will last remains to be seen, but clearly a new historical phase appears to be unfolding. To elucidate these changes, we classify communist activity as follows: states with ruling communist parties, states with legal communist parties in opposition, and states with banned communist parties.

States with Ruling Communist Parties. In Mongolia some communist leaders and writers began unprecedented denunciations of Stalin and former Mongolian leaders like Choybalsan and Tsedenbal, who were close to Stalin or ruled in the Stalinist style. As *glasnost'* spread throughout that country, the party's system of local governance came under attack. The press also admitted that the economy had been stagnating and that the advancing Gobi Desert had caused pastoral productivity to fall drastically in recent years.

In North Korea Kim Il-song continued to prepare for the transfer of power to his son and heir, Kim Chong-il. In September 1988 some 160-odd countries, including most of the socialist bloc countries, convened in Seoul for the 24th Olympiad, giving North Korea its worst diplomatic defeat. A number of personnel shifts occurred in party and government, including the replacement of the Korean People's Army chief of staff O Kuk-yol by Choe Kwang, a Politburo member and former chief of staff who had been fired in the late 1960s. The party leadership also called on the people to engage in a vigorous campaign of hard work for 200 days a year to accelerate production in all sectors of the economy. Reports of consumer goods and food shortages as well as various economic difficulties continued to leak out of the country. Yet various contacts between parties of both North and South Korea continued in 1988, culminating in an alleged agreement in Pyongyang in February 1989 between Chung Ju-yung, honorary chairman of South Korea's Hyundai conglomerate, and the head of Pyongyang's Taiwong Bank, Choe Su-gil, to build a resort on North Korea's eastern side in the Kumgang Mountains.

The PRC economy overheated in 1988, and worried leaders decided to impose price controls on key raw materials and to strengthen controls on funding and resource allocation in the third quarter of the year to roll back an inflation estimated at more than 25 percent for various categories of consumer goods and raw materials. Meanwhile, population grew at the higher-than-expected rate of 1.4 percent, strongly indicating that the one-child policy had not worked and that the country would not be able to meet the target of only 1.2 billion people at the end of this century.

Although no significant personnel changes occurred in either the party or the government, the party leadership seemed determined to separate party from government functions. Party cells were to be replaced by working committees, whose main tasks were to lead and direct the work of the organs directly under the party center. Such streamlining was supposed to gradually allow state and collective enterprises and government bureaus to be free of party interference. In the past nine years the party's Organization Department had enrolled 12.85 million new members, bringing party membership to 47 million. Persons below the age of 35 account for two-thirds of the total number recruited every year.

To replace the current procedure of the state building and assigning apartments, a new housing reform was announced that would distribute apartments through work units, which would sell according to market demand. The program began in 1988 with several cities serving as experimental centers. By 1990 all cities are expected to be carrying out this new reform.

Disturbances rocked Tibet in early 1988, and violent demonstrations by Chinese students and citizens against African students studying in Chinese universities in January 1989 strained Beijing's relations with many African states. Meanwhile, Chinese from Taiwan continued to visit the mainland, and numerous meetings and negotiations were held to finalize by 1990 the Basic Law, the rules of governance by which Hong Kong would be governed in 1997.

Throughout 1988, Vietnam's communist party continued to press for a revitalization of spirit and society. Although a reform plan to streamline the economy had been introduced the year before, little seemed to have changed, and poverty remained widespread, with per capita income still only around U.S. $309. Nearly half of the state's budget went to the military. The ruling Politburo of thirteen members had formed factions labeled by outsiders as the Reformers (Nguyen Van Linh, Vo Van Kiet, and Mai Chi Tho), the Conservatives (Do Muoi, Vo Chi Cong, and Nguyen Duc Tam), the Militarists (Le Duc Anh, Doan Khue, and Dong Sy Nguyen), and the Bureaucrats (Nguyen Co Thach, Tran Xuan Bach, Dao Duy Tung and Nguyen Thanh Binh). Those in the Militarist and Bureaucrat factions frequently switched their support to the Reformer or Conservative factions, depending on the issues being debated. The party's general secretary, Nguyen Van Linh, complained at the Fifth Plenum of the Sixth Congress in June 1988 of widespread corruption, incompetence, and lack of dedication among cadres and officials. Although the party leadership emphasized personnel matters, recruit-

ment, indoctrination, and training, it continued to evaluate and expel undesirable members from the party's ranks. Vietnam gradually removed some troops from Cambodia, but tensions with China remained high, with several naval clashes occurring in the South China Sea over sovereignty claims of some 52 islands in that area.

States with Legal Communist Party Opposition. Bangladesh, India, Nepal, Sri Lanka, Japan, Australia, and New Zealand allow communist parties to be active as long as they comply with existing laws. Nepal's various Marxist-type parties continue to jockey for influence, with their leaders continually changing. In Sri Lanka, the traditional Marxist parties are declining in popularity and influence as "new left" organizations supported by rural youth begin to emerge. In Japan, the communist party continues to attract mostly protest vote supporters, with few new members committed to the party's doctrine. The party devoted most of its political energy to an unsuccessful attempt to block a new tax reform bill proposed by the ruling Liberal Democratic Party. The party's aging leader and spokesman, Kenji Miyamoto, remained in charge. In New Zealand, the various local communist parties stepped up their criticism of the Labour government's free-market economic policies, which were alleged to have caused a rise in unemployment.

States with Banned Communist Parties. Burma, Thailand, Malaysia, Singapore, Indonesia, Pakistan, the Philippines, the Republic of China, and the Republic of Korea have outlawed communist parties.

In March 1988, student riots, the worst since 1974, rocked Rangoon, and although the military suppressed those demonstrations, the former Socialist Program Party formed a new but weaker National Unity Party. On 19 October the new party leadership ceased calling Burma a "Socialist Republic" in favor of the country's original name, the Union of Burma. After the riots, many Rangoon students fled into the jungles, and some even linked up with the banned communist party and its various military units. Most students, however, joined other insurgent organizations, so that the communist party's gain was probably minimal. In mid-September communist troops, with heavy artillery and some modern weapons, attacked the Mong Yang area; they continued these attacks until late October, when government troops finally drove them off.

In Thailand, the economy continued to prosper through 1988 as that state's effective political leadership and policies attracted foreign investment and enterprise while expanding exports and domestic economic growth. As income distribution improved and living standards rose, the country was no longer threatened by a communist insurgency. Little information surfaced about the leadership and activities of the Thailand Communist Party; probably fewer than two hundred people serve the party in the southern provinces. Meanwhile, the Thai government continued to negotiate with its neighbors concerning the refugee problem and the violence along that country's border with Cambodia.

In Indonesia, a major public debate erupted after the publication of a book by Sugiarso Surojo, a former intelligence officer who claimed that Indonesia's founding father, Sukarno, had been a dedicated Marxist since his student days in the 1920s and was deeply involved in the abortive coup of 1965. In the spring, the government carried out a vigorous campaign against suspected communist infiltration into state organs and the media that continued into the fall. Some senior officials lost their jobs because of suspected communist links.

In Malaysia, the inspector general of police estimated in early March that there were about 1,400 communist guerrillas operating in the Malaysian jungles even though more than 900 had surrendered to Malay and Thai authorities in 1987. There was no verification of his claim, but frequent reports appeared in the press about communist guerrilla activity in the jungles along the Thai border. Meanwhile, there was no evidence of any communist party organization in Singapore.

In the Philippines, the communist party continued to make war on the government. Yet it suffered several important setbacks in 1988, including the capture of some top leaders and severe splits between regional leaders. The Catholic Church steadily withdrew its support from the party, as did some trade unions. Captured communist party documents reveal that the party's annual budget in 1988 was about U.S. $2.6 million, with considerable income from so-called legal projects, businesses, and development projects. The New People's Army guerrilla manpower was reported at around 24,000 in November, and its main military activities shifted from southern to central Luzon.

Soviet Activity in the Region. As a follow-up to Mikhail Gorbachev's diplomatic overtures in Asia, Soviet foreign minister Eduard A. Shevardnadze met with his counterpart in Tokyo in late December in a bid to get Soviet-Japanese relations moving again. In this effort, however, he failed. The Northern Territories remained the chief stumbling block to any agreements between the two countries. Shevardnadze told Prime Minister Noboru Takeshita that a trip to Japan was on Gorbachev's schedule but did not announce a date. Shevardnadze visited Beijing in early February 1989, where his efforts proved successful; both countries agreed that Gorbachev would meet with Deng Xiaoping sometime before mid-1989 in Beijing.

Ramon H. Myers
Hoover Institution

Australia

Population. 16,260,436

Parties. Communist Party of Australia (CPA): Socialist Party of Australia (SPA); Communist Party of Australia–Marxist-Leninist (CPA-ML); Socialist Workers' Party (SWP); Association of Communist Unity (ACU); Socialist Labor League (SLL); International Socialists (IS); Spartacist League of Australia and New Zealand (SLANZ)

Founded. CPA: 1920; SPA: 1971; CPA-ML: 1964; SWP: 1972; ACU: 1985; SLL: 1972; IS: 1971

Membership. CPA: 1,000; SPA: 500; CPA-ML: 300; SWP: 400; ACU: 50; SLL: 50; IS: 75; SLANZ: 50

Leadership. CPA: Run by National Committee; Brian Aarons, Dennis Freney (spokesmen); SPA: Peter Dudley Symon (general secretary), Jack McPhillips (president); CPA-ML: Bruce Cornwall (chairman); SWP: Jim Percy (national secretary)

Status. Legal

Last Congress. CPA: Twenty-ninth, 6–8 June 1987; SPA: Sixth, 3 October; SWP: Eleventh, 2–6 January 1986; CPA-ML: Seventh Congress, October

Last Election. 11 July 1987; official government report says communist party polled 0.3 percent of the national vote.

Publications. CPA: *Tribune* (weekly; editorial collective), *Australian Left Review* (quarterly); SPA: *The Guardian* (weekly; Anna Pha, editor), *Youth Voice* (monthly); CPA-ML: *Vanguard* (weekly; Marcus Clayton, editor), *Australian Communist*; SWP: *Direct Action* (weekly; Steve Painter, editor), *Resistance* (occasional); ACU: *People's Cause* (bimonthly; Bill Brown, editor); SLL: *Workers' News* (twice weekly; Mike Head, editor); IS: *Socialist Action* (monthly)

The year 1988 marked yet another decline for the formal communist groupings in Australia. Nevertheless, these parties' residual influence was evident in the united front protests against the visiting Allied fleet (United Kingdom and U.S. Navy) that visited Australian ports in October. The communist party weekly reported protests in Townsville, Queensland; Portland, Victoria; Adelaide, South Australia; Cairns, Queensland; and Melbourne, Victoria (*Tribune*, 24 October). The HMS *Ark Royal* and the USS *Ingersoll* received no assistance docking at the port of Melbourne (Melbourne, *Age*, 17 October). Opposition to the visit of the U.S. ships to the Australian Bicentennary Naval Review occasioned few popular demonstrations but led to dramatic advertisements by a large number of elite opinion makers (*Australian*, 26 September). The demonstrations, particularly the prevention by the Moscow-aligned Seamen's Union of the docking of the carrier *Ark Royal*, led to a review of defense arrangements with Australia by the Margaret Thatcher government (Adelaide, *Advertiser*, 19 October). A conservative weekly reported that the labor union responsible for refusing tugboats to the Allied ships was led by officials long involved in a plethora of Soviet fronts (*Newsweekly*, 28 October).

Apart from this incident, Australia's communist element did not directly affect public policy. Ironically—unrelated to the influence (or lack of it) of their local communist mouthpieces—the generally improved image of the USSR under Mikhail Gorbachev made Moscow's image more acceptable, and Soviet activity in Australia was considerably boosted during this past year.

Following a worldwide pattern, rather than using their fronts, the Soviets sent numerous delegations to Australia. These peace, trade union, youth, cultural, and party delegations were matched by an increased number of visits by official government delegations. Last year Canberra welcomed the first visit by a Soviet foreign minister, Eduard Shevardnadze, followed this year by the

highest-level visit to Australia by a USSR official—the July visit of Soviet deputy prime minister Vladimir Kamentsev (*WSJ*, 28 September). Despite previous Australian concern about Moscow's involvement in fishing pacts with nearby South Pacific states, much of the government-to-government contact involved an on-again off-again proposal for the USSR to undertake fishing research in Australian coastal waters. Senator Gareth Evans, the Labor government's new foreign minister, signaled that it would no longer oppose the island states' developing relations with the USSR (*Sydney Morning Herald*, 26 September).

Australia also experienced interest from other senior communist bloc leaders, with President Nicolae and Madam Elena Ceauşescu of Romania visiting Australia from 11 to 17 April (*FBIS*, 11, 17 April). Chinese premier Li Peng visited Australia in mid-November (*FBIS*, 17 November).

There was no perceptible increase in electoral support for Marxist parties, but the improved Soviet image meant that Moscow was seen as more interested in arms reduction than the United States. According to a Saulwick poll, however, the USSR was still seen as imperialist by 45 percent of the people in Sydney (*Sydney Morning Herald*, 17 October). Although pro-Soviet sentiment in Australia is low, official government peace researcher Andrew Mack claims that there was a slight drop in support for the Australia–New Zealand–United States (ANZUS) security pact (down to 67 percent). A Defenctrac poll showed only 39 percent supported the joint facilities, with 51 percent opposed. Moreover only 24 percent were supportive of port visits, with 26 percent unsure and 50 percent opposed! (*Bulletin*, 6 September). Visits by the U.S. Navy to Australian ports, including visits by carrier battle groups for rest and relaxation, are a key issue that all Australia's communist factions unite in opposing. Just before his death, legendary British traitor and State Security Committee (KGB) general Kim Philby signaled Moscow's interest in decoupling Australia from this naval link with the United States. In an interview with author Phillip Knightly, Philby said that David Lange, the prime minister of New Zealand, "had the courage to ban nuclear ships from New Zealand waters. Now we have no reason to target New Zealand with our intercontinental missiles and indeed we have ceased to do so. I'm sorry I cannot say the same about Australia" (Melbourne, *Herald*, 5 January). Visiting Soviet Peace Committee director Yuriy Drozda, in Australia with four other Soviet Peace Committee members, scorned the joint U.S.-Australian facilities at Pine Gap, Nurrungar, and North West Cape "because they do not contribute to verification of nuclear arms control and hosting arrangements" (*FBIS*, 18 May).

Australia was increasingly used as a focal point for the activity of Soviet fronts such as the World Federation of Democratic Youth (WFDY), which held a major meeting in Australia in May that was extensively reported in the official organ of the Central Committee of the pro-Moscow SPA, the *Guardian* (11, 18 May). The International Union of Students also held a major meeting in Sydney in September, noted in the quarterly paper of the youth section of the SPA *Youth Voice* (October). Yet not all visits of Soviet representatives were made without cost. In order to secure an official invitation from the Australian Council of Trade Unions (ACTU), the Soviet trade unions were forced to assign their September visit to learning about democratic trade unionism from their contemporaries down under (*Newcastle Herald*, 5 October).

Nor should one understate the influence of remorseless official Soviet cultural activity. Melbourne and Sydney both were visited by the fourteenth Soviet film festival, which attracted widespread favorable publicity. A more precisely targeted visit—the government-run Moscow Jewish Theatre—was surprisingly successful at influencing a turnaround in attitudes of a previously strongly anti-Soviet element in Australian society.

Moscow began the year with a press conference that cleared up its previously qualified support for the South Pacific Nuclear-Free Zone (Moscow had said if any country such as Australia permitted the transit of nuclear-capable ships Moscow would be freed of obligations under the treaty) (*FBIS*, 5 February). Canberra did not take up a proposal by visiting French admiral Emile Threaut that Australia cooperate in an anti-Soviet defense pact in the Pacific (*FBIS*, 22 March). Australia, however, although adopting a more generous view of the USSR, did back the United States on major issues; former Foreign Minister Bill Hayden supported what he described as a "proportionate" U.S. action in the gulf to secure the passage of shipping from interdiction by Iran (*FBIS*, 9 April). Prime Minister Robert Hawke rejected Soviet premier Gorbachev's proposal—made in a speech in Krasnoyarsk—that the USSR would give up its facilities at Cam Ranh Bay in Vietnam if the United States would close down its naval base at Subic Bay in the Philippines (*FBIS*, 19 November).

Both Hawke and Hayden, however, signaled that they were favorably disposed to port access for Soviet fishing trawlers (*FBIS*, 17 June), although Deputy Prime Minister Lionel Bowen did indicate that there were security risks in allowing Aeroflot landing rights for crew changes of these trawlers (Channel 9, "TV Sunday Program," 24 July).

The proposal stalled because of mounting opposition and because the Soviets suddenly increased the number of fishing vessels from two to eight that they wanted to operate in northern Australia (*Sydney Morning Herald*, 2 November). Because the Australian government saw the possibility of linking the Soviet port access proposal with guarantees about commodity sales to the USSR, there was a strong likelihood by year's end that the deal would proceed. A severe problem with Australia's balance of trade was behind this desire to secure Soviet commodity markets for Australian exports, and Australian trade delegations visited Moscow in 1988 in the wake of Prime Minister Hawke's December 1987 visit. The Soviet Union ranks only thirteenth among markets for Australian goods, importing $697 million ($U.S. 559 million) in 1987, most of it wool. That figure was 30 percent off the level in 1986, mainly due to a drop in sales of Australian wheat to Moscow, from nearly $600 million to $87 million ($U.S. 481 million to $70 million) (*FBIS*, 11 October).

Moscow invited the usual stream of sympathizers, such as the Association of Communist Unity–controlled Building Workers' Industrial Union (*Age*, 10 August) and peace delegations, including noncommunists such as Australian democrat D. Bretherton. Left-wing Labor senator Olive Zakharov was asked to the USSR in August to witness the destruction of SS-21 missiles at Sayozek in Kazakhstan—the first step in the implementation of the historic intermediate-range nuclear forces (INF) agreements between the USSR and the United States (*Labor Star*, December). Moscow also succeeded in planting disinformation stories in respectable local media. For instance, a Melbourne evening newspaper picked up the widely identified Soviet disinformation report that Brazilian babies were being killed and their organs used in the United States for organ transplants (Melbourne, *Herald*, 8 August). A conservative professor, citing "a South African source," unwittingly nationally broadcast another key Soviet disinformation theme—that AIDS had been invented by demented germ warfare scientists on the U.S. government payroll at Fort Detrick in Georgia (Australian Broadcasting Corporation, "Notes on the News,"

4 April). But Moscow suffered a severe setback with the identification in late October of its acting ambassador Valery Zemskov as the highest-ranking KGB officer ever posted to Australia (Adelaide, *Advertiser*, 20 October). A week-long front-page controversy was sparked by an excerpt from an article by John Barron in *Reader's Digest* that maintained that Zemskov was in fact a member of the highly secret Special Reserves of the KGB. His cover blown, Zemskov was withdrawn "for promotion" at the end of the year.

Besides the Zemskov fiasco, Moscow also saw Australia refuse to admit the deputy head of the Soviet Chamber of Commerce, Igor Kamiyev, who was to have headed a seven-person trade delegation to Australia (*FBIS*, 12 May). Canberra also stopped the visit of Soviet professor Edward Ivanjian, "a specialist in the Asia Pacific Region and head of publications at the Institute of U.S. and Canadian Studies" (*Tribune*, 9 November). Ivanjian was to have addressed a 29 October seminar of the Australian/USSR Friendship Society on "the role of the Soviet Union in the Asia Pacific Region," which was addressed by Zemskov. The Soviet embassy also attracted persistent unfavorable publicity for its illegal, high-frequency transmissions and aerials in its Canberra diplomatic compound (*Canberra Times*, 28 December).

One of the Soviet Union's highest objectives in Australia—reunification of the disparate communist parties—received a setback last year as the pro-Cuban SWP and the CPA, the largest remaining communist grouping, fell out over the aims of a new left party charter. However, the SWP and the even more doctrinaire SPA are clearly preparing for amalgamation, with renewed talks, reporting of each other's conferences, and extensive support of each other's meetings. Independently, the CPA and the ACU, a small pro-Moscow-based communist grouping that retains an influential number of union officials and disenchanted Marxists to the left of the Australian Labor Party (ALP), have signed a joint declaration committing themselves to the establishment of a new Marxist political party by 1990 (Adelaide, *Advertiser*, 15 March 1989). National officers of the CPA remained unannounced and, together with the wooing of Marxist and radical environmentalists associated with the single-issue grouping called the Rainbow Alliance, seemed to be the basis for a relaunched new left party (*Australian Left Review*, June/July). But apart from some of the tiny Trotskyite sects, the communist groupings demonstrated their increased fealty to

Moscow and were rewarded with substantial advertising—the CPA theoretical quarterly took full-page ads for the pro-Moscow SPA's New Era bookshops (*Moscow News*, July). The significance of these moves is not yet clear. However, the Kremlin has a stake in both developments and in the year ahead will undoubtedly press for a future consolidation into a single pro-Soviet party.

The CPA. Given its past record, the CPA is frustrated at its current lack of influence. It retains a number of significant officials in building, metal, teachers', mining, and transport unions, but its overall membership has declined to about a thousand. Its organs, the weekly *Tribune* and the quarterly *Australian Left Review*, continue to appear, but even this basic task seems an effort. Communist party circles continue to talk of expanding the left press by amalgamation. One successful new party effort that seems to have attracted support from the nonaligned left was the launch of a left book club (*Tribune*, 15 April). In recent years, the CPA has been involved in the radical feminist movement, the homosexual/lesbian lobby, and the peace movement, where it has significant influence in People for Nuclear Disarmament (PND). Its influence in them is, however, hard to evaluate.

Opposition to any joint military cooperation between the United States and Australia remained a top goal of the CPA (*Tribune*, 19 October, 9, 30 November). It supported the rather unsuccessful march on the joint U.S.-Australian communications base at North West Cape in western Australia. Professor Dimitriu Volovoi, deputy editor in chief of *Pravda*, was guest of the pro-Moscow *Guardian* newspaper, but feelings toward the USSR were sufficiently positive for him to be interviewed in the CPA weekly *Tribune* (30 November). Perhaps the clearest indication of the CPA's enthusiasm for the new regime in Moscow was the launching of a booklet about *perestroika* published by the CPA called *The Fruits of* Glasnost'. The booklet was launched by *Pravda* correspondent Alexei Ivkin. (*Tribune*, 30 November.) Dennis Freney, the editor of *The Fruits of* Glasnost', was keen to emphasize, however, that "since at least 1968, the CPA had taken an independent stand on all issues concerning the Soviet Union" (*Financial Review*, 5 December).

Solidarity work with the Communist Party of the Philippines (CPP) remained high on the CPA's agenda, and, together with other anti-U.S. elements, the CPA sent several cadres to join a peace brigade to the Philippines. This brigade—some three hundred non-Filipinos, including some eighty Australians—organized a series of protests in Manila, including an unsuccessful march on the U.S. bases at Subic Bay and Clark Field. The communist weekly *Tribune* devoted a large amount of coverage to the Philippines, giving a full-page interview to visiting Professor Roland Simbulan, who was in Australia to attend a conference at Monash University, attacking Washington's low-intensity conflict strategy in the Philippines (*Tribune*, 31 August). The involvement of Australian church and aid organizations in providing money to fronts of the communist parties of the Philippines became a matter of public controversy in Australia following an official complaint from the Corazon Aquino government to Canberra.

Given the current inactivity in the South Pacific, the World Federation of Trade Unions (WFTU) has sought greater assistance from the CPA and the ACU for front activity in the Indian Ocean region.

The ACU. The ACU is a pro-Moscow communist faction that split from the SPA, the official Australian pro-Soviet communist party. Its small numbers understate the role its members have in important unions such as the Building Workers' Industrial Union (BWIU), the Seamen's Union, and the Miners' Federation. The ACU split from the SPA when its trade union bosses refused to subordinate their industrial attitudes to SPA party directives. The ACU, like the CPA, still supports (albeit critically) the official social contract between the Australian Labor government and the ACTU. The SPA opposes this accord and is against the BWIU's collaboration with attempts by the state ALP administration to abolish the Maoist Builders-Laborers' Federation.

Much to the chagrin of the SPA, the Soviets continued to invite the ACU to many front meetings. Brian McGahen attended the international meeting for nuclear weapons–free zones held in the German Democratic Republic (*Tribune*, 3 August). Pat Gorman, editor of the Miners' Federation weekly *The Common Cause*, "was the only Australian journalist at the 19th CPSU conference." Gorman was interviewed by both Radio Moscow and *Trud*, the state-run daily newspaper of the Soviet Union. Like other SPA and ACU cadres, he services a functionary Soviet front organization and is an executive member of the International Organization of Journalists (*Survey*, July). One aspect of the ACU's activities, previously underestimated, is its key role in the Australian-USSR Friendship As-

sociation, which has branches in all Australian states and many provincial centers. In fact, the ACU seems to have a bigger role in the Australian-USSR Friendship Association than the SPA. Some measure of its strength was the recent announcement— in a publication associated with the ACU—by the Australian-USSR Friendship Association national executive, together with its Sydney branch, that it will raise $250,000 to purchase a small building as an office and function center (*Survey*, August). Five Australian children were apparently sent by the ACU to the International Banner for Peace Assembly held in Bulgaria (*Survey*, September). At the initiative of the West Australian branches of the pro-Moscow BWIU and the Federated Engine Drivers and Firemens' Association (FEDFA), the West Australian Labor Council adopted a proposal to call an international union conference of Indian Ocean rim countries (*Social Action*, November). Although the Australian trade union movement is linked with the International Confederation of Free Trade Unions (ICFTU), WFTU, the Soviet front, has a number of supporters in Australia. The main links are through the ACU-CPA unions, particularly the BWIU.

The SWP. The SWP, confirmed in its five-year split from Trotskyism, is now firmly aligned with both Cuba and the Soviet Union. Within Australia this takes the form of an alliance with the pro-Moscow SPA, which reported a joint statement on a process of unity in both political program and common activities (*Direct Action*, 1 June). Further evidence of this was the proposed joint conference of the SPA and the SWP, to be held in early January 1989, called the conference of Socialist Reconstruction and Renewal (*Direct Action*, 30 November). The SWP-SPA held a joint meeting on industrial restructuring and foreshadowed the disaffiliation of unions from the Australian Labor Party as a way of breaking the Labor government's industrial accord (*Direct Action*, 20 July).

The SWP noted with approval the Sixth National Congress of the pro-Moscow SPA and referred to the adoption and publication of a joint statement by SPA and SWP executives in May (*Direct Action*, 11 October). The SWP and the SPA gave a test run to the electoral support for a joint SWP-SPA ticket when they ran in the Victoria state elections as "a Socialist alliance." Candidates in two working-class seats polled 3.5 percent and 6.5 percent, respectively (*ibid.*).

The SWP is increasingly involved with other pro-Soviet networks in Australia, with the high point being the address by Vladimir Tsaregradsky, the Soviet consul general in Sydney, on the occasion of the 71st anniversary of the Bolshevik Revolution. The function was organized by the SWP, the SPA, and "Spanish and Chilean communist parties in Australia" (*Direct Action*, 8 November). Earlier, Marina Bardina and Vera Sobleva, a delegation from the international department of the Soviet women's committee that was touring Australia as a guest of the Union of Australian Women, were given a highly laudatory full-page interview in the SWP's official organ (*Direct Action*, 25 October). A measure of the SWP's extraordinary shift to a faithful mouthpiece of Moscow was a double-page obituary for Kim Philby, who the SWP lauded as "a master spy and communist" (*Direct Action*, 25 May).

The SWP, closely identified with Cuba, continues to regularly advertise in *Granma*, the Cuban English-language communist organ, and in *Baric-cada*, the publication of the Nicaraguan Sandinistas. Last year in an important development, the SWP company The Pathfinder Press Asia Pacific copublished with the Jose Marti publishing house, the state publisher of Fidel Castro's communist regime, the collective writings of Ernesto (Che) Guevara for worldwide distribution. The SWP remains involved in the Australian-Cuban Friendship Association and plays a key role in Central American communism with its solidarity front the Committee in Solidarity with the Caribbean and Central America. From midyear on the SWP promoted the sixth annual work brigade to Cuba. On this work brigade Australian revolutionaries pay $3,350 to work and be indoctrinated by Castro's cadres (*Direct Action*, 20 July).

The SPA. The SPA, the official pro-Soviet communist party, held its Sixth Congress in early October. Messages of solidarity were sent on behalf of the Central Committee of the Communist Party of the Soviet Union (CPSU) (*Pravda*, 30 September), by the Central Committee of the Bulgarian Communist Party (*Rabotnichesko delo*, 30 September), and by the Central Committee of the East German Socialist Unity Party of Germany (*ND*, 30 September). The date (3 October) of the end of the Sixth Congress in Sydney was reported only in Moscow (*Pravda*, 4 October). Delegates from the CPSU, the Communist Party of Greece, and the Socialist Unity Party of New Zealand attended the conference as fraternal guests (*Youth Voice*, October). The SPA continued to produce its weekly news-

paper, *Guardian*, and sell Soviet propaganda at subsidized prices in its New Era bookshops.

Its youth section, the Young Socialist League (YSL), was given an increasingly important function—participating in a coalition of student groups that ran the newly created National Union of Students. The YSL also played a leading role in the National Preparatory Committee for the World Federation of Youth and Students (WFYS), which was to take place in North Korea. Dorothy Costa, national secretary of the YSL, took part in a round-table meeting on 3 June hosted by the Mongolian Revolutionary Youth Union (*Guardian*, 22 June). A delegation from the Korean Preparatory Committee led by Cho Gon Hyong, who is the deputy director of Korean Airways, visited Australia as part of the buildup to the WFYS (*Youth Voice*, October). Two children, members of the Young Pioneers, participated in a camp organized by the Soviet Union in Artek (ibid.).

The SPA continued its solidarity work with pro-Moscow factions among the Latin American, Middle Eastern, and Greek ethnic communities in Australia and continued to play an important function in the Eastern bloc friendship associations, apart from the Australian-USSR Friendship Association, where its rival, ACU, seemed more active. But, most important, the YSL was the real organizing force behind the WFDY's regional meeting, which took place in Sydney (*Guardian*, 18 May). The YSL was also assigned to host the Second International Student Roundtable Meeting "for a secure, nuclear-free, and independent Pacific," which took place in Sydney in September (*Youth Voice*, October).

The SPA's opposition to the joint U.S.-Australian facilities could be seen in the key Soviet ideological monthly, *World Marxist Review*. Hanna Middleton, a member of the Central Committee of the SPA, noted that there had been a marked change in attitude toward the USSR and that although some still raise questions about the moral equivalence of the superpowers, most members of the peace movement see the United States as intransigent: "it has become considerably more difficult for those who try to advance an anti-Soviet position in the peace movement" (*WMR*, June). Peter Symon, general secretary of the SPA, noted the anti-U.S. aspects of regional struggles in Palau in the context of the antinuclear developments associated with the South Pacific nuclear-free zone (the Rarotonga treaty). *Youth Voice* (October) reported the long trek to North West Cape, the joint Australian-U.S. facility.

The SPA is heavily involved in the peace movement through key activists in the Congress for International Cooperation and Disarmament (Victoria) and in branches of the Australian Peace Committee in other states. Although its numerical presence is small, it is a tribute to the effectiveness of many years of ideological activity that the peace movement in Australia sees the United States as the enemy, despite Soviet activities in Afghanistan and Vietnam in recent years.

The CPA-ML. Australia's most secretive party seems to have changed leadership, with Bruce Cornwall replacing Neil McLean as party secretary, although there was no report of this in any CPA-ML publication. The party's main trade union outpost, the militant Builders-Labourers' Federation, continues to decline. Documents from the Seventh National Congress of the CPA-ML were published in the *Australian Communist* (no. 151). The CPA-ML participated in many of the extreme left's campaigns against visiting U.S. ships (*Vanguard*, 27 July, 7 September). The party weekly noted the major memorial meeting addressed by prominent doctors, unionists, and even a Labor Party senator for the late General Secretary E.F. (Ted) Hill, who died on 1 February (*Vanguard*, 17 February). Clarrie O'Shea, another leading cadre and a major figure in the tramways union, also had his parting noted (*Vanguard*, 21 July). Tom Paine, the last remaining Australian to have heard Lenin in Moscow in 1922, was also eulogized (*Vanguard*, 11 May). CPA-ML, with a peculiar concentration on Japanese investment in Australia and involvement in the region, persistently campaigned against "Japanese imperialism" (*Vanguard*, 6 April, 13 August, 20 November). On the 50th anniversary of Australian wharf laborers' opposition to pig iron exports to Japan, the cultural attaché at the Chinese embassy attended the reunion (*Vanguard*, 30 November). Like other communist factions, the CPA-ML vociferously opposed the joint Australian-U.S. facilities and sent a group of trade unionists to an international solidarity affair with the Philippines communist party trade union satellite, the May First Movement (*Vanguard*, 27 July). The CPA-ML continued to favor "left unity" (*Australian Communist*, April). But its support was not urgently sought by other communist groupings.

Although the Marxist parties remain small and their attempts at unity have yet to reach a satisfactory conclusion, they retain influence in the media and in academic life.

They have considerable assets in the trade union movement, and because most Australian trade unions are affiliated with the governing ALP, their policies may be transmitted into the forums of the ALP. This is reflected in the socialist left faction, a coalition of Marxists and non-Marxists that represents about 35 votes out of the 99 at the Labor Party's Federal Conference, its supreme governing body.

The Marxist left is totally opposed to the pro-Western foreign and defense policies of the current Labor Government, but because of its organizational presence in the trade union movement, it is in a quandary. It does not want to appear to be acting in a way that would bring about the defeat of the Labor government, as this would reduce its support in the trade union movement. Its best chance of recruitment and progress toward unity could arise under a future conservative government, should it adopt strong antiunion policies.

Michael Danby
Melbourne, Australia

Bangladesh

Population. 109,963,551
Party. Communist Party of Bangladesh (CPB)
Founded. 1948 (as East Pakistan Communist Party; banned in 1954; re-emerged in 1971 following the establishment of Bangladesh)
Membership. 9,911 (claimed; Dhaka, *New Nation*, 6 January); actual membership estimated at 5,000
General Secretary. Saifuddin Ahmed Manik
Secretariat. 12 members
Central Committee. 40 members
Status. Legal
Last Congress. Fourth, 7–11 April 1987
Last Election. 3 March; CPB observed an opposition boycott of the election and did not field candidates.
Auxiliary Organizations. Trade Union Centre, Cultural Front, Chatra Union, Khetmozdur Samiti, Mahila Parishad, Jubo Union
Publication. *Ekota* (in Bengali)

The Bangladeshi political scene remained chaotic throughout 1988 as opposition coalitions waged strikes and demonstrations in support of their "one-point demand" that Bangladeshi president Hussain Muhammed Ershad resign as a prelude to fresh elections held under a neutral, caretaker government. To compound matters, Bangladesh was battered by a devastating flood in August that imperiled a fragile economy already crippled by weeks of political *hartals* (work stoppages).

Although the CPB hoped to capitalize on the regime's misfortunes, the party began the year at a political disadvantage. In November 1987, Ershad responded to mounting opposition calls for his ouster by proroguing parliament, declaring a national emergency, and scheduling another national election for early 1988 (*YICA*, 1988). Faced with these actions, the CPB not only forfeited its six hard-won seats in parliament but was also proscribed. The ban on CPB activities was never enforced rigorously and was lifted well in advance of national elections in March.

Party Developments. The CPB Central Committee met in Dhaka in early January to chart political strategy. The first order of business was to formalize the succession of Saifuddin Ahmed Manik as CPB general secretary. Manik had been acting general secretary since October 1987 when his predecessor died of a heart attack while in Moscow. From all outward appearances the succession went smoothly. The Central Committee endorsed Manik's leadership, the CPB hierarchy remained largely intact, and party cadres maintained their well-deserved reputation as a disciplined organization (a rarity in Bangladeshi politics). Two members were added to the twelve-man secretariat, and the Central Committee was expanded to 40 members. The CPB claimed 9,911 members, almost a twofold increase over the membership claimed at the Fourth Party Congress in 1987. The new membership figure is probably exaggerated because candidate members normally serve long apprenticeships.

No significant changes in enrollment or political activities were noted in CPB front organizations during the year. Six CPB fronts cater to select constituencies such as peasants (Khetmozdur Samiti), workers (Trade Union Centre), intellectuals (Cultural Front), women (Mahila Parishad), students (Chatra Union), and youth (Jubo Union). The party organ, *Ekota*, continued its editorial assaults on the Ershad regime and lent unswerving support to Soviet foreign policy pronouncements. Although

the CPB was generally supportive of Mikhail Gorbachev's reform efforts in the Soviet Union, the ideological struggles that raged within the Soviet party had no appreciable impact on CPB policies. The CPB remains a highly centralized organization in the classic Leninist mold (*New Nation*, 6 January).

On the political front, the Central Committee session reiterated the party line enunciated at the Fourth Party Congress that called for a "national democratic revolution" waged by "progressive, liberal democratic forces." Under this formula, the CPB pledged to continue its antiregime program as part of an eight-party, left-of-center alliance headed by the powerful Awami League (AL). The CPB was painfully aware, however, that leadership squabbles and disagreements over tactics within the coalition had detracted from the campaign to force Ershad from office. In particular, the CPB had grown weary of AL leader Sheikh Hasina Wazed's inability to mend political fences with the seven-party, right-of-center alliance headed by her archrival, Begum Khaleda Zia, and her Bangladesh National Party (BNP). The CPB realized that opposition disunity allowed Ershad to dominate the political debate and set the electoral agenda. From the CPB's standpoint, opposition bickering also played into the hands of rightist forces such as the Islamic fundamentalist coalition led by the cadre-based Jamiat-i-Islami.

At his maiden press conference following the Central Committee meeting, Manik pledged that the CPB would forgo any chance of re-entering parliament by honoring an opposition boycott of elections scheduled for 3 March. Moreover, Manik declared the party's support for the Liaison Committee, a political body cobbled together by three opposition alliances to coordinate antiregime activities. Manik, however, put some distance between the CPB and the existing alliance structure by indicating a desire to strive for the unification of leftist, pro-Moscow forces, presumably under the CPB banner. Although the CPB failed in 1988 to construct an ideologically coherent alliance of Marxist parties, Manik's comments clearly opened the way for the CPB to sever its tactical alliance with the AL if the CPB's "bourgeois" partners did not provide effective leadership. (Ibid.) Observers speculated that a realignment of leftist forces—a long-standing CPB objective—would group the CPB with the pro-Moscow wing of the eight-party alliance and an already existing five-party coalition of minor leftist parties. Although the Kremlin stood to gain from such a realignment, the political obstacles in forging a left-wing alternative to AL-BNP dominance proved insurmountable.

In October, Central Committee secretary Shankar Basu expressed CPB disenchantment with the alliance system by noting that the "bourgeois-democratic parties in Bangladesh, despite their apparent popularity, have been losing their former political influence." The CPB, he admitted, was "not yet in a position to head the movement against the authoritarian regime, but, given a unity of left forces within the national democratic front, the communists will become a serious counterweight to the bourgeois influence in it" (*WMR*, October). Throughout the year, the CPB stressed an independent political identity by championing long-standing CPB planks such as radical land reform and the renationalization of formerly state-owned enterprises sold to the private sector. Despite its frustration at following the political lead of "bourgeois" parties, the CPB stuck to its tactical objective of eventually winning a share of power by peacefully contesting elections. As last year's electoral drama unfolded, however, the CPB remained a minor (albeit disruptive) actor on the Bangladeshi political stage.

Domestic Political Developments. Bangladeshi opposition parties began the year in a hopeful mood as Ershad vowed to stage parliamentary elections with or without their participation. The bitterly divided alliances reasoned that an effective boycott would render the elections meaningless, deny Ershad political legitimacy, and conceivably drive him from office. Alternatively, some opposition schemers hoped the army might spare the nation a protracted political struggle by staging another coup and installing a caretaker government to oversee elections. In July 1987, Sheikh Hasina and Begum Zia agreed to cooperate in forcing Ershad from power. Their political truce proved short-lived. On 27 January, security forces in Chittagong opened fire on an AL demonstration, killing fourteen party activists. When Begum Zia declined to participate in Hasina's call for a "mass uprising" to commemorate the "martyrs," AL-BNP "unity in action" all but collapsed. AL and CPB cadres then organized mob attacks on government facilities in Chittagong and staged their own *hartals* (*Sangbad*, 28 January).

Undeterred by opposition threats, Ershad forged ahead with his controversial election plans. In a run-up to parliamentary balloting, local union *parishad*

elections were suspended on 10 February because of widespread voter intimidation and violence. As a last-ditch effort, the AL-BNP alliances attempted to rally international public opinion against what they regarded as a sham election. Leading opposition spokesmen traveled to Washington to plead for U.S. congressional pressure on Ershad—a tactic Ershad thought treasonous. Simultaneously, Sheikh Hasina addressed a World Peace Council gathering in Prague and buttonholed Soviet officials in Moscow. This resort to international lobbying was tantamount to an admission that the opposition did not have the political muscle to wreck the election and force Ershad out.

Elections held on 3 March handed Ershad a hollow victory. The opposition called for an election-day general strike to symbolize a national vote of no confidence in the regime. Ershad thwarted the plan by decreeing a three-day national holiday to coincide with the election. Voter turnout was sparse. Most observers agreed that the election was tainted by widespread fraud on the part of Ershad's operatives. Despite a massive deployment of security personnel, the press reported more than one hundred deaths in the campaign (the government reported seven killed). To no one's surprise, Ershad's Jatiya party won two hundred and fifty-two seats in the three hundred-seat parliament; a handful of insignificant parties and independents won the remainder (*NYT*, 5 March).

Parliament convened on 20 March as the boycotting opposition alliances staged another crippling *hartal*. Although the series of agitations that rocked the country attracted considerable public support, Ershad managed to weather the crisis by retaining the confidence of his main base of support, the 80,000-man army. Some opposition leaders such as Begum Zia have in the past attempted to unseat Ershad by sowing disaffection within the military. Ershad, however, has been adept at cultivating the army's support by carefully monitoring the political pulse of the rank and file and weeding out ambitious officers who posed a potential challenge. By all accounts, the CPB commands virtually no support at any level of the military.

In June, opposition forces took to the streets again when Ershad introduced into parliament a constitutional amendment that recognized Islam as the state religion. All major opposition parties, particularly the CPB, vigorously condemned the legislation as a betrayal of the secular heritage of the 1971 liberation struggle. Even the Jamiat-i-Islami, an organization dedicated to the construction of a theocratic state, rejected the move as a cynical manipulation of religion designed to rally domestic support for the regime. Although opposition criticism of the legislation attracted considerable support in urban areas, the agitation was largely ignored in the countryside, where 75 percent of the population resides. Ershad's rubber-stamp parliament enacted the measure after a perfunctory debate.

Opposition political momentum ground to a halt in August when the worst flood of the century inundated 75 percent of the country and left an estimated 25 million people homeless. Owing to the magnitude of the calamity, the opposition was hardly in a position to press ahead with planned strikes and demonstrations. The opposition was further demoralized when Ershad won domestic and international acclaim as the army performed admirably in rushing food and medicine to the stricken population. By the time the floodwaters receded, the opposition campaign to topple Ershad was in disarray.

The opposition was unable to regain the political initiative throughout the remainder of the year. Lacking a cohesive political platform and effective leadership, the opposition was relegated to the political wilderness. By year's end, there was speculation that Ershad might call a midterm poll in the expectation that some parties would break opposition ranks, contest the election, and reclaim their parliamentary seats as a loyal opposition. The CPB, for its part, was undecided whether to accept the challenge or alter the party line in the pursuit of a semblance of leftist unity that has historically eluded the party.

Foreign Affairs. In recent years, the CPB has dropped its vociferous criticism of the Chinese party, no doubt at Moscow's behest. Within days after passage of the constitutional amendment making Islam the state religion, General Secretary Manik traveled to Moscow for consultations. Although Moscow lent propaganda support to CPB and opposition agitations, Moscow has also tried to maintain correct relations with the Ershad government. The CPB's close affiliation with Moscow, however, remains a liability for the party. Ershad

and much of the Bangladeshi public are deeply suspicious of Soviet support for rival India and other Kremlin allies. By contrast, China is widely regarded as a steadfast friend of Bangladesh.

Douglas C. Makeig
U.S. Department of Defense

Note: The opinions expressed in this article are the author's own and do not necessarily reflect those of the U.S. government or any U.S. government agency.

Burma

Population. 39,632,183
Party. Burmese Communist Party (BCP)
Founded. 15 August 1939
Membership. 3,000 (based on 1978–79 party documents); estimated armed strength, 8,000–15,000
Chairman. [Thakin]* Ba Thein Tin (74, Sino-Burman)
Vice-Chairman. [Thakin] Pe Tint (72, Burman)
Politburo. [Thakin] Ba Thein Tin, [Thakin] Pe Tint, Khin Maung Gyi (61), Myo Myint (64), Tin Yee (66), Kyaw Mya (73), Kyin Maung (66, Chinese)
Secretariat. Khin Maung Gyi (61)
Central Committee. 29 members: Aye Hla, Aye Ngwe, [Thakin] Ba Thein Tin, Bran Ba Di, Khin Maung Gyi, Kyauk Mi Lai, Kyaw Mya, Kyaw Myint, Kyaw Zaw, Kyin Maung, Mya Thaung, Myint Min, Myo Myint, Ni Tu Wu, Pe Thaung, [Thakin] Pe Tint, Po Ngwe Sai, Po Tint, [Sai] Aung Win, San Tu, [Saw] Ba Moe, Saw Han, Soe Hein, Soe Lwin, Tin Yee, Tint Hlaing, Tun Lwin, Ye Tun, Zaw Mai
Status. Illegal

---

*Honorifics are in brackets. The remainder of the name is almost always one unit—there is no family name for most Burmese nationalities. As many unrelated Burmese may thus share identical or similar names, the honorifics are an important aid to identification.

Although many honorifics are obvious, identification of honorifics is not always easy, particularly where the non-Burman nationalities are concerned. For example in the case of [Saw] Ba Moe and Saw Han above, Saw in the latter case is an element of the name; in the former, it is an honorific. Thus, there is no attempt to distinguish honorifics in the text of the analysis.

Last Congress. Third, 9 September–2 October 1985

Last Election. N/a

Auxiliary Organizations. Communist Youth Organization (ca. 2,500 members); Women's Unions (ca. 33,000 members); Peasants' Unions (ca. 88,000 members), based on a 1978 party document. Membership statistics noted were 1978 BCP claims, described in the source as incomplete.

Publications. *People's Power* (*Pyeithu Ah Nar*). First issue reported 1987. No copies are known to have reached the West. Frequency and format are unknown. The BCP broadcasts over the Voice of the People of Burma (VOPB), apparently located near the Sino-Burmese border inside Burma.

A serious weakening in the position of the Rangoon government during 1988 may well have presented the BCP with its greatest opportunity for progress since the height of the late 1940s insurgency. Popular unrest was probably ignited by the September 1987 government demonetarization of most paper currency. Explained as necessary to control the black market, this move effectively eliminated 70 to 80 percent of the population's cash savings. Bloody suppression by the military of successive disorders beginning in March 1988 further spurred popular alienation from the regime.

A government investigation into police actions during 12–17 March student riots in Rangoon, the worst since 1974, led to the resignation of the minister in charge of police on 19 July and then to the resignation, after 24 years in power, of Ne Win on 23 July. Popular resistance to Ne Win's successor, Sein Lwin, forced his resignation on 12 August amid increasing public disorder. Civilian Maung Maung, named president 19 August and also unable to restore order, was replaced by a military junta led by General Saw Maung on 18 September. As the military forcefully suppressed demonstrations, the former unitary government of the Burma Socialist Program Party (BSPP) was reorganized into a substantially weaker National Unity Party. The country was officially renamed on 19 October, dropping Ne Win's "Socialist Republic" and returning to its original Union of Burma.

Leadership and Organization. Government military pressure in 1987–88 reportedly forced the move of the BCP leadership from Pang Hsang (Wan Long) north (about 70–100 kilometers) to the village of Yawng Prit, about 15 kilometers from the Chinese town of Ximeng. The current location of the VOPB broadcasting facility is now northeast of the new headquarters. Party leader Ba Thein Tin is in deteriorating health and undergoing medical treatment in a border area (Rangoon, *Working People's Daily*, 25 January; *FBIS*, 3 February). In his absence and with the illness of Deputy Chairman Pe Tint, the effective BCP leader is said to be party secretary Khin Maung Gyi.

Of the BCP's two district organizations in Tenasserim division, the Mergui district unit was noted in a government broadcast claiming the surrender of one of its members (Rangoon Domestic Service, 8 March; *FBIS*, 10 March).

BCP troop strength was estimated during the year by two sources at between eight thousand and ten thousand troops (Hong Kong, AFP, 17 February; *FBIS*, 17 February; *Insight*, 20 June). As usual with such estimates, their factual basis is probably minimal.

Party Internal Affairs. There is indirect evidence that the party's financial situation may have improved somewhat. Since about 1978 the party, like many other Burmese insurgencies, has drawn part of its income from the trade in opium from which heroin is refined. A large portion of the opium-growing area in Burma, perhaps as much as 80 percent, is in BCP-controlled territory (*NYT*, 31 March). The 1987–88 crop was estimated by the U.S. government at a record 1,275 tons, and preliminary estimates for 1988–89 indicate the new crop will be about 20 percent larger, thanks in part to ideal weather. Rangoon claims to have reduced the 1988 harvest to 864 tons through eradication; however, the Western suspension of military and antinarcotics aid to Rangoon subsequent to the September military coup and the diversion of Burmese military attention from the insurgents to keeping order in the cities will certainly reduce government pressure on opium growers and shippers.

A recent shift in opium-smuggling routes is also to the BCP's advantage. Smuggling through Thailand, the traditional route, is increasingly impeded both by Thai government efforts and by Burmese unrest. Among Thai enforcement successes, a customs seizure of 1,280 kilograms of heroin, probably of Burmese origin, on a freighter at Bangkok is believed to be a world record (*Bangkok Post*, 13 February; *FBIS*, 17 February). Thai border police also seized a heroin refinery and 140 kilograms of heroin near the Burmese border on 5 August. The refinery, which had only been in operation for ten days, was believed to have been supplied with raw heroin by the BCP. (*Bangkok Post*, 6 August; *FBIS*, 8 August.) Thailand also closed the border for varying periods after April, both to control smuggling and to contain disorders inside neighboring Burmese territory.

However, police in Hong Kong, long a major transshipment point for Southeast Asian heroin, report that this year for the first time, more than half the heroin seized there arrived overland from China rather than by the traditional sea route from Thailand (*WP*, 6 December). Most of Burma's border with China—over which these drugs must flow—is controlled by the BCP. Smugglers started using the China route in the early 1980s, and the flow has been increasing "very rapidly" over the last two to three years, according to Hong Kong police (ibid.). Chinese customs officials' inexperience in drug detection and nearly unrestricted border crossings by ethnic minorities have probably encouraged this change (Hong Kong, *South China Morning Post* [Business Post], *FBIS*, 19 July).

VOPB broadcasts monitored during the past year have concentrated on propaganda oriented toward antigovernment feeling among the general population, continuing a general trend over the past several years away from the former emphasis on ideological programs. Statements early in the year continued the call for armed revolution against Ne Win: "we must turn the gun on the military government" (VOPB, 9 February; *FBIS*, 11 February). The 28 March statement commemorating the "armed revolution" gave the BCP program as "(1) Abolish the one-party BSPP dictatorship and form a provisional government; (2) Abolish the present constitution and draft a new constitution; (3) Basic tasks to be completed by the provisional government are "(a) end the civil war, (b) restore full democratic rights to the people, (c) rebuild the unity of the national minorities, (d) improve the standard of living of the people . . . (e) pursue an independent and neutral policy in foreign relations" (VOPB, 1 May; *FBIS*, 3 May).

Beginning in May, the BCP began adjusting its line to the protests in Rangoon. In mid-May, VOPB broadcast a detailed account of the March demonstrations, including the text of the student demands (VOPB, 19, 21 May; *FBIS*, 24, 26 May), and called for "commanders and soldiers" of the Burma Army "to join the struggle against the BSPP one-party dictatorial government" (VOPB, 26 May; *FBIS*, 1 June). The time lapse between Rangoon events and the BCP reaction closed somewhat in subse-

quent months. A 28 August statement called government concessions to demonstrators "genuine victories won at great cost by the students and people" but warned that the government intended to maintain its control of the armed forces, implementing concessions only "within the framework of the state Constitution, which endorses the BSPP one-party dictatorship," and intended to "divide the people through brutal suppression" (VOPB, 4 September; *FBIS*, 6 September).

A new six-point program was presented in a 10 September statement: (1) "complete abolition of the BSPP one-party system and the military bureaucratic machinery"; (2) "restoration of full democratic rights to the people of all nationalities"; (3) "talks . . . with all political forces . . . opposed to the . . . BSPP"; (4) "drafting . . . of a common work program" by all opposition organizations "and individuals"; (5) "holding of general elections . . . only under circumstances where the military bureaucratic machinery has been completely dismantled . . ."; and (6) "a new parliament elected in general elections to draft a new state constitution" (VOPB, 17 September; *FBIS*, 19 September). On 18 September, the BCP warned "blatant and brutal suppression by the BSPP military is about to resume." Calling for the formation of a "patriotic army," the BCP promised its "all-out support" and ended with the slogans "Arm the people in every way possible! No enemy can overcome the people with arms!" (VOPB, 21 September; *FBIS*, 20 September.) A VOPB broadcast of an alleged transcript of Burma Army communications just before the coup accused Rangoon of ordering the army to handle protesters "roughly" and "shoot to kill" (VOPB, 28 September; *FBIS*, 29 September).

The BCP appears to have picked up recruits from among the student dissidents who fled the cities after the military coup; however, compared to the approximately six thousand students joining various insurgent organizations, the BCP gain was probably minimal. A 10 October government statement estimated five students were with the BCP; Burmese student sources estimated four hundred students had joined the BCP (Hong Kong, AFP, in English, 10, 12 October; *FBIS*, 12, 13 October).

There were reports that the BCP was behind antigovernment students (Hong Kong, AFP, in English, 12 August; *FBIS*, 12 August), that communist sympathizers were taking part in demonstrations (Tokyo, *Kyodo*, in English, 23 August; *FBIS*, 23 August), and that soldiers operating in the cities were told their targets were BCP insurgents (BBC

World Service, in English, 21 September; *FBIS*, 20 September; Hong Kong, AFP, in English, 22 September; *FBIS*, 23 September). A Rangoon newspaper commentary later specifically asserted that "the momentum and direction" of prodemocracy demonstrations was "controlled by underground communist cadres who were in well-placed positions. It would be naive to believe" that the course of the demonstrations "was entirely spontaneous," the account noted, citing the "meticulous precision" of protests. "In no way could ordinary students with ordinary dissatisfaction [have] matched the militancy and activity of the . . . BCP cells . . . specially nurtured and prepared for . . . agitation and militant activities." (Rangoon, *Working People's Daily*, 12 November; *FBIS*, 30 November.)

There is evidence of BCP contact with dissident student groups. An eyewitness (and self-described former student) was the author of a VOPB broadcast account of the March disorders in Rangoon (VOPB, 19, 21 May; *FBIS*, 24, 26 May). A representative of the All-Burma Students' Union, in Thailand for contacts with Burmese students, described student contact with a "party leader named Cho Saw" who offered them BCP support, but "we rejected this," he said (Bangkok, *Khao Phiset*, in Thai, 21–27 September; *FBIS*, 30 September). An outside observer commented that, although the continuation of organized student activities after the June riots testified to "an astute underground coordination nationwide, leaflets passed out by the demonstrators show a range of apparently independent leaders" (*CSM*, 11 August).

A prominent opposition leader publicly expressed concern over communist infiltration among the dissidents, although the accusation must be discounted, to some degree at least, as a product of opposition infighting. Former Brigadier General Aung Gyi described rival opposition leader Aung San Suu Kyi as "surrounded by communist party members" (Tokyo, NHK Television Network, in Japanese, 1 September; *FBIS*, 2 September). The formation by the two, along with former General Tin U, of the National League for Democracy did not end this attack. On 3 December, the Central Council of the League announced that Aung Gyi, its then chairman, had been dismissed from the league after rejection of his demand that eight alleged communists be expelled from the council. Aung Gyi described the incident as a confrontation between communists and anticommunists where communists had prevailed, resulting in his ouster as well as that of thirteen of his supporters. In contrast,

Aung San Suu Kyi called the outcome "a triumph of democratic principles." (Hong Kong, AFP, in English, 3 December; *FBIS*, 5 December.)

Although not evidence of BCP penetration, it is notable that the Unity and Development Party, registered by the government on 6 October, has as its official patron Thakin Soe, the former chairman of the Red Flag faction of the BCP (Rangoon Domestic Service, in Burmese, 6 October; *FBIS*, 7 October). Soe was captured by the Burmese Army in 1970 and subsequently released in an amnesty.

Considering the significant damage done to nationalist support for the regime both by previous Ne Win policies and by the heavy-handed military suppression of disorders this year, it is a valid question whether there has been an increase in popular sympathy for the BCP. A Rangoon-based diplomat asserted that government forces suffered higher losses than usual in clashes with the BCP and with other insurgents because "they failed to receive customary warnings from local villagers" (Hong Kong, AFP, in English, 26 October; *FBIS*, 27 October). A former student leader in Thailand said that his group is prepared to work with any group seeking to restore democracy and included the BCP "provided they do not seek to exploit the situation in the country" (Bangkok, *The Nation*, 1 September; *FBIS*, 1 September). "But," he continued, "they must realize that the majority of the Burmese people are fed up with the one-party system and socialism."

This aversion to socialism and to authoritarian rule is a repeated theme among the Burmese opposition, and thus assertions that communists controlled all or even most of the disorders are almost certainly incorrect. The majority of published statements indicate that substantial mistrust of the communists remains. A student dissident asserted,

We admit that we are very much afraid of the communists because they have a strong military. But we absolutely would not allow them to establish their party [as published] or to have power because the BCP and the BSPP are as alike as father to son. There is no difference in their evil . . . But in the future we know that we will have to fight them and wipe them out. We don't want dictatorship and socialism of any kind. (Bangkok, *Khao Phiset*, in Thai, 21–27 September; *FBIS*, 30 September.)

A foreign observer noted that "students appear to have no interest in the support of the insurgent BCP and the many ethnic rebel armies." He quoted a student: "These rebels have guns which they have obtained from foreign countries. This could lead in the future to a dependence on these foreign powers, which we don't want." (*FEER*, 18 August.)

The Insurgency. Before Ne Win's resignation, outside observers were commenting that the government had achieved more success against the insurgents over the past year than in the previous ten years. "The communists, driven back to border areas, can stage terrorist attacks at most, according to a foreign diplomat." (*Insight*, 20 June.) A major government offensive began after the BCP attacked Burmese army posts in northern Shan state near the Chinese border in November 1986 and "that pressure never stopped." In January 1987, as part of a campaign that would reopen the Chinese border to official trade (see below), the Burmese captured the border town of Panghsai (Kyu-hkok), opposite Wandingzhen (Wanting), where the Burma Road crosses the frontier. Panghsai, a border trading post and reputedly for years the BCP's most important source of revenue, as well as the largest (about six thousand to seven thousand persons) settlement in BCP territory, had been in BCP hands since 28 March 1970. In August 1987, the Burmese overran the headquarters of the BCP 101st Military Region in Kachin state. Burmese officials talked of moving east of the Salween River into the heart of BCP territory. (Hong Kong, AFP, in English, 17 February; *FBIS*, 17 February.) The reported shift of BCP headquarters followed Burmese army advances to within a two-to-three-day march from Pang Hsang (Wan Long).

By early September 1988, however, the military was forced to deny rumors that troops were fleeing the front lines as a result of internal disorder (Maymyo Defense Forces Radio, in Burmese, 14 September; *FBIS*, 15 September). Both communist and ethnic insurgents claimed successes against government troops in late September and early October (Hong Kong, AFP, in English, 15 October; *FBIS*, 18 October). A government spokesman in late October, although downplaying the level of fighting, admitted that the army was "somewhat spread out because of law-and-order restoration work in the towns" but asserted it was "still in a position to effectively contain the insurgency" (Hong Kong, AFP, in English, 26 October; *FBIS*, 29 October).

Although the military was affected by the disorders, available evidence does not indicate notable losses of territory by the government to the BCP. The most significant battle during the latter part of the year was evidently the BCP attack on the Mong Yang area, which began 14 September and in which the communists reportedly employed heavy artillery and "new modern weapons" (BBC World Service, in English, 29 September; *FBIS*, 29 September). However, in engagements lasting until about 20 October, the army appears to have driven off a series of BCP assaults (Rangoon Domestic Service, in Burmese, 24 October; *FBIS*, 25 October; VOPB, 2 November; *FBIS*, 3 November). The government firmly denied foreign reports of the loss of the ruby-mining center of Mogok and of other towns along the Burma-Chinese border (Rangoon Domestic Service, in Burmese, 30 September; *FBIS*, 4 October), and the commencement of Sino-Burmese cross-border trade through the latter area (see below) appears to confirm this denial. In a possible renewed effort to reassert control over the border trade, the BCP claimed a "crushing" win over a government troop column about twenty miles east of the Burma Road on 13 December (VOPB, 25 December; *FBIS*, 27 December).

Attempts by various insurgencies to repenetrate central Burma in October were indicated in a government report (Rangoon Domestic Service, in Burmese, 21 October; *FBIS*, 24 October). Although no specific insurgent organizations were named, BCP elements may well have been involved—probably for the first time since 1978—in an attempt to reoccupy an area from which they were driven in 1975.

Auxiliary and Front Organizations. No information was available on the activities of BCP auxiliary organizations during 1988. The BCP is allied with a number of ethnic insurgent organizations, among which are several smaller bodies believed to have been planned by the BCP as fronts for individual ethnic minorities. In most cases their exact nature and current status is postulated rather than certain. Probable front organizations include the Shan State Nationalities Liberation Organization (SSNLO) led by Tha Kalei, the Kayah New Land Revolution Council (or Party), the Karenni People's United Liberation Front led by Than Nyunt, and the United Pa-o Organization. Two of these—the SSNLO (VOPB, 9 October; *FBIS*, 13 October) and the Kayah New Land Party (VOPB, 24 September; *FBIS*, 27 September)—were mentioned during the year in BCP battle reports.

In addition, the BCP currently has alliances with other ethnic insurgent organizations that do not owe their existence to the BCP. Notable are the 1976 pact with the Kachin Independence Army (KIA) led by Brang Seng and the 1986 cooperation agreement with the National Democratic Front (NDF), an alliance of ten ethnic insurgent groups, including the largest and most significant.

The BCP's ethnic alliances are not without problems. An alliance with the Shan State Army (SSA) concluded in 1974 was abrogated by the SSA in 1981 after four years of increasing problems, including internal SSA splintering. The most prominent of these splinter groups was the northern faction led by Sai Lek and still allied with the BCP. This faction is probably the "Shan State Army" noted in one 1988 battle report (VOPB, 8 December; *FBIS*, 9 December). Brang Seng, whose KIA is part of the NDF, asserts that the NDF cooperates with the BCP militarily but distances itself from the communists politically (Tokyo, *Kyodo*, in English, 19 August; *FBIS*, 19 August). Brang Seng's own long-standing tie with the communists leaves him a dubious BCP critic, although other NDF leaders also emphasize that their BCP link is confined to "military matters" (*Bangkok Post*, 14 March; *FBIS*, 15 March). Earlier in the year, the NDF was seeking to upgrade this military coordination with the BCP (Bangkok, *The Nation*, 16 January; *FBIS*, 21 January). However, the Karen National Union of Bo Mya—along with the KIA, one of the two largest members of the NDF—opposes the BCP alliance. This was probably the major factor in Bo Mya's 1987 replacement as NDF leader. Bo Mya has stated that the Karens have no intention of fighting alongside the BCP. The BCP and the BSPP "are the same in the sense that they are both dictatorial-rule parties," he told Japanese correspondents (Tokyo, *Kyodo*, in English, 16 September; *FBIS*, 20 September).

International Positions and Activities. The BCP's party-to-party relationship with China—key to its survival for two decades—was unacknowledged by either side during 1988. A serious problem for this link was implied in reports (noted above) that smuggling of opium and heroin across China has surged in recent years. Beijing has responded to U.S. appeals for help in curbing the narcotics trade and assisted in recent drug seizures in the United States involving Chinese and Hong Kong connections (*NYT*, 31 March). In their internal efforts, the Chinese are hindered by lack of experience in coping with what, to the current regime, is a new problem. Any attempt to enlist BCP help in stopping the drugs at the source will be hindered by reduced Chinese leverage with the Bur-

mese communists (due to the withdrawal of Beijing aid over the past decade) and the BCP's consequent dependence on smuggling, particularly drug smuggling, to support itself.

A major limiting factor on the Chinese-BCP relationship is the state-to-state link between Beijing and Rangoon. Until July, the latter relationship was characterized by frequent exchanges of official visits, including this year the Burmese deputy prime minister and foreign minister. Among the travelers in the other direction, a Yunnan province delegation was probably most significant, signing on 5 August a precedent-setting agreement on cross-border trade that took effect 1 October (Beijing, Xinhua, in English, 7 August; *FBIS*, 8 August). The agreement regularizes a tacit understanding that has functioned for about two years. According to the Rangoon government in December, traders are now using the old Burma Road that was reopened through former BCP territory by a 1987 government offensive (noted above) (Rangoon Domestic Service, in Burmese, 9 December; *FBIS*, 12 December). An official Burmese estimate projects the trade at $300 million for 1988–89 (Xinhua, in English, 2 December; *FBIS*, 7 December), but unofficial estimates indicate it could reach $1.5 billion both ways.

Chinese press coverage of the Burmese unrest was initially blunt regarding the roots of the crisis: "government policy failed and the economy collapsed" (Beijing International Service, in Burmese, 17 August; *FBIS*, 18 August). "It's widely accepted that the worsening situation is rooted in the BSPP's bungling of the country's economy, the crackdown on the student movement, and its [the BSPP's] ignorance of public opinion" (Beijing, Xinhua, in English, 24 August; *FBIS*, 24 August). Beijing's tone moderated after Saw Maung began to control the "unruly masses" (and demonstrated increased sensitivity to foreign press criticism). Military policies in the subsequent month "pacified the touch-and-go situation. The grave confrontation between the government and the opposition factions is somewhat relaxed for the time being." (Beijing, *Renmin Ribao*, 20 October; *FBIS*, 26 October.)

Thai-Burmese relations continue close, spurred by Bangkok's concern over cross-border spillover of Burma's ethnic unrest, as well as over BCP activities near the Thai border and the possibility of a BCP linkup with Thai communists. Thai seizure of a BCP-supplied heroin refinery has been noted. The refinery was probably linked to a BCP-allied ethnic Wa insurgent group, which also threatened a cross-border route planned for newly legalized Burmese teak exports to Thailand (*Bangkok Post*, 28 March; *FBIS*, 25 March). This was a subject of discussion during Chawalit's April visit to Rangoon (*Bangkok Post*, 22 April; *FBIS*, 22 April).

Thai visitors to Burma in early 1988 included Crown Prince Maha Wachiralongkon and army Commander in Chief General Chawalit Yongchaiyut. Subsequent to the September coup, Thai foreign minister Sitthi Sawetsila, under public pressure, postponed a planned trip by a deputy foreign minister (*Bangkok Post*, 15 November; *FBIS*, 15 November), but soon afterward, on 14 December, a military and police delegation led by General Chawalit visited Rangoon to discuss border problems, including minority groups and the BCP. This was the first visit by a senior official of any country to Rangoon since the military coup, although Thai prime minister Chatchai Chunhawan noted that it did not mean Thai recognition of the Saw Maung government (Bangkok Domestic Service, in Thai, 13 December; *FBIS*, 14 December).

On his return, Chawalit noted he suggested common efforts by the Thai and Burmese governments to solve minority problems, but "in fact General Saw Maung and the Burmese people do not give much importance to the Burmese minority groups. It's only a small percentage of threat. The main threat is the BCP" (*Bangkok Post*, 15 December; *FBIS*, 15 December). Regardless of the restriction of relations with Burma by other countries, Thailand will maintain close ties in view of continuing problems along the two countries' common border, according to Thai foreign minister Sitthi (Bangkok Domestic Service, in English, 23 December; *FBIS*, 23 December).

Charles B. Smith, Jr.
U.S. Department of State

Note: The views expressed here are the author's own and do not necessarily represent those of the Department of State or the U.S. government.

Cambodia
(formerly Kampuchea)

Population. 6,685,592. Average annual growth rate is 2.25 percent.

Party. People's Revolutionary Party of Kampuchea (PRPK)

Founded. The PRPK traces its origin to the Khmer People's Revolutionary Party (KPRP), which was formed on 30 September 1951 with the establishment of a provisional Central Committee, pending the party's first congress. Recent Vietnamese histories, however, cite the founding date as June 1951.

Membership. 8,000–10,000 (*Sudestasie*, no. 50, 1987; *FBIS-East Asia*, 14 October)

General Secretary. Heng Samrin (b. 1934, former Democratic Kampuchean political officer and commander of the Fourth Division, assistant chief of the General Staff and member of the party Executive Committee of the Eastern Zone from 1976 to May 1978, when he became one of the leaders of an ill-fated rebellion in the Eastern Zone against Pol Pot. Fled to Vietnam in June 1978 and returned to Cambodia with the invading Vietnamese army in December 1978 as president of the Central Committee of the Kampuchean National United Front for National Salvation. Concurrently chairman of the Council of State.)

Politburo. 9 full and 4 alternate members: Heng Samrin (chairman, Council of State); Hun Sen (b. 1951, chairman, Council of Ministers; minister of foreign affairs); Say Phuthang (b. 1925, chairman, PRPK Central Control Commission; vice-chairman, Council of State); Bou Thang (b. 1938, vice-chairman, Council of Ministers); Chea Sim (b. 1932, chairman, National Assembly; chairman, Kampuchean United Front for National Construction and Defense); Chea Soth (b. 1928, vice-chairman, Council of Ministers); Men Sam-an (b. 1953, chairwoman, PRPK Central Organization Commission); Mat Ly (b. 1925, vice-chairman of the National Assembly; chairman, Kampuchean Federation of Trade Unions);

Ney Pena (minister of interior); Chang Seng (b. 1935, alternate Politburo member; vice-chairman, PRPK Central Control Commission); Nguon Nhel (b. unknown, alternate Politburo member; chairman, Phnom Penh Provisional Party Committee); Sar Kheng (b. 1951, alternate Politburo member, elected at the seventh plenum of the PRPK Central Committee in July; chief, Cabinet of the party Central Committee); Say Chhum (b. 1945, alternate Politburo member, elected at the seventh plenum of the Central Committee in July; vice-chairman, Council of Ministers; minister of agriculture)

Secretariat. Heng Samrin, Hun Sen (relieved of position during July or August), Bou Thang, Men Sam-an, Ney Pena, Sar Kheng, Say Phuthang (elected at the seventh plenum of the PRPK Central Committee in July), Say Chhum (elected at the seventh plenum of the PRPK Central Committee in July).

Status. Sole authorized political party of the regime in Phnom Penh. PRPK leaders serve concurrently as officials of the government of the People's Republic of Kampuchea (PRK).

Last Congress. Fifth, 13–16 October 1985 in Phnom Penh. Attended by 250 delegates from 22 subordinate party committees representing provincial, municipal, military and sectoral PRPK entities. (The Fourth National PRPK Congress was held in May 1981 and was attended by 162 delegates.)

Last Election. National Assembly, May 1981. The election, a single-party contest unchallenged by any political opposition, seated 117 of the 148 candidates for the National Assembly. The remainder of the candidates were fielded by mass organizations and other formal, organized interests recognized and legitimized by the ruling party.

Auxiliary Organizations. Kampuchean Afro-Asian People's Solidarity Organization Committee (chair: Khien Kanharit), Kampuchean Center of the Asian Buddhist's Council of Peace (chair: Tep Vong), Kampuchean Committee for the Defense of Peace (chair: Yit Kamseng), Kampuchean Federation of Trade Unions (chair: Mat Ly), Kampuchean Journalists Association (chair: Chey Sophon), Kampuchean People's Revolutionary Youth Union (secretary: Sun Sundoeun), Association of Revolutionary Youth in Kampuchea, Kampuchean Red Cross (chair: Phlek Phirun), Kampuchean Revolutionary Women's Association (chair: Mean Sam-an), Kampuchean United Front for National Construction and Defense

(KUFNCD) (chair of Presidium: Heng Samrin; chair of National Council: Chea Sim)

Publications and Media. *Pracheachon* (People), weekly publication of the PRPK Central Committee founded in 1985, editor in chief, Som Kimsuor; *Kangthap Padevat* (Revolutionary Army), weekly publication of the PRK Army; *Phnom Penh*, weekly publication of the Phnom Penh Municipal PRPK Committee; *Kampuchea*, weekly publication of the KUFNCD. Sarpordamean Kampuchea (SPK) is official news agency of the PRK; director general, Em Sam-an. SPK publishes *Daily Bulletin* in English, Cambodian, and French and *Angkor*, a monthly magazine, in Cambodian. Voice of the Kampuchean People (VOKP) Radio, director, General Kim Yin; Kampuchean Radio and Television Commission, director Kim Yin.

Central Committee. 31 full members and 14 alternate members. Full members: Bou Thang (b. 1938, vice-chairman, Council of Ministers; chairman, Kampuchean People's Revolutionary Armed Forces General Political Department; vice-chairman, KUFNCD); Chan Phin (b. 1930, chairman, Central Committee's Economic Commission through at least July); Chan Seng (b. 1935, vice-chairman of the PRPK Central Committee Control Commission); Chay Sangyun (b. unknown, commander, Third Military Region of the Kampuchean People's Revolutionary Armed Forces); Chea Sim (b. 1932, chairman, National Assembly); Chea Soth (b. 1928, vice-chairman, Council of Ministers); El Vansarat (b. unknown, chief, General Political Department of the Kampuchean People's Revolutionary Armed Forces; deputy minister of defense); Heng Sam Kai (b. 1930, brother of Heng Samrin; secretary of the Svay Rieng Provisional Provincial Party Committee); Heng Samrin (chairman, Council of State); Ho Nan (b. unknown, female, appointed minister of industry in August); Hul Savoan (b. unknown, commander, Fourth Military Region of the Kampuchean People's Revolutionary Armed Forces); Hun Sen (b. 1951, chairman, Council of Ministers; minister of foreign affairs); Keo Kimyan (b. unknown, first deputy minister of defense; relieved of the post of chief of the general staff of the Kampuchean People's Revolutionary Armed Forces in August); Khoy Khunhuor (b. unknown, chairman, PRPK Central Committee Propaganda and Education Commission); Kim Yin (b. 1928, director general of the Kampuchean Radio and Television Commission); Kong Korm (b. 1941, appointed minister of the State Affairs Inspectorate in August); Koy Buntha (b. 1952, relieved as minister of defense and appointed minister of social action and war invalids in August); Lak On (b. unknown, female, secretary of the Ratanakiri Provisional Provincial Party Committee); May Ly (b. 1925, vice-chairman, National Assembly; chairman, National Federation of Trade Unions); Mean Sam-an (b. 1956, chairwoman, Kampuchean Revolutionary Women's Association); Men Sam-an (b. 1953, chairwoman, PRPK Central Committee Organizational Commission); Ney Pena (b. unknown, relieved as minister of interior and appointed chairman, PRPK Central Committee Propaganda and Education Commission in August); Nguon Nhel (b. unknown, secretary, Phnom Penh Provisional Party Committee); Rung Phlamkesan (b. unknown, secretary, Koh Kong Provincial Party Committee); Sam Sundoeun (b. 1951, first secretary, People's Revolutionary Youth Union of Kampuchea; chairman, Kampuchean-Vietnamese Friendship Association); Sar Kheng (b. 1951, chief, cabinet of the PRPK Central Committee); Say Chhum (b. 1945, vice-chairman, Council of Ministers; minister of agriculture); Say Phuthang (b. 1925, chairman, PRPK Central Committee Control Commission; vice-chairman, Council of State); Sim Ka (b. unknown, vice-chairman, PRPK Central Committee Control Commission; chairman, Kampuchean-Soviet Friendship Association); Som Kimsuor (b. 1949, female, editor in chief, *Pracheachon*); Yos Son (b. unknown, chairman, PRPK Central Committee External Relations Commission; president, Kampuchean Committee for Afro-Asian Solidarity).

Alternate members: Chea Chanto (b. unknown, minister of planning); Chhay Than (b. unknown, minister of finance); Chheng Phon (b. unknown, minister of information and culture); Hun Neng (b. unknown, secretary, Kompong Cham Provincial Party Committee); Kham Len (b. unknown, member, Council of State); Lim Thi (b. unknown, secretary, Kandal Province Provisional Party Committee); Neou Sam (b. unknown, secretary, Siem Reap-Oddar Meanchey Provincial Party Committee); Pen Navut (b. unknown, minister of education); Ros Chhun (b. unknown, general secretary, KUFNCD); Sam Sarit (b. unknown, director, General Department of Rubber Plantations); Say Siphon (b. unknown, vice-chairman, Kampuchean Federation of Trade Unions); Som Sopha (b. unknown, deputy secretary, Stung Treng Provisional Provincial Party Committee; member, Provisional People's Revolutionary Committee of Stung Treng Province); Thong Khon (b. unknown, chairman, Phnom Penh Municipal People's Revolutionary Committee; deputy secretary, Phnom Penh Municipal Provincial Party Committee); Tea Banh (b. 1945, vice-chairman, Council of Ministers; appointed minister of national defense in August)

Leadership and Party Organization. During 1988 the party organization remained a bare-bones organization that depended on partial tables of organization at the central and provincial levels and extremely underdeveloped subprovincial chapters and branches. Throughout the year, the party Central Committee advertised internal organizational reform, membership recruitment, and the improvement of cadre as key themes for PRPK development.

The seventh session of the PRPK Central Committee added two alternate members to the Politburo (Sar Kheng and Say Chhum) and elected two new members to the Secretariat (Say Chhum and Say Phuthang). Hun Sen had been quietly and unceremoniously dropped from the Secretariat by August. Late in the year a senior PRK official told a Western correspondent that Hun Sen was relieved of his Secretariat position in part to enable him to devote his time exclusively to the resolution of the Cambodian conflict and in part to check what some Politburo members saw as an aggregation of power and advantage by Hun Sen.

In an August cabinet shuffle Politburo member Ney Pena was relieved of his post as minister of the interior and appointed chairman of the PRPK Central Committee Propaganda and Education Commission. Sin Song replaced him as minister of the interior. Tang Saroem was appointed minister of trade; Ung Phan replaced Tea Banh as minister of communications, transportation, and posts; and Tea Banh became minister of defense. A total of five nonmembers of the Central Committee held cabinet positions as a result of the August shuffle, one more than was the case before the cabinet change. The majority of cabinet positions remained in the hands of Central Committee members. With the exception of Ney Pena's replacement of Koy Khunhuor as chairman of the Propaganda and Education Commission, Central Committee commission-level leadership remained unchanged.

The August cabinet shuffle brought Tea Banh, an alternate member of the Central Committee, to the position of defense minister and relieved Central Committee member and Deputy Defense Minister Ke Kimyan of his concurrent position as chief of the general staff of the Kampuchean People's Revolutionary Armed Forces. He was replaced by Pol Saroeun, who was also appointed to a vice-ministerial slot in the defense ministry. Pol Saroeun, chairman of the PRPK Committee in Takeo province from at least 1979, had not held any prior military positions. His accession to the general staff position may have been the result of the Politburo's hope that he could bring his extensive provincial-level experience to bear on the high rate of defections, low morale, poor training, and lack of proper equipment that plagued provincial and local armed force units (BBC Far Eastern Commentary by Jacques Bekaert, 22 August). These changes and several other shifts within the Ministry of National Defense left the military underrepresented within the Politburo and the Central Committee and in the peculiar circumstance of having a defense minister (with alternate Central Committee membership) outranked by two vice-ministers of defense, El Vansarat and Keo Kimyan (with full Central Committee membership). Two other vice-ministers of defense (Nhim Vandy and Soy Keo) did not hold Central Committee membership, while the Third and Fourth Military Region commanders were full members of the Central Committee, an imbalance that suggested that future adjustments to the Central Committee were in store.

For the most part, provincial party secretaries elected in late 1985 and early 1986 continued to hold their jobs through the first half of 1988. In October, regional congresses of provisional provincial party committees began to elect new party secretaries and committees. During the year the regime sought to upgrade the provincial party structures, self-admittedly characterized by committees that were severely under strength, weak subordinate commune-level structures, and inadequate leadership. Regional groupings of provisional provincial party organizations were defined and conferences held to study and popularize organizational management and training improvements. Such regional party meetings were conducted under the chairmanship of a regional party center, defined as the geographic fulcrum for provincial party organizations. Those centers were apparently intended to serve as the catalysts for systematic reform and as models of functional provincial political organizations. (*FBIS-East Asia* [EAS], 4 March.)

The membership of the PRPK, which hovered at between 5,000 and 7,500 during the mid-1980s, increased to between 8,000 and 10,000 from 1986 to 1988. In an interview with a BBC correspondent in November, Hun Sen stated the party had 20,000 members, though a later Phnom Penh Domestic Service transmission suggested that the PRPK membership included "tens of thousands" of "rightful members" in addition to many alternate members and mass organization members. (Phnom Penh Domestic Service, in Cambodian, 27 November.) Public statements by PRK officials in 1988 called attention to substantial growth in local party membership, especially in Phnom Penh, and to the proliferation of chapter-level party organizations established throughout the countryside. The party-controlled media highlighted the growth of the capital city party organization and the development of party organizations in communes and wards subordinate to the municipality and in enterprises and factories. In 1984 Phnom Penh contained 92 party chapters. In mid-October, party General Secretary Heng Samrin cited the existence of 120 chapters with one thousand municipal members as a measure of the party's growth in a speech to the First Regional Party Congress held in Phnom Penh. (*FBIS-EAS*, 14 October.)

The sixth and seventh plenary sessions of the party Central Committee inventoried a two-year long effort to upgrade cadre training and organizational interaction of party chapters and core groups and a long-term project to build villages and communes into more effective planning and decision-making levels. The latter project would require heightened party activism and cadre intervention in local economic affairs and security matters. Public statements by party leaders emphasized the consistent attention given to basic party-building tasks. For example, in a late April speech, Chea Sim, Politburo member and chairman of the National Assembly, stressed the primacy placed by the regime on village- and commune-level force expansion for the party, as well as for mass organizations, governing bodies, and militia. In mid-June, during a visit to Kampot province, Heng Samrin focused on the tandem imperatives of militia and regional force expansion and party growth and advertised a midyear Politburo resolution and Secretariat directive devolving increased authority to the provincial- and municipal-level party and state organizations. (*FBIS-EAS*, 20 June.) He repeated the themes of village and commune consolidation and improved ideological and political training for cadre and mass organization expansion in a mid-September speech to a meeting in Siem Reap-Oddar Meanchy province (*FBIS-EAS*, 27 September). Later, the cadre training project was widened to include a call for generally improved popular education and proselytization.

The core group (Krom Snoul) continued to identify potential party members and to prepare them as candidates for regular membership in the absence of strong and capable youth organizations, the more conventional testing ground for future party members. According to media accounts, the central-level bodies of the People's Revolutionary Youth Union of Kampuchea and the Association of Revolutionary Youth in Kampuchea engaged in more systematic recruitment and cadre development work.

Domestic Party Affairs. Two Central Committee plenary sessions and several special Politburo sessions were held in 1988. The plenary meetings focused on organizational reform within the party and on domestic economic policies. During 18–24 January General Secretary Heng Samrin chaired the sixth plenum, which reviewed the work of the two previous years, ruled on the "main orientation" of the tasks set for 1988, and acted on decisions regarding alterations in the functioning and management of state economic units and branches. Those decisions were a terse acknowledgment that the broad contours of the Vietnamese economic reform program—cessation of central subsidies, autonomization of economic units, limitation of central planning and central authority over production units, and reorganization of management habits and practices—would be at least partially replicated in the PRK. (*FBIS-EAS*, 26 January.) The plenary session emphasized the recruitment and training of cadre and core group members, the activation of party chapters, and the fostering of cooperation between party chapter-level organizations. According to later articles in the party's publication, the plenum placed high priority on promoting political education and ideological work among party members, cadres and troops. (*FBIS-EAS*, 31 March.) The Central Committee's seventh plenary session, which ran from 3 to 6 July, took stock of the work of the first six months of 1988, reviewed the intended targets for political work in the second half of 1988, and elected two new alternate members to the Politburo and two new members to the Secretariat. The plenum "debated and unanimously approved" the establishment of joint state-private economic entities, thereby accepting the introduction of the

basic form of economic innovation at the core of the earliest Vietnamese reforms.

The themes of internal organizational and economic policy reform were stressed at several midyear and third-quarter meetings, including the First National Congress of Cadres, held in May, and a cluster of midyear calls on provincial party committees by key central leaders. In a mid-September party school meeting in Siem Reap-Oddar Meanchy province, General Secretary Heng Samrin expounded on these central ideas and specified five tasks for the PRPK: (1) developing mass organizations and concomitantly widening popular political and ideological training courses, (2) consolidating villages and communes and strengthening local units of the armed forces, (3) specifying realistic targets and plans for infrastructure construction, (4) strengthening communication and local defense fortifications, and (5) undertaking coordinated local security and defense work through appropriate organization of local resources (*FBIS-EAS*, 27 September).

In the last quarter of 1988, central party functional departments, military regions, ministries, and provisional party committees called a series of meetings. Those meetings, chaired or addressed by central party figures, reviewed the decade-long course of party and governmental policies and articulated strong support for the agenda of district-level party and militia development projects. The provincial party congresses of regional centers and subprovincial meetings heard reviews of draft political reports and elected new party committees and committee secretaries. (*FBIS-EAS*, 24, 25 October.) The first and second army region meetings, chaired by Bou Thang and attended by selected provisional provincial party committee secretaries, evaluated the political work of the party organizations in provincial and regimental units. A mid-October Central Committee conference focused on strengthening communal administration, and the late October First Congress of District Cadres held in Phnom Penh stressed "core cadre" recruitment, training policies, and the responsibilities of PRPK organizational commissions at all levels. Heng Samrin addressed the district cadre congress and stressed the need to refine and revise the functional definition of provincial-, district-, and ward-level party chapter responsibilities.

The government of the PRK also undertook modest organizational changes and several ministerial-level personnel shifts during the course of the year. The fourteenth session of the National

Assembly in early February approved a resolution ratifying the previous appointments of three vice-chairmen of the Council of Ministers and the transfer of a minister. A late May Council of State meeting gave ex post facto approval to several changes in assignments within the Council of Ministers. An August communiqué of the Council of State announced the dissolution of the Office of Economic and Cultural Cooperation with Foreign Countries and the establishment of a General Directorate for Tourism under the authority of the Council of Ministers. The communiqué noted the retirement of four ministers and appointments and transfers affecting eleven ministers and deputies. (*FBIS-EAS*, 21 June, 22 August.) On 17 June the Office of the Council of Ministers held the Second Working Conference of Services, Ministries, and Institutes at the provincial and municipal level. The conference, attended by Vietnamese "experts" attached to the Council of Ministers, focused on ministerial functions, the implementation of government decisions, and the coordination and improvement of local and provincial government. (*FBIS-EAS*, 21 June.) Finally, the regime paid continued attention to provincial- and subordinate-level governance, urging special efforts to improve the leadership and performance of People's Revolutionary Committees and devolving increased but unspecified authority to those levels (*FBIS-EAS*, 20 June).

In 1988 the governing apparatus of the PRK put in place the legislative paraphernalia required to run a restrained economic reform campaign that echoed the themes of the Vietnamese program of reform: decentralization of planning, autonomy for functional economic units, increasingly unfettered internal trade, reduced subsidies to state enterprises, and systematic increases in the production of consumer items. The fourteenth session of the First National Assembly (2–8 February) formally approved the report on the state budget for 1986, reviewed the government's financial situation for 1987, and discussed 1988 budgetary and state plan targets (*FBIS-EAS*, 5 February). A late May meeting of the Council of State undertook to amend a constitutional article on trade activities in addition to reviewing the Council of Ministers' first quarter evaluation of socioeconomic achievements and approving changes in assignments within the Council of Ministers. The fifteenth session of the National Assembly (7–11 July) outlined plans for correcting the imbalance in income and expenditure in the 1988 state budget and reviewed local administrative work

and party building. A late August decision by the Council of Ministers authorized the formation of a Committee for Building New Development Zones, areas that would receive special concentrated doses of infrastructure development and agricultural development assistance and would serve as the anchors for national reconstruction. Takeo and Battambang were singled out as test zones. (*FBIS-EAS*, 25 August.)

Auxiliary and Front Organizations. Mass and front organizations remained weak and underdeveloped during the course of the year. In several major speeches Politburo member Chea Sim, chairman of the National Assembly and the KUFNCD National Council, spoke of continued grass roots work toward the integration of party, government, and mass organizational systems at the village and commune level. He also endorsed a comprehensive "national reconciliation" policy calling for the blending of workers, intellectuals, ethnic groups, and clergy into organized citizen groups that would help expand commune and village militia units. (*FBIS-EAS*, 6 May, 28 July.) In a 27 October speech to the Fourth Front Congress of Prey Veng province, Chea Sim described the mass and front organizations as links between party and government organizations and the citizenry and stressed "intellectual, religion, and ethnic work" by front organizations. He noted that to facilitate the work of such organizations, "it is imperative that the party committee and authorities at all levels immediately eliminate their scorn, if any, for the role played by mass organizations" (*FBIS-EAS*, 28 October). In a speech before a provincial front congress in late 1988, Chea Sim reviewed the regime's efforts to co-opt religious groups and the modest track record of accomplishments, including the publication of prayer books, the institution of radio and television programs featuring religious events and prayer, and continued organizing work among religious groups. The government had formalized its relationship with religions in ministerial decisions and defined a role for front organizations in monitoring ordination and in supervising the participation of religious interests in political activities. (*FBIS-EAS*, 17 May.)

The overall leadership of the KUFNCD, elected in December 1981, remained essentially stable under Chea Sim's chairmanship. The National Council organized the May Day of Hatred Against the Pol Pot–Ieng Sary Clique; undertook preparations for the celebration of the tenth anniversary of National

Day, commemorating the 7 January 1979 victory over the Pol Pot regime; and participated in central government–coordinated preparations to mark the important Indochina anniversaries and agreements.

On 17 June trade union representatives from various central institutions, ministries, and sundry offices held preparatory sessions for the Second National Congress of Trade Union representatives. On 23 August the Central Committee of the Kampuchean Federation of Trade Unions (KFTU) organized its ninth session. During 1–3 October the KFTU held its Second National Congress. The congress elected a new executive committee consisting of 49 members, including an eleven-person permanent committee chaired by May Ly. Three vice-chairmen were elected: Say Siphon, Chhim Nguon, and Duong Savang. (*FBIS-EAS*, 4 October.)

The Second Congress of the Kampuchean Revolutionary Women's Association convened during 9–11 September and elected a new 37-member central committee. Mean Sam-an was re-elected chair of the association. (*FBIS-EAS*, 12 September.)

In early October the Youth Union's Central Committee and the governing body of the Youth Association held a joint three-day meeting in Phnom Penh (*FBIS-EAS*, 6 October).

International and Regional Issues. The PRK sustained its basic international relations in 1988, stressing the integrated character of the trilateral Indochina connection and advertising the increasing sophistication of relations with Moscow. The two trends were set in the context of Vietnam's declared intentions to withdraw its total troop presence from Cambodia by December 1989 or January 1990 and continued Soviet efforts to usher along regional negotiations on Cambodia.

The year's schedule was crowded with visits between Cambodian delegations and its two Indochinese partners and the ceremonious signing of protocols, agreements, and other officious documents underscoring the existence of an Indochinese link. Key contacts of commission-level party entities emphasized the efforts of the parties to continue high-level relations. The continuous exchange of ministerial-level visits and the routinized contacts of the three Indochinese countries underscored the continuous nature of Cambodia's connections with Vietnam and the functioning character of the Indochinese triangle. Protocols on goods exchanges for the year, special agreements on projects, and trilateral projects were trumpeted in the media and were intended to signal the PRK regime's

commitment to bilateral and trilateral economic cooperation and a shared conception of security relations and strategic imperatives. Conferences and meetings of the three Indochinese foreign ministers were held at strategic times to endorse key positions on the resolution of the Cambodian conflict and to emphasize the consultative nature of the relationship. For example, on 11 July an extraordinary conference of Indochinese foreign ministers, held in Phnom Penh, reviewed the People's Army of Vietnam's (PAVN) withdrawal plans, focused on the early July Association of Southeast Asian Nations' (ASEAN) foreign ministers' conference communiqué, and reaffirmed the Ho Chi Minh City communiqué of 29 July 1987 that stood as Hanoi's starting point for peace discussions.

The Soviets sought to maintain a constant rhythm of high-level and substantive contacts with the PRK during the year. Moscow representatives convened with Hun Sen at critical junctures during regional discussions on the Cambodian conflict and briefed him on developments in Soviet relations with Washington and Beijing. For instance, in late January Hun Sen met with Foreign Minister Eduard Shevardnadze to discuss the results of his second meeting with Prince Sihanouk and stopped in Hanoi for consultations with Foreign Minister Nguyen Co Thach. In mid-March a deputy foreign ministers' conference brought together Indochinese and Soviet officials to "exchange views" on a solution to the Cambodian problem. In early June, Soviet special envoy Boris Chaplin traveled to Phnom Penh to brief Heng Samrin on the U.S.-Soviet summit meeting. The Soviet-PRK meetings on regional and international issues provided important symbols of regime legitimacy for the PRK and signaled Moscow's approval of the manner in which the key PRK negotiator had acquitted himself in discussions with representatives of the noncommunist Cambodian resistance. Such contacts also reinforced Moscow's intention to maintain a separate and direct track to the PRK leadership. In addition, the Soviets dispatched party and government delegations to sustain central committee and ministerial-level contacts and to perpetuate agreements and protocols on assistance programs and project development.

In 1988 the key players in the Cambodia conflict edged closer toward mutual accommodation, manifesting increasing moderation in their positions and a renewed willingness to negotiate. China offered its own peace proposal in July in a major break with the long-standing practice of deferring to and speaking through the Coalition Government of Democratic Kampuchea (CGDK). Moscow appeared intent on nudging Hanoi toward an early resolution of the conflict, in part as a consequence of the priority placed on restoring relations with China, in part to establish itself as a credible regional player in the eyes of ASEAN, and in part to put an end to an expensive aspect of the Vietnamese-Soviet relationship. Thai foreign minister Sitthi Sawetsila and Vietnamese foreign minister Thach met on three separate occasions, once before the Djakarta informal meeting and twice in August, to discuss Cambodia and bilateral issues. ASEAN worked hard to facilitate continued regional discussions. A constellation of meetings, including two sessions between Hun Sen and Sihanouk, and the midyear Djakarta informal meeting sustained the impressive regional momentum. The Vietnamese promise to withdraw 50,000 troops by December prodded the principals toward efforts to address intractable issues.

Hun Sen met with Sihanouk in Paris for the second time on 20 January for two days of talks. The two discussed a specific schedule for the PAVN withdrawal, the formation of a coalition government, the governing structure of a postsettlement Cambodia, and the role of international controls and guarantees. Hun Sen refused to table a specific timetable for withdrawal, sustaining the Vietnamese line that troops would be withdrawn by the end of 1989 or the beginning of 1990. Hun Sen also demanded the dissolution of the Khmer Rouge army before the withdrawal of PAVN forces. He argued that any future government of Cambodia must be formed within the existing PRK framework and that elections must be organized not by a quadripartite government but by a committee formed within the framework of the existing PRK structure. Sihanouk demanded PAVN withdrawal without dismantling the Khmer Rouge army. Sihanouk called for the creation of a quadripartite government of national reconciliation that would run elections under international supervision. Hun Sen rejected the need for an international peacekeeping force.

The second Hun Sen–Sihanouk talk produced some signs of flexibility. Sihanouk implied that local and provincial administrative structures could continue to exist while the central state was dismantled. The prince endorsed equal representation in national ministries. Although Hun Sen and Sihanouk remained far apart on the sequence of events that would lead to the establishment of a coalition government and although Hun Sen rejected the prince's

argument for dissolution of the PRK, some observers noted that Hun Sen seemed prepared to negotiate formulas for the distribution of power in advance of national elections. Additionally, in late January the Phnom Penh regime signaled its willingness to deal directly with Khmer Rouge representative Khieu Samphan and explicitly ruled out dealing with other Khmer Rouge figures.

In the months following the Paris meeting, Phnom Penh stressed its inclination to deal in a reasonable and businesslike fashion and highlighted the natural basis of cooperation that existed between the PRK and ANS forces. Phnom Penh responded to Sihanouk's 30 January resignation, and his early February cancellation of the April meeting scheduled with Hun Sen by publicly reiterating the regime's blessing for the Hun Sen–Sihanouk channel. By late February, in the aftermath of a secret meeting between the prince and Khieu Samphan, Sihanouk returned to the resistance coalition, though he still adhered to the status of "indefinite leave" that he had announced in May 1987. Through March, Hun Sen gave steady support to the idea of resuming discussions with Sihanouk, while strongly defending the PRK positions on the establishment and composition of a coalition government, international supervision, and the question of the role of the Khmer Rouge in a postsettlement government. In a late March interview Hun Sen cautioned against allowing the process to drag out endlessly and noted that alternatives, including "partial solutions"—an oblique reference to the possibility of a separate and bilateral peace between the prince and Hun Sen—existed in the face of Khmer Rouge refusal to participate in negotiations. Following a 1 April meeting between Sihanouk and Chinese foreign minister Wu Xueqian in Beijing, the prince rejected Hun Sen's proposal for a third round of talks. Hun Sen worked hard to recover from that rebuff. In press interviews Hun Sen repeatedly offered to meet with Sihanouk at the convenience of the prince and gave considerable play to the possibility of a "partial solution" in the face of continued Khmer Rouge recalcitrance.

In early May, Indonesian foreign minister Ali Alatas, who replaced Mochtar Kusumaatmadja in March, announced his effort to revive his predecessor's plans to organize an informal conference to resolve the Cambodian conflict. The initiative stemmed from a meeting between Mochtar and Thach during July 1987 in Ho Chi Minh City. Alatas worked extremely hard to set a date and an agenda and to assure attendance by the four Cambodian factions plus the Vietnamese. On 9 July, Hun Sen communicated his decision to attend the Djakarta Informal Meeting, one day before Sihanouk's resignation as president of the CGDK. Sihanouk rejected new overtures by Hun Sen to schedule another Paris session and stood by his public comments of June, made during his visit to Beijing, that he would "unconditionally" approve any agreement reached by the other three Cambodian factions at the Djakarta Informal Meeting.

Sihanouk did not participate in the meeting but was present in Djakarta during the talks that seated Vietnamese, Cambodian, and ASEAN representatives together for the first time to discuss resolving the Cambodian conflict. The informal meeting yielded a proliferation of proposals, including a five-point proposal from Sihanouk endorsing an international conference under U.N. auspices to guarantee the neutrality of Cambodia and an international control commission to supervise the withdrawal of Vietnamese troops and the elections. Hun Sen tabled a seven-point proposal emphasizing the cessation of military assistance to the anti-Vietnamese resistance forces and the establishment of a national reconciliation council composed of the four Cambodian parties, headed by Sihanouk, and responsible for organizing general elections. Hun Sen endorsed the establishment of an international control commission and the convening of an international conference. Sihanouk rejected the national council proposal. Democratic Kampuchea (DK) representative Khieu Samphan refused to sign the conference communiqué, which was endorsed by the other three Cambodian factions. The Djakarta meeting was hailed as a milestone for getting the principals involved in discussions, but the advantage was generally agreed to have been with the Vietnamese, who were able to equivocate on the matter of a firm timetable for troop withdrawal and the cessation of assistance to the resistance forces and to utilize the leverage that came from their status as a "dialogue partner," which did not require them to confront the CGDK parties in direct talks.

Following the Djakarta Informal Meeting, Phnom Penh invested considerable energy in increasing the credibility and strength of its seven-point proposal. A two-day session of the Afro-Asian People's Solidarity Organization in Phnom Penh strongly endorsed the proposal and urged the "vacant seat solution" for the upcoming United Nations General Assembly (UNGA) session. The early September Non-Aligned Foreign Ministers' Conference in Nicosia further celebrated Phnom Penh's diplomatic proposals. A series of high-level visits from Moscow and Hanoi reinforced the PRK position and affirmed Soviet and Vietnamese confidence in Phnom Penh. By early September, the regime had turned its attention to preparing for another meeting between Hun Sen and Sihanouk and positioning itself for the UNGA debate over the draft resolution on Cambodia.

At the mid-October session of the Djakarta informal meeting working group, boycotted by the Khmer Rouge, Vietnam continued to insist on including external issues only in the larger group session, leaving internal issues to the Cambodian factions. Hanoi also sought to strengthen the link between PAVN withdrawal and preventing the restoration of Pol Pot by calling for cessation of aid to the resistance simultaneous with withdrawal of Vietnamese troops. The Vietnamese insisted that the Cambodian factions meet separately to discuss internal issues and that the format of the talks should follow a two-stage format of the original Djakarta informal meeting. ASEAN participants strongly countered Hanoi's positions. The working session set a second informal meeting for January 1989.

In early November, the UNGA took up a revised draft of the ASEAN resolution on Cambodia, which included a statement about the necessity of universally condemning the brutality of Khmer Rouge rule. The resolution on Cambodia gained 64 cosponsors and was adopted with a record-breaking 122 votes, 5 more than were cast in support of the resolution of the forty-third UNGA in 1987.

During 6–7 November Prince Sihanouk met Hun Sen. They were joined by Son Sann, president of the Khmer People's National Liberation Front (KPNLF), on 7 November, and the three agreed on the need for an international conference and on the necessity of forming a "commission of experts at the ministerial level" composed of representatives of the PRK and the two noncommunist resistance factions of the CGDK to continue working-level discussions. Sihanouk, Hun Sen, and Son Sann also agreed to meet again in late 1989 but failed to reach agreement on the most important issues: the PRK insistence that withdrawal of PAVN forces be linked to a cessation of aid to the noncommunist resistance, Phnom Penh's refusal to dismantle the PRK and form a coalition government before elections, and rejection of an international peacekeeping force that was opposed by Vietnam and the PRK but strongly favored by the noncommunist resistance. Hun Sen was measurably more assertive during the November meeting; his more insistent manner and his inclination to be less deferential to Sihanouk prompted the prince to re-evaluate the extent to which the bilateral talks with the PRK would afford him maneuverability and allow him to contour the process of diplomacy to his advantage. In mid-December Sihanouk met with Khieu Samphan to discuss Khmer Rouge professions of a more conciliatory posture on the diplomatic initiatives and willingness to participate in talks between the resistance and the Phnom Penh government. A Djakarta informal meeting working-group session convened in late December and set a schedule for a second informal meeting in early 1989. Sihanouk maintained his steadfast opposition to entertaining a fourth meeting with Hun Sen and denounced his interlocutor in strong terms for his unwavering support of Hanoi's regional interests. In mid-December Vietnam announced preparations for the withdrawal of elements of six PAVN divisions from Cambodia totaling about eighteen thousand troops. Hanoi claimed to have fulfilled its promise to reduce its in-country military presence by 50,000, although the arithmetic at the basis of that claim was disputed in many quarters. Nevertheless, with the exception of the Khmer Rouge, who continued to argue that the Vietnamese withdrawal was an elaborate rotation of troops involving the seeding of PRK ranks with PAVN in Cambodian uniforms, ASEAN seemed prepared to acknowledge that Hanoi had drawn down a significant number of troops and urged continued withdrawals according to a timetable.

Party. Party of Democratic Kampuchea (PDK). The PDK is the successor to the Kampuchean Communist Party (KCP), the instrument of rule under Pol Pot from April 1975 to December 1978 when the Vietnamese invaded Cambodia and displaced the brutal democratic Kampuchean regime.

Founded. The PDK traces its origin to the Khmer People's Revolutionary Party (KPRP), which was founded on 30 September 1951 with the establishment of a provisional central committee, pending the party's first congress. According to a party history issued under the authority of the Eastern Zone Military-Political Service in 1973, the decision to form a Marxist-Leninist party was made at the second congress of the KPRP in September 1960. The organization was renamed the Workers' Party of Kampuchea at that time. A 1977 speech by Pol Pot suggests that September 1960 was the first congress of the KCP, though the party did not

bear that name until a September 1966 Central Committee decision authorizing the change in nomenclature. The KCP designation endured until the nominal dissolution of the party in 1981.

Membership. Unknown

General Secretary. Since the dissolution of the KCP in 1981, the position of general secretary has not been publicly mentioned. Pol Pot was general secretary up to 1981 and was retired in August 1985 from his leadership role in the Democratic Kampuchean faction in an orchestrated effort to improve the group's image in the context of the tripartite Coalition Government of Democratic Kampuchea, founded in 1982.

Politburo. Possibly no longer functioning

Secretariat. Possibly no longer functioning

Central Committee. Possibly no longer functioning

Status. The KCP was officially dissolved in December 1981 in a calculated effort to facilitate the formation of an anti-Vietnamese coalition between the remnants of the Democratic Kampuchean (DK) regime, the Khmer People's National Liberation Front (KPNLF) of Son Sann, and Sihanoukist forces that remained hesitant about joining a coalition with the brutal DK to oppose Hanoi's occupation of Cambodia. A tripartite partnership aimed at opposing the Vietnamese military presence in Cambodia was established in mid-1982. The DK, or Khmer Rouge in the appellation preferred by Prince Sihanouk, has remained the dominant partner in the coalition with the most disciplined, best-organized, and most completely supplied army. The KCP was replaced by the PDK, an organization that replicated the leadership structure and high command relationships that characterized the KCP while publicly professing to have discarded the iconoclastic commitment to radical communism. The August 1985 public retirement of Pol Pot from his leadership roles further underscored the flexible nature of the organization. Pol Pot was widely viewed as still exercising considerable behind-the-scenes power, and the fundamental KCP structures were widely assumed to have remained intact and unaltered by the cosmetic changes. In 1986 Pol Pot was reported to be terminally ill in Beijing, though his current whereabouts, health, and status within the PDK remain unknown. The PDK controls a system of refugee and insurgent base camps along the Thai-Cambodian border and operates in southeastern Cambodia in the vicinity of the Great Lake (Tonle Sap) and near Phnom Penh.

Last Congress. The third and last party congress was held in Phnom Penh on 14 December 1975.

Last Election. 20 March 1976, for the People's Representative Assembly of Democratic Kampuchea. Elected were 150 peasants, 50 workers, and 50 soldiers.

Auxiliary Organizations. The Communist Women's Organization and the Alliance of Democratic Kampuchean Youth have probably been defunct since the fall of Pol Pot's regime in December 1978.

Publications and Media. The PDK maintains a radio broadcasting station called the Voice of the National Army of Democratic Kampuchea (VONADK) that operates clandestinely.

Leadership and Party Organization.

The PDK's organizational chart and the composition of the political high command remained shrouded in a secrecy equivalent to that which cloaked the Angkar organization, which ruled Cambodia from 1975 to 1979. In 1988 Khieu Samphan, the vice president of DK in charge of foreign affairs, continued to function as the party head, an ambiguous title that was sometimes replaced by the designation chairman of the DK side in official DK documents. Khieu Samphan presided over the management of diplomacy and the definition of DK foreign policy strategy, though apparently he consulted closely with the party's shadowy political high command on critical decisions. For example, Khieu Samphan suddenly departed New York before the UNGA vote on the ASEAN draft resolution on Cambodia and returned to the DK headquarters for consultations when it became clear that the new language, which called for a "nonreturn to the universally condemned policies and practices of a recent past," was going to attract a significantly higher level of cosponsorship and support than previous years' resolutions. Ieng Sary, one of Pol Pot's long-time and closest associates who was named a member of the CGDK Coordinating Committee for Economy and Finance in 1982, retained significant authority within the Khmer Rouge inner circle. He seems to have functioned as an overlord for foreign policy and military strategy. His wife, Ieng Thirith, held substantial power in the realm of foreign affairs, according to some observers (*Bangkok Post*, 26 February). Son Sen, deputy premier for national defense under Pol Pot, held the position of supreme commander of the National Army of Democratic Kampuchea (NADK). He was appointed a member of the CGDK Coordinating Committee for National Defense in 1982. Khieu Samphan and Son Sen were rumored to have formed an alliance representing a more moderate, conciliatory faction of the DK that was opposed by the followers and soldiers of the barbaric Ta Mok (also known as Chhit Choeun), vice-chairman of the NADK Military Committee. Through at least March, Ta Mok was the commander of six divisions in Siem Reap and Kompong Cham provinces consisting of about seven thousand men. (*Bangkok Post*, 4 March.) According to unconfirmed reports, Ta Mok was given command over the entire southeastern region and relieved of responsibilities for the northeastern region in a restructuring of the Khmer Rouge military organization late in the year (*The Nation*, 17 October). In the months following the April 1975 seizure of power by Pol Pot, Ke Pauk (also known as Tat Pok) commanded the military region that encompassed Phnom Penh. In 1988 Ke Pauk served as deputy general secretary of the NADK. Finally, Nuon Chea, chairman of the Standing Committee of the DK People's Representative Assembly from 1979 and a major but little-known power within the party's command, seems to have been involved in formulating long-term political strategy and postsettlement contingency plans (*Bangkok Post*, 7 May).

The PDK experienced some significant defections in 1988. In June, Thuch Rin, a former colleague of Ta Mok's in the southeastern zone during the 1970s and the DK minister of education and culture since at least 1982, contacted Prince Sihanouk at his residence in Pyongyang and made known his desire to join the prince's forces (*Bangkok Post*, 9 June). In March, the commander of one of the battalions subordinate to Division 912, one of the six divisions under Ta Mok's overall command, defected along with a handful of troops to the Sihanouk National Army (ANS). The battalion commander was reportedly the highest-ranking DK officer to have defected to date (*Bangkok Post*, 4 March).

The Khmer Rouge army, with a strength of between thirty thousand and forty thousand, remained the source of the DK's real power. In 1988 the NADK appeared able to replace its troop losses but was not capable of substantial force expansion. The DK was amply armed by China with basic infantry weapons, rocket-propelled grenades, and mortars and was thought to have extensive caches in the interior. Its primary strength was its tightly disciplined organization and experienced, effective leadership. Son Sen has been described by knowledgeable DK defectors as a capable military strategist, and Pol Pot continued to command a great deal of respect among the troops. The NADK's 1988 emphasis was on political action in the interior. The army avoided large-scale attacks on Vietnamese and PRK forces during the course of the year and accorded a much higher priority to diplomatic and political activities. In 1988, the DK began to target the noncommunist forces as its primary adversary, actively obstructing the efforts of the ANS and the armed forces of the KPNLF to penetrate into the interior. Several episodes of DK attacks against noncommunist resistance personnel in the vicinity of the Great Lake precipitated Sihanouk's resignations from the CGDK.

Domestic Affairs. The NADK fielded an average of 20,000–22,000 armed troops for actions inside of Cambodia at any one time during 1988, with the rest of the Khmer Rouge forces remaining in satellite camps along the Thai-Cambodian border. The DK military presided over these camps in a draconian manner. Site Eight, located south of Aranyaprathet and west of Sisophon, was a cluster of four camps. Four additional DK camps—Samrong Kiat, Huay Chan, Na Trao, and O-Trao—were located on Siem Reap-Oddar Meanchy province's northeastern border with Thailand, east of the ANS Site B. Two other DK camps, Bo Rai and Ta Luan in Thailand's Trat province, flanked the KPNLF camp called Sok Sann (*Asiaweek*, 29 July).

The Khmer Rouge–controlled civilian camps on Thai soil, inhabited by about 60,000 residents in 1988, were supplied by the U.N. Border Relief Organization (UNBRO), which was routinely denied access to the camps for the purposes of monitoring aid distribution. Allegations of conscription of civilians to serve as porters and the rigid discipline imposed on the camps by heavy-handed and often violent DK camp commanders, brought into focus long-standing issues of jurisdiction over civilian populations, rights of access to the camps by nongovernmental organizations (NGOs) seeking to monitor the distribution of humanitarian assistance, the rights of individuals appealing for relocation to camps controlled by the noncommunist factions of the CGDK, and the policies of the Thai government and its border security forces toward civilians under DK control. In June 1988 the International Committee of the Red Cross negotiated the release of 150 Khmer Krom in Site Eight, according to the U.S. Lawyers' Committee for Human Rights, but in general the draconian regime in the camps militated

against opportunities for free transfers. Some reports suggested that a limited amount of free market activity had been allowed in Site Eight, without altering the strictly regulated lives of civilians in the camps (Lawyers' Committee for Human Rights, *Protection Issues in Thai-Cambodia Border Camps*, 1988).

In October-November, PAVN and PRK artillery pounded civilian DK camps on the Thai side of the common border, in the vicinity of Pailin and posts south, and in the Phnom Melai area to prevent the NADK from advancing civilian populations into forward positions on Cambodian soil and to deter further NADK probes in the Phnom Melai area.

Auxiliary and Front Organizations. There was no information concerning PDK auxiliary or front organizations available in 1988.

International Views, Positions, and Activities. The DK faction was at a progressively worsening disadvantage during the year as the key regional players in the search for a resolution to the Cambodian conflict sought to maintain the pace of meetings that had begun in late 1987 with the Hun Sen–Sihanouk Paris meeting. The DK confined itself to reactive diplomacy in a manner that cast it as potential spoiler of any agreement between the Sihanoukists and the PRK and as unalterably opposed to any formula for discussion devised by the ASEAN countries. The periodic gestures of conciliation by the DK were efforts to recover from increasing isolation in the aftermath of miscalculations of regional and world response to strong and intransigent DK positions on the issues of participation in a postsettlement Cambodia.

In mid-January the DK faction made its position on the scheduled Hun Sen–Sihanouk talks clear: it would not join the negotiations with the PRK unless Vietnam agreed to be present. On 16 January a DK spokesperson told Thai reporters that although the DK had no objection to KPNLF president and CGDK premier Son Sann's proposal that the Vietnamese commit themselves to a promise of withdrawal in writing, this was not sufficient for DK leader Khieu Samphan. The DK spokesperson made these remarks in the aftermath of a 16 January meeting between Sihanouk's son, Prince Norodom Ranarith, commander in chief of the ANS; Son Sen; and KPNLF representative Im Chhudet. The three representatives of the coalition government convened to reinforce the image of unity in the face of centrifugal diplomatic forces and to publicly note the battlefield progress of the armed components of the coalition against the Vietnamese. The communiqué of the meeting noted consensus on the issue of planned joint tactical and strategic offensives but failed to mention the group's view of the diplomatic situation and did not reach an accord on the agenda for the Hun Sen–Sihanouk meeting. On 20 January the prince met with Hun Sen without a Khmer Rouge representative. Although the meeting produced no final communiqué or any agreement of substance, the PRK seized the opportunity to reinforce its position on the need to ensure the "nonparticipation" of Pol Pot and undefined associates in a postsettlement coalition. That position was shared by Prince Sihanouk, who was unalterably opposed to a return to power of a reconstituted DK but simultaneously inclined to recognize the necessity of factoring some portion of the Khmer Rouge into the political calculus of a coalition.

Throughout the year China, the key supporter of the DK, maintained the unconditional withdrawal of PAVN forces from Cambodia as the nonnegotiable centerpiece of its position and gave undiminished support to the formation of a coalition government under Sihanouk that did not exclude the DK faction from power. However, China demonstrated flexibility during the year and took steps to distance itself from the Khmer Rouge. Most important, in early July China floated a peace proposal in a major break with the long-standing practice of deferring to and speaking through the CGDK. The Chinese offer reiterated the demand for a Vietnamese troop withdrawal, endorsed the creation of a quadripartite coalition under Sihanouk, and described a scheme according to which each party would be granted a veto over the participation of the other three factions' candidates in a coalition. Significantly, China proposed a freeze on military forces of all Cambodian factions, suggesting that Beijing's intention was to cut off support to the Khmer Rouge, probably in the context of an end to Vietnamese support to the PRK. Phnom Penh took vigorous exception to the Chinese proposals, but by the end of the year China explicitly endorsed the tandem decrease of Chinese assistance to the resistance in concert with the drawdown of PAVN troops in Cambodia.

The DK spent a good deal of energy trying to recover from China's effort to maximize its maneuverability and from setbacks resulting from Khieu Samphan's inflexible demeanor during the Djakarta Informal Meeting. To allay growing suspicions that the DK was planning a strategy that would position them to seize power following PAVN's departure on

15 August, the DK faction broadcast a proposal for the settlement of the Cambodian conflict. That proposal closely paralleled Sihanouk's plan articulated at the Djakarta Informal Meeting. The DK called for: (1) a cease-fire to be observed by all armed factions following the initiation of a Vietnamese withdrawal; (2) simultaneous dissolution of the PRK and the CGDK; (3) the establishment of a four-party Cambodian army under a quadripartite high command with the formation of a single army as a "future goal"; (4) the convening of an international conference of the five permanent members of the U.N. Security Council and a delegation from the council to set out effective means of preserving Cambodia's independence, neutrality, and territorial integrity; and (5) a treaty of nonaggression between Cambodia and Vietnam. Essentially, the DK called for the establishment of an international organization to "ensure" that the DK did not "dominate" the other parties and proposed the simultaneous efforts of that committee to "ensure" that the DK did not return to Vietnam by force of arms. The proposal replicated a Chinese plan and was said by some observers to have been born in Beijing, suggesting that China anticipated the need for a more accommodating and reasonable DK in advance of the Sino-Soviet talks. The proposal seems to have been a DK effort to get the ball quickly out of its court before the 29 August Sino-Soviet meeting.

In September the DK mounted a full court press against the ultimately successful ASEAN effort to support a UNGA resolution on Cambodia that condemned the DK. In late October the DK was purposefully absent from a working session of the Djakarta informal meeting, a calculated snub directed at ASEAN and the participating Cambodian factions. Following that meeting, in an attempt to compensate for assuming that boycotting the session would put the DK in a position of diplomatic advantage, the Khmer Rouge announced that it was willing to accept an international peacekeeping force as part of a political settlement. The decision, issued as an addendum to the 15 August peace plan, was announced in a document signed by Khieu Samphan and read over the VONADK radio on 21 October (*FEER*, 3 November). In mid-December, Khieu Samphan met with Sihanouk in Paris to discuss the renewed DK willingness to participate in the working sessions of the Djakarta Informal Meeting.

Lewis M. Stern
Washington, D.C.

Note: The views expressed in this paper are those of the author alone and do not reflect the official policy or position of the Department of Defense or the U.S. Government.

China

Population. 1,088,169,192 (excluding Taiwan)
Party. Chinese Communist Party (Zhongguo gongchan dang; CCP)
Founded. 1921
Membership. 47 million (Xinhua, 22 June; *FBIS*, 23 June)
General Secretary. Zhao Ziyang (69)
Standing Committee of the Politburo. 5 members: Zhao Ziyang, Li Peng (60; acting premier since 24 November 1987), Qiao Shi (64; first secretary, Central Commission for Inspection Discipline; member of Secretariat; vice-premier), Hu Qili (59; in charge of propaganda; member of Secretariat), Yao Yilin (71; vice-premier; minister, State Planning Commission)
Politburo. 17 full members: Wan Li, Tian Jiyun, Qiao Shi, Jiang Zemin, Li Peng, Li Tieying, Li Ruihuan, Li Ximing, Yang Rudai, Yang Shangkun, Wu Xueqian, Song Ping, Zhao Ziyang, Hu Qili, Hu Yaobang, Yao Yilin, Qin Jiwei. Alternate member: Ding Guangen
Secretariat. 4 full members: Hu Qili, Qiao Shi, Rui Xingwen, Yan Mingfu. Alternate member: Wen Jiabao
Central Committee. 175 full members and 110 alternate members; first plenum, 2 November 1987; second plenum, 15–19 March; third plenum, 26–30 September
Central Military Commission. Chairman: Deng Xiaoping; first vice-chairman: Zhao Ziyang; permanent vice-chairman and secretary general: Yang Shangkun
Central Advisory Committee. 200 members. Chairman: Chen Yun; vice-chairmen: Bo Yibo, Song Renqiong
Central Commission for Discipline Inspection. 69 members. First secretary: Qiao Shi; deputy secretaries: Chen Zuolin, Li Zhengting, Xiao Hongda
General Office. Director: Wen Jiabao; deputy directors: Feng Lingan, Xu Ruixin, Yang Dezhong, Zhou Jie
Department of International Liaison. Director: Zhu Liang; deputy directors: Jiang Guanghua, Li Shuzheng, Li Chengren, Zhu Shanqing

Department of Organization. Director: Song Ping; deputy directors: He Yong, Liu Zepeng, Lu Feng, Meng Liankun, Zhao Zongnai
Department of Propaganda. Director: Wang Renzhi; deputy directors: Gong Yuzhi, Li Yan, Wang Weicheng
Department of United Front Work. Director: Yan Mingfu; deputy directors: Li Ding, Song Kun, Wu Lianyuan
Work Committee for Government Organs. Secretary: Chen Junsheng; deputy secretary: Wang Chuguang
Work Committee for Party Organs. Secretary: Wen Jiabao; deputy secretary: Gu Yunfei
Central Party School. President: Gao Yang
Status. Ruling party
Last Congress. Thirteenth, 25 October–1 November 1987
Last Election. 1987
Auxiliary Organizations. Communist Youth League of China (50 million members), led by Song Defu; All-China Women's Federation, led by Chen Muhua since September (replacing Kang Keqing); All-China Federation of Trade Unions, led by Ni Zhifu; Chinese People's Political Consultative Conference (CPPCC), the party's leading united front organization, led by Li Xiannian since April (replacing Deng Yingchao); eight democratic or satellite parties.
Publications. The official and most authoritative publication of the CCP is the newspaper *Renmin Ribao* (People's Daily), published in Beijing. The theoretical journal of the Central Committee, *Hongqi* (Red Flag), published its last issue in June. It was superseded by the new biweekly theoretical journal *Qiushi* (Seeking Truth), under the Central Party School, which published its first issue on 1 July. Influential in recent years is *Liaowang* (Outlook), the weekly publication of Xinhua (The New China News Agency; NCNA), the official news agency of the party and government. The daily paper of the People's Liberation Army (PLA) is *Jiefangjunbao* (Liberation Army Daily). The weekly *Beijing Review (BR)*, published in English and in several other languages, carries translations of important articles, editorials, and documents from these three publications and from other sources. *China Daily*, the first English-language national newspaper in the People's Republic of China (PRC), began official publication in Beijing and Hong Kong on 1 June 1981. It began a New York edition in June 1983.

Domestic Affairs. Although U.N. economists forecast a pessimistic world economy for 1988, expecting it to grow by only 3 percent instead of the 3.5 percent they had predicted two weeks before the October 19, 1987, stock market crash, they expected that China would continue to be the world's fastest growing economy during the year. The Chinese economy expanded by 7.4 percent in 1986, nearly 10 percent in 1987, and was expected to grow 8 percent in 1988, according to the U.N. economists. (AP; Honolulu, *Star-Bulletin*, 11 January.)

Finance Minister Wang Bingqian confirmed that China's gross national product (GNP) increased in 1987 by 9 percent (*China Daily*, 23 January; *FBIS*, 26 January).

By midyear, according to the State Statistics Bureau, China's GNP had reached 557.5 billion yuan (roughly U.S. $148.7 billion), up 11 percent over the same period in 1987. Gross industrial output increased by 17.2 percent in the first half of 1988 compared to the same period in the previous year (*BR*, 1–7 August).

However, China's population had increased 1.4 percent in 1987, exceeding the planned rate for the second year in a row (the 1986 growth rate also was 1.4 percent, up from 1.1 percent in 1985), prompting calls for stricter enforcement of the one-child policy (*People's Daily*, 14 January; Honolulu, *Star-Bulletin*, 15 January). Several months later, Peng Peiyun, minister in charge of the State Family Planning Commission, said that China's population could reach 1.27 billion by the end of the century, exceeding the 1.2 billion target that had been set early in 1980 (before the 1982 census), a target that "probably did not reflect a realistic picture of our population situation" (Beijing, *China Daily*; *FBIS*, 1 November).

He Jingzhi (64) resigned as deputy head of the Propaganda Department in January. It was also thought that the position of Wang Renzhi, head of the Propaganda Department who had led the campaign against bourgeois liberalization in early 1987, was also in doubt (Hong Kong, *Ming Pao*; *FBIS*, 6 January). By year's end, however, Wang remained in his position.

Jiang Jingguo (Chiang Ching-kuo), president of the Nationalist Government in Taiwan since 1978 and son of the late Generalissimo Jiang Jieshi (Chiang Kai-shek), died of a heart attack on 13 January. Vice President Li Denghui (Lee Teng-hui) was sworn in as president (Taipei, AP; Honolulu, *Star-Bulletin*, 13 January). Li Denghui was subsequently elected chairman of the Kuomintang on 8 July (Taipei, NCNA, 8 July; *FBIS*, 11 July).

The Nationalist Party on Taiwan approved on 3 February a sweeping plan that will eventually permit Taiwanese to elect all members of the Legislative Yuan. The number of seats elected on Taiwan would be increased while elderly members would be encouraged to retire voluntarily in both the 312-seat Legislative Yuan and the 934-seat National Assembly, the electoral college. Only 73 seats of the Legislative Yuan and 106 seats of the National Assembly are currently held by members elected on Taiwan. (Annie Huang, Taipei, AP; Honolulu, *Star-Bulletin*, 3 February.)

Jiang Qing (74) was reported to be suffering from throat cancer and is jailed in a building opposite the office of the Central Discipline Inspection Commission on Zhang Zizhong Road in Beijing. Her daughter Li Na often visits her. Zhang Chunqiao, also still imprisoned, is said to have lung cancer. Wang Hongwen, in Qincheng Prison, is in poor health. (He Fang, "Reference News," *Cheng Ming*, Hong Kong, 1 February; *FBIS*, 2 February.) Chen Boda (83) was reported to be on parole because of his advanced age and declining health (Beijing, *Zhongguo xinwen she*, 9 February; *FBIS*, 9 February).

On 19 January, price controls were reimposed on key raw materials, indicating major failures in the ambitious reform effort to phase out central planning and allow the marketplace to set prices. Two sets of regulations setting price ceilings on oil, gas, electricity, steel, timber, coal, rubber, farm chemicals, and other major raw materials as well as on shipping, railway, and air transport were published in the *People's Daily*. The rules were being implemented to combat "wildly" rising prices in 1987 that resulted in "market chaos" (*The Honolulu Advertiser*, 20 January).

On 30 January, Xinhua reported that Liu Binyan would be allowed to travel to the United States in March to give lectures at Harvard University and the University of California. Meanwhile, astrophysicist Fang Lizhi was promoted from fourth- to second-grade academician of the Chinese Academy of Social Sciences. Both Liu and Fang were expelled from the CCP in January 1987. Later in 1988, Fang was again in the news, this time demanding that he be put on trial after hearing that Deng Xiaoping had reportedly criticized him by name and called for Fang to be put on trial for allegedly spreading false information. Fang had commented on Chinese corruption (specifically regarding overseas bank accounts of Chinese officials) during his visit to Australia in August (Tokyo, *Kyodo*; *FBIS*, 5 October).

It was reported on 26 February that an important article written by Deng Xiaoping in 1941 on the relationship between the party and the government was to be published soon. The article, entitled "Party and the Democratic Political Power Against Japanese Aggression," maintains that the party should not place itself above the government. It says that the "party should guide and supervise the government and focus its responsibility on political principles instead of monopolizing and interfering in everything. The party only has the right to order party groups and party members in the government but does not have the right to overrule the government." (Liu Rui-shao, Beijing, *Wen Wei Po*; Hong Kong, *FBIS*, 27 February.)

Xinhua announced on 29 February that the Central Committee had decided to set up a research center of the CCP Central Committee for the Reform of the Political Structure, with Bao Tong as its director. The center will draft documents for the Central Committee. (*FBIS*, 29 February.)

At the end of February, a concrete measure to separate party from government functions was announced. Party cells are to be replaced by working committees whose responsibilities are somewhat different from the displaced cells. The principal tasks of the working committees are to lead and direct the work of the organizations directly under the party center and the government departments. The new units make up only a fraction of the original cells, and their composition and power is supposed to be much more restricted. They are to concentrate on party work, including appropriate educational and administrative duties, and examine, supervise, and approve the work of party secretaries and assistant secretaries. They are supposed to streamline party structures at various levels and free the running of enterprises and government bureaus from party interference. Wen Jiabao, the alternate member of the five-man party Secretariat, was named to head the working committee under the Central Committee, while Chen Junsheng, the general secretary of the State Council, heads the government's party working committee. (David Chen, Hong Kong, *South China Morning Post*; *FBIS*, 1 March.)

In early March, the State Council decided to implement a housing reform throughout the country over the next three to five years. The reform, regarded as an important element in the overall reform program, would replace the state building apartments and distributing them through work units with the sale of apartments according to the demands of the emerging socialist planned commodity economy. The program is to begin in 1988 with the selection of several cities or counties to pilot the housing reform. By 1990, almost all cities are expected to carry out housing reform. (Beijing, Xinhua, 9 March; *FBIS*, 10 March.)

The Second Plenary Session of the Thirteenth Central Committee was held from 15 to 19 March, with 171 members and 107 alternate members in attendance. Also attending were members of the Central Advisory Commission, the Central Commission for Discipline Inspection, and "responsible comrades concerned" on a nonvoting basis. The plenum adopted Zhao Ziyang's Politburo work report and also the names of leading personnel of state organs and of the CPPCC, to be recommended to the Seventh National People's Congress (NPC) and the Seventh CPPCC, respectively. (Beijing, Xinhua, 19 March; *FBIS*, 21 March.) Just before the second plenum on 14 March, the party convened a meeting with non-CCP party members and other notables to discuss the personnel selections for the impending NPC and CPPCC meetings in keeping with the policy of carrying out "consultations and dialogue among the people" (*BR*, 28 March–3 April).

The first session of the Seventh NPC was held in Beijing from 25 March to 13 April. Of the 2,970 newly elected and approved delegates to the new NPC, 684 are workers and peasants, 697 are intellectuals, 733 are party or government officials, 267 serve in the PLA, and 49 are returned overseas Chinese. Of the total, 1,986 are CCP members. Of the total, 15 percent represent the minority ethnic groups, compared with 13.5 percent in the previous NPC. Women deputies number 634, accounting for 21.3 percent, an increase over previous representation. The average age is 52.9 years, which is slightly younger than before, and the educational level has improved, with 56 percent of the new deputies having received higher education. (*BR*, 28 March–3 April.)

Acting Premier Li delivered the Report on the Work of the Government at the opening session (complete text in *FBIS-China Daily Report Supplement*, 28 March). Li summarized the work of the preceding five years, noting an average annual economic growth rate of 11.1 percent. The per capita net income of peasants increased from 270 yuan in 1982 to 463 yuan in 1987, with an average annual growth rate of 8.6 percent, adjusted for price increases; that of urban residents increased from 494.5 yuan in 1982 to 916 yuan in 1987, with an average annual growth rate of 6.3 percent, adjusted for price increases. Foreign trade saw an average annual increase of 14.7 percent, with the total import and export volume reaching $82.7 billion in 1987. But Li also acknowledged problems including the rise of prices, which has led to the lowering of the standard of living for some urban residents and the continued irrationality of the price system.

For the future, Li projected a 7.5 percent average annual growth rate to the year 1992, roughly the same as set forth in the current Seventh Five-Year Plan. He said that the following guideline is to be firmly grasped:

Regard reform as dominating the overall situation and integrate reform and development still more closely, so that the two can match and stimulate each other still better; seriously implement the strategy of long-term stability in economic development; focus still more on the development and reform of science and technology and education; speed up the development of the export-oriented economy in the coastal regions; further promote the economic prosperity of the whole country and enhance the level of modernization; while speeding up and deepening the economic structural reforms, actively and steadily carry out political structural reforms; step up the building of socialist democracy and the legal system, to consolidate and develop the political situation of stability and unity; vigorously step up the building of socialist spiritual civilization centered around economic construction, to provide the ideological guarantee and brain power support for economic construction; and gradually form an excellent social atmosphere suited to the demands of socialism.

Li Peng's report was endorsed by a resolution of the NPC, but only after more than one hundred changes were made in it, prompted by suggestions made by the delegates. Aside from dozens of changes in wording, there were added more-detailed analyses, explanations, and demands concerning agriculture, transport and communications, education, intellectuals, and regional autonomy in minority nationality inhabited areas (Xinhua, Beijing, 13 April; *FBIS*, 13 April).

On 8 April, the NPC elected Yang Shangkun president of the PRC and Wan Li chairman of the NPC's Standing Committee. Also elected were nineteen vice-chairmen, the general secretary, and

135 members of the NPC Standing Committee. The latter were selected from 144 candidates, making this the first time in the history of the NPC that there was a competitive election for its Standing Committee.

On the following day, it elected Li Peng premier and Yao Yilin, Tian Jiyun, and Wu Xueqian, vice-premiers. Also, Yang Shangkun and Zhao Ziyang were elected vice-chairmen of the Central Military Commission. Additionally, Ren Jianxin was elected president of the Supreme People's Court, and Liu Fuzhi, procurator general of the Supreme People's Procuratorate. (*BR*, 18–24 April.)

On 12 April, the NPC appointed 44 State Council members. The new council consists of the premier, three vice-premiers, nine state councillors, and one general secretary, as well as 39 ministers, the governor of the People's Bank of China, and the auditor general. The council members were, on average, younger and better educated than those appointed in 1983. The average age of the thirteen principal leaders is 61. (*BR*, 25 April–1 May.)

Among the several resolutions passed by the NPC were those on the State Council's plan for National Economic and Social Development in 1988 (and the report on the draft plan delivered by Vice-Premier Yao Yilin), on the state budget for 1988 (and the report on the implementation of the 1987 state budget and the draft 1988 state budget delivered by State Councillor Wang Bingqian), on the work of the Sixth NPC, on the "Law of the People's Republic of China on Industrial Enterprises Owned by the Whole People," on the "Law of the People's Republic of China on Chinese-Foreign Contractual Joint Ventures," on the establishment of a committee to draft the basic law of the Macao special administrative region (SAR), and on approving the establishment of Hainan province and the Hainan special economic zone. Haikou was designated the seat of the provincial government, which will administer three cities and sixteen counties as well as the Xisha, Nansha, and Zhongsha islands and the reefs and waters around them. (Ibid.)

Premier Li Peng and his three vice-premiers faced a press conference attended by more than four hundred Chinese and foreign reporters following the conclusion of the NPC session. Some of the questions were tough (even some of the Chinese journalists were aggressive), and the new premier was subsequently criticized for a less than adroit handling of some of them. (See Marlow Hood, "New Prime Minister Li Finds It Tough at the Top,"

Hong Kong, *South China Morning Post*; *FBIS*, 14 April.)

The draft of the basic law for the projected Hong Kong SAR was published both in China and in Hong Kong on 28 April with the objective of soliciting views from the public. The draft, consisting of a preface, ten chapters with 172 articles, and three annexes, had taken nearly three years to complete (full text in *BR*, 9–15 May).

On 5 April, Huang Xinbai, a member of the State Education Commission who is in charge of Chinese students abroad, denied reports that China will drastically reduce the number of students it allows to study overseas, especially in the United States. He said that he expected that the numbers of both state-financed and privately financed students would stay the same. (Beijing, AP; Honolulu, *Star-Bulletin*, 6 April.)

The government issued an extraordinary warning on national television on 11 June urging universities to control campus unrest and punish severely those who violate school discipline (Beijing, *WP* Service; Honolulu, *Sunday Star-Bulletin*, 12 June). But student unrest remained a prominent feature of life. Authorities did move swiftly to deal with the murderer of a graduate student at Beijing University in June, which had resulted from lax security on campus. There was little disposition to respond to economic grievances or political demands.

China gave complimentary coverage of the swift return by Taiwan authorities of a hijacked CAAC Boeing 737 airliner to the mainland in mid-May. The plane was returned to Xiamen less than twelve hours after the hijacking, with its eleven crew members and 105 passengers. (Beijing, Reuters, 14 May; *NYT*, 15 May.)

In June, the Central Committee's Organization Department revealed that the party had enrolled 12.85 million new members over the past nine years, bringing the membership to 47 million. Persons below the age of 35 account for two-thirds of the total recruited every year; by the end of 1987, 27 percent of the party membership belonged to the 18–35 age group. Although applicants for party membership have increased each year, numbering eight million in 1987, there is concern that some persons are admitted into the party because of their educational level or personal fame "to the neglect of their political and ideological quality." (Beijing, Xinhua, 22 June; *FBIS*, 23 June.)

The inaugural issue of *Qiushi* was published on 1 July, the 67th anniversary of the CCP. This new theoretical journal is under the Central Party School and displaces *Hongqi*, which was under the Central Committee and which, it is said, made it "inconvenient" at times to discuss some problems. (Juan Chi-hung, Beijing, *Wen Wei Po*, Hong Kong, 1 July; *FBIS*, 1 July.) Later in the year it was announced that beginning in March 1989 a new party magazine, *Dangjian yanjiu* (Studies on Party Building), would begin publication, to be run by the Party Building Research Center of the Central Committee's Organization Department. (Beijing, *People's Daily*, 5 November; *FBIS*, 9 November.)

Beijing's reaction to the Thirteenth Congress of the Kuomintang (KMT) Party on Taiwan, held 7–13 July, was a measured one. In reference to the continued stress on the "three no's policy" (no contact, no negotiation, and no compromise) and other rhetoric against the CCP, Zhao Ziyang commented that leaders of the KMT made remarks not in line with the current situation. "We expected them to make such remarks," Zhao said. "They had to do so, but they did also have some positive ideas." It was noted that the KMT leadership's draft statement on policies toward the mainland was criticized at the congress for being too conservative. In the end, the KMT agreed to allow Taiwanese residents to continue to visit relatives on the mainland, with restrictions relaxed somewhat according to circumstances. Also, the applications of mainlanders to visit sick relatives or attend funerals on Taiwan are to be handled on a case-by-case basis. The reshuffle in personnel at the congress was bigger than the policy adjustments. Although the policymaking core of the KMT remained basically the same, twelve new individuals joined the 31-member standing committee of the Central Committee, reducing its average age from 71 years to 67 years. Meanwhile the average age of the newly elected 180-member central committee fell from 69 years to 58 years. The elections were by means of ballot, and many reform-minded younger members enjoyed strong support. (Xiao Jing, *BR*, 25–31 July.)

Professor James Hsiung reported high-level interest in Beijing in forming a coalition government while renouncing the use of force if the KMT did not proceed with independence. Although Professor Hsiung denied being a messenger on this matter, KMT authorities rejected the idea. (See Terry Cheng, Hong Kong, *South China Morning Post*, 18 August; *FBIS*, 22 August.)

In the meantime, a nongovernmental Taiwan Studies Society was founded in Beijing to promote research on Taiwan and encourage academic exchange between the mainland and the island. Huan

Xiang, general secretary of China's Institute of International Affairs, was named director of the new society. Chen Yicun, president of the Institute of Taiwan Studies of the Chinese Academy of Social Sciences, and Wong Man-fong, deputy general secretary of the Hong Kong branch of the NCNA, are also on the staff of the society (*FBIS*, 22 August). It had been reported in June that Wu Xueqian had joined the Taiwan Affairs Group of the Central Committee and would take charge of the work on Taiwan affairs of the State Council and relevant government departments (Li Ta, Hong Kong, *Kuang Chiao Ching*, 16 June; *FBIS*, 17 June).

Beijing noted with interest a proposal put forward after the KMT's Thirteenth Party Congress by the 33-member KMT Central Evaluation Committee headed by Chen Li-fu. It proposed "reunification of China through Chinese culture" and joint establishment of a committee to promote an industrial plan to develop economic cooperation before finally proceeding to reunification by means of "consultation on political coalition." (See *BR*, 19–25 September; Chen Long, "Take the Mission of Revitalizing China as a Common Understanding," *Shijie jingji daobao*, 5 September; *FBIS*, 22 September.)

Soon afterward, the CPPCC National Committee in Beijing established the Association for the Promotion of the Peaceful Reunification of China. Eight chairmen were elected to the new organization, along with 24 advisers and 48 standing council members. Xu Shangyuan was named general secretary and Jin Xiaoqi, deputy general secretary. It issued a constitution and a declaration on reunification. It also sent a telegram of sympathy to Hu Chiu-yuen, a Taiwan legislator and honorary president of the China Reunification League, who was at the time visiting the mainland without authorization and who had just been expelled from the KMT for having done so. (Beijing, Xinhua, 22 September; *FBIS*, 26 September.)

Interestingly, the overseas edition of the Beijing weekly *Outlook* was quoted as saying in its 30 October issue: "If everyone regards China's reunification as their duty, then all problems can be resolved through negotiation. Even the problems of the military (threat of invasion) and the Four Cardinal Principles, repeatedly raised by the Taiwan authorities, can be discussed." This may have been the first intimation by a PRC publication that the Four Cardinal Principles were "negotiable." (Tokyo, *Kyodo*, 29 October; *FBIS*, 31 October.)

At the end of October, it was reported that nearly 330,000 Taiwan residents had visited the Chinese mainland since the ban on visiting was lifted by Taiwan authorities in November 1987 (Beijing, Xinhua; *FBIS*, 31 October). On 12 September, the first Taiwan passenger ship arrived in Shanghai; its passengers left Jilun (Keelung) Port on 9 September, then sailed to Naha, Okinawa, where they transferred to the vessel that took them to Shanghai. (Beijing, Xinhua, 12 September; *FBIS*, 13 September.)

In late July, Xinhua reported that the Central Committee had agreed to a proposal made by its Organization Department to gradually dissolve the leading party groups in all organizations under the State Council. The Central Committee recently agreed similarly to a proposal by the Central Discipline Inspection Commission to gradually dissolve the discipline inspection groups under the leading party groups and posted by the CDIC in organizations under the State Council. (Beijing, Xinhua, 31 July; *FBIS*, 1 August.)

Xinhua reported in August that the structural reform-related establishment and readjustment of all organizations and institutions directly under the Central Committee had been basically completed. The organs under the Central Committee were now reported to be the General Office, the Organization Department, the Propaganda Department, the United Front Work Department, the International Liaison Department, the Political Structural Reform Research Office, the Rural Policy Research Center, departments of the Central Advisory Commission, departments of the Central Commission for Discipline Inspection, the Work Committee of departments under the Central Committee, the Work Committee of the state departments of the Central Committee, the Central Party School, *Renmin ribao*, the party History Research Center, the party Literature Research Center, and the Central Compilation and Translation Bureau.

These reforms were said to have been carried out in accordance with the basic principle of separating the functions of the party from those of the government and with the object of changing functions, drawing a clear-cut line of demarcation between the responsibilities of the party's work organizations and the government organizations, streamlining the relations between the party work departments, improving the relations between the party and mass bodies, and forming a compact and highly efficient working system. (Beijing, Xinhua, 21 August; *FBIS*, 22 August.)

The new party History Research Center replaces

the previous unit. Also dissolved was the Commission for Collecting Party Historical Data. Hu Sheng, president of the Chinese Academy of Social Sciences, heads the new party History Research Center. (Beijing, Xinhua, 20 August; *FBIS*, 22 August.)

The Politburo met in Beidaihe 15–17 August and decided on a preliminary strategy on economic reform in the next five years aimed at solving the "glaring problems" in the price structure, reducing state interference in business, and attacking public corruption and waste (Beijing, *WSJ*, 19 August; Beijing, *China Daily*, 20 August; *FBIS*, 22 August). But the announcement, by reaffirming commitment to further price liberalization, reportedly led to eight days of panic. Retail prices in cities during July were up 24 percent from a year ago, and this was an official statistic that probably understated inflation by as much as half. Throughout China, consumers wary of the rapidly increasing inflation withdrew bank deposits in order to buy TV sets, refrigerators, and washing machines. This was accompanied by a general breakdown in financial discipline among enterprises and local governments.

Within days, the State Council announced a freeze on major price increases for 1988 and 1989.The State Council's move in responding directly to the public's alarm contradicted the Politburo's decision. It also confirmed speculation that Zhao Ziyang's effort to push forward with price reform was encountering stiff resistance. (Adi Ignatius, Beijing, *WSJ*, 1 September.) Zhao undoubtedly suffered some political losses in these developments; he and his advisers had underestimated the problem. (See also Robert Delfs, Beijing, *FEER*, 29 September.)

An internal Central Committee circular distributed in August to newspapers and broadcast media carried a warning not to report foreign events in any way that might aggravate domestic unrest. This appeared to be another indication of official concern regarding domestic unrest in China because of inflation and corruption. (Marlowe Hood, Beijing, *South China Morning Post*, 6 September; *FBIS*, 8 September.) A conference of heads of public security departments and bureaus at the end of June decided on a series of measures to deal with increasing serious public security problems, including establishing select mobile armed police forces in the major cities and regions; organizing patrol police in a number of cities; releasing personnel from the armed police of all provinces, autonomous regions, and municipalities to establish mobile forces; and enhancing the work of collecting information and increasing the capacity of its transmission (Hong Kong, *Wen Wei Po*, 28 August; *FBIS*, 29 August).

The Central Committee convened a "democratic consultative conference" in Beijing from 13 to 17 September for leading persons of the various satellite parties and other notables and a forum for economists based in Beijing from 13 to 15 September to solicit opinions on a tentative plan for price and wage reform. (Beijing, Xinhua, 17 September; *FBIS*, 19 September.)

A party central work conference was convened 15–21 September, attended by 217 leading officials from central departments of the party, government, and army and from the provinces, autonomous regions, municipalities, and the military regional commands. The conference decided that during the next two years the focus of reform and construction would be on improving the economic environment and rectifying the economic order. (Beijing, Xinhua, 22 September; *FBIS*, 22 September.) On 24 September, the Politburo endorsed this theme and the work report that expressed it, which was to be delivered to the impending Central Committee plenum.

The Thirteenth Central Committee held its Third Plenary Session in Beijing, 26–30 September, attended by 165 full members and 103 alternate members. Members of the Central Advisory Commission and the Central Commission for Discipline Inspection, as well as leading officials from relevant departments, also attended on a nonvoting basis. Zhao Ziyang's report to the plenum on 26 September dealt with three major issues—improving the economic environment and rectifying the economic order, promoting comprehensive reform systematically and under unified leadership, and strengthening party leadership. (Full text is in *BR*, 14–20 November.)

The communiqué of the plenum also indicated that the emphasis on reform and construction in the next two years is to improve the economic environment and straighten out the country's economic order. It explained that a major effort is required to reduce total social demand and curb inflation to put an end to confusion in economic activities, "especially in the sphere of circulation." Approved in principle was a preliminary program for price and wage reform that is to be implemented over the next five years. Also, close attention is to be given next year to enterprise reform, in order to separate government administration from enterprise management and to further improve the contract responsibility system. Experiments are to be made in implementing the share-holding system "with public ownership remaining predominant," and new enterprise groups were to be developed on a trial basis. (Beijing, Xinhua, 30 September; *FBIS*, 30 September.)

On 23 September, the PLA adopted a new military ranking system, which was soon conferred on officers at the various levels. This followed the conferral of ranks on several million enlisted men over the previous several days. New uniforms and rank insignia were to be worn by almost all PLA personnel by 1 October. (Beijing, Xinhua, 22 September; *China Daily, FBIS*, 23 September.) Earlier, on 1 August, more than 100,000 PLA officers changed from military uniform to civilian attire, becoming the first group of civilian staff in the PLA (Beijing, Xinhua, 30 July; *FBIS*, 2 August).

In September the Central Disciplinary Inspection Commission published guidelines on dealing with violations of party discipline that had been issued in July 1987 for circulation within the party only. The new publication was regarded as another effort to increase the "transparency" of party work. It followed by two months the announcement by the Ministry of Supervision of its provisional regulations on dealing with corruption, bribery, tax evasion, blackmail, and other violations of administrative discipline, after it had set up corruption report centers and hotlines for reporting corruption throughout the country. (Hu Sigang, Beijing, *China Daily*, 9 September.)

Some 1,974 procuratorates, including 26 at the provincial level and 130 at the prefectural level, have opened such centers since the first one appeared in Shenzen in March. By the end of September, more than 44,000 cases had been reported by citizens to these new facilities. Over half of the cases involved economic crimes such as embezzlement, bribery, tax evasion, profiteering, and speculation, while 3,300 of them, it is reported, dealt with the violation of the democratic rights of citizens. (Beijing, Xinhua, 19 October; *FBIS*, 20 October.)

In October, the party newspaper reported that the CCP expelled more than 25,000 "degenerate" members in 1987, while a total of 150,000 were punished with party discipline. In the six years between 1982 and 1987, 177,000 members were expelled from the party. (Beijing, *People's Daily*, 12 October; *FBIS*, 14 October.)

On 13 October, Xinhua announced that a review of thousands of state companies was in the offing as part of a campaign against corruption. Party and government officials were barred from managing companies, and government departments were banned from setting up companies with their operating funds; those already operating were to be disbanded. (Beijing, Reuters, 13 October; *NYT*, 14 October.)

Also in October, the State Council announced a decision to tighten control over the purchasing power of party and government bodies above county level, people's organizations, state and collective institutions, and capital construction firms with a staff of more than 200 persons. Spending is to be cut this year and next by at least 20 percent of last year. Spending quotas are to be given and subjected to an administration planned by the state. Also, the number of commodities under special state control will be increased from 19 to 29 items, including automobiles, sofas, carpets, air conditioners, cassette and video recorders, cameras, and various electronic appliances. Moreover, institutions and enterprises are to cease using high-class tourist hotels for meeting places and banquets. (*BR*, 31 October–6 November.)

On 11 October, Zhao Ziyang presided over another forum called by the Central Committee to solicit opinions and suggestions from leaders of the non-CCP parties on "some vital issues the country now faces." Zhao said that such meetings were to be held at irregular intervals every year. (Beijing, Xinhua, 11 October; *FBIS*, 12 October.)

On 16 October, the Institute of High-Energy Physics of the Chinese Academy of Sciences, located in the western outskirts of Beijing, reported another major nuclear technology breakthrough. China's first high-energy accelerator, an electron-positron collider, successfully became operational on its first try that morning. The project, regarded as China's largest scientific research engineering project, was initiated on 7 October 1984. (Beijing, Xinhua, 19 October; *FBIS*, 20 October.)

It was reported in November that Dazhai, the village in Xiyang County, Shanxi Province of the slogan "Learn From Dazhai" fame, had made great efforts in recent years to eliminate "leftist factors" and set up a new management system. A household contract responsibility system was established in the spring of 1983. In 1987, the total income of the villagers was more than 800,000 yuan, and their per capita pure income, 653 yuan. These figures were said to be, respectively, 3.3 and 2.5 times those of

1978. The latter percentage figure incidentally, is the same as the average per capita income increase for rural areas as a whole for the 1978–87 period. (*BR*, 7–13 November, 14–20 November.)

Minister of Personnel Zhao Dongwan announced on 26 October that China is drawing up new provisional regulations on state civil servants and will submit them for public discussion and examination at an appropriate time. He noted that China has adopted a series of reforms in personnel management since 1979, "but all this falls short of the requirements for the furtherance of both economic and political structural reforms" and hence the need for a comprehensive, well-coordinated reform of the personnel system. The new civil service system will be introduced nationwide within ten years and is to be adopted by central and provincial levels of government before 1992. (Beijing, Xinhua, 26 October; *FBIS*, 27 October.)

Another massive anti-Chinese demonstration took place on 5 March in Lhasa in which at least nine people were killed. The incident cast doubt on the success of Chinese efforts to restore calm following the violent riots of the previous October. The March rioting, which spread to Qinghai province north of Tibet (Daniel Southerland, Beijing, 10 March; *LAT*, 11 March), led Chinese authorities to restrict access to Tibet for foreign reporters and individual tourists. In an effort to reach a solution, the Dalai Lama in June conceded that, in return for otherwise complete autonomy for Tibetans, China could retain control over Tibet's foreign policy and defense (Karl Wilson, Hong Kong, *South China Morning Post*, 16 June; *FBIS*, 16 June). Beijing followed this in September with a proposal for talks with the Dalai Lama, allowing him to choose the time and place, to formally renounce Tibetan independence. In late October, the Dalai Lama responded that talks could be held in Geneva in January 1989 (Hong Kong, AFP, 29 October; *FBIS*, 31 October). However, on 10 December, another riot took place in Lhasa in which one lama was killed and thirteen other people were injured, underscoring the continuing restiveness in Tibet (*BR*, 19–25 December).

Auxiliary and Front Organizations. The Seventh National Committee of the CPPCC held its first session in Beijing, 24 March–10 April, for the most part concurrently with the Seventh NPC. Li Xiannian, the 79-year-old former president of the PRC, was elected chairman of the CPPCC's Seventh National Committee. A total of 28 people were

elected vice-chairmen. Zhou Shaozheng was re-elected general secretary. A total of 280 members were elected to the standing committee. (*BR*, 18–24 April.) The CPPCC has a membership of 350,000, about 64 percent of whom are not members of the CCP (*BR*, 4–10 April).

The Communist Youth League (CYL) held its twelfth national congress, 4–8 May, with about two thousand delegates in attendance, representing 56 million CYL members nationwide (*BR*, 16–22 May). Song Defu (42) was re-elected first secretary of the CYL at the plenum of the new CYL Central Committee on 11 May (Beijing, Xinhua, 11 May; *FBIS*, 11 May).

The All-China Women's Federation held its sixth national congress from 1 to 6 September, with 1,069 elected delegates and another 114 specially invited women present. Nearly three-quarters of the delegates were members of the CCP, while another 24 belong to the CYL. Chen Muhua was elected chairwoman. (Beijing, Xinhua, 31 August, 6 September; *FBIS*, 1, 7 September.)

The All-China Federation of Trade Unions (ACFTU) held its eleventh national congress 13–26 October. China's 530,000 grassroots trade union organizations reportedly have a combined membership of 130 million workers (*BR*, 7–13 November). Of the 93,365,000 ACFTU members, 1,500 attended the congress. On 26 October the congress elected a new 229-member executive committee, chosen by secret ballot from among 240 candidates. At the first meeting of the new eleventh ACFTU executive committee on the following day, Ni Zhifu was re-elected president, along with seven vice presidents and a nineteen-member presidium. (Ibid.)

Various satellite parties held major meetings during the year. For example, the China Democratic League held its sixth national congress in October, with 880 delegates present. Reportedly, more than 300 of the league's 81,000 members belong to either the NPC or the CPPCC. It was also reported that the number of members of the eight satellite parties had reached about 270,000 by the end of 1987. (Beijing, Xinhua, 8 October; *FBIS*, 11 October.) The China Democratic League elected 250 members and 50 alternate members to form its new central committee (Beijing, Xinhua, 16 October; *FBIS*, 19 October).

International Views and Positions. Foreign investment in China rose slightly in 1987 from 1986. The Ministry of Foreign Economic Relations and Trade said that China had approved the establishment of 2,230 foreign-invested enterprises with a total contract value of U.S. $3.68 billion, a rise of 1.3 percent. However, in 1987, investment from Hong Kong fell to less than 70 percent of the total after having been more than 80 percent of the total in the entire 1979–85 period. (Ellen Salem, *FEER*, 4 February.)

In the first half of 1988, China's total import and export values exceeded U.S. $43.2 billion, 22.4 percent higher than in the same period of 1987, according to Chinese customs figures released on 8 July. China's trade deficit dropped from U.S. $1.97 billion to U.S. $1.15 billion during the same period. However, the trade deficit is estimated at U.S. $910 million if the value of nontrade commodities is excluded. The trade deficit in 1985 had been U.S. $14.9 billion, U.S. $12 billion in 1986, and U.S. $3.75 billion in 1987, although 1987 actually saw a trade surplus of U.S. $1.88 billion, if the import and export values of nontrade commodities are deducted. (*BR*, 25–31 July.)

China's foreign exchange reserve reached $15.23 billion at the end of 1987, an increase of $4.85 billion over 1986 (Beijing, *People's Daily*, 10 October; *FBIS*, 14 October).

The overseas edition of the *People's Daily* said that China has built a new modern naval base in what is described as the largest artificial harbor in the Far East. The facility took eleven years to build and has four berths, two docks, and an operation area of 128,000 square meters. The location was not disclosed. (Beijing, Xinhua, 11 February; *FBIS*, 11 February.)

Foreign Minister Qian Qichen explained China's positions on a number of international issues at the Forty-third Session of the U.N. General Assembly on 28 September (excerpts in *BR*, 24–30 October).

China conducted a successful test in carrier rocket launching at sea between 14 and 27 September. The carrier rocket was launched by a China-made nuclear submarine from beneath the surface of the water. (Xinhua, 27 September; *FBIS*, 27, 30 September.)

A total of 445 Chinese athletes took part in the Twenty-fourth Olympic Games in Seoul, Korea. The Chinese athletes won five gold medals, eleven silver medals, and twelve bronze medals. (Beijing, Xinhua, 3 October; *FBIS*, 11 October.)

Relations with the Soviet Union. Sino-Soviet relations had been gradually improving in recent years, but 1988 saw a dramatic improvement, with

agreement reached by year's end on a summit meeting in 1989 between Deng Xiaoping and Mikhail Gorbachev.

A summit had been pursued by Gorbachev since 1985, but the Chinese regularly rebuffed the suggestion. The year 1988 began on the same note. In an interview with *Liaowang*—his first ever with a Chinese news organization—the Soviet general secretary repeated his proposal of 27 November 1987 (which had been rebuffed) to meet with Deng Xiaoping. He called a summit meeting with China a "logical development" in improving relations between the two countries. In view of the apparent seriousness of Soviet intentions to withdraw from Afghanistan during 1988, some thought that Gorbachev's proposal would be appealing to Deng. (Combined News Services, *The Honolulu Advertiser*, 11 January.) However, this was not the case. The Chinese Foreign Ministry responded by saying "Chairman Deng Xiaoping has made quite clear the conditions for a high-level meeting between China and the Soviet Union. It is the strong aspiration of the international community that Vietnam should withdraw all its troops from Kampuchea (Cambodia) promptly" (Beijing, AP; Honolulu, *Star-Bulletin*, 12 January).

In fact, Chinese leaders, furious with *Liaowang* for running the unauthorized interview with Gorbachev, banned all other publications from republishing the piece. The government was embarrassed by the article and reportedly forbade Chinese reporters from conducting interviews with foreigners without prior official permission. (*Honolulu Advertiser*, 16 January.)

In *Pravda* on 23 January, influential commentator Vsevolod Ovchinnikov wrote that both the Soviet Union and China "have the possibility to facilitate the success of the negotiations between Prince Sihanouk and Hun Sen (their second round of talks was on 20–21 January) to promote contacts between the opposing sides." He added that he saw no sense in linking a Sino-Soviet summit to 1990, when Hanoi has promised to withdraw its troops from Cambodia. (Sophie Quinn-Judge, Moscow, *FEER*, 4 February.) Soviet deputy foreign minister Igor Rogachev told reporters on his arrival in Beijing for talks on 27 August that he thought a breakthrough on the Cambodia issue was imminent, although his Chinese counterpart, Tian Zengpei, more cautiously said, "We hope to make some headway." (Beijing, AP; Honolulu, *Sunday Star-Bulletin & Advertiser*, 28 August.)

On 29 February, a Chinese Foreign Ministry

spokesman said that former Soviet foreign minister Andrei Gromyko's recollection and related description of his visit to China in 1958 in his recently published memoirs do not square with the facts (Beijing, Xinhua, *FBIS*, 29 February). On 2 March, spokeswoman Li Jinhua stepped up the criticism, saying that "many of the recollections and descriptions in Gromyko's memoirs relating to the history and the present state of Sino-Soviet relations do not square with the facts." Gromyko says in his memoirs that Mao Zedong had proposed during Gromyko's secret 1958 visit that U.S. troops be lured into China and then wiped out by Soviet nuclear weapons. (Beijing, AFP; *FBIS*, 2 March.)

The initial Chinese comment on the historic Soviet party conference in Moscow (26 June–2 July) bluntly noted that although Soviet leaders recognize the need for political and economic change, they are confronting serious difficulties and resistance (Edward A. Gargan, Beijing, 29 June; *NYT*, 30 June).

The Chinese have been undertaking their own review of Stalin, which led to the publication in the no. 5 issue of *Shulin* of the full text of Khrushchev's secret report to the Twentieth CPSU National Congress in February 1956 denigrating the crimes of Stalin. This unedited report had yet to be made known to the Soviet public. Also the no. 8 issue of *Shijie Zhishi* gave a detailed account of the great purges of the 1930s. (Chiu Sheng, "China, Too, Is Reassessing Stalin," *Ta Kung Pao*, Hong Kong, 30 June; *FBIS*, 1 July.)

In his speech on 16 September in Krasnoyarsk in eastern Siberia, Gorbachev said that the Soviet Union stands for the full normalization of relations with China and is ready to start preparations without delay for a Sino-Soviet summit meeting. Gorbachev said that last month's talks on Cambodia had "expanded in a certain way the zone of mutual understanding on this issue and contributed to improving Soviet-Chinese relations." (Beijing, Xinhua, 16 September; *FBIS*, 19 September.) An important turning point had been reached.

The third round of Sino-Soviet boundary talks ended in Moscow on 31 October after an agreement was reached on the alignment of the major part of the eastern boundary line between the two countries. Both sides agreed to continue talks on the areas that remain in dispute. The two sides also began discussing issues along the western boundary line during the eleven-day session. The Chinese delegation was led by Deputy Foreign Minister Tian Zengpei. (Moscow, Xinhua, 31 October; *FBIS*, 31 October, 2 November.)

Hence, on 14 October, Deng Xiaoping revealed during his meeting with visiting Finnish president Mauno Koivisto that he would hold a summit meeting with Soviet leader Gorbachev sometime during the next year (Seth Faison, Beijing, *South China Morning Post*; *FBIS*, 14 October).

Additional momentum was given this plan as a result of a successful visit to Moscow by Chinese foreign minister Qian Qichen on 1–3 December. Qian, who was the first Chinese foreign minister to visit the Soviet Union since Zhou Enlai in 1956, met with his Soviet counterpart Eduard Shevardnadze. At a press conference in Moscow, Qian described the talks, which focused on Cambodia and on the normalization of Sino-Soviet relations, as having been "resultful." (*BR*, 12–18 December.)

Relations with the United States. The year began on a somewhat tense note. A Chinese Foreign Ministry spokesman announced on 31 December 1987 that two Chinese diplomats who had been recently expelled from the United States for "engaging in activities incompatible with their diplomatic status" were victims of a frame-up (*BR*, 11–17 January). Also darkening the relationship was Chinese unhappiness with recent U.S. criticism (congressional and private sources, not the Reagan administration) of Chinese human rights abuses in Tibet. The Reagan administration, however, had been critical of Chinese arms sales to Iran, particularly Silkworm missiles that were seen as a threat to U.S. forces in the Persian Gulf, and had stopped its liberalization of high-technology exports last year as a consequence. The slow pace of U.S. steps to ease these restrictions irritated the Chinese. Furthermore, a legal challenge in the United States to a U.S. Defense Department rule led to the admission by the department that although it was trying to develop military cooperation with Beijing, it has secretly kept China on a list of hostile nations without informing the Department of State, which regards China as "friendly and nonaligned." The Pentagon explained that China was "incorrectly deleted from the list in 1987 and it will be returned to the list in the next edition." The court case in question challenged whether U.S. regulations favored China over Vietnam. (Nayan Chanda, Washington, *FEER*, 4 February.)

On 2 February, China and the United States signed a four-year agreement limiting the annual growth rate for China's textile exports to the United States to 3 percent. China has become America's largest supplier of textiles and apparel even though a relative newcomer to the textile export industry. Shipments in major import categories such as cotton, silk, and ramie had been growing at an annual rate of 19 percent, far outdistancing growth by established exporters such as South Korea and Hong Kong. Nevertheless, China accused the United States of protectionism for imposing quotas on Chinese textiles. The two countries also differ widely on the status of their bilateral trade. The United States claimed a deficit of $3.5 billion in 1987, whereas China claimed a deficit of $1.8 billion. However, the Chinese trade figures do not include the large amount of goods it sends to Hong Kong for shipment to the United States. (Beijing, AP; Honolulu, *Star-Bulletin*, 2 February.)

Foreign Minister Wu Xueqian, in a rare news conference on 6 April, said that China's growing arms sales abroad were conducted responsibly and that strict measures had been undertaken to prevent Iran from acquiring Chinese missiles. Western observers estimate that China sells about $2 billion worth of weapons abroad each year, ranking it among the top five arms exporters in the world. Wu said that his recent visit to the United States dissipated "the bad atmosphere" that had developed between the two countries in the past year. (Kathy Wilhelm, Beijing, AP; Honolulu, *Star-Bulletin*, Honolulu, 6 April.)

The estimated 1,500 Americans who reside in Beijing were warned on 9 June by the U.S. embassy of a possible attack by terrorists from an unidentified third country. The embassy had been informed of the Middle East–related threat by high-level public security officials. On 11 June, the Chinese government said that it would ensure the safety of foreigners in China, whether they are stationed there or visiting. (Beijing, AP; Honolulu, *Sunday Star-Bulletin & Advertiser*, 12 June.)

On 22 June, Hu Qili, during the visit of Gus Hall, general secretary of the Communist Party of the United States (CPUSA), announced that relations had been restored between the CCP and the CPUSA, terminating the 20-year suspension of such relations (Beijing, Xinhua; *FBIS*, 22 June).

Secretary of State George Shultz visited China in July, meeting Deng Xiaoping who acknowledged that the development of U.S.-China relations in recent years has been relatively smooth. Shultz said that his discussions with Chinese leaders on Cambodia were "very fruitful and worthwhile." He discussed the China reunification issue with Zhao Ziyang. (*FBIS*, 18 July.)

Relations Elsewhere. In Indochina, despite sharp military engagements between China and Vietnam both along the border and in the South China Sea, the focus of concern remained Cambodia, where China sought Vietnamese military withdrawal from the country and the establishment of a coalition government in Phnom Penh. Meetings earlier in the year in Paris between Prince Sihanouk, representing the resistance coalition in Cambodia, and Hun Sen, the prime minister of the Phnom Penh regime, shifted to an informal regional "cocktail party" meeting in Bogor, Indonesia, in late July. Beijing agreed with Sihanouk's proposal, which projected a four-way provisional government in which there would be international supervision of the Vietnamese withdrawal and maintenance of peace. (*Asiaweek*, 15 July.) China also implied for the first time a softening of support for the Khmer Rouge by proposing a freeze on the military contingents of the resistance factions and suggesting that they not interfere with the voting process. The Khmer Rouge subsequently did not appear to reject the Bogor informal agreement that their regime not be allowed to return to power. (*Asiaweek*, 5 August.) During his visit to Beijing in late August and early September, Soviet vice–foreign minister Igor Rogachev agreed with the Chinese and ASEAN idea of a coalition government and on international supervision to monitor the power transfer, although the Vietnamese had not assented to the latter provision. (*Asiaweek*, 16 September.) China inaugurated an oceanographic station in the Spratly Islands in early August (Beijing, *People's Daily*; *FBIS*, 16 August).

China played a role in bringing about a cease-fire in the military confrontation between Laos and Thailand in January over territory in the Rhom Klao area. This success, along with a general improvement in relations, led to the exchange of ambassadors between China and Laos in May. The Chinese undertook to cease supporting insurrectionary forces in Laos. (*WP*, 24 May.)

Qian rejected an invitation by South Korea to establish diplomatic relations. Nevertheless, during the year both governments sought to broaden the relationship between the two countries, to the chagrin of both North Korea and Taiwan. Sino-South Korean trade continued to expand, the total of which was expected to reach $2.5 billion this year. As noted above, China participated in the Olympic Games held in Seoul.

The Chinese government and media criticized a remark by a Japanese cabinet minister, Seisuke

Okuno, on 22 April that "Japan has never been an aggressor nation." Prime Minister Noboru Takeshita subsequently acknowledged the 1972 Japan-China joint statement expressing Japan's responsibility for the sufferings it brought about on the Chinese people during wartime. (Tokyo, Xinhua; *FBIS*, 11 May.)

During his visit to China in August, Prime Minister Takeshita signed an accord designed to boost economic cooperation by encouraging Japanese businesses to invest in China. Takeshita referred to the agreement as "a new starting point." He said that Japan would lend China another 810 billion yen between 1990 and 1995. This will be the third major loan made to China by the Japanese government and is 10 billion yen greater than the total of the two previous loans of 1979 and 1984. (*BR*, 12–18 September.) As of the end of 1987 Japanese investment in China accounted for only 8.7 percent of total foreign investment in China, but the amount of Japanese investment during the first six months of 1988 was nearly double the figure for the same period in 1987. (Beijing, *LAT* Service; Honolulu, *Sunday Star-Bulletin & Advertiser*, 28 August.) China and Mongolia signed a treaty on the border system and on a solution to border issues between the two countries in Beijing on 28 November (*BR*, 12–18 December).

Indian prime minister Rajiv Gandhi visited China on 19 December, signaling a major improvement in Sino-Indian relations. Only a year ago the situation along the border had been tense and marked by a notable military buildup. Trade, which had been resumed in 1977 after having been suspended for fifteen years, reached a volume of only U.S. $144 million in 1986–87. But a new Sino-Indian trade protocol of 1988 set no ceiling on quotas and was aimed to encourage the increase of bilateral trade. Since 1981, China and India have held eight rounds of talks on the unsettled boundary question on an official basis, but little substantial progress has been registered (*BR*, 12–18 December). Both China and India agreed during Gandhi's visit to establish a group to take up the difficult border dispute. Both sides declared the visit a triumph and said that the boundary question was not to stand in the way of a new course of expanded ties that will end the cold war of two decades. (Jim Abrams, Beijing, AP; Honolulu, *Star-Bulletin*, 22 December.)

The section of the Karakoram highway lying on the Chinese side of the border linking China and Pakistan was completed and opened to traffic (Beijing Radio, 2 October; *FBIS*, 3 October).

The year ended on an unfortunate note. A week of racial violence in Nanjing began on 24 December when African students brought Chinese girlfriends to a dance, leading to a brawl followed by violent protests by thousands of Chinese youths who destroyed property in the students' dormitories. Afterward, 140 African students fled to the railway station but were prevented from leaving the city and taken instead to a factory guest house outside the city. Several U.S. students who had been with them were subsequently released. On 1 January 1989, several hundred police forced their way into the guest house, reportedly using truncheons and electric cattle prods. Several students were isolated as "troublemakers." (Nanjing, AP; Honolulu, *Sunday Star-Bulletin & Advertiser*, 1 January 1989.)

Stephen Uhalley, Jr.
University of Hawaii

India

Population. 816,828,360
Party. Communist Party of India (CPI); Communist Party of India—Marxist (CPM)
Founded. CPI: 1928; CPM: 1964
Membership. CPI: 479,000; CPM: 450,000
General Secretary. CPI: C. Rajeswara Rao; CPM: E. M. S. Namboodiripad
Politburo. CPI: 9 members: C. Rajeswara Rao, Indrajit Gupta, Indradeep Sinha, Jagannath Sarkar, N. Rajashekara Reddi, N. E. Balaram, M. Farooqi, A. B. Bardhan, Homi Daji; CPM: 12 members: E. M. S. Namboodiripad, B. T. Ranadive, M. Basavapunnaiah, Harkishan Singh Surjeet, Jyoti Basu, Samar Mukherjee, E. Balanandan, Nripen Chakravarty, Saroj Mukherjee, V. S. Achuthanandan, L. B. Gangadhara Rao, A. Nallasivian
Central Committee. CPI: National Council, 125 members; CPM: 70 members
Status. Legal
Last Congress. CPI: Thirteenth, 12–17 March

1986, in Patna; CPM: Thirteenth, 27–31 December, in Trivandrum

Last Election. 1984. CPI: 2.71 percent, 6 seats; CPM: 5.96 percent, 22 seats (out of 509 contested in 544-seat Parliament); CPM also dominates left-front governments in two Indian states (Kerala and West Bengal).

Auxiliary Organizations. CPI: All-India Trade Union Congress, All-India Kisan Sabha, All-India Student Federation; CPM: Centre for Indian Trade Unions, Kisan Sabha, Students' Federation of India

Publications. CPI: *New Age* (Pauly V. Parakal, editor); Indian-language dailies in Kerala, Andhra Pradesh, West Bengal, Punjab, and Manipur; CPM: *People's Democracy* (M. Basavapunnaiah, editor); Indian-language dailies and theoretical journals in Andhra Pradesh, Kerala, and West Bengal

The CPM. In December 648 CPM delegates and 50 fraternal delegates from sixteen countries gathered for the Thirteenth Party Congress. The venue for the colorful communist pageant was Trivandrum, the capital of Kerala and stronghold of the CPM-dominated Left Democratic Front (LDF) government. E. K. Narayanar, the LDF chief minister and CPM state party boss, spared no expense in hosting the congress. The city was festooned with huge propaganda posters and pictures of Marx, Lenin, and Stalin. Whereas the CPM still regarded Stalin as a member of the communist trinity, pictures of Mao—once a prominent feature at CPM gatherings—were nowhere to be seen. The noncommunist press noted that the CPM had pressured local businessmen to make cash contributions to the gala. By the time the opening gavel fell on 27 December, Trivandrum shopkeepers had exhausted their supplies of red cloth used for bunting (*India Today*, 15 January 1989). "If colour could be a measure of revolutionary fervor," one reporter observed. "Trivandrum today perhaps has more of it than Petrograd in 1917" (*Telegraph*, 29 December).

Although delegates voted unanimously to adopt the lengthy political resolution moved by Politburo member Ranadive, there was considerable behind-the-scenes wrangling over the tactical line the party should follow in the next election. One faction led by General Secretary Namboodiripad advanced a long-term strategy of building a "left and democratic alternative" to Congress-I. Under this formulation, ousting Rajiv Gandhi from power was only one tactical objective. A second and possibly more important objective was to construct an ideologically cohesive alliance of "antimonopoly, anticapitalist, and antifeudal forces." As Namboodiripad told the delegates, "The mere removal of Rajiv Gandhi will not be enough. The requirement of the day will be broad unity on the basis of a radical socioeconomic programme internally and anti-imperialism externally" (*Telegraph*, 1 January 1989). The upshot of this strategy was to preclude CPM cooperation with communalist parties, particularly the Hindu revivalist Bharatiya Janata Party (BJP), as well as with "bourgeois" parties willing to share a platform with the BJP. Parties suspected of compromising with communalist forces include the Lok Dal, Telegu Desam, and Assam Gana Parishad. Because the first two parties are constituents of the National Front, adoption of the Namboodiripad formula could limit or possibly preclude CPM cooperation with a sizable chunk of the noncommunist opposition.

CPM's alternative electoral strategy, dubbed the "all in opposition unity" line, was advanced by Ranadive and West Bengal party boss Jyoti Basu. They agreed that the despised BJP must be isolated in the larger interest of defeating the "agents of communalism and imperialism." They were unwilling, however, to jettison secular, bourgeois parties that would share an electoral platform and seat allotments with the BJP. In contrast to Namboodiripad's preoccupation with preserving ideological purity, the supporters of Ranadive and Basu placed equal emphasis on the immediate task of enhancing CPM electoral fortunes at the expense of Congress-I (ibid.).

The resolution adopted by the congress generally adhered to the line Namboodiripad laid down. The CPM agreed to work cautiously with opposition combines only as long as its constituent elements maintained a "secular, democratic character" (code words for treating the BJP as a political untouchable). The resolution recognized that the electoral victory of "right reactionaries" would be worse than a Congress-I return to power. Ideally the CPM hoped to fashion a "third front" composed of communist and left-wing forces that challenged Congress-I *and* the BJP. Party insiders conceded, however, that an alliance modeled after CPM state ministries in Kerala and West Bengal could not dislodge Congress-I at the national level. To make an impact, CPM needed the cooperation of noncommunist parties that commanded support in the Hindi heartland (*Hindu*, 2 January 1989).

Predictably, CPM speakers were unsparing in

their criticism of Gandhi's domestic policies. Ranadive, in his keynote speech, lambasted Gandhi for "compromising with communal and successionist forces and sacrificing national unity to gain electoral advantage" (*Indian Express*, 28 December). Ranadive accused Gandhi of coddling Sikh separatists in Punjab, Gurkha secessionists in West Bengal, and tribal insurgents in Tripura. Gandhi's economic policies were also castigated. According to CPM, the country faced multiple crises such as soaring inflation, rising unemployment, peasant landlessness, and a mounting debt repayment burden. Speakers railed against Gandhi's economic liberalization program that purportedly benefited the rich and opened the country to exploitation by multinational corporations. CPM remedies—radical land reform, stepped-up nationalization of private industry, military and economic support from socialist countries—broke no new ground.

The Thirteenth Party Congress made few organizational changes. Namboodiripad was elected to a fourth term as general secretary. The party's geriatric Politburo (average age over 70) added two members: Gangadhara Rao and A. Nallasivian. The election of two non-Bengalis to the Politburo probably reflected the party's sensitivity to charges that the CPM "red fort" in West Bengal dominated party affairs. The CPM Central Committee also accepted three new members. Lastly, the congress approved the formation of a five-man Central Secretariat. This intermediate tier in the CPM hierarchy will operate between the twelve-man Politburo and the 70-member Central Committee. Modeled after similar structures in the Soviet party and the rival CPI, the new secretariat was charged with implementing Politburo decisions and overseeing party functioning on a daily basis. Its members include Sunil Moitra, S. Ramachandran Pillai, P. Ramachandra, Sitaram Yechury, and Prakash Karat (*Times of India*, 30 December).

After adopting the political resolution and confirming the party leadership, the CPM congress closed its doors to the press to discuss internal party operations. According to fragmentary evidence gleaned by reporters, the 70-page political organization report expressed strong disapproval of the failure to expand the party's base of support beyond West Bengal and Kerala. The party claimed 450,000 members, an increase of 100,000 since the 1985 party congress. The "red fort" states, however, accounted for the lion's share of the growth. The report reaffirmed the CPM commitment, first advanced at the 1979 Salkia plenum, to expand the party apparatus into the Hindi belt. The economically depressed state of Bihar was targeted as the party's best hope for a political breakthrough in the region. In southern India, the CPM pledged not to oppose noncommunist ministries in Andhra Pradesh, Karnataka, and Tamil Nadu as part of a strategy of building on CPM strength in neighboring Kerala. The report claimed that CPM front organizations had registered seven million new members since 1985. Combined membership of CPM fronts totaled 22 million. Here again, most of the growth was in West Bengal, where the CPM continued to entrench itself, particularly in rural areas. Finally, the report noted no appreciable decrease in circulation for the various party organs. To spread the party's message, the congress authorized the establishment of a CPM news agency (*Times of India*, 1 January 1989).

On the international front, the CPM lived up to its reputation as a maverick communist party. Delegations from the Soviet Union and China attended the congress. One reporter noted that "though the Soviets and the Vietnamese were the clear favourites [of the congress], Bengal delegates appeared to prefer the Chinese team" (*Telegraph*, 29 December). Earlier in the year, CPM delegations conducted routine consultations in Beijing to strengthen ties with the Chinese party and to urge Chinese officials to work with Gandhi in reaching a peaceful settlement to the Sino-Indian border dispute. The party congress praised Gandhi's statesmanship in conducting an official visit to China the week before the congress, the first Sino-Indian summit in 30 years. General Secretary Namboodiripad warned prospective opposition partners such as Janata Dal not to make a campaign issue of Gandhi's accommodative policy toward China (*Telegraph*, 28 December).

The CPM stepped gingerly around the Soviet party. The party resolution praised Mikhail Gorbachev's policies of *perestroika* and *glasnost*; however, some West Bengal cadres regarded Soviet reforms as "an accommodation with capitalism" or even "revisionist" (ibid.). The appearance of Stalin's icon at the congress underscored the fact that sections of the CPM had serious reservations over the direction in which Gorbachev was leading his country. As late as May, the CPM denounced Gorbachev's anti-Stalin campaign—a posture the party conveniently avoided at Trivandrum. Soviet delegation head Gennadi V. Kolbin dismissed the Stalin controversy and insisted that individual communist parties were free to arrive at their own conclusions. In response to grumblings that the Soviet party was hedging its bets in India by maintaining party ties with the CPI and Congress-I, Kolbin pleaded that the Kremlin sought rapport with a broad spectrum of secular, anti-imperialist parties (*Telegraph*, 3 January 1989). In the final analysis, CPM organizers skillfully avoided the Byzantine debates over ideology that had plagued the party in the past. In domestic affairs the Thirteenth Party Congress eschewed divisive revolutionary rhetoric in favor of hard-nosed debates over political strategy and organization; in the international arena the central theme was "world peace," a noncontroversial slogan intended to unite the divergent communist elements in attendance.

In regional party affairs, CPM state organizations encountered a variety of challenges in 1988. In the pivotal state of West Bengal, the CPM is the senior partner of a four-party Left Front ministry that has survived in power for eleven years. Its partners (Revolutionary Socialist Party [RSP], Forward Bloc, and CPI) complained that CPM growth was increasing at their expense. Electoral support for their common adversary, Congress-I, stabilized at about 42 percent of the vote. The smaller parties accused CPM chief minister Basu of bypassing them in the allocation of state resources and seat allotments. During local *panchayat* elections in February, Basu became exasperated with his Marxist partners and allowed CPM candidates to stand for election against all challengers. The specter of intracommunist bickering led one columnist to compare the Left Front with "Calcutta's trams, an antiquated system that creaks along to its destination under the weight of more passengers than it can carry" (*India Today*, 31 October).

In October complaints over Basu's leadership surfaced when Jatin Chakraborty, the RSP minister of public works, accused his CPM chief minister of channeling state purchases of electrical equipment to a company that employed Basu's son. Basu, widely regarded as incorruptible, bristled at the charge, forced Chakraborty's resignation, and solicited the national party to come to his defense. Although the Bengal Lamps controversy did not precipitate an open breach in the Left Front, the episode pointed to growing rifts within the state's Marxist ranks. There were numerous reports during the year that simmering hostility toward CPM degenerated into physical clashes between rival Marxist cadres (ibid.).

In Kerala CPM coalition partners include CPI, RSP, Janata, and Congress-S. As in West Bengal, CPM detractors complained that a CPM shadow government, not the LDF ministry or the permanent civil service, made all important decisions in the state. The CPM, it was alleged, was packing the bureaucracy and courts with its own supporters. Since replacing a weak Congress-I coalition in 1987, Kerala's LDF ministry has been subjected to mounting criticism for its failure to come to grips with unemployment, communal violence, and a rising crime rate. Chief Minister Narayanar's standard response was to blame Gandhi for starving the state of central government funds, a charge often echoed in West Bengal. By year's end, the CPM hoped that the propaganda and profits generated by the Trivandrum party congress would bolster the LDF image.

The embattled Left Front ministry in the northeastern state of Tripura did not survive the year in office. Ethnic Bengalis, who constitute about 70 percent of the state's population, are the mainstay of CPM support. The state's tribal minority had been waging an insurgency against Bengali settlers and the Left Front ministry. On the eve of state elections in February, Gandhi toured the state to determine whether local authorities were capable of maintaining security in the face of insurgent threats to disrupt the elections. Mindful of the wholesale slaughter inflicted by tribesmen during a 1984 election in Assam, Gandhi declared the state a "disturbed area." Under this mechanism, New Delhi took over administration of the state and gave security forces a free hand in bringing lawless elements to heel. Gandhi promptly dispatched eight thousand army troops and 22,000 paramilitary personnel to the state to oversee the balloting. Simultaneously, his Congress-I state apparatus engineered an electoral alliance with the tribal-based Tripura Upajati Juba Samiti (TUJS) (*India Today*, 29 February).

Gandhi's intervention in defiance of the Left Front's protests won the support of the tribal minority and, more important, convinced fearful Bengali settlers that Congress-I was prepared to crush the insurgents and ensure the peace. By comparison, the Left Front appeared hesitant and weak. CPM chief minister Chakravarty condemned the introduction of troops as an "undemocratic step" and criticized Gandhi for courting the insurgent vote. The army's presence ensured a heavy voter turnout and a minimum of violence. When the votes were tallied, the Congress-I/TUJS coalition had secured 31 of 59 parliamentary seats, enough to dislodge the Left Front from power. The CPM setback in

Tripura provided the Trivandrum party congress with additional evidence of Gandhi's supposed "authoritarian" leadership style (ibid.).

The CPI. CPI electoral support is spread thinly across India, though the party does command pockets of support in Hindi-speaking states. Lacking a regional stronghold, the CPI has had to contest elections on the coattails of the CPM and noncommunist opposition parties. Since the late 1970s, CPI has followed the CPM lead in opposing Congress-I domestic policies while endorsing the general lines of Indian foreign policy. The strategy has had limited success. CPI controls only six seats in the national parliament; in Kerala and West Bengal, the CPI is a junior partner in CPM-dominated ministries. Only a handful of CPI legislators have managed to win office in other states.

Despite its weak electoral position, the CPI is a disciplined organization that remains a political force to be reckoned with. The CPI labor front, the All-India Trade Union Congress, controls large sections of the workforce in nationalized industries. Many of these enterprises rely heavily on Soviet purchases of their output. The CPI also publishes a wide variety of educational and propaganda materials that are either subsidized or supplied outright by the Soviet Union. Soviet political support for the CPI (offset in recent years by the Kremlin's courtship of CPM and Congress-I) gives the party organizational muscle it would not otherwise have.

The CPI grappled with many of the same political dilemmas encountered by the CPM. During quarterly strategy sessions of the National Council, the party's inner circle began framing the draft political resolution that will be presented at the CPI Fourteenth Party Congress scheduled for Calcutta in March 1989. Like the CPM, the CPI seeks to isolate the BJP and contest elections with opposition partners deemed sufficiently secular and anti-imperialist. Gupta, the second in command of the CPI hierarchy, is reportedly in line to succeed Rajeswara Rao as general secretary.

In an article in the party organ *New Age* entitled "Why the Left Opposes Rajiv Gandhi's Policies" CPI Politburo member Daji outlined the themes on which the CPI will probably contest the 1989 election. Leveling a blistering attack on Gandhi's "dalliance" with communalists, Daji claimed the Congress-I government "stinks with new exposures every day of corruption in high places." In economic policy, Gandhi's "open door invitation to foreign capital and transnationals . . . was undermining the national policy of self-reliance. The public sector," he opined, "is being slowly dismantled." (10 April.)

Several weeks later another hard-hitting article in *New Age* elaborated on the national security implications of Gandhi's economic policies. Although careful to praise Gandhi for pursuing close ties with the Soviet bloc, the author lamented, "Recently some vacillations have come to the fore . . . like allowing American penetration of our defense industry in the name of acquiring technology. This is fraught with grave dangers. The democratic movement needs to be extremely vigilant about such vacillations" (1 May). The ingenious combination of "anti-imperialism" and economic self-sufficiency could become a CPI campaign staple.

Throughout the year the CPI and the CPM attempted to mend their differences by identifying areas of agreement and sponsoring joint rallies. In March the two parties organized a massive *bharat bandh* (work stoppage) to showcase their ability to mobilize supporters for political action. As many as one million supporters—the largest demonstration in recent memory—converged on New Delhi to call for Gandhi's resignation. In July the CPI and the CPM sponsored a sparsely attended rally in the Punjabi city of Jullunder. The convention urged central security authorities to stamp out Sikh terrorism at all costs. The CPI, in particular, had good reason to call for tough police measures. For years the terrorists have targeted CPI cadres for assassination. At the national level, the CPI and the CPM regularly convene a coordinating committee to iron out differences and improve communication.

Attempts to forge communist unity in advance of elections foundered as both parties engaged in political mudslinging. In September CPM heavyweight Harkishan Singh Surjeet questioned whether the CPI was a bona fide communist party. In an article in the pro-Moscow newspaper *Patriot* he wrote, "If the [Indian] communist movement had not split [in 1964], the CPI would have degenerated into a third-rate undivided force and there would have been none to bear the banner of the working class" (12 September). The attack prompted a CPI rejoinder in *New Age*, where CPI Politburo member Rajashekara Reddi noted little progress in communist unity in recent years. He then dredged up the hoary history of the 1964 split, the CPM's lingering "devotion to Maoism," and the party's insufficient respect for the Soviet party. "The main obstacle to communist unity," he wrote, "is the narrow-minded attitude of the CPM leadership to such unity. They glorify the split and perpetuate it...We hope the CPM leaders would do a bit of introspection" (25 September). The CPI and the CPM seemed unable to come together or to part company once and for all. In a telling commentary on communist unity efforts, the CPI did not send a delegation to the CPM congress in December.

On the international front, a CPI delegation visited China in March, the first such contact in almost 30 years. The Chinese party assumed the traditional Soviet position of encouraging the CPI and the CPM to settle their differences. Both sides admitted that disagreements arose during the talks, but both agreed to continue the dialogue. It is unclear whether a Chinese delegation will attend the CPI party congress in March. The CPI continued to lend unswerving support to Gorbachev's reforms and to every facet of Soviet foreign policy. When Gorbachev conducted a whirlwind visit to India in December, however, Indian communists were not accorded the customary audience with the Soviet leader. The Soviets pleaded that time constraints did not allow such a meeting. Observers speculated that, with national elections on the horizon, the Soviets were more concerned with bolstering Gandhi's electoral fortunes than catering to his domestic communist critics.

Other Communist Parties. Small communist parties exist on both the left and the right of the CPM and the CPI. On the right is the All-India Communist Party (AICP), established by S. A. Dange, a Lenin Peace Prize recipient who left the CPI in a disagreement over its decision to abandon the united front policy with the Congress Party. The AICP has been virtually ignored by the Soviets because of its anemic electoral performance. Moreover, its separate existence conflicts with the Kremlin's long-standing desire to unify Indian communists. In 1986 the moderate Communist Marxist Party emerged in Kerala when the national CPI leadership refused to sanction alliances with communal parties. The party is not a constituent of the LDF ministry and shows few signs of life. Yet another CPI renegade, the Indian Communist Party, was formed in 1987 by Central Committee member B. M. Kalyanasundaram. His death this past year will probably spell the end of the short-lived organization. The CPM has not suffered mass defections in recent years, although the CPI occasionally claims that disaffected CPM cadres are gradually returning to the parent party (see, for instance, *New Age*, 7 August).

To the left of the CPI and the CPM are a profusion of radical Maoist parties and underground cells, collectively known as Naxalites. India's ultra-leftists have lost the appeal they once enjoyed during the heyday of China's Cultural Revolution. Some parties continue their violent activities, while others have joined the political mainstream and field candidates in local elections. The most notorious band is the People's War Group operating in the Telengana region of Andhra Pradesh. Other pockets of Naxalite support can be found in backward tribal districts of West Bengal, Bihar, and Tamil Nadu. Without the backing of China or other foreign powers, Indian Maoists have been reduced in recent years to a local security menace.

Douglas C. Makeig
U.S. Department of Defense

Note: The opinions expressed in this article are the author's own and do not necessarily reflect those of the U.S. government or any U.S. government agency.

Indonesia

Population. 184,015,906
Party. Indonesian Communist Party (Partai Komunis Indonesia; PKI)
Founded. 1920
Membership. 1,000–3,000, with less than 10 percent engaged in organized activity (*World Factbook*, 1988)
General Secretary. Tomas Sinuraya, Moscow wing; Jusuf Adjitorop, Beijing wing
Leading Bodies. N/a
Status. Illegal
Last Congress. Seventh Extraordinary, April 1962
Last Election. N/a
Front Organizations. None identifiable in Indonesia
Publications. *Tekad rakjat* (People's will), published abroad, no data on editor

During 1988, Indonesian officials cited the appearance of former party activists in leadership positions in provincial political councils as one symbol of the feared resurgence of the PKI. Publication of a book in which the late President Sukarno was described as a dedicated Marxist touched off widespread public debate over the lessons of recent Indonesian history.

Leadership and Party Organization. Sinuraya, secretary of the party's Central Committee, and Satiadjaya Sudiman, listed as member of leadership, PKI, are the identifiable leaders of the pro-Moscow wing of the exiled party (*WMR*, September, May). There are no hard data on the number of PKI adherents of either the Moscow or the Beijing wing of the exiled party. Early in the year Indonesia's intelligence chief said that several young Indonesians abroad had recently joined the party; of the 35 Indonesians who attended the International Congress of Communist Parties in Budapest in January, many were new faces previously unknown to the security services. (*FEER*, 3 March.)

There is no way to estimate the number of PKI supporters in Indonesia. Some 33,000 former PKI detainees released in 1973 are still listed in Category B—under surveillance and prohibited from joining the armed forces or political parties or serving as teachers, religious leaders, journalists, or government functionaries. The 500,000 Category C ex-detainees include those involved in the failed 1948 communist uprising at Madiun. Some Category Cs are permitted to work in government agencies but remain subject to official surveillance (*Kompas*, 4 June; *FBIS*, 10 June).

At least two former party leaders were executed in mid-November 1987. One was Sukarman, a former Politburo member arrested in 1968 and convicted in 1976; the other was identified only as Soewandi. (*WMR*, May; *New Yorker*, 6 June; Reuters, 31 October.) On 16 October, Giyadi Wignysuharyo and Sukarjo, two former guards of President Sukarno said to have been directly involved in the assassination of generals in the 1965 coup attempt, were executed twenty years after their conviction (Djakarta, *Berita Buana*, 1 November; *FBIS*, 7 November). A government spokesman explained that the delay between conviction and execution was to give the condemned men an opportunity to renounce their behavior and to seek information about the widespread PKI network. A leader of Indonesia's Legal Aid Foundation urged clemency for the eleven aging party members still on death row. (Reuters, 9 December.)

Domestic Party Activities. Information about the activities of the banned PKI remains inferential.

A vigorous campaign against suspected PKI infiltration into government and the media began just before the March parliamentary session and continued through the October congress of Golkar, the ruling government party. Some observers speculated that the campaign was a political ploy by the army aimed at ensuring that Sudharmono, after he was elected vice president, would not also retain the chairmanship of Golkar. Whatever its origins, the campaign gained momentum and several senior officials lost their jobs on suspicion of having communist links (*FEER*, 10 November).

The campaign, which began with generalized warnings against PKI infiltration, was fanned by reports that the chairman of a Golkar regional executive council in Payakumbuh, West Sumatra, who was also a member of the provincial assembly, was a former PKI member (*Tempo*, 9 April; *FBIS*, 12 May). Although dismissed from office and declared a communist activist, no legal action was taken against him (*Djakarta Post*, 18 October; *FBIS*, 20 October). In April, two former PKI members were reported trying to establish a new political party, and shortly before the Golkar congress, another regional party official was uncovered as a former PKI member. *Jayakarta*, an independent daily linked to retired armed forces officers spearheaded the campaign with daily interviews with retired generals who warned of the communist threat and the PKI's ability to operate without tangible organizational form. (*Tempo*, 9, 23 April, 7 May; *FBIS*, 12 May; *Financial Times*, 1 November.)

A government spokesman dismissed the possibility of PKI men in strategic positions because all officials in top posts had passed security clearance. As for the PKI man in a key post in Payakumbuh, the official said that such clearances are not always perfect. Category C ex-detainees were allowed to work in government agencies because the government still needed their specialized skills. Government spokesmen sought to restrain the spate of charges of communists occupying strategic government posts and urged the press and public not to make random accusations but to send written reports to the authorities. (*Tempo*, 7 May; *FBIS*, 12 May.) Announcing plans to recheck the dossiers of all former detainees linked to the September 1965 abortive coup, Minister Sudomo said that although some PKI remnants had gone back to their old political activities, those activities had not yet reached an alarming state (*Kompas*, 4 June; *FBIS*, 10 June). Vice President Sudharmono, reacting to rumors that he had past leftist links, took the unusual step of holding a press conference to deny any involvement with communism. He then told the opening session of Golkar that he would no longer remain its chairman. (Reuters, 25 October; *FEER*, 10 November.)

President Suharto's speech opening the Golkar congress stressed the dangers of communism and its inappropriateness for Indonesia. He warned against allowing the return of communism and of liberalism with its system of free competition and reminded his audience of the upheaval and tension those ideas had caused in Indonesia before the introduction of the present new order. (BBC, Djakarta Home Service, 20 October.)

It was in this charged atmosphere that widespread debate was touched off by a book in which Sugiarso Surojo, a former intelligence officer, claimed that Indonesia's founding father, Sukarno, had been a dedicated Marxist since his student days in the 1920s and was deeply involved in the abortive coup of 1965. The author of *Who Sows the Wind, Reaps a Tempest* said he was moved to write the book in reaction to the revival of the Sukarno image in the 1987 election campaign when bands of youths in red costumes paraded pictures of the late president. (*FEER*, 6 October; *Tempo*, 8 October; *FBIS*, 13 October.) In a letter to the editor of *Tempo*, former government minister Oei Tjoe Tat, characterized by the authorities as a banned leftist, suggested that those who now insist on putting "Bung Karno on trial" should study current books about him by foreign scholars, many of whom have called him the greatest Indonesian patriot. The attorney general said the book was un-Indonesian because it spoke ill of a dead elder but chose not to ban it because it did not cause public unrest. Although several ministers agreed with him, others, including Suharto, took pains to remind the public that Sukarno was constitutionally relieved of the presidency following parliamentary censure of his role in the coup. President Suharto devoted his Armed Forces' Day speech to an attack on communism and called on the nation to review its recent history to avoid a repetition of the mistakes of the past. The failed coup of 1965 was a national tragedy, Suharto said; by acknowledging past mistakes, the country could prevent the same mistake. "The lesson to be learned from past history can thus bring a positive meaning and not be a continuing burden." (Hong Kong, AFP, 5 October; *FBIS*, 6 October.) The governor of the National Defense Institute, General Subiyakto, said the strong reaction to the book was

proof that communism still has strong influence in Indonesian society (BBC, 31 October).

The independent daily *Merdeka* was censured by the government for running an editorial on the anniversary of the coup attempt that "clearly clouded" the PKI's involvement in the coup (*Merdeka*, 6 October; *FBIS*, 13 October). The editorial, "Reviewing History," said the coup was the result of a confrontation of international forces on Indonesian soil and that the United States had targeted Indonesia. Although acknowledging that the coup involved the communists, the editorial referred to "complicated interactions and contradictions such that the mind cannot easily digest them" (*Merdeka*, 30 September; *FBIS*, 13 October). The government statement censuring the paper commented that "the trial sessions of the Extraordinary Military Tribunal, open to the public, where PKI leaders admitted that it was the PKI that planned, masterminded, and launched the abortive coup on 30 September 1965, are proof that can easily be digested by the mind" (*Merdeka*, 6 October; *FBIS*, 13 October).

In June, President Suharto ordered that stern action be taken against publications espousing communism, Marxism, or Leninism (*Merdeka*, 2 June; *FBIS*, 8 June). On 9 August, the attorney general announced that he had banned three books because they propagated communist ideas. The banned books were the novel *Gadis Pantai* by Pramudya Ananmta Toer, said to contain propagandist dialogues opposing the authorities, discrediting religion, and encouraging revolutionary acts; the novel *Siti Mari* by Mufti, said to propagate animism and atheism; and *Teologi Pembebasan* by Wahono Miliprawiro, charged with propagating Marxism. An earlier book by Pramudya, *Rumah Kaca*, was also banned because the stories were said to imply social discrimination, although it does not mention communism specifically. (Djakarta Domestic Service, *FBIS*, 9 August.) In October, the information minister announced that the government was investigating several national press publications for allegedly employing former communists or for articles "permeated" with communist teachings (AFP, *FBIS*, 6 October). At the same time, 37 Information Ministry employees were dismissed on the grounds of being former communists, and the minister of public works announced that his ministry was investigating 744 employees for the same reason (*FEER*, 20 October).

International Views, Positions, and Activities. The PKI's two principal leaders abroad, Sinuraya and Sudiman, continued to appear as the spokesmen of the party's pro-Moscow wing, publishing in *WMR* and taking part in *WMR*-sponsored meetings. As noted above, 35 Indonesians attended the International Congress of Communist Parties in Budapest in January.

Sinuraya participated in the *WMR* roundtable discussion "The Struggle for Peace, Security, Democracy, and Social Progress in the Asia-Pacific Region and the Communists." In his speech "Don't Harbor Illusions," he identified the nuclear arms race "fanned by the Pentagon" as the common issue facing the people of Asia. In Indonesia, he said, the party is frustrated in its efforts to rally public opinion in support of mass actions for peace because all the forms of mass action, such as demonstrations, rallies, and festivals, are outlawed by the military regime and because the mass media are mostly controlled by the military regime and pro-imperialist circles. "Working underground, our small and weak party still lacks its previous ability to organize the popular masses for open and huge mass actions," he said. To be able to attract the masses, the PKI believes it must show the interrelation between the cause of peace and the cause of improving social life and establishing democracy. Sinuraya concluded that success depends not only on the actions of the parties in each country but also on their interaction throughout the region. (*WMR*, September.)

Sudiman's article "To Ease Regional Tensions" reflected the questions posed for the PKI by the Indonesian government's increasing economic and trade ties with the bloc. Obliged to note with approval the recent talks between Indonesia's foreign minister and Soviet leaders, he affirmed the PKI's endorsement of peaceful coexistence and cooperation of countries with different social systems. But he pointed to the Association of Southeast Asian Nations' (ASEANs') close ties to the capitalist West and "their biased and conservative attitude to the socialist world . . . Will the governments of the region's countries be able and ready to throw off not only the economic and political but also the psychological yoke in order to pursue a consistent and independent foreign policy?" he asked. Although agreeing that the development of relations between the ASEAN countries and the socialist world "objectively assists in the normalization of the overall political situation in Southeast Asia," he concludes that this cannot be interpreted to mean a possible end to the class struggle. (*WMR*, May.)

Sudiman took part in *WMR*'s international symposium in Prague on Lessons of Socialist Orienta-

tion, where he posed the question: is it correct to characterize as national democratic those regimes that try to dominate communist parties or downright persecute them? (*WMR*, June).

The Indonesian government's approach to resumption of full diplomatic ties with the People's Republic of China (PRC) continued to reflect widespread suspicion that the PRC had a major role in the 1965 coup attempt. The official position remained that until the PRC admits and apologizes for its involvement in the 1965 coup initiated by the PKI and gives its promise to avoid such involvement in the future, Indonesia will not resume full relations. (*Antara*, *FBIS*, 19 February.) In his accountability speech to the parliament on 1 March, President Suharto reiterated that position, and asked that the PRC confirm that it would not help remnants of communist elements in Indonesia and would extradite Indonesian nationals now residing in China if Djakarta so requested. PRC deputy foreign minister Liu Shuqing said the Indonesians could return to Indonesia if they were willing to do so, but it was difficult to force them to go back to Indonesia because they had not violated Chinese laws. He said there were about one thousand Indonesians residing in China, most of them elderly and ailing. He said they had come to China for medical treatment but after the 1965 aborted coup did not want to return to Indonesia. He denied that a number of PKI members had attended the recent congress of the Chinese Communist Party (CCP). Liu said that the last time representatives of foreign communist parties were invited to a CCP congress was in 1956. Asked whether China recognized the PKI, Liu said that there was no problem of recognition because his country did not have any contacts with the PKI. (*Antara*, 13 April; *FBIS*, 14 April.) Liu's comments provoked several editorial comments, one of which challenged his statement that the government of China had not known about the attempted coup until after the event. "As far as we know," the editorial stated, "the Chinese government in Beijing called all Indonesian leaders who had been previously invited to Beijing and informed [them] of a new government in Djakarta and asked them to sign a declaration of support." (*Indonesia Times*, 15 April; *FBIS*, 22 April.) Another paper commented that because the exiled PKI leaders living in Beijing received special treatment and facilities from the PRC government and the CCP, it was logical to conclude that PKI remnants in Indonesia would receive similar assistance, presumably from the

CCP, once the PRC opened an embassy in Djakarta (*Suara Pembaruan*, 13 April; *FBIS*, 22 April).

Wu Xingtong, spokesman for the International Liaison Department of the CCP Central Committee, told a press conference that the CCP now has no relations with the PKI. The CCP only maintains moral relations with communist parties in Southeast Asia and other countries, he said. Such moral relations between political parties in different countries are a normal phenomenon, he continued, adding that the PRC does not interfere in another party's or another country's internal affairs by capitalizing on its relations with that country's political party. (*Zhongguo Xinwen She*, 17 May; Beijing International Service in Indonesian, *FBIS*, 18 May.)

A Philippine newspaper reported indications of increased cooperation between former PKI members and the Communist Party of the Philippines (CPP). The PKI members reportedly joined in a CPP campaign against U.S. bases in the Philippines. More interesting, the report said the PKI members involved were formerly in the pro-Beijing wing but had switched to the pro-Soviet wing. Therefore they have "become mediators between the Soviet side and the CPP" due to "sensitive" Soviet-CPP relations. (*Berita Buana*, 24 October; *FBIS*, 27 October.)

Jeanne S. Mintz
Washington, D.C.

Japan

Population. 122,626,038
Party. Japan Communist Party (Nihon Kyosanto; JCP)
Founded. 1922
Membership. 470,000 (*World Fact Book*, 1988); industrial workers are 65.6 percent of the members; 38.3 percent are women (*WMR*, April).
Central Committee Chairman. Kenji Miyamoto
Presidium Chairman. Hiromu Murakami
Central Committee. More than 200 members
Status. Legal
Last Congress. Eighteenth, 26–28 November 1987

Last Election. July 1986; 9 percent of popular vote in House of Representatives, 12 of 250 seats in House of Councillors, 27 of 512 seats in House of Representatives
Auxiliary Organizations. All-Japan Student Federation, New Japan Women's Association, All-Japan Merchants' Federation, Democratic Foundation of Doctors, Japan Council of Students, Japan Peace Committee, Gensuikyō (Japan Council Against Hydrogen and Atomic Bombs)
Publications. *Akahata* (Red banner), daily circulation 550,000, Sunday circulation 2,500,000, total readership over 3,000,000 in addition to frequent special issues and a poster called *Akahata Photo News* published twice a month in 90,000 copies; *Bulletin* (of the Central Committee of the JCP), information from abroad; *Gakusei shimbun* (Student newspaper), weekly; *Shōnen shōjo shimbun* (The boys' and girls' newspaper), weekly; *Zen'ei* (Vanguard), theoretical journal; *Gekkan gakushū* (Monthly studies), *Josei no hiroba* (Women's tribune), *Gurafu konnichiwa—Nihon kyōsanto desu* (Hello, we are the JCP), *Asu no nōson* (The countryside tomorrow), *Bunka hyōron* (Cultural review), *Keizai* (Economics), and *Rōdō undō* (Workers' movement)—all monthlies; *Sekai seiji: Rompyō to shiryō* (International politics: critical reviews and materials), fortnightly

During 1988, the JCP remained a Eurocommunist party, as it has been for some years. It stayed internationalist in its perspective and activities, though its contacts were not particularly intense with other Eurocommunist parties. Relations, as has been the case for some years, were strained with the People's Republic of China; ties were better with the Soviet Union. The JCP continued to oppose "bloc politics," advocating (and practicing) the independence of communist parties.

The JCP continued to do well at the polls, though there was no important election in Japan during 1988. Because this does not conform to the party's popularity in opinion polls or its success in recruitment, the explanation is that the JCP is a protest party and thus receives considerable protest votes. Party leaders announced a 500,000 membership goal in 1977; this goal is still to be reached. The share of younger members is down. According to party directives, 50 percent of members do not read party documents.

The prospects for the JCP's working together with other opposition parties to form a "united front" or to try to win an election and form a coalition government are fewer than in previous years. In recent years, the JCP has claimed, with some justification, that it is the only "progressive" party and that the other opposition parties in reality support many right-wing policies. Even the Japan Socialist Party (JSP), along with other opposition parties, has aligned against the JCP. Although this makes the JCP unique, it also reduces its already dim hope of ever winning political power.

The JCP, which still devotes considerable energy to antinuclear and peace movements, in 1988 spent much time blocking a tax bill proposed by the ruling Liberal Democratic Party (LDP) and on a scandal involving not only the LDP but the other opposition parties.

Party Leadership and Meetings. Kenji Miyamoto, at 80, remains the JCP's top leader and spokesman and was active throughout the year, notwithstanding his age. Tetsuzo Fuwa, elected to the newly created post of vice-chairman of the Central Committee in 1987 following a stroke, was Miyamoto's second. Fuwa was also active throughout the year. Hiromu Murakami, as Presidium chairman, runs the party's day-to-day operations.

The second plenum of the Central Committee of the JCP convened 26 May for three days at party headquarters in Tokyo. Central Committee chairman Miyamoto gave the introductory speech; Presidium chairman Murakami presented the presidium report.

In his speech Miyamoto discussed the new Noboru Takeshita cabinet, which he described as a "loyal successor" to the Yasuhiro Nakasone government. He pointed disparagingly to the growing U.S.-Japan security relationship and efforts to encourage China to favor the alliance, using the pretext of the threat of growing military power in the region. He also discussed the Takeshita government's effort to pass a new, indirect tax, the "power program" between the JSP and Komeitō Party, and their "making up" with the other opposition parties in an "anticommunist alliance." Miyamoto accused the LDP of violating its campaign promises regarding taxes and called for dissolution of the Diet and a general election to decide the tax issue. He accused the other opposition parties of cooperating with the LDP and of splitting the opposition and the antinuclear weapons movements. (*Bulletin*, June, p. 4.)

Speaking on the world situation, Miyamoto drew attention to "favorable conditions" on the international scene: the signing of the intermediate-range nuclear forces (INF) treaty, rising demands within the antinuclear peace movement for the elimination of nuclear weapons, nonnuclear victories in New Zealand and Denmark, and the withdrawal of Soviet troops from Afghanistan. Miyamoto declared that a number of dogmas "have begun to come apart." Here he referred to the general crisis of capitalism theory, the practice of regarding a specific party as the world leader, unconditional support for that party as the touchstone for proletarian internationalism, and the parroting of slogans put forward in Communist Party of the Soviet Union (CPSU) documents. (Ibid.)

Miyamoto applauded the Kremlin's decision to get out of Afghanistan and noted that the invasion was a "major political error" and one that the JCP had warned about. He pointed out that the JCP and the CPSU had signed a joint statement before the invasion in which the two subscribed to the policy of "allowing each country the right to determine independently the course of social progress and not exporting revolution." (Ibid.) Miyamoto recalled "abuses heaped on the JCP" in past years for not supporting the Kremlin's policies vis-à-vis Afghanistan (ibid).

In the context of expressing his approval of *perestroika*, Miyamoto underscored past points of difference with the CPSU, particularly regarding issues that now vindicate the JCP view: JCP refusal to call the Soviet Union a "developed socialist country," its position that the elimination of nuclear weapons can be pursued during an anti-imperialist struggle (that it does not have to follow), criticism of the view that the CPSU must be regarded as the "vanguard of the world communist movement," and the infallibility of the CPSU (*Bulletin*, June). Miyamoto also chided the policy of *glasnost'* as failing to lead to a publishing of the JCP's "correct" views (ibid).

Miyamoto blasted the CPSU for its recent summit talks with the JSP and what he called the "beautification" of the JSP by Soviet leaders. He pointed out that the JSP, based on the 1980 JSP-Komeitō accord approving of the U.S.-Japan military alliance and its support of LDP policies, made it an "imperialist party" that should not be praised by the CPSU. (*Bulletin*, June.) Miyamoto declared that the JCP is the only "vanguard party" whereas the JSP regards the JCP as an enemy party. Further attacking the JSP, he quoted from Mikhail Gorbachev's speech in Vladivostok regarding the Soviet Union's advocacy of disbanding military groupings as being in contraposition to the JSP's position. (Ibid.) He also suggested that the CPSU's relationship with the JSP is an international matter, not just a matter of relations between the two parties (*Bulletin*, June).

Regarding INF, Miyamoto asserted that the JCP and the CPSU agreed that the treaty did not eliminate the need to struggle against the "cling to nuclear weapons forces" advocates, that further work must be done to solidify public opinion in all countries for the elimination of nuclear weapons, that the Hiroshima-Nagasaki appeal should continue, and that international joint efforts must be made to support a second Wave of Peace. (Ibid.) The JCP applauded consultations based on the 1984 JCP-CPSU joint statement on these issues.

Other important JCP meetings in 1988 included a rally against the consumption tax in September and the Twenty-ninth *Akahata* Festival in October. At the latter meeting Central Committee chairman Miyamoto criticized the "LDP's consumption" tax and the Japanese imperial system. In the context of the emperor's deteriorating health, he declared that "the emperor is the person responsible for the barbarous politics of that dark age and equally he is the person who cannot be freed from the highest responsibility for the war of aggression." (*Akahata*, 10 October.) Miyamoto called for a national election as a referendum regarding the consumption tax and urged *Akahata* workers to get ready for elections next year (ibid.).

Domestic Affairs and Issues. The major domestic issues for the JCP during 1988 were the formation of a national union organization that excluded the JCP, relations with the other opposition parties, the consumption tax, and Japan's defense policy. JCP leaders also made an issue of police authority to use wiretaps against party members and the Recruit scandal that involved the other political parties, especially the ruling LDP.

The formation of the Japanese Private Sector Trade Union Confederation (Rengō) from 62 already existing unions with a total membership of 5.5 million continued to threaten JCP union support because Rengō bans dealings with the JCP (see *YICA*, 1988). Also, industry unions that join Rengō can only back—one or all—the four anticommunist opposition parties. However, according to Yoshinori Yoshioka, former editor in chief of *Akahata* and a JCP foreign affairs expert, Rengō formed at an unpropitious time in view of low wage increases (*FEER*, 14 January, p. 18). He predicted that Rengō's "right-wing leadership" will alienate the labor movement and that many will refuse to officially

"sign on" when the time comes and may even join with the United Labor Union Council (Toisu Rosokon), which supports the JCP (ibid.). Yoshioka also opined that changes in the labor front and the dissolution of unions that have automatically supported the JSP or the Democratic Socialist Party would lead to power struggles with Komeitō for trying to tear union support away from the other two. This could only work to the advantage of the JCP, he said. (Ibid., p. 19.)

Its bad relations with the other opposition parties has made the JCP seem unique, and if Rengō fails to unify Japan's unions the JCP will probably benefit. The success of Rengō, however, will likely result in a coalition of labor unions that eschew the JCP. The final results are yet to be seen.

The JCP's feud with other opposition parties accelerated during the year. Recriminations were especially strong toward the JSP as JCP leaders assailed even the left wing of the JSP, the Socialists Association. A JCP spokesman referred to it as a group of "flunkyist followers" that engaged in "slandering the JCP." (*Akahata*, 25 December 1987.) Party leaders pointed out that the JSP had "veered to the right since 1980," aligning with the LDP against the JCP and other progressive forces. This, according to the JCP, justified its working with and supporting the National Progressive Forces, which were "established seven years after the JSP's alliance with Komeitō against the JCP." The National Progressive Forces, the JCP claims, comprise 2,850 organizations with a combined membership of 4.5 million people. (*Bulletin*, February.)

During 1988 the JCP continued to rail against the government's policy of higher defense spending and what party leaders called a "violation of the Constitution." They particularly cited exceeding the 1 percent of gross national product barrier—a limit set some years ago by the LDP. JCP leaders attacked the ruling LDP, mentioning Prime Minister Takeshita by name, for flaunting the Three Nonnuclear Principles and Japan's "nuclear-free policy" and called Takeshita a liar in reference to these issues. (*Akahata*, 13 June.) JCP leaders also assailed the policy of nuclear deterrence, peace through strength, and the U.S.-Japan defense alliance (*FBIS*, 16 August).

Regarding the INF treaty, the JCP declared that the United States decided to sign the treaty for two possible reasons: "the need to cope with antinuclear public opinion and the people's struggle in the United States" and "selfish calculations by the Reagan administration" (meaning it would help the Republicans win the election) (*Akahata*, 13 June). The JCP applauded the INF but stated that it should go much further and advocated more complete disarmament and the ending of military blocs in the world (ibid.).

The JCP continued to oppose the new indirect tax, a consumption or value-added tax, proposed by the LDP. JCP leaders contend that the tax is unfair and that it is an additional tax burden placed on poor people. The party called for the dissolution of the House of Representatives and a general election to decide the issue. (*FBIS*, 16 June.) When the vote was finally taken the JCP boycotted the session (along with the JSP) (*Japan Times*, 17 November). The other opposition parties voted against the bill, which passed anyway.

Late in the year, the JCP became active in investigations of wrongdoing in the the Recruit scandal—a case involving the Recruit Cosmos Company selling shares to politicians before they were put on the market. Mitsue Higashinaka, JCP member of the House of Representatives, called the Recruit case the "largest political scandal in Japan's history" and demanded a thorough investigation. (*Japan Times*, 3 December.) Higashinaka accused former Prime Minister Nakasone as well as other high officials of the LDP currently in office (ibid.). At the same time, he pointed out that no member of the JCP was implicated in the scandal, which also hit the other opposition parties.

In a special Diet investigating committee meeting, JCP and JSP Diet members were allowed to question witnesses. JCP representatives said after the meetings that the failure of officials of Recruit Cosmos to disclose the names of purchasers of its stock before it was publicly floated broke the Diet's Testimony Law and deserved criminal investigation. (*Japan Times*, 20 November.) JCP spokespersons also accused the LDP of dragging its feet in the investigation (ibid.). Meanwhile the party published a list of shareholders of the First Finance Company, voicing suspicion that this company contemplated distributing its shares to politicians, bureaucrats, and other influential people as Recruit Cosmos had done (*Japan Times*, 19 November).

The JCP won points with the public on both the tax issue (even though taxes were to be reduced overall) and the Recruit Cosmos scandal. The media also sided with the JCP on its demands for investigations in the Diet regarding the scandal and its criticism of LDP leaders. (*Japan Times*, 2 December.)

When Emperor Hirohito became ill in September, the JCP refused to sign registers wishing him well and started a campaign against the "glorification of the emperor." The JCP was the only political party to take this stand. On 25 September the JCP paper declared that the emperor held the "highest responsibility for the war of aggression" and "dark politics suppressing human rights" during World War II (*Akahata*, 25 September). The LDP's weekly newspaper rebutted the JCP's charges and charged that the JCP lied when it stated it would uphold a system supported by the people. LDP leaders also asserted that the JCP sought to overthrow the Constitution.

Chairman Miyamoto replied at a JCP rally on 9 October that the JCP had opposed the imperial system since the party was established 66 years ago. He charged that it was the LDP that wanted to revise the Constitution and suppress the freedom of the people. The JCP subsequently opposed government efforts to sponsor imperial rites as part of the state duties of the new emperor. (*Japan Times*, 9 November.)

In the Okinawa prefectural assembly and other local governments, JCP members protested against government offices expressing sympathy for the emperor. The JCP's position was the inappropriateness of this sympathy in view of the emperor's "responsibility for World War II." (*Japan Times*, 28 September.)

The JCP continued to protest surveillance of the party and in one case called for agents of the Public Security Investigation Agency to be prosecuted for abuse of authority. This case involved the agency videotaping people entering and leaving the JCP's headquarters in Yoyogi. (*Japan Times*, 19 November.) The surveillance was noticed by JCP members and attracted press attention when an agent bumped into an elderly lady in the street and injured her (ibid.). A Tokyo district court judge inspected the condominium used in the taping and found notes on JCP members expected to run in the next election. Agency officials said the investigation was covert but not illegal. (*Japan Times*, 19 November.) Finally, the Tokyo district public prosecutor's office said it lacked justification for indicting any police official (*Japan Times*, 15 December).

Elections. The JCP entered the year as the fourth largest party in the more important house of the Diet, the House of Representatives. The JCP held 16 seats, compared with the LDP's 144, the JSP's 42, Komeitō's 23, and the DSP's 12. The JCP ranked fifth in the House of Councillors with 27 seats after the LDP with 302, the JSP with 86, Komeitō with 57, and the DSP with 29. In local assemblies the JCP was the largest opposition party with 3,919 seats, having performed well in the April 1987 nationwide local elections. (See *YICA*, 1988.)

There were no national or nationwide local elections during 1988, so the JCP's electoral strength remained essentially as it was. Polls of voter preference indicated a drop in support for the ruling LDP, though the beneficiary was the category of uncommitted voters. The JCP ranked fifth in popularity but garnered only 2.3 percent of the electorate voting support. (*FBIS-East Asia*, 30 June.)

However, the JCP won a major election victory to fill a House of Councillors seat vacated in Osaka in February when JCP candidate Hidekatsu Yoshii won 455,064 votes compared to the LDP candidate's 425,740 (*FEER*, 17 March, p. 40). The JCP's win was explained by a variety of factors including a scandal involving a senior LDP leader accused of tax evasion. The other opposition parties were linked to the LDP in the voters' minds in part as a result of the JCP publicizing secret deliberations within parliamentary steering committees that excluded JCP members because they routinely published details of the confidential meetings in *Akahata*. JCP leaders propagated the image of the JCP as the only clean party in Japanese politics and the standard-bearer of democracy. (Ibid.) JCP leaders, however, attributed their victory to their opposition to Prime Minister Takeshita's value-added tax proposal (*Washington Times*, 29 February).

The JCP also claimed victories in local elections in Furukawa City, Kubokawa Town, and the off-year village assembly election on Miyakejima Island (*Bulletin*, June, p. 6). Its leaders claimed that the party had made progress in struggles relevant to the next Lower House and Upper House elections (ibid.).

Auxiliary Organizations and Splinter Groups. The JCP supports and/or maintains contacts with a number of affiliated organizations, the most important of which are its youth organizations and several antinuclear groups (see previous volumes of *YICA* for details). The party does not maintain ties, and few if any contacts, with other communist groups in Japan, including the Shiga clique—a small communist group that was once part of the JCP. The JCP also eschews connections with radical leftist organizations, particularly the Red Army and other terrorist groups, though the

association in the public mind is damaging to the JCP.

During 1988 the JCP rendered special support to the World Council Against Atomic and Hydrogen Bombs. JCP spokespersons assailed the JSP for dropping out of the organization in 1986 and establishing a new organization called the International Test Ban Day Action in Hiroshima. (*Akahata*, 2 August.) JCP leaders went on to condemn the Partial Nuclear Test Ban Treaty, which was celebrating its 25th anniversary. Party leaders pointed out that the Soviet Union had signed the treaty after condemning all of its provisions, that it helped preserve the superpowers' nuclear monopoly, and that it weakened various antinuclear and peace movements throughout the world. (Ibid.) The party also repeated its contention that the treaty had led to the most serious arms race since the end of World War II. JCP spokespersons argued against any effort to revise the treaty as "not meeting the demand of the movement . . . for prevention of nuclear war and elimination of nuclear weapons" and becoming a "tool for division of the movement." (*Akahata*, 2 August.)

The JCP's public image in Japan suffered during 1988 as a result of its association with the Japanese Red Army and other terrorist organizations, which attracted considerably more attention than usual. The JCP, which avoids such organizations and explicitly repudiates terrorism, was linked by tenuous connections and circumstantial evidence to such groups.

In January the Red Army sent a letter (from the Middle East) to a bookstore in Japan promising retaliation for the rearrest and incarceration of Osamu Maruoka, who was released from prison in September 1977 in exchange for kidnapped passengers on a Japan Airlines plane in Dhaka (*Japan Times*, 5 January). Maruoka was picked up in November 1987 for violation of passport regulations and suspected involvement in terrorist activities to disrupt the election in South Korea in December 1987 and the Olympic Games in 1988 (*YICA*, 1988). He was subsequently accused of involvement in communist activities in the Philippines and underground activities in Tokyo, Osaka, and Kyushu and the Anti-War Democratic Front—a support network of the Japanese Red Army (*FBIS*, 16 February). The Japanese Red Army—which was formed from the Japan Communist League in 1969—by virtue of having the word communist in its name and by the JCP's alleged recent support for the communist movement in the Philippines, implicated the JCP by association (see *YICA* 1988 for details on JCP aid to the Philippine communist movement).

The JCP was further tainted in March when Kim Hyonhui, a North Korean woman, confessed on television to the bombing of a Korean Airlines (South Korea) plane in November 1987 that killed all 115 people on board. At the time a South Korean intelligence agency confirmed that her picture had appeared in 1972 in a photo magazine published by the JCP. (*FBIS*, 7 March.) The photo was taken by a JCP correspondent in North Korea. Although the JCP connection was only coincidental and no one accused the JCP or its leaders, there was, no doubt, guilt by association in the public mind. In any event the JCP made special efforts to justify its position that it believed that North Korea was responsible for the downing of the plane. Central Committee chairman Miyamoto himself put forward the JCP's position. (*Akahata*, 24, 27 January.) *Akahata* also published an editorial regarding the Kim confession, again attacking North Korea for plotting the bombing (*Akahata*, 2 February).

Further public attention focused on the Japanese Red Army in April when one of its members was arrested in the United States (in New Jersey) carrying bombs in his car. The suspected terrorist, Yu Kikumura, was said to be a member of Black Helmet, a group that joined with the Japanese Red Army in 1971. Kikumura was thought to have connections with the Popular Front for the Liberation of Palestine and with the Libyan government, leading to speculation that he was in the United States to plan a terrorist attack at the economic summit meeting in Toronto in June or the Democratic convention in July. (*Washington Times*, 15 April.) Reports also linked the Red Army to the Provisional Irish Republican Army, Abu Nidal, North Korea, Carlos the Jackal, and terrorist training camps in South Yemen (*Washington Times*, 13 January).

The Japanese Red Army got more attention in April when fingerprints of its members were found at the scene of a Naples bombing that killed five persons outside a U.S. servicemen's club (*Washington Times*, 28 June). The Red Army denied responsibility for the attack but did say that it supported the action (*Japan Times*, 21 April). At this time the National Police Agency in Japan issued ten thousand posters with pictures and descriptions of fourteen alleged Red Army terrorists (*Japan Times*, 22 April).

In May Japanese police arrested another Red Army member, Yasuhiro Shibata, who hijacked a Japan Airlines plane in 1970 (*FBIS*, 11 May). Shibata had been in North Korea, and was believed to have received special training there, and may have had plans to disrupt the Olympic Games in Seoul in the fall (*FBIS*, 16 May). These and other events prompted the Japanese government to initiate a number of meetings with police agencies in South Korea to prevent terrorist attacks during the September Olympics. (*FEER*, 30 June, pp. 18–20.)

International Views and Activities. The JCP continued to be an active party in terms of international contacts and interests. Its relations with the Soviet Union were lukewarm in 1988; its relations with China remained cold. It sent a number of delegations abroad during the year and received a number of visitors in Tokyo. The JCP kept a neutral and independent stance in terms of blocs. In January a JCP delegation led by Central Committee vice-chairman Fuwa visited India and Denmark (*FBIS*, 14 January). Fuwa's visit to India was at the invitation of the Indian Communist Party.

In February Central Committee chairman Miyamoto escalated the party's criticism of North Korea for the November 1987 bombing of a Korean Airlines (South Korea) plane. He described North Korea as a "dishonest socialist state" and detailed why he was certain that North Korea committed this act of terrorism, which the party reported uncertainty about at first. (*Akahata*, 24 January.) He further declared that it was an "illusion" that a socialist country can never be guilty of wrongdoing, adding that it is wrong for socialist countries to defend everything done by other socialist countries. He also said that North Korea forces its people to devote their lives to their "lord"—apparently a reference to North Korean president Kim Il-song. (*FBIS*, 19 February.) North Korea replied that the JCP and *Akahata* "had better behave prudently, clearly mindful of what a shameful and base act it is for them to side with the puppets bereft of reason after being coaxed by the imperialists" (*FBIS*, 17 March). The JCP responded by delineating North Korean terrorism, citing the Rangoon bombing of a temple that killed several members of the South Korean cabinet, the "arrogant hegemonistic attitude of the Worker's Party of Korea . . . in the shooting and capturing of a Japanese fishing boat in July 1984," and numerous other incidents (*Akahata*, 18 January). The article also made reference to the "atrocious hegemonism" and the "exorbitant interference" of the Worker's Party of Korea (ibid.).

In March JCP leaders held consultation talks

with representatives of the CPSU in Tokyo on ways of improving relations and promoting the anti-nuclear and peace movements (*FBIS*, 15 March). This was the second such talk. In April a JCP delegation headed by Koichiro Ueda, deputy chairman of the Presidium, traveled to the Soviet Union for talks (*FBIS*, 29 April). This was followed by a trip by Central Committee vice-chairman Fuwa in May to meet Soviet general secretary Gorbachev and discuss the promotion of peace and antinuclear campaigns (*FBIS*, 5 May). Gorbachev expressed the view in his talks with Fuwa that the INF treaty would be ratified and declared that a nuclear-free world, a program launched by the Soviet Union in January 1986, would be pursued in the future. Both leaders agreed that a nuclear-free world will test the ability of capitalism to develop in conditions of demilitarization; both agreed about the growing importance of the Asia-Pacific region and the U.S. response to Soviet interests there through greater military pressure. Gorbachev reaffirmed the significance of the joint statement made by the two parties in 1984. (Ibid.) Fuwa presented Gorbachev with the JCP's two-stage solution for resolving the territorial dispute over islands referred to in Japan as the Northern Territories. He also told Gorbachev that praise of the JSP in the CPSU's official gazette was "a mistake" and that the JSP is anticommunist and has endeavored to split the antinuclear movement in Japan. (*FBIS*, 6 May.)

Although formal relations between the JCP and the CPSU were more hospitable, relations were far from smooth. The two disagreed about the Soviet Union's "beautification" of the JSP (see above), Afghanistan, and a number of other issues. Ill feelings were also shown when the JCP published a detailed criticism of the book *The Japanese Communist Party: A Sketch of History* by I. I. Kovalenko, deputy chief of the International Department of the Central Committee of the CPSU. The JCP called the book unfair and charged the author with omitting causes of JCP-CPSU disagreement, such as Moscow's relations with the Shiga clique and its "great power chauvinism." (*Akahata*, 2 May.) The article concluded by saying that the book could give "an extremely grave, harmful and negative meaning to present and future relations" (ibid.).

In September, ostensibly not unrelated to its problems with North Korea, the JCP said that it would give "political recognition" to the government of South Korea. It further asserted that South Korean President Roh was "chosen through a direct

national election"—apparently signaling a revision of its stance that the South Korean government is a military dictatorship. (*Washington Times*, 11 October.) The JCP subsequently sent four of its Diet members and four reporters from *Akahata* to observe the Olympic Games (ibid.). At this same time, however, the JCP issued a statement advocating that the Japanese government recognize both Koreas (*FBIS*, 26 September).

In February it was reported that a JCP "front organization"—the Japan, Asia, Africa, Latin American Solidarity Committee—was launching a fund-raising drive on behalf of the African National Congress (ANC) and was warning Japanese businessmen to be "more cautious" in trading with South Africa (*Washington Times*, 17 February). In May the Japanese Foreign Ministry announced that the ANC would open an office in Japan to be staffed by J. Mansila, who was sponsored by JALA and who had represented the ANC in Sweden (*Washington Times*, 25 May). South Africa subsequently warned Japan against "providing a haven" to the ANC, which it said was a terrorist organization whose members are trained in Libya, Moscow, and North Korea (ibid.).

John F. Copper
Rhodes College

Korea
Democratic People's Republic of Korea

Population. 21,983,795
Party. Korean Worker's Party (Choson Nodong-dang; KWP)
Founded. 1946 (a united party since 1949)
Membership. 2.5 million
General Secretary. Kim Il-song
Standing Committee of the Politburo. 3 members: Kim Il-song (Democratic People's Republic of Korea [DPRK] president), Kim Chong-il (Kim

Il-song's son), O Chin-u (minister of People's Armed Forces)

Politburo. Full members: Kim Il-song, Kim Chong-il, O Chin-u, Yi Kun-mo, Pak Song-chol (vice president), Yi Chong-ok (vice president), Hong Song-nam, So Chol, Yon Hyong-muk (premier), Kim Yong-nam (foreign minister), Ho Tam, Kang Song-san, So Yun-sok, Kye Ung-tae, Chon Pyong-ho; candidate members: Hyon Mukwang, Kim Pok-sin, Choe Kwang, Kang Huiwon, Cho Se-ung, Hong Si-hak, Chong Chun-ki, Yi Son-sil, Han Song-yong

Secretariat. Kim Il-song, Kim Chong-il, Kang Song-san, Yon Hyong-muk, Ho Tam, Kye Ungtae, Hwang Chang-yop, Ho Chong-suk, Chon Pyong-ho, Chae Hui-Chong, So Kwan-hui, Choe Tae-pok, Chi Chang-ik, Pak Nam-ki, Kim Chungnin

Central Committee. 145 full and 103 candidate members

Status. Ruling party

Last Congress. Sixth, 10–15 October 1980, in Pyongyang

Last Election. 2 November 1986. 100 percent participation reported for Eighth Supreme People's Assembly, all 706 candidates on the slate elected.

Subordinate and Auxiliary Organizations. General Federation of Trade Unions of Korea, Union of Agricultural Working People of Korea, Korean Democratic Women's Union, Socialist Working Youth of Korea, Friends' (Chongdogyo religion) Party, Korean Democratic Party, Committee for Peaceful Reunification of the Fatherland, many others

Publications. *Nodong sinmun* (Worker's daily), KWP organ, *Minju Choson* (Democratic Korea); *Kulloja* (The worker), party theoretical organ; *Choson inminkun sinmun* (Korean People's Army news); many others. English-language publications include the *Pyongyang Times* and *Korea Today*; in Japan *The People's Korea* generally follows the North Korean line. The official news agency is the Korean Central News Agency (KCNA).

For North Korea, 1988 was a year of domestic unease and international setbacks. Kim Il-song continued to prepare to transfer power to Kim Chong-il, his son and heir, but there were hints of political dissent and indications the economy was faltering. At the same time, 160 countries—including most of the communist world—celebrated the games of the Twenty-fourth Olympiad in Seoul, marking perhaps

the greatest defeat for Pyongyang's diplomacy since the Korean War. The Olympics seemed a major watershed, signaling the willingness of the communist world to accept open—if still limited—ties with South Korea.

Leadership and Organization. Kim Chong-il was the center of attention again in 1988, writing keynote articles on Army Day (KCNA, 24 April) and Karl Marx's birthday (KCNA, 5 May) and giving "on-the-spot guidance" in Chagang province (Pyongyang Domestic Service, 14 April), in Siniuju, a city on the Chinese border (Pyongyang Domestic Service, 26 June), and in North Hamgyong Province (KCNA, 6 July). *Kimchongilia*, a begonia presented to the Dear Leader by a Japanese horticulturist, was celebrated as an especially magnificent flower and given a place beside *Kimilsongia*, an orchid reportedly grown in 200 areas in North Korea (Pyongyang Domestic Service, 10 April; KCNA, 20 April). The breeder of *Kimchongilia* was granted an honorary doctorate by the North Korean government (KCNA, 12 October). In September, Kim Chong-il—not his father—greeted Chinese president Yang Shangkun and Soviet KGB boss Viktor Chebrikov when they arrived in Pyongyang for the celebration of the 40th anniversary of the DPRK (KCNA, 8 September). Late in the year, Kim Kyong-hui, Kim Chong-il's sister, was made a member of the Central Committee (KCNA, 2 December).

The family celebration intensified as the DPRK prepared to celebrate its 40th anniversary on 9 September. An editorial in *Nodong sinmun* lavished praise on the Great Leader for bringing North Korea to the "zenith of its prosperity" (*Nodong sinmun*, 29 August) and called on the people to rejoice in achievements attained despite difficult circumstances. Kim Il-song's anniversary address noted his country's difficulties but stressed his regime's success in overcoming them (KCNA, 9 September). Delegations from all communist and many Third World countries attended the festivities. Czechoslovakia's Gustáv Husák was the only Soviet bloc party leader to show up, but most parties sent high-level Politburo members. China sent its head of state, Yang Shangkun, but reports that Soviet president Gromyko would attend turned out to be false. KGB chief Chebrikov came instead, reportedly because the Soviets wanted a hard-line voice to warn Pyongyang against any attempts to disrupt the Olympics (Seoul, *Yonhap*, 8 September).

The regime's posturing contrasted with gleanings from the press suggesting regime dissatisfaction with popular attitudes. There was no direct evidence of a claim that North Korea was embroiled in a power struggle (David Chen, *South China Morning Post*, 5 March). In February, however, a long *Nodong sinmun* article called for revival of the "spirit of Mt. Paektu" (Kim Il-song's legendary wartime camp and the official birthplace of Kim Chong-il) and expressed concern that the masses had not been adequately indoctrinated into the revolutionary struggle (*Nodong sinmun*, 2 February). The author wrote of "trials" and "difficulties," concepts also prominent in Kim Il-song's New Year's address (KCNA, 1 January) and complained that people were not firm in their faith. "Because of this, we say that the fighting spirit of the martyred anti-Japanese revolutionaries is a spirit which is more indomitable and stronger than that displayed in the peace days." Failure to inherit the tradition of struggle, it was alleged, would cause the party—and the country— to lose its way.

The party organ returned to this theme the next week (*Nodong sinmun*, 10 February), expressing concern that people did not understand the essence of the Korean revolution, that revolutionaries might forget their "fundamental mission," and that the cause of the working class depended on inheriting the leader's guiding ideology. This article again implied that times were difficult and stressed the need for unity even during "changing circumstances." On 15 February, a day before Kim Chong-il's 46th birthday, yet another long *Nodong sinmun* special article declared that unity was a prerequisite to socialist construction and warned that "a party apart from the popular masses is like oil floating on water and the popular masses without the leadership of a party and leader become rabble." The Politburo's 20 February letter announcing the 200-Day Battle for greater productivity also touched on this theme:

History shows that whenever the offensives of counterrevolutionary forces become intense, two utterly contradictory tenors appear. While cowards and those who are weak in their convictions in the revolution betray the revolution and go down the road of surrendering to the enemy, genuine revolutionaries lead the revolution to a greater upsurge, upholding the banner of the revolution higher and countering the enemy's offensives.

On 13 April, *Nodong sinmun* implied the existence of problems in the leadership, warning North Koreans to "resolutely reject all other forms of union except comradely union based on the leader's idea and will." The Korean people, according to the author,

will victoriously advance, as in the past, by defending and protecting the Great Leader no matter how fierce a storm they may encounter . . . However, one will face difficulties and ordeals . . . the revolutionaries can trust no one but the Party and the Leader and the revolutionary comrades with whom they are fighting together upholding the leader.

Nodong sinmun then warned against those who were "scared in the face of the enemy's last-ditch offensive." The article even seemed to carry a warning against would-be defectors: "If anyone holds disloyal feelings to the motherland which bore him and brought him up or betrays his motherland when it is in danger and tries to save his life only, no people of any country will regard him as one who has conscience."

Kim Yu-son, a candidate member of the Central Committee and head of North Korea's national Olympic committee, repeated these themes— particularly the warning against "cowards and counterrevolutionaries"—in an article in the May issue of *Kulloja*, the party theoretical journal. In addition, he warned against the emergence of "liberal" tendencies in society. In July, *Nodong sinmun* again stressed the importance of revolutionary indoctrination of the younger generation and spoke of the country's "strained situation" (*Nodong sinmun*, 5 July). Pyongyang party chief Kang Hui-won, writing in *Kulloja* in August, repeatedly referred to difficulties and strains, asserting that "we have a long way to go before consummating the cause of the party." In September, KCNA warned again that "the situation of our revolution is more strained and complicated than ever before" (KCNA, 2 September). *Nodong sinmun* stressed the necessity of undertaking "continuous revolution" in the face of "storms and trials" (*Nodong sinmun*, 25 October).

International attention was drawn to the succession in September, when Kim Pyong-il—Kim Il-song's son by his second wife—was appointed ambassador to Hungary (Budapest, MTI, 6 September). Reporters speculated that Kim Chong-il's leadership was facing domestic criticism and that his half-brother had been removed from the country to forestall his emergence as a rival. Pyong-il's dispatch to Hungary on the eve of that country's exchange of permanent missions with South Korea may have been a way of discrediting Kim Chong-il's half-brother as well as keeping him from the center of power. Kim Pyong-il was recalled from Budapest in protest of Hungary's action (Tokyo, *Kyodo*, 15 October) and appointed ambassador to Bulgaria (KCNA, 13 December).

In any case, there was no evidence of any major threat to Kim Chong-il. On 25 September, *Nodong sinmun* printed the text of a speech he had given to "senior" Central Committee members exactly one year before entitled "Let Us March Forward Dynamically Along the Road to Socialism Under the Unfurled Banner of the Anti-Imperialist Struggle." It appeared to be the international relations companion piece to an important talk on domestic affairs published on 15 July 1987. This time, the younger Kim stressed the contradictions of international capitalism and denied that time had proven incorrect predictions of its demise. He criticized socialist states for "deviations" from internationalist positions and insisted that the role of the party had to be strengthened, not weakened, to prevent working people from succumbing to the blandishments of capitalism's propagandists. Kim complained that "great mistakes" were made by communist countries after their establishment, a comment that—in the North Korean context—seems less likely to imply criticism of Stalinism than of more recent experiments with market forces in China and the Soviet Union (*Nodong sinmun*, 25 September).

North Korea underscored its orthodoxy a few days after Mikhail Gorbachev and the newly elevated Vadim Medvedev moved the Soviet Union closer to principles of market economics and away from the concept of irreconcilable class struggle. A signed article in *Nodong sinmun* stated that the destiny of a socialist state "depends entirely on the leading role of the party" (KCNA, 6 October). The author stressed the importance of the party's primacy over the state and of the party's control over all aspects of social life.

The regime, in the midst of these rumblings, shuffled some ranking personnel. It appeared the Kims were still fumbling to put together an effective economic management team, but it was not clear that these appointments would make any real difference in North Korea's hypercentralized decision-making process.

In February, former Premier Kang Song-san was appointed party boss in North Hamgyong province to replace Cho Se-ung, who became a vice-premier and chairman of the Construction and Building Materials Industry Commission (Pyongyang Domestic Service, 12 February). Kim Hwan once again became a vice-premier and chairman of the Chemical and Light Industry Commission. His predecessor on that commission, Kim Tal-yon, became chairman of the State Planning Commission. Hong Song-nam apparently was removed as a vice-premier, and Vice-Premier Kim Yon-hyok relinquished his chairmanship of the Construction and Building Materials Industry Commission. Yim Chun-chu, a North Korean vice president, died on 27 April at the age of 76.

Further changes took place in June (Pyongyang Domestic Service, 2 June). Hong Song-nam was once more identified as a vice-premier and named chairman of the State Planning Commission in place of Kim Tal-hyon, who—after only a few months on the job—became chairman of the Committee of External Economy. He subsequently was given the additional portfolio of the Foreign Trade Ministry in place of Choe Chong-kun, who was "dismissed" (KCNA, 7 October). Kim Pok-sin became chairwoman of the Light Industry Committee, which split off from the Chemical Industry Committee headed by Kim Hwan. Vice-Premier Cho Se-ung was relieved of his responsibilities as chairman of the Construction and Construction Materials Commission. That body was split up, with Chu Yong-hun becoming chairman of the Construction Materials Committee and Cho Chol-chun becoming minister of construction. Minor ministerial shifts were announced in September (KCNA, 14 September).

More personnel changes were announced at the thirteenth plenum of the KWP Sixth Congress (Pyongyang Domestic Service, 11 March). Kye Ung-tae was promoted from candidate to full Politburo member. Nine individuals were promoted from candidate to full Central Committee membership: Choe Man-hyon, Chang Chol, Kang Kwang-chu, Kim Kyong-pong, Sin Sang-kyun, Yi Sok, Yi Mong-ho, Kil Chae-kyong, Kwon Hui-kyong, Yi Chong-yul, and Pyon Hyong-yun. In addition, Kim Tal-hyon and Yun Sung-kwon were made full Central Committee members. The following 21 people were elected candidate members: Yun Chi-ho (who later died [KCNA, 1 August]), Won Hung-hui, Kang Tong-yun, Han In-sul, Yim Tong-uk, Choe Hui-pyok, Chong Song-taek, Kang Sok-chu, Kim Chong-suk, Kim Won-chin, Yi Yong-kyun, Hwang Sok-kyu, Kim Tong-won, Han Tok-su, Choe Pyong-ho, Kim Pyong-pal, Tong Sun-mo, Chi Chang-se, Yim Pong-yong, Chon Yong-hun, and Pak Yong-chan. Maeng Tae-ho became a member of the Central Auditing Committee.

This plenum, the first since December 1986—the longest interval between meetings since the sixth congress—was followed by another in late November (KCNA, 3 December). Chon Pyong-ho became a full Politburo member and Han Song-yong took his place as a candidate member. Pak Nam-ki and Kim Chung-nin were elected Central Committee secretaries. As noted above, Kim Kyong-hui—Kim Chong-il's full sister—was made a full Central Committee member. In addition, Yi Tong-song, Kim Yun-u, Yi Kyong-hui, Paek Se-yun, and Yi Yong-mu became Central Committee candidates.

An eventful year ended with the sacking of Premier Yi Kun-mo and his replacement by former First Vice-Premier Yon Hyong-muk (KCNA, 12 December). Kim Il-song presided over a meeting of the Supreme People's Assembly at which Yi was "recalled" for health reasons.

The most intriguing personnel shift in 1988 was the replacement of Korean People's Army chief of staff O Kuk-yol by Choe Kwang, a candidate Politburo member who had been chief of staff until he was sacked in the late 1960s. Choe gave up his position as a vice-premier to assume his military duties. This change had taken place by 21 February, when Choe saw off Defense Minister O Chin-u on the latter's departure for meetings in Moscow (KCNA, 21 February). O Kuk-yol appears to have been dropped from the Politburo, judging from his placement at the KWP plenum in March, on the funeral committee for Yim Chun-chu (Pyongyang Domestic Service, 11 March, 27 April), and at the April meeting of the Supreme People's Assembly (*Nodong sinmun*, 6 April). In addition, his ranking on these occasions suggested he was not placed on the party Secretariat, as some published reports had suggested (e.g., Seoul, *Korea Times*, 3 April).

It is difficult to tell whether O Kuk-yol's demotion was a setback for Kim Chong-il, as speculated by some press commentators (see Tokyo, *Sankei shimbun*, 23 March). O clearly had risen along with the Dear Leader, rising from 109th to 16th in the leadership between 1970 and 1980. Choe Kwang, a veteran of the anti-Japanese struggle, just as clearly was associated with the father rather than the son. But one should not be too quick to draw conclusions from this change—O Kuk-yol appeared at the party plenum and at Yim Chun-chu's funeral, albeit in a lower rank, and thus appeared to retain nearly as much respect as Choe Kwang had after *he* had been sacked as chief of staff in the 1960s. Perhaps O—

like so many North Korean functionaries—will one day return to prominence.

The change in military chiefs may be related to hints of military displeasure with the use of soldiers as construction troops. The media's hyperbolic praise of "soldier-builders" (Pyongyang Domestic Service, 15 February) suggested some disgruntlement. The reappointment of a respected military veteran may have been intended to demonstrate the old guard's commitment to the decision—presumably by Kim Chong-il—to divert thousands of troops to such huge construction projects as the Kwangbok Street athletic complex.

Alternatively, Choe's return could correspond to the modernization of North Korea's armed forces. Some observers believe he was fired originally because he was an "expert" in the age of a Red Army. Perhaps—with the introduction of new Soviet weapons since 1984 and in view of South Korea's military modernization program—Choe Kwang's views are back in style. Choe visited Soviet allies Czechoslovakia and Poland in September (KCNA, 18–22 September).

Choe's re-emergence could also have been related to the return to health of Defense Minister O Chin-u. O Kuk-yol had acted in O Chin-u's stead when the latter dropped from public view from September 1986 until August 1987. O Chin-u, or even the Kims themselves, may have been displeased with O Kuk-yol's performance during that period and decided to remove him, at least temporarily, from the highest levels of the leadership.

General Chon Mun-sop, another member of the old guard and a former minister of public security who had not appeared in public since 1986, was rehabilitated at the same time as Choe. He was one of those present at the airport in February when O Chin-u left for Moscow. Chon also was present when O departed for China on 16 May, at which time he was identified as a deputy defense minister. Meanwhile, Colonel General O Chae-won, a Central Committee member and director of the elite Mangyongdae Revolutionary School, died in late November (KCNA, 1 December).

Domestic Developments: The Economy. North Korea's unsettled personnel situation probably was connected to continuing economic troubles. As already noted, Kim Il-song opened 1988 with a speech stressing the need to overcome "many-fold difficulties and trials." His New Year's message seemed somber compared with the 1987 version, with greater emphasis on economic problems. Kim stressed first and foremost the need to expand and strengthen the country's power, coal, and metallurgy production. He called for the accomplishment of the ten long-term economic objectives of economic construction, goals established in 1980 and apparently still not attained. Kim next pointed to the need to develop chemical and light industries and "provide an adequate solution to the problems of food, clothing, and housing." He then praised the construction of the Sunchon vinalon (synthetic textile) plant, the Sariwon potash fertilizer project, and the Kwangbok Street athletic complex. He appealed to cadres to "radically increase" transport capabilities and returned again to the food problem with a demand for a "new turn" in agricultural prodution. He noted that "the tasks facing us this year are enormous."

Media commentaries repeated his stress on traditional economic centralization, with preference for grandiose construction projects and increased production of raw materials and basic goods (KCNA, 4 January). According to Pyongyang Domestic Service on 12 January, "if key industries (power, coal, and metallurgy), as the backbone of the people's economy, are not ceaselessly developed, the economy cannot be developed at a high speed." Managers were ordered to accomplish their goals more quickly, even as their tasks became "more difficult."

On 20 February, this notion became the economic theme of the year. In an unusual development, the Politburo drafted an open letter to the Central Committee—and thence to the people—calling for a 200-Day Battle designed to accelerate production in all sectors before the celebration of the DPRK's 40th anniversary on 9 September (eight days before the opening ceremonies of the Seoul Olympics (Pyongyang Domestic Service, 21 February). This letter continued to paint a somber picture of the country's condition, speaking of the "arduous and rugged" path yet to be trod. The letter contained specific economic goals:

Accelerate power plant construction to generate 1.2 million kilowatts of new capacity.

Expand important facilities in underdeveloped North Hamgyong province, including "second-stage" construction at the Kimchaek iron and steel complex and expansion of the Musan mining complex. In addition, the letter called for a new steel plant with a two-million-ton production capacity.

Complete construction of the Sunchon vinalon factory adequate to permit production of 100,000 tons of fabric. The army was specifically assigned to complete this goal "without fail."

Accelerate the first stage of construction of the Sariwon potash fertilizer plant.

Complete projects at the Kwangbok Street athletic complex "at an early date."

Accelerate progress in agriculture, in particular expanding irrigation of dry fields.

Ameliorate the country's transportation problems. In July, Kim Chong-il spoke of "strains" in rail transport and urged improvement of road and maritime systems.

Fill all other quotas at the same time functionaries are meeting the new demands.

The media periodically reported on progress in the 200-Day Battle, praising enterprises and projects that overfulfilled their quotas (see KCNA, Pyongyang Domestic Service, 7 March, 15 March, 6 May, for example). When the Battle was over, the media declared victory, specifically claiming that the electric power–generating goals had been met and that overall industrial production had risen 22 percent in comparison with the same period in 1987. The regime claimed that coal production had risen 22 percent, iron ore 17 percent, railroad freight turnover 27 percent, auto carriage 30 percent, large cargo shipping 45 percent, and machine tool production 11 percent. In addition, Pyongyang reported a "bumper" agricultural harvest, a 28 percent increase in seafood, and a 25 percent increase in fish production (KCNA, 14 September).

But there were indications of shortfalls. Pyongyang party boss Kang Hui-won, a candidate Politburo member, continued to stress the country's difficult times in a major address six days into the Battle (Pyongyang Domestic Service, 26 February). He called on citizens to "defeat the piled-up difficulties and ordeals" and declared that "today the internal and external situation of our revolution is more complicated and strained than ever before." He repeated word for word the passage quoted above about "cowards and counterrevolutionaries" and called for undying loyalty to the leader. A 15 April editorial in *Nodong sinmun* spoke repeatedly of difficulties, urging its readers to turn "misfortune to fortune." An article in the February issue of *Kulloja* accused some economic managers of using resources "indiscreetly" and harming the effort to increase productivity and improve the standard of living. In September, the regime reported only a "dramatic" increase in steel production and implied that railroad construction between Pyongyang and Kaesong and preparation of the Kwangbok Street athletic facilities had not been completed (KCNA, 14 September).

North Korea then launched a second 200-Day Battle, perhaps an indication of dissatisfaction with the results of the first one (KCNA, 4 September). In contrast to the first Battle, this time the regime did not establish specific production goals (KCNA, 14 September). An editorial late in the year called for better work in the machine tool and electronics industries, noting that "victory" in the struggle to meet production goals was "not certain" (*Nodong sinmun*, 14 December).

Kim Chong-il himself expressed impatience with supply and production problems. During an August visit to the Musan mining complex he expressed dissatisfaction with its productivity and with the pace of construction of new facilities (Pyongyang Domestic Service, 21 August). A few days later he urged managers at the Sangwon cement complex to improve their supply organization and ensure that workers are adequately fed (Pyongyang Domestic Service, 30 August).

An article by Kim Tal-hyon implied the existence of opposition to the regime's allocation of resources to grandiose building projects at the expense of basic human needs (*Kulloja*, February). Kim acknowledged the importance of solving food, clothing, and housing problems and admitted that "we face many difficult and complicated tasks in the course of solving them." But he insisted the Sunchon vinalon project—a complex designed to produce synthetic fabric and nitrogen fertilizer—was a "decisive factor" in meeting national needs. In an indication of morale problems, Kim urged workers to consider Kim Il-song's teachings as the "loftiest demands in life" rather than "an order or obligation."

Human factors apparently were not the only reasons for concern. The media noted climatic problems and congratulated corn farmers for overcoming "unfavorable spring weather conditions" (KCNA, 30 May). Following a visit to North Korea, an official of the organization of pro-Pyongyang Koreans living in Japan said bad weather had adversely affected the food supply for the past three years but denied press speculation of food shortages (KCNA, 14 September).

The March Central Committee plenum virtually ignored economic problems. According to the media, the Central Committee instead considered scientific and educational work, problems of public health, and "organizational problems"—a probable reference to personnel changes. The third session of the Eighth Supreme People's Assembly also apparently did not concentrate on the Battle but limited itself to promulgating the 1988 budget. Finance Minister Yun Ki-chong announced that state revenue reached 30,337,200,000 won—101 percent of the state plan and 106 percent over 1987 expenditures but only 91.3 percent of 1987 planned revenues (Pyongyang Domestic Service, 5 April). Expenditures were 30,085,100,000 won—99.3 percent of the plan. For 1988, she announced plans for a balanced budget, with revenues and expenditures pegged at 31,852,100,000 won. Yun credited troop reductions in 1986 and 1987 with the regime's decision to allocate only 12.2 percent of the 1988 budget to defense expenditures, "far less" than spent on defense in 1987.

According to Professor Suh Dae-sok of the University of Hawaii, who visited Pyongyang in June, North Korea decided to transform the eastern city of Nampo into a free port on the model of China's special economic zones (Seoul, *Korea Herald*, 26 June). There was no evidence, however, that the North was interested in the kind of economic reform of which Chinese special economic zones were a part.

North Korea's relations with its international creditors did not improve in 1988. In June, Pyongyang requested rescheduling of its debt to foreign banks. The North reportedly repaid $5 million to Western banks and promised to pay 30 percent of the $900 million falling due in 1991 (*Yonhap*, 3 June). Austria, for one, was unimpressed with this development—and with Pyongyang's repayment history—and closed down North Korea's trade office in Vienna (Vienna, *Die Presse*, 19 October). In December, Sweden refused to accept a token payment on a $133 million loan (Reuters, 13 December).

The Olympics. North Korea's campaign against the Seoul Olympics faltered badly in 1986 and 1987. Allegations of North Korean terrorism made matters worse as 1988 began, and the successful execution of the games from 17 September to 2 October culminated in, from Pyongyang's standpoint, an unmitigated diplomatic disaster. The Olympics—and the attendant growth of contacts between South Korea and the communist world—almost certainly spurred Pyongyang to refer to the "complex" international situation (*Nodong sinmun*, 5 July). The North looked to the 1989 World Youth Festival, awarded to Pyongyang under the auspices of the World Federation of Youth and Students, as a potential face-saving festival capable of competing with the Olympics in terms of ceremonial display (Beijing, Xinhua, 9 May).

The Soviet Union, China, the East European states (except Albania), Vietnam, and Laos all had announced their intentions to attend the Olympics by 17 January, the International Olympic Committee's (IOC's) deadline for national positions. This gave an immediate boost to South Korea's prospects for expanded relations with the East because Aeroflot and other bloc airlines scheduled flights to Seoul and because the communist states sent Olympic attachés to protect their delegations' interests. (*Yonhap*, 25, 27 January, 10–13 May.)

Soviet and East European officials went to Seoul several times before the games to discuss preparations. In addition, Soviet boxers competed in an international competition in Seoul in March (Moscow International Service, 23 March), and Soviet, Hungarian, and Yugoslav athletes attended a soccer competition in Seoul in June (*Yonhap*, 19 May). The Soviets sent gymnasts to a bilateral competition against South Koreans in Seoul a few weeks before the games (*Yonhap*, 3 August). South Korean athletes also competed in communist countries before the Olympics. Soviet boxing officials invited South Korea to send a boxing team to compete in Moscow in June (*Korea Times*, 15 March), and Moscow welcomed a South Korean team to the International Goodwill Pentathlon Competition (*Korea Herald*, 3 June).

Overall, 160 national Olympic committees selected teams for Seoul, making the 1988 games the best-attended ever—and the first since 1972 not marred by a major boycott movement. Only Cuba, Nicaragua, Ethiopia, Albania, Madagascar, and the Seychelles joined North Korea in refusing their Olympic invitations.

Pyongyang's embarrassment over its connection to terrorism increased in May with the capture in Japan of Shibata Yasuhiro, one of nine Japanese Red Army (JRA) members who had fled to North Korea after hijacking an airliner in 1970. Japanese officials determined that Shibata had entered Japan using a false passport probably provided by North Korea and alleged that he was a North Korean agent intent on disrupting the Olympics (Tokyo, *Kyodo*; *Yonhap*, 12 May). The Japanese press linked

Shibata with other JRA members arrested around the same time in Japan and the United States (Tokyo, *Asahi shimbun*, 11 May) and reported that Kim Il-song had decided in 1986 to send them "home" (Tokyo, *Sankei shimbun*, 11 May). Two of Shibata's colleagues in the 1970 hijacking implied their connection with North Korea and the Olympics by telling Japanese reporters that they would pursue Olympic cohosting "to the end" (*Asahi shimbun*, 24 May).

North Korea responded defensively, calling reports of its culpability "groundless slander" and claiming it had merely acceded to Shibata's wish to travel outside North Korea (KCNA, 12 May). Pro-Pyongyang Koreans living in Japan claimed Shibata had returned to Japan because he was "homesick" (*Kyodo*, 15 May). Kim Il-song himself reportedly assured visiting Mozambique president Joaquim Chissano that North Korea would not disrupt the games (*Kyodo*, 24 May). On 23 May the Foreign Ministry issued an angry denunciation of U.S., Japanese, and South Korean allegations of North Korean complicity in terrorism (KCNA, 23 May). The next day, *Nodong sinmun* demanded Japanese papers "stop the false, fabricated report against us." Kim Il-song, in a banquet speech honoring visiting Czechoslovak leader Miloš Jakeš, insisted the North still believed cohosting was possible and called his visitor's attention to South Korean popular support for his position (Pyongyang Domestic Service, 27 May). Pyongyang claimed the South was using the northern "threat" to mask preparations to repress the popular "struggle" against No Tae-u (VNA, 2 June).

In the end, Pyongyang failed to provoke violent opposition to the Seoul Olympics, which—despite the usual controversies over judging and drugs and occasional friction between tourists and security officials—were an enormous success. South Korea drew the attention of the world while North Korea sulked in isolation. Shortly after the closing ceremonies, Pyongyang media quoted an equally sullen Fidel Castro's strong criticism of those communist countries whose athletes went to Seoul (KCNA, 7 October).

North Korea's embarrassment over the Olympics was compounded by indications some Third World countries did not support the 1989 Pyongyang World Youth Festival. *Komsomolskaya pravda* expressed skepticism that the North would attract as many participants as the previous festival in Moscow, primarily because many smaller states could not afford to send delegates "to the other end of the earth" and because of the limited access to Pyongyang by air (Moscow, *Komsomolskaya pravda*, 14 May). The piece went on to claim North Korea's relatively limited network of diplomatic relations was an obstacle to universal attendance. More ominously, the article hinted that some attendees at a preparatory meeting in New Delhi were not enthusiastic over the choice of venue. According to the author, "there are quite a few shades of opinion regarding the DPRK," some of them "quite hostile." Indeed, the joint communiqué adopted in New Delhi termed the discussions "a useful exchange of views" indicating the existence of differences of opinion (KCNA, 21 May). As 1988 ended, it was unclear whether North Korea would attract the numbers of participants necessary to make the Youth Festival a credible counter-Olympics.

North-South Relations. The Olympics imbroglio overshadowed other areas of North-South relations, even though the two held their first direct talks since 1985. North Korea spent much of the year trying to exploit South Korean domestic divisions. Each Korea received defectors, with the North reporting the February arrival in Pyongyang of a South Korean "transport officer" (KCNA, 10 February) and the South trumpeting the April defection of an employee of North Korea's Ministry of Public Security (*Yonhap*, 1 May). The latter told a news conference in June that old guard military and political leaders oppose Kim Chong-il's succession. He also alleged that "many ordinary people" are against the younger Kim (Reuters, 8 June). The defector, in addition, claimed that North Korean officials had been involved in 69 cases of smuggling in 36 foreign countries from 1971 to 1987 (Seoul Domestic Service, 8 June).

In contrast to 1987, Kim Il-song's 1988 New Year's address contained little new on North-South relations. In a return to a well-worn formula, he proposed a meeting between North and South Koreans "from all walks of life," including opposition politicians and the leaders of social organizations as well as government officials. Subsequent commentary attacked the South's refusal to accept the offer but showed little of the negotiating flexibility that marked Pyongyang's approach to dialogue in 1987. The North-South atmosphere was not improved when a South Korean editorial called Kim's proposal "preposterous" (*Seoul simbun*, 7 January).

On 13 January Son Song-pil, the head of North Korea's Red Cross, telephoned his South Korean counterpart to inform him that Pyongyang would be sending an official letter containing Kim's proposal (KCNA, 13 January). Pyongyang broadcast this letter when the South refused to accept it (KCNA, 14 January) and suggested the two sides hold a preliminary meeting at Panmunjom on 19 February.

The issue became moot the next day when South Korea announced the results of its interrogation of the surviving member of a couple allegedly responsible for the 29 November 1987 destruction of Korean Airlines flight 858. Seoul declared the woman was a North Korean agent, acting under direct orders from Kim Chong-il. She confessed to this crime publicly and held a live press conference that attracted widespread international attention (Seoul Television Service, 15 January). Seoul not only ignored the North's proposal for a 19 February meeting but announced its launch of an international diplomatic offensive against Pyongyang (*Yonhap*, 15 January). South Korea demanded a North Korean apology, scrapped its policy directive of September 1987 permitting limited diplomatic contact with North Korean officials (the United States announced similar action), and took its case against Pyongyang to the United Nations and the International Civil Aviation Organization. South Korea also called for international diplomatic and trade sanctions against the North (Dow Jones, 16 January). This public offensive continued in February when a South Korean newspaper quoted Sin Sang-ok and Choe Un-hui as saying the younger Kim had indicated to them his responsibility for the attempt on the life of President Chun Doo Hwan in Rangoon in 1983 (*Korea Times*, 16 February).

North Korea responded by denying involvement in the incident. Pyongyang claimed the South Korean government had committed the deed to divert domestic political opponents from their struggle against the regime and to ensure No Tae-u's election as president (KCNA, 15 January). The North also claimed the South had timed the disclosure of its conclusions to distract world opinion from North Korea's proposal for a North-South meeting (Pyongyang Domestic Service, 16 January). The head of North Korea's observer mission made these same points at the United Nations' debate on the issue the next month (KCNA, 12 February).

The Soviets and Chinese reported the North's position in their media (Xinhua, TASS, 15, 16 January) but did not go out of their way to denounce the South's diplomatic campaign. Both powers also published factual reports of the South Korean case against the North (TASS, Xinhua, 15 January).

There is no evidence, however, to support claims in the South Korean press that North Korea sent emissaries to Moscow and Beijing carrying apologies for the bombing (*Yonhap*, 11 February).

North Korea tried to limit the international damage from the woman's confession by drawing the world's attention to the 1988 version of Team Spirit, the yearly U.S.-South Korean joint military exercise. In late January, Defense Minister O Chin-u denounced the "war maneuvers" and issued warnings of a thermonuclear holocaust on the peninsula (KCNA, 27 January). North Korea vowed "retaliation" for the exercise (Pyongyang Domestic Service, 29 January), and a Japanese newspaper claimed North Korean troops were massing along the demilitarized zone (DMZ) (*Sankei simbun*, 6 February).

It soon became clear that North Korea intended to stage an intense rhetorical reaction to Team Spirit, perhaps to show potential Olympic participants the dangers of attending events in South Korea. The North accused the South of shooting across the DMZ on 19 and 26 February (KCNA, Pyongyang Domestic Service, 19, 26 February) and claimed further "provocations" on 23 April (KCNA, 23 April). On 29 March and 29 April (KCNA, 30 March, 29 April), the North accused South Korean vessels of entering its territorial waters. On 20 March, near the height of Team Spirit activity, Kim Il-song ordered a "complete combat mobilization posture" (Pyongyang Domestic Service, 20 March). Pyongyang claimed the U.N. command had committed over 36,000 armistice violations in recent months. South Korea, for its part, accused North Korean troops of a shooting incident on 18 March (Seoul Domestic Service, 18 March). In May, North Korea called a meeting of the Military Armistice Commission at Panmunjom, at which it accused the U.N. command of violating the armistice agreement by introducing heavy weapons into the DMZ (KCNA, 9 May). The U.N. command denied having committed any violations and claimed North Korea was attempting to create a tense atmosphere in order to undermine the Olympics (Reuters, 21 May). The North responded by accusing the U.N. command of committing "over 7,800" violations in May (KCNA, 23 June). Pyongyang charged the U.N. command with another cease-fire violation on 5 July (KCNA, 6 July).

This exchange of rhetoric did not prevent a parallel North Korean effort to convince South Koreans and others of its sincere desire to resume North-South dialogue. The North held meetings of its delegation to proposed preliminary talks (Pyongyang Domestic Service, 4 February) and sent another message through the Red Cross reminding Seoul of Kim's New Year's proposal (KCNA, 9 February). Politburo member Ho Tam criticized the South for not agreeing to the 19 February meeting and offered to reschedule the session for 28 March (KCNA, 20 February). Stronger North Korean denunciations followed the latter date, but the North made clear its offer was still open (Pyongyang Domestic Service, 10 April).

The South meanwhile launched a limited rhetorical counteroffensive. No Tae-u renewed his call for North Korean participation in the Seoul Olympics and said he was ready to meet Kim Il-song to discuss Korean reunification (*Kyodo*, 1 March). In May, Pak Se-chik, president of the Seoul Olympic Organizing Committee, offered to go to Pyongyang to discuss Olympic preparations with North Korean officials (*Kyodo*, 16 May). The South indicated for the first time that it could accept joint North-South U.N. representation and even sought international support for its position (*Korea Herald*, 25 May). South Korean foreign minister Choe Kwang-su expressed his willingness to meet with his North Korean counterpart if both attended the General Assembly (*Yonhap*, 8 June).

Japanese press sources carried rumors that secret North-South talks were already taking place (*Sankei shimbun*, 7 May), speculation encouraged two days later when South Korea's minister of national unification said that such contacts had in fact been held (*Yonhap*, 9 May). But the South walked back from that position (*Yonhap*, 14 May) and denied published reports that Ho Tam had secretly visited South Korea in April (*Sankei simbun*, *Yonhap*, 17 May). North Korea denied the reports three days later (KCNA, 20 May). The South also denied Japanese reports that presidential adviser Pak Chol-on had visited Pyongyang in April (*Yonhap*, 14 June). Nevertheless, the publicity encouraged the impression that North Korea was willing to talk to the No regime, and, therefore, that a change in South Korea's government was not needed to ensure North-South dialogue.

Seoul had every reason to encourage this view in the wake of the government's defeat in the legislative elections. Opposition leaders Kim Tae-chung and Kim Young-sam had demanded North-South talks and criticized the government for not trying hard enough to ensure North Korean Olympic participation.

The South Korean legislative elections. Pyongyang—probably intent on ruining Seoul's credentials as an Olympic host—decided to encourage civil strife in the South in anticipation of a victory by the ruling party. On 13 April, the South Korean National Democratic Front appealed for workers to "rise in unison in strikes" to launch a "typhoon" against the elections. On 23 April, VNA called on workers to use all the weapons of struggle, economic and political, legal and illegal, violent and nonviolent. The North, however, still urged militants to avoid actions—such as firebombing public buildings—that might alienate the masses (VNA, 5 June). This approach was in sharp contrast to the situation before the presidential election when North Korea had cautioned student radicals to refrain from direct action and to support the workers' struggle for economic reform.

After the votes were counted, however, Pyongyang could not easily attack an opposition victory as undemocratic or avoid the conclusion that the ruling party had lost despite continued disunity among its opponents and was hard-pressed to deny the conclusion that change could come about in South Korea without a violent uprising. Not surprisingly, the North's first reaction—which took three days to appear—was to hail the "crushing defeat" suffered by the president's party despite "the worst violence and fraud ever in history" (KCNA, 29, 30 April, 5 May). But the North virtually ignored the opposition and did not celebrate its triumph, probably because Pyongyang wanted to avoid the suggestion that the process was a step forward for democracy in South Korea.

Pyongyang differentiated—even before the election—among opposition elements to establish that the concept of a "loyal opposition" was unacceptable. On 23 April, a *Nodong sinmun* commentary criticized those "conservative politicians" who put their own egos ahead of the national interest. The author advised South Koreans to "discard the fantasy and expectations of bigoted conservative factions who only pursue power." This piece seemed to express the North's fear that a regularized political process could cause some to "discard the anti-U.S., antimilitary struggle rule." In contrast, this article praised the role of religious dissidents who were not tempted by the lure of National Assembly seats.

The opposition victory seemed only to sharpen North Korean disapproval of opposition politicians. Interestingly, Kim Tae-chung became the main target for North Korea's wrath. *Nodong sinmun* noted Kim Young-sam's offer to meet Kim Il-song but ignored a similar appeal by Kim Tae-chung (*Nodong sinmun*, 6 May). North Korea was particularly incensed by what it perceived as Kim Tae-chung's willingness to delay investigations into the 1980 Kwangju incident and into corruption under Chun Doo Hwan until after the Olympics. VNA accused Kim of "betrayal" of his constituents and of his campaign promises (VNA, 5 May) and demanded he apologize to the nation for his improper behavior (VNA, 10 May).

The North's praise for religious dissidents increased along with its criticism of Kim Tae-chung. In particular, KCNA praised Mun Ik-hwan and other clergymen for their letter to North and South Korean leaders in support of Olympic cohosting (KCNA, 13, 15 May).

Further dialogue feelers. Pyongyang also carried forward its approval of a campaign by South Korean student leaders for a meeting and athletic competition with their North Korean counterparts. This idea had originated in posters appearing on South Korean campuses in early April (Seoul, *Korea Herald*, 2 April). Pyongyang Domestic Service broadcast a letter from students at Kim Il-song University to the Student Council and president of Seoul National University accepting the proposal—the South Korean Red Cross had refused to transmit the letter from Panmunjom (*Yonhap*, Pyongyang Domestic Service, 4 April). The North denounced Seoul's attitude and noted that South Korean students posted the North Korean letter on campus walls (KCNA, 5, 7 April).

North Korea returned to this issue on 17 May with a mass rally in Pyongyang. The next day, Red Cross chairman Son Song-pil telephoned his South Korean counterpart requesting permission to transmit a letter from participants in this rally to South Korean students (KCNA, 18 May) "accepting" a 10 June meeting between students from both sides.

Permission was rejected, of course, leading to harsher rhetoric from Pyongyang. In separate comments, Kim Il-song and Politburo member Ho Tam—while repeating their willingness to meet with South Koreans from all walks of life—said they could not in good conscience agree to a meeting between government officials alone because it would be a betrayal of that "majority" of South Koreans who oppose their government (KCNA, 28, 30 May). This marked a distinct hardening of the North's line from a softer version that included the offer to talk with South Korean authorities as long as the South Korean people approved.

The two sides intensified their propaganda struggle after South Korean students rioted on 10 June as a result of being turned away by police from a meeting with their North Korean counterparts. North Korea's delegation waited for an hour at Panmunjom and then held a news conference castigating Seoul for its attitude (KCNA, 10 June). At the same time, South Korean officials claimed they would consider a student meeting but only after a government-to-government meeting (*Yonhap*, 10 June). North Korea, in turn, criticized Seoul for trying to prevent the growth of North-South channels outside its control (KCNA, 10–13 June). North Korea supported the announcement by South Korean student radicals that they would again attempt a march to Panmunjom on 15 August (KCNA, 12, 15 June).

The Koreas talked past each other for the next few weeks. No Tae-u called for a "German-style" basic treaty between the two Korean states as a first step toward reunification. South Korea tried to preempt further demonstrations by calling for a "grand march" the length of the peninsula by 500–1,000 students from each side, culminating in sporting events and an exchange of visits (Seoul Domestic Service, 28 June).

The North ignored this proposal in favor of demands by radical South Korean students for student meetings unfettered by association with the Seoul regime (KCNA, 28 June). The South's "German solution" was unacceptable to the North because the 1972 agreement institutionalized the existence of two German states.

Relations with the Soviet Union. The Soviet Union reportedly delivered several new weapons systems to the North as counters to South Korean military modernization efforts and, perhaps, as compensation for the Soviet presence at the Olympics and increasing economic ties between South Korea and the Soviet bloc. According to Japanese press reports citing Japanese Defense Agency sources, the Soviets delivered MiG-29 high-performance aircraft (Tokyo, NHK, 18 June), a fighter far superior to anything else in the North's inventory of older Chinese and Soviet planes. In addition, North Korea received its first SU-25 ground attack fighters (*Sankei shimbun*, 24 January). In May, Japanese sources reported the North had up to ten SU-25s (*Yonhap*, 4 May). The 1988 edition of the U.S. Department of Defense publication *Soviet Military Power* said North Korea also had "reportedly" received SA-5 long-range, medium–high altitude antiaircraft missiles and improved versions of the SA-2 and SA-3. Press reports claimed the SA-5s were deployed close to the DMZ, prompting U.S. and South Korean concerns about the safety of South Korean airspace during the Olympics. (*Washington Times*, 7 June.) General Menetrey, commander of U.S. forces in South Korea, also noted North Korea's possession of ZSU 23-4 antiaircraft batteries (*Tong-a Ilbo*, 27 May). In April, North Korea and the Soviet Union announced an expansion of civil air service between their two capitals (KCNA, 22 April).

The two sides continued their steady stream of bilateral contacts in 1988:

In January, Soviet deputy premier Silayev received Kye Hyong-sun, North Korean minister of machine building (*Pravda*, 28 January).

As noted above, North Korean defense minister O Chin-u visited Moscow in late February, where he met with Soviet defense minister Yazov but apparently did not see Gorbachev (KCNA, 21–26 February).

In April, General P. G. Lushev, Soviet first deputy defense minister, visited Pyongyang, where he met with O and was received by Kim Il-song (KCNA, 22 April).

North Korean vice president Yi Chong-ok stopped over in Moscow after his trip to Zambia (*Pravda*, 25 April).

North Korean naval vessels and Admiral Kim Il-chol, North Korea's naval chief, visited Vladivostok between 29 July and 2 August (KCNA, 2 August), as they had in 1986.

Kim Pok-sin, vice-premier and a candidate Politburo member, led a trade delegation to Moscow in November (Pyongyang Domestic Service, 26 November).

Soviet foreign minister Shevardnadze visited Pyongyang briefly in December, meeting with both Kim Il-song and Kim Chong-il (KCNA, 23 December). In his banquet speech Shevardnadze noted the need for "a lot of work" to increase the effectiveness of bilateral economic relations. He also claimed that "more favorable conditions" exist for a peaceful solution to the Korean issue, underscoring the virtues of Moscow's contacts with Seoul.

There were fewer exchanges between North Korea and the East Europeans, but new Czechoslovak party boss Jakeš visited Pyongyang in

May (KCNA, 27 May), and North Korean Polit-buro member Ho Tam attended a conference on nuclear-free zones in East Germany, where he was received by Erich Honecker (East Berlin, ADN, 22 June).

Kim Il-song visited Soviet ally Mongolia, travel-ing by train through Chinese and Soviet cities (KCNA, 27 June–2 July). This visit repaid the trip to Pyongyang by Mongolian party leader Batmonh in 1986 when the host's appearance at the airport to greet his guest dispelled reports—given credence by South Korean officials—that Kim Il-song had been assassinated.

In May, vessels from the Soviet Pacific fleet paid what is becoming a yearly visit to North Korea. This time, the Soviets sent the *Novorossiysk*, a Kiev-class antisubmarine warfare vessel, and two other ships to Wonson. Admiral Khvatov, Pacific fleet commander, met with Kim Il-song, O Chin-u, and other officials (KCNA, 12–16 May).

On the negative side, the Soviet Union continued to exhibit some impatience with North Korea's eco-nomic troubles. In late 1987, *Izvestiia* painted a grim picture of life in Pyongyang, noting empty streets and shops with bare shelves (*Izvestiia*, 27 December 1987). The article stressed the North's penchant for grandiose monuments and implied it was hard for one accustomed to Soviet reality to understand what he or she sees in Pyongyang. In addition, *Izvestiia* drew the reader's attention to the "impressive" economic development of South Korea.

An article in *Ekonomicheskaya gazeta* frankly criticized the North's economic performance (Moscow, *Ekonomicheskaya gazeta*, March). The author wrote of Pyongyang's failure to implement ambitious economic plans, the unsatisfactory level of cooperation between the center and local offi-cials, and the fact that "no new forms have been introduced in the sphere of science and technology." In addition, *Ekonomicheskaya gazeta* complained that North Korea delivered less than 10 percent of the sewn goods it had pledged to export to the USSR in 1987. Although Soviet officials reportedly were partly to blame, "both sides ended up losers." A subsequent article in *Pravda* repeated the theme that the North's economic development was not "smooth" (*Pravda*, 8 September). In contrast, *Kom-somolskaya pravda* printed a piece extolling the potential for trade with South Korea and praising

the "unquestioned prestige" of South Korean work-manship (*Komsomolskaya pravda*, 27 October).

Exchanges in April and May underscored the rough spots in Soviet–North Korean economic rela-tions. Soviet first deputy premier Murakhovsky traveled to Pyongyang, where he met with Kim Il-song and other officials (KCNA, 28 April). The two sides reportedly discussed "urgent" matters of trade and economic cooperation. CPSU secretary Biryukova visited North Korea in mid-May and met with Kim Il-song, with whom she discussed ways of making economic cooperation "more effective" (TASS, 19 May). *Pravda* noted that "questions were examined" relating to economic cooperation and stressed the importance of ensuring "timely, com-plete fulfillment of existing agreements" (*Pravda*, 18 May).

Soviet, East European, and Vietnamese willing-ness to expand ties with South Korea was an even greater point of contention with North Korea in 1988. Communist tourists joined athletes and offi-cials at the Olympic Games, and the Soviets even permitted a South Korean passenger ship to pick up tourists and their automobiles at a Soviet port (*Korea Times*, 7 April). Six Soviet diplomats served consular functions in Seoul during the games (*Korea Herald*, 17 August), and their chief met with No Tae-u (*Yonhap*, 4 September). Soviet artists and performers were the hits of the Olympic cultural festival. Soviet officials not only commented on the good feelings caused by the Olympics (*Yonhap*, 4 October) but even expressed regret for the Soviet downing of Korean Airlines flight 007 in 1983 (*Yonhap*, 5 October).

North Korea expressed its overall frustration with its socialist friends in late October. An official Foreign Ministry statement alluded to the 19 Sep-tember *Nodong sinmun* attack on Hungarian–South Korean relations, bitterly criticizing Budapest for its "betrayal of socialism" and threatening to sever bilateral ties (Pyongyang Domestic Service, 27 Oc-tober). At the same time, the North held a sym-posium on the Two Koreas Plot and criticized those who played into the hands of U.S. efforts to pro-mote cross-recognition (KCNA, 26 October; *Nodong sinmun*, 27 October).

Relations with China. A relatively quiet year in Sino–North Korean relations may have signaled continuing bilateral problems. China, for example, was even less supportive than the Soviet Union of North Korea's position on Korean Airlines flight 858. Beijing took a public position against terrorism in any form and noted statements made by both Koreas virtually without comment (Xinhua, Beijing International Service, 16 January). In addition, the Chinese noted North Korean denunciations of U.S. sanctions but did not criticize them (Xinhua, 25 January; AFP, 28 January). China did oppose U.S. and South Korean calls for a U.N. Security Council consideration of the matter (AFP, 11 January), and there was no evidence to support the allegation that China had demanded an explanation for the Korean Airlines incident from Kim Chong-il (Tokyo, *Kendai Chosen*, 2 April).

Some international journalists speculated that relations between China and North Korea were not good. On 17 January, *Sankei shimbun* claimed China had promised the United States not to send troops to North Korea's aid if Pyongyang launches an invasion of the South. Hong Kong and Japanese sources reported a "cooling" of relations, perhaps because of Chinese opposition to the dynastic succession. These articles reported a breakdown of negotiations for Chinese use of North Korean ports and facilities to facilitate trade between China and Japan (*Kyodo*, 8 March; Chung Chu in Hong Kong, *Hsing tao wan pao*, 10 May). The Hong Kong reporter also claimed China had reduced arms deliveries to the North.

In February, reports surfaced that a Chinese ammunition train had exploded in northern North Korea, killing 120 and injuring 5,000. South Korean television claimed the train had been sabotaged by elements opposed to Kim Chong-il (Seoul, Korean Broadcasting System, 2 February). China dismissed the story as "pure lies" (AFP, 3 February).

As in the case of Soviet–North Korean relations, bilateral strains in 1988 probably reflected signs of expanding Sino–South Korean relations. Seoul television quoted Japanese press sources as saying the South Korean ambassador to the United States traveled to China four times in 1987 (Seoul, Korean Broadcasting System, 15 May; Tokyo, *Mainichi shimbun*, 16 May). In February according to *Yonhap*, an official Chinese trade mission gave the first "exclusive" briefing to a South Korean businessman in Hong Kong (*Yonhap*, 3 February). At the same time, the Japanese press reported rumors that Kim Man-che, South Korean economic planning minister and former deputy premier, had recently traveled to China (Tokyo, *Nihon keizai*, 3 February). In the summer, an article in a Hong Kong journal claimed Beijing had decided on a gradual introduction of direct bilateral trade (Hong Kong, *Cheng ming*, 1 July).

A Chinese spokesman denied his government would establish official relations with the South (Xinhua, 6 April), but the Japanese press alleged that Li Peng was to inform Kim Il-song about direct Sino–South Korean trade during a visit to North Korea scheduled for 1 May (*Kyodo*, 8 April). This visit did not take place, indicating either that it was never scheduled or that differences between the two sides had grown to the point that a visit would not produce good results. Although Li repeated that China would not establish diplomatic relations with South Korea (*Kyodo*, 2 July), other Chinese officials said South Korean trade and investment was "welcome" (*Yonhap*, 20 July). Late in the year Pong Yiren, executive vice-chairman of the National People's Congress, said that South Korea and China were engaged in direct trade (*Kyodo*, 6 December). The South Koreans announced the opening of trade offices in Beijing and Jinan in the same statement that declared a similar agreement regarding Moscow and Vladivostok (*Yonhap*, 18 October). According to a Hong Kong newspaper, China and South Korea also agreed to direct flights between Seoul and Shenyang (Hong Kong, *South China Morning Post*, 29 September).

Pyongyang, clearly unhappy over China's policy, could do nothing to reverse it and publicly played down its displeasure. North Korea betrayed its nervousness by quoting Li Peng to the effect that China would not recognize the South (KCNA, 5 November). Later that month, Pyongyang stressed its unwillingness to trade with Taiwan, by implication criticizing China's willingness to trade with South Korea (*Nodong sinmun*, 27 November).

Officially, of course, Beijing and Pyongyang claimed relations were good. In January, Yang Dezhi, the general who had commanded Chinese "volunteers" during the Korean War, published memoirs reminding Chinese and Koreans of the struggle they had shared (Xinhua, 22 January). High-level visits were exchanged in the spring, giving both sides the opportunity to put a positive public spin on relations:

So Yun-sok, KWP Politburo member and party boss in South Pyongan province, visited Beijing in April and heard Zhao Ziyang express the conviction that bilateral relations would "constantly develop" (KCNA, 3 April). So also met with Li Ximing, CCP Politburo member and

Beijing party secretary (Beijing, *Renmin Ribao*, 2 April).

At the same time, Kim Il-song met with visiting Jiangsu party secretary Han Peixin in a "friendly and cordial" atmosphere (KCNA, 4 April).

A few days later, Zhao met with a delegation headed by Hyon Chun-kuk, director of the KWP's International Department (Xinhua, 8 April) and a group of North Korean broadcasters (Pyongyang Domestic Service, 9 April).

The next month, vice-premier and candidate Politburo member Kim Pok-sin led a high-level trade delegation to China, where she met with Zhao and vice-premier and CCP Politburo member Wu Xueqian (Pyongyang Domestic Service, 13 May; Xinhua, 14 May).

CCP Politburo member Li Ruihuan visited North Korea in June and was received by Kim Il-song (Xinhua, 9 June; KCNA, 15 June).

In July, Wan Li, chairman of the Chinese National People's Congress, greeted a delegation headed by Kim Pong-chu, head of the North Korean General Federation of Trade Unions (Xinhua, 14 July).

North Korean foreign minister Kim Yong-nam visited China in November (Xinhua, 3 November), meeting with Qian Qichen, Zhao Ziyang, and Li Peng.

The two sides also exchanged high-level military visits. In April, O Chin-u and Choe Kwang received Zhang Zhongxian, political commissar of the Guangzhou Military District (Beijing International Service, 9 April; KCNA, 14 April). O Chin-u went to Beijing and Qingdao in May. He met with Deng Xiaoping, Yang Shangkun, Defense Minister Qin Jiwei, and other officials (Xinhua, KCNA, 16–19 May). The most notable point about O's visit may have been Deng Xiaoping's use of it to call for further Chinese economic reforms. The domestic audience was undoubtedly Deng's main target, but he may have also been giving advice on a future direction for the troubled North Korean economy. In July, North Korean Air Force commander Cho Myong-rok visited Beijing at the invitation of Wang Hai, his Chinese counterpart (KCNA, 21 July).

Relations with Japan. Fallout from the Korean Airlines bombing and allegations of North Korean collaboration with Japanese Red Army terrorists poisoned the already poor bilateral atmosphere. In addition, there was no progress toward resolving the fate of Japanese seamen held in North Korea.

Japan found itself at the center of Korean tensions when the surviving member of the couple accused of blowing up Korean Airlines flight 858 confessed to the deed (*Kyodo*, 15, 16, 18 January). The woman and her partner had posed as Japanese father and daughter on their travels, and some reports alleged the attack was part of a joint terrorist campaign conducted by the North and the Japanese Red Army. Prime Minister Takeshita specifically implicated the North in the crime (*Kyodo*, 16 January), and the Japanese Security Agency reopened investigations of missing persons on the strength of the claims—by Sin Sang-ok and Choe Un-hui among others—that North Korea had abducted Japanese citizens and forced them to give language instructions to terrorist trainees (*Korea Times*, 20 January; *Kyodo*, 3 February).

The government imposed sanctions two days after Kenji Miyamoto, the chairman of the Japanese Communist Party, said he believed North Korean agents were responsible for the bomb aboard flight 858 (*Kyodo*, 24, 25 January). As late as 22 January, the government had only "advised" citizens to reconsider travel to the North (*Kyodo*, 22 January) but on 26 January announced a ban on exchanges of official visits and of transit via Japan of flights destined for North Korea. Control over entry to Japan of North Korean citizens was "intensified" (*Kyodo*, 26 January). No economic sanctions were announced, and the government left open the possibility of unofficial visits by North Korean delegations.

North Korea responded immediately and predictably, declaring sanctions of its own against Japan on 1 February (*Nodong sinmun*, 1 February) making it clear there would be no further talks on releasing the crew of the *Fujisan Maru*, who had languished in North Korea since their capture in 1983. Japan "deplored" this counterpunch (*Kyodo*, 2 February) and denied entry to Yokohama of a North Korean vessel (*Kyodo*, 7 February). Another North Korean ship was admitted to Yokohama and Niigata port, but its crew was denied shore leave (*Kyodo*, 10 February). The same policy was invoked against a North Korean ship that visited Kobe in April (*Kyodo*, 1 April).

The Japanese sanctions, however, were not uniformly applied, and the South Koreans worried they would be lifted after the Olympics (*Korea Herald*, 29 March). In March, Japan announced it would deny visas for all North Koreans seeking to promote bilateral trade (*Asahi shimbun*, 9 March), and pro-Pyongyang Koreans denounced Tokyo's intention to ban re-entry to Japan of Koreans who visited their homeland—five Chosen Soren (the organization of pro-Pyongyang Koreans living in Japan) deputies did not attend the SPA meeting in April for fear they would not be allowed to return to Japan (KCNA, 4 April). Indeed, in June the port of Shimonoseki refused docking rights to a North Korean ship carrying 300 Korean residents of Japan returning from a visit to ancestral graves in North Korea (*Kyodo*, 27 June). The ship, however, found refuge in Kitakyoshu—the port closest to South Korea—a few days later, prompting a South Korean protest to Tokyo (*Yonhap*, 3 July).

On the other hand, on 20 April the Japanese announced they would permit ten North Koreans to conduct business talks in Japan. Tokyo also said it would allow North Korean officials to present a Korean wolf to a Japanese zoo. (*Kyodo*, 26 April.) The North, however, expressed its pique at Japan's sanctions policy by withdrawing the gift.

The most publicized exception to Japan's sanctions turned out to be an embarrassment to both sides. Japan announced it would admit a North Korean to the Asian table tennis championships—even though some on the delegation were government employees—on condition the North Koreans would not take part in any activities embarrassing to the Japanese government (*Kyodo*, 26 April, 6 May). The North may have read this decision as the first major crack in Tokyo's sanctions policy, and the president of the North Korean Table Tennis Association issued a statement welcoming the development (*Kyodo*, 9 May). Once in Japan, however, the team attended a welcoming reception given by Chosen Soren, which Japanese justice officials viewed as a violation of the conditions under which the visas were granted. The reception was unceremoniously broken up (*Kyodo*, 19 May). In protest, the North Korean team withdrew from the competition and went home (*Kyodo*, 20 May). North Korea strongly denounced Japan's action, and the head of its table tennis team called on international sports organizations to refuse to stage events in Japan (KCNA, 21 May).

The sanctions issue further damaged chances for progress toward releasing the *Fujisan Maru* crewmen. The issue already appeared stalemated when, in early January, Pyongyang refused a Japanese request for a meeting with the prisoners (*Kyodo*, 6 January). A plea from the Japanese Red Cross for reconsideration of the fifteen-year sentence meted

out to them on the basis of espionage charges (*Kyodo*, 12 January) was drowned by the fallout from the Korean Airlines flight 858 revelations. Japanese foreign minister Uno promised to keep trying to secure their release (*Kyodo*, 27 January), but Japanese socialist spokesmen accused the government of endangering the prisoners' health by invoking short-sighted sanctions against the North (*Kyodo*, 28 January). The North Korean Red Cross underscored these concerns when it declared the seamen's health had remained poor since first deteriorating in June 1987 (*Kyodo*, 17 February). In April, a North Korean Foreign Ministry spokesman declared that the *Fujisan Maru* problem "cannot be solved" (KCNA, 4 April).

The table tennis flap postponed tentative efforts to revive a dialogue on the issue (*Kyodo*, 23 May), and the North subsequently reiterated that progress would be impossible until Japan lifted its Korean Airlines flight 858–related sanctions (*Kyodo*, 22 June). Japan acknowledged this linkage, and a cabinet spokesman said his government would not lift sanctions before the Olympics—leaving open the possibility Tokyo would reconsider its options later in the year (*Kyodo*, 1 July). A few days later, Japan took advantage of South Korean president No's favorable nod toward better U.S. and Japanese relations with North Korea to call for "official talks" with Pyongyang on the *Fujisan Maru* problem (*Kyodo*, 8 July).

Despite the poor climate, North Korea left the door open for an eventual improvement in bilateral relations. Foreign Ministry officials told the Zambian foreign minister that they hoped relations with Japan would improve (Tokyo, *Jiji*, 8 March). In March and April, the North issued permits to Japanese fishing boats to operate within North Korea's 200-mile economic zone (*Kyodo*, 8 March, 12 April).

The Japanese decided finally to lift their sanctions the day before the Olympic opening ceremony (*Kyodo*, 16 September). The press speculated that Tokyo hoped the North Koreans in return would release the hapless *Fujisan Maru* crewmen. And, indeed, the North announced the latter had been released from jail but remained in North Korea pending resolution of the status of the North Korean seaman who had defected to Japan (*Kyodo*, 16 September). Japan granted the latter asylum in December, perhaps indicating Japanese confidence that the North would decouple the two issues or Japanese weariness with the impasse (*Kyodo*, 16 December). Indeed, the North responded with editorial criticism but did not immediately threaten the safety or status of their captives (KCNA, 22 December).

North Korea's relations with Japanese communists and socialists suffered badly in 1988. In a remarkable development, the Japanese Communist Party (JCP) issued a far stronger denunciation of the North's role in the flight 858 affair than had the Takeshita government. Kenji Miyamoto, JCP chairman, explicitly contradicted a weak editorial in the 16 January edition of *Akahata*, the party organ, and stated flatly, "we believe North Korean agents did it" (*Kyodo*, 24, 25 January). On 18 January, *Akahata* published an attack on the KWP's "barbarous model of hegemonism," calling the incident an "outrageous intervention" in civil commerce. In September, the JCP announced de facto recognition of South Korea, dismissing Kim Il-song's claim to be the sole legitimate Korean leader as "against historical reality" (*Kyodo*, 10 September). The JCP said Tokyo in return should recognize North Korea. Further evidence of JCP–North Korean tension emerged in October, when a JCP spokesman accused the North of preventing his party's participation in an international conference in Pyongyang (*Kyodo*, 21 October).

The JCP contrasted its policy with the Japan Socialist Party's (JSP's) vacillation. The JSP retained good relations with the North in 1988 but also seemed interested in contacts with the South. JSP officials visited North Korea and supported Pyongyang's contention that Japanese sanctions ensured that the *Fujisan Maru* crewmen would not be released soon (*Kyodo*, 1 July). On the other hand, party leader Doi Takako hinted publicly she was interested in expanding JSP relations with South Korea (see *Kyodo*, 11 April). The JSP seemed to go through internal ferment in May when a story in the party organ alleging that a former South Korean prime minister had "confessed" to U.S., Japanese, and South Korean responsibility for flight 858 led to domestic and South Korean demands for a retraction and apology (*Shakei shimbun*, 24 May). Two days later the JSP not only apologized but fired the paper's editor (*Kyodo*, 26 May). In June, the JSP set up a commission to review its policy toward South Korea (*Kyodo*, 2 June), and Doi told reporters she hoped to travel to Seoul "at an early date" (*Kyodo*, 13 June). In October, former JSP chairman Ishibashi led a delegation of ten party members on an unofficial visit to Seoul at the invitation of South Korean opposition politician Kim Young-sam (*Kyodo*, 12 October). Ishibashi met with President

No Tae-u as well as opposition leaders (*Yonhap*, 14 October).

Relations with the Third World. It appeared for a time that North Korea might become at least peripherally involved in efforts to settle the Cambodian problem. In late 1987, Prince Sihanouk had proposed meeting Cambodian premier Hun Sen in Pyongyang. The prince, however, continued to vacillate, alternately canceling (AFP, 4 January) and rescheduling (AFP, 19 January) these plans. It looked as if the meeting might be on when Phnom Penh reported Hun Sen's agreement to it (Phnom Penh, *SPK*, 25 January), but Sihanouk finally scuttled it, claiming Hun Sen had demanded a prior dissolution of Khmer Rouge forces (Xinhua, 7 February). As usual, Sihanouk came to North Korea after visiting China in April and remained in a palace near Pyongyang for two months (KCNA, 15 June). He paid an official courtesy call on Kim Il-song on 5 April (KCNA, 5 April), and the two old friends shared a banquet a few days later (Xinhua, 8 April). Sihanouk paid a visit to Kim and his wife on 15 April, Kim Il-song's 76th birthday (Pyongyang Domestic Service, 15 April), and Kim saw Sihanouk off in June (KCNA, 18 June). Interestingly, there is no evidence the Prince saw Kim Chong-il. Sihanouk returned for a short visit in August (KCNA, 2 August).

Olympic and terrorist fiascos left North Korea relatively isolated in 1988. Only Fiji actually broke off relations with the North after flight 858 (*Yonhap*, 10 February), but most Third World countries refused to support North Korea's Olympics boycott—and, as noted above, some may have disapproved of the choice of Pyongyang for the 1989 World Youth Festival. Nigerian Mahamane Sani Bako visited Seoul in June, announcing his country's support for the Olympics and South Korea's unification policy and asking for economic aid (*Yonhap*, 9 June).

Not surprisingly Cuba, the North's chief Olympics supporter, was Pyongyang's designated hero. Hwang Chang-yop, KWP secretary, met with Fidel Castro in Havana in March (Pyongyang Domestic Service, 2 March). One media commentary specified that the primary thrust of efforts by "U.S. imperialism" to gain military superiority and destroy the socialist system was Washington's "anti-DPRK, anti-Cuban campaign" (KCNA, 4 May).

There were some noteworthy North Korean diplomatic exchanges with other Third World states in 1988. President Mengistu of Ethiopia—the North's other major supporter on the Olympics—visited

Pyongyang in July (KCNA, 28 July). President Kaunda of Zambia had visited Pyongyang in early May (KCNA, 4 May) after a preparatory visit by Foreign Minister Mwananshiku. President Chissano of Mozambique did the same (KCNA, 20 May). Both presidents saw Kim Il-song, and both were shown around town by Vice President Yi Chong-ok. R.M. Kawawa, general secretary of the Revolutionary Party of Tanzania, came to Pyongyang in May (KCNA, 30 May), and Angolan president Dos Santos visited North Korea in October (KCNA, 26 October). Seychellois president René followed a few days later (KCNA, 7 November). Kim Il-song also received Iranian deputy foreign minister Mansouri in April (KCNA, 26 April) and Romesh Chandra, president of the World Peace Council, in May (KCNA, 11 May). Burkina Faso foreign minister Palm paid a visit to Kim Il-song in June (KCNA, 20 June). Shailendra Kumar Upadhyaya, his Nepalese counterpart, did the same in December (KCNA, 9 December).

North Korean officials also visited the Third World in 1988. Yi Chong-ok and North Korean foreign minister Kim Yong-nam made trips to Africa in 1988. Kim also met with Castro before addressing a meeting of nonaligned foreign ministers in Havana (KCNA, 30 May). He also visited Thailand and Nepal in October (KCNA, 26 October) and Iran in December (KCNA, 26 December). Premier Yi Kun-mo went to India (KCNA, 17 February) and Iran (KCNA, 20 June), while Supreme People's Assembly Standing Committee chairman Yang Hyong-sop visited Pakistan, Malaysia, and Singapore in May (KCNA, 30 May) and Thailand at the end of the year (KCNA, 26 December). On 29 December, Vice President Pak Song-chol left to represent North Korea at the celebration of the 30th anniversary of Fidel Castro's assumption of power (KCNA, 29 December).

David B. Kanin
Washington, D.C.

Laos

Population. 3,849,752. Average annual growth rate is 2.21 percent.
Party. Lao People's Revolutionary Party (Phak Pasason Pativat Lao; LPRP)
Founded. 22 March 1955
Membership. 40,000
General Secretary. Kaysone Phomvihane (68, Lao-Vietnamese, premier)
Politburo. 13 members: Kaysone Phomvihane, Nouhak Phoumsavan, Souphanouvong (president), Phoumi Vongvichit (acting president), Khamtai Siphandon, Phoun Sipaseut, Sisomphon Lovansai, Sisavat Keobounphan, Sali Vongkhamsao, Maichantan Sengmani, Saman Vi-gnaket, Oudom Khatti-gna (alternate), Chounmali Saignakon (alternate)
Secretariat. 9 members: Kaysone Phomvihane, Khamtai Siphandon, Sisavat Keobounphan, Sali Vongkhamsao, Maichantan Sengmani, Saman Vi-gnaket, Oudom Khatti-gna, Chounmali Saignakon, Somlak Chanthamat
Central Committee. 50 full members, 9 alternate members
Status. Ruling and sole legal party
Last Congress. Fourth, 13–15 November 1986, in Vientiane
Last Election. 1975; all 46 candidates were LPRP approved.
Auxiliary Organizations. Lao Front for National Construction (LFNC), Lao People's Revolutionary Youth Union, Federation of Trade Unions, Federation of Lao Women's Unions, Unified Buddhist Organization
Publications. *Pasason* (The people), LPRP central organ, published in Vientiane (daily); *Alun mai* (New dawn), LPRP theoretical journal, published in Vientiane (quarterly); the official news agency is Khaosan Pathet Lao (Pathet Lao News Agency; KPL)

The LPRP held a plenum early in 1988 at which a number of important decisions must have been made affecting subsequent developments, both domestically and internationally. Of these, the most significant by far was the decision to proceed with the holding of popular elections, the first since 1975. Two rounds were held to elect people's councils at the district and provincial levels; a third round, for the people's council at the central level, had to be postponed to 1989. Other decisions at the plenum accelerated the liberalization of the economy already under way for the past two years. In external affairs, the plenum introduced what was described on the occasion of a major anniversary as a "new conception" in relations with Vietnam and Cambodia. One possible manifestation of this "new conception" was the withdrawal of Vietnamese troops from Laos, confirmed by Laotian spokesmen to foreign journalists in May.

Party Leadership and Organization. In the first official mention in more than a year of the health of Souphanouvong, the veteran Pathet Lao leader and founding president of the Lao People's Democratic Republic (LPDR), KPL said on 2 February that he "is now gradually getting better," and he attended the three-day annual regular meeting of the Supreme People's Council (SPC) opening on that date (KPL, *FBIS*, 2 February). Souphanouvong suffered a stroke in 1986, according to unofficial accounts, and has not been participating in official functions. However, he joined acting President Phoumi Vongvichit in sending messages to Prince Norodom Sihanouk on the occasion of talks among the Cambodian factions. Adopting an extremely warm personal tone in his message, Souphanouvong recalled the two leaders' wartime meetings "in Phnom Penh, in the former liberated zone of Laos, in Hanoi, in Guangzhou, etc." and added "I myself and other Lao leaders were of the opinion that how sad it was to witness the upheaval inflicted upon your country due to genocidal forces." (KPL, *FBIS*, 4 February.)

Major General Kampha Chaleunphonmisai, a member of the LPRP Central Committee (CC) and a deputy minister of national defense, was killed in a helicopter crash on 14 March (Radio Vientiane, *FBIS*, 15 March). The crash of the Soviet-built MI-6 helicopter reportedly occurred near the scene of border fighting with Thailand, as the general was en route to Vientiane to participate in a medal award ceremony, and killed 23 other persons. (AFP, *FBIS*, 17 March.)

Domestic Party Affairs. The fifth plenum of the LPRP Fourth Congress was convened from 28 December 1987 to 17 January (Radio Vientiane, *FBIS*, 29 January). The plenum adopted a resolu-

tion "in which care is taken to widen the people's socialist democracy and freedom—the prerequisites for successful socialist building," according to a report of a nine-day seminar on general election affairs that opened in Vientiane on 1 April (KPL, 2 April; *FBIS*, 6 April). The report revealed that preparations were already under way to organize popular elections.

The initial instructions to party committees at all echelons issued by the LPRP CC Secretariat stated that the elections to people's councils in three successive rounds should be completed by the end of 1988 (Radio Vientiane, 12 May; *FBIS*, 17 May). This schedule proved overly ambitious, however. After holding the first round of elections for district-level people's councils as planned on 26 June, LPRP leaders, citing drought in the southern provinces, postponed the second round for provincial- and municipal-level people's councils from 23 October to 20 November and were unable to complete the process with a third round at the national level before the end of 1988.

The LPDR has not held any popular elections since November 1975, when balloting was hastily contrived in the "newly liberated zone" in an effort to lend some aspect of legality to the proceedings of the National People's Congress, which met the following month to abolish the monarchy and to proclaim the LPDR and appoint its leadership. Since that time the decisions of the LPRP have been the only law. Work on a constitution has been going on in a committee of the SPC, but progress seems to have been laborious. An SPC delegation discussed this work with the Supreme Soviet Presidium in March (TASS, 21 March). One of the first tasks of the national-level people's council, when elected, will presumably be to ratify this document as has been suggested by LPDR officials (*FEER*, 24 November).

Until 1985, Laos did not even have a population census. Appropriate election laws and procedures have had to be worked out from scratch. It is hardly surprising, therefore, that the whole process took longer than had been initially anticipated by the LPRP leadership. The fault lay with the organizers, whose lack of initiative was severely criticized in postballoting review, and not with the voters, who reportedly turned out in large numbers to fulfill their democratic duties.

The general election law was still only in draft form on 24 February when a one-week conference of participants from state and public institutions was opened by Sisomphon Lovansai, a Politburo member of the LPRP and the acting chairman of the SPC (KPL, *FBIS*, 24 February). In its final form, the election law was passed by the SPC at an extraordinary one-day session on 19 April (Radio Vientiane, 20 April; *FBIS*, 22 April). At this session, the SPC also passed a Law on the SPC of the LPDR and a Law on the Establishment of People's Councils and People's Administrative Committees at Various Levels.

This last was in fact an amendment of a law that had originally been passed by the SPC on 31 July 1978 (Radio Vientiane, 28–30 April; *FBIS*, 4 May). It consisted of 48 articles that defined the relationship between people's councils and the administrative committees of LPRP cadres that have overseen implementation of LPRP resolutions at all levels since 1975. People's councils have heretofore existed mainly in theory. In the words of Sisomphon, "though they can still be seen in certain areas, they are merely organizations and no concrete activities have been carried out." (Radio Vientiane, 29 August; *FBIS*, 1 September.)

No explanation has been forthcoming as to why the 1978 election law was never implemented. In 1978, however, there was widespread insecurity resulting from the resistance activities of guerrilla groups operating from Thailand. Vietnam's invasion of Cambodia, the third side of what the respective parties refer to as the "special relationship" in December 1978, and the establishment of the People's Republic of Kampuchea under Vietnamese auspices may also have been reasons for the failure to hold popular elections and clarify the constitutional setup in the LPDR.

Article 1 of the Law on the SPC of the LPDR states that "the SPC of the LPDR serves as the supreme representative organization of the laboring people of various tribes and the supreme state power organization of the LPDR." (Radio Vientiane, 2 May; *FBIS*, 6 May.)

Passage of the election law was followed immediately by a string of decrees from acting President Phoumi and Premier Kaysone setting an election schedule and establishing a national election committee charged with actually organizing the balloting. All seven members of the standing committee of this national election committee were high-ranking party members. (Radio Vientiane, 23 April; *FBIS*, 25 April.) Party oversight of the candidates for election was ensured by instructions issued by the LPRP Secretariat:

Party committees must appropriately guide and direct people's council elections at their own levels in accordance with practical conditions in their respective localities. The most important thing is that they must guide the Lao Front for National Construction; mass organizations such as youth, women, and trade unions; economic and cultural organizations; and national defense and public security maintenance organizations to consider and make public the political qualifications of candidates running in elections.

As for political qualifications, the candidates must maintain a line of thinking that explicitly distinguishes friends from foes, and a certain ability level for implementing the line and policies of the party and state. (Radio Vientiane, 12 May; *FBIS*, 17 May.)

A radio broadcast urged that the political standards of candidates "must be in alignment." It added "this means that they must possess the clear-cut class stand of the laboring people." (Radio Vientiane, *FBIS*, 16 May.)

Preparations for the first round of elections were said to be complete by 8 June (KPL, *FBIS*, 8 June). In the voting on 26 June, 1,793,032 people over the age of 18 were said to be eligible. There were in all 4,462 candidates running for 2,410 district-level seats, broken down as follows by the number of candidates for the number of seats in each province: Attopeu, 109 for 74; Bokeo, 113 for 59; Bolikhamsai, 203 for 102; Champassak, 342 for 212; Houa Phan, 247 for 130; Khammouane, 292 for 122; Luang Namtha, 205 for 113; Luang Prabang, 349 for 183; Oudomsai, 497 for 245; Phong Saly, 224 for 110; Saravane, 212 for 135; Savannakhet, 585 for 262; Sayaboury, 171 for 101; Sekong, 98 for 55; Vientiane province, 325 for 189; Vientiane municipality, 258 for 182; and Xieng Khouang, 238 for 136. (Radio Vientiane, 26 June; *FBIS*, 27 June.)

The LPRP drew lessons from the first round in preparing for the second. In its instructions issued on 6 August for the second round, the LPRP CC Secretariat blamed a lack of coordination between the party leadership on the one hand and the LFNC and other mass organizations on the other for voters in many localities not adequately knowing the background of the candidates. "That was one of the causes why many key cadres with full qualifications failed to get elected as people's representatives." (Radio Vientiane, 10 August; *FBIS*, 16 August.) Some party committees, moreover, failed to pay close attention to guiding work in carrying out the election and "considered that the election was solely the task of the election committees." In a supporting editorial, *Pasason* criticized the LFNC committees at grassroots levels for "lacking a sense of responsibility and initiative." (Radio Vientiane, 5 September; *FBIS*, 8 September.)

In the rescheduled second round on 20 November, for which preparations were basically complete 12 November, there were 898 candidates. Of these, 54 were women. The oldest candidate was 66 and the youngest 24. (KPL, 12 November; *FBIS*, 14 November.) In this round, 651 seats on province-level people's councils were contested, the size of each council varying from 31 to 45 depending on "the significance of the province's position in the fields of economy, society, politics, and national defense and public security and the total population of the province" (Radio Vientiane, 21 November; *FBIS*, 21 November). In early 1989, the electoral committees having drawn the appropriate lessons during meetings held in December, the third round would take place. In this process, the SPC would be enlarged from 46 to 79, according to LPDR officials quoted in Western media. (*FEER*, 24 November.) Premier Kaysone made the following comment in casting his ballot:

Democracy means that our people can consult with one another. It is not what we call nepotism. Our people, be they old or young or of either sex, have the right to consult with one another. Anyone can express his own opinion. Any sound, good views are always acceptable to all. (Radio Vientiane, 20 November; *FBIS*, 29 November.)

Under the new economic and financial policies decided on by the LPRP, companies and factories are expected to make a profit, prices are to be determined by the costs of production and the law of supply and demand, and workers are to be paid according to their productivity. Private traders are again allowed to operate, and competition among trading firms is no longer illegal. Checkpoints at provincial borders have been lifted, allowing goods to move more freely. Provinces can trade directly with foreign countries. A new law on foreign investments was endorsed by the SPC. (Radio Vientiane, 29 July; *FBIS*, 3 August.)

In a government reorganization, the Ministry of Finance was merged with the State Planning Commission to form a new Ministry of Economics, Planning and Finance, with Sali Vongkhamsao as minister. Phao Bounnaphon, the former minister of transport and communications, was named head of the newly formed Ministry of Foreign Trade and

Economic Relations. Oudom Khatti-gna was named minister of transport, and Saman Vi-gnaket was named minister of education. The Public Health Ministry was combined with the Social Welfare Committee to form the new Ministry of Public Health and Social Welfare, with Khambou Sounixay as minister. (*FEER*, 24 November.)

National road 9, now completely asphalted, was ceremoniously handed over to the LPDR by visiting Soviet vice-chairman of the Council of Ministers Vladimir Kuzmich Gusev at Se Thamouak in Savannakhet province on 19 November (KPL, 21 November; *FBIS*, 23 November). Also handed over was a 150-bed Soviet-built hospital in Vientiane (KPL, 20 November; *FBIS*, 30 November).

Without any explanation, the Catholic bishop of Pakse and the parish priest of his cathedral were released after eight years in prison (*Eglisi*, 4 November). The celebration of the LPDR's national day on 2 December, which marked the 13th anniversary of the regime, was "not on a big scale this year" (KPL, 29 November; *FBIS*, 30 November).

Auxiliary Organizations. The Lao People's Revolutionary Youth Union (LPRYU) held its Second National Congress in Vientiane on 13–15 July. Mrs. Thongvin Phomvihane, who is LPRP general secretary Kaysone's wife, delivered a political report and was re-elected as the first secretary of the organization's 35-member executive committee. (KPL, 16 July; *FBIS*, 18 July.) The LPRYU has 254,740 members in 5,787 grass-roots cells (KPL, *FBIS*, 23 June). On the occasion of her 50th birthday, Mrs. Phomvihane was awarded the Komsomol's highest order in recognition of her endeavors for peace and strengthening of friendship and solidarity among nations by Soviet ambassador to Laos Yuriy Mikhheyev (KPL, 30 January; *FBIS*, 2 February).

The sixth plenum (First Congress) of the Federation of Lao Women's Unions (FLWU) closed in Vientiane on 19 June after four days of work with the attendance of more than 60 delegates (KPL, 20 June; *FBIS*, 21 June). The organization held its Second National Congress in Vientiane 13–14 October attended by 255 delegates representing 496,032 members. Mrs. Onchan Thammavong, LPRP CC member and vice president of the FLWU, presented a political report. (KPL, 13 October; *FBIS*, 18 October.) A 37-member CC was elected. The LPRP CC Politburo announced that Aunt Khampheng Boupha, chairwoman of the first CC of the FLWU, had been appointed a member of the SPC standing committee. (Radio Vientiane, 14 October; *FBIS*, 18 October.)

International Views and Activities. The withdrawal of Vietnamese troops from Laos was first reported in March by foreign journalists quoting diplomats in Hanoi and Vientiane. Diplomats and aid workers who traveled to Bolikhamsai province in late December 1987 reported seeing four or five freshly abandoned Vietnamese army camps. Visitors to Xieng Khouang province in January reported seeing a convoy of 85 army trucks, full of soldiers and towing antiaircraft guns, heading toward the Vietnam border. The number of troops withdrawn was said to be four to five thousand. (*FEER*, 24 March.) Vietnamese troops in rotating units have been in Laos continuously since 1961, when fighting between the U.S.-backed Royal Army and the Pathet Lao escalated sharply, leading to an international conference on the "neutralization" of the country. After the cease-fire of February 1973 and the seizure of power by the LPRP in December 1975, the continued presence of Vietnamese troops was justified by the "threat" posed to Laos by China. The 1977 treaties between the LPDR and Vietnam provided a legal cover for this presence.

In an editorial in *Pasason* in February that reviewed implementation of the resolutions of the Fourth Congress, mention was made of a "new form of our relations and cooperation with Vietnam" in connection with "an experiment on building the strategic area at Lak Sao in Khamkeut District," Khammouane province. "It is a new form of building technical-economic groups in the mountainous rural region by combining the economy with national defense," the paper wrote. (Radio Vientiane, 10 February; *FBIS*, 23 February.)

In March, hailing "the victory of Boten battle front" (see below) in an editorial timed to coincide with an award ceremony in Vientiane, *Pasason* significantly failed to mention, even in the customary guarded manner, support from Vietnam in the conflict with Thailand. "The victories at the Boten battle were the victory of the heroic Lao nationhood, the heroic Lao army, the result of our efforts to be independent and self-sufficient and the strong will to fulfill our revolutionary tasks," the editorial said. (KPL, *FBIS*, 15 March.)

The first mention of a Vietnamese troop withdrawal by an official LPDR spokesman came in May. In a news conference in Vientiane for Western journalists, Deputy Foreign Minister Souban Salit-thilat said on 23 May that a "significant" contingent had withdrawn and had begun withdrawing in 1987. (*WP*, 24 May.) Significantly, the LPDR normalized its relations with China less than a month later; on 13 June, Liang Feng, the ambassador extraordinary and plenipotentiary of the People's Republic of China (PRC), presented his credentials to acting President Phoumi Vongvichit (KPL, 14 June; *FBIS*, 16 June).

On 22 November, Souban told a group of foreign journalists visiting Vientiane that "there are no Vietnamese soldiers in Laos." (AFP, *FBIS*, 23 November.) However, this claim was disputed by Lieutenant General Narudon Detpradiyut, director of the Thai Supreme Command Information Office, who maintained that there were still 20,000 of the original 40,000–60,000 Vietnamese troops in Laos, most of them engineers and most combat units being in the areas of Savannakhet, Champassak, and Luang Prabang. (Bangkok, *Naeo Na*, 25 November; *FBIS*, 28 November.) This evaluation concords with intelligence estimates that Vietnamese troops were still firmly entrenched in Cambodia and Laos near the junction of their common border with Thailand astride an infiltration route used by resistance groups in both countries (see below) (*FEER*, 1 December).

On 5–6 July Vietnam's foreign minister Nguyen Co Thach visited Vientiane at the invitation of the LPRP CC and the LPDR government as the special envoy of Nguyen Van Linh. He and Kaysone exchanged views "on recent developments in the world and Southeast Asia and on the tasks of national construction and defense of the two peoples." (Radio Hanoi, 6 July; *FBIS*, 7 July.)

On 6–7 February a scientific research conference of party historians was held in Vientiane. According to a joint communiqué, Sisana Sisan, chief of the Commission for the Study of the History of the LPRP, read a report on the Lao people's movements of revolutionary struggle under the leadership of the Indochinese Communist Party (ICP) and on the evolution and development of the Khmer People's Revolutionary Party (KPRP). Chey Sophon, head of the Commission for the Study of the KPRP, read a report on the evolution of the Cambodian revolution under the leadership of the ICP. Nguyen Van Phung, head of the Institute for the Study of the History of the Vietnam Communist Party, read a report on certain necessary issues concerning the history of the ICP that must be studied thoroughly. (Radio Vientiane, 8 February; *FBIS*, 29 February.)

The LPDR's relations with Thailand started 1988 on a note of armed confrontation but ended more positively with the visit to Vientiane of the new Thai prime minister amid professions of peace from both sides. The issue this time was a dispute over an area claimed by the LPDR as part of Boten district in Sayaboury province and by Thailand as part of Chat Trakan district in Phitsanulok province. The rival sovereignty claims arise from the ambiguity of topographic nomenclature in the Franco-Siamese Treaty of 1907, which both countries recognize as defining the border. The 1907 treaty had no map annexed.

Sporadic shooting and mining incidents had occurred since May 1987 in the area, which has importance for logging and apparently smuggling activities. However, in December 1987 the fighting escalated sharply, with the bringing to bear of large troop concentrations and heavy weapons and aircraft. (*FEER*, 28 January.) The Lao side shot down a Thai plane and captured two pilots. The casualties suffered on both sides apparently outnumbered those in prevous fighting along the border farther north where three villages are in dispute, and feeling ran high with popular demonstrations taking place in both capitals.

Consultations by military leaders on both sides, with some help from former Thai prime minister General Kriangsak Chamanan, who reportedly paid a secret visit to Vientiane (AFP, 18 February; *FBIS*, 22 February), led to the conclusion of an agreement in Bangkok between Lao People's Army chief of staff General Sisavat Keobounphan and Thai Army commander in chief General Chawalit Yongchaiyut for a cease-fire effective 19 February and mutual disengagement of forces (Radio Vientiane, *FBIS*, 18 February). This was followed almost immediately by a visit to Vientiane by General Chawalit (KPL, *FBIS*, 24 February). Meanwhile, a Lao-Thai military committee began work inside the disputed area to ensure compliance with the cease-fire (Radio Vientiane, *FBIS*, 23 February).

Although the cease-fire continued to hold, several rounds of talks by Foreign Ministry officials failed to resolve the territorial dispute, and the LPDR informed U.N. secretary general Javier Perez de Cuellar of its case (KPL, 30 April; *FBIS*, 3 May). It was not until a change of government in Bangkok that prospects opened for substantive talks at the diplomatic level. Then, during a further visit to Bangkok by General Sisavat in October, the new Thai prime minister, General Chatchai Chunhawan, gave a fresh spur to the talks. Chatchai himself accepted an invitation from LPDR premier Kaysone to visit Laos. The visit occurred on 24–25 November in an atmosphere of considerable expectation.

The two prime ministers signed a joint communiqué in the VIP lounge of Wattai Airport. Chatchai's visit was described as "an extremely important step in the consolidation and strengthening of the relations, cooperation, and mutual understanding between the governments and peoples of Laos and Thailand." The communiqué expressed satisfaction at the effectiveness of the cease-fire and announced the appointment of a joint border committee to hold negotiations. Kaysone also accepted an invitation to visit Thailand. (KPL, 26 November; *FBIS*, 28 November.)

The two sides "unanimously agreed" that the issue of Lao refugees in Thailand was one that had caused problems for the two countries, and therefore "the two sides agreed to cooperate with each other and with the U.N. High Commissioner for Refugees in solving this problem." According to the LPDR, there are some 90,000 refugees from Laos in Thailand—60,000 hill tribe people and 30,000 lowland Lao. (Radio Vientiane, 21 November; *FBIS*, 30 November.) That this large refugee population has served as a recruitment base for anti-LPDR guerrillas is well known and may do so in the future to the extent that the Vietnamese troop withdrawal and the measures to liberalize the economy have the effect of decreasing the regime's unpopularity at home. During the last visit by a Thai prime minister to Laos in 1979, Prime Minister Kriangsak and Premier Kaysone pledged to avoid interference in the other country's affairs, a phrase that was widely interpreted to mean that each country would not harbor bases for guerrillas operating against the other. LPDR spokesmen often quote this pledge as the basis for neighborly relations.

The persistence of guerrilla activities may constitute an even more serious problem in Lao-Thai relations than the border disputes. The LPDR media constantly warn the population to be vigilant against "exiled Lao reactionaries, commandos, and bandits." Thus, for example, Radio Vientiane reported the award of a certificate of commendation to a village in Champassak province—near the strategic triborder junction—for tracking down enemy elements and "searching and seizing all arms and provisions caches stashed away in the vicinity of the village by the enemies." (Radio Vientiane, 13 November; *FBIS*, 15 November.) This implies that the guerrilla groups are well organized, and indeed a

Bangkok newspaper carried an interview with the leader of one such group (*Bangkok Post*, 19 February).

Hmong guerrillas were reported to have ambushed a convoy of fifteen trucks on Route 13 between Vang Vieng and Luang Prabang at Christmas 1987 (AFP, 10 January; *FBIS*, 11 January). A bomb, also thought to be the work of resistance elements, exploded in front of a building housing Soviet experts in Vientiane on 17 November; although not reported by LPDR media, the story became widely known because the incident occurred only 200 meters from the Thai embassy and figured in official communications with Bangkok (Bangkok, *The Nation*, 20 November; *FBIS*, 21 November).

Guerrilla activities and the unresolved border disputes with Thailand notwithstanding, 1988 marked a year of lessening tensions in the LPDR's external affairs. The movement toward a negotiated settlement of the Cambodian problem, which the LPDR leaders feel to be closely connected with their own interests, especially opened a brighter perspective in Vientiane. Kaysone devoted a large section of his political report to the SPC annual meeting to tracing the progress toward a Cambodian settlement. (Radio Vientiane, 2 February; *FBIS*, 18 February.) As Souphanouvong's message to Prince Sihanouk made clear, the Lao would have no problem in accepting the volatile prince as a main actor in such a settlement. Also, the normalization of relations with China has helped clear the atmosphere.

Relations with the United States also continued their slow but steady improvement in 1988. The LPDR handed over to the United States remains of U.S. citizens missing in Laos that were salvaged from the excavations by LPDR personnel of plane crash sites in Savannakhet and Saravane provinces during December 1987 and January 1988. "The Lao side's positive response to this U.S. humanitarian issue shows the sincerity of the LPDR government in improving relations with the United States," Radio Vientiane said on the occasion (Radio Vientiane and *FBIS*, 17 February). Two joint Lao-U.S. excavations were reported later on. They took place in Tchepone district, Savannakhet province, in May and in Nong district in the same province in December (KPL, *FBIS*, 8 November).

Deputy Foreign Minister Souban arrived in Washington on 9 June for a three-day visit after having addressed the special U.N. session on disarmament (KPL and *FBIS*, 15 June). He met with government officials and with Ann Mills Griffith, executive director of the League of Families of POWs/MIAs. (*Newsletter of the League of Families of POWs/MIAs*, 15 June.)

On 22 November Souban said that the LPDR was moving satisfactorily on both the missing in action and drug fronts, despite a State Department charge that Laos was trafficking in narcotics "as a matter of policy" (*WP*, 30 August). Souban told reporters that U.S. charges that some Laotian officials were involved in trafficking were true but that those involved had been arrested and tried. "We dismantled two laboratories in June in Oudomsai," he said, and the governor of the province was sentenced to seven years in jail (AFP, 23 November; *FBIS*, 25 November).

The World Bank granted a loan of $25.8 million to the LPDR for use in rural electrification projects in southern Laos (KPL, 15 February; *FBIS*, 19 February). The World Bank carries gross national product per capita in the LPDR as $160 (*The World Bank Atlas*, 1988).

Kaysone's travels in 1988 took him to the Soviet Union, where he spent from 27 July to 31 August on holiday at the invitation of the Communist Party of the Soviet Union CC (Radio Vientiane, *FBIS*, 27 July). He returned to Vientiane on 30 September after visits to East Germany, Bulgaria, and Mongolia (Radio Vientiane, *FBIS*, 30 September). Kaysone was in Hanoi for medical tests in March (AFP, *FBIS*, 4 March).

Arthur J. Dommen
Bethesda, Maryland

Malaysia and Singapore

Population. Malaysia: 16,309,306; Singapore: 2,645,443
Party. Communist Party of Malaya (CPM); North Kalimantan Communist Party (NKCP)
Founded. CPM: 1930
Membership. Peninsular Malaysia: about 1,200

armed insurgents on Thailand side of international boundary; about 150 inside Malaysia; Sarawak: 42; Sabah: insignificant. Singapore: 200–500; Barisan Sosialis infiltrated by communists. (*World Fact Book*, 1988.)

General Secretary. CPM: Chin Peng

Politburo. No data

Central Committee. Abdullah C.D., chairman

Status. Illegal

Last Congress. CPM: 1965 (last known)

Auxiliary Organizations. CPM: Malayan People's Army (MPA); Malay Nationalist Revolutionary Party of Malaya (MNRPM)

Publications. CPM: No regular periodicals known; Voice of Malayan Democracy (VOMD), clandestine radio station. MNRPM: *Suluh Rakyat*.

Leadership and Party Organization. Chin Peng, whose death has been reported frequently during the past ten years, was still referred to as general secretary of the CPM at the third plenary session of the party's Twelfth Central Committee held on 10 August. Abdullah C.D., chairman of the CPM's principal front organization, the MNRPM, was elected chairman of the CPM Central Committee at that meeting. The press announcement on the meeting understandably did not say where the meeting was held; neither did it state how many attended or who the principal attendees were.

The meeting amended the party's constitution to provide that the plenary session of the party's Central Committee shall elect the Central Committee Politburo, its chairman, general secretary, and vice–general secretary; issue important decisions of the party; and be entitled to dismiss or accept new members or candidate members of the Central Committee if deemed necessary. The plenary session is organized by the Central Committee Politburo. These proposed amendments were to be presented to the upcoming Central Committee plenary meeting for ratification. (VOMD, 22 August; *FBIS*, 23 August.)

The impression created by this press announcement of an active, vigorous party contrasted markedly with other news about the party and its supporters during the year. On 1 January, Thai army sources said the CPM had requested another month to consider the army's proposal that the insurgents stop their armed struggle in exchange for official permission to settle permanently on Thai soil. At that time, about 400 CPM guerrillas were reportedly still active along the border of Yala province.

The CPM members reportedly feared they might be sent back to Malaysia, although Thai government policy continues to allow CPM members who lay down their arms to remain in Thailand. (*Voice of Free Asia*, 1 January; *FBIS*, 5 January.)

During the year, there were reports of small numbers of guerrillas surrendering to Thai forces including three members of the CPM 10th regiment who surrendered in mid-January (*Bangkok Post*, 16 January; *FBIS*, 21 January). There were also frequent reports of guerrillas killed or arrested by Malaysian security forces. Details in some of these reports suggest a degree of continued CPM organization. For example, a leader of the 1st Armed Task Force killed in Selangor was a member of a regional Central Committee. He was 41 years old and had joined the CPM in 1975. (RTM Television Network, 1, 4 March; *FBIS*, 7 March.)

In early March, Malaysia's inspector general of police estimated there were about 1,400 communist guerrillas operating from Malaysian jungles after more than 900 surrendered to Malaysian and Thai authorities in 1987. Twelve hundred of those terrorists were said to be operating along the Malaysian-Thai border, 150 in the Malaysian peninsula, and 42 in Sarawak. Most of the remnants of the communist units in the peninsula were believed to be in Selangor, Perak, and Pahang. The police inspector general warned the public to be constantly on the alert against a real threat of a communist attempt to seize power by militant means. (*Bernama*, 6, 7 March; *FBIS*, 7 March.) Small bands of terrorists reportedly failed in their attempts to establish a base in Negeri Sembilan because of the unwillingness of the local population to support them, and the only *Orang Asli* (aborigines) assisting the terrorists were said to be doing so under coercion (*Berita Harian*, 31 March; *FBIS*, 13 April; *Bernama*, *FBIS*, 5 May). In Sarawak, some of the 42 remaining communist terrorists reportedly wished to surrender but were prevented from doing so by their leader. A special branch official said that, except for their leader, many of the communist remnants in Sarawak are still young and could carry on with their struggle for a long time. (Kuala Lumpur International Service, *FBIS*, 13 October.)

There were no indications of CPM organization or leadership in Singapore, although the Singapore government said there was new evidence of CPM links to the people arrested in 1987 for allegedly participating in a Marxist conspiracy (*FEER*, 5 May).

Domestic Party Activities. The year 1988 was one of some political turmoil in Malaysia, including a deep split in the long-time ruling party, the United Malays National Organization (UMNO) and the dismissal of the chief justice and several other Supreme Court justices (*CSM*, 14 January; *WSJ*, 5 February; *NYT* 27 October). A broadcast on the CPM's clandestine radio station about the split in UMNO gave a reasonably low-keyed account of these events (VOMD, 2 March; *FBIS*, 3 March). At the beginning of the year, Malaysia's deputy home minister, Datuk Megat Junid Megat Ayub, said that the CPM had adopted new tactics to screen its efforts to attract recruits from the business and professional classes. He said that the recruiters were masquerading behind bogus businesses and trading houses after recognizing that their traditional program of recruiting among workers and farmers was ineffective. (*Washington Times*, 18 January.) On another occasion, he said that communists had "tried to infiltrate the social movement in the country by exploiting local sentiments" (Kuala Lumpur International Service, *FBIS*, 3 March). Later in the year he said that among those the government had arrested under the Internal Security Act (ISA) in October 1987 were two or three communist agents who had infiltrated the trade union movement. These agents, who were ordinary members of the union, had managed to join the unions without the union leaders' knowledge, according to the deputy minister. The agents were trained to be cadres by two communist parties in two neighboring countries, he claimed. Their task was to organize demonstrations and instill anti-government feelings. The deputy minister said that the government had evidence that the agents had participated in a popular uprising against President Ferdinand Marcos in the Philippines in 1986. In his statement to the press, the minister also said that no politician detained under the ISA in 1987 was a communist agent. (*Bernama*, *FBIS*, 9 September.)

The government's White Paper on security, issued in March to explain its reasons for the arrest and detention of more than 100 public figures six months earlier, reiterated the argument made at the time of the arrests: that the police had to act in a situation of mounting racial and religious tensions that Marxist sympathizers were exploiting. The report said that some Catholic church workers were Marxists who believed in the Marxist "liberation theology." One of the detained church social workers was quoted as having said under interrogation that they had formed an urban rural mission to organize estate and factory workers and squatters with the "aim of forming a mass-based people's movement" to radically challenge existing social structures and government policies. The report said that university campuses were also a Marxist target and that two university lecturers, Mohamed Nasir Hashim and Chee Heng Leng, among the detainees had worked toward a "dictatorship of the proletariat." A radical Malay student, Mohamed Yunus Lebai Ali, reportedly said under interrogation that CPM general secretary Chin Peng, whom he had met in Beijing in 1980, had encouraged him to revive militant activity among Malay students. According to the report, Yunus also claimed that Chin financed his studies in London, where he met Tan Wah Piow, believed to be the mastermind behind the alleged Marxists detained in 1987 in Singapore. A government statement said that Yunus told authorities that Tsui Hon Kwong, a former student colleague of Tan's who now lives in Hong Kong, was instructed by Chin to arrange for Yunus's finances and had supplied Yunus with funds over the next three years. (*FEER*, 7 April, 5 May; see *YICA*, 1988.) The VOMD's commentary on the White Paper chided the government for not revising its own policies rather than blaming those arrested for arousing dissatisfaction among the people (VOMD, 9 June; *FBIS*, 17 June).

In Singapore, where nine of those accused in 1987 of being Marxist conspirators (see *YICA*, 1988) retracted their televised confessions and eight were promptly rearrested, there were new government charges of the group's links to the CPM. Trade and Industry Minister Lee Hsien Loong, commenting on a statement by one of the former detainees, said that "the plot" was about "the overthrow of the government and the establishment of a Marxist state" (Singapore, *Sunday Times*, 24 April; *FBIS*, 25 April). Singapore government officials said that Lim Li Kok, a bookshop owner who was one of the original detainees but not one of those rearrested, told authorities she had supplied locally published books on economics and politics to Tan Wah Piow, who had then passed on the books to the CPM. She also said that Tan had helped five fellow students, said by the government to be CPM members, to gain political asylum in Europe after working for the CPM's radio station that operated in southern China until 1981. One of the five students, now living in Paris, denied that she or her four fellow students had ever been members of the CPM or had any connection with the CPM. Some observers thought that the Singapore government's statements, issued after the rearrests in April, marked a shift in the terms of the perceived Marxist threat posed by the detainees. The role of Catholic church workers, a centerpiece of the government's case against the detainees in 1987, was downplayed somewhat in its 1988 statements. One of the four priests forced to step down from his activities in the Singapore diocese after the 1987 arrests told a newspaperman that the government "tried to sell this idea that there were Marxists in the church last year, but it didn't work. So they have reverted to the hidden hand of the CPM. No one knows anything about the CPM so it is much more difficult to refute." (*FEER*, 5 May.)

Auxiliary and Front Organizations. The CPM's principal front organization, the MNRPM, continued to focus its appeal on Malaysia's Malay Muslim majority. An editorial in *Suluh Rakyat*, an MNRPM publication, on the question of revising the Malaysian constitution vigorously supported the proposal to establish a royal commission to conduct the revision. In particular, the editorial endorsed the recommendations made by the Deputy Paramount Ruler, His Royal Highness Perak Sultan Azlan Shah, noting that "the sultan previously served as lord president and is thoroughly knowledgeable in constitutional affairs." The editorial praised Malaysia's blend of parliamentary democracy with constitutional monarchy and the traditional role of the paramount ruler and sultans "as guardian of the sovereign rights of the Malays and symbol of the unity" of the country's multiracial people. The prime minister was accused of seizing power for matters pertaining to Islam, which, under the present constitution, rests with the sultans, not the government. Under the present government, the editorial said, "the sacredness of Islam has been desecrated and religion has been politicized." (VOMD, 7 April; *FBIS*, 13 April.)

International Activities. There is no information about CPM or affiliated organizations' activities in international communist forums.

Jeanne S. Mintz
Washington, D.C.

Mongolia

Population. 2,067,624
Party. Mongolian People's Revolutionary Party (MPRP)
Founded. 1 March 1921
Membership. 88,150 (*WMR*, February); 30.3 percent women; 33.2 percent workers; 16.8 percent Agricultural Association members; 50 percent intelligentsia
General Secretary. Jambyn Batmonh (62)
Politburo. 7 members: Jambyn Batmonh (chairman, Presidium of People's Great Hural), Dumaagiyn Sodnom (premier), Bat-Ochirym Altangerel, Bujyn Dejid, Demchigiyn Molomjamts, Tserendashiyn Namsray, Bandzaragchin Lhamjab; 2 candidate members: Sonomyn Lubsangombo, Paavangiyn Damdin
Secretariat. 6 members: Jambyn Batmonh, Tserenpilyn Balhaajab, Paavangiyn Damdin, Bujyn Dejid, Demchigiyn Molomjamts, Tserendashiyn Namsray
Central Committee. 85 full members; 65 candidate members
Status. Ruling party
Last Congress. Nineteenth, 28–31 May 1986, in Ulan Bator
Last Election. 22 June 1986; of 370 seats in People's Great Hural, 346 (93.5 percent) went to members or candidate members of the MPRP.
Auxiliary Organizations. Mongolian Revolutionary Youth League (269,000 members), Ts. Narangerel, first secretary; Central Council of Mongolian Trade Unions, B. Lubsantseren, chairman; Committee of Mongolian Women, L. Pagmadulam, chairwoman
Publications. *Unen* (Truth), MPRP daily organ, published Tuesday–Sunday; MONTSAME is the official news agency.

Leadership and Party Organization. The MPRP's top leadership did not change significantly in 1988. Foreign Minister Mangalyn Dugersuren was replaced by Tserenpilyn Gombosuren on 22 June (MONTSAME, 22 June; *FBIS*, 23 June). Although there was some speculation that Dugersuren was removed because of his opposition to the

MPRP's moves to improve relations with China, he was subsequently appointed Mongolia's ambassador to the United Nations on 29 August.

The other major change was a government reorganization in January. Six state commissions and committees were combined into two: the MPRP State Committee for Planning and Economy headed by Puntsagiyn Jasray, deputy chairman of the Council of Ministers; and the MPRP State Committee for Science, Technology, and Higher Education headed by Munhoorjiyn Dash, former head of the State Committee for Science and Technology. (MONTSAME, 2 January; *FBIS*, 26 January.) The reorganization is the Mongolian version of *perestroika* and accompanies the government's admission of widespread failure in the economy. (*FEER*, 11 February, 30 June.)

Domestic Affairs. More significant than changes in leadership this year was the attitude adopted toward past leaders. In line with Soviet criticism of Joseph Stalin and his successors through Leonid Brezhnev, the Mongolian party began the unprecedented denunciation of both Stalin and former Mongolian leaders. In April MONTSAME carried the reminiscences of a Soviet poet who told of Stalin's persecutions of Mongols who were driven into Siberia. (MONTSAME, 12 April; *FBIS*, 26 April.) Writers to Mongolian publications demanded that Stalin's statue be removed from public places. Mongolian leaders also began to denounce Choybalsan and Tsedenbal. In his report at the fifth plenum of the Nineteenth Central Committee in December, Batmonh charged that Choybalsan had created a personality cult that violated party democracy and allowed the "administrative method of management" to take the upper hand. (Radio Ulan Bator, 22 December; *FBIS*, 27 December.)

Just before the plenum, *Unen* carried articles and letters pointing out that Choybalsan had made some contributions but had also committed serious crimes. *Unen* noted that of the first seven revolutionary leaders of Mongolia, all but Choybalsan died "prematurely." Choybalsan was also implicated in the purge and death of thousands of other party officials during the mid- and late 1930s. Another article claimed that Choybalsan's purges of the armed forces left the army in a weakened condition and that only the battle of Halhin Gol (in which Soviet and Mongolian forces fought the Japanese to a draw) put an end to Choybalsan's destructive im-

pulse. (Radio Ulan Bator, 19 December; *FBIS*, 22 December.)

Batmonh also strongly criticized Tsedenbal's record. Although Tsedenbal contributed to economic development and improvement of Mongolia's international ties, he concentrated power in his own hands, violated party democracy, and weakened collective leadership by making unilateral decisions. (Radio Ulan Bator, 22 December; *FBIS*, 27 December; Radio Beijing, 24 December; *FBIS-China*, 29 December.) Batmonh and other top leaders of the MPRP were promoted during the period of Tsedenbal's leadership; thus, their denunciations of him may eventually reverberate on their own political fortunes.

The political fortunes of some Mongolian officials were cast into doubt by new, unprecedented revelations. In line with the new spirit of *glasnost'*, the People's Great Hural and local hurals came in for criticism. A *Unen* poll found that only 20 percent of those polled evaluated the work of their deputies positively; 40 percent did not know the name of the person who represented them. *Unen* also stated that too many officials were deputies and suggested that officials should constitute no more than 20 percent of deputies to hurals at all levels. (MONTSAME, 8 August; *FBIS*, 17 August.)

Judging by Mongolia's *glasnost'*, the economy has not been faring well. MONTSAME reported in February that "accelerated economic development has not been adequately coupled with vigorous social policies," which resulted in agricultural stagnation. (MONTSAME, 18 February; *FBIS*, 23 February.) The Mongolian press admitted, in fact, that there were fewer livestock in 1988 than in 1970, a situation that led to the announcement that Mongolia was to reduce its supply of meat to the USSR by 17,000 tons (MONTSAME, 11 November; *FBIS*, 16 November). In March the MPRP news agency reported that a conference of farmers concluded that "the results of the past year give no cause for satisfaction." Grain and vegetable production were underfulfilled by 13.1 percent and 10.6 percent, respectively. (MONTSAME, 11 March; *FBIS*, 16 March.)

The government introduced some measures to cope with serious economic problems. In March the Council of Ministers adopted a resolution that encourages the development of private cooperatives. (MONTSAME, 28 March; *FBIS*, 31 March.) The People's Great Hural and the Council of Ministers also debated a new enterprise law that will presumably allow greater flexibility in industrial management when implemented (MONTSAME, 11 August; *FBIS*, 12 August; MONTSAME, 22 September; *FBIS*, 27 September). Such reform is uncertain because it is unknown how far the authorities will actually allow these measures to go.

Last year's revelation that the advancing Gobi Desert had caused a 60 percent decline in pastureland productivity apparently contributed to new measures to deal with the environment. The second plenum of the Mongolian Society for Nature and Environmental Protection stressed that more urgent reforestation was needed to combat the devastation of pastures (Radio Ulan Bator, 3 May; *FBIS*, 5 May). Mongolian environmentalists also joined with their Soviet counterparts to explore means for saving Lake Baykal and Lake Hobsgol, and a Mongolian journalist commented that "Hobsgol Lake, which is a symbol of purity and eternity for every Mongol, should remain forever as part of our people's soul" (MONTSAME, 7 July; *FBIS*, 13 July).

The struggle against rodents and field vermin grew in urgency. A report in December stated that one-third of the nation had been overrun by the field vole, that 4.5 million hectares had been lost, and that large numbers of buildings and watering holes had been rendered useless in thirteen of the nation's eighteen aymags. Locusts were also causing considerable damage. (*Novosti Mongolii*, 11 November; *FBIS*, 23 December.) Another setback for the economy was the waste of energy. The trade union newspaper *Hodolmor* reported that the country was importing trucks, cars, and motorcycles from the Soviet Union, causing a rapid upsurge in fuel consumption. Because of its low price, much fuel was being wasted, adding to the country's economic burden (Radio Ulan Bator, 21 December; *FBIS*, 28 December).

Not all the economic news was bad. An August report indicated that auxiliary food production and food markets in some areas were yielding a better supply and adding to farmer income (MONTSAME, 9 August; *FBIS*, 10 August). The Erdenet complex is adding a new factory that will produce felt and felt boots. Some enterprise managers are now chosen by the workers rather than appointed from above (MONTSAME, 15 July; *FBIS*, 18 July). A Chinese visitor to Erdenet observed that the copper-molybdenum ore-processing plant employs 5,400 workers of whom 1,400 are Russians (Beijing, *Shijie zhishi*, 16 November; *FBIS-China*, 13 December).

Some of Mongolia's economic news seemed to cast doubts on Ulan Bator's relationship with the Soviet Union. In April, P. Haadgar, deputy minister of agriculture, praised Mongolia's "virgin lands" project of the late 1950s, which he credited with laying the foundation for Mongolia's agricultural development (MONTSAME, 21 April; *FBIS*, 26 April). A similar program in the USSR is widely regarded as one of Khrushchev's harebrained schemes. Similarly, MONTSAME reported a letter from D. Batsuh, who holds a Ph.D. in economics, stating that Mongolia should solve its own problems rather than rely on foreign advisers and now that Mongolia had learned much from Soviet colleagues, it was "high time to make our own efforts to realize our possibilities in life." (MONTSAME, 19 December; *FBIS*, 20 December.)

The MPRP took steps to strengthen its legal system. In July *Unen* singled out law enforcement agencies as having serious shortcomings, including delays in investigations, unjustifiable periods of detention, and the conviction of the innocent. (MONTSAME, 28 July; *FBIS*, 3 August.) Subsequently, revisions in the Ministry of Public Security were announced, notably in personnel policy (Radio Ulan Bator, 18 August; *FBIS*, 23 August). *Unen* complained that too many problems and issues were being hidden under the excuse of "state secrets" and noted that lawlessness had not decreased since 1983. Rather, economic crimes had increased. The paper insisted that more be done to correct this situation. (MONTSAME, 23 August; *FBIS*, 25 August.)

Criticism was also leveled at the Academy of Sciences. *Unen* charged that the academy adhered to a "passive" approach in considering new problems and rewarded some academicians with high titles they had not earned. (MONTSAME, 8 July; *FBIS*, 13 July.) The MPRP was hardly passive with respect to the new issue of AIDS, however. In August the AIDS Research Center reported that it had improved its budget and its expertise and had conducted tests on 2,000 people. (MONTSAME, 13 August; *FBIS*, 15 August.) By December, 16,000 people had been tested and no cases of AIDS in Mongolia had been detected (Radio Ulan Bator, 1 December; *FBIS*, 5 December). Unfortunately, drug and alcohol addiction remain serious problems (Radio Ulan Bator, 28 October; *FBIS*, 7 November).

International Views and Affairs. The continued thaw in Sino-Soviet relations favorably affected Mongolia's relations with the People's Republic of

China (PRC). In February, the consular treaty negotiated in 1987 became effective. (PRC State Council Bulletin, 30 March; *JPRS-China*, 22 March.) The same month border trade talks between the two sides were held, and a few months later a new agreement was concluded. Xinhua reported that trade between the two countries would increase by 6 percent. (Xinhua, 5 November; *FBIS*, 7 November.) Moreover, Beijing and Ulan Bator successfully concluded negotiations on a new border treaty that was signed on 28 November (Xinhua, 28 November; *FBIS-China*, 29 November; Radio Ulan Bator, 1 December; *FBIS*, 5 December). In October, General Arbay, commander of Mongolia's border and frontier forces, stated that positive changes were occurring along the Sino-Mongolian border but that there had been incidents (Radio Ulan Bator, 3 October; *FBIS*, 4 October). The new treaty was designed to implement procedures for solving frontier problems and signified a definite upturn in relations.

A delegation from the People's Great Hural reciprocated a 1987 visit by a delegation from the PRC National People's Congress. Headed by L. Rinchin, its chairman, the delegation met with several top Chinese leaders and toured Chinese cities in September. (Xinhua, MONTSAME, 13–19 September; *FBIS*, 13–22 September.) In July, a PRC friendship delegation headed by Zhang Wenjin visited Ulan Bator and met with Altangerel (MONTSAME, 27 July; *FBIS*, 29 July). Mongolia also concluded a joint railway agreement with China and the USSR in September. The warming relationship was also evidenced by favorable comments about China's reforms in the Mongolian press and generally laudatory treatment of China in Foreign Minister Gombosuren's speech before the U.N. General Assembly in October. (Radio Ulan Bator, 8 October; *FBIS*, 11 October.)

Mongolia endorsed Mikhail Gorbachev's September speech in Krasnoyarsk, stating that it would contribute to the elimination of tension in the Asia-Pacific region. Batmonh personally stated that Mongolia would give full support to Soviet initiatives that would strengthen peace and security. (Radio Ulan Bator, 27 September; *FBIS*, 29 September.) Although Mongolia is not known to have publicly taken a stand on prospects for further reductions of Soviet forces in Mongolia, the implication of Batmonh's statements is that the MPRP will not present strong resistance.

Nevertheless, the MPRP remains at odds with China on some issues, notably Cambodia, where Ulan Bator has firmly supported Hanoi's approach. At several points during the year, Ulan Bator conveyed veiled criticisms of China's continuing support for Pol Pot and endorsed negotiations between the Hun Sen regime in Phnom Penh and Prince Sihanouk. (Radio Ulan Bator, 31 October; *FBIS*, 16 November.) During a visit to Ulan Bator by Laotian leader Kaysone Phomvihan, Batmonh endorsed the "peace initiatives and tireless efforts of Laos, Vietnam, and Kampuchea aimed at bringing back to normal the situation in Southeast Asia" (Vientiane, KPL, 3 September; *FBIS*, 6 September).

Close ties were maintained with other communist states. Romanian leader Nicolae Ceausescu visited Ulan Bator in April and Miloš Jakeš of Czechoslovakia and Kim Il-song of North Korea made state visits in June. The first president of India to visit Mongolia, Ramaswamy Venkataraman, arrived in July. Batmonh made state visits to Poland and the German Democratic Republic in October. In February, the MPRP announced that assistance from the Council for Mutual Economic Assistance (CEMA) member countries had increased by 41.6 percent, and in December the Mongolian delegate to CEMA announced that the organization was being restructured to improve support for developing countries, notably Cuba, Vietnam, and Mongolia. (Radio Ulan Bator, 6 December; *FBIS*, 13 December.)

Mongolia's newly established relations with the United States showed some momentum. The first U.S. ambassador to Ulan Bator, Richard Williams, presented his credentials to Batmonh in September. Williams was accompanied by Vernon Walters, U.S. ambassador to the United Nations, who held discussions with Mongolian leaders on bilateral and international affairs. (MONTSAME, 13–14 September; *FBIS*, 14, 15 September.) Batmonh sent a congratulatory message to George Bush on his election as president of the United States, and Mongolia's youth newspaper carried a favorable article on the new U.S. president (MONTSAME, 17 November; *FBIS*, 18 November).

As in past years, Mongolia continued to adhere closely to the Soviet lead in foreign and domestic policy questions. Besides consistently praising Gorbachev's new proposals for force reductions between the superpowers, Mongolia's leadership increasingly began to implement its own versions of *glasnost'* and *perestroika*.

William R. Heaton
Dumfries, Virginia

Nepal

Population. 18,252,001

Parties. Nepal Communist Party—Marxist (NCP-Marxist); Nepal Communist Party—Marxist-Leninist (NCP-ML); Nepal Workers' and Peasants' Organization—pro-Beijing (B); Nepal Communist Party—Maoist (NCP-Maoist) with three factions supporting China's disgraced Gang of Four; Nepal Communist Party/pro-Moscow (NCP/M), with four factions; Janabadi Morcha (Democratic Front)

Founded. NCP-Marxist: 1949; NCP-ML: 1978; Janabadi Morcha: founded in 1980 as radical democratic organization but turned Che Guevarist in 1985

Membership. 10,000 (estimated), with neutralist Marxists, Marxist-Leninists, and Maoist factions accounting for almost 75 percent of the members

Leadership. NCP-Marxist: Man Mohan Adhikary, Mrs. Sahana Pradhan (Pushpa Lal's widow); NCP-ML (neutralist since 1988): Radha Krishna Mainali, Mohan Chandra Adhikary; Nepal Workers' and Peasants' Organization-B: Narayan Man Bijukchhe "Rohit"; NCP-Maoist: Nirmal Lama, Mohan Bikram Gharti, Kiran (pseud.); NCP-M (Rayamajhi faction): Dr. Keshar Jung Rayamajhi, (Manandhar faction) Bishnu Bahadur Manandhar, (Varma faction) Krishna Raj Varma, (Tulsi Lal faction) Tulsi Lal Amatya; Janabadi Morcha: Ram Raja Prasad Singh

Politburo. 9 members in NCP-Marxist; no data on other factions

Secretariat. No data

Central Committee. 35 members in NCP-M (Rayamajhi faction); 35 members in NCP-Marxist faction; no data on other factions

Status. Proscribed

Last Congress. 1961: the Third and last presplit Congress; 1975: NCP-Maoist, Mohan Bikram Gharti and Nirmal Lama convened Fourth Congress; 1986: NCP-M Manandhar faction held its Fifth Congress

Last Election. 1986. N/a

Auxiliary Organizations. NCP-Marxist: Nepal Progressive Students' Union; Nepal Progressive Democratic Youth Association; NCP-ML: All-Nepal National Free Students' Union; People's Front; NCP-M: Nepal National Student Federation, Nepal National Youth Federation. In addition, all the communist groups have infiltrated government-sponsored labor and peasant organizations.

Publications. NCP-Marxist: *Naya Janabad* (New democracy); NCP-ML/B: *Nepal Patra*, *Barga Sangharsha* (Class struggle), *Mukti-Morcha* (Liberation front); NCP-Maoist: *Mashal* (Torch); NCP-M: *Samikshya Weekly*. *Daily Diary Weekly* and *Dristi Weekly* publish news and views of all communist factions.

Leadership and Organization. The history of the NCP is a history of factionalism. But despite these factions and the organizational weakness of the NCP, these groups remain capable of attracting increasing numbers of Nepalese to their ranks, thus making it possible to portray themselves as a powerful alternative to the present order if they could form a single unified party. So far, however, party unification is unimpressive.

The first split in the pro-Moscow group reportedly occurred in 1982 when B.B. Manandhar broke from Dr. Rayamajhi's party to form his own party. B.B. Manandhar's party split in 1983 when one of its leaders, Krishna Raj Varma, left the group, blaming the Manandhar group for the split in the anti-imperialist movement in Nepal. By 1985 Dr. Rayamajhi's group had become ineffective among pro-Moscow communists. Nonetheless, this group still talks of unity and calls other groups to join their "parental group." Unity talks between several leftist groups continued throughout 1988.

The NCP-Marxist, which emerged in 1987 as a result of the merger of two neutralist factions, follows the Communist Party of India—Marxist's line, does not embrace either Beijing or Moscow, and attempts to extend its contacts with both the Chinese and the Soviet communist parties. Its leaders—M.M. Adhikary and Mrs. Sahana Pradhan—made a week-long visit to the Soviet Union in mid-September 1988 at the invitation of the Soviet communist party (*NPD*, 19 September).

The NCP-Maoist group, formerly led by Mohan Bikram Gharti, is now divided into the Fourth Congress, the Mashal, and the Bahumat Mashal. The leaders of these factions, respectively, are Nirmal Lama, Mohan Bikram Gharti, and Kiran (pseud.). The first split in this group occurred in 1983 when Nirmal Lama and Jaya Govinda Shah convened a conference of their own and expelled Mohan

Bikram Gharti from the party. Gharti, in turn, led his own group and identified it as *mashal* (torch). In 1986, the Mashal was further divided; the group that quit the original Mashal formed the Bahumat Mashal (majority torch). The conflict in the group evidently appeared in the post-Mao era when Gharti accused the post-Mao Chinese leadership of abandoning the fundamental principles of communism. Now all these groups seem to follow Gharti's opinion regarding post-Mao China, including the view that true communism does not exist anywhere in the world. These factions still reportedly place their faith in the thought and activities of China's disgraced Gang of Four. The continuation of the split, however, seems to be partly due to personality clashes but mainly due to internal policy differences regarding participation in Panchayat elections. These factions reportedly have contacts with the Revolutionary Communist Party of the U.S.A.

The NCP-ML, an offspring of the Indian Naxalite movement, has emerged as more influential than any other communist group in Nepal, already reportedly establishing a strong organization in more than 60 of its 75 districts. Since the mid-1980s this group has abandoned its policy of violence in favor of utilizing Panchayat organs in the cause of revolution. Beginning in 1988 it reversed its policy of regarding the Soviet Union as "enemy number one" and "social-imperialistic." It now regards the Soviet Union as a great socialist country and the Soviet communist party as a fraternal party. Some observers believe this group abandoned its pro-Beijing policy to give its new policy—utilizing the Panchayat organs by participating in its elections— a greater leverage. The group may also have expected some financial assistance from the Soviets, which is crucial for any electoral politics.

With NCP-ML's abandonment of the pro-Beijing line in 1988, there now remains only one pro-Beijing group in Nepal which is led by Narayan Man Bijukchhe "Rohit," also known as the Rohit group, which functions under the name of Nepal Workers' and Peasants' Organization and which is influential in Bhaktapur district and surrounding areas. This group differs from other Maoists in that it relies basically on the legal or systemic means to promote its ideology and depends on local and communal factors. A member of the National Panchayat representing Bhaktapur district, eight miles east of Katmandu, is sponsored by the Rohit group.

Janabadi Morcha (Democratic Front), which made major headlines in the summer of 1985 by exploding bombs in different parts of the country, is led by Ram Raja Prasad Singh, a lawyer and former national legislator. The Morcha is violence-prone, extremely antimonarchist and places its faith in Che Guevara–type revolution. The rank and file in this group come from Nepal's Terai, and it is headquartered in an undisclosed location in India. In 1987, a special court sentenced four persons, including Ram Raja Prasad Singh, to death in absentia. Mr. Singh, however, is still at large. There were some reports of alleged arms deliveries by this group to the Dang district in Western Nepal (*NPD*, 4 July).

Domestic Party Affairs. The main issue dividing the communist party since the mid-1950s has been the problem of identifying the main enemy and creating a united front against that enemy. Sino-Soviet disputes appeared to be the issue only in the mid-1960s, especially since the beginning of the Cultural Revolution in China. The Maoists belonging to the Fourth Congress and the Mashal group regard the king and the NC as enemies of equal proportions and hence reject the idea of any form of united front with the NC. The NCP-ML, also known as the Naxalites, regard the monarchy as enemy number one and at the same time rule out the possibility of a united front with the NC, which they regard as a puppet of both international comprador capitalism and the reactionary Indian government. By 1986, however, this group changed its line and participated in a political process that it previously described as enemy number one. In June 1988, however, this group was reported to have been involved in a "conspiracy" to start a violent movement in Dang district of western Nepal. The group's leader, Radha Krishna Mainali, who was released from jail in October 1987 after serving fourteen years, was reported to have visited Dang district allegedly to supervise the proposed revolution. The authorities, however, arrested Mainali and seized minutes of a meeting of the NCP-ML group (*NPD*, 4 July). In a September statement, the party stressed that a unified communist party must become a disciplined and popular national party to hasten the triumph of revolution in Nepal (*NPD*, 12 September). Meanwhile, Jhapa district court was ordered to auction the properties of some NCP-ML leaders, including Chandra Prakash Mainali, who were involved in the 1972 Naxalite terrorism in Jhapa district (ibid., 28 November).

The NCP-Marxists appear to be guided by the ideology of radical socialism, not Marxism-Leninism. Its program envisages the replacement of the Panchayat system by a democratic system rather than the overthrow of the monarchy. It advocates a broad-based united front of all progressive and democratic elements, including the NC, to achieve its objectives. The pro-Soviets see different roads to democracy and hence advocate both covert and overt strategy.

The NCP-Marxists and Tulsi Lal Amatya faction of NCP/pro-Moscow held a public meeting to mourn the National Stadium stampede tragedy. The police intervened in the meeting and briefly arrested a large number of persons, including Man Mohan Adhikary, Tulsi Lal Amatya, and Mrs. Sahana Pradhan (*NPD*, 4 April). The Politburo of the NCP-Marxists called for a "joint front" of all outlawed political parties to fight the Panchayat system and declared that Marxists do not favor utilizing the Panchayat elections for political purposes (ibid., 8 February, 9 May).

The NCP Mashal group made a statement condemning all other leftist groups' talk of unity as "rightist opportunism" and reiterated its commitment to Maoism (*NPD*, 9 May). The general secretary of the Fourth Congress group expressed satisfaction that "the communist force has today become the only force fighting for fundamental political and economic change in Nepal (ibid.). Its leader, Nirmal Lama, demanded an election to the Constituent Assembly to let the elected representatives draft the constitution themselves. The B.B. Manandhar and Krishna Raj Varma groups of the NCP/pro-Moscow continued to call for unity among different political groups (*NPD*, 8 February and 7 March).

The pro-Beijing group, led by Narayan Man Bijukchhe "Rohit," was in the headlines in late August and early September following the lynching death of Karna Prasad Hyonju, a former National Panchayat member, during an earthquake relief operation in the Bhaktapur district. The authorities arrested Rohit and nearly 175 followers of Rohit including Govinda Duwal, who was also a member of National Panchayat (ibid., 5 September). Rohit and Duwal are still in jail awaiting trial.

The leaders of the three factions of the pro-Moscow party decided to contest the by-elections to the National Panchayat from the Myagdi district. The NCP-ML, Rohit, and Maoist Fourth Congress factions also decided to participate in the by-election, while the Marxist and Mashal groups decided to boycott. In the by-election the participating communist groups did not fare well.

Auxiliary and Front Organizations. Three new leftist front organizations—All-Nepal National People's Front (Mashal group), Nepal Progressive Democratic Youth Association (Marxist), and People's Front (NCP-ML)—appeared in Nepal in 1988. All describe as their objective mobilizing workers and peasants in the cause of the restoration of democracy and a people's revolution (*NPD*, 4, 11 January, 9 February). In Jhapa district, the authorities raided the local office of the All-Nepal Peasants' Association, an affiliate of the Marxist-Leninist group, and seized membership forms, seditious leaflets, and plans for a violent movement (ibid., 22 February). The Ninth National Conference of the All-Nepal National Independent Student Union was held in March and attended by 1,000 delegates from 59 districts. Leftist members of the National Panchayat—Padma Ratna Tuladhar, Som Nath Pyasi, and Jagrit Prasad Bhetuwal—were among those attending the conference (*NPD*, 21 March). In April, five leftist student organizations called for a general strike to condemn the government for failing to avoid the stampede at the National Stadium (ibid., 4 April). Meanwhile, the Fourth National Conference of the Nepal Progressive Students' Union (Marxist front) was inaugurated by M.M. Adhikary; foreign fraternal delegates were also reportedly present (*NPD*, 18 April). A similar conference of the Nepal Revolutionary Students' Union was inaugurated by Narayan Man Bijukchhe "Rohit" (ibid.). The leftist joint student front achieved victory in the student union elections on 17 of the 25 campuses in Katmandu Valley and other major campuses outside Katmandu (*NPD*, 2 May).

International Views, Positions, and Activities. A change was recorded in the attitude of the NCP-ML group toward the Soviet Union. In a statement the group described its past policy of criticizing the Soviet Union as "erroneous." The Fourth Congress and both factions of the Mashal are critical of both China and the Soviet Union. The NCP-Marxists supported the opposition movement in Bangladesh and the struggle of the Palestinian people for a homeland and welcomed the intermediate-range nuclear forces treaty signed by Reagan and Mikhail Gorbachev in Washington in December 1987 (ibid., 8 February). The Mashal group pledged its support to the Tamils of Sri Lanka in their "legitimate" struggle for a separate and independent state (*NPD*, 9 May).

The Soviet communist party supports the B.B. Manandhar and K.R. Varma factions. In fact, Soviet embassy officials occasionally participate in the meetings of the Varma and Manandhar groups. There is no indication of any covert or overt Chinese support to the divided pro-Beijing groups. Maoists have established relations with the Revolutionary Communist Party of the U.S.A.

M.M. Adhikary, Mrs. Sahana Pradhan, B.B. Manandhar, Mohan Bikram Gharti, and Nirmal Lama have remained notable figures and newsmakers of the Nepalese communist movement.

Chitra K. Tiwari
Arlington, Virginia

New Zealand

Population. 3,343,339
Parties. Communist Party of New Zealand (CPNZ); Socialist Unity Party (SUP); Socialist Action League (SAL); Workers' Communist League (WCL); People's Alliance (PA)
Founded. CPNZ: 1921; SUP: 1966; SAL: 1969; WCL: 1980; PA:1988
Membership. CPNZ: 50; SUP: 300; SAL: 50; WCL: 50; PA: 100 (all estimated)
Leadership. CPNZ: Harold Crook (secretary); SUP: George Jackson (national president); SAL: Russell Johnson (national secretary); WCL: Graeme Clark; PA: Jim Delahunty and Sue Bradford (spokespersons)
Status. All legal
Last Congress. CPNZ: Twenty-third, 1984; SUP: Eighth, 22–24 October 1988; SAL: Eleventh, 26–31 December 1986; special conferences 28–31 December 1987 and 4–6 June 1988; WCL: Fourth, October 1988; PA: Inaugural conference, 4–6 June 1988
Last Election. 15 August 1987 (parliamentary), no representatives elected; 11 October 1986 (local government), no representatives elected
Auxiliary Organizations. SUP: Youth in Unity, Workers' Institute for Scientific Education (WISE), Peace Council New Zealand, New Zealand–USSR Society; SAL: Young Socialists, Socialist Forum, Latin American Solidarity Committee, Cuba Friendship Society, Committee for a Workers' Front, Nicaragua Must Survive Com-

mittee; CPNZ: New Zealand–Albania Society; PA: People First (Wellington), Left Alternative (Auckland)
Publications. CPNZ: *People's Voice* (fortnightly); SUP: *Tribune* (fortnightly), *Socialist Politics* (every two months); SAL: *Socialist Action* (fortnightly until 15 July 1988 when it ceased publication; SAL members were encouraged to purchase the weekly *Militant*, which was published in New York and airfreighted to New Zealand), *Socialist Action Review* (periodically); WCL: *Unity* (every three weeks)

Internationally, New Zealand during 1988 significantly extended its relations with the Soviet Union and the People's Republic of China. Domestically, the various local communist parties stepped up their criticism of and campaigns against the Labour government's free market economic policies and the resulting and continuing increase in unemployment. They welcomed as a victory the sacking of Labour's minister of finance, Roger Douglas, by the prime minister, David Lange, on 14 December.

The CPNZ. The first Central Committee meeting in thirteen months was held on 4 July and endorsed a report entitled "Our Marxist-Leninist Agenda," a lengthy ideological statement on the role of the CPNZ in the light of recent national and international developments.

The CPNZ throughout 1988 was vehemently critical of the Labour government, which it held responsible for New Zealand's serious and escalating unemployment. In March the CPNZ adopted the slogan "Bring down the Labour government." A number of CPNZ members led by Willie Wilson took part in a march against unemployment that traversed the length of the North Island and culminated in a demonstration outside Parliament on 2 November. During the march the CPNZ sold 3,944 copies of the *People's Voice* and distributed 50,000 leaflets.

In September Harold Crook, the party's secretary, and Barry Lee, another member of the National Secretariat, visited Albania, where the CPNZ and the Albanian Party of Labor found themselves in "complete agreement around Marxist-Leninist principles and policies" (*People's Voice*, 10 October).

The SUP. Much of the SUP's organizational activity during 1988 revolved around its Eighth National Conference, held 22–24 October. A special issue of *Socialist Politics*, the SUP's two-monthly journal of Marxist-Leninist theory and practice, was issued in March and contained six chapters that were to be discussed throughout the party preparatory to the conference. There was an introduction by the editor and acting General Secretary Marilyn Tucker and a final section on "Money Raising in Mass Work." In between were four draft statements on politics, the national question in New Zealand, women, and unemployment. Tucker noted that the SUP's "Central Committee has been critical of the party's inability to get to grip with" the "tremendous, new challenges" it was facing and that the SUP had to become an initiator of change and not just respond to it. Of particular concern was that, "having previously won a leadership position in the trade union movement, our failure to give direction in this period of upheaval was a significant factor, though not the only one in that movement's aimlessness in the recent period." The main issue facing the workers of New Zealand was unemployment, but "the Maori people face a situation of dual oppression" and there is an "increasing feminization of poverty."

Preparatory regional conferences were held throughout New Zealand during the early part of 1988, with special schools for party youth, women, and unionists to discuss matters of particular importance to them. The Eighth National Conference was attended by observers from Australia, the German Democratic Republic, the People's Republic of China, and the USSR. The draft statements were adopted, and it was reported that $53,872 had been contributed to the 1987 Fighting Fund, which had a target of $55,000. Another campaign had been undertaken to raise $25,000 for desktop publishing technology to produce the *Tribune*.

Marilyn Tucker, who had been acting general secretary for two years, was confirmed as SUP general secretary. The other four members elected to the Central Executive were George Jackson (president), Ken Douglas (chairperson), Joe Tonner (assistant general secretary) and G.H. "Bill" Andersen. The Central Committee consisted of those five plus Dave Arthur, Richie Gillespie, Doug McCallum, Frank McNulty, Jack Marston, and Bernie O'Brien, with four candidate members, Jan Farr, Joe Te Pania, Simon Wallace, and Graeme Whimp.

At a function on 26 August to celebrate Jackson's 80th birthday, Soviet ambassador to New Zealand Yuri Sokolov made a presentation to Jackson and informed him that at the SUP's national conference Jackson would be awarded the Order of People's Friendship by the Presidium of the USSR Supreme Soviet.

During the year the SUP consolidated its influence within the New Zealand trade union movement, particularly through Ken Douglas, the SUP's national chairperson who also is president of the New Zealand Council of Trade Unions (CTU), and Bill Andersen, the chairman of SUP's Auckland Regional Committee and an SUP Central Executive member, who heads the Northern Drivers' and Distribution unions, serves on the CTU's national executive, and in June was elected the first president of the Auckland Regional Coordinating Committee of the CTU.

Tucker, Andersen, and Douglas attended in June a conference of Communist Unity in Australia, which resolved to take more definite steps by June 1989 to form a united Marxist party in Australia.

The SAL. Seventy people, including activists from Australia, Britain, Canada, and the United States, attended a special conference of the SAL in Hamilton on 28–31 December 1987. The SAL's national secretary, Russell Johnson, addressed the gathering on the effects of the October 1987 world stock market crash on semicolonial countries such as Mexico and the Philippines. The other speakers were Michael Prairie, co-editor of *New International* and a leader of the Revolutionary Workers' League of Canada; Mike Tucker, editor of *Socialist Action*; Mac Warren, Socialist Workers' Party of the United States; Joe Hawke, leader of the Maori land struggle for Bastion Point in Auckland; John Minto, International Secretary of the antiapartheid Halt All Racist Tours organization; and Keith Locke, coordinator of the Philippines Solidarity Network.

During January, 27 people from New Zealand helped harvest coffee in Nicaragua and later addressed meetings throughout New Zealand. In Auckland the speakers were joined by the Labour government's associate minister of foreign affairs, Fran Wilde, M.P.

A conference of socialist workers and youth was organized by the SAL in Wellington on 4–6 June to discuss Cuba and the Philippines and the building of a communist organization in New Zealand industry.

On 15 July *Socialist Action* announced that it was temporarily ceasing publication and that in future the *Militant*, published weekly in New York, would be flown to New Zealand and distributed instead. The announcement came as a surprise because a concentrated attempt to increase the circulation of *Socialist Action* during the first half of 1988 had apparently been successful, with an additional 1,197 subscriptions reportedly being taken out in the first four months.

The WCL. The WCL's Fourth National Conference in October reaffirmed the party's opposition to the Labour government's free market economic policies and endorsed attempts to forge greater cooperation among left-wing groups. It decided that to achieve "the principle of women's self-determination within the WCL" at least half the party's national committee should be women and that where appropriate there should be women only meetings and decisions. The year 1990 was to be designated "a year of struggle against racism and for Maori self-determination" (*Unity*, 14 October).

Earlier in the year the editors of *Unity*, celebrating the paper's 10th year of publication, attacked the divisions in the New Zealand left caused by "a tendency to mechanically import overseas models of struggle and society, sectarian attitudes to other progressive forces, and inappropriate forms of internal organization [that] have helped consign it to the margins of political life" (*Unity*, 12 February).

During the year the WCL supported a number of broad-based left meetings and activities such as the March Against Unemployment in October and November and a debate—on the value of working to change the Labour party from within—between two former Labour presidents, Margaret Wilson and Jim Anderton, M.P., and the WCL's David Steel and Auckland trade unionist Bruce Fowler. The WCL also obtained a fortnightly radio program on alternate Sundays at 12:30 on Wellington's Radio Access.

In June Jack Manson died. A former baker, freezing worker, watersider, and driver, Manson was born in Dunedin, fought in Italy during World War II, and came to prominence in New Zealand's political left during the 151-day waterfront strike of 1951 when he was a member of the strikers' finance committee. In 1959 he returned from an international conference in Romania critical of Nikita Khrushchev and was partly responsible for persuading the CPNZ to side with China in the Sino-Soviet dispute. As chairman of the Wellington District Committee of the CPNZ he remained loyal to the Chinese alliance when the CPNZ shifted its allegiance from China to Albania. Manson and the rest of the Wellington Committee were expelled from the CPNZ and most thereafter supported the WCL, formed in 1980.

The PA. At a conference at Wellington High School on 4–6 June the PA, a new left-wing political organization, was formed. The 65 people present were largely drawn from three groups that had contested the 1987 general election: Left Alternative (Auckland), People First (Wellington), and Socialist Alliance (Christchurch).

There was a clear division between the Socialist Alliance and People First, which included a strong representation of WCL members. It was decided not to form a political party because a similar national conference of left-wing groups, which in 1986 formed the Socialist Alliance, had subsequently split into factions, some favoring electoral participation and others hard-line activism.

The Left Alternative and People First organizations, however, decided to merge into a people's alliance and work toward preparing a people's charter for presentation at a future conference, probably in 1989. The intention was to consolidate as far as possible a left-wing alternative to Labour for the 1990 elections.

One of the Left Alternative leaders, Sue Bradford, subsequently organized the March Against Unemployment from Te Hapua in the north to Wellington during October and November and later in November, with twenty other hecklers, wrecked a meeting being addressed in Auckland by Roger Douglas, the controversial minister of finance in the Labour government. Bradford (36), is married with four children and is the Auckland-based coordinator of a national unemployed network known by its Maori name Te Roopu Rawakore. Active in the militant socialist Progressive Youth Movement during the anti–Vietnam War protests, Bradford later studied Chinese at Auckland University before spending six months during 1980–81 in China. She was also active and arrested during the violent anti-Springbok rugby football tour protests of 1981.

New Zealand and the Soviet Union. In February, New Zealand's minister of recreation and sport, Peter Tapsell, M.P., and the chairman of the Hillary Commission for Recreation and Sport, Sir Ronald Scott, visited Moscow to discuss an agreement between New Zealand and the USSR for a wide range of sporting exchanges between the two countries involving teams, individual athletes, coaches, and experts in sports medicine.

The Soviet Union in February unconditionally ratified the Raratonga treaty, a declaration by 13 South Pacific forum members, including New Zealand, that their region of the world was a nuclear-free zone. The treaty, which came into force on 11 December 1986, does not affect the transit of vessels carrying nuclear weapons but does seek to prevent the production, testing, or storing of nuclear weapons in the South Pacific. In November, the Soviet Academy of Sciences hosted an Asian-Pacific peace conference in Vladivostok attended by invited representatives from 30 countries including New Zealand.

A New Zealand parliamentary delegation led by Kerry Burke, M.P., speaker of the House of Representatives, visited the USSR in May. In the delegation were two other Labour M.P.s, Trevor Mallard and Noel Scott, and two National Party M.P.s, George Gair and John Luxton. As guests of the USSR Supreme Soviet, the five M.P.s visited Moscow, Leningrad, Tashkent, and Tbilisi before spending a week in Poland as the guests of the Polish government.

The New Zealand parliamentarians' visit went ahead despite the concurrent refusal by the New Zealand government of an entry visa to New Zealand for a senior Soviet trade official. Igor Kanaev, chairman of the Committee for Trade Promotion of the Soviet Chamber of Commerce and Industry, was to have led a seven-member trade delegation to Australia and New Zealand but for undisclosed reasons was refused visas by both countries.

A visit to the USSR by New Zealand's deputy prime minister, Geoffrey Palmer, in July, was postponed when Palmer had to return to New Zealand because of the sudden illness of Prime Minister David Lange. The visit was seen as recognizing the Soviet Union's developing role in the Pacific, the important trading relationship between the two countries, and a common interest in nuclear disarmament.

Prime Minister Lange, during a visit to the United Nations in New York in September, met at the Soviets' request with Soviet foreign minister Eduard Shevardnadze. They discussed arms reductions and nuclear-free zones in the Asia-Pacific region and the desirability of expanding economic, political, and cultural ties between New Zealand and the USSR.

The sale to the USSR of 60,000 tons of New Zealand butter for N.Z. $150 million was announced in October, and discussions continued between New Zealand and the Soviet Union on a bilateral agreement to govern potential commercial arrangements for New Zealand companies to service the Soviet Union's Pacific fishing fleets. It was envisaged that up to 200 deep-water Soviet fishing vessels could be provisioned and serviced in New Zealand. This would require the Soviet airline Aeroflot being granted landing rights to fly into New Zealand up to 10,000 crew members a year.

That proposal was discussed further when Palmer, accompanied by a delegation of New Zealand businessmen, made his postponed visit to the Soviet Union in November. Palmer subsequently announced that the signing of any agreement with the Soviet Union to service its Pacific fishing fleet was still many months away, but he also expressed his hope that there would be a considerable increase in Soviet–New Zealand trade and in joint venture enterprises, particularly in the Soviet Far East.

Palmer visited Leningrad, Moscow, Khabarovsk, and Vladivostok and held talks with Soviet foreign minister Shevardnadze; Valentin Falin, head of the CPSU Central Committee's International Department; and Vladimir Kamentsev, Soviet deputy prime minister and minister responsible for external trade and who, from 1979 to 1986, was USSR minister of fisheries. Palmer also delivered a lecture on international law at the Institute of State and Law in Moscow, invited the Soviet Union to station a journalist in New Zealand again, and invited Kamentsev to visit New Zealand in 1989.

Soviet visitors to New Zealand during 1988 included in June a 32-strong delegation of Soviet politicians, academics, and trade union officials. The group was led by Tatyana Ivanova, first deputy chairman of the Supreme Soviet of the Russian federation.

The New Zealand–USSR Society held a Labour weekend symposium in October. Professor Anatoly Bursov, the chairman of the Philosophy department at the USSR's Diplomatic Academy, spoke on foreign affairs with an emphasis on peace and ecology, and Alexei Kunitsyn, senior research fellow in the Institute of the USA and Canada at the USSR Academy of Sciences and newly elected vice president of the USSR–New Zealand Society in Moscow, spoke on current economic reforms in the USSR.

In December, Soviet and New Zealand scientists reached a first-ever agreement to collaborate in Antarctic research, with special attention to climatic change and the ozone layer. Mike Collins, New Zealand's acting director of the Department of Scientific and Industrial Research, said that Soviet scientists would benefit from access to New Zealand's Scott Base facility while New Zealand scientists would have access to Soviet bases and would work in the Ross Sea with Soviet oceanographers on Soviet research ships. The pooling of research programs would mean more Soviet research vessels would use New Zealand for provisioning, Collins predicted.

New Zealand and the People's Republic of China.

Diplomatic and trade relations between New Zealand and China continued to develop cordially during 1988. In May the leader of the House of Representatives, Jonathan Hunt, M.P., led a seven-person Labour Party delegation to China to renew contacts with the Chinese Communist Party first made during a similar visit by former Labour Party president Margaret Wilson in 1985. Later in the year, former Labour Party leader Sir Wallace Rowling, recently returned from three years as New Zealand's ambassador to the United States, accepted an invitation from the Chinese government to pay his third visit to China.

Not only the Labour government but also the National Party opposition in the New Zealand Parliament showed an interest in advancing New Zealand–Chinese relations. The leader of the National Party, Jim Bolger, M.P., accompanied by the opposition spokesman on overseas trade, Warren Cooper, M.P., visited Beijing, Xian, and Guangzhou from 25 August until 1 September at the invitation of the Chinese People's Institute of Foreign Affairs (CPIFA). Bolger and Cooper had talks concerning bilateral trade, China's economic reforms, and international affairs with Chinese vice-premier Wu Xueqian, vice-ministers Zhu Qizhen (foreign affairs), Liu Zhongli (finance), and Wang Pinqing (economic affairs), and CPIFA president Han Nianlong.

In November the prime minister of China, Li Peng, accompanied by a 90-strong party including four ministers and two vice-ministers, paid a four-day state visit to New Zealand, during which Li and New Zealand prime minister Lange signed an investment protection agreement between the two countries.

New Zealand has thirteen joint venture investments in China, and China has also to a small extent invested in New Zealand industry. Since diplomatic relations were normalized between the two countries in 1972, total trade has increased from N.Z. $13.2 million to N.Z. $544 million. China was New Zealand's fifth-largest trading partner and the largest market for New Zealand wool, which constituted 77 percent of New Zealand's total exports to China, for the year to June 1988 (*NZ Herald*, 21 November).

Barry Gustafson
University of Auckland

Pakistan

Population. 107,467,457
Party. Communist Party of Pakistan (CPP)
Founded. 1948
Membership. Under 200 (estimated)
General Secretary. Ali Nazish
Status. Illegal
Last Congress. First, 1976 (clandestine)
Local Bodies. No data
Publications. None

The year 1988 was a watershed one in the political history of Pakistan. In August the eleven-year rule of Pakistani strongman General Zia ul-Haq ended abruptly when an aircraft carrying Zia, the U.S. ambassador, and high-ranking Pakistani military officers mysteriously crashed, killing all aboard. To the surprise of many observers, Zia's constitutional system survived the crisis. The military resisted the temptation to seize power, and an interim caretaker government fulfilled its constitutional obligation to stage national elections. In November Pakistani voters elected a Pakistan People's Party (PPP) government headed by Benazir Bhutto, the daughter of former Prime Minister Zulfiqar Ali Bhutto, who was overthrown in a 1977 coup and subsequently hanged by Zia. By all acounts, Benazir's arrival in power marked the beginning of a new political era in Pakistan. The past year was also a critical juncture in Pakistani foreign policy. In April, the Soviets decided to cut their losses in the long struggle for Afghanistan by agreeing to withdraw all troops by 15 February 1989.

The tiny CPP remained a minor political player throughout the year. Despite the historically weak appeal Marxism has always had in Pakistan, leftists connected with the CPP and a profusion of regionally based, pro-Moscow parties had reason to celebrate the PPP electoral victory. The left clearly hoped that a more liberal political environment under a PPP government would allow the fragmented communist movement to organize and agitate in the open. Moreover, the proposed Soviet withdrawal from Afghanistan allowed the left to free itself of the politically unpopular task of defending Soviet actions in the region.

Party Affairs. With an estimated membership of two hundred, the CPP remains a clandestine organization with few accomplishments to show in over 40 years of existence. The CPP has been proscribed since 1954. Successive Pakistani governments, both civilian and military, have vigorously suppressed the CPP—a policy that may change under the new Bhutto government. The party does not openly support front organizations or publish a party organ, and there is no information on internal party organization. There are only two figures who risk identifying openly with the CPP. The first is Ali Nazish, the elderly CPP general secretary, who has guided the party since the early 1960s. The second, more visible party stalwart is Jam Saqi, the CPP Central Committee secretary, who occasionally gives interviews and issues press releases. Both leaders are from Sind, probably the only province where the CPP maintains a political foothold.

Before Zia's death, Jam Saqi had outlined the CPP program in an interview with *Unsere Zeit*. The CPP, he claimed, fully backed the Movement for the Restoration of Democracy (MRD), an umbrella organization of opposition parties formed in 1981 to spearhead the movement to remove Zia from office. Although not a formal member of the MRD, the CPP operated in tandem with the Marxist constituents of the alliance. These parties include the Quami Mahaz Azadi, the Pakistan Socialist Party, the Pakistan Progressive Party, and the Awami National Party. Saqi maintained the CPP had earned "semilegal status" because of its consistent (though unsolicited) participation in MRD agitations. CPP applications for full membership in the alliance had been rebuffed by the PPP, the most powerful member of the MRD. Saqi outlined a five-point CPP program that included (1) land reform, (2) the elimination of unrestricted subcontracting of workers, (3) self-determination for Pakistan's "five nationalities" (Punjabis, Baluch, Sindhis, Pathans, and *mohajirs*, Muslim immigrants originally from India), (4) a "genuinely independent" foreign policy (i.e., a curtailment of security ties with the United States), and (5) a tripling of the minimum wage. Saqi condemned the Zia regime and the United States for interfering in Afghanistan's internal affairs. For good measure, he also accused Pakistani generals, Afghan "bandits," and the Central Intelligence Agency of cornering the South Asian heroin market (3 July).

Domestic Political Developments. On 29 May President Zia set the stage for the coming electoral battle when he dismissed the government of Prime Minister Mohammed Khan Junejo and dissolved the national assembly that was elected on a nonparty ballot in 1985. Junejo, a mild-mannered Sindhi landlord with few political enemies, was handpicked by Zia to head his hybrid system of nonpartisan Islamic government. Most observers believed the dismissal was triggered, in part, by Junejo's handling of an official inquiry into an ammunition dump explosion that occurred in Islamabad in April. More than four hundred bystanders were killed in the blast. Junejo wanted to pin blame on the army for siting the facility in a populated area—a finding that Zia and his senior commanders found unpalatable. Junejo's dismissal also left his Muslim League supporters in parliament without a leader.

Zia's death in the plane crash on 17 August left the nation shaken. His constitutional successor, national assembly speaker Ghulam Ishaq Khan, assumed the presidency and pledged to hold elections within 90 days. The new army chief, General Mirza Aslam Beg, later admitted that the military seriously considered imposing martial law to avert a political crisis. Beg and his commanders, however, decided to allow the political process to run its course. Ishaq Khan declared a national emergency and established a makeshift emergency council, composed of senior cabinet officials and three service chiefs, to see the country through the crisis.

In October an official board of inquiry released the findings of its investigation into the plane crash. According to the report, the crash was probably the handiwork of unnamed saboteurs who released an incapacitating gas in the cockpit, causing the flight crew to lose control of the aircraft. Pakistani officials pointed accusing fingers at the Afghan, Soviet, and even Indian secret services—innuendos that were vehemently denied by all three governments. The cause of the disaster will probably never be proved conclusively.

Zia's sudden departure from the political scene threw the election into disarray. Zia's supporters in the national assembly cobbled together a nine-party coalition dubbed the Islamic Democratic Association (IDA). The alliance standard-bearer, Punjab chief minister Nawaz Sharif, soon faced a revolt by Junejo and his supporters, who bolted the IDA. The MRD, for its part, saw Zia's passing as a golden opportunity. Although the PPP was relatively confident of victory on the strength of its own following (provided the election was not rigged), Benazir Bhutto was careful to include the MRD constituent parties in PPP election plans. This decision bene-fited the small left-wing parties that stood virtually no chance of winning a share of power without PPP backing. Opposition prospects were significantly enhanced in October when the Supreme Court nul-lified Zia's regulation mandating elections on a non-party basis. Heading into an election with the ad-vantage of party labels and confronting a divided ruling coalition, the PPP and its electoral partners sensed victory.

Voter turnout for the 16 November balloting was a respectable 40 percent. By most accounts, the balloting was not marred by the widespread fraud and violence that usually characterize Pakistani elections. The PPP won a plurality of national as-sembly seats (93 of 205) on the strength of 45 percent of the popular vote; the IDA captured 54 seats, and the balance of seats were held by regional parties, independents, and Islamic fundamentalists. The results of provincial elections held three days later were mixed. The PPP was able to form uneasy coalition ministries with the pro-Soviet Awami Na-tional Party in the Northwest Frontier Province, with the IDA in Baluchistan, and with a local *moha-jir* party in Sind. In the critical province of Punjab, where over half the population resides, Nawaz Sharif's IDA formed a ministry on the strength of a slim majority.

Although the PPP fell short of a commanding majority either at the center or in the provinces, President Ishaq Khan gave the nod to Benazir Bhutto to form a government. Once in power, the PPP promptly engineered the election of Ishaq Khan for a five-year term as president, a position of considerable power and influence. To allay the mili-tary's fears of wholesale reversals of Zia's carefully laid policies, Bhutto pledged not to seek reprisals against officers connected with the former martial law regime or to alter established policies affecting the defense budget, Afghanistan, Islamic institu-tions, or nuclear weapons development. In an ad-dress to the nation on 2 December, the 35-year-old female prime minister (the world's first woman to head an Islamic government) stated: "We are marching on a journey toward a progressive Paki-stan, a democratic Pakistan, and an exploitation-free Pakistan."

One of Bhutto's first acts in office was to release political prisoners, some of whom had languished in prison throughout the Zia era. The move was designed primarily to benefit PPP activists who, like Bhutto and her family, had run afoul of martial law edicts. Also released, however, were a number

of freewheeling Marxists. In addition, radicals who had fled Pakistan to safe haven in Western Europe during the dark days of martial law started return-ing to the country. By year's end there was specula-tion that Bhutto was preparing to arrange the return of her exiled brother, Murtaza, who had been living in Syria after masterminding the 1981 hijacking of a Pakistani jetliner. Although the new PPP govern-ment was careful to project itself as responsible and moderate, the Pakistani left clearly interpreted Bhutto's arrival in power as a new political lease on life. Currently, however, Marxist influence in Pakistan is confined to small pockets of followers in the three minority provinces, a few trade unions, leftist student groups, intellectual circles, and a left-wing fringe of the PPP itself.

Foreign Policy. Exasperated by the futile strug-gle to maintain a communist client regime in power in Kabul, Soviet leader Gorbachev moved swiftly in 1988 to staunch what he once termed the "bleeding wound" of Afghanistan. (For a full discussion of events leading up to the Soviet withdrawal, see separate chapters on Afghanistan and the Soviet Union in this volume.) At a conclusive round of U.N.-brokered negotiations held in Geneva in April, the Soviets agreed to withdraw half their troops by mid-August; the remainder would leave by February 1989. After a series of consultations between Washington, Islamabad, Beijing, and the various Afghan resistance parties, the United States pledged to continue providing military assistance to Afghan partisans via the Pakistani arms conduit as long as Moscow kept supplying the Kabul regime. The Soviets then attempted to fashion an Afghan coalition government in which the communists would retain a share of power. As a last resort, the Soviets even began negotiating directly with Af-ghan guerrilla organizations. Pakistan spurned all face-saving formulas put forward by Moscow and stuck to the text of the Geneva agreement. In the final analysis, the Soviets had no alternative but to begin their withdrawal with no assurance that their Afghan clients would survive the anticipated onslaught of rebel forces. Most informed observers expect the regime to collapse or capitulate within a few months after the Soviet withdrawal is completed.

President Zia was a passionate defender of the Afghans' struggle against Soviet domination. With-out Pakistan's matériel and moral support, the insur-gency would have been condemned to a desperate rearguard action with virtually no chance of success. Zia's death raised the possibility that Pakistani resolve on the Afghan issue might waver. Bhutto, however, made no discernible changes in Afghan policy. As Soviet troops began their withdrawal across the Amu Darya River, the PPP government hoped that a popular Afghan government would soon come to power, thereby inducing the three million Afghan refugees living in Pakistan to return home. Both Pakistan and the Soviet Union signaled a desire to improve bilateral relations once the Afghan issue was resolved.

Pakistan's close and enduring relations with China remained a cornerstone of Pakistani foreign policy. China is held in high esteem because of its consistent support for Pakistan, regardless of the political character of a given regime in Islamabad. Shortly after assuming power, Bhutto announced her intention to travel to Saudi Arabia and China, Pakistan's most cherished allies.

Douglas C. Makeig
U.S. Department of Defense

Note: The opinions expressed in this article are the author's own and do not necessarily reflect those of the U.S. government or any U.S. government agency.

Philippines

Population. 63,199,807
Parties. Communist Party of the Philippines (Marxist-Leninist) (CPP); Communist Party of the Philippines (Partido Komunista ng Pilipinas; PKP)
Founded. CPP: 1968; PKP: 1930
Membership. CPP: 32,000 (estimates range from 30,000 to more than 45,000); PKP: 5,000 (estimates as high as 8,000)
Leadership. CPP: Jose Maria Sison (chairman); PKP: Felicismo C. Macapagal (chairman); Merlin Magallona (general secretary)
Central Committee. CPP: Regular members: Jose Maria Sison, Benito Tiamzon, Antonio Tujan, Jose Luneta, Wilma Austria-Tiamzon, Arturo Tabara, Leo Velasco, Salvador Bas, Satur Ocampo, Antonio Zumel, Ricardo Reyes, An-

tonio Cabanatan, Randel Echanis, Prudencio Calubid, Carolyn Malay-Ocampo, Sotero Llamas, Julius Viron; alternate members: Elizabeth Principe, Eugenia Topacio, "Bart Paredes," Herminio Pasedes, Josefino Corpuz, Nilo De la Cruz, Adel Silva, Miel Laurenaria, Jesus Nacion, "Gundo," Federico Guanzon, Ruben Balistoy. Captured in 1988: Tomas Dominado, Nicholas Ruiz, Rafael Baylosis, Benjamin De Vera, Jorge Madlos, Francisco Pascual, Ignascio Capegsan, Enrico Esguerra, Romolo Kintanar (later escaped). PKP: Felicismo C. Macapagal, Merlin Magallona, Alejandro Briones, Jesus Lava, Jose Lava, Aurora Evangelista
Status. CPP: illegal; PKP: legal
Last Congress. CPP: Expanded plenum of Central Committee Executive Committee, February; PKP: Ninth, December 1986
Auxiliary Organizations. CPP: New People's Army (NPA), National Democratic Front (NDF). Under its National United Front Commission, the CPP controls or influences many other organizations, listed here by sector. Religious: Christians for National Liberation (CNL); Association of Major Religious Superiors, which created the National Secretariat of Social Action (NASSA); Ecumenical Movement for Justice and Peace; National Ecumenical Forum for Church Response; Ecumenical Partnership for International Concerns (EPIC); Mindanao Interfaith Pastoral Center (MIPC). Education, Youth: Nationalist Youth (Kabatang Makabayan, KM); League of Filipino Students (LFS); National Union of Students of the Philippines (NUSTO); Association of Concerned Teachers (ACT); Youth for Democracy and Nationalism (KADENA); Association of Nationalist Teachers (KAGUMA). Labor: May First Movement (Kilusang Mayo Uno, KMU); Peasant Movement of the Philippines (Kilusang Magbubukid ng Pilipinas, KMP); Federation of Small Fisherman; Small Farmers' Association (SFAN); National Federation of Sugar Workers. Women: Patriotic Movement of Women (Makabayang Kilusan Ng Bagong Kababaihan, MAKIBAKA); Mothers and Relatives Against Tyranny (MARTYR); General Association Binding Women for Reforms, Integrity, Equality, Leadership, and Action (GABRIELA). Human Rights: Task Force Detainees (TFD); Philippine Alliance for Human Rights Advocates (PAHRA). Professional: Philippine Educational Theater Association (PETA); Medical Action Support Group (MAG); Movement of Attorneys for Brotherhood,

Integrity, and Nationalism (MABINI); Concerned Artists of the Philippines (CAP); Confederation for Unity, Recognition, and Advancement of Government Employees (COURAGE). General Political: New Nationalist Alliance (Bagong Alyansang Makabayan, BAYAN); People's Party (Partido ng Bayan, PnB); Alliance for New Politics (ANP); Volunteers for Popular Democracy (VPD); Philippine Rural Reconstruction Movement (PRRM). CPP foreign auxiliaries and solidarity groups: United States: Alliance for Philippine Concerns (APC); Philippine Workers' Support Committee; Friends of the Filipino People in Honolulu; Church Coalition For Human Rights In The Philippines; Canada: Canada-Asia Working Group; Austria: Philippine-Austrian Committee; Belgium: Philippine Group-Gent; Britain: Philippine Resource Center; Philippine Support Group; Denmark: Danish-Philippine Group; Italy: Friends of the Filipino People in Italy; Solidarieta con il Popolo Filipino; Ireland: Filipino-Irish Support Group; Netherlands: Filipino People's Committee (Komite ng Sambayanang Pilipino, KSP); Dutch Philippines Group (FGN); Simbayan; Sweden: Swedish-Filipino Association; Switzerland: Samahang Pilipino; Gruppe Schweiz-Philippinen; West Germany: Aktionsgruppe Philippinen (AGPHI); Japan: Resource Center for Philippine Concerns; Australia: Philippine Action Support Group; New Zealand: Philippine Solidarity Network. PKP: Association of Agricultural Laborers; National Association of Workers (Katipunan); Philippine Committee for Development, Peace and Solidarity (PCDPS). CPP and PKP joint membership: Forward-Looking Organization of Women (FLOW); Freedom from Debt Coalition; National Movement for Civil Liberties.

Publications. CPP: *Ang Bayan* (The nation), monthly; NDF: *Liberation*, monthly; NPA: *Pulang Bandila* (Red flag), bimonthly; Alex Bocayao Brigade: *Ang Partisano* (The partisan); *Taliba ng Bayan*, biweekly; *Larab*, monthly, published in Samar; *NDF Update*, bimonthly, published in the Netherlands; *Filippijnenbulletin*, monthly, published by Dutch Philippine Group; *Pintig*, irregular, published by Aktionsgruppe Philippinen; *Philippines Brief*, irregular, published in Australia by Philippine Action Support Group; *Philippines Update*, monthly, published in New Zealand by Philippine Solidarity Network; *Solidardad II*, quarterly, published in Japan by the Resource Center for Philippine Concerns

CPP. In 1988 the CPP continued to pursue its war, posing a most serious political-military threat to Philippine democracy. However, it suffered several setbacks, including the capture of many top leaders, splits in regional leadership levels, and loss of support in the Catholic Church and in the union movement. Captured documents have provided an unprecedented picture of party structure, finances, and international relations. The CPP also began to pursue a broad-based political strategy—including unprecedented cooperation with the PKP. Internationally, the CPP continued to move closer to the Soviet bloc while continuing to receive political and financial support from a large solidarity network.

Leadership and organization. Although he has been based in Europe for 1987 and 1988, CPP cofounder Jose Maria Sison has apparently regained his former job of CPP chairman (*FBIS*, 9 August). It is widely assumed that his new pseudonym is "Armando Liwanag," who is referred to as chairman of the CPP Central Committee in the July 1987 issue of *Ang Bayan*. Sison's exact role is unclear, though he seems to be regarded as party theoretician and is actively promoting ties with other communist parties. Sison's leadership was apparently confirmed by a three-week expanded plenum of the Executive Committee of the CPP Central Committee in February. Sison may resume full leadership when he returns to the Philippines but does seem to exert some influence over leadership questions from abroad (*FBIS*, 9 August). Captured CPP documents indicate some internal opposition to Sison (*FBIS*, 5 May, 27 September). It is possible that Sison may have been chosen chairman to paper over deeper splits in the Central Committee (CC).

Sison has had high public visibility, including a long four-part interview in the leftist news weekly *National Midweek* (*FBIS*, 21 July). After much pressure by the Armed Forces of the Philippines (AFP), on 21 September President Corazon Aquino ordered the cancellation of Sison's passport, even though he vehemently denies regaining the CPP chairmanship (*FBIS*, 21 September, 17 October). Benito Tiamzon appears to hold the position of "acting chairman" in Sison's absence. CC members Satur Ocampo and Antonio Zumel, who gained much publicity in 1986 and 1987, have been much less visible in 1988, perhaps indicating diminished status in the CC.

The most dramatic leadership turnover has been at the CC level. Twelve new alternate members apparently were elevated at the February CC Executive Committee plenum, but eight members were captured by the AFP: 4 February, Tomas Dominado, Nicholas Ruiz (*FBIS*, 4 February); 29 March, General Secretary Rafael Baylosis, Benjamin De Vera, Romolo Kintanar (*FEER*, 14 April); 20 June, Francisco Pascual (*Washington Times*, 22 June); 7 July, Jorge Madlos (*Philippine Daily Enquirer*, 11 July); Enrico Esguerra (*FBIS*, 15 August); 6 November, Ignacio Capegsan (*FBIS*, 7 November). NPA leader Romolo Kintanar escaped from Camp Crame, in Manila, on 12 November; Francisco Pascual attempted an escape on 12 October (*NYT*, 13 November; *FBIS*, 19 October).

The most spectacular arrests were those of Baylosis, De Vera, and Kintanar, coinciding with the 29 March anniversary of the NPA. Just as important, the AFP also captured 23 functional and territorial staff cadres dealing in financial matters, international affairs, and the staff of *Ang Bayan* (*FBIS*, 15 November). Although an important setback to the CPP, these arrests are not viewed as backbreaking.

The leadership of the six CPP territorial commissions saw significant turnover: Prudencio Calubid (replacing Salvador Bas), Kommid (Mindanao Commission); Manuel Calizo (replacing Arturo Tabara), Visayas Commission; Satur Ocampo (replacing Jose Luneta), Southern Luzon Commission; Francisco Pascual, Central Luzon Commission; Leo Velasco (replacing Ignacio Capegsan), Northern Luzon Commission, and "Carol," National Urban Commission (*FBIS*, 15 July, 15, 18 November; *Manila Chronicle*, 17 July).

In March the AFP revealed that the CPP had reduced the number of its functional national commissions from eight to six. These commissions and their leaders are National United Front Commission, leader unknown; National Organizations Commission, Antonio Tujan; National Research and Propaganda Commission, Antonio Zumel; National Commission on Overseas Work, Sixto Carlos; National Commission on Ethnic Minorities, unknown; and National Military Commission, Benito Tiamzon (*FBIS*, 14 March).

A chart of the National United Front Commission from the documents captured in March indicates it is divided into four major groupings. The Multi Sectoral Campaign and Alliance Department (MSCAD) includes groups like BAYAN and the National Movement for Freedom, Justice, and Democracy; contains a Human Rights Committee; and controls CPP interests in the new National Movement for Civil Liberties. The Middle Forces De-

partment (MFD) contains several sectoral bureaus covering the church, health, teachers, scientists, news media, lawyers, and businessmen. The National Democratic Front (NDF) Secretariat controls the monthly magazine *Liberation*, the NDF International Office, an International Solidarity-International Liaison group, and the Media Liaison Committee. Under a grouping called Legal Political Forces (LPP) the CPP controls a Congress Group and a Volunteers for Popular Democracy Group that includes the Institute for Popular Democracy and the Philippine Rural Reconstruction Movement.

Captured documents also revealed the structure of the CPP's International Department. It is divided into seven committees staffed by foreign-based CPP members that cover the United States and Canada, Western Europe, Asia-Pacific, Eastern Europe, Latin America, the Middle East, and a final committee that is thought to cover either the Communist Party of the Soviet Union or the Chinese Communist Party (*New York City Tribune*, 22 December).

Domestic affairs. There was growing evidence in 1988 of intraparty rifts (*FBIS*, 22 June). It is alleged that Baylosis, De Vera, and Kintanar may have been betrayed by Benito Tiamzon, who is said to have barely escaped capture (*FBIS*, 5 April). Former NPA leader and failed PnB Senate candidate Bernabe Buscayno criticized the 1986 boycott and continued "sparrow" killings in Manila (*FBIS*, 20 April). In a candid interview, captured CC member Ignacio Capegsan expressed his disappointment over the lack of consensus on strategy, claiming that cadres promote various revolutionary models, like the Russian and Nicaraguan, which impedes the party's progress. He said that the CC is divided informally into geographic factions (*FBIS*, 16 November). Capegsan is reported to have been stripped of his CC position for financial and marital indiscretions (*FBIS*, 26 July). But he claimed he left the "movement" in 1986 when he saw the futility of the CPP's boycott of the February 1986 election and implied criticism of the CPP's "militarist" faction (*FBIS*, 15 November).

Strong opposition to "militarist" policies forced a split in the Negros Island Regional Party Committee (NIRPC). In March former NIRPC Executive Committee secretary Nemesio Dimafiles was captured, having broken away from the party in 1987 over opposition to increased NPA attacks (*Daily Globe*, March 3). By midyear several other top cadres had "resigned" over personal and policy issues—mainly disagreement with the policy of increased NPA violence, which they see as decreasing public support (author interview, 16 July). The assassination of one of their number by the NPA in early July prompted the "resignees" to publicly attack the CPP (*FBIS*, 19 July). Some of these cadres expect further retaliation. The AFP revealed that as many as 855 CPP members and activists were killed in the Mindanao purge of 1985 to 1986 (*Philippine Star*, 18 July).

Despite such internal opposition to NPA violence, CPP hard-liners appear to be in control. The April issue of *Ang Bayan* called for "bigger military drives" (*FBIS*, 20 April). Documents from the February plenum, captured with Baylosis and De Vera, indicate the CPP has proposed tactics that reinforce "the primacy of armed struggle." These documents also indicate that the CPP views itself as having reached the threshold of the "strategic counteroffensive"; the last substage of the "strategic defensive" stage (*FEER*, 28 July). The documents also indicate the CPP is organizing an independent network of companies to acquire and ship heavy weapons such as rocket grenades, mortars, and surface-to-air missiles.

Captured documents also provided an unprecedented view of CPP finances, which are apparently well managed and include foreign bank accounts. The CPP's 1988 budget was about 55.2 million pesos (U.S. $2.6 million). In 1987 income came from "legal projects," businesses, and development projects (69 percent); "revolutionary taxation" (22 percent); "solidarity groups" and foreign donations (7 percent); and dues and donations (2 percent). (Ibid.) Senator Ernesto Maceda claimed the CPP was collecting 300 million pesos (U.S. $15 million) a year in "revolutionary taxes"; other estimates place this figure at 150 million pesos (*FBIS*, 26 July, 2 August).

In June the AFP estimated NPA strength to be 25,800 guerrillas, but this figure declined to 24,430 by November (*FBIS*, 17 November). According to the AFP, these were deployed in about 73 guerrilla fronts that either influenced, infiltrated, or threatened 19 percent of the country's 41,693 barangays—roughly 20 percent of the countryside. Through November, the war resulted in 3,334 deaths in 2,274 insurgency-related incidents. This would indicate a slight reduction from the 3,812 total deaths recorded for 1987. Most of the incidents were in rural areas, but 95 soldiers, 74 policemen, 44 government officials, and 419 suspected civilian informers were killed in urban areas (Philippine News Agency, 7 December).

NPA attacks were less dramatic than 1987 but continued the new trends of attacking economic targets and foreigners. In February, two South Korean engineers were released after 89 days of captivity and a reported ransom payment of $750,000 (*FBIS*, 9 February). NPA leaders in Negros threatened to attack U.S.- and Canadian-funded assistance projects (*FBIS*, 22 April). In August guerrillas overran a government-owned geothermal plant (*Daily Globe*, 6 August). In early December NPA guerrillas attacked several farms in Negros, burning sugar cane fields (AFP, Negros News and Features, 20 December). Although the NPA did not attack more U.S. servicemen, the May issue of *Ang Bayan* warned "All U.S. troops in installations in the country are military targets of the NPA."

The main focus of NPA activity in 1988 seems to have shifted from southern to central Luzon (*Manila Bulletin*, 14 July). The importance of central Luzon was highlighted in the May issue of *Ang Bayan*. In May, it was reported that NPA attacks in Manila by the Alex Boncayao Brigade (ABB) had risen 15 percent over 1987 (*FBIS*, 24 May). On 28 March ABB "sparrows" assassinated Prospero Oreta, mayor of a Manila suburb and relative of President Aquino (*WP*, 29 March). Press reports indicate increased tension in provinces around Manila like Quezon, and Bataan province is reported to still be under "effective control" of the CPP (*FBIS*, 18, 23 March; *Manila Chronicle*, 17 July).

Regarding political interaction with the government, the CPP did not participate overtly in the 18 January local elections as it had in the congressional elections of 1987. But the party did exert widespread influence, reportedly killing 22 candidates, kidnapping 13, and, according to the Commission on Elections chairman Ramon Filipe, supporting 15,000 out of 150,000 candidates (*FBIS*, 21 January). On 21 July the Catholic Bishops' Conference of the Philippines proposed a resumption of peace talks with the NDF. This was welcomed by Aquino but initially opposed by Defense Secretary Fidel Ramos. (*Manila Chronicle*, 17 July.) In an early November statement, the CPP CC Executive Committee rejected the bishop's initiative to renew dialogue with Aquino (*FBIS*, 15 November).

There was sharp debate in the government over who was winning the war. In her 25 July state of the nation address Aquino said this "may be remembered as the year that the insurgency was broken"

(*WP*, 26 July). However, an AFP report for the first quarter of 1988 that was leaked by opposition politicians stated the AFP lost all but one of 15 "decisive engagements" (large battles) with the NPA (*FBIS*, 25 July). However, it is clear that the AFP has regained the momentum in its war against the CPP in areas like Davao, Mindanao, and Negros. Its continued success in Davao is due largely to controversial "vigilante" groups like the Alsa Masa. In Negros, its success is due largely to CPP alienation of public support and increased public support for the AFP, particularly by sugar planters who have funded a new militia unit and additional police stations in the capital city of Bocolod.

In 1988 the AFP introduced new tactics that may improve its performance. The first is the Special Operations Team (SOT), a small unit that lives in a CPP-affected area and seeks to win back the population through education, responding to local demands, and providing protection. When finished, the SOT is then to be replaced with a Civilian Armed Forces Geographical Unit (CAFGU) composed of reservists and local volunteers to act as a territorial defense militia. The latter is intended to replace the "vigilante" groups. Aquino ordered the disbandment of the "vigilantes" on 25 July.

Auxiliary and front organizations. Opposition to U.S. military facilities in the Philippines and criticism of Aquino's human rights record were major themes for CPP fronts in 1988. They led frequent protests in front of the U.S. embassy that often led to skirmishes with police. Starting at the end of December several CPP fronts including the KMU, KMP, BAYAN, ACT, GABRIELA, and the Ecumenical Partnership for International Concerns were organizing a series of activities for about 200 foreign "Peace Brigade" volunteers to protest the U.S. military facilities (*News Weekly*, 7 December).

CPP fronts continued to lose support in some sectors, largely due to more effective government counterpropaganda. The government made widespread use of a videotaped interview, made in Belgium in March 1987 by the Belgian Labor Party, of Jose Maria Sison and his wife Juliet in which Mrs. Sison linked several groups to the CPP. These groups included the Kilusang Mayo Uno (May First Movement, KMU); Kilusang Magbubukid ng Pilipinas (Peasant Movement of the Philippines, KMP); Alliance of Concerned Teachers; GABRIELA; League of Filipino Students; BAYAN; and the PnB. (*FBIS*, 8 September.) In early Novem-

ber Sison denied that he had confirmed such groups were CPP fronts, but by late November, the AFP was hinting that it might outlaw the groups named by Mrs. Sison (*FBIS*, 4, 18 November).

A *Liberation* article on Christians for National Liberation (CNL) asserts that it is so strong in some rural areas that it feels confident enough to seek the cooperation of the local Catholic bishop (*Liberation*, March–April). But CPP elements were dealt a significant setback when Cardinal Jaime Sin went on the offensive, acknowledging the church's problem with communist infiltration (*WSJ*, 14 March). Sin supported the reorganization of the National Social Action Secretariat (NASSA), which had been accused of channeling foreign donations to CPP fronts (*National Catholic Register*, 21 February). On 15 July about 2,000 people protested communist infiltration of the Negros Catholic Diocese (*Philippine Daily Inquirer*, 17 July).

Cardinal Sin also criticized the leftist bias of the human rights monitor, Task Force Detainees (AFP, 4 February). The Aquino government was the target of intense criticism on the human rights issue, particularly over its inability to solve the killings of several leftist leaders. Amnesty International and the New York–based Lawyers' Committee for Human Rights issued reports highly critical of the Aquino government for this and for her support for "vigilante" groups. (*FEER*, 17 March.)

The CPP also lost support in the trade union movement. In December the 50,000-member United Lumber and General Workers' Union disassociated itself from the KMU because of its "hidden agenda" (*Philippine Star*, 19 December). In July, the National Federation of Sugar Workers (NFSW) of Negros, one of the most powerful KMU unions, was identified as a CPP front by two "resigned" CPP members, including former NFSW vice president Edgar Estacio (*Daily Globe*, 23 July). On 7 August, the Philippine constabulary filed charges against eleven KMU leaders for "illegal association" with the CPP (*Malaya*, 22 August). On 6 October, the Bocolod police chief filed a complaint against the NFSW leadership accusing them of being CPP members (*Daily Star*, 7 October).

The CPP is now seeking to recover its political losses by pursuing a broader-based political front strategy. In August the PnB revealed it was investigating the possibility of joining the Liberal Party, led by Senate speaker Jovito Salonga; the PDP-Laban Party, led by Senator Aquilino Pimentel; and the LDP Party, led by House Speaker Ramon Mitra

(*FBIS*, 9 August). The PnB fielded only fifteen full slates of candidates in the January local elections (*NYT*, 17 January).

For the first time there is significant cooperation between fronts of the PKP and CPP. In the women's-sector CPP, PKP fronts and noncommunist groups have formed the FLOW coalition (*Morning Star*, 5 April). CPP and PKP front leaders are also present in the new National Movement for Civil Liberties and the new Freedom From Debt Coalition. These two groups also include noncommunist leftists and, in the case of the Freedom From Debt Coalition, 21 congressmen and Senator Wigberto Tanada (*Philippine Daily Inquirer*, 5 May). With this evolution of front tactics, the CPP gives up the degree of control it has over its own fronts but has a better chance of regaining middle-class support lost by boycotting the February 1986 presidential election.

International views. Captured documents confirmed that the CPP is seeking formal relations with the Communist Party of the Soviet Union (CPSU), after which it expects material support. One document from the February plenum states, "If party-to-party relations are ever established with the Soviet Union, this has great implications for diplomatic, material and financial support." These documents indicate that in 1987 Sison proposed talks that would lead to party-to-party relations with East Germany, Hungary, Cuba, Bulgaria, and Vietnam. By the February 1988 plenum, Vietnam was said to have had "no definite stand" on the request, and Hungary, Yugoslavia, and East Germany said they would respond by mid-1988. (Captured document dated 21 February.) It was widely reported in the Philippine press that Sison wrote a letter to Soviet general secretary Mikhail Gorbachev in September 1987 to propose a meeting to discuss party-to-party relations (*FBIS*, 16 September). But during the February plenum it was stated that Soviet relations with the PKP continued to be a major impediment to formal party-to-party relations (*Asian WSJ*, 13 December).

On several occasions Soviet officials denied they were assisting the CPP. Former Foreign Minister Andrei Gromyko did so to a visiting Philippine Senate delegation in July (*FBIS*, 12 July). Foreign Minister Eduard Schevardnadze repeated the denial during his first visit to Manila in late December, a major advance for persistent Soviet efforts to court Manila (*FEER*, 5 January 1989).

NDF international representative and ex-priest Luis Jalandoni advanced CPP relations with two communist parties that are close to Moscow. In December 1987 Jalandoni addressed the Twenty-sixth Congress of the French Communist Party, stating "we deeply appreciate your consistent political and moral support for our national liberation struggle, for the NDF, our New People's Army and other patriotic organizations" (*FBIS*, 16 March). In April Jalandoni signed a formal agreement with El Salvador's Soviet- and Cuban-supported Farabundo Martí National Liberation Front to "fight U.S. domination of our respective countries" (*Malaya*, 30 April).

During a 14 to 16 April visit to the People's Republic of China (PRC) by President Aquino, Premier Li Peng refused to end moral support to the CPP, saying "When you ask us not to give moral support, that is difficult" (*Asiaweek*, 29 April). In September the PRC ambassador to Manila stated its "moral relationship" with the CPP was not meant to interfere in Philippine affairs (*FBIS*, 23 September). The PRC sharply curtailed its material support to the CPP when relations were established with the government of Ferdinand Marcos, but party-to-party relations continue.

Increased attention was focused on CPP international "solidarity" activities (*FBIS*, 26 July). One captured document indicates that 1,753 foreigners went on CPP-controlled "exposure tours" in 1986 and 1987 (*FEER*, 19 May). Documents captured from a January 1987 meeting in Manila of the International Department's Asia-Pacific (ASPAC) Committee indicate that solidarity groups in Japan, like the Resource Center for Philippine Concerns, promote links between the Japanese union federation Sohyo and the KMU and that there are "working relations" between BAYAN and the Japan Socialist Party.

The ASPAC country report for Australia states an intention to open an NDF office. It notes solidarity activities are coordinated by the Philippine Action Support Group and that there "are also a number of ALP [Australian Labor Party] members recognizing and supporting in whatever way they can the NDF" (*News Weekly*, 10 August). Solidarity activities in Australia appear to be led by Joy Balazo, a Filipino citizen representing the Ecumenical Partnership for International Concerns. In September and October Balazo toured New Zealand seeking support for the December "peace brigade" to the Philippines to protest U.S. military facilities (*Philippines Update*, August).

Elsewhere in Asia the CPP was said to be recruiting supporters among Filipinos working in Hong Kong (*FBIS*, 12 July). Captured evidence indicates that the CPP cooperates with the Indonesian Communist Party and may even have had NPA guerrillas trained in Malaysia (*FBIS*, 27 September; *FEER*, 28 July).

Foreign Secretary Raul Manglapus complained to diplomats from Japan and Australia about foreign support to the CPP. This resulted in Japan denying a visa to PnB activist Nelia Sancho (*FEER*, 28 July). On 29 November Australian foreign minister Gareth Evans warned Australians going to participate in a Philippine "peace brigade," organized by CPP fronts, not to associate with the CPP (*News Weekly*, 7 December).

BAYAN general secretary Zenaida Uy toured the United States beginning in September (*Philippine-American News*, 5 December). Her tour was coordinated by the Los Angeles–based Alliance for Philippine Concerns, named as a CPP solidarity group in one captured CPP document. The U.S. State Department denied a visa to NPA founder Bernabe Buscayno so he could not speak at the fourteenth annual conference of the Committee to Advance the Movement to Democracy and Independence, founded by the Union of Democratic Filipinos (KDP) (*Washington Times*, 24 May). During the 1970s the KDP raised money for the NDF and the NPA but now considers itself to not be in the "mainstream" of the Philippine radical left (*National Midweek*, 17 February).

By one AFP estimate, the CPP was able to raise $15 million from foreign sources in 1987 (*FBIS*, 1 September). The United Methodist Church of the United States gave a $12,129 grant to GABRIELA (*United Methodist Reporter*, 24 June). The Dutch government's National Commission for Development Aid gave $28,500 to the Dutch Philippine Group in 1987 (*Manila Times*, 8 September). An Australian report stated that of the $129,000 given annually to Philippine projects by the Australian Council of Churches, one-third ends up in the hands of the NPA (*West Australian*, 7 May).

More understanding of how the CPP uses fronts to funnel foreign funds was gained from National Council of Churches of the Philippines (NCCP) employee Noel Villalba, a suspected member of the International Department's Asia-Pacific Committee, who was arrested in late June. Philippine military records trace Villalba's involvement with the communist movement back to 1971. In a handwritten statement, Villalba described how money is skimmed from projects approved by the NCCP by CPP members in the NCCP. Up to 60 percent of individual project funds can be diverted for use by the CPP (*Daily Globe*, 12 July). Villalba later denied statements attributed to him, saying they were made under torture (*Daily Globe*, 13 July).

PKP. This year the PKP began to raise its profile. For the first time it has begun to cooperate substantively with the illegal CPP, signaling that a rapprochement is beginning to overcome the bitter 1968 split between the two parties.

Leadership and organization. Felicismo C. Macapagal is now chairman of the PKP, with Merlin Magallona as general secretary (*WMR*, January; *Neues Deutschland*, 20 June). A new addition to the PKP Politburo is Aurora Evangelista (*WMR*, September).

Domestic Affairs. The PKP held its Ninth Congress in December 1986 (*WMR*, January). The program adopted at that congress includes a long list of socialist economic policies and opposition to U.S. military facilities (*IB*, January). But in an interview in the 5 April issue of the British communist party's *Morning Star*, PKP CC member "Reynaldo Dimal" was highly critical of the Aquino government. He accused her government of "surrender" to U.S. interests, said Aquino's land reform is "meaningless," and was critical of elite domination of politics. Dimal noted a new PKP attitude toward the CPP. "The PKP does not make an issue of armed struggle versus legal struggle with the CPP." This was a major issue in the 1968 CPP-PKP split. Dimal also noted that the CPP is now shifting to emphasize legal struggle, a transition the PKP made over a decade ago. Dimal stated that the PKP has long called for "unity of all left, anti-imperialist, patriotic, and democratic forces" and is "gratified to see that this principle is being recognized more widely today."

However, there was also evidence that PKP and CPP interests may still conflict at the local level. A spate of gun battles in Angeles City, outside Clark Air Base were reported to stem from turf battles between NPA and old PKP "Huk" factions (*Daily Globe*, 11 July).

Auxiliary organizations. Dimal explained that CPP and PKP front organizations now cooperate jointly and in conjunction with noncommunist leftists. Examples of joint cooperation include that between the PKP's Association of Agricultural Laborers and the KMP. Examples of more broadly based PKP-CPP initiatives that also include non-communist groups are FLOW, whose vice president is Leonor Briones; the National Movement for Civil Liberties; and the Freedom From Debt Coalition.

International Views. In several statements, the PKP was critical of the continued U.S. military presence in the Philippines (*FBIS*, 11 April, 23 June; *WMR*, September). On the other hand there was much praise for Soviet peace and disarmament initiatives. But PKP chairman Macapagal said Sino-Soviet normalization was proceeding "disappointingly slow" (*WMR*, January). The PKP is still substantially funded by the Soviets.

Richard D. Fisher, Jr.
Asia Studies Center, The Heritage Foundation

South Pacific Islands

Populations. Federated States of Micronesia: 76,050; Fiji: 740,761; French Polynesia: 190,939; Kiribati: 67,638; Marshall Islands: 40,609; Nauru: 8,902; New Caledonia: 150,981; Palau: 14,106; Papua New Guinea: 3,649,503; Solomon Islands: 312,196; Tonga: 99,620; Tuvalu: 8,475; Vanuatu: 154,691; Western Samoa: 178,045

The South Pacific region contains 22 island states and six million people. Since 1984, the South Pacific has received increased attention from the USSR and even unlikely surrogates such as Libya. This has complicated international security relations in the South Pacific, contributing little to development needs of the island states.

No country in the South Pacific has a formal communist party, Soviet aligned or otherwise, but Soviet front organizations, particularly in the youth, student, and labor areas, have reached out to even the smallest states. Two major re. 'on l front meetings were held in 1988, and both took pla. in

Sydney, Australia. They were part of the regional buildup for the June 1989 World Federation of Democratic Youth (WFDY)/International Union of Students (IUS) project—the World Festival of Youth and Students (WFYS).

The first of these meetings, chaired by WFDY president Walid Masri, took place in Sydney on 7–8 May. According to the official organ of the Central Committee of the Moscow-aligned Socialist Party of Australia (SPA), *The Guardian*, this Regional Youth Forum for Peace and Disarmament in Asia and the South Pacific included regional delegates from Papua New Guinea, Fiji, Vanuatu, and Kiribati. Delegates from 29 organizations were purportedly represented and issued a declaration in conformity with local goals of Soviet foreign policy such as banning visits by nuclear-capable ships and the liquidation of all sea-launched cruise missiles (both of which would only affect the U.S. Navy).

In early September the Second International Round Table Meeting for a Secure Nuclear-free and Independent Pacific gathered representatives from all over the South Pacific. Students came from Papua New Guinea, Vanuatu, New Zealand, Western Samoa, the Philippines, and Kiribati. A delegation of three attended from Fiji's University of the South Pacific. This was a buildup to the WFYS as well as an effort to establish a permanent network with the communist League of Philippino Students, which acted as a "clearing house for the new network" with assistance from the IUS (*Youth Voice*, October).

The South Pacific region now receives more aid per capita than any other region in the world. More recently, Soviet fisheries' deals with Kiribati and Vanuatu have led to a further commitment of Western aid, most notably Japan's Kuranari Doctrine of 1987, which will see Japan become a major donor to the region. There is a clear concern that the frustration of the island states' economic aspirations could provide the Soviets with opportunities for entrée into the region.

The 1984 evaluation of academics Richard Herr and Bob Kiste, experts on South Pacific affairs, still stands:

This opportunity for a Soviet or surrogate entrée would be indistinguishable from any purely commercial arrangement initially and could be defended by the recipient island state as exclusively economic...
The insidiousness of this danger derives from the fact that...the prospects for even an approximation of the one acceptable solution to this problem, moderate economic self-sufficiency, is remote for perhaps a

majority of the FICs [Forum Island Countries]. (*The Potential for Soviet Penetration of the Pacific Islands: An Assessment*, 1984).

Because fishery contracts can constitute a significant proportion of the island states' national incomes, the potential for economic leverage by the Soviet Union is great. The Soviet foreign minister hinted during a Canberra visit in 1987 that he expected political influence to follow from such economic contacts. Evidence that the Soviets are pursuing fishery arrangements for other than commercial reasons can be found in the fact that despite having lost an estimated $20 million on its fishing activities around Kiribati, the Soviet Union went on to negotiate a similar agreement with Vanuatu, whose waters are less prolific in tuna and are best fished by long-liners, whereas the Soviet fleet consists almost entirely of purse seiners. Fortunately, these agreements have not been renewed as they expire. The Soviet Union may, however, be seeking to renew its agreement with Kiribati.

Fisheries deals with the Soviets have served to undermine strategic denial and the sense of a regional security community. Again in the words of Herr,

The growth of Soviet access to the region since August 1985 could be interpreted as signaling the demise of strategic denial as a practical doctrine for regional security . . . it may indicate that the islands' sense of mutual responsibility has been eroded to the extent that some states may be prepared to pursue their own interests regardless of the effects on their neighbors.

Both Kiribati and Vanuatu came in for considerable regional criticism as a result of their dealings with the Soviet Union.

In 1987 the U.S. and South Pacific Forum concluded a multilateral treaty with the Forum Fisheries Agency governing licensing and royalties arrangements that will be worth $60 million to the island states over the next five years. This more than anything will undermine Soviet attempts to use fishing as leverage to enter and influence South Pacific politics.

The South Pacific Nuclear-Free Zone (SPNFZ) Treaty, an initiative of the Australian and New Zealand Labour Governments, is primarily aimed at prohibiting French nuclear testing and the dumping of nuclear waste in the region, which have been the main antinuclear concerns of the island states. The treaty leaves open to individual signatories the question of nuclear ship visits. The refusal of the United States, Britain, and France to accede to the treaty's protocols because of the precedent it might set has generated some ill will toward these Western states on the part of island leaders. The islands are for the most part keen supporters of the Australia/New Zealand/United States (ANZUS) alliance and have been disturbed by New Zealand's ban on nuclear weapons and its implications for regional security. The dispute between New Zealand and the United States has generated some uncertainty in the islands about their future security. It is not surprising, therefore, that the Soviet Union has been an enthusiastic supporter of the SPNFZ Treaty and has signed its protocols. Fiji, Vanuatu, Papua New Guinea, and the Solomons have all imposed bans on nuclear visits on various occasions.

The Soviet Union has nonresident diplomatic relations with Fiji, Nauru, Papua New Guinea, Tonga, Vanuatu, and Western Samoa. Libya's involvement in the region has included diplomatic and political ties with Vanuatu and support for radical elements of the Front for Liberation of National Kanak Socialists and the Organsasi Papua Merderka (Free West Papua Movement, OPM). This involvement has been mostly rhetorical to date, although some Kanak, OPM, and Barak Sope cronies have been to Tripoli for security training and indoctrination. In 1987 Australia expelled its resident Libyan People's Bureau, which covered the South Pacific, because of activities of Libyan diplomats in the region.

The People's Republic of China (PRC) has an active aid program in the region. Its main concern has been to counter Soviet and Taiwanese diplomatic influence. To this end, it has established nonresident diplomatic relations with Fiji, Kiribati, Vanuatu, and Western Samoa and resident relations with the Solomons and has made overtures to most of the other island states. The new Chinese ambassador, Zhang Wei, was one of the first to meet the new Papua New Guinea prime minister, Robbie Namaliu (*FBIS*, 3 October). The PRC offered to set up two TV stations following unsatisfactory negotiations with two Australian commercial networks (*FBIS*, 2 February).

In terms of foreign relations, the Polynesian and Micronesian countries are much more conservative than the Melanesian countries. The emergence of the Melanesian Spearhead Group as a subregional bloc within the South Pacific Forum may undermine regional solidarity on foreign policy questions, in particular on the desirability of links with non-Western powers external to the region. However, there is still a good deal of deference to Australia and New Zealand in the conduct of the region's approach to foreign affairs and security matters.

Since New Zealand's abandonment of the important ANZUS security treaty, Australia has stepped up a Defence Cooperation Program (DCP) in conjunction with the island states that will amount to $20.633 million in 1988–89. The DCP involves such projects as the Pacific Patrol Boat Program, which provides seven island states with a total of twelve patrol boats.

The Melanesian states (Papua New Guinea, Fiji, the Solomon Islands, Vanuatu, and New Caledonia) are the most populous and resource-rich in the region. Aid is approximately 27 percent of the gross domestic product of the Solomon Islands and Vanuatu and only 3 percent in Fiji.

The Polynesian states (Western Samoa, American Samoa, the Cook Islands, Tonga, Tuvalu, French Polynesia, and Niue) have an average population size of only 55,000 and a resource base restricted to a few agricultural goods and fish. These countries are the most aid-dependent in the region, aid that they obtain in most cases from their close association (in some cases semi-independent status) with the former colonial power (France, the United Kingdom, and New Zealand).

The Micronesian states (including Kiribati, Nauru, and the Federated States of Micronesia) are among the smallest of the region's states and are also heavily aid-dependent.

Papua New Guinea (PNG). The 1975 constitution of PNG provided for a 109-member parliament. PNG politics are characterized by numerous political parties, usually very narrowly constituted (sometimes limited in membership to the parliamentary representatives). Despite a procapitalist approach to development, political and economic pork barreling is widespread.

A key foreign policy problem faced by PNG is the OPM uprising against Indonesian authority in West Irian Jaya. Indonesia has implemented a program of transmigrating its people from densely populated islands such as Java to less-populated areas such as West Irian, which is the immediate cause of the uprising. PNG shares a border with Indonesia, and refugees from the uprising (some ten thousand) are now encamped just inside PNG. Any intensification of fighting in West Irian could generate a significant refugee problem for PNG and has already led to cross-border incursions by the Indonesian military in pursuit of OPM rebels. The border issue has been the source of some tension in Indonesian-PNG relations, although a 1987 Treaty of Mutual Respect, Friendship and Co-operation between the two countries has helped smooth relations. Some twenty OPM fighters have allegedly received military training in Libya.

In July there was a peaceful transition of power in PNG, the South Pacific's largest democracy, from Pais Wingti to Prime Minister Namiliu. There is no formal communist party in PNG, although Moscow has sought recruits for its front organization among unionists and students. Students from PNG will attend the major Soviet recruiting project, the World Festival of Youth and Students to be held in Pyongyang, North Korea, in July. Representatives of the PNG Students' Association attended a WFDY forum in Sydney (*Youth Voice*, June, July) and the subsequent IUS front meeting in Sydney in September (*The Guardian*, 21 September). The PNG Trade Union Council is suspicious of pro-Soviet activities and even of the left-tilting Pacific trade union community.

In August Prime Minister Namiliu proposed the opening of a Soviet embassy. This followed a visit to Port Moresby in March by Yeugniy Somotekin, Moscow's ambassador to Australia, who is accredited to PNG. Port Moresby and Moscow have had formal diplomatic relations since 1976 (*FBIS-East Asia*, 4 March). PNG's decision to host a resident Soviet mission, the first in the region, has been strongly criticized by the head of PNG's Department of Defence.

Following persistent questions in Parliament, the PNG government decided to delay the opening of the Soviet embassy, calling for significant developments in trade and technical aid before any permanent mission was established. The parliamentary motion also called for a strengthening of the capacities of the national intelligence organization before the Soviets opened up in Port Moresby (*FBIS*, 7 September). However, by year's end it looked like the USSR would soon open a legation in PNG. (The only Soviet-aligned organization in PNG is the students' association of the university, which is affiliated with the IUS.) Following a worldwide pattern, the Soviets in midyear sent a delegation from the USSR, rather than one of their fronts, for a tour of PNG. Representatives of PNG students attended a whole range of meetings including bureau meetings of the WFDY and IUS in preparation for the World Festival of Youth and Students. Gabriel Ramoi, a former student politician who is active in the Soviet fronts, lost his position as communications minister in a cabinet reshuffle in July even before the Wingti government was defeated at the elections.

The PNG delegation visited the PRC (*FBIS*, 29 September), and PNG participated in the ministerial-level delegation of South Pacific countries that visited China following a Pacific nations' conference in Japan (*FBIS*, 29 August).

Fiji. The demise of established democratic institutions in Fiji is fortunately not typical of the region. Only New Caledonia has a complex racial situation that poses a threat to the political stability of that terrritory.

It is noteworthy that the election of the Labour–National Federation Party Government was assisted by Australian far left trade unionist John Halfpenny, who assisted in the formation of the Fiji Labour Party.

In 1968, the University of the South Pacific (USP) was opened in Suva, Fiji. The university has eight thousand students throughout the region and is invaluable in supplying the region with graduates and facilitating contact between the islands' elites. It is funded 70 percent by Fiji and 10 percent by external assistance, with the remainder coming from the rest of the region. Of considerable concern is the fact that both the USP students' association and the PNG students' association are affiliated with the IUS, the Prague-based Soviet front organization.

Despite the military-conservative nature of the Fiji regime, a Soviet trade delegation led by V. Golanov arrived in Suva as part of a four-nation tour that included Tonga, Vanuatu, and PNG (*FBIS*, 18 April). Following the discovery of a 12-ton container load of East bloc arms in Sydney en route to the western Fijian port of Loluka that had arrived from Hodeida, North Yemen, police and troops raided the premises and arrested 25 people and seized 165 AK-47 rifles, rocket launchers, grenades, and ammunition (*FEER*, 16 June). Mohamed Kahan, a Fijian Indian, was sought in connection with the cache of arms (*FBIS*, 3 June). Western intelligence services privately blamed India for shipments of Soviet arms to Fiji, allegedly for a countercoup against the ethnic Fijian-dominated military government (*FBIS*, 10 June). Two hundred troops combing Fiji's rugged western interior netted only about one-third of the ten tons of Czech-made arms allegedly smuggled into Fiji in April (*FBIS*, 27 July). Two Soviet heavy machine guns were subsequently uncovered (*FBIS*, 6 Sep-

tember). Although the ban on foreign journalists and other restrictions on democratic liberties remained in force (*FBIS*, 6 October), the end of the year did see the suspension of the international security decree and a gradual easing of tensions.

Solomon Islands. Independence in 1978 saw the Solomons adopt a constitution that provides for a unicameral Parliament containing no more than 50 and no less than 30 members elected every four years. The Parliament elects the prime minister and cabinet. Solomon Island politics have been turbulent in recent years, and there are strong indications that there may be a change in government. The Solomons have diplomatic ties with Taiwan, and the Taiwanese maintain a resident mission in Honiara. The country's National Union of Workers is affiliated with the World Federation of Trade Unions (WFTU), a Soviet front. Moves by this trade union to form a labor party are said to have been helped by Libya. The Solomons have been the main advocates of the Melanesian Spearhead Group, a subregional bloc within the South Pacific Forum.

The Solomon Islands' prime minister, Ezekiel Alebua, brought in the experienced Sir Peter Kenilora as foreign minister; even this will do little to assist his government's image, which is under threat from a democratic opposition. Local irritation at the alleged illegal presence of two U.S. tuna boats in territorial waters led to talks with the United States (*FBIS*, 15 March). But the Solomons' main international orientation as part of the Melanesian Spearhead Group was prompted by opposition to French activities against indigenous Kanaks in New Caledonia. The increasingly erratic government expelled twelve Australian businessmen and had an expatriate adviser threaten the Australian high commissioner. Solomon Mamalaoni, the opposition leader, alleged that his and government ministers' phones were being tapped. This and other incidents relating to the Solomons' leadership involvement with an eccentric Australian business group have made a change in the country's political leadership probable, although no major change in foreign policy is likely to result. A former Solomon Islands foreign minister, Dennis Dulay, warned the country's government about regional Soviet activities. *Glasnost'* meant that the Soviets were likely to become stronger and more regionally ambitious, he warned, pointing to the opening of a Soviet embassy in Port Moresby (*FBIS*, 9 October). As with every country in the region, there is no formal communist party in the Solomon Islands.

The Solomon Islands National Union of Workers remains affiliated with the WFTU and had another delegation in Moscow in October. However, generally pro–Soviet Union activity has declined with the renewed involvement of the International Confederation of Free Trade Unions in the region. The Pacific trade union community has been in voluntary abeyance, especially as island unions take more practical assistance from a Brisbane-based arm of the Commonwealth Trade Union Council.

Western Samoa. The Legislative Assembly of Western Samoa has 47 members including the speaker. Forty-five members are elected by the traditional ruling class of landholders, who constitute about 10 percent of the population. Only two members are popularly elected. Western Samoa is a devoutly Christian society, which helps ensure its pro-Western orientation. Western Samoa has seen some political instability in recent years due to economic difficulties, leading to three changes of government in 1982 alone.

There was little political turbulence in this conservative island society. However, individuals continue to participate in Soviet front meetings, particularly of the WFDY and WFTU, as well as to attend occasional regional meetings of the fronts in Australia. An unnamed delegate attended the IUS regional meeting in Sydney in September, according to the newspaper of the youth section of the pro-Moscow Socialist Party of Australia, *Youth Voice* (October).

Cook Islands. In the South Pacific, Moscow's fishing deals have come to nothing, but the Soviets have other avenues. In January the Soviet oceanographic research vessel *Akademik Oparin* arrived in Rarotonga in the Cook Islands following earlier activity by another "research" vessel there. (The real value of these vessels is the research they do for the Soviet navy, particularly for its extensive submarine force.) In early March the Soviet ambassador to New Zealand, Yuri Mikhailovich Sokolov, also visited the Cook Islands (*WSJ*, 28 September). New Zealand is responsible for the Cook Islands' foreign affairs and defense arrangements.

Vanuatu. Formerly a British-French condominium, Vanuatu became a republic in 1980 and has had a turbulent political history. Its unicameral parliament has 39 members. Postindependence politics have been dominated by the Vanuatu Party led by Prime Minister Walter Lini. The Vanuatu Party is a well-organized and disciplined political machine, which accounts for some of its success. The main opposition party is the francophone-based Union of Modern Parties (UMP).

Vanuatu is the most radical and only nonaligned state in the region. Its foreign policy stems in large part from its bitter decolonization experience and the beliefs associated with Melanesian socialism, which have some currency in Vanuatu, PNG, and the Solomons. Nonalignment has seen Vanuatu attempt to achieve balance in its external relations by cultivating diplomatic links with the Soviet Union, Cuba, Libya, Poland, Vietnam, and North Korea, as well as with the West. In 1987 Vanuatu signed a one-year fisheries agreement with the Soviet Union worth $1.5 million.

The Libyan connection perhaps has been the most damaging, both externally and internally. Vanuatu has facilitated contact between FULK (the radical wing of the Kanak Socialist National Liberation Front), the OPM, and Libya, thus presiding over extraregional interference in two of the region's most likely areas of instability, and has been criticized by the rest of the region for doing so.

Barak Sope, who has the most developed Libyan links and is the secretary general of the ruling Vanuatu Party, led a riot against the Lini government on 16 May with the assistance of his Libyan-trained bodyguards. One person died and many were injured in the riot. Sope was subsequently sacked from his government and party posts. Sope and a handful of dissident Vanuatu Party supporters joined with UMP members of Parliament in a walk-out in an unsuccessful attempt to deny the government a parliamentary quorum. He has since formed the breakaway Melanesian Progressive Party. Following the 16 May riot, Australia provided tear gas and riot control equipment to the Lini government in case of further disorders.

The failure of Sope's efforts to bring down the government by parliamentary means saw him enlist the support of the Vanuatu president Sokomanu (who is also Sope's uncle) in dismissing the government and installing Sope as interim prime minister. The president had no constitutional authority to do so, and Prime Minister Lini described the action as an attempt at a political coup. Sope and Sokomanu were immediately arrested on charges of sedition and have been found guilty. The Sope experience and the expulsion of the Libyan People's Bureau from Canberra has caused Lini to reconsider his country's involvement with Libya and led to the cancellation of plans to establish a people's bureau in Port Vila. Vanuatuan students reportedly attended meetings of two Soviet fronts in Australia in May and September, respectively (*The Guardian*, 8 May; *Youth Voice*, October).

Tonga. Since the Russian scare in 1976 (a result of Soviet offers of assistance to Tonga), the region has not experienced a shortage of Western aid. Australia quadrupled its assistance to the region in following years and pressured other Western countries to follow suit. Tonga is a conservative country and highly supportive of Western interests in the region, although the crown prince of Tonga saw fit to visit the Soviet Union in February 1987. There appears to be no progress on Soviet foreign minister Eduard Shevardnadze's claim, made in Canberra in March 1987, that Moscow would open relations with Nukeulofa.

Kiribati. Kiribati achieved independence in 1979, and President Tabai has held office since then. It has a 35-member House of Assembly. The opposition Christian Democratic Party (CDP) emerged over the issue of fisheries deals with the Soviet Union, to which it is opposed, and the CDP attempted to pass a no-confidence motion against the government. Since the 1987 election, a number of CDP members of Parliament have formed the Neutral Party, which now often holds the balance of power.

Another Soviet research vessel, the *Akademik Korolev*, was the subject of some controversy during a visit to the Kiribati capital of Tarawa. Following a friendly reception on Christmas Island, the Soviet ship arrived earlier than scheduled at the Kiribati main island. It was boarded by police and government officials and not allowed into Tarawa's Betio Lagoon (Radio Australia, 11, 12 October).

Palau. The death of the second president, Lazarus Salii, by shooting, meant continuing political turbulence in the U.S. Trust Territory (*FBIS*, 20 August). In April the Palau Supreme Court ruled that the island's antinuclear constitution meant that a vote of 73 percent for a 50-year compact of free association with the United States was insufficient to overrule the constitution, which requires a 75 percent vote to change it (*FEER*, 19 May). A large majority of local people support entry to the compact, which gives the United States certain military strategic rights in return for an aid package of $450 million over fifteen years (*NYT*, 4 August). These attempts were vociferously opposed by a local minority and their overseas supporters. A number of individuals associated with opposition to the treaty with the United States appeared as Palauan representatives at various meetings in the Soviet bloc and of World Peace Council and WFDY fronts.

Nauru. An independent republic since 1968, Nauru's Parliament has eighteen members elected every three years. The Parliament elects the president, who chooses a six-member cabinet. Politics in Nauru are dominated by the fact that its phosphate reserves, which make it the wealthiest island state, will be exhausted in the next few years.

President Hammer de Roburt confirmed a report from the Soviet news agency TASS (*FBIS*, 4 February) that Nauru and the Soviet Union have established diplomatic links. Moscow's ambassador to Canberra is accredited to other South Pacific states, and Nauru's imminent dissipation of its sole resource, phosphate, has led to plaintive appeals for Soviet aid.

Tuvalu. After independence in 1978, Tuvalu acquired a unicameral parliament of twelve members. The prime minister is elected by a majority of its members. Tuvalu is also very anti-Soviet and rejected a $2 million fishing contract with the Soviet Union in 1985 (Tuvalu's gross national product in 1983 was only $4 million).

Trust Territory of the Pacific Islands. In the wake of World War II, the United States was mandated the islands of Micronesia by the United Nations. Long-running negotiations over decolonization—concluded in the last few years—will see the islands broken up into four states. The northern Marianas have become a commonwealth of the United States; its people are not U.S. citizens. The Republic of Palau, the Marshall Islands, and the Federated States of Micronesia have signed compacts of free association with the United States. Under these agreements, the United States promises to provide massive economic assistance to the islands in return for unhindered military access and the denial of military access to other countries.

Michael D. Danby
Melbourne, Australia

Sri Lanka

Population. 16,639,695
Parties. Communist Party of Sri Lanka (CPSL, pro-Moscow); Janatha Vimukthi Peramuna (JVP, Maoist)
Founded. CPSL: 1943; JVP: 1968
Membership. CPSL: 5,000 (estimated); JVP: unknown
General Secretary. CPSL: Kattorge P. Silva
Politburo. CPSL: 11 members including Silva and Pieter Keuneman (president); JVP: Rohana Wijeweera (leader), Upatissa Gamanayake (deputy leader)
Status. CPSL: legal; JVP: proscribed
Last Congress. CPSL: Thirteenth, 22–26 March 1987
Last Election. CPSL: 1977, parliamentary, 2.0 percent, no seats (1 member elected in by-election). 1982, presidential, did not run a candidate but supported a coalition (United Socialist Alliance) that did. Ossie Abeygoonasekera received 4.6 percent of the vote. JVP: 1977, parliamentary, did not contest; 1982, presidential, 4.2 percent.
Auxiliary Organizations. Federation of Trade Unions (24 affiliated unions), Public Service Workers' Trade Union Federation (100 affiliated unions), Communist Youth Federation, Kantha (women's) Peramuna
Publication. *Aththa* (major daily newspaper, 28,000 circulation)

The continued decline of the traditional Sri Lankan Marxist parties and the continued rise of the new left marked Sri Lankan society in 1988. The CPSL and its ally, the Lanka Sama Samaja Party, continued to be unable to exercise influence in Sri Lankan government. On the other hand, the JVP intensified its campaign of violence against the government and anyone else who supported the 1987 Indo-Lanka accords. In the process, they created a serious threat to the stability of the political system.

The CPSL. In early 1988, the communist party joined the Trotskyite Lanka Sama Samaja Party, the Sri Lanka Mahajana Party (SLMP), and the Nava Lanka Sama Samaja Party to form the United Socialist Alliance (USA). The coalition was formed to bolster the electoral support of the old left and to counter the effects that the Sri Lankan system of proportional representation and its rewards for large parties will have on smaller parties.

Despite violence, the government went ahead with plans to create provincial governments. The USA decided to contest the provincial council elections even though the main opposition party, the Sri Lanka Freedom Party (SLFP), boycotted them on the grounds that provincial governments were only needed in the Tamil areas and that their introduction throughout the rest of the country was a waste of money and unwanted by the Sinhalese people. In the provinces dominated by the Sinhalese ethnic group, the only serious opposition to the United National Party (UNP) was the USA. Two other parties, the Liberal Party and the Muslim Congress, also contested but were not an important factor in the outcome. In April and June the UNP won control of each of these seven provincial council elections. The elections were marked by allegations of fraud on behalf of the UNP. In addition, the threats of the JVP in the southern province resulted in a voter turnout of less than 8 percent in Hambantota district.

The weakness of the old left was displayed in the presidential elections held on 19 December. The USA candidate, Ossie Abeygoonasekera, received only 4.6 percent of the vote. The election was won by the governing party's current prime minister, Ranasinghe Premadasa. with 50.4 percent of the vote. Former SLFP prime minister Sirimavo Bandaranaike received 44.9 percent of the vote in the three-way contest. Voter turnout was a disappointing 55 percent, which was considerably lower than the 85 to 90 percent turnout that has marked earlier national elections. The JVP threats and voter intimidation were especially prevalent in the south where voter turnout was extremely low.

SLFP candidate Sirimavo Bandaranaike claimed that supporters of the UNP had threatened her supporters, and in some cases army soldiers had prohibited voters from entering the polling areas or closed the polling booths completely. A Supreme Court challenge to the election failed, and Prime Minister Premadasa was expected to be inaugurated on 2 January 1989.

The JVP. The JVP, which had led an insurrection in 1971 against the United Front government of Sirimavo Bandaranaike, re-emerged in 1987 with a campaign of assassinations that began in August after the Indo-Lanka accords.

During the 1971 insurrection, the JVP espoused a Maoist ideology. When it became legalized in the late 1970s, it promoted nonviolent change and reform. However, in 1983, the party was banned and its leadership went into hiding. The party began rebuilding its rural network and emerged as a violent threat to the government in 1987. Today, its ideology is less Maoist and more nationalist. The party supports the protection of the Sinhalese ethnic group and thus opposes the introduction of any Indian influence in Sri Lanka, including the introduction of Indian troops in Sri Lanka to police the Indo-Lanka accords and the treaty's provisions that allow India to veto some Sri Lankan government foreign policy decisions. They have also opposed concessions to the Tamil ethnic minority in the north and east of the island. This includes opposition to the uniting of the northern and eastern provinces into a single provincial council.

JVP support comes from young people, many of whom have become disillusioned with the UNP government of Junius Richard Jayawardene, which has governed the country since 1977. Its main base of support is among rural youths in the southern province of Sri Lanka and in the newly colonized irrigation schemes in Polonnaruwa and Moneragala districts in the center of the island.

JVP attacks have been focused on members of the UNP government and members of the USA. Both the USA and the UNP support the Indo-Lanka accords as a means to resolve the ethnic civil war. The campaign of assassinations has been directed at local- and national-level politicians. The most prominent attack was the murder of the leader and founder of the SLMP, Vijaya Kumaratunga, on 16 February. The JVP later began a campaign of intimidation against candidates and voters in the provincial council elections. A large number of candidates and voters were killed. The JVP also tried to disrupt the presidential election, threatening voters and calling for a general strike to shut down the capital city of Colombo. The intimidation of voters was successful in the southern province, the stronghold of the movement, but largely failed in other areas of the country.

The Ethnic Conflict. The JVP violence has overshadowed the Tamil insurrection. Indian troops contained the last remaining violent Tamil group, the Liberation Tigers of Tamil Eelam (LTTE), in the dense jungles of Vavuniya and Mullaitivu districts.

Although the LTTE still has support in other Tamil areas, they have not been able to exercise the military control that they were able to before the arrival of the Indian forces in July 1987. Nevertheless, the Indian military has been unable to defeat the LTTE.

The continued violence in the Tamil areas prevented elections for a combined eastern and northern provincial council until 19 November. The LTTE boycotted the elections, but two former guerrilla groups contested them along with the UNP and the Muslim Congress. No elections were held in the northern province. No more than one party decided to contest any of the electoral districts, and the Eelam People's Revolutionary Liberation Front (EPRLF) and the Eelam National Democratic Liberation Front received all of the seats. In the eastern province, the dominant party in the north, the EPRLF, won the elections and formed the provincial government.

Prospects for the Future. The new leadership in Sri Lanka offered the brightest hope to the country in more than five years. The government of UNP leader Jayawardene, which had been viewed as extremely corrupt and had lost its legitimacy in the eyes of many Sri Lankans, prolonged itself in power by holding a referendum in 1982 to prolong the life of Parliament for seven more years. Election fraud discredited the results of the election and undermined the legitimacy of the government. In addition, 82-year-old President Jayawardene has been considered by many to be weak and ineffective in his last years in power. Prime Minister Premadasa offers new hope to resolve the two insurrections in the country. The JVP, in the past, has always been careful to avoid criticizing him and his populist politics, which appeal to many rural people. In addition, he was popular with many Sinhalese nationalists because of his opposition to Indian troops in the country. It was expected that he would ask the Indian military to leave the country soon after his inauguration. However, it was still uncertain whether this would appease the JVP and its supporters or the leadership of the Tamil insurrection in the north.

Robert C. Oberst
Nebraska Wesleyan University

Thailand

Population. 54,588,731
Party. Communist Party of Thailand (CPT)
Founded. 1942
Membership. 250; 500 armed strength (estimated)
General Secretary. Thong Jaensri (unconfirmed; possible pseud.)
Politburo. Thong Jaensri (general secretary [?]), Waithan Sunthuwanit, Nop Presoetsom
Status. Illegal
Last Congress. Fourth, March and April 1984, clandestine
Last Election. N/a
Publications. *Thong Thai* (Thai flag), *Prakai fai* (The flame), and intermittent underground publications

In 1988 Thailand continued its remarkable economic growth and sustained period of political stability. The kingdom became a model of how effective leadership, generally conservative economic policies, and an educated and increasingly technologically sophisticated citizenry can bring about economic growth, a more equitable distribution of resources, and a higher standard of living. Thailand's growth rate was estimated to reach 9 percent in 1988.

New institutions were established that partially replaced the personalistic rule of the past. These new institutions included interest groups, political parties, nongovernment associations, and decentralized ministerial units run by technocrats.

In the face of public awareness and acceptance of these institutions, since 1985 military factions have no longer attempted to seize power by means of a coup d'état. Elections have become the legitimate means for transferring power. There has been no successful coup since 1977. The likelihood of unconstitutional intervention by the military has decreased with the rise of legitimate procedures for succession.

Because Thailand is no longer threatened by internal communist insurgency or by external aggression, the military's rationale for controlling the society has been reduced. The appointment of Chatichai Choonhavan as prime minister following

the 24 July elections is the culmination of the democratization of the polity as he became the first leader since 1976 who was an elected member of Parliament.

The Thais elected a new Parliament following the dissolution of Prime Minister Prem Tinsulanond's administration. About 64 percent of the Thais voted for candidates for Parliament from among fifteen political parties. A coalition of five leading parties was formed with agreement that Prem would once again be invited to lead the new government. In a surprise decision, Prem declined the offer. The coalition then turned to the leader of the party winning the most seats, former General Chatichai Choonhavan, a famous military, political, and business personality.

Chatichai was elected a member of Parliament from Khorat province. He served as deputy prime minister and minister of industry under Prem and was foreign minister under Kukrit Pramoj. He is close to both business and military interests, and he pledged to continue the essentially conservative domestic and anticommunist foreign policies of the previous administration.

Prime Minister Chatichai in his capacity as the director for prevention of communist activities presided over the annual meeting of the Internal Security Operations Command (ISOC) in October. In his opening speech, he stated that the Thai government was victorious over the communist movement and that in 1988 there were no significant armed struggles, with the exception of small-scale armed insurgency in the south.

Army commander General Chawalit Yongchaiyut, the architect of the "politics over military" doctrine that is considered a major reason for the demise of the CPT, also spoke to the same meeting, stressing that international relations were such that the possibility of a third world war was never so remote. In Thailand, however, he noted that the outlawed CPT had not given up its goal of revolutionizing Thai society. He repeated the theme that he had reiterated for many years: that the CPT has merely changed its method from armed struggle— in which it had been defeated in the earlier 1980s— to recruiting and mobilizing its members and sympathizers to form a "united front" to work for a socialist revolution (*The Nation*, *FBIS*, 26 October).

General Chawalit suggested that the CPT is now trying to politically exploit the "weak political party system" and the "inability of the government" to resolve several chronic national problems since the end of the armed struggle in the early 1980s. The

CPT claims, and ISOC tends to believe, that the communists are having "great success" in organizing a new "united front" that is "superior in quality" to the one that existed at the start of the armed struggle and "deadlier in destructive potential" than an armed struggle itself. He noted that this is so because the general public is oblivious of its hidden threat. (Ibid.)

General Chawalit criticized those who claim that ISOC is trying to revive the so-called communist ghost to enhance its influence and budget allocations. He stated that there is no such thing as a "communist ghost"; there is only a "spectre of communism," just like the one Karl Marx and Friedrich Engels wrote about at the beginning of their *Communist Manifesto* in 1848: "A spectre is haunting Europe, the spectre of communism." He stated that when ISOC and he are talking about the continued communist threat, they are not trying to revive the "communist ghost" but are trying to remind the country and the people to continue their vigilance against communism by making democracy work.

The ISOC conference members listed their three top priorities in the current fiscal year: (1) Continuing the strategic offensive at the national level by emphasizing democratic development of the system of constitutional monarchy; (2) Developing rural areas to bridge the gaps between the rural and the city people, such as the "Green Isan development plan and other rural projects initiated by King Phumipol Adunyadej; (3) Preventing a revival of the armed struggle of the CPT.

More specifically, ISOC will continue to monitor CPT urban activities because some CPT members have remained active, collecting information and meeting with former CPT members who have defected to the government. An ISOC spokesman said surveillance continues against members of Parliament (M.P.s) who are former CPT members to learn about their activities. General Chawalit said that officials "should keep an eye on opposition M.P.s to see if they are committing any misdeeds" (*Bangkok Post, FBIS*, 25 August).

Little information was available in 1988 regarding leadership of the CPT. The southern branch was restructured in order to revive its underground antigovernment activities, according to a spokesman of the Fourth Army Region. He put the CPT's strength in the south at between 175 to 190 men under arms, but this figure was unconfirmed. (*Bangkok Post, FBIS*, 25 August.)

Communal tensions between Muslims and Buddhists in the southern provinces raised concerns about a resurgence of communist insurgency, common banditry, and Muslim separatist terrorism, particularly the Pattani Liberation Organization (Pulo) and Barisan Nasional Revolusi (BRN). The separatist groups had lost support during the mid-1980s; from a peak of about 1,800 armed men in 1981, Pulo and BRN are said to command no more than 300 men between them today (*FEER*, 28 April). Increased violence in the south during the year was sparked by a conflict over the wearing of the *hijab*, the Islamic women's headdress. The conflict was temporarily resolved when a decision on the legality of the issue was postponed.

After the arrest of eighteen leading CPT members in April 1987, thirteen were eventually released after renouncing communism. The remaining five suspected leaders of the CPT, including Politburo member Nop Presoetsom, were charged in May with violating the Anti-Communist Act. Charges were also filed against Chitchanok Sophonphan, an aide of Politburo member Waithun Sunthuwanit; Sompong Whichitchaiphan; Wirot Bunphet, a Loei provincial committee member; and Onsi Inthawutchai.

In an unprecedented move, the Thai army negotiated with China about establishing a war reserve stockpile, the first communist war stockpile in a noncommunist country. The stockpile proposal was worked out in Beijing by General Chawalit in November as a result of a series of border clashes between Thai, Vietnamese, and Laotian troops. General Chawalit also signed a major arms deal involving 30 Chinese-made tanks and 800 armored personnel carriers. Both the Association of Southeast Asian Nations and the Indochinese countries criticized the moves as an unnecessary buildup of weapons.

Relations with Vietnam were improved after Chawalit became prime minister and announced that he wanted to turn the Vietnam battleground into a trading market. He announced he would visit Vietnam in early 1989, the first prime minister to do so since the Vietnam War. At the same time, the Thai permanent representative to the United Nations submitted a letter to the U.N. secretary general about the violation of Thailand's sovereignty and territorial integrity by Vietnamese forces in Cambodia. He documented 100 violations of Thai territorial integrity in July alone. The government reiterated its stand that ties between the two nations could not be normalized until Vietnam had withdrawn its troops from Cambodia.

The year began with intense armed and aerial

battles between Laos and Thailand over a disputed piece of territory in Ban Romklao. The dispute was lessened when Prime Minister Chatichai and his Laotian counterpart, Kaysone Phomvihan, agreed in November to the formation of a joint committee to solve the border problems. The announcement of the Joint Border Committee resulted from a formal visit by Chatichai to Vientiane. The joint communiqué also included agreements to solve the Laotian refugee issue and to develop telecommunications networks and hydroelectricity.

As in the past two years, reliable information on the CPT is scarce because the party has been decimated and the armed struggle has ceased. The year 1988 saw Thailand improve its relations with its communist neighbors and with the communist superpowers, consistent with the nation's "omnidirectional" foreign policy.

Clark D. Neher
Northern Illinois University

Vietnam

Population. 65,185,278
Party. Vietnam Communist Party (Viet Nam Cong San; VCP)
Founded. 1930 (as Indochina Communist Party)
Membership. 2,120,000 (5th Plenum communiqué, June): 20 percent female (estimated); about 99 percent ethnic Vietnamese; average age, mid-50s; 40 percent *ban co* (poor peasant); 25 percent peasant/farm laborer; 15 percent proletariat; 20 percent other
General Secretary. Nguyen Van Linh (b. 1915)
Politburo. Nguyen Van Linh, Vo Chi Cong (b. 1912), Do Muoi (b. 1917), Vo Van Kiet (b. 1922), Le Duc Anh (b. 1910?), Nguyen Duc Tam (b. 1920), Nguyen Co Thach (b. 1920), Dong Sy Nguyen (b. 1920?), Tran Xuan Bach, Nguyen Thanh Binh, Doan Khue, Mai Chi Tho (b. 1922), Dao Duy Tung
Secretariat. Nguyen Van Linh, Nguyen Duc Tam, Tran Xuan Bach, Dao Duy Tung, Tran Kien, Le Phuoc Tho, Nguyen Quyet, Dam Quang Trung,

Vo Oanh, Nguyen Khanh, Tran Quyet, Tran Quoc Hoang, Pham The Duyet
Central Committee. 124 full and 49 alternate members
Status. Legal
Last Congress. Sixth, 15–18 December 1986
Last Election. 19 April 1987, Eighth National Assembly, 98.8 percent, 496 seats, all VCP-endorsed (*Indochina Chronology*)
Auxiliary Organizations. Vietnam Fatherland Front (Nguyen Huu Tho, chairman), Ho Chi Minh Communist Youth Union (Ha Quang Du, general secretary)
Publications. *Nhan dan* (The people), VCP daily, Ha Dang, editor (also CC member); *Tap chi cong san* (Communist review), VCP theoretical monthly; *Quan doi nhan dan* (People's army), army newspaper, Ha Xuan Truong, editor

The people of Vietnam, party members and public alike, were presented with continual intimations of momentous socioeconomic change in their society during all of 1988, as they had been promised the previous year. This began with New Year's Day messages from individual Politburo members and continued unabated through to the end of December with National Assembly reportage. The theme was consistent: demands by party leaders that there be immediate and drastic improvement in the management of the society's various institutions, particularly economic, accompanied by spectacular state policy promulgations to accomplish quickly that which the leadership demanded. What was needed and could not be achieved, the communicational outpouring indicated, would be renovation (*doi moi*) of the society in the spirit of openness (*coi mo*) that would do for Vietnam what *perestroika* and *glasnost'* were accomplishing in the USSR. This vast mobilization and moral exhortation program, most ambitious in a decade, had been launched by the Sixth Party Congress in December 1986. It took most of 1987 to translate the congress's intent into a coherent campaign of development. But it seemed as 1988 began that Vietnam's postwar economic stagnation was at last going to end. Even more than the previous year, 1988 in Vietnam was a year of expectation.

Yet it was evident at the end of 1988 that remarkably little change had actually eventuated and that virtually nothing had taken place that could clearly be labeled significant progress. The great reform plan—to streamline economic and production institutions, to decentralize much of the economic and even some of the political decisionmaking, to re-store the party to its earlier centrality, and through all this to re-energize the entire society—remained largely that, a plan on the drafting boards.

Vietnam's central problem remained its poverty. With a per capita income of $309 it was one of the world's poorest countries, ranking 151st in the economist's poverty index of the world's 156 coun-tries. It was an economy permanently mobilized for a war it could ill afford, with perhaps as much as half of its national budget being allocated to military purposes, leaving little for operating the economic sector and virtually nothing for true economic de-velopment. There was an unhealthy dependence on outsiders (chiefly on USSR–Council for Mutual Economic Assistance [CMEA] economic aid insti-tutions), virtually no hard currency reserves, and one of the world's worst trade deficits. Finally it was saddled by a top-level leadership singularly un-qualified to deal with knotty economic problems (only two of the thirteen Politburo members have the equivalent of a high school diploma) and unwill-ing to trust economic decisionmaking to anyone outside of the Politburo.

The major reason for this lack of forward move-ment—this inability to effect change in a country where there is universal desire for change and in which no one any longer defends the status quo—was the ongoing unresolved political struggle within the Politburo, which was a product of a yet uncompleted generational transfer of political power, a struggle accompanied by complex doc-trinal infighting over the degree of risk in changing domestic and foreign policies in the name of reform and renovation. As is common with Leninist gov-erning systems, this political turbulence at the top had the net effect of paralyzing lower-level party and state policymaking organs. As the year began most Hanoi watchers generally agreed that reform was in fact under way in Vietnam. If it did not precisely match the phenomena of *glasnost'* and *perestroika* in the USSR, it was at least akin to it. At year's end many Vietnam specialists were no longer sure. It was argued by some that General Secretary Nguyen Van Linh and his band of reformers were (or had become) mere front men for their ostensible opposition, the conservatives, and that what was actually transpiring in Hanoi was a charade, the status quo dressed up in the garb of reform to ingratiate Hanoi with Moscow's aid givers. Only this thesis, it was argued, could explain the midyear advent of the new premier, Do Muoi, an old-guard conservative.

It did seem clear as the year 1988 closed that Hanoi had put reform on hold. It also seemed prob-able that this was a temporary condition and that history was continuing to push Vietnam inexorably toward change and reform. The question that re-mained was when this indeterminate condition would end and the march toward progress be re-sumed. No one could be sure, but clearly it would not be until the ongoing reformer-conservative struggle for political power, doctrinal at root, had been resolved and the next generation of leaders fully installed.

Leadership and Party Organization. The central fact of political life in Vietnam's ruling party circles during 1988 was the continuing turbulence engendered by Sino-style factional infighting. It was a condition triggered by the personnel and policy changes ordered by the Sixth Party Congress (December 1986) and the Eighth National Assem-bly meeting the same month. Many of the party's old guard departed, although a number of them lin-gered on as Politburo "consultants" whose contin-uing influence was difficult to determine. About 50 percent of the new party Central Committee and about 60 percent of the current National Assembly members were first-timers. Younger, if not young, leaders were gradually moving into positions of power, part of the ongoing generational transfer of political power. There was a rise in influence of technocrats, economists, and others with occupa-tional specialization—party provincial secretaries and "professional" generals in the military. What might be called a "southern predominance" devel-oped in the new emerging political leadership in that virtually all of the major Politburo figures re-maining have had their careers long bound up with the south, if they are not themselves southern. Pre-sumably this meant a leadership that better under-stood the south and was better able to tap its eco-nomic potential. The leadership turbulence extended below the Central Committee level. An estimated one-third of all the provincial party secre-taries in what had been South Vietnam were re-placed during 1988 as were about 40 percent of the party leadership at the district/village/enterprise levels.

Probably these personnel changes, which con-tinued throughout the year, were not extensive enough to alter the fundamental character of the top leadership. The Politburo remained in the hands of individuals skilled in leadership mobilization and motivation techniques but unschooled in a society's peacetime needs and largely ignorant of the science of economics.

What seemed clear at year's end was that no longer was there serious doctrinal argument among top party leaders of the early postwar years—labeled by outsiders as ideologue versus pragmatist. It had not been won by the pragmatists as much as it had metamorphosed into a new set of arguments over the nature and pace of changing policies in the economic sector and the meanings these have for national security and foreign affairs. The pragmatists had become "renovationists" (and might fairly be called reformers) while the ideologues became ultracautious pragmatists (and might be termed conservatives, or neoconservatives). What separated them primarily was the question of orthodoxy in economic change, specifically the degree of willingness to bend longstanding doctrine to fit new needs. The reformers were more willing to innovate, experiment, take risks in the economic sector. The conservatives saw the reformers as pressing programs rashly, not fully taking into account their effect outside of the economic sector. There was in this doctrinal dispute much that united—the common perception that the Vietnamese economic machine simply must be gotten into gear and running and, beyond that, true economic development begun—hence there was no reason to believe that the long-standing principle of collective leadership would not continue to serve as the basic operational code of the Politburo.

The selection of Do Muoi as prime minister in June (see biography) came as a disappointment to those who had hoped that acting Premier Vo Van Kiet, a reformer, would be retained. The National Assembly vote on Do Muoi, 296 to 200, was a reasonably accurate index of the existing leadership division between conservative and reformer. It indicated that although the conservatives still outnumbered the reformers it was not by much, meaning that compromise would be required in all political decisionmaking. Because all factions continued to hold to the principle of collective leadership, any numerical advantage the conservatives might have in a Politburo "vote" did not have the meaning it would have elsewhere. There was general agreement among most Hanoi watchers that the thirteen members of the ruling Politburo were divisible into at least four factions: reformers, conservatives (or neoconservatives), military (commonly termed *modernizers*), and bureaucrats (or "economists"):

Reformers: Nguyen Van Linh, Vo Van Kiet, and Mai Chi Tho

Conservatives: Do Muoi, Vo Chi Cong, and Nguyen Duc Tam

Military: Le Duc Anh, Doan Khue, and Dong Sy Nguyen

Bureaucrats: Nguyen Co Thach, Tran Xuan Bach, Dao Duy Tung, and Nguyen Thanh Binh

According to this analysis, doctrinal infighting was not simply between the reformers and the conservatives but was a four-way struggle in which the military and bureaucrat "swing" forces would "vote" reformer or conservative depending on the specific issue. Although every member of the Politburo had an opinion on reform, those for whom it was a central issue—the reformers and the conservatives—were in the minority (with three "votes" each). The reform issue—disputation over policy proposals having to do with change (and continuity) and with acceptable risk to be taken—was only one of the important issues. Others were (a) economic allocation of resources (having most meaning to the People's Army of Vietnam (PAVN); (b) economic assistance (having to do with foreign economic relations/USSR relations); (c) economic planning/decentralization (wisdom of moving away from the orthodox socialist economic model); (d) foreign relations (having chiefly to do with serving Vietnam's national security interests relevant to Cambodia); and (e) "democratization," which chiefly involved the idea of the party sharing political power with nonparty members and which does not represent as challenging an issue as it does in the USSR and elsewhere.

Since Sino-based, Leninist-modified factionalism as the style of politics practiced in Hanoi remained unchanged, what was under way during the year was a struggle to establish a new doctrinal matrix among the power-sharing factions. Specific political events during the year served chiefly to demonstrate that the reformer-conservative struggle had become a temporary standoff in which Nguyen Van Linh as reformer and Do Muoi as conservative each sought to become the bridge between the factions, building consensus and arbitrating policy disputes as Ho Chi Minh did during his long tenure. Neither had succeeded in this by year's end.

Pham Hung, the stalwart old-guard prime minister (actually there is no such title in the Socialist Republic of Vietnam [SRV]; the post officially is chairman of the Council of Ministers), died 10 March after having been in the post only nine months. He was replaced by Do Muoi (see biographic sketch below). Clearly the appointment of conservative Do Muoi was forced on Nguyen Van Linh by a coalition of conservatives and other Politburo factions.

Death also claimed Truong Chinh during the year. This old-guard defender of the orthodox, the most intellectually influential ideologue in Vietnamese party circles over the years, died 30 September at the age of 80. He had been one of the Politburo "retirees" of 1987 who stayed on as a "Politburo consultant," but apparently he was politically influential up to the time of his death.

Other deaths during the year included Dang Hoi Xuan, SRV minister of public health who was killed 9 September in the crash of an Air Vietnam plane outside Bangkok and Nguyen Xuan Linh, SRV National Assembly Standing Committee secretary who died in early March; he was an influential member of the Truong Chinh faction.

On the state side, under party supervision, the SRV vice-premiership system was reorganized in early July. Under the new arrangement, Premier Do Muoi assumed responsibility for defense and the campaign to control economic inflation. Under him were: Vo Van Kiet, the principal vice-premier responsible for administration of the economy and increasing productivity; Nguyen Co Thach (foreign relations); and Vo Nguyen Giap (development of technical education). Nguyen Khanh was named chef d'cabinet to Do Muoi (and removed as vice-premier). The Do Muoi vice-premier vacancy was not filled, hence the number of vice-premiers was reduced from six to four. Doan Duy Thanh was named minister of the newly formed Ministry of External Economic Relations, which merged the Ministry of Foreign Trade and the State Commission for External Economic Relations. Dao Ngoc Xuan in late March was named to head the all-important SRV State Planning Commission when Kiet was named acting chairman of the SRV Council of Ministers.

Domestic Party Affairs. The VCP during 1988 remained in what only could be termed a semicrisis condition, a characterization made of it by none other than the party general secretary, Nguyen Van Linh. At the fifth plenum (Sixth Congress) in June he described at length the "party's slide into the muck of degeneration and degradation." He listed as lesser sins inadequate ideological training, excessive bureaucratic centralism, inattention to party business, and "mandarinism" (distancing oneself from the people) and as greater sins, breach of discipline, bribe taking, and embezzlement. There was, Linh said, a general rise in corruption, incompetency, and lack of dedication. At the plenum and throughout the year Linh stressed the breakdown of cadre discipline and the general confusion among rank-and-file party members. The party's "institutions of leadership" and the party "ideological thought," he said, were not equal to the revolutionary task faced; the party had not "renovated [*doi moi*] itself as required, had not met the demands and aspirations of the people" (Radio Hanoi, *FBIS-East Asia* [EAS], 22 June). All of this was verified by other reports emanating from Vietnam during the year.

The fifth plenum (Hanoi, 14–20 June) was devoted to internal "party building" matters, as they are termed, that is party organization and cadre leadership at the basic or grass-roots level, indoctrination and retraining of cadres, and personnel policies involving promotions and assignments. Much of the plenum was marked by spirited debate over the party's role in the task of lifting Vietnam by its economic bootstraps. The challenge here, Linh said, was an "ideological task"—to return the party to its institutional centrality of the wartime years when it enjoyed a reputation for being nearly infallible. The party must again become the leader, the goad, the model of behavior for economic development, he said, ridding itself of its present image as "fifth wheel on the cart." Restoring the party to its rightful place as the center of all things, Linh indicated, can not be accomplished simply by making the claim of primacy. The "ideological task" requires that the party be able to supply answers to the question troubling all Vietnamese—the organization and operation of the economy. The party, Linh indicated, must supply a clear and credible strategy for economic development, one that will work. In addition to offering a systematic vision for the future, the party cadre system must be renovated, improved, made more competent and meaningful, and possessed of greater rectitude, eliminating "degenerate elements" and enforcing the criterion for measuring cadre behavior or the degree of "actual contribution to renewal (i.e., reform) of the party by the individual."

Actions taken by the plenum included (1) VCP Central Committee Secretary Dao Duy Tung was raised from candidate to full member of the Politburo (now thirteen full members, no alternate members); (2) tenure of party secretaries was limited to ten years; (3) in upcoming party committee elections, including to the Central Committee, "one-third of the membership must be replaced"; (4) Ha Trong Hoa (Thanh Hoa province party secretary) was removed from the Central Committee for "mistakes in his work" (Radio Hanoi, *FBIS-EAS*, 21 June; *Pravda*, *FBIS-Soviet Union*, 22, 25 June).

Observance of the 58th anniversary of the founding of the VCP (3 February) was conducted in a distinctly understated manner compared with earlier years. The theme, particularly in provincial capital observances, was party "purification." General Secretary Linh addressed a high-level party conference in Ho Chi Minh City in which he stressed the need "for the people to control the party cadres" and called for intensified efforts by all against "negativism," the catchall phrase for what is wrong with the society (Radio Hanoi, 6 February; *FBIS-EAS*, 9 February).

This sober treatment underscored a serious intent to press the Politburo's emulation campaign begun in September 1987 and labeled Campaign to Purify and Raise the Combative Strength of Party and State Organizations and Invigorate Social Relations, known less formally as the "accountability campaign" and even less formally as the "general purge." The campaign's twin goals were to cleanse and to improve; thus it was directed in part at "degenerate and degraded" members and in part at "mediocrity in the party ranks . . . those members who are blasé about party discipline." (*Quan doi nhan dan*, 10 August.) Politburo circulars during the year contained specific orders to "purify" rank-and-file membership. Dutifully, provincial party secretaries reported back the results, of which these reports are typical: Binh Tri Thien: 115 evaluated then expelled; Cao Bang: 506 expelled, another 391 disciplined; Cuu Long: 164 members investigated for corruption and 63 expelled; Dac Lac: 10 local party organizations and 557 members disciplined; Hai Hung: 2,353 disciplined, 750 expelled, 16 percent of rank and file disciplined or under investigation; Lang Son: 120 province/district cadres disciplined for corruption, 46 of them jailed, 70 members also expelled; Quang Ninh: 20 senior officials expelled for bribe taking, selling fuel on black market, and coal speculation; Tay Ninh: 92 cadres disciplined. *Nhan dan* (23 August) reported that probably about 20 percent of all provincial/city party officials would be replaced during the year.

A tabulation of provincial-level statistics as reported by the press indicated that the campaign was centered in the south and that a disproportionate number of southern officials were being expelled or disciplined. The statistics also indicated that, on a nationwide basis, about 10 percent of all party members were judged unqualified for membership for various reasons, of which 2 percent were grievously so and were expelled, while the other 8 percent were salvaged through various rectification measures. Only one-third to one-half of all party members were judged adequate or better. Poor health and age were also debilitating the party, the surveys indicated. One survey of village party members found only 37 percent "efficient, capable, and qualified" and 42 percent "of advanced age or in poor health." The party membership in 1975 stood at 1,490,000. By June 1988, it had recruited 940,000 new members and lost (removed, retired, died) 310,000, leaving a membership of 2,120,000.

The stringent measures adopted by the Politburo drew a commendation from Moscow. *Pravda* correspondent M. Demogratiskikh (*Pravda*, 14 January) reported in approving terms "the purging of party organs and state apparatus is proceeding in an exacting and businesslike manner." He cited specific examples of the expulsion from the party of senior cadres but gave no total figure of the number expelled.

A six-month report on the purification campaign was issued 12 June (reported in *Nhan dan* (13 June), which said the campaign had "won widespread and unanimous support from a large number of party cadres, members, and people" and had "yielded initial results."

The purification campaign if nothing else was unflagging. It was given renewed emphasis by a Politburo Resolution Four (8 August) that added new stringent measures of "inspection and control work," the general term for monitoring party/state activity. Although the campaign chiefly involved moral exhortation, behind it could be seen a struggle between the reformers and the conservatives and behind that the remnants of the doctrinal struggle between the pragmatists and ideologues. Much of the struggle at this level turned on the issue of "democratization" supported by the reformers/pragmatists and opposed by the conservatives/ideologues. Some of the "purification" apparently involved instances in which the campaign to reform was abused by individuals who slandered cadres and officials in the name of democratization and openness.

Party congresses were held at the district/ward level in September as part of a systematic effort to move party people into more central and activist positions in the People's Councils, the lowest level of government in Vietnam. Following these summer congresses, party provincial secretaries gathered in Ho Chi Minh City 17–19 October to review affairs following provincial-level congresses during the summer. An overhaul of provincial-level central committees was announced. On average about one-third of the southern party provincial secretaries were replaced and about 40 percent of the party leadership at the district/village/enterprise levels.

Auxiliary and Front Organizations. The Vietnam Fatherland Front (VFF), the VCP's mass organization, held its Third Congress in Hanoi 2–4 November, attended by 580 delegates and 26 observers from fourteen foreign countries. Nguyen Huu Tho was elected president of the VFF Central Committee Presidium. Tho, a longtime front organizer, was chairman of the now defunct National Liberation Front of South Vietnam (Viet Cong); from 1981 to 1987 he served as chairman of the SRV National Assembly replacing Huynh Tan Phat. The congress was devoted chiefly to discussion of VFF "mobilization and motivation tasks," that support VCP programs and policies, the VFF's function within the system.

The Vietnam Confederation of Trade Unions' Sixth National Congress was held in Hanoi 17–20 October and attended by 839 delegates, representing some four million members in Vietnam, and 32 foreign delegations. Nguyen Van Tu was elected chairman; Cu Thi Hau and Nghiem Xuan An were named vice-chairmen. A fifteen-person secretariat was selected as well as a twelve-person Control Committee headed by Cu Thi Hau. Congress business was devoted to reports and discussion of the responsibilities of Vietnamese workers in overcoming Vietnam's economic difficulties.

Vietnam's two noncommunist political parties, the 42-year-old Socialist Party and the 44-year-old Democratic Party, were disbanded in 1988. The Socialist Party (sometimes called the Radical Socialist Party) traced its lineage back to the Indochina Socialist Party formed in the early 1930s under the encouragement of the French Socialist Party. It fragmented into several Vietnamese socialist groups, including one formed in Hanoi 22 July 1945 as an organization for "patriotic and progressive intellectuals." Its final congress was held in Hanoi 21–22 July under the gavel of General Secretary Nguyen Xien. The party's activities were absorbed by the VFF and professional organizations.

There were a number of political parties in early Vietnam that used the term *democratic* in their name. The Hanoi-based organization of that name was formed 30 June 1944 and joined the Viet Minh. In the later years the Democratic Party catered to those bourgeois elements in North Vietnam who for various reasons were not eligible for membership in the VCP. In the same manner the Socialist Party catered to Vietnamese intellectuals. The Democratic Party, under General Secretary Nghiem Xuan Yem, dissolved itself at its 18–20 October congress in Hanoi, giving as the reason that it was "no longer capable of operating in a way that meets the requirements of the revolutionary task."

International Views and Activities. Vietnam's general foreign relations position continued poor throughout 1988. Some of the difficulties were lack of international support for the SRV in its quarrel with China over the Spratly Islands; the USSR's more conciliatory position on Cambodia and its gestures toward China, neither of which are regarded in Hanoi as in Vietnam's best national interest; the lack of development and improvement of relations with the United States; and growing behind-the-scenes quarrels in the SRV Foreign Ministry over foreign policy.

Few new foreign policy decisions were actually made during the year, and in fact there was virtually no change in policy at all. This was chiefly attributable to the ongoing internal political turbulence in Hanoi that mitigated against making initiatives or change of any sort on the international level. The country remained regionally isolated, surrounded by hostile neighbors. Its cold war with China continued unabated, threatening at times to escalate into a hot war over the Spratly Islands. Vietnam's dependency on the USSR/CMEA, which both Vietnamese and Soviets appear to consider excessive, continued unchanged. It was also one more year of failure by Vietnam to attract more than token foreign economic investment and aid from capitalist countries, despite the midyear promulgation of a new foreign investment code. There was a drawdown of PAVN forces from Cambodia and still in effect, as far as anyone knew, was the SRV promise that all of its forces would be withdrawn by May 1990. In general with respect to foreign relations, the leaders in Hanoi appeared to consider themselves locked into an external situation over which they had no appreciable control but not one they found unendurable.

The Cambodia "peace process" occupied a good

deal of the SRV Foreign Ministry's attention during the year as it did other governments of the region. High point of the year in this respect was the Djakarta Informal Meeting (at Bogor, Indonesia) 24–28 July, attended by SRV foreign minister Nguyen Co Thach. From Vietnam's viewpoint the meeting settled virtually nothing, as was true of other Cambodian developments during the year. As the year ended the central problem for Vietnam was not the withdrawal of its forces or the danger of a return of Pol Pot per se but how to assure that the future government in Phnom Penh would not become a threat to Vietnam's national security; of necessity Vietnam understood that this would require a governing arrangement, presumably a coalition government, that was acceptable to the other outside interested parties, chiefly China and Thailand. Vietnamese statements on Cambodia during the year indicated that although the leadership understood the requirements for the peace process, it did not think there was much that could advance the process under the general requirements set down at Bogor, which were a timetable for the withdrawal of PAVN, a cease-fire/end to resistance activity, recruitment (and funding) of outside peacekeepers, devising a mechanism for provisional rule, the subsequent establishment of the new government/constitution based on free and supervised elections, the disarming/sequestering of all military forces and creation of a new single Khmer armed force, and installing a mechanism of outsider enforcement/guarantees.

In keeping with previous assurances, the PAVN drawdown in Cambodia continued during the year. Some 50,000 troops departed Cambodia in 1988—listed by Hanoi officials as men of the 4th, 5th, 307th, 309th, 315th, and 339th divisions (Radio Hanoi, *FBIS-EAS*, 1 December). It was not possible to verify this report through independent sources.

The quarrel between Vietnam and China over the sovereignty of the archipelago (some 51 islands) in the South China Sea known as the Spratly Islands (*Truong Sa* in Vietnamese, *Nansha* in Chinese) continued to simmer throughout 1988, growing ugly from time to time with naval clashes. On the night of 31 January, according to the Hanoi version, four Chinese warships provocatively engaged in maneuvers with two Vietnamese freighters and then sunk them along with a third later; the Chinese version was that the Vietnamese vessels had challenged a routine Chinese naval patrol operating in Chinese waters. On 6 August Vietnam lodged a diplomatic complaint in Beijing over Chinese naval exercises near the Spratly Islands, which it said "do not conform to solving the territorial dispute through negotiations." The Chinese replied the exercises were required to "respond to Vietnam's confrontations." Vietnam repeatedly called on the Chinese to negotiate the dispute, and the Chinese repeatedly replied there was nothing to negotiate.

Moscow spokesmen on several occasions, when asked, said the USSR was concerned over the dispute and wanted the claimants to settle their differences peacefully. Soviet foreign minister Gerasimov at a Moscow news conference in March described the Vietnamese position as "taking constructive steps in resolving differences with China not by force but through negotiations," a position supported by the USSR (*Pravda*, 28 March). Western press reports said that the USSR had given Hanoi intelligence about Chinese naval activity from its electronic monitorings and satellite reconnaissance (*FEER*, 24 March).

Vietnamese officials during the year were not sure what to make of Soviet moves in the Cambodian peace process or of the bilateral Sino-Soviet discussions about their relationship. The Hanoi press during the year gave a low-key treatment to the developments that seemed to indicate a generally improved Sino-Soviet relationship, probably indicating further uncertainty as to whether this would jeopardize Vietnam's interests in any serious way. Vietnam officials also were not sure what to make of repeated Chinese assertions that the "third obstacle," that of Cambodia, remained an impediment to improved Sino-Soviet relations. This was because the exact nature of the "obstacle" was never made clear—that all PAVN forces must be withdrawn from Cambodia or merely that Beijing officials must be convinced that Moscow had done all in its power to persuade Vietnam to withdraw its troops.

Soviet-Vietnamese bilateral relations during the year remained intimate, turning largely on Soviet economic assistance programs. USSR deputy foreign minister Igor Rogachev in an interview by Radio Moscow (14 January) described the association as "capacious and intensive . . . made complex by the Kampuchea problem." In travels throughout the region in March, Rogachev's statements were vague, chiefly to the effect that peace in Cambodia depended on "international understanding."

A high-level delegation headed by Politburo candidate member Georgii Razumovsky spent five days in Hanoi (24–29 April) for official party-to-party talks on "strategies for economic development," techniques for "overcoming negative phenomena," and methods for improving internal party organization and cadre performance (TASS, 24 April, *Pravda*, 29 April). Most of the routine meetings between Vietnam and the USSR during the year involved economic matters. In the Gerasimov interview cited above, the Soviet official said that the USSR currently had 250 economic aid projects under way in Vietnam and that the "trade turnover" between the two countries was 1.3 billion rubles. In August, on the anniversary of the start of formal Vietnamese-USSR economic relations (1955), the Vietnamese press tabulated assistance as 440 Soviet projects completed or under way and said that in 30 years imports from the USSR had increased 200-fold and exports to the USSR had increased 30-fold. USSR/CMEA trade currently accounted for 80 percent of all of Vietnam's foreign trade (Radio Hanoi, *FBIS-EAS*, 2 August).

VCP general secretary Linh was in Moscow in mid-July, met with General Secretary Mikhail Gorbachev (20 July), and, according to Vietnam press reports, discussed Soviet military aid to Vietnam, estimated to be running at about U.S. $2 billion per year; according to Moscow press reports the two discussed PAVN withdrawal from Cambodia (the meeting came shortly before the Djakarta Informal Meeting on Cambodia) (VNA, *FBIS-EAS*, AFP, 15 July; TASS, *FBIS-Soviet Union*, 20 July). Vietnam's State Council chairman Vo Chi Cong paid a highly visible state visit to the USSR (19–26 September) marked by lavish Soviet hospitality—wined and dined by host Andrei Gromyko and conferred with General Secretary Gorbachev—a concerted Soviet effort to soften a major conservative figure in Hanoi politics. A joint communiqué (14 September) said the "two sides informed each other of activities aimed at . . . socialist restructure and renovation and effecting socialist democracy and openness." Observers note that Cong's trip came amid reports of growing Sino-Soviet rapprochement and was reminiscent of the last time a Vietnamese head of state visited Moscow—1982, when Moscow made a surprise offer to begin talks with the Chinese (*FEER*, *FBIS-Soviet Union*, *FBIS-EAS*, 27 September; joint communiqué: *Pravda*, *FBIS-Soviet Union*, 25 September).

U.S.-Vietnamese semidiplomatic activity during the year underwent a series of zigs and zags, chiefly because of doctrinal infighting in Hanoi. Most activity involved resolution of the casualties issue and the possibility of U.S. diplomatic recognition of Vietnam. There were visits to Vietnam by U.S. graves registration personnel and the turnover

of a number of remains of U.S. servicemen. However it was clear that the outgoing Reagan administration would leave the decision on formal diplomatic recognition of Vietnam to the incoming Bush administration.

The SRV Council of State (5 August) established a State Commission for Cooperation and Investment and charged it with "creating favorable conditions for the new Foreign Investment Law." On 5 September, the final version of the new law was promulgated (having been passed by the National Assembly 29 December 1978). Analysis of the new 113-article code by foreign economists indicated it was more liberal than those of most other socialist societies, allowing considerable decisionmaking latitude and administrative independence to foreign investors in matters relating to production schedules and shipment. Enterprises could be wholly foreign owned; initial taxation would be as low as 10 percent for the first four years. However, there remained the question of implementation of the code (VNA, 15 September; Jean-Claude Chapon, AFP, *FBIS-EAS*, 29 September).

Biography. *Do Muoi.* The SRV National Assembly 22 June elected Do Muoi chairman of the SRV Council of Ministers (in protocol terms, prime minister of Vietnam). He had long been a well-entrenched but low-profile member of the upper-level party hierarchy, an old-guard type, clearly identified with the conservative/ideological elements of the party. He had held various state and party posts from the earliest years, many of them in the economic sector, and his detractors would have said that he as much as any single leader in Vietnam was responsible for Vietnam's postwar economic failure; kinder commentators would say that he merely shared the blame equally with others.

Do Muoi always commanded respect as an organizer and a disciplinarian and had an untarnished reputation for integrity as a maintainer of communist idealism, scourge of the corrupt, the incompetent, and the slack. He was said to be of short temper, with little patience for anything less than perfection. Although his record in the economic sector stood against him, he achieved administrative successes over the years in troubleshooting problems in flood control, typhoon aftermath, and, in the mid-1980s, emergency rice shipments from south to north. He was a "northerner" in the full meaning of that word as it is applied to Vietnam, which could be counted both a political plus and a minus.

On the basis of his rather voluminous writings and speech making, it could be said that Do Muoi's economic philosophy was essentially "Stalinist," that is, concentration on heavy industry, large-size agricultural production units, highly centralized planning, use of moral exhortation more than individual incentive as chief motivating force, and minimal role for the market in economic activity. Possibly some of his views were tempered by administrative experiences in the 1980s.

Although a somewhat obscure figure abroad, Do Muoi has traveled extensively in Vietnam and probably was more tireless in stumping the boondocks than any other Hanoi figure. He also traveled extensively abroad but almost entirely to socialist countries.

According to his official biography Do Muoi was born as Pham Van Thien on the outskirts of Hanoi (Dong My village, Thanh Tri district) in 1917. He joined the party as a youth, was active in the Popular Front movement of the 1930s, and was incarcerated by the French during World War II. He broke out of Hoa Lo prison in Hanoi in 1945, according to his official biography. His revolutionary career in Ha Dong province began in 1945. Early in the Viet Minh war he held a succession of provincial-level party posts and later moved into PAVN political commissar positions (eventually to equivalent rank of brigadier general). He was involved in the occupation of Haiphong at the end of the Viet Minh war. His first post in the new SRV government was vice-minister of commerce (1956), followed by a series of assignments, chiefly in the domestic trade sector. Do Muoi was inactive from 1961 to 1968 (age 44 to 53) for reasons never revealed. In 1969 he was assigned to the construction sector and held a variety of posts (he was the Vietnamese liaison official to the USSR team that built Ho Chi Minh's mausoleum and to the Cuban team that built the Thanh Loi hotel). After the war he was directly responsible for planning the initial socialist transformation effort (1976–1979) and if he is indictable for past performance it would be for this grievous failure. He became vice-premier in December 1969 and a Central Committee member and Politburo alternate member in March 1982 and a full Politburo member and Central Committee secretary in 1986. He was a National Assembly delegate from 1980 to date. In the past decade Do Muoi was identified with the Council of Ministers (vice-chairman in 1981) rather than with a particular ministry or mission.

Little is known about his personal life.

Douglas Pike
University of California at Berkeley

EASTERN EUROPE AND THE SOVIET UNION

Introduction

That one can no longer consider the USSR and Eastern Europe as a monolithic bloc could be seen from reactions to *perestroika* and *glasnost'* by the individual regimes, which extended from liberalization to complete rejection of the Soviet model. Personnel changes in 1988 suggest that the CPSU general secretary will have several more-experienced advisers. Vadim A. Medvedev, promoted to head the new ideology commission, served as chief of the Central Committee department for liaison with the East European ruling communist parties during the preceding two years. Vladimir A. Kriuchkov, new State Security Committee (KGB) head, had dealt with Hungarian affairs between 1954 and 1967 when he transferred to foreign intelligence operations. Nikolai V. Talyzin returned to become chief representative to the Council for Mutual Economic Assistance (CMEA), which he had been three years earlier.

The Soviet Union. The Nineteenth National Communist Party of the Soviet Union (CPSU) Conference, the first such meeting since 1941, adopted resolutions that will introduce changes in the political system. (These, of course, had been approved in advance by the party leadership.) Proposed by Mikhail Gorbachev in January 1987, the conference did not open until 28 June 1988. Many, if not most, of the delegates reportedly had negative attitudes toward reforms.

Hence it proved impossible for Gorbachev to renew the Central Committee or change the CPSU rules. He did, however obtain approval for popularly elected soviets and a more powerful presidency for himself, but both the party and governmental executive committees would be headed by the same CPSU apparatchiks.

On the other hand, the Nineteenth Conference was permeated with a freedom of expression not permitted during the preceding six decades. Discussion of the economy, the media, the law, human rights, and nationalities at times became heated. In his own interventions and closing on 1 July, Gorbachev played the role of a moderate, which contrasted with his three-and-a-half-hour opening speech. In summary, despite the example being set by *glasnost'*, all delegates understood that "democratic centralism" would remain the basis for decisionmaking. Six resolutions were adopted without any problems whatsoever.

Gorbachev broke the power of the CPSU Secretariat on 30 September at a Central Committee plenum. The new apparatus includes six commissions, each headed by a national secretary with specific responsibilities that do not overlap with other units. The general secretary's deputy, Igor K. Ligachev, was demoted by being moved to chair agriculture. KGB chief Viktor Chebrikov lost that position when he was named to head the legal commission. Winners were the new chief ideologist Vadim A. Medvedev and international commission chairman Aleksandr N. Iakovlev. The following day, Gorbachev became titular chief of state at a 44-minute session of the USSR Supreme Soviet in place of Andrei A. Gromyko.

Eastern Europe. Although no increase had been registered in the overall hard currency debt for the region, individual country growth rates ranged from 0.9 percent in Hungary to 4.3 percent in Poland. Exports to Western Europe increased by 6 percent, which suggests that some of the CMEA member states would prefer to shift their trade away from the Soviet bloc. After 40 years, the East European economic organization seems to be headed toward a dead end.

Only the Warsaw Treaty Organization (WTO) holds the region together, with USSR troops stationed in four of the countries and many more divisions in the Soviet Union proper. Gorbachev's statement on 7 December before the United Nations, that 500,000 men under arms will be disbanded over the next two years, affects the garrisons in East Germany, Poland, Czechoslovakia, and Hungary only marginally.

The 50,000 to be withdrawn from those countries is less than 10 percent of the 565,000 now stationed there. However, all of the WTO members, except Romania, did announce that they would cut indigenous armed forces and defense budgets. If they follow the USSR example, a one-tenth cut will not make much difference. The Brezhnev Doctrine, on the basis of which Czechoslovakia was occupied by Soviet troops in 1968, has not been abrogated to date.

Apart from the above economic and military constraints, most East European communist party bosses are hesitant to follow Gorbachev's domestic political reforms because they do not know whether he can remain in power. The situation in the individual countries looked as follows during the year under review:

- Poland's prices for food and other essentials doubled or even tripled when inflation between 70 and 88 percent is included. General Wojciech Jaruzelski dismissed six Politburo members, bringing in eight new faces before Christmas. He refused to choose between continuation of socioeconomic decline and political pluralism, although roundtable discussions with Solidarity finally got under way in the first week of February 1989.

- East Germany, in contrast, has political stability and a net material product that is the envy of the region. However, the other model to the West, the unknown successor to 77-year-old Erich Honecker, and the lack of popular support make the future uncertain. Nevertheless, Moscow will remain more important than Bonn to the regime in East Berlin. If *perestroika* fails in the USSR, one should expect a spillover effect in the German Democratic Republic.

- Czechoslovakia also borders on the West and, hence, is of prime geopolitical importance to the Soviet Union. Its leadership has been slow to introduce reforms, now scheduled for 1991. Memories of USSR tanks, which had entered Prague almost two decades earlier, were revived when Miloš Jakeš became the new leader last December. He had supervised the purge of about 500,000 communist party members after the invasion. In mid-January 1989, his riot police clubbed and dispersed some two thousand peaceful marchers commemorating a student who burned himself to death in protest against the Soviet occupation.

- Bulgaria's leader also announced that a decision on basic reforms would be postponed until 1991. Todor Zhivkov is slightly older than Honecker and has twice purged potential successors, during the middle and end of last year. Nevertheless, reforms ultimately will be implemented by a society that finds the fundamental Marxism of its leaders an impediment to progress. By tradition pro-Soviet, there is little reason if any why the next leader should not emulate Moscow with enthusiasm.

- Romania is the least enthusiastic about any kind of reform; change can only come after the death or removal of Nicolae Ceauşescu. Even then, commitments to the communist system, a nationalism that enhances legitimacy, and personalized power should remain. Any new leadership probably will adhere to autonomy in foreign affairs, although it may draw closer to CMEA. Only a change in the current policy of persecuting ethnic minorities, destroying their villages, and forcibly moving them to shoddy apartments would give the new leader respectability in the West.

- Hungary, reputedly the showcase of Eastern Europe, revealed a different picture—delays in reform measures, inflation, a decline in living standards, and social tensions—at the May 1988 communist party conference. Although the new leader, Károly Grósz, predicted that a multiparty system would be out of the question in his lifetime, a law on private associations was adopted by his parliament in early 1989. If another one regulating their activities is approved before August and if there is no crackdown, competitive elections may take place during 1990.

- Yugoslavia is the larger of the two non-WTO countries, although it holds associate CMEA membership. Here too inflation (250 percent), unemployment, strikes, and ethnic disruption have continued. At the very end of last year, the cabinet resigned in conflict with parliament for the first time since the communists seized power after World War II. Disintegration has not taken place only because of agreements on a (1) strong defense to preserve sovereignty, (2) regional self-sufficiency versus a weak center, and (3) free enterprise at microlevels with socialist ownership at macrolevels. This last principle assured almost $1.5 billion in new loans from the International Monetary Fund and the World Bank during 1988.

- Albania, neither a member of CMEA nor of WTO, finally seems ready to enter the twenty-first century. It has had no relations with the Soviet Union since 1961. Mismanagement, economic stagnation, and repression were inherited by Ramiz Alia when he succeeded the autocratic Enver Hoxha. The current leader has moved slowly to reverse these trends, although reform does not touch system fundamentals. Without political change, as yet unanticipated, economic reforms alone cannot succeed.

So what is the prognosis for Eastern Europe? Despite some change, the communist regimes remain more similar than different. None has indicated any intention to abandon one-party rule or the centrally planned economy. However, a trend seems to be spreading toward professional qualifications rather than communist party service for certain positions in government. Most of the regime decisionmakers now realize that progress cannot be achieved without a realistic pricing system, at least some decentralization, and incentives for workers.

The future of Eastern Europe will continue to depend on the USSR. Apart from military occupation forces in the majority of WTO member states, all CMEA economies depend on raw materials imported from the Soviet Union. The latter produces most of the crude oil (93.4 percent), iron ore (97.5 percent), and natural gas (93.4 percent) available in the region, not to mention a preponderance of cotton, electricity, and even grain. All of these commodities are exported to the USSR's client states.

Richard F. Staar
Hoover Institution

Albania

Population. 3,147,352. (*The World Factbook*, p. 2)
Party. Albanian Party of Labor (Partia ë Punes ë Shqipërisë; APL)
Founded. 8 November 1941
Membership. 147,000 claimed: 39.8 percent workers; 25.5 percent cooperativists (peasants); 31.3 percent white-collar workers. Women constitute 32.2 percent of the membership (*Zeri i popullit*: 4 November 1987).
First Secretary. Ramiz Alia

Politburo. 13 full members, most of whom occupy other high government positions as well: Ramiz Alia (first secretary, president of the republic, commander-in-chief of the armed forces), Adil Çarçani (prime minister), Besnik Bekteshi (deputy premier), Foto Çami (member of Secretariat), Lenka Çuko (member of Secretariat), Hekuran Isai (deputy premier, minister of interior), Hajredin Çeliku, (member of Secretariat), Rita Marko (deputy chairman of the Presidium of the People's Assembly), Pali Mishka (first secretary, Korçë party district), Manush Myftiu (deputy premier), Prokop Mura (minister of defense), Muho Asllani (first secretary, Shkodër party district), Simon Stefani (member of Secretariat); 5 alternate members: General Kiço Mustaqi (deputy defense minister, chief of the General Staff), Llambi Gjegprifti (minister of industry and mines), Vangjel Çerava (deputy premier), Qirjako Mihali (first secretary, Durres party district), Piro Kondi (first secretary, Tiranë party district).
Secretariat. 5 members: Ramiz Alia, Foto Çami, Lenka Çuko, Simon Stefani, Hajredin Çeliku
Central Committee. 85 members, 46 alternate members
Status. Ruling party
Last Congress. Ninth, 3–8 November 1986
Last Parliamentary Elections. 1 February 1987, all 250 candidates of the Democratic Front. Only one ballot was declared invalid. (*Zeri i popullit*, 3 February 1987.)
Auxiliary Organizations. Albanian Democratic Front, Nexhmije Hoxha, chairwoman; Central Council of Trade Unions (UTUA), approximately 610,000 members, Sotir Koçollari, chairman; Union of Labor Youth of Albania (ULYA), Mehmet Elezi, first secretary; Albanian War Veterans, Shefqet Peçi, chairman; Pioneers of Enver, elementary school organization
Main State Organs. Council of Ministers (24 members, including 2 members without portfolio, Alfred Uçi and Ajet Ylli, who serve as chairmen of the Committee for Culture and Arts and the State Committee for Science and Technology, respectively (*Zeri i popullit*, 21 February 1987).
Publications. *Zeri i popullit*, daily organ of the Central Committee of the APL; *Rruga ë partisë*, monthly theoretical organ of the Central Committee of the APL; *Zeri i rinisë*, daily organ of the ULYA; *Bashkimi*, daily organ of the Democratic Front; *Puna*, weekly organ of the UTUA; *10 Korrik* and *Lluftetari*, biweekly organs of the Ministry of Defense (circulated in the armed forces); *Nen-*

dori, literary monthly, organ of the Albanian Writers and Artists' League; *Laiko vema*, organ of the Greek minority. The Albanian Telegraphic Agency (ATA) is the official state news service.

The APL, the youngest communist party in the Balkans, was founded on the initiative of the Comintern after the German invasion of the Soviet Union. Two Yugoslav agents, acting on Josip Broz Tito's behalf, visited Tiranë in the fall of 1941 to survey the scene and explore the possibilities of creating an organization to lead the resistance against the Axis powers in that part of the Balkans. The two emissaries found only two dozen communists (each pretending to represent a larger group of followers) who were at odds over the desirability of engaging in any resistance and thus going against the dominant national feeling. (Dmitris Mihalopoulos, *Scheseis Ellados Alvanias*, Salonica, 1987, pp. 161–62.) The first emissary, Miladin Popović, a Montenegrin from Kosovo who was fluent in Albanian, was preparing the ground to form a party when he was arrested by the Italian authorities. His alibi—a butcher buying livestock—did not check out (Nikos Argyrocastritis, *Ho Slavocommunismos Sten Alvania, 1877–1946*, vol. 1, Athens, 1956, p. 142). During his time in Tiranë, however, he succeeded in eliminating the anti-Comintern group Zjari, which had been established by Anastas Llulo, a shady character with connections to Greek Trokskyite circles. Popović was eventually smuggled out of prison and joined his newfound Albanian comrades. Tito, unsure about the fate of his agent, dispatched to Tiranë a second operative, Dušan Mugoša, a member of the Central Committee of the Kosovo branch of the Yugoslav Communist Party. Mugoša stayed in Tiranë for approximately three weeks, spending most of his time instilling a sense of discipline among the self-proclaimed communists and telling them how to take advantage of the power vacuum that was bound to be created in the country with the inevitable defeat of the Axis. (Vladimir Dedijer, *Jugoslovensko-Albanski Odnosii, 1939–1948*, Belgrade, 1948, pp. 86–97.) The two Yugoslavs pointed out to their Albanian pupils Balli Kombetar, a nationalist organization that was waiting in the wings to take up arms at the appropriate moment.

On 8 November 1941, the day after the anniversary of the October Revolution, the two dozen or so Albanian communists, heeding the advice of Tito and the Comintern, succeeded in founding the Albanian Communist Party and its provisional Central Committee. Enver Hoxha, the son of a mullah from Gjirocastër and recipient of a royal scholarship to study law in France, was chosen as provisional secretary. There is disagreement as to who constituted that provisional Central Committee. Hoxha, in his book *Kur Lindi Parti* (When the Party Was Born), p. 220, lists the following members besides himself: Qemal Stafa, Koçi Xoxe, Tuk Jakova, Kristo Themelko, Ramadan Çitaku, and Gjin Marku. According to Argyrocastritis (op. cit., p. 136), a prominent intellectual from Gjirocastër and an associate of Hoxha until 1945, missing from Hoxha's account are four members of the founding Central Committee—Ymer Dyshnika, Liri Gega, Bedri Spahiu, and Kadri Hazbiu—who were purged between 1960 and 1981. The Albanian Communist Party was renamed Albanian Party of Labor at its first congress in 1948.

On 29 November 1941, a date carefully chosen to coincide with the anniversary of the declaration of Albanian independence in 1912, the newly established party created an Albanian communist youth organization with a five-member Central Committee, headed by Qemal Stafa as general secretary. Among its members were Nexhmije Xhungili (later Madame Hoxha) and Misto Mame, the son of a wealthy Greek merchant who had often given shelter and money to Enver Hoxha (Argyrocastritis, p. 136). Hoxha characteristically edits two critical facts from his account of the founding of the Albanian Communist Party: first, he takes full credit for its establishment, not recognizing any role for the Yugoslavs; second, he omits four participants from the Tiranë gathering. Koçi Xoxe and Tuk Jakova (the only Catholics among the founders) are mentioned in the Hoxha account only as convenient scapegoats for whatever went wrong in the party's history.

A distinguishing characteristic of the Albanian Communist Party, which sets it apart from other ruling parties, is its instability at the top and the propensity of the late Hoxha to govern via the *Sigurimi* (security police) and the politics of permanent purge. Hoxha, who maintained the top position longer than any other European communist leader, copied Stalin's leadership style in every respect, including the latter's paranoia. A total of seven major and brutal (even by Albanian standards) purges of top leaders and cadres, or approximately one every six years, had been undertaken and carried out on his orders since 1948. The last one involved his prime minister for 28 years, Mehmet Shehu, along with a dozen other top officials. Shehu reportedly was shot during a meeting of the Central Committee. His death precipitated a massive cadre turnover and paved the way for the post-Hoxha era in Albanian politics. Shehu's deputy, Çarçani, was appointed prime minister. Alia, a Hoxha protege (and Madame Hoxha's student at the Institute of Marxist-Leninist Studies), became first secretary following Hoxha's death in April 1985. Under their leadership, the process of opening to the West, initiated by Shehu, continued in a more rational and predictable manner.

Following the assassination of Shehu, Hoxha carried out his last major purge of party cadres and senior military officers suspected of being followers of the late prime minister. There are no specific numbers of people purged in the anti-Shehu campaign; figures vary from four hundred to thousands. Recent Albanian refugees to Greece, some of whom served in prisons with Shehu's followers, give the number of victims as "several thousands" (sworn affividavit of a refugee, 28 September, in author's possession).

Alia legitimized his full control of the party at the Ninth Congress held in Tiranë, 3–8 November 1986. Although groomed for that position by Hoxha, he has been slow in establishing his own style of leadership. Conservative personalities under the influence of the late dictator's widow seem to slow attempts toward relaxation of domestic controls and meaningful openings to the rest of the world. During 1988, however, there has been an intensive debate about the future of Albanian politics and the role of the party in the economic and social life of the country. The contradictory positions taken by key party members (particularly Çami and Kondi) suggest that Alia does not set the pace in the ideological debate.

The Fifth Central Committee Plenum, held on 1–2 March, dealt with the problem of culture and the role of the party in shaping it. The main report to this plenum was given by Çami, an academician known for his unpredictability, who was critical of the lack of standards in artistic and literary works (ATA, 2 March; *FBIS*, 3 March). At the end of his report he came out for the maintenance of "class struggle" in the work of Albanian writers and warned against trends in literature that are being complicated by the new "world situation." As he noted, "at present, the class struggle in the field of culture is very complicated and fierce. It can be hidden neither by the slogans of deideologization of culture nor by the convergence of bourgeois and socialist cultures that have been enlivened particu-

larly in the context of the revisionist *perestroika*" (ibid.).

Alia, who spoke at length during the same plenum, echoed some of Çami's basic themes but went further in arguing for better definition of standards and merit in art and culture. The first secretary expressed concern about the "leveling of values in literature and art," which in his opinion "is due to weaknesses in literary and artistic criticism, [and] to its generalized judgments" (ATA, 3 March; *FBIS*, 7 March). Alia took issue with those who favor "leveling values" in the name of antielitism and rejected the "massification of culture" in the name of egalitarianism. As a corrective measure he recommended that "conditions be created for talented people to work for the benefit of socialism and the country" (ibid.). Contradicting Alia's position on the need for distinction and merit in artistic achievement, Madame Hoxha deplored the unevenness in cultural levels in various parts of the country. Writing in *Bashkimi* in her capacity as chairwoman of the Democratic Front, she criticized the persistence of cultural variations in the country, despite income equality: "Even though family incomes in the villages of the Pogradec and Pukes districts are almost the same . . . there is a large difference in their cultural levels" (*Bashkimi*, 17 June). Madame Hoxha drew the same parallels between villages of Gjirocastër (Greek inhabited) and villages around Tiranë, which are lagging behind in "cultural outlook." Furthermore, she saw regression in culture when families maintained the bourgeois tendency of spending "too much on weddings and funerals, men spending too much for alcohol and most having no taste in furnishing the interiors of their houses" (ibid.). The implication is that "leveling equality," even in culture, is preferable to elitism. Meanwhile, the cult of her late husband is kept alive and reinforced in almost daily rituals. Ceremonies marking the anniversaries of his birth and death are attended by most members of the Politburo and the government and are usually led by his widow (ATA, 11 April; *FBIS*, 14 April), and the publishing houses continue to issue Hoxha's collected works. The 62nd volume came out on 29 November with more planned (ATA, 29 November; *FBIS*, 30 November).

The top echelons have been relatively stable since Hoxha's death, despite apparent ideological conflicts that pit conservatives (Stalinists) against moderates who apparently have no recognizable standard bearer. A major article in *Zeri i popullit* (13 January) pointed to the persistence of leftist sectarianism and outmoded criteria by which party cadres are selected. Its author (a senior editor of the Central Committee organ), Halil Lalaj, decries sectarian manifestations, which often parade under "the magnification of class struggle" (*RAD Background Report*, no. 14, 5 February; *Zeri i popullit*, 13 January). The author questions the method of selection of party candidates, which includes "going into a prospective candidate's distant past, instead of being judged on the basis of present responsibility, age, and professional skills."

Although the year passed without any significant changes involving the top party ranks (and the government as whole), Alia initiated a massive turnover in cadres and party functionaries, supposedly to achieve economic and governmental efficiency. In several editorials that preceded changes in cadre utilization, the party daily, *Zeri i popullit*, blamed most of the economic problems on the inefficient bureaucracy and cadres who felt too comfortable in their positions to be innovative or bold. Thus, by a Politburo decree (*Zerit i popullit*, 12 June), the tour of duty of all cadres "dealing directly with the vital requirements of the working people" will be limited to five years in any given position. In conformity with this decision, "all heads or officials in charge of cadre, housing, labor and residence permit bureaus, who are working in central organs, in the districts and enterprises, and who have completed five years of duty are to be replaced within the month of June" (ibid.). This drastic step, with its potentially far-reaching implications, affected a minimum of 70,000 people in senior administrative positions, most of whom owed their status and jobs to Hoxha's notorious nepotism. Alia reiterated the position that "cadre policy" remains a party monopoly, but he also affirmed his view that efficiency and competence must be rewarded.

Zeri i popullit and *Rruga ë partisë* repeatedly mentioned something drastic coming in the area of cadre deployment. On 28 March the paper pointed out that in excess of 1,300 highly skilled people are working outside of their expertise (e.g., 64 biochemists in Durrës working in a plastics factory), a terrible waste of talent and resources. In a speech to the party organization of Vlorë, Alia decried the fact that at least 30,000 inadequately educated people still hold senior jobs, whereas a lot of educated people were employed in tasks that made no use of their skills (*Zeri i popullit*, 23 March).

Rotation of cadres was given a high priority in all mass media and took the form of a major drive reminiscent of the Chinese and Albanian cultural revolutions of the mid-1960s. The first agency targeted for cadre transfers was the Ministry of the Interior, which controls the dreaded *Sigurimi*. According to *Zeri i popullit*, priority in transfers was given to those who were "subject to pressures" for favors, but as far as the Ministry of Interior is concerned, there might have been more important reasons. This agency has a history of instability at the top, as indicated by the fact that all interior ministers since 1948 have been purged or executed, allegedly because they were hatching conspiracies. The current minister assumed the position after his predecessor, Feçor Shehu, vanished (presumed dead) after his uncle's death. Cadres of this ministry were "expected to volunteer" for duty outside the urban centers. At least "150 people volunteered for border duty as base commissars, according to news stories" (*Zeri i popullit*, 17 June). The Ministry of Health was also under pressure to implement the cadre rotation, which it went about in a wholesale way (ibid.). Although the reasons given for this policy were based on "needs" of the economy and state, there is little doubt that Alia is engaging in his own version of *perestroika*, despite formalistic denunciations of the Mikhail Gorbachev version. Apparently, Alia, starting to clean house in the cumbersome bureaucracy, opted to do it from a level below the top party and state organs. The transfer of *Sigurimi* people, obviously a priority, suggests a continuation of a policy initiated by Hoxha to root out remnants of the Shehu state apparatus, whose strength lay in the civil service, the military, and the security apparatus. There is still a perception among top Albanian officials that a comeback by Shehu followers cannot be excluded.

Domestic Affairs. The domestic political debate during 1988 was dominated by strenuous efforts to spark productivity and increase exports, for Albania has serious problems in securing hard currency reserves. From the criticism aimed at enterprises and managers, which culminated in the drastic transfer of senior cadres from urban centers, one can safely argue that the economy continues to be the main preoccupation of the Alia regime and perhaps its weakness.

Niko Gjizari, chairman of the State Planning Commission, admitted the failure of the 1988 state plan in meeting goals set for productivity and exports. The shortcomings, Gjizari argued, are the result of a tendency "that has also been encountered in previous years, that leads enterprises and cooperatives, districts or ministries, to ask for more, even above their quotas, without contributing more to the accumulation of funds or foreign currency earnings" (*Bashkimi*, 30 May).

Gjegprifti, a young candidate member of the Politburo and former mayor of Tiranë, assumed the position of minister of mines and industry (a post he had previously held from March 1981 to November 1982), underscoring the weaknesses of the extractive industries. Another change of some significance was the appointment by a decree of the Council of Ministers of a newcomer, Ismail Ahmeti, as construction minister and Farudin Hoxha (a member of the Academy of Sciences) as Minister to the Presidium of the Council of Ministers (decree no. 7201, *Zeri i popullit*, 28 February), a new position of as yet unknown significance. Despite changes, exhortations, and propaganda campaigns, the government and high party organs seem dissatisfied with the level of production in oil and chrome extraction, two main earners of foreign currency. In early June, the Politburo held extensive discussions of the problems and their causes, and efforts were made to link the cadre rotation to the decline in productivity. The party organ lamented the fact that "despite all efforts, reliability of production from existing wells remains unsatisfactory" (*Zeri i popullit*, 23 June).

Alia, who has made it an annual ritual to address major political issues via the Korçë party organization (Korçë was where Hoxha first joined a communist cell under the sponsorship of Pillo Peristeri), dealt with the economic issues from an ideological/propaganda perspective. In a fashion that can easily be misconstrued as frankness, Alia blamed some of the shortcomings on poor propaganda efforts by the party! "It must be said," Alia stated, "that in some cases our propaganda and meetings gloss over things. For instance, one talks about the imperialist-revisionist blockade, but without saying how it is evident in our development, whether it hampers it and how" (*Zeri i popullit*, 10 November). As evident even from slogans painted on walls, the Albanian government continues to propagate the notion that most of its problems are caused by an "economic blockade" imposed by the imperialists and revisionists. In that respect, little has changed since Hoxha's departure, except that it is more difficult to sell the idea of a blockade to the Albanian people, who now listen to foreign radio and television broadcasts. Alia, however, was not deterred from arguing before the Korçë party organization that a "blockade" still has propaganda value. But for good measure, he warned the party and state authorities in the region to tighten their belts. Korçë, he said,

"consumes 600-700 million leks worth of raw materials, fuel, and electricity every year. The overwhelming majority of these materials consist of exportable items or imported materials." (Ibid.) Reduced consumption, he advised, will improve exports and increase reserves of hard currency. In general the emphasis of the party and government officials during the year was on economic problems, reduction in consumption, increase in exports, improvement in the status of hard currency and, still, on "go it alone."

Economic Issues. The economy dominated the political agenda of the government. Openly admitted failures to meet quotas were a recurring theme in the Albanian press and in public statements by high officials. The UTUA organ pointed to the persistent inability of various districts to meet their objectives in variety and quantity of goods produced. Out of a total of 26 districts, exactly half of them did not meet their quotas by midyear (*Puna*, 15 July). One district, Tropoje, had a dismal midyear performance, fulfilling its plan by only 64 percent of expectations. Making matters worse, the government noted a tendency on the part of managers to "produce goods that carry weight," while ignoring other smaller items (ibid.). Furthermore, the economic situation was complicated, according to the party's theoretical journal, by the practice of managers to play fast and loose with "statistical data" (*Rruga ë partisë*, no. 6, June, p. 56) (i.e., they did not provide reliable statistics to gauge performance).

The Eleventh Legislative Session of the People's Assembly, which examined the results of the 1987 state plan and approved the 1988 budget, was informed by Gjizari, chairman of the State Planning Commission, of serious shortfalls in most areas of economic activity, particularly agriculture (*Zeri i popullit*, 30 December 1987). Andrea Nako, the minister of finance, also noted serious problems in the state budget, "which resulted in only 95 percent fulfillment of planned state revenues and 91 percent of the targeted income in agricultural cooperatives" (*RAD Background Report*, no. 7, 21 January 1987). Both Gjizari and Nako blamed part of the failures on (a) poor economic management and (b) natural causes.

Economic issues occupied the proceedings of the Sixth Congress of Agricultural Cooperatives held in Tiranë during mid-November. Themie Thomai, the minister of agriculture, implored the participants to adopt new scientific methods in agriculture and to consider new incentives to spark productivity. With 700,000 people working in agriculture, the minister looked for ways of reducing dependence on the central authorities for social security in the countryside and recommended adoption of the "Elbasan model" of incentives. Elbasan (central Albania) agricultural managers have wide latitude in the distribution of income among cooperativists after they have delivered their quotas to the state (*Zeri i popullit*, 22 November). Indirectly, however, Thomai pointed to the main cause of low agricultural productivity: 75 percent of the arable land is managed by 460 large production centers that also control 80 percent of the country's livestock (ibid.), negating incentives and affecting productivity. Indicative of the difficult times in Albanian agriculture is a renewed effort by state authorities to come down hard on "cheaters of public land." Apparently, the instinct to own a piece of land has not been eradicated in Albania. According to *Bashkimi* (30 July p. 1), the sneaky peasants "blithely move the fence an inch in one day, and a yard the next" to increase their private plots. Expropriation of "public land" by individuals has not escaped the attention of the procurator general's office; the Tiranë prosecutor's agents inspected various areas around the capital and found at least "12,000 square meters of land used by private wheeler-dealers" (*Zeri i popullit*, 12 November). "It is amazing," the party organ stated, "that even some communists are among the speculators" (ibid.). With agriculture in a difficult situation, the Albanian exporting industry had serious problems in meeting its goals—more than 40 percent of industrial exported goods are of agricultural origin (*Zeri i popullit*, 22 November).

Indicative of a difficult economic situation was the fact that Gjizaris's report to Parliament avoided giving percentages for performance (except in the most general sense), and for the first time changes in the proposed budget occurred during debate of items in the legislative session. On the recommendation of the chairman of the Finance Committee of Parliament, expenditures for a railroad project were cut by 50,000,000 leks and administrative expenditures reduced by 27,000,000 (*RAD Background Report*, no. 7, 21 January). Gjizari's approach to the economic difficulties was taken directly from the Hoxha book of economics: limit consumption to production, limit expenditures to income, and limit imports to what exports would permit.

Auxiliary and Mass Organizations. The major mass organizations—Women's Union of Albania

(WUA), Union of Labor Youth of Albania (ULYA), and Trade Unions (UTUA)—were mobilized, as usual, to implement the economic and social agenda of the party. The ULYA Central Committee Plenum, held in late March, was attended by Çami, the Politburo member who routinely represents that body in practically all major meetings of auxiliary organizations. He used the opportunity to criticize the failure of youth and party leaders to instill socialist consciousness among the youth (*Zeri i rinisë*, 30 March).

Lisen Bashkurti, secretary of ULYA, repeated what Çami noted and criticized local youth organizations for inadequate attention to serious social problems caused by improper upbringing of young people. In her view, "attempts to properly educate the youth in socialist behavior have been a failure because they are not specific enough" (*Zeri i rinisë*, 30 March). A proper role for local organizations, in Bashkurti's view, would be to function as a social control entity: "as long as there is unbecoming behavior and extravagant dress on the Durrës beach and other alien symptoms, this means that the youth organizations and committees in these districts have not been doing their jobs properly" (ibid.).

Çami was the Politburo representative to the Trade Unions General Council meeting, in which its chairman, Koçollari, gave the main report. Predictably the chairman of the 600,000-member umbrella organization took to task local chapters for failure to meet production goals (*Puna*, 19 February). Çami, too, used the opportunity to chide the UTUA leadership for its inability to instill a sense of pride in the workers and to encourage socialist emulation. "Many professional organizations," he said, "pay more attention to decorating the enterprises' emulation display stands than to solid work encouraging emulation and competition between basic production units and among the masses of workers" (ibid.).

The Women's Union of Albania held its Tenth Congress in Tiranë during 6–10 June. Lumturi Rexha, chairwoman of the organization, gave the keynote address. The congress was attended by delegations from Third World countries, Vietnam, and North Korea. Ten foreign delegations (including those from the United States and Canada) attended the congress. Romania was the sole East European state to send an official group. Rexha's report dealt with the progress made by Albanian women and with the activities of the 700,000-member organization (ATA, 6 June; *FBIS*, 16 June). According to her, "women make up 33 percent of the party membership and over 40 percent of all elected officials," but in some regions they are still bartered for dowry.

Social Problems. As in previous years, party and government authorities seem troubled by their inability to deal with several categories of social issues. However, one could not fail to note an unusual openness in discussing these issues and their solutions. At least four sets of issues seem to preoccupy the authorities: (a) youth problems complicated by the intrusion of "alien manifestations," (b) persistence of old traditions, including religious practices, (c) persistence of dishonesty and theft of socialist property, and (d) low productivity.

Youth problems have been a favorite subject of Professor Hamid Beqeja, a noted psychologist at the University of Tiranë, who believes that honest discussion of issues is a better way to deal with problems of the young than dogmatic admonitions. But, as he notes, "old taboos are especially strict regarding problems of morality" (*Zeri i popullit*, 17 June). Beqeja takes issue with those who refuse to see the complexity of bringing up young people and who behave "like ostriches that stubbornly close their eyes for fear that the sun will burn them" (ibid.). He wonders why sex education is a taboo in Albania. "It is surprising, not to say regrettable," he wrote in *Zeri i popullit*, "that even the simplest biological and hygienic aspects of this subject [sex], quite apart from its social and ethical dimensions, are not discussed, not merely in the family, but in schools and mass media." Beqeja lays the fault for current attitudes toward youth on old taboos and on those who have fixed notions about socialist morality. "Upholders of these old taboos," he wrote, "attempt to drive young people into a state of pedantic dependence and automatic subjugation" (ibid.).

Çami, who seems to be everywhere in the social debate in Albania (occasionally he contradicts himself), talked quite openly about youth attitudes as well, but he sees the problem differently than Professor Beqeja. In his view, revival of old customs and foreign influences are at the core of youth misbehavior. The Politburo member lists a litany of unacceptable traits displayed by the young "in the area of ethics: breaches of discipline, low productivity and poor quality, destructiveness, misuse, and even theft." Even more troubling, Çami said,

We are talking about that very uncultured behavior toward girls and women and old people, about the base and banal vocabulary used even by university students, about unruly behavior causing concern to people on buses, trains, movie theaters, sports fields, and other public places; and we are talking about the revival of some old customs concerning betrothals, weddings, and funerals. (*Zeri i rinisë*, 30 March.)

Stefani, another Politburo member, joined the debate on antisocial behavior displayed not only by youth but also by adults. He conveniently blames most of the problems "on the capitalist-revisionist world which surrounds us" (*Zeri i popullit*, 13 May). The capitalists and revisionists, he said, "constitute a source of nourishment of petit bourgeois psychology and a malevolent activity that attempts to spread a mood of liberalism, to encourage degeneration and to strike against socialist property in various ways" (ibid.). Stefani's solution to these problems is for the "organs of justice and police to promptly detect wrongdoers."

Old customs seem to be an unsolvable problem in contemporary Albania. As in previous years, the authorities are frustrated by the refusal of people to abandon religious practices and traditional weddings, which include the use of matchmakers (*Zeri i popullit*, 26 June).

Theft of socialist property continues to plague the authorities, particularly when party officials and bureaucrats are involved. Whistle-blowers have no better fate in Albania than they do anywhere else. The party newspaper takes note of the situation in the country where "righteous workers" have been punished by demotions or transfers whenever they reported misappropriation of socialist property. "Instead of being thanked for their honest efforts," the paper wrote, "they are victimized" (*Zeri i popullit*, 12 June). Apparently expropriation of socialist property is pervasive. The UTUA paper reports the callous attitude of a shoe shine boy in Korçë who collected money from seven customers, put it in his pocket, and gave no receipts. "That is a crime," the paper lamented, and concluded that the "bourgeois psychology" is the main culprit in perpetuating the seeds of apathy vis-à-vis socialism. (*Puna*, 18 March.)

Human Rights Violations. Despite the relative openness in post-Hoxha Albania and the expanded opportunities for outsiders to travel there, the country remains a gross violator of basic human and religious rights. Reporters who visited Albania during the year said that tourist guides do not even use the terms B.C. ("before Christ") in their explanation of historical sites. Instead, they use the expression "before our time." A German newspaper

(*Luxemburger Wort*, 21 July) wrote that Alia continues the practice of demolishing houses of worship that had survived the Hoxha era. Correspondent H. Gstrein observed, "During the last three years even those houses of worship, which until Hoxha's death had been left standing as warehouses, have been leveled in the Albanian cities." This has happened to the Jesuit church in Skutari and the Orthodox seminary in Durrës. (Ibid.) The latter was a coal depot for twenty years, while the former has been used as a basketball court.

Taking note of the situation, the U.N. Human Rights Commission by a vote of fourteen in favor, six abstentions, and four against, expressed "grave concern about the constitutional and legal measures adopted by Albania to forbid religion in any form, including its teaching, practice, texts, and symbolisms" (Economic and Social Council, Resolution 8/XXIII, 31 August). But in the interest of tourism, the Albanian authorities have not been shy in using old photographs of Byzantine cathedrals; for maximum propaganda (and confusion) songs about Enver and communist heroes are sung in tones of church hymnology (*Luxemburger Wort*, 21 July; *FBIS*, 21 September).

Foreign Relations. The Alia regime, under the pressure of economic needs, continued the policy established by Shehu in the late 1970s for broadening contacts with the rest of the world, particularly the West. During 1988 the pace of expansion of relations with European countries—both East and West—quickened, and for the first time since 1961 Albania has participated in multilateral, regional meetings. However, the Tiranë government has not formally changed its policy vis-à-vis the two superpowers, even though the tone of its tirades against Moscow and Washington has been milder. A dramatic change occurred in February when Foreign Minister Reiz Malile attended the Belgrade meeting of Balkan foreign ministers, where common interests were discussed. The proceedings of this meeting were factually and favorably reported in the Albanian press, with the party newspaper taking the lead in declaring the event to be in "the interest of good-neighborliness and cooperation in the Balkans" (*Zeri i popullit*, 28 February). In June, Albania participated in a meeting at Sofia, Bulgaria, where an agenda for future meetings on specific issues was decided (ATA, 28 June; *FBIS*, 30 June). Six meetings, to deal with such items as environment, economic research, industrial cooperation, energy, and so forth, were agreed upon (*Zeri i popullit*, 29 June). They will be held in various Balkan capitals. In January, Tiranë will host a meeting at the level of deputy foreign ministers to discuss "regional and bilateral issues" (ATA, 14 November; *FBIS*, 15 November).

Aside from participation in the Belgrade and Sofia meetings, Albania has entered the road of normalizing relations with the Eastern bloc as well. In January, Sofia and Tiranë decided to raise their diplomatic representation to ambassadorial level (BBC, Current Affairs, 27 January). The first Albanian ambassador since 1961 presented his credentials to President Todor Zhivkov in late August. The Bulgarian leader, known for his pro-Moscow docility, used the opportunity to praise the Albanian model and to assure the new ambassador of the "availability of untapped opportunities for promotion of reciprocal ties" (BTA, 5 September; *FBIS*, 5 September). In September, Gjizari, chairman of the State Planning Commission, visited Bulgaria in connection with a trade fair and was received by Zhivkov and Prime Minister Georgi Atanasov. Their discussions revolved around "means for increased cooperation." During the second half of 1988, Albanian delegations participated in numerous other activities in Bulgaria such as the Eightieth Conference of the Interparliamentary Union, the centenary celebration of Sofia University, and a meeting of environmentalists (*RAD Background Report*, no. 207, 14 October).

Normalization of relations with the communist bloc took a step forward during Malile's visit to New York to attend the Forty-third Session of the U.N. General Assembly. During his stay, he met with eighteen foreign ministers, seven of whom were from communist-ruled countries, including China's foreign minister Qian Qichen. While in New York, Malile pursued "normalization" of relations with Hungary and East Germany (GDR). As a result, diplomatic ties were reestablished with East Berlin, while (ironically) relations with the Federal Republic of Germany were expanding at a pace unprecedented in Albania's history (BBC, CARIS report, nos. 89/87, 11 December). A trade protocol was signed with the GDR, which envisions exporting basically the same goods (agricultural items, petroleum by-products, handicrafts, etc.) Albania exports to other countries and importing direly needed machinery and chemicals (ATA, 3 November; *FBIS*, 9 November). That same month, relations with Budapest were raised to the ambassadorial level (ATA, 25 November; *FBIS*, 28 November).

Indicative of the improvement of relations with

the communist-ruled states is the new Albanian practice of attending embassy functions at ministerial level. Even relations with Yugoslavia have improved considerably; in a change of mood, the Albanian foreign minister and several of his colleagues attended a reception at the embassy in Tiranë on the occasion of Yugoslavia's national day. (In previous years, Deputy Foreign Minister Sokrat Pliaka or the protocol chief would have done the honors.) (ATA, 26 November; *FBIS*, 28 November.) More important, for the first time the Yugoslav ambassador to Tiranë was granted permission to visit the Macedonian minority in the Korçë region (ATA, 19 November). (Formerly, the Albanian government had refused to even recognize the existence of a Macedonian minority within its borders.) Another indication of changing times in the Balkans is Albania's willingness to let members of its literary elite and scientific community participate in regional and international gatherings. Androkli Kostollari, head of the Albanian National Committee for Balkan Studies, accompanied by two other Albanian specialists, attended the association's gathering in Bucharest, Romania. Ismail Kadare, Albania's most prominent writer (who weaves into his novels the ideological conflicts Hoxha had with his patrons), visited several West European countries and upon return wrote rather frankly about the questions people ask about Albanian society (*Bashkimi*, 17 April, 3 May). Furthermore, an Albanian biochemist and the director of the Institute of Monuments visited Zagreb and Rome, respectively, to acquaint themselves with new ideas in their respective fields (*RAD Background Report*, no. 106, 10 June).

Albanian–West German relations. Relations between Bonn and Tiranë have grown dramatically during the past year, when high-level visits from both sides took place. In June, a far-reaching agreement on economic, industrial, and technical cooperation covering such areas as agriculture, energy, transportation, construction, and trade was signed in Bonn between the two countries. Farudin Hoxha, the Albanian minister to the Council of Ministers, traveled to West Germany for the occasion and was received by Foreign Minister Hans-Dietrich Genscher and other high-level officials (ATA, 2 June; *FBIS*, 6 June). In August, a West German parliamentary group, headed by Dr. Hans Stercken, the chairman of Bundestag's Foreign Relations Committee, paid a visit to Tiranë and promised his hosts that "the parliament will go after" the executive

branch to promote further relations between the two countries (ATA, 22 August; *FBIS*, 26 August).

The most telling sign of the status of West German-Albanian relations is the growth in trade. During 1987 bilateral trade stood at DM 56,500,000. By mid-September 1988, Albanian exports to West Germany had increased by 30 percent, while imports from Germany increased by only 12 percent. This disparity is deliberate; Albania is in dire need of hard currency reserves, and deutsche marks are now preferred to American dollars (*RAD Background Report*, no. 194, 22 September). That same month, Albanian foreign minister Malile visited Bonn, where he discussed "further growth in relations" (BBC, CARIS report, nos. 68/88, 15 September). However, despite Genscher's "encouragement" Albania still refuses to participate in the European Cooperation and Security Conference, remaining the sole state on the continent not abiding by the Helsinki accords (*RAD Background Report*, no. 194, 22 September).

Albanian–West European relations. With West Germany setting the pace other West European states have entered the Albanian scene seeking trade and, above all, trying to help Albania break out of its political isolation and xenophobia. French, Austrian, Swiss, and Italian delegations have made their appearance in Tiranë and left after a ritual press conference at the airport expressing their approval of the "progress Albania has made" under its model of socialism.

In July, a Swiss delegation, headed by Rudolph Raichling, chairman of the National Council of the Swiss Confederation, visited Tiranë. He was received by top officials, including the prime minister, and discussed "issues of mutual interest and possibilities of cooperation, particularly in the food industry sector" (ATA, 26 July; *FBIS*, 29 July). French and Japanese officials, too, ventured to Tiranë during the past year in search of trade and cultural cooperation. In January, a group of French parliamentarians visited Tiranë (ATA, 24 January; *FBIS*, 28 January), and a month later, Didier Bariani, the French state secretary to the minister of foreign affairs, paid an official visit (Tanjug, 25 January; *FBIS*, 27 January). Takujiro Hamada, the Japanese deputy foreign minister, arrived in the Albanian capital on 17 August to explore the possibility of "further development [in relations], particularly in the fields of economic, trade, scientific, and technological exchanges" (ATA, 17 August; *FBIS*, 18 August).

Relations with Austria continued in an upward direction as well. Deputy Foreign Minister Sokrat Pliaka paid an official visit to Vienna and was received by Chancellor Franz Vranitzky, Interior Minister Karl Blecha, Foreign Minister Alois Mock, Chairman of the Federal Chamber of Commerce and President of the Republic Kurt Waldheim (*Zeri i popullit*, 9 November). For a relatively insignificant figure, Pliaka was given high-level access in Austria. The most visible outcome of his trip was the acceptance of his invitation to Austrian Foreign Minister Mock to visit Albania, turned down on budgetary grounds. A more important matter from Albania's perspective was the appointment of an Austrian ambassador to Tiranë, which remained unresolved. Currently the Austrian ambassador to Belgrade is also accredited to Albania (*Wiener Zeitung*, 20 September; *FBIS*, 22 September). To facilitate trade and tourism, the two countries agreed to establish direct flights by the Austrian airline Alpenair to Tiranë. Albanian authorities have finally discovered the value of tourism for their economy.

During 1988 the governments of Albania and Italy sought to improve relations, despite the presence of the six-member Albanian Popa family in the Italian embassy at Tiranë, who have been there since December 1985 seeking political asylum and the right to leave the country (*YICA*, 1986). In May, a cultural agreement with Rome was signed covering a wide range of areas (*Zeri i popullit*, 20 May; *NYT*, 20 June). But Italian-Albanian relations were given another twist when Italian newspapers reported a cozy relationship between Italian smugglers and Albanian authorities that allegedly provides a safe haven for contraband ships (*La Stampa*, 7 January; *Il Giornale*, 23 December 1987; *RAD Background Report*, no. 3, 14 January). For the Albanian authorities, this is a quick way to bolster hard currency reserves. Evidence of closer relations with Rome was the October visit to Tiranë of Italian minister of labor Rino Formica—the first such visit to Tiranë since the incident with the Popa family (ATA, 17 October; *FBIS*, 18 October).

Greek-Albanian relations. Relations between Athens and Tiranë continued on an upward trend during 1988. The Andreas Papandreou government and the Greek communist party (which had close relations with its Albanian counterpart during the war and resistance period) have provided assistance to Tiranë's efforts to improve its image in the eyes of Greek public opinion. Following termination of the state of war (which the opposition party, New Democracy, promised to reverse if elected to power, *YICA*, 1988), the Greek socialist government has been trying to expedite the expropriation of properties owned by Greek nationals in Albania and transfer the funds to the Albanian government. Instrumental in this display of socialist internationalism is Greek foreign minister Karolos Papoulias, who counts among his secondary school classmates several high-level Albanian officials of Greek nationality.

At the diplomatic level, several visits by important government officials occurred during 1988. In early March, Ioannis Papantoniou, the deputy minister of national economy of Greece, visited Tiranë to sign a protocol for economic, industrial, and scientific cooperation. While in Tiranë he was received by several high-level Albanian officials including Deputy Premier Vangjel Çerava (ATA, 4 March; *FBIS*, 7 March). In June, a Greek merchant marine group, headed by Vasilios Papadopoulos, the secretary general of the Ministry for the Merchant Marine, also visited Tiranë, where he held talks with Albanian minister of transportation Luam Babameto (ATA, 2 June; *FBIS*, 6 June). No specific issues were resolved during the visit. The details for establishing a ferry boat connection between Corfu and Sarande, agreed upon during Papoulias's second visit to Albania in the fall of 1987, were not ironed out (*YICA*, 1988). The most critical issue—reunification of families and open visits by members of the Greek minority—has not even been considered for discussion during the numerous visits, except in the most propagandistic manner. During 1987 (the year for which accurate figures are available), five hundred people from Albania were allowed to visit relatives in Greece (*NYT*, 20 June). Approximately the same number visited Greece during 1988, but the number of Greek communists and assorted leftists visiting Albania has increased dramatically. The number of ordinary Greek tourists has also increased, but they are carefully selected by the Albanian embassy in Athens. Critics of the Albanian regime need not apply.

Malile, the traveling Albanian foreign minister, paid an official visit to Athens in April—the first such visit by an Albanian foreign minister—in return for a similar visit by his Greek counterpart a year earlier (*YICA*, 1988). While in Athens, Malile was received by the prime minister, the president of the republic, and numerous other high-level officials. No surprises were announced during his visit, but the official Albanian press and radio praised the state of relations between the two countries and predicted their further growth (*Zeri i popullit*, 19 April). Malile conveyed to Prime Minister Papandreou a personal message from his Albanian counterpart, Adil Çarçani, and an invitation to visit Tiranë. The invitation was accepted, but the visit did not take place as planned because of Papandreou's health and political problems. In August, Karolos Papoulias traveled unexpectedly to the southern city of Sarandë, where he met again with Malile (ATA, 1 August; *FBIS*, 1 August). Apparently, relations in some areas between Greece and Albania have gone beyond the ordinary. Unpublished documents show that Greece imported at least 75,000 kilograms of high-explosive materials from Albania to be used in the production of 105-millimeter shells for export to Iran and Iraq (application by Greek Shell and Munitions Industry to the Ministry of Defense, 3 July 1986). The type of explosives imported from Albania were designated in the application as T-248/C8-11-74, Type I.

Albanian-Turkish relations. Relations between Albania and Turkey continue to grow, reflected by numerous high-level visits in both directions and by increases in economic, cultural, and agricultural exchanges. The foundations of these relations, as stated by officials of both sides, are to be found in their historical links and their shared Muslim culture.

Setting the pace of high-level contacts was a multimember Albanian delegation to Turkey headed by Marko, Politburo member and deputy chairman of the People's Assembly. Underscoring its significance, the foreign minister of Albania, the chairman of the People's Assembly, and a dozen other officials of ministerial rank saw them off at the Tiranë airport. (ATA, 22 March; *FBIS*, 23 March.) While in Turkey the Albanian delegation visited several cities and met with senior Turkish officials, including President of the Republic General Kenan Evren (ATA, 24 March; *FBIS*, 25 March). A month later, Vito Kapo, the Albanian minister of light industry, paid an official visit to Ankara, where she was received by high-level Turkish officials including Prime Minister Ozal (ATA, 7 April; *FBIS*, 8 April).

In August, Turkish foreign minister Mesut Yilmaz visited Tiranë and declared that "there are no problems in the relations between the two countries" (ATA, 5 August; *FBIS*, 5 August). The Albanian party newspaper declared the discussions a

success and exuberantly announced that the visit by Yilmaz "serves the consolidation of Albanian-Turkish relations" (*Zeri i popullit*, 6 August). Knowing the state of relations between Athens and Ankara, Tiranë tries to keep relations with Greece and Turkey on an even keel.

Albanian-Yugoslav relations. As relations between Serbs and Albanians in Kosovo deteriorated (*WP*, 20 November; *NYT*, 22 November), relations between Tiranë and Belgrade improved noticeably. As stated earlier, Albania participated in the Belgrade conference of foreign ministers and subsequently pursued more contacts with her northern neighbor (*RAD Background Report*, no. 185, 12 September). In a major speech at the northern city of Dibër, Alia showed some impatience with Belgrade's procrastination in signing a cultural agreement, which had been initialed two days before the Belgrade meeting of foreign ministers (ibid.). Two weeks later, an Albanian delegation visited Belgrade to finalize the cultural agreement, which defines the principles for all types of exchanges between the two countries (ATA, 7 September). With or without a formal agreement, exchanges picked up in pace during 1988. Ismail Kadare and Dritero Agolli, chairmen of the Writers' and Artists' Union, participated in the Bor Conference of Balkan Writers 15–17 September (ATA, 7 September; *FBIS*, 8 September), and several sporting events involving teams from both countries also took place (*Rilindjia*, 28 August). On 29 June, a border trade agreement, similar to one with Greece, was signed between the two countries to facilitate exchange of goods between border regions (ATA, 30 June; *FBIS*, 30 June). Overall there was a noticeable de-escalation of Albanian attacks on Yugoslavia about the situation in Kosovo. Several critical articles in the Albanian press were carefully aimed at regional authorities in Serbia and Macedonia (rather than Belgrade) for mistreating the Albanians within their jurisdiction. One paper, for example, took note of the discussion in the Macedonian party meeting of the issue of "large Albanian families," which "supposedly threaten to change the demography of the Republic." The organ of the Democratic Front calls such talk "neo-Malthusian" politics (*Bashkimi*, 4 January). Another paper pointed to the "revival of crossbearers," a clear implication of Serbian anti-Muslim attitudes, which indicate a "broadening of the anti-Albanian campaign among the Serbs" (*Zeri i popullit*, 21 May). Thus it seems that the Tiranë government has been rather astute in seeking good relations with Yugoslavia while feeling free to attack components of its federal system (Macedonia and Serbia). However, there were several diatribes against Yugoslav revisionism, which Tiranë ideologues see as the core cause of the disarray in the communist bloc (*Zeri i popullit*, 28 July). In fact, the official organ of the APL Central Committee blames Yugoslav theoreticians for the latter developments in the USSR. "The Soviet Union's counterrevolutionary turn started precisely with the reconciliation with Yugoslavia" stated a major editorial (ibid.).

Albania and the superpowers. Albania made no move to re-establish relations with either of the two superpowers. However, a noticeable de-escalation in the rhetoric pervaded the Albanian press and public pronouncements during the year. As has been observed, the Alia regime is in a dilemma concerning the future course of its foreign policy (Elez Biberaj, "Albania After Hoxha" in *Problems of Communism*, November–December 1985). The dilemma is real as far as USSR-Albanian relations are concerned. On the one hand, Tiranë has normalized relations with all East European states beginning with the most staunch pro-Moscow regimes of Zhivkov and Erich Honecker, but on the other hand it continues to assert its orthodox Marxist-Leninist line.

Formally and in absolute terms, Albania has rejected the Soviet economic and political experiment and dismissed Gorbachev as a social imperialist who finally admits the mutuality of Soviet and American interests at the expense of the socialist camp (*Rruga ë partisë*, no. 5, May; *Zeri i popullit*, 14 July). The visit to Washington of Marshal Sergei Akhromeyev, among other items, was used as "clear evidence" of interest convergence by the two superpowers (*Zeri i popullit*, 14 July). As far as *perestroika* is concerned, the Albanian ideologues dismiss it as Gorbachev's attempt to "provide a theoretical basis for the strategy of strengthening Soviet socialist imperialism" (*Zeri i popullit*, 24 June). Furthermore, *glasnost'* is simply his "means to crown the bourgeois ideals" (ibid.). In this context, another source denounces as "tricks" the Soviet regime's invitation to the public to write "letters to the editor" exposing social and other problems. In its view, they are "psychological diversions [by which] the Gorbachevians are trying to foster the illusion that the new political line is the product of extensive public discussion" (*Bashkimi*, 23 July). It must be noted, however, that the Albanian attacks

against Moscow were kept at the ideological-theoretical level. Predictably, Tiranë took issue with Gorbachev's decision to rehabilitate Nikolai Bukharin and other victims of Stalinism and once again praised Stalin for his "revolutionary vision" (*Zeri i popullit*, 15 June; *Lluftetari*, 23 June).

Although the Tiranë regime assumed a relatively hard line on ideological issues with Moscow, Soviet spokesmen and commentators remained determined to ignore all such attacks and repeatedly wrote about Albanian politics factually and often in a complimentary fashion (*New Times*, no. 21, 21 May; *Pravda*, 28 July). As in previous years, the Soviet-Albanian Friendship Society, which was revived in 1985, organized numerous activities on the occasion of important Albanian anniversaries. Nina Smirnova, a Soviet commentator, decided to go to the roots of the Tiranë-Moscow break and dealt extensively with the 1961 events that led to it, doing her best to blame it all on Khrushchev. As she put it, "it was an overreaction on our part on the stand taken by the Albanian leadership. In response to the Albanian side's fanning of ideological differences, we broke off diplomatic relations" (*New Times*, 21 May). This was the closest Moscow ever came to apologizing to Albania. Moscow's peace offensive toward Tiranë continued unabated during 1988.

Official attitudes toward the United States remained more or less static. However, Albania substantially relaxed travel restrictions for American citizens of Albanian origin, and for the first time, even people who had escaped from the communist regime were allowed to visit relatives. At the political level, Tiranë launched attacks on American imperialism (often simultaneously with attacks against Moscow) for its aggressive policies toward Central America, the Middle East, and Europe (*Bashkimi*, 22 July).

Despite the ideological posturing vis-à-vis the superpowers, the relaxation is noticeable. The Ronald Reagan–Gorbachev meetings were reported factually, and not until days after their occurrence were "ideological interpretations" added to "explain" their significance (ATA, 2 June; *FBIS*, 3 June). American domestic developments were reported quite factually and with diminished anti-imperialist rhetoric. In the spring a film series titled Film, Society, and Age opened with the American movie *They Shoot Horses, Don't They?* The youth newspaper praised it as a realistic portrayal of American life "where not everybody makes it, no matter how hard he/she works, or how honest he/she might be" (*Zeri i rinisë*, 9 April). The fact that an American film was screened for such an occasion is significant, but even more significant is that an important series opened with a Hollywood production.

To keep matters in ideological perspective, Albanian commentators kept up their demands that the two superpowers leave the Mediterranean "because neither the Soviet Union nor the United States are Mediterranean powers" (*Zeri i popullit*, 2 November). The Albanian government denounced the United States for its Persian Gulf policy on numerous occasions and formally welcomed the declaration of a "Palestinian state" (*Zeri i popullit*, 19 November).

Party Relations. Albania continued its established policy of not having party-to-party relations with Eastern Europe or the Soviet Union. However, this year the number of so-called "Marxist-Leninist" visitors also dropped. A large delegation of the APL Central Committee, headed by alternate Politburo member Kondi, attended the Seventh Congress of the Brazilian Communist Party (ATA, 8 May; *FBIS*, 9 May). Alia received Raoul Marko, first secretary of the Central Committee of the "orthodox" Spanish Communist Party (ATA, 23 February; *FBIS*, 25 February), and the Canadian Marxist Terence Bacon (ATA, 8 April; *FBIS*, 14 April). It is interesting to note that the Tiranë regime no longer uses the term "Marxist-Leninist" when referring to splinter parties, implying that these groups are the sole communist parties in their respective countries.

Nikolaos A. Stavrou
Howard University

Bulgaria

Population. 8,966,927 (July) (*The World Fact Book*)
Party. Bulgarian Communist Party (Bŭlgarska komunisticheska partiya; BCP)
Founded. Bulgarian Social Democratic Party founded in 1891; split into Broad and Narrow

factions in 1903; the Narrow Socialists became the BCP and joined the Comintern in 1919.
Membership. 932,055. According to information presented at the Thirteenth Party Congress in April 1986, 44.36 percent of the membership was classified as industrial workers, and 16.31 percent, as agricultural workers (BCP Central Committee Report to the Thirteenth Congress, BTA, 5 April 1986; *FBIS*, 8 April). Bulgaria no longer publishes data on ethnic minorities; Turks and Gypsies, the two largest minority groups, are believed to be underrepresented in the party in proportion to their numbers among the general population.
General Secretary. Todor Khristov Zhivkov (b. 7 September 1911)
Politburo. 9 full members: Todor Zhivkov (chairman, State Council), Georgi Atanasov (b. 1933, prime minister), Milko Balev (b. 1920, member, State Council), Dobri Dzhurov (b. 1916, minister of national defense), Grisha Filipov (b. 1919), Pencho Kubadinski (b. 1918, member, State Council; chairman, Fatherland Front), Petŭr Mladenov (b. 1936, minister of foreign affairs), Ivan Panev (b. 1933), Dimitur Stoyanov (b. 1928), Yordan Yotov (b. 1920); 6 candidate members: Petko Danchev (b. 1949, chairman, Association of Biotechnical and Chemical Industries), Petŭr Dyulgerov (b. 1929, chairman, Central Council of Trade Unions), Andrey Lukanov (b. 1938, minister of foreign economic relations), Stoian Ovcharov (b. 1942, minister of the economy and planning), Grigor Stoichkov (b. 1926, deputy prime minister), Georgi Yordanov (b. 1931, minister of culture, science, and education)
Secretariat. 8 members: Milko Balev, Grisha Filipov, Emil Khristov (b. 1924, member, State Council), Dimitur Stanishev (b. 1924), Dimitur Stoyanov, Vasil Tsanov (b. 1922), Yordan Yotov, Kiril Zarev (b. 1926)
Central Committee. 204 full and 134 candidate members
Status. Ruling party
Last Congress. Thirteenth, 2–5 April 1986, in Sofia; next congress scheduled for 1991.
Last Election. 8 June 1986. All candidates ran on the ticket of Fatherland Front, an umbrella organization (4.4 million members) comprising most mass organizations. Fatherland Front candidates received 99.9 percent of votes cast. Of the National Assembly's 400 members, 276 belong to the BCP and 99 to the Agrarian Union; 25 are unaffiliated (most of these are Komsomol members). The

Bulgarian Agrarian National Union (BANU, 120,000 members) formally shares power with the BCP and holds 3 of the 27 seats on the State Council; has places in the ministries of justice, public health, and social welfare; and fills about one-sixth of the people's council seats. BANU leader Petŭr Tanchev's post as first deputy chairman of the State Council makes him Todor Zhivkov's nominal successor as head of state.

Auxiliary Organizations. Central Council of Trade Unions (CCTU, about 4 million members), led by Petŭr Dyulgerov; Dimitrov Communist Youth League (Komosomol, 1.5 million members), led by Andrey Bundzhulov; Civil Defense Organization (750,000 members), led by Colonel General Tencho Papazov, provides training in paramilitary tactics and disaster relief; Movement of Bulgarian Woman (30,000 members), led by Elena Lagadinova, stimulates patriotism and social activism.

Publications. *Rabotnichesko delo* (*RD*; Workers' Cause), BCP daily, edited by Radoslav Radov; *Partien zhivot* (Party Life), BCP monthly; *Novo vreme* (New Time), BCP theoretical journal; *Otechestven front* (Fatherland Front), front daily; *Dŭrzhaven vestnik* (State Newspaper) contains texts of laws and decrees. Bulgarska telegrafna agentsiya (BTA) is the official news agency.

The Bulgarian public responded to the influence of Soviet *perestroika* and *glasnost'* with unprecedented independent political initiatives that provoked the Zhivkov regime to institute a repressive crackdown. Two members of the Politburo who were believed to favor more extensive liberalization in the country were purged. Bulgaria ended the year with Zhivkov still clearly holding the reins of power but increasingly isolated from the reform-minded intelligentsia.

Leadership and Party Organization. Despite signs of division in the party leadership and dissatisfaction in Moscow, Zhivkov continued to demonstrate his mastery of the Bulgarian political scene by purging two of the most influential members of the Politburo. At age 77, he continued to enjoy vigorous health and gave no sign that he intends to relinquish power in the foreseeable future.

Chudomir Alexandrov had been considered by many observers to be Zhivkov's probable successor. Fifty-two years old and well educated, he seemed to represent Bulgaria's new "technocratic generation,"

and after the BCP's Thirteenth Congress in 1986 he was one of the four men who were members of both the Politburo and the Secretariat. At the close of the BCP Central Committee Plenum (19–20 July), which was devoted to the restructuring of intellectual life, it was announced that he had resigned from these positions "at his own request." The July plenum (see below) was a major setback to the supporters of *glasnost'* and reform in Bulgaria; it seemed likely that Alexandrov was a victim of the closing of conservative ranks in the party leadership. Stanko Todorov, a Politburo member since 1962, also gave up office "at his own request." Todorov, age 67, had a long career as a Zhivkov protégé but had reportedly become disillusioned by Zhivkov's inconsistent attitude toward reform. Although he made few public statements, his wife had a long reputation as a supporter of liberal causes and was one of the most active participants in the independent movement for the environmental defense of Russe (see below). It was reported in the Chinese press that she had been expelled from the party, and it is likely that her activities were involved in Todorov's dismissal.

The July plenum also dismissed Stoian Mikhailov as a Central Committee secretary. This was not surprising because Zhivkov had already subjected him to sharp public criticism for allowing a decline in the party's control of intellectual life. Like Alexandrov, Mikhailov was a link to the "technocratic generation." He had come to party work from academic life and was reportedly quite popular among the intelligentsia. Both he and Alexandrov were removed from the Central Committee in December. Their downfall represented one more example of the party leadership retreating from the forces set in motion by the Mikhail Gorbachev era.

Svetlin Rusev, who had been chairman of the Artists' Union, was also expelled from membership in the Central Committee by the plenum. Rusev had taken a prominent part in the Russe affair and, like Mikhailov, had been publicly attacked by Zhivkov before the plenum.

At the BCP Central Committee plenum in December, Ognyan Doynov, who had been criticized for past economic failures, resigned from the Politburo. His protégé Stoian Markov also gave up his Politburo candidate membership. The plenum added two full members, promoting Dimitur Stoyanov from candidate membership and electing Ivan Panev, leader of the Sofia party organization. Stoyanov, who had held the post of minister of the interior since 1973, was also named to the party

Secretariat. (*Sofia News*, 21 December.) He was generally expected to take over Chudomir Alexandrov's role as supervisor of party organizations and cadres. The December plenum also added two candidate members: Stoian Ovcharov and Petko Danchev (*Sofia News*, 21 December). Ovcharov's promotion had been expected ever since his appointment as minister of the economy and planning in August 1987. Danchev, like Ovcharov, is a specialist in biotechnology and heads the Association of Biotechnological and Chemical Industries. He is also expected to play a prominent role in economic administration.

Despite the changes in the Politburo and Secretariat, they remained completely dominated by Zhivkov's cronies. Six of the Politburo's ten members are 68 or older, and two of them, Dzhurov and Yotov, have ties to Zhivkov that go back to the World War II partisan movement. In the months after the plenum Yotov seemed to take over Mikhailov's responsibility for ideological and cultural affairs and became the most visible party spokesman next to Zhivkov himself.

When Dimitur Stoyanov was made a member of both Politburo and Secretariat, he gave up the post of minister of the interior. He was replaced in this position by Georgi Tanev (*Sofia News*, 21 December). Tanev had been appointed minister of transport only three months previously but before had headed the party organization in the Kurdzhali district, the area of the largest concentration of ethnic Turks, where he earned a reputation for forcefulness.

Some issues of structural reform in the party were raised at the National Party Conference held 28–29 January. Although the proposals were far less radical than those advanced at the Central Committee plenum in June 1987 (see *YICA*, 1988), Zhivkov did suggest that the posts of state and party leadership should not be held by the same individual and that party officeholders be limited to two, or in exceptional cases three, terms. The conference took no immediate action on these or other proposals, deferring them to the BCP's Fourteenth Congress in 1991. (*RD*, 2 February; *FBIS*, 8 February; *Sofia News*, 3 February.)

The crash of a Balkan Airlines flight in Sofia and a major rail collision near the capital prompted the firing of Transport Minister Vasil Tsanov and three of his deputies amid charges of poor organization and discipline. Tsanov, a member of the BCP Central Committee who had held the post since 1973, was replaced by Georgi Tanev on 22 September.

When Tanev took over the Interior Ministry in December, he was replaced at transport by Trifon Pashev (b. 1936), who had headed the party organization in the Mikhailovgrad district. Two other ministerial changes were made in December. Professor Radoi Popivanov (b. 1913) retired as minister of public health and social welfare and was replaced by Dr. Mincho Peichev (b. 1936). Georgi Menov (b. 1933) replaced Aleksi Ivanov as minister of agriculture and forestry (*Sofia News*, 21 December). All four men involved in the last two changes were members of the BANU leadership.

Internal Affairs. *Social and political developments.* Events in the USSR and Zhivkov's apparent embrace of *glasnost'* and *perestroika* at the July 1987 plenum stimulated a level of public activism that was unprecedented for Bulgaria. Calls for a fuller and more honest evaluation of the past, voiced last year by some members of the literary intelligentsia, continued and gathered momentum. The English-language *Sofia News* inaugurated the series Remembrance, which was devoted to examining "the fate of Bulgarian political emigrés in the USSR and of the functionaries of the international communist and workers' movement who were repressed during the years of the personality cult." It began with the memoirs of Krustiu (Christian) Rakovski's niece, who recounted the story of her uncle's arrest in 1938 and called on historians to discover the truth about his death. Such discussions tarnished the legend of Georgi Dimitrov, head of the Comintern from 1935 to 1943, who was involved in the purges of many foreign communists. Later in the year the USSR announced that it would open Comintern archives to investigators from Eastern Europe, promising fresh revelations about the founder of Bulgaria's communist state.

Some organs of the press, particularly *Trud*, the trade union daily, exposed cases of high-level corruption. A small but persistent dissident organization, formed in January 1987, continued to draw international attention to the Bulgarian regime's violations of the Helsinki Accords. *Le Monde* (20 February) reported that four professors at the University of Sofia had been fired and expelled from the party after protesting Zhivkov's personality cult and the government's failure to institute genuine reforms. And many "voluntary associations" appeared that were independent of party influence. Their formation was first observed among young people, who ignored Komsomol activities in favor of spontaneously forming clubs devoted to Western rock stars and fashions. But far more ominous from the point of view of the government was the emergence of the ecological movement focused around the city of Russe.

In 1982 a Soviet-built chlorine and sodium combine was opened at Giurgiu on the Romanian side of the Danube. Owing to its methods of operation and to prevailing winds, it immediately created a major health problem for the approximately 200,000 inhabitants of Russe, Bulgaria's fourth largest city, where the incidence of lung disease and birth defects rose to catastrophic levels. The government, asserting its close, fraternal relations with Romania, maintained that the problem would be resolved in a cooperative spirit but was apparently unable to persuade the Romanians to reduce the level of pollution or even to acknowledge responsibility. Spontaneous demonstrations reportedly broke out in Russe during the fall of 1987, followed by the formation of a committee for the defense of the city that gained broad support. Although the committee's full membership cannot be determined, it included prominent members of Bulgaria's artistic and scientific elite and even important party figures. Among its leaders were Neshka Robeva, the coach of Bulgaria's world champion rhythmic gymnastics team and a deputy in the National Assembly; the artist Svetlin Rusev, director of the National Gallery of Fine Arts; and Sonia Bakish-Todorova, the wife of Politburo member Stanko Todorov. The committee also clearly had the support of the journals *Literaturen front* and *Narodna kultura* and of many spokesmen in the medical community, including Dr. Evgeni Nazarov, chief physician of Russe's municipal hospital. In December 1987 and January 1988 the committe held an art exhibition in Russe called Ecology—Russe '87, which displayed the works of local artists who depicted in the most graphic terms the suffering of the region and its people. The exhibit was accompanied by scientific and medical data on the levels of chlorine pollution in the air and on land and the rising incidence of lung disease and birth defects among the population. The exhibit was described by *Narodna kultura*, which also reprinted the statistical evidence. Soon afterward, the Union of Bulgarian Artists published an appeal to the country's intellectuals to take action to save a city living "in a state of chemical warfare" and warned of a "loss of faith" in the government's ability to improve the situation. It also quoted letters from Russe mothers comparing the city to Chernobyl or Bhopal and pleading with authorities to "save the lives of our children." Several days before a scheduled

meeting of the Bulgarian and Romanian prime ministers on 20 February, a mass demonstration was held in Russe that occasioned a strongly worded article in *Literaturen front* attributing the unrest in the city to the suffering of its population and to the government's efforts to suppress exposure of the situation and "not permit even a small outlet to relieve the people's souls from all the accumulated pain." (RFE, *Situation Report*, 11 February, 8 March.)

The public initiative for the defense of Russe, unprecedented in communist Bulgaria, clearly accelerated the regime's retreat from political and cultural reform. In late March a series of purges began in the intellectual community. (It may not be coincidental that these purges followed the publication in *Pravda* of the Nina Andreeva letter, which was critical of Gorbachev's reforms.) Damian Obreskov, editor in chief of *Trud*, was removed from his post, and the *Trud* journalist Georgi Tambuev, author of a hard-hitting series on corruption, was fired and subsequently expelled from the party. Evtim Evtimov was forced to resign as editor of *Literaturen front* amid charges that he had committed "literary-sociological demagoguery." Rusev was dismissed as director of the National Fine Arts Gallery. Robeva led Bulgaria's women gymnasts to the summer Olympics in Seoul but later announced her retirement to devote herself to the training of small children. (RFE, *Situation Report*, 27 May.)

These purges were followed by the announcement that a Central Committee Plenum would be held to discuss restructuring in intellectual life. Subsequently came the All-Army Party Conference at which Colonel Orlin Orlinov, editor of the military journal *Bulgarski voin*, attacked "the 'patriots' and 'humanitarians' who . . . are trying to deceive the whole people by pretending to be the only ones who really care for Bulgaria." The party and government, he continued, do not need moral admonitions but discipline, action, and the implementation of the party's program. Members of the creative intelligentsia in the military were lauded for using their talents to stimulate love for the motherland and for communism (*Narodna armiia*, 29 April; *FBIS*, 3 May). At the end of April, Zhivkov issued his "Considerations" on this problem, setting some clear limits on permissible activities. According to this document, problems now receiving attention in the USSR had long ago been dealt with in Bulgaria, specifically at the April 1956 Plenum that marked the beginning of Bulgarian de-Stalinization. Some elements in the Bulgarian intelligentsia, Zhivkov continued, mistakenly believed that the experience of Soviet reconstruction would automatically be transferred to Bulgaria. This was especially true regarding some "sensational" aspects of the past that were being revealed in the Soviet Union. But, he continued, restructuring must proceed in accordance with specific conditions prevailing in each country, so that despite Bulgaria's tradition of looking to Soviet experience, there was no need to repeat specific Soviet measures. The Bulgarian media should understand that *glasnost'* and restructuring mean "to support the new" and that the country does not need "complaints, moaning, and groaning that form an incorrect attitude towards restructuring."

On the issue of independent associations, Zhivkov stated that Bulgaria welcomed the idea of "socialist pluralism" but that it had to be *socialist* pluralism. Any deviation from this principle, he warned, would invite anarchy and would not be tolerated. Zhivkov was particularly severe in his criticism of the Union of Bulgarian Artists, whose governing board took "fateful decisions" concerning Bulgaria's relations with another state, and he added that "restructuring in these conditions is impossible."

Zhivkov called on the party to direct "socialist pluralism," stating it was a "time-honored tradition" that the party be the initiator of voluntary associations. He was severely critical of the party organizations in the cultural unions that had allowed the situation to get out of hand. And he denounced Central Committee Secretary Stoian Mikhailov in charge of ideological affairs for failing to ensure party leadership. He concluded by stating that the party welcomed the growing activization of public consciousness with its more intense discussions and dialogues but that "the tone must be met by the party, by the Central Committee." (*Sofia News*, 4 May.)

The plenum, held 19–20 July, endorsed Zhivkov's positions and announced the dismissals of Alexandrov, Todorov, and Mikhailov (described above). The principal address was given by Yotov, who echoed Zhivkov's "Considerations." Although a number of speakers pointed to real difficulties and shortcomings in the organization of Bulgaria's educational, cultural, and scientific institutions, actual reforms were deferred to future "congresses" that would deal with each area individually. (RFE, *Situation Report*, 29 July.)

The government heralded the creation of two "independent" committees: one devoted to the defense of the environment and the other to the pre-vention of human rights abuses. The membership of these committees was filled with prominent names, indicating that their activities would be kept within safe bounds (*Sofia News*, 8 June).

Seven individuals were placed on trial for a series of bombings that occurred in 1984. Three were sentenced to death by firing squad, and the others received prison sentences of one to five years. Although the press reported little about the motivation for the bombings, it is likely that they were a form of protest against the forced Bulgarization of the country's ethnic Turks. (*Sofia News*, 27 April; RFE, *Situation Report*, 27 May.)

Elections. The elections for mayors and regional and municipal councils, held on 28 February, were supposed to have been the first conducted under new regulations providing for multiple candidacies. In any event, more than one candidate was on the ballot in only one race out of five. In the rest, there was either no opposition or local elections commissions disqualified all but a single nominee. Approximately 99 percent of the registered voters cast ballots, with successful candidates receiving 89 percent of the vote. Of the more than 50,000 councillors elected, it was reported that 61 percent belonged to the BCP, 13 percent to the BANU, and 26 percent were independents. (BTA, 29 February; *FBIS*, 1 March; *Sofia News*, 2 March.)

Economy. According to the government's annual report, Bulgaria's domestic net material product grew during 1987 at a rate of 5.1 percent. The report did not clearly describe how this figure was arrived at, and it was not consistent with the growth rates given for various sectors of the economy. For example, total industrial production was said to have increased 4.1 percent, and yet agricultural production actually declined 3.8 percent. The problems in agriculture were attributed both to poor weather and to poor planning and organization. The low procurement prices set for grain and some other crops led agricultural managers to "misunderstand their freedom of choice under the new conditions of restructuring" because they apparently reduced the amount of sown acreage. (*RD*, 27 January; *FBIS*, 4 February.) Quarterly reports issued during the year stated that the 1988 economic performance was exceeding expectations.

In September, Zhivkov published a Politburo memorandum on the reorganization of agriculture that called for "the individual worker, the family, or the voluntarily formed collective" to become the basic unit of production. They would earn their living by selling the products of land leased to them for periods of up to 50 years. The land would be leased by the existing agro-industrial complexes (AICs). The memorandum stated that the AICs would continue to exist, although they are in need of "radical reform," and that the self-managing agricultural brigades created last year might or might not be continued. The memorandum called for a nationwide discussion of agricultural reform and announced that a Central Committee Plenum would tackle the issue. (RFE, *Situation Report*, 15 November.)

In January, the Krumovgrad AIC withdrew from the Association of the National Agro-Industrial Union complaining that its excessive bureaucracy drained off profits. At the end of the year, the decision to go it alone was pronounced a success, with the complex greatly increasing its efficiency and its workers dividing substantially increased bonuses (*Sofia News*, 13 January, 14 December).

Legislation adopted last year allows Bulgarian enterprises to bid for hard currency to purchase equipment from the West. The first auction, of $1 million supplied by the National Bank, saw bids as high as twelve levs to the dollar, with others approximating the black market rate of five to six levs (the official exchange rate is .85 levs to the dollar). The high profits earned through the sale will likely persuade enterprises possessing a surplus of hard currency to put it on the market in future auctions. (RFE, *Situation Report*, 29 July.)

In October the prices of several goods were sharply increased, prompting rumors of large-scale price hikes. Various brands of coffee increased 50 to 100 percent in price, sugar 50 to 80 percent, and the price of newspapers and magazines approximately doubled. Although Minister of Economy and Planning Ovcharov stated early in the year that prices in Bulgaria would eventually have to be pegged to the world market (*Sofia News*, 10 February), the government stated that this would be done very gradually and hastened to reassure the public that no other major price increases would be imposed this year (RFE, *Situation Report*, 24 October). The rise in the prices for newspapers and periodicals resulted from a reorganization of the press aimed at making journalistic enterprises self-financing and decreasing the need for state subsidies (RFE, *Situation Report*, 15 November).

AIDS. According to a government report issued in January after the testing of 365,799 people, 54 Bulgarian citizens were found to be carrying the AIDS virus. Because most of these cases were acquired through contact with foreigners, the government introduced mandatory testing for all Bulgarians who had been out of the country for more than one month and for all foreigners staying in Bulgaria for more than one month. The report stated that among the "high-risk" groups tested were 5,368 female prostitutes, 2,849 homosexuals, and 403 drug addicts. (*Sofia News*, 20 January.)

Auxiliary Organizations. A plenum of the central committee of the Dimitrov Communist Youth League, held on 15 January, made a number of organizational changes, Komsomol territorial units were altered to correspond to the national administrative reorganization carried out last year. The plenum also created five councils to specialize in work among young people in the following categories: industrial workers, agricultural workers, high school students, university students, and scientific workers. (*Narodna mladezh*, 16, 19 January; *FBIS*, 21 January.)

The Movement of Bulgarian Women hosted a delegation of International Women for a Productive Summit led by Margaret Papandreou, wife of the Greek prime minister. The women's groups discussed issues of peace and disarmament (BTA, 28 March; *FBIS*, 29 March). On 20 October the movement held its Fourth National Conference. After hearing an address by Zhivkov, the conference reelected Lagadinova as chairperson of its governing committee. (Sofia Domestic Service, 20 October; *FBIS*, 21 October.)

Tanchev, head of BANU, visited the Middle East and met with state leaders in Jordan, Iraq, and Egypt (*Sofia News*, 17 February). Tanchev also traveled to Italy for meetings with the leadership of the Christian Democratic Party (*Sofia News*, 24 February). A meeting of BANU's Supreme Council on 29 April heard an address by Zhivkov on restructuring. The council gave its strong approval and pledged BANU's full support for the BCP program (*Sofia News*, 4 May).

International Affairs. During the year Bulgaria continued to try to shed its image as a supporter of international terrorism. On 8 April the State Council ratified the International Convention Against the Taking of Hostages and accepted the obligation to extradite or punish perpetrators of terrorist acts arrested on its territory (*Otechestven front*, 8 April; *FBIS*, 13 April). Bulgarian athletes scored notable successes at the summer Olympics in Seoul, but their performance was tarnished when the weight lifters withdrew following the failure of some of them to pass drug tests.

The Soviet Union. Rumors persisted of mutual dislike between Gorbachev and Zhivkov. *Frankfurter Allgemeine Zeitung* (23 August) reported that the USSR had been given only a few hours notice before the purge of Chudomir Alexandrov, who had been meeting with Soviet leaders in Moscow only weeks before his dismissal. The purge was followed by several meetings between Zhivkov and high-ranking Soviet officials in Bulgaria, but nothing of substance about them was reported. On the surface, Bulgaria's relations with the Soviet Union remained very close. In September, Soviet Politburo member Lev Zaikov spent five days in Bulgaria meeting with Zhivkov and signing a comprehensive agreement on cooperation among party, trade union, and youth organizations (*RD*, 15 September; *FBIS*, 19 September). In March, Viktor Sharapov replaced Leonid Grekov, who had served a normal term, as ambassador to Bulgaria (RFE, *Situation Report*, 8 April).

Other East European and Balkan countries. In the past Bulgaria generally avoided participation in multinational or regional approaches to Balkan issues, preferring to deal with its neighbors on a bilateral basis and stressing its alliance with the USSR as the cornerstone of its foreign policy. Consequently, Bulgaria's enthusiastic participation in the conference of Balkan foreign ministers, held in Belgrade during 24–26 February, represented a new departure. Bulgarian diplomats recognized this and described it as a result of Soviet initiatives to reduce tension in Europe between the North Atlantic Treaty Organization and the Warsaw Pact. The conference avoided the difficult areas of territorial and ethnic disputes and focused instead on the development of regional cooperation in trade, communications, environmental protection, tourism, and cultural affairs. The conference communiqué called for a further series of meetings devoted to specific issues to be held during the course of the year. (*Sofia News*, 2 March; RFE, *Situation Report*, 8 March.) The first of these, held in Sofia during 21–23 June, was attended by deputy foreign ministers and was devoted to establishing a framework for further cooperation. It approved the creation of a research institute on Balkan economic cooperation to be opened in Athens and scheduled a series of meetings of experts on various issues for this and the coming year. (*Sofia News*, 29 June; RFE, *Situation Report*, 29 July.)

An important by-product of the Balkan foreign ministers' conference was the signing of a separate protocol between Bulgaria and Turkey aimed at reducing the level of hostility between the two states that resulted from the forced Bulgarization of the Turkish minority that Sofia carried out in 1984 and 1985. Since then, Turkey has adopted a belligerent attitude and sought to mount an international campaign, particularly among the Islamic nations, in defense of Bulgaria's ethnic Turks. This campaign had little success, and the Turkish government apparently decided to settle for minor concessions. According to the protocol signed by Petŭr Mladenov and Turkish foreign minister Mesut Yilmaz, two Bulgarian-Turkish commissions would be established: the first to discuss "humanitarian issues" and to prepare a declaration on good-neighborliness, friendship, and cooperation and the second to discuss issues of trade, transport, and communications. (BTA, 23 February; *FBIS*, 24 February; *Sofia News*, 2 March.) Both commissions began discussions "in an atmosphere of understanding and cooperation" during May (BTA, 12 May; *FBIS*, 13 May). Bulgaria allowed 64 children of Turkish descent to be united with their parents in Turkey and agreed to allow the Bulgarian-born weight lifter Naim Suleymanoglu, who defected to Turkey in 1986, to compete in the Olympics under the Turkish flag (RFE, *Situation Report*, 8 March). Although talks on various issues continued during the year, the improvement in relations suffered a setback in September when a member of Bulgaria's National Assembly defected to Turkey. Seydiye Tahiroglu (who had been forced to take the name Sevda Taskova during the period of forced Bulgarization) explained that she had been sent to the National Assembly against her will and agreed to serve only when she learned that deputies are given diplomatic passports. She used hers to take her son and husband to Greece and then to Turkey, where she denounced Bulgaria's policy of forced assimilation. (RFE, *Situation Report*, 24 October.)

Since the election of the Panhellenic Socialist Movement (PASOK) government, Bulgaria has had unusually warm relations with Greece. During 22–23 February, Greek prime minister Andreas Papandreou visited Sofia, where he was received by Zhivkov. The two leaders reportedly discussed the expansion of trade and tourism and pledged to work for greater cooperation between the Council for

Mutual Economic Assistance (CMEA) and the European Economic Community (EEC) (BTA, 23 February; *FBIS*, 24 February).

The issue of Macedonia has soured Bulgaria's relations with Yugoslavia in the past. This year polemics on the question were strikingly absent from the press in both countries, and the Bulgarian media were very circumspect in reporting on Yugoslavia's internal difficulties. In October, Zhivkov received Gligorie Gogovski, president of the Executive Council of the Macedonian Republic. They discussed measures to improve Bulgaria's economic relations with Yugoslavia and with the Macedonian republic in particular (BTA, 27 October; *FBIS*, 28 October).

In the wake of the protests in Russe, Bulgaria and Romania agreed to establish a joint commission to investigate the problem of chlorine pollution (RFE, *Situation Report*, 8 March).

Bulgaria's relations with Albania continued to improve. In January the two countries raised their diplomatic missions to ambassadorial status (BTA, 25 January; *FBIS*, 26 January).

Miloš Jakeš, general secretary of the Central Committee of the Czechoslovak Communist Party, met with Zhivkov in Sofia during 20–21 April. The two leaders discussed general problems of restructuring and democratization and signed an agreement on economic, scientific, and technical cooperation through the year 2000 (*RD*, 21 April; *FBIS*, 25 April).

Polish leader Wojciech Jaruzelski made a one-day visit to Bulgaria on 30 September. After his meeting with Zhivkov, the two heads of state signed agreements on interparty cooperation in the fields of ideology, science, and culture through the year 2000 and on economic, scientific, and technical cooperation to the year 2005 (BTA, 30 September; *FBIS*, 3 October).

Western Europe and the United States. West Germany is Bulgaria's largest Western trading partner. In November Richard von Weizsaecker, president of the Federal Republic, and Foreign Minister Hans-Dietrich Genscher came to Sofia, returning the visit Zhivkov made to Bonn the previous year. The two sides agreed to establish four working groups on humanitarian, cultural, and economic cooperation and on developing relations between the EEC and the CMEA. They also agreed to open national cultural centers in Sofia and Munich. (*Sofia News*, 23 November.)

Prince Albert of Belgium led a delegation to Sofia at the end of October for talks on expanding economic contacts. He discussed with Zhivkov the role of Belgian banks and businesses in developing the Bulgarian economy, particularly in the areas of joint enterprises and consortia (BTA, 25 October; *FBIS*, 27 October).

Contacts between American and Bulgarian officials increased significantly during the year. Deputy Secretary of State John Whitehead visited Sofia twice, and Foreign Minister Mladenov held private talks with Secretary of State George Shultz following his speech to the U.N. in October. On these occasions both sides expressed the hope for a continued improvement in relations, but no specific measures were announced. Andrey Lukanov, candidate member of the Politburo and minister of foreign trade, visited the United States in May, conferring with Secretary Shultz in Washington and holding a press conference on Bulgarian restructuring in the offices of the *Wall Street Journal* in New York. He went on to visit several other American cities, meeting with local business groups to promote expanded Bulgarian-American trade (BTA, 2 May; *FBIS*, 3 May). Approximately fifty Bulgarian enterprises joined a Bulgarian-American Trade and Economic Council. Konstantin Glavanakov, deputy minister of foreign economic relations, was elected chairman of its Bulgarian section (BTA, 20 October; *FBIS*, 24 October). At year's end Bulgaria became the last member of the Warsaw Pact to end jamming of broadcasts by Radio Free Europe (*WP*, 28 December).

Other countries. Ali Salim al-Biedh, general secretary of the Central Committee of the Yemeni Socialist Party, visited Bulgaria during 12–16 May. He and Zhivkov announced their common views on Middle Eastern issues and called for continued improvement in economic and cultural ties between Bulgaria and the People's Democratic Republic of (South) Yemen (BTA, 16 May; *FBIS*, 17 May).

Bulgaria extended recognition to the Palestinian state proclaimed by the Palestine Liberation Organization (PLO) and raised the status of the PLO mission to Sofia to embassy level (*Sofia News*, 14 December).

Bulgarian tourism authorities approved the operation of direct charter flights between Bulgaria and Israel. An Israeli-owned company was expected to begin selling package tours in the summer of 1989 (*Ha'aretz*, 8 August; *FBIS*, 11 August).

A Bulgarian delegation led by Politburo member Kubadinski visited China in May to attend the

Eighth Congress of the Chinese Communist Party and to follow up Zhivkov's visit to China last year. An agreement was signed between Bulgaria's Fatherland Front and the National Council of the Chinese People's Political Consultative Committee that provided for regular exchanges of working groups and delegations (BTA, 20 May; *FBIS*, 27 May).

John D. Bell
University of Maryland, Baltimore County

Czechoslovakia

Population. 15,620,722
Party. Communist Party of Czechoslovakia (Komunistická strana Českoslovanska; KSČ)
Founded. 1921
Membership. 1,705,490 (*Rudé právo*, 3 September 1987)
General Secretary. Miloš Jakeš
Presidium. 15 full members: Ladislav Adamec (federal prime minister), Vasil Bil'ák, Jan Fojtík, Karel Hoffmann, Gustáv Husák (president of the republic), Alois Indra, Miloš Jakeš, Ignác Janák, Josef Kempný, Ivan Knotek, Jozef Lenárt, František Pitra, Miroslav Štěpán, Karel Urbánek, Miroslav Zavadil; 3 candidate members: Josef Haman, Vladimír Herman, Miloslav Hruškovič
Secretariat. 8 secretaries: Mikuláš Beno, Vasil Bil'ák, Jan Fojtík, František Hanuš, Karel Hoffmann, Miloš Jakeš (general secretary), Jozef Lenárt, František Pitra; 7 secretariat members: Zdeněk Hoření, Marie Kabrhelová, Josef Mevald, Vasil Mohorita, Jindřich Poledník, Rudolf Rohlíček, Miroslav Štěpán
Control and Auditing Commission. Jaroslav Hajn, chairman
Central Committee. 135 full and 62 candidate members
Status. Ruling party
Last Congress. Seventeenth, 24–28 March 1986, in Prague; next congress scheduled for 1991
Slovak Party. Communist Party of Slovakia (Komunistická strana Slovenska; KSS); membership: 436,000 full and candidate members; Jozef Lenárt, first secretary; Presidium: 11 mem-

bers; Central Committee: 91 full and 31 candidate members
Last Election. 1986, 99.94 percent, all 350 National Front candidates; 66 percent of seats reserved for KSČ candidates
Auxiliary Organizations. Revolutionary Trade Union Movement (Eleventh Congress, April 1987), Cooperative Farmers' Union, Socialist Youth Union (Fourth Congress, October 1987), Union for Collaboration with the Army, Czechoslovak Union of Women, Union of Fighters for Peace
Main State Organs. The executive body is the federal government, which is subordinate to the 350-member Federal Assembly, composed of the Chamber of the People (200 members) and the Chamber of the Nations (150 members). The assembly, however, merely rubber-stamps all decisions made by the KSČ Presidium and Central Committee.
Publications. *Rudé právo*, KSČ daily; *Pravda* (Bratislava), KSS daily; *Tribuna*, Czech-language ideological weekly; *Predvoj*, Slovak-language ideological weekly; *Život strany*, fortnightly journal devoted to administrative and organizational questions; *Práce* (Czech) and *Práca* (Slovak), Revolutionary Trade Union Movement dailies; *Mladá fronta* (Czech) and *Smena* (Slovak), Socialist Youth Union dailies; *Tvorba*, weekly devoted to domestic and international politics; *Nová mysl*, theoretical monthly. Československá Tisková Kancelář (ČTK) is the official news agency.

The KSČ developed from the left wing of the Czechoslovak Social Democratic Party, having co-opted several radical socialist and leftist groups. It was constituted in Prague and admitted to the Communist International the same year. Its membership in the Comintern, however, was an uneasy one until in 1929 the so-called Bolshevization process was completed and a leadership of unqualified obedience to the Soviet Union assumed control. During the First Czechoslovak Republic (1918–1939), the KSČ enjoyed legal status, but it was banned after the Munich Agreement. After the war, it emerged as the strongest party in the postwar elections of 1946, although it did not poll a majority of votes. In February 1948, the KSČ seized all power in a coup d'état and transformed Czechoslovakia into a communist party-state of the Soviet type. The departure from Stalinist practices started later in Czechoslovakia than in other countries of Central and Eastern

Europe, but it led to a daring liberalization experience known as the Prague Spring of 1968. A Soviet-led military intervention by five Warsaw Pact countries in August of the same year ended the democratization course and imposed on Czechoslovakia the policies of so-called normalization—a return to unreserved subordination to the will of the Soviet Union and the emulation of the Soviet example in all areas of social life. Unqualified obedience to the Soviet power center, however, need not be identical with the pursuit of the present conservative, antireformist course; this became obvious in 1987.

Party Internal Affairs. The year 1988 was an important one in the history of the KSČ not so much on account of what the party undertook but rather what it endeavored to avoid, ignore, or postpone; for this reason the observers of the political scene in Central and Eastern Europe closely followed the events in Czechoslovakia. The Czechoslovak communist party-state stayed on its cautious conservative course which it had embarked on after the Soviet-led military intervention of August 1968. This course was often defined by its proponents as one of "normalization," but in the rapidly changing situation in the Soviet Union and other countries of the Soviet bloc it was perceived as an absurd anomaly. Although Czechoslovakia's reputation was that of a "model satellite" since the forcible interruption of the liberal reforms introduced by KSČ first secretary Alexander Dubček, it was among the most reluctant followers of the new line initiated by Mikhail Gorbachev in the USSR. In reality, of course, there was no inconsistency in the KSČ position: it continued to adhere to the principles established by the now defunct Brezhnev team, who twenty years earlier had put the present party bosses into positions of power.

The dilemma facing the leadership of the KSČ in 1988 was serious and had several aspects, above all, the question of its true allegiance. On this point there could be hardly any doubt: it continued to belong to the Soviet Union. Unconditional loyalty to the USSR in 1988, however, would negate or put into doubt the very beliefs in the name of which the present leaders had assumed their functions in April 1969 and take away the regime's tenuous raison d'être. Open opposition to the Soviet reform trend, although theoretically conceivable (precisely because of Gorbachev's implicit renunciation of the Brezhnev Doctrine), would require seeking substantial domestic support that could only be obtained at the price of considerable concessions to the population at large. Such concessions would be tantamount to—but probably in excess of—those made by the Dubček team during the brief period of the Prague Spring. The leading group of today, with General Secretary Jakeš at the head, would probably not survive their impact. Thus the practical result of these contradictory factors and pressures was a stalemate or a slow, dilatory adjustment to the new situation.

The individual decisions and statements made by various party leaders and organs during the year reflected this complex attitude. In his New Year's address, President Gustáv Husák, who shortly before had relinquished the post of secretary general but retained the top executive function in the state, endorsed the *perestroika* program of Mikhail Gorbachev. However, he stressed its economic part without commenting in detail on its political component and passed in silence Gorbachev's call for *glasnost'* (*NYT*, 2 January). Presidium member and federal Prime Minister Lubomír Štrougal, however, gave an interview to a group of West German journalists in which he declared that "things [in Czechoslovakia] must change, even if it means temporary crises" (*Frankfurter Rundschau*, 22 January). Husák also commented on an earlier interview of former KSČ first secretary Dubček in the Italian Communist Party daily *L'Unità* (10 January) and stated that in his opinion "this country [Czechoslovakia] needs reforms" but that "the political leadership has until now always failed in this task" and that Dubček in 1968 "was too weak a man for that kind of historical period." He even indicated that "a differentiated process of rapprochement" between the reformers of the Prague Spring and those of *perestroika* had already begun (*Frankfurter Rundschau*, 26 January). This apparently more conciliatory position was also adopted by Central Committee secretary Jan Fojtík in his interview with Hungarian television where he admitted that "the Prague Spring was, indeed, a process of renewal and democratization." He added, however, that "a group in the leadership failed to live up to the expectations." (MTI, in English, 5 February.)

These more moderate assessments of the liberalization period of 1968 were in sharp contrast to other comments from the KSČ, such as the editorial in *Rudé právo* published on the 20th anniversary of the Central Committee (CC) meeting that elected Dubček to his leading function (4 January), which charged that the Prague Spring had actually aimed at "dismantling socialism." Also, the party media emphasized at the start of the year that there was no similarity between the reform program of Dubček and *perestroika* in the USSR (Radio Prague, 3 January). The 40th anniversary of the communist coup d'état, celebrated in February, provided another opportunity to articulate the leadership's views on sensitive contemporary issues. General Secretary Jakeš declared at a meeting of five hundred party officials at Prague Castle that *perestroika* was "the continuation of the revolution under new conditions." He added, however, that there was "a chasm of difference between the restructuring process in the USSR and our country today and the intentions of the right-wing elements in 1968" (*Rudé právo*, 25 February). Jakeš elaborated on these points in a later interview given to *Time* magazine (18 April). Honoring two prominent architects of the "normalization" course—President Husák and CC secretary Jan Fojtík on their 75th and 60th birthdays respectively—Jakeš underscored his will to continue the given line (Radio Prague, 7 January; *Rudé právo*, 9 April).

The plenary session of the CC, held 8–9 April, brought some changes in the composition of the party governing bodies but none that seemed to indicate an impending shift in the policies. The postponement of two diplomatic visits to Prague—Austrian federal chancellor Franz Vranitzky and U.S. Information Agency director Charles Wick—at the request of the Czechoslovak government with explicit reference to the forthcoming CC session, made foreign commentators wonder whether a major modification of the political course might be in the making. This did not materialize, however. At the session, Antonín Kapek, Presidium member and secretary of the influential Prague municipal party committee, and Josef Havlín, the CC secretary in charge of culture and education, were relieved of their functions. Presidium candidate members Fojtík and Janák became full members. Hanuš, regional party secretary in central Bohemia, became CC secretary; at a subsequent meeting of the CC of the Communist Party of Slovakia (KSS), Lenárt relinquished the post of KSS first secretary and was replaced by Janák. Josef Haman was no longer a KSČ Central Committee secretary but remained a candidate member of the Presidium. Poledník was released from the function of CC secretary and became a member at large of the Secretariat. Mohorita, chairman of the Socialist Youth Union, and Štěpán of the Prague Municipal KSČ Committee also became CC Secretariat members (*Rudé právo*, 10 April). The departing officials

as well as the three newcomers were all firmly committed to the "normalization" line.

A series of district party conferences following the CC plenum did not bring any significant change in KSČ politics, merely rubber-stamping the decisions made in Prague. That the CC meeting preceded these conferences—as it always had—testified to the unchanged concept of "party democracy," a "democratic centralism" of Stalinist vintage (*Rudé právo*, 23 April). Before these events, the party announced the expulsion of two, and reprimands of several, high officials involved in the "Babinský case" (*Rudé právo*, 20 February). Stanislav Babinský, the principal defendant in the trial that prompted the party sanctions (see also *YICA*, 1988), claimed that many more top party leaders were implicated in this illegal business (private entertainment at the expense of the state) including Foreign Minister Bohuslav Chňoupek and Peter Colotka, Presidium member and federal deputy prime minister. Their resignations and retreat from political life in October 1988 (see below) may have partly been in connection with the Babinský affair.

The Czechoslovak version of *perestroika*, even stripped of its political component, did not make much headway during the year. General Secretary Jakeš stated in early June that "nothing much has changed yet" and that "restructuring must become a matter of virtually every citizen" to overcome what he called "stagnant waters" (Radio Prague, 7 June). On the following day, the party main daily carried in a prominent place a "letter by a simple Czechoslovak worker" complaining that "central bureaucrats" were preventing the state enterprises from exercising their autonomy and that economic reform in Czechoslovakia was facing the same difficulties as *perestroika* in the USSR (*Rudé právo*, 8 June). Later in the year, Bořivoj Málek, a scientist and inventor, described in a radio interview how, owing to bureaucratic procedures, it took about eighteen years for a new discovery to be produced (Radio Prague, 8 August). In spite of numerous grievances and criticisms, the regime did not appear willing to admit that many problems were due to the suppression of the reformist program of 1968. In frequent polemics with the main protagonist of the reform course—former First Party Secretary Dubček, who reiterated his views on several occasions in Western media (*Life*, June; Rome, *Avanti*, 5 July; Austrian television, 7 July; *Stern*, 8 August) and in a speech at the University of Bologna, where he received an honorary doctorate (AP, 13 November)—Czechoslovak official spokesmen continued to affirm that the period of the Prague Spring had been one of deviations and dangerous crises and that Dubček was guilty of "conceit and megalomania" and thus became "a figure for foreign manipulation" (*Rudé právo*, 16 July).

A small concession to Gorbachev's call for *glasnost'* by the KSČ in 1988 was the Measures to Improve the Information System Inside the Party released by the CC Secretariat in the spring (*Život strany*, 23 May). These measures were supposed to give the rank and file more access to hitherto confidential information and data. Whether this would help restore the shaken confidence of the party members in their present leaders was unclear. In November, Miroslav Válek, minister of culture of the Slovak Republic, declared that Czechoslovakia's restructuring needed firm guarantees to enlist the cooperation of the population. Válek conceded that the mass expulsions from the party in 1970, with the concomitant wave of job dismissals, had traumatized the society. He also suggested that the grievances articulated by various dissident groups such as Charter '77 should be carefully listened to ⌐n analyzed (*Rudé právo*, 15 November). The fol-)wing day, General Secretary Jakeš, in his address ɔ the KSČ regional organization in Hradec ƙrálové, advanced the idea that the participation of he broad strata in the reconstruction efforts might)e better assured if executive posts in the govern- nent and civil service were also open to noncom- nunists (Radio Prague, 16 November). His pro- posal, if serious, would make significant inroads into the system of *nomenklatura*, more scru- pulously applied in Czechoslovakia than in any other communist party-state.

Major decisions on the highest levels of the party, however, seemed to contradict these isolated manifestations of flexibility and insight. The CC plenary meetings of 10–11 October carried out a number of changes in the tenure of the various party funtions, followed by a change in the federal gov- ernment. In the party Presidium, Prime Minister Lubomír Štrougal and Deputy Premier Peter Colo- tka submitted their resignations. Five new members were elected to the Presidium: Knotek, Pitra, Štěpán, Urbánek, and Zavadil, thus enlarging the supreme executive body of the KSČ from twelve to fifteen members. Josef Mevald and Rudolf Rohlí- ček were co-opted as members of the Secretariat replacing Pitra and Poledník (Radio Prague, 12 October). A new federal government was con- stituted shortly afterward with Adamec as prime

minister, Jaromír Johanes as minister of foreign affairs, and František Kincl as minister of the inte- rior. They replaced Štrougal, Bohuslav Chňoupek, and Vratislav Vajnar, respectively (*Svobodné slovo*, 13 October). Considering that all newly elected officials belonged to the centrist or even right-of- center tendency, the recast of the two most impor- tant party and state organs did not suggest any significant modification of the current political line. Some commentators, among them dissident Rudolf Slánský, son of the former KSČ general secretary (executed in 1952), viewed it as a conservative victory that would set back the country's develop- ment (*L'Unità*, Rome, 21 October).

Domestic Affairs. The regime's policies con- cerning internal issues exhibited a similar reluc- tance toward needed reforms as it did toward the management of party affairs, occasionally punctu- ated by small concessions in various fields. A year of a number of important anniversaries, 1988 pro- vided several occasions for a confrontation between the conservative position of the KSČ leadership and the broad public, which began to articulate alter- native views on many problems. The three most significant dates were the 40th anniversary of the communist coup d'état (25 February), the 20th an- niversary of the Soviet-led military intervention against the reformist course of Dubček (21 August), and the 70th anniversary of Czechoslovak indepen- dence (28 October). In all three cases, public opin- ion forced the regime into a defensive, if not apolo- getic, stand. The precariousness and inconsistency of the regime's position became especially clear in connection with the anniversary of the founding of the Czechoslovak Republic in October. After hav- ing initially claimed that Czechoslovak indepen- dence in 1918 had been an offshoot of the Russian Bolshevik Revolution of 1917 and that the First Czechoslovak Republic had been a reactionary bourgeois-capitalist state where the working class suffered oppression at the hands of T. G. Masaryk and Beneš (*WMR*, May), the party entirely reversed itself. Shortly before 28 October, Fojtík, party chief ideologist, admitted in his speech at the CC plenum that the interpretation of the events of 1918 by the KSČ had been "one-sided" in the past (*Svobodné slovo*, 12 October). As a concrete step toward re- dress, the government made 28 October again a national holiday (since 1948 it had been remem- bered as the anniversary of the first round of na- tionalization, but it had been a working day). Com- memoration festivities, held in Czechoslovakia as well as abroad, were sponsored by Czechoslovak diplomatic representatives. A second-rank governmental delegation deposited a wreath at the grave of Masaryk in Lány (*Rudé právo*, 28, 29 October).

There were no signs, however, that these concessions to precommunist traditions would be paralleled by meaningful changes in political institutions. Not even reforms such as those introduced in the Soviet Union by the national conference of the Communist Party of the Soviet Union (CPSU) in May (election of nonparty members into the legislature, several candidates competing for every party and state office, etc.) were suggested or contemplated. General Secretary Jakeš became chairman of the National Front in which the KSČ continues to hold two-thirds of all seats and thus also a two-thirds majority in all legislative bodies at the federal and state levels (Radio Prague, 3 February). The call by Deputy Chairman Tomáš Trávníček for "more real participation of the individual components of the National Front in policymaking" (Radio Hvězda, 11 February), echoed by Fojtík at the 10th KSČ CC plenum (*Svobodné slovo*, 12 October), could only be viewed as rhetoric. The example of Soviet reform was followed only in a purely formal way, insofar as the number of ministries and central administrative bodies was reduced by 30 percent (Radio Prague, 26 March, 19 April). The changes in the composition of the party top administrative bodies decreed by the 9th plenum in April also entailed some changes in the national government. These, however, were not radical in any sense, and neither were those carried out after the 10th plenum; they rather confirmed the continuity of the conservative course (*Rudé právo*, 22 April; *Svobodné slovo*, 13 October).

A few steps intended to improve communist Czechoslovakia's image in the free world were undertaken in 1988. In January, Václav Štafek, chairman of the Foreign Relations Committee of the federal Parliament, pleaded for "contacts with all compatriots abroad who have a sincere and honest attitude toward our Republic," which—as he explicitly stated—would also mean revising the official assessment toward emigration after 1948 (ČTK, 20 January). At the request of the KSČ Presidium, the federal Ministry of the Interior submitted proposals to the federal Assembly that purported to simplify the procedures "dealing with unification of families, travels by Czechoslovak citizens to nonsocialist states, and problems resulting from unauthorized emigration" (Radio Prague, 15 April). A simplification concerning travel to the West in general was effected (Radio Prague, 30 April), but the allocation of hard currency to individual travelers remained a principal obstacle. Another gesture of conciliation could be seen in the decision to discontinue the jamming of the Radio Free Europe broadcasts shortly after the Soviet Union stopped jamming the programs of Radio Liberty. Jamming the Czech- and Slovak-language broadcasts of Voice of America and other official agencies of the Western countries (*Deutsche Welle*, *Radiodiffusion Française*) had already been abandoned. Voice of America established official contacts with Czechoslovakia in 1987 and was granted the use of Czechoslovak programming and transmitting facilities.

Public health care, traditionally a point of pride with communist party-states, came under repeated fire, as it was argued that Czechoslovakia was falling behind world standards (*Práce*, 30 August). A main reason for concern was the rapidly deteriorating environment. Jan Vodehnal, minister of agriculture and nutrition of the Czech Republic, admitted that the general public regards the degree of the contamination of basic foodstuffs, such as milk and meat, as almost catastrophical (*Mladá fronta*, 4 August). Other government spokesmen found that "the officials are responding rather reluctantly to the frightening reports circulating among the public [about the poisoning of food]" (*Zemědělské noviny*, 19 August). Although the general awareness of various ecological threats became keener in 1988, little was undertaken by the regime. Two regions of the country, northern Bohemia where the air pollution from the use of soft coal reached alarming proportions (*Mladá fronta*, 12 November 1987) and southwestern Slovakia with the capital city of Bratislava (*Pravda*, Bratislava, 4 February), seemed to be the center of attention for the ecologically conscious. In the environs of Bratislava, a controversial joint Hungarian-Czechoslovak dam project between the towns of Nagymáros and Gabčíkovo was, in the opinion of its critics, causing irreparable damage to the water and the forests. This dispute, which began in 1986, continued in 1988 (*Nové slovo*, 19 February). There was also widespread uneasiness about the safety level of the nuclear plants, especially after the Chernobyl incident in the USSR. Czechoslovak energy experts conferred with Soviet deputy premier Ivan Silayev on this problem in Prague early in the year (ČTK, 22 February). The purpose of this meeting might also have been to pacify public opinion. A resolution on environmental protection, adopted by the federal government in the summer, banned the construction of new nuclear facilities that lacked adequate environmental safeguards (Radio Prague, 26 July).

The armed forces. Owing to their special significance in domestic and international politics, the Soviet troops deployed in Czechoslovakia since the military intervention of 1968 played an equally important role as the Czechoslovak army proper. According to Western sources, the strength of the Soviet garrisons in Czechoslovakia was estimated at 83,000 in 1988 (Bonn, *Soldat und Technik*, January). These units belonged to the so-called Central Group of Forces of the Red Army and were believed to be better trained and equipped than their Czechoslovak counterparts. In 1988 they stood under the command of Colonel General Edvard A. Voroblev. The tactical nuclear missiles at their disposal—39 SS-12s—are now targeted for removal as part of the Soviet disarmament program. The short-range missile withdrawal began in February (ČTK, 24 February), shortly after the meeting of the foreign ministers of the Warsaw Pact in Prague, where Eduard Shevardnadze briefed his colleagues on his talk with U.S. secretary of state George Shultz (Radio Prague, 23 February). This step and Gorbachev's intention, in January 1989, to reduce Soviet military presence in all countries of Central and Eastern Europe are important political gestures, especially to Czechoslovakia.

In connection with the 1968 agreement about the "temporary location of Soviet units in the Czechoslovak territory," Marshal Viktor Kulikov, General Anatolii Gribkov, and Marshal Nikolai Ogarkov visited Prague and were received by General Secretary Jakeš (Radio Prague, 23 June; ČTK, 2 September). The Soviet military presence caused not only problems of fundamental political nature but also friction with the local population. The inhabitants in the neighborhood of Soviet military bases often complained about the troops' behavior: noise, drunkenness, mass buyouts of all available commodities, as well as the commanders' interference with the peaceful life of the communities, especially ruthless invasions of people's privacy in search of deserters and other miscreants (*Ze zásuvky i z bloku*, 17 June). The Czechoslovak army itself participated in joint exercises with the Soviet units in Bohemia in March to which 43 observers from 22 countries were invited (Radio Prague, 27 March). Later in the year, domestic maneuvers code-named *Šumava* (Bohemian Forest) 1988 took place involving seventeen thousand men; delegates from nineteen signatory states of the Helsinki Agreement on European Security were present (ČTK, 6 June).

The lack of interest among eligible young men in pursuing a military career—reflected in the low number of applicants to officers' schools—persisted in 1988 (Bratislava, *Práca*, 10 June). The military has never enjoyed high occupational prestige in Czechoslovakia, but this was even more true in 1988. In March, a petition by 60 well-known personalities, including writer Václav Havel and former Foreign Minister Jiří Hájek, was submitted to the Conference on European Peace and Security in Vienna, pleading for recognition by Czechoslovak authorities of the right of conscientious objectors not to serve in the military, which was guaranteed by the Helsinki Agreement (Prague, AFP, 18 March). The year 1988 also saw a group of ten U.S. inspectors on the missile sites in Czechoslovakia verifying compliance with the Intermediate-range Nuclear Forces (INF) treaty (ČTK, 21 July). In May, federal Defense Minister Milan Václavík went to Vienna to discuss with his Austrian colleague Robert Lichal "questions of common concern in the area of security policies" (Radio Prague, 9 May).

The economy. The Czechoslovak economy, like the economies of other communist party-states, confronted in 1988 a number of serious problems that, again like the rest of the Soviet bloc, provided arguments for the reform of the system. However, the urgency of these problems being notably lower in Czechoslovakia than, for example, in neighboring Poland, the relatively better performance of the economy was invoked by the leadership to counteract its lack of popularity and its slowness in adopting the model of the Soviet reform program, especially such political aspects as *glasnost'*. Given that the Czechoslovak version of *perestroika* (in Czech *přestavba*, which means "reconstruction," not "restructuring") was the fourth major economic reform program since 1948, the skepticism of the population as to its ultimate success was commensurate with the establishment's reluctance. In public statements, of course, the spokesmen of the regime unreservedly endorsed the economic component of the restructuring program. Party chief ideologist and Presidium candidate member Jan Fojtík claimed in an extensive article published early in the year that "an anachronistic system of bureaucratic centralism and related deformations of socialist democracy" continued to be major obstacles to the development of socialism in Czechoslovakia

(*Hospodářské noviny*, 8 January). The main KSČ daily saw "the unchanged economic environment within which the experimenting enterprises have to operate" as being "the primary barrier to a more efficient application of the experiment" (*Rudé právo*, 7 March).

Following a government decision, the new state enterprises adopted a two-pronged system of self-financing while remaining subject to central planning (Radio Hvězda, 11 February). This approach created difficulties because the managers of the state firms were denied full authority over their plants but had to face all the financial risks (*Rudé právo*, 15 July). Also because of the purely quantitative production targets imposed on them by the central planning board, they had to meet these targets regardless of their costs and balance sheets (*Rudé právo*, 16 June). This method was also in conflict with the very principles of economic reform as spelled out in the Law on the Enterprises promulgated by the Federal Assembly (Radio Prague, 14 June). Preserving the institution of central planning was essential to the regime, even at the price of imperiling the entire process of reconstruction, so "the party's leading role could be thoroughly safeguarded," which in 1988 appeared to be the main concern of the KSČ leadership (*Život strany*, no. 1, 3 January).

Although this contradiction was a serious impediment to the professed reform, other factors were also blamed for its slow progress: sabotage by officials of the central governing bodies who "used refined and effective methods to block the economic measures" (Radio Prague, 11 September); "those responsible for Czechoslovakia's economic plight now want to preside over the reforms but can hardly expect people to trust them" (*Rudé právo*, 7 October); and deeply ingrained wage egalitarianism that prevented differentiated compensation based on individual performance and caused low productivity of labor" (Miloš Jakeš in *Time*, 18 April). Some even thought that the reforms were not radical enough. The party Presidium in January called for more privately run businesses, services, or small cooperatives (*Rudé právo*, 7 January). Valtr Komárek of the Economic Forecasting Department of the Academy of Sciences declared that the nationalization of small crafts and services effected after the seizure of power by the KSČ in 1948 had been "sheer nonsense" (*Hospodářské noviny*, 14 October).

The assessment of the prospects of economic reform and the future of the Czechoslovak economy gave rise to a sharp exchange between the conservative elements in control and other, more open quarters. A study by the Academy of Sciences commissioned in 1987 confronted the official view represented by Jaromír Obzina, deputy prime minister and chairman of the State Board for Scientific, Technical and Investment Development, with those of three leading economists: Václav Kupka, Michal Spak, and Jan Klacek. Obzina asserted that Czechoslovakia by the year 2000 would be technically independent from the industrially developed countries of the world; the economists in the study argued that "a simple look into the economic future [of Czechoslovakia] can suggest only stagnation and indebtedness." They pointed out that "even the hoped-for steady growth figure of 3.5–4 percent, if it materialized, would not improve the international position that Czechoslovakia had held since the mid-1980s" (*Rudé právo*, 28 March; *Investiční výstavba*, no. 1, January). Actually, the predicted growth rate proved to be too optimistic. After the midyear economic report was published in July, the performance of the national economy was severely criticized by Václav Vertelář, first deputy chairman of the State Planning Board, as "inadequate and ridden with disproportions" (Radio Prague, 26 July). Shortly afterward, the growth figures were revised downward, from 3.5 percent to 2.2 percent in 1989 and 3 percent in 1990 (*Rudé právo*, 29 July). These developments, together with Czechoslovakia's deteriorating foreign trade, weakened the regime's argument for staying the conservative course.

Culture, youth, and religion. In contrast to what happened in the centers of official culture, such as the Writers Union, during the liberalization period of the 1960s, in 1988 these centers did not display much creative originality or take the lead in the implementation of *glasnost'*. Independent thought in 1988, as in earlier years, was almost exclusively the domain of unofficial science, art, and literature as characterized by samizdat publications (see the section in this essay on Dissidence). A new cultural periodical *Kmen*, sponsored by the Czech Writers' Union, began to appear in January. Although not outspokenly conservative or dogmatic, it avoided taking positions on politically sensitive issues of arts and sciences and later in the year carried a subtle but unmistakable attack on the new freedom and plurality in Soviet culture and politics. The attack came from the pen of Eva Fojtíková, labeled the emergence of uncensored ideas and works as "an uncontrolled eruption of emotions," flooding the literary market with "humbug" and promoting "nihilistic attitudes to the past." She saw "the current state of Soviet culture as considerably chaotic" (*Kmen*, no. 33, 18 August).

KSČ general secretary Jakeš criticized the state of social sciences in Czechoslovakia and appealed to scholars "to become courageous and mature joint creators of the party's policies" (Radio Prague, 13 April). Most sociologists, however, found this to be a rather hollow gesture until and unless the present emphasis on conservative conformity, part of the "normalization" drive, was abandoned (*Ze zásuvky i z bloku*, June).

There seemed to be far more action in the realm of religious life. Church spokesmen and informal groups of believers articulated their demands for more freedom of religion, and the regime seemed to modify its position, at least verbally. Although there were not many institutional concessions to Catholics and Protestants and the structures supporting the antireligious drive remained in place, the representatives of the political establishment often used more hospitable language when dealing with religion. Western observers and media turned their attention at the start of the year to a spectacular initiative by Catholic Christians who submitted a 31-point petition for greater respect of religious rights. This petition had been prepared by a group of believers in Moravia in December 1987 and signed by several hundred thousand citizens (about 350,000 according to the Radio Free Europe/Radio Liberty report of 1 March). It received full support from Cardinal František Tomášek, the Czechoslovak primate (Prague, AP, 19 January). The regime's reaction to this unprecedented proof of the vitality of religion, even after more than four decades of relentless persecution, was one of visible embarrassment. The party daily *Rudé právo* and its Slovak appendage, *Pravda*, attacked the petition as being "the voice of a secret church in the service of anticommunism" (12 February). They argued that this action was aimed at "disturbing the course of the talks between the representatives of the Czechoslovak state and the Vatican delegation" (Bratislava, *Pravda*, 13 February), an allusion to the negotiations that Archbishop Francesco Colasuomo was conducting with the Federal Secretariat for Religious Affairs (Radio Prague, 18 January). Chairman Vladimír Janků, deputy minister, said after their conclusion that they had "contributed to a deeper understanding of questions of common in-

terest" but that "some émigrés" were not interested in an improvement of church-state relations (Radio Prague, 4 February).

Official media went to great lengths to claim that no restriction of religious activities had ever taken place in Czechoslovakia or was intended by the government (ČTK, 2 February). Miroslav Válek, minister of culture of the Slovak republic, asserted at a meeting with clergymen that the state was willing "to explore all possible solutions of church problems" (Radio Bratislava, 1 February). However, several occurrences during the year indicated that the political establishment continued to view religiosity as a threat to the system. The unusually large attendance at a mass in honor of Blessed Agnes of Bohemia, celebrated by Cardinal Tomášek after which the believers peacefully demonstrated for religious freedom, elicited annoyed and scornful comment from the regime's media (Radio Prague, 6 March). The annual pilgrimage to Levoča in northeastern Slovakia, which attracted large numbers of believers, was disturbed by police harassing participants as well as Western reporters and observers (Vienna, *Die Presse*, 4 July). In March, police in Bratislava arrested about two hundred people who were nonviolently demonstrating for religious rights. Police also manhandled a BBC correspondent, which led to a formal protest from the British government (Reuters, 26 March). A group of 40 Hungarian activists and intellectuals declared their solidarity with the Bratislava demonstrators (Budapest, AFP, 27 March). The continuation of this hostile behavior on the part of the state organs prompted Cardinal Tomášek to send an open letter to federal Premier Štrougal in which he pointed out that the petition for religious liberty—which by then had been signed by more than a half million persons—represented the true voice of the people and should be taken seriously (Prague, AP, 3 May). In a pastoral letter to all Catholics, the cardinal encouraged believers to endure in their struggle against the repressive policies of the state (Radio Vatican, 7 May).

The talks between the Czechoslovak government and the Vatican resumed in Rome in the spring (Radio Prague, 12 April). They led to an agreement concerning part of the agenda, but other questions remained open. Three new bishops were appointed. A concession by the regime to the church could be seen in the government representatives dropping their original demand that at least one of the new bishops be a member of the proregime organization, *Pacem in Terris*. Two bishops, Jan Lebeda and

Antonín Liška, were consecrated in Prague and the third, Jan Sokol, in Trnava, Slovakia (ČTK, 11, 12 June). The ceremony of their consecration was attended by many thousands of believers (Vienna, *Die Presse*, 12 June).

As for other religious faiths and denominations, the synodal senior of the Evangelical Church of Czech Brethren, Jan Hromádka, was introduced into his function at the start of the year (Radio Prague, 4 January). In February, 45 American rabbis—the largest delegation of Jewish dignitaries to visit Czechoslovakia since the end of World War II—came to Prague "to acquaint themselves with the life of the Jewish communities." They reported "no sign of religious suppression and no hindrances to the development of these communities" (Radio Prague, 17 February).

However, the fundamental position of the regime on religion does not seem to have changed, despite the partial improvement of church-state relations. The institutes of "scientific atheism," attached to the party and to the school system, continued their activities in 1988. Although the official argument— propagating atheism does not imply suppressing religious freedom—might appear plausible, other facts testify to persistent religious persecution, including discouraging religious education, banning believers from all higher-level jobs and careers, and, most of all, the incompatibility of party membership and religious affiliation (which, because of *nomenklatura*, automatically excludes the faithful from any public office or civil service career). The difficult position of all religious groups in Czechoslovakia was described in an article that Dr. Erika Kadlecová, former head of the Secretariat for Religious Affairs, now a dissident, wrote for the Italian communist party daily *L'Unità*. She called the petition for religious rights "an unprecedented phenomenon in a politically inert and socially anaesthetized country like Czechoslovakia." In her view it was "not so much an explosion of Catholic religious feeling as a light of civic hope" (*L'Unità*, Rome, 30 March). Ruthless police and court actions against more outspoken believers went on unabated. Slovak Catholic Ivan Polanský, after six months of detention, was condemned by the regional court in Banská Bystrica to four years in prison for publishing and distributing religious literature (Bratislava, *Pravda*, 14 June). Two months later, his appeal was rejected by the Supreme Court of the Slovak Republic (Radio Bratislava, 29 August).

This evidence notwithstanding, regime spokesmen kept claiming that unrestricted religious freedom existed in Czechoslovakia (ČTK, 2 February; Vladimír Janků on Radio Prague, 4 February). Ladislav Adamec, the new federal prime minister, in a statement made after his nomination, declared that his government wished "to establish the best possible relations with churches and believers" (*Rudé právo*, 11 November).

The impact of the official ideology on young people—whatever little grip the state-supported organizations, such as the Socialist Youth Union, may have had—was weakening and eroding. The interest and the allegiance of Czechoslovak youth had long since shifted to areas beyond party and governmental control, comparable to that observed in the realm of art and literature. Although the spontaneous activities of young people were on the whole nonpolitical—centering on sports and popular music—their emancipation from the regime's tutelage was in itself highly political and preceded by many years the constitution of various independent centers of culture and the samizdat publications. Deeply rooted traditions of precommunist youth ideas and movements played an important role in this emancipation, among them that of the Czechoslovak Scouts. Regime media on several occasions complained that the Scout spirit was still alive among those who should be dedicated Pioneers (*Tribuna*, no. 21, 21 May; *Mladá fronta*, 23 April). Unwelcome influences did not seem to be limited to the past, however. Popular figures of Western modern music, such as Beatle John Lennon, continue to be worshipped by Czech and Slovak boys and girls, to the dismay of the regime's spokesmen. The latter were concerned not only about the beat-style music being a formidable competitor to socialist youth culture but also of direct political consequences. They accused the "Lennonists" (who chose this name to distance themselves from the "Leninists") of "oversimplifying the complexity of international class struggle and promoting false pacifism" (*Mladý svět*, no. 4, January).

Dissidence. If all independent public activities uncontrolled by the regime are included in the term—as they have to be, considering the totalitarian nature of the Czechoslovak state—dissidence in 1988 both expanded and gained in intensity. Its growth was reflected not only in the frequency of various dissident manifestations but also in the increasing number of independent groups, organizations, centers, and publications. Charter '77's agenda continued to be the center of public attention. Its spokesmen for 1988 were historian Miloš Hájek, psychologist Bohumír Janát, and computer technician Stanislav Devátý (*Informace o Chartě*, no. 1). In January, Charter '77 appealed to Czechoslovak and European public opinion to show their solidarity with the Romanian population "who suffer under the arbitrary personal rule of Nicolae Ceauşescu" (Charter document no. 2). This solidarity was expressed by brief simultaneous strikes in Prague, Budapest, and Warsaw in accord with Hungarian and Polish civil rights groups (AFP, 1 February). The international cooperation of dissidents was also documented by a plea, on behalf of the Hungarian minority in Eastern Europe, that was addressed to the Czechoslovak government to support the interests of ethnic minorities at the forthcoming conference on European peace and security (Helsinki treaty) in Vienna. Charter '77 endorsed the plea and delivered the pertinent documents to Prime Minister Štrougal (Charter document no. 74, 15 December 1987). In a similar gesture of solidarity, 70 Czechoslovak rights activists pleaded with General Wojciech Jaruzelski for the release of two Polish dissidents (Vienna, *Die Presse*, 4 June). In turn, sixteen thousand Polish citizens signed a petition in support of Czechoslovak Catholics who demanded more religious freedom (Warsaw, UPI, 6 June). In July, 26 prominent Polish and Czechoslovak dissidents issued a joint statement urging the governments of communist-ruled countries to implement a five-point program of human rights (Prague, AP, 10 July). After the brutal treatment by the police of the participants in the spontaneous manifestation commemorating the 70th anniversary of national liberation, six hundred Hungarian personalities of all walks of life sent a letter of protest to President Husák (Budapest, DPA, 21 November). Also promoting the international solidarity of dissidents, the new independent samizdat paper *Lidové noviny* (named after a well-known liberal daily founded at the turn of the century but discontinued in 1952) published an interview with Arvo Valton, Estonian writer and human rights champion (*Lidové noviny*, no. 1). The same paper later carried an exclusive interview on the political and economic situation in Yugoslavia with Milovan Djilas (*Lidové noviny*, no. 9). In October, both U.S. presidential candidates, George Bush and Michael Dukakis, gave short interviews to *Lidové noviny* (no. 10).

Among the newly constituted independent groups, Western media reported Democratic Initiative, Initiative for Social Defense, Movement for Civil Liberty, The Masaryk Society, T. G. Masaryk Association, and Independent Peace Association (Prague, Reuters, 16 April, 11 May, 8, 14, 15 October). The Association for Friendship with the USA was denied incorporation in 1987 but was reconstituted in 1988 (*Magazin Společnosti přátel USA*, no. 2, 30 June). A group was also set up to promote the erection of a monument to the victims of Stalinist terror (*Informace o Chartě*, 13 July). Two Czechoslovak dissidents attended a conference on Prague Spring and dissidence in the Soviet bloc in Nijmegen in the Netherlands in September (*De Tijd*, 18 September).

Western interest in the fate of Czechoslovak dissidents was demonstrated by the contacts that political and diplomatic representatives of Western nations established with individuals and groups while on official visits in Czechoslovakia. Thus members of the delegation of the Federal Republic of Germany, headed by Chancellor Helmut Kohl, met with Jiří Hájek, former minister of foreign affairs and Charter spokesman, in Prague (Prague, DPA, 27 January). John Whitehead, U.S. deputy secretary of state, talked with leading human rights activists, among them playwright Václav Havel (Prague, AP, 8 February). British undersecretary of state David Radford protested the Czechoslovak government's rough treatment of Czechoslovak activists who had been guests at the British embassy in Prague (Reuters, 5 March). French minister of foreign affairs Roland Dumas, visiting Czechoslovakia in September, met with Chartists Jiří Hájek, Miloš Hájek, and Peter Uhl (Prague, AFP, 20 September). Also French president François Mitterrand received Czechoslovak rights defenders at a breakfast at the French embassy and was briefed by them about the situation in the country. Václav Havel and Miloš Hájek were among his guests. (*NYT*, 10 December.) When Pavel Wonka, the leader of the Committee for the Protection of Unjustly Persecuted Persons, died after a long imprisonment, the European Parliament in Strasbourg called for an impartial investigation into the cause of his death. Czechoslovak authorities allowed U.S. physician Robert Kirschner to perform an autopsy on Wonka. Dr. Kirschner found "no evidence of any acute injuries as might have been inflicted by torture" (AP, 5 May; *Le Monde*, 20 May). Wonka was buried in Vrchlabí in northern Bohemia with many foreign participants at the funeral services and under close police surveillance but without incidents (Vienna, *Die Presse*, 6 May).

Numerous anniversaries of important historical

events gave dissident groups an opportunity to promote public awareness of various political problems facing the society at large. Recalling the seizure of power by the KSČ 40 years earlier, the spokesmen of Charter '77 saw the current situation of Czechoslovakia as testifying to "the defeat of the victors and the victory of the vanquished" and urged everybody to keep in mind the countless innocent victims of the failed communist utopia (Charter documents, 20 February). As the 20th anniversary of the Soviet-led military intervention approached, the group called Democratic Initiative issued a statement calling on the Soviet leadership to repudiate the principles on which the 1968 intervention had been based. It also exhorted the KSČ to remove Gustáv Husák and Vasil Bil'ák from their functions, as a first condition to improve the political climate (Prague, AP, 24 July). The Italian socialist daily *Avanti* carried a series of articles by leading dissidents and exiles commenting on the events of the Prague Spring and the invasion (Rome, *Avanti*, 15 May). In March, a special statement issued by Charter '77 pressed for a public discussion in all Warsaw Pact countries that had taken part in the intervention (Prague, AP, 23 March). On 21 August, the anniversary of the invasion, a large gathering formed at Václavské Square in the center of Prague to demonstrate against the Soviet interference with the reform efforts of Prague Spring. A group of dissidents unfolded a banner condemning the Soviet act and calling for the withdrawal of Soviet troops from Czechoslovak territory (*NYT*, 22 August). A few days later, dissident writer Václav Havel expressed the same demands in an address to more than five thousand people at the annual folk festival in Lipnice in East Bohemia (Samizdat report, 3 September).

A special statement by Charter '77 and four other dissident groups was released on the 70th anniversary of national liberation (Prague, AP, 28 October), which also provided the occasion for many more activities. Charter '77, in cooperation with the Helsinki Watch center, located in Vienna, planned a historical seminar in Prague in November to discuss the foundation of the Czechoslovak republic in 1918. Although the party and the government had decided that 28 October would again be remembered as a national holiday, official permission to hold the seminar was not given. As soon as the seminar started, it was broken up by the police and the foreign participants deported (Prague, AFP, 11 November). The authorities also issued a stern warning against any public manifestations on this occasion and ordered a temporary internment of all known dissidents. These preventive measures notwithstanding, a demonstration of many thousands of people took place in Prague 28 October. A strong police contingent dispersed the crowd, which reassembled in another part of the city. Many people were wounded and arrested (*NYT*, 29 October). The KSČ Presidium later denounced these manifestations as "the work of émigré groups and U.S. diplomats" (*Rudé právo*, 4 November). Six independent civil rights groups thereafter sent a letter to *Rudé právo* protesting this allegation (*NYT*, 5 November).

In December, on the 40th anniversary of the signing by Czechoslovakia of the U.N. Universal Declaration of Human Rights, the government permitted a demonstration to be held in Prague sponsored by Charter '77 and other allied groups. About six thousand people turned up, and the main speaker was Václav Havel. This reversal of the official policy on spontaneous public gatherings elicited interest from foreign observers. It was speculated that this conciliatory gesture might have been recommended by Moscow to impress the European Conference on Peace and Security, then meeting in Vienna. The Soviets were known to be anxious to host the next meeting of this body in Moscow in 1991 (*NYT*, 11 December). The definite policy of the present KSČ leadership on the human rights movements and dissident groups in general was difficult to gauge. Earlier in the year, the secretariat of the Central Committee issued a circular letter to regional and district party organizations on the problem of dissidence. The document identified the individual groups by name and classified them according to the perceived degree of their hostility to the regime. It urged KSČ officials "to mobilize every single communist to a political and ideological struggle" against these "internal and external enemies of socialism." In this context, party media emphasized that "without the Western media, this infantry of betrayal would have no significance whatsoever" (*Rudé právo*, 2 June). The practical policy based on these analyses, however, showed the same inconsistency as the party policies on most other major issues in 1988.

Foreign Affairs. The most visible initiative undertaken by the Czechoslovak government in the field of foreign policy in 1988 was to create "a zone of confidence and good neighborly relations" between the countries of the North Atlantic Treaty Organization (NATO) and the Warsaw treaty in

Europe. The proposal was first mentioned by General Secretary Jakeš in his speech to party officials on the anniversary of the February 1948 coup d'état (Radio Prague, 24 February). It was then discussed by Foreign Minister Bohuslav Chňoupek at a meeting with the heads of the diplomatic missions of the NATO member nations (ČTK, 7 March). The idea was to establish a belt, free of nuclear and chemical weapons, that extended along the borders of Norway, West Germany, East Germany, and Czechoslovakia. As the proposal was received only lukewarmly by NATO members, especially the United States, Czechoslovak spokesmen (e.g., Ambassador Houštecký in Washington, D.C.) insisted that it was not only a disarmament proposal but also one of "confidence and security measures" in the critical regions. Was Czechoslovakia seeking to create a situation that would enable it to dismantle, without much loss of face, the Iron Curtain? No one could answer this question with certainty. A zone of confidence in Central Europe was also the topic of a discussion that Jaromír Johanes, the first deputy minister of foreign affairs, had with Jürgen Sudhoff, state secretary in the foreign office of the Federal Republic of Germany, in Bonn, in the summer (ČTK, 27 July). However, the item gradually disappeared from the diplomatic agenda and media focus as the year advanced.

Contacts with the United States were more frequent and touched on more areas than in previous years. At the start of 1988, the U.S. and Czechoslovak governments agreed on the procedures to be followed during the inspections on the Czechoslovak territory foreseen by the INF treaty (Radio Prague, 5 January). Edward Rowny, President Reagan's special adviser on arms control, visited Czechoslovakia in late summer (Radio Prague, 7 September). In January, a U.S. congressional delegation, led by Representative Tom Lantos from California, was received by Deputy Foreign Minister Jaromír Johanes and KSČ Presidium member Vasil Bil'ák (Prague, UPI, 18 January). On this occasion, Bil'ák argued that the apparent slowness in the adoption by Czechoslovakia of the Soviet reforms was a sign of growing independence from the Soviet Union; "something over which," Bil'ák said, "the United States should rejoice." Shortly afterward, U.S. deputy secretary of state John Whitehead came to Prague on his tour of Central and Eastern Europe and met with President Husák and Foreign Minister Chňoupek. Whitehead found that since his previous visit progress had been made in Czechoslovak-U.S. relations but that "serious

concern remained in the United States about Czechoslovakia's human rights record" (Prague, AP, 8 February). A delegation of the federal Assembly, classified as "unofficial," reciprocated the U.S. congressional visit in early summer, touring several major U.S. cities (Radio Prague, 25 June). On return, one participant, Deputy Richard Nejezchled, gave an unusually balanced, unbiased account of his impressions of America in an interview for the press (Rol'nícke noviny, 8 July). Another group of U.S. congressmen stopped in Prague on their orientation trip to Europe and met with KSČ Presidium member Miroslav Štěpán in the fall (Radio Prague, 16 November).

Czechoslovak-British contacts in 1988 began with the visit to Prague of a high-ranking official, Deputy Foreign Secretary Renton (Rudé právo, 3 February), but became somewhat marred later in the year. The British Foreign Office felt obliged to protest twice to the Czechoslovak government: first against the harassment of the rights activists invited to the British embassy for dinner (5 March) and second when the police in Bratislava manhandled a British reporter covering the peaceful manifestation for religious freedom (26 March). On the latter occasion, the Czechoslovak party press compared British junior foreign secretary David Mellor to Lord Runciman, special envoy of Prime Minister Neville Chamberlain in 1938, who during the Munich crisis took the side of the Sudeten German irredentists. The climate between the two countries deteriorated further when, as a retaliation for the expulsion of three Czechoslovak diplomats from London on charge of espionage, the Czechoslovak Foreign Ministry ordered two British diplomats to leave Czechoslovakia (ČTK, 28 September). Contacts with France developed on the highest level. In September, Prague hosted French foreign minister Roland Dumas during a three-day official visit. Dumas stated that he had undertaken the trip to Czechoslovakia "not only with the view to bilateral relations but also with regard to France's general policy towards the socialist states" (Prague, AFP, 20 September). His visit was followed at the end of the year by that of President Mitterrand, who, in a speech at the gala dinner given in his honor, openly expressed his sympathies for the suppressed reform movement of the Prague Spring of 1968. The KSČ daily reprinted his remarks uncensored (Rudé právo, 9 December). At a press conference before his departure from Prague, Mitterrand declared that "a closer web of ties [between Czechoslovakia and France] could be woven only when the human rights record of the former improved (*NYT*, 10 December). Italian minister of labor Salvatore Formica paid an official visit to Czechoslovakia in early summer (Radio Prague, 2 July). Czechoslovak federal deputy prime minister Matej Lúčan went to Italy for a three-day visit two months later (Radio Prague, 20 September). In October, General Secretary Jakeš received in Prague Spanish senate chairman José Frederic de Javarjal (ČTK, 5 October). Among the representatives of the smaller West European countries, Dutch minister of foreign affairs Hans van den Broek paid a visit to Czechoslovakia in the spring (Radio Prague, 22 April). A delegation of the federal Assembly, led by First Deputy Chairman Jan Marko, went to Brussels and Strasbourg in February, to meet with the members of the European Parliament (Radio Prague, 6 February).

As for Czechoslovakia's immediate Western neighbors, the Federal Republic of Germany (FRG) and Austria, contacts and mutual visits were quite frequent in 1988. The series was initiated by West German federal chancellor Kohl, who came to Prague at the beginning of the year. On the agenda of his talks with the government and party representatives were peace and security in Central Europe; technical cooperation; trade; joint efforts to avert the threat to the environment, especially acid rain; and humanitarian issues of all kinds. The importance of the talks was underscored by Czechoslovakia and West Germany, respectively, in 1988 assuming the chairmanship of the Council for Mutual Economic Assistance (CMEA) and the European Economic Community (EEC). Negotiations involving these two economic communities had been under way for a considerable time. Kohl met with Premier Lubomír Štrougal, who declared himself open to any proposal that could "create an atmosphere of confidence" and "help remove outdated stereotypes" (*Rudé právo*, 27 January). Kohl said that he wanted his visit "to be a milestone on the path to good neighborliness" that would "contribute to the construction of the Europe of tomorrow, guaranteeing the peoples a peaceful future and respect of human rights." He deplored the atrocities perpetrated in Czechoslovakia by the Nazis and called Lidice (a village exterminated by the SS troops in 1942) and the infamous Jewish ghetto Theresienstadt (Terezín) "two monuments against atrocity and inhumanity" (Prague, AP, 26 January). In April Prague hosted Johannes Rau, prime minister of the West German state Nordrhein-Westfalen, who was received by KSČ general secretary Miloš Jakeš

(*Rudé právo*, 29 April). As a sign of improved Czechoslovak–West German relations, the party and the government positively evaluated the visit of Czechoslovak foreign minister Chňoupek in Bonn in the summer. Chňoupek held talks with his West German collague Hans-Dietrich Genscher and Chancellor Kohl. On this occasion binational working groups were constituted to deal with questions of common concern, such as border traffic, emigration of ethnic Germans to the FRG, youth exchange programs, setting up a West German cultural center in Prague and a Czechoslovak cultural center in a principal West German city, and a visit in the near future by the president of the FRG, Richard von Weiszaecker, to Czechoslovakia (*Frankfurter Allgemeine Zeitung*, 31 August). Deputy Foreign Minister Jaromír Johanes praised the present state of Czechoslovak–West German relations as a model of rapport between countries with different socioeconomic systems (Radio Prague, 3 August).

The most important official contact between Czechoslovakia and Austria in 1988 was the visit to Prague by federal Chancellor Franz Vranitzky. The visit, originally scheduled for the second half of April, was postponed because of the Central Committee plenary session (although the reason was not explained in detail) and took place from 26 to 28 June. The climate between the two countries had for a long time been unfavorably influenced by border incidents due to the existence of the Iron Curtain, the unwillingness of the regime to allow contacts between Czechoslovak and Austrian Catholics and the growing apprehension of Austrian environmentalists about the Czechoslovak nuclear plants and other ecologically threatening projects near Austrian territory. Prime Minister Štrougal expressed the view that these issues could be satisfactorily settled and that the good relations between Austria and Hungary should be emulated (Vienna, *Kronenzeitung*, 22 June). The official communiqué at the end of Vranitzky's visit contained a similar hope (Radio Prague, 28 June). A delegation of the Austrian parliament visited Prague and Bratislava in the fall. The Austrian deputies discussed with their Czechoslovak hosts a number of environmental and economic issues (Radio Hvězda, 17 October). In November, the new Czechoslovak foreign minister, Jaromír Johanes, met with the Austrian and Hungarian ambassadors to discuss the joint world fair to be held in 1995 (ČTK, 21 November). In the same month KSČ Presidium member Vasil Biľák traveled to Vienna where he held talks with Chancellor Vranitzky and President Kurt Waldheim (*Die Presse*, nitzky and President Kurt Waldheim (*Die Presse*, 19 November). The meeting between Interior Minister Vratislav Vajnar and the Austrian government, represented by Chancellor Vranitzky and Foreign Minister Alois Mock, in Vienna in February drafted an agreement on cooperation in preventing crime (Radio Prague, 17 February).

Diplomatic contacts with other Western countries included the visit to Prague by Greek president Christos Sartzetakis, the first by a Greek representative of this rank since the end of World War II (ČTK, 28 May). Premier Štrougal went to Brazil on an official visit to promote trade between the two nations (Radio Prague, 10 May). Shintaro Abe, Secretary general of the ruling Liberal Democratic Party of Japan, came to Prague for a brief visit and met with KSČ general secretary Jakeš (Radio Prague, 2 May). Foreign Minister Chňoupek traveled to Cairo in April and met with his Egyptian colleague Ahmed Abdel Meguid. A joint statement issued on this occasion condemned Israeli actions in the territory of the West Bank (Radio Cairo, 28 April). This was the first contact with Egypt on the cabinet level since the break between Egypt and the Soviet Union in 1974. In June, Yassir Arafat, the leader of the Palestine Liberation Organization, arrived in Prague for a two-day "official friendly visit" (ČTK, 27 June). In November, Czechoslovakia noted as valid the declaration of an independent Palestinian state (Radio Prague, 18 November). The overtures toward the Arab world, however, did not prevent the Czechoslovak leadership from seeking a renewal of ties with Israel, which were broken off under Soviet pressure after the Six-Day War in 1968. Foreign Minister Chňoupek took the opportunity of the 43rd session of the U.N. General Assembly in New York to have an extensive talk with Israeli foreign minister Shimon Peres (AP, 27 September). Although some commentators (e.g., Israeli radio) expected that formal diplomatic relations would be resumed before the end of year, this did not happen. The party leadership appears to lag behind other parties of the Soviet bloc, such as Poland and Hungary, in this respect.

A slow disengagement from the Brezhnev era in international politics also continued in relation to "deviant" communist states and parties, such as Albania and China. In May, the Yugoslav press reported that economic ties between Czechoslovakia and Albania would be expanded and that diplomatic relations, severed in the 1960s, would be renewed at the ambassadorial level (*Rilindja*, 20

May). Indeed, shortly afterward, Foreign Minister Chňoupek met with his Albanian counterpart Reiz Malile—also at the U.N. session in New York—to discuss these plans (Radio Prague, 29 September). Wei Jian Xing, the Chinese minister of supervision, came for a working visit to Czechoslovakia in June (ČTK, 10 June). Jan Risko, head of Czechoslovak Radio, traveled to China to conclude the first cooperation agreement between the Czechoslovak and Chinese broadcast corporations (Xinhua, 13 June).

As for contacts with other communist countries, there was a visit to Prague by Soviet deputy foreign minister Anatolii Adamishin (Radio Prague, 26 February). Romanian prime minister Constantin Dăscălescu made an official friendly visit to Czechoslovakia in March and met with his colleague Štrougal, who sharply criticized shortcomings in economic cooperation between the two countries (Radio Prague, 23 March). Romania was known among CMEA members as the staunchest opponent of all economic integration plans. In May, a delegation of the Bulgarian parliament traveled to Czechoslovakia under the leadership of National Assembly chairman Stanko Todorov and received by President Husák and Prime Minister Štrougal (ČTK, 18 May). Czechoslovak defense minister Milan Václavík held talks in Havana with Cuban president Fidel Castro (Radio Havana, 27 March). Castro, who in 1968 endorsed, with some qualifications, the Soviet intervention in Czechoslovakia and recently expressed his unwillingness to follow Gorbachev's example, may have appeared to the present KSČ leaders as more congenial than most other heads of communist party-states.

Foreign trade and debt. The relatively low per capita foreign indebtedness of Czechoslovakia (second lowest in the Soviet bloc) has for a long time been one of the regime's major arguments for continuing its economic policies, in contrast to reforms effected in the neighboring communist party-states, especially Hungary. At the turn of 1988, the gross foreign debt stood at U.S. $3.7 billion, which was $500,000,000 less than in 1987. However, in view of the urgent need to modernize production to become competitive in international markets, new loans in convertible currencies are indispensable to Czechoslovakia. In official statements, government spokesmen appeared confident that "only limited borrowing" from the West would be necessary (Radio Prague, 26 July). International economic experts estimate, however, that the modernization of the Czechoslovak industry will require between

$150,000,000 loan awarded by a consortium of West German, Austrian, and Japanese banks would seem only a modest advance on these outlays (*Rudé právo*, 31 July). Postponing the required investments, however, might jeopardize Czechoslovakia's chances of securing an adequate share in the international division of labor, all the more in the critical period at the threshold of the 1990s when the EEC will begin to emerge as a powerful single agent in world markets.

Part of the economic reconstruction program in 1988 was simplifying the exchange rate system of the Czechoslovak currency, which hitherto had varied according to the trade partner and the nature of the transaction. The koruna will now have a uniform exchange value (Radio Prague, 31 August). Following an agreement signed with the Soviet Union, the convertibility of both currencies was introduced and the exchange rate of the ruble was fixed at 10.4 koruny (Radio Prague, 21 March), making the U.S. dollar equal to 6.23 koruny. An agreement about the use of national currencies in bilateral trade with Bulgaria, where previously the accounting had been made in Soviet rubles, was also reached in 1988. In the summer, Prague hosted the 44th meeting of the prime ministers of the member nations of CMEA. Štrougal urged the signatory countries to overcome, by "quicker and bolder" economic reforms, the stagnation, low production cooperation, and slow advance of technology (Radio Prague, 7 July). KSČ Presidium member Jozef Lenárt returned to this subject in an article in *World Marxist Review* wherein he proposed an integration of member states' national economies of CMEA, comparable to that achieved by the EEC, as the best remedy for current problems (*WMR*, no. 10, October). This point was first made by economist Jaromír Matějka at the start of the year. Matějka saw CMEA falling behind the EEC not only in level and quality of economic performance but also degree of integration and cooperation (Radio Prague, 7 January). The hard realities of the individual member nations' economies, however, made such recommendations appear rather untimely. In fact, 1988 brought, on the part of the Soviet bloc countries, various protectionist measures reinforcing economic nationalism and the policies of Socialism in One Country. Czechoslovakia imposed severe limits on the export of goods purchased by tourists from other CMEA nations, which elicited strong criticism in Poland and the Soviet Union (Radio Warsaw, 19 November; Radio Moscow, 22 November). Justifying these measures, regime spokesmen argued that it was not Czechoslovakia's duty "to solve the distribution problems of other socialist countries" (Radio Prague, 23 November). Czechoslovak tourists visiting Hungary were subject to limitations on exchanging koruny for Hungarian forints. This measure had been in force before 1988.

The impact on the Czechoslovak economy of its neighbors' economic difficulties was intensified by the dependence of Czechoslovakia on the trade with CMEA. In 1988, 80 percent of Czechoslovak foreign trade was conducted with communist countries, half with the Soviet Union. This was the result of a deliberate, long-term policy started in the 1950s. No change in the volume of trade with the USSR was expected in 1988 (Radio Prague, 1 February). It was not clear from the statements of the KSČ leaders whether the economic reconstruction now in progress implied a modification of the foreign trade pattern. The accent on greater competitiveness of Czechoslovak products seemed to indicate such intentions. Contacts were made during the year with several Western countries with a view to stimulating foreign trade. French minister of industry Alain Mandelin made a one-day visit to Prague and talked with Prime Minister Štrougal about bilateral economic cooperation (Radio Prague, 2 February). Another round of talks with French trade representatives took place toward the end of the year, when Minister of Foreign Trade Jan Štěrba received in Prague a group of trade officials and businessmen from France (ČTK, 21 November). At about the same time, Deputy Prime Minister Jaromír Obzina discussed the possibilities of enlarged Czechoslovak-British trade with British trade minister Alan Clark (Radio Prague, 23 November). After the visit of Foreign Minister Chňoupek to Bonn in August, the West German Kommerzbank signed an agreement with the Czechoslovak government on expert counseling and financing for joint industrial ventures (*Frankfurter Allgemeine Zeitung*, 31 August). The Austrian company Warimpex established a joint venture with the Czechoslovak state travel agency ČEDOK to remodel Czechoslovak hotels and build new ones. The volume of Austrian-Czechoslovak trade exceeded U.S. $1.3 billion, second only to trade between Czechoslovakia and West Germany. The leading Viennese bank, Creditanstalt Bankverein, opened a branch office in Prague in 1987 (*Die Presse*, 22 May). First Deputy Minister of Foreign Trade František Langer paid an official visit to Australia at the beginning of the year (*Rudé právo*, 22 tralia at the beginning of the year (*Rudé právo*, 22 January). The Mixed Commission for Cooperation between Czechoslovakia and the U.N. Industrial Development Organization approved a five-year operation plan in Vienna (Radio Prague, 2 February). After the official visit of Czechoslovak premier Štrougal to Belgrade (Radio Hvězda, 17 June), Yugoslav minister of foreign trade Nenad Krekić repaid his visit in September and discussed with Štrougal in Prague the details of economic cooperation between the two countries (*Rudé právo*, 8 September).

Concerning economic relations with the countries of the Third World, it was reported that Algerian prime minister Abdelhamid Brahimi concluded, during his three-day visit in Czechoslovakia, an agreement on the delivery of Algerian natural gas in exchange for Czechoslovak assistance in building industrial plants in Algeria (ČTK, 18 February). Economic questions were also on the agenda of the official visit by Indian president Ramaswamy Iyer Vankataraman to Prague (Radio Hvězda, 22 September). A trade delegation came to Czechoslovakia from Iran for a session of the Mixed Commission for Economic and Technical Cooperation (Radio Prague, 9 March), and a trade protocol covering the exchanges in 1988 and 1989 was signed with Afghanistan (Radio Prague, 29 April). A session of the Czechoslovak-Egyptian Committee for Economic and Scientific-Technological Cooperation took place in Prague in July (ČTK, 10 July). In September, Foreign Trade Minister Štěrba paid a working visit to Syria (Radio Prague, 2 September). The foreign minister of Mozambique, Pascoal Manual Mocumbi, made a working visit to Czechoslovakia, including discussions on economic cooperation (Radio Prague, 3 May).

International Party Contacts. The relations between the KSČ and the other parties of the world communist movement, ruling as well as in opposition or illegal, had since 1968 been influenced by the Soviet military intervention. These relations ranged from close to cool, if not hostile, according to the party's position on the invasion and its ideological justification, the so-called Brezhnev Doctrine. With the dramatic reversal of Soviet policies in the mid-1980s, the leadership of the KSČ began to perceive its sister parties also in terms of their stands on *perestroika* and *glasnost'*. Here, however, the correlation was negative: the more enthusiastic the party's espousal of the Soviet reform line, the

cooler the attitude of the KSČ was likely to be. Thus, from the Czechoslovak perspective, Gorbachev's initiatives became another factor promoting solidarity or division within the communist world. This factor was more or less symmetrically superimposed on the earlier pattern of sympathies and mistrust; whichever party endorsed the Soviet intervention in 1968 was also likely to sympathize with the reluctance of the current KSČ leaders to adopt the Soviet reform model. There were exceptions: Hungary, which participated in the military action against the Prague Spring, preceded and even outdid the Soviet reform efforts; Romania, which rejected the intervention and did not share in it, also rejected *perestroika* and especially *glasnost'*. In Czechoslovakia these complex circumstances often created curious situations. For example, the regime and the dissidents found themselves in agreement when both condemned the harsh economic and minority policies of Nicolae Ceauşescu, although the regime could not forgive Romania's refusing to legitimize the Soviet intervention (which implied the illegitimacy of the current KSČ governance); the dissidents saw in the persecution of the ethnic minorities and dissidents in Romania only a variant of the "normalization" policies of Husák and Jakeš. (Charter document, no. 2, 2 January; *Rudé právo*, 24 June; *Mladá fronta*, 30 August.)

Despite—or perhaps because of—the differences between the present KSČ leadership and the Communist Party of the Soviet Union (CPSU) under Gorbachev, the rapport with Moscow was in 1988 the most important component of a web of interparty links that the Czechoslovak party entertained. General Secretary Jakeš went on a two-day visit to the USSR at the beginning of the year (*Rudé právo*, 11 January) and met with Mikhail Gorbachev. Their talks, according to the official communiqué, covered "a wide range of questions touching on the domestic policies of both parties and states and the situation in the world at large" (Radio Hvězda, 12 January). Observers concluded that the talks were aimed at eliminating the frictions in Czechoslovak-Soviet relations. The emphasis in Jakeš's dinner speech in the Kremlin on "the need to respect specific conditions in Czechoslovakia" (TASS, in English, 11 January) sounded somewhat odd from the head of a team that had been forced on his party and nation by the very power from which he proposed to seek independence. Later in the year, Jakeš received in Prague Alexandra Biryukova, secretary of the CC of the CPSU (Radio Prague, 23 September). In November, Alexander

Czechoslovakia and met with Jakeš (Radio Prague, 11 November). He also gave an interview to the KSČ daily in which he urged "unrestricted publication of different opinions on all issues" (*Rudé právo*, 16 November). In April, Anatolii Dobrynin, secretary of the CPSU CC and former Soviet ambassador to the United States, came to Prague to take part in a conference on the editorial and ideological problems of the journal *Problems of Peace and Socialism*. On this occasion he met with Jakeš. In his opening address at the conference, Dobrynin pointed out that the international communist movement had for a long time witnessed an "explosion of polemics" and "sharpening of relations among parties and even splits between them" (Radio Prague, 11 April; TASS, 12 April).

The gradual improvement of relations between the USSR and the People's Republic of China spilled over into Czechoslovak-Chinese relations. Presidium member Vasil Bil'ák traveled to Beijing where he held talks with party General Secretary Hu Gili (Radio Prague, 22 March). The Chinese communist party sent a delegation to Prague, led by Wang Renzui, the head of the propaganda department (ČTK, 22 April). General Secretary Jakeš went to China on a five-day visit in May. When Zhao Ziyang, his host, stressed that it was essential for a socialist society "to ensure that the population should know what is going on and be able to help decide important issues," Jakeš replied that, while the problems of China and Czechoslovakia might be the same, the ways of dealing with them are different—an implicit defense of the KSČ's unwillingness to embark on the path of political reforms (Beijing, AP, 24 May).

Vasil Bil'ák and Michal Štefanák, head of the CC Department for International Affairs, participated in a meeting of the secretaries of CCs of ruling communist parties in Havana (Radio Prague, 25 February). The talks between General Secretary Jakeš and his East German colleague Erich Honecker in Berlin in March were reported to have taken place "in an atmosphere of brotherly friendship, trustful openness, and agreement." On this occasion, Jakeš decorated Honecker with the highest Czechoslovak award, the White Lion medal, first class, the first conferred on a German national (*Rudé právo*, 11 March). The cordiality of this meeting was no surprise; observers had long assumed that the dislike and mistrust of the Soviet reform course were similar in Prague and in East Berlin and would bring these two regimes, also similar in their lack of legitimacy in the eyes of their subject populations, closer together. Jakeš later traveled to Bucharest for a working visit and met President Nicolae Ceauşescu, with whom he discussed the modalities of cooperation between the two nations up to the year 2000 (Radio Prague, 27 April). The hard, conservative stance of the Communist Party of Romania under Ceauşescu, in itself congenial with the general position of the KSČ, did not outweigh the disagreement between the two leaders concerning their views of the Soviet military intervention in Czechoslovakia in 1968. Jakeš probably felt more at ease when he received in Prague the representative of the Communist Party of Bulgaria, Politburo member Grisha Filipov, who came to Czechoslovakia for an official visit in the fall (Radio Prague, 18 October). Bulgaria in 1988 seemed to be on a similar wave length with Czechoslovakia concerning political reforms and *glasnost'*. As the anniversary of the Soviet-led invasion of Czechoslovakia approached, these more-implicit than explicit agreements and disagreements surged to the surface.

Several interesting views and comments on this highly controversial issue could be gleaned from the world communist press. Among the most intriguing was an extensive feature story with illustrations in the *Moscow News*. The article came from Soviet journalists who in 1968 were in Czechoslovakia and witnessed the invasion as well as the reaction of the Czechoslovak population. They categorically refuted the claim of the so-called Soviet White Book (allegedly also compiled by "a group of Soviet journalists"), that "faithful Marxist-Leninists in the KSČ" had invited the invaders. They emphasized and documented by photos, taken during the invasion days, that the response of the Czechs and the Slovaks was uniformly negative (*Moscow News*, 25 August). Less suggestive but also pertinent were the comments on the 1968 crisis by Leonid S. Yagodovsky from the Institute of the Economics of the World Socialist System in Moscow (*Argumenty i fakty*, no. 33) and by academician Oleg Bogomolov (Soviet Television, 25 June). Yagodovsky admitted that "the Brezhnev leadership had from the start been biased against the reforms initiated by Alexander Dubček." Bogomolov declared that any further application of what is known in the West as the Brezhnev Doctrine is inconceivable.

Rozsoe Nyers, member of the politburo of the Hungarian Workers' Party, gave an interview to the British Broadcasting Company about Hungary's role in the 1968 intervention. He said that "the Hungarian leadership at that time was uncertain and

Hungarian leadership at that time was uncertain and was not united on this matter. In Nyers's opinion, "the intervention in Czechoslovakia—and the halting of the Czechoslovak reform process—was an unfavorable event both for Czechoslovakia's internal development and for the international reform process in the socialist world" (BBC, Central Talks and Features, report no. 53/88, 19 August). Georges Marchais, general secretary of the Communist Party of France, stated that "the intervention was a grave error, with deeply regrettable consequences" (Paris, L'Humanité, 22 August). The Communist Party of Italy, which over the past twenty years had made itself a champion of the cause of the abortive Czechoslovak reform, remembered the anniversary of the Soviet invasion by opening the pages of its central daily organ to Dubček and other protagonists of Prague Spring. An interview with Dubček (Rome, L'Unità, 10 January), elicited comments from Czechoslovak dissidents Zdeněk Jičínský, Rudolf Slánský, and Jan Štern, who called on the present leadership of the CPSU to explicitly "disown the 1968 invasion" (L'Unità, 14 January).

The present KSČ leadership seems to avoid contacts with those communist quarters in the world where the sensitive issue of the Prague Spring and its suppression by the Soviets was likely to be raised. "Comradely visits" outside the Soviet bloc were in 1988 oriented toward such parties as the communist parties of Greece and Syria (Radio Prague, 24 January). A party delegation from Afghanistan arrived in Prague in February (Radio Hvězda, 14 February). Of some interest was the visit by KSČ Presidium member Jan Fojtík with the leaders of the Social Democratic Party (SPD) of West Germany in Bonn (Radio Prague, 14 April). Although this contact, made on the invitation of the German SPD, did not imply the rehabilitation or legalization of the Czechoslovak Social Democratic Party, which was eliminated in 1948, such a step by the KSČ appeared more significant in the context of recent statements by the leaders of the CPSU concerning social democracy in general. Vadim Zagladin, first deputy chief of the International Department at the CPSU CC, having somewhat earlier called the communist parties and the social democratic parties "two wings of one great movement," perhaps one could read more into the KSČ's chief ideologist's trip to Bonn than a mere diplomatic gesture.

Biography. *Miloš Jakeš.* Miloš Jakeš was born into a poor peasant family in the Česky Krumlov area in August 1922. After graduating from school he was trained in electrical engineering and was employed as an installation worker and then industrial designer at the Svit factory in Gottwaldov. While working on these jobs he completed a course at the Higher School of Industry.

In June 1945, soon after Czechoslovakia was liberated by the Soviet Army, Miloš Jakeš joined the communist party. He carried out party functions at the Svit factory, served on the KSČ district and regional committees in Gottwaldov, was active in the youth organization, and was the first secretary of the district and regional committees of the Czechoslovak Union of Youth and a Presidium member and secretary of its Central Committee.

After graduating from the Higher Party School under the CPSU Central Committee, Miloš Jakeš was appointed head of a department in the KSČ Central Committee. In 1961 he was put in charge of the Central Office for the Affairs of National Committees. In 1963 he worked as first deputy chairman of the Central Office for Local Economic Development and in 1966–1968 as deputy interior minister in charge of civil administration.

In March 1968 Miloš Jakeš was elected chairman of the KSČ Central Auditing Commission on which he had served since 1966. During the open offensive of the anti-socialist and counterrevolutionary forces he firmly upheld the interests of the party and the people and was active in the drive to overcome the crisis in the party and in society and to clear the backlog of problems.

Miloš Jakeš became a member of the KSČ Central Committee, an alternate member of its Presidium, and a Central Committee secretary in 1977 and a full member of the Presidium, a Central Committee Secretary, and chairman of the KSČ Central Committee Commission on the National Economy in 1981. He has been a member of the House of the People since 1971 and a Presidium member of Czechoslovakia's Federal Assembly since 1981. The Central Committee of the Communist Party of Czechoslovakia elected Miloš Jakeš its general secretary at the plenary meeting in December 1987. (*WMR*, February, p. 70.)

Zdeněk Suda
University of Pittsburgh

Germany
German Democratic Republic

Population. 16,596,875
Party. Socialist Unity Party of Germany (Sozialistische Einheitspartei Deutschlands; SED)
Founded. 1918 (SED, 1946)
Membership. 2,324,995 members and candidates (*Neues Deutschland* [ND], 11 January 1989); 58.1 percent workers, 4.8 percent peasants and farmers in cooperatives, 22.4 percent intelligentsia, 14.7 percent others (*ND*, 18 April 1986)
General Secretary. Erich Honecker (76)
Politburo. 21 full members: Erich Honecker (chairman, State Council), Hermann Axen (72), Hans-Joachim Boehme (57; first secretary, Halle region SED executive), Horst Dohlus (63), Werner Eberlein (68; first secretary, Magdeburg region SED executive), Kurt Hager (77; member, State Council), Joachim Herrmann (60), Werner Jarowinsky (61), Heinz Kessler (68; defense minister), Guenther Kleiber (57; deputy chairman, Council of Ministers, and permanent representative to the Council for Mutual Economic Assistance [CMEA]), Egon Krenz (51; deputy chairman, State Council), Werner Krolikowski (60; first deputy chairman, Council of Ministers), Siegfried Lorenz (57; first secretary, Karl-Marx Stadt region SED executive), Erich Mielke (81; minister of state security), Guenter Mittag (62; deputy chairman, State Council), Erich Mueckenberger (78; chairman, Central Party Control Commission), Alfred Neumann (79; first deputy chairman, Council of Ministers), Guenter Schabowski (59; first secretary, Berlin region SED executive), Horst Sindermann (73; chairman, Council of Ministers), Willi Stoph (74; chairman, Council of Ministers, and deputy chairman, State Council), Harry Tisch (61; member, State Council, and chairman, Free German Trade Union Federation); 5 candidate members: Ingeborg Lange (61), Gerhard Mueller (57; first secretary, Erfurt region SED executive), Margarete

Mueller (57; member, State Council), Gerhard Schuerer (67; deputy chairman, Council of Ministers, and chairman, State Planning Commission), Werner Walde (62; first secretary, Cottbus region SED executive)
Central Audit Commission. Kurt Seibt, chairman (80; president, German Democratic Republic [GDR] Solidarity Committee)
Secretariat. 11 members: Erich Honecker, Hermann Axen (international relations), Horst Dohlus (party organs), Kurt Hager (culture and science), Joachim Herrmann (agitation and propaganda), Werner Jarowinsky (church affairs, trade, and supply), Egon Krenz (security affairs, youth, and sports), Ingeborg Lange (women's affairs), Günter Mittag (economics), Guenter Schabowski (Berlin), Werner Krolikowski (agriculture)
Central Committee. 165 full and 53 candidate members, as of 15 June
Status. Ruling party
Last Congress. Eleventh, 17–21 April 1986
Last Election. 8 June 1986, 99.94 percent of vote, all 500 seats won by National Front candidates.
Auxiliary Organizations. Free German Trade Union Confederation (FDGB), 9.5 million members, Harry Tisch, chairman; Free German Young (FDJ), 2.3 million members, Eberhard Aurich, first secretary; Democratic Women's League of Germany (DFD), 1.5 million members, Ilse Thiele, chairwoman; Society for German-Soviet Friendship (DSF), 6.3 million members, Erich Mueckenberger, president
Publications. *Neues Deutschland*, official SED daily, Herbert Naumann, editor in chief; *Einheit*, SED theoretical monthly; *Neuer Weg*, SED organizational monthly; *Junge Welt*, FDJ daily; *Tribune*, FDGB daily; *Horizont*, foreign policy monthly. The official news agency is Allgemeine Deutscher Nachrichtendienst (ADN).

The politics of consolidation and transition shared center stage in the GDR during 1988. Many signs of continuity were present. On the foreign policy front, East Germany continued to pursue new diplomatic initiatives in East-West relations, including a May visit to Washington by Politburo member Axen. The GDR leadership also gained considerable attention in late June through its sponsorship of an international meeting on establishing atom free zones in Central Europe. But, as always, domestic considerations played a more important role in shaping GDR politics and society. Despite continued public disagreement with the Soviet Union on the need for far-reaching reform in East Germany, Honecker continued to dominate the political scene. Change however was in the air, as East Germany's leaders found themselves confronted by a ground swell of popular dissatisfaction with a malfunctioning economy, continued religious persecution, and decades of environmental neglect.

Leadership and Party Organization.

Honecker's grip on political power remained unchanged in 1988. There had been speculation in the West (*Deutschland Archiv* [*DA*], March) that the long-serving party leader (since 1971) might step aside before the next party congress in 1991. At the seventh plenum of the the the SED (1–2 December), however, Honecker abruptly announced that the forthcoming Twelfth Party Congress had been brought forward a year. Why? Ostensibly because Honecker wants to have the next meeting (now scheduled to take place 15–19 May 1990) to coincide with the new five-year plan (*DA*, December).

But at 76 Honecker's departure over the next several years appears increasingly likely. One Western report (*Spiegel*, 9 January 1989) suggests that the long-serving party chief appeared to be losing his voice and attention span at year's end. Meanwhile, two noteworthy shifts in the SED leadership took place in 1988. On 3 November it was announced that Central Committee member Christa Zellmer had been chosen to replace the late Hans Joachim Hertwig as first secretary of the party district organization in Frankfurt (Oder). A more important event in the SED leadership took place earlier in the year with the sudden death of politburo member Werner Felfe on 7 September (*DA*, March; *ND*, 8 September) from a heart attack. A full politburo member since 1976, Felfe was Central Committee (CC) secretary for agricultural economics (*Landwirtschaft*) at the time of his death. His departure removes one of a handful of younger leaders considered possible successors to Honecker. His agriculture portfolio on the CC has since been taken over by Politburo member Krolikowski. But at year's end, a new Politburo member had yet to be named.

In the aftermath of Felfe's death, the strongest contenders for party leadership are considered to be Krenz, Schabowski, and Lorenz. A less likely possibility is Modrow, who has the reputation of being a cautious advocate of economic reform (RFE, 26 July). The results of a series of local and regional party elections, held between 12 September and 12 November, resulted in few surprises. A follow-up report by the CC secretariat says, for example, that only 23 candidates for local party secretary failed to receive the necessary votes (Bonn, *Bundesminister fuer innerdeutsche Beziehungen: Informationen*).

Domestic Affairs. *Sociopolitical Changes.* Although the SED leadership vigorously denied throughout 1988 that major segments of the population were becoming disenchanted, reality indicated otherwise. Reformist literature entering the GDR from the Soviet Union created special difficulties for the party last year. In February, for example, customs officials barred three issues of the German edition of *New Times* containing segments from Mikhail Shatrov's *And on, and on, and on*, a play critical of Stalin (*Economist*, 26 November). Throughout the year, ideological spokesmen made veiled critiques of Soviet journals that featured increasingly scathing critiques of the Stalinist period and the need for more grass-roots democracy in the Soviet Union. On 19 November, GDR authorities took even more drastic action against Soviet publications by imposing a total ban on the magazine *Sputnik*, which in German translation had enjoyed widespread readership in GDR schools. The catalyst behind this action was an article provocatively suggesting that Stalin and Hitler shared some common characteristics. In justifying the ban, the SED daily *Neues Deutschland* (*ND*, 25 November) asserted that comparing "Hitler with Stalin is unacceptable." These actions hardly took place in isolation, however. Over the same time period the East German Ministry of Culture abruptly withdrew five Soviet films from circulation after they had been listed in the program of the East Berlin film festival (*DA*, December).

But these events were only reflections of underlying shifts in GDR society. Civilian assertiveness frequently met with official repression in 1988 but not enough to discourage activist groups from pressing forward. In a preview of what the year would have in store, a human rights group took the unprecedented step of staging a parallel rally to the official yearly remembrance commemorating the executions of Karl Liebknecht and Rosa Luxemburg on 17 January 1919. The response was swift. Some 120 people were subsequently arrested. In response to growing West German and domestic pressure, the authorities partially reversed themselves a week later by sending 54 of these people West. The remaining detainees were subsequently released (*DA*, March).

More conflictual social relations in the GDR

have also been reflected in the role of the Protestant church. Honecker began to mend relations with the country's Protestant churches in the late 1970s, and over the past several years, the SED has achieved limited success in establishing common ground on such matters as the renovation of religious landmarks. For all that, ties between party and church reached a new level of tension in 1988. In a throwback to the Stalin era, officials blocked access to the Sophia Protestant church in East Berlin (*CSM*, 8 March) in early March. The ostensible reason was to discourage alleged "misuse" of church property by human rights groups. In late April, authorities prevented circulation of several regional Protestant weeklies because they discussed such sensitive subjects as emigration (RFE, 3 May).

The depth of official concern about deteriorating church-state relations was reflected in an SED secret document on church ties that came out of a meeting between Politburo member Jarowinsky and Bishop Werner Leich, chairman of the Federation of Evangelical Churches in the GDR on 19 February (*Frankfurter Allgemeine* [*FA*], 14 November). Although he lauded progress in church-state relations, Jarowinsky also uttered some blunt warnings to his religious counterpart. Referring to the use of churches for human rights gatherings, he warned, "The limit of what can be tolerated has been surpassed, the opposition groups have gone too far." Similar threats were made later in the year by Politburo member Mittag (*Tagespiegel*, 9 September). Such words did not, however, stop church authorities from calling for greater official tolerance for opposition voices. Reflective of this position were statements made by leaders of the Federation of Evangelical Churches in the GDR at its national synod in Dessau during mid-September. Commenting on the sensitive status of would-be emigrés, the federation's vice chairman, Manfred Stolpe, said that the church had a "coresponsibility" for taking care of such people (RFE, 22 September).

Despite their efforts, however, the authorities have come to recognize that crackdowns against dissent stimulate more criticism and rebellion. In limited but increasingly visible ways, the SED displayed signs of flexibility and greater openness in 1988. Stefan Heym, a longtime thorn in the SED's side, enjoyed a partial rehabilitation last year. A decade ago, Heym got into serious difficulty for defending the folksinger Wolf Biermann, and the expectation was that such pressure would force "East Germany's best-known nonperson" to emigrate West (*Economist*, 10 September). Traditional

GDR sensitivity to Western opinion may have convinced the SED that allowing Heym to remain in the GDR as an in-house dissident might improve East Germany's tarnished image. Indicative of Heym's new status was a highly complimentary biographical sketch carried in *Neues Deutschland* on the occasion of his 75th birthday in April (*DA*, May). The SED also appears to be inching toward a more honest rendering of German-Soviet relations during the Stalin era. "Our party deeply regrets and decisively condemns violations of legality and Stalin's personality cult," said the SED Politburo in its report on the sixth meeting of the Central Committee (*ND*, 12 November).

East German intellectuals have been considerably more circumspect in criticizing Stalin and calling for major ideological changes than have their Soviet counterparts. There are significant exceptions, however, including the "discovery" and subsequent publication of a manuscript condemning the Stalin era by the late culture minister Johannes R. Becher in the philosophy journal *Sinn und Form* (*DA*, July). In a particularly damning sentence, Becher wrote that socialism, far from "ushering in a happy future, gave birth to an era whose tragic content cannot be compared with previous periods." Living people are also being heard from. In a July interview in the West German magazine *Vorwärts*, the philosopher Juergen Kuczynski sharply criticized the backwardness of East Germany's economy and its shackled press. "Naturally there are still many remnants from Stalin's time among us," he said (*DA*, September).

The year 1988 also witnessed a more forthcoming SED posture on the Holocaust and more general policies toward Jewry. Until recently, the GDR had adamantly refused to make specific payments to survivors. Its argument was that East Germany was an antifascist state and bore no legal or moral responsibility for Hitler's crimes. But in early June, the ice broke. In separate meetings with representatives of East and West Germany's Jewish communities, Honecker made a commitment to pay up to $100 million in compensation to Holocaust survivors (RFE, 10 June). East Germany's new reconciliation policy toward world Jewry was also reflected in a series of official ceremonies in East Berlin throughout the fall. The events began on 29 September with a commemoration service cohosted by the national council of the National Front and the Association of Jewish Communities in the GDR. This was followed by an exhibition of Jewish contributions to German history at the Ephraim Palace in

East Berlin. The culminating event was the holding of a special commemorative session on Crystal Night in the GDR People's Chamber (Volkskammer) on 8 November (*DA*, December).

The new spirit of rapprochement has been extended to East Germany's small Jewish community as well. It has not been an easy path. Reduced to approximately 3,000 persons, this group largely consists of survivors from the Third Reich. In the past, the SED attempted to win their support by emphasizing the common bond of suffering between Jews and other persecuted groups during the Third Reich. At least for the party, this supposed bond has been strengthened by the presence of Jews in the SED's hierarchy. But these efforts have been largely nullified by the GDR's vocal propaganda campaign against Israel and its militant support for Arab countries. The sudden resignation of Isaac Neumann, a Polish-born U.S. rabbi, from his post in East Berlin this past spring hardly improved matters (RFE, 9 May).

But Honecker's efforts to make amends nevertheless bore some fruit in 1988. The government paid for the restoration of a synagogue in Prenzlauer Berg and committed itself to turning a nineteenth-century temple on Oranienburgstrasse into a memorial. These and other conciliatory actions have been taken for a number of reasons, but clearly the GDR's desire to improve economic relations with the United States is probably the most immediate one. Washington has consistently told East Berlin that prospects for expanded ties largely depend on the GDR's readiness to act on "unresolved financial issues," which means that the GDR must pay reparations to Holocaust victims (RFE, 20 October). For this reason, Edgar Bronfman's three-day visit to East Berlin in October was a watershed. As president of the World Jewish Congress, Bronfman was given special treatment by his East German hosts, including presentation by Honecker of the Star of People's Friendship (Stern der Völkerfreundschaft) on 17 October (*ND*, 18 October). Pronouncing himself satisfied with his host's more conciliatory positions on honoring Holocaust victims and payment of reparations, Bronfman called for the granting of most-favored nation treatment for the GDR.

Economic Affairs. The GDR's economic performance in 1988 was decidedly mixed. Compared with other Eastern European countries, East Germany continued to set the pace in terms of standard of living, technological development, and the ability to service external debts. Climatic conditions also improved. An extraordinarily cold winter during 1987 had created significant difficulties in the energy and transportation sectors and a resulting drop in production. Comparatively speaking, the January–March period of 1988 was relatively mild (*DA*, October; RFE, 8 August).

Notwithstanding these considerations, the GDR economy confronted severe, increasingly serious problems in 1988. According to the West Berlin-based German Institute of Economic Research (DIW), GDR growth last year was 2.7 percent, the lowest since 1982. The DIW maintains that GDR economic performance was hampered by serious delays in deliveries and unrealistic plan targets. Although GDR leaders are not about to throw in the towel after hearing the DIW report, they have also been making critical noises about the malfunctioning of their economy. Reflective of the new sobriety were the comments of Politburo member Eberlein at the fifth party plenum in December 1987 (*DA*, January; RFE, 8 August). Directly challenging the official optimism, he called on the party to "present an unadorned picture" of the real situation and to resist the tendency to "gloss things over."

Indeed, in a number of respects, East Germany's economic situation worsened last year because of long-standing labor and energy shortages, lagging technological modernization, and an archaic transportation infrastructure. There were also growing indications of deep-seated consumer dissatisfaction (*Spiegel*, 19 December). Reasons for such concern were not hard to find. This year's grain harvest was officially reported under plan by 1.4 million tons, along with major shortfalls in sugar beet production (*FBIS*, 1 December). Consumer goods production increased last year, but in Honecker's words, these successes have been marred by "production and contractual backlogs" (*FBIS*, 14 December). He reported that, out of 205 positions in the state's supply plan, 95 were not completely filled by the end of October (ibid.).

Despite official rejection of Soviet-style *glasnost'* in the political arena, Honecker and his Politburo colleagues displayed a marked readiness in 1988 to employ Mikhail Gorbachev's *glasnost'* in attacking major economic ills.

These official concerns were reflected in Honecker's remarks at a 12 February CC conference for district secretaries in East Berlin (*DA*, March). His criticisms included inadequate plan fulfillment, poor quality of components, and growing public dissatisfaction with the quality and supply of consumer goods; so it went throughout the year. At the sixth and seventh CC plenums, 9–10 June and 1–2 December, Honecker continued to hammer away at the dual themes of technological renewal and consumer dissatisfaction (*DA*, August; *FBIS*, 2 December).

On the energy front, 1988 brought mixed economic news. As a resource-poor country, the GDR's international debt position significantly worsened in the wake of huge energy price increases a decade ago. Although energy independence is an unrealistic goal, East German industry has undertaken a major effort to drastically curtail energy use. At the last CC plenum, Honecker reported major savings in raw material use. Projected oil imports from the USSR have been cut back by two million tons annually. The next five-year plan (1991–95) calls for saving the equivalent of at least 80 billion tons of unprocessed brown coal (*FBIS*, 2 December). But in comparison with Western industrial countries, energy consumption in the GDR remains high. As a result, independent sources question East German claims that total energy use is down (*Plan Econ Report*, 30 September). In the meantime, East Germany's growing environmental movement cannot but have been alarmed by Honecker's year-end announcement that refining of brown coal is to be further intensified (*FBIS*, 2 December).

Confronted with limited financial resources and unwilling to adopt free market reforms, the SED has launched a series of highly publicized "rationalization initiatives." The goal is to demonstrate that groups of well-trained, highly motivated people can achieve major productivity breakthroughs within the framework of centralized planning. At the seventh CC plenum, Honecker devoted special attention to the Schwedt initiative where, under the motto "fewer people produce more," a number of combines were reportedly able to achieve high productivity and quality ratings by their own efforts without the assistance of additional technology and manpower.

So, notwithstanding domestic and international pressures to reform, East Germany's leaders ended 1988 with a ringing endorsement of centralized planning and control. The mood was appropriately captured in Honecker's year-end statement that "the GDR's people have achieved a standard of living that is unprecedented in their history" (*FBIS*, 14 December).

Foreign Policy. *Intra-German relations.* By virtually any standard, East Germany's relations with West Germany have significantly improved over the past several years (*Die Zeit*, 20 January 1989), and 1988 was no exception as the two governments continued to expand bilateral cultural, economic, and political contacts. Not that the atmosphere was free of tension. Traditional East German sensitivity about domestic dissent occasionally spilled over into the intra-German arena. In late January, for example, the SED daily *Neues Deutschland* charged that GDR dissident groups were funded by contacts in West Berlin with ties to the West German intelligence service. Seen in broad outline, however, the past year once again underlined the importance assigned by the SED to robust ties with the Federal Republic of Germany.

This state of affairs is reflected in the growth of travel between the two Germanies. Official GDR sources report that in 1988 a total of 6,746,853 trips to West Germany, including West Berlin, were made by East German citizens; this compares with 5,059,860 trips in 1987 (*FA*, 5 January 1989). Of that number, more than a million were estimated to have been made by people under retirement age; close to 30,000 GDR citizens emigrated to West Germany over that period (RFE, 30 December). Moreover, requests for travel to the West that are turned down must now be accompanied by an official explanation for refusal, and such people may reapply. It bears noting that issuance of these new regulations comes sixteen years after they were formally agreed on by the two Germanies (*FA*, 15 December).

On the official level as well, practical breakthroughs were also achieved. These include a new regulation allowing West Berliners to make overnight visits to East Berlin (1 March); an accord to exchange segments of land on both sides of the divided city signed between the GDR and West Berlin (31 March); initiation of a student exchange program (18 May); in the first visit by a West German environmental minister to the GDR, the two governments' announcement of their joint commitment to tackle common German pollution problems (13 July); and a West German agreement to make a yearly payment of 860 million deutsche marks to the GDR until 1999 for use of the autobahns linking West Berlin and the Federal Republic of Germany (14 September).

Indicative of this warming trend was the number of by now routine trips made by high-ranking West German officials to the GDR last year. The list included Free Democratic Party leader Otto Graf Lambsdorff; Hans-Jochen Vogel, chairman of the Social Democratic Party (SPD); Voelker Ruehe, deputy head of the ruling parliamentary group in Bonn; Rita Suessmuth, then health minister; Martin Bangemann, then economics minister; Klaus Toepfer, environment minister; Oscar LaFontaine, prime minister of the Saarland; and Mayor Eberhard Diepgen. Chancellor Helmut Kohl also made a private trip to the GDR last year.

On a broader canvas, 1988 also reflected a fundamental consensus between the two Germanies on matters involving European security and arms control. Honecker emphasized this point in a speech before SED district secretaries on 12 February: "We highly value the Federal Republic's contribution" to reductions in middle- and short-range nuclear weapons" (*DA*, May). East German efforts to expand the scope of German-German cooperation in this area were also reflected in an August proposal by GDR defense minister Heinz Kessler to have meetings between respective heads of the two countries' defense establishments, an idea repeated by Honecker the following month. West Germany, however, demurred. Likewise, West German Chancellor Kohl turned down an invitation to participate in a GDR sponsored international meeting for atom free zones, held in East Berlin during 20–22 June (*DA*, August).

Discussions between the West German SPD and the SED on intra-German and broader European security concerns bore more fruit. The stage for this wide-ranging discussion was set in August 1987 with publication of a joint SPD-SED statement entitled "The Battle of Ideologies and Common Security" (*DA*, January). The dialogue continued last year, but at least on the SPD side there were signs of dissatisfaction. In an interview given to German radio on 11 September, Erhard Eppler, a moving force behind the dialogue, obliquely criticized the SED's insistence that discussion of security issues between the two political parties be confined to the search for "peace," rather than a broader effort to overcome ideological and political barriers within and between the GDR and the Federal Republic (*DA*, October).

East and West. Large elements of continuity occasionally interrupted by elements of change describes GDR foreign policy on the regional and global levels. There was little of substance to report in Honecker's approaches toward Eastern Europe. Underlining the GDR's increasingly strong sense of national independence, Honecker broke ranks with Gorbachev and other bloc leaders by ostentatiously praising Romanian leader Nicolae Ceauşescu when he made a visit to East Berlin in mid-November. Earlier meetings in 1988 between Honecker and his Hungarian and Polish counterparts, Károly Grósz and Wojciech Jaruzelski, appeared to yield little in terms of substance or expanded political cooperation (*DA*, August, October).

Likewise, few significant changes took place in Soviet-GDR relations. The SED's rejection of Gorbachev-style *glasnost'*, if anything, appeared to harden and was reflected in a variety of ways. In late June, for example, *Neues Deutschland* published an article praising former East German leader Walter Ulbricht, who at the end of his career became increasingly unpopular with Moscow (*NYT*, 30 June). This more nationalistic line was also reflected in Honecker's remarks about the right of each socialist state to chart its own course of development. "German communists never aimed at applying the Soviet system in their country," he said (ibid.). Such verbal militancy, however, was balanced by continued East German support for Gorbachev's foreign policy and arms control initiatives.

Regarding the West, the GDR broke new ground last year when Politburo member Axen made an "unofficial" visit to Washington in May, the first such trip by a high-ranking East German official to the United States (RFE, 5 May; *DA*, June). Organized by the Washington-based American Institute for Contemporary German Studies, the high point of his stay was a 45-minute meeting with Secretary of State George Shultz. There is good reason to believe that Axen's meeting with Shultz and various other U.S. officials during his sojourn helped set the stage for the GDR's subsequent announcement of its readiness to honor Jewish claims. The following month, the State Department's number two person, John Whitehead, participated in an international meeting at Potsdam, East Germany.

Building a profile in the West has been a major East German foreign policy goal for the past several decades. The record-setting performance at the Seoul Olympics and Honecker's various trips to France and Spain marginally added to that profile. At a minimum, no one in the West, or the East for that matter, could say at the end of 1988 that they had never heard of the German Democratic Republic.

John M. Starrels
Joint Economic Committee, U.S. Congress

Hungary

Population. 10,588,271
Party. Hungarian Socialist Workers' Party (Magyar Szocialista Munkáspárt; HSWP)
Founded. 1918 (HSWP: 1956)
Membership. 816,622 (*Pártélet*, November); 32.1 percent women, 40.2 percent industrial workers, 7.2 percent collective farm workers, 44.7 percent intellectuals and white-collar workers, 7.9 percent other occupations. Approximately 80 percent of the members joined the party after the 1956 revolution. The average age of the members is 46.6.
General Secretary. Károly Grósz (58, worker)
Politburo. 11 members: János Berecz (58, historian), Judit Chehák (48, physician), Károly Grósz (58, worker), Csaba Hámori (40, technical intelligentsia), Pál Iványi (47, technical intelligentsia), János Lukács (53, intelligentsia), Miklós Németh (40, economist), Rezsö Nyers (66, political economist), Imre Pozsgai (55, intelligentsia), István Szabó (64, farmer), Ilona Tatai (53, technical intelligentsia)
Secretariat. 6 members: Károly Grósz (general secretary), János Berecz, György Fejti (42), János Lukács, Pál Iványi (46, technical intelligentsia), Mátyás Szürös (55)
Central Committee. 108 members (listed in *FBIS*, 13 May)
Status. Ruling party
Last Congress. Thirteenth, 25–28 March 1985
Last Conference. Second, 20–22 May
Last Election. June 1985; 387 seats (35 national list, 352 multicandidate constituencies). Approximately 70 percent of deputies are HSWP members.
Auxiliary Organizations. Patriotic People's Front (PPF), general secretary, István Huszár; Communist Youth League (CYL), 700,000 members, general secretary, Imre Nagy; National Council of Trade Unions (NCTU), 4,399,00 members, general secretary, Sándor Nagy; National Council of Hungarian Women, chairwoman, Mrs. Lajos Duschek
Publications. *Népszabadság* (People's freedom), HSWP daily, editor in chief, Gábor Borbély; *Társadalmi szemle* (Social review), HSWP theoretical monthly, editor in chief, Katalin Radics; *Pártelet* (Party life), HSWP organizational monthly, editor in chief, Sándor Lakos; *Heti világgazdaság* (World economy weekly), editor in chief, Iván Lipovecz; *Magyar hirlap* (Hungarian news), semigovernment daily, editor in chief, Zsolt Bajnok; *Magyar nemzet* (Hungarian nation), PPF daily, editor in chief, István Soltész; *Népszava* (People's word), NCTU daily, editor in chief, Tamás Pálos; Hungarian Radio, president, István Hajdú; Hungarian Television, president, Gyula Bereczki. The official news agency is Magyar Tavirati Iroda (MTI), and its general director is Sándor Burján.

On 24 March 1918, Béla Kun, Endre Rudnyánszky, Tibor Szamuely, Károly Vantus, Ferenc Münich, and Ernö Por founded the Hungarian section of the Russian communist party in Moscow. On their return from Russia to Hungary they established the Party of Hungarian Communists (Kommunisták Magyarországi Pártja) on 24 November 1918 in a private apartment in Buda. Kun was chosen chairman, and his former fellow prisoners of war with the addition of some Hungarian left-wing socialists made up the Central Committee of the new party. Amid general anarchy in Hungary, induced by external and internal factors, the party seized power on 21 March 1919 and proclaimed the Hungarian Soviet Republic (*Magyar Tanácsköztársaság*). Despite its brutal terror, the communist dictatorship lasted only 133 days. After the fall of the Soviet republic, the party was outlawed. Throughout the interwar period, the party remained an insignificant force in Hungary's political life. The conquest of Hungary by the Red Army in the spring of 1945 heralded the return of a handful of Hungarian communists from their Soviet exile. Mátyás Rákosi, Ernö Gerö, Mihály Farkas, József Révai, Zoltán Vas, and a few others who survived Stalin's terror had made up the leadership of the Hungarian Soviet Republic of 1919. Rákosi and the other leading communists, facilitators of a policy dictated by Stalin, moved with ruthless determination toward the inauguration of a Soviet-type one-party regime in Hungary. By June 1948, under the protective umbrella of the Red Army and through the skilled combination of terrorist methods such as show trials of political opponents based on trumped-up charges and the forced merger of various political parties into the Hungarian Communist Party, this small group of dedicated Stalinists emerged as the sole custodians of all political, economic, and ideological power in Hungary.

Thus began the rapid degeneration of Hungary from a political nation into Hungarian-speaking producers of steel and consumers of grain within the greater Stalinist empire. The stage was also set to transform Hungary's cultural life into a replica of the Soviet literary scene. Révai, whose Stalinist loyalties frequently clashed with the ideas of his liberal intellectual upbringing, rallied around him some young people who, in addition to being fanatical party men, were of considerable talent and ability. Their motive in embracing Marxism-Leninism-Stalinism was an all-consuming desire to lift Hungary out of the stagnation of two world wars into the era of industrial modernization and material well-being. Stalin was their hero and the Soviet Union their model. For this Révai-Jugend, Khrushchev's secret speech on the true nature of Stalinism was an eye-opener, and the subsequent denunciation of Rákosi's policies by the Central Committee of the Hungarian Workers' Party in July 1956, a shattering experience. Suddenly they saw the chasm between their positions and the realities of daily life. With the same passion with which they had embraced communism, they now wanted to bridge the gap between themselves and the people. The ensuing confrontation between these writers and the party bureaucrats developed into a full-fledged struggle for freedom and democracy that in 1956 was to involve the whole Hungarian nation.

During the weeks that followed the suppression of the revolution, the leaders against the Soviet oppressors and the newly installed János Kádár regime were the workers. In view of the reign of terror by both the Soviet army and the reformed Hungarian State Defense Agency (*Államvédelmi Hatóság*) and the Kádár regime's disinformation campaign against the revolution, the Central Workers' Council became the only voice of opposition in Hungary.

Edict number 4 of 1963 of the Presidium of the People's Republic on the General Amnesty put an end to the Kádár regime's brutality. From 1963 on, Hungary's history has been a continual search for consolidation and stabilization of the political situation by both the regime and the people. To accomplish this objective, Kádár made a crucial move. Because he could not embrace the true message of 1956 and was equally unable to revive the myth of an innocent and perfect type of communism, he decided to depoliticize Hungarian society. At the beginning, Kádár's scheme of exercising power was

not without success. Viewed from the perspective of the Rákosi era, it broadened the average citizen's room to maneuver and meant that the people were not compelled to be active in politics. Hungarians who stayed away from adverse political activities were left alone. Helped by massive Western aid, the Hungarian economy appeared to improve, thus providing the Kádár regime with an additional modicum of success. In the early 1970s Hungary represented the only concrete success of the West in the Council for Mutual Economic Assistance. However, at the end of the 1970s, Hungary was left with a foreign debt of $7 billion (currently $18 billion), a backward economy unable to compete in the world market, an ideologically and politically bankrupt party and state bureaucracy, and a population that demanded more wealth and freedom.

Party Affairs. The year 1988 confronted a seriously divided and confused HSWP and its leadership with the very same problems that had been threatening the political, economic, and social fabric of Hungarian society for the previous ten years. Foreign debt and the budget deficit continued to rise sharply. Agricultural and industrial output stagnated. The indicators of economic efficiency declined. In political terms, Hungarians spoke freely and openly about their contempt for Kádár in particular and the party in general. Their opposition to and hatred of the regime was an open secret in the country. For the younger members of the party's top leadership, it became clear that Kádárism failed and that unless Kádár was removed, both the party and Hungarian society would continue to pay a terrible price.

Thus, in early January Hungary's critical situation facilitated an unlikely political alliance between János Berecz and Károly Grósz for Kádár's position. As a result of a tension-filled three-day party conference on 20–22 May, Kádár, Hungary's party leader since 25 October 1956, was replaced by then President of the Council of Ministers Grósz as general secretary of the HSWP. The composition of the party's highest governing body, the Politburo, was also radically altered at the conference. A newly elected Central Committee removed eight Politburo incumbents, including Kádár, and elected six new members to replace them. Dropped from the Politburo were György Aczél, Kádár, Sándor Gáspár, Ferenc Havasi, György Lázár, László Marothy, Károly Németh, and Miklós Ováry. New members are Iványi, Lukács, Németh, Nyers, Pozsgai, and Tatai. The new Politburo has eleven members with an average age of 52. The new 108-member Central Committee comprises 38 newcomers. Of the eight members removed from the Politburo, only Aczél, Kádár, and Marothy were re-elected to the Central Committee. The 986 delegates at the conference also approved, with four votes against, nine abstentions, the final version of the conference's position paper on party and political reform.

On the basis of this position paper, the new communist leadership was charged with the difficult task of strengthening and preserving the political monopoly of the party by initiating and implementing limited political and economic reforms. In his speech at the conference, Grósz, the new general secretary, clearly stated that in order to accomplish this objective, the party must assure the unity of political centralization. By combining the two top positions of party and government, he indicated that he intends to tighten the organizational discipline of the party and the government simultaneously. Within this political framework Grósz launched a vigorous campaign to improve the economy through modest reforms without actually altering the political situation.

However, his strategy of Kádárism without Kádár was doomed to fail, for Kádárism was not and is not designed to withstand prolonged depression. While Grósz was trying to deal with Hungary's critical economic situation, large segments of the population started to create the framework for expanded political participation outside the party. Thus, the popular movement for political pluralism forced the new leadership to deal with the two cardinal questions of political liberalization and economic reform. As far as the party is concerned, the results cannot give rise to self-satisfaction. Lacking a unified and acceptable strategy, Hungary's new leaders are torn between their ingrained conservatism and the obvious need for genuine political reforms as a precondition for additional economic sacrifices on the part of the people. Instead of trying to resolve this apparent contradiction, Grósz has preferred to remain ambiguous. Alternating between ominous warnings and self-criticism, he seems to acknowledge past political errors and the faults and deficiencies of economic planning but criticizes those within and outside the party who demand essential changes. His political schizophrenia was particularly manifest at a 29 November meeting of ten thousand party activists in Budapest. Replying to questions about independent groups, he criticized in the strongest terms "hostile counterrevolutionary forces" and "extremist reactionaries"

for disturbing Hungary's "international relations" and trying to undermine the army and the "forces of public security." He reassured his audience that the party intends to take a "firm stand" against these groups and individuals. At the same time, he appeared to extend an olive branch to those who want to avoid open confrontation with the party. (*Népszabadság*, 30 November.)

Equally ambiguous is the language used by Berecz, the secretary in charge of ideology and propaganda. In his speech to the Central Committee on 1 November, Berecz lashed out at both the Stalinist faction within the party and the liberal groups within and outside the party. He vowed that the party will counter such practices. (*Népszabadság*, 2 November.)

In contrast, Pozsgai, a newcomer to the Politburo, speaks of the desirability of politically competing with the communist party, which, according to him, must exist in a truly pluralistic environment. Pozsgai is supported in his more liberal views by another Politburo member, Rezsö Nyers, who stated in an interview with Radio Budapest that new legislation in Hungary provided for "the possibility of a socialist society developing a natural political system." (Kossuth Rádió, 18 November.) A new law—debated intensively throughout 1988 and passed by parliament on 11 January 1989—on association and assembly has already received various interpretations (*Népszabadság*, 23 August). Kálmán Kulcsár, the new minister of justice, claimed that the new law "recognizes the possibility of a multiparty system," whereas Berecz stated that this question will be decided by a separate, future law (*Népszabadság*, 3 December; *Magyar hirlap*, 29 December).

Although political developments in Hungary were in flux throughout 1988, the forces demanding real political and economic reform have gained strength and momentum. Conversely, the party in general and Grósz in particular are losing control over the situation. The reorganization of the Politburo in May 1988 did not eliminate a single problem facing the party. A more sophisticated strategy aimed at granting limited political pluralism will not avert the impending economic, social, and moral collapse of Hungarian society. What Hungary needs is real and genuine political reform as the precondition for a sustained economic renewal.

Economic Affairs. Despite encouraging developments in foreign trade in 1988, Hungary's economy was characterized by an accelerating decline.

At the November meeting of the Central Committee of the HSWP, the overall state of the economy was termed "unsatisfactory." The statement issued by the Central Committee listed several new and old reasons that rendered the full implementation of last year's government program impossible. Interest payments on foreign loans, the hostile environment of East bloc trade, and mismanagement of the economy in general and Hungary's financial resources in particular were blamed for another disappointing year of economic failures. What the statement failed to point out was that these problems of the country's economy are due to the party's refusal to change the political framework within which, after all, the economy dysfunctions. (*Népszabadság*, 3 November.)

In addition, the statement displayed little enthusiasm for radical economic reform. Even the new law on business associations was treated in a rather offhand fashion at the conference. This law, which entered into force on 1 January 1989, regulates, among other things, the forming of companies by state and private offering of stocks and the financing of limited liability companies through the sale of shares. Moreover, companies that are privately or foreign owned can employ up to five hundred workers. Private stock companies can be formed with a minimum capital of ten million forints (approximately $185,000). The minimum threshold for limited liability companies is one million forints (approximately $18,500). (*Magyar közlöny*, no. 47.)

A closely related second law also came into force on 1 January 1989 that deals with the taxation of business associations. The law mandates a 50 percent general tax on companies with a net annual profit of three million forints or more. Companies that make less net profit than that will be taxed at the rate of 40 percent. These high rates of taxation indicate that the political intent of the new legislation was to cover Hungary's current account deficit rather than launch a new, bold offensive of economic modernization. Also, as the Association of National Enterprises (Vállalkozók Országos Szövetsége) pointed out in its comprehensive criticism of both laws, their fatal shortcoming is that they do not contain any provision on real wages adjusted to inflation. A promise made by Grósz in 1987 concerning such a law remained unfulfilled by the government in 1988. Equally troubling is the decision taken by the Central Committee at its November session to liberalize import regulations. Because the existing restrictions on hard currency imports helped to create the 1988 surplus in hard currency

trade, this decision could be self-defeating. By the same token, fledgling private companies will certainly find stiff competition from Western firms difficult to overcome. (*Magyar közlöny*, no. 61.)

At present, Hungary's economy is at a standstill. In the first three quarters of 1988, production of the state and cooperative industrial enterprises was essentially the same as in the same period in 1987. Production in the basic material sectors increased by 3.2 percent. The production of the processing industry remained the same. Production in the energy sector decreased by 2.8 percent. Machine industry production increased by only 0.3 percent. In the light and food industries production also decreased, and domestic industrial sales went down by 1.4 percent. However, industrial exports to hard currency markets increased by 6 percent. The value of retail trade turnover between January to September 1988 increased by 10.5 percent, but its quantity decreased by 5.4 percent. Domestic sales of food and beverages decreased by 1.9 percent and miscellaneous industrial articles, 2.9 percent. Finally, the consumer price index increased by an average of 15.9 percent. The greatest increase took place in the price of food, clothing, services, heating, and household energy supplies. (*Népszabadság*, 2 November.)

Social and Cultural Affairs. In 1988, a hopelessly divided leadership faced growing pressure from below to move toward genuine political pluralism. The inability of this leadership to resolve their disagreements and to forge a unified strategy contributed to the overall uncertainty and instability in Hungary. As a consequence, a multitude of groups, formal and informal associations, and a broad range of *samizdat* publications began to emerge throughout the country. Apparently torn between their hope of co-opting the more moderate elements of these emerging groups and their ingrained hostility toward any form of dissent, Hungary's leaders' reaction to this proliferation of pluralism wavered between benign tolerance and police brutality. Generally, the leadership's tolerance outweighed the number of violent reactions. For example, the authorities, overall, exhibited understanding toward numerous protests organized by various groups against the officially supported Gabcikovo-Nagymaros dam system in which on occasion more than twelve thousand demonstrators participated. Although some members of the Politburo expressed strong suspicion that the majority of the participants had hostile political motives beyond their sudden concern for the environment, the party- and government-controlled media provided extended coverage of the protestors' position.

Another issue that met with official approval was protesting Romania's treatment of its Hungarian minority. Thus on 27 June, a demonstration by more than 30,000 people was widely reported by the Hungarian press and radio and shown in detail on Hungarian television. (*Népszabadság, Magyar nemzet, Magyar hirlap*, 28 June.) Demonstrations aimed at commemorating the revolution of 1956 or gatherings expressing displeasure with the Soviet Union, however, were dealt with in a decisive manner. On 23 October, the anniversary of the Hungarian revolution, the police banned all demonstrations by any group. Individuals that tried to circumvent the ban were beaten and taken to police headquarters. Similarly, a symbolic and peaceful protest demonstration on 7 November, the annniversary of the October Revolution in Russia, an official holiday, was quickly dispersed by the police. Marosan, the new government spokesman, made it clear that "the festive nature" of this day "cannot be brought into doubt." (*Soviet East European Report*, 15 November.)

Elemér Hankis, director of the Institute of Sociology of the Hungarian Academy of Sciences, classified the Federation of Democratic Youth (Fiatal Demokraták Szövetsége), the organization that staged the protest, as the "most militant and strongest" independent movement in Hungary and "the party's staunchest opponent" (*Danas*, 31 May). Founded in March 1988 by law students, the federation specifically bars members of the official CYL from participation. Its nineteen-point manifesto, which includes calls for free elections, a multiparty system, a re-evaluation of 1956, reviving the traditional Kossuth crest to replace the current one, real freedoms, and the withdrawal of all Soviet troops from Hungary, is clearly unacceptable to the leadership. This official position was echoed by Berecz on Hungarian television on 19 October. A prominent Hungarian weekly charged that the federation was subjected to "police measures" because of its unwillingness to register with the authorities (*Magyarország*, 21 October).

Another youth organization, the National Council of Hungarian Youth (Magyar Ifjak Országos Tanácsa), however, received official recognition. Claiming that the CYL had "lost the confidence of young people," the council vowed to operate within the framework of the existing legal system. Another feature of this organization attractive to the au-

thorities is that it reached out and successfully co-opted previously "illegal" and "semilegal" groups, such as the 405 Club of the Technical University of Budapest and the Catholic Association (*Magyar hirlap*, 22 July). Other newly founded democratic organizations include the March Front, the Openness Club, the Hungarian Democratic Forum, the Szárszó Front, and the Alliance of Free Democrats.

Although in existence since March, the March Front deliberately maintained a low profile until its formal inception in September. The March Front membership includes such diverse political personalities as Nyers and Miklós Vásárhelyi, spokesman of Imre Nagy during the revolution of 1956, and Mihály Bihari, Zoltán Király, and László Lengyel, recently expelled members of the HSWB. Accordingly, members differ about the objectives of the front. Whereas Nyers sees in the organization a vehicle to "rethink socialism" and to promote a "democratic consensus" (Kossuth Radio, 17 September), Vásárhelyi defined the goal of the organization as helping to create democratic pluralism (*Corriere della sera*, 11 October).

The Openness Club was the brainchild of Pozsgai, member of the newly constituted Politburo. Formally recognized in October, the club started promoting freedom of speech and of the press as early as January (*Mozgó világ*, July). The Hungarian Democratic Forum appears to be a free-for-all intellectual movement. Because the forum moderated its position on a host of issues, it enjoys a certain degree of official support. (*Magyar nemzet*, 14 November 1987; *Heti világgazdaság*, 16 September.) The Alliance of Free Democrats is another loose coalition dominated by populist intellectuals. In reality, there is little difference between the alliance and the democratic forum. (Kossuth Radio, 13–14 November.) The Szárszó Front, formally established in September, views itself as a political heir to the Smallholders' Party of 40 years ago. Two environmental groups, the Danube Circle and the Blues, have for several years mounted an increasingly aggressive campaign against the Gabcikovo-Nagymaros dam system to no avail (Kossuth Radio, 17 October).

There are two left-wing associations currently active in Hungary. The Alternative Association promotes a "long-term concept of the future of socialism." Claiming that Stalinism was "actually right-wing," the association urges the authorities to introduce genuinely socialist institutions into politics and the economy. (Kossuth Radio, 22 October.)

The other organization is the Ferenc Münich Society, named after the former prime minister of Hungary. The society, which opposes liberalization, has attracted since its inception on 9 December, active and retired party workers, police and army officers, and members of the HSWP's paramilitary arm, the Workers' Guard (Munkásörség) (*The Washington Times*, 3 January 1989).

Foreign Affairs. In an article published on 17 December in the party daily *Népszabadság*, Mátyás Szürös defined the leitmotiv of Hungarian foreign policy as a contribution to the country's social and economic restructuring. He noted with satisfaction that although domestic developments alternated between progress and setbacks, Hungary's foreign policy was characterized by continuity and renewal. The overriding objective of Grósz's visits to the United States, Canada, Austria, and France was to maintain and, if possible, foster the favorable image of Hungary as the most liberal state in the Warsaw Pact. He was less successful in his second objective, namely, facilitating more trade between the West and Hungary. In the United States Grósz tried to reassure his hosts that Hungarian political and economic reforms will continue. Showing a degree of independence from Moscow, Hungary established official relations with the Republic of Korea (ROK) in September. At the end of December, Sin Tongwon, first deputy foreign minister of the ROK, visited Hungary at the invitation of his Hungarian counterpart, Gyula Horn. At the end of their two-day meeting, they signed an investment protection agreement. According to the official Korean news agency, Yonhap, the two countries will announce an agreement on ambassador-level diplomatic relations when Gyula Horn visits Seoul in January 1989 (MTI, in English, 28 December). Closer to home, Hungary signed an agreement with the European Economic Community that will make the latter's market more accessible for Hungarian goods. Commenting on the agreement, Szürös pointed out that Hungary could serve as a bridge between Eastern and Western Europe. (*Népszabadság*, 7 December.)

Communist Affairs. As Berecz stated, the HSWP is "happy to witness the emergence of the new philosophy in East-West relations" (*Külpolitika*, English supplement, 7–8 March). At the same time, party leaders expressed satisfaction over developments in the Soviet Union (*Népszabadság*, 3 July). Sporadic criticism directed at the Council for

Mutual Economic Assistance did not affect Hungary's political loyalty to Moscow.

In July, Grósz visited Moscow on his first trip abroad as general secretary and held talks with Mikhail Gorbachev, Egor Ligachev, and Nikolai Ryzhkov. These meetings focused on Grósz's upcoming visit to the United States and Canada and bilateral political and economic relations. Within the framework of political relations they also discussed the possibility of Soviet troop reductions in Hungary. (*Népszabadság*, 5–7 July.) Hungary's troubled relationship with Romania further deteriorated in 1988. In addition to the objectionable treatment of the more than two million Hungarian nationals living primarily in Transylvania, Hungary protested the destruction of Hungarian villages throughout Romania. A meeting in Arad between Grósz and Nicolae Ceaușescu failed to reconcile the differences between the two parties. (*Népszabadság*, 1 September.) Hungary's relationship with North Korea became strained because of developments with South Korea. Relations with other communist countries developed satisfactorily in 1988.

Government and Mass Organizations. In 1988, the notion that a successful reform of the economy could not be realized without an essential transformation of the existing political institutions became universally accepted. Most important, the political significance of a new constitution that will reflect the changes in the functions and roles of the government, the parliament, and the judiciary became apparent. One major area that needs revision, according to Dr. Kálmán Kulcsár, the new minister of justice, concerns the basic principles of political and social power in Hungary. In this context, the question of political pluralism will have to be addressed in practical terms. Another area of political concern is a detailed division of power among the individual branches of government and the HSWP. Because the role of parliament was perceptibly enhanced in 1987 and 1988, constitutional guarantees to safeguard and expand the pre-eminent political status of the legislature must be adopted. As part of this process, the 21-member Presidential Council, which acts as a substitute parliament and as a collective head of state, will have to be abolished. By the same token, the powers of the courts must also be reinforced and fundamentally expanded. Proposals include creating a constitutional court modeled on the U.S. Supreme Court and the Federal Constitutional Court of the Federal Republic of Germany. To protect citizens from arbitrary actions by central and local government agencies, a separate administrative court system must be introduced. Other proposals suggest that judicial independence must be absolutely protected by the new constitution against political meddling by the party and the government.

For the time being, Németh's new government is in an extremely difficult situation. In addition to being charged with solving Hungary's severe economic problems, the young prime minister must counter mounting public cynicism toward both the party and the government. Although speeches by Németh and other leaders have dealt primarily with the economy, members of parliament and independent organizations addressed with increasing frequency the burning political problems of pluralism and trust.

The three major auxiliary organizations of the HSWP continued to persist in their attempts to formulate programs independent of the party. This trend undoubtedly indicates intense pressure from the increasingly radical memberships, which took positions openly contradicting those of the party throughout 1988. As a result, CYL, Hungary's official youth organization, is undergoing a severe crisis of confidence. Over the past five years its membership declined from 920,000 to 700,000. Csaba Hámori, a member of the Politburo, was replaced as the CYL's general secretary by his deputy Nagy in late November. Hámori, who in the past was an obedient servant of the leadership, embroiled himself in a political controversy by stating that communism is "utopian" and that the steps leading to communism are not worked out "scientifically" (Kossuth Radio, 17 September). He, in turn, was criticized by veteran Kádárist György Aczél for his statements (*Népszabadság*, 28 September). Following Hámori's controversial remarks, the CYL reverted to closed meetings because debates became "passionate" and members leveled "personal attacks" at each other (Kossuth Radio, Magyar Television, 8 October).

Miklos Radványi
Library of Congress

Poland

Population. 37,958,420
Party. Polish United Workers' Party (Polska Zjednoczona Partia Robotnicza; PZPR)
Founded. 1918, Communist Workers' Party; 1948, PZPR
Membership. Approximately 2.2 million
First Secretary. General of the Army Wojciech Jaruzelski
Politburo. Wojciech Jaruzelski, Władysław Baka, Kazimierz Barcikowski, Stanisław Ciosek, Kazimierz Cypryniak, Józef Czyrek, Czesław Kiszczak, Iwona Lubowska, Zbigniew Michałek, Alfred Miodowicz, Marian Orzechowski, Wiktor Pyrkosz, Mieczysław Rakowski, Gabriela Rembisz, Janusz Reykowski, Florian Siwicki, Zdzisław Świątek. Alternate members: Zdzisław Bialicki, Manfred Gorywoda, Marek Hołdakowski, Janusz Kubasiewicz, Zbigniew Sobotka
Central Committee Secretaries. Wojciech Jaruzelski, Władysław Baka, Stanisław Ciosek, Zygmunt Czarzasty, Józef Czyrek, Zbigniew Michałek, Leszek Miller, Marian Orzechowski, Marian Stępień
Status. Ruling party
Last Congress. Tenth, July 1986
Last Election. 1985; the regime claimed that 78.81 percent of eligible voters participated; all 460 seats
Auxiliary Organizations. United Peasant Party (ZSL); Democratic Party (SD)
Publications. *Trybuna ludu* (*TL*), party daily; *Nowe drogi* and *Ideologia i politika*, party monthlies; *Życie partii*, fortnightly party organ; *Tygodnik powszechny* and *Słowo powszechne*, Catholic publications. Polska Agencja Prasowa (PAP) is the official news agency.

The year 1988 will be remembered as another unhappy time of social conflict and economic decline. It was a year of confrontation between communist authorities and Polish society that included two waves of strikes organized by a new generation of workers and the perpetuation of an indecisive program for socioeconomic reform. Poland may be the most liberal country in the Soviet bloc: opposition against the communist government is vocal and widespread. However, the regime's hostility toward Solidarity and the Roman Catholic Church has prevented the authorities from negotiating a solution to the country's massive problems. In 1988, political moves by General Jaruzelski left no room for legalization of Solidarity or for granting constitutional status to the church. Democratization of the political system, a precondition for social and economic reforms, has been postponed. Current policies erode the standard of living and preclude institutional guarantees for pluralism and restructuring the economy. The authorities in Warsaw, repeating the mistakes of the past four decades, have pushed the country toward a cyclical pattern of economic decline, political stalemate, and social upheaval.

Communist rule has resulted in historically unprecedented failures. Socioeconomic ills include a poverty comparable only to the Third World, the highest mortality rate in Europe, environmental pollution that has forced authorities to declare the Nowa Huta steel plant in the Kraków district an "area of ecological disaster," inflation that exceeded 120 percent, rampant alcoholism, and mass emigration to the West that is draining the nation's human resources. The government's approach to reform and social regeneration excludes participation by the vast majority of people. The present level of pluralism in Poland tolerates de facto opposition and permits the legal functioning of some political and economic associations defined as "clubs." However, this is insufficient to reverse Poland's decline.

Economic reforms are impossible without simultaneous political changes. The traditional communist preference for a totalitarian model has enabled Jaruzelski's regime to stay in power at the price of isolation and an inability to mobilize society to work. For this reason, the economy is stagnant and the population, apathetic. It is not surprising that the authorities have no legitimacy and are afraid to yield any tangible political concessions. But this situation cannot last forever, and the question is whether the regime is able to establish a coalition government in a peaceful manner or if another full-fledged national revolt will become necessary to accomplish real change.

It is important to realize that the protracted crisis in Poland could have been solved eight years ago. Concessions to the moderate forces of the opposition would have restored trust in the government and focused national attention on the economic and social decay. The essence of the Polish drama is the inability of the authorities to extricate the nation from the crisis. Official propaganda has reduced the issue to economic failure, but the Polish crisis is political in character. In the words of Lech Wałęsa, winner of the Nobel Peace Prize and leader of the outlawed union Solidarity, "The government's program for economic reforms goes along with that of Solidarity, but Solidarity is also fighting for the democracy to which Poles aspire. Solidarity is the people, Solidarity is indispensable to the life of the country and nothing can be done without its cooperation" (AFP, *FBIS-Eastern Europe [EEU]*, 6 June).

The Party. Two separate themes dominated the agenda of the ruling communist party in Poland: personnel changes and sterile ideological debates. The seventh plenum of the Central Committee reorganized the Politburo and the Secretariat, curtailing the influence of the dogmatic faction. Those demoted from the Politburo included Marian Woźniak and Włodzimierz Mokrzyszczak. Chief political commissar General Józef Baryła, Tadeusz Porębski, and Stanisław Ciosek resigned their seats on the Secretariat. Stanisław Bejger, a nonvoting Politburo member, was removed from his post and later dismissed as the party leader at Gdańsk for his failure to prevent strikes in early May. Also, Henryk Bednarski was fired from the chairmanship of the Central Committee ideological commission. Of those who resigned, only Ciosek was promoted to deputy membership in the Politburo as replacement for Bejger. Other promotions included Władysław Baka, who was named to the Politburo and the Secretariat with responsibility for economic reforms; Marian Orzechowski, Mieczysław F. Rakowski, and Bogusław Kołodziejczak were appointed to the Secretariat. Rakowski had already been a member of the Politburo, and Orzechowski took over chairmanship of the Central Committee ideological commission responsible for preparing the Third All-Poland Theoretical and Ideological Conference scheduled for 1989. (Warsaw Domestic Service, 14 June; *FBIS-EEU*, 15 June; *NYT*, 16 June; RFE *Research*, 30 June.)

These changes indicated a pragmatic liberal tilt on the new Politburo and Secretariat, the highest bodies of the ruling communist party. As always personnel changes preceded a shift in the political course taken by the party. Moreover, personnel changes are an indirect admission of political setbacks. It also became evident that every official serves at Jaruzelski's pleasure. He has no propensity to indulge in the personality cult preferred by Stalin and the older generation of communist leaders. However, in the Stalinist tradition, Jaruzelski maintains direct command over key sources of power and keeps in check every leader working for him. The military flow of power established during martial law is yet to be dismantled, and the Polish leader acts as a policeman while pretending to be a reformer.

The eighth plenum of the Central Committee met at the end of August following the second wave of social unrest. The party leadership failed to reexamine policies that were rejected by the November 1987 referendum. Instead, the Central Committee attacked the so-called Solidarity myth and the strike ringleaders. General Jaruzelski recognized that the "situation is complicated" but credited the party for securing stability of the "Polish socialist state." In the name of socialist pluralism, he made careful overtures towards the Roman Catholic Church, the official unions, and other social groups but reminded his audience that the ultimate responsibility for the fate of Poland is in the hands of the party. Solution to the Polish problem, according to Jaruzelski, is in "strengthening and continuing the supreme principles of the political line of the party [and] above all, boldness—boldness in breaking down long-standing stereotypes, obstacles, and barriers" (Warsaw Domestic Service, 27 August; *FBIS-EEU*, 29 August). Like many times before, neither the assessment of the situation nor recommended remedies had anything in common with reality. The opposition, which exists and is supported by the majority, has no place in the official political milieu.

In September the government of Zbigniew Messner was forced to resign and was replaced by the cabinet of Mieczysław F. Rakowski. At the same time, General Jaruzelski promised that the last 1988 plenum of the Central Committee "should be something in the nature of a jolt." (Warsaw Domestic Service, 17 November; *FBIS-EEU*, 18 November.) When the tenth plenum finally convened at the end of December, the results were unclear and confusing. The meeting started with a purge of individuals blamed for economic and political failures, including Zbigniew Messner, who lost the power of Politburo member. The new premier, Mieczysław Rakowski, was relieved from the post of Central Committee secretary but retained his membership on the Politburo. Stanisław Ciosek, a veteran "liberal" communist specializing in relations with trade unions, was promoted to full Politburo membership. (Warsaw Domestic Service, 21 December; *FBIS-EEU*, 22 December.)

Jaruzelski's address to the plenum contained nothing "in the nature of a jolt." Instead, he repeated the themes of previous speeches. His unyielding view that the party "is and will remain the key political force of socialist Poland" was reiterated together with assurances that the party is neither "capitulating" nor "slowing down." (Warsaw Domestic Service, 20 December; *FBIS-EEU*, 21 December.) In the speech summarizing the plenum, General Jaruzelski concluded that after all, the Polish situation is not bad compared with some Third World countries. His imagination wandered so far as to assume that by cutting expenses on social welfare, Poland could become another "Asian Tiger." At the end, the Polish leader identified only one weakness in the current political program: "we do not sufficiently utilize support and popularize initiative."

But the possibility of an agreement with the opposition was cautiously outlined at the plenum by Premier Rakowski, who recognized the "conciliatory attitude of Wałęsa" and Solidarity's inclination to "arrive at agreement with the country's chief political force, our party and allies" (Warsaw Domestic Service, 21 December; *FBIS-EEU*, 22 December). On 22 December, the tenth plenum suspended its activity for "consultations with the working class" on the subject of trade union pluralism in Poland. By the end of the year, no decision had been made regarding the future legal status and political influence of Solidarity.

Ideological debate. Official deliberations have focused on a model of pluralism as Poland's political prototype for the future. In practice the question is how to reconcile the 1976 constitutional provision granting the communist party a political monopoly with a democratic system of government that calls for a multiplicity of political and social organizations.

The Poles are careful to differentiate between the so-called bourgeois pluralism, considered to be confrontational and a by-product of class division, and socialist pluralism, open for prosocialist forces only. In principle, the monopoly of the communist authorities would not be threatened by allowing various social groups to organize independently from the authorities. Independent social organizations committed to the principles of socialism, a form of loyal opposition, should not violate the constitution.

The road to pluralism in Poland must include two basic steps. First, the authorities should entirely abolish censorship except in matters of national security and when dictated by moral principles. Second, the citizens should be permitted to form social groups representing their political ideas. These groups would become autonomous partners with the communist party and participate in political bargaining within the general framework of the system.

This approach to pluralism in Poland is endorsed by the authorities but with some important exceptions. From the perspective of the communist party, socialist pluralism is a form of "reborn" socialism. Consequently, the party claims the right to choose or create its political partners rather than to legalize existing grass-roots organizations like Solidarity. The authorities promote the idea of dialogue and accord, yet they are unwilling to restrain their own power. The union is seen as violating two preconditions for an accord. First, from the legal point of view, the union has been defined as a sociopolitical movement ineligible for trade union status. Second, Solidarity's goals—according to the authorities—clash with the constitutional system in Poland, rendering the organization socially destructive in the eyes of the authorities. Jerzy Turowicz, chief editor of the Catholic *Tygodnik powszechny* (20 October), observed that

> If it is necessary to expand the social base of and reform the government system, to attract to political life independent committees which remain outside the political system or even oppose it, and to include members of these committees in representative bodies and in the power apparatus, this must not be done by advance, arbitrary individual selection or by appointing a kind of opposition. Independent political forces which are outside the political system should be able to set up their own organizations, to publish their own programs, to enjoy free access to the mass media, and to exert a real influence on public opinion in order, if possible, to enable their representatives to share in the system of political power.

The regime is busy erecting new political structures that are closely tied to the party, such as the Patriotic Council of National Rebirth. This strategy of winning social credibility is fundamentally dishonest and manipulative. "We are dealing with a more or less patient monologue by the authorities," observed one commentator. For communist authorities, society is "a rhetorical figure devoid of reality." (*Konfrontacje*, April.) The definition of socialist pluralism is subordinated to the principle of "leadership of the communist party" and maintenance of the party's superiority in the country.

The coalition method of governing promoted by the party is designed to consolidate various social forces under the communist hegemony. The party searches for new tactics that would reaffirm its monopoly of power and provide for greater flexibility in daily management of national affairs. Specifically, General Jaruzelski has redefined the role of the government—its structure and functions, its representative, administrative, and judicial bodies—while leaving the supremacy of the party intact. He hopes that broadening the freedom of choice available to the government will achieve stability of the system. The coalition government would be allowed to articulate demands, check bureaucracy, and avoid duplication of administrative structures. The party's model of socialist pluralism is confined to the principles of democratic centralism. Basically, it is an updated version of the united or single-front political façade hiding the communist monopoly.

The current version of ideological adjustment offers no room for grass-roots democracy in the form of a multiparty system and, in consequence, falls short of popular expectations. The regime continues to suppress Solidarity, while attempts to reestablish the prewar Polish Socialist Party and the Christian Democratic Party have been turned down by the authorities. As a Polish political scientist explained,

> What is happening is a defense of the party's more important role—that of the sole, dominant political force—by giving up some of its decision-making powers in some areas . . . That means other forces will now be allowed to participate, but only if they first recognize the supremacy of the party. (*WP*, 19 November 1987.)

As a result, the political reforms offered by Jaruzelski's regime have been rejected by society. The party has not freed itself of its Stalinist frame of mind, and the system under socialist pluralism is the same as it was during the past four decades. This is a mistake of historical proportion similar to the decision to build heavy industry in the age of electronics and the imposition of Russian totalitarianism on a nation culturally rooted in individualistic and Christian traditions.

Internal Affairs. The creative forces of society exist outside the party, and the main preoccupation of the communists is to maintain political power. The party is experiencing a prolonged structural and ideological crisis, which, according to its spokesmen, include

Weakness and low level of influence by many primary organizations

Failure of members to identify with the party

Absence of an unequivocal ideological interpretation of social, economic, and political processes

Low level of commitment by party members

Insufficient party influence and low prestige among workers, peasants, and young people

Poor results in recruiting new members among those categories

Bureaucracy and ineffective action in party organizations

Sharp distinction between party and nonparty members (*TL*, 10 November).

A declining ability of the regime to mobilize society was exemplified by the June local election. This experiment with democracy was designed to include Solidarity, but the party never relinquished control over the nomination procedure. Eventually, only 700 "opposition" members competed in 108,000 races. Local election committees often had to search for candidates as the public ignored the campaign. The turnout was stated to be about 56 percent, the lowest since the first postwar elections in 1947. (*WP*, 20 June; *CSM*, 21 June.) Following this defeat a secret report prepared by Mieczysław Rakowski, a Politburo member since December 1987 and premier since September 1988, stated

that socialism has arrived at a historic point. It will either find in itself sufficient creative power, courage, and imagination to liberate itself from ideas that are no longer useful as well as from antiquated judgments, or it will condemn itself to a slow death. Should there be no power of renewal, we must assume that the future of our system will be marked by convulsions and revolutionary explosions that will increasingly be initiated by enlightened people. (*Der Spiegel*, 18 July; *FBIS-EEU*, 19 July.)

But the "traditional" communists see themselves as a driving moral-political force that is promoting unprecedented reforms, undoing the damage inflicted by former party leader Edward "Gierek's voluntarism and Solidarity's extremism," fostering a program of broad democratization, developing self-government in various spheres of social life, increasing the role of the Sejm (parliament), establishing a constitutional tribunal, granting greater freedom of speech and press, and promoting dialogue with society (*FBIS-EEU*, 7 March).

The party has learned to keep its distance from everyday policies and has erected a shield protecting the Politburo from criticism due to failures of economic reforms and other officially sponsored programs. The new role of the government is to find ways of implementing the party's political and economic initiatives. On 19 September, General Jaruzelski selected Rakowski as the new head of the government to replace Messner. Messner had become premier in November 1985 when General Jaruzelski resigned this post to concentrate attention on party affairs. Messner's background as an economist closely associated with heavy industry would play a critical role in the implementation of the second stage of economic reforms. The disastrous results and another outbreak of social unrest, the worst since 1981, terminated his political career. More precisely, Messner became a scapegoat of the party that claims to promote realistic programs of reform that had been mismanaged by the government. In his resignation speech, Messner stated cynically that "one should be aware of the fact that the overthrowing of governments will not substitute for the achievements of social and economic goals" (*WP*, 20 December).

The resignation of the entire Council of Ministers without any prior warning came unexpectedly. Only two months earlier the government had received a full vote of confidence for implementing economic reforms during 1987. However, two new rounds of strikes in May and August, plus an inflation rate of over 60 percent during the first half of the year, placed the party's economic program in doubt. In April only 8 percent of the population supported the government's economic policies; 40 percent expressed their discontent, and 44 percent expressed resignation. (*Słowo powszechne*, 8 April; *FBIS-EEU*, 26 April.)

Instead of admitting its mistakes, the party turned against the government. Several members of parliament implied that the responsibility for failures lay beyond the government, but only one deputy (Mikołaj Kozakiewicz from the United Peasant Party) made it explicit, saying that "the government is not sovereign; it is directly subordinated to the political leadership of one party alone" (RFE *Research*, 7 October).

When the Polish communist party selected Rakowski to replace Messner it admitted that the central issue was political rather than economic. Rakowski is an experienced politician who combines liberal and conservative perspectives. He was born in 1926 at Kowalewko, a village in Bydgoszcz voivodship in northern Poland. His father was executed by the Germans in September of 1939. The young Rakowski spent the war years in Poznań working at the railroad repairs depot. After the war, he joined the Polish People's Army, where he became a political education officer. He left the army in 1949 and studied journalism at the Higher School of Social Science and later political science at the Institute of Social Sciences of Warsaw University, earning a Ph.D. in 1956. At the same time, he worked for the Central Committee of the communist party as an instructor in its propaganda department.

His appointment in 1958 as editor-in-chief of *Polityka* was the first step in his national career. *Polityka* became known for its controversial approach to such themes as liberalism and democracy. Rakowski operated on the edge of what was permissible without stepping beyond the limits of loyalty to the party. His association with General Jaruzelski dates back to the 1980–81 period, when he represented the government during negotiations with Solidarity. In February 1982, General Jaruzelski appointed him a deputy premier. However, Rakowski lost this post in November 1985 and was demoted to the politically insignificant position of deputy chairman of the Sejm. At the same time, he was publicly attacked by the USSR for his supposedly anticommunist and anti-Soviet views. His political comeback can be attributed both to his skills and to the popularity of his analysis of the Polish situation. Jan B. de Weydenthal explains that Rakowski's "strong dislike of Solidarity as well as an almost pathological hatred of Lech Wałęsa" is combined with advocacy of "'socialist renewal' as the main strategy of exercising power." He continues

This concept accepts changes in the style of party and government operations but emphasizes the need for continuity in both the current institutional framework of the political system and the party's leading role in that system. It evolved in response to the emergence of Solidarity and other autonomous public bodies in 1980 and has provided the lens for all party activities

ever since. (RFE *Research*, *RAD Background Report*, 28 September.)

Rakowski is a pragmatic communist, flexible on ideological and economic issues but firm on the essentials of the system. His opposition to genuine pluralism has been well known, making Rakowski rather unwelcome by a society looking for a politician inclined to relegalize Solidarity. The initial reaction to his choice as Poland's next premier was that his government would be a transitional regime until a final decision concerning the future of Solidarity is taken.

The liberal-conservative hybrid represented by Rakowski surfaced when he moved in favor of "roundtable" talks among various groups including the outlawed union. This hard-line approach assumed that the union is only a minor element of the opposition and a closed chapter of Polish history. At the same time, Rakowski invited the "constructive" opposition to take ministerial posts in his new government. "The search for a broad agreement," stated Rakowski, "does not lead to Wałęsa . . . and a few others who consider themselves leaders of the opposition. We are looking for the active participation of a lot of people who have a totally different view than the current leadership of Solidarity" (*WP*, 28 September).

Rakowski's concept of political change involves greater responsibility by the government for directing daily political affairs of the nation and continuing emphasis on destruction of Solidarity, rather than creative initiative to break the eight-year-long political deadlock. This is the model of a system that would combine relatively liberal economic and social policies with a tough political superstructure resembling the fascist regime in Spain under Francisco Franco. Rakowski, in a *Der Spiegel* interview 5 September, said "I do not believe that Poland's future depends on whether the Solidarity trade union exists or not. What is much more important is the question of how the social and general climate in enterprises will develop." (*FBIS-EEU*, 8 September.)

But even the "constructive" opposition turned down the offer to join the government (*NYT*, 14 October). The first move toward broadening the social base for the regime failed, as society adopted a wait-and-see attitude while looking for clear signals on how Rakowski would approach the issue of national reconciliation. Those who declined his invitation to join the cabinet were Andrzej Stelmachowski, leader of the Catholic intellectuals and a professor of law; Lech Trzeciakowski, professor of history from Poznań; Grzegorz Białkowski, a physicist and rector of Warsaw University; and Aleksander Paszyński, private businessman from Warsaw. (*NYT*, 10 October.) The purpose of Rakowski's "coalition" was to outmaneuver Solidarity and reduce the Polish problem to economics.

Last spring and summer Poland was again paralyzed by a wave of strikes at shipyards, coal mines, and steel mills. Strikes erupted at the Gdańsk shipyard during the end of April and again at the end of August in response to drastic price increases for food and clothing. The strikes were not initiated by Solidarity but by the younger workers who later accepted Wałęsa's leadership. Stanisław Kwiatkowski, the official government pollster, concluded that "20 year olds have entered the political scene sooner than we expected. They embody an almost exact replica of the problems of the 30 year olds, but their radicalism is of a different type. They don't have leaders, and they are political illiterate. They are difficult to control." (*WP*, 24 August.) This might have convinced the regime that, after all, Solidarity is the lesser evil in comparison with young radicals. The unrest involved about 75,000 workers, caused over 11 billion zlotys damage; de facto martial law was declared in some parts of Poland as local leaders were authorized to reinforce police control of factories, isolate strikers from the local population, introduce a curfew, and introduce accelerated judicial procedures against the strikers. (*NYT*, 23 August.)

The strikes demonstrated both the strengths and weaknesses of Solidarity. The union provided new evidence of its popularity among fellow-workers. It became apparent again that internal stability cannot be achieved without Solidarity's participation. However, the young generation, impatient with peaceful methods, was reluctant to recognize the union supremacy. Solidarity's ability to mobilize millions of workers has declined sharply. Bogdan Lis, its leader in the Gdańsk region, admitted that "the strike was a kick both to the authorities and us. It showed them that the possibility of social outburst exists. It showed us that we had lost touch with the new generation of rank and file." (*CSM*, 28 July.)

The domestic situation improved at the beginning of September when Wałęsa asked the strikers to resume work in exchange for the regime's promise to start negotiations with Solidarity. The authorities argued that the economic damage caused by the strikes was detrimental to both sides and proposed talks without any preconditions, that is,

without prior recognition of the union. The strikers' prime demand was put aside in exchange for "roundtable" meetings. Initial contacts between Wałęsa and General Czesław Kiszczak, a member of the ruling Politburo and minister of internal affairs, produced an agreement that full-scale negotiations on "the functioning of the state and public life, speeding up development of the national economy, and the shape of the Polish trade union movement," should begin in mid-October. (*WP*, 17 September.) The public expected a landmark decision formally legalizing Solidarity. Writing for the Catholic *Tygodnik powszechny*, Ryszard Bugaj concluded,

> For the first time since August 1980, a real opportunity has been created to reach a compromise. The opportunity is there, because, as it seems, four conditions have been fulfilled: (1) some segments of those in power have realized that the stability of the system can be guaranteed only if it undergoes considerable modernization; (2) the opposition communities have discerned prospects for acquiring a legal position and real influence on the process of solving social and economic problems; (3) neither those in power nor the opposition are able to count on massive public support if they reject an honest compromise; and (4) even far-reaching changes must be the precondition of a compromise and will certainly not encounter a categorical external opposition.

Soon it became evident that once the strikes had ended, the government could see no reason to move beyond procedural issues. Negotiations broke down when the authorities objected to including two prominent activists, Jacek Kuron and Adam Michnik, among the delegates. Both were charged with "aggressive anticommunism," and Solidarity accused the government of "interference in the internal matters of an independent union." (*NYT*, 26 October.) Wałęsa noted that "there are many signs that the position of the authorities has changed, and that sufficient political will is lacking to resolve the basic issues" (*NYT*, 28 October).

The prospect of facing a union ten million strong alarmed the authorities, who must have estimated that the political consequences of stopping the talks would be easier to handle than a revival of this once-powerful organization. Containment of Solidarity has once again become the paramount task of the government. Premier Rakowski fought back by deciding to close the Lenin shipyard, the cradle of Solidarity.

In 1987, the yard had a deficit of 1.7 billion zlotys and received 5.6 billion zlotys in subsidies from the government. However, another shipyard in Gdynia reported an 8.9 billion deficit, obtained 11.6 billion in subsidies, and was not designated for immediate closure. (*NYT*, 1 November.) Selection of the Lenin shipyard was a move designed to dislodge Solidarity. The Secretariat of the Episcopate characterized this decision as "a political act that is not conducive to the idea of an agreement." (*FBIS-EEU*, 16 November.)

The situation was unclear by the end of the year. On 9 November, *Le Figaro* reported that the liquidation procedure would take over one year and that a mutually acceptable solution is likely to emerge in the future. The Polish radio, on the other hand, stated that the shipyard would be reorganized into three limited liability partnerships. However, on 15 December, the government plenipotentiary for employment and social conditions arrived at Gdańsk to facilitate a search for alternative employment. (PAP, *FBIS-EEU*, 16 December; Warsaw Domestic Service, *FBIS-EEU*, 27 December.)

Signs of a thaw in state-union relations surfaced at the end of the year following Wałęsa's visit to Paris in December. Jerzy Urban, spokesman for the government, praised Wałęsa and other leaders of Solidarity for rejecting strikes as a political weapon. Wałęsa's statements, according to Urban, "reflect the intention of accord, and our intentions are the same." (*Rzeczpospolita*, 14 December; *FBIS-EEU*, 19 December.) There is hope for "roundtable" talks and eventual legalization of Solidarity in 1989. Following the meeting of Solidarity's leadership with more than 60 Polish intellectuals, a "citizen's council" was established to coordinate the union's relations with the authorities, and Wałęsa described prospects for dialogue as only "dotting the i's." (DPA, 18 December; *FBIS-EEU*, 19 December.)

This change in the hard-line attitude initially adopted by Rakowski came about after a highly publicized television debate between Wałęsa and Alfred Miodowicz, head of the official union. The majority of Poles declared Wałęsa the winner, a fact that Rakowski did not question but attributed to Wałęsa's moderate political platform. Speaking at the tenth plenary session of the Central Committee, Rakowski admitted that "a new political situation came into being in Poland after the Miodowicz-Wałęsa TV discussion." This "generally conciliatory attitude of Wałęsa" was attributed to the "necessity of staying in time with a majority of society, a changing international situation making the West less interested in domestic conflicts in Poland, and finally, renewed interest of the church for national agreement." (PAP, 21 December; *FBIS-EEU*, 22 December.) Rakowski's interpretation is highly self-serving, but his description of Solidarity as a "constructive opposition" creates a tangible foundation for a political breakthrough in Poland.

The Church. For years, relations between church and state in Poland have been complicated by the issue of a legal status for the church and diplomatic relations between Warsaw and the Vatican. In principle, the regime is inclined to make ideological and legal concessions in exchange for political support. Under the present circumstances, however, the church has chosen to keep its distance from the authorities and avoid "an unholy alliance between the baton stick and the cross. By becoming an ally of this unpopular state, the church risks its support from the people." (*Tygodnik powszechny*, quoted in *CSM*, 29 July.)

The church continues to adhere to the doctrine of political neutrality as long as the regime is unwilling to implement a national agreement. "Insofar as the Polish nation is concerned," explained Jozef Cardinal Glemp, "the Catholic Church does not identify itself with any political faction. While spreading the gospel of unity and love, the church has its eye on the prospects of a nation as a whole and on the prospects of the state." Referring to the August strikes, he added that "what our country needs most of all is order, peace, and a rapprochement of the two sides in the conflict." (*Słowo powszechne*, 29 August; *FBIS-EEU*, 13 September.)

Nevertheless, the Episcopate, with its appeals for law and order, has facilitated the regime's task of stabilizing the internal situation. Strikes and revolts will not improve the internal situation because the government "is always able to print more and more paper money, but it will never be able to print milk, meat, and bread, because these goods have to be produced by manual labor." The Catholic doctrine assumes that work is the duty of every citizen and that all parties in the domestic conflict should "relinquish ambitious, resentful attitudes, and humbly see on the part of the authorities as well as the workers the way of service to all the homeland and not just one social group." (*Słowo powszechne*, 29 August; *FBIS-EEU*, 13 September.)

The role of the church in Poland expanded during 1988 to include an official role in the country's relations with the USSR. At the end of 1987, Cardinal Glemp received an invitation from the Russian

Orthodox Church to attend a symposium commemorating 1,000 years of Russian Christianity. He declined this invitation but visited Moscow and Kiev in June to witness ceremonies marking the occasion. Later, in September, the primate traveled to Belorussia to visit several Polish communities in territories annexed by the USSR in 1939. It is estimated that over two million Poles live in territories similarly incorporated after World War II.

Both visits should be seen as preparation for the pope's visit to the Soviet Union. John Paul II had expressed a desire to visit Lithuania in 1984 and celebrate the 600th anniversary of Christianity as well as the Polish-Lithuanian union. His request was turned down by Moscow, but at the end of 1988, USSR authorities made several conciliatory gestures toward the Vatican. Archbishop Julionas Steponavicius was freed from internal exile and permitted to visit Rome, and the Cathedral of Saint Casimir in Vilnius was reopened after serving for 32 years as a state museum. The Vatican, however, approached the Soviet gesture with some skepticism: "The Lithuanians are asking for drastic change, even independence," observed a Vatican official, "and so giving them their cathedral was an easy, symbolic concession" (*NYT*, 26 October).

The invitation of Father Mieczysław Krąpiec, a professor at the Catholic University in Lublin, to lecture Mikhail Gorbachev on sovereignty was unprecedented. The Soviet leader was told that the Brezhnev doctrine had medieval roots, but Father Krąpiec went on to say,

> It seems that the statements made by Mr. General Secretary M. Gorbachev are consistent with the concept of the sovereignty of man, nations, and states when they stress partnership in decisionmaking and in solving various problems. Mankind would feel more secure if this fact were especially confirmed in some way. (*Przegląd katolicki*, 24 July; *FBIS-EEU*, 27 July.)

One can only speculate about Warsaw's motives for having a priest lecture Gorbachev on nonintervention. Could it be that Father Krąpiec was speaking on behalf of the Polish government?

Since the death of Stefan Cardinal Wyszyński in May 1980, the Roman Catholic hierarchy in Poland has been split internally. The moderate attitude of Cardinal Glemp has brought him the nicknames "Comrade Glemp" and the "Red Cardinal" to illuminate his allegedly conciliatory policy toward the authorities. Several Polish bishops and many younger priests are known for their militant support of Solidarity and striking workers. The radical priests still hold masses for the homeland to commemorate victims of communism and celebrated the 70th anniversary of Poland's independence on 11 November. This split, however, has no damaging effect on the church's ability to play a key political role in the country. The next generation of church leaders will be far more assertive, demanding a higher price for settlement with the regime. Supposedly, Cardinal Glemp has been offered up to 90 seats in the Sejm and legalization of a new Christian Democratic Party. (*NYT*, 29 July.)

The Sejm. It was a busy year for the Polish parliament. The party has a comfortable majority in the Sejm, able to pass any legislation it may wish or to block constitutional changes. However, the communist programs are sharply criticized by independently minded deputies willing to stress social impact rather than the statistical achievements of various reforms. Also, there is an honest tendency to expose the real capacities of the national economy and to critically evaluate the leadership skills of the people in power. Frank exchanges of views and verbal clashes are routine.

Among the legislative acts of the Sejm was an amendment concerning an electoral law for people's councils. Under the new legislation, a maximum of 10 percent of the councillors will be elected from the official (voivodship) list and the names of candidates will be arranged in alphabetical order. Up to three candidates will be allowed to run for one seat in each electoral precinct. (PAP, 10 March; *FBIS-EEU*, 11 March.) The right to nominate candidates was extended to all legally existing social organizations, including citizens' meetings convened by town and village citizen self-governments, regional groups, and professional, creative, and cooperative associations.

Also, a constitutional amendment has been approved adding a fourth type of property, communal property, to the already existing state, cooperative, and private forms of ownership. The purpose of this change is to free the central authorities in Warsaw from financial responsibility for local governments. The people's councils are entitled to make investments and are solely responsible for the maintenance of health, educational, cultural, sports, tourist, and recreational facilities. (PAP, 19 June; *FBIS-EEU*, 20 June.)

All legislative acts in Poland come under scrutiny of the constitutional tribunal, which began its work in January 1986. It has reviewed seventeen laws, ten governmental decrees, and two ministerial orders. In the end, nine of these acts were returned for changes or rescinded. (*Rzeczpospolita*, 16 March.) The need to change Poland's 1952 constitution is suggested frequently because the current document is "burdened by the brand of history, the brand of the era in which it had been framed," the brand of Stalinism. The most likely date for enactment of a new constitution is 3 May 1991, the bicentennial of the historical 3 May Constitution. (Warsaw ITD, 28 February; *JPRS-Eastern Europe Report*, 18 May.)

In addition, the Sejm recently enacted an "alternative service" law offering conscientious objectors work in civilian organizations. Officially, there are now 86 "pseudo-pacifists." However, statistics show that there are some 100,000 Jehovah's Witnesses who refuse to be drafted. Poland now complies with the international treaty on human and political rights. (*Żołnierz wolności*, 8 August.)

The crime rate has always been high and continues to rise. According to General Czesław Kiszczak, minister of internal affairs, there are two parallel trends in today's crime. The positive side of the trend is the 15 percent reduction since 1986 in the number of offenses committed in public places. However, there has been nearly a 10 percent increase in robberies and thefts. The detection rate ranges from 56 to 78 percent. In 1987, there were 152,000 cases of drunk driving and 7,699 alcohol-related road accidents that killed 1,435 people and injured 8,231. (Warsaw Domestic Service, 17 June; *FBIS-EEU*, 20 June.) The overall crime index for 1987 was 1,350 per 100,000 inhabitants, including 36,427 road accidents, and 17,000 drug addicts (*TL*, 23 February). In 1987, a second AIDS-related death occurred among Poland's 29 AIDS patients. So far, close to 120,000 Poles have been screened for AIDS. (RFE *Research*, 23 June.)

A special problem for the authorities is the youth. Almost half of Polish society is under 30, and about three million are pupils in secondary schools. It is disturbing that about 70 percent of the young people would like to emigrate to the West; fewer than half think of the socialist system favorably, and about the same number are of the opinion that it pays to work (*Rzeczywistość*, 10 January). Over 600,000 Poles have left the country since 1981—three-fourths of them under 35 years old. This number includes thousands of physicians, engineers, scientists, and managers. (*WSJ*, 10 May.)

One catastrophic issue involves the availability of housing. In 1986, the government provided the same number of apartments as in 1966. Waiting time for an apartment is over twenty years, or half a century in more desirable places such as Warsaw. Over eight million young people are waiting for their own apartment. Many sociologists regard the housing shortage as the main source of social conflict. "These people will never accept the situation of waiting twenty years for apartments for the opportunity to settle down, and a violent explosion may follow, because young people have always been the shock troops of all uprisings and revolutions." (*Nowe drogi*, 21 December 1987.) In February, the official trade union organized a Congress of People Without Housing. It was determined that Poland needs at least four million new apartments and houses over the next ten years; approximately 189,000 are being constructed annually. (RFE *Research*, 8 February.)

Social problems have a devastating impact on the Polish people, who, according to a known writer, "continue their obscurantist myths, egalitarian attitudes, and disgruntled slogans. Poverty will continue to be a virtue, prosperity a vice, resourcefulness a crime, and passivity the right attitude. Populism and conservatism have found a quiet and secure haven in our country." (Eustachy Rylski, *Przegląd tygodniowy*, 3 January; *FBIS-EEU*, 25 January.)

Suicides have increased two-and-a-half times, fourfold among young people in the last four decades. Only during the sixteen months between August 1980 and 13 December 1981—the time of high expectations associated with Solidarity—did the suicide rate drop, by 35 percent. Among public officials, however, the suicide rate increased during the same time, showing irritation with the union. Currently, although the suicide rate is on the rise among the population at large, the trend among those in power is declining. (*Polityka*, 4 June.)

The Economy. The steady decline of the economy has continued for ten years. At the end of 1987, the regime introduced the second stage of economic reforms by reducing the standard of living to about 78 percent of the 1978 level. (*WSJ*, 10 May.) Statistical information provided by the Polish government shows the produced national income in 1987 increased by 2 percent in comparison to 1986, or 1 percent per capita. The sold production of the socialized industry grew by 3.3 percent, the labor productivity increased by 3.8 percent, and the overall central annual plan was realized by 100.3 percent. Polish exports to Soviet bloc countries totaled 10.9 billion rubles, an increase of 5.9 percent, whereas imports exceeded 10.5 billion rubles and increased 1.1 percent. Exports for hard currency totaled $7 billion, or an 8.4 percent increase. Imports totaled $5.8 billion, marking a 7 percent increase. The currency surplus held by the population exceeded 3,776 billion zlotys at the end of 1987, that is 534 billion (16.5 percent) more than a year earlier. In the middle of 1988, economic indicators pointed to a 6.4 percent growth in exports and a 15.7 percent growth in imports. (Statistical Communiqué on Poland's Socioeconomic Situation in 1987 in *FBIS-EEU*, 3 February; PAP, 8 August; *FBIS-EEU*, 9 August.)

Polish indebtedness to Western creditors increased dramatically in 1987 because of the devaluation of the dollar. By the end of 1988 it should exceed $40 billion, or over 70 percent of the country's annual national income. However, the authorities in Warsaw are optimistic. The amount of Western debt is expected to increase until 1991 and then stabilize at a level of $43–$44 billion. (*TL*, 11 July.) It is not the first time that the authorities have published unrealistic forecasts concerning reduction of the Western debt or consistently overestimated the country's ability to increase exports of goods that are in demand in the West. They can rely, however, on hard currency sent home by compatriots permanently or temporarily living abroad. This export of Polish labor brings about $1.4 billion annually, which is more than the balance of foreign trade. (*Prawo i życie*, 12 March; *JPRS-Eastern Europe Report*, 2 May.)

Inflation for 1988 exceeded 120 percent because the unofficial value of the dollar increased from approximately 1,800 zlotys in 1987 to about 4,000 at the end of 1988. The shortage of consumer goods necessary to balance the purchasing potential of the population is worsening despite frequent price increases.

Another fundamental weakness of the Polish economy involves production of defective goods and a disregard for safety standards. On 15 June, *Rzeczpospolita* reported that 46.1 percent of manufactured goods and 23.9 percent of food articles had to be withdrawn from the market because of poor quality. Also, approximately 40 percent of the food delivered to market contains dangerous levels of toxic substances. The Central Office of Statistics calculates that the damage due to low-quality production exceeds 105 billion zlotys.

After five years of excellent harvests, agricultural production declined by 6 percent in 1987, which prompted the regime to legalize the Foundation for the Development of Polish Agriculture set up with help from the Rockefeller Brothers' Fund. This "self-supporting" enterprise received $350,000 to promote the export of ham to the United States. (*NYT*, 21 February.) In addition, Poland succeeded in obtaining a loan from the World Bank amounting to $17.9 million to stimulate export of frozen fruit and vegetables. (*NYT*, 11 November.)

The "promarket" reorientation of the Polish economy received some encouragement at the end of September when a law authorizing all sectors of the economy to issue, buy, and sell bonds cleared the Sejm. This move should create a 5,000 billion zloty money market out of so-called forced savings, that is, cash unsupported by goods held by public and private sectors. (RFE *Report*, 11 November.) The most significant change, however, came on 7 December when the Sejm drafted a piece of sweeping legislation stating simply that "taking up and performing economic activities is free and permitted to anyone on equal rights under conditions defined by law" (PAP, 12 December; *FBIS-EEU*, 13 December). This law, effective 1 January 1989, introduced equality for all forms of ownership. Engagement in economic activities in agriculture and manufacturing requires only a notification of the authorities. Meanwhile, limits on the size of private enterprises and convertibility of the zloty to hard currency has also been eliminated. This green-light approach to private business is a personal victory for Mieczysław Wilczek, the minister of industry in Rakowski's cabinet and one of the most successful and affluent private entrepreneurs in the country.

This "get-rich" campaign has powerful adversaries who sense the gradual erosion of communism and political capitulation of the party. "Traditionalists" like Piotr Karpiuk predict social inequality, unemployment, and discrimination against the socialist sector of the economy. (*Nowe drogi*, July 1987.) Accustomed to nonmarket distribution of goods, Poland's red barons distrust spontaneous socioeconomic processes that take away their power and privilege.

Foreign Affairs. Soviet leader Gorbachev's six-day visit to Poland in July was described as a "historic event" of global significance. Gorbachev's *perestroika* and Jaruzelski's renewal were hailed as evidence of change and the flexibility of socialism. Another purpose of the visit was to fill so-called blank spots in history between the two nations. These blank spots include the Soviet-Nazi partition of Poland in August 1939, the Katyn massacre of Polish officers in 1941, the treatment of the Polish army of General Władysław Anders in the Soviet Union during World War II, the circumstances of the communist takeover of Poland, the refusal to help the Warsaw Uprising in 1944, the kidnap-murder of Polish underground leaders after World War II, and the heavy-handed Soviet rule in Poland—especially during the Stalinist period. (RFE *Report*, 15 May 1987.) Designed to mark a new era in friendly relations, the trip stressed equality, partnership, and a new openness between the two neighbors. In Gorbachev's own words, "Today, equal rights, independence, and the joint solving of the problems before us are an undeniable rule of our relations. They are becoming free of paternalism and are fully geared to voluntary partnership based on interests" (*Rzeczpospolita*, 13 July; *FBIS-EEU*, 18 July). The Brezhnev doctrine of limited sovereignty—fully endorsed by Gorbachev during his 1986 visit—would be replaced by an alliance of equal states. However, the Soviet leader made it clear that equality applies only to the "roads of transition to the new quality of socialism" (*Przegląd tygodniowy*, 24 July; *JPRS-Eastern Europe Report*, 31 August).

The trip, however, elevated the high degree of distrust and misunderstanding by the Soviet leadership concerning Poland. The blank spots were hardly addressed, and instead, the USSR leader focused on the Nazi crimes committed against the Polish nation. The Katyn massacre, perhaps one of the most emotional and politically sensitive issues in Polish-Russian relations, was entirely ignored, as well as the question of the 1968 Soviet invasion of Czechoslovakia. In addition, the USSR leader was visibly isolated from the public. Gorbachev's visit to Kraków's main square, for example, was eclipsed by an entourage of secret police and communist party functionaries, ensuring that no embarrassment could come to the general secretary from anticommunists. Visiting the Adolf Warski shipyard in Szczecin, Jaruzelski and Gorbachev avoided mentioning Solidarity. Instead, both leaders stated that the events of 1980–81 were the initial phase of reform now implemented by the Polish regime. Gorbachev's misconception of the internal situation in Poland reached its culmination when the USSR leader stated on television that the Polish people "were lucky at this stage of history there has appeared a man" like General Jaruzelski (*WP*, 15 July). It is apparent that Gorbachev's visit was merely limited to an exchange between two ruling communist parties. Normalization of Polish-Russian relations has yet to be affected by *glasnost'*.

British prime minister Margaret Thatcher's arrival in Poland differed considerably from the artificially monumental visit of the Soviet guest. The first lesson that Thatcher lectured Polish officials on was political and economic issues, saying,

> You will only achieve higher growth, only release enterprise, only spur people to greater effort, only obtain their full-hearted commitment to reform, when people have the dignity and enjoyment of personal and political liberty, when they have the freedom of expression, freedom of association, and the right to form free and independent unions. (*WP*, 4 November.)

After the official meeting with Premier Rakowski, the British prime minister proceeded to lay a wreath at the grave of Father Jerzy Popie-łuszko. She also traveled to Gdańsk to meet Wałęsa and other leaders of Solidarity. In short, Thatcher went to Poland determined to communicate with the broad spectrum of society. Her support for the opposition was unequivocal. "We regard Solidarity," she explained during a press conference, "as going beyond the normal trade union relationship. It is the expression and focus of the opposition in this country, so it has that character and quality. As such, it is a very important group of people." (RFE *Research*, 11 November.)

For the Polish authorities Thatcher is a symbol of economic recovery and a tough policy toward labor unions. Her visit was designed to add legitimacy to Jaruzelski's political maneuvering in Poland, especially his uncompromising views on Solidarity. But the British leader would not allow the Polish authorities to compare the democratic and totalitarian regimes.

The arrival of West German foreign minister Hans-Dietrich Genscher in Warsaw in January had almost a symbolic character: to illustrate to the world that a reconciliation between the regime and West Germany is not completely inconceivable and to confirm West German commitment to respect the existing territorial and political order on the European continent. Economically, the Polish authorities hoped to expand access to West German markets and credits, but the visit did not result in signing of any specific agreements between the two countries. (DPA, 13 January; *FBIS-EEU*, 14 January.) Besides meetings with Polish officials, Minister Genscher also met with Wałęsa and Cardinal Glemp and visited the grave of Father Popiełuszko. This "private" aspect of his visit improved the image of West Germany among the Polish people and was welcomed by Solidarity.

Little progress has been made in Polish relations with the United States as both sides appear to be waiting for domestic changes favorable to mutual contacts. This wait-and-see attitude became evident during U.S. deputy secretary of state John C. Whitehead's visit to Poland in October 1988. In his opinion, "the lack of any national accord at all" is the principal source of political and economic difficulties, and Poland should not expect U.S. economic assistance before genuine normalization at home. Most likely, U.S.-Polish relations would not proceed beyond formalities until opposition forces are granted legal status. (*TL*, 9 May; *FBIS-EEU*, 18 May; *PAP*, 14 October; *FBIS-EEU*, 17 October.) The Polish side, on the other hand, hopes that the new George Bush administration will show more compassion for Poland's economic problems.

Noticeable progress has been made in Poland's relations with Israel. In April, the Polish government organized an international conference to commemorate the liquidation of about 3.5 million Polish Jews by the Nazis and the 45th anniversary of the Warsaw Ghetto uprising. The state of Israel was officially represented by Deputy Prime Minister Yitzhak Navon, Minister of Justice Avraham Shariv, and six members of the Knesset. Israeli officials awarded 97 Poles the Yad Vashem medal, given to non-Jews for saving Jews during the Nazi occupation. Polish officials condemned anti-Semitism in Poland, apologizing in particular for the expulsion of Jews in 1968. (*NYT*, 18 April.) But Solidarity recognized that Poles, in general, had "behaved indifferently during the Holocaust" (RFE *Research*, 29 April).

Organizing this celebration, the Polish government expected to gain moral authority at home and abroad. But as Dr. Marek Edelman, former deputy commander of the Ghetto Uprising and now the most distinguished Jewish leader living in Poland, remarked during the ceremonies, the Polish regime is a "totalitarian government" and "the uprising was a fight for dignity and freedom. The government does not recognize such values, so it has no right to organize such celebrations." (Ibid.) This occasion undoubtedly contributed to a better understanding between Poles and Jews, but it was the opposition rather than the authorities that scored a moral victory. A reconciliation between both nations is already well advanced, especially among the post-World War II generation, as several leaders and many followers of Solidarity are of Jewish origin.

Biography. *Stanisław Ciosek.* Ciosek was born in 1939 in Pawlowice, to a family of teachers. He has a degree in economics. He has been a member of the PZPR since 1959. He began doing social work in the students' union of the Higher School of Economics in Sopot. From 1960 to 1961, he was deputy chairman of the district council of the Polish Students' Union in Gdańsk and then became chairman. In 1963, he became secretary of the Supreme Council of the Polish Students' Union; from 1966 to 1969 he was deputy chairman of the union, and from 1969 to 1973 he was chairman of the union.

From 1973 to 1975, he was chairman of the Federation of Socialist Unions of Polish Youth. From 1975 to 1980, he was first secretary of the Jelenia Góra party committee and chairman of the Jelenia Góra People's Council, after which, from 1980 to 1985, he was secretary of the Council of Ministers' Sociopolitical Committee and deputy chairman of the Committee for Trade Union Cooperation. From 1983 to 1984, he was also minister of labor, wages, and social affairs.

From 1971 to 1980, he was a deputy member of the Central Committee, and from 1980 to 1981 he was a full member. The 10th Congress made him a Central Committee secretary. In June 1988 he was made a candidate member of the Politburo. Since 1986, he has been chairman of the PZPR Central Committee Commission for Law, Order, and Moral Health. In 1968, the PRON National Council made him its general secretary. He has been a deputy in the Sixth, Seventh, and Eighth Sejms. He belongs to the Joint Commission of Government-Episcopate Representatives. (*FBIS-EEU*, 4 January 1989.)

Arthur R. Rachwald
United States Naval Academy

Romania

Population. 23,040,883
Party. Romanian Communist Party (Partidul Comunist Român; RCP)
Founded. 8 May 1921
Membership. 3,709,735 (31 December 1987). Party members make up 23 percent of the adult

population of Romania and 33 percent of the employed population. The social composition of the party is 55 percent workers, 16 percent peasants, 20 percent intellectuals, and 9 percent pensioners and housewives. Of the total party membership, 35 percent are women. During 1987, 116,041 individuals joined the party; of them 66 percent are workers; 14 percent, peasants; and 19 percent, intellectuals. Almost 50 percent of the new party members are women (*Scînteia*, 1, 2 April; *WMR*, June).

General Secretary. Nicolae Ceauşescu

Political Executive Committee (PEC). 19 full members, 7 of whom are members of the Permanent Bureau: Nicolae Ceauşescu (general secretary of the RCP; president of the Socialist Republic of Romania; chairman, National Defense Council; and chairman, Supreme Council on Socioeconomic Development), Emil Bobu (Central Committee [CC] secretary for party organization; chairman, Council on Problems of Economic and Social Organization), Elena Ceauşescu (first deputy prime minister; chairman, National Council of Science and Instruction), Constantin Dăscălescu (prime minister), Manea Mănescu (vice president, State Council), Gheorghe Oprea (first deputy prime minister); Gheorghe Rădulescu (vice president, State Council); other full members: Virgil Cazacu, Lina Ciobanu (deputy prime minister), Ion Coman (CC secretary for military and security matters), Nicolae Constantin (chairman, Central Collegium of the RCP), Ion Dincă (first deputy prime minister), Miu Dobrescu (chairman, Central Council of the General Confederation of Trade Unions), Ludovic Fazekas (deputy prime minister), Paul Niculescu, Constantin Olteanu (CC secretary for propaganda and media; member, State Council), Gheorghe Pană (chairman, Committee for People's Councils' Affairs), Ion Pătan, Dumitru Popescu (rector, Ştefan Gheorghiu RCP Academy); 25 alternate members: Stefan Andrei (deputy prime minister), Radu Balan (chairman, State Planning Committee), Nicu Ceauşescu (RCP first secretary, Sibiu County), Gheorghe David (minister of agriculture), Suzana Gâdea (chairwoman, Council of Socialist Culture and Education), Mihai Gere (chairman, Council of Working People of Hungarian Nationality), Maria Ghitulica (vice president, State Council), Nicolae Giosan (chairman, Grand National Assembly), Neculai Ibanescu (deputy prime minister), Mihai Marina, Ilie Matei, Vasile Milea (minister of national de-

fense), Ioachim Moga, Ana Mureşan (minister of domestic trade; chairman, National Council of Women), Elena Nae, Marin Nedelcu, Cornel Pacoste (deputy prime minister), Tudor Postelnicu (minister of internal affairs), Constantin Radu (first secretary, Bucharest Municipal Party Committee; chairman, Municipal People's Council [Mayor of Bucharest]), Ion Radu (deputy prime minister), Ion Stoian (CC secretary for international relations), Iosif Szasz (vice-chairman, Grand National Assembly), Ioan Toma (first secretary of the CC, Union of Communist Youth; minister of youth), Ioan Totu (minister of foreign affairs), Ion Ursu (vice-chairman, National Council of Science and Instruction), Richard Winter

Secretariat. 9 members (with presumed areas of responsibility): Nicolae Ceauşescu (general secretary), Vasile Bărbulescu (agriculture), Emil Bobu (party organization), Ion Coman (military and security matters), Silviu Curticeanu (chief of staff), Constantin Olteanu (propaganda and media), Ion Sirbu (the economy and control of party and state bodies and staff activity), Ion Stoian (international relations), Gheorghe Tanase (cadres)

Central Committee. 286 full and 161 alternate members

Status. The RCP is the only legal political party in Romania.

Last Congress. Thirteenth, 19–22 November 1984, in Bucharest; next congress is scheduled for 1989.

Last Elections. 17 March 1985 for members of the Grand National Assembly (parliament). Of the 15,732,095 registered voters who participated in the election, 97.8 percent voted for candidates of the Socialist Democracy and Unity Front (SDUF). Next parliamentary elections are scheduled for 1990.

Auxiliary Organizations. SDUF, the RCP's political front organization, selects candidates for local and national government office: Nicolae Ceauşescu, chairman; Manea Manescu, first vice-chairman; Tamara Maria Dobrin, chair of the Executive Bureau. General Confederation of Romanian Trade Unions (7 million members): Miu Dobrescu, chairman of the Central Council. Union of Communist Youth (Union Tiniteretul Comunist, 4 million members): Ioan Toma, first secretary of the CC. National Council of Women: Ana Muresan, chairwoman. Councils of Working People of Hungarian and German Nationalities:

Mihai Gere, Eduard Eisenberger, respective chairmen.

Publications. *Scînteia,* RCP daily (except Monday), Ion Mitran, editor in chief; *Era socialistă,* RCP theoretical and political biweekly; *România liberă,* SDUF daily (except Sunday); *Lumea,* foreign affairs weekly; *Revista economică,* economic weekly. Agerpres is the official Romanian news agency.

The RCP was founded in Bucharest on 8 May 1921, after the splitting from the Social Democratic Party over the question of affiliation with the Communist International. For the next three years the RCP was subject to police harassment and restrictions on its activities, and in April 1924 it was outlawed. Even before it was banned, the RCP was unsuccessful in attracting support. In 1922 its membership was reported to be two thousand, and the highest estimate of its numbers during the interwar period was only five thousand.

Many factors contributed to its failure to win support. During the first decade of its existence, the RCP suffered from a highly factionalized leadership, and it was a full decade before the Soviet Union was able to establish control. The most serious obstacles were the party's subservience to the Soviet Union and its hostility to Romanian national aspirations. After World War I, Romania acquired Bessarabia from Russia and Transylvania from Hungary, both of which were inhabited by large ethnic Romanian populations but also included were significant numbers of non-Romanian minorities. The Soviet Union refused to accept the loss of Bessarabia, and the RCP was forced to adopt policies favoring its return. The hostility of the Hungarian minority to Romania's annexation of Transylvania was a source of instability that the Soviets wanted to exploit. The RCP was thus required to support "national self-determination" for Transylvania (that is, its separation from Romania); this placed the RCP squarely at odds with Romanian national aspirations. As a result, the small RCP was dominated by ethnic minorities and had little appeal to Romanians.

The party came to power as a result of the occupation of Romania by the Soviet army during the final year of World War II. The Soviet occupation forces required that the insignificant RCP be included in successive coalition governments. With the support of Soviet troops and with RCP control of a core of militant forces in the major population centers, the party gradually seized the dominant

role in the coalition governments. It acquired additional credibility when it won the support of Dr. Petru Groza, a political leader who had participated in Romanian governments during the 1920s. The RCP-dominated regime, with the help of the occupying Soviet army, suppressed the traditional political parties and "won" the elections of 1946. When it was fully in power, the RCP banned all other political parties. The final stage was the merger of the RCP with the remnants of the Social Democratic Party in 1948. The new organization—the Romanian Workers' Party (Partidul Muncitoresc Român, RWP)—was the only legal political organization. The leaders of the former Social Democratic Party took a minor role in the new organization, and the RCP leaders quickly completed their total domination of the RWP and the country.

During this period, the communist leadership was involved in a bitter internecine struggle between two principal factions. The Muscovites, who spent most of the interwar years in Moscow, were led by Ana Pauker and Vasile Luca, while the Nativists, most of whose members spent those years in Romania, were headed by Gheorghe Gheorghiu-Dej. In 1952 Gheorghiu-Dej gained the upper hand, purged his opponents, and established uncontested control of the party.

Although ethnic Romanians came to play the dominant role in the party's leadership, particularly after the purge of the Jewish Pauker and the Hungarian Luca, the party was still dominated by the Soviet Union and continued to be seen by most Romanians as an alien institution inimical to Romanian interests. Gheorghiu-Dej carefully followed the accepted Soviet pattern, and Romania became a model Stalinist satellite. Agriculture was collectivized, which further alienated the peasantry, and a program of Stalinist industrialization was implemented at considerable economic and personal cost. Party control was established over intellectual and cultural life, which assumed the drab uniformity of "socialist realism."

After Stalin's death in 1953 and the rise of Nikita Khrushchev to power in the Soviet Union in the mid-1950s, Gheorgiu-Dej began to take steps that would ultimately lead to important economic and political differences with the Soviet Union and to a redefinition of the relationship between the RCP and the Romanian people. Initial Soviet efforts toward the economic integration of Eastern Europe in the late 1950s and early 1960s were stubbornly resisted by Gheorghiu-Dej. Although the Soviet proposals had a certain economic rationale, the RCP, doggedly pursuing a Stalinist policy of economic nationalism, proceeded to construct a series of heavy-industry projects that the Soviets strongly opposed.

The significant differences between the Soviet Union and China in the early 1960s provided Romanians with an opportunity to expand their autonomy from the Soviet Union in interparty affairs. This reached its high point in the April 1964 Statement of the RCP Central Committee, which asserted the sovereignty and independence of each party and affirmed the principle of noninterference of parties in each other's internal affairs. This foreign policy provided an opportunity for the party to develop genuine national support.

These policies were initiated under the leadership of Gheorghiu-Dej, RCP leader from 1944 until his death in 1965, but they have been continued and extended by his successor, Ceauşescu, who has dominated the RCP and Romania since 1965. His rise and long association with Gheorghiu-Dej began at the end of World War II. After the death of Gheorghiu-Dej in 1965, Ceauşescu's power was confirmed at the Ninth RCP Congress (at which the RWP was renamed the RCP). In international relations, Ceauşescu continued the policies of international autonomy begun under Gheorghiu-Dej. The high point of these policies came in 1967–68 when Romania, unlike the rest of the Soviet bloc, maintained diplomatic relations with Israel, established diplomatic relations with West Germany before the Soviet Union approved Ostpolitik, and moved closer to the nonaligned bloc. Ceauşescu's vigorous denunciation of the Soviet-led invasion of Czechoslovakia in August 1968 marked the apogee of Romanian defiance of the Soviet Union but also emphasized the limits of deviance. Although the RCP under Ceauşescu has continued to pursue an international policy that reflects a degree of autonomy from the Soviet Union, it has also carefully avoided pushing that policy to the point of provoking Soviet military intervention. Although USSR threats and actions have established clear limits to his foreign policies, Ceauşescu's international policies remain the principal source of his legitimacy with the Romanian people.

Between 1965 and 1971—the same time that he achieved the greatest flexibility and autonomy in international relations—Ceauşescu also pursued a certain liberalization in the economy and in cultural policy. Since then, however, he has pursued a rigid, centralized economic policy involving substantial investment in heavy industry and limited production of consumer goods. This, plus the lack of investment and poor organization in agriculture, have contributed to periodic food shortages and growing popular dissatisfaction. Under Ceauşescu's economic policies, Romania incurred substantial foreign debts and repaying them has been difficult. A massive effort to cut imports and expand exports to repay all foreign debt by 1990 has contributed to the economic hardships. In the cultural and educational sphere, he has demanded rigid ideological consistency. Although the RCP has maintained a degree of autonomy from the Soviet Union, because of Ceauşescu's mismanagement of the economy and his rigid, Stalinist domestic policies, it has lost much of the popular support, authority, and legitimacy that it won during the 1960s.

Leadership and Party Organization. Ceauşescu has maintained his control of the party through strict concentration of power in his own hands. He has prevented the development of any internal centers of opposition by giving important positions to members of his own family and long-trusted associates and by shifting subordinates from one position to another at regular intervals.

As genuine popular support for Ceauşescu and the RCP has waned, the party leader has encouraged an artificial ritual of personal adulation. The personality cult began with his 55th birthday in 1973 but reached a new climax in January 1988 when Ceauşescu celebrated his 70th birthday. In an effort to enhance the image of Ceauşescu and the party, on 26 January the State Council approved the broadest amnesty in 23 years in honor of the festive occasion. The Romanian Academy organized a Solemn Session dedicated to Ceauşescu at which seven papers were presented praising his "patriotism and revolutionary abnegation," his contribution to science and culture, and his "personality, which intertwines, in a creative synthesis, scientific thinking with concrete political activity" (*Scînteia*, 23 January). The RCP CC likewise hosted a festive observance of Ceauşescu's birthday that "dwelt on the heroic revolutionary activity of Comrade Nicolae Ceauşescu, the great hero among the heroes of the nation, the architect of modern Socialist Romania [who] has devoted more than 55 years with matchless patriotic, communist dedication to the cause of the Romanian party and people" (*Scînteia*, 25 January).

For his birthday, Ceauşescu received the decoration Hero of the Socialist Republic of Romania for the third time. This award, established in 1971, is the highest Romanian award; in the last eighteen years, it has only been awarded to Nicolae Ceauşescu three times and to his wife, Elena, once (RFE, *Romanian Situation Report*, 26 January). He also received international attention. The Soviet Union awarded him the Order of Lenin, which was actually presented later in the year when Soviet president Andrei Gromyko visited Bucharest (*Pravda*, 26 January, 10 May; *Scînteia*, 26 January, 10 May). East Germany conferred on Ceauşescu the Order of Karl Marx, and Czechoslovakia likewise gave him its highest honor, the Order of the White Lion First Class with Chain. East Germany and Czechoslovakia—the two East European countries to give him this honor—have both opposed Soviet reforms, as has Romania.

The effort to generate the appearance of vast international interest and affection for Ceauşescu, however, ran into some problems. When countries did not respond appropriately to the official Romanian request for messages for Ceauşescu's birthday, the public relations apparatchiks dusted off old statements and printed them as new congratulations. A telegram from the Swedish king was revealed as bogus by the Swedish press (Stockholm, *Aftonbladet*, 27 January), the British government protested a fabricated message from Queen Elizabeth II, and the Spanish government protested another concocted one from King Juan Carlos (*LAT*, 24 January; Reuters, 29 January; *WSJ*, 16 February).

This personality cult for the party chief also extends to his wife, Elena. Her 69th birthday on 7 January was marked by a panegyrical letter to her from the RCP CC (*Scînteia*, 8 January) and by a report that the Russian version of her scientific volume *Researches in Polymer Chemistry and Technology* had been published by the Soviet Academy of Sciences (Agerpres, 5 January). The most extreme examples of adulation, however, were poems written in her honor that appeared in connection with her birthday (RFE, *Romanian Situation Report*, 28 January). For the first time in her political career Elena Ceauşescu delivered the main speech at celebrations marking 23 August, the Romanian National Day (*Scînteia*, 21 August).

Ceauşescu's reliance on his family has been a principal means of maintaining his grip on the party and the government. The nepotism under Ceauşescu has reached heights unknown in the rest of Eastern Europe and even provoked Soviet leader Mikhail Gorbachev to criticize the Ceauşescu dynasty indirectly by pointedly remarking on, during a visit to Bucharest, the nepotism of the Brezhnev era in the Soviet Union (*Scînteia*, 27 May 1987). Elena Ceauşescu is a full member of the PEC as well as first deputy prime minister and chairman of the National Council of Science and Instruction. The most important post she holds, however, is head of the RCP cadre commission, which oversees all party personnel matters. The youngest son of the couple, Nicu Ceauşescu, is an alternate member of the PEC. For several years he served as first secretary of the Union of Communist Youth, but in late 1987 he was appointed RCP first secretary of Sibiu County. There is no doubt that the career change represents his father's continuing efforts to promote his career. In recent years, the party leaders of Romania's 40 counties have been key officials of Ceauşescu's regime. Other members of Ceauşescu's family that hold key party and government positions include his brother Lieutenant General Ilie Ceauşescu, who is deputy defense minister responsible for party control of the armed forces. Another brother, Nicolae A. Ceauşescu, is head of the cadres department at the Ministry of Internal Affairs, which has responsibility for the secret police, and a third brother, Ion Ceauşescu, is first vice-chairman of the State Planning Committee and a member of the Council of Ministers. It is significant that most of the family members in key positions are responsible for personnel.

In addition to relying heavily on members of his own family, Ceauşescu, continuing his policy, during 1988 rotated a number of ministers, county party first secretaries, local government leaders, and other officials from one position to another. For example, the head of the Bucharest municipal party and government organizations, Constantin Olteanu, became CC secretary for Propaganda and Media. Constantin Radu was moved from the post of deputy prime minister to replace Olteanu as mayor of Bucharest. CC secretary Radu Balan was rotated to the post of chairman of the State Planning Committee. At the CC plenum that reviewed cadre policy in March, Ceauşescu again reiterated, "We must constantly apply rotation principles to the promotion of cadres" (*Scînteia*, 30 March). Rotation prevents any RCP leader from establishing a solid geographic or organizational base from which to challenge the incumbent party leader. The only constituent for aspiring RCP officials is Nicolae Ceauşescu.

Domestic Party Affairs. The tenor of internal party affairs during 1988 was set at the RCP's National Party Conference in Bucharest, which was held in mid-December 1987. Traditionally, the RCP has held a National Party Conference, which is almost as large an event as a congress, midway between party congresses, which take place every five years. The conference was held at a difficult time for Ceauşescu and the party. Soviet leader Gorbachev was critical of the RCP for its opposition to reform, Romania was being criticized internationally for its violation of human rights, and the conference opened just one month after major worker protests had taken place in the Romanian industrial center of Brasov. In his major speech to the conference, Ceauşescu vehemently reaffirmed his antireformist stand and pledged to continue his policies of ideological orthodoxy (RFE, *Romanian Situation Report*, 13 January).

During 1988, three CC plenary sessions were held. Increasingly, the CC has become a formal forum similar to the Romanian Parliament, which meets infrequently to ratify decisions made by higher party bodies. A clear indication of this is the fact that each of the three CC sessions (28–29 March, 28 June, and 28–30 November) were immediately followed by a session of the Grand National Assembly (30 March, 29 June, and 1 December). The Political Executive Committee, which meets monthly in formal sessions, has become the body where discussion and debate takes place, though the PEC has also been a forum for Ceauşescu to issue his periodic ex cathedra pronouncements.

The procedure that was followed in approving the final version of the 1988 economic and social plan for Romania indicates the general decline in significance of the CC and other party organs. The PEC determined that the 1988 plan should be presented to the CC for approval, but two months later Ceauşescu, as president of Romania, signed the decree directing ministries to begin work on implementing the plan, though it had not been approved by either the CC or the Grand National Assembly. Some months later, when the Grand National Assembly "approved" the plan already being implemented, Prime Minister Constantin Dăscălescu listed those organizations that had given prior approval of the plan, but the CC was not mentioned (RFE, *Romanian Situation Report*, 29 March).

Auxiliary Organizations. No unusual developments or major changes involved the RCP's principal auxiliary organizations during 1988. The most noteworthy activity was the intensifying dispute between Romania and Hungary over treatment of the Hungarian minority in Transylvania (see be-

low). In this context, the Councils of Romanian Working People of Hungarian Nationality and German Nationality held meetings in June to reaffirm "the consistent policy of the RCP and Romanian state to guarantee the full equality of all citizens." As the controversy intensified, local units of these organizations were mobilized to reaffirm the Romanian position in the dispute. The Union of Communist Youth rejected an appeal by the Hungarian Communist Youth League on the Hungarian minority issue.

Domestic Affairs. *Ideological antireformism.* A dominant theme in Romanian domestic affairs in 1988 was opposition to the reforms that were blossoming in the Soviet Union under the leadership of Gorbachev. Differences between the two party leaders on this issue have been evident for some time, but during 1988 Ceauşescu broadened his antireformism. Initial Romanian opposition to Soviet-inspired reform focused primarily on the economic sphere; in 1988 increasing antireformism was voiced in ideological terms. For example, at the November RCP CC plenum, Ceauşescu emphasized that action must be taken to "perfect" socialist society but "by no means should we open the path to capitalist forms." He was equally unyielding in demanding no diminution of the leading role of the party: "We should take resolute steps against any liquidationist trends of weakening the party's role" (*Scînteia*, 29 November). Ceauşescu also suggested during a speech in April that "rightist deviations" were more dangerous in the present stage than "leftist deviations" (*Scînteia*, 4 May).

The economy. Ceauşescu's continuing pursuit of the rigid antireformist hard-line in domestic political and economic affairs came despite clear signs of domestic unrest and greater estrangement from Romania's allies in the Council for Mutual Economic Assistance (CMEA). In November 1987, several thousand workers in the industrial city of Brasov ransacked the city hall in protest against harsh living conditions, two months of pay cuts for nonfulfillment of the plan, and the prospect of another winter of food and energy shortages (RFE, *RAD Background Report*, no. 231, 4 December 1987). The situation was brought under control through a combination of tough action by the military, security forces, and local police and concessions to workers in the form of advance payments from the enterprise profit-sharing funds and the promise of a 10 percent pay increase to take place between 1988 and 1990. There were other indications of domestic unrest and dissent during 1988, as well as evidence of tough action by officials to maintain order (RFE, *Romanian Situation Report*, 13 January, 23 June, 20 July).

Ceaușescu did keep the promise to increase workers' salaries. In June, legislation was approved to increase wages by 10 percent in three steps between 1 August and the second half of 1989 (*Scînteia*, 30 June). At the same time pensions were also increased. Because these increases are contingent on fulfillment of plan targets, as has been Romanian practice since 1983, the effect may be more promise than reality. Plan targets are generally unreasonably high (RFE, *Romanian Situation Report*, 23 June).

No consideration was given to any reform of the highly centralized economic system, despite repeated criticism of economic performance in 1988. Throughout the year, monthly PEC sessions reviewed economic performance and found it wanting (*Scînteia*, 4, 5 February; *Revista Economica*, 12 February). Ceaușescu's sweeping analyses of the economic problems and the specific directives issued during his periodic tours of factories and farms focused on the need to implement central directives. Despite concerns with worker unrest, however, reports from Romania throughout the year indicated the continuation of serious food and energy shortages. The PEC and State Council decisions on energy production and consumption issued in October indicated that there would be slightly increased electricity available to households in the winter months, but the situation showed little improvement (*NYT*, 18 February; *Manchester Guardian Weekly*, 8 May; *Le Monde*, 4 November; *Die Presse*, 5–6 November; RFE, *Romanian Situation Report*, 2 December).

The pressure to meet high economic targets has exacted a toll from the environment. Two major problems came to light this year, principally because of their impact on neighboring countries. First, serious air pollution from a Romanian chemical plant in the city of Giurgiu has periodically affected the Bulgarian city of Ruse, which has a population of 200,000 and lies just across the Danube River from the Romanian city. Several noxious chlorine emissions occurred in the fall of 1987 and early 1988. The most serious emission, in February 1988, provoked a major protest demonstration involving some two thousand people in the Bulgarian city. Bulgarian media have reported serious problems with the quality of life in Ruse: the

poisonous pollution has damaged vegetation, and there have been sharp increases in lung and skin diseases and birth defects. Romanian media have generally ignored the problem, but Bulgarian officials have publicly pressed for remedial action (RFE, *Bulgarian Situation Report*, 8 March; RFE, *Romanian Situation Report*, 29 March).

A second major environmental problem, never fully described but obviously serious, resulted in high-level dismissals and reprimands for the officials involved. On 17 June, the PEC dismissed Chairman of the State Planning Committee Stefan Birlea, Foreign Trade Minister Ilie Vaduva, and other lesser officials for "serious violations of the country's laws and abuse of power." The dismissals were linked to the storage of hazardous industrial wastes—apparently dangerous chemicals from Western Europe—that were shipped to Romania for storage at the Black Sea port of Sulina. The storage of these materials was said to have had "serious consequences." How serious is not known, but Radio Moscow (16 July) reported that Soviet satellite photographs of the Black Sea facilitated "the rapid discovery of sources of pollution." Sulina is very near the Soviet border. Those reprimanded included Prime Minister Dăscălescu, his first deputy, Gheorghe Oprea, three deputy prime ministers, as well as ministers, and other officials. Among the group of those dismissed or reprimanded were two full members of the PEC and three alternate members. In July seven people directly involved in the matter were sentenced to between eleven and eighteen years in prison for their responsibility in the affair.

A massive centrally directed effort to eliminate the burden of foreign debt has been one important reason the Romanian economy has been under such pressure and consumer goods have been in such short supply. (A Soviet commentary discussed the "tension" caused by Romania's debt repayment effort; *Pravda*, 5 January.) Considerable progress was made during 1988 to retire the Romanian debt. Near the end of 1988, Romanian trade officials announced that gross foreign debt had been reduced from some U.S. $10 billion in 1981 to only $2.5–$2.8 billion (Reuters, 12 December). These figures are consistent with Western ones. The *1987 Annual Report of the International Bank for Reconstruction and Development* (World Bank) reported that at the end of 1986 Romania had a foreign debt of U.S. $6.639 billion. Romanian trade officials noted that because Romania was owed $3 billion by Third World countries, its net foreign debt was nil (RFE,

Romanian Situation Report, 29 December). Despite the improvement in its international debt situation, however, Ceaușescu, in his speech to the CC in November, specifically avoided promising any improvement in living standards and called for a continued high rate of investment (*Scînteia*, 29 November). This suggests that the same policies of forced industrialization will continue, despite the growing evidence that investment is not yielding results that are commensurate with the input.

Rural systematization. In March at the All-Country Conference of People's Councils' Chairmen, Ceaușescu launched his plan of "village systematization," a massive scheme to reduce Romania's thirteen thousand villages to less than half that number by the year 2000. The plan calls for the rural population to be concentrated in some 5,500 "agro-industrial centers," in which peasant families will live in residential apartment buildings grouped together in a community (*Scînteia*, 4 March). A special commission for implementation of the scheme was created by the RCP PEC in May headed by Prime Minister Dăscălescu (*Scînteia*, 7 May).

The new program had three major goals. First, the restructuring is intended to increase land available for cultivation by adding the 660,000 acres on which the villages to be destroyed now stand. The second goal, which is not stated explicitly, is to do away with the remnants of private property in the countryside by incorporating privately cultivated plots into the state and collective farms, thereby bringing them under full control of the state plan. This would satisfy the ideological goal of fully "socializing" agriculture, but it would also result in a decline in agricultural output because privately cultivated land produces a disproportionate share of the fruit, meat, and milk produced in Romania. Furthermore, it is a move directly opposite to the direction currently being taken by the Soviet Union, China, Hungary, Poland, and Yugoslavia.

Third, this scheme's ideological dimension is consistent with Ceaușescu's belief in the communist dogma of the superiority of industrialization and urbanization. It fits his love of grand schemes of social engineering to create the "new socialist man" and is emphasized by the Song to Romania cultural centers that are to be built in each new agro-industrial town. The program would also weaken religion in the countryside: when villages are destroyed, churches would also be leveled, and it is unlikely that new houses of worship would be built in the new state-planned towns.

The most controversial aspect of the plan was its impact on Romania's ethnic minorities. Although Romanian officials gave assurances that it would not weaken or destroy minority nationalities, the systematization clearly would result in wholesale destruction of Hungarian and German churches, cemeteries, historical buildings, and traditional villages. The program would also disperse minority communities and merge them with ethnic Romanian villages, thus diluting the minority proportion of the population and undermining its right to schooling in the mother tongue and the use of the minority language. Furthermore, the emphasis on socialist culture implemented through the Song to Romania cultural centers can hardly be seen as a vehicle to preserve minority cultures. (RFE, *Romanian Situation Reports*, 23 June, 23 August, 16 September, 14 October, 9 November.)

As the scale and extent of this massive plan became known, it provoked a major international outcry. The first countries to react were those with ethnic ties to the minorities most affected in Romania—Hungary and West Germany. As the extent of the Romanian plans became known, however, the protests escalated to include the governments of most countries of Western Europe and the United States. Private individuals, academicians, writers, cultural figures, human rights organizations, and others joined the protests. Although the destruction of minority cultures continued to be the principal concern of the protests, the massive dislocation of Romania's rural population came to be seen as a gross violation of human rights of both the minority and the Romanian nationalities. (RFE, *RAD Background Report*, no. 129, 9 July; RFE, *RAD Background Report*, no. 212, 20 October.)

In the face of the international outcry, Romanian officials strongly defended the economic rationale for rural systematization and denied any intention of adversely affecting the national minorities. In his speech to the RCP CC at the end of November, Ceaușescu again demanded that the program be implemented "unflinchingly" (*Scînteia*, 29 November). At the same time, however, there were signs that the Romanians were proceeding with greater caution. During the latter part of the year reports on the resettlement program indicated that fewer villages would be eliminated, that the process would be gradual rather than immediate, and that the program would take over a decade to complete. Romanian officials also explained that "many of the villages" would be "consolidated administratively" rather than being physically destroyed (RFE, *Ro-*

manian Situation Reports, 14 October, 29 December). Only time will tell whether this apparent backpedaling represents a permanent change in plans or only a temporary tactical retreat for public relations purposes.

Foreign Affairs. Just as Ceauşescu's dogmatic and Stalinist domestic policies have created significant internal difficulties for the regime, his foreign policies have alienated his Soviet and East European allies as well as his former supporters in the West. In its effort to resist Moscow's domestic reforms, Romania has isolated itself from the Soviet Union and most states of Eastern Europe, and its rigid, unyielding position on human rights has isolated Romania from erstwhile supporters in Western Europe and the United States. It is ironic that as the USSR has moved toward arms control with the United States and as East-West relations have improved significantly—actions that Romania has vigorously advocated since the early 1960s—Ceauşescu has become increasingly isolated from both sides. For Romania, the consequence of the East-West rapprochement is that Romania is no longer needed to play the role of international mediator. International conditions have shifted dramatically in the last few years, but Romania has not adjusted its thinking or its policies. Despite the growing international isolation into which Romania sank during 1988, Ceauşescu acted as if nothing had changed. There were more personal visits than usual to Asian and African capitals, as well as a frenzy of discussions with both sides in the Israel-Arab dispute in a futile effort to maintain the image of Ceauşescu as the international mediator.

Relations with the Soviet Union. Although some countries of Eastern Europe (most notably, East Germany and Czechoslovakia) have not accepted Gorbachev's reforms in the economic, social, and political realms, Romania appears to be almost alone in its rejection of Gorbachev's foreign policy. The Soviet Union has cautiously moved toward a rapprochement with the West based on important concessions in the area of human rights, but Romania has vigorously rejected any such policy. In the Helsinki Review Conference in Vienna, Romania was the lone holdout delaying agreement among the 35 participating countries.

These differences with the Soviet Union were highlighted during two high-level visits. In May, President of the Supreme Soviet Andrei Gromyko visited Bucharest. In a speech published the day that

Gromyko's visit was announced, Ceauşescu denounced "rightist deviation" and "recipes for improving socialism" (*Scînteia*, 4 May). During the visit, Romanian media heavily censored Gromyko's discussions of Soviet reforms and *glasnost'* (*Scînteia*, 11–15 May; *Pravda*, *Izvestiia*, 11–16 May). While in Bucharest, Gromyko presented Nicolae Ceauşescu with the Order of Lenin, which had been awarded in connection with Ceauşescu's 70th birthday in January. The Soviets, however, pointedly disapproved of Elena Ceauşescu's role: she was excluded from official discussions, and the Soviet press failed even to mention her name (RFE, *Romanian Situation Report*, 26 May).

In October, Nicolae and Elena Ceauşescu paid an official visit to Moscow at the invitation of Gorbachev. The differences over reform and human rights appeared to be as sharp as ever, although the two leaders avoided the pointed exchanges that have marked some of their previous meetings. Gorbachev, critical of the economic mismanagement and human rights violations in Romania, noted that "the success of each socialist state will be a common ideological achievement, but the failure of any one can, alas, mean a common setback" (*Pravda*, 6 October). Ceauşescu at the same time reaffirmed his view that "the revolutionary process unfolds in each country under different conditions" (*Scînteia*, 6 October). Noncontroversial economic issues figured prominently in the talks. One curious feature of the visit was the end of the Soviet boycott against Elena Ceauşescu; she participated—for the first time—in the official talks (RFE, *Romanian Situation Report*, 9 November).

Relations with Hungary. In 1987 Hungarian-Romanian relations deteriorated seriously, but during 1988 those already bad relations grew worse. The principal source of conflict was the Romanian treatment of its Hungarian minority in Transylvania. In a situation unprecedented in communist Eastern Europe, large numbers of Romanian citizens—many, though not all, of Hungarian ethnic background—fled Romania and sought refuge in Hungary. Hungarian radio reported that during 1987 more than twelve thousand people, mostly ethnic Hungarians from Romania, were given residence permits in Hungary (Radio Budapest, 3 December). Refugees continued to flee to Hungary in large numbers throughout 1988, with some reports indicating as many as 40,000 refugees (*Manchester Guardian Weekly*, 8 May; *WP*, 1 April; *CSM*, 17 August).

The Romanian policy of rural systematization caused a further deterioration of relations between Budapest and Bucharest. On the Hungarian side, official protests were made to Romanian authorities, the Hungarian media (newspapers, radio, and television) continued massive criticism of Romanian policies toward the Hungarian minority, and there were spontaneous demonstrations by Hungarian organizations. On 27 June the largest demonstration in Hungary since the Hungarian Revolution of 1956 was staged in Budapest. Although organized by a number of independent groups, it clearly had the tacit approval of Hungarian authorities. According to Hungarian media some 50,000 to 100,000 Hungarians participated. Protesters carried signs bearing the names of ethnic Hungarian, German, and Romanian villages that were to be leveled in the systematization campaign. There were also signs with slogans such as "Hitler, Stalin, Ceauşescu" and "End the Dictatorship." The protesters marched to the Romanian embassy to present a statement asking Romania to honor international agreements on the rights of ethnic minorities. Embassy officials refused to receive the statement, whereupon the group sang the Hungarian national anthem and dispersed (RFE, *Hungarian Situation Report*, 8 July).

The Romanian response was swift and strong. The next day, at an RCP CC plenum in Bucharest, speakers denounced the "chauvinistic, anti-Romanian, and antisocialist actions" in Hungary. Ceauşescu compared contemporary communist Hungarian policies toward Romania with those of the Fascist dictatorship of Admiral Miklos Horthy during World War II. The same day, the Romanian government closed the Hungarian consulate in the city of Cluj-Napoca in Transylvania and demanded that its staff leave Romania within 48 hours (*Scînteia*, 29 June).

The Soviet Union, although obviously discomfited over the dispute between two of its allies, declined to mediate and urged both countries to resolve the dispute on a bilateral basis. At the same time, however, the Soviet Union supported a Hungarian proposal to establish a commission on human rights and ethnic minority rights under the Warsaw Pact. Despite official neutrality on this thorny issue, the Soviet position was closer to that of Hungary. Romania argued that the issue was an internal one, whereas Hungary urged resolution of the matter through bilateral discussion. The Soviets supported the call for a bilateral resolution of the dispute. The other countries of Eastern Europe likewise avoided involvement in the matter, but East European media gave greater coverage to official Hungarian statements, put forward factual references to Hungarian grievances against Romania, and ignored Romania's claims that minority conditions were excellent (RFE, *RAD Background Report*, no. 161; RFE, *RAD Background Report*, no. 162, 18, 19 August).

In an effort to resolve the differences, Ceauşescu proposed to his Hungarian counterpart that the two party leaders meet to discuss outstanding issues. The eight-hour meeting took place on 28 August in the Romanian border town of Arad. The meeting, which was the first meeting between party leaders of the two countries in eleven years, took place just a few weeks after Károly Grósz had become leader of the Hungarian party. The discussions, however, failed to deal with the real points of difference over treatment of the Hungarian minority. The top agenda item for the Hungarians was the rural systematization program, but the Hungarians won only the promise that they could send a delegation to Romania at a later time to see how the program was being implemented. At Romanian insistence the issue of reopening the Cluj-Napoca consulate was dropped from the agenda. Reports on the talks were sparse, but the Romanians remained intransigent on the nationality issues and the Hungarian leaders were criticized for failure to achieve any progress (*Népszabadság, Magyar hírlap, Magyar nemzet*, 29 August; RFE *Romanian Situation Report*, 16 September; RFE, *Hungarian Situation Report*, 23 September).

In Romania, the summit was followed by a major campaign to support Ceauşescu's anti-Hungarian position. Just after the meetings, Ceauşescu reported on his discussions with Grósz to the party leadership, which approved the position he took (*Scînteia*, 4 September). The party daily (*Scînteia*, 4 September, 2 October) accused the Hungarian media of distorted reporting, said Romanians were "outraged" by the Hungarian media's "gross attempts to falsify Romanian realities and denigrate Romanian policies," and accused the Hungarian media of echoing "hostile, chauvinistic and nationalistic circles and groups." Local organizations in Transylvania met at the end of September to denounce Hungary and to oppose the reopening of the Hungarian consulate in Cluj-Napoca. The Hungarians, meanwhile, were getting better international attention for their position. *Le Monde* (9 November), for example, published an interview with Grósz that explained the Hungarian view.

Another sign of the low level of relations came in November when Romania ordered the expulsion of the commercial counselor in the Hungarian embassy in Bucharest. The Romanian government accused him of distributing inflammatory leaflets against Romania and its leadership. The diplomat left Romania the following day, but Hungary rejected the accusations as unfounded. A few days later, in a formal response to the expulsion, Hungary ordered a diplomat at the Romanian embassy in Budapest to leave the country. It is unprecedented for two Warsaw Pact allies to engage in this reciprocal expulsion of diplomats.

All Hungarians feel strongly about the treatment of the Hungarian minority. In the era of *glasnost'*, the Hungarian government is increasingly in the position of having to respond to popular sentiment on such an emotional issue. At the same time, with freedom of information and association increasingly exercised in Hungary, private individuals and groups are finding it easier to encourage action on these matters. Likewise in Romania, the Hungarian ethnic issue is one on which all ethnic Romanians can unite. In view of the abysmal living conditions and the increasing international isolation, stirring up the nationality issue is one way for the Ceauşescu regime to maintain a measure of popular support and enthusiasm. Embattled Romania must circle the wagons against internationally supported Hungarian irredentism.

Other East European countries. Romania's isolation from the other members of the Warsaw Pact was not limited to its differences with the Soviet Union over reform and its conflict with Hungary over treatment of the Hungarian minority. In multilateral relations, Romania continued to maintain its distance from the other countries. In July, Romania refused to join the other nine members of the Soviet-led CMEA in an agreement to establish a "common market." In October, the Warsaw Pact agreed to establish a Parliamentary Cooperation Council, but Romania refused to join the other six pact members in the organization.

Bilateral relations with other states were also not the best. Ties with Bulgaria were strained over Romanian air pollution affecting Bulgarian communities (see above). This issue was an important one in the discussions between Romanian prime minister Dăscălescu and his Bulgarian counterpart. The talks were held in the Bulgarian city of Ruse, the city most affected by Romanian pollution. Nicolae Ceauşescu also met with Bulgarian party leader

Todor Zhivkov in July during a Warsaw Pact summit in Warsaw. Even Yugoslavia, a country with which Romania has traditionally had good relations in the past, was critical of the treatment of the Serbian minority in Romania, and Bucharest was criticized by a senior figure in the Presidium of the Yugoslav party (*Borba*, 16 June, 30 July; RFE, *Yugoslav Situation Report*, 9 September).

The two East European countries with which Romania has been closest—Czechoslovakia and East Germany—are also opposed to Soviet reforms. Both honored Ceauşescu with their country's highest honor on his 70th birthday in January, and both party leaders exchanged official state visits with Ceauşescu—the only two such visits involving Ceauşescu and his East European counterparts in 1988. In April Ceauşescu hosted Czechoslovak CP general secretary Miloš Jakeš in Bucharest (*Rudé právo*, *Scînteia*, 28 April), and in November Ceauşescu was the guest in East Berlin of Erich Honecker, general secretary of the East German CP (*Neues Deutschland*, 18, 19, 20 November; *Scînteia*, 18–21 November).

Relations with the West. In the late 1960s and 1970s, Romania enjoyed good relations with Western Europe and the United States, in large measure because of its demonstrative autonomy from the Soviet Union. Since the late 1970s, however, relations have begun to deteriorate with Western countries because of Romania's human rights abuses. Trends in the Soviet Union have exacerbated these developments. The general improvement of East-West relations has minimized the importance of Romanian autonomy, and human rights have become more of an irritant as a result of the Soviet Union's new openness, which was particularly evident in 1988 with the increase in Soviet Jewish emigration, a new Soviet willingness to deal with human rights, and the decision to hold a human rights conference in Moscow. In 1988 the issue of human rights was the major reason for a sharp deterioration in relations between Romania and Western countries. The Romanian plan for rural systematization produced a major international outcry, but there were other reasons that human rights became such an important and negative issue in Romania's relations with the West.

The focus of the criticism of Romania was the Review Conference in Vienna of the Conference on Security and Cooperation in Europe (CSCE). Romania's human rights record was the subject of strong and sustained Western criticism in this forum throughout the year. In June, as the Review Conference was working toward a final document, Romania declared "unacceptable" most of the human rights provisions of the draft final document submitted by the neutral and nonaligned states. The Romanian foreign affairs weekly (*Lumea*, 28 July) criticized these countries for "their shift in favor of the West." Romania's isolation was particularly evident because it was the only Warsaw Pact country to object to the draft. Romania submitted its own human rights proposals and announced that it would not accept any major agreements concerning human contacts and the free flow of information. The Western countries reacted by accusing Romania of seeking to prevent implementation of the human rights provision of the Helsinki accords. Romania's absolute intransigence brought the Review Conference to a halt. Austrian vice-chancellor and foreign minister Alois Mock, on behalf of the host government, appealed to Romania to alter its uncompromising position on human rights in order to permit the conference to make progress. The Romanian government responded that there was no need to go beyond the 1983 Madrid document on humanitarian questions, a view that was harshly criticized by Western representatives. The U.S. representative said Romania's resistance to progress on human rights was unacceptable to the "vast majority" of the states at the conference and urged Romania to "reconsider the outrageous position it has taken." The net effect of the adamant Romanian stand—the opposite of what the government desired—focused additional international attention and criticism on Romania's human rights policies.

Romania's human rights record was also criticized in an unusual series of international demonstrations that were held throughout the West and in Eastern Europe. On the basis of an appeal from the Czechoslovak human rights group Charter 77, 1 February was marked by a series of simultaneous demonstrations in Czechoslovakia, Hungary, Poland, and the Soviet Union as well as in Great Britain, France, West Germany, the United States, and elsewhere of solidarity with the Romanian people and against the Romanian government. In November, Romanian émigré and human rights groups held demonstrations to commemorate the first anniversary of the Brasov workers' uprising and to condemn Ceauşescu's human rights policies. In addition to demonstrations in a number of Western cities, protests were also held in Budapest and Wroclaw, Poland. President Ronald Reagan sent a message to the American demonstrators criticizing the abuse of human rights by Romania.

During the year, Romania exacerbated its difficulties with clumsy and heavy-handed policies. Western journalists were a particularly counterproductive target of Romanian sanctions. In May the Netherlands protested to Romania for arresting a Romanian dissident who criticized his government in an interview with Dutch television. The same month two Romanian intellectuals were arrested because of contacts with French journalists. In June a high-ranking Swedish diplomat canceled a trip to Bucharest to protest Romania's refusal to grant entrance visas to two Swedish journalists. In September the French Foreign Ministry protested the temporary detention by Romanian police of a French journalist who had visited dissidents in Bucharest, and in November Romanian authorities arrested and expelled another French journalist after he attempted to visit a dissident. The Western press reported extensively on these incidents.

Another action by Romanian officials drew international attention to its human rights abuses. A Romanian U.N. official was invited to present a report on human rights and youth to the U.N. Subcommittee on the Prevention of Racial Discrimination and Persecution of Minorities. When he failed to appear in Geneva, the Romanian government said he was ill and could not attend, but he sent a message to the subcommittee reporting that he and his family had been placed under police surveillance, that his passport had been suspended, and that his mail and foreign telephone calls were being interrupted. The subcommittee requested that U.N. secretary general Javier Pérez de Cuéllar take up the case with Romanian authorities. Dutch and Norwegian delegates threatened to take Romania to the World Court on the matter. The affair continued for weeks, again generating much negative publicity for Romania (*NYT*, 6, 9 August; RFE, *Romanian Situation Report*, 23 August).

In an effort to go on the offensive on human rights and get back at Hungary for the anti-Romanian demonstrations, Romania proposed that the United Nations adopt a resolution specifying the responsibility of countries and their mass media to combat chauvinistic, racist, or other activities that monger hate between peoples. The General Assembly adopted this resolution in December, but it did little to help Romania's badly tarnished image.

U.S.-Romanian relations. Relations with the United States, already cooling because of Romania's human rights policies, deteriorated sharply during 1988. In early February U.S. deputy secretary of state John Whitehead visited Bucharest for meetings with top Romanian officials to explain the importance the United States attaches to human rights and individual freedom (*NYT*, 7 February). The timing of the visit was important because the House of Representatives had already voted to suspend most-favored nation (MFN) status for Romanian exports to the United States, and Senate consideration of the legislation was imminent. The talks had little effect because the Romanian government refused even to make a gesture on human rights. Shortly afterward the Senate voted to deny Romania MFN benefits. Before the legislation became law, Romania announced that it would renounce MFN status (*NYT*, *LAT*, *WP*, 27 February). On 5 June, President Reagan announced that he would let MFN status for Romania expire, and an agreement ending the preferential tariff status was signed 22 June (*WP*, 25 June).

Also during 1988 the Congress, in renewing the charter for the Overseas Private Investment Corporation, removed Romania from the list of countries eligible for this program of U.S. government guarantees and insurance for trade and international economic cooperation (U.S. Congress, House of Representatives, *Miscellaneous International Affairs Authorizations Act of 1988*, 100th Congress, 2d session, Report 100-594 [Washington, D.C.: 3 May], p. 7).

The cost of these actions to Romania in purely economic terms will be substantial. Estimates of the cost in lost exports from Romania to the United States as a result of the revocation of MFN status were placed as high as $300 million a year. Trade between the two countries in 1986 gave Romania a surplus of $588 million, with U.S. imports from Romania of $839 million and exports to Romania of only $251 million. (*NYT*, 27 June 1987.)

U.S. government officials on several occasions publicly criticized Romania's human rights record. Secretary of State George Shultz described Romania as "the worst country" in Eastern Europe "on the scale of internal repressiveness." The rural systematization was called "a gross violation of human rights" by Deputy Secretary of State Whitehead (interview on Hungarian television, 22 July). In August the U.S. Senate unanimously approved a resolution condemning Romania's rural systematization plans as "new, gross abuses of human rights." In October the House of Representatives adopted a resolution condemning the Romanian

government's violations of human rights, focusing on plans to raze villages and restrictions on religious rights and emigration.

In October Deputy Secretary Whitehead paid another visit to Bucharest and met with Ceaușescu. Again he raised U.S. concerns with village systematization, religious rights, and family reunification. Again the Romanians refused to change their policies.

Ceaușescu as statesman and mediator. Despite the growing isolation of Romania from both its Soviet and East European allies and the West, Ceaușescu attempted to continue his role of international statesman and mediator. Perhaps because of the growing problems in relations with East and West, Ceaușescu did more international globetrotting than usual and seemed to be more active in discussions of the Middle East with Palestine Liberation Organization (PLO) and Israeli representatives. None of these activities were particularly productive in economic or political terms, but they had a domestic public relations value, which the Romanian media skillfully exploited.

Ceaușescu's foreign travel—beyond trips to East Berlin, Warsaw, and Moscow—was to Asia and Africa. There were no trips to Western Europe or North America because of Romania's intransigency on human rights. There were reports that Romanian officials requested an invitation for a Ceaușescu visit to Helsinki, but the request was rejected (*Helsingin sanomat*, 8 August).

Nicolae and Elena Ceaușescu made two trips to Africa in 1988. The first, in March to West Africa, included stops in Ghana, Liberia, and Mauretania. Despite the serious food and consumer goods shortages and the economic problems in Romania, Ceaușescu provided food assistance to Mauretania (Reuters, 15 March). There were also reports that Romania had provided military equipment to Liberia (AP, 11 March), another country with serious human rights problems. The second African trip in September included a visit to East Africa with stops in Kenya and Tanzania and a brief stopover in Cairo for meetings with Egyptian president Husni Mubarak.

The year also included two major trips to Asian countries, although the Ceaușescus' last Asian trip was in May 1987. The traveling Ceaușescus' first Asian journey of 1988 included Indonesia, Vietnam, Australia, and Mongolia. The 32-member delegation also made an unannounced stopover in Karachi, Pakistan, for meetings with the Pakistani president. On 15 October—just ten days after the Ceauşescus returned from their trip to Moscow—they left on another Asian junket to the People's Republic of China and North Korea.

In addition to his international travel, Ceauşescu attempted to keep his status as international statesman alive with a series of discussions on the Middle East with PLO representatives and Israeli government officials. PLO chief Yassir Arafat was in Romania for talks four times at Ceauşescu's invitation (March, June, September, December). Ceauşescu also met in June with the leader of the Democratic Front for the Liberation of Palestine and in July with George Habash, head of the People's Front for the Liberation of Palestine. In November, shortly after the PLO declared the establishment of a Palestinian state, Ceauşescu recognized it.

Contacts with the Israeli government were primarily through Ceauşescu's subordinates. The RCP CC secretary for foreign affairs met with Foreign Minister Shimon Peres. In May Deputy Prime Minister Nicolae Constantin met with Premier Yitzak Shamir and Foreign Minister Peres. In July a special envoy from Ceauşescu told Israeli leaders that PLO leader Arafat was ready to hold direct talks with Israeli leaders (*Jerusalem Post*, Radio Budapest, 10 July). In July Israeli trade minister Ariel Sharon was received by Ceauşescu. The frequency and level of Romanian contacts with Israel were lower than with the PLO. Now that the Soviet Union and other East European countries are dealing directly with the Israelis and the PLO is talking directly to U.S. officials, Romania's role as a mediator has been further eroded.

Despite Ceauşescu's support for the PLO, Romania was harshly criticized by a leading PLO official on the Hungarian minority issue. Salah Khalaf, second in command at the PLO, said in an interview on Hungarian television that Romania was treating ethnic Hungarians in Transylvania "as cruelly" as Israel was treating the Palestinians and that Romania's policies promised "no good for Ceauşescu's mediation" in the Arab-Israeli conflict (Radio Budapest, 22 August).

Robert R. King
Washington, D.C.

Union of Soviet Socialist Republics

Population. 285,200,000 (TASS, 25 April)
Party. Communist Party of the Soviet Union (Kommunisticheskaia Partiia Sovetskogo Soiuza; CPSU)
Founded. 1898 (CPSU, 1952)
Membership. 19,468,786 (*Pravda*, 14 April); 585,000 new admissions, 1987; workers, 45 percent; collective farmers, 11.8 percent; white-collar workers and others, 43.2 percent
General Secretary. Mikhail S. Gorbachev
Politburo. (Unless otherwise indicated, nationality is Russian; first date is year of birth, second is year of election to present rank.) 12 full members: Mikhail S. Gorbachev (b. 1931, e. 1980, chairman of the Presidium [president], Supreme Soviet), Viktor M. Chebrikov (b. 1923, e. 1985, chairman, party commission on legal policy), Egor K. Ligachev (b. 1920, e. 1985, chairman, party commission on agriculture), Vadim A. Medvedev (b. 1930, e. 1988, chairman, party commission on ideology), Viktor P. Nikonov (b. 1929, e. 1987, deputy chairman, party commission on agriculture), Nikolai I. Ryzhkov (b. 1929, e. 1985, chairman [prime minister], Council of Ministers), Vladimir V. Shcherbitskii, Ukrainian (b. 1918, e. 1971, first secretary, Ukrainian Central Committee), Eduard A. Shevardnadze, Georgian (b. 1928, e. 1985, foreign minister), Nikolai N. Sliun'kov, Belorussian (b. 1929, e. 1987, chairman, party commission on social and economic policy), Vitalii I. Vorotnikov (b. 1926, e. 1983, chairman of the Presidium, Supreme Soviet of the Russian Soviet Federated Socialist Republic [RSFSR]), Aleksandr N. Iakovlev (b. 1923, e. 1987, chairman, party commission on international affairs), Lev N. Zaikov (b. 1923, e. 1986, first secretary, Moscow city party committee) Note: Chebrikov and Ryzhkov were listed in Soviet sources as Ukrainian before their appointments to chairs in the KGB and to the party Secre-

tariat, respectively, in November–December 1982; they have since been listed as Russian. 8 candidate members: Aleksandra P. Biriukova (b. 1929, e. 1988, deputy chairman [deputy prime minister], Council of Ministers), Anatolii I. Luk'ianov (b. 1930, e. 1988, first deputy chairman of the Presidium [vice president], Supreme Soviet), Iuri D. Masliukov (b. 1937, e. 1988, first deputy chairman [first deputy prime minister], Council of Ministers), Georgii P. Razumovskii (b. 1936, e. 1988, chairman, party commission on party building and personnel), Iuri F. Solov'ev (b. 1925, e. 1985, first secretary, Leningrad *oblast'* party committee), Nikolai V. Talyzin (b. 1929, e. 1985, deputy chairman [deputy prime minister], Council of Ministers), Aleksandr V. Vlasov (b. 1932, e. 1988, chairman, RSFSR Council of Ministers), Dmitrii T. Iazov (b. 1923, e. 1987, minister of defense)

Secretariat. 8 members: (*indicates members of Politburo): *Mikhail S. Gorbachev (general secretary), *Viktor M. Chebrikov (police and legal affairs), *Egor K. Ligachev (agriculture), *Vadim A. Medvedev (ideology), *Viktor P. Nikonov (agriculture), *Nikolai N. Sliun'kov (economy), *Georgii P. Razumovskii (cadres), Oleg D. Baklanov, Ukrainian (b. 1932, defense industry)

Central Committee. 307 full and 107 candidate members were elected at the Twenty-seventh CPSU Congress. The Central Committee is organized under 6 commissions and 21 departments; key department heads include Valentin M. Falin (b. 1926, international), Ivan I. Skiba, Ukrainian (b. 1937, agriculture), Nikolai E. Kruchina (b. 1928, adminstration of affairs), Aleksei D. Lizichev (b. 1928, main political directorate of the armed forces).

Status. Ruling and only legal party

Last Congress. Twenty-seventh, 25 February–6 March 1986, in Moscow

Last Election. Supreme Soviet, 4 March 1984; more than 99.4 percent of vote for CPSU-backed candidates, all 1,500 of whom were elected; 71.4 percent of elected candidates were CPSU members.

Defense Council. This is the inner circle of leadership concerned with national security affairs; only the chairman is publicly identified. Chairman, Mikhail S. Gorbachev; probable members, as of 1 January 1989: Eduard A. Shevardnadze, Aleksandr N. Iakovlev, Marshal Dmitrii T. Iazov, Lev N. Zaikov. Possible members or associates: Nikolai I. Ryzhkov; Vladimir A. Kriuchkov (b.

1924), chairman, Committee for State Security (KGB); Valentin M. Falin; Colonel General Mikhail Moiseiev (b. 1938), chief of staff and first deputy minister of defense.

Government. 107 members of the Council of Ministers, including two first deputy chairman (first deputy prime ministers), 11 deputy chairmen (deputy prime ministers), 15 ex officio deputy chairmen (prime ministers of the Union republics), 54 ministers, and 24 chairmen of state committees. Key members of the government not identified above include Vsevolod S. Murakhovskii, Ukrainian (b. 1926, first deputy chairman, Council of Ministers, and chairman, State Committee for the Agro-Industrial Complex), Boris L. Tolstykh (b. 1935, deputy chairman for science and technology, Council of Ministers), Lev A. Voronin (b. 1928, deputy chairman, Council of Ministers, and chairman, State Committee for Material and Technical Supply).

Auxiliary Organizations. Communist Youth League (Kommunisticheskii Soiuz Molodezhi; Komsomol), 39.5 million members, led by Vladimir Mironenko, Ukrainian (b. 1953); All-Union Central Council of Trade Unions (AUCCTU), 132 million members, led by Stepan A. Shalaiev (b. 1929); Voluntary Society for the Promotion of the Army, Air Force, and Navy (DOSAAF), led by Admiral Georgii M. Egorov (b. 1918), more than 65 million members; Union of Soviet Societies for Friendship and Cultural Relations with Foreign Countries

Publications. Main CPSU organs are the daily newspaper *Pravda* (circulation more than 10 million), the theoretical and ideological journal *Kommunist* (appearing 18 times a year, with a circulation over 1 million), and the semimonthly *Partiinaia zhizn'*, a journal of internal party affairs and organizational matters (circulation more than 1.1 million). *Kommunist vooruzhennykh sil* is the party theoretical journal for the armed forces, and *Agitator* is the same for party propagandists; both appear twice a month. There is also a weekly information sheet for propagandists, *Dokumenty i fakty.* The Komsomol has a newspaper, *Komsomolskaia pravda* (6 days a week), and a monthly theoretical journal, *Molodaia gvardiia.* Each USSR republic prints similar party newspapers in local languages and usually also in Russian. Specialized publications issued under the supervision of the CPSU Central Committee include the newspapers *Sovetskaia Rossiia, Sel'skaia zhizn', Sotsialisticheskaia industriia, Sovetskaia kul'tura,* and

Ekonomicheskaia gazeta and the journal *Politi-cheskoe samoobrazovanie*. Telegrafnoe Agentstvo Sovetskogo Soiuza (TASS) is the official news agency.

When Mikhail Gorbachev assumed office as general secretary of the CPSU in March 1985, the USSR was enmeshed in a general systemic crisis that defied easy solutions. At home, the economy was plagued by waste and inefficiency, poor adaptation to modern technology, and chronic agricultural shortfalls. A deadening social malaise seemed to have sapped the country's vitality, reflected in rampant alcoholism, rising crime rates, extensive corruption, and a growing lack of confidence that the Soviet regime could satisfy even modest expectations of the populace. Abroad, the USSR confronted an extreme diplomatic isolation unmatched since the early 1930s.

The all-around crisis of the system invited a program of sweeping reform. But Soviet society, in the epoch of "mature socialism," had shown itself highly resistant to change. Moreover, given the closed nature of the Soviet system, any program of revitalization would have to be carried out by officials who had participated in the politics of decline and who were associated in some degree with failed policies. There was, however, one major asset for the new leadership that was partially a product of the decline.

The stagnation of leadership in the late Leonid Brezhnev years had contributed immeasurably to the crisis, and the instability linked with unsettled succession in the first half of the 1980s had prevented any wide-ranging assault on the system's problems. The immobility at the top had left in place an aging corps of leaders, particularly at the system center. The actuarial tables dictated a generational turnover, and, given the general secretary's powerful influence in *nomenklatura* appointments, this necessity could be utilized to infuse somewhat fresher blood into the moribund officialdom and open the way to new approaches. In the following years, Gorbachev would take full advantage of this opening.

At the outset, Gorbachev did not have a single client or protégé in the central party leadership (full and candidate Politburo members and members of the Secretariat). Accordingly, he had to rely heavily on figures propelled to the top by Iurii Andropov such as Ligachev, Ryzhkov, and Chebrikov—men who could feel that Gorbachev owed more to them than they did to him. Personal authority building, a

critical task for any new general secretary, was further complicated by the fact that Gorbachev was the youngest member of the upper leadership.

Gorbachev set about his Herculean labors with a zest and flair rarely, if ever, seen in Soviet politics. His plan of attack had four interrelated aspects: to make sufficient inroads in the "levers of command" via personnel placement so that his authority would be clearly established, to seize control of the system agenda, to change the style of the Soviet leadership in order to rehabilitate its image at home and abroad, and to formulate and execute a broad program to restore vigor to the ailing system.

A new style was evident almost at once, and Gorbachev used the "bully pulpit" of the general secretary's office to gain control of the agenda. The other objectives were more difficult. Everything depended on Gorbachev's accumulation of organizational power, and this would necessarily be a fairly lengthy process. But over the following three-and-one-half years, he forged steadily ahead. Despite increasingly overt opposition to his proposals for reform, nearly all plenums of the Central Committee resulted in increments of Gorbachev's dominance over the central organs of the party. Carefully meshing his policy formulation with the expansion of his organizational power, Gorbachev gradually developed a rounded program to cope with systemic problems.

The general secretary's program was grounded in the twin concepts of *glasnost'* (openness or publicity) and *perestroika* (restructuring). The main purpose of *perestroika* was revival of the economy, and, in Gorbachev's view, freer communication under *glasnost'* was essential for the success of *perestroika*. Specifically, *glasnost'* was intended to bring such public pressure to bear upon lower levels of the bureaucracy that expected opposition to reform would be dissipated. As the program of economic reform developed, it included such elements as greater independence and responsibility for individual enterprises, emphasis on incentives for workers, some private enterprise in the service sector and the consumer goods industry, a variant of "family farming," and organization of joint ventures with foreign capitalist firms.

But *perestroika* was not confined to the economy. Gorbachev's first signal success was in the realm of foreign policy. Institutions in this area were the system structures most vulnerable to penetration by a new leader. In a series of dazzling coups in 1985–86, Gorbachev gained dominance over the foreign ministry and the Central Committee's (CC) International Department. The foreign ministry was re-organized, new ambassadors were appointed to all major embassies, and Anatolii Dobrynin was put in charge of the International Department. Détente was revived as Gorbachev went to the summit five times within a three-year period with U.S. President Ronald Reagan and concluded an unprecedented sweeping agreement on intermediate nuclear missiles in 1987. Skillfully executed overtures produced thaws in relationships with a number of countries, including China, and arrangements were made to extricate the USSR from the quagmire in Afghanistan. Long-range priorities remained in doubt as Gorbachev steered a middle course between the "America first" option—said to be supported by Dobrynin—and the "borderlands" strategy, which downplayed ties with the United States—openly advocated by Iakovlev, party secretary.

At home, *perestroika* ran headlong into a thicket of daunting problems. The nuclear accident at Chernobyl in April 1986 was a major setback but less inhibiting than the reluctance of various interests to part with established ways. The piecemeal introduction of reform produced some confusion, and the streamlining of economic organization, especially in agriculture, yielded disappointing results.

Workers were generally skeptical of reforms that threatened job security and promised little in the way of tangible early returns. Managers were loath to accept new responsibilities, and higher-ranking economic administrators resisted erosion of their power. Gorbachev was caught in a cross fire between conservative resistance to his program and the pressure of those who thought that reform was proceeding too slowly. These tensions came to a head with the explosive October 1987 CC plenum and the public humiliation and dismissal as Moscow party chief of Boris El'tsin, one of the strongest supporters of *perestroika*, in the following month.

Glasnost' was perhaps even more controversial than *perestroika*. The Soviet public was treated to a wider range of information than before, although criticism of the central party leadership remained off-limits. A more objective picture of events and conditions in the West was depicted, and writers were given latitude to fill in the "blank pages" of Soviet history. The Josef Stalin era naturally became the main focus of attention, and the flood of revelations dismayed conservatives who saw this new freedom as a threat to system legitimacy. Even Gorbachev seemed surprised by the tendency of *glasnost'* to go beyond its intended purpose and

assume a momentum of its own; he sometimes added his voice to those urging caution. The most important negative effect of *glasnost'* had been the surfacing of nationalist tensions, which was one area that could not be ignored by Gorbachev or his critics.

By the fall of 1987, open opposition to Gorbachev's reform program was apparent even at the top levels of leadership. Party secretary Ligachev had become the rallying point for all those disoriented and disaffected by reform, and Chebrikov, head of the KGB, lent important support. Meanwhile, the setbacks on the *perestroika* front had convinced Gorbachev that revival of the economy and forward social movement could not be achieved without major structural reform of the political system. Thus, his two major objectives for the new year were the curbing of opposition and putting in place the mechanism for major political reform.

The general secretary was to have striking success in both objectives. The Nineteenth Party Conference, in June and July, featured an open discussion of issues not witnessed in the USSR since the 1920s and some outspoken criticism of reform. Yet, despite some apparent success of entrenched party resisters in packing the ranks of the conference delegates, Gorbachev got most of a revised and toned-down wish list presented at the meeting's outset. A reform package was approved that included proposals for a new national legislature, a more powerful presidency, election of officials in open contests and by secret ballot, and the turning over of many day-to-day functions of running the country from the party to the soviets and government officeholders. These proposals were subsequently endorsed by the Supreme Soviet and the CC.

Gorbachev's relentless drive for organizational power climaxed in a dramatic victory at the September CC plenum. The CC apparatus was reorganized under six commissions, and several opponents were removed from the leadership or downgraded. Ligachev was demoted to chairmanship of the new agricultural commission, and Chebrikov was named head of the legal commission, being replaced as head of the KGB by Kriuchkov, reportedly close to Gorbachev. However, Chebrikov would presumably be the Politburo's supervisor of the security agency. Protégé Medvedev emerged as a rising political star, assuming leadership of the commission on ideology. One surprise was the departure of Dobrynin, which left Iakovlev as the undisputed party supervisor of foreign policy. Andrei Gromyko "retired" and, on the day following the CC plenum, stepped down from the presidency, being replaced by Gorbachev. The general secretary's confidant Luk'ianov moved from the Secretariat to the vice presidency to manage the transition to the new governmental scheme scheduled for 1989.

Implementation of economic reform proceeded during the year, with barely perceptible progress. There was more tinkering with the ministerial structure, and the reorganized *Gosplan* was recognized as a major disappointment, leading in January to the naming of a new head for the agency drawn from the "military-industrial complex." One of Gorbachev's pet projects, the reorganization of agriculture, was an even greater flop. The State Committee on the Agro-Industrial Complex (*Gosagroprom*) had reportedly led to more bureacratic entanglement, rather than less, and had become a standing joke. The expansion of cooperatives and the new leasing arrangements in agriculture held promise of an early improvement in the standard of living, but, for the present, shortages and discomfort plagued the Soviet consumer and widespread grumbling continued.

More serious was the escalation of nationalism during the year. In the south, bloody ethnic clashes accompanied a dispute over the status of Nagorno-Karabakh, an Armenian enclave in the Azerbaijan Soviet Socialist Republic, and by December the Armenian capital of Erevan was under virtual martial law. In this region, conflict among the subordinate nationalities tended to neutralize the threat to central authority. This was not the case in the Baltic republics.

Demands for autonomy, spearheaded by Estonia, mounted to a crescendo in the fall with proposals for republican control over most governmental and economic functions and even veto power over Soviet legislation. Moscow rejected the demands as unconstitutional, but Gorbachev sounded a conciliatory note, admitting past mistakes in treatment of ethnic minorities and promising a CC session in 1989 to deal specifically with the nationalities question. Nevertheless, the nationalities problem emerged as the most pressing issue confronting the Soviet leadership, and serious doubts were raised about Gorbachev's ability to maintain the thrust for systemic reform if nationalist agitation threatened the existing federal structure of the USSR. Reformist members of the intelligentsia, attuned to the continuities of Russian history, were reminded that Alexander II had faced problems similar to those of Gorbachev and that the crucial

event in his turn away from reform after 1866 had been the abortive Polish uprising.

Again, external affairs gave less cause for concern than did the domestic scene. Gorbachev and Reagan met in Moscow in May and again in New York in December. No major agreements were concluded, but relations between the superpowers remained on an even keel, despite continuing divisive issues. The improved Soviet record on human rights and the planned withdrawal from Afghanistan contributed to the harmonious atmosphere of Moscow-Washington contacts and to upgrading the Soviet image in other Western countries. Afghanistan was still a problem, however, and the pullout of Soviet troops stalled as rebel harassment of the departing forces intensified and as Moscow denounced continuing support by the United States and Pakistan for the foes of the puppet Kabul regime. But the softer Soviet stance on Afghanistan facilitated a growing détente with China, capped by expectations for a summit meeting between Soviet and Chinese leaders in 1989.

Perhaps the most satisfactory area was Western Europe, whose leaders were strongly supportive of Gorbachev's domestic plans. The Soviets had lined up the equivalent of $9 billion in credits from consortiums of Western banks, an impressive payoff for Gorbachev's normalization approach vis-à-vis the region. But some Westerners were troubled by reports that the increase in the Soviet military budget had doubled in 1986–87 as against the 1981–85 period and by the deployment of an array of sophisticated weaponry when the Soviets admitted for the first time that their budget was in deficit.

Gorbachev sought to assuage such concerns in his speech to the U.N. General Assembly in December, promising a cut of 500,000 in Soviet troop strength, a reduction of 10,000 tanks, and a "clearly defensive" military deployment in Europe.

The general secretary's New York visit was another public relations triumph, but grim news from home forced cancellation of scheduled stops in Havana and London. The massive earthquake in Armenia caused up to 100,000 deaths, and the enormous economic dislocation wrought by the disaster added a further complication for the restructuring program.

At year's end, Gorbachev appeared to have attained new heights of personal authority, but major problems still confronted the leadership. The future of reform remained problematic.

Leadership. Party leader Gorbachev continued the process of consolidation of power during the year and used the plenums of the CC both for this purpose and to push his reform program, which had encountered serious difficulties in the previous year. Between these meetings, there was evidence of discord in the upper leadership. In the course of the year, Gorbachev's secure organizational base enabled him to deflate the critics at this level. But there were indications that recalcitrance in the upper leadership was only the tip of the iceberg, and many observers concluded that the scheme for a more powerful presidency was primarily designed to surmount opposition within the party.

In his six-hour speech at the January CC plenum, Gorbachev focused his drive for renewal on the ruling party for the first time. He devoted much of the speech to the "stagnation" that was a legacy of the Brezhnev period and charged that "the leading bodies of the party and state" bore responsibility for it. Clearly implied by his prolonged description of the negative effects of earlier policies and by the absence of assertions that these had been overcome was the conclusion that the party was continuing to hamper forward movement. As an antidote, the general secretary proposed multicandidate elections and secret balloting for local and provincial party offices, leaving open the possibility that such procedures might be applied to the upper leadership as well.

Gorbachev did not openly chastise his critics but was obviously referring to his opposition when he said that "we are often asked whether we are not making too sharp a turn." Dismissing the question, the general secretary sought, as he had often done in the past, to link his reform proposals to an idealized version of pristine Leninism, from which later leaderships had allegedly departed (*Pravda, NYT*, 28 January).

The January plenum had been merely a sounding board for Gorbachev's ideas. To give momentum to his drive for political reform, the general secretary needed to deepen his organizational grip at the party center. A move of some consequence in this direction was made at the February plenum of the CC when Razumovskii, party cadres secretary, was promoted to candidate member of the Politburo. Razumovskii had long been closely associated with Gorbachev and had been the party leader's chief agent in personnel matters since his assumption of the cadres post in 1985. Razumovskii's elevation was widely viewed as a further check on "second

secretary" Ligachev, whose responsibility in the personnel area was probably now at best nominal.

The February plenum also elected D. Masliukov (50), newly appointed first deputy premier and head of *Gosplan*, as a candidate Politburo member. Talyzin, his predecessor at *Gosplan*, retained his candidate membership. As expected, El'tsin, the deposed Moscow party chief, lost his place among the candidate members (*Pravda*, 19 February).

Zaikov, the new Moscow party leader, kept his place on the Secretariat, where he had served as supervisor of the defense industry since 1985. However, Baklanov (56), USSR minister of general machine building and a specialist in the defense industry, was added to the Secretariat, apparently to take over full responsibility for supervision of arms production (*RL Research*, 18 February; *NYT*, 19 February). It seemed likely that a transition period was envisioned, such as in 1976 when armaments czar Dimitri Ustinov retained his seat on the Secretariat for a time after being named defense minister.

Despite Gorbachev's gains at the February plenum, frictions in the leadership continued. With the June party conference looming, the conservatives evidently dug in their heels for a last-ditch stand, perhaps encouraged by the indications of midlevel resistance to further political restructuring. Ligachev was again the point man for the resisters and apparently committed a tactical blunder that accelerated his political slide downhill. On 13 March, just as Gorbachev was leaving on a trip to Yugoslavia, *Sovetskaia Rossiia* published a letter purportedly written by Nina Andreeva, a Leningrad chemistry teacher, that defended Stalin's leadership and sharply attacked the critical reexamination of Soviet history under *glasnost'*.

The letter, which reportedly had been rejected by three publications in fall 1987, had apparently been heavily edited by the editors of the newspaper. Giulietto Chiesa, a correspondent of *L'Unita*, the Italian communist party's newspaper, claimed to have seen a copy of the original letter and reported that only five of the eighteen pages written by Andreeva were included in the revised version published by *Sovetskaia Rossiia* (*L'Unita*, 23 May; *RL Research*, 5 June). Some accounts had Ligachev directing the entire operation, beginning with approval of publication in the newspaper. In any event, Ligachev subsequently praised the letter, which he called (perhaps more accurately) an "article," and recommended it as a model for use in party discussions. Over the following two weeks, the letter was widely reprinted.

On his return from Yugoslavia on 13 March, Gorbachev launched a spirited counterattack. He reportedly convened a special meeting of the Politburo to discuss the matter, with Ligachev, traveling outside Moscow, absent. The ruling group was said to have approved a mild reprimand for Ligachev and a stronger one for Valentin Chikin, the editor of *Sovetskaia Rossiia*.

Three weeks after appearance of the letter, *Pravda* denounced the piece in a full-page editorial, calling it "an attempt at revising party decisions on the sly" (*Pravda*, 5 April). Gorbachev praised the *Pravda* editorial as setting the record straight, and *Sovetskaia Rossiia* reprinted it without comment on 6 April. At midmonth, the RSFSR organ issued a full-scale recantation, the editors saying that they had "not demonstrated enough responsibility, a sufficiently balanced approach" and "the understanding that the letter leads one away from the revolutionary renewal of society through democracy and openness" (*Sovetskaia Rossiia*, 15 April).

The 15 April *Sovetskaia Rossiia* turnabout may have been precipitated by continuing public evidence of discord among the hierarchs. On 13 April, in a speech in Tashkent, Gorbachev said that *perestroika* had "frightened some people" who "simply lost their bearings." He also told a group of visiting American businessmen that *perestroika* had produced "an acute confrontation, I would even say, clash of views." But on the same day, in a speech in Cheboksary, Chebrikov expressed quite different opinions:

Today we openly lay emphasis on shortcomings and negative phenomena and with a very good reason, to expose their root causes. However, this is only one side of the question. The other side is that we should by no means permit the belittling of the positive example, but should propagate more actively advanced experience and labor achievements of the people who personally put into practice the transformations outlined by the party (*NYT*, 14 April).

One week after the Gorbachev and Chebrikov speeches, Soviet officials said that Ligachev had at least temporarily relinquished his role as supervisor of press and television. According to unconfirmed reports, Ligachev had been ordered to take a vacation, with his ideology portfolio to be assumed in his absence by Iakovlev (ibid., 20 April). Nevertheless, at the Lenin anniversary celebration on 22 April, Ligachev took his customary place at Gorbachev's right. But the anniversary speaker was Gorbachev's close associate Razumovskii, who delivered a speech strongly supportive of the general secretary's reform program (TASS, 22 April; *Pravda*, 23 April).

As the dust settled on the Andreeva affair, other events of the time, unnoticed earlier, seemed to provide evidence of an old-fashioned power struggle in the Kremlin. While Gorbachev was in Yugoslavia, Ligachev's name began appearing in media reports out of alphabetical order and ahead of his Politburo colleagues (TASS, Radio Moscow, 18 March). On 2 April, Vasilii Sitnikov was dismissed as first secretary of Irkutsk *obkom* in the wake of an attempted airline highjacking (*Pravda*, 30 May), but this was not immediately reported in the central press. Sitnikov, reportedly a Ligachev client, was apparently a scapegoat in an early skirmish in Gorbachev's campaign against the "second secretary"; his sacking appeared to have been a "first shot across Ligachev's bow" (*RL Research*, 22 April).

There were some signs that Gorbachev had not landed a knockout punch in the Andreeva affair and that the conservative opposition at middle levels of the party was resisting more strongly than ever. Preparations for the Nineteenth CPSU Conference in June lagged, and local and regional organization officials appeared to have gained control of delegate selection in many places, shutting out reformers (*NYT*, 9 June). A CC plenum in May promoted Vladimir Popov, head of the Soviet Writers' Union and at best lukewarm on *glasnost'*, to full CC membership (*Pravda*, 24 May). However, theses on the party conference approved at the meeting included a proposal for limiting terms of officials, a measure strongly pushed by reformers (ibid., 26 May).

The party conference brought into the open the controversy simmering within the party but endorsed proposals for reform agreed upon beforehand by the Politburo (see below). Although there were hints of tension within the leadership, the party hierarchs maintained a facade of amity, and Ligachev again occupied his customary place during most of the sessions, with protocol precedence just below Gorbachev.

Another rallying plenum of the CC was held in late July to follow through on the conference. No breakthroughs were reported, but accounts of the plenum also indicated no sign of overt opposition to the general secretary. Approval was given to a Supreme Soviet session in November to promulgate constitutional changes, and elections for the new national legislature were scheduled for March 1989 (*Pravda*, 30 July).

Following the plenum, evidence of turmoil within the leadership continued to mount. Gorbachev left for his summer vacation, and, just as he had done in March (and in late summer of the previous year), Ligachev used the occasion of the leader's absence to attack his policies. In a speech in Gorky on 5 August, Ligachev rejected the idea that the USSR should move in the direction of a market economy and questioned the idea of general global interests transcending the traditional "two camps" approach to world affairs. "We proceed from the class character of international relations," Ligachev said, adding that "any other presentation of the problem sows confusion among Soviet people and among our friends abroad" (*Sovetskaia Rossiia*, 6 August; *RL Research*, 16 August).

A response followed quickly. Speaking in Riga on 10 August, Iakovlev said that "it is hardly possible to maintain commodity-money relations and financial autonomy while at the same time denying the market the right to exist" (*Pravda*, 11 August). Two days later, in Vilnius, Iakovlev decisively scorned Ligachev's "two camps" rhetoric on international relations: "Marxism is the understanding of common human interests from the viewpoint of history and the perspective of the development of mankind, not just certain of its countries and classes, peoples, and social groups" (Central Television, 12 August; *RL Research*, 16 August).

The situation had by now reached a point where the public evidence of disharmony within the leadership was damaging the general secretary's image at home and abroad. In late September, he struck with startling swiftness to bolster his position. A plenum of the CC was called on less than three days' notice, with a Supreme Soviet meeting to follow on the next day. Foreign Minister Shevardnadze had to hurry home from New York, where he was attending the fall session of the U.N. General Assembly. The call for a gathering of the two bodies was the most dramatic domestic political development in Moscow since the fall of Khrushchev and evoked memories of the CC shootout in the summer of 1957; Western observers anticipated a showdown. Although there was some speculation that Gorbachev was in trouble, one clue pointed in the opposite direction: if the CC was summoned to deal with personnel questions, there would be no point in also convening the Supreme Soviet unless the departure of President Gromyko was anticipated.

The outcome was another major step in the consolidation of organizational power by the general secretary. Six presumed resisters were ousted or demoted, and five certain Gorbachev supporters were promoted. At the same time, the CC apparatus was reorganized under six commissions. The commission scheme had been endorsed by the Nineteenth CPSU Conference in July, but the timing of the plenum suggested a coup by Gorbachev to avoid giving the opposition enough time to organize a counterstroke.

The commissions were assigned to four sitting full Politburo members, one new full member, and one candidate member. The commissioners named were Iakovlev, foreign affairs; Ligachev, agriculture; Chebrikov, legal affairs; Medvedev, ideology; Sliun'kov, economy; and Razumovskii, party organization. Medvedev, who had served as party secretary for relations with ruling communist parties since the Twenty-seventh CPSU Congress, was moved directly to full Politburo rank without passing through candidate status (*Pravda*, 29 September).

It was not immediately clear how the commission system would affect the existing departmental structure of the CC. Medvedev, at a press conference following the plenum, said that the creation of the six commissions would streamline the party's administrative machinery, part of Gorbachev's campaign to remove the party from the day-to-day management of nearly all aspects of Soviet life (*NYT*, 29 September). But should the departmental setup be retained, the new modus operandi might not differ very much from that previously prevailing, with certain CC secretaries, usually Politburo members, supervising the work of several departments.

Gromyko (79) "retired" after 41 years service in top positions in the Soviet system, and Mikhail Solomentsev (74), chairman of the party Control Committee, was also dropped. The exits of the two oldest Politburo members had been foreshadowed by an attack on them by a delegate at the Nineteenth CPSU Conference. Party secretary Vladimir Dolgikh (64), reportedly a key figure in the late desperate attempt to stop Gorbachev in the spring of 1985, was also sacked. His retention to this point indicated some checks upon Gorbachev's consolidation of power because, as long-time Secretariat supervisor of the nuclear industry, he would have been a convenient scapegoat for the 1986 Chernobyl disaster.

Three candidate members were added to the Politburo: Vlasov, head of the Interior Ministry, slated to move to the premiership of the RSFSR; Luk'ianov, Gorbachev's onetime schoolmate at the

Moscow State University law school and Secretariat overseer of the police, who was scheduled to assume the vice presidency; and Biriukova, party secretary for light industry, tabbed for a deputy premiership. Biriukova thus became the first woman to hold Politburo rank since Ekaterina Furtseva was dropped from the ruling body in 1961 at the conclusion of the Twenty-second CPSU Congress. The veteran Piotr Demichev, first vice-chairman of the Supreme Soviet Presidium under Gromyko and a candidate member for more than two decades, was dumped to make way for Luk'ianov's transfer.

A major surprise was the "retirement" of Dobrynin (69) as party secretary and head of the International Department. Dobrynin had supervised the reorganization of the Foreign Ministry in 1986 and been one of the chief architects of the new course in foreign policy. When reputed hard-liner Falin (62), chairman of the Novosti press agency and former ambassador to West Germany, was announced as new head of the International Department three weeks later (TASS, AP, 20 October), some doubts were raised about the completeness of Gorbachev's victory. However, close examination of Falin's public statements revealed a clear correspondence with the views of Iakovlev: strong criticism of the United States, downplaying the superpower connection, and greater emphasis on relations with Western Europe and "borderlands" states.

Boris Pugo (51), party chief of Latvia and an outspoken proponent of *perestroika* and *glasnost'*, was named as Solomentsev's successor to the chairmanship of the party Control Committee (*Pravda*, 1 October). With control and auditing structures scheduled for fusion under the projected party reorganization, it seemed likely that Pugo would emerge as a powerful figure in the future.

Some observers noted certain indications that Gorbachev had not been able to deliver a knockout blow to his critics. Pugo was not elected to even candidate Politburo membership as might have been expected, and Razumovskii was not promoted to full membership. Most important, Ligachev and Chebrikov retained full Politburo membership. There was some speculation that Gorbachev might have preferred to keep the two men on the Politburo for a time to avoid the appearance of a sharp break that would further alienate party conservatives. But it was more likely that the balance of forces within the ruling body precluded their ouster. Past experience indicates that it is far easier for a general secretary to demote than to expel a Politburo mem-

ber, and, after all, the changes actually made amounted to the most extensive shakeup of the top leadership since Nikita Krushchev's victory over the "antiparty" group in 1957.

Most significantly, the switch in functional responsibilities of Ligachev and Chebrikov represented a clear plus for Gorbachev. Chebrikov would probably serve as Politburo supervisor of the KGB, but he had lost day-to-day control of the agency, which passed to Kriuchkov, who had accompanied Gorbachev to Washington for the summit meeting in 1987 (see below). Ligachev was transferred to the usually politically unprofitable sector of agriculture, apparently without real control over farming; party secretary Nikonov retained administrative oversight in this area. Ligachev's role as a supernumerary was further indicated two weeks later when he was absent from an important meeting on agriculture that was attended by Gorbachev, Nikonov, and other leadership figures (*CSM*, 13 October). It appeared that Ligachev was being set up to serve as scapegoat for agricultural failures without real power to control events.

The reassignment of Vorotnikov was more difficult to evaluate. There was speculation that his election as chairman of the Presidium of the Supreme Soviet of the RSFSR (*Izvestiia*, 4 October) was intended to facilitate the transition to the new constitutional structure, with Vorotnikov set to remain as the key party figure, while serving as president of the largest republic. But there were strong arguments against such a conclusion. If Vorotnikov, who had reportedly become increasingly disenchanted with the reform program, was to occupy such a role, there seemed no pressing urgency for the shift at this point. In any case during the interim period, real control of RSFSR affairs would lie in the hands of the new premier Vlasov, a close associate of the general secretary.

Of special note was the fact that Gorbachev had eliminated or reduced most of the independent figures who had reportedly supported his election in 1985. Geidar Aliev had been ousted in the fall of 1987. Now, two independents—Gromyko and Solomentsev—had been dropped, and two others—Ligachev and Chebrikov—had been shorn of their power bases. Vorotnikov, another probable early backer among the independents, for the present at least, occupied a sinecure. The power of the independents had become the single greatest impediment to Gorbachev's ascendancy over the party center, and his success in curbing them was probably the most important result of the plenum.

When Gorbachev assumed the presidency on 1 October with his confidant Luk'ianov as vice president, the circle was virtually complete. Some outside observers, critics within the USSR, and even a minority of *perestroika* supporters began to view Gorbachev's structural reforms as a grand design for the amassing of personal power. He had been remarkably successful, but there appeared to be an inherent tension in the combination of the strategies of "revolution from above" and "revolution from below." How could his thrust for something akin to "one-man rule" be squared with "democratization"?

However, Gorbachev had carefully calibrated and meshed his moves on various fronts. Now he took another giant step. The victory at the September plenum gave him the additional clout needed for his reductions of the armed forces, announced at the United Nations in December (see below). But this apparently stirred up a hornet's nest among the military brass, adding one more alienated group to the ranks of the resisters. Gorbachev's strategy for consolidating power had been quite similar to Khrushchev's, and some Western observers saw the same pattern of unresolved conflicts involving powerful interests that ultimately brought Khrushchev's political demise. Whether structural reform of the system would be extensive enough to neutralize such potential powder kegs remained to be seen.

Nineteenth CPSU Conference. The long-awaited party conference was a milestone less for the fact that it was convened (a novelty in the "mature" socialist system, as the first such gathering since 1941) or for its resolutions (which provided for extensive structural change in the political system but were essentially proposals approved in advance by the leadership) than for the popular reactions set in motion by the organizing of the conclave and the atmosphere attending its deliberations.

The conference had occupied a central place in Gorbachev's plans for revitalizing the Soviet system, and projecting this vehicle of reform had been a struggle, as preparations became mired in the growing conflict between reformers and resisters. First proposed by Gorbachev at the CC plenum of January 1987, it had been set for summer 1988 at the June 1987 CC plenum.

As originally conceived, the conference was designed to achieve two major objectives for Gorbachev: revision of the party rules and an infusion of new members into the ranks of the CC. The latter

point was particularly important. At the June 1987 plenum, Gorbachev noted that "changes in the composition of the central bodies of the party" had been one of the concerns of party conferences in the past (*Partiinaia zhizn'*, no. 13, July 1987), and indeed these meetings of an earlier era had the right to renew up to 20 percent of the membership of the CC.

Gorbachev had evidently become convinced that the party itself was the most important inhibitor of reform, surpassing even the economic bureaucracy. Despite the flurry of personnel changes in his first year as general secretary that provided many "automatic" changes in the CC membership, 60 percent of that body elected at the Twenty-seventh CPSU Congress consisted of holdovers. This led to a problem. By June 1988, some fifty members of the CC, about one-sixth of the membership, fell into the category of "dead souls"—those who had been deprived of positions entitling them to seats in the CC but who still retained membership in that body. Thus, the CC was a bastion of conservatism; Gorbachev's spectacular success in using the powers of his office for cadre renewal was not fully reflected in the composition of its membership. This no doubt accounted for some trimming of the sails by party leaders as his reform program developed.

The theses approved by the May 1988 plenum (*Pravda*, 27 May) showed that the general secretary would not achieve these primary objectives. There would be no renewal of the CC, the conference would not have the right to change the party rules, and there would be no general re-examination of the qualifications of party functionaries. But stymied on this front, Gorbachev had another plan. If general reform of the party had to be postponed and if the economic bureaucracy was recalcitrant, then another center of power, largely independent of the party, could be created to supervise the economy. A refurbished structure of soviets could serve this purpose; a powerful president, presumably the party leader, would dominate this complex "separation of powers" system by leading the party, commanding the government, and heading the all-Union legislature.

The conservatives in the leadership evidently acquiesced in the plan—popularly elected bodies with real powers—under the assumption that they might be able to manipulate the elections and the operations of the governing structures. But they must have had misgivings about the powerful presidency, the first occupant of which would almost certainly be Gorbachev. This was perhaps a price paid for Ligachev's overstepping of the bounds in the Andreeva affair. One aspect of the approved plan that clashed with the general "separation of powers" theme was that local and regional party leaders could serve as heads of the projected executive committees in their areas, a proposal that Gorbachev would defend at the conference. It was not clear whether this was Gorbachev's idea to assure that lower-level party leaders would still bear responsibility for functioning of the system in their areas or whether it was a concession to the conservatives.

Preparations for the conference offered a marked contrast to the machinelike organizing of party meetings in the past; in view of the turmoil engendered, it was a miracle that the conference was held at all. In the spring, the election of delegates was running at least a month behind schedule, a snag partially attributed by some Kremlin watchers to the Andreeva affair. Gorbachev had to intervene, following his return from Yugoslavia, to get the preparations back on track. Reformers were dismayed by the apparent widespread success of lower-level party officeholders in packing the ranks of the conference, with some prominent outspoken proponents of *perestroika* excluded.

In some places, hundreds and even thousands of people attended rallies protesting the process of delegate selection, an unprecedented burst of popular participation believed stimulated by Gorbachev or his confederates in the CC as part of the general counterattack against Ligachev and his allies. In a clear strike against the presumed leader of the conservatives, the election of Fedor Loshchenkov in the Volga city of Iaroslavl was overturned (*Pravda*, 17 June; *RL Research*, 23 June). Loshchenkov, a government minister and former first secretary of the Iaroslavl party *obkom*, was known to be a close associate of Ligachev.

The infighting continued right up to the opening of the conference. On the weekend before the start of the meeting, *Ogonek* charged that the conference delegates included "people who have compromised themselves in the area of bribe taking" (the delegates in question were from Uzbekistan); this was due, the article said, to "the imperfect system of selecting and electing delegates" (*Ogonek*, 25 June). On the same day, *Pravda* published an attack on the radical historian Iurii Afanas'ev, rector of the History and Archives Institute (*Pravda*, 25 June). Afanas'ev had compiled a collection of critical essays, including pieces by Andrei Sakharov and Tat-

iana Zaslavskaia, which was distributed to all delegates (*CSM*, 27 June).

Depite their spirited tussle with conservatives to set the atmosphere of the conference, the mood of the reformers was generally downbeat. The watering down of proposals at the May CC plenum and the exclusion of such prominent figures as Zaslavskaia, the playwright Aleksandr Gel'man, and the economist Gavriil Popov (*RL Research*, 23 June) led many to believe that the conference would be an exercise in futility and a probable setback for Gorbachev.

As it turned out, the conference had at least one positive result: it was an epochal breakthrough for *glasnost'*. In terms of freedom of discussion, nothing comparable had been permitted in the USSR for more than sixty years. Soviet citizens were astonished to witness on their television delegates engaged in frank, sometimes heated debate and were particularly impressed by the exchanges between the party leader and ordinary delegates. Although the latter may not have been as spontaneous as they appeared at first blush, the ambience of the meeting conveyed to the man in the street the spirit of *glasnost'* as nothing had done since the inception of the campaign for "openness."

The debates touched a wide variety of subjects, including the economy, the role of the media, the legal system, human rights, and nationalities in addition to the proposals for political restructuring. An early focus of contention between reformers and conservatives was the role of the media, with the latter sharply critical of alleged "excesses." The writer Iurii Bondarev compared the present leadership course to an airplane pilot "who has taken off but does not know where he is going to land." But these charges and the defense of *glasnost'* by a few reformers failed to attract the attention commanded by three exchanges between Gorbachev and the delegates and the speeches of El'tsin and Ligachev.

Mikhail Ul'ianov, actors' union leader, delivering a speech critical of the role of the apparatus in controlling the press, said that the regional press was less supportive of *glasnost'* than were the national newspapers. Gorbachev interrupted and criticized "some of the wild stuff" issuing from the central press. In response to a pointed question from Ul'ianov on whether the party leader favored "elevation of the role of the press," Gorbachev rejected the idea of giving the press to "the domination of one group after another," implying an unwillingness to promote popular controls that might break the hold of *glasnost'* opponents over certain publications (*Pravda*, 30 June). When Viktor Postnikov, head of a collective farm in the Stavropol area, said that bureaucrats ought to be "stripped of their functions," Gorbachev interrupted to reject a purge of bureaucrats "from the top" and recommended instead public pressure to change their behavior (ibid., 1 July). When Vladimir I. Mel'nikov, first secretary of Komi *obkom*, called for the removal of "those who were active in the past pursuing the policy of stagnation" from the central party and government organs, Gorbachev broke in to inquire whom he was speaking about. In reply, Mel'nikov identified by name Politburo members Gromyko and Solomentsev, *Pravda* editor Viktor Afanas'ev, and Georgii Arbatov, head of the Institute of the USA and Canada (Moscow Television, 30 June; *Pravda*, 1 July).

The latter two exchanges were probably stage-managed, and the Mel'nikov incident prefigured the departures of Gromyko and Solomentsev, as had been widely expected at the time. All the verbal encounters served useful political purposes for Gorbachev. In these and other interventions and in his closing speech, Gorbachev carefully positioned himself as a moderate in contrast to the generally forceful tone of his wide-ranging, three-and-one-half hour opening speech in which he had said that "we have no right to let socialism founder on the rocks of dogmatism and conservatism" and that "the next few years will determine the fate" of the Soviet Union (*Pravda*, 29 June). Having had to compromise with the conservatives on the reform program, he could project an image as the one person able to hold back the swelling tide of discontent that, without him, could engulf the resisters in a revolutionary upheaval.

There was plenty of evidence of such rumblings. On one day alone, 30 June, an outpouring of complaints about the backwardness of the Soviet economy and other matters led Gorbachev to deliver an angry half-hour rebuke imploring the delegates to concentrate on the main business of the meeting, political reorganization (*NYT*, 1 July). On the previous day, a startling event occurred when Zaikov, Moscow party chief and holder of the number three protocol rank in the party, was jeered from the podium for being too long-winded and self-serving. Not to be outdone in rambunctiousness, conservative delegates erupted with catcalls of "*Ogonek, Ogonek*" during a speech criticizing that journal's avant-garde posture (*WP*, 1 July).

The El'tsin-Ligachev show was given one more run and again had the highest ratings among Muscovites. El'tsin begged for rehabilitation in view of the posthumous restoration of honor to Nikolai Bukharin and other old Bolsheviks; his request was rebuffed, and he had to endure more insults from his old foe Ligachev. But the former Moscow party chief did not confine himself to a personal plea. Even in disgrace, he continued to speak for a certain sector of opinion in the party, calling for more financial accountability within the CPSU and limited terms for its officials. That El'tsin was elected as a delegate occasioned some surprise and his inclusion among the speakers even more. For some this was striking evidence of democratization. Other observers speculated that Gorbachev had engineered El'tsin's appearance to provide a useful radical foil that would make the party leader look more like a centrist on controversial issues.

Ligachev's speech was interesting for the light it shed on leadership politics and prevailing currents in the broader struggle within the party over policy. Although not renouncing his position as leader of the conservative forces, Ligachev spoke as a man on the defensive. He sought to dissociate himself from Stalinism by noting that some of his own relatives had been shot or arrested during the purges. Ligachev reaffirmed his support for *perestroika* but urged a "cautious approach" in its pursuit. On *glasnost'*, he gave "full and total support" to those speakers who had been most critical of the policy. His strongest criticism of the media concerned the tendency to depict a divided leadership: "we have no factions, no reformers or conservatives, but many would like there to be such."

In response to the attack on Gromyko and Solomentsev, Ligachev revealed some intriguing details about the events of March 1985. The senior secretary indicated that he, Chebrikov, Solomentsev, Gromyko, and an "important group of *obkom* first secretaries" had played the crucial role in averting the "real danger" of "radically different decisions" (*Pravda*, 1 July). In other words, the election had been a close thing; without the actions of Ligachev and his comrades, there would have been no Gorbachev era. Implied was the continuing need of these important figures to maintain the unity of the party leadership that Ligachev claimed existed, despite media reports to the contrary. Ligachev was explicitly stating that Gorbachev owed a debt to him and to the others. This reminder may have been another false step by the senior secretary; such dependence is something that any long-term general secretary must seek to extricate himself from in the process of consolidating personal power.

Although a tentative date of 1 July had been set for the end of the conference proceedings, when the meeting was adjourned with many speakers remaining to be heard, widely divergent conclusions were drawn. But it was generally agreed that whatever the impression created by the freewheeling debate, the realities of decisionmaking under "democratic centralism" remained intact. The major formal result of the conference was the passing of resolutions incorporating virtually unchanged the main proposals put forward by Gorbachev in his opening speech. However, the final session saw the first openly divided votes since the early years of the Soviet state.

The six resolutions passed on the conference's final day covered political reorganization, economic perestroika, glasnost', the legal code, nationality questions, and bureaucratic obstacles to change. Most important, the conference approved a new relationship between the party and other elements of the system, endorsed the development of a new legislative structure, and agreed to the transformation of the presidency into a powerful executive office. The delegates assented to specific measures that would transfer some power from the party to popularly elected legislatures and assure that the party should not supplant government, state, or other organizations through the exercise of old "command-and-injunction" methods. One measure emphasized that "delimiting functions performed by the party and state bodies and restoring in full power the soviets at all levels is of key significance." Competitive, multicandidate elections for party offices were mandated, and a maximum term of ten years was set for elected party and government officials. However, the limited terms would not be retroactive to the time current officeholders assumed their jobs. It was also proposed that the party Control Committee and the Central Auditing Commission be abolished and replaced by a single body, a Central Control and Auditing Commission of the CPSU, to be elected at party congresses. Reorganization of the party apparatus "in the near future" and its reduction in size were approved in vague terms.

The conference proposed revision of the constitution to provide for a new parliamentary body, the Congress of People's Deputies, with authority to set the main lines of policy. Two-thirds of the members would be popularly elected; one-third elected by public organizations, providing a mixture of representative and corporate elements in the legislature. The congress would elect a much smaller body—a Supreme Soviet in "permanent session"—that would meet twice a year for lengthy periods, with power to enact legislation. The congress would elect a president holding broad executive authority, with power to appoint the government, direct foreign and defense policy, and oversee the domestic operations of the government (International Herald Tribune, 2 July; NYT, 2, 5 July; LAT, 2 July; WP, Pravda, 5 July; RL Research, 6 July).

The conference resolutions were only recommendations; actions by the CC and the Supreme Soviet followed later in the year to put the proposals into effect. But the momentum of change had been accelerated, and the reformers, if somewhat disappointed in the results, could take comfort from the indications that glasnost' might well be irreversible. But democratization would depend on structural reform and on the creation of a division of power that would sustain it. The conference pointed toward a fundamental change of the political system, but the USSR was moving into uncharted waters, with the outcome of the voyage uncertain. The new program might be sabotaged in its implementation by the maneuvering of incumbent officials (the usual fate of reform in the past), or the endemic passivity of the political culture might prove fatal to a framework geared toward modernization. Perhaps the biggest stumbling block would be the nationalities problem; at the conference, the most resistance had been from ethnic representatives of the outlying republics, wary of their role in the restructured order.

If the scheme for structural reform worked in accord with its paper appearance, Gorbachev might amass sufficient personal power to force through further, more radical changes. But if he depended on outside interests rather than his party base, his perch atop the system might be quite precarious. If the party were weakened, the way might be open for the system's coercive forces to unite with disaffected elements in the party to overthrow Gorbachev and reverse the current thrust of policy. The resolution on "socialist legality" and legal reform pointed toward checks on the KGB. Military reform had been ignored at the conference, but the generals had taken a back seat during Gorbachev's tenure. A further setback for Frunze Street was in the offing. The reform program promised far greater curbs on the party apparatus than the reorganization by Khrushchev that incited midlevel party officials to support that leader's ouster. However, if all went well for Gorbachev's grand design, it was at least conceivable that a reinvigorated party could emerge as a more potent organization than before, with its "leading role" in the society intact.

Whatever the future might bring, the events of the year through the conference demonstrated that, for the present, both the reform program and Gorbachev's political fortunes hinged on further inroads by the general secretary into the "levers of command" at the top of the system. This imperative would soon be addressed by the party leader at the September CC plenum (see above).

Party Organization and Personnel. Party organizations encountered challenges from two directions during the year. On the one hand, it was necessary to deal with the legacy of the Brezhnev years; the vitality of the party as an institution had been eroded by the stagnation of that period. On the other hand, the party was expected to be the vanguard of *perestroika* while grappling with the definition of its future role. Corruption and nationality issues combined with the effects at lower levels of the political struggle at the top meant that the "stable good weather" for cadres projected by Ligachev at the Twenty-seventh CPSU Congress was often difficult to find.

The Ukraine continued to be one of the party's storm centers. At a tumultuous plenum of the Ukrainian CC in January, several leading figures of the Ukraine's party and government drew heavy fire, as did the republican Politburo and Secretariat. The assault was led by Vladislav Mysnichenko, first secretary of Kharkov *obkom*, reportedly one of Gorbachev's favorite regional leaders in the republic (*Pravda*, 26 January). Immediately following the plenum, the CPSU CC singled out the Kiev city party organization for special criticism, noting shortcomings on *perestroika* and democratization (ibid., 31 January).

An April resolution of the CC said that the most important criterion for party membership should be a person's attitude toward *perestroika* and called for the process of selecting new members to become more democratic and open (TASS, *RL Research*, 15 April). The resolution reflected some of the criticisms put forward by *Moscow News* in a hard-hitting article a month earlier (*Moscow News*, 18 March).

One week after the CC resolution, Razumovskii delivered a forceful proreform speech as the keynoter of the Lenin anniversary celebration. The party's personnel overseer, a close associate of Gorbachev, spoke at length about the need for "democratization," saying that *perestroika* requires "a se-

rious renovation of the party." He seemed to imply that opposition to *perestroika* was linked with Stalinism, a ploy that the Gorbachev forces were now finding useful in putting their opponents on the defensive. The party, Razumovskii said, "must have the courage to rid itself of those notions of socialism that bear the imprint of certain conditions, particularly those developed during the period of the cult of personality."

Razumovskii ventured into dangerous ideological ground with a reference to the concept of alienation under socialism, which is central to the revived debate on the "contradictions of socialism" and poses troubling questions about the validity of the Soviet model of development. The cadres secretary maintained that the economic reforms under *perestroika* would put an end to the idea that, under socialism, the proletariat experiences "alienation." Razumovskii also spoke approvingly of the development of informal groups that had arisen in the USSR; he was the highest-ranking member of the leadership to publicly discuss this phenomenon (Radio Moscow, *RL Research*, 22 April; *Pravda*, 23 April). Lacking the usual balanced approach of such ceremonial addresses, Razumovskii's speech appeared to be a trumpet call for reformers in Gorbachev's counteroffensive against conservative elements in the leadership that had been launched in late March (see above).

Although leadership rhetoric emphasized general issues of reform, important specific personnel changes most often reflected nationality turmoil or the continuing struggle for organizational control within the leadership. Following ethnic riots over the issue of Nagorno-Karabakh, the party leaders of Azerbaijan and Armenia were dismissed. Karen S. Demirchian, first secretary in Armenia since 1974, had been frequently at loggerheads with the new Moscow leadership and a target for much criticism in the central press. Kiamran I. Bagirov, head of the Azerbaijan party since 1982, had been politically weakened by ongoing revelations of official corruption in his republic. Their replacements were far removed from the displaced leaderships. In Armenia, Suren G. Arutiunian (49), a deputy premier who had served six years as a functionary in Moscow, took the reins. In Azerbaijan, Abdul-Rahman Vezirov, a diplomat serving as ambassador to Pakistan, was named CC first secretary. TASS issued the usual statement that both departing leaders had resigned for "reasons of health" (TASS, 21 May; *Pravda*, 22 May).

At the beginning of the year, Inamzhon

Usmankhodzhaev, first secretary of the Uzbekistan communist party, an Andropov appointee in office since 1983, stepped down "due to retirement for reasons of health" and was replaced by Rafik Nishanov (52), a former diplomat serving as president of the Presidium of the Uzbek Supreme Soviet (TASS, *Pravda vostoka*, *RL Research*, 13 January). Usmankhodzhaev had been unable to cope satisfactorily with the messy situation in the republic in the wake of the long rule by Sharaf Rashidov. Following his dismissal, Usmankhodzhaev became the target of a press campaign dealing with continuing corruption in Uzbekistan. In March, three suspects in the investigations of corruption in the republic—the former head of the Uzbekistan Interior Ministry, a former first deputy premier, and a former regional first secretary—were all reported to have committed suicide (*Komsomolskaia pravda*, 15 March), further evidence of the strange tendency for physical and psychological maladies to assume epidemic form among ousted officials in the southern republics.

Another diplomat was drafted to take over the leadership in restive Estonia. Vaino I. Väljas, ambassador to Nicaragua, was elected as CC first secretary, replacing the veteran Karl Vaino (*Sovetskaia Estonia*, 17 June; *FBIS*, 12 July). After Pugo was named as chairman of the CPSU Control Committee, J. J. Vagris, chairman of the Presidium of the Latvian Supreme Soviet, moved into the post of Latvian party first secretary (*Pravda*, 5 October).

Several changes were made in the CPSU CC *apparat*, notably the long-expected departure of Brezhnev's close associate Nikolai Savinkin (74) as head of the Department of Administrative Organs, which among other things oversees the KGB. Unofficial sources in Moscow reported that Savinkin's replacement was Aleksandr Soshnikov, a deputy chief of the department (*RL Research*, 24 June). The well-known advocate of political reform Georgii Shakhnazarov moved from deputy head of the CC Department for Liaison with the Communist and Workers' Parties of the Socialist Countries to a position as adviser to General Secretary Gorbachev on relations with the socialist countries (TASS, 19 March; *RL Research*, 22 March).

Aleksandr F. Gudkov (58), first secretary of Kursk *obkom*, "retired" in January and was succeeded by A. I. Seleznez, director of a section of the CPSU CC Department of Party Organizational Work (*Pravda*, 10 June).

The disturbances in Nagorno-Karabakh led to the firing of that province's party chief, B. S. Kevorkov, a Russian, and his replacement by G. A. Pogosian, an Armenian and first vice-chairman of the province's Soviet executive committee (*Bakinskii rabochii*, 24 February). Similarly, the ethnic rioting in Sumgait occasioned the replacement of *gorkom* first secretary D. M. Muslim-zade by F. S. Gadzhiev, chairman of the Nakhichevan Autonomous Republic Council of Ministers. Muslim-zade was also expelled from the CPSU (ibid., 17 March).

The Gorbachev-Ligachev contretemps set in motion by the Andreeva affair apparently was the real cause for the dismissal of Vasilii I. Sitnikov (61) as first secretary of the Irkutsk province party committee (*Pravda*, 30 May). It was probably also responsible for the replacement of two *obkom* first secretaries—Iurii Khristoradnov (59) in Gorky and Iurii V. Petrov in Sverdlovsk—who had allegedly been involved in reprinting the controversial article (*Bakinskii rabochii*, 17 June). Khristoradnov was granted a "soft landing," moving to the chairmanship of the USSR Supreme Soviet Council of the Union; Petrov was dispatched as ambassador to Cuba (*Izvestiia*, 16 July). New first secretaries were G. M. Khodyrev, promoted from second secretary, in Gorky; Leonid F. Bobykin, head of the CPSU CC Light Industry and Consumer Goods Department, in Sverdlovsk; and V. I. Potapov, moved up from second secretary, in Irkutsk.

When Fedor T. Morgun, veteran first secretary of Poltava *obkom* in the Ukraine, moved to Moscow as chairman of the USSR State Committee on Environmental Protection, he was succeeded by A. S. Miakota, chairman of the Poltava province Soviet Executive Committee (*Pravda*, 13 April).

Leonid A. Borodin (65) retired as first secretary of Astrakhan *obkom*, and Ivan N. Diakov, a close associate of CC secretary Razumovskii, shifted from the second secretaryship of Krasnodar *kraikom* to fill the post (ibid., 1 June). Following the death of Donetsk province party chief Vasilii P. Mironov (63) (*Pravda*, 13 June), second secretary A. Iu. Vinnik was promoted to first secretary of the *obkom*, one of the more important party posts in the Ukraine (ibid., 23 June).

Government. The Supreme Soviet was much more active than usual as Gorbachev's escalating pace of reform required the nominal legislature to give its sanction to a barrage of proposals. Its most important actions came in December, when changes in the Soviet constitution and electoral laws were approved to give effect to the resolution on political reform adopted at the Nineteenth CPSU Conference. Elections to the new Congress of People's Deputies were set for 26 March 1989 (*Izvestiia*, 2 December).

The provision for one-third of the congress deputies to be elected by public organizations continued to draw criticism on several grounds: that the organizations are party-dominated and thus subject to manipulation, that it would have the effect of giving some persons two or more votes, and that it would weaken the political power of the outlying republics and thus the ethnic minorities. However, the general issue of the rights of the constituent republics was put off for what Gorbachev called the "second stage" of political reform (Knight-Ridder Newspapers, 4 December).

At its 1 October session following the dramatic CC plenum that shook up the leadership, the Supreme Soviet elected Gorbachev to succeed Gromyko as chairman of the Supreme Soviet Presidium (president) and named Luk'ianov as first vice-chairman. Aleksei K. Antonov was dropped as a deputy prime minister, and Talyzin was moved down from first deputy prime minister to fill Antonov's place, also being appointed as USSR representative to the Council for Mutual Economic Assistance (CMEA). Biriukova moved from the CC Secretariat to a deputy premiership. Kriuchkov, head of the KGB's first chief directorate for foreign intelligence, was confirmed as successor to Chebrikov, who had been shifted to the CC Secretariat as chairman of the security agency (*NYT*, 2 October).

Two other meetings of the Supreme Soviet were livelier, displaying the first traces of something akin to opposition in the parliament in more than fifty years. In May, the Supreme Soviet postponed consideration of a draft law on private business after some members demanded repeal of a new business tax. In October, the ritual unanimity of Soviet legislative sessions was cracked when some members voted against two disputed pieces of legislation, forcing vote counters to leave their seats in the Kremlin meeting hall and search for the nays. Thirteen members voted against a decree that would require advance permission for street demonstrations, and 31 opposed extending the powers of special Interior Ministry troops used to break up public demonstrations (ibid., 29 October).

A milestone was reached on 10 January when the Council of Nationalities district number 37 held the first contested election for deputy. Sergei M. Ka-

tilevskii (34), Russian and a communist, defeated another party member, Vitalii F. Zakharov (43), Ukrainian (*Izvestiia*, 15 January).

In ministerial ranks, a major change was made in February when Talyzin was replaced as head of *Gosplan* following a steady drumbeat of criticism directed against the planning agency. He was succeeded by Deputy Premier Masliukov, a defense industry specialist who had seved as first deputy chairman of *Gosplan* from 1982 to 1985. It was widely believed that Masliukov's appointment reflected Gorbachev's oft-stated objective of utilizing military and defense industry expertise in restructuring the domestic economy. In line with the importance of his new assignment, Masliukov was also promoted to first deputy prime minster (*Pravda*, 7 February; *Izvestiia*, 8 February).

Talyzin was named head of the Bureau for Social Development and retained his first deputy premiership. Some observers concluded that this was merely a lateral transfer and not a demotion, particularly since he retained his seat as a nonvoting member of the Politburo. It appeared that he was assuming the functions formerly performed by Geidar Aliev, who had "retired" as first deputy premier the previous October. However, on 1 October, Talyzin was reassigned to the less prestigious deputy premiership for CMEA affairs, and he now seems to have experienced a phased "soft landing." The functions he had exercised during the interim period were turned over to Biriukova.

Two days after the shuffle involving Talyzin and Biriukova, a more important shift was announced. Vorotnikov moved to the heretofore ceremonial post of chairman of the Russian Federation's Supreme Soviet Presidium, and Vlasov, head of the Interior Ministry since January 1986, was appointed as prime minister of the RSFSR (TASS, 3 October; *Izvestiia*, 4 October). Long associated with Gorbachev in southern Russian politics, Vlasov had been one of the party leader's more prominent clients even before Gorbachev's assumption of the general secretaryship in 1985. Promoted to candidate membership on the Politburo at the 30 September CC plenum, Vlasov became only the second official with Politburo status younger than Gorbachev (Razumovskii is the other). His appointment maintained the tradition of assigning someone with a background as a regional secretary in the RSFSR as the republic's premier; he had served as party chief of the key Rostov province from 1984 to 1986.

The well-travelled Konstantin Katushev, once

the "boy wonder" of the Gorky automobile works and in the mid-1970s considered as a possible long-term successor to Brezhnev, received a new title. He was appointed USSR minister of foreign economic relations, a position created after the abolition of the USSR Ministry of Foreign Trade and the USSR State Committee on Foreign Economic Relations (*Izvestiia*, 17 January).

Zagash Kamalidenov, Kazakh party secretary for ideology and a former head of the republican KGB, was elected chairman of the Presidium of the Supreme Soviet of Kazakhstan (*Kazakhstanskaia pravda, RL Research*, 10 February). Kamalidenov had an earlier stint as a CC secretary under Dinmukhamed Kunaev, his two terms in the Secretariat having been sandwiched around his tour as republican KGB chief. His work was reviewed as mixed by party leader Gennadii Kolbin at the January plenum of the Kazakh CC. But as one of the few prominent ethnic Kazakhs who had survived the recent wave of purges, he looked like a possible successor in the republican party leadership in the event of Kolbin's transfer to a higher post in Moscow.

In the continuing reorganization of the governmental apparatus, the Ministry of Machinery for Light Industry and the Food Industry and Household Appliances was abolished in February (*Izvestiia*, 25 February). In the same week, Igor V. Koksanov was appointed USSR minister of the shipbuilding industry (ibid., 22 February). Two weeks later, another revision of the ministerial structure was announced. A Union-republic USSR State Committee for Public Education was created, combining the former ministries of Education and Higher and Specialized Secondary Education and the State Committee for Vocational and Technical Education (*Pravda, Izvestiia*, 9 March).

Other new members of the Council of Ministers included Fedor Morgun, chairman of the USSR State Committee for Environmental Protection (*Izvestiia*, 14 March); Vitalii K. Doguzhiev, USSR minister of general machinery (*Pravda*, 27 March); Mikhail I. Busygin, USSR minister of the timber industry; and Aleksandr S. Isaev, chairman of the USSR State Committee on Forests (*Izvestiia*, 28 March).

Following the resignation of Marshal Sergei Akhromeev in December, Colonel General Moiseiev (50), commander of the Far Eastern military district, was appointed first deputy minister of defense and armed forces chief of staff (*Krasnaia zvezda*, 17 December). Former Deputy Interior Minister Iurii Churbanov was sentenced to twelve

years in prison for accepting bribes (*Izvestiia*, 31 December).

Economy. Economic reform had been the centerpiece of Gorbachev's program to revitalize the USSR and still retained its primacy, despite the strong emphasis now accorded to political reform. *Glasnost'* and structural reform of the political system were regarded by Gorbachev and his associates as essential for economic revival; the latter, in turn, had been consistently described by the general secretary as necessary for the USSR to remain a great power. However, the linkage of all these elements seemed clearer programmatically than in practice, and failures in the economic sphere threatened a negative spillback into the political arena, where Gorbachev was kept busy extinguishing brushfires.

The figures on 1987 economic performance were disappointing but did increase the pressure for further economic reforms, which Gorbachev pushed vigorously during the year. The increase in aggregate growth of national income in 1987 was 2.3 percent over the previous year against a planned target of 4.1 percent; the rate of growth was significantly lower than the average during the Eleventh Five-Year Plan, 1981–85. Although capital investment grew 4.7 percent against the scheduled 4.3 percent average envisioned in the current five-year plan, there was a substantial drop from the 8 percent growth achieved in 1986.

Industrial production rose only 3.8 percent against a planned rise of 4.4 percent. All branches of the fuel and energy complex met their targets, but more than two-thirds of the quotas for high-technology products remained unfulfilled. There were shortfalls in consumer goods production and in most agricultural products, although grain production was up slightly, to 211.3 million tons. Labor productivity was claimed to have risen 4.1 percent against a planned increase of 4.5 percent, but in the agricultural sector the growth was only 2.5 percent, well below the average figures for both the Tenth and Eleventh Five-Year Plans (*Ekonomicheskaia gazeta*, no. 5, January; *Pravda*, 24 January; *RL Research*, 11 February). Some of these results could be attributed to the attempt to emphasize quality while seeking to boost production. But the qualitative results were probably even more disappointing than those registered by the traditional quantitative indicators.

Gorbachev added a somber note at the February plenum of the CC when he asserted that the low growth rates of the early 1980s had been achieved because of inflated world prices for exported Soviet oil and increased retail sales of alcoholic products. In effect, the Soviet economy had stopped growing (*Pravda*, 19 February; *RL Research*, 22 February).

Meanwhile, economic reform proceeded with a forward movement in enunciation of plans and promulgation of decrees, with at best a mixed record as to results. Some 60 percent of industrial enterprises went over to *khozraschet* (self-financing), a major component of Gorbachev's economic plans, on 1 January (*Izvestiia*, 29 December 1987).

In the agricultural sector 56,000, or more than half, of the collective and state farms and processing enterprises also began operating on *khozraschet* principles on 1 January (TASS, 26 January; *FBIS*, 28 January). This presumably figured in calculations that the target for grain production—235 million tons (equaling the spectacular record of the 1978 crop)—could be met (*Sel'skaia zhizn'*, 13 April; *FBIS*, 21 April). However, the press spotlight on continuing problems in agriculture during the year indicated that achievement of the goal was highly unlikely.

The incentive schemes for workers introduced earlier had apparently failed to affect the economy. At both the February CC plenum and in his major speech to the party conference in June, Gorbachev complained that managers were reluctant to implement bonuses for individual productivity for fear of offending members of the work force (*Pravda*, 19 February, 29 June). Economic planners repeatedly asserted that economic reform would lead to increased social stratification in terms of income, but deep-rooted egalitarian sentiments were difficult to alter.

These popular attitudes also worked against the reforms promoting private business ventures, cooperatives, and family-owned enterprises. Many potential entrepreneurs were reluctant to go into business for fear of a public backlash, in addition to a natural wariness born of the fate of the New Economic Policy in the 1920s. Evidence of adverse public reaction was taken into account by Gorbachev in remarks at a Moscow ball bearing factory in March. Promising a progressive income tax, the general secretary complained that some cooperatives "take advantage of shortages and engage in open money grubbing" (ibid., 8 March). The progressive tax was subsequently proposed with rates ranging up to 90 percent, but the highest rates were scaled down before implementation because of protests by economists. The law authorizing certain private business enterprises, limited by a prohibi-

tion against hiring of personnel other than the owners' family members, went into effect on 1 May (*Izvestiia*, 2 May) with apparently limited early effects. The cooperatives did have some positive impact in the restaurant and other service industries, but early successes were most noticeable in Estonia, whose culture was more geared to Western-style individualism than other areas of the country.

The record on *khozraschet* was perhaps the most discouraging aspect of the early returns on reform. The Law on Enterprises, enacted 30 June 1987, was a change from the old allotments and planned targets to a system of *goszakaz* (state orders) for production requested by the ministries and *Gosplan*. These orders were expected to account for 50 to 70 percent of the output of enterprises, with the remainder consisting of orders secured by direct contracts with customers. In practice, the ministries found they could retain control by increasing the state orders; by midyear, these were said to amount to about 80 percent of output, with some *goszakazy* demanding up to 103 percent of a firm's production (*Pravda*, 30 June). As the leadership recognized the extent of the sabotage, plans were made to limit these state orders (*Izvestiia*, 29 October), but reform had already suffered a serious setback. Some observers concluded that most managers were not entirely unhappy with this state of affairs because *khozraschet* imposed new risks and responsibilities that these officials were not eager to assume.

Even if the undermining by central officials could be checked, at least one major problem, price reform, which had been postponed for two years (although Gorbachev hinted at the June party conference that it might come sooner), would remain. The most intractable obstacle was the enormous subsidies, particularly in food and housing, to which the Soviet consumer had long been accustomed. Unless these subsidies were eliminated, there could be no general price reform and no consistent allocation of resources tied to the cost of production. But price reform entailed serious political costs. It would mean at least a temporary substantial increase in the cost of living for the average Soviet consumer and a decline in individual real income for most citizens and would surely provoke popular protests that could seriously threaten political stability. Thus, Gorbachev and the reformers approached this explosive issue with understandable caution.

The key to reform was clearly movement toward a market economy. But full commitment to the market would entail a sacrifice of the essentials of Soviet socialism. The question then was how much of a market economy could be tolerated, and opinions on this varied widely even among commited adherents of *perestroika*. Following Gorbachev's apparent victory at the September CC plenum, Medvedev, the new ideological overseer, called for major departures geared to the market approach. Speaking to a gathering of political scientists from communist-ruled countries, Medvedev said that low-level experiments with cooperative ownership and small entrepreneurs should be extended to heavy industry (TASS, 5 October; *NYT*, 6 October).

Several measures were taken between June and September to give effect to initiatives pushed by Gorbachev at various earlier meetings. In June, the USSR central savings bank announced creation of a new source of credit for Soviet entrepreneurs (*Sotsialisticheskaia industriia*, 8 June; *RL Research*, 15 June). In August, the USSR Council of Ministers adopted three resolutions calling for cooperatives and individual labor to play leading roles in developing the consumer sector and for ministries responsible for defense industries to increase their production of consumer goods (*Izvestiia*, 21, 23, 24 August; *RL Research*, 29 August). But the most spectacular reform measures of the year affected the agricultural sector.

The State Committee for the Agro-Industrial Complex (*Gosagroprom*) attracted at least as much criticism as had *Gosplan*, and it is probable that Murakhovskii, the agency's director, was saved from the fate of Talyzin, the state planning commission's head, only because he had been Gorbachev's first patron in the CPSU. Now Murakhovskii introduced the most radical change in the organization of agriculture since Stalin's brutal collectivization drive. It was announced in August that individual farmers would be permitted to lease land for up to fifty years and to buy tractors and trucks from the state (TASS, 26 August; *WP*, 27 August).

The budget for the next fiscal year, adopted by the Supreme Soviet at its October session, gave priority to helping the long-suffering Soviet consumer and contained provisions designed to promote the fuller implementation of *khozraschet*. It was announced that state-run farms and factories will be shut down if they do not make a profit, and Finance Minister Boris Gostev disclosed that a deficit of 36.3 billion rubles ($58.6 billion) was anticipated for the coming year. Gostev said that similar budgets had been run in previous years but had

never been publicly revealed (*Izvestiia*, 28 October).

With more wrenching dislocations promised for the coming year, the adverse impact of reform on many workers was already evident. In July, the State Committee on Statistics announced that almost one million factory workers had lost their jobs since the beginning of the year, although all were assured other employment (Radio Moscow, AP, 27 July). More distressing was that Soviet living standards had declined over the previous decade and that this trend was continuing even as Soviet workers were being called on for greater efforts. Gorbachev directly confronted the rising tide of discontent in a September encounter with citizens in the Siberian city of Krasnoiarsk that was televised on "Vremia," the main Moscow television news program. On his first stop after landing at the Krasnoiarsk airport, the Soviet leader was met by a contentious crowd shouting complaints about shortages of food and housing (*NYT*, 13 September).

The December earthquake in Armenia added one more burden to the already hard-pressed Soviet economy. The reconstruction promised by Gorbachev and Premier Ryzhkov would mean the subtraction of massive sums from other sectors of the economy, and much of Armenia's production of highly specialized industrial equipment would be lost indefinitely.

Glasnost'. The Soviet media continued to report events at home and abroad on a more objective basis than previously, a trend confirmed in December by the full and frank reportage on the disaster in Armenia. This aspect of "openness" seemed to produce little friction in official circles. More contentious were revelations and interpretations of past events within the USSR and the expression of opinions concerning present regime policies. Here the erratic course of *glasnost'* partially reflected the tug of war between Gorbachev and Ligachev. More important was the inherent tension between centralized political structures and processes of democratization. Once a measure of cultural diversity has been permitted, it is difficult to put the genie back into the bottle, particularly because *glasnost'* and *perestroika* are so closely linked.

The most radical proponents of reform could invoke the name of Gorbachev when expressing their ideas, and opponents of Gorbachev could cloak their hostility in words of concern about stability and continuity. The inability of the political leadership to regulate fully the processes of *glasnost'* permitted the freest discussion of ideas since the imposition of Stalin's dictatorship but also brought into the open dark forces from Russia's past and it contributed to the resurgence of national animosities.

The country was in an era of upheaval like that of the 1860s, the 1920s, or the late 1950s, when barriers lowered, new possibilities opened up, and the future seems open-ended. Some Western observers thought that this period would have a different denouement than the earlier ones, that things had gone too far for a return to the ways of the past. Others were more pessimistic, noting that the machinery for repression remained in place and wondering if *glasnost'* could survive either the failure of *perestroika* or political setbacks for Gorbachev.

At the beginning of the year, reformers were somewhat wary about the future of *glasnost'* in the aftermath of the El'tsin affair, especially in view of KGB chief Chebrikov's role in the humiliation of the most outspoken defender of *perestroika* for voicing criticisms of the Soviet system to foreign journalists. Gorbachev's first declaration of the year on matters of *glasnost'* did little to allay such concerns.

In a speech to representatives of the Soviet media, ideological institutions, and creative unions on 8 January, Gorbachev expressed confidence concerning the future of *glasnost'* and denied that the "phraseology" used in rebuffing El'tsin was "a blow to restructuring." However, he cited Lenin's statement that "literature is an all-party task" and said that this applies to the press. He denounced left-wing critics who used "ultra-*perestroika*" phraseology in their attempt to push restructuring too fast and said that the USSR was entering a new stage of restructuring in which the Soviet media would be expected to devote their attention primarily to economic issues. Gorbachev asserted that *glasnost'* in the press has no limits if it is serving "the interests of socialism." Determination of this would presumably be made by the party leadership, and the party leader left little doubt of the intention to control processes of *glasnost'* from above (TASS, 12 January; *RL Research*, 13 January). The meeting was attended by Ligachev. Iakovlev was noticeably absent; it was claimed that he had been ill since the Washington summit (*Süddeutsche Zeitung*, 12 January).

In March, a special commission to review banned early Soviet literary works delivered a preliminary report. Vladimir Solodin—head of the commission and chief of *Glavlit*, the Soviet censorship agency—announced removal of the ban on several thousand early Soviet authors, including works by Bukharin and Aleksei Rykov. Solodin said that works by writers who left the USSR in recent years might also be made available "if their content is not anti-Soviet" and if they do not "run counter to provisions of the Soviet constitution." The commission report was welcomed by advocates of *glasnost'* but served as a reminder that the authorities would still determine what could be published and that, despite "democratization," *Glavlit* remained on the scene and active (*Sovetskaia kul'tura*, BBC Caris, 23 March).

In the same week, *Komsomolskaia pravda* published several articles in response to the publication in December by *Novii mir* of several poems by Nobel Prize–winner Yosif Brodsky. The articles avoided direct political accusations against the emigré poet but consisted mainly of personal invective with anti-Semitic undertones (*Komsomolskaia pravda*, 15 March; *RL Research*, 28 March).

The selective tolerance of dissent was spotlighted in May following the organization of an "opposition" political party—the Democratic Union—by a handful of self-described radicals. A police crackdown ensued, with the arrest of more than two dozen of the members of the fledgling group. When Sergei Grigoriants, editor of the unofficial magazine *Glasnost'*, who was not a member of the group and was openly skeptical of its prospects, agreed to meet with a delegation from the "opposition party," he was arrested, along with three others, including a Democratic Union organizer (*NYT*, 9 May). On 17 May, Valeria Novodvorkaia, another Democratic Union organizer, was arrested and sentenced to fifteen days for taking part in an unauthorized demonstration. And in the same week *Glasnost'* was closed down when police confiscated Grigoriants's printing equipment and destroyed his files and manuscripts (ibid., 18 May). These actions were widely interpreted as an ominous signal on the eve of the Moscow summit meeting between Gorbachev and President Reagan.

Despite evidence of a hostile climate at the top following the El'tsin affair, "informal" political groups continued to arise, with some of them encouraged by the authorities (*RL Research*, 27 January). Independent "unofficial" journals, mostly *samizdat*, also continued to proliferate but were mostly ignored by the authorities. The suppression of *Glasnost'* indicated that there were limits to the toleration.

The main battles of *glasnost'* were, however, fought in the official media. In some areas, official publications became sounding boards for demands for greater autonomy and for criticism of Moscow's nationalities policies. At the center, the expression of diversity reached a crescendo on the eve of the Nineteenth National Party Conference, apparently triggered by publication of the CC-approved "theses" for the conference. The most relaxed control over expression came in early June, when the daily newspaper of the Young Communist League reported on a meeting between several informal political clubs and the historian Iurii Afanas'ev. Proposals voiced at the meeting included creation of a permanent legislative commission to oversee the police and the KGB, abolition of internal passports and residence permits, elimination of all privileges of the *nomenklatura*, and enactment of a law declaring that the CPSU has authority only over its members (*Komsomolskaia pravda*, 7 June).

Debates in the official media not only concerned present policies and the future course of the USSR but also the Soviet past; filling in the "blank pages" of the country's history was the main preoccupation of some writers. That these two aspects of *glasnost'* were closely related as the context for discussions of present policies was inevitably the consideration of the earlier development of the Soviet system. The central media aligned into two rather distinct camps on the issues, with *Novii mir*, *Ogonek*, *Sovetskaia kul'tura*, and *Moscow News* spearheading the drive for more "openness" and *Pravda*, *Sovetskaia Rossiia*, and some other periodicals usually on the other side.

Filling in the "blank pages" of Soviet history naturally concerned, first of all, the years of Stalin's tyranny. Revelations about the Stalin era abounded during the year, meeting stiff resistance from conservatives who maintained that too close a look at the past threatened the foundations of legitimacy of the Soviet regime. Rebuffed in the Andreeva affair, the conservatives maintained their rearguard action and were as outspoken as ever at the party conference in June. Nevertheless, the exposure of Stalinism continued, reaching floodtide in August when Soviet television screened the documentary "Risk-2," which equated Stalin with Hitler as a demented autocrat (*WP*, 4 August). Professional historians, led by Afanas'ev, entered the fray, with considerable help from Akhmed Iskenderov, the new editor of *Voprosy istorii*. In his first editorial in the journal, Iskenderov set a course for the publication to assume a leading role in the objective rewriting of Soviet history (*Voprosy istorii*, no. 2, February). One indication of the depth of the re-

examination of the past came at the end of the school year when examinations in Russian and Soviet history were canceled because of "the unsatisfactory state of available textbooks" (*Harriman Institute Forum*, November).

One of the most ticklish aspects of the Stalin era—the Nazi-Soviet pact—was uncovered in full detail. Remarkably, the secret protocols to the treaty were published in Estonia in July and in *Sovetskaia Rossiia* in August, following the appearance in June of an article by Stalin's official biographer, General Dimitri Volgokonov, which was highly critical of the treaty (*Pravda*, 20 June).

Posthumous rehabilitation of leading victims of Stalin's terror proceeded during the year and included Bukharin, Rykov, Zinov'ev, and Kamenev (ibid., 6 February, 8, 14 June, 19 August). The rehabilitation of Bukharin had been considered a touchstone by the more ardent reformers, and the favorable image of the old Bolshevik projected by the media on several occasions during the year added a special touch. A positive depiction of Bukharin was particularly important for Gorbachev because much of the party leader's economic program was similar to the policies pursued under the New Economic Policy, of which Bukharin was the principal spokesman in the 1920s.

Even Trotskii left the ranks of nonpersons. In January, the literary journal *Znamiia* published the new play *Onward, Ever Onward* by Mikhail Shatrov, which portrayed Trotskii as a victim of Stalin. An earlier play by Shatrov, *The Brest Peace*, which also depicted Trotskii in a favorable light, had opened the previous November with Gorbachev present at the premiere. Three conservative historians lashed out at Shatrov's newest work in a *Pravda* article, charging that it presented a negative picture not just of Stalin but of the building of socialism in the USSR and that it portrayed Lenin as a weak and passive character (*Pravda*, BBC Caris, 16 February). By September, the political climate had changed to such an extent that *Pravda*, which had been considered a conservative bastion earlier in the year, published another article by Volkogonov, Stalin's biographer, that gave Leon Trotskii credit for playing a key role in the Bolshevik Revolution and the Civil War and acknowledged that he had been "the most popular leader after Lenin." However, the article was entitled "The Demon of Revolution," and an editor's preface called Trotskii a Judas (*Pravda*, 10 September).

A full rehabilitation of Trotskii was unlikely, for further upgrading his image could not serve a political purpose for Gorbachev in view of Trotskii's opposition to the New Economic Policy, his insistence on the primacy of world revolution, and his dictatorial methods when in power. But his reappearance as a prominent figure in official Soviet history, which began when Gorbachev touched lightly on his role in a major speech at the commemoration of the 70th anniversary of the Bolshevik Revolution in November 1987, was ideologically important for the party leader. Trotskii's analysis of Stalinism as a bureaucratic deformation of Bolshevism was essentially the same as Gorbachev's critique. The ideological foundation of Gorbachev's leadership—selected passages from the writings of Lenin—conveyed the impression that the founder of the Soviet state was an advocate of a democratic form of socialism. Later leaders, starting with Stalin, had departed from the original blueprint of Bolshevism, according to Gorbachev's reading of history; *perestroika* and *glasnost'* were legitimate expressions of socialism, providing a way for return to the true course of pristine Leninism. This interpretation conveniently overlooked Lenin's persecution of political opponents, his fostering of a centralized structure of rule, and his role in creation of the apparatus of a police state.

Two Soviet writers began to confront this contradiction and breached the taboo on criticism of Lenin in articles in avant-garde journals. In April, the historian Nikolai Popov wrote in *Sovetskaia kul'tura* that the concentration of excessive power in the hands of the communist party started under Lenin but that he had recognized the danger of this tendency too late to reverse it. Two months later, the journalist Vasilii Seliunin wrote in *Novii mir* that Lenin personally justified the systematic use of terror in managing the Soviet state but concluded that by 1921 he understood the "erroneous nature of the economic policy of war communism" (*Novii mir*, no. 7, June; *NYT*, 8 June).

In December, *glasnost'* penetrated perhaps the most conformist sector of Soviet society—the public schools. On the eve of a national education conference to consider reforms, Gennadii Iagodin, chairman of the State Education Committee, said that students will be allowed to choose elective courses and that teachers will be able to teach once-banned classics of twentieth-century Russian literature (AP, 19 December).

Nationalities. In a year of considerable domestic turmoil in the USSR, nationality issues produced more friction than any others. *Glasnost'* had provided an arena for the airing of ethnic grievances, and in several of the outlying republics, unofficial groups were organized to serve as vehicles for the expression of minority demands. In two areas, these discontents assumed critical dimensions, requiring constant attention by the Soviet leadership throughout the year. In the south, Azerbaijan and Armenia squared off in a revival of ancient rivalry, and in the north the Baltic states were aflame with anti-Soviet agitation.

Nagorno-Karabakh *oblast'*, an enclave within Azerbaijan SSR with a population that is more than 75 percent Armenian, sparked the controversy between the two southern republics. The province had been under the administrative control of Azerbaijan since 1923, but a rising chorus of protest culminated in January in a petition signed by 75,000 Armenians demanding annexation of Nagorno-Karabakh by Armenia SSR.

The petition was rejected by the CPSU CC and massive public demonstrations followed in both Nagorno-Karabakh and Armenia. By late February, more than one million people had participated in protests and strikes in Erevan (Armenia's capital), and in a two-week period beginning 13 February, some 120,000 were reported to have demonstrated daily in Nagorno-Karabakh's main city, Stepanakert (ibid., 25 February). The old feud between Christian Armenians and predominantly Muslim Azeris resumed in full force; ethnic clashes resulted in the deaths of several Armenians in Nagorno-Karabakh.

On 23 February, Nagorno-Karabakh party first secretary B. S. Kevorkov, a Russian, was relieved of his duties "for shortcomings in his work" and replaced by Genrikh Pegosian, an Armenian (*Bakinskii rabochii*, 24 February). On 27 February, in response to an appeal from Gorbachev and his promises of a satisfactory settlement, organizers in Erevan agreed to a month-long suspension of protests (*NYT*, 28 February). But at the end of February, clashes in the city of Sumgait in Azerbaijan resulted in the deaths of 31 persons according to official reports. Unofficial sources put the number at more than one hundred, mostly Armenians; in the following month, official accounts described the disorders in Sumgait as a "pogrom" against Armenians. On 18 March, the Azerbaijan Party CC dismissed several leading officials in Sumgait, including the city party chief D. M. Muslim-zade, for "failure to curb outrages" and "irresponsible attitudes" toward the "safeguarding of public order" (*Bakinskii rabochii*, 19 March). An Armenian political group subsequently claimed it had proof that

536 people had been killed in the Sumgait violence (AFP, 24 June; *FBIS*, 27 June).

Armenian party leader Karen Demirchian apparently sided with the protesters in his republic, perhaps hoping to use revived nationalism as a lever against his critics in Moscow. In May, he was ousted along with Kiamian M. Bagirov, first secretary of the Azerbaijan CC. Their replacements were Suren G. Arutiunian, vice-chairman of the republic Council of Ministers, in Armenia and Abdul-Rahman Vezirov, USSR ambassador to Pakistan, in Azerbaijan (*Pravda*, 22 May).

The February truce provided only a temporary respite. In July, widespread protests and violence flared again. Meanwhile, the Armenian Supreme Soviet made a futile request to the Azerbaijan Supreme Soviet for cession of the disputed territory and then appealed to the USSR Supreme Soviet. Following an acrimonious eight-hour session during which both Armenian and Azerbaijani delegates were subject to repeated angry interruptions by Gorbachev, the USSR Supreme Soviet rejected the demand (*Izvestiia*, 19 July), and the authorities braced for more violence. Troops and tanks had already been employed during the July unrest, which led to an ugly confrontation between protesters and military personnel at the Erevan airport. Now forces in the troubled areas were beefed up for the expected reaction to the USSR Supreme Soviet decision, and more violence followed. Responding to the growing crisis, Moscow's mediator, Arkadii I. Volskii, brought together the party leaders of the two republics for a meeting in Stepanakert.

On 2 August, an agreement between the two leaders was announced. The decision of the USSR Supreme Soviet on Nagorno-Karabakh was accepted by both sides, and an intensive effort was promised to resolve the region's political, economic, and social problems (*LAT*, 3 August). Nevertheless, unrest continued. Defying a ban on public demonstrations, a throng of more than 100,000 gathered in Erevan to protest in early September, and a change of mood toward the central CPSU leadership was evident. Placards displaying pictures of Gorbachev that were seen in earlier demonstrations had disappeared, replaced by angry complaints about the Soviet leader (*NYT*, 5 September). Stepanakert was soon paralyzed by a general strike (AFP, *FBIS*, 15 September; *NYT*, 16 September). Meanwhile, violence claimed lives on both sides of the republics' border. Moscow, toughening its stance, declared a state of emergency in Stepanakert and sent armored forces to occupy the

central part of Erevan, where most public facilities had been closed down. Adding to the problems of the leadership, demonstrations occurred on the same day in Tbilisi, capital of Soviet Georgia, to register various grievances (*NYT*, 23 September).

Soviet authorities claimed that order had been restored in Armenia, with more than twelve hundred soldiers deployed in central Erevan and Nagorno-Karabakh under martial law. The Armenian Foreign Ministry reported that factories, stores, schools, and offices had begun to reopen in the republic's capital (*LAT*, 24 September; *NYT*, 3 October). The tough new measures did stem general disorder; but sporadic acts of violence persisted, and refugees continued to flow in both directions across the border. When the devastating earthquake struck Armenia in December, many of the victims were refugees from the Azerbaijan SSR. The disaster apparently did little to stem the ethnic animosity, as reports of violence by both sides coincided with the organizing of relief efforts, including allegations that the houses of several Armenians in Baku had been burned down when troops were removed from that city to help cope with the emergency in Armenia.

Gorbachev cut short his visit to New York after news of the earthquake reached him and spent several days in Armenia accompanied by his wife, Raisa, and Premier Ryzhkov; full assistance for Armenia's reconstruction was promised. But relations between the party leader and the Armenians, which soured when Gorbachev vented his frustrations at the July Supreme Soviet session, deteriorated further. The general secretary charged that the Karabakh Committee, which had helped organize the mass rallies in Erevan, had thwarted some of the government's rescue plans and spread rumors like the one that Armenian orphans would be sent to other republics. A spokesman for the Armenian protesters responded that Gorbachev's charge was "just false." But the organizing group had become a principal target for the authorities; in December, five members of the committee were arrested and given 30-day "administrative" sentences (*WP*, 22 December).

In the Baltic states, nationalist resistance to Moscow assumed definite organizational structure during the year and affected the internal functioning of the CPSU in all three republics. Demands for greater autonomy for the Baltic states escalated to the point where the Soviet leadership, in November, drew a sharp line and faced down representatives of the republics. Despite the historical and cultural differences among the three republics, nationalist controversy during the year displayed three common features: (1) taking advantage of the opportunity afforded by *glasnost'* to fill in "blank pages" of Soviet history, specifically the occupation of the independent states in 1940, the Nazi-Soviet pact that made it possible, and the deportations during World War II; (2) utilizing the debates over political restructuring as a forum for the presentation of proposals for a new status for the republics; and (3) expressing the pent-up frustrations and resentments over the migration of Russians into the area.

Early in the year, the authorities took a hard line on developments in Lithuania. Police and civilian auxiliary officers patrolled various areas to prevent demonstrations marking the republic's twenty years of independence, and heavy restrictions were placed on press coverage (ibid., *CSM*, 17 February). In Estonia and Latvia, the authorities were more flexible, and intellectuals took the lead in pressing demands for the right to travel abroad and for restrictions on immigration into the republics (BBC Caris, 20 June). Pugo, Latvia's party chief and an avowed supporter of *glasnost'* and *perestroika*, seemed most successful in riding the tiger of rising nationalism and was rewarded in October with promotion to chairmanship of the CPSU Party Control Committee. But Estonian communist party chief Karl Vaino fell by the wayside, apparently losing his job because he failed to contain the agitation (*Sovetskaia Estonia*, 17 June; *FBIS*, 12 July). Ringaudas Songaila, the new party leader in Lithuania who was elected in November 1987, was generally considered to be ineffectual, and the party leadership in Vilnius played a generally passive role after February as the proponents of autonomy rallied their forces (*RFE Research*, 31 August).

The forthcoming party conference inspired mass meetings in the republics, and Estonia, which had been given responsibility for management of seven areas of its economy at the end of April, took the lead in pressing demands. Vaino Väljas, the newly installed republic party leader, led the party conference delegation and pledged to secure greater self-government and financial autonomy for Estonia (BBC Caris, 22 June).

The conference resolution on nationalities was regarded as something of a victory for national groups. On 9 July, 100,000 Lithuanians attended a rally in Vilnius to hear a report from the Lithuanian party conference delegates, who spoke of favorable results in developing greater autonomy for the Soviet republics and expansion of their rights, greater recognition of national languages, and measures aimed at environmental protection. The rally marked a breakthrough on cooperation among the nationalities; speakers included members of the Estonian Popular Front and the Belorussian Initiative Group. The Belorussian representative took matters beyond local interests by calling for a referendum on the issue of Nagorno-Karabakh (ibid., 11 July).

Publication of the secret protocols of the Molotov-Ribbentrop pact in July and August provided additional fuel for demonstrations on the 49th anniversary of the agreement that had sealed the fate of the Baltic states (RFE *Research*, 26 August). Despite the party conference resolution, the movement for greater autonomy in the three republics gave no sign of slowing down. The situation had become serious enough by August to warrant dispatching Iakovlev to Latvia and Lithuania, where he met with party activists, representatives of the media, scholars, and workers. Iakovlev showed sympathy for national concerns and emphasized that the status of the republics and nationalities would be dealt with at the CC plenum on interethnic relations expected to take place in early 1989. However, Iakovlev sharply rejected proposals that would cut off the economy of a republic from the Soviet economy as a whole, apparently referring to suggestions that Estonia be turned into a special economic zone with its own currency and immigration control (RL *Research*, 31 August).

Perhaps the most impressive development of the year was the rise of alternative political organizations with the potential for functioning in opposition to the communist party. Again, Estonia took the lead, forming a Popular Front in April and setting up a similar organization in Latvia and the Lithuanian Movement for *Perestroika*, which was more openly anti-communist. By October, the Estonian Popular Front claimed more than one hundred thousand members (*NYT*, 9 October). The Estonian and Latvian movements held congresses during the first week of October attended by prominent regional CPSU figures. In Estonia, party leader Vaino Väljas, just back from a conference in Moscow with Gorbachev, invited the Popular Front to put up its own candidates for election and to promote ideas that may differ from the communist agenda (ibid., 2 October). In Lithuania, Anatolii Gorbunov, the newly installed activist president of the republic and at 45 one of the youngest major officials in the USSR, endorsed the reform proposals of the Popular Front and the demand for an end to central government policies that involve transfer of Latvians to jobs outside the republic and bringing of non-Latvians in (*LAT*, 9 October).

Legislatures of the three republics in September and October decreed the flying of the old nationalist flags and gave official status to the native languages in preference to Russian. Moscow seemed willing to tolerate such "national in form" deviations but in November quashed more radical political demands. On 16 November, the Estonian Supreme Soviet, by a vote of 258 to 1, with five abstentions, declared its right to veto all-Union laws passed in Moscow and called for a treaty to "determine the further status of Estonia in the composition of the Soviet Union" (AP, 16 November). After officials in Moscow sternly rejected the Estonian proclamation, the parliaments of Lithuania (ibid., 19 November) and Latvia (*NYT*, 23 November) shelved plans to issue similar declarations. In the following week, the USSR Supreme Soviet Presidium offically ruled against the Estonian legislative act, and President Gorbachev said that it was "in deep contradiction with the Constitution of the USSR and must be rejected as mistaken, not having any legal force." However, opposition to the proposed constitutional changes that were to be approved by the USSR Supreme Soviet a few days later, particularly the one on the mode of representation for the Congress of People's Deputies, remained strong, and massive protests were organized by the independent political groups (AP, 26 November). As he had in the matter of Armenian demands on Nagorno-Karabakh, Gorbachev largely forfeited strong early support for *perestroika* by his adamant stand against revision of the basic federal structure of the USSR, but given the political reality of continued Russian dominance of the Soviet system, he had probably displayed the greatest flexibility possible.

A major step toward the Moscow leadership's most daunting nightmare on problems of ethnic relations—collaboration among the subordinate nationalities—was taken in midyear. On 11 and 12 June, representatives of non-Russian national movements in the Ukraine, Lithuania, Estonia, Latvia, Georgia, and Armenia met in Lvov to found a Coordinating Committee for Patriotic Movements of Peoples of the USSR (RL *Research*, 22 June).

The commission, set up the previous year to defuse Tatar protests, presented its report and exhibited the same reluctance to tamper with the forms of national interaction established by Stalin that had guided the leadership's action on other issues. The commission granted thousands of Crimean Tatars the right to return to their homeland 44 years after Stalin's deportations but rejected demands for revival of the Tatar autonomous republic in the Crimea (*WP*, *NYT*, 10 June). The commission promised a greater government effort to ensure equal treatment for Crimean Tatars in employment, housing, and education and expanded programs to teach the Tatar language (*LAT*, 10 June). Tatar spokeswoman Elvira Ablaeva criticized the report on the grounds that without autonomy none of the national rights of the Crimean Tatars could be guaranteed (RL *Research*, 10 June).

Using *glasnost'* for the purposes of ethnic politics was not confined to the subordinate nationalities. Activities of the Russian nationalist group *Pamiat'* (memory) assumed an even uglier aspect than before. During the summer, *Pamiat'* was reported to be holding weekly hate rallies in downtown Leningrad, with authorities turning a blind eye to the gatherings. At a July demonstration, one speaker called for the immediate deportation of Jews and other "alien races" to "their historical motherland." Another speaker suggested declaring war on people who "concealed their ethnic origin under a Russian name" (*Moscow News*, 5 August).

Responding to the threat from the extreme right, Gorbachev, at the June plenum of the Central Committee, called for strengthening the law against both the incitement of national enmity and the preaching of racial and national exclusivity and contended that nationalist passions benefit all anti-*perestroika* forces (*Pravda*, 30 July; RL *Research*, 1 August).

Auxiliary and Front Organizations. The Public Commission for Humanitarian Questions and Human Rights was established in November 1987 under the chairmanship of Fëdor Burlatskii, apparently reflecting a more flexible stance on human rights by the Soviet leadership. However, the main purposes of the new organization seemed to be upgrading the USSR's image in the West and preempting criticism on human rights by dissidents and the new informal groups. In an interview in December 1987, Burlatskii admitted that the commission's activities would be directed mainly toward "international cooperation" rather than monitoring human rights violations in the USSR (*Sovetskaia Rossiia*, 27 December 1987).

In late January, the commission hosted a delegation of the International Helsinki Federation for Human Rights, which is based in Finland, at a meeting in Moscow (*CSM*, 29 January). Western delegates were initially impressed with evidence of "pluralism" in the USSR (AP, 29 January). However, an admission by Mikhail Krutogolov of the Institute of State and Law of the USSR Academy of Sciences that the USSR had "blatantly exaggerated social and economic rights" in the past was not reported in the Soviet media, and the official press also ignored the presence at the conference of Lev Timofeev, head of Press Club *Glasnost'*, who had been allowed to speak at the insistence of Western delegates over the objections of Burlatskii. The meeting was further marred by police breaking up a meeting between some Western delegates and members of Soviet informal groups (RL *Research*, 11 February). Burlatskii, in an interview two weeks after the conference with Western human rights activists, redirected his focus to domestic issues, saying that two major aims of the commission were changes in legislation on religion and churches in the USSR and fundamental reforms of the Soviet legal system (*Izvestiia*, 12 February).

The Komsomol appeared to be faring badly in comparison with unofficial political clubs. In a February interview, Komsomol head Viktor Mironenko acknowledged problems, including a lapse into "bureaucracy and self-importance," but insisted that the organization would recover its position as the unquestioned molder of orthodox Marxist-Leninists (*NYT*, 7 February). Two months later, Mironenko admitted that Komsomol membership had fallen by 4 million (from a 1982 high of 42 million), with a decline of approximately 2 million in 1987 alone, but said that in the first three months of 1988, the membership had started to "increase by a very little" (Moscow Television Service, 16 April; *FBIS*, 20 April). In another interview in April, the Komsomol chief pointed to considerable improvement in "the atmosphere of Komsomol life. The work has become much more difficult," he said, "but this promotes the advancement of enterprising people who are ready to assume personal responsibility and are capable of organizing work in the new way" (*Pravda*, 2 April).

The Soviet Artists' Union held its first congress since 1983 in January amid signs of serious disarray in the organization due to internal dissent and the growing alienation of young painters (AFP, *FBIS*, 19 January). Indicating that, despite *glasnost'*, the CPSU leadership intended to continue to determine the main lines of officially sanctioned cultural activity, fifteen prominent party figures—full and candidate members of the Politburo and CC secretaries—were featured at the meeting. The roster included the disgraced El'tsin, then still a candidate member of the Politburo, who assumed his regular place among the honored guests (Moscow Domestic Service, *FBIS*, 19 January).

International Views, Positions, and Activities. The USSR continued to face the problem, abroad as well as at home, of the disparity between limited resources and overextended commitments. Domestic costs of the thrust to superpower status had been high, and internal crisis put a premium on revised or innovative policies to reduce the burden. Moreover, there was recognition that the earlier priority of military means in foreign policy had been in some respects counterproductive. Yet the many-sided pressures confronting the leadership did not induce general retreat or a circling-the-wagons defensive stance. On the contrary, Gorbachev continued to pursue an activist foreign policy designed to maintain or enhance the USSR's role in world affairs. But the emphasis now was on economy of means: the Soviets sought to maintain via diplomacy and public relations a position in the world that could no longer be maintained on the bases of traditional objective indicators of national power.

Perestroika had a more positive impact on foreign affairs than on the home front. The new style in diplomacy had yielded spectacular results, and the Soviets persevered in its exercise during the year, with Gorbachev the leading practitioner. The old style of confrontation and relative inflexibility associated with the name of Andrei Gromyko was criticized severely, particularly by Foreign Minister Shevardnadze. Foreign observers agreed that the new style was far more effective; indeed, the contrast in results was palpable. From a position of stark isolation in March 1985, the USSR had risen to a role of chief initiator of events in the international arena.

That many initiatives were simply playbacks of earlier Western proposals did not gainsay the Soviet achievement; a country in evident decline had become the protagonist on the world stage of a remarkable drama largely scripted in Moscow. An appreciative international audience responded with cries of "author, author," and scriptwriter Gorbachev took his bows with alacrity. The Soviet chieftain had become the world's most popular political figure, surpassing American president Reagan and other Western leaders in public opinion polls in both the United States and Western Europe. This international prestige was a powerful asset in

Gorbachev's drive for personal hegemony within the USSR.

The domestic-external link worked both ways. *Glasnost'* was the most effective tool in altering the USSR's international image, and outsiders were startled by the new realities of "openness" within the country. But the new course in foreign policy extended beyond matters of image and technique. The USSR displayed a striking flexibility on a wide range of substantive issues: arms control, Afghanistan, competition between the blocs, relations with East European states, and the roles of the Soviets and their Vietnamese ally in Southeast Asia. With "peace breaking out all over," it was often overlooked by euphoric Westerners that decisions were based on careful calculations of Soviet national interest and that convergence of interests between the USSR and other major powers was still subject to severe limitations.

But the USSR had traditionally defined national interest, at least in its public rhetoric, in terms of Marxism-Leninism. Soviet ideology, which legitimized external policy and achievement of international goals in line with that ideology, shored up the foundations of the regime's domestic legitimacy. Accordingly, many foreign observers looked closely for signs of ideological change, believing that without it the new Soviet course in foreign affairs would be largely cosmetic, leading to a probable reprise of Brezhnevian détente. Here, too, the Soviets could not merely convey a new image for foreign consumption. Questioning so much of the Soviet heritage in the unfolding of domestic *glasnost'* and *perestroika* was bound to raise serious questions about the validity of previous approaches to the outside world.

Soviet grappling with the ideological aspect of foreign policy during the year did not go unnoticed. The old calls for world revolution, the demonological analysis of capitalism, the time-honored "two camps" rhetoric, and—perhaps most significantly—the slogan of "proletarian internationalism" were missing, and their absence was duly noted and successfully challenged by Ligachev. The year was marked by some important events pointing toward doctrinal evolution. In March, during his visit to Yugoslavia, Gorbachev fleshed out his apparent abjuration of the Brezhnev Doctrine in the previous November. In April, party secretary Dobrynin told an audience in Prague that the Soviets had wrongly assessed the staying power of capitalism. In April, Vadim Zagladin of the CC International Department frankly admitted that the

Soviets had erred on Afghanistan and said that the international working class was not confined to the communists but also included social democrats and other forces. In August, Iakovlev flung back Ligachev's "two camps" challenge with a paean to the "common interest of mankind," also a frequent theme of Gorbachev's speeches and writings.

The search for a more convincing rationale for Soviet world policy appeared to be inspired in large measure by the thinking of Iakovlev. His statements and those of Gorbachev seemed to put forward a vision of a technologically interdependent world that transcended national boundaries and class differences. That such a footing would mean the dumping of much ideological baggage seemed no great loss. Socialism had fared poorly in the economic competition with capitalism, and the Soviet version of Marxism-Leninism had largely played out as an energizing force at home and abroad. But the trend toward ideological revision raised serious questions about the future basis of legitimacy of the Soviet regime and the position within it of the CPSU, still committed to the "leading role of the party" and, despite political reform, continuing to operate under the principle of "democratic centralism." The demotion of Ligachev surely did not end the questioning on this point by skeptics within the CPSU.

Iakovlev had long been known as an advocate of a foreign policy strategy that de-emphasized relations with the United States and gave priority to important "borderlands" areas, particularly Western Europe and China. This position was apparently challenged by Dobrynin, whose main focus was on superpower relations. Major events of the year pointed superficially toward the continued primacy of the U.S. connection supposedly favored by Dobrynin. Gorbachev and Reagan met at a largely ceremonial summit in Moscow in May and at a brief minisummit featuring fellowship and gourmet food on an island in New York harbor in December. Between these meetings, both sides moved to implement the provisions of the intermediate-range nuclear forces (INF) treaty and cooperated on various matters, including the breakthrough agreement on Namibia and Angola. The Soviets welcomed U.S. assistance following the Armenian earthquake in December, and cooperation on this disaster was a tangible confirmation of Gorbachev's rhetoric on international interdependence. But the departure of Dobrynin in September signaled the assumption of an even more powerful role for Iakovlev in foreign policy, and Dobrynin's replacement by the openly anti-American Falin at the International Department increased the probability that the heyday of Soviet-American détente had passed.

The "retirement" of Dobrynin was not exclusively the result of a power play by Gorbachev's deputy Iakovlev; there was a certain logic in the changing of the guard. Dobrynin was doomed by the success of the policies that he advocated, for the further arms control between the superpowers proceeded, the less necessary was the United States to USSR foreign policy. To the extent that removal or reduction of nuclear weapons on the European continent made less credible the U.S. deterrent, the more likely were West European states to seek new arrangements with the USSR, necessitating Moscow's greater concentration on the area. Further, the U.S.-Soviet rapprochement had been greatly facilitated by the personal relationship between Reagan and Gorbachev, which was unlikely to be duplicated when Reagan's successor took the reins of office. During his campaign for the presidency, George Bush indicated greater reservations about Soviet policy, both domestic and foreign, than any voiced by Reagan in the twilight of his tenure.

From Moscow's standpoint, the stance of the Bush administration vis-à-vis the USSR would make much less difference than that of its predecessor, given Gorbachev's success in Western Europe and U.S. budgetary constraints. The Soviet leader's spectacular offer of unilateral military cuts in Europe, made to the U.N. General Assembly in December, further solidified his standing in Western Europe and made problematic the modernization of NATO forces on the continent. If West Europeans were not yet willing to accept the Gorbachev line about "our common European home," they were generally receptive to the cooing noises emanating from the Kremlin. The most impressive payoff for Gorbachev's policy of normalization in Europe was the inflow of Western capital. Close observers of international money transfers wryly noted that the total of loans made or promised by West European banks during the year plus direct aid to the Sandinistas from Norway and Sweden was almost identical to the annual Soviet outlay in military and economic aid for Cuba and Nicaragua. In effect, Western Europe was financing the Soviet presence in Central America and the Caribbean.

The USSR's agreement to withdraw forces from Afghanistan also helped in upgrading the Soviet image in Western Europe and had benefits for relations with China and other states. It was a measure of the success of Gorbachev's diplomacy that the Soviet admission of error on Afghanistan and Moscow's attempt to disengage from its own "Vietnam" enhanced the USSR's status as a world power and improved its relations with most other key actors in international politics.

Eastern Europe was quieter than expected, and Gorbachev played his card of personal diplomacy in the region with some success. But regime leaders watched warily for possible spillover effects from the reform and domestic turbulence in the USSR and for the impact on their economies, most of which were hard-pressed, of re-emphasized CMEA integration.

Soviet willingness to remove stumbling blocks inhibiting rapprochement seemed about to pay off in relations with China, and it appeared likely that Gorbachev would visit Beijing for a summit meeting with Chinese leaders in the new year. But China, as usual, was playing a balancing game and offset the opening to the USSR by cozying up to Moscow's longtime quasi-ally India. The rash of problems convulsing China's economic reform added grist to the mill for Gorbachev's critics in Moscow.

Favorable prospects for improved relations with Japan ran aground on the perennial issue of the northern islands. Another U.S. ally, the Philippines, experienced a more serious Soviet courtship. In December, Foreign Minister Shevardnadze traveled to Manila and indicated Soviet willingness to dismantle the naval base at Cam Ranh Bay to allay Filipino security concerns.

In the Third World generally, Moscow displayed a realistic approach, no longer automatically endorsing all revolutionary movements with a national liberation stamp or urging defaults by debtor nations. The record of socialism in the Third World had been generally dismal, and the "two-track" strategy of the 1970s—support for armed struggle in the Third World while practicing détente with the major capitalist powers—was not tenable in the late 1980s. Although continuing to support the strategically important Marxist regimes in Cuba and Nicaragua, the USSR moved to disengage from economically unsound commitments such as those in Afghanistan, Angola, and Cambodia that conflicted with broader policy goals.

Overall, the USSR seemed to be gearing itself for the adjustment to an increasingly multipolar world. The real change in world politics was not in Soviet policy but in the distribution of power. As Moscow fine-tuned its policy to meet the challenge of the ongoing diffusion of power (largely economically grounded), the United States was caught in a leadership transition with its strategy for the future unclear. Nevertheless, the long-range prospects for the modernized Soviet diplomatic machine hinged on political and economic developments within the USSR. Gorbachev had consistently maintained that domestic restructuring was imperative for the USSR to function as a great power into the twenty-first century. Significantly, he had not tied restructuring to superpower status or to a dominant role for the USSR in world politics. But if the domestic reform program were to go awry, it was doubtful that Moscow could long play the more limited but pivotal great power role envisioned in Gorbachev's grand design.

U.S.-Soviet Relations. Limitations on nuclear arms and verification continued to be the main focus of attention at the outset of the year. A twenty-member U.S. team carried out a five-day inspection of the Semipalatinsk test range in Kazakhstan, followed two weeks later by a visit of Soviet inspectors to the U.S. test range in Nevada (*NYT*, 31 January). In Geneva, representatives of the two sides discussed new measures for verification of two 1970 test treaties. As a new round began in the strategic arms reduction talks (START), the USSR proposed elimination of the Strategic Defense Initiative (SDI) as a condition for cutting intercontinental nuclear forces in half; the proposal was promptly rejected by the United States (AP, 15 January).

The day after the new rebuff on SDI in Geneva, Gorbachev said that Western military strategists who back SDI and seaborne cruise missiles are trying to circumvent arms control and dismissed fears that the INF treaty would put Western Europe in danger (TASS, 15 January; *Pravda*, 16 January).

The INF treaty continued on course in Moscow, with backing from the Soviet military. Testifying before a committee of the Supreme Soviet considering ratification of the treaty, Chief of Staff Marshal Sergei Akhromeev implicitly admitted the real reason for Soviet acceptance of the "zero option"—that the installation of SS-20 missiles had backfired on the USSR. Akhromeev said that the U.S. missiles earmarked for destruction could "reach Moscow in ten minutes, or even less" and that the Soviet missiles involved in the pact could not strike U.S. territory (AP, 19 February).

Continuing U.S. expressions of concern about human rights in the USSR, particularly by President Reagan, drew sharp rejoinders from Moscow. When U.S. secretary of state George Shultz visited

Moscow in April, Gorbachev delivered an angry tirade about the "confrontational" U.S. attitude "geared to interference in our internal affairs" and said that it might lead to a situation "such as will make it no longer possible to solve any further issues" (TASS, 22 April). Because it came in the aftermath of the Andreeva affair, there was some suspicion that the outburst was primarily aimed at a domestic audience. But the two days of talks between a Soviet team, including Shevardnadze and Dobrynin, and the U.S. delegation, topped by Shultz and national security adviser Colin Powell, produced little movement on arms control and regional issues dividing the two countries (*LAT*, 23 April).

As negotiations proceeded in Geneva and the two capitals, it appeared unlikely that any START agreement would be ready for signing at the Moscow summit. But a more pressing concern was the possibility that the summit would be a complete washout, due to a delay in ratification of the INF treaty by the U.S. Senate. Led by Senator Jesse Helms, a Republican from North Carolina, opponents of the treaty stalled ratification with proposed amendments. Five days before Reagan's scheduled arrival in Moscow, Shultz went to Capitol Hill to plead for ratification (*NYT*, 24 May); formal approval came just in time for the signing in Moscow.

When the Soviet and U.S. leaders met in Moscow, human rights issues provided some sparks. Reagan met with 90 dissidents and refuseniks at Spaso House and visited the restored Danilov monastery, making strong human rights pitches at both places; a TASS commentator decried the "exploitation" of the subject of human rights "for purposes of stepping up hostility in international relations" (TASS, 30 May; *FBIS*, 31 May). Gorbachev rebuked Reagan for "sermonizing" and interfering in domestic affairs (*NYT*, 31 May). The Soviets also staged a news conference in Moscow at which U.S. political and social activists complained about abuses against minorities in the United States (AP, 30 May), and *Pravda* (30 May) published a large picture of a black American standing in a soup line across from the White House.

Despite the contention over human rights, the general atmosphere of the summit was quite convivial, particularly the meetings between the two leaders. A news highlight of the affair was a walkabout by Gorbachev and Reagan in Red Square, where they conversed with citizens (*NYT*, 1 June).

The main formal business of the summit was the signing by Gorbachev and Reagan of the document putting the ratified INF treaty into effect. The two sides were again unable to agree on SDI, and there was only limited progress on START. However, the two leaders did sign one provision of START, an agreement to notify each other of the time, place, and intended targets of missile tests (AP, 31 May). Agreements were also signed by the foreign ministers and other officials on search and rescue at sea, the setting up of a joint navigational system, the conduct of a joint experiment into nuclear test ban verification, scientific and technological cooperation, and other matters (TASS, 31 May; *FBIS*, *Pravda*, 1 June).

Gorbachev and Reagan agreed that it was still possible to have a START agreement before the end of the U.S. president's term of office, and both expressed confidence in future U.S.-Soviet relations. However, the results of the summit were probably fewer than Gorbachev anticipated. His strong push for deep arms reductions, vastly increased trade ties, joint space programs, and other concrete results were turned aside by the Americans (*NYT*, 5 June).

After the summit, contacts continued in several arenas. Defense Minister Iazov met with U.S. secretary of defense Frank Carlucci for the third time during the year (they had met at Bern, Switzerland, in March and at the Moscow summit in May), with indications that the place of the military in Soviet economic and political life was becoming a subject of sharp debate within the USSR. At a conference on Soviet foreign policy in Moscow in late July, Foreign Minister Shevardnadze called for a law requiring that all departments concerned with military and military-industrial activity be "under the control of the supreme nationwide elected bodies," and other foreign policy specialists were proposing cuts in Soviet conventional forces. Meanwhile, Chief of Staff Marshal Sergei Akhromeev, who had visited the United States in July and was showing a high political profile, emerged as the leading opponent of cuts in Soviet forces (BBC Caris, 1 August). All of this had important implications for the superpower relationship, and Iazov went to great lengths to reassure the U.S. defense chief by a lavish display of Soviet "openness." Carlucci was allowed to inspect various Soviet weapons systems, including the missile-launching cruiser *Slava* at the Sevastopol naval base. After seeing Carlucci off for Turkey, Iazov told reporters that "we parted not only as colleagues, but as good friends" (AP, 4 August).

In September, Shevardnadze and Shultz met in the United States before the fall U.N. General As-

sembly session to discuss arms control negotiations and the Soviet withdrawal from Afghanistan (ibid., 8, 23 September). Meanwhile, a new round of arms control talks was underway in Geneva, focusing on preparation of protocols on verification of treaties limiting nuclear tests to 150 kilotons. At the outset of the talks, chief Soviet delegate Igor Palenykh expressed the belief that the negotiations would "become a milestone event" in the U.S.-Soviet dialogue on nuclear disarmament (AP, 27 August). Also in August, a U.S. group led by Nuclear Regulatory Commission (NRC) chairman Lando Zech inspected the Chernobyl nuclear reactor involved in the April 1986 explosion, and an NRC spokesman said that the U.S. team and Soviet officials had arrived at agreements paving the way for further cooperation on sensitive nuclear power issues (ibid., 8 September).

The December meeting between Gorbachev and Reagan underscored the steady warming trend in relations between the U.S. and USSR but was overshadowed by the Soviet leader's dramatic speech to the U.N. General Assembly earlier in the day that announced forthcoming major cuts in Soviet forces in Europe (see below). Following the luncheon and talk on Governors Island in New York, Reagan declined to say whether the troop withdrawals would stimulate Soviet-U.S. talks on further force reductions (*NYT*, 8 December).

Before the minisummit, Soviet deputy foreign minister Vladimir Petrovskii had listed an ambitious agenda for the talks, including arms negotiations, Central America, Afghanistan, and the Middle East (*WP*, 3 December). However, the Reagan administration sought to dampen expectations about the meeting, and as it turned out the main business seemed to be fond farewells between Gorbachev and Reagan and photo opportunities for the two heads of state plus U.S. president-elect Bush. The combination of the brevity of the meeting, U.S. unreadiness for Gorbachev's spectacular gambit at the United Nations, Reagan's lame-duck status, and Bush's unwillingness to make commitments before assuming the presidency worked against concrete results. However, Soviet officials said that the New York meeting went "extremely well," and a key Kremlin aide told Western reporters that Gorbachev hoped to make arrangements for a formal summit meeting with Bush in the first half of 1989 in the United States (ibid., 15 December).

The Armenian earthquake that cut short Gorbachev's visit to the United States confirmed the growing rapprochement between the two countries, which had been furthered by the cessation of Soviet jamming of U.S. broadcasts a month earlier. American supplies and relief personnel poured into the devastated area, and the usual checks on incoming foreigners were all but totally suspended. The Soviets publicly welcomed the aid and spared no details about the desperate need for outside assistance. The striking contrast between the efficiency of U.S. and other Western relief efforts and the inadequacy of Soviet personnel, particularly army forces assigned to relief work, was an object lesson to the Soviet public on the need for *perestroika*. Americans were impressed by evidences of changed attitudes among the Soviet leaders, such as premier Ryzhkov's attending a meeting on victims with Mother Teresa (*Time*, 2 January 1989) and Elena Bonner's report that her husband, Andrei Sakharov, a visitor to the United States in November, had been asked by Gorbachev and Iakovlev to help mediate the conflict between Armenia and Azerbaijan (*NYT*, 29 December).

Western Europe. Soviet policy toward Western Europe was designed to facilitate transition to a new strategic balance, to erode U.S. influence on the continent, and to secure aid from the advanced capitalist economies for economic recovery and technological upgrading of the USSR. With the superpower nuclear standoff and the sharp division of Europe no longer tenable as supports of policy, a fluid situation had been created that provided a tough testing ground for the new Soviet diplomacy.

The Soviets followed up on Gorbachev's renewed push for a nuclear-free zone in the European north as indicated in his October 1987 Murmansk speech and sought to improve relations with Sweden, disturbed in recent years by evidence of Soviet naval incursions into Swedish waters and the effects of the Chernobyl nuclear explosion. Premier Ryzhkov visited the Stockholm and Goteborg areas in January, stressing trade ties and arranging a number of export and import contracts. But the main business of the visit touched more pressing concerns. Ryzhkov concluded agreements on the principles governing the demarcation of waters in the Baltic Sea, on the prompt notification of nuclear accidents, and on the exchange of information on nuclear installations (*Pravda*, 14 January; *Izvestiia*, 15, 18 January). Similar agreements were signed during a brief Ryzhkov visit to Norway.

Attention quickly turned to the Federal Republic of Germany (FRG), which was central both in geography and in Soviet policy aims; the FRG contin-

ued to be the main target of Soviet initiatives on the continent throughout the year. In January, USSR foreign minister Shevardnadze visited the FRG and met with FRG chancellor Helmut Kohl, Foreign Minister Hans-Dietrich Genscher, Economics Minister and Free Democratic Party (FDP) chairman Martin Bangemann, and Christian Social Union chairman Franz-Josef Strauss. Shevardnadze's talk with Bangemann focused on bilateral economic relations and featured praise by the Soviet foreign minister for the role of the pivotal FDP in "shaping the relationship between the two countries" and its contribution to "constructive *Ostpolitic*." Agreements were signed on regular consultations between foreign ministers, economic cooperation, and issues connected with the opening of consulates in Munich and Kiev, and arrangements were made for regular meetings on legal and humanitarian matters. FRG foreign minister Genscher, a longtime ardent proponent of détente, said that he favored further development of all-around ties between the two countries at various levels (TASS, 17, 18 January; *FBIS*, 19 January).

In February, Aleksei Altunin, USSR deputy premier, conferred in Moscow with Heinz Ruhnev, board chairman of Lufthansa (TASS, 18 February; *FBIS*, 29 April), and in March, Ryzhkov met in the Soviet capital with F. W. Christians, board chairman of the Deutsche Bank (*Pravda*, 20 March), which was to play a major role in the flow of FRG credits to the USSR arranged during the year.

In May, Ryzhkov welcomed FRG economics minister Bangemann to Moscow for talks on FRG cooperation in the USSR's economic restructuring, with particular emphasis on support for the modernization of Soviet light and food industry enterprises (*Izvestiia*, 17 May). A week after the Bangemann visit, FRG ambassador Andreas Meyer-Landhut appeared on the Moscow newscast "Vremia" and spoke effusively about the improved state of Soviet-FRG relations (Moscow Television Service, 23 May; *FBIS*, 24 May).

Bernhard Vogel, president of the Bundesrat and minister-president of Rhineland-Palatinate, was in Moscow in July as the guest of the Supreme Soviet Presidium. In his talks with Vogel, USSR president Gromyko denied that the USSR was trying "to drive a wedge" between Western Europe and the United States and said that the four-power agreement on West Berlin "in no way limits the possibilities for the development of relations between the FRG and the GDR" (*Pravda*, 12 July). Two weeks later, Genscher visited Moscow; a few days after the FRG foreign minister's departure, Mathias Rust, the young West German pilot who had landed on Red Square in May 1987, was released from prison and allowed to return home (BBC Caris, 3 August; AP, 4 August). Rust's release was widely interpreted as a goodwill gesture preparatory to Chancellor Kohl's scheduled visit.

The FRG leader arrived in Moscow in October accompanied by Genscher and four other cabinet ministers, 50 business and banking figures, and four hundred aides and journalists. The main business of the visit was the signing of a $1.6 billion agreement on credits for Soviet economic development (*NYT*, 24 October; *Pravda*, 25, 26 October). The flow of Western credit to the USSR was expected to total some $8 billion for the year, and on 18 October the U.S. Senate voted 64 to 2 for a nonbinding resolution calling for talks between the United States and its allies about the security implications of the massive loans (*NYT*, 19 October).

The economic aspects of the Kohl visit were all but eclipsed by a flap over political prisoners. Kohl said that the Soviets had promised to "release all persons whom the West considers to be political prisoners" by the end of the year, and a senior FRG official said that Shevardnadze had made the promise to Genscher. Soviet Foreign Ministry spokesman Gennadii Gerasimov declined to confirm that any such assurances had been given, and there was controversy over the definition of "political prisoner" and the numbers involved. Gerasimov said that only "dozens of persons" fell into the category of political prisoners, but Western human rights organizations and unofficial Soviet groups estimated that there were at least two hundred to three hundred prisoners of conscience in prison camps, internal exile, or psychiatric hospitals in the USSR (*WP*, 27 October).

Other continental countries received less attention than the FRG, but Moscow kept a close watch on nuclear weapons issues. In May, the Soviet media sharply criticized United Kingdom foreign secretary Sir Geoffrey Howe for his "condemnation" of Denmark's refusal to allow nuclear weapons on its territory in peacetime (*Pravda*, 14 May) and lashed out at the British "Defense White Paper" that proposed modernizing existing nuclear weapons and substituting cruise missiles for other systems (Moscow Domestic Service, *FBIS*, 22 May). In July, the canceling by Portugal of a treaty providing for construction of a tracking station in Almodovar as part of the SDI program drew warm praise from Moscow (Radio Moscow, 6 July; *FBIS*, 12 July).

Although Great Britain was perceived as less attuned to Soviet objectives than some other West European countries, there were some bright spots for the Soviets, notably the marked increase in cultural exchanges, and on the occasion of the official farewell for departing United Kingdom ambassador Sir Bryan Cartledge, USSR president Gromyko praised Britain for its support of the INF treaty. However, sharp criticism of Britain (and of Prime Minister Margaret Thatcher personally) continued over London's pronuclear defense policy and its resistance to most Soviet proposals on arms control in Europe (BBC Caris, 27 July). But Gorbachev had established a good personal relationship with Prime Minister Thatcher, confirmed by the warmth of their 1987 meetings in Moscow in March and in London in December. Another round of talks was scheduled between the two leaders to follow Gorbachev's U.N. visit, but the London stopover had to be canceled when the Soviet president rushed home because of the earthquake in Armenia (*Pravda*, 9 December). Soviet officials said that an attempt would be made to reschedule the London trip for early 1989.

The most important development in the Soviet "peace offensive" and campaign for normalization vis-à-vis Western Europe was Gorbachev's speech to the U.N. General Assembly in December. United States policymakers had anticipated a major proposal by Gorbachev, but his wide-ranging U.N. speech contained such radical concessions that much of official Washington was stunned. Gorbachev told the General Assembly that over the next two years the USSR would reduce its military forces by 500,000 men and ten thousand tanks, disband about half of its tanks in Eastern Europe, and withdraw six tank divisions from East Germany, Czechoslovakia, and Hungary. Total Soviet forces from the Atlantic to the Urals would be reduced by 8,500 artillery systems and eight hundred combat aircraft. Soviet divisions remaining in Eastern Europe would be reorganized so that their posture would be "clearly defensive." Gorbachev also promised to bring home "a major portion" of USSR forces in Mongolia and put forward a new proposal for peace in Afghanistan, including a 1 January ceasefire. All cuts were presented as unilateral, not contingent on reductions by other countries. (*NYT*, 8 December.)

The reductions announced by the Soviet leader—motivated in part by the need to redirect resources and manpower to the ailing Soviet economy—would leave the USSR with a quantitative edge of about two and one-half to one in all major weapons systems in Europe. Nevertheless, Western observers generally considered the cuts significant, and Prime Minister Thatcher hailed the action as "an important step towards securing a better balance of forces in Europe in view of the Soviets' present overwhelming superiority" (ibid.). One immediate effect of the announcement was a negative impact on modernization of NATO forces in Europe, especially since FRG foreign minister Genscher, perhaps the most influential diplomat in NATO, seemed strongly opposed to any major move in that direction.

Although Gorbachev's dramatic announcement seemed a clear triumph for Soviet European policy, it had its domestic costs. On the same day as Gorbachev's U.N. speech, the resignation of Chief of Staff Marshal Sergei Akhromeev was announced with the shopworn explanation that it was for "reasons of health." Actually, a behind-the-scenes struggle had been going on in Moscow for months over the issue of military cuts, and General Iazov, minister of defense, had evidently tried to whip the generals into line over the opposition of Akhromeev. Following Gorbachev's speech, a stream of letters from Soviet Army officers critical of the reductions appeared on the pages of *Krasnaia zvezda* (*WP*, 18 December).

Eastern Europe. This region was uncertain about its position in the new order unfolding on the continent. Gorbachev remained a popular figure, with hopes among the masses and the intelligentsia that his reforms in the USSR would have a pronounced effect on the regimes of the region, but most party and government leaders resisted Moscow's lead on internal democratization. Meanwhile, the economies continued to undergo severe strains, and even the East Germans experienced a decline in living standards. Ambitious Soviet plans for enhanced economic integration remained largely on paper, but most regime leaders seemed willing to go along with Moscow's proposals so long as they were not forced to follow Gorbachev's lead on domestic political reform. Immediately after the Nineteenth CPSU Conference, Premier Ryzhkov represented the USSR at the Forty-fourth Executive Meeting of CMEA (*Pravda*, 6 July) and apparently tried to push integration further with no substantial results.

In the first quarter of the year, Moscow seemed to direct its attention away from the northern tier of states toward those further south. Within the bloc, Hungary and Romania presented special problems.

Hungary had been in the forefront of economic reform, but the restructuring of its economy seemed to be going awry. Although the Soviets resisted copying Budapest's plans, the failure of Hungary's reform program could be used as a negative example by resisters in the USSR, and the situation had to be watched closely.

In late 1987, economic crisis and popular protests raised doubts about the future of communist rule in Romania. The country's longtime leader, Nicolae Ceauşescu, responded to the turmoil by tightening authoritarian control and spurned Gorbachev's lead on reform, moving in the opposite direction on all fronts. Not only was Bucharest out of step with Moscow, but it was threatening bloc cohesion with its domestic policies, as Hungary protested treatment of the Magyar minority in Transylvania. Although its sympathies were clear, Moscow followed a strict hands-off policy in regard to Romania's internal affairs and even declined to offer its services as mediator in the Hungarian-Romanian dispute. However, the Soviets reportedly supported a Hungarian proposal for a commission on human rights and ethnic minorities within the Warsaw Treaty Organization (RFE *Research*, 18 August).

Gromyko visited Budapest in February to mark the 40th anniversary of the signing of the Soviet-Hungarian Treaty of Friendship (*Pravda*, 24, 27 February). An unfortunate reminder of the imposition of Stalinist rule on Hungary and reportedly cool toward Gorbachev's reforms, the Soviet president was largely ignored by the Hungarians.

The issue of the Magyar minority in Transylvania was kept off the agenda when Gromyko visted Bucharest in May. The joint communiqué on the visit indicated vague agreement on "progressive forms" of bilateral economic cooperation including the formation of joint enterprises (ibid., 14 May), but Gromyko was given something less than an enthusiastic reception. The only formal agreements signed were minor ones, dealing with cultural exchanges and sports.

The travels of Gorbachev were closely followed throughout the region. When the Soviet leader visited Yugoslavia in March, he displayed a keen interest in the country's nationalities problems, not surprising in view of the rising ethnic unrest at home, and seemed to look favorably on economic reform within Yugoslavia. The Soviet-Yugoslav declaration at the end of the visit endorsed "socialist self-management" as a guarantee against "administrative-bureaucratic distortions of socialism" (*Pravda*, 19 March). However, in a speech in Belgrade on 15 March, Gorbachev said that "we have to maintain a regulating role at the center to safeguard against mistakes, especially in such a large country as the Soviet Union" (*WP*, 16 March).

More important for the countries of the region was the declaration's treatment of relations between socialist states. In his Moscow statement of November 1987 and in his book *Perestroika*, Gorbachev appeared to back away from the Brezhnev Doctrine, and the declaration provided some confirmation of a new Soviet approach, although it was less specific than earlier statements by Soviet spokesmen other than Gorbachev. Some observers were disappointed that the declaration did not contain explicit repudiation of earlier interventions or an unqualified promise to forego use of force in all circumstances (RFE *Research*, 29 March). However, the document did state that each party is accountable "to the working class and people of its own country" and called for "mutual respect for different paths in building socialism." The declaration also noted that neither the Soviet nor the Yugoslav party intended "to impose its concepts of social development on anyone" and affirmed that countries were entitled to independence and equal rights "regardless of their sociopolitical system, the convictions they are guided by, the forms and nature of their international alliances, or their geographic position" (*Pravda*, 19 March).

Political and economic crisis within Poland provided a depressing backdrop for Gorbachev's visit to that country in July, and the Soviet leader's strong support for the country's increasingly unpopular leader, General Wojciech Jaruzelski, made the trip a somewhat risky venture in public relations. However, the Soviet leader's personal diplomacy and walkabouts again seemed to carry the day. Accompanied by his wife, Raisa, Gorbachev made 21 public appearances in Warsaw, Kraków, and Szczecin, evoking a favorable public response, including many autograph hunters demanding the Soviet leader's signature on copies of *Perestroika*.

In Kraków, the Gorbachevs visited the Church of St. Mary as guests of Auxiliary Bishop Jan Szkoden, apparently endorsing recent moves toward cooperation between the regime and the church in Poland and maintaining the more tolerant attitude toward religion recently displayed by the Soviet leadership at home, particularly in regard to celebration of the millenium of Christianity in Russia. In Szczecin, Gorbachev spoke to 3,000 workers at the Adolf Warski shipyard and praised the workers

for their support of Soviet restructuring. But in his address to the Polish *Sejm* and elsewhere, Gorbachev avoided any direct reference to the banned Solidarity union or to the controversy over revelations about the Katyn Forest massacre. (*NYT*, 14, 15 July; Warsaw Television Service, 14 July; *FBIS*, 15 July; *Pravda*, 14, 15 July; *Time*, 25 July.)

The joint statement at the end of the visit emphasized the "consonancy of the restructuring carried out in the Soviet Union and the course of socialist renewal pursued in Poland." The statement was even more explicit about noninterference in domestic affairs than the Soviet-Yugoslav declaration of March: "Soviet-Polish relations are based on full respect for the sovereign right of each country to independently determine the methods and forms of building socialism, the pace of sociopolitical transformations, the approaches to solving problems, and overcoming contradictions" (*Pravda*, 15 July).

However, the apparent tolerance of diversity in domestic affairs was completely absent in regard to external policy: "In international affairs, the CPSU and the PPR regard the organic combination of their initiatives with the common coordinated line of socialist states as standard practice" (ibid.).

The whirlwind of activity in Poland preceded the Warsaw Pact summit meeting at Warsaw. According to the final communiqué, the session had mainly dealt with military matters, presumably related to Gorbachev's various tentatives regarding force reductions in Europe (*Pravda*, 17 July).

The Hungarian response to economic ills was to push for reform—apparently encouraged by the Soviets—as Gorbachev's domestic reform program shifted into high gear. Following his July meeting with Gorbachev in Moscow, Hungarian party boss Károly Grósz said that the Soviet leader had displayed an interest in adopting some of Hungary's pioneering economic and political reforms (*NYT*, 10 July; BBC Caris, 12 July).

Afghanistan. In the first week of the year, Foreign Minister Shevardnadze said that the USSR hoped to remove its troops from Afghanistan by the end of 1988 and indicated that the withdrawal would not depend on the creation of an acceptable transition government. Shevardnadze also said that the United States had agreed to cut off aid to Afghan guerrillas as part of a withdrawal package. The foreign minister's statement marked the first time Soviet authorities had said publicly that removal of the USSR's 115,000 troops was not conditional on the makeup of the government left behind (*NYT*, 7 January).

As *glasnost'* at home forced several admissions by prominent officials that the invasion had been a mistake, the Afghan-Pakistani talks resumed at Geneva in February. Within two months, it appeared that the negotiations were finally bearing fruit. On 7 April, Gorbachev and the Afghan leader Najibullah met in Tashkent and issued a statement that the last obstacles to a settlement had been removed and that, if a formal agreement were signed "within the shortest period," the Soviet withdrawal would begin on 15 May (*NYT*, 8 April). The agreement was signed in Geneva on 14 April between Afghanistan and Pakistan, with the United States and USSR as guarantors (ibid., 15 April). According to the terms, the United States would be allowed to continue supplying weapons to the Islamic guerrillas during the Soviet withdrawal "at an equal and balanced level" with the arms supplied by the USSR to the Afghan government. Half the Soviet troops would be withdrawn within three months following the 15 May start of the exodus, and the remainder would leave by 15 February 1989.

The departure of Soviet troops began on schedule in May, but movement of units was inhibited by harassment from the guerrilla forces, which also stepped up campaigns against the puppet Kabul regime. The increasingly precarious position of Najibullah's army made it seem unlikely that the Geneva timetable would be met. Shevardnadze met in Moscow with Pakistani foreign minister Yaqub Khan the first week of August, accused the Pakistanis of violating the Geneva accords by continuing to arm the mujahedeen, then flew to Kabul for emergency consultations with the Afghan government (BBC Caris, 5 August). However, the Soviet press depicted the withdrawal as proceeding normally, with troops continuing to leave south Afghanistan and with all Soviet soldiers out of the city of Kandahār (*Pravda*, 5 August).

On 30 August, the U.S. State Department said that the Soviets had conducted aerial raids in and around Kundūz (*WP*, 31 August). The USSR confirmed this report on the following day, saying that the action was necessary to protect troops withdrawing from Kataghan, a northern Afghan province bordering on the USSR, but denying that the combat missions were a violation of the Geneva accords, as charged by the United States (*NYT*, 1 September).

In early November, U.S. officials reported that the Soviets had sharply escalated the war in Afghanistan, bringing long-range missiles into the country for the first time and using sophisticated fighter-bombers in intensive operations against advancing rebels in southern Afghanistan (Newhouse News Service, 2 November). On 4 November, the USSR suspended troop withdrawals, blaming the West for violations of the Geneva accords (*Pravda*, 5 November).

Still caught in the Afghan imbroglio, the Soviets pursued every possible avenue for completion of the withdrawal without humiliation. The first meeting between the Soviets and representatives of the Afghan rebels was held 3–5 December in Taif, Saudi Arabia, where Soviet officials negotiated with the seven-party guerrilla alliance supported by the United States and Pakistan. On 11 December, a rebel spokesman announced that a representative of the Pakistan-based resistance would meet with USSR envoy Iulii Vorontsov within two weeks, and a spokesman for the Iran-based rebels said that a Soviet offer of negotiations was being considered (AP, 12 December).

Carrying the peace drive to a wider arena, Gorbachev made a settlement in Afghanistan the major emphasis of his 7 December U.N. General Assembly speech, proposing a four-point plan: a complete cease-fire as of 1 January 1989, cessation on the same date of all supplies to the belligerents, the sending of a U.N. peacekeeping force to Afghanistan and demilitarization of the country (*NYT*, 8 December). The Gorbachev plan was generally well received at the United Nations but was rejected by the United States.

On 30 December, Najibullah announced a unilateral cease-fire as of 1 January, and on the following day the Soviet Foreign Ministry said that Soviet troops would cease fire on New Year's Day. Najibullah said that the Muslim insurgents would be given four days to accept the truce. Soviet first deputy foreign minister Aleksandr Bessmertnykh met with the U.S. and Pakistani ambassadors in Moscow on 30 December and urged that their governments support the proposed truce; Moscow also expressed willingness to stop supplying the Kabul regime with arms. The new truce proposal was rejected by both U.S. secretary of state Shultz and the Afghan rebels (AP, *NYT*, 1 January 1989). However, in his weekly radio talk, U.S. president Reagan expressed confidence that the USSR would meet its February target date for the withdrawal of all troops from Afghanistan (AP, 1 January 1989).

China. Sino-Soviet relations, thawing since Gorbachev's July 1986 statement at Vladivostok, continued a slow warming trend during the first half of the year, with an increase in various kinds of contacts and a further lowering of tensions on the border. This improvement could be traced to the new Soviet flexibility on the three issues that Beijing had identified as the crucial impediments to a resumption of normal relations—Afghanistan, Cambodia, and the Soviet military presence on China's northern frontier. However, none of the issues had been entirely removed from the agenda, and at midyear prospects were uncertain. The twelfth round of Sino-Soviet political consultations at Moscow ended in June with only an agreement to hold another round of meetings at Beijing in the spring of 1989 (*FEER*, 4 August).

Nevertheless, the push for rapprochement continued, with the Soviets eager to arrange a summit meeting that would make it possible for Gorbachev to practice his brand of personal diplomacy in Beijing. The Chinese had insisted that substantial progress on all three big issues was a precondition for such a meeting of leaders. The beginning of the Soviet withdrawal from Afghanistan and removal of one motorized rifle division from Mongolia were major steps toward eliminating two obstacles, but the Cambodian issue was more complex because the USSR could only apply pressure to Hanoi, not control events in Southeast Asia. When U.S. secretary of state Shultz visited Beijing in July, he was told that a positive Soviet role in arranging a settlement in Cambodia had become the only precondition for scheduling a summit meeting between the USSR and the People's Republic of China (PRC) leaders (WP, 22 July).

Soviet deputy foreign minister Igor Rogachev traveled to Beijing in late August for talks on the Cambodian issue (TASS, 27 August; *FBIS*, 29 August). After one week of discussions Rogachev said that "we have a very clear mutual understanding" and that the governments had agreed that they should take steps to bring peace in Cambodia but indicated that differences remained over how to achieve a settlement (*LAT*, 3 September; *Pravda*, 4 September).

Gorbachev took another major step toward normalizing relations in a December U.N. General Assembly speech with proposals on Afghanistan and, more important from Beijing's standpoint, a promise to remove "a major portion" of the USSR's forces from Mongolia (*NYT*, 8 December).

Evidently the Chinese leadership concluded that satisfactory progress had been made on all major issues, and officials in Beijing and Moscow now considered a Gorbachev summit trip to Beijing in the new year as highly probable. However, the PRC, still maneuvering to avoid the appearance of either anti-Sovietism or a tilt toward Moscow, made overtures to India, long noted for its pro-Soviet, anti-Chinese orientation in foreign affairs. For the first time since 1960 Chinese and Indian leaders met when Prime Minister Rajiv Gandhi was welcomed to Beijing for talks with Premier Li Peng. The two leaders discussed the border dispute between the two countries, economic exchanges, and the possibility of establishing consulates in Shanghai and Bombay (AP, 19 December). At the conclusion of the visit, it was announced that the two countries would establish a joint commission on the border problem (ibid., 22 December).

Japan and the Pacific. In addition to the major issues and strategic concerns that had long separated the USSR and Japan, there were the usual minor irritants. In May, Japanese police complained that Soviet officials had refused to cooperate with investigators looking into a fire aboard a docked Soviet liner that killed at least eleven people (AP, 18 May). However, there were indications of an evolution of thinking on both sides about the overall relationship between the two countries.

In July, former Japanese premier Yasuhiro Nakasone visited Moscow and had a two-and-a-half-hour session with Gorbachev, reportedly touching on numerous divisive issues. Following Nakasone's visit, press accounts from Moscow stated that the CPSU Politburo had decided to "add a Japan-Soviet summit to the Soviet Union's timetable of international activities" (*FEER*, 18 August). The Soviets now looked to the economic potential inherent in closer ties between the USSR and Japan. On the Japanese side, Soviet movement on the major issues important to Beijing also created a favorable impression in Tokyo. Public opinion polls in Japan showed that the number of Japanese who regarded the USSR as peace-loving had more than doubled recently and that a majority of respondents were interested in better trade and political relations (ibid., 6 October).

Attempting to take advantage of the newly favorable climate, the Soviets dispatched Foreign Minister Shevardnadze to Tokyo in December (*Pravda*, 18 December). He met with Japan's foreign minister for lengthy discussions on economic matters and the status of the Kuril Islands. However, the talks reached an impasse when the Japanese set return of the northern islands as a precondition for increased trade (*NYT*, 21 December).

Undeterred by his rough reception in Tokyo, Shevardnadze moved on to Manila to up the ante in his dealings with Pacific states. At the conclusion of the USSR foreign minister's visit, Filipino foreign minister Raul Manglapus reported that Shevardnadze had held out the possibility of a Soviet withdrawal from the Cam Ranh Bay naval base in Vietnam, a move that would greatly lessen the Philippines' security dependency on the United States. But Manglapus said that Shevardnadze told him the USSR hopes to strengthen relations with the Philippines without harming Manila's ties with the United States (AP, 22 December).

Elsewhere in the region, the Soviets continued their political fishing in South Pacific waters. A conference at Canberra, Australia, in March considered the security implications of Soviet fishing agreements and political initiatives toward the small island states of the South Pacific. Former U.S. national security adviser Zbigniew Brzezinski said that "political influence is the first step toward military influence" and contended that the Soviets' long-term goal was the removal of U.S. military facilities and port access in the South Pacific. The USSR's fishing treaty with Vanatu lapsed in January, but the Soviets moved on a bigger target, slating a May visit by a trade delegation to Papua New Guinea (*CSM*, 1 April).

India. Despite its concentration on more pressing foreign policy matters, Moscow did not neglect its longtime close relationship with India. In July, it was reported that the USSR had bested Italian and West German competitors by offering a lower price for, and was about to close a deal with India on, the sale of an undisclosed number of highly advanced MI-28 helicopters (Xinhua, 4 July; *FBIS*, 7 July). India's president Ramaswamy Venkataraman was welcomed to Moscow in July for talks with USSR president Gromyko and other officials. The Soviet media reported that the discussants emphasized "the proximity or coincidence of the two countries' positions on the fundamental international problems" and stressed Venkataraman's satisfaction with recent Soviet actions on Afghanistan (*Pravda*, 7 July).

Near and Middle East. As elsewhere, the Soviets displayed a high degree of flexibility and a more moderate attitude toward erstwhile opponents, an approach aided by the shelving of revolutionary rhetoric. The new Soviet diplomatic stance was most evident in regard to Israel, and Moscow devoted most attention to the Israeli-Palestinian conflict.

In March, when Foreign Minister Shevardnadze met a delegation of the Arab League's Committee of Seven in Moscow, the Soviets appeared to be on a traditional track, condemning Israel in the strongest terms for its "repressive policy" toward the Palestinians and for "mass violations of human rights" and calling for Israeli troop withdrawal from all occupied Arab territories and the "realization of the Palestinian people's national rights." However, the Soviet press reported that the conferees also affirmed "the right of all states and peoples of this region to a secure existence." This statement, which implied recognition of Israel's independence and security needs, was subscribed to by the representative of the Palestine Liberation Organization (PLO) at the meeting, perhaps a harbinger of things to come (ibid., 19 March).

At the meeting of the Socialist International in Madrid in May, Soviet observer delegates strongly supported the demand for an independent Palestinian state and condemned Israel's "repressive practices" against the Palestinian Arabs and the "state terrorism" involved in the assassination of Palestinian deputy military chief Khalil al-Wazir, reportedly by Israeli commandos. However, the Soviet delegates sounded out Israeli labor party leader Shimon Peres about his party's willingness to support a Middle East settlement through an international conference including the Soviets (Kuwait Kuna, *FBIS*, 23 May).

A more overt step toward a new relationship with Israel came in July when the Soviets issued visas for an Israeli consular delegation to visit Moscow (*NYT*, 20 July), officially for the purpose of reviewing the handling of Israeli affairs, mostly the issuance of visas for emigrating Soviet Jews by the Dutch embassy. A similar Soviet delegation had been in Israel for a year. The Soviet action was generally viewed as a move toward restoring diplomatic relations, although both sides acknowledged that normalization would be a slow process. On the day the Israeli delegation arrived in Moscow, USSR Foreign Ministry spokesman Vadim Perfiliev restated the Soviet position that Arab-Israeli peace talks were a prerequisite for re-establishing diplomatic relations between the USSR and Israel. However, the Soviets continued to maintain that the Arabs must recognize Israel's right to exist and no longer insisted that Israel withdraw from all occupied territories before the restoration of diplomatic relations between Moscow and Tel Aviv (*LAT*, 29 July).

When PLO leader Yassir Arafat was denied entry to the United States to address the U.N. General Assembly, the Soviets joined in the general condemnation of Washington. But the resulting brouhaha gave the Soviets a new opportunity to play a role—as honest broker—in negotiations among the various parties. The Soviets reportedly exerted tremendous pressure on Arafat to speak the exact phrases demanded by U.S. secretary of state Shultz as a condition for U.S. negotiations with the PLO. Stung by the U.S. reversal on dealings with the PLO, Israel's premier Yitzhak Shamir was said to be vigorously pursuing the restoration of diplomatic relations with Moscow (AP, 21 December). However, since Shamir continued to publicly reject negotiations with the PLO and since Moscow adhered to its position that Israeli-Palestinian talks were a precondition for diplomatic recognition, the restoration of formal ties appeared to be an elusive goal. At the end of the year, the politics of the region remained extremely complex but Moscow was perhaps a bit closer to its goal of getting back into the Mideast peace process.

Another Soviet initiative for normalization in the region had no immediate result but again demonstrated Moscow's assumption of a broker's role as a means of playing a more active role in the region. The USSR sought to bring about a reconciliation between Egypt and Libya that would lead to the restoration of diplomatic relations between those countries. Vladimir Poliakov, USSR Foreign Ministry section chief for the Near East and North Africa, met with Egyptian president Hosni Mubarak in June and reportedly put forward proposals for such a reconciliation (*al-Itthad*, 27 June; *FBIS*, 29 June).

The renewed confrontation between the United States and Iran and the start of the Soviet withdrawal from Afghanistan provided the setting for an improvement in relations between Moscow and Teheran. In May, Iran was still blasting the USSR for its shipment of arms to Iraq but on 9 June announced the formation of a joint shipping company to operate in the Caspian Sea. This followed closely an agreement to develop land, sea, and air transportation linking Iran, Bulgaria, and the USSR (RL *Background Report*, 10 June). The intricate interweaving of connections in the restyled Soviet diplomacy was demonstrated later in the year when the closer relation between Moscow and Teheran facilitated overtures to the Iran-based Afghan guerrillas.

Africa South of the Sahara. The Soviet role in the dramatic breakthrough on settlement of the conflicts in Angola and Namibia provided a striking illustration of the new Soviet realism on the Third World and appeared to mark another step back from the goal of promoting revolution in undeveloped areas. In July, South Africa, Angola, and Cuba accepted the fourteen-point Principles for a Peaceful Settlement in Southwest Africa (*WP*, 21 July), but a further five months were required to work out all details of the settlement.

The USSR played a major role in achieving the agreement and reportedly exerted heavy pressure upon Cuba and Angola to adopt flexible positions in the negotiations leading to the formal agreement in December. Representatives of Cuba, Angola, and South Africa signed an agreement in Brazzaville on 13 December (ibid., 15 December), and a further official signing took place in New York two weeks later.

Under the agreement, 3,000 of the 50,000 Cuban troops were to leave Angola, and a U.N. peacekeeping force of 9,000 was to move into Namibia by 1 April 1989. By 1 July 1989, South Africa was to remove all but 1,500 of its 50,000 troops from Namibia. By 1 November 1989, elections were to be held in Namibia and 25,000 Cuban troops were required to be out of Angola, with the remaining 25,000 moving north of the Benguela railroad. By 1 July 1991, the last 25,000 Cubans were to be withdrawn from Angola. Jonas Savimbi's National Union for the Total Independence of Angola (UNITA) was not a party to the agreement and vowed to continue fighting unless UNITA were included in an Angolan government (*Time*, 26 December). But the agreement did provide for disengagement of the superpowers from the region's conflicts and promised to get the Cubans out of that part of Africa.

U.S. assistant secretary of state Chester Crocker, whose policy of "constructive engagement" had been much maligned by critics in Washington, was the star of the Brazzaville ceremony and was generally credited as the main architect of the pact. Less prominent in Brazzaville but also a key figure in the settlement was USSR deputy foreign minister Anatolii Adamishin. The agreement was widely hailed as an example of the new spirit of cooperation between Washington and Moscow. Adamishin said that the agreement was "very good in the broader context of Soviet policy, if you want, the new thinking of Comrade Gorbachev" and conceded that "I personally don't think they are going to build socialism in this part of the world" (*WP*, 15 December).

Latin America. The wide-ranging new Soviet diplomacy affected Latin America, with the USSR moving to develop links with several countries of the region. In May, an agreement on cooperation in science and technology related to agriculture was signed between the USSR State Agro-Industrial Committee and the Mexican Ministry of Agriculture and Hydraulic Resources (TASS, 11 May; *FBIS*, 12 May). In August, a USSR Supreme Soviet delegation headed by Presidium deputy chairman Zagash Kamalidenov visited Ecuador (*Pravda*, 10 August). Also in August it was announced that the USSR would sell or lease airplanes to Aero-Peru, the Peruvian state airline (*El Comercio*, 6 August; *FBIS*, 15 August).

Moscow's special interest in Brazil was signaled by the appointment of Leonid F. Kuzmin (58), a senior specialist in Latin American affairs, as ambassador. Kuzmin, chief of the southern zone department of the USSR Foreign Ministry, served as ambassador to Peru from 1975 to 1983 (*Insight*, 10 October). Deputy air minister Lieutenant General C. Rosa Filho visited Moscow in August (*Krasnaia zvezda*, 30 August), and an agreement on exchange of military attachés was signed when Brazil's president Jose Sarney traveled to the USSR in October. Sarney, the first Brazilian president to visit the USSR, was warmly welcomed to Moscow by Soviet president Gorbachev. Plans were reportedly being considered for a Gorbachev tour of Brazil, Argentina, and Uruguay or Mexico in 1989 (*WP*, 19 October).

The main Soviet interest in the region continued to focus on Nicaragua and Cuba. The strategic importance of the two Marxist regimes precluded Soviet disinterest, but the domestic economic problems of the two countries made for increasingly thorny relations as the Soviets faced mounting pressures on their own economy. The new economic cooperation agreement between the USSR and Nicaragua, signed in January, provided for $294 million over a three-year period, a cutback from the previous accord (RL *Research*, 30 March). The Cuban economy was in shambles, and the annual Soviet subsidy of about $7 billion was given more grudgingly than before, particularly in view of

Fidel Castro's frostiness toward Gorbachev and his adamant resistance to Soviet-style restructuring. Gorbachev had intended to visit Cuba following his appearance at the United Nations in December to see for himself the conditions in the essential yet irritating allied state, but the Armenian earthquake intervened. Soviet officials said that Gorbachev would try to reschedule the visit for sometime in the next year (*NYT*, 9 December).

Party International Contacts. The flexibility and ecumenical approach to dealings with other parties that had characterized the Gorbachev era was even more pronounced during the year, and personnel changes at the top levels of the CPSU apparat promised not less, and possibly more, of the same in the future. The appointment of Falin to succeed Dobrynin as head of the International Department did not foreshadow a change of direction, and the selection of Medvedev to fill the already eroded ideological portfolio of Ligachev symbolized a decisive rejection of the "two camps" approach favored by the former second secretary.

Ideological disputes and the Soviet record of interventionism had been central to splintering the world communist movement over the previous four decades. CPSU spokesmen sought to repair some of the damage by ideological pronouncements during the year, renouncing any claim to Soviet infallibility and supporting the idea of "different roads to socialism," closely following the domestic theoretical justification for restructuring. The altered stance on relations with communist parties and other "progressive" forces did facilitate contacts but raised serious questions about the ideological foundations of the CPSU's role in international affairs. A general doctrinal approach to contemporary world socialism reflecting the practical activity of the CPSU under Gorbachev had still to be worked out, but, just as in domestic affairs, admissions of past errors were so far-reaching as to bring into question the concept of "scientific socialism" and a "leading role" for the CPSU in processes of global political change. The tendency toward pragmatism and the downplaying of revolutionary rhetoric served useful purposes in the pursuit of near-term Soviet foreign policy goals, but no galvanizing idea for communist activity had surfaced to substitute for the outmoded or discredited traditional precepts of the Soviet version of Marxism-Leninism.

The communiqués on Gorbachev's visits to Yugoslavia and Poland, with their stress on noninterference in domestic affairs, attracted most attention, but statements of lower-ranking officials were generally more explicit. During the spring, remarks by two senior CPSU foreign policy specialists dramatically departed from traditional positions. On 12 April, CC secretary Dobrynin, addressing the opening session of a conference in Prague on the work of the journal *Problems of Peace and Socialism*, said that three problems were affecting the development of the communist movement in Western countries: capitalism had "proved to have a much greater durability than was earlier thought"; socialism had not provided people in Western countries with "a convincing example of thorough democratization of society" or "radical solutions" to economic problems; and polemics within the communist movement had produced "a sharpening of relations among parties and even splits between them" (TASS, AP, 12 April; RL *Research*, 15 April).

In late May, Vadim Zagladin, first deputy head of the CPSU CC International Department in an interview with the Czechoslovak weekly *Tvorba*, said that communists in the past were dogmatic, made major mistakes, and suppressed human rights. He admitted error on Afghanistan and attributed this to an attempt to skip stages of social development. Zagladin acknowledged that "the majority of countries who freed themselves from the yoke of colonialism in fact chose the capitalist road." On relations among "progressive" forces, Zagladin said that the working class could no longer "be a class for itself" but rather must be "a class for the entire society, for all mankind." Further, he noted that "one must not forget that the working class movement is not exclusively communist; the communists themselves constitute only a minority. The social democrats and socialist movements are also working class" (*Tvorba*, 25 May; RFE *Research*, 6 June).

The new flexibility and "openness" served the CPSU well in Eastern Europe by simultaneously reassuring nervous leaders of bloc parties and encouraging proponents of the domestic economic restructuring needed to support the USSR's own *perestroika* program. Gorbachev conferred with leaders of all the bloc parties at the Warsaw Pact summit in July (*Pravda*, 18 July) and, in line with his stated position on noninterference, evidently made no attempt to deal with the widely divergent domestic policies of the region's ruling communist parties. Given the unsettled political and economic situation within the USSR, doctrinal tendencies were closely aligned with practical political limita-

tions; polite encouragement was the order of the day. This was the tactic of Premier Ryzhkov during a visit in April to Budapest, where he discussed *perestroika* with Hungarian party general secretary János Kádár and Hungarian prime minister Károly Grósz and, in his public appearances, criticized "economic stagnation" among the bloc countries (Radio Budapest, 20 April; RL *Research*, 22 April). But a jarring note to the general atmosphere of *glasnost'* was also sounded by Ryzhkov. In Prague for the CMEA executive session in July, he said that the CPSU still agreed with the assessment of the 1968 events in Czechoslovakia issued by the Czech and Slovak party organizations in 1970 (Radio Prague, 8 July; RFE *Research*, 13 July).

When Grósz assumed the leadership of the Hungarian party, he apparently sought to dispel his image as a reluctant reformer by keeping the Hungarian economic model in line with, or a step ahead of, Moscow's. In July, immediately following the Nineteenth CPSU Conference, he traveled to Moscow for a meeting with Gorbachev (*Pravda*, 5 July). On the eve of his departure from Budapest, he said that the tasks facing the Soviet and Hungarian parties were "similar" and that Soviet *perestroika* "creates favorable historical conditions for us, too" (AP, 3 July). Following the meeting with Gorbachev, Grósz said that the Soviet leader had expressed an interest in adopting some of the Hungarian reforms in the USSR (*NYT*, 10 July; BBC Caris, 12 July).

The other bloc countries were, in varying degrees, more resistant to Soviet style restructuring, and Gromyko, in his dual capacity as Politburo member and head of state, was often assigned to deal with the hardest cases. In January, Gromyko conferred with East German foreign minister and SED CC member Oskar Fischer in Moscow (*Neues Deutschland*, 29 January), and in May he went to Bucharest for talks with the inveterate foe of restructuring, Romanian party chief Nicolae Ceauşescu (*Pravda*, 11, 13 May).

SED party control commission chairman and Politburo member Erich Mueckenberger visited the Ukraine in April and met with Ukrainian party secretary and Politburo member Iurii N. El'chenko; Vladimir A. Ivashko, Ukrainian CC Politburo member and first secretary of Dnepropetrovsk *obkom*; and other Ukrainian party officials (*Pravda ukrainy*, 20 April; *FBIS*, 3 May). A delegation of CPSU party workers headed by Iurii P. Voronov, head of the CPSU Culture Department, visited the

German Democratic Republic in January (*FBIS*, 13 January).

Miloš Jakeš, the new Czechoslovak party first secretary, was kept busy dealing with the CPSU. In January, he traveled to Moscow for talks with Gorbachev (TASS, 15 January; *FBIS*, 19 January). In April, he met with CPSU CC secretary Dobrynin in Prague (Radio Prague, 11 April; RL *Research*, 15 April), and in July, he conferred with USSR premier Ryzhkov in Prague on the results of the Nineteenth CPSU Conference (*Pravda*, 9 July). In August, Jakeš again journeyed to the USSR for talks with top CPSU officials (*Leningradskaia pravda*, 16 August; *FBIS*, 15 September). Czechoslovak president and former party leader Gustáv Husák discussed the USSR's domestic restructuring process with Gorbachev in Moscow on 12 March (TASS, 12 March; *Pravda*, 13 March).

When a delegation from the Danish Communist Party visited the USSR in February, the official communiqué emphasized the Soviet initiative for a nuclear-free zone in Northern Europe (TASS, 29 February; *FBIS*, 1 March). Pugo, first secretary of the Latvian CP, headed a CPSU delegation that visited Sweden in May at the invitation of the Left Party-Communists of Sweden (TASS, 15 May; *FBIS*, 19 May).

The Soviet attempt to disengage from the war in Afghanistan provided the backdrop for contacts with Afghan party leader Najibullah during the year. Gorbachev met with him at Tashkent in April to discuss the impending announcement of the Geneva accords (*NYT*, 8 April), and the two party chiefs met again in Moscow in June (RL *Research*, 10 June). Komsomol first secretary Viktor Mironenko traveled to Kabul in April and congratulated Afghan youth "on the great victory made possible by the successful implementation of the national reconciliation policy" (*Komsomolskaia pravda*, *FBIS*, 20 April). In the first week of August, USSR foreign minister and Politburo member Shevardnadze flew to Kabul to discuss the precarious situation of the Afghan government with Najibullah (BBC Caris, 5 August).

CC secretary Dobrynin greeted a delegation from the Progressive Party of the Working People of Cyprus on its May visit to the USSR (*Pravda*, 23 May).

Brutents, deputy head of the CPSU International Department, visited Ethiopia in May at the invitation of the Workers' Party of Ethiopia Central Committee (ibid., 3 May). A delegation of the Yemen Socialist Party was in the USSR, 8–18 August, and met in Moscow with officials of the CPSU CC General and International departments (TASS, 18 August; *FBIS*, 23 August).

Two party delegations were in the USSR in July. One, from the Portuguese communist party, met with various CPSU officials, 10–18 July, to discuss *perestroika* and the work of the Nineteenth CPSU Conference. Another, from the Cambodian communist party led by party secretary Men Sam-An, visited Alma Ata for talks with officials of the Kazakh communist party and, on 18 July, met with CPSU CC secretary Medvedev in Moscow (*Pravda*, 19 July).

Kaysone Phomvihan, general secretary of the Lao People's Revolutionary Party Central Committee, vacationed in the USSR during the month of August as a guest of the CPSU CC (ibid., 1 September).

CPSU CC secretary Dobrynin met with Jorge Risquet Valdes-Saldaña, Cuban party secretary and Politburo member, in May for talks concerning negotiations on a settlement in Southwest Africa (Moscow Domestic Service, 10 May; *FBIS*, 11 May). Gorbachev was scheduled to meet with Castro in December, but the trip to Havana had to be postponed due to the earthquake in Armenia (*Pravda*, 9 December).

Viktor I. Smirnov, candidate member of the CPSU CC and second secretary of the Moldavian party CC, led a CPSU delegation to the Eleventh Congress of the Ecuadorean Communist Party in July (ibid., 20, 21 July). S. M. Nesterenko, second secretary of the Turkmen party CC, led the CPSU delegation to the Twenty-third Congress of the People's Progressive Party of Guyana (*Pravda*, 28 July).

Biographies. *Vladimir Aleksandrovich Kriuchkov.* Kriuchkov, a Russian, was born in 1924 and joined the communist party in 1944. He graduated from the Moscow All-Union Judicial Institute in 1949 and from the Higher School for Diplomats at the USSR Foreign Ministry in 1954. During World War II, he worked in defense plants and from 1944 to 1946 was a Komsomol official in Barrikadi *raion* and in the city of Stalingrad. From 1946 to 1954, Kriuchkov worked in procuracy offices in Stalingrad city and *oblast'*.

In 1954 Kriuchkov moved to the diplomatic service as third secretary of the Soviet embassy in Hungary. As a subordinate of USSR ambassador Iurii Andropov, he played a role in the suppression of the Hungarian uprising in 1956. After Andropov returned to Moscow to head the CC Department for Liaison with the Communist and Workers' Parties of the Socialist Countries, he chose Kriuchkov as chief of the sector of that department concerned with Hungary. When Andropov was named chairman of the KGB in 1967, he took Kriuchkov with him to serve as head of the secretariat of the KGB's First Chief Directorate (foreign intelligence). Subsequently, Kriuchkov was promoted to first deputy head and then, in 1974, to head of the First Chief Directorate. In 1978, while retaining the latter post, he was accorded the rank of deputy chairman of the KGB.

Kriuchkov accompanied CPSU general secretary Gorbachev to the Washington summit meeting in 1987. On 1 October, following the transfer of KGB chief Chebrikov to the CC Secretariat and to chairmanship of the newly created party commission on legal affairs, Kriuchkov was appointed KGB chairman.

Kriuchkov has been a member of the CPSU CC since the Twenty-seventh CPSU Congress in 1986.

(Sources: *Pravda*, *NYT*, 2 October; Albert L. Weeks, *The Soviet Nomenklatura*, Washington, 1987, p. 97; RL *Research*, 1, 9 April 1986.)

Vadim Andreevich Medvedev. A Russian, Medvedev was born 29 March 1929 at Makhonkovo in the Iaroslavl region. He graduated from Leningrad State University in 1951 and became a member of the CPSU the following year. His early career was spent at educational institutions in the Leningrad area. An instructor at Leningrad State University, 1951–56, he was named an assistant professor at the Leningrad Institute of Rail Transport in 1956. He served as head of a faculty at the Leningrad Technological Institute, 1961–68, and in 1968 returned to Leningrad State University as a professor of economic science.

Medvedev was summoned to Moscow in 1970 to become deputy head of the Propaganda Department of the CPSU CC, where he worked closely with Iakovlev before the latter's appointment as ambassador to Canada in 1973. In 1978, he was appointed as rector of the CPSU CC Academy of Social Sciences and in 1983 was promoted to the position of head of the Department of Science and Educational Institutions of the CPSU CC.

Following the Twenty-seventh CPSU Congress in 1986, Medvedev was appointed secretary of the CPSU CC responsible for relations among ruling communist parties, and he also supervised science and education, including the merger of academic research with civilian-technical and military-technological innovation. In this position, he was identified as a strong supporter of Gorbachev's initiatives for *glasnost'* and *perestroika*, leading to a major new role when reorganization of the CPSU apparatus was announced at the CC plenum of 30 September 1988. Medvedev was elected a full member of the Politburo and named to head the new commission on ideology.

Medvedev was elected to the Central Auditing Commission at the Twenty-fifth CPSU Congress in 1976 and was elected a member of the CC at the Twenty-seventh CPSU Congress in 1986. He was named to membership on the Commission on Science and Technology of the USSR Supreme Soviet Council of the Union in 1984. He has been a corresponding member of the USSR Academy of Sciences (Economics Department) since 1984 and holds the Order of the October Revolution. He has traveled widely in Eastern Europe and has also visited Western Europe.

(Sources: RL *Research*, 24 February; *Pravda*, *NYT*, 1 October; *Pravda*, 7 March 1986; Boris Lewytzkyj, *Who's Who in the Soviet Union*, Munich, 1984, p. 210; Weeks, *Soviet Nomenklatura*, p. 6.)

R. Judson Mitchell
University of New Orleans

Yugoslavia

Population. 23,580,148

Party. League of Communists of Yugoslavia (Savez Komunista Jugoslavije; LCY). The LCY is the only political party in the Socialist Federal Republic of Yugoslavia (SFRY). However, there are communist party organizations in each of the six republics—Slovenia, Croatia, Bosnia-Hercegovina, Montenegro, Macedonia, and Serbia—and in the two autonomous provinces—Kosovo and Vojvodina—as well as within the Yugoslav armed forces (JNA).

Founded. April 1919, as the Socialist Workers' Party of Yugoslavia; disbanded and replaced by the Communist Party of Yugoslavia (CPY) in June

1920. The CPY took the name League of Communists of Yugoslavia at the Sixth Party Congress in November 1952.

Membership. 2,079,613 (1987)

President of the Presidium. Bosko Krunić (59), a Serb from the autonomous province of Vojvodina. Replaced in June by Dr. Stipe Šuvar (52), a Croat from Croatia.

Secretary of the Presidium. Radiša Gačić (50), a Serb from Serbia (second half of a two-year term). At this time there are 8 appointed executive secretaries: Slobodan Filipović, Stefan Korosec, Marko Lolić, Vukašin Lončar, Boris Mužević, Stanislav Stojanović, Uglesa Uželac, and Ljubomir Varoslija. The number of executive secretaries varies as needed.

Presidium. 23 members representing the republics, autonomous provinces, and the LCY organization in the JNA. Fourteen members of the Presidium hold that job between party congresses. However, there are 9 ex officio members who take part in Presidium meetings by virtue of being presidents of their own territorial League of Communists (LC) or heads of the JNA party organization. Since these presidencies rotate on different schedules—on a one-year or two-year basis—the makeup of the ex officio members can change within any given year. Members: Slovenia, Stefan Korosec and Franc Setinc (resigned); Croatia, Ivica Racan and Stipe Šuvar; Bosnia-Hercegovina, Ivan Brgić and Milanko Renovica (resigned); Montenegro, Marko Orlandić and Vidoje Zarković; Macedonia, Milan Pančevski and Vasil Tupurkovski; Serbia, Dušan Čkrebic (present status undetermined) and Radiša Gačić; Kosovo, Kol Shiroka (resigned); Vojvodina, Boško Krunić (resigned). Ex officio members: Slovenia, Milan Kucan; Croatia, Stanko Stojčević; Bosnia-Hercegovina, Milan Uželac; Montenegro, Milan Radović; Macedonia, Jakov Lazarovski; Serbia, Slobodan Milošević; Vojvodina, Milovan Sogorov; Kosovo, Azem Vlasi (resigned); party organization in the army, Vice-Admiral Petar Simić

Central Committee. 165 members: 20 from each republic, 15 from each of the two autonomous provinces, and 15 from the army's party organization

Status. Ruling party

Last Congress. Thirteenth, June 1986

Last Elections. 1986. The Yugoslav parliament has two chambers: a 220-member Federal Chamber and an 88-member Chamber of Republics and Provinces. Elections are conducted by the Socialist Alliance of the Working People of Yugoslavia via a complex delegate system. In May, Dušan Popovski (Macedonia) became president of the assembly; Spasoje Medenica (Montenegro) became vice president. The term of office is currently one year.

Auxiliary Organizations. The Socialist Alliance of the Working People of Yugoslavia (Socijalistički savez radnogo naroda Jugoslavije; SAWPY) is a mass umbrella organization that includes all major political/social organizations as well as individuals. SAWPY provides the political machinery for conducting elections and mirrors the tensions of the LCY. There is also the Confederation of Trade Unions of Yugoslavia (SAVEZ Sindikata Jugoslavije; CTUY) and the League of Socialist Youth of Yugoslavia (Savez socijalisticke omladine Jugoslavije; LSYY).

Government Bodies. An 8-member collective state presidency was elected in May 1984 for five-year terms. The president and vice president serve for one year, and these positions rotate among the membership. In May 1988, Raif Dizdarević (61) from Bosnia became president of the SFRY, and Stane Dolanc (62) from Slovenia was elected vice president. Other members of the presidency are Josip Vrhovec, Croatia; Sinan Hasani, Kosovo; Lazar Mojsov, Macedonia; Veselin Djuranović, Montenegro; Radovan Vlajković, Vojvodina; and Nikola Ljubičić, Serbia. LCY president Stipe Šuvar meets with the state presidency as an ex officio member. Day-to-day government is in the hands of a 29-member Federal Executive Council (FEC) that is selected for four years and headed by Prime Minister Branko Mikulić (60). There are two vice-premiers: Miloš Milosavljević and Janez Zemljaric. Among the most important federal secretaries are Budimir Lončar, foreign affairs; Colonel General Veljko Kadijević, defense; Dobroslav Čulafić, internal affairs; Svetozar Rikanović, finance; and Nenad Krekić, justice. The prime minister and the entire FEC resigned on 30 December. They will remain in office until a new government is formed.

Publications. Main publications of the LCY are *Komunist* (weekly) and *Socijalizam* (monthly); SAWPY's main publication is *Borba*, a daily newspaper. Other major dailies include *Politika* and *Politika ekspres* (Belgrade), *Večernji list* and *Vjesnik* (Zagreb), *Delo* (Ljubljana), *Oslobodjenje* (Sarajevo), *Nova Makedonija* (Skopje), and *Rilinda* (Pristina). Prominent weeklies are *NIN*

(*Nedeljne informativne novine*; Belgrade) and *Danas* (Zagreb). The boldest youth weekly newspapers are the Slovene Youth Organization's *Mladina*; the Belgrade University's *Student*; and the Zagreb University's *Studentski list*. Much controversial religious material appears in the biweekly Catholic journal, *Glas koncila*. Controversial philosophical and social issues often appear in Belgrade's biweekly *Književne novine*.

Leadership and Party Organization. The year 1988 was difficult for the LCY. The republic party organizations not only drifted apart, but they began publicly to quarrel with one another. In virtually every republic, the Tito era leaders had retired or been removed from positions of power, thereby eliminating any cadre basis for interrepublic party cooperation. The new generation of leaders seemed more intent on building republic-centered political machines and warring with one another than in dealing effectively with the nation's pressing problems. Overall, in 1988, the LCY lost considerable political clout and public confidence. At the federal level, the presidency of the LCY was held until 30 June by Krunić, a Serb from Vojvodina. He was succeeded by Dr. Šuvar, a Croat and Zagreb University sociologist. The replacement of the top leadership followed the traditional annual rotation schedule and did not represent any intentional policy shift. The top officeholders in the LCY change every year, and the positions are rotated among members from one republic or province to another by a predetermined schedule.

Krunić's mandate as head of the party can be characterized as primarily conciliatory and directed toward achieving party unity. During the first half of the year, the federal party did little to interfere with Serbian party chief Milošević's concentration of power in Serbia and refrained from outright involvement in Slovenia's party affairs. For example, the fourteenth session of the Central Committee, which convened in Belgrade during May, dealt with traditional questions relating to Yugoslavia's deteriorating economic policy and the declining membership base of the LCY. The fourteenth session endorsed both government attempts to reschedule Yugoslav foreign loan repayments and the need to have the economy conform better to market forces (Tanjug Domestic Service, 11 May; *FBIS* 13 May).

From 29 to 31 May, the LCY held an extraordinary party conference to which more than eight hundred delegates were elected by secret ballot. This meeting, chaired by Krunić, dealt with the theme of party unity and the revitalization of party efforts to "pull the country out of the social and economic crisis" (*Pravda*, 30 May; *FBIS* 8 June). The conference, which accomplished little in the way of concrete actions, appeared to strengthen the realization that the party had lost control over the national policy agenda and become fractionalized into petty republic and provincial enclaves. Calls were repeatedly made to convene a special party congress, but these were pointedly rejected by the leadership (*Politika*, 2 June; *FBIS*, 10 June). More important, much of the leadership of the LCY, including Krunić and Renovica (Krunić's immediate predecessor), were criticized by name and accused of ineptitude, corruption, and abuse of power (*Borba*, 2 June; RFE *Research*, 7 June). Many of these condemnations were initiated by Serbian delegates to generate internal Serbian public support for Milošević's Serbian reform efforts. Their more immediate impact, however, was to help isolate the federal party leadership from the membership and to reduce its credibility.

In conformity with party procedures, Krunić surrendered his office to Dr. Šuvar during the fifteenth session of the Central Committee held in Belgrade on 29–30 June. To a great extent, this plenum recognized that the extraordinary conference in May was a failure and that the party leadership was incapable of reversing the deterioration (Tanjug Domestic Service, 29 June; *FBIS*, 12 July). As had occurred during the conference, this plenum witnessed a great many critical and often personality-directed attacks among the participants.

A sizable number of resignations from the Central Committee had been expected at the May conference. Stane Dolanc, a Slovene and a former close associate of Tito, publicly stated his intention to resign if requested to do so (Tanjug Domestic Service, 3 July; *FBIS*, 5 July). Franc Setinc, a member of the Presidium from Slovenia, submitted his resignation because "our methods of work are destroying us without producing results," and he stated that radical changes are necessary to carry out reform (*Borba*, 1 July; *FBIS*, 20 July). Neither Dolanc's offer nor Setinc's resignation were accepted at that time.

The only significant resignation that occurred was by Dr. Radovan Radonjić, chairman of the LCY Ideological Commission, which is responsible for party discipline and democratic centralism. This resignation symbolized the temporary failure of the party leadership's reform efforts. As Radonjić stated, his resignation was a voluntary recognition of his failure to implement what he had pledged at the Thirteenth Congress (Tanjug Domestic Service, 3 July; *FBIS*, 12 July). The failure was echoed by Josip Vrhovec (Croatia), who referred to recent demonstrations in front of the Central Committee building where shouts of "thieves, thieves, out!" could be heard. It was seconded by Ante Marković who stated that there would be no reform without a change in the leadership team (*Borba*, 2–3 July; *FBIS*, 14 July).

In this crisis-ridden environment, Dr. Šuvar (Croatia) was elected by secret ballot to the LCY presidency. He recognized that his task was overwhelming and that the league was running out of time to attempt solutions (Tanjug Domestic Service, 29 June; *FBIS*, 12 July). Dr. Šuvar is arguably one of Yugoslavia's most consummate political infighters. He has been known to speak his mind and to take very controversial positions. Although many consider him to be unnecessarily abrasive, he has been most effective in building coalitions and in isolating the adherents of extreme political views. Šuvar gained prominence in Croatia in the early 1970s with his opposition to the nationalist movement in Croatia and achieved notoriety when, as Croatian education minister, he implemented the widely unpopular education reforms in the late 1970s. His election to the party leadership of Croatia in 1985 was seriously contested, an unprecedented action at that time, but he moved swiftly to broaden his coalition. Unlike his predecessors, Šuvar is from the postwar generation and represents a distinct break from the stale Titoist party traditions.

The problems of the LCY intensified immediately following Šuvar's election at the end of June. During July throughout Serbia a flood of mass demonstrations occurred daily that were orchestrated by Milošević, in an attempt to force the LCY to support Serbian demands in Kosovo at the scheduled July plenum. Serbian party support for the demonstrations represented a dangerous and unprecedented trend in postwar Yugoslavia and was vehemently opposed in the autonomous provinces of Vojvodina and Kosovo (*Dnevnik*, 18 July; *FBIS*, 25 July). The demonstrations became worrisome and engendered protests to the federal Central Committee from Dragoslav Marković, a former Serbian party leader, and others who were concerned that the demonstrations were "nourishing irrational nationalist feelings and passions" (Belgrade Domestic Service, 8 September; *FBIS*, 13 September). By

late July, the presidency ordered the demonstrations to cease.

On 29 July, a twenty-hour marathon session of the Central Committee (sixteenth session) on the problem of Kosovo was held, and its deliberations were broadcast live throughout Yugoslavia. During the session, the Serbian and Kosovan party leaders came to an impasse on their contrasting viewpoints, and relatively little was accomplished (Belgrade Domestic Service, 29 July; *FBIS*, 1 August). The session was characterized by intense emotional exchanges in which "some members were called names in public such as traitor of the people, member of the fifth column, separatists, and similar things," and a special commission chaired by Vinko Hafner (Slovenia) was formed to investigate the matter (Tanjug Domestic Service, 30 July; *FBIS*, 1 August). Šuvar prophetically closed the session with a warning that if the Kosovo national problem were not soon resolved, it would degenerate into a Yugoslav nationalist problem (*Delo*, 2 August; *FBIS*, 5 August).

This party drama intensified throughout the summer with a new flood of Serbian protest marches and sympathy strikes. The Belgrade party apparatus called for the expulsion of Marković from the party and for the scheduling of a special congress of the LCY (Tanjug, 6 September; *FBIS*, 7 September). Serbian demonstrators began to demand resignations from other republics, particularly in Slovenia (*Borba*, 28 September; *FBIS*, 30 September). The vehemence of the attacks resulted in the resignation of Franc Setinc, a respected moderate Slovenian Presidium member, who called attention to the "madness which is obviously pushing us all towards disaster and which we are doing little to stop" (Tanjug Domestic Service, 26 September; *FBIS*, 27 September). An influential Croatian news weekly even accused Serbia's Milošević of "anti-constitutional radicalism" (*Danas*, 30 August; RFE, 9 September).

The most significant party event of the year occurred during the seventeenth session of the Central Committee 17–19 October. This session, chaired by Šuvar, was forced by escalating violence and disorder to face the challenge to party unity represented by Milošević and the Serbian communist party. In the two weeks before the session, Milošević's supporters again took to the streets. One crowd forced the resignation of the Vojvodinan party leadership in Novi Sad. More ominously, other groups mobilized in Titograd and attempted to force the resignation of the Montenegrin leadership. These mob actions backfired on Milošević, however, when the other republics joined forces to condemn the street demonstrations and attempts by Serbs to extend their influence outside their own republic.

When the seventeenth session began, there were high expectations that up to one-third of the Central Committee would be forced to resign and that the Serbian party would be severely disciplined. The primary focus of attention was the debate between the Serbs and Kosovans during which neither side gave ground or appeared ready to even consider a compromise. At the session, four members of the Presidium resigned, including Renovica from Bosnia who was party chief from 1986 to 1987, Krunić from Vojvodina who was party chief from 1987 to 1988, Šetinc, a Slovene, and Široka, a Kosovo Albanian (RFE, 11 November).

The Central Committee's decision to take an unprecedented vote of confidence in its Presidium was the most controversial element of the session. In secret balloting among the ten remaining members, Čkrebić, a Serbian member, failed to receive the necessary majority from the Central Committee. This act was interpreted (correctly) as a repudiation of Milošević. Macedonian Presidium member Vasil Tupurkovski even called the vote a "victory for an unprincipled coalition" (*Borba*, 21 October; *FBIS*, 25 October).

Controversy did not end with the lack of confidence expressed by the Central Committee in Čkrebić. Milošević, for example, argued that the decision was not binding and would only be valid with the concurrence of the Serbian Central Committee. On 18 November, Čkrebić, on the advice of the Serbian committee, withdrew his resignation, thereby directly challenging the federal party and its Central Committee (Zagreb Domestic Service, 18 November; *FBIS*, 21 November).

The long-term deterioration in the capacity of the LCY to effect policy change has had an impact on membership and morale within the organization. Membership declines occurred in all republics and provinces during 1987, and total membership fell to 2,099,613, which was a drop of 77,476 from the peak reached in 1983 (*Borba*, 1 March; *FBIS*, 9 March). This membership decline was not localized. Of 69,028 party cells in 1986, 49,201 (71 percent) did not admit a single new member. As many as 92.5 percent Slovenian cells, 80.2 percent in Montenegro, 79.6 percent in Croatia, 76.5 percent in Serbia proper, 73.5 percent in Vojvodina, 65.8 percent in Bosnia, 64.2 percent in Macedonia,

and 61.6 percent in Kosovo did not admit a single new member.

During 1987, the Vojvodina party registered its largest annual decline in the past four years, losing 4 percent of its total membership compared with 1986 (*Borba*, 29 June; *FBIS*, 18 July). In 1987, three-quarters of all Vojvodinan party cells did not admit any new members, and over the past three years, 40 percent of party cells in the province had not added a single member (Tanjug Domestic Service, 15 June; *FBIS*, 23 June).

Preliminary 1988 data from Slovenia indicate a precipitous exodus from the party, at least in that republic. During the first four months of 1988, there was a 3.4 percent decline in the total Slovenian party membership (*Borba*, 12 July; *FBIS*, 18 July). Social science research and anecdotal evidence suggest strong member dissatisfaction with the party, a decline in party self-respect, disgust over social inequalities, and abuse of privileges by party leaders (*Danas*, 26 January; *FBIS*, 5 April).

The real story about the fragmentation of the federal LCY in 1988 can be seen in developments within the Serbian communist party. The expulsion of Dr. Dragiša Pavlović, former head of the Belgrade party, and the removal of Ivan Stambolić, former political chief in Serbia, coupled with wholesale purges of the editorial board of the highly respected *Politika* news organization and Belgrade's television network, demonstrated the extent to which power in Serbia was concentrated in Milošević's hands. The widespread protest marches organized by Milošević, which occurred throughout the summer and fall despite repeated admonitions from the central party leaders, underlined the weakness of the federal LCY. The resignation of the Vojvodinan party apparatus because of the street demonstrations in October removed any contention that the federal party apparatus could control, or even seriously affect, events within a republic's jurisdiction. Finally, the inability of the national party leadership to work in concert to discipline Milošević and his faction during the seventeenth party session in October, despite serious provocations and extensive disregard for democratic centralism, underscored fears that confederalism had become a reality in the party.

Domestic Affairs. Deterioration in government affairs continued throughout 1988 and resulted in the resignation of Prime Minister Mikulić and his entire cabinet on 30 December. Mikulić had survived a parliamentary attempt to bring down his government in the spring only to see a series of his economic and inflation control packages rejected repeatedly by the federal parliament. In May, according to custom, Raif Dizdarević succeeded Lazar Mojsov as head of the federal collective presidency. Dizdarević, however, was forced to shift his attention from the acute economic problems to the growing political unrest in much of the country.

Government affairs. Despite tremendous difficulties, Prime Minister Mikulić's government remained essentially intact throughout the year. The major personnel change occurred in the Defense Ministry, with Colonel General Kadijević replacing the controversial Admiral Branko Mamula, who retired.

In May, the Slovenian and Croatian parliamentary delegations formally requested a motion of confidence following Mikulić's two-year interim evaluation (Tanjug Domestic Service, 10 May; *FBIS*, 12 May). After considerable political maneuvering, the Slovenian-Croat coalition was not able to recruit new members, and on 14 May the motion of no confidence failed by 64 to 23 in the Chamber of Republics and Provinces and by 125 to 64 in the Federal Chamber (Belgrade Domestic Service, 14 May; *FBIS*, 16 May). Although the very attempt to force the resignation of the cabinet was unprecedented in postwar Yugoslav history, the move was purely symbolic, with no alternative programs being proposed. However, even those delegates who defended the government only did so from a reluctance to introduce more chaos into the system immediately before delicate negotiations with the International Monetary Fund (IMF) (*Borba*, 16 May; *FBIS*, 2 June).

There were repeated demands for the government to resign throughout the summer and fall. On the positive side, Mikulić's government remained united despite the interrepublic squabbling that existed in the party and within other political institutions. The government also successfully completed a series of debt renegotiations and was able to guide the constitutional amendments through to passage. Nevertheless, few could defend a government that had brought about an inflation rate of about 240 percent, an unemployment rate approaching 20 percent, and a drop in the standard of living by 25 percent. Finally, in late December, the Federal Assembly refused to approve the budget, and the government chose to step down on 30 December.

Economy. Economic issues dominated government behavior during the first half of the year. In 1987, there were 1,570 strikes involving 365,000 workers, approximately double the 1986 figures (Tanjug Domestic Service, 4 January; *FBIS*, 5 January). The number of strikes in 1988 not only maintained the high levels of 1987 but became more intense and more political in the demands that were made (Tanjug Domestic Service, 2 March; *FBIS*, 3 March). Compared with 1987, when work stoppages were nearly always inspired by low personal income resulting from government economic stabilization policies (*Politika*, 14 March; *FBIS*, 18 March), the 1988 work stoppages, particularly in Serbia, Montenegro, and Macedonia, often developed into political demonstrations and were more serious in nature (Tanjug Domestic Service, 2 August; *FBIS*, 3 August). For example, in early July, some four thousand workers from a Borovo shoe factory stormed the Federal Assembly building demanding a 100 percent pay increase and changes in the government leadership. They also clashed with police and were forcibly evicted from the parliament building (*WP*, 7 July). Similar demonstrations occurred with increasing frequency throughout the year in republics throughout the country (Tanjug Domestic Service, 19 September; *FBIS*, 20 September).

Strikes by public employees, particularly teachers, also increased in intensity and frequency (Tanjug Domestic Service, 5 September; *FBIS*, 6 September). The demands became increasingly strident during the course of the year, and demonstrations in front of the Federal Assembly became commonplace. By 1 July 799 strikes had been recorded with more than 150,000 workers involved (Tanjug in English, 5 September; *FBIS*, 6 September).

Many other economic measures continued to show negative trends. Unemployment marginally increased in 1987 to 1,087,094 (*Politika*, 8 March; *FBIS*, 17 March), and it is expected that unemployment will increase dramatically as the Federal Executive Council's program of restructuring the economy takes hold (Tanjug Domestic Service, 14 July; *FBIS*, 21 July). These economic measures, which eventually led to the resignation of the prime minister and the cabinet, were designed to encourage market factors in Yugoslav economic life and to stimulate more competition, but these occurred at the expense of bankruptcies of inefficient firms.

In 1986 inflation was approximately 85 percent and nearly doubled in 1987, to 167 percent (Tanjug, in English, 11 April; *FBIS*, 11 April). In August 1988, inflation rose to an annual rate of 189 percent and concluded the year at approximately 250 percent, far above the planned rate of 95 percent (*Borba*, 22 August; *FBIS*, 24 August). Production through July dropped 1.8 percent compared with 1987, and personal income fell by 8.4 percent in the first six months of the year and by nearly 25 percent at year's end. Finally, one-sixth of all economic enterprises in the country were operating at a loss that was 132 percent greater than that for the same period in 1987 (*Politika*, 25 August; *FBIS*, 9 September).

On the positive side, Yugoslavia recorded a substantial trade surplus in 1988, compared with a trade deficit in 1987 (*Borba*, 30 April–1 May; *FBIS*, 6 May). During the first half of the year, exports were 16 percent higher than the previous year, and much of that increase was registered among the industrially developed countries (Tanjug, in English, 15 July; *FBIS*, 19 July).

At various times during the year, the Federal Executive Council (FEC) negotiated agreements with the IMF and banks to reschedule $8 billion of its $21 billion external debt. New credits granted to the Yugoslav economy during the year totaled $1.25 billion, of which $410 million was granted by the IMF, $250 million by the Bank for International Settlements, $150 million by the World Bank, and $340 million by various Western governments (Tanjug, in English, 21 September; *FBIS*, 23 September). In late October, an additional $180 million debt repayment was deferred by the Federal Republic of Germany (*Borba*, 20 October; *FBIS*, 1 November).

The pacesetting loan from the IMF entailed considerable negotiation and committed the FEC to a strong anti-inflation program and another austerity plan (*WP*, 29 May). Under the FEC-IMF agreement, nearly 40 percent of the value of industrial production remained under direct price controls (Tanjug Domestic Service, 14 July; *FBIS*, 21 July). In addition, personal income levels were strictly limited, causing considerable popular dissatisfaction and directly contributing to the waves of strikes and protest marches throughout the country (*Borba*, 12 September; *FBIS*, 14 September). As with previous plans, the austerity measures addressed only the issue of foreign debt and did little to encourage additional investment and heightened productivity.

Serbian centralization. According to the 1974 constitution, Serbia is a republic with two autonomous provinces. Both provinces were given a considerable degree of self-rule by that constitution; each has its own government ministries, judicial system, LCY organization, and representation in all government and party leadership bodies. One province (Vojvodina) is a relatively wealthy area that is primarily populated by Serbs with a substantial Hungarian minority. The other province (Kosovo) is populated largely by ethnic Albanians (85 percent) and is the most underdeveloped region in Yugoslavia. Perversely, Kosovo is also the historical and emotional center of the Serbian nation. This conflict between demographic realities and historical legacy is responsible for much of the political conflict within contemporary Yugoslavia.

In the spring of 1981, serious Albanian nationality riots broke out in Kosovo province. These outbreaks were eventually quelled by federal authorities under the direction of then Interior Minister Stane Dolanc, a Slovene and the likely choice for the federal presidency in 1989. Serbian authorities, at that time led by Marković, initially exercised considerable patience and tried to avoid the appeals for vengeance from Yugoslavia's Serbian communities. Despite serious provocations and repeated demands for retribution from Serbs in Kosovo, Serbian government and party officials through 1986 continued to defuse the situation and work through constitutional mechanisms.

In 1986, a new and younger Serbian leadership team consisting of Dragiša Pavlović (LCY head in Belgrade), Ivan Stambolić (president of the Serbian Republic), and Milošević (president of the Serbian LCY) was elected and displaced the older and more cautious Marković group. This new troika initially concentrated its attention on economic reform but found itself increasingly isolated from public support in the republic and incapable of initiating change.

By late 1987 the Serbian coalition had dissolved, and Milošević discovered that his thinly disguised appeals to Serbian nationalism and the Kosovo problem had strong public support in Serbia. Milošević used this support and the moderate stance of both Pavlović and Stambolić against his former colleagues. By the beginning of 1988, Milošević had not only eliminated his competitors but had gained control over the Politika publishing company, Serbia's most influential publisher, and the Belgrade television network. Milošević, in short, had emerged as Serbia's uncontested national leader.

After gaining control of the Serbian party, government institutions, and media organizations, Milošević imposed constitutional changes on the two provinces to restrict their autonomy and place them under direct Serbian control. These efforts were strongly resisted by the leadership in both provinces, particularly by the Vojvodinan party, which was headed by Krunić, president of the LCY.

In the waning days of Krunić's mandate, Milošević organized Serbian-Montenegrin marches throughout Serbia. Requests to conduct a similar demonstration in early July at Novi Sad, the capital of Vojvodina, were rejected by the party and government leaderships of the province, and intense public attacks from Serbia were directed against the Vojvodina leaders. In September–October, however, the demonstrations ballooned in size, frequency, and intensity. Seventy-thousand demonstrators marched in Titovo Užice, and 300,000, in Niš (Tanjug Domestic Service, 24 September; *FBIS*, 26 September). Sixty-thousand assembled in Smederevo, and another 100,000, in Kraljevo (Tanjug Domestic Service, 22 September; *FBIS*, 23 September). By 24 September it was estimated that more than 2.5 million people had participated in one or more protest meetings (Belgrade Domestic Service, 24 September; *FBIS*, 26 September).

On 6 October, a crowd estimated at 100,000 besieged the Vojvodina party headquarters in Novi Sad and successfully demanded the resignation of the provincial party and government leaderships (*NYT*, 7 October). On 7 and 8 October, violent demonstrations took place in Titograd, the capital of Montenegro; angry mobs demanded the mass resignations of the republic's government. Dizdarević, the state president, responded by addressing the nation on television, advising the Montenegrin government not to concede to mob rule, and threatening to use the army and declare martial law in Titograd (Belgrade Domestic Service, 9 October; *FBIS*, 11 October). The crowds were eventually dispersed by the police, but the entire Montenegrin government resigned three weeks later on 26 October (TASS, 26 October; *FBIS*, 26 October).

In late November, following the Milošević-induced resignations of much of Kosovo's leadership, major street demonstrations occurred involving up to 150,000 people. Strong vocal opposition to the resignations was expressed as well as condemnation of the constitutional amendments (Tanjug, 19 November; *FBIS*, 21 November). Huge counterdemonstrations were organized in Belgrade, and some Serbian officials threatened tough police action if the Kosovo demonstrations did not immediately cease (*NYT*, 24 November).

This was the first time in postwar Yugoslav history that party officials and government leaders had resigned in the face of crowd pressure. It marked the end of autonomy for the provinces and placed these Serbian provinces in Milošević's hands. With these events Serbia, if not all of Yugoslavia, has entered a distinctively new phase. The absence of a strong federal response highlights the centrifugal nature of current Yugoslav politics and government.

Slovenian pluralism. While events in Serbia moved that republic toward a more centralized state, Slovenia, Yugoslavia's most developed and prosperous republic, was moving toward a much more pluralistic and tolerant political and social environment. The Slovenian movement has also generated considerable controversy and conflict among the republics. The centrifugal forces present in Yugoslavia are made most apparent by the contrast between events in Serbia and Slovenia.

In the early part of the year, the Yugoslav armed forces (JNA) responded sharply to the attacks of *Mladina*, the Slovenian Youth Organization's weekly newspaper. It was the army's contention that the editors of *Mladina* were engaging in a series of unfounded and unscrupulous attacks on the integrity of the armed forces and that much of the content of *Mladina*'s charges were close to treasonous (*Narodna armija*, 18 February; *FBIS*, 3 March). Throughout 1987 and into the early part of 1988, *Mladina* charged that Admiral Branko Mamula, the current defense minister, was a "merchant of death" and that the ministry was corrupt. In addition, the journal questioned the efficacy of the military to resist invasion; it implied that the ministry was an institution of Serbian hegemony and argued that the military might directly and openly become involved in internal Yugoslav domestic politics. Probably *Mladina*'s greatest sin was its accusations of corruption at the highest levels of the military, particularly Admiral Mamula. Although the corruption charges were vociferously denied, little doubt remained that some of the military hierarchy may have profited from their positions in the armed forces (*Vjesnik*, 8 March; *FBIS*, 15 March) and that the integrity of the Yugoslav JNA had been tarnished.

Some issues of *Mladina* were banned by Slovenian authorities (*Borba*, 21 March; *FBIS*, 24

March), but the more typical responses of the Slovenian Socialist Alliance and much of the Slovenian party leadership were to support freedom of the press and the right of *Mladina* to publish (*Borba*, 2–3 April; *FBIS*, 8 April). In fact, repeated JNA attempts to pressure the Slovenian prosecutor to bring charges against the editorial board of *Mladina* were strenuously rejected by Slovenian civil authorities (*Politika*, 10 July; *FBIS*, 26 July).

In mid-May, *Mladina* published a sensational article allegedly based on the stenographic record of the 29 March meeting of the LCY Central Committee. The alleged transcript charged that the JNA had planned a military putsch in Slovenia to end political liberalization and that only the steadfast resistance of the Slovene party leaders prevented the coup attempt (AFP, in English, 19 May; *FBIS*, 19 May). On 31 May events took a bizarre turn. JNA officials arrested the editor of *Mladina* and two accomplices for possession of military secrets. The arrests were made without the knowledge and approval of the civilian leadership in Slovenia (Tanjug, in English, 15 June; *FBIS*, 15 June), and the arraignment and trial were conducted by a military court in secret, initially without representation of a defense attorney. The most explosive and politically inept part of the judicial proceedings was that the military judge mandated the proceedings be conducted in Serbian rather than Slovenian, which was the language of the defendants (Ljubljana Domestic Service, 20 July; *FBIS*, 21 July).

The outcry was immediate and dramatic. The civilian and party leadership of Slovenia condemned the army's behavior, the Slovene legal association supported the accused (*Borba*, 11–12 June; *FBIS*, 15 June), street demonstrations occurred in Ljubljana, and thousands of individuals and more than five hundred organizations joined a human rights committee to resist army pressure (Ljubljana Domestic Service, 7 July; *FBIS*, 8 July). Even the Slovene Assembly expressed deep concern and formally required the Slovenian government to investigate the legality of the proceedings (Belgrade Domestic Service, 29 September; *FBIS*, 30 September).

Overall, the arrests and trials have served to unite the Slovene political and party leadership with the people and to exacerbate tension between Slovenia and Serbia (*WP*, 10 June). The events are particularly worrisome because this is the first time since Rankovic's forced retirement in 1966 that the army has directly involved itself in internal political affairs and has publicly opposed the civilian,

elected leadership of a republic (RFE, 7 June). The events have served to make the Slovene leaders popular heroes, just as Milošević had become in Serbia, and to underscore the gross differences between Serbian centralism and Slovenian liberal pluralism (*Delo*, 10 September; *FBIS*, 15 September). The Yugoslav challenge in future months will be to discover a method by which both popular political cultures can work harmoniously toward a common end.

Dissent. With relatively few exceptions, dissent is tolerated in Yugoslavia and expressed in a wide variety of forums, for much of what would be characterized as dissent among Yugoslavia's communist-ruled neighbors is considered legitimate political activity in this federated nation-state. Discussions about dissent are further complicated in Yugoslavia because each republic and province defines dissension differently. For example, investigations of official corruption tend to be tolerated in Serbia and Croatia but are repressed in Macedonia and Bosnia. Opposition to Milošević's policies is considered dissent in Serbia but is tolerated in other republics. On the one hand, the political environment of Slovenia is so open that support for the central government in Belgrade would be considered dissent in that republic. On the other hand, Kosovo Albanians have virtually no freedom of expression or rights to assembly.

Yugoslav dissent has achieved new forms and widespread appeal in recent months. Numerous street demonstrations have occurred; crowds have demanded resignations of public figures and called their leaders thieves and worse. Some crowds in Serbia have demanded guns to use against the Albanians in Kosovo, and even party chief Šuvar called for the abolition of party monopoly.

Repression of dissent is extraordinarily difficult for Yugoslav authorities. With few exceptions, (i.e., national security), federal authorities have no power to suppress dissent. Censorship of publications can be conducted only by republic authorities, and the ban is valid only in the territory of the republic introducing the ban. As a result, a journalist has almost complete freedom to write about events in other republics, and citizens possess similar freedom to read and discuss these events (*Danas*, 12 January; *FBIS*, 30 March). Even Milovan Djilas, Yugoslavia's most prominent social critic, was invited to speak publicly by the youth organization at the University of Maribor in Slovenia.

The year 1988 did witness some milestones and reverses for the establishment of what some Yugoslavs refer to as the civil society. The right to strike has been officially recognized in some republics: in Slovenia and Croatia, party members were encouraged to participate in strikes when necessary (*WSJ*, 16 March). In prior years, strikes (referred to as unauthorized work stoppages) were of very short duration, and were directed against the elected management of the enterprise. As noted earlier, in 1988 the strikes were more numerous, of longer duration, and often directed against government policy. The strike, in short, has reasserted its role as a political weapon in Yugoslavia.

The most noteworthy change is that Yugoslav dissent has become a mass phenomenon. The Human Rights Protection Committee in Ljubljana, in response to events in Slovenia, achieved a membership in excess of 60,000 and full support from hundreds of organizations and societies (Ljubljana Domestic Service, 29 June; *FBIS*, 15 July). The Serbian Writers' Association called for the introduction of a multiparty system (RFE, 2 May), and nearly every newspaper has engaged in public polemics against what it perceives as the misguided policies of other papers (*Oslobodenje*, 22 July; *FBIS*, 29 July).

Not everything indicates free rein to dissent. The army crackdown on *Mladina*'s editors certainly indicates that there are limits. Periodically, newspapers and journals are banned (Tanjug, 28 January; *FBIS*, 29 January). Most discouraging of all, however, is that the courts have been very reluctant to expand individual freedom or to interpret the statutes and constitution to facilitate dissent and to protect the dissenters. In March, for example, the Constitutional Court of Yugoslavia refused to rule on whether Article 114 of the criminal code, an article that could imprison dissenters for a minimum of one year, was unconstitutional (*Borba*, 10 March; *FBIS*, 17 March).

Constitutional amendments. For the third consecutive year, Yugoslavia has been going through the ponderous process of recommending, discussing, and deliberating about a series of constitutional amendments. The process has pitted the provinces of Kosovo and Vojvodina against the republic of Serbia and virtually every republic against one another. The discussions have involved huge numbers of groups and joint statements from nearly every society, association, and enterprise unit in the country. In an effort to be conciliatory, however, the breadth of the proposals and changes were relatively narrow and will not help Yugoslavia emerge from its current economic, social, and political crises (*Duga*, 14 May; *FBIS*, 21 July).

It is not surprising that the amendments eventually surfaced with such a limited scope. Each republic used the drafting process to protect its own circumstances. Serbia, for example, pushed for a stronger chief executive (*Student*, 15 April; *FBIS*, 22 June), and Slovenia rejected fourteen proposed amendments, including demands for a stronger executive (*Borba*, 24 May; *FBIS*, 3 June). The LCY despaired over the coordination process that was necessary (Tanjug, 5 July; *FBIS*, 12 July) and abandoned much of its involvement to cope with the Milošević challenge to the party.

The absence of a pathbreaking document did not imply little controversy. Slovenia, for example, openly announced its readiness to veto the entire package if concessions were not forthcoming (*Borba*, 20–21 February; *FBIS*, 7 March), and Vojvodina's reservations about accepting the constitutional amendments in August precipitated the Serbian-inspired mass demonstrations and the eventual resignation of the Vojvodina and Kosovo party and government leaderships in October and November.

Relatively few political structural changes were introduced. The members of the Federal Chamber, one of the two houses of the Federal Assembly, would be elected, on the basis of districts, by direct and secret ballot rather than on the delegate system. The membership of the other chamber, the Chamber of Republics and Provinces, would continue to be selected by the republics and provinces. Some relatively minor budgetary procedural issues were introduced, and the JNA was guaranteed a source of income and a minimum level of financial support on the basis of the gross social product.

One fundamental area of change concerned further adaptations to a market economy and support for the private sector. Permissible private landholdings would increase from the current 10 hectares (25 acres) to 30 hectares (75 acres) (Tanjug, in English, 27 March; *FBIS*, 29 March). Neglect of employment responsibilities by workers could lead to dismissal, thereby potentially restoring some industrial discipline to the economy. The right to strike was formally recognized (Tanjug, in English, 4 August; *FBIS*, 5 August). Foreigners would be given the right to invest capital and repatriate their profits, and Yugoslav citizens could invest in stocks and bonds issued by Yugoslav firms and share in the risks and profit (*Vjesnik*, 10 August; *FBIS*, 26 August).

Considerable pressure was extended to ensure that the amendments would be adopted by 29 November (Yugoslav Republic Day). Little public enthusiasm for the constitutional process materialized, however, and the general consensus among those participating was that the amendment process had failed and that considerable political capital had been expended in the process (*Duga*, 14 May; *FBIS*, 21 July). The only noteworthy events regarding the amendment process near the end of the year were that Slovenian authorities resisted the funding provisions of the army until the very end, and mass rallies were held in Kosovo by Albanians to voice their opposition to the constitutional changes.

Auxiliary organizations. Paralleling the centrifugal tendencies of the LCY, Yugoslavia's other sociopolitical organizations have continued to draw apart from one another. SAWPY, a united front organization, illustrates most profoundly the differentiation that affects all of organized Yugoslav society. Overall, most Yugoslavs consider SAWPY to be moribund, and few consider it to be a modern, popular, progressive movement (Tanjug, 6 July; *FBIS*, 12 July). In some parts of Yugoslavia, SAWPY is strictly under the thumb of the LCY and functions only as a transmission belt agency (*Danas*, 2 February; *FBIS*, 12 April). In Serbia and Croatia, for example, SAWPY republic organizations have tended to attack the concept of social movements and have distanced themselves from the antinuclear, proenvironmental, pacifist, and human rights organizations.

In other areas, notably Slovenia, SAWPY has been extremely resourceful in reaching out and absorbing the new social movements and in providing moral encouragement and practical assistance. The Slovenian SAWPY and its leadership, for example, have been very outspoken and critical of the JNA and its conduct of the *Mladina* trials in Ljubljana. It also has been leading the fight to revise the federal criminal code to protect individual rights (Ljubljana Domestic Service, 15 July; *FBIS*, 18 July). In addition, the Slovenian SAWPY has been leading the movement to revitalize SAWPY nationally and to transform it into a truly mass movement capable of conducting internal debates and providing a constructive opposition force to the government (Tanjug, 23 May; *FBIS*, 24 May).

An interesting illustration of the Slovenian SAWPY outreach activities was the formation of a Slovene Peasant Union in May, attended by more than one thousand delegates. Among other points, the conference stated its lack of confidence in the federal government, demanded direct elections in which the union would nominate candidates, and threatened a general strike of livestock producers if meat prices were not immediately raised (*Delo*, 13 May; *FBIS*, 17 May). The Peasant Union also affiliated itself with the Slovene SAWPY. Unfortunately, the other republic and province SAWPY organizations have been reluctant or hostile to embrace the more critical social forces within their republics.

Compared with previous years, CTUY has been noncontroversial. The unions asked for and received constitutional amendments that would permit strikes, union leadership of strikes, industrial discipline, and consistent regulations regarding enterprise bankruptcies. No union actions were taken, however, to reverse the long decline in union membership or to strengthen membership identification with the unions.

The battle between the Yugoslav Socialist Youth Federation and its Slovenian affiliate continued. The federal leadership attacked the stand of *Mladina*, the Slovenian youth organization journal, for its antiarmy activities. The federal leadership was most troubled by the insistence of the Slovenian organization that Janez Jansa, one of the indicted *Mladina* editors, be accepted as a candidate for the Slovenian youth organization presidency (Belgrade Domestic Service, 15 July; *FBIS*, 18 July). The Slovenian association shocked the federation with its call for an abolition of the one-party system (*Borba*, 14 October; *FBIS*, 17 October). Following the pattern of earlier years, other republic youth organizations have allowed the Slovene affiliate to set the agenda and then gradually endorsed the Slovene body's program. The cessation of the traditional youth day celebration, youth support for the environmental movement, and acceptance of reforms in the criminal code all followed this pattern.

Foreign Policy. No major changes occurred in Yugoslav foreign policy during 1988. The two major initiatives that did occur—namely, the Balkan nations' meeting at Belgrade in February and Mikhail Gorbachev's visit to Yugoslavia in March—served to reinforce Yugoslavia's public commitment to nonalignment and did not introduce any new complicating factors in Yugoslav foreign policy processes.

The meeting of the Balkan representatives occurred in Belgrade from 24 to 26 February and included the foreign ministers of Yugoslavia, Albania, Bulgaria, Greece, Romania, and Turkey (Tanjug, in English, 23 February; *FBIS*, 23 February). Although the conference did not directly result in important new agreements, it was significant in that (1) Albania broke its self-imposed exile and participated in a regional conference for the first time and (2) this was the first time that all the countries had met at such a high level (Tanjug, in English, 28 February; *FBIS*, 29 February). The agenda was apparently quite extensive and may signal the advent of considerably more bilateral and multilateral economic and cultural cooperation (Tanjug, in English, 26 February; *FBIS*, 29 February). The very fact that this meeting occurred is an important achievement for the Yugoslav Foreign Ministry.

Gorbachev's five-day visit to Yugoslavia in March is the other event that attracted world attention. Gorbachev and his wife, Raisa, were warmly received, engaged in extemporaneous discussion with residents wherever they traveled, and spoke openly with workers in Belgrade, Dubrovnik, and Ljubljana. The most significant aspects of the visit, however, were the long-term economic cooperation agreements, Gorbachev's address to the Yugoslav Federal Assembly, and the Yugoslav-Soviet Declaration of Principles. Combined, these three events served to remove all significant obstacles to the further development of Yugoslav-Soviet bilateral ties and reassured Yugoslav officials that they would be able to deal with their internal difficulties without external interference from the USSR.

In the economic sphere, the Soviet-Yugoslav plan for economic cooperation to the year 2000 recognized the need to address the significant balance of payments deficit ($1.2 billion) that the USSR had incurred with the Yugoslavs (*Ekonomicheskaia gazeta*, 13 March; *FBIS*, 1 April). It linked Soviet raw material prices, primarily petroleum, to world levels, thereby removing a major irritation for Yugoslav officials, and it assured Yugoslavia of a market for a significant share of its equipment, machinery, and technological export capacity (*Aussenwirtschaft*, 25 May; *JPRS*, 22 July).

Gorbachev's address to the Yugoslav Federal Assembly on 16 March was well received by the delegates and represented a masterful political performance (*NYT*, 17 March). In the speech, Gorbachev assumed full responsibility for the Tito-Stalin split and apologized for it. He modestly criticized the resistance that opposes Soviet *perestroika*,

praised the efforts of the United States to reduce nuclear weaponry, supported cooperation in the Balkans, supported demilitarization of the Mediterranean, and extended full willingness to disengage from regional conflicts such as Afghanistan (*Pravda*, 17 March; *FBIS*, 17 March).

The content of the USSR-Yugoslav declaration, which was announced immediately before Gorbachev's departure, was even more significant in that it rejected the Brezhnev Doctrine and prohibited the Soviet Union from repeating invasions similar to those in Hungary during 1956 and Czechoslovakia in 1968 (*NYT*, 19 March). Particularly noteworthy is the document statement that "no one has a monopoly over the truth, the two sides declare that they have no pretensions of imposing their concepts of social development on anyone" (Tanjug, in English, 18 March; *FBIS*, 18 March). In short, the USSR publicly pledged not to meddle further in Yugoslav internal politics.

In addition to the Balkan meeting and Gorbachev's visit, the Yugoslav government maintained its usual intense pattern of international visits. Prime Minister Mikulić visited Canada in February, Hungary and the Federal Republic of Germany in April, and Japan in May. The primary purpose for these meetings was economic cooperation; trade and debt relief were the major agenda items.

The calls by the prime minister were supplemented by other high-level visits to the United Kingdom in March, Spain and the People's Republic of China in April, the United States in May, Libya and South Korea in September, and West Germany in November. Complementing these visits were official missions from a host of countries to Yugoslavia. Dignitaries from South Korea and Thailand and Indian prime minister Rajiv Gandhi visited Yugoslavia in July.

Currently, the only major international trouble spot for Yugoslavia is in its relations with Albania. Although Yugoslavia and Albania have signed a new cultural agreement and although Albania was welcomed to the Balkan foreign ministry conference, the level of tension between the two states is high (RFE, 26 February). From Tiranë's perspective, Yugoslavia is a military superpower, and from Yugoslavia's perspective, the Albanian ethnic unrest in Kosovo is encouraged and supported by Albania. Neither side can trust the other, and the mutuality of interests between them is very limited. For the time being, however, both Belgrade and Tiranë seem willing to reduce the intensity of their polemics (RFE, 12 September).

Overall, Yugoslav foreign policy developments have continued a trend that has been evident since Tito's death in 1980. Yugoslavia maintains its commitment to nonalignment but is gradually reducing its global role in the movement. In addition, the federation is becoming more involved in regional matters and is assuming a more realistic level of foreign policy activity directed toward economic stabilization and protection of its own basic interests.

Biographies *Raif Dizdarević* (62) has been president of the SFRY state presidency since May 1988. His term will end in May 1989. A Bosnian Muslim born in 1926, he joined the partisans in 1943 and at war's end was a member of the state security forces. He served in the diplomatic corps in Bulgaria, the Soviet Union, and Czechoslovakia. From 1972 to 1974, he was the assistant federal secretary for foreign affairs. During 1974–78, he was president of the Bosnian Trade Union Federation and became president of the presidency of Bosnia-Hercegovina from 1978 to 1982. He served a one-year term as president of the National Assembly from 1982 to 1983 and was the foreign minister until 1987. Dizdarević was elected to the post of vice president in late 1987. (Sources: Tanjug, in English, 15 May; *FBIS*, 16 May; RFE, 19 May.)

Stane Dolanc (63) is vice president of the state presidency (May 1988 to May 1989) and is likely to be elected to the position of president on the completion of his term of office. He was born in Slovenia in 1925 and graduated from the faculty of law in Ljubljana. Dolanc joined the partisans and the League of Communists in 1944. He was also a close associate of Tito during his later years and held numerous public offices including positions in the federal Ministry of the Interior, the state presidency, and in various federal and republic party offices. (Sources: Tanjug, in English, 15 May; *FBIS*, 16 May.)

Colonel General Veljko Kadijević (63) serves as the minister of defense. A Croat, Kadijević was born in 1925 and joined the partisans and the party in 1943. From 1981 to 1985, he served as assistant federal secretary of national defense and since 1985 as the deputy minister of defense. Kadijević has not been a vocal social critic but has built his reputation on his management skills. (Source: RFE, 19 May.)

Dr. Stipe Šuvar (52) is now serving as president of the LCY Central Committee presidium (June 1988 to June 1989). A Croat, Šuvar holds a doctorate in law and is a professor of sociology at Zagreb University. He has been active in youth and university organizations and has served as editor for the Croatian theoretical party journal *Naše teme* and the Yugoslav party journal *Socijalizam*. In the latter 1970s, he held the position of education minister in Croatia and was elected to the presidency in an unprecedented contested election in 1985. The outspoken Šuvar has published extensively on theoretical party issues and sociological concerns. (Source: *Ko je ko u Jugoslaviji*, 1970.)

Jim Seroka
Pennsylvania State University at Erie

Council for Mutual Economic Assistance

Division and Conflict on Its 40th Anniversary

The Council for Mutual Economic Assistance (CMEA), which celebrated its 40th anniversary in January 1989, is an international governmental organization. Its active members include the Soviet Union, Bulgaria, Czechoslovakia (ČSSR), the German Democratic Republic (GDR), Hungary, Poland, Romania and three non-European countries: Cuba, Mongolia, and Vietnam. Albania, although formally a member, has not participated in the CMEA since December 1966. The supreme policymaking body is the Council, convened once a year. The CMEA Executive Committee and Secretariat are responsible for day-to-day management of the organization.

Overview: Problems and Prospects. In response to the European Recovery Program, CMEA was established at a conference in Moscow on short notice and without any formal preparations. In a brief communiqué it was announced that (1) CMEA would be open to all European countries, (2) its decisions would not be binding, and (3) meetings would be held periodically in capitals of member states (Zbigniew M. Fallenbuchl, Toronto, *International Journal*, no. 1, Winter 1987–88). A formal charter was adopted at the 12th Council session in 1959, ten years after CMEA had been established.

Because of its unique features—the highly uneven distribution of power and the communist domestic system—the status of CMEA is not comparable with other international economic organizations. It is not a customs union because tariffs have no impact on the foreign trade of its members. Because of the dominance of planning as a mechanism for allocation, stimulation, and coordination of economic activity in member countries, CMEA does not qualify as a common market. Member countries have not transferred their rights of sovereignty to the CMEA so it is not a supranational organization. One author classifies CMEA as an international protection system (Vladimir Sobell, *The Red Market*, Aldershot, U.K., 1984). Indeed it is not a trade-stimulating arrangement, although the antitrade bias can be traced to domestic economic systems and not to CMEA itself.

CMEA is comparable with international governmental organizations such as the United Nations. In contrast, however, its purpose is not universal. It is focused on providing a framework for economic interaction among its member countries.

The distinctive features of CMEA as an international economic organization stem from the political and economic dominance of the Soviet Union, the great disparity in economic and technological levels among member economies, and the institutional traits of individual domestic economic systems. The USSR accounts for about 70 percent of total gross domestic product (GDP) within CMEA. Most intra-CMEA transactions in goods and services by other members are with the Soviet Union. As the USSR towers over the other members of the "socialist community," the pattern of intra-CMEA interaction is radial, that is, bilateral ties between individual members and the Soviet Union overshadow multilateral links. Moscow's hegemonic position rests on its military and economic dominance, which has been exercised inter alia through the Warsaw Treaty Organization and CMEA, both of which provide the USSR with the mechanism for fostering cohesion of the alliance.

The Soviet Union, one of the largest producers and net exporters of natural resources in the world,

has traditionally been the major supplier of energy and raw materials to other CMEA members. As a result of industrialization—characterized by a complete disregard of their endowment in natural resources and by excessive consumption of energy and raw materials (Paul Marer, "The Political Economy of Soviet Relations with Eastern Europe" in Sarah Meikeljohn Terry, ed., *Soviet Policy in Eastern Europe*, New Haven, 1984, pp. 158–60)—the East European CMEA members have become critically dependent on Soviet resources. Thus political and military dependence has been complemented by an economic one.

The parallelism of economic development is an outcome of similar institutional arrangements in communist societies and Soviet demands on its junior allies. The East European CMEA members are dependent on supplies of raw materials from the USSR and on access to the West for technology. With the latter, they are able to produce manufactured goods of better quality. This satisfies Soviet demand but is not sufficient to meet world standards. Eastern Europe thus obtains from the USSR goods that can be sold in international markets, paying for them with goods that are mostly noncompetitive in those markets. This arrangement has been increasingly criticized by Moscow.

CMEA members have had neither incentives nor opportunities to develop multilateral ties with other than the Soviet Union. The striking feature of CMEA has been the growth of integration along the lines of the radial pattern centered around the USSR and, in contrast, the dependence of smaller East European CMEA members on the West.

As can be seen in Table 1, the shares of trade of smaller East European countries with one another significantly decreased between 1971 and 1985. The average (unweighted) share of their mutual imports, for example, fell from 46 percent in 1971–75 to 38 percent in 1981–85, whereas imports from the Soviet Union increased from 54 to 62 percent. The share of noncommunist trade partners in their total exports increased in the same period from 33 to 38 percent. This significant shift in trade patterns was triggered to some extent by an improvement in terms of trade for energy and raw materials vis-à-vis manufactures in intra-CMEA trade.

The Soviet trade share of non-European CMEA members increased even though Cuba and Mongolia increased their deliveries of raw materials to the Eastern European countries (Horst Brzezinski, "Economic Relations Between European and the

Table 1: Soviet Union and Noncommunist Shares in Intra-CMEA Trade
of East European CMEA Members
(five-year averages in percentages of total trade)

		To/FROM THE USSR			To/FROM NONCOMMUNIST STATES		
		1971–75	*1976–80*	*1981–85*	*1971–75*	*1976–80*	*1981–85*
Bulgaria	Exports	71	72	74	21	24	27
	Imports	68	74	78	25	20	22
ČSSR	Exports	49	52	60	30	28	26
	Imports	49	52	61	31	29	23
GDR	Exports	52	51	58	27	27	35
	Imports	54	56	63	35	34	33
Hungary	Exports	54	55	62	30	41	44
	Imports	54	55	60	37	48	47
Poland	Exports	57	58	60	40	41	44
	Imports	54	59	64	49	47	39
Romania	Exports	51	47	49	51	54	55
	Imports	47	45	48	54	58	50

SOURCE: Author's calculations from German Institute for Economic Research data in European Parliament *Working Documents* A 2-187/86.

Less-Developed CMEA Countries," in *East European Economies: Slow Growth in the 1980s*, vol. 2, Washington, D.C., 1986, pp. 302–28). Trade turnover with the CMEA economies also accounts for a significantly larger portion of their trade, ranging in the 1980s between around 70 percent (Cuba) and 97 percent (Mongolia).

The second general factor is the developmental gap between technological and economic levels of the European and the non-European CMEA members that reflect the north-south division in the international political economy. No economic grouping in the world is characterized by such disparities, and the objective of CMEA (Article 1 of its charter) is the gradual evening out of development levels in all participating countries. At the Forty-fourth CMEA Council session (Prague, 1988), the delegate from Vietnam called for "making conditions and the level of development even for all members" (Dragan Vukevic, Belgrade, *Borba*, 12 July; *FBIS-Eastern Europe* [*EEU*], 19 July). Because of the absence of reliable estimates for per capita gross national product (GNP) in the non-European member countries, it would be difficult to assess to what degree this objective is being met.

Judging by the fact that there has been little progress in evening out the level of East European economies, it is inconceivable that the gap was reduced between them and Cuba or Vietnam. As can be seen from Table 2, the dispersion as measured by the ratio of standard deviation to average per capita GNP of East European CMEA members dropped between 1970 and 1980 and only in 1987 returned to its 1970 level. Because there are no GNP estimates for non-European CMEA countries based on the same methodology used for data in Table 1, no similar calculations could be made for CMEA as a whole.

CMEA membership, however, introduces potential areas for conflict similar to those between north and south in other international fora. Non-Europeans are encouraged to specialize in subtropical products and raw materials; for instance, bilateral agreements signed with Cuba in 1988 promise CMEA assistance in developing the engineering industry and consumer goods production in exchange for sugar, citrus fruits, and nickel. Similar arrangements exist between other CMEA countries and Vietnam. Eastern Europe has been recently under considerable pressure from Moscow to pick up part of the Soviet burden. This makes little sense from Eastern Europe's viewpoint and therefore contributes to tensions within CMEA (Vukevic, *Borba*, 12 July).

The third factor that makes CMEA unique is the absence of market mechanisms. The economic system of command planning that emerged in the Soviet Union in the 1930s and was adopted by other

Table 2: Per Capita GNP in East European Member States in 1970, 1980, and 1987 (constant 1987 dollars)

	1970	1980	1987	1987*
Bulgaria	$5,272	$ 6,669	$ 7,222	137
ČSSR	7,306	8,985	9,715	133
GDR	7,636	10,346	11,860	155
Hungary	6,112	7,668	8,260	135
Poland	5,444	7,056	6,890	127
Romania	3,587	5,490	6,358	177
Average	5,893	7,702	8,384	143
Standard deviation	1,353	1,581	1,895	
Ratio of standard deviation to the average	.23	.20	.23	

* (1970 = 100)

SOURCE: Author's calculations from data in I. W. International Financial Research Inc., *Economic Growth in Eastern Europe, 1970 and 1975–1987*, New York, 1988.

communist-ruled countries is devoid of contractual relationships, interdependencies between buyers and sellers, and autonomous economic agents responding to price signals. This system continues today, with some modifications, and follows a different logic than the market system. Its logic is politics—the primacy of political considerations over those of economic efficiency. Rather than autonomous activities geared to finding the most efficient ways to produce goods and services, as is the case in the market economies, its modus operandi is state control. Therefore in contrast to societies where interaction of state and market pushes toward international integration, the politically dominated communist system confines economic activity to its national boundaries.

The logic of this economic system, which is based on administrative directives, has been extended to relations among communist countries. As the Soviet economist R. Grinberg has noted, "the administration-by-edict system of economic management that has grown up in each of the socialist countries has been accurately reproduced in relations within CMEA too" (*Izvestiia*, FBIS-Soviet Union [*SOV*], 16 January). However, this reproduction has never been completed, as there is no supranational planner. The decisions concerning intra-CMEA relations are thus an outcome of bargaining among its governments. Bargaining, a dominant mechanism of allocation, is constrained by the primacy of security interests and the use of world market prices in intra-CMEA transactions. It is also critically dependent on the Soviet ability to suppress the national interests of smaller CMEA members.

That the communist economic system is devoid of market competition has profoundly affected the organization of inter-CMEA relationships. From the point of view of external economic interaction, the system displays a strong bias in favor of autarky. Uninformed planners cannot identify areas in which they have comparative advantage. Domestic producers insulated from both foreign and domestic consumers have no incentive to look actively for marketing opportunities. The absence of financial and commodity convertibility in turn fosters a propensity to structural bilateralism in intra-CMEA relations, to borrow an apt phrase from Jozef van Brabant (*Bilateralism and Structural Bilateralism in Intra-CMEA Trade*, Rotterdam, 1973).

Structural bilateralism is the result of the state's foreign trade monopoly or, more generally, restricting public economic policy instruments in both the national and the CMEA arena to administrative tools. As a result, there are few effective mechanisms to encourage specialization and active participation in the international economy because specialization within CMEA would entail unbalanced trade flows, which would be against the economic interests of the trading partners. Credits and other financial devices using the transferable ruble cannot provide this kind of incentive. Iurii Shiriaev, director of the CMEA International Institute of Economic Problems of the World Socialist System, succinctly noted, "A guiding principle in such cases [bilateral cooperation agreements] was not effectiveness [efficiency], but the formal need to balance mutual deliveries. A feeble link-up between the value sides of cooperation curtailed the possibilities of taking advantage of international [CMEA] credits." (Moscow, *Social Sciences*, no. 3.)

Under those institutional constraints, there is little incentive to open the economies. It is quite telling, for example, that the volume of intra-CMEA exports increased about 20 percent between 1980 and 1986, whereas total exports of highly developed Western economies increased by more than 30 percent in the same period (*Życie gospodarcze*, Warsaw, no. 35).

The extremely low mobility of factors of production should stimulate larger trade flows than occurs in economies characterized by relatively unfettered movements of capital and labor. Except for unplanned trade deficits, which have to be financed ex post facto and credit transactions limited to some jointly undertaken projects, there is little capital flow. With the exception of joint investment programs, labor is highly immobile within CMEA. This low mobility of capital and labor has not been conducive to increased intra-CMEA trade. (Paul Marer and John M. Montias, "CMEA Integration: Theory and Practice," in *East European Economic Assessment*, part 2, *Regional Assessments*, Washington, D.C., 1981, p. 168.) In the end, trade intensity of the CMEA economies is well below the levels of market economies at a similar per capita GNP. Thus even the low mobility of factors of production does not compensate for the antitrade bias of CPEs.

Without the introduction of convertibility of national currencies and a market mechanism in domestic economic systems, this antitrade bias cannot be overcome unless national sovereign rights over all areas of economic policy are transferred to a supranational planning authority. Except for Nikita Khrushchev's ill-fated attempt, the Soviet Union has not sought to subjugate its client states to a single, all-encompassing plan but has apparently sought to strike a balance between the region's viability and the capacity to control its "junior allies." Economic interaction tends to be organized on a government level, with each state retaining considerable discretion over the areas in which it wants to cooperate with other member countries. But one may argue that, in the areas directly affecting Soviet security interests, this discretion has been significantly curtailed.

The alternative to supranational planning would be organizing intra-CMEA interaction on a market basis, that is, with a price mechanism and convertibility of national currencies. In this vein, the pro-reform shift in Moscow has also affected CMEA. Mikhail Gorbachev's assessment that central planning is accountable for a "precrisis situation" apparently applies not only to the Soviet Union but also to CMEA (*Pravda*, 26 June 1987). The last four years have witnessed a spate of public policy declarations from CMEA sessions that promise an overhaul of the administrative mechanism of cooperation and efforts toward the gradual introduction of conditions for the unfettered movement of production factors, goods, and commodities among member countries. It remains to be seen whether this goal will be vigorously pursued. What is clear, however, is that CMEA on its 40th anniversary faces major

restructuring if it is to serve Soviet interests by putting planned economies on the path of efficient economic development.

Because USSR interests have been the major driving force behind the evolution of the "socialist economic community," without major restructuring in the Soviet Union, economic and political rules of the intra-CMEA order will remain unchanged. As Hungarian prime minister Miklós Németh put it, "In the European Economic Community there is no one country with outstanding economic potential like the Soviet Union in the CMEA. So in our integration the Soviet Union has a determining role, and without the progress of the Soviet reform one cannot imagine a radical reform in CMEA." (*Népszabadság*, 8 July; *JPRS-Eastern Europe Report* [*EER*], 10 August.)

Institutional Framework and Scope of Activity. The communiqué from the founding meeting of the CMEA, which was held in Moscow in 1949, indicated that the following countries participated: the Soviet Union, Bulgaria, Czechoslovakia, Hungary, Poland, and Romania. It also contained the provision that all other European countries were invited to join (Fallenbuchl, *International Journal*, no. 1). This provision was removed at the 16th CMEA session held in Moscow during mid-1962.

As of January 1989, there were eleven full members of CMEA. Albania joined in 1949 but, since the announcement by the Albanian delegation at the fifteenth session of the Council in Warsaw (December 1961), has not participated in CMEA activity or paid its dues (Richard F. Staar, *Communist Regimes in Eastern Europe*, 5th rev. ed., Stanford, Calif., 1988, p. 292). The newly established GDR joined the organization in 1950 and Mongolia, in 1962. During the 1970s, two communist-ruled Third World countries became full members of CMEA: Cuba (1972) and the Socialist Republic of Vietnam (1978). Despite the strong support of the GDR, the application of Mozambique was rejected in 1981. Probably because the economic cost has exceeded political and military benefits to the Soviet Union, other allies in the Third World were discouraged from applying for full membership. Contrary to the expectations of some analysts in the 1970s, Laos, Afghanistan, and Cambodia were not incorporated as full members to CMEA.

The organizing principle underlying membership in the organization is that of "interested party," that is, members retain full discretion over their participation in CMEA programs. Full membership, however, is not the only affiliation status envisaged by the CMEA charter. The other forms include limited participant status, cooperant status, and observer status. The only country that has limited membership status is Yugoslavia; the agreement was signed in 1965 at the Nineteenth Council session in Prague. Yugoslavia participates in several programs of the CMEA, and its representatives attend meetings of the policymaking CMEA Council.

Three countries—Finland (1973), Mexico (1975), and Iraq (1976)—ratified cooperant status agreements with CMEA. These countries do not have centrally planned economies and are not empowered to conclude foreign trade agreements on behalf of private corporations. For this reason, their involvement in CMEA activity consists of sending mixed government-business delegations to explore business opportunities. They may sign "directional" agreements with various bodies of the CMEA, but their implementation is not binding. These countries do not participate in Council meetings.

Another designation for interaction with the CMEA is observer status. Since 1978 the observer status group has included the following nine countries: Afghanistan, Angola, Cambodia, Ethiopia, Laos, Mozambique, Nicaragua, North Korea, and South Yemen. Apparently not all of them have retained this status. Among the observers of the Forty-fourth Council session held in Prague (July 1988), there were no representatives from either Cambodia or North Korea; all the others sent official delegations. The status of Afghanistan is not clear, but the signing of the protocol of the CMEA Commission on cooperation with Afghanistan in Kabul on 2 April (TASS, *FBIS-SOV*, 5 April) may indicate its upgrading to a cooperant status. According to this agreement, "concrete objects and fields of cooperation between the CMEA and Afghanistan were defined" (ibid.).

Granting status within CMEA tends to reflect the relations between a country's government and the Soviet Union. The People's Republic of China, for example, held observer status at one time. Others like Guyana, Chile under Salvador Allende, and Egypt were said to have been considering obtaining this status (Marer and Montias, "CMEA Integration," p. 150). Because CMEA is not a supranational organ, a special status governing the affiliation of a country with CMEA is secondary to its already established political or economic links with the Soviet Union.

The institutional framework of CMEA is not a carbon copy of command planning hierarchies characteristic of the Soviet Union and most other CMEA members, although it has many of the same traits. In the absence of markets and autonomous activity to establish links across borders, interdependence can only be promoted and coordinated by explicit action of the states involved. As a result, there is a myriad of functional and branch organs within a centrally administered framework.

Chart 1 shows the organizational structure of CMEA. The session of the Council, the supreme policymaking body, has been convened over the past two decades at least once a year. CMEA members are represented by prime ministers or party first secretaries. The resolutions of the Council are reviewed by members. If approved, they serve as a framework for bilateral or multilateral negotiations. The agreements set the stage for implementation, monitored and supervised by appropriate permanent commissions or committees. Given the "self-interested" party provision, the CMEA is structured in such a way as to provide a framework and facilities for bilateral negotiations.

In addition to the organizations on the chart, there are a host of various institutionalized activities such as conferences of nongovernmental organizations with some ties to CMEA; the seven annual CMEA conferences to consult on trade, patents, and so forth, which reportedly were abolished in 1988; and various intragovernmental ad hoc groups. According to one estimate, about one hundred thousand people were involved in CMEA and CMEA-related activities during the 1970s (Marer and Montias, "CMEA Integration," p. 151).

The Executive Committee, Secretariat, committees, permanent commissions, and functional organizations form the core of CMEA planning and negotiating machinery. The Executive Committee, whose members are permanent representatives with the rank of deputy prime minister, is in charge of cooperation within CMEA. The Moscow-based Secretariat meets four times a year and supervises and is responsible for the implementation of the Council's recommendations. It also provides policy input for Council sessions.

Council committees, the organizational innovation of the 1971 Integration Program, are designed to promote coordination of research and development effort and to develop productive structures in member countries through establishing organizational facilities for joint planning. There are now six

Chart 1: CMEA Organization, 1988

Member States

Council (1949)

Council Committees

Executive Committee (1962)

Secretariat
(departments)
1. Planning—1971
2. Science and Technology—1972
3. Foreign Economic Relations—1988
4. Agro-Industrial Complex—1988
5. Engineering—1985
6. Electronics—1988
7. Fuels and Materials—1988

Permanent Commissions	Functional Organizations	International Economic Associations	Bilateral Intergovernmental Commissions
1. Metallurgy (Moscow), 1956	1. International Bank for Economic Cooperation (Moscow), 1964		
2. Chemical Industry (Berlin), 1956	2. International Investment Bank (Moscow), 1971		
3. Transportation and Civil Aviation (Moscow), 1988	3. Institute for Standardization (Moscow), 1962		
4. Light Industry (Prague), 1963	4. Institute for Economic Problems (Moscow), 1972		
5. Telecommunications and Posts (Moscow), 1971	5. Administration of Electric Power System (Prague), 1964		
6. Environmental Protection	6. Freight Bureau (Moscow), 1963		
7. Electrical and Atomic Energy (Moscow), 1988	7. Railroad Car Pool (Prague), 1964		
8. Statistics, 1988			
9. Currency and Finance, 1988			
10. Legal Affairs, 1988			
11. Standardization, 1988			

SOURCES: Staar, *Communist Regimes*, p. 301; Sobell, *Red Market*, p. 19; *RAD Background Report* no. 37; RFE, RL, Munich; *FBIS-SOV*; *Hospodářské noviny*, no. 106 (1988), Prague.

committees, four of which were established during the 1980s.

Permanent commissions are the regional equivalent of branch ministries in member countries, although some of them are in charge of functional issue areas such as environmental protection and public health. Although they are responsible for creating international economic associations, they are not empowered to make decisions binding on all CMEA members unless a country becomes a member of a CMEA international economic association. INTERMETAL, the CMEA equivalent of the West

European Coal and Steel Community, for example, can pass resolutions binding on all members (Staar, *Communist Regimes*, p. 298). Because the international economic organizations are subject to the national jurisdiction of the country in which their headquarters are located, they are not part of the CMEA institutional structure. However, they do have a close relationship with permanent commissions.

The scope of activities of the functional organizations is indicated by their names. Two CMEA banks deserve a short comment, however. The International Bank for Economic Cooperation (IBEC)

performs bookkeeping operations associated with transactions among members. It also grants trade credits and is empowered to deal with external financial institutions. The International Investment Bank (IIB) helps finance investment in member countries as well as in joint CMEA projects. Credits are mainly in transferable rubles. Thanks to IIB's borrowing in the international capital markets, some loans are in convertible currencies. Beginning in 1988, the IIB has become involved in financing microintegration, that is, joint ventures and direct production contracts among enterprises (TASS; *FBIS-SOV*).

The institutional structure of CMEA has evolved considerably since the 1950s, its evolution mirroring the changing priorities and areas targeted for regional coordination. Until the adoption of the Comprehensive Program in 1971, the CMEA bureaucratic apparatus had been enlarged by adding new organizational bodies that were to foster coordination along branch lines.

With the adoption of the Integration Program, however, the thrust of organizational activity in the 1970s shifted to functional issue areas, which meant that the functional issues of integration received higher recognition within CMEA. Three Council committees charged to perform key line functions were established: the Committee on Cooperation in Planning, the Committee on Scientific Technological Cooperation, and in 1974 the Committee on Cooperation in Material and Technical Supply. The first two still exist; the third was reportedly closed in 1987–88 (*RAD Background Report*, no. 37; RFE, RL, Munich, 8 March).

Committees empowered with wider responsibility replaced either some of the then existing permanent commissions or bureaus. For example, the Permanent Commission on Research and Development was transformed into the Committee on Cooperation in Research and Technology, whereas the Bureau of the Executive Committee was upgraded to the Committee on Cooperation in Planning. Its members were the chairmen of the respective national planning commissions, thus introducing an extra link between the Executive Committee and the national economic decisionmaking process. This enhanced the notion of a single super plan for the CMEA yet "fell well short of being a supranational planning agency," as Sobell observed (*Red Market*, p. 17). Member governments were apparently unwilling to transfer their decisionmaking authority to the CMEA.

Neither the organizational reform that followed the adoption of the Comprehensive Program for Integration nor the proliferation of various intragovernmental commissions and bilateral cooperation agreements led to increased coordination of development plans or contributed in any measurable way to production specialization and multilateral trade. At Soviet insistence, the view that the integration mechanism was basically flawed became accepted among policymakers of most CMEA countries. Németh, secretary of the Hungarian communist party, in an interview with the Soviet weekly *Ekonomicheskaia gazeta* (no. 6), gave the following assessment:

> We feel that the stabilizing influence of CMEA countries' cooperation has declined over the last decade. In their mutual ties, most countries strove not to increase exports but to solve the balance problems on the basis of additional imports. Nor has there been a proper solution to questions of the development, production, and reciprocal deliveries of the latest equipment and technology needed to reduce energy and materials intensiveness and to improve the structure of production in general. (*FBIS-SOV*, 18 February.)

The assessment that CMEA is in need of repair prompted convening the Forty-third Extraordinary Session of the Council in mid-October 1987 at Moscow. The session called for "restructuring" the mechanism of public economic policy coordination and for specializing and cooperating in production. It made decisions to foster direct ties among enterprises and research institutions from different countries. It also promised an increased effort to change the financial arrangements underpinning intra-CMEA trade and specialization. To facilitate these goals, the organizational framework was to be significantly changed.

It is not clear what the organizational changes will be. Greater reliance on mechanisms of market provenance should reduce the administrative burden of CMEA organs so they can become more involved in setting legislative and financial frameworks for cooperation among country members. Interviews and various documents issued by CMEA indicate that this is indeed the direction that CMEA "reformers" strive to take. Viacheslav Sychev, CMEA secretary, declared that the Executive Committee "has decided to delegate decisionmaking on all practical matters of economic interaction to their national managerial bodies in various sectors, first of all their economic organizations which cooperate either directly or through joint ventures." (TASS,

FBIS-SOV, 4 February.) The success of reducing the bureaucratic load of CMEA hinges on a genuine reform of the financial system underlying intra-CMEA interaction, that is, on supplementing the administrative mechanism with the market mechanism.

The year 1988 witnessed fierce reorganizational activity. The "branch structure" as represented by permanent commissions was streamlined. Their number fell from 24 in 1987 to 13 by the end of 1988. Some of them were abolished altogether, and others were merged; some of their functions were assumed by new committees. However, full information is not available as to their current status. The communiqués on funding new CMEA organs do not give details as to which permanent commissions have been affected by the reorganization. Two new permanent commissions were established: one for cooperation in environmental protection and the other on cooperation in electricity and nuclear power. The latter was the result of a merger of two commissions dealing with these matters (Sobell, Munich, RFE, RL, 8 March). The resolution of the forty-fourth session also called for the fusion of the CMEA permanent commissions for the oil, gas, and coal industries and for geology. It is not clear whether they merged in 1988.

As part of the reorganization, two new committees were established: a committee on cooperation in foreign economic relations and a committee on cooperation in the sphere of agro-industrial complexes. The former is to supervise "work on perfecting price formation, contractual standards and general terms of reciprocal trade." (TASS, *FBIS-SOV*, 15 February.) The latter's main function includes "coordinating economic and scientific and technical policy . . . on the most important problems of scientific and technical progress in the agro-industrial complex for the entire cycle from scientific research work to the production and sale of output" (*Sel'skaia zhizn*, *FBIS-SOV*, 21 January). In Prague on 21 September the committee convened a meeting during which decisions were reached to establish a new system of scientific information—the so-called Agroproinform for agriculture, forestry, and the food industry.

Streamlining also affected the CMEA Secretariat. At its one-hundred and twenty-sixth session in February in Moscow, the Executive Committee approved measures for reorganizing the Council Secretariat. According to the final communiqué, "the Secretariat activity is to focus on the ongoing analysis of the state of cooperation, the preparation of economic analyses, and forecasts" (*Pravda*, 8 February). Other documents also emphasized that the Secretariat would pay more attention to "the fulfillment of adopted resolutions." Some departments were to be enlarged, in particular those responsible for intersectoral matters, and "new departments, for example the fuel and power and metallurgy ones, will be formed," said Sychev, secretary of the CMEA, in an interview with Soviet journalists (TASS, 4 February; *FBIS-SOV*, 5 February).

Some of these organizational measures had already been implemented. The CMEA Executive Committee's report that was submitted to the forty-fourth session in Prague in July informed the participants that the CMEA apparatus was "organizationally simplified and that the number of tenured positions for employees of the CMEA Secretariat was reduced by almost one-third" (*Rudé právo*, 6 July; *FBIS-EEU*, 15 July).

The institutional changes introduced over the last two years were designed to improve information flows, to make the CMEA organs more active in encouraging cooperation, and to monitor the actual implementation of the resolutions adopted by the sessions. Thus far they have fallen short of introducing the machinery that would assure the implementation of the "better thought out" recommendations, and any progress in streamlining and reducing the CMEA bureaucracy may be illusory. If Romanian prime minister Constantin Dăscălescu is right in claiming that there is a tendency "of some ministries and central bodies in our countries to replace the dissolved CMEA bodies by new organizational forms outside the council, which should actually examine the same problems that were examined by the former bodies" (*Scînteia*, 8 July; *FBIS-EEU*, 14 July), then one bureaucracy is being replaced by the other.

The CMEA institutional framework, although designed to extend domestic planning activity to a regional level, does not delegate the authority to execute plans directly to CMEA. Most interaction is subject to bilateral controls by the respective national planning bodies, whereas calls for multilateral cooperation and coordination are subject to the CMEA institutions. The introduced changes may improve the organization's ability to track new opportunities but can do little to create sustained interest among economic actors in cooperation. Thus they will be another source of frustration to those keen on "socialist integration" unless they are assisted by measures enabling integration at the level of firms.

Policy Instruments, Areas of Integration, and "Restructuring."

According to its charter, CMEA is charged with coordinating efforts designed to promote socialist economic integration, stimulating economic and technological progress, and gradually evening out the level of economic development of the CMEA country members (*Osnownie dokumenty Soveta Ekonomicheskoi Vzaimopomoschchi*, vol. 1, Moscow, 1981, pp. 10–11). Because of the absence of supranationality and the limitations inherent in the administrative mechanism of coordinating and stimulating economic activity, the organization faces several obstacles in the pursuit of these objectives. It has to seek consensus of its members or limit its efforts to the "interested" member countries. The implementation of the adopted agreements is not a "grass-roots" spontaneous process in response to economic stimuli, as is the case in the West, but requires an explicit *administrative* action by the state.

The institutional devices and public economic policy instruments that have evolved over the past 40 years represent attempts to overcome the difficulties involved in the economic opening of centrally planned systems. It is scarcely surprising that the tools used to achieve CMEA's declared objectives belong to the realm of administrative planning and management. The mechanisms and tools used to promote integration include preplan frameworks or programs, five-year trade agreements, joint investment projects, target plans, cooperation and specialization agreements, joint ventures, and five-year plan coordination. In view of the ongoing reassessment of the economic role of Eastern Europe by the Soviet Union, all these tools have been carefully scrutinized by the CMEA organs since 1985.

Historically, one of the first instruments was exchange of information between chairmen of planning agencies and other party and government officials on the content of five-year plans. Its purpose was to reduce parallelism in capital projects because industrial development strategies remained highly similar in the CMEA economies. However, because it is impossible to demonstrate that developmental strategies would produce even more parallelism without this type of coordination than has been actually observed, the effectiveness of this instrument is difficult to assess. As was pointed out earlier, the institutional body in charge of coordination—the CMEA Committee for Cooperation in

Planning, founded in 1971—does not have supranational authority.

Another mechanism is direct ties among firms and joint ventures. Although the first enterprise jointly owned by member countries' firms was established in 1959 (Marer and Montias, "CMEA Integration," p. 151), joint ventures remained rare until recently. Promotion of direct ties and joint ventures as a form of cooperation has been a hallmark of Soviet policy toward the CMEA since Mikhail Gorbachev was appointed general secretary. In 1986–88, those microties were established mainly between the Soviet Union and other countries, thus reproducing a radial pattern characteristic of the CMEA. In 1987 for instance, 116 Hungarian and Soviet enterprises established direct ties and 19 joint enterprises and two associations were set up (*Ekonomicheskaia gazeta*, no. 6; *FBIS-SOV*, February). According to former Polish prime minister Zbigniew Messner, "more than 200 production enterprises, 190 trade organizations, and 100 R&D organizations established direct links with the Soviet partners" (Warsaw, *Rzeczpospolita*, 6 July). Coal and energy enterprises from the GDR concluded agreements with twelve Soviet enterprises in 1987–88 (East Berlin, *Presse-Informationen*, 6 May; *JPRS-EER*, 15 July).

The effectiveness of this instrument, which removes direct control of a CMEA member government over some areas of an enterprise activity, hinges on the compatibility between bilateral arrangements and the domestic system of the appraisal of enterprise performance. Because in most CMEA countries bonuses and rewards are somehow linked to an enterprise's financial performance, the problem of convertibility hinders cooperation. A partial solution is the use of domestic currencies. Recently, several CMEA countries (Bulgaria, Czechoslovakia, Hungary, and the Soviet Union) either signed or negotiated bilateral agreements to settle accounts in their respective domestic currencies.

Although agreements on specialization date back to the early 1950s, a major step to make them a leading tool of integration began after the adoption of the 1971 Complex Program. Having carefully examined empirical data on specialization agreements, authors from The Rand Corporation concluded that they have neither increased multilateralization of economic ties nor improved technological innovativeness (Keith Crane and Deborah Skoller, *Specialization Agreements in the Council for Mutual Economic Assistance*, Santa Monica,

Calif., 1988, pp. 59–60). In spite of these short-comings, specialization agreements are a part of CMEA interaction.

Long-term target plans designed for selected sectors of the economy have been developed in an attempt to integrate the perspective plans of the member countries on a sectoral basis. In one respect, they are similar to the comprehensive programs in that they provide a framework for bilateral and multilateral agreements on trade within these sectors, joint projects, and specialization and cooperation in production, science and technology, and other areas.

In the 1970s joint investment projects were the core of integration efforts to develop supplies of important industrial raw materials. The largest undertaking so far has been the Orenburg project (constructing a natural gas complex in Orenburg and a 1,700-mile gas pipeline to the Soviet western border). Its total cost (about $6 billion) absorbed about half the expenditures on joint projects in 1976–80 (Marer, "Political Economy of Soviet Relations with Eastern Europe," p. 163). The second largest undertaking was a pulp mill at Ust Ilim. Those two projects were jointly planned and built by the participating countries. The project belongs to the country in which it is located, and in exchange for secured supplies at negotiated prices, the participants provide investment goods, labor, and hard currency. Joint projects are often financed through the IIB. No undertakings on the scale of the Orenburg projects were carried out in the 1980s.

Major programs set the basic long-term priorities that CMEA members are to incorporate in their developmental plans and specify the basic rules and procedures to be established in their interaction. In CMEA there were two such programs; the third one is to be completed in 1989. The first, the Comprehensive Program for the Further Extension and Improvement of Cooperation and the Development of Socialist Economic Integration by CMEA Member Countries (hereafter CP) was adopted at the Twenty-fifth Council session in Bucharest in July 1971. Although the document referred to the "improvement of commodity money relations," its thrust was on cooperation in planning in selected spheres of the economy. It laid the framework for joint resource development projects, mainly in the Soviet Union with the participation of interested countries.

The second program was the Comprehensive Program for CMEA Country Members' Scientific and Technical Progress Through the Year 2000 (hereafter STP). STP was adopted in December 1985 at the Forty-first Council session in Moscow. Its preparations started in early 1984 in response to external developments like the launching of the Strategic Defense Initiative (SDI) and Eureka programs in the United States and the European Community (EC) and the sanctions imposed on the Soviet Union in the aftermath of the imposition of martial law in Poland. The basic priorities of STP are similar to those of the Eureka program. STP focuses on five major areas, which when developed will make CMEA a technological community. These areas, ranked according to their priority in the program, include

1. Computerization and "electronization" of the economy
2. Increased automation of production processes
3. Acceleration in the development of nuclear energy
4. Development of new materials and technologies for their production
5. Biotechnology

STP was conceived of as a vehicle that would assist the CMEA economies in the transition from extensive and intensive patterns of economic growth and that would assist the Soviet Union in its goal of changing the composition of its exports to the CMEA economies by increasing the share of manufactures at the expense of oil prices, which have been declining. The program—initially consisting of 93 (later expanded to 94) projects in which all full members and Yugoslavia were to participate—had two special features. First, it directly addressed a well-known shortcoming of a centrally planned economic system—the structural inability to convert research and technical knowledge into efficient technologies and new products. The program called for the development of agreements that would "encompass all stages of the process—science, technology, production marketing." (Sofia, *Robotnichesko delo*, 8 March; *FBIS-SOV*, 7 March.)

Second, its implementation called for microintegration, that is, the establishment of direct across-the-border links between research institutions and enterprises. Projects were supervised and coordinated by so-called head organizations, usually research institutions with no links with the industrial sector.

The realization of STP has run into a problem

familiar to bureaucratically managed economic activities. STP's complexity has clearly exceeded the management capacity of the CMEA organs and led to the establishment of networks of tremendous complexity. By the end of 1987, 285 cooperation agreements and 900 contracts for specific research projects had been signed by ten participating countries (*Rudé právo*, *FBIS-EEU*, 6 May), and about 1,500 organizations were involved in their implementation (ibid.). Given this complexity, it is not surprising that most contracts were either not completed or fell behind schedule. In addition, the products that were eventually developed were below international technical standards.

The coordination problem that creates often insurmountable difficulties for a single national planning board has been magnified by the necessity to control all stages of technology or product development processes under different national jurisdictions. As a Czech official noted, it was "virtually impossible to coordinate the program from the center to the minutest detail." (*Rudé právo*, 6 May.)

Even assigning priority to the STP projects "in the plans of individual countries so that these projects receive 'most-favored treatment' in the mechanism of CMEA cooperation," as a Soviet official argued (Nikolai Sliunkov, CPSU Politburo member, Budapest, *Népszabadság*, 4 June; *FBIS-EEU*, 24 June), would not prevent the STP from faltering. The program was too broad (*Planovane hospodartvi*, no. 2), and therefore preferential treatment would water down to "most-favored treatment," which would not bode well for its implementation. In addition, the absence of convertibility and procedures for pricing research and development would undermine the program and give preference to bilateral rather than multilateral cooperation (which actually happened). (Ibid.)

The problems with STP were acknowledged in the official documents of the CMEA Council sessions in Moscow (1987) and in Prague (1988) as well as in the CMEA Executive Committee. In its report to the participants of the forty-fourth session in Prague (June 1988), the CMEA Executive Committee frankly admitted that "thus far, we have not succeeded in overcoming the serious difficulties which have for a long time accompanied cooperation in production...based on the outputs of the Comprehensive Program for Scientific Technical Progress and agreements on direct relations" (*Rudé právo*, 6 July; *FBIS-EEU*, 15 July).

To cope with these shortcomings, several solutions were suggested including (1) pooling the research and development resources of the member countries, (2) establishing large international institutions staffed on a competitive basis and endowed with up-to-date scientific equipment (*Rudé právo*, 14 June; *FBIS-EEU*, 16 June), and (3) the selection of head organizations on the basis of competitive bidding.

The winds of reform blowing from Moscow and growing frustration with the STP's implementation triggered a thorough examination of the factors accountable for the problems of organizing interaction among the CMEA members. The Forty-third CMEA Council session obliged the Secretariat to develop a new approach to socialist integration. A comprehensive program, which became known as the Collective Concept of International Socialist Division of Labor in the Years 1991–2005 (hereafter DL), was submitted and adopted at the forty-fourth session. In contrast to the previous two programs, DL included not only general statements calling for intrabranch specialization and new forms of cooperation but also "proposals for dividing into stages the restructuring of the mechanism of multilateral cooperation and the integration of socialist economy."

DL seeks to extend the ties among CMEA members beyond government ones. It identifies three levels of cooperation: (1) the government level where a framework for public economic and scientific-technological policies is set, (2) the intermediate level between representatives of the leading sectors, and (3) an enterprise level. Although the first and, to a lesser extent, the second have been the core of the traditional mechanism, the third one revives the idea of microintegration dating back to the 1971 comprehensive integration programs. By granting enterprise management the authority to deal with foreign firms, DL challenges the sacrosanct principle of the state monopoly over foreign economic relations.

The DL program, however, recognizes the existing constraints, and to alleviate them it promises a gradual introduction of decentralizing measures that should result in a "joint socialist market." Direct administrative tools of control are thus supplemented by indirect tools of public economic policy. It is hoped that this will set a new framework for spontaneous cooperation fueled by the self-interest of enterprise management in member economies.

The proposals for restructuring do not call for abolishing planning. Instead they recommend a new formula of fusing plan with market and call for concerted economic policies and coordination of plans at the level of industrial firms that is made possible by "upgrading the methods of pricing, widening monetary functions of the transferable ruble, and the use of national currencies to service direct ties" (TASS, *FBIS-SOV*, 12 July).

Because of formidable technical and political obstacles, the joint socialist market will not emerge soon. In the meantime, CMEA has to rely on administrative mechanisms to implement a concept of international socialist division of labor and to attain the declared goal of closing the economic and technological gap with the EC countries by the year 2005. The draft of this program, which was adopted by the CMEA Committee on Cooperation in Planning at its forty-first session in Sofia in March, stresses the use of traditional policy instruments. It emphasizes "specialization and cooperation in production, especially in engineering, electrical engineering, chemistry, and the consumer goods industry" (ČTK, 24 March; *FBIS-EEU*, 25 March).

The Evolution of the Soviet Approach. The history of CMEA reflects the evolving domestic political system in the Soviet Union. At the same time, it mirrors USSR responses to external challenges, its perceptions of global and regional interests, and the ability to use junior allies to pursue its goals without undermining their political stability and economic viability. CMEA has never been the only mechanism of Soviet dominance; it has, however, proved a useful conduit for establishing rules and procedures that regulate economic interaction between the Soviet Union and other communist countries.

The founding of CMEA in January 1949 was not prompted by a Soviet search for an institutional instrument through which Moscow would be able to impose its preferences on newly established communist countries in Eastern Europe. It was Stalin's terror, the presence of Soviet advisers in key positions in economic and repressive apparatus, and the direct management of some enterprises in all countries except Poland that allowed Moscow to shape economic developments according to its preferences. All decisions concerning which countries should specialize in what products and to what areas capital should be allocated were made by the Soviets. Thus the Soviet Union had direct access to East European resources that were used to rebuild and promote Soviet economic development. The unrequited transfers from Eastern Europe to the Soviet Union between 1945 and 1955 were estimated at $14 billion, the same amount that was transferred

from the United States to Western Europe under the Marshall Plan (Marer, *Political Economy of Soviet Relations with Eastern Europe*, p. 156).

In view of the abundance of channels through which the Soviets could exercise direct control, CMEA was a symbolic response to the Marshall Plan and to West European economic integration. The communiqué issued at the time of its formation explicitly mentioned the Western boycott of

> trade relations with the countries of people's democracy and the USSR because these countries did not consider it appropriate that they should submit themselves to the dictatorship of the Marshall Plan . . . In light of these circumstances, [to] establish . . . wider economic cooperation between the countries of people's democracy and the USSR, the conference considered it necessary to create the Council for Mutual Economic Assistance. (Michael Kaiser, *Comecon: Integration Problems of the Planned Economies*, London, 1965, pp. 1–12.)

The communiqué, however, did not stipulate a mechanism for integration nor was there any mention of coordinating economic policy and development programs, which indicates that Moscow at that time did not attribute any practical significance to CMEA.

Its creation reflected Stalin's concept of a separate "world socialist market" as a viable alternative to the capitalist one that was doomed to disintegrate (Joseph Stalin, *Economic Problems of Socialism in the USSR*, New York, 1952, pp. 24–27). In more practical terms, this was only one component of the Soviet policy aimed at preventing the West from controlling political developments in Eastern Europe.

Yet even during Stalin's period CMEA turned out to be a useful instrument for Soviet policy in Eastern Europe. Its mere establishment dealt a mortal blow to various schemes of subregional integration envisaged by Czechoslovakia, Bulgaria, and Hungary in the late 1940s, and the Soviets obtained an extra channel for monitoring economic relations in CMEA countries because all bilateral commercial agreements had to be registered with CMEA. It also provided Moscow with institutional machinery for fostering the development of radial patterns of economic interaction organized around the Soviet Union at the expense of multilateral links.

Because of the political instabilities in Eastern Europe triggered by de-Stalinization and climaxed by the Polish upheaval and Hungarian Revolution in

1956, there was a significant change in the foundation of Soviet–East European relations. Khrushchev, seeking to find substitutes for Stalin's commands that were based on coercion, introduced the concept of a socialist commonwealth that accorded the East European regimes limited freedom in choosing their own roads to socialism. This shift toward a more subtle form of control over Eastern Europe also increased the importance of CMEA to the Soviet Union.

To maintain cohesiveness and to assure political stability in East European countries, the Soviet Union had to limit its aspirations for total control and put an end to the blatant exploitation of its junior allies. Khrushchev's regime sought to maintain control by introducing clearly defined rules that would be acceptable to all CMEA members. The charter of CMEA was negotiated and formally adopted in 1960. The prices, previously set arbitrarily in bilateral negotiations, became subject to a clearly defined rule adopted at the ninth CMEA session in Bucharest in 1958. According to this rule, known as the Bucharest formula, the CMEA members set prices of traded goods on the basis of five-year average world market prices. (Until 1975, the prices were revised every five years.) Because it was difficult to find world equivalents for some goods in particular manufactures, the formula left room for bargaining. Had the previous arrangements been maintained, in the absence of the Soviet coercion the bargaining would have been less constrained.

In 1961–64, the Soviet Union attempted to introduce a radical program of intersectoral regional integration that would have added the dimension of supranationality to CMEA. The program, dubbed by Khrushchev the "international socialist division of labor," aimed at establishing a fully integrated, centrally planned socialist commonwealth directed from Moscow. Member countries were to eschew their sovereignty over economic development that would then be subject to a single regional plan. Less-developed members of the CMEA (e.g., Bulgaria and Romania) were to specialize in agriculture and in the production of low-processed manufactures.

The project brought to the surface East European fears of a return to the levels of Soviet domination under Stalin. Because of the opposition of Romania, which had gone so far as to publicly challenge Soviet intentions (Marie Lavigne, *Les Economies Socialistes*, Paris, 1979, pp. 377ff.), and the likely although more discreet opposition of other members, the program disappeared in its

original ambitious version from the Soviet agenda after Khrushchev's fall in 1964. It left as its legacy a preference for intrasectoral as opposed to intersectoral approaches to coordination, an increased CMEA bureaucracy, and the Principles of International Division of Labor among the Socialist Countries. Several specialized organizations were established (e.g., International Bank for Economic Cooperation in 1964) as well as a host of new, permanent, mainly industrial commissions; between 1960 and 1963 their number almost doubled, from 10 to 19 (see Chart 1).

In an apparent effort to find a substitute for the proposed integration policy, CMEA adopted a nonbinding procedure of exchanging information on investment programs to avoid parallelism in the development of industrial structures. It was argued that ex ante coordination of capital investment projects would increase complementarity and thus expand the availability of products for intra-CMEA trade. Because of the difficulties involved in selecting projects for international specialization in the absence of prices reflecting relative scarcities and meaningful exchange rates, CMEA members tended to choose similar products.

The Leonid Brezhnev era as viewed through the lenses of the CMEA was not marked by stagnation but by "caution, stability, piecemeal methods, and technocratisation," as Sobell (*Red Market*, p. 11) noted. In 1964–68 the CMEA issue was not very high on the Soviet agenda. The new Soviet leadership was first preoccupied with consolidating its power and then surprised by Prague Spring in 1968. In the aftermath of military intervention, intrabloc relations, CMEA included, moved to the top of the political agenda. As Marer and Montias observed, the Soviet Union wanted "to promote the cohesiveness of the CMEA network through which it could maintain its dominion without resorting to coercion...and [probably] a system of regional integration that would place external limits on the economic reforms undertaken by any East European country" (*Political Economy of Soviet Relations with Eastern Europe*, p. 162). This would suggest that the Soviet leadership was interested in developing a more extensive network that would make individual countries more dependent not only on the Soviet Union but on each other.

This new Soviet approach resulted in the Comprehensive Program for the Further Extension and Improvement of Cooperation and the Development of Socialist Economic Integration by the CMEA Member Countries at the twenty-fifth session of the

Council in Bucharest in July 1971. The document, the result of compromises among various visions of integration held by different countries, was conceptually incoherent and internally inconsistent. It called for comprehensive integration without identifying mechanisms and instrumentalities that would assure this goal. It retained the principle of interested party, that is, of the nonbinding character of the CMEA's decision, while stipulating organizationwide specialization. As John Hannigan and Carl McMillan succinctly noted, "The CP [Comprehensive Program] was in fact a compromise which sought to reconcile two opposing views: integration through comprehensive, supranational planning and integration through decentralized, market-determined integration" ("Joint Investment in Resource Development: Sectoral Approaches to Socialist Integration," in *East European Economic Assessment*, p. 264).

Taking into account that no country made any significant progress in introducing market-oriented measures (with the possible exception of Hungary), it came as no surprise that an administrative approach, focused on selected lines of production, prevailed over a decentralized one. In other words, some domestic plans were extended into intragroup dimensions, and new organizational links at the lower levels of governments of member countries were established. The constraining effect of structural bilateralism caused by the lack of convertibility of CMEA currencies on inter-CMEA trade was partially mitigated by specialization agreements. Contrary to anticipations of the comprehensive programs, joint development projects became the most visible form of CMEA regional integration.

The oil shock of 1974 and the expanding demand of smaller CMEA members for Soviet raw materials and energy significantly changed the matrix of intrabloc relations. During the 1960s when the prices of raw materials and energy were either falling or stagnating, the Soviet Union was ready and willing to meet East European demands that arose from inefficient industrial use and investment bias in favor of raw materials and energy-intensive sectors. The situation changed in late 1973 when the Organization of Petroleum Exporting Countries (OPEC) successfully effected an almost fivefold increase of the price of oil (Persian Gulf oil increased from $2.48 per barrel in 1972 to $11.65 per barrel on 1 January 1974). Between 1972 and 1974 the prices of manufactures rose by 43 percent, whereas the prices of energy and raw materials rose by 250 percent.

Given the Soviet specialization in raw materials and energy and the East European specialization in manufactured goods, this dramatic reversal of terms of trade between raw materials and manufactures changed priorities in their commercial policies. The Soviet Union wanted to reap hard currency benefits from the sale of oil and other raw materials on international markets, while the East Europeans wanted to secure their supply. As a consequence of the oil shock, the opportunity cost of oil exports to CMEA significantly increased for the Soviet Union. At Soviet insistence, the 1975 Moscow agreement amended one provision of the 1958 Bucharest arrangement: the prices were to be revised every year instead of every five years. This new arrangement provided CMEA members with a protective shield against worldwide energy scarcities at Soviet expense because the sale of oil to non-CMEA countries would generate foreign revenues several times higher.

Leaving aside the consequences for political stability of overhauling the Bucharest formula, the Soviet "lost revenues" were compensated for by several developments. First, thanks to its improved terms of trade with the noncommunist world, the Soviet Union enjoyed large windfall gains estimated at $50 billion for 1973–1980 (Marer, *The Economies and Trade of Eastern Europe*, discussion paper, no. 6, Bloomington, Indiana, 1988). Second, the Soviet Union caught a large share of the dramatically expanding arms market in the OPEC countries. Third, it curtailed growth rates of its oil supplies in the 1970s, which fell to zero in the 1980s. Fourth, taking advantage of its newly acquired bargaining strength, the Soviet Union was in a position to sway East European CMEA members to increase their assistance to non-European members, that is, Mongolia, Cuba, and Vietnam as well as some pro-Soviet regimes in the Third World (ibid.). Finally, under the pressure of the declining availability of Soviet supplies of raw materials, some CMEA countries became interested in carrying out the provisions of the Comprehensive Program concerning joint investment programs.

The joint investment programs, which consisted in developing a Soviet resource base and infrastructure to transport basic fuels and raw materials and cofinanced by the interested CMEA countries, became the nucleus of regional integration in the 1970s and advantageous to both the Soviets and the East Europeans (Hannigan and McMillan, "Joint

Investment in Resource Development," p. 265). Eastern Europe would obtain secure, long-term access to raw materials that otherwise would have to be purchased for scarce hard currencies. The Soviet Union, in turn, would obtain much-needed assistance in developing resource bases and transport facilities in the remote Siberian regions. A significant portion of the output would be used for domestic consumption and export to the West.

This change in the CMEA countries' priorities also served Soviet political objectives. The joint investment projects added a seemingly permanent long-term dimension to the existing radial network of bilateral arrangements that tie CMEA countries to the Soviet Union. On top of East European increased diversion of exports from other markets—mainly domestic and potentially from other CMEA countries—to the Soviet Union, triggered by the declining terms of trade, the new pattern locked the CMEA economies even tighter to the Soviet Union. The lack of coordination of the purchases of Western technology and know-how reduced the potential for developing multilateral ties. This in turn exacerbated structural dependence on the Soviet Union. In addition, pressures to introduce economic reforms to adjust to the international economy were considerably weakened because of the CMEA "protective shield." This declining interest was also fueled in part by Soviet resistance to decentralizing economic reforms, as illustrated by the case of Hungary in the 1970s. The other reason was the newly gained access of East European countries to Western private financial markets, the consequence of petrodollar recycling following the first oil shock. The latter combination enabled East European regimes to postpone economic reforms.

Under these circumstances, it is scarcely surprising that "not a single one of the important provisions [of the Comprehensive Program for Integration] proclaimed there [in Bucharest] has been carried out thus far," as Polish economist Jerzy Kleer observed (Warsaw, *Polityka-Eksport-Import*, no. 8). Indeed with the exception of joint projects in the Soviet Union, the provisions for market-oriented financial and currency settlements, which were quite innovative, were not implemented because their implementation would entail economic reforms in the Soviet Union. There were neither short-term economic incentives nor the political willingness to promote multilateral links when the Soviet domination was not in danger.

The circumstances shaping the posture of the Soviet Union and other members toward the issue of regional integration changed in the 1980s. Because of the expanding costs of servicing international debt and the Western credit squeeze, the economic situation of East European countries deteriorated. The recession in the West and the increased cost of Soviet oil—only partly mitigated by the Soviet willingness to run trade deficits with its CMEA partners—exacerbated the balance of payments problems (*Osteuropa Wirtschaft*, no. 2).

The East European balance of payments crisis in the early 1980s revealed the weaknesses of the intra-CMEA framework. As a result of the absence of coordination in the purchases of capital equipment and technology from the West, a "secondary [imported] parallelism emerged," to borrow an apt description from Soviet economist Shiriev (Moscow, *Social Sciences*, no. 3). There was neither coordination of economic policies designed to cope with external financial problems among CMEA members nor "mutual" economic assistance in the time of crisis. Cuts in Western imports and the stagnation of Soviet deliveries of basic fuels and raw materials dampened exports to other than Soviet Union–CMEA member economies. Among the first casualties of economic problems were the CMEA specialization agreements, as a Rand study noted (Crane and Skoller, *Specialization Agreements*, p. 48). CMEA did not provide a buffer that would dampen the impact of external disturbances. As one author observed, CMEA proved irrelevant during this period (Fallenbuchl, *International Journal*, no. 1). This realization became widespread among policymakers, in particular from those countries that were hit hardest, Hungary and Poland.

Yet it was not until Gorbachev's ascension to power that the issue of socialist integration re-entered Moscow's political agenda. This new interest in CMEA was triggered by the deteriorating economic performance, the growing technological gap between the CMEA economies and the West, and falling hard currency revenues. As a result of depressed world prices of oil and other raw materials, the Soviet terms of trade with the West sharply decreased. In addition, Middle East importers of Soviet arms curtailed their purchases because of significantly reduced oil revenues. In consequence, the buffer that allowed the Brezhnev regime to cushion the political impact of the stagnating domestic economy vanished. It became apparent to the new Soviet leadership that nothing short of significant changes in the ways of managing the economy and modernizing the productive structure would prevent the crisis.

Seeking assistance for the modernization drive, the Soviet leadership turned to CMEA for support. In stark contrast to the de facto benign neglect throughout most of the 1970s, the Soviets became committed to restructuring the mechanism of coordination and cooperation within the bloc. Five sessions of the Council held between 1985 and 1988 were devoted to a critical appraisal of every aspect of CMEA. They did not result in any significant actual changes, as various CMEA documents readily admit; for instance, the final communiqué of the forty-fourth session reads inter alia: "The economic cooperation of the CMEA countries does not as yet properly encourage a greater efficiency of their economies" (*Pravda*, 8 July).

However, all the drawbacks and obstacles to integration were revealed in the new spirit of *glasnost'*. The "market" ideas that had been circulating among East European economists, particularly Hungarians and Poles, since the Khrushchevian debate on socialist international division of labor were given an official seal of approval during the Forty-third Extraordinary Session of the Council convened in Moscow 13–14 October 1987 and the forty-fourth session in Prague, 6–8 July. The Soviet prime minister declared that "to us, the integrated market is not a fashionable buzzword but an important direction of development of the integrative process" (Warsaw, *Polityka*, no. 29).

The creation of an integrated market, assuming that political obstacles are overcome, is a long-time process. The signing of a joint declaration on the establishment of official relations between the EC and CMEA at the Kirchberg International Conference Center in Luxembourg on 25 June will not affect their economic relations in the near future. In the meantime, the Soviets have to content themselves with minor changes in the mechanism of cooperation that consist of supplementing administrative policy instruments with decentralized financial measures. In addition, the Soviet Union has used the CMEA institutional machinery to force East Europeans to adopt a common aid program for the non-European CMEA members. This program was discussed at the Forty-fourth CMEA Council session in Prague in July.

Conclusion: Potential for Conflict. On its 40th anniversary, CMEA is in crisis; it has become an impediment to economic reforms and restructuring. Hungarian Politburo member Németh suc-

cinctly observed that "we can already see clearly that the support and stabilizing effect which CMEA represented for the Hungarian economy ten to twenty years ago is sometimes becoming the opposite. Conflicts of interest have appeared in the cooperation which can hardly be bridged over with the present system of tools." (*Népszabadság*, 7 July; *JPRS-EER*, 10 August.) This observation applies not only to Hungary.

The crisis is a manifestation of two interrelated phenomena. The first is the inherent inefficiency of the mechanism of organizing foreign economic interaction under command planning by CMEA. The second phenomenon is the "discovery" by Gorbachev and other communist leaders that CMEA has been of little assistance to the Soviet Union and other members in solving their economic problems.

Although the shortcomings of command planning and of CMEA as a mechanism of foreign trade among its members have been known for years, the Soviet "precrisis" situation and the poor economic performance of other CMEA members triggered a re-examination of the CMEA institutional framework. The new joint socialist market program, if implemented, would require radical reforms of domestic economic systems and would transfer some national sovereign rights to CMEA. The transformation of CMEA from a traditional international government organization to a supranational organization could cause conflict among member countries. It remains to be seen whether Moscow will be able to suppress conflicting interests.

The Soviet "precrisis" situation has changed the major component that shaped CMEA activity, that is, the Soviet economic posture to the CMEA countries. Its evolution was marked by a transfer of resources to the Soviet Union in the 1950s, more equitable relations in the 1960s, and increased Soviet opportunity costs in the 1970s. There was little political risk in tapping East European resources to offset the Western embargo in the 1950s. Opportunity costs of providing Eastern Europe with energy and raw materials were minimal when buyers dominated the international commodity markets in the 1960s. These costs substantially increased in the 1970s but were compensated for by several favorable developments in the world markets of the Soviet Union. The trade pattern involving the exchange of Soviet hard currency exportables for internationally noncompetitive East European manufactures was then acceptable to Moscow. As viewed from the Kremlin, this was "an effective but cumbersome" arrangement, to paraphrase Michael

Marrese ("CMEA: Effective But Cumbersome Political Economy," *International Organization*, no. 2, Spring 1986).

Because of poor economic performance and adverse developments in the international markets (depressed prices of energy and basic fuels), this trade pattern has become less acceptable now. The Soviet Union would like Eastern Europe to provide world-quality manufactures, to increase imports of Soviet machinery, and to assist the Soviet Union in its efforts to restructure the economy. Gorbachev and other Soviet officials have warned their allies against using CMEA as a "garbage can" (*NYT*, 4 January). Soviet prime minister Nikolai Ryzhkov's statement in a speech at the Moscow CMEA session—that all future increases in the Soviet exports to other CMEA partners should come from the sales of capital equipment—has been incorporated in a CMEA draft of a collective long-term plan. According to this draft, the Soviet Union is to increase machine building exports by 400 percent by the year 2005.

Under the present circumstances, these new Soviet demands are unlikely to be met, however. Eastern Europe is in no position to improve the quality of their exports to the Soviet Union for at least three interrelated reasons. First, seeking to adjust to balance of payments disequilibria in the early 1980s, most of them drastically curtailed investments and imports of Western technology in the 1980s. As a result, the technological quality of their manufactures and their international competitiveness is lower than it was in the 1970s (Kazimierz Poznanski, "The Competitiveness of Polish Industry and Indebtedness," in Paul Marer and Wlodzimierz Siwinski, eds., *Creditworthiness and Reform in Poland*, Bloomington, Indiana, 1988, pp. 46–52).

Eastern Europe exports mainly raw materials and low-processed goods to the nonsocialist world, which accounts for about 70 percent of its exports. The share of high-technology products in exports to the West, for example, fell from 1.2 percent in 1980 to 0.6 percent in 1986; at the same time this share in exports of the Third World increased from 9.8 percent to 13.2 percent (*Życie gospodarcze*, no. 35). Thus highly processed products are in short supply in Eastern Europe.

Second, meeting the Soviet request for high-quality products would entail a significant restructuring of East European economies. Over a period of 40 years their investment programs have been designed to replace hard currency imports and to pay for Soviet deliveries of raw materials. As Hungarian prime minister Németh wryly observed, "we carried out investments worth many tens, even hundreds of billions of forints, which did not shift the structure of Hungarian production in a modern direction, for at the time these were based on a secure [Soviet] market" (*Népszabadság*, 7 July; *JPRS-EER*, 10 August). Changing this structure would require stepping up investment outlays and Western imports. Given their strenuous balance of payments position and domestic political tensions, none of these options is within easy grasp.

Third, Soviet pressures for higher-quality products may lead to cuts in East European imports of low-quality products from the Soviet Union. For instance, Hungarians want to replace the Soviet Union as their major iron ore supplier because its low-grade content is allegedly accountable for the low international competitiveness of their steel products (*NYT*, 4 January). Many other areas offer East Europeans the possibility of retaliation by demanding from the Soviet Union low-processed products meeting international standards. Their bargaining position will certainly improve if the Soviets insist on increasing their share of capital equipment in exports to Eastern Europe.

Thus the only alternative seems to be a market-oriented restructuring of both the domestic systems of the CMEA members and the CMEA integrative framework. Yet in spite of a declared commitment at the forty-fourth CMEA session to establish a joint market, there are formidable obstacles. The conviction of the necessity of radical reforms is not shared by all CMEA member governments. Although only Romania did not endorse "provisions for gradual restructuring" of DL, other members are not necessarily enthusiastic about the reform. Only the Hungarian and Polish governments have so far introduced measures that may lead to a mixed economy. Others either debate the measures to be introduced (the Soviet Union, Mongolia, and Bulgaria) or pay lip service to restructuring (Czechoslovakia, the GDR, and Cuba).

As a Hungarian participant in the CMEA session noted, "one can observe in the conference hall that we do not mean the same thing by the words of reform—price, convertibility, bank, market" (*Népszabadság*, 7 July). In the implementation stage, one may thus expect a lot of "silent" resistance that may effectively subvert innovative measures. Because the establishment of a common market calls for a market-oriented convergence of national economic mechanisms, it does not bode well for the prospects of reforming CMEA.

Neither does the growth in political tensions among CMEA member governments. There has been open conflict between Romania and Hungary over discrimination against the Hungarian minority in Romania. The Polish government has clashed with the GDR over the sea-lanes in the Szczecin gulf and with the GDR and Czechoslovakia over pollution. All East European CMEA members have become involved in a virtual customs war directed against foreign visitors from socialist countries. By introducing Draconian customs measures that are to take effect on 1 February 1989, the Soviet Union became a partner in the conflict. The competition on the same markets and for the assistance of the same Western financial institutions has also contributed to the increased tensions. Therefore a spontaneous emergence of a joint market is unlikely.

The alternative would be Soviet unilateral action to impose a new, "restructured order" in CMEA. However, the Soviet Union neither has a well-defined vision of this new order nor can risk the political instabilities that such an action might trigger in some CMEA countries. In addition, its economic leverage over the other CMEA countries has probably been eroded by the fall in energy prices, its own growing supply constraints, and overall economic stagnation. For these reasons, the restructuring of CMEA is likely to remain lower on the Soviet political agenda than convincing the West to make a financial and technological contribution to *perestroika* in the Soviet Union.

Bartlomiej Kaminski
University of Maryland

Warsaw Treaty Organization

The Warsaw Treaty Organization (WTO) was established in 1955 and was extended to the year 2005 in 1985. Despite General Secretary Mikhail Gorbachev's policies of *perestroika* (restructuring), *glasnost'* (openness), and "new political thinking," Soviet control over its East European pact has not lessened. The proposals announced at the various WTO fora were Moscow's policies. The pact's ubiquitous officials and media representatives accelerated their promotion of arms reductions, nuclear-free zones, peace, détente, and the idea of a "common European home" (to exclude the United States and Canada)—all designed to influence West European and world public opinion. Press conferences were conducted following the numerous WTO meetings, and officials, including military and even Committee for State Security (KGB) officers, made themselves available for interviews to more effectively propagate Moscow's policies. Militarily, WTO officials, although admitting to asymmetries and imbalances in certain weapons systems, claimed "rough parity" in WTO and North Atlantic Treaty Organization (NATO) conventional armaments. However, WTO did advance prospects for arms control negotiations with seemingly greater willingness to exchange information and verification measures. Overall, Moscow's objective appeared to be to separate the United States and Canada from Western Europe and to denuclearize Europe, which would give enormous military and political advantage to the Soviet Union and pose serious security problems for the United States, Western Europe, and the free world.

Military Developments. The secretary of defense declared that despite its "new look" the Soviet Union was continuing its arms buildup and was the "major threat" to the security of the United States and its allies (Department of Defense, *Annual Report to Congress, Fiscal Year 1989*). The joint staff reported that Warsaw pact military strength "far exceeds" its defensive needs (*Military Posture FY 1989*). According to a NATO comparison of WTO-NATO military figures in the Atlantic-to-Urals area, as of January WTO superiority is as follows: ground forces (3,090,000 to 2,213,593), main battle tanks (51,500 to 16,424), combat aircraft (8,250 to 3,997), artillery pieces (43,400 to 13,857), anti-tank weapons (44,200 to 18,240); other categories show similar WTO superiority (NATO, *Conventional Forces in Europe: The Facts*, November). General Secretary Gorbachev's December announcement before the U.N. General Assembly of troop cutbacks (see below) had no immediate impact on current military strength.

Modernization of all Soviet strategic nuclear forces continued. Intercontinental ballistic missile (ICBM) strength was essentially the same, with about one hundred new mobile SS-25 launchers and some ten rail-based SS-24s. Submarine-launched ballistic missiles (SLBMs) were strengthened by one *Typhoon*-class strategic missile-carrying nuclear submarine with twenty SS-N-20 missiles and one *Delta IV*-class with sixteen SS-N-23s. Three older submarines were retired. The 3,000-km-range SS-N-21 submarine-launched cruise missile (SLCM) was fitted to a *Yankee*-class nuclear-powered guided missile submarine and six nuclear-powered submarines (SSNs). The SLCM SS-NX-24 was being tried in a *Yankee*-class submarine. Production of the *Backfire* continued, with additional bombers deployed. The *Blackjack*, the most modern bomber, was demonstrated to Secretary of Defense Frank Carlucci in August and may be operational. (International Institute for Strategic Studies [IISS], *The Military Balance, 1988–1989*.)

Under the U.S.-Soviet intermediate-range nuclear forces (INF) treaty, Moscow was obliged to eliminate three times as many launchers and twice as many missiles as Washington. In the November 1987 data exchange, the USSR submitted 405 SS-20 missiles and launchers deployed at 48 bases; 118 launchers and 245 missiles were not deployed. Moscow showed 65 SS-4 missiles, with 105 in storage. The biggest surprise to IISS was the large number of SS-23s deployed—82 launchers with 167 missiles. Western figures on SS-12s were close to the Soviets, with two missiles for each launcher. Neither SS-12s nor SS-23s were in production. By 1 June Moscow had transferred launchers and missiles to destruction areas: withdrawn launchers: 16 SS-4s, including closing a base in the southern Ukraine; 78 SS-12s, including all those in the German Democratic Republic (GDR) and the Czechoslovak Socialist Republic (ČSSR), leaving only two brigades and one unit in the Far East; and one brigade of 18 SS-23 launchers from the Belorussian Military District (ibid.).

Modernization of Soviet conventional forces continued, with the modern main battle tanks (MBTs) (T-64B, T-72, and T-80) increased, the T-62 decreased, and reactive armor retrofitting continued. A new turretless tank with a 135-mm gun was reportedly tested. Each of the five armies in the Group of Soviet Forces in Germany (GSFG) evidently does have an independent tank regiment with 148 MBTs, a situation that may exist in other Soviet armies. Units with infantry fighting vehicles (BMPs) are increasing, indicating that all motor rifle divisions in GSFG have two instead of one BMP-equipped regiments. Considered as most significant are increases in self-propelled (SP) artillery, to about 9,000. The number of MT-LB armored personnel carriers/artillery tractors increased considerably. Air defense troops were strengthened, and the number of fighter aircraft increased by about 500, mostly MiG-23s and 100 more MiG-31s. A new *Foxbat* variant, the F, which was designed to attack air defense systems from a long-range standoff position, may be entering service. The year witnessed continuation of a slowdown in naval construction. New ships were one *Victor*-III SSN, one *Sovremennii*, and two *Udaloi* missile destroyers; three *Sverdlov* cruisers were retired. (*The Military Balance, 1988–1989*.)

In December 1987 Moscow finally admitted to about 50,000 tons of chemical warfare weapons—substantially fewer than Western estimates and claiming none outside its borders. About 60,000 men constitute the Soviet chemical forces. (Ibid.)

Few significant developments occurred in non-Soviet WTO armed forces. Ground forces remained essentially unchanged. The ČSSR received some 203-mm 2S7 SP guns and 240-mm 2S4 SP mortars, now having four of each weapon. The GDR had 50 more 122-mm 2S1 SP guns and was considered capable of organizing four reserve divisions. Hungarian ground forces were reorganized to simplify the command structure and improve logistics. Rather than the standard army/division/regimental structure, Budapest established a corps/brigade structure with a corps having three to five brigades and corps support units similar to divisions; brigades have three to five battalions of tank and motor rifle units. The former six divisions were all rated Category B. The Polish navy was modernizing slowly. To its force of 3 *Whiskey*-class submarines were added one *Foxtrot* and one *Kilo*-class, with one *Whiskey* retired. The surface fleet received one *Kashin*-class guided-missile-equipped destroyer, renamed *Warszawa*, and earmarked as a flagship. The Romanian navy received one *Kilo*-class submarine, its first since 1967. The air forces continued their modernization, with Bulgaria showing an increase of 30 Su-25s and five MiG-23s; the ČSSR 15 Su-25s; Hungary, 35 MiG-23s; and the GDR, 35 Mi-24 *Hind* helicopters. (*The Military Balance, 1988–1989*.)

In his 7 December address to the United Nations Gorbachev declared a unilateral Soviet troop reduction of 500,000, along with substantial armament reductions, within two years. By 1991 six tank divisions will be withdrawn from the GDR, Czechoslovakia, and Hungary and disbanded. Soviet forces in these countries will be reduced by 50,000 men and five thousand tanks. In the European USSR and Eastern Europe, Soviet reductions would consist of ten thousand tanks, 8,500 artillery systems, and eight hundred combat aircraft. (*Facts on File*, 9 December.) NATO foreign ministers meeting in Brussels welcomed Gorbachev's announcement, but Secretary General Manfred Woerner said the cutbacks "reduce but clearly do not eliminate Soviet superiority and do not establish a stable balance" (*NYT*, 9 December).

The Political Consultative Committee (PCC). The PCC, which is made up of WTO party leaders, held its conference 15–16 July in Warsaw amid speculations about a partial withdrawal of the 565,000 Soviet troops in the GDR, the ČSSR, and Hungary, especially the 65,000 in Hungary. The State Department said it had "increasing indications that the Soviets may be contemplating an early decision to pull forces out of Hungary" (*NYT*, 9 July). This WTO summit issued three documents: a communiqué, a statement on armed forces and conventional arms reductions in Europe, and a document on ecological security, none of which referred to Soviet withdrawals.

The communiqué noted favorable trends in international life, hailed the U.S.-USSR INF treaty, stressed the significance of continued dialogue, and appealed to NATO and the Conference on Security and Cooperation in Europe (CSCE) participants to conclude major agreements on reducing armaments and armed forces, thus strengthening security and stability. The PCC identified as priorities a treaty on a 50 percent reduction of U.S. and Soviet strategic offensive arms, a ban on nuclear weapons testing, a convention on eliminating chemical weapons, and the reduction of armed forces and conventional armaments in Europe, as well as military spending. (*Pravda*, 17 July; *FBIS*, 18 July.)

Party leaders reaffirmed the pact's position exchanging information on armed forces and armaments in Europe and verifying the information by on-site inspections. They called for elimination of the existing asymmetries and imbalances on the all-European scale and in individual regions and for substantial cuts in the armed forces and conventional armaments in Europe. (Ibid.)

The PCC again proposed comparing NATO and WTO military doctrines and convening talks on freezing and reducing military spending. The leaders favored separate negotiations on reducing and eliminating tactical nuclear weapons in Europe, including nuclear components of dual-capable systems. They recalled their zonal proposals, reaffirmed their idea of a "common European hope," and repeated their position on the dissolution of both alliances. The communiqué reconfirmed the need for all countries to respect the principles of national independence and sovereignty, nonuse of force or the threat of force, inviolability of borders and territorial integrity, peaceful settlement of disputes, noninterference in internal affairs, equality, and other principles and aims of the U.N. Charter, the Helsinki Final Act, and generally recognized norms of international relations (*Pravda*, 17 July; *FBIS*, 18 July).

The PCC issued a separate detailed statement on arms that called for substantial cuts in armed forces and conventional armaments in Europe, from the Atlantic to the Urals, with negotiations convening in 1988. The first phase of the talks should reduce at "roughly equal collective levels" the armed forces and conventional weapons of the two alliances. Imbalances and asymmetries would be eliminated by withdrawing forces from the reduction states and subsequently disbanding them. The arms and equipment to be reduced would be eliminated at designated sites or converted to peaceful uses, with the possibility of "temporary" storage of certain arms and equipment under international verification. (*Pravda*, 16 July; *FBIS*, 18 July.)

In the second phase each side would reduce its armed forces by approximately 25 percent, or about 500,000 men, and reductions would continue in the third phase. Throughout the process measures would be adopted to reduce and eliminate the risk of a surprise attack; these would include creating zones between alliances from which destabilizing arms would be eliminated or reduced. Concurrently, confidence-building measures limiting military activities in the zones would be negotiated. (Ibid.)

The PCC proposed an exchange of "relevant initial data," essential to the negotiations, that would identify imbalances and asymmetries in the armed forces and conventional armaments on European and regional scales. This would be accomplished early in the negotiations or even before the talks commenced. A verification regime would contain not only national technical means—a favorite means of WTO negotiators in the past—but "on-site inspections without right of refusal" and exit-entry points applicable during the process of reduction and elimination phases. The leaders provided for an international verification commission and reaffirmed their proposal for negotiations in the near future on eliminating tactical nuclear weapons, including dual-capable systems, to reduce the risk of war and create a more stable Europe. They perceived a close relationship between the Atlantic-to-Urals reductions and CSCE's examination of unresolved issues such as air forces and navies. (*Pravda*, 16 July; *FBIS*, 18 July.)

At a Moscow press conference following the PCC session, Viktor Karpov, head of the department on arms control in the Soviet Foreign Ministry, stressed as a new feature the PCC's proposal on an information exchange on the armed forces and conventional armaments in Europe that would take place "before" an agreement on limitations is concluded. WTO members, he said, would thus guarantee not to repeat the Mutual and Balanced Force Reduction's (MBFR's) impasse over data. (TASS, 18 July; *FBIS*, 19 July.)

PCC's document on ecology—Consequences of the Arms Race for the Environment and Other Aspects of Ecological Security—reflected a problem characterized in their communiqué as "exceptionally urgent" in densely populated Europe. The document surprised observers, but WTO countries lag badly in environmental protection. Also, serious ecological problems gave officials an opportunity to promote an "all-European home." The document portrayed the arms race as a dangerous source of environmental damage. Although a nuclear war would be an ecological catastrophe, any war would inflict heavy damage on the environment. The production, stockpiling, and transportation of weapons; the construction of military installations; and military exercises all affect the environment. The PCC pointed out the importance of pursuing disarmament, holding international dialogues, and adopting a document by 1992—the twentieth anniversary of the U.S. conference on the environment. (*Pravda*, 17 July; *FBIS*, 18 July.)

A press conference was held following the session by Polish deputy foreign minister and PCC general director Henryk Jaroszek, but nothing new was added (PAP, 16 July; *FBIS*, 18 July). However, the Hungarian representative, General Secretary and Premier Károly Grósz, revealed that he had raised the human rights issue at the meeting and that his recommendation to establish a working commission to handle humanitarian questions was accepted. Grósz also said that the session discussed a reorganization of the pact. (MTI, 16, 17, 18 July; *FBIS*, 18, 19, 21 July.) As for the possibility of Soviet troop withdrawal from Hungary, Grósz reportedly acknowledged to Giovanni Spadolini, president of the Italian Senate, that there was truth to the reports (Radio Budapest, 18 July; *FBIS*, 19 July). These developments were not included either in the PCC documents or in subsequent public comments, except by the Hungarian leader.

Foreign Ministers. The first meeting in 1988 of the WTO Foreign Ministers' Committee was held 29–30 March in Sofia. Soviet foreign minister Eduard Shevardnadze briefed the participants on the progress of U.S.-Soviet nuclear talks in Geneva and on his 21–23 March discussions in Washington with President Ronald Reagan and Secretary of State George Shultz. (BTA, 29 March; *FBIS*, 29 March.) The ministers issued two documents: a lengthy communiqué and a repetitious appeal to NATO and CSCE members. The far-ranging communiqué stressed the "urgent need" for progress in disarmament and for creation of a nuclear-free, nonviolent world. The ministers viewed the INF treaty as a first step that should be followed by agreements on the reduction of strategic offensive weapons; the prohibition of nuclear tests; the elimination of nuclear, chemical, and other weapons of mass destruction; and a reduction of armed forces and conventional arms in Europe. They considered Moscow's withdrawal of its OTR-22 missiles from the GDR and the ČSSR before the INF treaty came into force as "a manifestation of goodwill in the nuclear disarmament process." The ministers voiced their countries' intentions to seek substantial cuts in armed forces and conventional arms from the Atlantic to the Urals in new negotiations, to include the exchange of "necessary" data and an effective system of verification and monitoring, and to remove, on a mutual basis, asymmetries and imbalances in Europe. They fully supported their members' disarmament proposals, such as nuclear-free zones, and favored extending reduction of military activities to the seas and oceans around the continent. The ministers restated the pact's long-held proposal to dismantle NATO and WTO. (*Pravda*, 31 March; *FBIS*, 1 April.)

The WTO foreign ministers "urgently appealed" to members of NATO and the 35 CSCE countries "to take advantage of the historic opportunity" toward disarmament to strengthen security and cooperation. They proposed to ratify the U.S.-USSR INF treaty; conclude a U.S.-USSR treaty on a 50 percent reduction in strategic offensive arms; ban nuclear weapons tests; eliminate chemical weapons; complete the mandate for the Atlantic-to-Urals negotiations "as soon as possible"; exchange data on

WTO and NATO armed forces and conventional arms in Europe and eliminate asymmetries and imbalances; commence talks on reduction of tactical nuclear weapons in Europe, including nuclear components of dual-purpose systems; implement WTO and NATO comparisons of military doctrines; expand CSCE's confidence- and security-building measures; create zones free of nuclear and chemical weapons; begin talks by naval states; declare a moratorium for one to two years on increasing military expenditures by WTO and NATO states; and activate practical and purposeful work at the Geneva Disarmament Conference. (Ibid.)

A press conference was held following the meeting by deputy foreign ministers of Bulgaria, Hungary, and the USSR to reflect on provisions in the communiqué. Soviet deputy Vadim Loginov said the Soviet Union was "hopeful" of signing a treaty on a 50 percent reduction of strategic offensive arms. (BTA, 30 March; MBFR, 31 March.) In a 30 March interview with ČTK, ČSSR foreign minister Bohuslav Chňoupek, noting the positive trends in U.S.-Soviet relations, characterized the disarmament advances as "irreversible" (FBIS, 31 March). According to its spokesman, NATO welcomed the foreign ministers' statements as they reflected the concerns of its members but stressed the necessity of concrete proposals at negotiating fora.

The pact's foreign ministers met 13 May in East Berlin for a briefing by Soviet foreign minister Shevardnadze on his discussions in Geneva with Secretary Shultz regarding the Moscow summit. The ministers, expressing hope for agreement on strategic offensive weapons, gave full support to the Soviet position on its negotiations with the United States. Radio Budapest's foreign political editor, Peter Nyarady, cited as "interesting" the fact that Romania was represented by its ambassador to the GDR rather than its foreign minister. There was no public explanation. (Radio Budapest, ADN, 13 May; FBIS, 16 May.)

The regular session of the Foreign Ministers' Committee was held 28–29 October in Budapest. In addition to a communiqué, the ministers issued a Statement on Confidence- and Security-Building Measures and Disarmament in Europe. The ministers favored continuation of the 35-member CSCE negotiations as early as 1988 and the beginning of the 23-member NATO-WTO Atlantic-to-Urals talks. The CSCE negotiations were to develop and expand constraining measures, such as banning large-scale military exercises; new measures, including prior notification of independent activities

by air and naval forces; and measures to increase openness and predictability of military activities. The ministers proposed eliminating military bases on foreign territories, repeated the pact's position on dissolving military-political alliances, and suggested an all-European summit, including the United States and Canada, to explore reducing armed forces and conventional armaments in Europe. (MTI, 28 October; Pravda, 29 October; FBIS, 31 October.)

Following the meeting, a press conference was conducted by Hungarian foreign minister Peter Várkonyi, who stressed that the statement on strengthening confidence had the force of an appeal. He said that Soviet foreign minister Shevardnadze briefed the ministers on Chancellor Helmut Kohl's talks in Moscow, with the Soviet news agency adding that Shevardnadze noted the importance of such dialogue to promote the European process. Várkonyi revealed that the ministers held fewer protocol discussions and more nonofficial but substantive discussions than previously, a tendency for the future. (Radio Budapest, TASS, 29 October; FBIS, 31 October.)

CSCE Follow-up Conference. Begun 4 November 1986, the Vienna-based CSCE negotiations discussed the relationship between theirs and the Atlantic-to-Urals talks. The 35 participants also continued to consider their 152 proposals that would build on the Stockholm document. On 28 April WTO delegations submitted a draft on security and cooperation in the Mediterranean, including lowering the military confrontation. (TASS, 28 April; FBIS, 29 April.) On 6 June the president of Poland, Wojciech Jaruzelski, sent a message to the U.N.'s Third Special Session on Disarmament that expanded on the July 1987 Jaruzelski Plan, which was intended to reduce and eliminate tactical nuclear weapons in Central Europe (PAP, 6 June; TASS, 18 June; FBIS, 7, 20 June). WTO's campaign for nuclear weapons–free zones continued with a mammoth 20–22 June meeting in East Berlin of 1,034 representatives from 113 countries (ADN, Neues Deutschland, 20, 21 June; FBIS, 22, 23 June).

MBFR Negotiations. The NATO-WTO negotiations on MBFR ended the year as they had started, without a treaty, after fifteen years of talks on reducing conventional armed forces in Central Europe. As usual, three rounds were held during the year, with the 492nd plenary session of round 46 concluding on 1 December. The positions of the twelve NATO and seven WTO negotiators both reflected their last proposals, NATO of 5 December 1985 and WTO of 20 February 1986 (see *YICA*, 1987 and 1988). The West continued to face "massive" Soviet forces in Eastern Europe and Western USSR, and the WTO had not reacted "constructively" to NATO's initiative. Thus, the East-West military confrontation in Europe remained unchanged as did the imbalance of conventional armed forces that prompted the MBFR negotiations fifteen years earlier. WTO officials continued to claim that Western technological advances offset any numerical imbalance in favor of the East. The negotiators appeared to bide their time, awaiting a decision of the two alliances in view of the newly mandated negotiations—the Conventional Stability Talks (CST). (*MBFR Press Transcripts*, January–December; Department of State, *Fundamentals of U.S. Foreign Policy*, March.)

Atlantic-to-the-Urals Talks. All 23 members of NATO and WTO began discussions in 1987 in Vienna to develop a mandate for new conventional arms negotiations covering all of Europe, from the Atlantic to the Urals (*YICA*, 1988). The CST negotiations were to be conducted within the framework of the CSCE process but would be autonomous in subject matter, participation, and procedures. The CST participants agreed on procedures, participants, objectives, methods, and verification and hoped to conclude the discussions by the end of 1988 (they did not) in order to begin the new negotiations. (*IB*, July.) A major problem blocking agreement on a mandate was dual-capable weapons.

The objective is to strengthen security and stability in Europe by a balance of conventional forces at lower levels. In its 2 March statement the NATO council stressed that "conventional imbalance in Europe remains at the core of Europe's security concerns, WTO having not only superiority in key weapons systems but possessing important asymmetries." (*Bulletin*, May.) Among other things, the council called for greater openness about military activities and exchange of detailed data about forces and deployments (ibid.).

For its part NATO issued *Conventional Forces in Europe: The Facts* (no date but released 25 November), an assessment of the strength of the NATO and WTO armed forces in Europe as of January. In CST, NATO intends to provide full details of its forces and requested WTO members to reciprocate. The

negotiators will attempt to eliminate disparities that give WTO "a capability for surprise attack and large-scale offensive action." (*Bulletin*, May.) The West may face a problem in getting WTO to admit superiority and to furnish detailed data. Although Marshal Viktor G. Kulikov, WTO commander in chief of the joint armed forces, admitted to "certain asymmetries," which they are prepared to eliminate, he reflected the pact's position that there is "a roughly equal balance in weapons." (Radio Moscow, 8 July; *FBIS*, 11 July.)

Commission on Disarmament Questions. At its May 1987 Berlin session, the PCC established a special disarmament commission to consider arms limitations and disarmament, especially nuclear, and to formulate joint proposals. The first session of the commission, at the deputy foreign ministers' level, was held 2–5 February in Warsaw and included senior defense representatives. The deputy ministers considered the U.S.-USSR treaty on the elimination of intermediate- and shorter-range missiles and additional actions in Europe and in the world to be "building a continuous and irreversible character to the disarmament problem, building a world without nuclear weapons." The meeting also examined the WTO-NATO Vienna consultations to prepare a mandate for talks on reduction of armed forces from the Atlantic to the Urals. The commission was to draft the general concept. (TASS, 5 February; *FBIS*, 9 February.)

The second session, held in Warsaw 10–12 May, discussed activities to speed up the negotiations on the reduction of armed forces and conventional weapons in Europe and the status of WTO-NATO consultations in Vienna on a mandate for the talks. The commission continued to develop a joint concept for future negotiations and preventions of threats of sudden attack. Other issues included arms limitation, disarmament, and confidence- and security-building measures. (Radio Warsaw, 12 May; *FBIS*, 13 May.)

The third session was held 17–18 October in Bucharest. The representatives analyzed the WTO-NATO mandate talks in Vienna to include the reduction of armed forces and conventional armaments. Confidence- and security-building measures in Europe were also discussed in accordance with PCC's proposals. (Agerpres, TASS, 18 October; *FBIS*, 19, 20 October.)

Military Council and Defense Ministers. The Military Council of WTO Joint Armed Forces meeting in Sofia 11–13 May was attended by the commander in chief of the joint armed forces and USSR marshal Viktor G. Kulikov, by representatives of the members' defense ministries, and by army General Anatolii Gribkov, chief of staff of the joint armed forces. The session coincided with the 33rd anniversary of the WTO. The council discussed enhancing the military strength of the joint armed forces, promoting and strengthening friendship among communist countries, and WTO's proposal to the West and adopted recommendations. (BTA, 11 May; *Narodna armia*, 12 May; TASS, 13 May; *FBIS*, 12, 16 May.) Public comments stressed the "defensive military doctrine" of WTO (e.g., *Pravda*, 14 May). A revealing comment appeared in the Bulgarian party organ during the meeting. Captain Ivan Genov, under "Weekly International Review," wrote that frequently commentaries had appeared about military preparations of the United States and NATO but seldom about WTO activities. He quoted Gribkov on maintaining WTO armed forces at combat readiness "to repulse any outside attack," adding that the West is continually increasing military preparations, necessitating their "increasing the defensive might of the allies to such a level as to exclude the military supremacy of imperialism over socialism." (*Rabotnichesko delo*, 16 May.)

During 5–8 July in Moscow the Defense Ministers' Committee, meeting for the second time in six months, examined military-political developments in Europe following the Reagan-Gorbachev summit and the state of the pact's joint armed forces. The session was chaired by army General Dimitrii T. Yazov, Soviet minister of defense, and attended by Soviet marshal Kulikov, commander in chief of the joint armed forces, and by Soviet General Gribkov. The committee unanimously approved the U.S.-Soviet INF treaty, the 50 percent reduction in strategic offensive weapons, and compliance with the 1972 antiballistic missile (ABM) treaty. The defense ministers also approved Moscow's withdrawal of its OTR-22 (SS-12s) from the GDR and the ČSSR before the treaty's ratification "as a token of goodwill in the general process of nuclear disarmament." They also approved the meetings of U.S. and USSR defense ministers as a "positive step in Soviet-American relations." The participants alleged that "certain NATO circles" plan on "compensating" for the intermediate- and short-range missiles that are being eliminated by "building and extensive modernization of other armaments" to disrupt the process of eliminating nuclear weapons

from Europe. The ministers further defined the process to improve their joint armed forces in line with their "defensive military doctrine" and the Stockholm document. They stressed further cooperation and combat collaboration of their armies and maintaining high levels of combat readiness to "defend socialism." (*Pravda*, 9 July; *FBIS*, 11 July.)

In an 8 July interview with Radio Moscow (*FBIS*, 11 July), Marshal Kulikov said that in the current "struggle for peace and détente," the defending of security must not only be by violent means but also through the new political thinking; the task is to strengthen defensive capability, improve operational and combat training, and carry out the decisions of the PCC. On his return to Budapest, Colonel General Ferenc Karpati, the Hungarian defense minister, said that the fact that the defense ministers met for the second time in six months, whereas years went by between past sessions, was due to "significant changes in recent months in military policy in other areas." Regarding the political and economic reforms and openness, Karpati said that Soviet military leaders act according to the CPSU conference, including applying economic reforms to the military. Reduction of military expenditures would be welcome in Hungary, he said. (Radio Budapest, 9 July; *FBIS*, 11 July.)

On 8 September an exchange of views took place in East Berlin between GDR minister of defense Heinz Kessler and General Gribkov on the military-political situation and the defense of pact armies. Noting disarmament successes, the two sides agreed that the NATO autumn maneuvers and efforts by "certain circles" to compensate for the medium-range missiles "would not be conducive to the further course of détente." (ADN, 8 September; *FBIS*, 9 September.)

The thirty-eighth session of the Military Council was held 3–5 October in Budapest. Participants included Marshal Kulikov and ranking officials of the ministries of defense. The council summarized the results of the 1988 training program, set goals for the upcoming military training year, and discussed other practical issues relating to the pact's armed forces. (MTI, 5 October; *FBIS*, 6 October.)

The 17–18 October regular session of the Committee of Defense Ministers was held in Prague and attended by all WTO defense ministers and the commander in chief and chief of staff of the joint armed forces. According to the chairman—army General Milan Vaclavik, ČSSR minister of defense—the agenda concentrated on WTO disarmament programs but also covered the Vienna follow-up conference and the political-military situation in the world. (TASS, Radio Prague, 18 October; *FBIS*, 19, 20 October.)

Military Exercises and Inspections. The Stockholm document provided for notification, observation, forecasting, and inspection measures to reduce the risk of military confrontation in Europe (*YICA*, 1988). WTO implementation of the provisions was "generally good." Early technical problems of WTO and NATO were being reduced, and "a more consistent pattern" was developing, with East meeting the letter and "in some cases" the spirit of the document (*Twenty-fourth Semiannual Report*, 1 October 1987–1 April 1988; *Twenty-fifth Semiannual Report*, 1 April–30 September 1988).

As of 31 December, eighteen inspections had been conducted under the Stockholm document, thirteen during 1988: 4–6 February the United States inspected a combined Soviet/Hungarian/ČSSR exercise in Hungary; 13–15 March the USSR inspected the Arrowhead Express exercise conducted by the United States and its allies in Norway; 9–11 April the United Kingdom inspected the Odessa MD airborne exercise in the USSR; 10–12 April the United States inspected a GDR/USSR unnotified exercise in the GDR; 1–3 May Bulgaria inspected the amphibious exercise Dragon Hammer, conducted by Italy/United States/allies in Italy; 25–27 July the United States inspected an unnamed Soviet/Polish exercise in Poland (U.S. Joint Chiefs of Staff).

During 12–14 August the Federal Republic of Germany (FRG) inspected an unnamed Soviet/GDR exercise in the GDR; 23–25 August Turkey inspected an unnamed exercise in the Trans-Caucasus MD; 7–9 September the USSR inspected Certain Challenge, conducted by United States/FRG/allies in the FRG; 5–7 October the USSR inspected a Home Defence exercise by the United Kingdom (UK) and 50 U.S. participants in the UK; 14–16 October the United States inspected an unnamed exercise in the Baltic MD in the USSR; 7–9 November Poland inspected Iron Hammer training areas of FRG/UK/few U.S. participants in the FRG; and 28–30 November the GDR inspected the Sachsentross exercise in the FRG (ibid.).

WTO officials utilized the presence of nonpact inspectors at the exercises to project a positive image of compliance with the Stockholm document and to portray a new defensive military doctrine. However, Western observers witnessed a continua-tion of offensive operations, including mass tank attacks. The ČSSR Defense Ministry used a pre-march exercise briefing for foreign military attaches in Prague "to denounce past NATO exercises as threatening to the Warsaw Pact states." During the ČSSR/USSR maneuvers, Soviet officials refused to provide the true unit designations of the participants or information on their normal locations. The U.S. observers noted that a portion of the February exercise in Hungary spilled beyond the notified area. During the Šumava 88 exercise, conducted in June by the ČSSR army, Prague for the first time gave written permission to observers to use personal binoculars, tape recorders, and cameras. Moreover, Czech officials refrained from derogatory remarks about NATO or the United States. However, true unit designations were still hidden and all observable demonstrations were setpieces (*Twenty-fourth Semiannual Report; Twenty-fifth Semiannual Report; NYT*, 4 November).

Moscow's allegation of noncompliance regarding the 7–9 September exercise in the FRG marred an otherwise positive record of inspections. Moscow charged the FRG with violating the forecast provisions of Stockholm by having more than 75,000 troops in a single exercise, which Bonn should have forecasted two years in advance. Both the United States and the FRG "strongly rejected" the allegation, showing that Moscow included allied forces in one exercise that was, in reality, several separate and unrelated activities. The U.S. inspectors were impressed with the cooperation of Polish officials. Romania conducted no forecasting exercises, and for the first time Bucharest sent observers to a U.S. military activity—Certain Challenge, held in the FRG in September (*Twenty-fifth Semiannual Report*).

For 1988 WTO members forecast 22 notifiable military activities—fourteen national and eight combined exercises. The USSR participated in eighteen, ten of which were conducted entirely by Soviet troops. WTO exercises began 29 January–6 February with Baratsag 88 (Friendship 88), north of Lake Balaton in Hungary, with 8,500 Hungarian, 2,500 Soviet, and 2,000 ČSSR troops employing 1,500 trucks, 198 tanks, 360 armored personnel carriers, 95 cannon, nine aircraft, 26 helicopters, and 170 armor-piercing weapons. The stated purpose was to prepare for defensive engagement in early battle operations. This was the first time a press conference—conducted by Lieutenant General Lajos Morocz, Hungary's state secretary of defense who commanded the maneuvers—accompanied the exercise's announcement, a result of "the openness of international affairs." Among the observers was Soviet General Gribkov, chief of staff of WTO's joint armed forces, and Colonel General Karpati, Hungary's minister of defense (*Twenty-fourth Semiannual Report*; Radio Budapest, 28 January; MTI, 28 January, 5 February; *FBIS*, 1, 5 February).

Moscow forecast an exercise for early February (it took place 1–6 February) of fourteen thousand troops in the Belorussian MD and another that was held 29 February–6 March of thirteen thousand troops in the Kiev MD (Joint Chiefs of Staff). A joint USSR/ČSSR exercise was held 22–27 March in the north Bohemian areas of Jáchymov, Bečov, Beňátky, Liberec, and Děčín. The seventeen thousand Soviet and three hundred Czech troops consisted of two partial divisions of the Central Group of Soviet Forces, including a tank regiment with modern T-72 tanks, artillery, motorized rifle units and a Czech rifle battalion. The exercise was designed to upgrade field training standards. Said to be defensive, the maneuvers included a counterattack by a tank regiment. In accordance with Stockholm, the exercise was watched by 43 observers from 22 states. (TASS, 15 March; Radio Prague, 25 March; ČTK, 25 March; *Rudé právo*, 28 March; *FBIS*, 17, 28 March, 1 April.)

Moscow forecast three national exercises during April: (1) three thousand airborne troops in the Odessa MD, conducted 8–13 April; (2) thirteen thousand men in the Carpathian MD, held 1–7 April; and (3) thirteen thousand troops in the Odessa MD, which took place 15–20 April (Joint Chiefs of Staff).

The second phase of Friendship 88 was held 8–15 April in the GDR with eleven thousand GDR, four thousand Polish, and seven thousand GSFG troops; three hundred tanks; 320 antitank missile launchers on armored vehicles; three hundred artillery pieces, 60 helicopters, and two hundred aircraft. The exercise, conducted in Havelberg, Potsdam, Niemegk, Magdeburg, and Gardelegen, was led by Colonel General Horst Stechbarth, deputy minister of national defense and chief of GDR's ground forces. Forty-four representatives from 23 CSCE states observed the exercises, which stressed halting the attacker, repulsing new thrusts, and reestablishing the original position. Soviet army General Boris Snetkov, GSFG commander in chief, attended a joint meeting concluding the exercise. Soviet army Major General Valerii Katko, referring to the U.S.-USSR INF agreement, said that the

Soviet Union had withdrawn and begun destroying its SS-22 missiles (ibid.; ADN, 8, 11, 12, 14, 15 April; *FBIS*, 12, 13, 15, 18 April).

During 6–10 June the ČSSR army conducted the Šumava 88 exercise with 17,459 troops in southern Bohemia in the areas of Strakonice, Česke Budějovice, Vyšší Brod, and Železná Ruda. Major General František Podesva, deputy commander of the western MD, headed the exercise in which two motorized rifle divisions practiced defensive and offensive operations that were witnessed by 36 observers from nineteen CSCE states (*Rudé právo*, 4, 10 June; Radio Prague, 7 June; *FBIS*, 8, 9, 15 June). Prague had forecast a thirteen-thousand troop exercise to be held later in June but subsequently informed the CSCE states that the activity had been reduced below the notification threshold (*Twenty-fifth Semiannual Report*).

The code-named Shield 88, a command and staff exercise, was held in northwest Poland 4–11 June and involved fourteen thousand Polish, ČSSR, GDR, and Soviet forces. CSCE signatories were notified. The purpose was to perfect command coalition cooperation in defensive operations. The maneuvers were directed by army General Florian Siwicki, Polish minister of national defense. Attending were defense ministers of WTO states; the commander in chief of WTO joint armed forces, Marshal Viktor Kulikov; and his chief of staff, General Gribkov. The president and commander in chief of the Polish armed forces, General Jaruzelski, paid a visit and conferred with the defense ministers (PAP, 4, 11 June; Warsaw TV, 6 June; ADN, 6, 8 June; *FBIS*, 7, 8, 13 June). During 21–28 July a joint exercise with 13,500 Soviet and five hundred Polish troops was held in northwest Poland led by the commander of the USSR North Group of Forces. The U.S. observers conducted an inspection (Joint Chiefs of Staff; PAP, 24 July; Warsaw TV, 25 July; *FBIS*, 25, 27 July).

Joint maneuvers were held 24–29 July in the GDR by 17,500 GSFG and 500 GDR troops in the Brandenburg, Luckenwalde, Eisenhuettenstadt, Peitz, Jessen, and Moeckern areas. Some forty observers from twenty CSCE member states were present. The exercise was led by Lieutenant General Aleksandr Chumakov, commander of an army of GSFG, and employed five hundred tanks, 330 guided antitank missile launchers mounted on armored vehicles, 230 artillery pieces, 40 helicopters, and fewer than two hundred aircraft. The purpose was to improve the training of staff and troops in defensive operations, repulsing attacks and counterattacking. (Joint Chiefs of Staff; ADN, 18, 24, 26, 29 July; *FBIS*, 18, 25, 27 July, 1 August.)

A joint GDR/USSR exercise was conducted 8–14 August in the GDR with 14,500 GSFG and 500 East German troops participating in the Burg, Jessen, Luebbenau, Teupitz, and Luckenwalde regions. The maneuvers were led by Lieutenant General Aleksandr Kozlov, deputy commander in chief of the GSFG. The objective was to improve troop leadership and the cooperation of the components in defensive operations. From 20 to 26 August, Moscow held a thirteen thousand-troop exercise in the Trans-Caucasus MD, and Bulgaria, 12–17 August held the Maritsa 88 exercise, its only military activity during the year requiring prior notification under the Stockholm document (Joint Chiefs of Staff; *Twenty-fifth Semiannual Report*).

Command staff exercise Autumn 88 under the leadership of army General Dimitrii Yazov, USSR defense minister, was conducted 15–23 September in the Ukraine, Moldavia, and the adjacent area of the Black Sea. The "token force" involved airborne and seaborne landings with Black Sea fleet ships. WTO and Yugoslavian defense ministers observed the activities. Notification figures furnished by Moscow to CSCE signatories were fourteen thousand for an exercise in the Odessa MD (Joint Chiefs of Staff; TASS, 15, 18, 23 September; *FBIS*, 19, 26 September; *Pravda*, 22 September).

Moscow notified the CSCE states that an exercise of more than 45,000 troops would take place in the Belorussian MD. The maneuvers were conducted 17–22 September in Dubrovo, Shatsk, Berezino, and Ulla. The purpose—to upgrade field training standards of the troops—involved dynamics, assault, and attack-approximating combat conditions. Both land and air forces, including tanks, helicopters, and motorized rifle troops, participated; the number cited by TASS was 21,000. Twenty-six CSCE states sent observers; Moscow forecast a fifteen thousand-troop exercise for the Baltic MD; it was held 10–16 October (Joint Chiefs of Staff; TASS, 9, 21 September; Moscow TV, 21 September; *FBIS*, 12, 22, 27 September).

A joint USSR/Hungarian exercise was conducted 15–20 October in Hungary, north of Lake Balaton, to improve command and cooperation. Commanded by Lieutenant General Yurii Vodolazov, first deputy commander of the Soviet Southern Army Group in Hungary, the maneuvers involved 16,500 Soviet and 500 Hungarian ground and air forces, including a Soviet motorized infantry division and a reduced armored division, as well as 321

tanks, 222 artillery pieces, 26 helicopters, and several aircraft. This was the first time foreign observers (36 from eighteen countries) had attended military activities in Hungary. (Joint Chiefs of Staff; *Izvestiia*, 9 October; MTI, 9, 18, 20 October; *FBIS*, 11, 20, 27 October.)

The last joint WTO exercise of the year was held in the GDR 17–22 October with 17,500 Soviet and 500 GDR troops. Under the command of Major General Aleksei Mityukhin, commander of a GSFG army, the maneuvers aimed to upgrade field training and to improve cooperation of the staffs and troops of the two countries. They were held in Wittstock, Gardelegen, Magdeburg, Zehdenick, and Feldberg. Seventeen states sent 33 observers, this being the sixth exercise in the GDR attended by observers since the Stockholm document (1 January 1987). The troops had 578 tanks, 537 launchers for antitank guided missiles on armored vehicles, 208 artillery pieces, 34 multiple rocket launchers, and 41 helicopters. Fewer than two hundred aircraft sorties were planned. One feature was the crossing of the River Elbe, near Sandau, by motorized rifle and tank units, with air support provided by fighter bombers and helicopters. (Joint Chiefs of Staff; TASS, 17 October; ADN, 17, 19, 22 October; *Neues Deutschland*, 22–23 October; *FBIS*, 19, 20, 27, 28 October.)

Differences Within the WTO. Serious economic problems led to Gorbachev's December announcement of military cutbacks. During the year, however, WTO defense spending continued, except in Romania. According to IISS, there was no indication that "the increase in the rate of defense spending has been cut since the beginning of Gorbachev's tenure" (*The Military Balance, 1988-1989*). This enabled the continued modernization of the pact's armed forces. Gorbachev's declaration was not received with alacrity by all WTO regimes. Hungary and Poland approved enthusiastically, but the ČSSR and GDR did not.

All regimes continued to maintain control, but if any were in danger, Moscow would likely have intervened. Despite the rhetoric about sovereignty, noninterference in internal affairs, and independent socialism, the Brezhnev Doctrine—the Soviet-proclaimed right of military intervention in any country when a communist system is threatened—was not rescinded.

Not all leaders were enamoured by Gorbachev's policies of *glasnost'* and *perestroika*. To most these posed a threat to their rule. The GDR held that

Soviet methods were not transferable. The ČSSR's Miloš Jakeš, who had opposed Alexander Dubček's reforms in 1968 and rejected his rehabilitation in 1988, dismissed the prime minister and others favoring restructuring. Nicolae Ceauşescu's pursuit of a Stalinist course was heading Romania on a disastrous course. Hungary seemed to be the exception.

The region was beset by restiveness, discontent, tension, and human rights violations. Even some communist leaders labeled Marxism-Leninism as an "outmoded ideology." The power of nationalism burgeoned onto the landscape during the year not only in Eastern Europe but within Soviet borders with its more than 140 nationalities. In the Baltic Republics of Lithuania, Latvia, and Estonia and in the Ukraine and elsewhere, demands not only for cultural but political autonomy were made. Russification begot intense resentment. Popular fronts were established in the Baltic states. After months of clashes the Armenian-Azerbaijani dispute was temporarily diffused by Soviet tanks. The Hungarian-Romanian dispute over minorities prompted General Secretary Károly Grósz to raise the question of human rights at the PCC conference. Bulgaria did not even acknowledge the existence of its large Turkish minority. Widespread labor unrest, including strikes, was epitomized by Poland's Solidarity movement, with its official recognition by year's end seemingly inevitable.

After decades, the USSR and other countries not only failed to create atheistic societies but faced open resurgence of religious power. This necessitated loosening long-resisted rights, especially in strongly Catholic Poland, to pacify, at least temporarily, potentially explosive situations. Budapest took another lead in inviting Pope John Paul II to visit Hungary. Religion and nationalism were often inseparable forces, and Moscow also kept a wary eye on the 50 million Muslims in the Central Asiatic Republics who opposed restructuring because it eliminated Moscow's free financial aid.

Despite the many changes stemming from openness and restructuring, there was no shred of evidence of systemic change, the essential ingredient for a real solution to enormous problems.

John J. Karch
Falls Church, Virginia

International Communist Organizations

WORLD MARXIST REVIEW

The Prague-based *World Marxist Review* (*WMR*), the Soviet-controlled international communist theoretical monthly, is the only permanent institutional symbol of unity for the world's pro-Moscow and independent communist parties (see *YICA*, 1984, for a fuller treatment). Aleksandr Subbotin and Sergei Tsukasov, both USSR citizens, continue to serve as chief editor and executive secretary, respectively, with Lubomir Hanak of Czechoslovakia serving as a second executive secretary.

The magazine holds conferences every three to four years; the last took place in April and was attended by representatives of 79 communist parties and fourteen other groupings. One participant, then Communist Party of the Soviet Union (CPSU) International Department (ID) first deputy chief Vadim V. Zagladin, stated that a broadening of the magazine's scope was being contemplated to "more extensively reflect the problems of the world and the communist parties" and to carry views of more than just "communists and forces close to them" (Prague radio, 13 April; *FBIS*, 14 April). Less than six months later another Soviet source boasted that the magazine, although remaining a communist publication, as a result of the meeting "has effected a resolute shift toward cooperation with broad forces representing the entire workers' and entire democratic movement so that its pages have become the venue for creative debate and the emergence of new ideas" (B. Ivanov in *Pravda*, 27 September). He added that "representatives of the social democrats, believers, pacifists, ecologists, and other social forces write in almost every issue" (ibid.). Although exaggerated—the trend had started even before the April conference and the diverse categories of authors are still not that all pervasive—this is certainly the direction that *WMR* has taken during the year. Chief Editor Subbotin confirmed these trends in an interview with Prague's *Rudé právo* on 14 September.

The second change Zagladin foresaw as a result of the conference was a "democratization" of the magazine. Specifically, the chief editor and editorial board were to be elected and the number of parties directly involved in the magazine's production was to be increased (Prague radio, 13 April). Each such party, incidentally, is represented on the Editorial Council, the body that presumably was to do the aforenoted electing. In contrast to Zagladin's first point—the broadening of viewpoints to be carried by the magazine—not one of these "democratic" changes in the staff organization seems to have taken place. There is no evidence of any elections for chief editor or editorial board membership, and the number of parties represented on the Editorial Council has actually diminished by one (participating parties are listed on page 2 of the British edition of *WMR*). This reduction was brought about by the withdrawal of the Italian Communist Party from the magazine, which was announced at the April conference (Prague, *Rudé právo*, 15 April). In a parallel move, the Japan Communist Party's representative to the conference complained about Soviet domination of the magazine and suggested that it cease publication (Tokyo, *Akahata*, 14 April). These actions represented little real change from the preexisting situation, however. In the words of the 15 April *Rudé právo*, the Italian participation had long been "merely formal." Exactly the same behavior on the part of the Japan Communist Party's Standing Presidium was noted in December 1981 (*Communism*, November–December 1982, p. 62). These formal moves by the two Eurocommunist parties took place when it was at least being contemplated that the magazine would become more open and democratic.

FRONT ORGANIZATIONS

Control and Coordination. The Soviet international communist front organizations that have been operating since World War II are counterparts of organizations established by the Comintern after World War I, and their function is the same: to unite communists with other political persuasions to support, strengthen, and lend respectability to USSR foreign policy objectives. Moscow's control is evidenced by the fronts' faithful adherence to the Soviet policy line and by the withdrawal patterns of member organizations (certain pro-Western groups

withdrew after the cold war began, Yugoslav affiliates left following the Stalin-Tito break, and Chinese and Albanian representatives departed as the Sino-Soviet split developed).

The CPSU controls the fronts through the ID (U.S. Congress, *The CIA and the Media*, Washington, D.C., 1978, p. 574), and ID sector chiefs have been publicly involved with front affairs— Yuliy F. Karlamov in the World Peace Council (WPC) and Giorgi V. Shumeiko in the World Federation of Trade Unions (WFTU) and the Afro-Asian People's Solidarity Organization (AAPSO) (*Problems of Communism*, September–October 1984, p. 73). Such officials appear to operate, however, through the Soviet national affiliate, which usually has a representative in the front's international headquarters. This individual is usually a member of the front's Secretariat, but in some cases he or she may be a vice president (*YICA*, 1981).

In addition to the CPSU's influence on the various fronts through the ID, there is more-direct coordination. First, since at least 1979 these fronts, defining themselves as "closely coordinating" nongovernmental organizations, have met periodically to formulate a joint policy (*YICA*, 1988). Second, the WPC, the largest and most important international front, provides positions for the leaders of other main fronts so that they can interlock with one another (ibid.). Finally, the *WMR* has a Problems of Peace and Democratic Movements Commission that apparently furnishes *WMR* representation to meetings of "closely coordinating" nongovernmental organizations (*YICA*, 1987). During the year, evidence of front/*WMR* cooperation was shown in the January and May issues, which carried information on joint WFTU/*WMR* seminars on "social injustice." The International Union of Students (IUS) president Josef Scala made a major policy statement in the July issue on behalf of his organization (as had General Secretary Johannes Pakaslahti for the WPC in the November 1987 issue).

The *WMR* is not considered a front because it is (with one recent exception) fully communist in composition, whereas the fronts cover the spectrum from organizations such as the WFTU (most of whose affiliates are communist) to the WPC (which has a fairly good balance of communists, socialists, "revolutionary democrats," and "independents") to the basically noncommunist Christian Peace Conference (CPC).

Note: In most of the front meetings described below, the local affiliate of the international organization concerned acted as cohost; for simplicity's sake, this fact will not be repeated each time such a meeting is mentioned.

Techniques. Just as Moscow and Havana—world and regional communist centers, respectively—predominated in front-related activities in 1987 (*YICA*, 1988), New Delhi and East Berlin did so in 1988. "Nonaligned" New Delhi hosted the largest and most important official front meeting of the year, the Seventh Congress of AAPSO (November), as well as the annual General Council meeting of the WFTU (October) and the second International Preparatory Committee meeting (May) for the forthcoming (1989) World Youth Festival at Pyongyang. To a large extent, this was a spin-off from the Asia-Pacific emphasis noted during 1987 (*YICA*, 1988) that continued on into 1988 (see below), that is, it marked the first time that an AAPSO congress, a WFTU General Council, or a World Youth Festival (cosponsored by the IUS and the World Federation of Democratic Youth [WFDY]) had met in Asia.

Just as New Delhi has the advantage (from a front standpoint) of being outside the bloc, East Berlin has the advantage of having a confused status in many people's minds while furnishing the controlled environment of a communist center. The German Democratic Republic (GDR) capital hosted an (ostensibly) government-sponsored meeting on nuclear weapons–free zones in June, attended by more than one thousand delegates, exceeding even the AAPSO congress in size. Although not an official front meeting, it had more top front leaders in attendance than had been documented at any other gathering during the year. (*Neues Deutschland*, 20 June.) Using the GDR Peace Council's speech to address its own preparatory committee (Helsinki, *Peace Courier*, no. 4), its subject matter was an important front theme (see below). GDR party chief Erich Honecker opened and closed the meeting, met with foreign delegations during its course, and held a reception for the attendees after it closed (East Berlin, ADN, 20, 22 June; *FBIS*, 21, 23 June). This was more reminiscent of Fidel Castro's behavior during the series of Havana conferences on debt in the summer of 1985 (*YICA*, 1986) than of Mikhail Gorbachev's more-limited involvement in the Moscow "personalities" and women's conferences of 1987 (*YICA*, 1988). More like the latter was Premier Rajiv Gandhi's mere keynoting of the aforenoted Seventh AAPSO Congress, itself a propaganda coup for the meeting's organizers, or General Noriega's less surprising address to the October Latin American Youth and Students' Conference called to support his stand against the United States. Honecker also addressed the Third World Youth Forum International Preparatory Committee meeting at East Berlin in November. Other front meetings in that city during the year were the Tenth Plenary Session of the Berlin Conference of European Catholics (BCEC) in June and the Tenth Conference of the Trade Union International (see below) of Building Workers in September; both were the highest-level meetings held by the respective organizations.

There were three examples during the year of worldwide fronts' attempting to increase their identification with subsidiary organizations they had spawned (originally, they seem to have distanced themselves from the new activities). Two were related to the WFTU General Council meeting wherein one major document called for a closer WFTU relationship with the Trade Union Internationals (TUIs, the eleven worldwide organizations set up by WFTU to deal with specific trades) (Prague, *Flashes from the Trade Unions*, 11 November). The day after the council meeting ended, the Asian-Pacific Trade Union Coordination Committee began its annual sessions. In the same city, the latter organization combined WFTU affiliates with leftist but non-WFTU unions to extend Soviet influence in the area (*YICA*, 1986). The latter case involves yet another New Delhi meeting and is a good example of the back-to-back technique used for front meetings in 1987 (*YICA*, 1988). Another back-to-back series occurred when AAPSO's Asia/Pacific Presidium meeting in Vientiane on 3, 4, and 5 August, was followed by its conference on Cambodia in nearby Phnom Penh on 6, 7 August. Note also that an even more closely entwined concurrent set of meetings took place in Havana on the part of two Latin American regional groupings: the third meeting of the Continental Front of Women (3–7 October) and a conference of Latin American peace movements (3–5 October).

The last example of a close linkage being forged between a parent front organization and its de facto subsidiaries occurred at the October Congress of the Federation of Latin American Journalists (FELAP) in Acapulco. The newly elected FELAP president, Armando Rollemberg, and deputy general secretary, Ernesto Vera, are, unlike their predecessors, vice presidents of the International Organization of Journalists (IOJ). (The re-elected FELAP general secretary, Luis Suarez, is also an IOJ vice president.) The Cuban citizen Vera, moreover, heads the recently established IOJ regional center in Mexico City, where FELAP headquarters is located. The former IOJ general secretary, Jiri Kubka, was recently appointed Czechoslovak ambassador to Mexico and attended the Acapulco congress (as did his IOJ successor). (Mexico City, *Excelsior*, 17, 20 October; Prague, *IOJ Newsletter*, no. 11, June.)

These efforts to tighten up the trade union and journalists' mechanisms were accompanied by an apparent loosening up of the Soviet-line peace movement amid its self-criticism for past one-sidedness. During the latter half of 1987, WPC general secretary Johannes Pakaslahti openly acknowledged that the one-sided stand of his organization had limited its effectiveness and called for cooperation, not confrontation, with other strands of the peace movement (Helsinki, *Peace Courier*, no. 8, 1987; London, *WMR*, November 1977). During 1988, Soviet ex-WPC secretary Tair Tairov, continuing and amplifying this line of argument, admitted that the WPC had developed into a mere instrument of Soviet policy and that too much emphasis had been placed on high-level conferences at the expense of "grass-roots" movements (Copenhagen, *Information*, 13–14 August; Helsinki, *Rauhan puolesta*, September; Sydney, *Tribune*, 5 October). The WPC's Soviet vice president, Genrikh Borovik, echoed these comments and claimed that the Soviet Peace Committee (SPC), of which he is chairman, had already developed relations with a broad spectrum of domestic political organizations (Moscow, *Mezhdunarodnaya zhizn*, no. 10; Helsinki, *Kansan uutiset*, 29 October). Tairov, explaining why the SPC could offer little help in getting the WPC on the right track, said that the Soviet body had not made much progress in *glasnost'* and that Borovik's election as SPC chairman was undemocratic (Helsinki, *Rauhan puolesta*, September; Moscow, *Komsomolskaia pravda*, 25 June). In any case, the November meeting of the WPC bureau proposed that the sessions of the organization's two largest bodies should have near-equal representation from non-WPC organizations (150 each for the Presidential Committee and four hundred WPC to three hundred non-WPC delegates to the forthcoming December 1989 Council) (Helsinki, *Peace Courier*, no. 12). Although Pakaslahti had been one of the public initiators of the campaign to open up the WPC, he was apparently maneuvered out of his job by the same bureau meeting (in the restructuring, which involved re-

ducing the size of all WPC bodies, no provision was made for the general secretaryship [ibid.]).

Another opening up was projected by the November AAPSO congress when it decided that henceforth the non-Afro-Asian associate members would be given a greater say in running the organization (including being elected to the AAPSO Presidium Bureau) (New Delhi, *New Age*, 4 December; *People's Democracy*, 11 December). The IOJ's desire to appear more open, despite its apparent increase in control over FELAP (see above), was seen in its opening up its *Democratic Journalist* to freer discussion (paralleling the aforenoted changes in the *WMR*) and its cosponsoring of the "first ever" conference of secular and church journalists in Prague in December (Prague, *Democratic Journalist*, no. 5; *Rudé právo*, 12 December).

As far as new fronts or semifronts go, the International Physicians for the Prevention of Nuclear War, with its Soviet and U.S. initiatives and copresidents, has become a model for other such organizations (*YICA*, 1988). But in 1988 the Swedes became an additional factor. The International Association of Lawyers Against Nuclear War, which started organizing in 1987 (ibid.), was officially inaugurated at an April meeting in Stockholm with Soviet, U.S., and Swedish copresidents (Moscow, TASS, 13 June; *FBIS*, 16 June). Somewhat similar to this, a new International Foundation for the Survival and Development of Humanity was formed in January with headquarters in Moscow and missions in the United States and Sweden; it has a Soviet chairman and a U.S. vice-chairman. (Moscow, TASS, 15 November; *FBIS*, 17 November.) Similar to the above in its Soviet-American aspect was the April Kabul meeting of "Soviet, American, and Afghan public figures" on the Afghan situation; in structure and personnel, however, it paralleled Castro's conference of "personalities" on the foreign debt in 1985 (*YICA*, 1986) and the Moscow meeting of important "personalities" in 1987 For a Nuclear-Free World, for the Survival of Humanity (*YICA*, 1988).

Themes. There were definite parallels between the WPC's *Programme of Action, 1988*, published in December 1987, and the WFTU General Council resolutions that came out in October (Prague, *Flashes from the Trade Unions*, 11 November). The functional themes of both (with one exception) were not only identical but were listed in the same order: (1) peace, security, and disarmament, (2) socioeconomic development, (3) human rights, and

(4) environmental concerns. (The *Programme of Action* added "culture and education for peace" in fourth place, relegating the environment to fifth.) These five categories provided five of the six points of the agenda for the April International Encounter for Peace, Disarmament, and Life, held in Merida, Venezuela, cosponsored by the University of the Andes, the WPC, and the United Nations Educational, Scientific, and Cultural Organization (UNESCO). The AAPSO congress declaration of November had "peace and disarmament" in first place followed by human rights, national liberation, and economic development provisions (New Delhi, *New Age*, 4 December). AAPSO seems to have given short shrift to environmental as well as cultural issues. A preliminary analysis by the WPC of its *Programme of Action, 1989* (promulgated in November) indicates that while disarmament, human rights, and environment remain top priorities, development has been downgraded and "culture and education for peace" may have disappeared altogether (Helsinki, *Peace Courier*, 1/89).

Under the "peace, security, and disarmament" rubric, the fronts emphasized their approval of the signing of the intermediate-range nuclear forces (INF) treaty in December 1987 (e.g., the AAPSO Presidium in January) and its exchange of ratifications in June (e.g., Prague's *Flashes from the Trade Unions*, 17 June). The WFTU's newsletter put the INF treaty in the context of "a decisive step towards ridding the world of all nuclear weapons by the year 2000" (ibid., 16 September). The latter idea, put forth by Gorbachev in 1986, had been the theme of two major front congresses in 1987 (see *YICA*, 1988). Similarly, in 1988 the BCEC held its June plenum under the motto "free of nuclear weapons by 2000 A.D."

Regional conflicts were the subject of an AAPSO conference in Kabul in March, and concern for such conflicts was expressed by the WPC Presidium at its Prague meeting that same month. As the Angolan, Iran-Iraq, and Afghan wars wound down during the year, this subject seemed to be getting less and less attention (though the WFDY at its December executive meeting in Kiev still made note of it). One conflict where little progress had been made, Cambodia, was the subject of an AAPSO meeting in Phnom Penh in August.

The most striking subdivision of the peace and disarmament theme in 1988 is the "nuclear-free zone/nuclear weapons–free zone/zone of peace" campaign. The East Berlin nuclear weapons–free zone conference was the largest (see above); the

other 1000-plus delegate meeting was the aforementioned October Havana Latin American women's meeting (Havana, *Granma Weekly*, 16 October). In addition, the following specific areas were emphasized:

South Atlantic as a Zone of Peace: subject of a June WFDY and a September WPC meeting, both in Brasilia

Indian Ocean as a Zone of Peace: subject of a WPC/AAPSO meeting in Antananarivo in April and emphasized at the WFTU Bureau meeting (Addis Ababa, March) and the AAPSO Asia-Pacific Presidium meeting (Vientiane, August)

Nuclear weapons–free Zone for Korea: subject of an October WPC meeting in Pyongyang

Nuclear-free Asia-Pacific: an emphasis of the WFTU bureau (Addis Ababa, March) and General Council (New Delhi, October) meetings as well as a WFDY Asia-Pacific youth meeting (Sydney, May)

There was also stress on the removal of bases in the Asia-Pacific region (chiefly in the Philippines, Japan, and Diego Garcia) at the Vientiane June AAPSO meeting, and an emphasis on limiting Pacific naval activities in the WPC's *Programme of Action, 1989.*

The "development" theme remained a favorite of the trade union fronts (*YICA*, 1988) and continued to be pursued in relation to disarmament (Western disarmament would release funds for Third World development) and nonpayment of foreign debts, which were said to hinder Third World development. The WFTU February conference in Paris on international economic security had workshops devoted to the development/disarmament relationship, more-equitable international economic cooperation, and Third World debt and hunger (Paris, *L'Humanité*, 25 February). The WFTU October General Council meeting called for a world trade union conference on development and for trade union action against "the consequences of the unpayable external debt" (New Delhi, *New Age*, 6 November). The WFTU-related Dublin Committee (*YICA*, 1986), at a June meeting in Geneva, called for a Disarmament for Development Fund to be set up under U.N. auspices (Prague, *Flashes from the Trade Unions*, 1 July), an idea reiterated by the WFTU General Council meeting. The foreign debt theme, first promoted by the Cubans vis-à-vis Latin

America in 1985 (*YICA*, 1986), focused on Africa at two WFTU conferences in Addis Ababa, one in December 1987 and the other the March bureau meeting. Foreign debt as it affected the Asia-Pacific region was emphasized at the annual meeting of the WFTU-related Asian-Pacific Trade Union Coordination Committee in New Delhi in October (New Delhi, *New Age*, 13 November). The New International Economic Order, which would embody the changes suggested by the fronts, had a new parallel in the New International Scientific Order, which was put forth by World Federation of Scientific Workers' president Jean-Marie Legay in January (Sofia, BTA, 23 January; *FBIS*, 25 January); presumably, scientific resources were to be diverted from military to peaceful uses under this rubric.

As befitted the 40th anniversary of the U.N. Declaration of Human Rights, the fronts emphasized the subject with, however, a narrow focus and a linkage to other major themes. As an example, the WPC's *Programme of Action, 1988* started out with "right to life and peace" and then emphasized "racism and apartheid," citing South Africa, Namibia, and Palestine. Palestine and South Africa were also the focus of both the September WFTU memorandum to the United Nations and the CPC's October Continuation Committee meeting in Gorlitz, GDR (Prague, *Flashes from the Trade Unions*, 30 September; Prague, *CPC Information*, 3 November). Palestine was also the subject of an AAPSO meeting in Nicosia in June and of a special session of the New Delhi AAPSO congress in November.

The WFTU tailored the issue to workers' rights, cosponsoring a symposium with the WMR on "the working class and social injustice" at some time before May, holding a conference on "human and trade union rights" in Sofia in June, and publishing articles on trade union rights in nearly half of its issues of *World Trade Union Movement* during the year (nos. 2, 3, 7, 8, and 11/12). The call of the Asia-Pacific young workers' conference held in Alma Ata in January for "the right to participate in trade union life and the building of a progressive society" (Prague, *Flashes from the Trade Unions*, 12 February) suggests that many of these so-called rights would be considered more as duties in Western societies. The AAPSO congress stressed rights associated with political and economic independence (a slap at transnational corporations [TNCs]) (New Delhi, *New Age*, 4 December). During the year the WFTU began publication of a *TNCs Bulletin*. Finally, IUS President Josef Scala in the July *WMR* noted the existence of an International Center

for the Defense of Student Rights, apparently modeled on the International Center for the Defense of Trade Union Rights, which had been set up in Prague in November 1987 (*YICA*, 1988).

The WPC's monthly *Peace Courier* carried articles devoted to ecological issues throughout the year (nos. 4, 5, 7/8, 10, and 12). In March the 10th Agricultural Workers TUI Conference emphasized the ecological issue and the WPC Presidential Committee meeting stressed environmental protection as a human right (again, linkage). The WPC/UNESCO April Merida (Venezuela) "International Encounter" had on its environmental agenda consideration of "the Third World as dump site of international contaminated waste material" (conference brochure). An August–September WPC seminar in Porto Alegre was devoted to the Amazon rain forest, and the no. 12 issue of *Peace Courier* attributed the rain forest depletion to the demand for more beef cattle grazing areas, in turn the result of the demand for hamburgers (again, the transnational corporations are the culprits!). And though WFTU's *World Trade Union Movement*, no. 11/12, devoted seven of its 33 pages to ecological issues, it appears that the WPC will continue to take the lead in this subject (e.g., indications are that its *Programme of Action, 1989*, has raised the subject to the organization's number three priority).

The WPC seemed to be almost the sole purveyor among the fronts of "culture and education for peace," though access to the materials of the World Federation of Teachers Unions (FISE) would no doubt reveal a concern about this matter. Even the WPC, however, did not give the subject much stress, in spite of the fact that the United Nations has declared 1988–1997 the World Decade for Cultural Development. One conference on the subject (Tubingen, May) we will note only to point out that WPC vice president Mikis Theodorakis played a leading role; with only 10 percent of its participants coming from outside West Germany, we are reluctant to consider it "fully international." (Prague, *World Student News*, no. 12.) The WPC also seems to have avoided stressing a front theme linked to that of culture and education, the New International Information and Communication Order (NIICO). This omission occurred even in a *Peace Courier* article, "The West Distorts Third World Reality" (Helsinki, *Peace Courier*, no. 12), the very situation the NIICO is purportedly designed to overcome. The NIICO was emphasized in the WFDY's bureau meeting of December 1987, and the IOJ's *Democratic Journalist* had articles devoted to it in

Major International Communist Front Organizations

Organization (president, general secretary, or equivalents)	Year founded	Headquarters	Claimed membership	Affiliates	Countries
Afro-Asian Peoples' Solidarity Organization (AAPSO) (Murad Ghalib, Nuri Abd-al-Razzaq Husayn)	1957	Cairo	no data	87	no data
Asian Buddhist Conference for Peace (ABCP) (Kharkhuu Gaadan, G. Lubsan Tseren)	1970	Ulan Bator	no data	15	12
Berlin Conference of European Catholics (BCEC) (Franco Leonori, Hubertus Guske)[1]	1964	East Berlin	no data	no data	45
Christian Peace Conference (CPC) (Karoly Toth, Lubomir Mirejovsky)	1958	Prague	no data	no data	ca. 80
International Association of Democratic Lawyers (IADL) (Joe Nordmann, Amar Bentoumi)	1946	Brussels	25,000	no data	ca. 80
International Federation of Resistance Movements (FIR) (Arialdo Banfi, Alix Lhote)	1951	Vienna	5,000,000	68	29
International Institute for Peace (IIP)	1957	Vienna	no data	no data	no data
International Organization of Journalists (IOJ) (Kaarle Nordenstreng, Dusan Ulcak)[1]	1946	Prague	ca. 250,000	no data	120+
International Radio and Television Organization (OIRT) (Sakari Kuru, Gennadij Codr)	1946	Prague	no data	no data	no data
International Union of Students (IUS) (Josef Scala, Georgios Michaelides)	1946	Prague	ca. 34,000,000[2]	117[2]	110[2]
Organization of Solidarity of the Peoples of Africa, Asia, and Latin America (OSPAAL) (Susumu Ozaki?, Rene Anillo Capote)	1966	Havana	no data	no data	no data
Women's International Democratic Federation (WIDF) (Freda Brown, Mirjam Vire-Tuominen)	1945	East Berlin	200,000,000	142	124
World Federation of Democratic Youth (WFDY) (Walid Masri, Gyorgy Szabo)[4]	1945	Budapest	150,000,000	ca. 270	123
World Federation of Scientific Workers (WFSW) (Jean-Marie Legay, Stan Davison)	1946	London	740,000	ca. 46	70+
World Federation of Teachers' Union (FISE) (Lesturuge Ariyawansa, Gerard Montant)	1946	East Berlin	26,000,000	124	79
World Federation of Trade Unions (WFTU) (Sandor Gaspar, Ibrahim Zakariya)	1945	Prague	ca. 214,000,000	92	81
World Peace Council (WPC) (Romesh Chandra, Johannes Pakaslahti)	1950	Helsinki	no data	no data	145[3]

1. East Berlin, *Neues Deutschland*, 20 June.
2. Prague, *World Student News*, no. 2 (membership figure includes newly incorporated secondary school students; number of affiliates apparently for university-level only).
3. Prague, ČTK, 18 March; *FBIS*, 21 March.
4. Budapest, *WFDY News*, no. 8–9.

three of its first eleven issues of 1988 (nos. 3, 4, 5). This suggests a specialized interest just like trade union rights in the case of *World Trade Union Movement* and ecology in the case of *Peace Courier*.

As in 1987 (*YICA*, 1988), Asia and the Pacific continued to be stressed by the fronts in 1988, as seen by the number of conferences that were held in that area. The WPC's *Programme of Action, 1988*

devoted more space to Asia and the Pacific than to any other geographic area. Gorbachev's 16 September Krasnoyarsk speech has been interpreted, much like his 1986 Vladivostok speech, as showing a renewed emphasis on the Asian-Pacific area (Helsinki, *New Perspectives*, No. 1/89, p. 17; *YICA*, 1988). The next World Youth Festival, the largest type of front meeting, will be held in Pyongyang in

July 1989, which indicates that the area will continue to be of paramount front interest.

Personnel. The footnoted names in the accompanying chart indicate the most important new leaders in front circles. Not noted was the fact that Murad Ghalib of Egypt was confirmed as president and Nuri Abd-al-Razza Husayn from Iraq was reelected as general secretary at the AAPSO's congress in November (New Delhi, *People's Democracy*, 11 December).

New IOJ vice presidents were Chou Chang Chun (North Korea), Leszek Gontarski (Poland), and Edgar Jaramillo (Ecuador) (Prague, *Democratic Journalist*, no. 10). New IOJ secretaries during the year were Konstantin Ivanov (Bulgaria?), Leena Pakku (Finland), Constantin Pisacaru (Romania?), and Bernd Rayer (East Germany) (Prague, *IOJ Newsletter*, nos. 2, 3, 15, 18). The IOJ Secretariat lacks Africans or Asians; thus Rayer has the African (and apparently the Arab) account whereas Pisacaru covers Asia (ibid., nos. 7, 18). By the first of 1989, however, the situation appeared to have been partially remedied by the appointment of Christopher Muzavasi (South Africa?) as an IOJ secretary (ibid., no. 1, 1989).

The presidents and vice presidents of the IUS and WFDY, unlike the other fronts, share, at least to some degree, in the day-to-day running of their respective organizations. The president, vice presidents, general secretary, secretaries, and treasurer of the IUS are in the Secretariat (Prague, *IUS Secretariat Reports*, no. 7–8, 1987; *World Student News*, no. 2). The same positions also constitute the WFDY bureau (Budapest, Twelfth Assembly of the World Federation of Democratic Youth, "Proposal for the Composition of the WFDY Bureau"). Vice presidents thus serve on the staffs of these organizations' magazines (e.g., Jose de la Rosa Castillo on *World Student News* and Abd-al-Basit Musa on *World Youth*), along with the usual component of the organizations' secretaries. The Soviets then, again uniquely, have not traditionally had secretarial slots in the IUS and WFDY (*YICA*, 1984, 1988); a vice president would do as well!

The lists of the *World Student News* Editorial Board would indicate that because Pius Dakora (Ghana) has replaced his countryman Philip Gardiner on that body, he has also replaced him as the Ghanaian IUS secretary (Prague, *World Student News*, no. 1, 1986, no. 11; *Problems of Communism*, March–April 1987). It also appears that Vesselin Valchev has replaced V. Zlatinov as Bulgarian

IUS secretary, though the latter had never been definitely identified in that position (ibid.; *World Student News*, no. 1, 1986). Mouhamadou M. Fall is the IUS's new Senegalese vice president and IUS secretary Gaston Grisoni is from Uruguay (ibid., no. 7, 1987, no. 4, 1987).

WFDY vice presidents Luis Cardoso (Portugal) and Matthew T. Rajajai (India) also sit on the *World Youth* Editorial Board (Budapest, *World Youth*, no. 3; Sydney, *The Guardian*, 18 May). Because S. Brostrom (Denmark) has replaced his countryman Henrik Andersen on the *World Youth* Editorial Board, he has probably also replaced him as the WFDY's Danish secretary (Budapest, *World Youth*, no. 11–12, 1986, no. 3; *Problems of Communism*, March–April 1987). The following 1988 board members of *World Youth* may also be occupying slots allocated to their respective countries on the WFDY bureau: vice presidents: A. Kovylov (USSR), C. de Negri (Chile); deputy general secretary: R. Lopez (Colombia); secretaries: V. Georgakakis (Greece), U. Brockmeyer or B. Grassler (GDR) (Twelfth Assembly of the World Federation of Democratic Youth; Budapest, *World Youth*, no. 3).

A comparison of the WPC's *New Perspectives*, no. 6, 1987, and no. 6, 1988, shows that the organization obtained the following new vice presidents during the year: Genrikh Borovik (USSR), Abou Camara (Guinea), Marcelino Jaen (Panama), Jorge Alberto Kreyness (Argentina), Sarwar Mangal (Afghanistan), Hugo Mejias Bricero (Nicaragua), and Ali Ameir Muhammad (Tanzania). How long these will last is not known in view of the fact that the WPC's bureau in November proposed that it contain only 30 vice presidents, not the 51 that sat on it up to that point (Helsinki, *Peace Courier*, no. 12). Whether the other 21 vice presidents would lose their positions altogether or merely their seats on the bureau was not clear. A comparison of the aforenoted two *New Perspectives* also indicated the following new members of its Editorial Board: Marjut Helminen (Finland) and Ray Stewart (New Zealand). And as noted above, Pakaslahti and the position of general secretary may be eliminated from the WPC.

The WFTU added a new secretary for Black Africa, Messeambia Koulimaya (Congo); Hans Christoph is the new FISE secretary for the GDR (Prague, *World Trade Union Movement*, no. 8; Pyongyang, KCNA, 8 September; *FBIS*, 9 September); and Jamil Shahada (Palestine), Antonio Jaimes A. (Mexico), Helga Labs (GDR), Rimm Papilov (USSR), and Michèle Baracat (France), were newly noted vice presidents of that organization (*Teachers of the Whole World*, East Berlin, no. 4, 1987). Newly identified AAPSO personnel were deputy secretary general S. S. al-Gampi (PDRY), and secretaries T. Schubert (GDR), S. Molifi (South Africa), and P. Spassov (Bulgaria, presumably replacing the Czech Ivan Pleshaty) (*Afro-Asian Solidarity*, Cairo, 3/4).

Wallace H. Spaulding
McLean, Virginia

THE MIDDLE EAST AND NORTH AFRICA

Introduction

A series of stunning and generally unforeseen major developments burst upon the political scene in the Middle East during 1988. In February Gorbachev announced the complete withdrawal of Soviet forces from Afghanistan within one year. Three months later Morocco and Algeria renewed diplomatic relations after thirteen years of Algerian support for the guerrilla war in the Western Sahara against Morocco. July brought Iran's sudden acceptance of the U.N.-sponsored cease-fire with Iraq. Soon thereafter came King Hussein's dramatic severance of legal and administrative ties to the Israeli-occupied territories of the West Bank and the Gaza strip. This step altered the dimensions of the Arab-Israeli conflict, helping to precipitate the Palestine Liberation Organization's declaration of an independent Palestinian state in the occupied territories, the upsurge of the *intifada* against Israeli occupation, and finally, in December, U.S. agreement to open a dialogue with the PLO following the latter's recognition of U.N. Resolutions 242 and 338, among other steps taken by the organization. Although less publicized, the failure of Lebanon's parliament to agree on a successor to retiring president Amin Gemayel in September removed that tortured country's remaining symbol of nationhood, edging it even closer to complete disintegration.

The communist parties of the region were, for the most part affected negatively by this wave of events. Far from playing a leadership role in their countries, with the exception of the isolated little People's Democratic Republic of Yemen, the parties merely reacted to major political forces at best as hangers-on and more often as illegal underground organizations. Furthermore, the parties' ideological vigor continued to be debilitated by the unfolding revelations of *glasnost'* and *perestroika*. As the mother church of communism recanted much of its standard gospel and laid bare the pervasive national failures resulting therefrom, reality overtook the old façade of Soviet progressiveness. Closer U.S.-Soviet relations further blurred Marxist dogma's distinctiveness. This effect was compounded, of course, by Soviet actions favoring the USSR's economic interests (particularly in its relations with the West) at the expense of radical states and revolutionary or liberation movements. Soviet withdrawal from Afghanistan was seen regionally in this light—an effort to improve economic relations with the wealthy Gulf states, the West, and the Islamic world overall. Also evident was Moscow's concern for the restiveness of its own large Muslim population, which lessened further the relative importance attached to the welfare of regional communist parties.

At the end of the year, the People's Democratic Party of Afghanistan (PDPA) more and more seemed doomed to play a sacrificial role in this process of the USSR's reorientation, as the final stages of the Soviet military withdrawal from Afghanistan progressed. Following the Soviet invasion of 1979, the PDPA was not, by Moscow's definition, a communist or even socialist party, but rather a ruling party in a state undergoing the "national democratic stage of revolution" (*YICA*, 1987 and 1988). This position provided the Soviets with an ideological salve for the pain of their withdrawal and gave the PDPA a theoretical basis for de-emphasizing its Marxist orientation in favor of Afghan tradition and nationalism. The PDPA's efforts, however, were manifestly unsuccessful. Party factionalism was evident throughout the year, and prior to the October plenum three top figures were dismissed from office (AFP, 25 October; *FBIS*, 26 October). In addition, several hundred people were arrested, including up to 50 party members. Out of 165 full and alternate party members, reportedly only 94 attended the plenum (*NYT*, 26 and 29 October).

An abortive coup attempt in the country's second largest city the following month was particularly embarrassing to the regime, as it was led by personnel of the supposedly loyal ministries of state security and interior and was intended to transfer power to the resistance forces (U.S. Department of State, *Afghanistan: Soviet Occupation and Withdrawal*, Special Report no. 179, December; TASS, 24 November; *FBIS*, 28 November).

High-level defections during the year further highlighted the dilemma the PDPA found itself in as it alienated its own hard-line factions through ever wider efforts to form a coalition government that would include factions of the guerrilla forces. None of the resistance groups was swayed from their goal of complete destruction of the PDPA and the Soviet-built ruling apparatus. Even a resort to obviously rigged and hastily staged National Assembly elections only deepened the sense of illegitimacy plaguing the regime. Initial published results gave the leftist groups a mathematically impossible 114.7 percent of the winning candidates; the portion of victorious candidates belonging to leftist groups was subsequently changed to 44 percent, giving "independents" 56 percent (*Kabul Times*, 24 April and 30 April). Apart from the fact secret ballots were disallowed, candidate lists were published only after polls opened, and many polling booths were unmanned, the resistance did not permit the elections in its areas of control (U.S. Department of State, ibid.). The final months of the year brought instances of open Soviet disillusionment with the regime and public contradiction in Soviet media of some of the more overly optimistic assessments by the PDPA.

Just as a complete Soviet military withdrawal from Afghanistan will undoubtedly bring new waves of bloodshed, the Iran-Iraq cease-fire prompted a campaign by the Khomeini regime to execute its internal enemies wholesale. The immediate motivation was retribution against the guerrilla opposition, the Mojahedin-e Khalq, whose underground had harassed the regime at home and abroad and, finally, conducted full-scale military operations within Iran from Iraqi bases. Given the Mojahedin's leftist orientation, all leftist prisoners were apparently targeted. Toward the end of the year the "Tudeh Party of Iran [asked] the United Nations, the human rights committee, and Amnesty International to take prompt action to save the lives of thousands of people whose only crime [was] having a different ideology..." (Clandestine Radio of the Iranian Toilers, December; *FBIS-NES*, 2 December). Although some Tudeh prisoners had been executed during the war, most were held by Teheran, partly as pawns to reduce Soviet military assistance to Iraq. The cease-fire removed that inhi-

bition, and with the need to finally face the human and physical dislocations of the long war, the regime apparently decided to eliminate disloyal elements. The Tudeh had been split earlier in the year when dissidents held a congress outside Iran and founded a new communist party, the Iranian People's Democratic Party, announced by a communiqué in Paris on 6 February (*Le Monde*, 9 February; *FBIS-NES*, 11 February). Despite this splintering, the loss of imprisoned members of the party, and draconian measures of repression taken by the government, party activities were not reduced, according to Tudeh claims. Clandestine activities by party cells included organizing strikes and protests, as well as efforts to form fronts with other revolutionary leftist organizations (*Tudeh News*, 17 and 27 February).

In the absence of more precise information, the effects of the executions on the Tudeh are difficult to weigh. Prisoners killed reportedly number in the thousands. One victim reportedly was Nurudin Kianouri, who led the Tudeh until 1983 (*Manchester Guardian Weekly*, 11 September). Soviet protest over the fate of the prisoners generally consisted of bland repetitions of the Tudeh's own published denunciations of Iran's actions (for instance, *Pravda*, 7 December; *FBIS-SOV*, 8 December). Moscow Radio's more forceful criticism questioned the "policy of moral and physical assassination," accusing Teheran of "sacrificing members of the Tudeh Party and the Fedaiyin Organization... to gain the trust and support of [U.S.] imperialism..." (Moscow Radio Peace and Progress, in Persian to Iran, 5 November; *FBIS-SOV*, 30 November).

While the Tudeh's link with the Mojahedin-Khalq was principally that of guilt by only the broadest form of association, the Iraqi Communist Party (ICP) had, since early in the war, concentrated its resources in the north of Iraq and formally joined with the Kurdish guerrilla parties against the Baghdad government. The ICP was thus identified with the guerrilla and Iranian aim of overthrowing Saddam Hussein's regime, and its destruction was assured once the cease-fire brought the end of Iranian support and freed Iraqi forces to regain control of Iraqi Kurdistan. As tens of thousands of Kurds escaped to Turkey and Iran, and many of those remaining were forcibly moved to Iraq's southern plains, and many thousands killed, the organized resistance was shattered (*Middle East International*, 9 September). Reliable information on the fate of ICP members is not yet available, but the party's situation was partially revealed by an appeal on the Kurdish resistance's radio in October to fighters to return to Iraq and join in the battle (*Hurriyet*, Istanbul, 2 October; *FBIS-NES*, 13 October). While the ICP has surely survived in some form, its postwar role seems sharply limited by the stigma of cooperation with Iraq's internal and external enemies while the country's back was to the wall during nearly nine years of war.

Although still suffering many of the divisive effects of its 1986 civil war, the ruling Yemeni Socialist Party of the Peoples' Democratic Republic of Yemen (PDRY) held its ground as the one Marxist party of the Middle East in control of a state. In contrast to the many ambiguities of Soviet policy toward the Gulf countries, Moscow's support for the PDRY seemed if anything upgraded, possibly in part to offset the image of Soviet military withdrawal from Afghanistan, which was seen as abandonment of the PDPA. Moscow's military resupply of the PDRY exceeded losses from the civil war to a degree prompting speculation about Soviet prepositioning of weapons for its own possible use (*CSM*, 11 March). An equally plausible Soviet motive is the provision of high-visibility military hardware to bolster the position of a YSP still beset with internal factionalism and tribal disputes. Military ties were dramatized by the defense minister's visit to Moscow in March and by the visit to Aden of Admiral Sidorov, deputy commander in chief of the Soviet navy, in May. Similarly, the PDRY's endemic financial stress, exacerbated by the civil war and reduced remittances from the 100,000 South Yemenis employed in Saudi Arabia, added to the importance of Soviet economic assistance. Petroleum represents the PDRY's most promising new source of earnings, and Soviet discoveries in 1987 led to contracts in January for development of the oil fields and a pipeline to enable export. The pipeline will be completed in 1990. In the meantime, the exchange of ministerial-level visits between Moscow and Aden drew attention to high expectations for the PDRY's oil sector.

Despite continuing border disagreements with all its neighbors that led to minor clashes with both Oman and Saudi Arabia, the PDRY pursued improved relations with these moderate Arab states and in February restored diplomatic ties with Egypt. This more moderate and accommodating PDRY was in harmony with the USSR's strong desire to gain acceptance as a responsible, as opposed to revolutionary, power in the Persian Gulf region. Moscow's opening of diplomatic relations

with Qatar in August bolstered this effort, particularly as it occurred at a time of tension between Qatar and the United States occasioned by Qatar's black-market purchase of a dozen U.S. Stinger anti-aircraft missiles (*NYT*, 1 August). While Moscow's long courtship of Saudi Arabia did not yet achieve such success, two specialists from the Soviet ministry of foreign affairs visited the Saudi deputy prime minister and foreign minister in February. As the Soviet's Saudi effort advanced, propaganda attacks by the small and shadowy Communist Party of Saudi Arabia (CPSA) against the kingdom moved from the obviously Soviet-linked *World Marxist Review* to outlets less closely connected with the Soviet Union. For instance, the review's March issue called for a broad front of "national patriotic forces" to replace the Saudi monarchy and to turn the Middle East and Indian Ocean region into a "zone of peace," a standard position taken in Soviet propaganda. In October, however, the CPSA's denunciation of the monarchy for the execution of four Shia saboteurs was carried by the clandestine Voice of Palestine radio rather than by a Soviet-controlled media (6 October; *FBIS-NES*, 7 October). Moscow's continuing classification of the Bahrain National Liberation Front (NLF/B) as a "national democratic party" rather than a full communist party (see *YICA*, 1986), on the other hand, is apparently considered a sufficient fig leaf to permit NLF/B statements in virtual Soviet mouthpieces like the *Information Bulletin* and *World Marxist Review*. However, the NLF/B's regular participation in meetings of delegations predominately from full communist parties and its claims of party activities in Bahrain, Saudi Arabia, Oman, and Iraq hardly conceal a Moscow-NLF/B link from the Saudis, from whose perspective Bahrain occupies a particularly sensitive and important place.

In contrast to the complete repression or state control encountered by most Marxist parties elsewhere in the Middle East, the Lebanese Communist Party (LCP) and the Organization of Communist Action in Lebanon (OCAL) operate openly within the semianarchic Lebanese mélange of shifting militia alliances. Both the LCP and OCAL have suffered heavy losses throughout the civil war because of their close links to Palestinian guerrilla groups and the enmity of Shi'ites to their atheism. But the communists, like most other groups, are deeply apprehensive about their fate should Lebanon's divisions worsen. The failure of parliament to replace President Amin Gemayel when his six-year term expired in September increased these fears. In late

1987, LCP general secretary George Hawi had urged political compromise, even though the new president would inevitably be "right-wing" rather than "progressive" (*IB*, January). The LCP's most prominent role is within the National Resistance Front, which opposes de facto Israeli occupation of its "security zone" in South Lebanon. When a party member, a twenty-year-old girl, shot and seriously wounded Antoine Lahad, commander of Israel's proxy, the South Lebanon Army, in November, the LCP achieved a major propaganda coup (*FBIS-NES*, 8 November). The LCP readily exploited the event through its own publishing outlets and radio station, which broadcasts eighteen hours daily (*WMR*, August).

Even before Jordan tightened security following King Hussein's severing of political and administrative ties to the Israeli-occupied West Bank, the Communist Party of Jordan (CPJ) regularly complained of political repression (*IB*, April). By August, Jordan's government had replaced the boards of directors of the country's three leading newspapers with its own appointees, a step which was partly responsible for the subsequent closing of Jordan's only English-language weekly (*Middle East Report*, January-February 1989). The major financial dislocations caused by the king's policy toward the West Bank—a sharp fall in the value of Jordanian currency and reduced remittances from abroad—added to an atmosphere of increasing government restriction likely to further reduce the scope of the CPJ's activities.

In Israel, the Communist Party of Israel (CPI), with the allied Democratic Front for Peace and Equality, held its own in the November general elections, garnering 3.7 percent of the vote and keeping the four seats it had previously held (out of 120 in the legislature) (*Jerusalem Post*, international edition, 6–12 November). Given the growing force of *intifada* in the occupied territories, there had been some expectation that Israeli Arabs, who constitute about 80 percent of CPI membership, would increase their support for the CPI, which has traditionally been an outlet for Arab grievances. But the voting turnout by qualified Arabs rose only to 75.6 percent from 72 percent in the previous election, and the CPI was not a major beneficiary of the increase (ibid., 6–12 November). In the occupied territories, the illegal but tolerated Palestinian Communist Party continued to be part of the secret Unified Command that apparently controls the uprising (*NYT*, 6 February). This committee includes representatives of Fatah, the Democratic Front for

the Liberation of Palestine, and the Popular Front for the Liberation of Palestine, among others. Committee representatives also participate in underground local committees, but it is by no means clear who is directing whom, or whether initiatives are generated locally more than by direction of the Unified Command. Fatah's struggles with the communists are of long standing, and the factionalism characteristic of the Palestinian movement does not appear to have diminished with the advent of *intifada*.

This factionalism is partly related to Syria's long effort to control the movement for its own political ends and prevent any settlement of the Arab-Israeli dispute not serving its purposes. Arafat's dispute with President Hafez Assad and Syria's consequent support for extremist PLO factions have complicated Soviet efforts to seize the initiative in the peacemaking process and have put Soviet and Syrian policies at cross-purposes. The Syrian Communist Party (SCP) faithfully follows Moscow's line and is a part of the ruling National Progressive Front, playing a formal rather than an activist role in Syrian politics. Independent activism by the SCP not only would disrupt Syrian-Soviet relations, but also stimulate the kind of bloody repression characteristically employed by Assad against his enemies. Syria's isolation in the Arab world, stemming largely from Damascus's alliance with non-Arab Iran during the war, began to bear bitter fruit after the cease-fire. Iraq soon began to support Christian forces in Lebanon opposed to Syria's political strategy there. Saudi aid to Syria lagged. Egypt's improving relations with the USSR and, especially, Egypt's re-entry into the Arab fold as a result of the war weakens Syrian leverage. The quickening pace of Soviet discussions with Israel as a facet of Moscow's aggressive pursuit of a peacemaking role is as upsetting to Assad as are Soviet pressures for debt repayment and footdragging in military matters (*Middle East International*, 24 June). In such an atmosphere, the chances that the SCP will assume a vigorous political role seem slim and will likely remain so until a very different Syrian regime has emerged.

Denied even the symbolic public role of the SCP, the Egyptian Communist Party is small and functions clandestinely, "Under difficult conditions . . . to strengthen their underground structures and to step up their ideological work" (*African Communist*, Fourth Quarter 1987). The Egyptian communist movement, moreover, is notoriously splintered, and in recent years its appeal has been greatly overshadowed by militant Islamic groups, as has happened elsewhere in the Middle East. As a direct consequence of *intifada*, students at Ayn Shams University staged massive protest demonstrations in January against the Israeli occupation. After peace had been restored by tear gas, Egypt's interior minister assigned responsibility jointly to communists and Muslim fundamentalists (*Manchester Guardian Weekly*, 17 January; *FBIS-NES*, 15 January). Most observers, however, identify the fundamentalists as the prime movers of the demonstrations. Although Egypt's refurbished image in the Arab world enhances its political stature at home, the country's staggering economic problems continue to create opportunities for opposition groups. Among these, the leftist banner is carried not by the ECP or other strictly Marxist parties, but by the legal National Progressive Unionist Party. Some of its members, including General Secretary Khalid Muhyi al-Din, are Marxists, but the party is an amalgam of various ideologies. The 1987 parliamentary elections gave NPUP only 2.2 percent of the vote, far short of the 8 percent needed for seats.

Algeria, long a shining beacon for the Middle Eastern left, was deeply shaken in early October by massive riots in which over 200 people died. Rioters' targets in Algiers were shops, hotels, government buildings, police stations, and offices of the ruling party, the National Liberation Front (NLF) (*Manchester Guardian Weekly*, 16 October). Although the illegal communist Socialist Vanguard Party (PAGS) was active before and during the riots, their principal organizers were Muslim fundamentalist groups capitalizing on the NLF's austerity measures, high prices, the housing shortage, and unemployment (*Middle East International*, 21 October). The religious rallying cries and garb of the leaders of the riots left no doubt about their inspiration by the Muslim Brotherhood and other fundamentalists. When the FLN's late-November congress dissolved the old FLN party in favor of a broad new front to include different groups, illegal groups like PAGS that had pressed for a multiparty system were marked for exclusion.

By contrast, the legal Moroccan communist Party of Progress and Socialism (PPS) operated freely within the parliamentary coalition of major opposition parties formed in late 1987. PPS general secretary Ali Yata conceded that his party's weakness required downplaying its own program in favor of common efforts with other opposition parties to form "some kind of patriotic and progressive front" (*Le Libéral*, Casablanca, 15 February). The PPS sought this unity in the context of Morocco's serious inflation and unemployment and its problems of housing, education, health care, and other needs. In neighboring Tunisia the Tunisian Communist Party (PCT) capitalized on the departure of former president Habib Bourguiba and the efforts of his successor, President Zine el Abidine Ben Ali, to invigorate the country's democratic process. The PCT became the only opposition party to participate in special parliamentary by-elections during January, but demanded the elections be declared invalid immediately thereafter because of alleged ballot-box stuffing by the ruling Destourian Socialist Party (*International Herald Tribune*, 26 January). The PCT subsequently boycotted by-elections in an effort to unify the Tunisian left and also opposed the government's proposed bill to reform election procedures (*al-Tarik al-Jadid*, 13–19 July). In its effort to remain in the political stream, however, the PCT agreed to participate in the coming 1988–89 elections based on President Ben Ali's pledge to hold fair elections and the PCT's demand for a national commission of all political parties to monitor future elections (*Pravda*, 9 August; *FBIS-SOV*, 11 August).

James H. Noyes
Hoover Institution

Afghanistan

Population. Unknown: estimated 14,480,863 (*World Fact Book*, 1988); refugee flow plus wartime casualties have reduced significantly a population that in 1978 was thought to number about 17 million.

Party. People's Democratic Party of Afghanistan (Jamiyat-e-Demokrati Khalq-e-Afghanistan, literally Democratic Party of the Afghanistan Masses; PDPA). The party has two basic and mutually antagonistic wings, Parcham (Banner) and Khalq (Masses), as well as numerous smaller factions that have developed since 1986.

Founded. 1965

Membership. Party membership claims appeared

to peak in May at 205,000, of whom 150,000 were in the armed forces, including army, police, and secret police (TASS, 14 May; *FBIS*, 16 May). The total membership was said to represent an increase of 30,000 over the preceding six months, when the probationary period as a candidate member was dropped as a requirement. Unlike earlier years, there were no reported gains in party membership by the end of 1988 (Radio Kabul, 23 October; *FBIS*, 24 October). All of the above figures are suspect; noncommunist intellectuals have stated that party membership in fact was rapidly declining in late 1988 (*CSM*, 6 December). Successes of the resistance and the commitment by the USSR to withdraw its troops by mid-February 1989 have seriously undercut the attractiveness of party membership. The progressive intellectual degradation of the party was indicated by the claim in March that before 1978, 95 percent of the party considered themselves intellectuals (*Kabul New Times* [*KNT*], 2 March), yet at the October 1987 Party Conference, only 36.9 percent of ranking party members who had joined since 1982 considered themselves intellectuals (*YICA*, 1988). Of the rest, 18.3 percent said they were workers, 26.5 percent peasants, and 3 percent craftsmen; 58 percent were under 30 years of age (ibid.).

General Secretary. Lt. Gen. Najibullah, also known as Dr. Najib, Mohammed Najibullah, Mohammed Najibullah Ahmadzai, and variations (aged about 43, Pashtun, studied but never practiced medicine) (*YICA*, 1987)

Politburo. 12 members: Najibullah, Sayed Mohammed Gulabzoi (about 44 years of age, Pashtun, airforce background, former minister of interior, now in Soviet exile), Najmuddin Akhgar Kawiani (about 39, pre-party background unknown, in charge of the Central Committee's International Relations Department, House of Representatives [HR] delegate for Balkh, chief of the HR's standing commission on international relations), Sultan Ali Keshtmand (53, Hazara, intellectual, dropped as prime minister of the Republic of Afghanistan [RA] but promoted to party secretary) (Bakhtar, 22 June; *FBIS*, 23 June), Suleiman Laeq (59, Pashtun, writer/media, minister of tribal affairs), Dr. Haider Masoud (50, [Tajik?], formerly media, now fulltime party worker in Central Committee's publicity and extention department, also HR delegate), Niaz Mohammed Mohmand (Pashtun, economics expert, HR delegate for Kunar, chief of HR agricultural land reforms and water commission) (*Kabul Times*

[*KT*], 26 June), Nur Ahmad Nur (52, Pashtun, intellectual, ambassador to Poland) (*KNT*, 19 March), Gen. Mohammed Rafi (about 43, Pashtun, military, vice president) (Radio Kabul, 3 June; *FBIS*, 6 June), Abdul Wakil (42, economist/teacher, foreign minister), Gen. Mohammed Aslam Watanjar (43, Pashtun, military officer, minister of interior) (U.S. Department of State, "Afghanistan: Soviet Occupation and Withdrawal," Special Report no. 179, December; hereafter referred to as "USDS report"), Lt. Gen. Ghulam Farouq Yaqubi (Pashtun, minister of state security). There are 4 alternate members: Mir Saheb Karwal (Pashtun), Farid Ahmad Mazdak (Tajik, secretary of the Democratic Youth Organization of Afghanistan [DYOA], and HR delegate for Kabul City), Gen. Nazar Mohammed (54, Pashtun, military officer), Shahnawaz Tanai (39, Pashtun, military officer, minister of defense). Two party stalwarts previously thought to be loyal to Najib, Dr. Saleh Mohammed Zeary and Abdul Zaher Razmjo, were summarily dismissed from the Politburo without official explanation (Radio Kabul, 19 October; *FBIS*, 20 October). (Except where noted, the sources for the above are *YICA*, 1988 and Anthony Arnold, *Afghanistan's Two-Party Communism: Parcham and Khalq*, Stanford: Hoover Institution Press, 1983.)

Secretariat. 12 members: Najibullah, Karwal, Kawiani, Keshtmand, Masoud, Mohmand, Nur, Sarferaz Mohmand (HR delegate from Nangarhar, Secretary of Nangarhar Province Party Committee (*KT*, 22 March), Ahmad Nabi (secretary of the Kandahar Province Party Committee), Mohammed Daoud Razmyar (secretary of the Kabul City Party Committee and HR delegate), Mohammed Khalil Sepahi (HR representative from Herat and secretary of the Herat Province Party Committee), Mohammed Sharif (governor of Balkh and secretary of the Balkh Province Party Committee). (Note: Zeary and Karwal were dropped. Nabi was listed as the provincial secretary of Kandahar Province in 1986, whereas the fact that the person [unnamed] holding that position was a member of the Central Committee Secretariat was announced only in late 1987; it is possible that Nabi was replaced between 1986 and late 1987 [*YICA*, 1988].)

Central Committee. Up to 118 full and 60 candidate members, but probably fewer due to reported purges

Status. Ruling party

Last Congress. First, 1 January 1965, in Kabul;

National Conferences, 14–15 March 1982, and 18–19 October 1987. Plena in 1988 were held on 27–28 January, 22 June, and 19 October.

Last Election. Elections to a newly formed bicameral National Assembly were held in April 1988, under provisions of the 1987 Constitution. The old Revolutionary Council was abolished to make room for the new body. It was claimed that 1.6 million Afghans, representing 74 percent of the enfranchised population, had elected 51 senators and 184 HR deputies. Voter turnout was 100 percent in the armed forces; 99.7 percent in the Ministry of Interior and Ministry of State Security (WAD). Of those elected, 22.6 percent (42 seats) were from the PDPA; 15.4 percent (28 seats) from the PDPA-dominated National Front (NF); 6 percent (11 seats) from registered opposition parties; and 56 percent (103 seats) had no party affiliation (*KT*, 30 April). The figures indicate that the RA considered only 2.2 million Afghans eligible to vote. Women were given the vote and were responsible for about 50 percent of the turnout in Kabul and 40 percent in Samangan Province, but the regime did not reveal the percentage of their overall participation. The ethnic breakdown of the combined House and Senate—48.7 percent Pashtun, 30.2 percent Tajik, 9.4 percent Uzbek, 6.4 percent Hazara, 2.7 percent Turkoman, 1 percent Baluch, and 1.4 percent other—was supposed to reflect in general the composition of the country's population (ibid.).

Auxiliary Organizations. The National Front (NF) (chairman: Abdul Rahim Hatef) had "more than one million members" (*KNT*, 3 March). The trade unions (president: Abdus Sattar Purdeli) claimed a marginal increase from 300,000 to 304,899 members in 2,987 primary organizations (*KT*, 22 May). The Democratic Youth Organization of Afghanistan (DYOA) (first secretary: Farid Ahmad Mazdak) claimed 280,000 members, of whom 49 percent were students, and 1,000 professional staff personnel in 5,000 primary organizations (*CSM*, 25 November; *FBIS*, 24 October). The Afghan Women's Council (AWC) (chairperson: Masooma Esmati Wardak) claimed 125,000 members (Bakhtar, 16 August; *FBIS*, 16 August). The Union of Journalists had a new president, Mohammed Hassan Bareq Shafiee, and a new Association of Woman Journalists was founded (*KT*, 27 June). The Union of Writers also had a new chairman, Dr. Mohammed Akram Usman (Radio Kabul, 17 March; *FBIS*, 18 March). The Association of Lawyers (chairman: Prof. Ghulam

Sakhi Masoon) had 1,045 members (*KNT*, 11 February). The National Reconciliation organization (chairman: Abdul Rahim Hatef) claimed 3,370 commissions that included more than 6,000 people from former opposition groups (Radio Kabul, 21 January; *FBIS*, 22 January). Tribal militias were said to total 40,000 troops (ibid.). Less information was published on fronts in 1988 than in previous years; for information on others, see *YICA*, 1988.

Publications. New in 1988: *Heywad* (Homeland), organ of the presidency (*KT*, 7 May). Old publications: *Anis*, daily, NF organ; *Haqiqat-e-Enqelabe Saur* (The Saur revolution truth), daily, Central Committee organ in Dari and Pashtu, Bareq Shafiee, editor in chief; Bakhtar, official news agency, Sarwar Yuresh, chief; *Haqiqat-e-Sarbaz* (The soldier's truth), Gen. Fakhri, editor; *Darafsh-e-Jawanan* (The banner of youth), Pashtu and Dari daily; *Dehqan* (Peasant); *Kabul New Times* (renamed *Kabul Times* on 22 March), English-language daily, Mohammed Seddiq Rahpoe, editor; *Storai* (Story), DYOA monthly; *Peshahang* (Pioneer), Pioneer monthly; *Zindagi Hezbi* (Party life), biweekly, Abdul Rahim, editor (*YICA*, 1988). The regime maintains a radio station and has a limited television network.

Background. In 1967, two years after its founding, the PDPA split into opposing wings: Parcham and Khalq. Both kept the PDPA name and both were loyal to Moscow, but each maintained a separate organization and recruitment program. Khalq, led by Nur Mohammed Taraki, the PDPA's founder, depended for support on the relatively poor rural intelligentsia and recruited almost solely among the Pashtuns, the dominant (then about 50 percent) Afghan ethnic group. Parcham, more broadly representative ethnically, was urban-oriented and appealed to a wealthier group of educated Afghans. It was led by Babrak Karmal, son of an Afghan general. Both groups focused their initial recruitment efforts on intellectuals, media employees, and especially teachers. When Mohammed Daoud overthrew the Afghan monarchy in 1973, the Parchamis at first collaborated with him and were obliged to refrain from aggressive recruiting. The Khalqis, however, remained in opposition and began an intensive recruitment campaign among the military in preparation for the PDPA coup that was to follow five years later. During this period, the Khalqis moved from parity with the Parchamis to significant numerical superiority.

Under Soviet pressure, Parcham and Khalq formally reunited in mid-1977, and their combined strength was enough to overthrow Daoud and establish the Democratic Republic of Afghanistan in April 1978. They almost immediately fissioned again, however, with Taraki sending the most prominent Parchamis into diplomatic exile as ambassadors and jailing or demoting most of those who remained in Afghanistan. When a Parchami plot to unseat Taraki was discovered in the summer of 1978, the ambassadors were recalled but disobeyed the order and fled into exile in Eastern Europe.

Meanwhile, popular resistance to Khalq's rigorous Marxist-Leninist rule grew rapidly and soon threatened to topple the new regime in spite of massive Soviet military aid. In September 1979, the Soviets attempted to force another artificial reconciliation between Parcham and Khalq, but their plan to place all the blame for the schism on Taraki's deputy, Hafizullah Amin, backfired when Amin himself seized power and murdered Taraki. Amin, however, could not pacify his rebellious people, and on 27 December 1979, Soviet troops invaded Afghanistan, shot Amin, and restored the Parchamis to power. Babrak became the new leader and tried to heal the breach with the Khalqis on the one side and the Afghan population on the other. In neither effort was he successful, and in May 1986 he suffered the first of several demotions in power. His successor, Najibullah, performed no better, and the regime maintained a tenuous hold on power only in a few main Afghan towns during daylight hours, thanks to a Soviet presence that slowly swelled from 85,000 combat troops in 1980 to about 120,000 by the end of 1984. Thereafter, the Soviet occupation force strength remained fairly constant until May 1988, when the first true withdrawals began.

Since the Soviet invasion, the PDPA technically has not been a communist or even a socialist (according to the Soviet lexicon) party, but merely the ruling party in a country undergoing the "national democratic stage of revolution." In 1987, regime spokesmen began emphasizing the nonsocialist nature of the regime, and these denials rang even louder in 1988. Despite their own continued unabashed allegiance to Marxism-Leninism as a creed, RA leaders acknowledged that the Afghan people did not share that philosophy. The PDPA's major goal during 1987–1988 was to gain enough legitimacy to permit its independent survival as a political force after Soviet troops had gone home. Steps taken in this direction during 1987 included the renaming of the nation, of its major front, and

even of its leader (*YICA*, 1988). The process continued into 1988, with the renaming of the English-language daily and the holding of elections to a new national legislature. Najibullah's program of national reconciliation, launched with great fanfare in 1986–1987 with the proclaimed goal of permitting non-PDPA groupings a share of political power, found expression in the 1987 constitution and the 1988 elections.

The achievement of legitimacy suddenly acquired urgency following Soviet leader Mikhail Gorbachev's declaration on 8 February 1988 that he would soon withdraw all Soviet military units, and his later promise that the withdrawal would be completed by 15 February 1989. As 1988 drew to a close, however, the prospects for survival in Afghanistan of any political grouping endorsed by the USSR seemed extremely dim.

Party Leadership and Organization. Although there were some significant personnel changes in the PDPA during 1988, the media devoted more space to the RA state apparatus. Individuals promoted to CC membership were usually named but those demoted were not, and some of the data were contradictory. None of the personnel shifts achieved the PDPA's two main goals: increasing its external legitimacy and decreasing its internal factionalism. In fact, pursuit of both goals simultaneously only exacerbated both problems.

At the January plenum, four alternate CC members were promoted to full CC membership, and two others bypassed the alternate stage to acquire full membership. Nine new alternates were also named. The meteoric progress of Abdul Zaher Razmjo's career brought him to the rank of CC secretary. In April, a hitherto unknown figure, Mohammed Wali, was given the sensitive post of chief of the cadres and personnel department of the CC.

At the next plenum, on 22 June, another four alternates became full CC members, and another two jumped directly into full membership. Another new CC secretary. Sultan Ali Keshtmand, was named, probably to compensate for his dismissal as prime minister. This plenum also saw one of the rare instances where an expellee was identified by name. He was Gen. Abdul Qader, former Politburo member and minister of defense, whose roller coaster career in the PDPA had been on a descending curve since 1984 and whose last post had been ambassador to Poland. He was not only dropped from the CC without explanation, but was also being considered for expulsion from the party.

Qader's replacement as ambassador was Nur Ahmad Nur, whose appointment may also have been a discreet demotion (Radio Kabul, 23 February; *FBIS*, 1 March). Nur still apparently held his longstanding memberships in the Politburo and the secretariat, but as an absentee his influence was clearly reduced.

The most dramatic changes in the topmost levels, however, occurred just before the October plenum, when three well-known figures were abruptly removed from the PDPA's political equation (AFP, 25 October; *FBIS*, 26 October): Sayed Mohammed Gulabzoi, the unacknowledged head of the PDPA's Khalqi faction, was suddenly bundled off to Moscow as "ambassador," even though the incumbent Afghan ambassador continued to function in that position after his arrival (*NYT*, 18 November); the just-promoted Razmjo, thought to be one of Najibullah's most trusted lieutenants, was summarily fired from the Politburo and secretariat (Radio Kabul, 19 October; *FBIS*, 20 October); and Saleh Mohammed Zeary, for decades known in party circles as "Quicksilver" for his ability to emerge on the winning side in any political conflict, was also dismissed from the Politburo and secretariat (ibid).

In the three days before the plenum, up to 300 people, including between 17 and 50 CC members, were arrested. Of a reported 163 full and alternate CC members, only 94 attended the plenum (*NYT*, 26 and 29 October). Details of the reason for the dismissals were lacking, but Najibullah shortly afterward referred to "some adventurist and short-sighted [party] elements" and their unspecified "open anti-state activities and provocations within the armed forces against the Republic of Afghanistan to seize power" (Radio Kabul, 23 October; *FBIS*, 24 October). The main bone of contention was reportedly the party's intention to offer even more concessions to the *mujahideen*, the Afghan resistance.

The following month there was an abortive coup attempt in Kandahar, Afghanistan's second largest city. WAD personnel, normally the most reliable regime supporters, led an attempt to yield the city to the resistance but failed; some 30 of the 400 who took part were killed (USDS report; TASS, 24 November; *FBIS*, 28 November).

These events demonstrated the party's inability to achieve legitimacy even within its own ranks. At the previous year's PDPA conference, which had as one of its main themes the need for party unity and loyalty, plans had been laid to hold a Second Party Congress in late April 1988 on the occasion of the tenth anniversary of the communist takeover. These plans were quietly shelved, and the anniversary celebrations were generally subdued. Ironically, the keynote address on unity at the 1987 party conference had been delivered by Zeary.

At Kabul University, the party's weakening hold was demonstrated by the abrupt cancellation in October of all political indoctrination courses (*CSM*, 28 November).

At the start of the year the government was still putting on a brave face, with the claim that it controlled "all provincial capitals and major districts, all 45 cities, 214 (sub?) districts, (and) 55 percent of all villages" (Bakhtar, 14 January; *FBIS*, 15 January). But a Soviet commentator claimed in November that PDPA organizations existed in only 900 villages (out of perhaps 23,000, or about 4 percent); he also noted that about 3,000 village self-defense formations supported neither the government nor the resistance and might end up strengthening the latter (*JPRS-UIA*-88-018, 23 November).

The party's pessimism about the future was revealed in its militarization. In February, Najibullah revealed that all PDPA and DYOA members would receive military training (*KNT*, 3 February). By August, 40 percent of the DYOA was under arms and virtually all PDPA civilians (52,000) had received some military training (Radio Kabul, 15 August; *FBIS*, 17 August). In September, Najibullah was advocating the formation of "partisan detachments, creating headquarters in the provinces..." (Radio Kabul, 2 September; *FBIS*, 6 September).

As the Party's prospects for survival in a post-Soviet Afghanistan dimmed, defections of ranking figures increased. In August, Najibullah's own brother Siddiqullah fled the country, to be followed in November by a cousin, WAD Brigadier Gen. Mohammed Gul. The latter asserted that many more leading figures would leave if they dared (AFP, 25 October; *FBIS*, 26 October). In November, Abdul Ghaffar Lakanwal, a former CC member, former minister of agriculture, and a deputy foreign minister, became the highest ranking defector to request asylum in the United States (*San Francisco Chronicle*, 18 November).

Domestic Affairs. The contradiction between the PDPA's twin goals of external legitimacy and internal unity was nowhere more clearly illustrated than on Afghanistan's domestic political scene. In order to project the image of a conventional political party, the PDPA had to make ever more convincing gestures showing that it was ending its monopoly of power and really intended to form a coalition government with its blood enemies in the resistance. The umbrella policy under which these moves were carried out was "national reconciliation." Its gestures, however, dismayed the PDPA's own hard-line factions to an ever greater degree, thus setting back the goal of party unity. Moreover, they were completely ineffective in dampening the resistance's enthusiasm for annihilating the entire party-state apparatus that had been built in Afghanistan under Soviet guidance.

In late 1987, a first demonstrative step toward renunciation of total PDPA control came with the re-emergence of two rump parties, the Organization of the Working People of Afghanistan (OWPA) and the Revolutionary Organization of the Working People of Afghanistan (ROWPA). These two groups had received publicity during 1986 as groups that had just merged with the PDPA, but in late 1987 they re-achieved ostensible independence. In early 1988 it was announced that one ROWPA leader had been appointed deputy prime minister and president of the state planning committee, another the minister of justice, and a third the minister of mines and industries (KNT, 7 January; Kabul Radio, 17 March; FBIS, 18 March). This came amid claims that 27 ministerial senior positions would be offered to the opposition if it joined the government. Later it became apparent that ROWPA was really a reincarnation of Settam-e-Melli, a Marxist-Leninist group that had split from the PDPA in 1968 because it opposed Pashtun domination of both Parcham and Khalq branches of the party (KNT, 28 January). No party admitted to being socialist or communist, however, and the PDPA declared that it was not even Marxist (Radio Kabul, 15 August; FBIS, 17 August).

(Note: Depending on the source, OWPA and ROWPA are sometimes known by their Dari acronyms SZA and SAZA, or as TOA and TROA, standing for the Toilers' Organization of Afghanistan and the Toilers' Revolutionary Organization of Afghanistan.)

Upon their re-emergence, OWPA and ROWPA immediately joined the PDPA in an "Alliance of Leftist Democratic Parties." Later, two other new entities, the Islamic Party (IP) and the Peasants' Justice Party (PJP), joined the alliance, In the elec-tions that followed, the PDPA did not run candidates in areas where any of the above were also running. Later, two more parties, these supposedly more truly oppositional, were also formed: the Ansarullah Union and the Fedayeen Self-Sacrificing Afghan People's Solidarity Movement. Various other splinter parties, many of them restricted to localities, were reportedly formed about this time (USDS report). Najibullah, in speaking of the PDPA's intention to share power, claimed that there were 12 active parties but did not name them (Bakhtar, 2 September; FBIS, 2 September).

At the same time, Najibullah's obscure grumbling about the new parties' "shortsighted party-political approach to national tasks . . . the enormous emphasis on efforts to achieve power" may have referred to some genuinely independent ambitions that were developing even within the leftist alliance. Both OWPA and ROWPA spokesmen openly criticized the PDPA for keeping a monopoly of political power. OWPA, which claimed to have formed its own militia in support of the government, said that "the party" (presumably PDPA) had refused to arm these detachments (KT, 5 and 9 September).

Meanwhile the spring elections for the National Assembly (Melli Shura) had been hastily organized and held, with predictably confusing and contradictory statistical results. The election commission was only formed on 17 March and the elections held 5–15 April. Contrary to election laws, there were no secret ballots; candidate lists were only published after the polls opened; many polling booths were unmanned; and children as young as thirteen were observed voting (USDS report). Although the PDPA technically won only 22 percent of the seats, its OWPA and ROWPA clones, the National Front, and various individual fronts insured a comfortable majority. In fact, when the first results published were added together they showed that the leftist groups had provided 114.7 percent of the winning candidates (KT, 24 April), although their share of the victorious candidates was later modified to 44 percent (81 seats), with 56 percent (103 seats) described as "independent" (KT, 30 April).

The government boasted that 54 of 229 HR polling stations and 18 of 62 Senate (Sena) polling stations had operated in opposition-controlled territories (Radio Kabul, 10 April; FBIS, 11 April), and 29 opposition candidates had been elected (Bakhtar, 8 May; FBIS, 13 May). Moreover, 13 Senate and 50 more HR seats (of a theoretical total of 427 for both houses combined) were being held vacant for the armed opposition. In fact, however, the resistance was solidly opposed to the elections and did not permit them in areas under its control (USDS report).

On 26 May the old rubber-stamp Revolutionary Council voted itself out of existence in deference to the new *Melli Shura*. Najibullah appointed a new prime minister, Dr. Mohammed Hassan Sharq, who was billed as nonparty but who in fact had been a regular regime collaborator, having served as ambassador to India (1980–1986) and most recently as minister of repatriation affairs. Sharq was widely reputed to be a longtime KGB (Soviet State Security) agent (*NYT*, 31 October).

Sharq put together a streamlined cabinet of 31 members, down from the 40 members it had had shortly before the elections. He claimed that sixteen members of the cabinet, "including me," were nonparty, but in fact all identifiable new ministers had collaborated with the regime in earlier years (Radio Kabul, 26 July; *FBIS*, 27 July). Several ministerial seats, including those of defense, information and culture, and Islamic affairs, were left open temporarily, apparently in the hopes that some real opposition leaders could be enticed into occupying them (USDS report). If so, the hopes remained unrealized. There were only fourteen carryovers from the previous cabinet, but of the seventeen newcomers, eleven were well-known leftists, and many of these were identified PDPA members. By the end of the year, the cabinet had grown to 33 with the appointment of known leftists as ministers of defense and information/culture.

Sharq did his best to appear politically neutral. He even stated at an October news conference that "the Afghan people have no more confidence in the People's Democratic Party of Afghanistan than they have in the opposition" (AFP Hong Kong, 12 October; *FBIS*, 13 October). He was given a high profile in Afghan media and went to New York to address the U.N. General Assembly in November. Most Afghans, however, appeared to have little use for him. At the end of the year, an Afghan trader in Kabul opined that perhaps 50 percent of the people were in favor of ex-King Zahir Shah, 30 percent were for resistance field commander Ahmad Shah Massoud, 10 percent were for Massoud's nominal superior in Pakistan (Rabbani), less than 10 percent were for Gulbuddin Hekmatyar (another exile leader), and one percent were for Najibullah (*CSM*, 7 December). Sharq's name did not even enter the conversation.

In their efforts to win popularity, the PDPA made especially strong appeals to women and religious figures. The drive for female support included founding a union of woman journalists and more than doubling the size of the AWC, which started the year with only 55,000 members. The fields where it was claimed that women played a significant role were education (22,000 teachers, 233,000 students, and 43 percent of the Ministry of Education), construction (more than 50 percent of construction brigades), medicine (300 doctors, 3,000 nurses), engineers (7,000), defense (5,000 in civilian defense forces), and skilled workers (4,000) (*KNT*, 8 March). Nevertheless, women made up only 3.6 percent of the PDPA apparat and 9 percent of the trade unions. After the expulsion of Anahita Ratebzada from the Politburo following Babrak's ouster in 1986, no women remained in the upper reaches of the party or state.

The PDPA worked equally hard to project an image of Islamic godliness. Najibullah made a long public speech on the occasion of each religious holiday. In February, he appointed an eleven-man Islamic consultative council tasked with propounding an Islamic but progovernment view of the national reconciliation policy, land and water reforms, taxes, bribery, and other matters (*KNT*, 1 March). Two weeks later he appointed a second such council, with seven members, to oversee education (*KNT*, 15 March). In a speech on Islamic matters, he claimed that eleven clergymen, including one vice premier, were on the Revolutionary Council, that "some" clergymen were mayors and provincial governors, that 1,400 clergy and religious scholars were mobilized in the NF and 1,092 were involved in local government (*KNT*, 1 March).

The government also pursued old policies of promising to restore property to its previous owners and encouraging private enterprise. There was frequent positive reporting about private business in government media, with statistics to show indirectly that the RA was not going socialist: 80 percent of the nation's domestic trade, 53.5 percent of its foreign exports, and 49.9 percent of its imports were reported to be in private hands, as were 308 newly established companies. Some 7,000 "national traders and others" were organized into 943 business firms, compared with just twelve state-owned trade institutions (Bakhtar, 19 July; *FBIS*, 21 July).

In January Najibullah extended for another six months the cease-fire he had twice proclaimed in the previous year. Like its predecessors, this gesture bore no relation to reality; the war if anything intensified, as Soviet troops began withdrawing. He also proclaimed new amnesties for draft dodgers and deserters. Death sentences on such renowned resistance field commanders as Ahmad Shah Massoud were lifted, apparently in the vain hope that this would entice them into collaboration with the government (Radio Kabul, 26 January; *FBIS*, 27 January).

As Soviet forces began their withdrawal from outlying districts, especially along the border with Pakistan, the government's troops were also obliged to pull back. Making the political best of a militarily hopeless situation, Kabul proclaimed these areas to be "peace zones" and then reacted with injured indignation when the resistance took them over. The government also, however, continued to count as "under government control" any settlement that was not definitely in resistance hands, provided only that its leaders voiced lip-service allegiance to Kabul. There was an explicit government policy of self-determination for such settlements, again a virtue deriving from necessity; once the Soviet retreat began, PDPA-appointed village leaders, almost to a man, died violently in office, defected to the resistance, or ran away to Kabul (interview with Olivier Roy, November).

Another tactic was the Afghan version of gerrymandering. For example, the new provinces of Nuristan and Sar-e-Pol were set up, apparently in the hopes of exploiting minority aspirations among the Nuristanis and Hazaras who lived in them (USDS report). The governor of Herat was appointed governor of Badghis and Ghor provinces as well. There were also planned amalgamations of provinces in the Pashtun areas where resistance conquest of one would lead the government simply to abolish and amalgamate the fallen area with a neighboring province where it still had control (*NYT*, 26 October).

Yet another part of the national reconciliation program was enticing Afghan refugees in Pakistan and Iran to return home. So-called "peace hotels" were set up to handle returning refugees, who were entitled to bring back duty-free such exotic items as air conditioners, freezers, two TV sets, video cassettes, and other consumer goods far beyond the means of most Afghans on either side of the border (*KNT*, 2 March). Meanwhile, the government said it had dispensed more than 25 million afghanis ($500,000 at the official rate) worth of goods to those returning (Bakhtar, 21 February; *FBIS*, 23 February). In fact, however, even by RA statistics refugee return was less than 5 percent; it was prob-

ably even less, because of the danger posed by millions of antipersonnel mines sown indiscriminately by the RA and Soviets over the years.

The military situation, which had begun on a relatively high note for the regime with the lifting of the resistance's siege of Khowst in early January, deteriorated rapidly thereafter. The army suffered heavy losses in its best units in the Khowst campaign and never fully recovered. Throughout the year, Najibullah repeatedly boasted that the government had 500,000 men under arms, but few believed his claim. Even the Soviet sources noted that the government's propaganda was "partly marked by indiscriminate optimism" (*Pravda*, 26 May; *FBIS*, 1 June). The chronic problems of desertion and draft dodging remained, despite the amnesty, profligate dispensation of medals, mass promotions to general in the officer corps, and pay raises for enlisted men up to tenfold of what they had previously received (*KNT*, 8 February). In addition, Najibullah decreed that PDPA civilians would be mobilized into their own military units, but this merely had the effect of depressing the already sagging morale of the party cadres (USDS report).

The resistance steadily increased in strength as the RA troops wilted. Its most dramatic success was the detonation of an arms and fuel depot in Kalagay, about 100 miles north of Kabul. The blast, set off by a chance rocket, killed about 700 Soviet soldiers and civilians and destroyed two-years worth of ammunition being stockpiled for the regime (*London Times*, 23 August).

Soviet operations continued to be brutal. Thus, Wardak Province's capital Kowte Ashraf, captured by the resistance in June, was flattened by artillery and air strikes that were directed by Soviet advisors (AFP, 6 July; *FBIS*, 6 July). Later, the resistance took the northern provincial capital of Kunduz, leading Najibullah to accuse party and state officials there of "flagrant treachery, shameful cowardice" (Radio Kabul, 23 October; *FBIS*, 24 October). Only massive air strikes by bombers based in the USSR permitted regime troops to retake the city (*CSM*, 1 September). These and other strikes caused heavy civilian casualties.

What remained of the Afghan economy was in shambles. The inflation rate in 1988 was 40 percent, compared to 30–35 percent in 1987. The currency was devalued by 25 percent during the year, and agricultural production probably fell (USDS report). Najibullah said that the war was absorbing 60 percent of the state budget (Bakhtar, 29 April; *FBIS*, 29 April). In March, Keshtmand acknowledged that state income had fallen by six billion afghanis during 1987 due to failures in the extraction and supply of natural gas (*KNT*, 16 March). In parallel with the political decentralization, he recommended that communities be given local economic independence. As in the case of political self-determination, however, the gesture was hollow: most Afghan communities were already out of Kabul's economic grasp.

Front Activities. Continuing the trend noted in 1987, most PDPA front groups kept a low profile during 1988. Statistics about the activities of the national reconciliation commissions and their activities were released at the start of the year but disappeared from the media thereafter. Similarly, AWC received periodic praise in the media until late June and then dropped from sight. The DYOA came in for heavy criticism in February, mainly for its failure to inculcate enough enthusiasm for military service into the youth.

One of the few front activities to get media attention late in the year was an International Islamic Conference held in Kabul in October and attended by delegates from India, Palestine, Egypt, Portugal, and Uganda (Radio Kabul, 26 October; *FBIS*, 27 October). Even this did not get extensive coverage, possibly because of the somewhat limited foreign representation.

One possible reason for the decline of the fronts was their formal divorce from immediate PDPA control. As of January 1987, the PDPA CC no longer had responsibility for the NF (and presumably for its member fronts), whose subordination was left unclear but presumably devolved on the state apparatus (*YICA*, 1988). Major fronts such as the DYOA, AWC, and trade unions continued to be run by old party hands, and there is no doubt that the PDPA also controlled the NF itself, despite the ostensibly "nonparty" status of its chief, Hatef. Nevertheless, with the development of a government that was billed as truly multiparty, the continued existence of such powerful groups that were obviously PDPA auxiliaries might have been seen as a potential embarrassment.

A second reason for the fronts' low profile may have been the PDPA's belief that the emerging "opposition" parties would serve many of the same functions and not be such unmistakable puppets. In support of this theory, at least six senators appointed by Najibullah had previously been prominent members of various fronts, though that fact was not mentioned when their new senatorial status was

announced. Even if this theory is correct, however, it appears that the PDPA grip on the parties is not as firm as it always has been on the fronts, and thus that the degree of PDPA control has lessened slightly.

But perhaps the overriding reason for the fronts' dormancy was the deterioration of the military situation. Only in Kabul and at various military strongpoints could prominent front personalities have a measure of personal security. Early in the year Najibullah mentioned three heads of national reconciliation commissions (two of them chiefs of provincial commissions) and five other prominent figures who had been assassinated in the recent past (Bakhtar, 16 January; *FBIS*, 20 January). It was indicative of the concentration of front members in safe areas that the DYOA, with a total membership of only 280,000 in November, collected 200,000 signatures from its members in Kabul alone during February, indicating that at least five out of seven DYOA members lived in the capital at that time (*CSM*, 25 November; Radio Kabul, 31 January; *FBIS*, 3 February).

International Views, Positions, and Activities. Although the start of 1988 saw some international PDPA activity, by year's end the party was much more noticeable for its international isolation than for its presence. Najibullah visited Cambodia 29–31 December 1987 on what was billed as a "party-state" visit, with the party aspect always in first place in the communist media's coverage (Radio Kabul, 31 December 1987; *FBIS*, 4 January 1988). This was the last time, however, that his party rank took open precedence over his state rank.

In late April, the tenth anniversary celebration of the "Great Saur Revolution" (the 1978 communist coup) continued to be boycotted by most of the world's political parties. Of those in the free world, only India's Congress Party sent representatives. The USSR, on the other hand, put its delegation under the command of Vladimir P. Orlov, chairman of the Presidium of the Russian Republic's Supreme Soviet; Orlov is doubtless a member of the CPSU, but his party rank was never revealed in the Afghan and Soviet coverage of this event (*San Francisco Chronicle*, 27 April). The CPSU was clearly distancing itself from the PDPA.

As the year progressed, Najibullah's own party title of general secretary faded ever further into the background, yielding first place to his rank of president even in coverage of party affairs. In both Afghan and Soviet news stories dealing with other matters, the party title was usually ignored completely. In only one case out of perhaps 150 where his name was noted in Soviet or Afghan media was he referred to as "comrade"—probably the result of editorial oversight (*Trud*, 22 July; *FBIS*, 28 July). Usually he was called the "Esteemed Najibullah."

In early May Najibullah went on a state visit to India, the only country to afford him such an honor in 1988. In June he went to the U.N. to address the General Assembly on disarmament issues and proceeded on to Cuba. A planned return by way of Czechoslovakia was shelved at the last minute, probably a result of coup rumors and unrest in Kabul. Later in the year there were probably other visits to Moscow (USDS report). If so, the Soviets were clearly unenthusiastic about publicizing them.

Taking over from the president as chief RA spokesman abroad was Hassan Sharq, who addressed the U.N. in early November (*NYT*, 6 November). This was the first time that an ostensibly nonparty RA official had been given such a responsibility, and it fueled speculation that the Soviets might have selected him to succeed Najibullah.

During the year, the USSR had taken various steps to maintain at least some influence in Afghanistan after the withdrawal of its troops. In March came the first evidence of a purported Soviet plan to amalgamate the nine northern provinces of Afghanistan into a rump state or new Soviet republic, where PDPA officials could find a home after the expected fall of Kabul. The evidence included the assignment of a vice premier as chief of a newly constituted Northern Zone that encompassed the nine provinces, the opening of a new university at Balkh, greater publicity for this region than heretofore, and intensified trans-border economic ties (*San Francisco Chronicle*, 27 April). The USSR has made no open commitment to such a development, which appears to be at most only a contingency plan for the time being. If feasible at all, the reported plan could only work if the resistance were rendered impotent by internecine squabbling after having driven the RA out of Kabul.

Another effort has involved intensified economic links between individual Soviet republics, oblasts, cities, and communities with all Afghan provinces. This program, begun in 1987, was sharply accelerated in 1988. The goal here seemed to be the retention of a Soviet economic stake via a program that would downplay the role of central bureaucracies on both sides, and that would emphasize personal and community relations in their place.

The attempted Sovietization of Afghan youth continued. At the start of the year, there were re-

portedly 8,500 Afghan students in the USSR, but by midyear this had risen to 10,000. In addition there were a reported 1,500 Afghan orphans being cared for in the USSR (*Bakhtar*, 27 January and 19 April; *FBIS*, 28 January and 19 April). This program has continued for many years and so far has not resulted in large numbers of pro-Soviet cadres.

None of these measures is believed likely to succeed, especially because of the continued Soviet use of harsh military tactics against Afghan civilians and the accelerating dissolution of the PDPA.

Soviet disenchantment with Najibullah and the PDPA became more and more evident during 1988. In July, Soviet Major Gen. Kim Tsagalov predicted that the Soviet withdrawal would be followed by a quick collapse of the Kabul regime (*London Times*, 25 July). This prediction was publicly denied by other Soviet military officers, but it is probably widely shared. In October, Soviet ambassador Nikolay G. Yegorychev, who had taken over only in the spring from his predecessor Mozhayev, was abruptly relieved of his duties and replaced by First Deputy Foreign Minister Yuli M. Vorontsov. Najibullah was reportedly called to Moscow at this time and may have been given a green light to unify the PDPA however he saw fit, a possible explanation for the arrests and sweeping changes that occurred at the October party plenum.

These measures, however, appeared only to accelerate the disintegration of morale in the PDPA, and in early November the USSR announced it was suspending the withdrawal of troops (ibid., 5 November). This announcement followed by only a few weeks the deployment against the resistance of MiG-27 fighter bombers, SCUD surface-to-surface missiles, and TU-26 (Backfire) bombers, none of which proved capable of turning the tide of battle.

The ultimate insult to the PDPA came when the USSR began negotiating directly and alone with the resistance leaders in Pakistan and Iran for terms that would allow a peaceful withdrawal of Soviet troops (*San Francisco Chronicle*, 28 November; *CSM*, 13 December). Although by year's end these negotiations had produced no known positive results, they seemed to symbolize Moscow's final loss of faith in Najibullah and the PDPA.

At the start of 1988, both the Soviet and the Afghan media had held out high hopes that the policies being pursued in Afghanistan would be a model for settling other regional conflicts in a manner satisfactory to the interests of socialism. Said Najibullah, "Today, the policy of national reconciliation is the way forward for some countries such as Cambodia, Nicaragua, Angola, Ethiopia, and so on who are fighting for revolutionary transformation, independence, and territorial integrity" (Radio Kabul, 1 January; *NYT*, 10 January). By year's end that statement rang hollow for the PDPA and many other Third World Marxist-Leninist parties. For the Afghan resistance, however, Najibullah's words were oddly prophetic: it was the PDPA's national reconciliation policy—and its unacceptability to the Afghan people—that has indeed been a help to the resistance in its relentless pursuit of those same goals, if not in the manner intended by Najibullah.

Ruth and Anthony Arnold
Novato, California

Algeria

Population. 24,194,777
Party. Socialist Vanguard Party (Parti de l'avant-garde socialiste; PAGS)
Founded. 1920 (PAGS, 1966)
Membership. 450 (estimated)
First Secretary. Sadiq Hadjeres
Politburo. No data
Secretariat. No data
Central Committee. No data
Status. Proscribed
Last Congress. Sixth, February 1952
Last Election. N/a
Auxiliary Organizations. No data
Publications. *Sawt al-Sha'b* (Voice of the people), issued clandestinely at infrequent intervals; editor unknown

Background. The Algerian Communist Party (Parti communiste algérien; PCA) was founded in 1920 as an extension of the French Communist Party. It has existed independently since October 1936. Although the PCA participated in the nationalist struggle against France, it was proscribed in November 1962, only four months after Algerian independence. In 1964 dissident left-wing elements of the legal National Liberation Front (FLN) joined with communists from the outlawed PCA to form the Popular Resistance Organization. In January

1966 this group was renamed the Socialist Vanguard Party. No regular party congress has been held since 1952, although the PAGS has held at least one national conference (in 1969) and in July 1981 held a meeting at which a ten-point general platform was adopted. In 1979 PAGS members achieved several positions of leadership in the Algerian national youth organization (UNJA) in an attempt to give student interests genuine representation independently of the FLN. That same year party members were elected to the executive commission and national secretariat of the Algerian national workers' union (UGTA). Barely tolerated by the Algerian government, the PAGS is recognized in the communist world as the official Algerian communist party.

Leadership and Party Organization. Although the precise membership of the PAGS Politburo and Secretariat is not known publicly, prominent members of the party—in addition to Sadiq Hadjeres—are believed to include Larbi Bukhali, a former party general secretary; Bashir Hadj 'Ali; Ahmad Karim; and 'Ali Malki. Both Hadjeres and Malki have contributed to the *World Marxist Review* and the *Information Bulletin* on behalf of the PAGS, and Malki is on the editorial board of the *World Marxist Review*.

Domestic Party Affairs. The PAGS has generally viewed the regime of President Chadli Benjedid, which has ruled Algeria since early 1979, as opportunist and reformist compared with the more militant regime of Houari Boumediene (1965–1978) (see *YICA*, 1983). The party opposes what it views as "the slide to the right" that has occurred in Algeria under the Benjedid regime. In the PAGS's view, this slide to the right has involved liberalization of the economy, weakening of the strong state sector established under the Boumediene regime, worsening of the living conditions of the working class, a housing shortage, and a growing gap between official institutions and the masses (see *YICA*, 1987).

The PAGS sought to capitalize on the wave of riots that shook Algeria for nine days in early October. The riots, which began in Algiers and soon spread to at least seven other Algerian cities, were the most serious domestic upheavals since the country's independence in 1962. For the first time, the army was called in to restore order. In the few months leading up to the riots, militant PAGS members, along with various underground Islamic fundamentalist groups, encouraged protests among workers, students, and white-collar government employees, who challenged the regime's authority and demanded better living conditions (*NYT*, 27 November). Most observers considered the PAGS to have links with the underground Islamic fundamentalist organization most responsible for the riots, the Popular Movement for Algerian Renewal (*Middle East International*, 21 October).

The young Algerians who rioted in October protested the regime's economic austerity measures, high prices and unemployment, and a housing shortage. The riots, which degenerated into violence on several occasions and in several cities, led to 150 deaths and left over 1,000 wounded and 3,000 under arrest.

On 9 October, at the height of the riots, the overseas branch of the PAGS in Paris issued a statement that gave the party's views of the October upheavals. The party rejected the regime's explanation that financial difficulties from falling oil prices and the burden of repaying a large and growing foreign debt caused the riots. The PAGS accused the regime of having squandered much of Algeria's oil revenues on luxury projects for the wealthy class. Members of this class were able, in recent years, to amass huge fortunes from speculation, theft, political racketeering, and corruption. The party argued that the country's number one problem was not, as President Benjedid declared, repayment of the foreign debt; instead, it was the improvement of the lot of workers and youth. (*La Tribune d'Octobre*, Paris, December.)

The PAGS offered, once again, its solutions for solving Algeria's financial crisis. These solutions included renegotiating the foreign debt; limiting the use of foreign exchange to the importation of basic foodstuffs and basic materials needed to allow factories to operate; freezing all prestige expenditures; and taxing the rich, especially those who have amassed fortunes at the expense of workers and the country. (Ibid.)

The PAGS identified one other cause of Algeria's October crisis: the absence of genuine democracy. The party accused the FLN of having stripped Algeria's mass organizations of any meaningful activity. As a result, workers try to organize themselves outside of official channels, and the youth is left to idleness and restlessness. With all avenues of dialogue closed and all demands considered as crimes, the PAGS is not surprised to see violent demonstrations and plundering. It declares that the Algerian people aspire to democracy and freedom of expression, and that they demand mass organizations that are genuinely representative. (Ibid.)

Finally, the PAGS expressed skepticism that the October riots resulted from opposition by conservative hard-liners to economic reforms in agriculture and state industries. The party argued that the Algerian economy did in fact need reforms, whose objective would be to improve the management of state industries. This would allow an increase in both the quality and quantity of production and would strengthen state industries by a fully democratic participation of workers in their management. (Ibid.)

While there is no evidence that the PAGS instigated the riots, the party did encourage the disturbances after they had begun, and PAGS members distributed antiregime leaflets in Algiers during the riots. The thrust of antiregime criticism heard among rioters was that the regime refused to share power, and that it had not sufficiently loosened up various levers of control. By contrast, the PAGS has argued consistently that the Benjedid regime has compromised the doctrinaire socialism of the Boumediene period. This criticism implied that the PAGS was even more out of step with popular sentiment than the Benjedid regime.

On 12 October, President Benjedid defused the riots by announcing a referendum for 3 November to approve a number of constitutional changes. These changes shifted more power to the prime minister and transferred authority from the ruling FLN to the hitherto weak People's National Assembly. In response the PAGS, along with other underground opposition groups, rejected the continuation of a one-party state and called for a boycott of the 3 November referendum. These groups, including the PAGS, accused Benjedid of attempting only superficial changes of the political system and of failing to address the underlying issues that provoked the October riots. (*Middle East International*, 4 November.)

The FLN congress, held in late November, declared that the FLN was no longer a party and would henceforth revert to being a broad-based front. The new FLN was expected to incorporate different political "tendencies" that would emerge during 1989. The illegal underground groups—including the PAGS—who urged a multiparty system, were, however, to be excluded from the broad-based front. (Ibid., 2 December.)

International Views, Positions, and Activities. The PAGS favors a foreign policy that would confirm positions that brought Algeria to the forefront of the Nonaligned Movement. These positions include effective support for national liberation struggles in Palestine, South Africa and Namibia, the Western Sahara, and elsewhere; promotion of a new world economic order; elimination of the indebtedness of exploited Third World nations; and increased cooperation and solidarity with the world socialist system in the struggle for peaceful coexistence and against the arms race.

In a statement dated 9 December 1988, the PAGS reacted with "relief and hope" to the conclusion, one day earlier, of the Soviet-American INF Treaty to eliminate intermediate- and shorter-range nuclear missiles. The party hailed the signature by CPSU General Secretary Mikhail Gorbachev and President Ronald Reagan of the historic treaty that paves the way into a new age of struggle for a world without nuclear weapons. The PAGS cited the Soviet peace offensive launched after the 27th Congress of the CPSU as a factor that helped to neutralize "the efforts of the U.S. government and the powerful American military-industrial complex to impose an escalation of tension on the world and forced the U.S. to sign the treaty." (*Sawt al-Sha'b*, 9 December 1987; *IB*, May.)

The PAGS argued that the INF Treaty was particularly significant for Third World countries. According to this argument, the arms race aggravates the structural crisis of capitalism, leading imperialist countries to shift an increasingly heavy burden onto Third World countries by manipulating commodity prices and raising interest rates on international loans. This helps explain the large degree of indebtedness among Third World countries. Therefore, the PAGS urges these countries to try to limit and eventually abolish the arms arsenal "in order to get rid of the stranglehold of indebtedness." Thus for Third World countries, the struggle to abolish arms has a double importance: human survival and economic development. (Ibid.)

Relations with the Soviet Union. In 1988 Algeria continued its pattern of sending high-level delegations to the Soviet Union. Belkacem Nabi, minister of energy, chemical, and petrochemical industries, headed an important delegation from his own ministry and the Algerian company Sonatrach that visited Moscow in mid-June. On 16 June, Nabi and Soviet Minister of Foreign Economic Relations Konstantin Katushev held talks that dealt with bilateral cooperation in the energy and petrochemical fields. The two ministers agreed in principle on the creation of a joint Algerian-Soviet company for producing fertilizers and chemicals, conditional on the continuation of bilateral technical talks aimed at accelerating cooperation in this field. (Algiers, Domestic Service in Arabic, 16 June; *FBIS*, 17 June.) At the same time, Gen. Abdallah Belhouchet, Algerian deputy minister of defense and chief of staff of the National People's Army, headed an important delegation of senior Algerian army officers that visited Moscow at the invitation of the Soviets. Belhouchet held talks with Marshal Sergey Akhromeyev, first deputy minister of defense and chief of staff. The talks included an exchange of views on Algerian-Soviet cooperation. (Algiers, Domestic Service in Arabic, 17 June; *FBIS*, 21 June.)

In January, it was announced in Algiers that Algerian and Soviet companies had concluded five large contracts for the supplying, from the Soviet Union, of $80 million worth of civil engineering equipment. Negotiations were continuing for the supply of an additional $20 million worth of site dumpers and self-propelling cranes. (Algiers, Domestic Service in French, 5 January; *FBIS*, 7 January.)

At the end of August, Algerian Minister of Culture and Tourism Boualem Bessaih visited Moscow, where he held talks with Petr Demichev, alternate Politburo member and first vice-president of the Supreme Soviet Presidium. After a review of bilateral cultural cooperation, both sides sought more active and broader contacts in culture and other fields. (TASS in English, 31 August; *FBIS*, 1 September.)

In addition, an FLN party delegation visited Yugoslavia in the spring. The delegation, led by Mohamed Cherif Messaadia, head of the FLN Central Committee Permanent Secretariat, held talks in Belgrade with a delegation of the League of Yugoslavian Communists (LYC) led by Bosko Krunić, president of the LYC Central Committee Presidium. (Algiers, Algerian Press Service in English; 31 March; *FBIS*, 4 April.) Messaadia also held talks with Secretary of the LYC Presidium Radiša Gačič and Yugoslav state president Lazar Mojsov (Belgrade, Tanjug in English, 31 March; *FBIS*, 4 April). The talks allowed a thorough exchange of views both on the internal development of the two countries and on many international issues, on which Algeria and Yugoslavia frequently hold identical views. During the concluding talks, the two parties agreed to intensify mutual cooperation and their joint contribution to the struggle for peace, for faster economic progress of the developing countries, and to turn the Mediterranean into an area of peace, stability, and cooperation. (Belgrade, Tanjug Domestic Service in Serbo-Croatian, 1 April; *FBIS*, 4 April.)

John Damis
Portland State University

Bahrain

Population. 480,383
Party. Bahrain National Liberation Front (NLF/B)
Founded. 1955
Membership. Unknown but believed negligible
Chairman. Yusuf al-Hasan al-Ajajai (not noted since 1983)
General Secretary. Saif ben Ali (noted from 1987)
Governing Committee. (Last known members of this apparently politburo-level body; list of names incomplete): Yusuf al-Hasan al-Ajajai (last noted 1983), Saif ben Ali, Abdallah Ali Muhammad al-Rashid, Muhammad Ali, Ali Nagi Abdallah, Badir Malik, Aziz Mahmud (last noted 1983), Yusuf al-Hasan (alternate member only)
Status. Illegal
Last Congress. Unknown
Last Election. N/a
Auxiliary Organizations. Bahrain Peace and Solidarity Committee (affiliated with the World Peace Council and Afro-Asian People's Solidarity Organization), Democratic Youth League of Bahrain (affiliated with the World Federation of Democratic Youth), National Union of Bahraini Students (affiliated with the International Union of Students), Women's Organization of the NLF/B (affiliated with the Women's International Democratic Federation), Federation of Bahraini Workers (affiliated with the World Federation of Trade Unions)
Publications. *Al-Jamahir* (The masses), *al-Fajr* (The dawn)

The NLF/B is apparently still regarded by the Soviets as a "national democratic party," a Marxist grouping falling short of full-fledged communist-

party status because of ideological and disciplinary shortcomings (see *YICA*, 1986). It continues, however, to participate in meetings where all the other delegations have full communist-party status (for example, the April conference of "Arab communist parties" calling for the end of the Iran-Iraq war) (*IB*, Prague, no. 14). It also continues to participate in meetings in which communist parties predominate, where it is kept company by other "nonkosher" groupings (for example, the Popular Unity Party of Yemen Arab Republic at the March conference of "the communist and workers' parties of the eastern Mediterranean, Middle East, and Red Sea countries," which applauded the February Soviet-Afghan agreement) (ibid., Toronto, June). And though there is still a good chance that NLF/B headquarters is in Damascus (see *YICA*, 1986), the front's *al-Fajr* claims to be published in Nicosia.

"Bahrain: 33 Years of Struggle for Independence and Progress," dated 15 February and published in the June *Information Bulletin* (Toronto), appears to have been the NLF/B's main statement of the year. It accuses the Bahrain government of being linked to imperialism abroad and of suppressing civil liberties at home. An example of the first is said to be foreign capital's ability to drain wealth out of the country, and of the second, the imprisonment, torture, and murder of members of the "patriotic movement." The statement calls for freedom for political parties and other organizations to operate and for the restoration of democratic bodies. Turning to foreign affairs, it blames "imperialism" for aggravating the Iran-Iraq war and calls for withdrawal of foreign navies from the Persian Gulf and a settlement based on Security Council Resolution 598. The war in Afghanistan is called "yet another excuse for granting new military privileges to imperialism and for an onslaught on democracy." It lauds the uprising of the Palestinians and calls for their alliance with the Syrians and "Lebanese patriotic forces."

Apparently written at about the same time, an article by the NLF/B's General Secretary Said ben Ali and alternate Governing Committee member Yusuf al-Hasan, published in the March *World Marxist Review* (London) gives a more detailed exposition along the same lines. Added emphases here were the alleged role of U.S. arms and bases in the Gulf states in exacerbating international tensions and diverting resources from economic development. The Iran-Iraq war was specifically blamed for emigration from Bahrain, water pollution in the Gulf, and the continued suspension of democratic liberties in the country. The article is critical of both Iraq and Iran but poses no specific solution for their conflict. Its most interesting aspect is its acknowledgement that "workers', youth, and women's organizations" are active in Bahrain (see also *YICA*, 1988), its claim that the NLF/B is "working to establish cooperation with the People's and Islamic Fronts for the Liberation of Bahrain," and its allowance of the possibility that even part of the bourgeoisie could join these "national forces" to press for common objectives. Finally, the article claims that since 1986 a "regional committee of youth, women, students, and trade unions in Bahrain, Saudi Arabia, Oman, and Iraq" has been active, but implied that a similar move toward joint action among "peace champions" in the area was not successful.

It was apparently the same Yusuf al-Hasan, the coauthor of the above-mentioned article, who attended the April meeting in Prague on the work of *World Marxist Review* (*Rudé právo*, Prague, 14 April); and thus in retrospect it would seem that he is also the one who represented the NLF/B at the 1987 Nicosia symposium sponsored by the *World Marxist Review* and *al-Nahj* (see *YICA*, 1988). The other internationally active NLF/B leader continues to be Abdallah Ali Muhammad al-Rashid; he is currently listed as his country's sole member of the Presidential Committee of the World Peace Council (WPC) (*New Perspectives*, Helsinki, no. 5), the largest and most important of the Soviet-line international communist front organizations, and he was featured in Czech media coverage of the March meeting of that body in Prague (ČTK, 20 March; *FBIS*, 21 March).

Wallace H. Spaulding
McLean, Virginia

Egypt

Population. 53,347,679 (July 1988)
Party. Egyptian Communist Party (al-Hizb al-Shuyu'i al-Misri; ECP)
Founded. 1921; revived in 1975
Membership. 500 (estimated)
General Secretary. (Apparently) Farid Mujahid

Politburo. Michel Kamil (chief of foreign relations), Najib Kamil, Kamal Muhammad Magdi (representative to the *WMR*); other names unknown
Central Committee. Farid Mujahid, Yusuf Darwish; other names unknown
Status. Proscribed
Last Congress. Second, early 1985 (possibly 1984)
Last Election. N/a
Auxiliary Organizations. Union of Egyptian Peasants; others unknown
Publications. *Al-Intisar* (Victory), main ECP newspaper, published about nine times a year; *al-Wa'i* (Consciousness), dealing with intraparty issues; *Hayat al-Hizb* (Party life), primarily concerned with party work; *Ideological Questions*, a theoretical journal. In the recent past, Egyptian communists in Paris have published *al-Yasar al-Arabi* (The Arab left).

Background. The Egyptian communist movement remains as splintered as ever. Besides the ECP, several groups have surfaced in recent years. These include the Revolutionary Current, the Egyptian Communist Party-8 January, the Egyptian Communist Workers' Party, the Popular Movement, the Armed Communist Organization, the Egyptian Communist Party-Communist Faction, a Trotskyite communist organization called the Revolutionary Communist League, and the Revolutionary Progressive Party. It is possible that some of these are merely descriptive labels rather than formal names of organizations, and it is not known whether there is any relationship between these groups and the ECP (or, in most cases, whether they continue to exist). All indications point to the relative insignificance of communist groups in comparison with the threat to the regime posed by militant religious movements or potentially even by the military. An antiregime organization called Egypt's Revolution, which came to the surface in 1987 and twenty members of which (including the son of the late President Gamal Abd al-Nasir) were charged in February with attacks on U.S. and Israeli diplomats, has been vaguely described as "leftist" (*NYT*, 18 February; MENA, 18 February; *FBIS*, 19 February), but there is no indication that it has a Marxist orientation.

Leadership and Party Organization. Little is known about the ECP's leadership and organization. Few party officials have been mentioned in available publications. Official statements by ECP leaders published abroad are mostly anonymous. The names most often mentioned are two Politburo members, Michel Kamil, obviously because of his position as the party's chief of foreign relations, and Kamal Muhammad Magdi, representative to the *WMR*. All indications point to the typical pattern of "democratic centralism," albeit in a rudimentary form resulting from the group's small membership and clandestine character.

Domestic Party Affairs. No information is available on meetings of party organs during the year. A statement issued by the Secretariat on 12 June 1987 is the only available indication of any meeting during that year (*IB*, January).

In the aftermath of massive demonstrations at Ayn Shams University protesting against Israeli rule in the West Bank and Gaza (put down with tear gas by the antiriot police [*Manchester Guardian Weekly*, 17 January]), Egypt's interior minister Zaki Badr accused both communists and Muslim fundamentalists of being involved and of hoping to use this issue to create chaos in their own country (Voice of Lebanon, Beirut, 15 January; *FBIS*, 15 January). An article in *African Communist* (London, 4th Quarter, 1987) describes Egyptian communists as working "under difficult conditions . . . to strengthen their underground structures and to step up their ideological work." The article singles out for mention the role of the party's theoretical journal *Ideological Questions*, each of whose five issues has dealt "in depth with a specific theme" such as Egypt's socioeconomic situation or the Palestine question (ibid.).

Magdi reported that Marxists in his country "still show much interest in problems of socialist orientation," particularly because of the socioeconomic reforms in Egypt after 1952. But he complained that even during the period of President Gamal Abd al-Nasir, changes were inadequate and that "the socialist ideas proclaimed were eclectic." He praised the emergence of "public and cooperative sectors" during that period, but pointed to the simultaneous growth of "the parasite stratum of bureaucrats" that limited progress to mere "*national democratic reforms*" (emphasis in the original). The ECP's dissolution in 1965 was deemed to have been "a bad mistake" in light of the Arab Socialist Union's failure to develop into anything more than "a loose and socially heterogeneous organisation." (*WMR*, June.)

Available ECP statements emphasized deterioration of economic conditions. An editorial in *al-Intisar* in November 1987 reiterated the ECP's refutation of President Anwar al-Sadat's claim that he was putting the country on the road to prosperity, which the editorial's author said does not result from "integration . . . with the world capitalist economy" but rather from "complex economic and social development . . . oriented toward well-being and social justice," especially for "the working masses." He described present conditions in terms of eroding wages and earnings, the increase of the national debt from $2 billion in 1970 to $45 billion by 1986, a 27.5-fold increase in the import of luxury items during the same period, a drop in the production of marketable goods, and a drastic drop in the value of Egyptian currency. He matched the inability to fulfill basic needs with "guaranteed profits for the parasitic strata, the big bourgeoisie, the Arab and other foreign investors, and the transnational corporations." (*IB*, March.)

A statement of the party's Central Secretariat on 12 June 1987 described the People's Assembly (the Egyptian parliament) as representing "the political and economic interests of the Egyptian big bourgeoisie and its parasitic section." The regime was accused of launching "a bitter attack on the working classes," especially in the context of trade union elections. The statement also deplored the "upsurge of religious passions and terrorist acts staged by the extremist religious groups," as well as the government's use of torture against those who were arrested in the aftermath of such incidents. Asserting that the government found these activities a convenient "excuse" to take away the people's "already scanty rights," the statement referred to limits on freedoms during the recent parliamentary elections and to plans for "a new terrorism law." (*IB*, January.)

Al-Intisar deemed Egypt's "clearly formed" class structure to be conducive to the completion of "the stage of the national-democratic revolution" (*IB*, March).

Auxiliary and Front Organizations. Little information has come to light about any auxiliary organizations of the ECP. Under current conditions, it seems safe to assume that children's and youth organizations do not exist. In the past, the party was actively concerned with organizing primarily students and workers. The party sponsors the Union of Egyptian Peasants (see *YICA*, 1988). At least as of the early 1980s, it was said to be "prominent" in organizations like the Committee for the Defense of

Workers and Democratic Women and Youth (*African Communist*, 1st Quarter, 1982).

The ECP's Central Secretariat called for the creation of "a united front of all honest trade union activists" to promote working-class interests and for attracting participation in "democratic organizations of workers, peasants and other social groups," as well as in the establishment of "a national democratic front incorporating all national patriotic, progressive and honest forces" (*IB*, January).

Much more important than the ECP or any other communist organization is the broad, legal leftist opposition front, the National Progressive Unionist Party (NPUP), whose general secretary is longtime Marxist Khalid Muhyi al-Din. (For a biography of Muhyi al-Din, see *YICA*, 1984.) Its deputy general secretary is Rif'at al-Sa'id. Some of the members of the NPUP are Marxists; others are Nasserites or other opponents of the nonsocialist pro-Western direction of the regime. The NPUP publishes the widely circulated weekly newspaper *al-Ahali* (edited by Muhyi al-Din and with the long-time prominent leftist intellectual, Muhammad Sid-Ahmad as managing editor). The party got only 2.2 percent of the vote in the 1987 parliamentary elections, and the application of the 8 percent rule prevented it from winning any seats. But there is no dispute that corruption and manipulation, as well as arrests of party supporters and other kinds of governmental interference, were factors in this defeat.

The NPUP joined the other opposition parties on 18 June in announcing a boycott of local council elections. These parties affirmed that the regular "rigging of elections" and other kinds of disregard for the constitution had put "the democratic process" in peril. The statement of the party leaders, including Muhyi al-Din, also criticized a new law regarding local government for "adopting the worst elections system, that of whole-party lists," depriving local councils of supervisory functions, and banning coalitions of parties during elections. (*Al-Wafd*, Cairo, 5 July; *FBIS*, 12 July.)

According to Sid-Ahmad, the "debacle" in the 1987 elections led to a "soul-searching debate" within the NPUP. He pointed to the past manipulation of the left—by both Nasir and Sadat—as having undermined it "as an independent electoral force" and reported that NPUP members were debating among themselves about whether a party made up of such diverse ideological groups could survive, particularly when Nasserist and communist parties are legalized. Stressing that such a pluralist party of the left is "in keeping with . . . *perestroika*," he also pointed to "the danger of external manipulation." (*Middle East Report*, Washington, January–February.)

For a leftist, Sid-Ahmad is highly respected in mainstream Western circles. He spoke on United States–Arab relations at a dinner in his honor sponsored by the Mid-America–Arab Chamber of Commerce in May 1987, following consultations at the Brookings Institute (*Mid-America–Arab Chamber of Commerce Bulletin*, Chicago, June/July 1987). (Also see his article, "Egypt: The Islamic Issue," in *Foreign Policy*, Washington, Winter 1987–88.)

Muhyi al-Din wrote of "the price of disavowing progressive ideals" since Nasir's death. While admitting that there had been "difficulties, mistakes, setbacks and retreats" even under Nasir, Muhyi al-Din saw that period as one of "progressive transformations" that were ended when "Sadat placed his bets on the 'fat cats'—representatives of parasitic capital." He recognized that Sadat's successor, President Hosni Mubarak has brought "certain changes," but in methods rather than substance. He insisted that the only way to reverse current economic deterioration is "by changing the *political course*" (emphasis in the original). (*WMR*, August.)

Muhyi al-Din complained that the "lack of a single national leadership of all Left forces" works against "mass pressure on the government." He reported that his party's effort to establish a Front of Struggle for Wider Democracy—a "broad alliance of Left forces" that will included the NPUP, the ECP, and the Arab Socialist Nasserite Party—"is now on the threshold of taking organisational shape" and that there are also the beginnings of cooperation with other opposition groups. (*WMR*, August.)

The NPUP ran over a thousand candidates in the trade union elections of October 1987, and 750 were elected to various committees, triple the previous number. Muhyi al-Din noted that opposition parties, including the NPUP, "hold a majority in the leadership of the lawyers' and veterinary surgeons' unions." (*WMR*, August.) The NPUP and the other "legal opposition parties as well as Muslim groups," have renewed the National Committee for the Support of the Palestinian and Lebanese People (*Middle East Report*, May–June).

On an international level, Muhyi al-Din stressed the priority of struggling to overcome Egypt's dependence on the United States and other capitalist states, which is the impediment to the kinds of change in "the *political course*" (emphasis in original) that would allow a breakaway from the present "economic deadlock" (*WMR*, August).

International Views, Positions, and Activities. The ECP participated in a meeting with representatives of eight Arab communist and workers' parties late in September 1987 that was concerned mainly, at least as one infers from the statement they issued, with the situation in Saudi Arabia (*IB*, January). A meeting of the ECP and nine other communist and workers' parties of the Arab East (*sic*, as those of Tunisia and Morocco were also represented) issued a statement expressing solidarity with the Palestinians in the Israeli-occupied territories on 15 December 1987. A statement on regional conflicts was issued by the ECP and twelve other communist and workers' parties of the Eastern Mediterranean, Middle East, and Red Sea countries on 10 March (*IB*, June). Seven Arab "Communist and Democratic Parties," including the ECP, issued a statement in April on the Iraq-Iran War and Iraq's war on the Kurds (*IB*, July). The ECP was represented by Magdi at a discussion of the work of the *World Marxist Review*, held in Prague during the same month (*IB*, June; the discussion is excerpted and summarized in *WMR*, June).

The annual editorial board meeting of *al-Nahj*, a journal published jointly by communist and workers' parties in the Arab world (presumably including the ECP) met 16–18 November 1987 in Damascus (see the communiqué in *IB*, February).

Al-Intisar deplored Sadat's termination of "the period of the liberation struggle" and "forcible switch . . . to the camp of states dependent on U.S. imperialism." This shift was blamed for the region's deepened divisions and deteriorated economic conditions. The article argued that increased conflict had belied Sadat's prediction that he was bringing peace to the region and maintained that the region had been "'reorganized' to suit the hegemonistic interests of imperialism." The "owners of petroleum," particularly Saudi Arabia, were described as now "in power, and . . . fully attached to the U.S. strategy of neoglobalism—extending their counterrevolutionary role as far as Nicaragua, Afghanistan, and Angola." (*IB*, March.) Joint statements of the ECP and other communist parties praised the Palestinian uprising, which was said to have frustrated the schemes of "Israel's ruling Zionist circles" and "the Jordanian regime." The same statement called for the convening of an international peace conference, with PLO participation, leading to full Israeli withdrawal and the rights of return and self-

determination for the Palestinians (*IB*, February). Another joint statement denounced the Saudi regime for "mass arrests and torture" and described the "carnage" wrought by guardsmen among "unarmed pilgrims" with the protection of "U.S. imperialism" (*IB*, January). A joint statement in April deplored the Iran-Iraq War for playing "into the hands of imperialism and Zionism only." The Iraqi regime was blamed for initiating the war and the use of chemical weapons, described as "a genocide campaign" that "in Iraqi Kurdistan . . . has assumed a mass racial character unprecedented in history," with "assistance from the Turkish regime." The statement called for "solidarity with the Iraqi people" against their "barbaric" rulers, but also blamed Iran for "continuing the war" and occupying Iraqi territory. (*IB*, July.) Still another statement, issued in March, greeted the recent understanding between the USSR and Afghanistan and the beginning of the Soviet withdrawal, condemned "attempts by third parties to interfere" in Afghanistan's internal affairs, and declared "firm solidarity with the Afghan people and its government" (*IB*, June).

Glenn E. Perry
Indiana State University

Iran

Population. 51,923,689
Party. Communist Party of Iran (Tudeh Party)
Membership. 1,000–2,000 hardcore members; 15,000–20,000 sympathizers.
First Secretary. 'Ali Khavari
Leading Bodies. No data
Status. Illegal
Last Congress. 1986, National Conference
Last Election. N/a
Affiliated Party. Fedayeen-e Khalq (majority)
Publications. *Rahe Tudeh* (Tudeh path), *Mardom* (People), and *Tudeh News* (in English)

Domestic Affairs. The brewing factionalism that plagued the Tudeh Party after it had been dismantled in Iran in 1983 came to a head in 1988. The expulsion of some members and alternate members of the Central Committee in May 1986 split the party (see *YICA*, 1986 and 1987). Tudeh dissidents held a congress in January 1988 outside Iran and founded a new communist party—the Iranian People's Democratic Party—according to a communiqué issued in Paris on 6 February (*Le Monde*, 9 February; *FBIS-NES*, 11 February). Although this historical division was partly triggered by the controversy over the new leadership, the Central Committee Plenum re-elected 'Ali Khavari first secretary of the Tudeh Party (*Pravda*, 23 February; *FBIS-SOV*, 24 February).

The split did not appear to impede the activities of the party cells within Iran, either. During its plenary meeting in January 1988, the Central Committee Plenum praised the intensification of the activities of the Tudeh groups in Iran and decided to make organizational changes that would better fit the conditions of the clandestine activities (*Tudeh News*, 17 February). One of the most important aims of the party cells is to form the "Front for Freedom and Peace" by forging unity of action with such other leftist revolutionary organizations as the Fedayeen-e Khalq (both majority and minority) and a group of Mojahedin supporters. The party's own activities included organizing protests and strikes among the workers. The party cells, according to its own publications, "are playing an important role in the continuous enhancement of the revolutionary movement amongst the workers" (ibid., 27 February). Besides organizing protests and strikes, the Tudeh cells gathered information on the internal situation in Iran; tried to form antiwar committees; and helped families of Tudeh political prisoners.

No aspect of the party activities inside or outside Iran in 1988 so preoccupied the Tudeh leadership as the fate of Tudeh political prisoners. Already of great concern to the party since 1983, political prisoners came to be of even greater concern in late 1988. The alarm bell rang as early as February, when the Supreme Judicial Council in Iran passed sentences of death on almost 70 political prisoners, including some Tudeh members (ibid., 17 February). In an attempt to call worldwide attention to the mistreatment of political prisoners in Iran, Ahmad Danesh, a member of the Central Committee of the party, managed to distribute from Evin Prison in Iran, where he had been imprisoned for five years, a letter dated 5 May. In it he charged that he had been subjected to torture, despite his services as a surgeon in treating patients who were political prisoners. He said: "I feel that today the slogan 'A good

Tudeh member is a dead one' has been promoted . . . to the level of an unwritten law . . ." (ibid., 6 July).

What transformed this slogan into deadly reality in July were the military operations of the leftist Mojahedin-e Khalq forces against the Tehran government from bases inside Iraqi territory. A U.N. report said on 2 November that human rights violations in Iran included "a wave of executions" of political prisoners, 200 of whom had been supporters of the Mojahedin-e Khalq; they were killed in Evin Prison on 28 July (*NYT*, 3 November). These executions had the appearance of revenge against anyone suspected of disloyalty to the government. But according to Amnesty International, most victims had been left-wing political activists and sympathizers, including members of the Tudeh Party (see *Amnesty International*, USA, 12 December; and *NYT*, 13 December).

The Central Committee of the Tudeh Party issued a statement on executions on 26 July. It said in part that on 20 July, Kiomars Zarshenas, a member of the Central Committee, and several other party members had been executed, and that another 55 political prisoners awaited execution. The Central Committee had also heard that Anoushiravan Ebrahimi, secretary of the CC of the Tudeh Party and a one-time member of the party's Executive Committee, had also been among those executed (*Tudeh News*, 17 August). The Politburo of the Central Committee sent out a bulletin in September, stating that a "renowned revolutionary, literary figure and journalist," Rahman Hatefi (Heydar Mehregan), a member of the Politburo at the time and a founding member of the Navid Organization, "had been murdered under torture in the Islamic Republic . . ." (ibid., 14 September). The Central Committee listed a number of other regular and Central Committee members who had been executed by 1 December, and the "Tudeh Party of Iran [asked] the United Nations, the human rights committee, Amnesty International, and all other humane forces in the world to take prompt action to save the lives of thousands of people whose only crime [was] having a different ideology." (Clandestine Radio of the Iranian Toilers, in Persian, December; *FBIS-NES*, 2 December).

Knowing how intimately both the internal situation in Iran and the developments in the Iraq-Iran war affected the fate of all opposition groups, members of the Tudeh Party keenly monitored events in these two areas. In regard to the internal situation, the party took note of a public dispute between President Khamenei and Ayatollah Khomeini over the powers of the central government. Perhaps with an eye to his rival, Prime Minister Musavi, who favors state intervention in the economy, Khamenei, who is a free-marketeer, argued on 1 January that Islamic law sets limits to governmental power. He was openly rebuked by Ayatollah Khomeini on 6 January, who claimed absolute powers for the Islamic government (Tehran Domestic Service, in Persian, 7 January; *FBIS-NES*, 7 January). To the Tudeh Party this edict of Khomeini further proved that Iran had "a medieval, despotic regime" (*Tudeh News*, 3 February). What the Tudeh Party completely ignored was the positive side of the decree. Khomeini's decree was intended to break the logjam on social and economic reform that had been created by the conservative members of the Council of Guardians, who had repeatedly vetoed bills passed by the Majlis.

To the Tudeh, however, Khomeini's "Islamic democracy is nothing but religious despotism" (ibid., 2 March). This attitude was reflected in its position on the Majlis elections as well. The Central Committee critically asked: "How can they be called free elections when the participation of political parties and organizations has been outlawed and the prisons are filled with the true defenders of people's rights?"—meaning leftist forces (ibid., 13 April). When Khomeini appointed the Majlis Speaker Hashemi-Rafsanjani commander in chief of the Armed Forces, the Tudeh Party took a dim view of the appointment, concluding that the Islamic Republic "is increasingly becoming unstable" (ibid., 6 July).

The Tudeh Party had always been critical of Iran's obstinate continuation of the war with Iraq after the Iranian forces had recovered Khoramshahr in May 1982, but in 1988 they criticized the Iraqi government as well. Iraq's use of chemical weapons triggered the Tudeh Party's condemnation of the Baathist regime in Iraq. The party joined the communist parties of Turkey and Iraq in a common denunciation of the use of chemical weapons. The three parties issued a joint statement on 19 April, specifically condemning Iraq's use of chemical weapons against its own Kurdish citizens in the town of Halabjah on 16 March. They also took the opportunity to "support the proposals put forward by the Soviet Union for the withdrawal of Western naval forces from the region . . ." (ibid., 25 May). Following the U.N. Security Council's condemnation of the use of chemical weapons on 9 May, the Majlis Speaker Hashemi-Rafsanjani said, "We hope not to be forced into using chemical weapons. But if we feel the need, Iran will not accept any responsibility concerning the outcome." The Tudeh Party latched onto this statement to assert that Iran shows its "utter disregard for human lives . . ." (ibid., 8 June).

Like everyone else, the Tudeh Party was taken by surprise when on 18 July, the Iranian government accepted the U.N. Security Council Resolution 598 of 20 July 1987. But the party's attitude was one of self-congratulation. To use the words of the Central Committee's statement of the same day: "The foreign mass media branded this act of the regime [acceptance of U.N. Resolution 598] as 'unexpected.' However, this was by no means surprising for our Party." (Ibid., 3 August.) The party's Politburo had said as early as 9 June that "time has proved the futility of the Iran-Iraq war to the people of our homeland . . . alienating the masses from the regime and driving increasingly large numbers of people into opposition." (*Morning Star*, London, 8 August; *FBIS-NES*, 11 August).

Despite its ideological blinders, the Tudeh Party's explanation of Iran's acceptance of the ceasefire in the war with Iraq was more comprehensive than most other accounts that simply emphasized Iran's military setbacks in explaining its acceptance, setbacks that began in April 1988, when the Iraqi forces unexpectedly recovered the Fao Peninsula. By contrast, the Tudeh Party suggested three main factors: "The people were no longer prepared to go to the war fronts for 'martyrdom'; the deep socioeconomic crisis had been deepened by effective Iraqi air strikes against Iranian ports and oil terminals; contradictions between the ruling factions had intensified and seriously affected the revolutionary guards and the army." Of the Iranian political actors who had persuaded Ayatollah Khomeini to accept the U.N. Resolution 598, the party singled out Majlis Speaker Hashemi-Rafsanjani and Ahmad Khomeini, the Ayatollah's son, who felt "deep anxiety . . . about the future of the regime after Khomeini's death." (Ibid.)

In essence, the Tudeh Party's analysis of postwar Iran was twofold. First, the party did not believe that even after the establishment of peace, the Iranian regime would be able to cope with the problems it faced. These included the creation of jobs for five million unemployed people, the reconstruction of cities and villages and industrial centers, the return of about three million war refugees to their homes, the provision of employment for hundreds of thousands of mobilization forces released from the armed forces, the revival of the bankrupt economy, and so on (ibid., 21 September). Second, in anticipation of factional confrontations, especially after Khomeini's death (*Tudeh News*, 9 November), the "progressive forces" had to attempt to mount a united challenge against the regime (*Morning Star*, London, 8 August; *FBIS-NES*, 11 August). For the party this was "the main issue," because after analyzing the strength of these forces it had concluded "that none of the progressive and democratic parties and organizations alone [could] present an alternative to the existing inhuman regime...A United Front is the only capable and effective force" (ibid., 21 September). The Tudeh Party, of course, having itself experienced a factional split in 1988, knows better than any other "progressive force" that rampant factionalism has always made it impossible to form such a united front.

Foreign Relations. The events of 1988 posed an extraordinary challenge to the Soviet Union's policy on Iran. They forced the Soviet leaders to simultaneously walk several complicated tightropes. Moscow was determined to pursue a number of seemingly contradictory foreign-policy objectives. In the end, the Soviet leaders appear to have done quite well, at least in the short run.

One of the dilemmas faced by the Soviet leaders was posed by the surge of suppression of the leftist forces in Iran, including the Tudeh Party, at a time when they were reluctant to criticize the Iranian government too harshly. Despite repeated frustrations since 1979, they were still determined to woo Iran; to persuade it to stop the war with Iraq; to seek its cooperation in settling the problem of Afghanistan; to keep up Soviet-Iranian pressure on Washington against the naval presence of Western powers in the Persian Gulf; and to expand commercial and economic relations with Tehran.

For the Soviet Union to have continued to ignore publicly the "mass execution" of Tudeh Party members was obviously no real alternative. The party had shown nearly half a century of loyalty to the Moscow brand of communist ideology. In responding to the Iranian execution of the Tudeh members, the Soviet Union had to do better than simply reproduce the Tudeh denunciations of the Iranian government in its media, as indeed *Pravda* did in one instance (ibid., 8 December). An acceptable alternative was provided by a U.N. report on human rights violations in Iran that was published on 3 November. Only two days later, with an eye to the U.N. report, Moscow Radio broadcast to Iran an unattributed commentary in Persian. Rhetorically,

the commentary asked, "What is the reason behind intensifying suppression in Iran...[when] the situation demands that the policy of moral and physical assassination be ended and that all society's forces be mobilized for postwar reconstruction?" (Moscow Radio Peace and Progress, in Persian to Iran, 5 November; *FBIS-SOV*, 30 November). And the answer was: "However, the truth is that those who favor monopolizing rule sacrifice the interests of the people for the sake of their own greedy interests. They consider freedom and democracy to be a threat to their collective interests. The ceasefire in the war with Iraq has given rise to new concerns among the enemies of democracy in Iran..." (ibid.). The commentary also charged the Iranian regime with pro-American tendencies. Allegedly, "by sacrificing members of the Tudeh Party and the Fedaiyin Organization," the Iranian government was trying "to gain the trust and support of [U.S.] imperialism..." (ibid.).

The Soviet Union's most important strategic objective in 1988, as in previous years, was to get Iran to stop the war. In 1987, Moscow's pressure on Iran had been confined to hints about Moscow's possible support for a follow-on resolution for an arms embargo against Iran (*YICA*, 1988). But in 1988, Moscow's pressure tactics went beyond hints of an embargo. On 14 January 1988, the Soviet ambassador to the U.N., Alexander Belonogov, reportedly said that an arms embargo resolution against Iran may "become absolutely necessary" at some time, although he told reporters that the secretary general of the U.N. should first have more talks with Iran and Iraq (*WP*, 14 January). The Soviet Union had already joined fourteen other Security Council members on 24 December 1987 in a public announcement of readiness to proceed with an embargo. This obviously had stopped short of an arms-embargo resolution. In 1988, Moscow was prepared to go along with an arms embargo if the Soviet Union could participate in a U.N.-sponsored naval force that would patrol the Persian Gulf, an idea opposed by the United States (*NYT*, 16 January).

The Iranian media suspected that a U.S.-USSR deal lay behind the Soviet pressure on Iran. Allegedly, "the Americans made promises of White House cooperation in solving the Afghanistan issue in exchange for the Russians' assistance in solving the Persian Gulf problems and the Iran-Iraq war." (Tehran Television Service, in Persian, 8 January; *FBIS-NES*, 12 January). The Soviet officials tried to prod Iran toward acceptance of the U.N. Resolution

598 by suggesting—as did the Soviet ambassador in his talk with the Majlis Speaker Hashemi-Rafsanjani—that "Iran's absolute acceptance of this resolution could make its use by the United States, and the need to issue a new resolution, meaningless" (Tehran Domestic Service, in Persian, 30 January; *FBIS-NES*, 1 February). While Rafsanjani thanked the Soviet ambassador for his country's opposition to the presence of U.S. and other NATO forces in the Persian Gulf, he did "not think it [was] enough," adding that the heavy burden of fighting against these forces "should not fall on Iran's shoulder alone" (ibid.). He was not hinting that Iran wanted Soviet military intervention in its behalf. He was belittling the importance of Soviet verbal support for Iran and for Iran's opposition to the presence of all foreign forces in Persian Gulf.

Although Iran appreciated the Soviets' effective stalling against the American drive for an arms embargo, it resented their continuing arms supply to Iraq. This old grudge deepened in 1988, when the "war of the cities" seriously strained Tehran-Moscow relations. Between 29 February and 18 April, about 180 Iraqi al-Hussein missiles rained down on Tehran and other Iranian cities, killing thousands of innocent people and pulverizing many homes and other buildings. On 2 March Ayatollah Khomeini, in an apparent reference to the Soviet arms supplies to Iraq, said that "of course our people will not forget who helps Saddam in his mischiefs, who orders him and who gives him missiles" (*WP*, 3 March). On 20 March President Khamenei also criticized the Soviet Union in general terms for its failure to stand beside Iran (Tehran Domestic Service, in Persian, 20 March; *FBIS-NES*, 23 March). On 24 March, Rafsanjani joined the chorus of criticism directed at the Soviet Union. He said that the current wave of Scud Bs had been manufactured in the Soviet Union in 1985 and 1986, and charged that the Soviets gave the Iraqis access to "facilities" where Iraq improved missile ranges from 340 to 500 kilometers (*WP*, 25 March). Although on 9 March the Soviet Union acknowledged that it had supplied Iraq with missiles, it insisted that Iraq had not been given permission to modify the missiles to extend their range (ibid., 10 March).

Soviet diplomacy within and outside the U.N. and the Soviet maintenance of a military balance between Iran and Iraq no doubt contributed eventually to Iran's acceptance of the cease-fire, which was the overriding objective of the Soviet Union in regard to the Iraq-Iran war. But Moscow had also hoped to gain political influence with both belligerents by trying to play the role of honest broker in the peace process. Reportedly, Soviet First Deputy Foreign Minister Yuliy Vorontsov had offered the good offices of the Soviet Union, but President Khamenei rejected direct negotiations with Iraq and called for U.N. mediation to bring about the cease-fire (*Kyodo*, Tokyo, in English, 23 July; *FBIS-NES*, 26 July).

The Soviet Union, however, seized upon the cease-fire to try to deepen its commercial, economic, and technical relations with Iran. The Iranian government, in effect, faced the challenge of a "twofold *perestroika*" (my appellation), postwar reconstruction, and belated social and economic development. Meetings between Soviet and Iranian officials on expanding economic ties were held in February. Tripartite agreements between Iran, the Soviet Union, and Bulgaria on transportation links were also reached in June. But not until after the cease-fire had gone into effect on 20 August, and the peace negotiations had begun on 25 August, were the Soviet-Iranian negotiations for expanding economic relations put into high gear. On 27 August, Soviet ambassador Vladimir V. Gudev and Iranian Minister of Economic and Financial Affairs Mohammad Javad Iravani took up issues concerning the upcoming eleventh session of the permanent Tehran-Moscow economic cooperation commission. The really important issue for the Soviet Union was its active participation in Iran's postwar reconstruction. The Soviet ambassador declared his country's readiness for active cooperation in postwar reconstruction and suggested that a Soviet delegation of experts visit Iran for that purpose (*FBIS-NES*, 29 August, taken from IRNA, Tehran, in English, 27 August). On 15 September, a Soviet economic delegation led by Deputy Foreign Trade Minister Veniamin Korolev arrived in Tehran. The timing was perfect; the delegation could visit the ongoing Fourteenth Tehran International Trade Fair (12–13 September) during its stay in Tehran. Although the purpose of the visit was declared to be preparing for the eleventh meeting of the Iranian-Soviet Joint Economic Commission, it was clear that what really interested the Soviets was "new topics." The Soviets used every opportunity during their visit to seek active participation in Iran's postwar reconstruction (*FBIS-NES*, 16 September, taken from IRNA, in English, 15 September).

The Soviet delegation timed its visit to the Tehran International Fair to coincide with the Soviet Union's national day. Korolev told Iran's deputy minister of economic and financial affairs, Ali Majidi, on 18 September that "we are eager to upgrade mutual economic, technical and cultural ties with Iran" (IRNA, in English, 18 September; *FBIS-NES*, 20 September). He said that the volume of trade between Iran and the USSR totalled $250 million in 1987, which was an increase from $100 million in 1986, and was expected to reach $350 million in 1988. He claimed that during the previous 25 years Iran had set up 120 industrial units with Soviet collaboration, and characterized the upcoming eleventh meeting of the joint economic commission as being "of great importance in view of the end of the Iraq-imposed war, establishment of peace and the beginning of the postwar reconstruction in Iran" (ibid.). Although Korolev met with a number of Iranian officials of comparable rank, his visit with Prime Minister Husein Musavi of Iran should be regarded as important in view of Musavi's reputation as an Iranian leader who is not enthusiastic about foreign participation in Iran's postwar reconstruction. On this occasion, however, he seemed quite enthusiastic. He called for the expansion of volume of bilateral trade and for the launching of several joint infrastructural projects as means of expanding economic ties in the postwar period (IRNA, in English, 21 September; *FBIS-NES*, 21 September).

In Moscow, on 5 December, the work of the eleventh meeting of the Iranian and Soviet intergovernmental commission finally began. For the first time, Railways Minister Nikolay Konarev of the USSR acted as chairman of the Soviet side; the Iranian delegation was headed by Economy and Finance Minister Mohammad Javad Iravani. On 6 December, Soviet Premier Nikolay I. Ryzhov told Iravani: "A new chapter had been opened in Tehran-Moscow ties," and called "on behalf of the Soviet leadership" for a deepening of political and economic relations (TASS International Service, in Russian, 6 December; *FBIS-SOV*, 6 December). Minister Iravani delivered a message from Prime Minister Musavi to the chairman of the USSR Council of Ministers, noting radical positive changes in the Soviet Union in the course of the current restructuring, which were being followed with great interest in Iran (ibid.). The heads of the delegations signed a protocol for boosting cooperation in ferrous metallurgy, heat and hydraulic power engineering, transport, industrial and housing construction, and transport links. Given the longstanding disruption of the export of natural gas from Iran to the Soviet Union, it is important to note that the two countries finally signed an agreement on re-

suming shipments (ibid., 9 December). But according to the Iranian oil minister Aqazadeh, no immediate export could take place because it would have to be gas that was in excess of domestic needs, and such a surplus would not be available until the Kangan refinery became operative in another year (Tehran Television Service, in Persian, 6 December; *FBIS-NES*, 7 December). The two countries also signed an agreement on building and operating a hydro-scheme on the border river Aras. In the meantime, the first Iranian vessel, *Eqbal*, entered the Soviet port of Odessa, carrying 40,000 tons of wheat from Argentina (Moscow Radio, in Persian to Iran, 13 December; *FBIS-SOV*, 15 December).

It appeared that besides the ending of the Iraq-Iran war in 1988, the decision of the Soviet Union to withdraw its forces from Afghanistan would also help remove the other main obstacle in the way of improving Soviet-Iranian relations. But by the end of 1988 the Soviet-Iranian differences over Afghanistan, although somewhat muted, were far from settled. In essence, the Iranians favored the emergence of an Islamic republic in postoccupation Afghanistan, while the Soviet Union wanted a pro-Soviet nonaligned regime on its southern border, one Islamic neighbor being bad enough.

The events of 1988 can shed light on the Soviet-Iranian differences over the future of Afghanistan. On 30 January, the Soviet ambassador to Iran told Rafsanjani that "we have decided on a final solution. Afghanistan's future will be determined today by those who are involved in the talks. Iran's active presence in solving this issue will also solve the problem of hundreds of thousand of Afghans [refugees] . . ." Rafsanjani replied, "At the beginning, and in a friendly manner, we told you that it would not be in your interest to have a military presence in Afghanistan. We do not have any plans regarding Afghanistan other than being friendly and neighborly. If you are determined to leave Afghanistan, we are prepared to help you leave so that the United States does not dominate Afghanistan after your departure." (Tehran Domestic Service, in Persian, 30 January; *FBIS*, 1 February.) The different viewpoints implicit in this exchange resurfaced during a discussion of political issues between Iran and the Soviet Union in November. A ranking Soviet official, Deputy Foreign Minister Aleksander Bessmertnykh, and the Iranian deputy foreign minister for Euro-American affairs, Mohammad Javad Larijani, held several rounds of talks in Tehran beginning on 10 November. The Soviet official and his entourage, during a three-day visit, discussed with Iranian officials the Iraq-Iran peace process, the presence of Western forces in the Persian Gulf, and the future of Afghanistan. Bessmertnykh himself characterized the talks as "fruitful," but the exchange between him and Rafsanjani would seem to reveal that Iran supported the Afghan Mojahedin, while the Soviet Union was more concerned about the fate of the Kabul regime (ibid., 14 November).

This interpretation is supported by the evidence of mutual Soviet-Iranian suspicion. On 27 February, soon after Gorbachev announced the decision to withdraw Soviet forces from Afghanistan, Ayatollah Montazeri, reputedly Khomeini's successor, told a group of "combative Afghan clergymen": "The Soviet Government should be aware that if it intends to make a show-piece exit, to place in power a particular group subservient to the Soviet Union, and if it does not allow the Afghan nation to determine its own fate, that would be another mistake by the Soviet Union" (ibid., 29 February). The Soviets were equally suspicious of Iran's intentions. On 10 December, in a commentary on Iran and Afghanistan, Aleksander Denisov warned that the Afghanistan problem still had a "negative impact" on Soviet-Iranian relations. He criticized Iran's past "slander of the Afghan leadership" and recalled "the astronomical sums that were sent through the Ministry of Islamic Guidance and the Islamic Propaganda Center to Afghan antistate groupings, or the fact that nearly 20 military training centers for Afghan rebels were set up in provinces bordering Afghanistan—that is, in Khorasan and Sistan va Baluchestan provinces." (Moscow Radio, in Persian to Iran, 10 December; *FBIS-SOV*, 10 December).

Although not a party to the U.N.-sponsored negotiations on Afghanistan, Iran has had every intention of influencing the shape of the political system that emerges after the completion of the Soviet withdrawal planned to take place by mid-February 1989. Iran's relations with the Afghan resistance groups give it the kind of leverage it needs. It fully controls about two million Afghan refugees on its soil and is host to an eight-party coalition of Afghan Mojahedin. It also has influence with the Pakistan-based seven-party alliance led by Burhanuddin Rabbani, as it has had with Hekmatyar Gulbuddin.

For the first time the Soviets and the Afghan Mojahedin held talks on 3–4 December in Taif, Saudi Arabia. Rabbani represented the Mojahedin, and First Deputy Foreign Minister Yuliy Vorontsov spoke for Moscow. On 24 December, Rabbani made an important visit to Tehran, where he tried to convince the Iran-based eight-party coalition of the Mojahedin to join future talks with the Soviets, and reported to Iranian leaders on the outcome of his discussions with the Soviets. On his arrival at Tehran's Mehrabad Airport, Rabbani said, "We give special importance to negotiations with Iranian officials and Afghan brothers based in Iran and we hope the talks would bear good results" (IRNA, in English, 24 December; *FBIS-NES*, 27 December). The Iran-based Mojahedin had already received a Soviet offer for direct talks with them, and they were studying it when Rabbani arrived. Besides Foreign Minister Ali Akbar Velayati and other Foreign Ministry officials, President Khamenei, Prime Minister Musavi, and Speaker Rafsanjani all received Rabbani. They applauded the Afghan resistance movement; advised him of the need for Mojahedin unity regardless of Sunni and Shia groupings; and, in one way or another, expressed the hope that an "Islamic government" would be established in Afghanistan.

The prospects of peace in the Iraq-Iran war and the settlement in Afghanistan during 1988 made this year quite different from any previous year of nearly a decade of unprecedented conflict in Southwest Asia. To the extent that the interests of the Soviet Union and the United States converged, the chances of resolution of regional conflicts by peaceful means improved. Yet, the superpower competition in the economic, and particularly the diplomatic field in effect increased. By the end of 1988, Moscow had achieved an unprecedented diplomatic presence in the region and was targeting Iran as the premier objective of its search for economic influence through Soviet participation in Iran's postwar reconstruction plans. The prospects of projecting Soviet economic and diplomatic influence into Iran were somewhat dimmed by the historical suspicion and contemporary ideological and political antagonism between Iran and the USSR. They were also partly counterbalanced by a remarkable economic and diplomatic re-entry into Iran by Western powers. In this regard, the United States was the only major industrialized democracy that failed to patch up its differences with Iran. Perhaps the administration of President George Bush will be able to break down American isolation from this strategic country by the end of 1989.

R. K. Ramazani
University of Virginia

Iraq

Population. 17,583,467
Party. Iraqi Communist Party (ICP)
Founded. 1934
Membership. No data
First Secretary. Aziz Muhammad (64, Kurd, worker)
Politburo. (Incomplete): Zaki Khayri (78, Arab/Kurd, journalist), Fakhri Karim
Last Congress. Fourth, 10–15 November 1985
Last Election. N/a
Auxiliary Organizations. No data
Publications. *Tariq al-Sha'b* (People's road), clandestine, published since 1982 in guerrilla-controlled Kurdish area; *Al-Thaqafah al-Jadidah* (The new culture) and its Kurdish counterpart, *Peri Noi* (New thought), both ideological journals; *Iraq Letter*, published abroad

Background. 1988 will go down in history as one of the worst years the ICP has experienced in its more than half a century of activity. The events of this year rank with the suppression of the ICP under the monarchy in 1947 or its bloody treatment at the hands of the Ba'thists in 1963 and 1968. Although the ICP made peace of a sort with the Ba'thists in 1973, that phase of its history did not entirely end until 1979. During the Iraq-Iran war, the ICP moved its activities primarily to northern Iraq where it sided with purely Kurdish groups in conducting guerrilla warfare against the government. An end to the war and the overthrow of Saddam Hussein and his regime were the ICP's chief goals. However, freed of military pressure from Iran, Saddam turned his battle-hardened forces on the Kurdish guerrillas in September, shattering their resistance and re-establishing government control over Iraqi Kurdistan. The Iraqi communists went down to defeat along with their Kurdish associates.

Leadership and Organization. The restructuring of the Central Committee carried out by First Secretary Aziz Muhammad at the Fourth Congress has remained in effect (see *YICA*, 1987). Concern that losers in the power struggle intended to set up a rival organization has dissipated. The dissidents

disagreed with the policy of trying to overthrow Saddam, limiting themselves to working for a democratic Iraq. Most of the dozen or so members of this group have been in exile for some years and have no following in Iraq. ("Iraq's Seventh Year," *Middle East Report* [*MERIP*], March–April.)

The military defeats inflicted on the Kurdish forces occurred in late August and September and were followed by large voluntary and forced movements of the Kurdish population. No information had surfaced as of December concerning the defeats' effect on the ICP leadership.

One former member of the ICP's Central Committee, who defected to the regime under torture in 1969, now serves as Iraq's representative to UNESCO (*NYT*, 6 July).

Domestic Affairs. The disaster that befell the Iraqi communists and their Kurdish allies in mid-1988 came about suddenly and unexpectedly. In the last half of 1987 and through the first quarter of 1988, Iraqi ground forces remained on the defensive. Concentrating on the south and central fronts where major Iranian attacks had occurred in previous years, the Iraqis conceded control of large parts of the northeast to Kurdish guerrillas. These forces, backed by Iran, continued to push deeper into Iraq and seized the district capital of Halabja in March.

The guerrillas showed signs of confidence in their position; a spokesman for the Kurdish Democratic Party of Iraq (KDP/I) said that pack trains moving from Iran west in the zone just south of the Iraqi-Turkish border met no Iraqi forces until near the oil pipeline in far western Iraq. He was concerned, however, that Turkey might respond to an Iranian military breakthrough by seizing parts of northern Iraq, including guerrilla-held territory. (*The Middle East*, April.) An Iraqi victory seemed unlikely.

A broad national front of all factions opposed to the Ba'thist regime continued to elude the ICP. It did, however, join with the principal Kurdish groups to resolve differences among the guerrillas. Six groups—the Party of Unified Kurdistan (PUK), the KDP(I), the Socialist Party of Kurdistan, the Kurdish Socialist Party, the People's Democratic Party of Kurdistan, and the ICP formed a coalition to fight the Baghdad regime. The announcement was made by PUK leader Jalal Talabani while he was in Damascus for meetings with President Asad of Syria. (IRNA, Teheran, 9 May; *Hurriyet*, Istanbul, 24 May; *FBIS*, 10 and 27 May.) This agreement was reached with difficulty and after long negotiation. The PUK had resisted the ICP's inclusion and, as the largest Kurdish force, it carried much weight. But the KDP(I)'s insistence that the ICP, with which it had been allied since 1980, be included eventually wore the PUK down. (*The Middle East*, April.) The KDP(I) and ICP share a goal of autonomy for Iraqi Kurds, while the PUK has traditionally favored Kurdish independence.

This coalition came together after the tide of war had begun to run strongly in Iraq's favor. An anticipated Iranian winter offensive in the south did not materialize. The Kurdish/Iranian seizure of Halabja prompted an Iraqi response that took the form of a poison-gas attack on the town that killed some 5,000 citizens. The Iraqis followed with an assault on PUK positions in the Qara Dagh district. (Voice of the Masses, Baghdad, 2 April; *FBIS*, 4 April.) A few weeks later the Iraqis drove Iranian forces out of Fao and followed that up with other successes on the ground. With Iran desperately short of money due to Iraq's attacks on its oil exports, civilian and military morale shattered, and recruitment by the armed forces lagging, Khomeini was persuaded to call for a cease-fire in July. When it went into effect, Iranian support for the Iraqi Kurds ceased.

Iraq promptly redeployed forces to the Kurdish area. It overwhelmed Kurdish resistance with massive firepower, poison gas, and air attacks. Some 70,000 Kurds fled to Turkey; 30,000 to Iran. In addition, Baghdad stepped up its policy of forced relocation of the Kurdish population, moving large numbers to settlements in the plains. Resistance collapsed. The antiregime alliance issued a call by radio through the Voice of KDP(I) asking Kurdish fighters to return to Iraq and take up the struggle; the ICP joined in the appeal. (*Hurriyet*, Istanbul, 2 October; *FBIS*, 13 October.) Specifics of the ICP's losses and its new situation have not yet emerged from the general picture.

International Relations. Publicized international activity by the ICP is sharply reduced from the levels recorded in the past several years. The party's association in March with other communist parties of the Eastern Mediterranean, the Middle East, and the Red Sea area in a statement supporting the Soviet decision to withdraw from Afghanistan stands in marked contrast with its silence on other issues (Statement in *IB*, July).

USSR-Iraqi relations followed the pattern of recent years in being good but not close. The USSR remained a major supplier of armaments for the Iraqis; it was the source in earlier years of the Scud-B missiles that Iraq altered to extend their range in order to hit Teheran (*WSJ*, 31 March). The USSR denied any complicity in the Iraqi missile strikes. (*Soviet Union and the Middle East*, vol. 13, no. 3.)

First Deputy Foreign Minister Vorontzov visited Iraq and Iran in mid-July, leaving the latter country the day before it accepted U.N. Security Council Resolution 598, which calls for an end to the fighting between the two countries (ibid., vol. 13, no. 7). The Soviets urged both sides to take pains to make the negotiations succeed. The Soviets gave Iraq the benefit of the doubt in treating the question of the use of chemical weapons in northern Iraq (ibid. no. 8–9:17).

John F. Devlin
Swarthmore, Pennsylvania

Israel

Population. 4,297,379 (not including territories occupied in 1967)
Party. Communist Party of Israel (CPI); also called New Communist List (Rashima Kommunistit Hadasha: RAKAH)
Founded. 1922
Membership. 2,000 (estimated)
General Secretary. Meir Vilner (70; member of the Knesset [parliament])
Politburo. 9 members, including Meir Vilner, David (Uzi) Burnstein, Benjamin Gonen, Wolf Erlich, Emile Habibi, David Khenin, Tawfiq Tubi (deputy general secretary and member of the Knesset), Tawfiq Zayyad (member of the Knesset and mayor of Nazareth); 4 alternates, including Zahi Karkabi (member of the Haifa Municipal Council)
Secretariat. 7 members, including Meir Vilner, Salim Jubran, Salibi Khamis, David Khenin, George Tubi (chief of the Central Committee's international section), Tawfiq Tubi, Jamal Musa
Central Committee. 31 members, including Nimer Marcus and L. Zakhavi; 5 candidates
Status. Legal

Last Congress. Twentieth, 4–7 December 1985

Last Election. 1 November 1988; 3.7 percent of the vote, winning 4 seats (with the Democratic Front for Peace and Equality [DFPE]), total number of seats in the legislature: 120

Auxiliary Organizations. Young Communist League, Young Pioneers, Democratic Women's Movement

Publications. *Al-Ittihad* (Emile Habibi, editor; Salim Jubran, deputy editor); *Zo Ha-Derekh* (Meir Vilner, editor); *al-Jadid* (Samih al-Qasim, editor); *Information Bulletin, Communist Party of Israel*; *al-Didd*; *al-Darb*

Background. Following a split in the Israeli communist movement in 1965 largely along ethnic lines, the disappearance by the late 1970s of the heavily Jewish Israeli Communist party (Miflaga Kommunistit Isra'elit; MAKI) left the mainly Arab, pro-Moscow RAKAH as the undisputed claimant to being the Communist Party of Israel (CPI). With Arab nationalist parties not permitted (although the joint Arab-Jewish Progressive List for Peace [PLP] emerged in 1984 to espouse the cause of Palestinian self-determination and thus to compete for the Arab vote), RAKAH has served mainly as an outlet for the grievances of the Arab (Palestinian) minority. It is estimated that about 75–85 percent of the party's vote comes from this sector of the population (Elie Rekhness, "Jews and Arabs in the Israeli Communist Party," in *Ethnicity, Pluralism, and the State in the Middle East*, ed. Milton J. Esman and Itamar Rabinovich [Ithaca, New York, and London: Cornell University Press, 1988], p. 130). The CPI-dominated DFPE got about 50 percent of the Arab vote in 1977 and 38 and 34 percent in 1981 and 1984 respectively. The DFPE has dominated most Arab town councils since the 1970s.

Leadership and Party Organization. The organization of the CPI is typical of communist parties in general and is described by party leaders as based on the principle of "democratic centralism." The congress normally meets at four-year intervals and chooses members of the Central Committee, the Central Control Commission, the Presidium, and the Secretariat. There are also regional committees, local branches (90), and cells. Cells are based on both residence and place of work. The CPI is said to be the best organized political party in Israel, which gives it an important advantage in its rivalry with the PLP for Arab votes.

According to George Tubi, "*Perestroika* is very important to the CPI," which "is conducting a broad discussion regarding its methods of work, its tactics and the forms used to publicise its positions." But he complained in highly ambiguous terms that this is causing "certain problems," with *perestroika* sometimes degenerating into "total permissiveness" and leading "some Communists at times [to] behave as if the principles of democratic centralism have ceased to exist." (*WMR*, September.)

About 80 percent of the members of the CPI are Arabs, although it claims that the two ethnic groups are represented in it about equally (Rekhness, "Jews and Arabs," p. 132). But Jews predominate in the top party organs, with "a traditional majority of one" on the Politburo and the Central Committee (ibid., p. 131). In recent years, the Jewish general secretary has been balanced by an Arab deputy general secretary. Similarly, a Jew, Wolf Erlich, heads the Central Control Commission, while the deputy chairman of that body is Ramzi Khouri, a member of the Acre municipal council and an Arab. Despite increased Muslim representation during the past two decades, Christians (largely Greek Orthodox) predominate among the Arab leaders (ibid., p. 137). Although the party has been noted as a nearly unique arena of Arab-Jewish amity, there are reports of dissatisfaction on the part of Arabs because of their inadequate representation at the top.

Domestic Party Affairs. The regular plenary session of the CPI Central Committee met at the beginning of February (TASS, 2 February; *FBIS*, 3 February; *Neues Deutschland*, Berlin, 3 February). No information is available on meetings of other party organs during the year.

The DFPE received 84,720 votes in the general election on 1 November, 3.7 percent of the total (*Jerusalem Post*, international edition, 6–12 November). This gave it four seats in the new Knesset, the same as before. The same four individuals—Vilner, Tawfiq Tubi, Charlie Biton (noncommunist), and Zayyad, who were again on the DFPE electoral list in that order (Jerusalem Domestic Service, 16 August; *FBIS*, 19 August)—were elected. This was only slightly more than the DFPE's percentage in the 1984 election. Some polls had predicted that the front would win six seats (*Yedi'ot Aharonot*, Tel Aviv, 21 October; *FBIS*, 25 October). It was clear that the Labor Party's involvement, as part of the government of national unity, in suppressing the uprising in the occupied territories would take away much of its usual support in the Arab sector (and not many Arabs could be expected to vote for even more hard-line parties) and work to the advantage of non-Zionist parties, including the DFPE, the PLP, and the newly formed Arab Democratic Party, headed by an Arab deputy formerly associated with the Labor Party (and still a potential partner in a coalition with Labor). Furthermore, the number of qualified Arab voters had increased by 65,000, reaching 320,000, which theoretically could have elected 20 members of the Knesset (*Jerusalem Post*, international edition, 16–22 October). And the turnout among qualified Arabs rose this year, but only to 75.6 percent (compared with 72 percent in the previous election and an overall voting rate of 79 percent (ibid., 6–12 November). The percentage of Arabs voting for non-Zionist parties rose from 48.7 percent in 1984 to 59.3 percent this year, but this included the Druze minority, who make up about a tenth of the Arab vote (and in fact is classified by the Israelis as a group distinct from Arabs), 80 percent of whom continued to vote for Zionist parties. The non-Zionist parties as a group also lost one or two seats because their mutual rivalry prevented them from concluding arrangements for sharing surplus votes. (Ibid., 13–19 November.) No figures are available on the percentage of Arab votes going to the DFPE, although a poll in September put it at 38.6 (*al-Hamishmar*, Tel Aviv, 9 September; *FBIS*, 13 September).

The influence of the PLO on the Arab vote in Israel is unclear. It formerly gave moral backing to both the DFPE and the PLP, with each of the latter claiming to be the preferred group. One spokesman for the PLP attributed his party's failure to get open PLO backing against the communists to a fear of antagonizing the USSR. Jubran dismissed the question of PLO influence on the election by asserting that, while the DFPE "is in full solidarity with the PLO and the Palestinian people," the Arabs of Israel do not need to be told for whom to vote. And this time the PLO indicated its preference for a broader range of Israeli parties, including the Labor Party, which one top PLO leader, Salah Khalaf, called "more progressive" than Likud. (*Jerusalem Post*, international edition, 16–22 October.) In fact, the PLO sought in various ways to encourage a Labor victory over the Likud, including obtaining a ruling from religious scholars in Saudi Arabia that directed Muslim Israelis to vote for candidates "most likely to make peace" (*CSM*, 17 October).

Much of the DFPE's attention, as usual, was devoted to the condition of the Arab population in Israel. According to Zayyad, the Arabs "breathe racism as a human being breathes air, 24 hours a day" (*Arab-American Affairs*, Summer [no. 25]). While emphasis continues to be put on the ongoing process of confiscation of Arab land and "the Judaization of Galilee," more attention during 1988 was devoted to the issue of governmental neglect. According to Central Committee member Nimer Marcus, Arab town and village councils are allotted "20–25 percent, at most, of the budget of the Jewish ones, and roads, sewage systems, and various social services are victims of extreme underfunding." He accused the authorities of trying to prevent the industrialization of Arab communities. (*WMR*, September.) A one-day strike in October shut down all services except schools in 45 Arab villages and towns in protest against such discrimination in funding, which had led to an inability to pay municipal salaries for two months, and in protest also against the demolition of Arab homes (*Jerusalem Post*, international edition, 16–22 October).

The issue of demolishing homes was the focus of a general strike and riots during November. The homes had been built illegally after confiscation of Arab land; failure to designate enough areas in Arab communities for housing at a time of rapid population growth allegedly left such illegal construction as the only solution. At an emergency meeting in the village of Taibe, Arab leaders not only declared the one-day strike but decided to form a delegation to present their grievances to the United Nations. (Ibid., 13–19 November.)

The CPI Arabic daily *al-Ittihad* was temporarily shut down during March (*Neues Deutschland*, 25 March; *The Middle East*, London, July).

The CPI's support for the uprising in the occupied territories notwithstanding (see below), its spokesmen expressed adamant opposition to the revolt's actual extension to Israel proper. Violent acts during various activities expressing support for the uprising were attributed to other groups. On the annual Day of the Land (March 30), in which the CPI has always played a leading role, communist stewards were present at all rallies in order to prevent the repetition of the violence that had occurred during December 1987 and January; this led to congratulations by President Chaim Herzog and condemnation by more militant Arab groups within Israel, like the Sons of the Village (*The Middle East*, July).

Auxiliary and Front Organizations. The CPI dominates the DFPE, which includes noncommunist partners: the Black Panthers (an Afro-Asian or Oriental Jewish group protesting discrimination by Jews of European origin, whose leader, Biton, was re-elected to the Knesset on the front's list on 1 November); the Committee of Arab Local Council Heads (which barely missed getting its candidate, Mayor Hashim Mahmud of al-Fahm, elected, as he was fifth on the list) (Jerusalem Domestic Service, 17 August; *FBIS*, 19 August); and the Nitzotz-Ashara organization, whose newspaper, *Derech Hanitzotz* (Way of the spark), and its Arabic counterpart, *Tariq al-Sharara*, were closed down for six months, starting 18 February, on charges of being linked to the Popular Front for the Liberation of Palestine (*The Middle East*, July), while one of its editors, Ya'aqov Ben-Efrat, was arrested on suspicion of misdemeanors connected to national security (IDF Radio, Tel Aviv, 17 April; *FBIS*, 18 April). In addition to its delegation in the Knesset, the DFPE is particularly well organized in Arab towns and villages. According to Vilner in March, the CPI was "pressing for the creation of a broad front" (TASS, 17 March; *FBIS*, 18 March), but he did not specify which groups he sought to bring in.

The CPI sponsors the active Young Pioneers and the Young Communist League. At least in the past, it sponsored or actively participated in the Committee Against the War in Lebanon, There is a Limit (an organization calling on Israeli servicemen to refuse to serve in Lebanon and the occupied territories), the Committee for the Defense of Arab Land, Mothers Against the War, Soldiers Against Silence, Women for Peace, the Israel-USSR Friendship Movement, the Israeli Association of Anti-Fascist Fighters and Victims of Nazism, and Arab student committees (whose members have long dominated at some universities).

Beginning in December 1987, a monitoring committee made up of local council heads, Arab members of the Knesset, religious leaders, and representatives of Arab organizations organized activities demanding equality for Arabs in Israel and supporting the uprising in the occupied territories (*Jerusalem Post*, international edition, 13–19 November).

International Views, Positions, and Activities. The CPI was represented at a discussion of the work of the *World Marxist Review* held in Prague on 12–15 April (*IB*, June, pp. 4–5). Central Committee member George Tubi participated in a discussion of *perestroika* in the USSR and its relationship to the international communist movement, sponsored by the same publication (*WMR*, September).

Vilner led a CPI delegation to Moscow in March at the invitation of the CPSU Central Committee (*Pravda*, 18 March; *FBIS*, 23 March). A delegation of DFPE local functionaries visited the USSR in August at the CPSU Central Committee's invitation (TASS, 25 August; *FBIS*, 26 August). Another delegation of CPI activists was in the USSR in September (TASS, 15 September; *FBIS*, 16 September). Vasiliy Osnach, a member of the Ukrainian Communist Party Central Committee, headed a delegation that visited Israel at the invitation of the Israel-USSR Friendship Movement in May (*Ha'aretz*, Tel Aviv, 17 May; *FBIS*, 19 May).

There were several contacts with East European leaders during the year. George Tubi visited Bulgaria in April (Sofia BTA, 4 April; *FBIS*, 5 April). A delegation of the GDR's Socialist Unity Party met with its counterparts in the CPI at the end of April (the first such GDR visit to Israel in two years) (*Ma'ariv*, Tel Aviv, 29 April; *FBIS*, 2 May; East Berlin ADN International Service, 4 May; *FBIS*, 6 May). Zahi Karkabi led a CPI delegation to Sofia in May (Sofia BTA, 20 May; *FBIS*, 24 May). Vilner headed another CPI delegation to Bulgaria in July (*Pravda*, 13 July; *FBIS*, 19 July). David Khenin met with Dimitur Stanishev while vacationing in Bulgaria later in the same month (Sofia Domestic Service, 28 July; *FBIS*, 29 July).

As an indication of the continuing normalization of relations between the CPI and China, Vilner received a New Year's greeting from the leader of the Chinese Communist Party for the first time (*al-Hamishmar*, Tel Aviv, 31 December 1987; *FBIS*, 4 January).

On the occasion of Vilner's 70th birthday, he received greetings from Mongolian party leader Jambyn Batmonh (Ulan Bator International Service, 25 October; *FBIS*, 27 October) and from Bulgarian Communist Party General Secretary Todor Zhivkov, who granted him the highest Bulgarian award, the Georgi Dimitrov Order (Sofia, *Rabotnichesko Delo*, 23 October; *FBIS*, 1 November).

A delegation representing the Central Committee of the Communist Party of Greece met with the CPI Central Committee in Tel Aviv in March and issued a joint communiqué (Athens Domestic Service, 11 March; *FBIS*, 15 March).

The CPI was represented at the meeting of communist and workers' parties of the Eastern Mediterranean, the Middle East, and the Red Sea countries in March (*IB*, June; for quotations related to the subject of Afghanistan, see the essay on Egypt in this edition of *YICA*). In November, the CPI issued a joint statement with the communist parties of Jordan and Palestine calling for speeding up a Middle East international conference (*IB*, March; for quotes see the essay on the Palestine Communist party in this edition of *YICA*).

At a meeting between a CPI delegation and PLO Chairman Yassir Arafat in Moscow in November 1987, the Israelis received a message from him to be conveyed to their government, announcing his acceptance of Security Council Resolution 242 (*CSM*, 19 January). A report in the Israeli press (*al-Hamishmar*, 19 February; *FBIS*, 23 February) that the two organizations agreed in the Moscow meeting to the CPI's representation in the occupied territories and in the Arab world generally by the PLO, and to the latter's representation in Israel by the CPI appears dubious, particularly in light of the PLO's subsequent position on the Israeli election (see above).

The beginning of the uprising in the occupied territories quickly evoked support by the Arabs in Israel. The Committee of the Heads of Arab Local Councils, in which the DFPE is heavily represented, met to designate 21 December as Peace Day and the occasion of a general strike for the Arab population (*WMR*, September). Despite the CPI's apparent attempt to keep the demonstrations peaceful, Arab areas in Israel became nearly indistinguishable from the revolting occupied areas, with downtown Nazareth closed by rioting for several hours (*The Middle East*, July). Another massive, but generally peaceful, demonstration occurred in Nazareth on 23 January. The uprising also inspired Arabs in Israel to protest discrimination against themselves. They also collected money to provide food and medicine for the people of the occupied territories. (*CSM*, 9 November.)

CPI spokesmen continued consistently to reiterate their support for a comprehensive, durable, and just peace based on complete Israeli withdrawal from the occupied territories, with self-determination of the population of those territories leading to an independent Palestinian state. The road to such a peace would be an international peace conference, with PLO participation. Vilner deplored "the recklessness of Israeli ruling circles' expansionist policy" (*Pravda*, 18 March; *FBIS*, 23 March). He attributed Israel's ability to continue such policies to the "support of U.S. imperialism" (Prague, *Rudé právo*, 26 April; *FBIS*, 29 April). He spoke of polarization in Israel with regard to the Palestinian issue, with "development in two directions"—on the one hand toward recognition of the need for peace, and, on the other hand, the growth of "ultrarightists and fascist forces" who support intensified "barbaric measures of oppression" (*Neues Deutschland*, 28 January; *FBIS*, 5 February). CPI leaders also repeatedly blamed Israel's economic problems on excessive military expenditures.

The USSR continued to receive praise. Vilner spoke of its "consistent course aimed at disarmament and the prevention of a nuclear catastrophe" (*Pravda*, 18 March; *FBIS*, 23 March). He declared that "*perestroika* and *glasnost*' are shaking the world," and even that human survival depends on the success of these policies (*WMR*, April). He also noted the recent "normalization of relations" between the CPI and the Communist Party of China (*WMR*, April).

Other Marxist Groups. For information on the Israeli Socialist Organization (Matzpen) and groups that have broken away from it, including the Revolutionary Communist League, see *YICA*, 1982 and 1984.

Glenn E. Perry
Indiana State University

PALESTINIAN COMMUNIST PARTY

Population. Over 4,500,000 (estimated) Palestinians, including 1.7 million in the West Bank and the Gaza Strip (*CSM*, 19 October, based on a new study by the West Bank Data Project), over 700,000 in Israel, and more than 1.4 million in Jordan (East Bank) (estimated)

Party. Palestinian Communist Party (al-Hizb al-Shuyu'i al-Filastini; PCP)

Founded. 1982

Membership. Accurate estimate not available

General Secretary. (Presumably) Bashir al-Barghuti (journalist); deputy general secretary: Sulayman al-Najjab

Politburo. Sulayman al-Najjab (member of the PLO Executive Committee), Na'im Abbas al-Ashhab; others not known

Secretariat. Sulayman al-Najjab; others not known

Central Committee. Dhamin Awdah, Mahir al-Sharif, Sulayman al-Nashshab, Ali Ahmad, Mahmud al-Rawwaq, Na'im Abbas al-Ashhab, Mahmud Abu-Shamas, Mahmud Shuqayr (representative of the PCP to the *WMR*); others not known (names on various lists not necessarily up-to-date)

Status. Illegal, but tolerated to a large extent in Israeli-occupied areas

Last Congress. First, 1984

Last Election. N/a

Auxiliary Organizations. Progressive Workers' Bloc (PWB)

Publications. *Al-Tali'ah* (The vanguard), weekly newspaper, Bashir al-Barghuti, editor; *al-Watan* (The homeland); *al-Kitab* (The writer), monthly magazine

Background. With the approval of the Communist Party of Jordan (CPJ), the PCP was organized in February 1982 (for the evolution of the PCP, see *YICA*, 1987, and Emile Sahliyeh, *In Search of Leadership: West Bank Politics since 1967* [Washington, D.C.: Brookings Institution, 1988], especially pp. 87–114). The party was to include communists in the Gaza Strip and the West Bank, members of the Palestinian Communist Organization in Lebanon, and all Palestinian members of the CPJ, except those living in Jordan, that is, the East Bank.

Leadership and Party Organization. Relatively little is known about the organization of the PCP. The First (constituent) Congress met in 1984 and adopted a program and rules for the party, as well as selecting the members of the Politburo, Secretariat, and Central Committee. No subsequent Congress has been reported. Several non-PCP publications refer to Barghuti as the party's leader (or as its leader in the occupied territories), but there is no evidence that he is necessarily the general secretary.

Palestinian Affairs. The PCP has been particularly active in the Israeli-occupied territories, but its activities extend to the Palestinian diaspora as well, though not to Jordan. Neither does it compete with the CPI in Israel proper. The party is evidently based in Damascus, as shown by statements issued from there.

Although the PCP is illegal in the occupied territories, it is in fact generally tolerated. Security concerns sometimes lead to crackdowns (and there have been reports of individuals arrested at times for possessing communist literature). At least in the past, this toleration has been explained in terms of Israel's wish to limit other groups and "not to antagonize the Soviet Union," as well as the influence of the CPI (which is doubtful), and the PCP's emphasis on political rather than military struggle (Sahliyeh, *In Search of Leadership*, p. 93).

Barghuti, who was once imprisoned by the Jordanians and was subjected to town arrest by the Israelis during the early 1980s, edits the weekly party newspaper *al-Tali'ah* in East Jerusalem. Published since 1976, it has "a high circulation among West Bank intelligentsia and students." The PCP has also published "a monthly literary and political magazine" entitled *al-Katib* (The writer) since 1980, in addition to its underground "official organ" *al-Watan* (The homeland).

Deputy General Secretary Sulayman al-Najjab, who is also the PCP's representative on the PLO Executive Committee, praised the session of the Palestine National Council (PNC) in Algiers in 1987—in which the PCP was given representation—as "an important stage in the history of the PLO." He described the PCP as "a counterweight" to some who are drawn to Camp David-type plans and "to right-wing and ultra-nationalist tendencies in the PLO." (*IB*, October.)

There was much evidence of rivalry between the PCP and other Palestinian organizations. Competition with the ideologically similar Democratic Front for the Liberation of Palestine (DFLP) became intense early in the year, but the relationship is said later "to have improved, largely by popular demand" ("The Significance of Stones: Notes from the Seventh Month," *Middle East Report*, September–October). Rivalry with Fatah, the largest guerrilla organization in the PLO, is long-standing and has considerably reduced communist influence during the past decade (Sahliyeh, *In Search of Leadership*, p. 113). A circular letter from the PCP Central Committee complained that Fatah had, in January, issued a communiqué "in the name of all organizations" that differed from what they had agreed to and then spread rumors "questioning the participation and role of our party in the uprising." The letter noted that the relationship between these organizations had improved but that "the problems and difficulties have not altogether disappeared." (*IB*, November.)

Islamic groups were another problem for the PCP. Al-Najjab complained of the "emergence of certain fundamentalist tendencies of the Khomeini type" but distinguished them from "the truly democratic religious forces" and asserted that his party is on "exceptionally good" terms with most religious movements (*IB*, October). The PCP Central Committee maintained that the importance of religious groups in the uprising has been exaggerated, and that, despite growth at the outset, this current "gradually retreated" (*IB*, November). PCP spokesmen repeatedly accused the Israelis of having issued fake statements in the names of both their party and the religious groups in which each attacked the other (*WMR*, July; *IB*, May).

While the uprising in the Israeli-occupied territories began spontaneously in December 1987, a Unified Command soon emerged that included representatives of the PCP as well as of Fatah, the DFLP, the Popular Front for the Liberation of Palestine (PFLP), and Islamic Jihad. This secret committee, which emerged two weeks after the beginning of the uprising (*NYT*, 6 February), periodically issues leaflets that direct the resistance activities. It carefully avoids calling on the population to do more than can in practice be sustained ("The Strengths of the *Intifada's* Unified Command," *Middle East International*, 9 September).

The PCP also participates in the underground local committees, whose composition, however, seems to vary from place to place. The Central Committee's circular letter explains that "each committee constitutes a fully-fledged leadership for its locality," and that members are easily replaced if arrested, while "specialized committees" concentrate on activities like blood donation and distribution of food (*IB*, November). The PCP allegedly "took the initiative in" the formation of these local committees, beginning in Gaza (ibid.).

PCP statements on Israeli policies and actions reflected the outlook of Palestinians generally. The occupation was described in terms of its "brutality" (*IB*, July), "violence and terror," and "rampant confiscation of Arab land and water sources" (joint statement, with Israeli and Jordanian counterparts, *IB*, March). One statement compared the Israeli settlers with the Ku Klux Klan in the United States (*IB*, May). With reference to Israel's Ansar-3 prison, Shuqayr spoke of "racism" and "torture-chambers" that violate the Fourth Geneva Convention (*WMR*, September).

PCP statements consistently called for a peace settlement with Israel that would involve its complete withdrawal from the occupied territories and establishment of an independent Palestinian state in keeping with the right of self-determination. Such a peace settlement would come about as a result of "a plenipotentiary international conference to be attended by all interested parties, including the PLO" (*IB*, January). Calling for acceptance of the principle of "an independent Palestinian state in exchange for peace" with Israel, al-Najjab declared that "the main job" of the PNC session in November was to offer a "clear political program . . . from a position of strength." He invoked the authority of the United Nations' partition plan of 1947. However, he questioned the feasibility of a Palestinian government in exile at the time, as it would threaten to create a power center rivaling the PLO Executive Committee. (Algiers Domestic Service, 13 November; *FBIS*, 14 November.) Communists in Gaza joined with other public figures there in calling on the PNC to accept a two-state solution (Jerusalem Television Service, 24 October; *FBIS*, 26 October).

Opposition was expressed to "capitulatory plans" backed by "the ruling quarters in Jordan and Egypt" (*IB*, January). One statement declared that "the uprising has laid the Camp David line to rest once and for all, making a return to the Amman accord totally out of the question," and that the people's sacrifices would not permit "some 'division of functions,'" any substitute for the PLO, or "some 'autonomy' plan" (*IB*, April).

Auxiliary and Front Organizations. The PWB, which is closely tied to the PCP, has long dominated the General Federation of Trade Unions in the occupied areas (see *YICA*, 1986, 1987, and 1988). Communists have also been involved in student, professional, youth, and women's groups (see Sahliyeh, *In Search of Leadership*, pp. 101–107). The PCP Central Committee claims that "the mass organizations that have been set up and led by the party over the last 20 years, such as the trade unions, the voluntary committees, the medical and agricultural relief organizations, the Union of Working Women Committees . . . , and others, have constituted the solid basis of many of the uprising's specialized committees" (*IB*, November).

The PLO is much like a government in exile, though it does not call itself that. Its supporters and its leadership span the political spectrum, and the inclusion of a PCP representative in its Executive Committee, which is analogous to a cabinet, would seem at least technically to qualify it as a popular front (or government of national unity) despite the peripheral role of the communists in the organization. The PLO's dominant component, Fatah, might itself be called a united front, since it avoids ideology in favor of pursuing a national cause. Its members are ideologically diverse, but it is dominated by centrists like Yasir Arafat. Fatah and the communists struggled with each other to control the Palestine National Front, which was formed in 1973 in the occupied areas, and each has blamed the other for its disintegration. The communists have accused Fatah of being dominated by rightists and of dependence on the support of conservative regimes in the Arab world (ibid.). Small groups like the PFLP and the DFLP—both of which are represented in the PLO—are Marxist, but are not considered communist.

International Views, Positions, and Activities. A PCP representative participated in a discussion of the work of the *World Marxist Review* in Prague during April (*IB*, June). Na'im Abbas al-Ashhab attended a *WMR*-sponsored international symposium on "socialist orientation in countries of Asia and Africa"—also held in Prague (*WMR*, June).

Ashhab and Central Committee member Mahmud Abu-Shamas were guests of the Polish United Workers' Party in Warsaw in June 1987 (PAP, Warsaw, 19 June, 1987; *FBIS*, 20 June 1987). Ashhab led a PCP delegation to the GDR in October of the same year; the delegation met with leaders of the Socialist Unity Party of Germany (East Berlin, 15 October; *FBIS*, 20 October).

Ashhab led a PCP delegation that visited Bulgaria in February (BTA, Sofia, 23 February; *FBIS*, 24 February). The delegation went on to Hungary in March (MTI, Budapest, 7 March; *FBIS*, 8 March).

The PCP Central Committee received a letter of solidarity from the director of the International Department of the Central Committee of the Workers' Party of Korea (KNCA, Pyongyang, 16 September; *FBIS*, 16 September).

The PCP issued a joint statement with other Arab communist and workers' parties in September 1987 (*IB*, January) and with other communist and workers' parties of the Arab East in December (*IB*, February). The PCP also joined in statements by communist and workers' parties of the Eastern Mediterranean, the Middle East, and the Red Sea countries on 10 March (*IB*, June) and with communist and democratic parties of Arab countries in April (*IB*, July). (For excerpts from these statements, see the profile on Egypt in this edition of *YICA*.) A joint statement of the communist parties of Jordan, Palestine, and Israel was issued in November 1987 (*IB*, March).

Nine Palestinian groups, presumably including the PCP, met in Libya in April to sign an agreement on support for the uprising in the occupied areas and on stepping up action abroad (Tanjug, Belgrade, 12 April; *FBIS*, 13 April). Al-Najjab and leaders of other Palestinian organizations participated in the celebrations of the anniversary of the Libyan Revo-

lution in Tripoli in September (Tripoli Domestic Service, 27 August; JANA, Tripoli, 30 August; *FBIS*, 30 August).

It was reported that Ahmad Ghunaym, a PCP official in southern Lebanon "disappeared under mysterious circumstances . . . after inspecting the party's positions in the Al-Qasimiyah area" in March (Voice of Lebanon, Beirut, 17 March; *FBIS*, 18 March).

Shuqayr visited Afghanistan, presumably early in the year (*WMR*, April). He reported on the "direct assistance" by the USSR that he had observed and on the U.S. and British weapons of the "counter-revolutionary forces" who had used them against civilian planes. He also observed that the People's Democratic Party of Afghanistan "has won the support of the masses and has kept advancing despite all the obstacles being erected in its way." He pointed to "the gross intervention" in Afghan affairs as "a manifestation of the neoglobalist policy of the United States." (*IB*, April.)

Relatively few statements dealt with broader international questions or those outside the region. United States imperialism was attacked mainly in the context of Middle Eastern issues, particularly in relation to support for Israel and conservative Arab regimes. Moves to lessen tensions were praised, but particularly lauded were Soviet peace initiatives that "aim to eradicate nuclear arms by the turn of the century," and "Soviet policies and initiatives . . . in the Middle East." There was also "unequivocal support for the broad renewal, openness and democratization now under way in all areas of Soviet life." (*IB*, March [joint statement with Israeli and Jordanian communist parties].)

Revolutionary Palestinian Communist Party (RPCP). Reports of a Revolutionary Palestinian Communist Party, presumably newly formed, surfaced during the year. Its general secretary, Arabi Awwad, and two of its Politburo members, Jiryis Qawwas and Abdullah Nimir, were received by Assistant General Secretary Abdullah al-Ahmar of the Ba'th party in Damascus in February. It was reported that the talks dealt with ways to support the uprising in the occupied areas and with relationships between the two parties. (Damascus, SANA, 2 February; *FBIS*, 4 February.) A meeting of the "leaders and cadres" of the RPCP and the Palestine National Salvation Front (PNSF), consisting of Syrian-backed factions, was held in Tripoli, Lebanon, in November to protest the resolutions of the PNC meeting in Algiers and to assert their

"people's historical right to fight for liberation, repatriation and establishment of their independent
Palestinian state on the whole of their national soil."
Calling for "shame and disgrace to the traitors and
defeatists," the RPCP and the PNSF adopted a six-
point program to unify various groups to work for
the implementation of the PLO's National Charter
through armed struggle and to strengthen alliances
with "the Arab liberation movement and the progressive nationalist Arab regimes" and "progressive
liberation forces in the world." ([Clandestine] al-
Quds Palestinian Arab Radio, 19 November; *FBIS*,
21 November.) (Awwad, who was deported from
the West Bank in 1973, was the leader of the Palestinian Communist Organization in Lebanon at the
time of the founding of the PCP; although his organization opposed the creation of the new party because of its support for the two-state idea, he later
joined it [Sahliyeh, *In Search of Leadership*, pp.
91, 97]).

Glenn E. Perry
Indiana State University

Jordan

Population. 2,850,482 (excluding the West Bank
and East Jerusalem)
Party. Communist Party of Jordan (al-Hizb al-
Shuyu'i al Urduni; CPJ)
Founded. 1951
Membership. Accurate estimate not available
General Secretary. Dr. Ya'qub Zayadin
Leading Bodies. No data
Status. Proscribed
Last Congress. Second, December 1983
Last Election. 1986
Auxiliary Organizations. None
Publications. *Al-Jamahir, al-Haqiqa*

After the partition of Palestine, the League for
National Liberation (the communist party of undivided Palestine since 1943) changed the party's
name in June 1951 to the Communist Party of
Jordan. The CPJ entered the Jordanian parliamentary election campaign of 1951 under the name of

the Popular Front, and three of its candidates were
elected. It campaigned on a practical platform that
called for legalizing political parties and trade
unions, land reform, and industrialization in order
to provide employment.

The Partisans for Peace also provided an outlet
for the CPJ that attracted establishment figures and
nationalists. In addition to its official organ, *al-
Muqawamah al-Sha'biyah* (Popular resistance), the
CPJ issued two others in 1952: *al-Jabha* (The front)
and *al-Raye* (Opinion).

The government clamped down by sentencing
the CPJ's general secretary, Fu'ad Nasser, to ten
years of rigorous imprisonment in December 1951.
Two years later it amended the Law to Combat
Communism, making any association with party
activities illegal and punishable by a jail sentence
ranging from three to fifteen years. Despite these
restrictions the CPJ entered the 1954 parliamentary
campaign under the name of the National Front,
organized mass demonstrations against the Baghdad Pact, and together with nationalist parties
helped create the atmosphere in which Jordan terminated the 1948 Anglo-Jordanian Treaty in 1956.
The CPJ polled 13 percent of the vote in the 1956
elections and was the first communist party in the
Arab East to be represented in the cabinet. A subsequent all-out offensive by King Hussein's army,
backed by the Eisenhower administration, led to the
ouster of the cabinet, imposition of martial law,
dissolution of the parliament, and imprisonment of
communist deputies and hundreds of communists,
most of whom remained incarcerated until the general amnesty of April 1965.

During the 1960s, the CPJ aligned itself with
Egypt and Syria in accordance with the prevailing
Soviet policy of cooperation with the national-
bourgeois regimes in the Third World. The party
benefited from the decision of the Jordanian government to establish full diplomatic relations with the
Soviet Union in August 1963, but it continued to
function clandestinely.

The party's 1964 program called for rapid industrialization, social-welfare legislation, and a nonaligned foreign policy for Jordan. It endorsed the
first Arab summit meeting of January 1964 and the
creation of the Palestine Liberation Organization
(PLO). But when its new official organ *al-Taqadum*
(Progress) published a front-page article that considered Arab solidarity a positive trend and regarded Jordan as progressive, a rift in the party
ensued. The elements responsible for the article
were purged as right-wing deviationists.

The 1967 Israeli occupation of the remainder of Palestine and the consequent rise of an independent Palestinian resistance based largely in Jordan provided impetus for the re-emerging of oppositional political forces in the country. The CPJ enjoyed a period of relative toleration by the regime, interrupted by occasional repression. Following the rift between King Hussein and Yasir Arafat in February 1986, and the U.S. aerial raid on Libya in April of the same year, student demonstrations at one of Jordan's universities (*al-Yarmouk*), in which many people were killed and injured, provided an opportunity for the government to crack down on the party. The government arrested the entire leadership of the CPJ in May 1986, blaming it for the student protests. The seventeen leaders were released on 4 September 1986, but the party remained officially banned.

Party Internal Affairs. Following a congress of the CPJ in 1970 in Amman, a rift in the party produced a faction led by Fahmi Salfiti and Rushdi Shahin. This left-wing faction operated under the name of the Communist Party of Jordan-Leninist Cadre and began to publish the newspaper *al-Haqiqa* (Truth—not to be confused with the journal of the same name published by the CPJ).

The CPJ congress in 1970 established the Ansar militia to contribute to armed Palestinian resistance against Israeli occupation. Two years later, Nasser was elected to the Palestinian National Council (PNC). In 1974, the CPJ published a transitional plan that influenced the posture of the Democratic Front for the Liberation of Palestine (DFLP) and ultimately the PNC decision to struggle for the establishment of an independent Palestinian state.

In late December 1981, the CPJ's Central Committee decided to authorize the Palestinian Communist Organization (PCO)—the leading component of the Palestine National Front (PNF) in the occupied West Bank and Gaza—to prepare for the establishment of an independent Palestinian communist party (*IB*, March 1982). The PCP, which continued the work of the PNF underground, was established on 10 February 1982 (*WMR*, February). In November 1985, the CPJ's Central Committee issued a major statement declaring that "the unity of the communists of Jordan . . . has been attained" in accordance with Fa'iq Warrad's initiative of 14 May 1985.

The Jordanian and Palestinian communist parties met in January 1987 and issued a joint communiqué decrying various attempts to water down the

Arab consensus on the question of Palestine and to generate alternative structures for a Palestinian settlement. The communiqué mentioned in particular the attempts to erode the decisions of the Rabat, Baghdad, and Fez Arab summit conferences, as well as to bypass the PLO via a Jordanian/Israeli condominium based on a functional compromise (*IB*, May 1987).

Domestic Attitudes and Activities. The CPJ leaders have consistently denounced the Jordanian regime for following a "course aimed at suppressing democracy and civil rights and liberties" (*IB*, April). In the first half of October 1984, the Central Committee of the CPJ held an enlarged plenary meeting and adopted resolutions against what it described as a reign of terror in Jordan. The Central Committee's December 1986 report stated that "the Rifai Government, more than any previous one, is tightening the screws on general human rights and freedoms" (*IB*, May 1987). Jordanian communists are represented in the General Secretariat of the Alignment of Popular and Trade Union Forces, as well as in the newly established Committee of Political Parties and Organizations. The program of the CPJ congress of December 1983 called on the party membership to work for the formation of a "broad national democratic front of workers, peasants, members of the petty and national bourgeoisie and revolutionary intellectuals in order to bring about national democratic rule" (*WMR*, July 1984). The party's strategy in the internal arena calls for a termination of the Amman Agreement of 11 February 1985 between Hussein and Arafat; it also calls for ensuring the freedom of assembly and association, which includes the right to organize trade unions, political parties, and to strike; it affirms that Jordanian resources should be utilized for industrialization in cooperation with "progressive" Arab countries; and it expresses commitment to pursuit of "a radical agrarian reform providing for the confiscation of large landed estates and their distribution among the poor peasantry; and the establishment of equality between the sexes together with the development of public programs to satisfy educational, health, and social security needs" (*IB*, February).

During the following year, the CPJ's Central Committee issued a report on local, regional, and international affairs, noting an intensified struggle between "socialism" and "imperialism" and factors that retard progress in the Arab world: militarization, the Iran-Iraq war, attempts to crush the PLO and weaken the Lebanese nationalist movement, and the military cooperation between the United States and some Arab states (*IB*, May 1987). The statement also referred to Jordanian concessions aimed toward normalization of relations with Israel, and vowed to support the restoration of PLO unity in order to counteract these moves by Jordan and also to resist the attacks on Palestinian camps in Lebanon by Amal (ibid.).

Auxiliary and Mass Organizations. Jordan's all-out offensive against the PLO in September 1970 and Israel's de facto annexation of the West Bank and Gaza Strip helped to spawn the indigenous nonviolent resistance inside the West Bank, under the banner of the PNF. Organized in August 1973, the PNF attracted a broad nationalist coalition reminiscent of the 1950s. The PNF organized against land expropriation and publicized various grievances under the 1949 Geneva Conventions in the Israeli Parliament through the Israeli Communist Party (RAKAH). It urged Arab businessmen not to pay taxes to the occupation authorities and organized mass demonstrations against Israeli expulsion of Palestinian leaders from the occupied territories. Israel clamped down on the PNF in April 1974 and placed many of its leaders in administrative detention. The Soviet newspaper *Pravda* reported the arrests in Jordan in connection with the Yarmouk University demonstrations (June 18, 1986), but identified those arrested as activist members of the JCP, the Jordanian-Soviet Friendship Society, the Jordanian Committee for Peace and Solidarity, and trade unions (*FBIS*, 19 June 1986).

International Activities and Attitudes. An article by Izhaq al-Khatib, member of the CPJ Politburo, published in October 1983 advocated a policy of close relations with the Arab national liberation movement (*WMR*, October 1983). The program of the congress of December 1983 recognized the serious difficulties facing the Arab national liberation movement, which it attributed to the "abandonment of radical positions by the majority of patriotic Arab regimes" and the inability of the petty-bourgeois regimes to preserve gains made in the 1960s.

During 1984, however, the CPJ began to distinguish between various Arab and Third World countries on the basis of the "degree of social development" attained by each country. In countries such as the People's Democratic Republic of Yemen and Ethiopia, the "national democratic revolution has achieved a reasonably high level of development."

These countries thus formed "vanguard parties guided by the theory of Scientific Socialism, Marxism-Leninism." In countries such as Jordan and Saudi Arabia, however, where the "national and revolutionary forces are crushed and persecuted," it has been necessary to form a broad coalition of nationalist and leftist parties. The 1985 literature of the CPJ, however, recognizes the difficulties facing that prospect: "The 'oil era,' the flood of 'petrodollars,' the growing influence of the oil producing countries of the Persian Gulf Cooperative Council [have] . . . led to an increase in pressure for capitulationist settlement options, and the growing threat of the United States establishing its control over the regime within the framework of the strategic alliance [with Israel]" (*IB*, February 1985).

In March 1988, the CPJ, together with other communist parties of East Mediterranean, Middle Eastern, and Peninsula/Gulf countries, issued a statement in support of the Soviet-Afghan agreement on Soviet withdrawal announced on 8 February 1988. The statement said that "the question of what steps should be taken as part of the national reconciliation effort or what government will be created in Afghanistan is a matter for the Afghans themselves" (*IB*, June). The statement also condemned attempts by third parties to interfere in the internal affairs of Afghanistan.

An article by Ya'qub Zayadin, general secretary of the JCP, surveyed international and domestic affairs during 1987, and outlined the party's position on those developments. With regard to the Arab Summit Conference of November 1987, which was held in Amman, the article expressed satisfaction with the manner in which the Palestinian question was handled, but criticized the summit's handling of the Gulf war and particularly the U.S. naval presence there, as well as the decision to reintegrate Egypt into the Arab community (*WMR*, June). Further, the article lauded Palestinian national unity, calling it an "objective necessity," and criticized U.S. and Israeli efforts to promote direct bilateral talks and separate deals as tactics aimed at "dodging the issue of an international conference on a Middle East settlement, a proposal put forward by the Soviet Union" (ibid.). The article emphasized that Jordan's political crises were aggravated by economic difficulties due to the decline of the oil boom. Consequently "GNP growth rates have diminished, and personal incomes have been on the wane . . . foreign debt is growing . . . the deficit of the national budget and, consequently, the government's domestic debt are increasing" (ibid.).

The article stated that the socioeconomic situation is closely linked to civil and human rights: "Martial law is still in effect, the Constitution has been virtually suspended, emergency trials and courts-martial have replaced ordinary courts." The JCP seems to be having a *perestroika* of its own, in that it links the achievement of its immediate objective—a national democratic revolution—to a broader social base: "In order to attain these objectives, the Jordanian communists are fighting tirelessly to rally together workers, peasants, the urban and rural petty-bourgeoisie, and the national bourgeoisie, which has no ties to foreign capital. The JCP is seeking broad cooperation with intellectuals, religious figures and all other forces fighting against imperialism, Zionism and reaction, for freedom, democracy, and social progress" (ibid.).

The party's organ *al-Haqiqa* published in March 1987 an important article decrying U.S. interference in Jordan's internal affairs. It cited two studies by the Agency for International Development that urged Jordan to abandon state-sector enterprises and subsequently to privatize them. The measure was seen as a move to increase Jordan's dependency on the United States by seeking to submit the "local market to international capital interests" and create a "blind allegiance to the system of international capitalist division of labor." (*IB*, July 1987.) Among the sectors targeted for privatization, the article mentioned the Public Transportation Department, the Telephone and Telegraph Department, and the Alia Civil Aviation Department.

Relations between the Soviet Union and Jordan continue to be limited to ceremonial visits often concluded with joint statements endorsing the need for an international settlement of the Palestinian question.

Naseer H. Aruri
Southeastern Massachusetts University

Lebanon

Population. 2,674,385 (July 1988)
Parties. Lebanese Communist Party (al-Hizb al-Shuyu'i al-Lubnani; LCP); Organization of Communist Action in Lebanon (Munazzamat al-'Amal al-Shuyu'i; OCAL)
Founded. LCP: 1924; OCAL: 1970

Membership. LCP: 14,000–16,000 (claimed); 2,000–3,000 (CIA estimate, *World Fact Book*, 1988); OCAL: 1,500 (author's estimate)
General Secretary. LCP: George Hawi; OCAL: Muhsin Ibrahim
Politburo. LCP: 11 members
Central Committee. LCP: 24 members
Status. Legal
Last Congress. LCP: Fifth, February 1987; OCAL: First, 1971
Last Election. 1972, no representatives
Auxiliary Organizations. LCP: Communist Labor Organization, World Peace Council in Lebanon, and a number of labor and student unions and movements
Publications. LCP: *al-Nida'* (The call) daily, publisher is 'Abd al-Karim Muruwwa; *al-Akhbar* (The news) weekly; *al-Tariq* (The road) quarterly. OCAL: *al-Hurriyya* (Freedom) weekly, publisher is Muhsin Ibrahim

Background. The LCP and OCAL (for more information, see *YICA*, 1987) continue to play a role in the loose coalition of pro-Syrian forces, in which the major organizations are the predominantly-Druze Progressive Socialist Party (PSP) and the Shi'ite Amal Movement. Both the LCP and OCAL have frequently found themselves on the defensive since 1982, especially as a result of attacks by Shi'ite militants who not only consider communism anathema, but continue to resent the close association between the communists and various Palestinian guerrilla organizations. (During the heyday of Palestinian influence in Lebanon, from the early 1970s to 1982, the Shi'ites came to abhor Palestinian domination of the areas where they lived.) LCP members, in particular, have been subject to both assassination and harassment, and in 1987 four Central Committee members were killed (*WMR*, December 1987; for more information see *YICA*, 1988). However, both organizations are continuing to play a role—in the case of the LCP, an important role—in resisting the Israeli occupation in south Lebanon, where Israel's "Security Zone" covers about 9 percent of Lebanese territory.

Leadership and Organization. George Hawi has served as the LCP's general secretary since 1979, and Muhsin Ibrahim has led the OCAL since its foundation in 1970.

Formal authority in the LCP is vested in the 24-member Central Committee, which, in turn, elects the 11-member Politburo. There were two plenary meetings of the Central Commitee, in January (*IB*, May) and in October (*FBIS*, 19 October).

The party congress, theoretically the highest organ of the LCP, is supposed to convene every four years, yet the LCP has held only five congresses since 1924. The Fifth Congress met 3–5 February 1987 (see *YICA*, 1988).

Domestic Views and Activities. The major political event of the year in Lebanon was the abortive attempt to elect a president to replace Amin Gemayel whose six-year term expired in September. After some very difficult years, the LCP seemed anxious for the respite that a successful election might bring. In late 1987, Hawi emphasized the need to accept a compromise solution to the Lebanese conflict, and he realistically acknowledged the sort of president a compromise would produce. He was under no illusions: "Naturally, he will be a right-wing president, but at least he will be a moderate, since with the existing alignment of forces, we cannot even hope for the election of a progressive president" (*IB*, January). Although the plenary meeting of the LCP's Central Committee in January admitted that it had "no clear notion" of the form in which a dialogue could be organized, it rejected the United States as a mediator, since the underlying goal of the United States is to prevent settlement of the conflict (*IB*, May). In March, Hawi, as well as Politburo members Nadim 'Abd al-Samad and George Batal, joined Walid Joumblatt, leader of the PSP, in calling for a halt to electoral deal-making with U.S. envoys (*FBIS*, 8 March). In April, the LCP Politburo announced its support for the candidacy of favorite-son Antoine al-Ashqar, a Christian member of the PSP (*FBIS*, 1 April).

In tandem with Syria, U.S. diplomacy was active throughout the year in an ultimately unsuccessful effort to find an acceptable presidential candidate. On 6 August, the LCP declared that it would only support a president who stands for the expulsion of Israel from Lebanon as a first priority. In addition, the party emphasized the need for a pure Arab Lebanon to maintain unique relations with Syria, and to eliminate the hegemony of the militia of the largely Maronite Christian Lebanese Forces (*FBIS*, 9 August). Joumblatt later withdrew Ashqar's candidacy and threw his support behind Syria's candidate, former president Sulaiman Franjieh (*FBIS*, 17 August). The LCP quietly fell in line behind Franjieh as well. Later, the LCP met with eleven other "nationalist" parties or factions, including Amal and the PSP, to call for an end to

political sectarianism and to demand an end to all forms of hegemony prior to the election (*FBIS*, 24 August).

After long discussion with U.S. envoys in September, Damascus finally agreed to drop Franjieh's candidacy in favor of Mikhail Daher, but the appearance of a U.S.-Syrian diktat insured opposition from the Lebanese Forces, the powerful Maronite militia. Instead of a new president, by late September Lebanon found itself with two rival governments: one led by army commander Michel 'Awn and the other by acting prime minister Salim al-Huss. Consistent with earlier LCP accusations, Hawi blamed the United States for unleashing a plot to foil the election and thereby partition Lebanon. In reaction to the U.S. ambassador's admission that Washington had committed some mistakes, Hawi reacted cynically: "It is strange and surprising that the new U.S. ambassador to Lebanon should begin his activities by admitting mistakes in U.S. policy. However, what is the use of this admission, which is similar to that of a doctor admitting a mistake after the patient has died?" (*FBIS*, 27 September). In Hawi's view, the United States planned the mistake.

The LCP is programmatically nonsectarian, and, as expected, the party reacted negatively to the unofficial partitioning of Lebanon into "Christian" and "Muslim" sectors. At the October plenary of the Central Committee, it was emphasized that Christian isolationism should be met by "the slogan of an Arab, democratic, and non-sectarian Lebanon," not by the slogan of a Muslim Lebanon (*FBIS*, 19 October). An LCP spokesman denounced Iraqi deputy prime minister Taha Yasin Ramadan for supporting the government of Michel 'Awn (*FBIS*, 12 October).

Throughout the year, the LCP emphasized its commitment to eliminating the consequences of Israeli aggression, strengthening ties with fraternal Syria, improving relations between the Lebanese and the Palestinian peoples, and implementing radical social and political measures (*Pravda*, 4 February). Politburo member Hasan Rifa'i described the LCP's "most important task" as the liberation of territories occupied by Israel, a reference to Israel's continuing presence in southern Lebanon. Rifa'i also stressed the need to unify all resistance forces and indicated the LCP's desire to assist the Lebanese army in "our regions" (*FBIS*, 28 December). In November, the LCP joined Amal, the PSP, the pro-Syrian segment of the Ba'th Party, the Syrian Social Nationalist Party—Dawud Baz wing, several Nasserist factions, and pro-Syrian Palestinian groups to form a joint operations room in West Beirut (*FBIS*, 9 November).

There are several groupings active in the anti-Israel resistance, including the Islamic Resistance Front, the National Resistance Front (NRF), and the Amal movement. The NRF was created in 1982, and the LCP remains the most active member of the front. In fact, the NRF carried out 124 attacks for the twelve months ending 16 September, and the majority were handled by the LCP (private communication). The most sensational attack, indeed one of the major events of the year, was the attempted assassination on 7 November of Antoine Lahad, the commander of the South Lebanon Army—the Israeli-created force that operates in the "Security Zone" created by Israel in 1985 when it withdrew the bulk of its forces from Lebanon. The would-be assassin was Suha Fawwaz Bisharah, a twenty-year-old woman from the southern village of Dayr Mimis, who wounded Lahad critically with two shots from a pistol. Bisharah had reputedly been an LCP member since 1982 (*FBIS*, 8 November).

As of December 1988 Lahad was still hospitalized, leaving the Israelis without an effective Lebanese commander for their proxy force. Bisharah was being held in the al-Khiam prison, and 30 persons, LCP members and their families, were expelled from the security zone for alleged complicity in the incident (*FBIS*, 5 January 1989). Bisharah has become a heroine for the NRF.

The vaguely socialist PSP is one of the foremost militias in Lebanon, and it has extended its protection to the LCP and to OCAL. In fact, Muhsin Ibrahim lives under PSP protection near the village of Beit al-Din in the Druze region. The leader of the PSP is Walid Joumblatt, whose late father Kamal was a recipient of the Order of Lenin. Joumblatt remains on very good terms with Moscow. A large Soviet arms shipment, sequestered by the Syrians since 1986, was reportedly released in 1988, and part of the shipment is likely to have ended up in the hands of the LCP and OCAL (*WP*, 19 September).

Until January, the Palestinian camps around Beirut and in the south had been under more or less continuous attack from the Shi'ite Amal movement, which was intent on preventing the re-establishment of an armed Palestinian presence in Lebanon. The LCP lent rhetorical support to the Palestinians, and accused Amal of exploiting Syrian support in order to lay siege to the camps (*WMR*, December 1987). However, the LCP tempered its support for Palestinian national rights with a restrained view of Palestinian prerogatives in Lebanon. Thus Hawi

asked: "Must Lebanon be a garden in which the Palestinian forces are free to pick any fruit they can reach using methods that harm the tree instead of taking care to preserve the garden and make it more fruitful?" (*IB*, January).

International Views and Contacts. In January, Joumblatt and Hawi, accompanied by LCP officials N. A. Samad, K. Brueh, A. Shuheib, and S. Takieddin, met in Moscow with Ye. K. Ligachev, member of the CPSU Central Committee, A. F. Dobrynin, CPSU CC secretary, and K. N. Brutents, deputy head of the CPSU CC International Department. The conferees emphasized that an international conference—a key goal of Soviet policy—is the only way to achieve a just settlement of the Middle East conflict. It was stressed that the PLO must participate in such a conference. With regard to the Lebanese crisis, the need for dialogue, as well as the important role that Syria has to play in normalizing the situation, was emphasized (*IB*, April; *FBIS*, 25 January).

Regarding the U.S. decision in December to initiate a dialogue with the PLO, the LCP noted that this represents a shift, but warned of pressure on the PLO to compromise (*FBIS*, 20 December).

The LCP remains a strong and consistent supporter of the Soviet Union, but there was some evidence of LCP discomfiture over the low profile that the Soviet Union has adopted in the region. "There is a fault or an imbalance in the region, as there is almost no confrontation by the Soviet Union and the world progressive forces of the U.S. onslaught. There is no doubt that the Soviet Union shoulders reponsibilities with respect to the priorities and issues it tackles." Rather than placing the blame on Moscow, however, the LCP indicated that culpability lies with the Arabs who "have placed their fate in the hands of the United States" (*al-Qabas*, 13 October).

For its part, the Soviet Union reacted carefully to events in Lebanon, trying to maintain a balance between the two sides. Soviet Ambassador Vasily Kolotusha stressed that the presidential elections were "primarily a Lebanese affair," and "stressed the Soviet Union's desires to see Lebanon emerge from this long state of crisis to a state of peace, political dialogue, and to hold elections on the date specified constitutionally" (*FBIS*, 10 August). After the Lebanese parliament failed to elect a new president, the Soviets declared: "We have no stand with regard to the two governments. The issue of the two governments only concerns the Lebanese, who must decide which of the two is the legitimate one" (*FBIS*, 30 September).

At the invitation of the Lebanese Consumer Co-operative Society, an economic cooperative delegation from the Central Council of Soviet Co-operatives visited Beirut (*FBIS*, 24 March). József Györke, deputy head of the Foreign Affairs Department of the CC of the Hungarian Socialist Workers Party, conferred in Budapest with Deputy General Secretary Nadim 'Abd al-Samad (*FBIS*, 1 February). Hawi was received by PCF CC secretary Maxime Gremetz at CC headquarters in Paris. Hawi spoke of the growing repression in the south, citing the 30-year sentence given to resistance fighter Anwar Yasin by an Israeli court (*L'Humanité*, 1 July). Nicolae Ceauşescu received Hawi in Bucharest (*FBIS*, 28 October). The CPSU CC sent birthday greetings to Hawi (*Pravda*, 5 November), as did Erich Honecker of the GDR (*Neues Deutschland*, 3 November).

The OCAL leader Muhsin Ibrahim visited Algeria and met with Politburo member Muhammad Cherif Messaadiya (*FBIS*, 21 January).

Publications. The principal LCP publications are the Arabic-language daily newspaper *al-Nida'*, the weekly *al-Akhbar*, and the quarterly *al-Tariq*. The party also publishes the weekly *Kanch* (The call) in the Armenian language. These publications contain articles on Lebanese political and socioeconomic issues, international and Arab politics, and Marxist-Leninist ideology. These organs often disseminate the news of illegal communist parties in the Middle East, although in recent years their publication or distribution has been disrupted because of the prevailing insecurity in Beirut. OCAL publishes the weekly *al-Hurriyya* jointly with the Democratic Front for the Liberation of Palestine, a component organization of the PLO. Both the LCP and OCAL also publish booklets and pamphlets.

The LCP has also operated a radio station, the Sawt al-Shaab (Voice of the People), since 1986 (*WMR*, October). The station broadcasts eighteen hours a day and is said to be the second most popular station in Lebanon (*WMR*, August).

Auxiliary Organizations. A number of other Lebanese communist and communist-dominated organizations have been mentioned in the news media from time to time. Among these, the more significant seem to be the Communist Labor Organization, the Organization of Arab Communists, the Revolutionary Communist Party (Trotskyist), the Lebanese Communist Union, the World Peace Council in Lebanon, and various "Friendship Committees" with East European countries.

Augustus Richard Norton
United States Military Academy

Note: Views expressed in this article are those of the author, and should not be construed to necessarily represent the position of the U.S. government or any of its components.

Morocco

Population. 24,976,168
Party. Party of Progress and Socialism (Parti du progrès et du socialisme; PPS)
Founded. 1943 (PPS, 1974)
Membership. 3,000–5,000 (estimated); PPS claims 10,000, plus 30,000 sympathizers
Composition. Unknown
General Secretary. 'Ali Yata
Politburo. 13 members: 'Ali Yata, Ismail Alaoui, Mohamed Ben Bella, Abdeslem Bourquia, Mohamed Rifi Chouaib, Abdelmajed Bouieb, Omar El Fassi, Thami Khyari, Abdallah Layachi, Simon Lévy, Mohamed Moucharik, Abdelwahed Souhail, Amina Lemrini
Secretariat. 4 members: Mohamed Rifi Chouaib, Omar El Fassi, Mohamed Moucharik, Abdallah Layachi
Central Committee. 71 members
Status. Legal
Last Congress. Fourth, 17–19 July 1987, in Casablanca
Last Election. 14 September 1984, 2.3 percent (official figure; estimate, less than 1 percent), 2 out of 306 seats
Auxiliary Organizations. Moroccan Youth of Progress and Socialism (Jeunesse marocaine du progrès ed du socialisme; JMPS)
Publication. *Al-Bayane* (daily), French and Arabic editions, 'Ali Yata, director

Background. The Moroccan Communist Party (Parti communiste marocain), founded in 1943 as a branch of the French Communist Party, was banned by the French protectorate in 1952. After three years of open operations in independent Morocco, it was again banned in 1959. It was renamed the Party of Progress and Socialism (PPS), which was granted legal status in 1974. In the 1976 municipal elections, the PPS won thirteen seats on the city council of Casablanca. It participated in the Moroccan national elections in the spring of 1977 and won one seat in Parliament. In the last municipal elections, held in June 1983, the PPS won only two seats on the Casablanca city council. In Morocco's last parliamentary elections, held in September 1984, the PPS won two seats in Parliament, where the party is presently represented by Yata and Alaoui.

Leadership and Party Organization. The PPS's Fourth National Congress, held in July 1987, re-elected 'Ali Yata as general secretary of the party, re-elected 56 of the 65 members elected to the Central Committee by the party's Third National Congress in 1983, and elected fifteen new members. The congress also elected a thirteen-member Politburo, which included the twelve men who had composed the previous Politburo plus the first woman ever elected to the PPS's Politburo. At the conclusion of the congress, the Central Committee elected a four-man secretariat, a six-man political control commission, and a four-man financial control commission.

Domestic Party Affairs. During a series of meetings in the summer of 1987 among the PPS and other Moroccan opposition parties, it became clear to all the participants that they held common positions on basic issues in the areas of domestic Moroccan affairs, the Arab world, and international politics. These meetings paved the way for the formation of a parliamentary coalition among the major Moroccan opposition parties, including the PPS, during the last two months of 1987. This coalition opposed the government's five-year development plan for the period 1988–1992, and it contributed to a parliamentary majority opposed to the government's 1988 budget. (See *YICA*, 1988.)

The PPS's coordination of position with other opposition parties carried over to the extraordinary session of parliament in January. During this brief parliamentary session, the opposition coalition proposed common amendments to the 1988 budget. Despite the government's claim that it desired a dialogue, it rejected all the amendments proposed by the opposition. Worse, a government minister declared that this was a "rejection founded on principle." General Secretary Yata complained that the government does what it wants without regard to the views of the opposition. Yata considers the present government to be uninterested in change, weak, and incapable of advancing democracy in Morocco. (*Le Libéral*, Casablanca, 15 February.)

The coordination of position during the extraordinary session of parliament in January encouraged Yata to believe that, in the foreseeable future, Moroccan opposition parties would be able to extend their coordination of policy beyond the parliamentary level, eventually leading to "some kind of patriotic and progressive front." To illustrate the broad potential of cooperation among opposition parties, Yata pointed out that the PPS and the Istiqlal Party held identical views on major domestic issues. (The Istiqlal Party was the leading political grouping during the critical years of the Moroccan independence struggle, from 1944 to 1956; though in the opposition, it is much more of a "nationalist" than a leftist party.) Both parties defend democratic freedoms of expression, assembly, and association; elected bodies that reflect the popular will; the safeguarding of essential elements of the state sector from privatization; and a national system of education that is universal, Arabized, and Moroccanized. (Ibid.)

Yata conceded that, by itself, the PPS did not exercise sufficient influence within Morocco to replace the government's program with its own platform. Thus it would be absolutely necessary that the PPS negotiate with other opposition parties to work out a common platform, a minimum program that all the opposition forces shared. He went on to specify that the major opposition partners that would share a common platform with the PPS would be the Socialist Union of Popular Forces (USFP) and the Istiqlal Party. (Ibid.)

In his report to the Fifth Plenary Session of the PPS Central Committee, held on 16 October in Casablanca, Yata discussed the internal situation of Morocco. Concerning economic affairs, he noted that recent improvements in the country's financial indices (inflation, growth rate, debt-service ratio) had resulted from such unstable and variable exterior elements as low oil prices, fluctuations of the dollar, remittances from Moroccans working abroad, and higher prices for phosphates and phosphoric acid. With the exception of agriculture, however, other elements of the Moroccan economy continue to suffer from several profound structural shortcomings, characterized by the weakness of productive forces, the inability of industry to satisfy the country's needs, and the growth of the external debt. (*Al-Bayane*, 21 October.)

Yata went on to argue that the Moroccan popular masses do not share in the economic gains claimed by the regime. The people's living conditions, housing, and their share of social rights, such as education and health, have not improved. Moroccans are forced to pay higher prices for basic necessities. The employment problem has become the clearest indication of the failure of the liberal economic policy dictated by international financial institutions—a policy of economic reform that entails the impoverishment of the masses. (Ibid.)

In the area of social issues, Yata criticized the growing housing shortage for Moroccans of low income. The government has reduced investments in public housing, entrusting this responsibility to the private sector. This results in speculation in housing in the interest of maximizing profits. Similar trends were cited in health care, where the situation has become deplorable: hospitals lack medicines, beds, and basic equipment; the sick are obliged to pay their own expenses; and the government has allowed the largest hospitals to become financially autonomous, leading to fees that sometimes exceed those in private clinics. In education there is a great need of classrooms, schools, and colleges to alleviate overcrowding. The government has abandoned the principle of universal education. These shortcomings in education will only aggravate a steadily worsening unemployment situation, such that over the long term Morocco risks becoming a nation of unemployed. In short, instead of increasing expenditures to deal with the social crisis, the government has cut back on such spending, to the detriment of basic rights of citizens. (Ibid.)

Auxiliary Organizations. The youth organization of the PPS—the Moroccan Youth of Progress and Socialism (JMPS)—held its second national congress 1–3 July in Rabat under the slogan "For School, Employment, and Democratic Rights." Though the organization's membership is not known, 550 elected delegates attended the three-day congress. Also attending the congress were foreign youth organizations from the Occupied (Palestinian) Territories, Algeria, the Soviet Union (Komsomol), Poland, Bulgaria, Romania, Czechoslovakia, and Hungary, as well as from other un-

identified countries. (*Al-Bayane*, 1 July.) On the closing day of the congress, Abdallah Nasser, a member of the national direction of the National Union of Algerian Youth (UNJA), hailed the normalization on 16 May of relations between Morocco and Algeria and declared that it was strongly supported by Algerian youth (ibid., 5 July).

At the congress, JMPS First Secretary Ahmed Salem Latafi presented a detailed report of the activities and work of the organization during the decade since its first congress in 1978. On the political level, Latafi identified three priorities for the JMPS: the mobilization of Moroccan youth for the right to work, the struggle against unemployment, and the inducing of the authorities to guarantee work for the employed; the problems of working youth and of the youth in schools and universities; and coordination with other youth organizations and progressive and national political forces to solidify the democratic rights of youth, including the right to vote at 18 years of age. On the last point, Latafi proposed an appeal to all Moroccan youth organizations to solidify this right in 1989, the year of Morocco's local and national parliamentary elections. (Ibid., 13 July.)

On the international scene, Latafi praised the Soviet contribution to the superpowers' reduction of their nuclear arms, expressed support for the Palestinian uprising (*intifada*) in the Occupied Territories, and proclaimed the satisfaction of all Moroccan youth with the steps taken toward the normalization of all aspects of Moroccan-Algerian relations. Further, he called on all North African youth to work out a unified plan of action that aimed at mobilizing youth to lead the struggle against "imperialist meddling" in the region and to contribute to the building of an Arab Maghreb where national and progressive forces would play a vanguard and constructive role. (Ibid., 12 July.)

International Views, Positions, and Activities. Along with all other Moroccan political parties, the PPS welcomed the re-establishment, on 16 May, of full diplomatic relations between Morocco and Algeria. The party observed that this event would not have been possible without some lessening in the level of regional tension. (*Al-Bayane*, 17 May.) In a statement issued the next day, Yata termed the resumption of relations "a great event, surely a historic event...that will allow, by way of negotiation and in a constructive spirit, the elimination and resolution of the disputes existing between the two countries" (*L'Opinion*, Rabat, 18 May).

In his report to the fourth session of the PPS Central Committee, held in Casablanca on 26 June, Yata stated the PPS's views on some major international issues. Stressing the importance of the resumption of Moroccan-Algerian relations, he stated that this event would be useful to Morocco's "central cause," the reintegration of the country's "southern Saharan provinces." Yata noted that the joint communiqué accompanying the re-establishment of relations contained many terms for which the PPS has long struggled. These terms included the confirmation of the validity of treaties and conventions concluded between the two countries, and support for the *intifada* in the Occupied Territories by every possible means until the Palestinian people obtain all their legitimate rights. Yata warned that after twelve years of tension arising from confrontation, difficulties inevitably will arise between Morocco and Algeria, fomented by those who judge their interests threatened by the bilateral rapprochement. (*Al-Bayane*, 30 June.)

Yata analyzed the implications of the Maghreb Summit held in Algiers on 10 June. This summit marked the first heads-of-state meeting ever for all five countries of the Maghreb—Morocco, Mauritania, Algeria, Tunisia, and Libya. He warned that in the setting up of the Arab Maghreb, the constitutional institutions of each country—with different origins, conceptions, and rules of operation—must be respected. At the present stage, the most important thing is to adopt common projects in many areas of the industrial, agricultural, social, or basic-equipment sectors in order to create among the five countries a unified infrastructure, the parts of which complement each other. Other important factors on the path to achieving the Arab Maghreb are the opening of roads, railways, and airline routes and the joint exploitation of mineral riches. (Ibid.)

Yata stressed that, at the present time, the five states of the Maghreb need to realize that many differences of views remain concerning different problems and internal and international issues. Respect for the national sovereignty of each state is necessary, as well as observance of the important principle of noninterference in the internal affairs of other states. Nevertheless, the adoption of the principle of unity of action, which is yet to be realized, imposes on each state a minimum of joint action in various sectors—economic, social, or others. The five states already share common positions on a number of important and vital questions. This commonality of views is evident in Arab affairs, especially support for the Palestinian cause and the

Palestinian people in their *intifada* until all their rights have been secured and their legitimate claims have been satisfied, above all the establishment of an independent state with Jerusalem as its capital. In African affairs, the five countries are in agreement in the economic domain and on solidarity with the African peoples. They support liquidation of the colonial system, elimination of apartheid in South Africa, independence of Namibia, and strengthening of African unity. Finally, the Maghrebi states share a common need for coordinated positions and joint action in order to meet problems posed by the European Common Market. (Ibid.)

Beyond Maghrebi coordination at the state level, Yata called for cooperation also among political parties, mass organizations, and cultural and professional associations. This would require organizing very large party meetings at the level of the masses and similar parallel meetings of other organizations and associations. At the same time, thought should be given to creating joint structures. An essential element, in this context, is the creation of a Maghrebi parliamentary institution composed of representatives of the national parliaments of the five countries, meeting twice a year, each time in one of the national capitals. Its role would only be consultative, to study problems and joint projects and to present suggestions, resolutions, and recommendations in many domains. Yata noted that the PPS had considered the subject of the Arab Maghreb in a conference that the party had organized in 1962, whose proceedings were published in a pamphlet entitled *Means and Steps in Setting Up the Arab Maghreb*. He suggested that the current relevance of the ideas that the party had put forward a quarter of a century ago was indisputable. (Ibid.)

Yata expressed the PPS's unqualified support for the extraordinary Arab Summit held in Algiers 7–9 June. He stated the summit had unified the Arab position calling for an international Middle East peace conference based on international law and United Nations decisions guaranteeing the rights of the Palestinian people, with the participation of the five permanent members of the Security Council and all parties concerned with the conflict in the region, including the Palestine Liberation Organization (PLO), which would have an equal status with, and the same rights as other parties. In this regard, Yata cited the call by Soviet leader Mikhail Gorbachev, at the end of his Moscow meeting with President Reagan in late May, for a unified Arab position. The PPS leader asserted that the Arab Summit will assist the convening of an international conference to resolve the Middle East crisis, and Arab unanimity on the Palestinian question will have strong influence internationally on the opinion of certain fringe groups that are not convinced of the utility of holding an international conference. In addition, this unanimity will spill over into other areas where it will help promote unity of ranks among Arabs and unite efforts to work in favor of causes common to Arab countries, especially the cause of the Palestinian people. (Ibid.)

Yata alluded to the "maneuvers undertaken by imperialism" and its repeated attempts to cause the summit to fail, and to the pressures on certain Arab regimes not to participate in the summit or to undermine it from within. All these efforts failed. Morocco played a large role in their failure by attending the summit and assuring its success and good progress. (Ibid.)

Turning, finally, to the East-West summit, the PPS leader singled out the INF treaty of December 1987 as the single most important event that had created a favorable climate in superpower relations. This was the first concrete result that fostered a climate of confidence and optimism about achieving other steps toward the final elimination of all nuclear arms and toward avoiding humanity's destruction in a nuclear cataclysm. This momentum carried forward to the Reagan-Gorbachev summit in Moscow, from 29 to 31 May, where some progess was made on a treaty to reduce the two countries' offensive strategic nuclear arms by 50 percent, and a final agreement was adopted covering the destruction of medium- and short-range warheads as a follow-up to the INF Treaty. (Ibid.)

In the PPS view, the most important result of the Moscow summit was the qualitative change that had taken place in Soviet-American relations. From the phase of confrontation and Cold War, carrying risks of a nuclear explosion, these relations have evolved toward understanding, peaceful coexistence, and the settlement of disputes by negotiation. The new conditions stemming from the improvement of relations between the superpowers will have important new consequences at many levels. They will spur countries advanced in the field of nuclear industry to restructure that industry toward peaceful and exclusively defensive objectives. At the same time, the new conditions will favor initiatives aimed at eliminating military bases and prohibiting foreign military presence in third countries. This is an indispensable condition for the preservation of national sovereignty and independence, and it will allow also large areas, especially Europe, Asia, and the North American continent, to be free of nuclear arms. The seas also will be rid of military fleets, especially the Mediterranean Sea and the Persian Gulf, a condition that will guarantee freedom of passage in straits and free trade, as in the case of the Strait of Gibralter. (Ibid.)

At the level of international visits, a two-member PPS delegation, composed of Politburo members Omar El Fassi and Simon Lévy, visited Madrid from 5 to 7 September at the invitation of the Spanish Communist Party (PCE). In Madrid, the PPS delegation held a political meeting with a three-member delegation from the PCE leadership, during which overviews of the political, social, and economic situations of the two countries were presented. The two parties issued a joint communiqué at the end of their meeting, in which the PPS expressed its positive appreciation of the position adopted by the PCE at its Twelfth Congress in February on the question of Ceuta and Melilla, the two Spanish enclaves on the northern coast of Morocco. On this question the PCE defends the territorial reintegration of Ceuta and Melilla into Morocco and proposes negotiations between the two countries with the aim of defining transition measures. The two parties agreed on the necessity for the European Economic Community to develop a policy of cooperation with the countries of North Africa in particular, and with the developing countries in general. While noting again the existence of important differences of opinion between them on the Western Sahara question, both parties nevertheless support the organization there of a free, regular, and unconstrained referendum on self-determination. (Ibid., 7 July.)

John Damis
Portland State University

Saudi Arabia

Population. 15,452,123
Party. Communist Party of Saudi Arabia (CPSA)
Founded. 1975
Membership. Number unknown but believed negligible
General Secretary. Mahdi Habib

Other Spokesmen Noted Since 1979. Abd-al-Rahman Salih, Salim Hamid, Abu Abdallah-Muhsin Abdallah, Hamad al-Mubarak (Politburo member)
Status. Illegal
Last Congress. Second, August 1984
Last Election. N/a
Auxiliary Organizations. Saudi Peace and Solidarity Committee (affiliate of the World Peace Council and Afro-Asian Peoples' Solidarity Organization), Saudi Democratic Youth (affiliate of the World Federation of Democratic Youth), Workers' Federation of Saudi Arabia (associate member of the World Federation of Trade Unions), Democratic Women's League of Saudi Arabia (affiliate of the Women's International Democratic Federation), Committee for the Defense of Human Rights—Saudi Arabia
Publication. *Tariq al-Qadyhin* (Path of the laborers)

The first quarter of 1988 saw a series of communist attacks on the Saudi government carried in the Soviet-dominated *World Marxist Review* and its companion, *Information Bulletin.* In a CPSA statement of September 1987, the rioting of Iranian pilgrims in Mecca in July 1987 was said to have been the excuse for the Saudi government to launch a campaign of "terrorism" and "political repression" against "various progressive, democratic, and religious national-patriotic forces" (*IB*, January). The party further asserted therein that "the extensive US-NATO military presence in the Persian Gulf emboldened the Saudi regime to organize the massacre [i.e., quell the disturbance] in Mecca" (ibid.). The worsening of Saudi-Iranian relations as a result of the Mecca incident and the alleged intensification of the Iran-Iraq war as a result of the U.S. presence in the Gulf area were said to be background factors contributing to the "repression campaign" (ibid.). (Many of the security measures undertaken by the government were apparently directed against Eastern Province Shias—coreligionists of the majority of Iran's population.) The general argument was repeated by Saudi spokesmen in the February and March issues of the *World Marxist Review*. In the latter issue the argument was added that, in light of previous Saudi aid to the Iraqi regime, Irangate showed that the government had a general interest in escalating the war.

In an apparent appeal to world public opinion, these documents call, as short-term goals, for release of political prisoners and the granting of democratic freedoms domestically and for withdrawal of U.S. and NATO forces from the Gulf and ending the Iran-Iraq war internationally (*WMR*, February; *IB*, January). The stated long-term goals in these respective spheres were to organize a broad front of "national patriotic forces" to replace the Saudi monarchy with a "democratic national government" and to transform the Middle East and Indian Ocean region into a "zone of peace" (*IB*, January; *WMR*, March).

The gradual Soviet withdrawal from identification with the CPSA line was logical as Soviet-Saudi diplomatic relations began to warm. The last item cited above appeared in the March 1988 issue of the *World Marxist Review* and thus was probably prepared in February at the latest. Late February saw a visit to the Saudi deputy prime minister and foreign minister in Riyadh by two specialists from the Soviet Ministry of Foreign Affairs. On 4 August the Kuwaiti *al-Ittihad*, quoting "Soviet sources," stated that restoration of Saudi-Soviet relations were foreseen for October and would coincide with Foreign Minister Shevardnadze's visit to Riyadh (neither occurred that month). Significantly, the next CPSA attack on the Saudi government (for the execution of four Shia saboteurs in October) was carried by the clandestine Voice of Palestine radio broadcast on 6 October rather than by an identifiably Soviet-controlled outlet (*FBIS*, 7 October). Such inhibitions, incidentally, did not apply to the supposedly communist-front Committee for the Defense of Human Rights—Saudi Arabia (see *YICA*, 1987), whose attack on the Saudi government appeared on 7 October in *Flashes from the Trade Unions* (Prague). The latter is the organ of the Soviet-dominated World Federation of Trade Unions, and it had carried one of this committee's broadsides in its issue of 29 January, also.

The CPSA was moderately active internationally during the year. It participated in the March meeting of "Communist and Workers' Parties of the Eastern Mediterranean, Middle East, and Red Sea Countries," at which the Soviet withdrawal from Afghanistan was lauded, and the April meeting of eastern Arab communist parties, at which an end of the Iran-Iraq war was called for (*IB*, June; *Flashes from the Trade Unions*, no. 14/88). Its Politburo member Hamid Mubarak served as a "fraternal delegate" to the March congress of the Spanish Communist Party (*Mundo Obrero*, Madrid, 25 February–2 March). He also represented his party at the April meeting in Prague on the work of *World Marxist Review* (*Rudé právo*, Prague, 15 April) and would thus seem to be CPSA's member of the magazine's editorial council (see *YICA*, 1988).

Wallace H. Spaulding
McLean, Virginia

Syria

Population, 11,569,659
Party. Syrian Communist Party (al-Hizb al-Shuyu'i al-Suri; SCP)
Founded. 1924 (as a separate party in 1944)
Membership. 5,000 (estimated)
General Secretary. Khalid Bakhdash (76); deputy general secretary: Yusuf Faysal (62)
Politburo. Khalid Bakhdash, Yusuf Faysal, Ibrahim Bahri, Khalid Hammami, Maurice Salibi, Umar Siba'i, Daniel Ni'mah, Zuhayr Abd al-Sammad, Ramu Farkha, Ramu Shaykhu (list of names not necessarily complete or up-to-date)
Secretariat. No data
Central Committee. Nabih Rushaydat, Muhammad Khabbad, Issa Khuri, R. Kurdi, A. W. Rashwani; other names unknown
Status. Component of the ruling National Progressive Front (NPF)
Last Congress. Sixth, July 1986
Last Election. February 1986; 8 out of 195 (presidential election in 1985)
Auxiliary Organizations. No data
Publication. *Nidal al-Sha'b*

Background. Seemingly no longer a serious threat and following a foreign policy that often paralleled that of the Ba'thist regime, the SCP gained quasi-legal status after 1966 and finally joined the Ba'th-dominated NPF in 1972.

The Syrian communist movement has undergone several schisms in recent years. Riyad al-Turk, who was chosen general secretary of one breakaway group in 1974, has been imprisoned without trial since 1980 and subjected to beatings and torture. Dozens of members of the proscribed Communist Party Political Bureau have been imprisoned without trial since the early 1980s, although many others were released in the mid-1980s (*Amnesty*

International Report 1987). Amnesty International adopted one of these, the writer Muhammad Khoja, as a prisoner of conscience in 1987 (*Index on Censorship*, London, July 1987). Yusuf Murad, a former member of the SCP Central Committee, formed another group, the Base Organization, in 1980. Many members of the Party for Communist Action and others who were suspected of having ties to that group have been imprisoned without charges during the 1980s, while a student named Haytham Kamil Mustafa who was arrested for his role in founding the Union for Communist Struggle was released in 1986 after being held for six years (*Amnesty International Report 1987*).

Leadership and Party Organization. Little is known about the dynamics of the SCP's leadership except that General Secretary Bakhdash has long been the dominant figure. There have been some divisions among the top leaders; for example, Politburo member Ni'mah (now a representative of the SCP on the Central Command of the NPF) broke with the party temporarily during the early 1970s. There were also some reports of dissent within the party during 1986. No information is available on meetings of party organs during the last two years.

Domestic Party Affairs. Politburo member Khalid Hammami told members of an international symposium in Prague that the concept of "revolutionary democracy" (meaning radical noncommunist regimes in the Third World, such as the one in his own country) as a substitute for "working class parties" had been proved erroneous. While not denying such regimes' radical approaches to the "revolution of liberation" or the "substantial anticapitalist potential of a segment of the revolutionary democrats," he concluded that Syria had "demonstrated . . . that that potential is limited"—that in fact Syria's previous listing "among the socialist-oriented countries" was a mistake (*WMR*, June). This statement is quite in keeping with previous indications in international forums of distaste for the socioeconomic aspects of the Ba'thist regime.

Auxiliary and Front Organizations. Little information (none of it current) is available on auxiliary organizations. The SCP presumably participates in such groups as the Arab-Soviet Friendship Society; the Syrian Committee for Solidarity with Asian and African Countries; the National Council of Peace Partisans in Syria; and the Syrian-Bulgarian Friendship Society.

The present Syrian regime is officially based on the NPF, which includes the SCP, the Arab Socialist Party, and the Socialist Union, in addition to the dominant Ba'th party, which is non-Marxist. The cabinet includes two members of the SCP, which is also represented in the central leadership of the NPF. This does not mean that the SCP has any significant influence, but rather that it has for the time being more or less abandoned revolution in favor of a largely formal role. The quiet position of the regime's partner also conforms to the wishes of the USSR.

Ba'thist Assistant General Secretary Abdullah al-Ahmar praised the two countries' mutual "friendship and cooperation" and declared it to be "firm, entrenched, and unchanging" (Damascus Domestic Service, 15 September; *FBIS*, 19 September). Fikryat Tabeyev, chairman of the USSR-Syria Society "praised Syria's courageous, wise policies" (Damascus Domestic Service, 4 April; *FBIS*, 6 April). The Syrian newspaper *al-Thawrah* (8 October; *FBIS*, 14 October) celebrated the eighth anniversary of the two countries' treaty of friendship and cooperation by stressing that the treaty had "entrenched and deepened" mutual ties that are of a "strategic nature."

Yet there are indications that not all is well in USSR-Syrian relations. Damascus is said to be uneasy about the possible tightening of Soviet arms supplies, tentative conciliatory Soviet moves toward Israel, and the danger that the USSR will downplay the Syrian role in Soviet policy in the region, as well as Soviet pressures to repay debts and lectures on domestic policies ("Cold Draught," *Middle East International*, 24 June). Syrian policies on several Middle Eastern issues, particularly those toward the PLO and Iraq, have long been at odds with Soviet positions.

As usual, during 1988 there were numerous exchanges of visits between delegations of Syrian state and Ba'th party officials and delegations of state and communist party officials from the USSR. Karen Brutents, deputy chief of the CPSU Central Committee's International Department, ended a visit to Damascus on 1 January (Damascus Domestic Service, 1 January; *FBIS*, 4 January). A CPSU delegation headed by Uzbek Communist Party Central Committee secretary Khan Khalmukhamedov held talks with Ba'th party officials in February (Damascus Domestic Service, 28 February; *FBIS*, 1 March). General Pikalov led another Soviet delegation in March (Damascus Television Service, 23 March; *FBIS*, 29 March). Fikryat Tabeyev, a member of the CPSU Central Committee and chairman of the Soviet-Syrian Friendship Society, arrived in Damascus later in the same month (SANA, Damascus, 28 March; *FBIS*, 1 April). A delegation from the Soviet Air Force headed by Marshal of Aviation Yefimov was in Damascus in April to discuss the possibility of supplying Syria with additional sophisticated aircraft (*al-Ittihad*, Abu Dhabi, 7 April; *FBIS*, 11 April). "Comrade" Ivanov, collegium member of the Soviet Ministry of Land and Water Reclamation, was in Damascus in April to discuss irrigation projects (Domestic SANA, Damascus, 16 April; *FBIS*, 19 April), as was a delegation of Soviet cosmonauts headed by General G. S. Titov (Damascus Domestic Service, 15 April; *FBIS*, 19 April). A Soviet friendship delegation headed by Tord Jikin, chairman of the State Committee for Printing and Publication, visited Syria in May (SANA, Damascus, 31 May; *FBIS*, 1 June). General Pikalov returned to Syria in June at the head of another military delegation, reportedly in connection with Soviet plans to supply Syria with SS-23 Spider missiles (*al-Ittihad*, Abu Dhabi, 8 June; *FBIS*, 13 June).

A Syrian parliamentary delegation visited Moscow in August (TASS, 31 August; *FBIS*, 1 September). Assistant General Secretary al-Ahmar stopped in Moscow in September and held talks on developing relations between the ruling parties of the two countries (Damascus Domestic Service, 5 September; *FBIS*, 7 September). A delegation of the Syrian Afro-Asian Solidarity Committee visited the USSR in September on the invitation of the Soviet-Asian Solidarity Committee (TASS, 25 September; *FBIS*, 28 September).

There were also exchanges of visits with socialist countries other than the USSR. A Syrian military delegation led by Ibrahim al-Ali, commander of the Popular Army, was in the German Democratic Republic in July (*Neues Deutschland*, 18 July), while Ba'thist Regional [i.e., country-level as opposed to national, i.e., pan-Arab] Deputy General Secretary Sulayman Qaddah led a delegation to that country in October at the invitation of the Socialist Unity Party of Germany (ibid., 20 October). A delegation from the Czechoslovak National Front held talks with their counterparts in the Syrian NPF and concluded a friendship and cooperation agreement with them (Damascus Domestic Service, 23 and 28 May; *FBIS*, 23 May, 2 June). A delegation of the Communist Party of Czechoslovakia, headed by

Vasil Bil'ák, secretary of the Central Committee, visited Damascus in January as guests of the Ba'th party (Damascus Televison Service, 24 January; *FBIS*, 25 January). The Romanian assistant minister of foreign trade held talks with Syrian Prime Minister Mahmud al-Zu'bi and other officials in Damascus in April (Damascus Domestic Service, 28 April; *FBIS*, 29 April). A Syrian Solidarity Committee delegation led by Ba'thist Central Committee member Abd al-Razzaq Awwad visited Budapest in March for talks with the chairman of the Hungarian Solidarity Committee and officials of various social organizations (*Népszabadság*, Budapest, 25 March; *FBIS*, 1 April). Assistant General Secretary al-Ahmar was in Cuba in September on the invitation of the Cuban Communist Party (Damascus Domestic Service, 20 September; *FBIS*, 21 September). In May, Pyon Yong-nip, envoy of North Korean President Kim Il-song, arrived in Damascus for talks with Syrian officials, including President Hafiz al-Asad (SANA, Damascus, 1 and 29 May, 2 June; *FBIS*, 1, 7 June). A delegation from the Communist Party of China, headed by Politburo member Li Ximing, visited Damascus in June as guests of the Ba'th Party; meetings were held with Ba'thist Party and Syrian governmental leaders, with the two parties concluding a two-year cooperation agreement (Damascus Domestic Service, 13 and 14 June; *FBIS*, 16 June). Official Syrian spokesmen and the newspaper *al-Ba'th* later adamantly denied Israeli claims that the two countries had concluded a missile deal (SANA, Damascus, 2 July; Damascus Domestic Service, 3 July; *FBIS*, 5 July).

Within the region, Haydar Abu Bakr al-'Attas, chairman of the South Yemeni Supreme People's Council Presidium, visited briefly in August (Damascus Domestic Service, 5 August; *FBIS*, 10 August). A Syrian parliamentary delegation spent seven days in Aden in July and August, and a protocol for cooperation between the national legislatures of the two countries was concluded (Damascus Domestic Service, 5 August; *FBIS*, 10 August). A (South Yemeni) Yemen Socialist Party delegation visited Damascus in October as guests of the Ba'th Party (Damascus Domestic Service, 21 October; *FBIS*, 25 October).

For reports of contacts with an apparently new Revolutionary Palestinian Communist Party, see the profile on the Palestinian Communist Party in this edition of *YICA*.

International Views, Positions, and Activities. Hammami, who, in addition to his other offices, is the SCP representative on the editorial council of the *World Marxist Review*, participated in an international symposium on "ways of socialist orientation in countries of Asia and Africa" in Prague (*WMR*, June) (see under "Domestic Party Affairs" in this essay).

The journal *al-Nahj*, published jointly by Arab communist parties, sponsored a conference in Damascus from 29 October to 2 November 1987. The government forbade the attendance of some Palestinian and Iranian delegations, in the latter case because of a request by the Iranian government (*Index on Censorship*, January).

The SCP participated in a statement by eight Arab communist and workers' parties made late in September 1987, whose focus was on the Saudi Arabian regime and the Persian Gulf War (*IB*, January). It joined in another statement by "Communist and Workers' Parties of the Arab East" on the subject of "Stronger Solidarity with the Palestinian People's Struggle in the Occupied Territories" on 15 December 1987 (*IB*, February); in a statement by thirteen communist and workers' parties of the Eastern Mediterranean, Middle East, and Red Sea countries on "The Way to Solve Regional Conflicts" (dealing with Afghanistan) on 10 March (*IB*, June); and in a statement by seven communist and democratic parties of Arab countries entitled "End the War and Terror" (on the Iraq-Iran War, mainly condemning the Saddam Husayn regime) (*IB*, July). For quotes from each of these statements, see the profile on Egypt in this edition of *YICA*.

Glenn E. Perry
Indiana State University

Tunisia

Population. 7,738,026
Party. Tunisian Communist Party (Parti communiste tunisien; PCT)
Founded. 1934
Membership. 2,000 (estimated); PCT claims 4,000

Composition. Unknown

General Secretary. Muhammad Harmel (59)

Politburo. 9 members: Muhammad Harmel, Muhammad Ennafaa, Abdelhamid Ben Mustapha, Hichem Sekik, Junaidi Abdeljawad, Abdelmajid Triki, Boujomaa Remili, Ahmed Ibrahim, Rachid M'charek

Secretariat. No data

Central Committee. 22 members: Ahmed Ibrahim, Ahmed Ben Younes, Junaidi Abdeljawad, Boujomaa Remili, Habib Kasdaghli, Rachid M'charek, Sadok Labidi, Tarak Chaabouni, Abdelhamid Larguech, Abdelhamid Ben Mustapha, Abdelmajid Triki, Abdelwahed Abassi, Ali Khmira, Muhammad Ben Della, Muhammad Marmel, Muhammad Ennafaa, Muhammad Lakhdhar, Muhammad Kallel, Muhammad Khelaifi, Mustapha Ouannen, Noureddine Metoui, Hichem Sekik

Status. Legal

Last Congress. Ninth, 12–14 June 1987, in Tunis

Last Election. 2 November 1986; boycotted by PCT

Auxiliary Organization. Tunisian Communist Youth

Publication. *Al-Tariq al-Jadid* (New path), weekly

Background. The PCT was founded in 1920 as a branch of the French Communist Party and became independent in 1934. The banning of the PCT in 1963 formalized a single-party state under the direction of the Destourian Socialist Party (PSD). In July 1981, the government lifted the ban on the PCT, ending the party's eighteen-year period of clandestine existence. The PCT was the only opposition party allowed to operate openly from July 1981 to November 1983, when President Habib Bourguiba legalized two other opposition parties (see *YICA*, 1984).

Leadership and Party Organization. The PCT's Ninth National Congress in mid-1987 re-elected Harmel as general secretary. It elected an enlarged nine-member Politburo to replace the six-member Politburo elected by the Eighth Congress in 1981 and a 22-member Central Committee to replace the 12-member Central Committee elected in 1981. Harmel and Politburo member Muhammad Ennafaa have occasionally contributed articles to the *World Marxist Review*.

Domestic Party Affairs. During 1988, the PCT tried in various ways to encourage the government

of President Zine el-Abidine Ben Ali to live up to its promises. Upon deposing the aging President Habib Bourguiba in November 1987, Ben Ali had promised to liberalize political laws to allow more freedoms for parties, end some press censorship, and run an open and democratic government (see *YICA*, 1988).

The first test case of the new regime's commitment to open and honest government came in five special parliamentary by-elections called in January to replace deputies who resigned after Ben Ali took over the reins of power. The PCT, as a show of support for, and faith in the new president's pledge of a "new era," was the only opposition party to take part in the special elections, held on 24 January. The following day, the PCT demanded that the elections be annulled because of election fraud. The party alleged that ballot boxes had been stuffed with ballots for the ruling PSD. (*International Herald Tribune*, 26 January.) The PCT also alleged intimidation by the regime. Because of these allegations, Ben Ali's pledge of renewal suffered a sharp setback. (*Middle East International*, 19 March.)

The new government's initial attempts in February and March to liberalize the political system fell far short of satisfying expectations and demands of the opposition. The PCT, along with other opposition groups like the Movement of Social Democrats (MDS), was bitterly disappointed by the government's proposals to change the laws governing political and journalistic freedom. The opposition groups rejected the draft law on political parties on the grounds that it was more repressive than its predecessor. Nor were they much more supportive of the new press code. (Ibid.) Well into the summer, the PCT and other opposition parties continued their policy of boycotting parliamentary elections until they saw genuine improvements (ibid., 22 July).

During the period from January to August, when the PCT was boycotting elections, the party attempted to join forces with the progressive elements of the opposition. In July, for example, when addressing a group of mine workers in the village of Erdayef, a small suburb of Gafsa, General Secretary Muhammad Harmel called for the unification of the Tunisian left. He cited the need to separate the ruling party—the PSD was renamed the Constitutional Democratic Rally (RCD) on 27 February—from the government. The experiment of elections under the new government showed that Tunisian democracy suffered from the sickness of electoral fraud. Therefore, he argued, all forces should unify to oppose the government's proposed bill for election procedures; they should search for a minimal concept of democracy that would allow all popular forces to participate in decision making. (*Al-Tarik al-Jadid*, 13–19 July.)

Harmel went on to argue that the opposition could play a positive role in pointing out mistakes and unmasking the self-serving and self-interested elements in society and the country. Thus the PCT appealed to all political parties to participate in discussions of all social and economic problems, and appealed especially to the ruling RCD to allow the opposition to participate in those discussions. Harmel criticized those individuals who called for cooperation with the RCD, because that would lead to exploitation of the political arena and the logic of the single party. The only solution for workers' interests and problems will come from the Tunisian left and especially the PCT. Harmel called on independent individuals to join and participate in opposition to the RCD. Maghrebi integration alone will not solve Tunisia's problems, nor will "reactionary types, like the Mufti of Tunisia, who like to attack the PCT." He concluded that the left needs to overcome sterile ideas and unify to try to solve the country's problems, especially the failures of capitalist economic policies. (Ibid.)

In July, the PCT complained bitterly about attacks against it from religious circles within Tunisia. The party reacted, in particular, to attacks by the Mufti of Tunisia, Cheikh Mokhtar Essallami, who accused the PCT of being an "infidel" organization. After declaring that these charges were without foundation, the party went on to accuse the government of providing funds to support attacks on the PCT from mosques and to denounce charges made by "retrograde" circles. (Ibid., 6–12 July.) As Harmel explained, "Those who speak of us in the name of religion do so in fact from a certain reading of Islam whose motivations are in fact social, political, or ideological, sometimes reactionary and retrograde" (*Réalités*, Tunis, 1–7 July). The irony in these attacks came from the fact that the PCT had been a staunch defender of the rights of the Islamic Tendency Movement (MTI), a mainstream Islamic movement that was the object of a major government crackdown in 1987 (see *YICA*, 1988).

On 25 July, Tunisia's Republic Day, President Ben Ali announced by-elections for the coming parliamentary year (1988–1989) and declared that he would personally ensure that these elections would be free of fraud. Then, on 31 July, at the end of the RCD's three-day extraordinary congress, Ben

Ali told his party's delegates that there could be no democracy without a multiparty system, the guarantee of freedom of expression, and fair elections. (*Middle East International*, 5 August.)

A few days later, the PCT decided to take part in the parliamentary by-elections. In a PCT Central Committee statement issued on 8 August, the party noted that this decision was based on Ben Ali's pledge to guarantee democratic elections and to prevent vote tampering. The PCT called on the government to give opposition parties the opportunity to expound their positions and programs through the mass media. To give concrete form to Ben Ali's pledges, political and administrative measures need to be adopted to ensure that the election campaign is democratic throughout. To this end, the PCT proposed the establishment of a national commission with the participation of all political parties to monitor the course of the elections. (Moscow, *Pravda*, 9 August; *FBIS*, 11 August.)

In a press interview during the summer, Harmel spelled out the PCT's short-and medium-term objectives in domestic policy. Through dialogue on economic and social questions, the party aims to call into question the current capitalist and liberal orientation that has failed in Tunisia and elsewhere. The PCT considers that the principles introduced into Tunisian politics by Ben Ali's assumption of power have a "positive impulse," but it is necessary to go further to take up basic questions—economic and social problems, like unemployment, that concern the daily life of the people, as well as the future of the country. The party has an alternative, but it should be discussed "with all partners." This alternative should be progressive and democratic. It will be the undertaking of the left and all national, progressive, and democratic forces. In this sense the largest possible alliance of forces is constantly on the agenda. (*Réalités*, Tunis, 1–7 July.)

For the present, the PCT recognizes its divergences from the government, especially on economic and social questions. But the party does not see itself as permanently in the opposition. One day, it will participate in the government when the conditions are right. For the moment, one must increase the standing of various authorities of civil society and accelerate and energize the construction of a democratic mass movement embracing politics, labor, and culture—a movement for both the satisfaction of immediate demands and a progressive alternative. (Ibid.)

On 22 April, President Ben Ali invited all Tunisian political and social forces to participate in the formulation of a "national pact" that "would define the common denominators and principles on which all Tunisians agree." The Tunisian president later explained that the proposed pact "is not a Government program nor a coalition plan...[but rather] a civilizational and national project" that defines the working methods and relations between different social partners. He stressed that the pact is not a substitute for the Tunisian Constitution. Rather, it is "a freely accepted moral commitment" that preserves the independence of all parties. Ben Ali explained further that the pact would cover such key points as the country's cultural identity, the democratic model it seeks to establish, its development objectives, and its foreign policy principles. (*Tunisia Update*, Washington, D.C., October–November.)

In a press interview in late June, Harmel declared that the PCT accepted the idea of the National Pact but was discussing its content and would eventually discuss its form. He added that the pact's content "should develop pluralism. We have experienced a historic period where consensus took the form of a mechanical 'unanimity.' The result was catastrophic and Tunisia experienced a political and intellectual impoverishment." (*Réalités*, Tunis, 1–7 July.)

On 6 September, Harmel met with President Ben Ali to discuss the content of the National Pact. Also attending the meeting were Muhammad Belhaj Amor, general secretary of the Party of Popular Unity, and Hédi Jilani, president of the Tunisian Union of Industry, Commerce, and Handicrafts (UTICA). At the conclusion of the meeting, Harmel stated that the PCT had two major requirements for the Pact: first, "pluralism and union autonomy, which imply the normal exercise of criticism by the democratic opposition, as well as the defense of the interests of the workers"; and second, "national solidarity, which the country needs in this new phase of its history." Harmel agreed with Ben Ali that the pact should avoid "programmatic" aspects that relate to the government's policy. In the PCT view, the pact should also avoid conceptions and expressions that have an ideological connotation and should stress principles that form the subject of convergences on the question of the country's development model. The party clearly reaffirmed Tunisia's Arab-Muslim identity and wanted to give that identity an advanced content oriented to the future rather than the past. Finally, the PCT wanted to develop rationalist aspects of the national heritage, as well as progressive aspects of modern Tunisia. (*La Presse*, Tunis, 7 September.)

The final form of the National Pact proved to be acceptable to the PCT. On 7 November, the first anniversary of the deposition of Bourguiba and the advent to power of the Ben Ali government, Harmel and other representatives of all major Tunisian political parties and social organizations signed the National Pact at the Parliament in the presence of the members of Parliament.

International Views, Positions, and Activities. In July, in the wake of the Maghreb Summit held in Algiers on 10 June, the party newspaper expressed the PCT's support for Maghrebi integration. It approved ongoing efforts among the five states of the Maghreb—Morocco, Mauritania, Algeria, Tunisia, and Libya—to clarify differences. The party hailed the improving relationship with neighboring Libya, a relationship that has often been troubling and even threatening in the past fifteen years. At the same time, the Maghrebi working committees had a sense of apprehension owing to the news of an impending union between Libya and Algeria, because this kind of union has in the past led to a polarization within North Africa. (*Al-Tarik al-Jadid*, 13–19 July.)

Despite these obstacles, the PCT view was that movement toward Maghrebi unification continued. The past few months witnessed some concrete decisions leading in this direction, namely those regarding the opening of borders and the free movement of workers and goods. The governments of the Maghrebi states also agreed not to yield to political pessimism. In the PCT's view, further developments do not require a political decision; rather, they should happen naturally. The party urged the Maghrebi countries to be serious and practical about cooperation and integration. This is necessary in order to meet the challenge posed by the European Economic Community, which has quietly supported Maghrebi integration even though the latter will in fact injure the fragile European economy. (Ibid.)

John Damis
Portland State University

Yemen

People's Democratic Republic of Yemen

Population. 2,425,620
Party. Yemeni Socialist Party (al-Hizb al-Ishti-rakiya al-Yamaniya; YSP)
Founded. 1978
Membership. 31,000 (including candidate members)
President of the Presidium of the Supreme People's Council. Haydar Abu Bakr al-'Attas (elected November 1986)
General Secretary. 'Ali Salim al-Bayd (elected 7 February 1986)
Assistant General Secretary. Salim Salih Muhammad (elected 7 February 1986)
Politburo. 11 members: Salih Munassar al-Siyayli, Salim Salih Muhammad, Haydar Abu Bakr al-'Attas, 'Ali Salim al-Bayd, Yasin Sa'id Nu'man, Muhammad Sa'id 'Abdullah, Sa'id Salih Salim, Fadl Muhsin 'Abdullah, 'Abdullah Ahmad al-Khamiri, Salih 'Ubayd Ahmad, and Muhammad Haydara Masdus. 3 candidate members: Haytham Qasim Tahir, Sayf Sa'il Khalid, and Salim Muhammad Jubran.
Central Committee. 77 members
Status. Ruling party
Last Congress. Fourth, 20–21 June 1987
Last Election. 1986, all candidates YSP approved
Publication. *Al-Thawra*, YSP Central Committee weekly

The People's Democratic Republic of Yemen (PDRY), also known as South Yemen, Southern Yemen, or (as is preferred by its government) Democratic Yemen, has pursued a path of "scientific socialism" in domestic policy and close alignment with the Soviet Union and other Eastern bloc countries in foreign affairs. The Yemeni Socialist Party (YSP), heir to the independence-winning National Liberation Front (NLF), is the only legal party in the state and has had no significant opposition since independence in 1967. The party itself, however,

has been riven with factionalism and infighting. Internal power struggles reached climaxes in 1969, 1971, 1978, 1980, and in the civil war of January 1986.

The constitution (adopted in 1970 and amended in 1978) specifies that the Supreme People's Council (SPC) is the highest authority. Elections to the council were first held in 1978, and members are elected for five-year terms. The SPC elects the president and eleven to seventeen members of the Presidium, to which the SPC's authority is delegated when the SPC is not in session. At first, the Presidium exercised considerable influence as a collegial body, but the president assumed unchallenged predominance as a result of the power struggle of 1971. The SPC also elects the prime minister and his cabinet, and the members of the Supreme Court.

As in other socialist states, real power rests within the party. The superiority of the party was firmly established as a result of events in 1978 that culminated in the execution of President Salim Rubayyi 'Ali and assumption of his position by a rival and the head of the party, 'Abd al-Fattah Isma'il. During the 1970s, several efforts were made to transform the ruling NLF into a true Marxist organization, and several other small legal parties were incorporated into it. Neither the Popular Democratic Union, a local communist party founded in Aden in 1961, nor the Vanguard Party (Baathist) had seriously challenged the NLF for power.

The First Congress of the YSP was held in October 1972, following the ouster of the party's moderates, and another was held in October 1980, after the defeat of the ultraradical faction. The Third Congress took place in October 1985 amidst considerable tension, and the Fourth Congress had to be postponed until June 1987 because of continuing fundamental differences.

Successive struggles for supremacy within the party have eliminated factions from both the right and the far left, as well as most of the original party leaders who fought in the war for independence. In January 1986, the country's pragmatic leader, 'Ali Nasir Muhammad (al-Hasani; prime minister, 1971–1985, and president, 1980–1986), sought to check the deterioration of his authority by eliminating his doctrinaire left-wing rivals. Although his supporters managed to kill four of the last five prominent founding members of the party, including former president and former party leader 'Abd al-Fattah Isma'il (al-Jawfi; ousted from power in 1980), 'Ali Nasir's opponents eventually won the resulting civil war. 'Ali Nasir, the fifth of these historic leaders, was forced to flee with his supporters; he maintains homes in the Yemen Arab Republic (YAR, North Yemen), Ethiopia, and Damascus.

The remaining nucleus of the Adeni regime, reduced to party lightweights and relatively unknown technocrats, has followed a pragmatic course and pursued many of 'Ali Nasir's policies, especially in foreign affairs, while refusing any dialogue with the exiled president.

Internal Affairs. For the first time in several years, Aden remained calm, at least on the surface. Tensions continued to linger, however, as a consequence of both the continued presence of 'Ali Nasir Muhammad and his followers in neighboring North Yemen and simmering rivalries between YSP factions. Ideological divisions remain between pragmatists and hard-liners, and a younger generation of committed Marxists, popularly known as *al-Fattahiyin* (followers of the late 'Abd al-Fattah Isma'il), appears to be gaining force in the provinces and army garrisons.

The hold of the Hadramis, who occupy the top positions of YSP general secretary, president, and prime minister, and that of the North Yemenis seemed increasingly vulnerable. The balance of power seemed to be held by the rival Yafa'i and al-Dali' tribes, who predominate in the armed forces. Among the latter is Col. Haytham Qasim Tahir, first deputy defense minister, army chief of staff, and hero of January 1986. Generally regarded as one of the Fattahiyin and close to the Soviets, rumors continue to circulate that he is a potential Soviet-supported coup-maker.

High-level government and party changes were minimal. The YSP Central Committee elected Muhammad Haydara Masdus as a full member of the Politburo on 7 September, and also chose Dr. Salih Muhsin as its secretary and Muthanna Salim Askar as its deputy secretary.

Dire economic straits continue to dog South Yemen, and per capita income is less than $500. The two most important sources of income are the estimated 100,000 South Yemenis working in Saudi Arabia, and the Aden refinery. However, remittances continued to spiral downward along with falling oil prices, and the refinery remained underutilized during 1988. Government budgets are chronically in deficit, and foreign aid from international donors and from the Arab Gulf states lags behind the growing external debt. The fighting in January 1986 forced the postponement of the country's third five-year plan until this year, and anticipated spending was scaled back to $1.7 billion.

Great hope is being placed on the expectation of income from oil exports within the next few years, and the National Yemeni Petroleum Company was created in November. The Soviet Union began construction of a pipeline extending from the oilfields, discovered in Shabwa governorate in 1987, to the coast. The pipeline is expected to be completed in 1990. The location of the oilfields in a border area near North Yemen and that country's oil deposits is another potential source of conflict between the two Yemens.

In the interim, the country was moderately successful in finding crude oil supplies for the recently modernized refinery in Aden. Kuwait renewed its agreement to provide nearly 29,000 barrels a day (b/d) towards the refinery's 170,000 b/d capacity. Iraq began providing 10,000 b/d in April; the volume of Iraqi crude oil was subsequently raised to 15,000 b/d. The first Iraqi tanker to transit the Strait of Hormuz since the cease-fire in the Iran-Iraq war docked in Aden in August.

Relations with 'Ali Nasir Muhammad and His Supporters. Two full years after the civil war of January 1986, there still was no solution to the problem posed by former president 'Ali Nasir and his supporters in North Yemen, who number between 20,000 and 60,000. The spate of executions in late December 1987, the result of Aden's mass trial of members of the 'Ali Nasir faction, provoked a new wave of hundreds of refugees fleeing to the north. Unlike past years, there were no significant third-party initiatives to bring the two sides together. The unsatisfactory status quo looks increasingly permanent, with a lasting negative impact on inter-Yemeni relations. The YAR government claims that it must find $10 million a month to take care of over 20,000 refugees who are not being looked after by their own families.

Foreign Affairs. There were no dramatic developments in foreign affairs. Relations with the Soviet Union, somewhat cool during 1986 and 1987, seemed to be on the upswing again, with military resupply and economic cooperation in the forefront. *Le Monde* observed in January that the Soviet military resupply seemed to have completely overcome the losses of material in 1986, and large maneuvers in the desert outside Aden were meant to demonstrate the superiority of the South's military capabilities over those of North Yemen. A report in the *Christian Science Monitor* (11 March) cited U.S. government officials as claiming that the Soviet resupply far exceeded South Yemen's requirements and conceivably could represent prepositioning of equipment and supplies for Soviet use. MiG-23 aircraft for the PDRY air force may have been included in the re-equipping.

Visits by Soviet officials to Aden and by PDRY officials to Moscow were numerous during the year. YSP general secretary 'Ali Salim al-Bayd underwent gall-bladder surgery in Moscow during February; he also made a private visit to the Soviet Union in August. The dean of the Soviet diplomatic academy visited Aden in February, while the Soviet and PDRY foreign ministries held consultations in Moscow, and the deputy minister of health visited Aden in March. The PDRY minister of culture and information held talks in Moscow in May on television and radio broadcasting. June visitors to Aden included the Soviet deputy ministers of the interior and fish industries. A YSP delegation held meetings in August at the CPSU Central Committee's General and International Departments, and Karen Brutents, candidate member of the CPSU Central Committee and deputy chief of its International Department led a delegation to Aden that month. A Soviet party-government delegation, headed by the deputy chairman of the council of ministers, took part in the celebration of the 25th anniversary of PDRY's 14 October Revolution and of the 10th anniversary of the founding of the YSP.

On the military side, the defense minister, Col. Salih 'Ubayd Ahmad, held talks in Moscow in March with his Soviet counterpart. Admiral Sidorov, the deputy commander in chief of the Soviet navy, visited Aden in April and in May a Soviet military delegation helped celebrate the fifteenth anniversary of the founding of South Yemen's People's Militia. Lt. Gen. Yuriy Ivanovich (Shomilikhin) paid a visit in November.

A disproportionate share of Soviet activity in the PDRY revolved around oil. Although a number of international oil companies hold concessions, the only discoveries during 1988 were those made in Shabwa governorate by Soviet Technoexport. Contracts for the overall development of Yemeni oilfields and for building the export pipeline were signed in January 1988, and follow-up protocols were signed in February and March. The Soviet ministers of oil industry and of construction of petroleum and gas industrial enterprises visited Aden in March.

Prime Minister Nu'man stopped in Moscow in July to meet with the Soviet petroleum industry minister, and the Soviet deputy minister of the petroleum industry inspected Shabwa oilfield sites in November. Soviet deputy prime minister Boris Yevdokimovich Shcherbina arrived in Aden on 21 November to familiarize himself with the development of the oil industry, as well as with PDRY gold production and the completion of the power station, all Soviet projects.

Economic cooperation was evident in other areas as well. The January meeting in Moscow of the Joint Yemeni-Soviet Economic Committee resulted in aid for fishery cooperatives in the Hadramawt, technical studies for a fishing complex on Socotra Island, and the modernization of the fish cannery in al-Mukalla. The imminent completion of the large thermal power station north of Aden, under construction since 1982, was signaled by the signing of a protocol in February. The provision of medical experts and the training of Yemeni personnel was agreed upon in March.

Numerous visits and agreements were exchanged with other communist countries. A Chinese communist party delegation visited Aden in March and Prime Minister Nu'man received the Chinese deputy minister of installations and chairman of the Chinese side of the Joint Yemen-Chinese Economic Committee in June. Talks were held in Pyongyang in June between delegations of the YSP and the Workers' Party of Korea. A joint YSP and PDRY government delegation went to Pyongyang in September to attend celebrations of the 40th anniversary of the founding of the DPRK.

In May, Defense Minister Salih 'Ubayd Ahmad visited Poland at the invitation of the Polish defense minister, and in September, a group from the Supreme People's Council became the first Yemeni parliamentary delegation to visit Poland. On 25 October, an agreement between the Democratic Yemen Peasants Union and the Union of Peasants in the German Democratic Republic to provide scholarships for training union cadres in East Germany was signed in Aden. A Hungarian delegation came to Aden in January, and a YSP group visited Bulgaria in March and April. In July, Prime Minister Nu'man attended the 44th CMEA session in Prague, while Foreign Minister 'Abd al-'Aziz al-Dali visited Czechoslovakia in September, and the Czech minister of national defense visited Aden in December.

Cuban-South Yemeni ties were particularly prominent. In May al-Bayd held talks in Cuba with President Fidel Castro (and also visited Nicaragua), and al-Dali attended the ministerial meeting of the Nonaligned Movement Coordinating Bureau in Cuba. A Cuban military delegation attended the June celebrations marking the fifteenth anniversary of the People's Militia. In August, the Cuban deputy interior minister visited Aden; the PDRY minister of fisheries went to Cuba; and the two countries' deputy ministers of the interior signed an agreement on cooperation.

In other ties to leftist states in the Third World, Foreign Minister al-Dali delivered a message from the YSP general secretary to Ethiopian president Mengistu in January. Muhammad Sa'id 'Abdullah Muhsin, a Politburo member and secretary of the YSP Central Committee, led a party delegation to the People's Republic of Mozambique in April. In the same month, a PDRY delegation joined the first anniversary celebrations of the Afghanistan revolution. An agreement on broadening inter-party contacts was concluded in Managua in August between the Sandinist National Liberation Front and the YSP.

Prime Minister Yasin Sa'id Nu'man disclosed in a November interview that the question of resumption of relations with the United States had been raised in an "unofficial context." Aden abruptly broke off ties in 1969, and a scheduled visit by a U.S. State Department team in 1978 never took place due to the outbreak of fighting in Aden. Reopening relations with the United States is a potentially explosive topic within YSP ranks, and Nu'man admitted that dissent over the issue had been expressed already in the Central Committee. That did not stop an agreement in early October for Sheraton to manage Aden's rebuilt luxury hotel, which had been severely damaged in the 1986 fighting.

On 9 February, the PDRY became the eleventh Arab state to restore diplomatic relations with Egypt, and in March a foreign-ministry delegation made the country's first official visit to Cairo since 1979. Elsewhere, General Secretary al-Bayd went to Khartoum at the end of September to meet with Sudanese prime minister Sadiq al-Mahdi. PLO chairman Yasir 'Arafat arrived in Aden in August to attend a graduation of Palestinian "cubs" and to meet with al-Bayd. 'Arafat returned in early November to brief Adeni leadership on the new Palestine National Council resolutions.

Ties with Syria remained close: Foreign Minister al-Dali went to Damascus at the end of July to meet with Syrian president Hafiz al-Asad. Prime Minister Nu'man and al-Dali met in Damascus with the Syrian foreign minister in October, and YSP assistant general secretary Salim Salih Muhammad visited Syria in October. Relations with Iraq seemed to have recovered completely from their disruption at the beginning of the 1980s. Deputy prime minister and minister of energy and minerals Salih Abu Bakr ibn Husaynun and Iraqi first deputy prime minister Taha Ramadan met in Baghdad in July; one tangible result was the increased volume of Iraqi crude oil designated for the Aden refinery.

Border incidents with all three of its neighbors did not seem to cause permanent harm to the PDRY's relations with Saudi Arabia, Oman, and the YAR. Reported border clashes between PDRY and Saudi troops during the summer seemed to be smoothed over during the visit of deputy prime minister and interior minister Salih Munassar al-Siyayli to Riyadh in October.

The relationship with Oman, begun in 1982 after years of animosity, continued to take root. The Omani minister of culture and national heritage represented his cousin the sultan at the celebrations of the PDRY's national day on 14 October. A border flare-up, less severe than the one in 1987 that caused the loss of several lives, threatened to derail the first-ever visit to Oman by a South Yemeni head of state. Nevertheless, President Haydar Abu Bakr al-'Attas arrived on 29 October in Muscat; the course of negotiations on the PDRY-Omani border were a major topic of discussion.

North and South Yemen continued to dance around their declared commitment to unity. Relations between the two Yemeni states, still scarred from Sanaa's support of 'Ali Nasir in the 1986 fighting, have also been troubled by border clashes prompted by the prospect of oil in disputed border areas. Nevertheless, some improvement in relations could be seen in 1988. An April summit between YSP general secretary 'Ali al-Bayd and YAR president 'Ali 'Abdullah Salih seemed to defuse the border problem and produced yet another timetable for imminent unification.

Al-Bayd made a return trip to Sanaa on 4 May to sign a joint agreement on reactivation of the Supreme Yemeni Council and other joint unity committees, to prepare the draft constitution for a unified state for submission to the two people's assemblies and then to a popular referendum, and to demilitarize a disputed border zone that might contain oil deposits, and to establish a joint-investment venture for the exploitation of that oil.

Simultaneously, the two countries' prime ministers signed an agreement to replace their separate border posts with joint posts, to remove restrictions on cross-border travel by Yemeni citizens (who would be allowed to use only identity cards), and to build new roads linking border areas. The agreement took effect in June. The oil ministers agreed in June to set up the Yemen Oil Company for Investments and Mineral Resources to carry out exploration and development in the joint-investment zone.

J. E. Peterson
Washington, D.C.

WESTERN EUROPE

Introduction

The fortunes of the communist parties in this region during this decade have undergone dramatic change. In 1981 the French Communist Party (PCF) had joined a coalition government with the socialists, led by François Mitterrand, and held four cabinet posts in one of the most important countries in Western Europe. Toward the end of 1983, the *World Marxist Review* concluded that "the ideas advanced by Europe's communists meet the innermost interests of the people" (November 1983). These needs were given specific definition by the coalition government as it nationalized major segments of French industry, including the country's leading banks. Indeed, the PCF emerged as a legitimate party in a democratic government and thus seemed to foreshadow the path to be followed by its counterparts elsewhere in the region.

By 1984, just one year later, interparty strife fractured the apparent cohesion of Western Europe's communist parties. The programs of social engineering and attempts at political transformation of society not only alienated the French electorate, but they greatly weakened the economy. The result was the PCF decision to withdraw from the coalition government as the French president and his prime minister drastically curtailed their program of socialization. By the end of 1988, the French communists were in disarray in the wake of their party's election defeat in 1986—the worst in sixty years—when they polled only 9.8 percent of the vote for election to the French National Assembly. They fared little better in 1988, when they received 11.3 percent of the vote in the French national election, following Mitterrand's re-election to the presidency for a second seven-year term.

As a legitimate party of government in France, the PCF had faced the challenge of reconciling its goal of achieving "socialism in French colors" with the necessity of acknowledging its inability to achieve that goal when forced to accept compro-

mise as a member of a coalition government. Thus confronted with a contradiction impossible to resolve, it had to make a choice: to explain why compromise was necessary or to resign. Either alternative meant a loss for the PCF. In addition, however, the experience of the PCF adversely affected both the credibility of its counterparts elsewhere in Europe and the confidence of the voters in the assurances of the communist parties that they were capable of acting as responsible members of democratic governments.

By the end of 1988, strong leadership in the West European communist movement had disappeared. The PCF experience had challenged other communist parties to demonstrate what constructive role they could play in their respective countries in the future. The result was reflected clearly in the outcome of national elections in Western Europe between 1985 and 1988. In each of the seven national elections held during 1985, the communist parties received fewer votes than they had in previous years. In the four national elections held in 1986, this poor record continued. In 1987 significant losses were suffered by the communist parties of Italy, Finland, Iceland, and Portugal. In the four national elections held during 1988, significant changes were recorded in France where the PCF received 11.3 percent of the vote (in 1986 it had obtained 9.8 percent), and in San Marino where the party increased its share of the vote from 24.3 to 28.7 percent.

The declining fortunes of Western Europe's communist parties were also affected by two factors over which they had relatively little control. The first of these involved the rise of market forces throughout the world in the second half of the 1980s, while Europe's communist parties watched the idea of socialism fade at the same time. This was not only true in Europe, but throughout the world, and most dramatically in the Soviet Union whose communist party had provided the model on which Western Europe's communist parties modeled themselves since 1945. The emergence of new leadership in the Soviet Union under Mikhail Gorbachev in 1985 proved to be the second factor. His domestic and foreign policies, as they were given spirit and substance between 1985 and 1988, presented a challenge to the cohesion of Western Europe's communist parties that was not only unexpected, but that was also impossible to foresee. Moreover, the challenge appeared so rapidly that adjustment to it was frustrating and complicated, and it resulted in the division rather than the union of the region's communist movements. By the end of 1987 it seemed clear that a return to competition, incentive, and free enterprise had a vastly greater appeal than the ephemeral promises of socialism. One year later, at the end of 1988 this trend was even more pronounced.

During the year, twelve of Western Europe's 23 communist parties were represented in their respective parliaments: Cyprus, Finland, France, Greece, Iceland, Italy, Luxembourg, Portugal, San Marino, Spain, Sweden, and Switzerland. With the exception of San Marino and Iceland, party members held no cabinet posts. Four national elections were held during 1988 (eleven were held in 1987; four in 1986; seven in 1985; one in 1984; and ten in 1983); they took place in Denmark, France, San Marino, and Sweden. Of the twelve parties with legislative representation, that of San Marino held the highest percentage of seats based on votes received (28.7), followed by Cyprus (27.4), Italy (26.6), Iceland (13.2), France (11.3), Portugal (11.0), Greece (9.9), Finland (9.4), Sweden (5.8), Luxembourg (4.9), Spain (4.6), and Switzerland (0.8). The eleven parties without legislative representation received between 0.1 (Great Britain) and 0.8 (Denmark) percent of the votes cast in the most recent parliamentary elections in their countries.

The reasons for this weakness were anticipated in 1985 by Aleksandr Zinoviev, who was expelled from the Soviet Union in 1978:

> If the Western Communists want to survive and to continue to have any influence over the masses, they are doomed to repudiate Marxist ideology. Their future, if they are to have a future, is in any case bleak indeed. They must either follow the dictates of Moscow or break up. There is no other choice; they must be either pro-Soviet or anti-Soviet. (Kevin Devlin, "Zinoviev Sees Bleak Future for Western Communist Parties," RAD Background Report, no. 61, 2 July 1985.)

What Zinoviev did not anticipate was the complexity of the predicament in which the leadership of the Soviet Union would place Western Europe's communist parties. To follow the direction given by Moscow in 1988 resulted in internal party strife between the conservative and liberal elements of the communist movement, which threatened to break them up; and to resist the promises of *glasnost'* (openness) and *perestroika* (restructuring), which were overwhelmingly endorsed by Western Europe's democratic parties, threatened to consign the communist parties to the background of contemporary European history. By the end of 1987 Western Europe's communist parties were caught in a dilemma that became even more frustrating in 1988: "[they must] either reassert their traditional philosophy, at the risk of losing more support, or move toward the social democratic center, at the risk of losing their identity." (William Echikson, "West Europe's Communists Running Out of Steam," *CSM*, 2 October 1987.)

In 1988 there was little that Western Europe's communist parties could offer their voters that was economically or politically attractive. They were caught in a classic contradiction in which either alternative open to them offered an unacceptable choice, namely, alienation of the voters. The notions and the realities of *perestroika* and *glasnost'* are thus having a highly disruptive effect on Western Europe's communist parties, since they are forcing liberal and conservative factions within the parties to confront each other so that one faction or the other will emerge with the responsibility to determine party policy. But irrespective of which elements will prevail in 1989 there is a "big question mark" that clouds the future of every communist party of Western Europe:

> They can recoil from the new challenges facing them and accept becoming bunker parties backed by a dwindling minority of voters. Alternatively, they can accept the painful changes involved in a true Westernization. This would mean, in effect, discarding class warfare and accepting to work within a democratic and modern capitalistic system. But if these parties should move that far, wouldn't they cease to be Communist? (Leo J. Wollemborg, "'Eurocommunism' is Choking in Gorbachev's Dust," *WSJ*, 19 September 1988.)

The activities of the PCF, and the challenges the party faces, are among the most interesting of the communist parties of Western Europe. The decade of the 1980s has seen the party's fortunes change dramatically and its popularity wax and wane. The PCF formally abandoned its support for a Union of the Left in 1985, following its withdrawal from the French government in 1984. In an effort to restore unity, party secretary Georges Marchais announced in 1986 that he would not be a candidate for the presidential elections in France, scheduled for May 1988. In spite of his efforts, however, the party remained divided and in 1986 suffered its worst defeat in elections to the French National Assembly since the end of World War II.

Internal division characterized party life during 1987 and 1988. Debates within the PCF "included charges that Stalinism had returned to plague the PCF, public demands for the resignation of Marchais, and an analysis by former PCF spokesman, Pierre Juquin . . . in which he argued that the party's decline was due to the leadership's refusal to make the appropriate analysis of, and adjust strategy to, fundamental changes in French society." (*YICA*, 1987.)

The result was the accusation leveled by André Lajoinie, chairman of the PCF caucus in the French National Assembly, that Juquin was "ultimately aiming to preserve capitalism" (*YICA*, 1987). During 1987, the rift developed into a dispute between Juquin and Lajoinie, both of whom sought to become the PCF candidate for the presidential election in 1988. At the end of 1987, party secretary Marchais succeeded in gaining sufficient support to expel Juquin from the PCF at the same time that the party's Twenty-sixth Congress, held in December, ratified Marchais's choice of Lajoinie as the party's candidate for the presidential election. Thus 1988 began with the re-election of Marchais as general secretary for a seventh term, as well as the re-election of all members of the Politburo. But as the year began the party faced continued prospects for division that did not bode well for a strong electoral showing in May.

During the election campaign Lajoinie argued that the coalition government of the French Socialist Party (PSF) and the PCF, formed in 1981 when François Mitterrand was first elected president of the French republic, had been a "mistake" (*Le Point*, 11 January), and the party newspaper, *L'Humanité* (18 April) concluded that "we lost our credibility as defenders of the underdog by joining a government that didn't carry out our policies." The dispute between Juquin's "reformists" and Lajoinie not only divided the party, but contributed to the worst defeat for the PCF in its 68-year history. Lajoinie polled 6.8 percent of the vote (in 1981 Marchais received 15.5 percent), and the 2.1 percent received by Juquin was widely regarded as insufficient to bolster reformist strength within the party. The party claimed that the poor showing did not reflect the

PCF's real influence in French political life. Yet the party had strongly supported participation in the democratic process in 1981. Thus, Marchais's conclusion that "the election of the President by universal suffrage is the most undemocratic of elections" stood in stark contrast to its previous position.

Following his re-election, President Mitterrand called for elections to the National Assembly in June. The voters returned 27 PCF deputies to the French parliament, with a total of 11.3 percent of the popular vote (in 1986 the party had obtained 9.8 percent of the votes and 35 of 577 seats). While the party lost seats, it nonetheless claimed victory by arguing that the return to single-member districts under the Chirac government artificially lowered its representation, and that the PCF's real representation should amount to 65 to 70 seats.

Although PCF leaders criticized those advocating leftist unity, they did arrive at a legislative modus vivendi with the PSF which formed a minority government under Michel Rocard. The Socialists changed the rules of the National Assembly, reducing from 30 to 20 the minimum number of seats required for recognition as an official parliamentary group, and PCF deputies voted with the PSF to elect former Socialist prime minister Laurent Fabius as president of the National Assembly. By the end of the year, however, whatever unity did exist seemed to be dissolving. In the autumn, PCF leaders and their trade union representatives of the General Confederation of Labor were embroiled in a test of nerves with the minority Socialist government of Michel Rocard over wage rates for public sector workers. The disagreement resulted in a series of strikes that disrupted mail, transportation, and other public services. As relations between the PSF and the PCF deteriorated, analysts across the political spectrum predicted substantially increased difficulties in forging sufficient leftist unity to preserve PCF offices in the municipal elections set for the spring of 1989.

The Communist Party of Italy (PCI) has argued since 1986 "that the old differences between the communist and socialist movements are not sustainable" (*YICA*, 1987). The efforts to set aside these differences did not produce a victory at the polls in 1987 of the magnitude the party expected. It won only 177 of 630 parliamentary seats, compared to the 198 seats obtained the previous year.

The PCI's losses in 1987 resulted in the continuation of a debate that ended in a reaffirmation of the opening to the noncommunist European left proclaimed at the 1986 congress in Florence. Following the party's further decline in municipal elections in May and June of 1988, the debate focused on how to chart a "new course" and to redefine the identity of the Communist Party of Italy. It also contributed to the resignation of Alessandro Natta as general secretary and to his replacement by Achille Occhetto. As the spokesman for the "new course," Occhetto argued that the PCI must achieve "the conquest of the center" in Italian politics, and urged that this be pursued with more "openness" (*trans-parenza*). He especially emphasized the need to publicize the proceedings of the meetings of the party's directorate, to elect "in the most open and direct way possible" all leaders at all levels of the party structure, and to adopt new rules that would permit the clear expression of majority and minority positions on policy issues. (*L'Unita*, 21 June.)

The PCI remained concerned throughout the year with the prospects for the communist movement in Western Europe. In the October issue of *World Marxist Review*, party member Gianni Cervetti emphasized the PCI position that "there is no point in speaking about a communist movement," but that the "forces of progress and renewal" in Western Europe supported the Soviet government's policies of *glasnost'* and *perestroika*. According to one observer of communist affairs, Kevin Devlin,

The warning was blunt and clear enough: if Gorbachev were ousted and perestroika abandoned, the PCI and other like-minded forces in Western Europe would break off relations with the CPSU. (Kevin Devlin, "The Communist Movement in 1988," RAD Background Report/249, 30 December 1988.)

This conclusion was put another way by Alessandro Natta, Occhetto's immediate predecessor as PCI general secretary, in a press conference following a lengthy meeting with Gorbachev in Moscow at the end of March. He emphasized that the PCI endorsed "a pluralist political system, we believe in the creative value of democracy; as I have said, ours are the choices of a party that functions in a Western reality." (*L'Unita*, 31 March.) Natta's concern also reflected the attitude taken by the party leadership as a whole, as it prepared in the latter half of the year for the Eighteenth Congress to be held in 1989. The document drafted by the party, preparatory to the congress, called for "a new chapter in the struggle for socialism" on the basis of "the crisis and exhaustion of past historical experiences," and it affirmed that "democracy is not a path to socialism but is the path of socialism." (Ibid., 25 and 26 November.)

Whether the PCI would be successful in its effort to unite the left in Italy in 1989, and in Europe as a whole, was doubtful at the end of the year. But the party leadership was sending the carefully drawn message that the path to socialism would not be dictated by the CPSU.

The Spanish Communist Party (PCE) has operated legally within Spain since 1977. Under the leadership of Santiago Carrillo, it was the leading advocate of Eurocommunism until 1981. In 1982, at the age of 37, Gerardo Iglesias succeeded Carrillo and served as general secretary of the party until 1988. Between 1983 and 1988 the PCE was plagued with internal dissension; the result is that the party has played a minimal role in Spanish politics. It is one of the most fragmented in Europe. Led by Ignacio Gallego, pro-Soviet dissidents withdrew from the Eurocommunist PCE in 1983 to form the Communist Party of the Peoples of Spain (PCPE) in 1984. A second group, led by Carrillo, was created in 1982 following his failure to be reconfirmed as the party's general secretary. Carrillo formally resigned from the PCE in 1986 and officially formed the Spanish Workers' Party–Communist Unity (PTE-UC) in 1987. All three parties campaigned in the most recent election in Spain, held in 1986, and the PCE, in a multiparty coalition of the left, including the PCPE, received 7 of 350 parliamentary seats.

Amid continuing argument in 1988 the PCE held its Twelfth Congress in February. In a move reflecting growing anxiety over a "lack of leadership," the congress replaced Gerardo Iglesias as general secretary with the former mayor of Cordoba, Julio Anguita (born in 1941). The party congress emphasized that although the PCE had successfully avoided a "very real threat of disintegration," it must focus on "ideological renewal" and bring together all communist groups in Spain in a coalition of the United Left. Thus Anguita stressed that the purpose was not to absorb or dissolve dissident groups, but to unite them with the common interest of designing programs to solve society's problems. During the year, the PCE therefore sought to develop a dialogue with the PCPE and with the PTE-UC. By the year's end, PCPE chairman and founder Gallego had been removed and party general secretary Juan Ramos supported the efforts to join with the PCE to strengthen the United Left. Carrillo, as the spokesman for the PTE-UC, rejected unity as advocated by the PCE and endorsed the concept of a federation of communist groups in Spain. While it was clear in December that efforts to achieve some form of communist-party unity would continue in 1989, it was impossible to predict whether these efforts would be successful.

The Portuguese Communist Party (PCP) has been served by Alvaro Cunhal (75 years of age) as general secretary since 1961. In a coalition of the left in elections held in 1987, the PCP won 30 of 250 parliamentary seats; it claims a membership of approximately 200,000. The party's political influence, however, has declined significantly since it garnered 19 percent of the vote in 1979. It remains one of the most Stalinist parties in Europe, and while it declared its solidarity with the Soviet Union during 1988, it has not enthusiastically endorsed the domestic and foreign policy positions of the Soviet government under Gorbachev. Within the party, however, a major difference of opinion emerged in the course of the year that was the subject of the party's Twelfth Congress in December.

In January a "Group of Six," younger members of the PCP, released to the Portuguese press proposals establishing a secret ballot, free and open discussion, and a rejuvenation of the party leadership as subjects of discussion at the forthcoming congress. The party's Central Committee condemned the public airing of these views as "divisive." Conservative elements within the PCP called for expulsion of the "Group of Six," while moderate members of the party's leadership recommended disciplinary measures short of a complete break.

This debate and struggle over the future direction of the party continued throughout the year. It was not resolved at the Twelfth Congress, but two interesting developments did occur. The delegates elected 54 new members to the Central Committee, and dropped 44 members, to underscore Cunhal's endorsement of "continuing renewal." While it did not reflect the "rejuvenation" advocated by the "Group of Six," who boycotted the congress, political observers in Portugal concluded that the congress may have marked a new era for the PCP since differences of opinion were openly aired. As with the PCE in Spain, however, the future direction of the PCP remained uncertain. Cunhal was re-elected as party general secretary, but faced continued pressure in 1989, to permit, if not endorse, open debate about the future views and positions of the PCP.

In Cyprus, Greece, Malta, San Marino, and Turkey, the communist parties do not play influential roles in the design of domestic and foreign policy, but in Cyprus and San Marino their importance is greater than, for example, in Spain or Portugal. The Communist Party of San Marino (PCS) is an extension of the Italian Communist Party, just as the country's other political parties reflect the views of their Italian counterparts. The party (PCS) claims a membership of 1,200 and is led by General Secretary Gilberto Ghiotti. In May 1988, San Marino held a national election in which the PCS increased its percentage of the popular vote by approximately 4 percent, for a total of 28.7 percent of the vote and 18 of 60 parliamentary seats (in 1983 it received 24.3 percent of the vote). This victory allowed the PCS to continue its coalition with the Christian Democratic Party (PDCS), and between them to hold 75 percent of the country's parliamentary seats. The government is headed by two captains-regent, elected for six-month terms from among Council members.

The Communist Party of Malta (CPM), established in 1969, has an estimated membership of 300 and did not participate in a national election until 1987. Of a total of 236,169 votes, the CPM received 119, of which 13 were cast for the party's general secretary Anthony Vassallo. As a consequence, the party's role in Maltese affairs is minimal, but it does maintain contacts with the communist parties of Europe, and especially with the Communist Party of the Soviet Union. This latter point is of special significance and reflects Soviet interest in the strategic position the island occupies in the Mediterranean. This concern prompted former Deputy Ambassador to the United Nations from the United States, Charles Lichenstein, to conclude in 1986 that "the democracies in the West must view with growing concern Malta's drift towards the Soviet sphere" (*YICA*, 1987). In 1988, however, the Maltese government under Prime Minister Fenech Adami, who replaced the Labor government in 1987, clearly rejected the Soviet government's proposal for the withdrawal of USSR and U.S. fleets from the Mediterranean. Indeed, Adami underscored his government's vision of a "Western European role . . . we will seek to become full members of the European Community" (*The Times*, Malta, 13 July).

In Turkey the communist party (TCP) is proscribed, and is the only communist party of Western Europe to operate illegally. Developments within Turkey during the year, however, suggested that Prime Minister Turgut Ozal's government may consider lifting the 60-year-old proscription in 1989.

In Cyprus, the Progressive Party of the Working People (AKEL) claims a membership of 15,000 and holds 15 of 56 seats in the Cypriot parliament. The AKEL received 27.4 percent of the vote in the most recent national elections, held in 1985. The party's popular support is drawn primarily from the Greek Cypriot majority, which comprises approximately 80 percent of the island's estimated population of 691,000. In municipal elections of May 1987, the AKEL received 32.5 percent of the Greek Cypriot vote, and its candidates for mayor were victorious in nine of the eighteen cities in the southern part of the island. A major change occurred in 1988 with the death of General Secretary Ezekias Papaioannou, who died in April after serving as head of the party since 1949. He was replaced by Dimitris Christofias who, at the age of 42, became one of the youngest general secretaries of a communist party in Europe.

The most significant political development during the year was the election of independent candidate George Vassiliou as president of the Republic of Cyprus in February. Vassiliou, with the support of the AKEL, was elected with 52 percent of the popular vote for a five-year term. As had Papaioannou, Christofias committed the AKEL to support the new president "in the implementation of his platform," and declared that the party "will struggle for a rapprochement between Greek and Turkish Cypriots" (Nicosia Domestic Service, 23 April). In response to his critics, President Vassiliou emphasized that the AKEL does not seek "the transformation of society" and supports cooperation among "parties or persons of different ideologies" (*World Marxist Review*, June). He thus sought AKEL support for his efforts to resolve constitutional and territorial issues in negotiations between Greek and Turkish Cypriots. These discussions were initiated in 1988 and were scheduled to continue in 1989. At the end of the year the AKEL endorsed his efforts, presumably with the expectation that this approach would exercise broad appeal among the island's voters.

The Communist Party of Greece (KKE) has been divided between pro-Soviet and Eurocommunist factions since the period of military government in Greece (1967–1974). In the 1980s rivalries within the Greek communist party became not only intense, but also extremely complex. The pro-Soviet KKE, with an estimated membership of 50,000, holds 13 of 300 seats in the Greek parliament, won in the 1985 national elections. The Eurocommunist faction, known as KKE-Interior (KKE-I), divided itself into two groups in 1987. The stronger of the two is known as the Greek Left and is led by Leonidas Kyrkos. The second group retained the appellation KKE-I and added the title Renovating Left under the leadership of Giannis Banias.

Since 1974 the KKE, headed by General Secretary Kharilaos Florakis, has taken domestic and foreign policy positions similar to those of Andreas Papandreou's governing Panhellenic Socialist Movement (PASOK). During his first term in office (1981–1985), Papandreou was supported by the KKE in positions critical of the European Community and NATO and supportive of an expanded role for the public sector at the expense of private enterprise. In 1985 Papandreou's government began to encounter economic pressures that resulted in renewed support for private enterprise for the purpose of combating an inflation rate of almost 20 percent, as well as in a wage and salary freeze. By the beginning of 1988, PASOK's popularity had declined from approximately 46 percent to 26 percent, and the KKE recognized an unusual opportunity to appeal to Greek voters via a broad alliance of the left. Thus, the KKE embarked on a program in early 1988 designed to achieve a gradual rapprochement between it and the left-wing political forces, and primarily the Greek Left under Leonidas Kyrkos, its general secretary declaring that "the solution lies only in firm alliance of the left forces relying on a common programme with a socialist outlook" (Kharilaos Florakis, *World Marxist Review*, January). To promote this alliance, KKE has toned down its criticism of the European Community (EC) and moved closer to the position of the Greek Left that is focused on gaining the most favorable terms for Greek membership and on closer cooperation with leftist forces within the EC itself, as well as acknowledging that private enterprise has a definite role to play in the Greek economy.

By the middle of the year, under the shadow of Papandreou's serious illness, Kyrkos, the leader of the Greek Left, indicated an interest in formation of an alliance of the left. By year's end, political observers in Greece noted the real possibility that the increasing numbers of disenchanted PASOK supporters may shun the party in the parliamentary elections scheduled for mid-1989 and vote for the candidates of the alliance of the left. If this strategy proves successful, the forces of the left in Greek politics, including the KKE, may exercise significant parliamentary influence in 1989.

The Communist Party of Great Britain (CPGB) has never been one of Britain's major parties, and at its peak in 1942 enjoyed a membership of only 42,000. The party's influence in British politics is minimal, and its membership has been dropping since 1980; indeed, in 1988 it stood at less than

10,000 members. In Great Britain's most recent national election, held in June 1987, the CPGB received 0.1 percent of the vote and its 19 candidates polled only 6,078 votes. The party has been without representation in the British parliament since 1950 and is represented in the House of Lords by one member, Lord Milford.

The long-standing conflict between the Eurocommunist leadership under General Secretary Gordon McLennan and the Stalinist minority, which controls the party newspaper *Morning Star*, continued throughout the year. The intraparty conflict in 1988 unfolded in the context of several consecutive years of stinging defeats for the political left in Britain. Recognizing that "Marx's classical working class . . . is a declining minority" (*YICA*, 1988), the Eurocommunist majority in control of the party is turning to the advocacy of broad alliances among leftist parties and groups. The decision in late 1987 to break the party's ties to *Morning Star* led to a permanent split in 1988, when the publishers of *Morning Star* and their supporters held their own congress in late April. About 150 delegates representing 1,600 dissident communists met in London and agreed to "re-establish" the Communist Party with the name "Communist Party of Britain," in contrast to the name "Communist Party of Great Britain." The consequences of this split were impossible to predict at the end of the year, but it seemed clear that neither faction would increase its following significantly, if at all, in 1989.

The Communist Party of Ireland (CPI) does not play a significant role in Irish political life. Although it did participate in local and national elections in 1987, it is without representation in parliament. The party's small base of support is concentrated in Belfast and Dublin, and its traditional views focus on the religious division of the country and on Ireland's economic problems. The party opposes terrorism in Ireland and supports the country's reunification on the basis of working-class solidarity designed to overcome the division between Catholics and Protestants.

The communist parties of Belgium, Denmark, Luxembourg, and the Netherlands exerted marginal influence on the political life of their respective countries in 1988. The Communist Party of Luxembourg (CPL), headed by René Urbany, claims a membership of 600. In the most recent national election, held in 1984, the party received 4.9 percent of the vote and occupies 2 of 64 parliamentary seats. Party leadership remains in the hands of the Urbany family, which founded the

party in 1921. The CPL plays no significant role in the European communist movement, but it received congratulatory messages on the occasion of its Twenty-fifth Congress held in April, that were symbolic of the approach taken by the Soviet Union toward Western Europe's communist parties. They included a message from the Central Committee of the CPSU that praised the "solidarity with our work in reconstructing Soviet society and with our foreign policy based on the new thinking" (*FBIS*, 26 April). Consistent with the position taken by the majority of Western Europe's communist parties, the CPL announced formation of a coalition of left-wing forces in Luxembourg, thus suggesting that 1989 would see an intensification of the effort to attract a broader political following.

The Communist Party of Denmark (DKP) has not been represented in the Danish parliament since 1979, when it failed to receive the minimum 2 percent of the vote required for proportional representation. Its political fortunes did not change in 1988, when it polled only 0.8 percent of the vote in Denmark's national election.

The party's chairman, Ole Sohn, was elected in April 1987 at the age of 32, to succeed DKP chairman Jørgen Jensen following his death in the same month. Sohn has sought to improve the party's electoral prospects by seeking electoral alliances with other radical socialist and Marxist parties under the motto "Forum for Democratic Renewal." This effort, however, has proved unsuccessful thus far, and the DKP has become an increasingly irrelevant peripheral observer and critic of Danish domestic affairs, a position which not only represents little change from the previous year, but which is unlikely to alter significantly in 1989.

The Belgian Communist Party (PCB) claims a membership of approximately 5,000 in a country with a population of almost ten million. Since the party lost its representation of two seats in the Belgian parliament in 1985, when it received 1.2 percent of the vote, it has been in steady decline. It has been slow to respond effectively to the issues of language and region in a country in which there is a clear division between the Flemish north and the French-speaking Wallons of the south and the francophone majority in Brussels. While Belgium's major parties recognized the necessity to structure their party organizations regionally and to revise the Belgian constitution in federalist directions, the PCB did not give its Flemish and francophone wings greater freedom from central control until 1986, and it was not until 1988 that the PCB endorsed the pursuit of tactical alliances with other leftist groups on a regional basis.

The consequences of rigidity are well illustrated by the outcome of the 1987 parliamentary election held in December, when the PCB received only 0.8 percent of the vote (in comparison to 2.3 percent in 1981). In the words of party chairman Louis Van Geyt, the PCB has been reduced to "a nonparliamentary role" in Belgian politics (*Drapeau Rouge*, 15 December 1987). Indeed, according to Van Geyt, the party's ineffectual collaboration with noncommunist political forces has produced the emergence of "social movements which championed peace, environmental protection, the cause of the dispossessed...and solidarity with the oppressed and exploited Third World Peoples...outside or next to the working class movements and historical left organisations rather than on their basis" [sic] (*World Marxist Review*, February). This indictment of the inability of the PCB to adjust to political realities not only left the party in a position of weakness at the end of the year, but also represented a major challenge for 1989.

The Communist Party of the Netherlands (CPN) has an estimated membership of 12,000 in a country with a population of almost 15 million. In its ideological and social composition, the CPN resembles other northern European communist parties. It exercises little influence on the political life of the Netherlands and holds no seats in the country's parliament. The CPN held its 1988 annual meeting in Amsterdam in March. This gathering resulted in a conventional declaration in support of nuclear-free zones and the abolition of all nuclear weapons in Europe. The main problems facing the party remained, first, the apparently irreversible decline into insignificance and, second, the split between the feminist and pacifist majority in the CPN and the old-style Stalinists who dominated the party's leadership until the late 1970s.

In October the CPN celebrated its seventieth anniversary, and party chairman Elli Izeboud announced that in the future the party would focus its attention on the arms race and environmental issues. But the party remained without a program that appealed to a significant segment of the population, and there were no indications at the end of the year that the CPN offered political alternatives that would increase its popular support in 1989.

In the Nordic countries of Iceland, Norway, Sweden, and Finland, the communist parties were active, but without major influence, with the exception of Iceland. The People's Alliance of Iceland

(PA) was founded in 1968 and has an estimated membership of 3,000 in a country with a population of approximately 250,000. Until 1983 the party regularly participated in coalition governments. In the 1987 national elections the party received another setback, polling 13.2 percent of the vote and winning only 8 of 63 seats in the Icelandic parliament (in 1983 it obtained 17.3 percent of the votes and 10 of 60 seats). As the new year began, the PA faced an uncertain future, the difficulties of which will be exacerbated by intraparty strife, as well as by the political challenge of the Women's Alliance, a major competitor for leftist women's votes.

In 1988 economic problems reignited inflation and presented Iceland's center-left government, led by Thorstein Palsson, with a severe fiscal crisis. The result was the collapse in September of the coalition among the Independence Party (moderate conservative; IP), the Progressive Party (agrarian liberal; PP), and the reformist Social Democrats (SDP). The consequence was the formation of a new coalition under Steingrimur Hermannsson (PP) with the SDP, the PA, and a one-man splinter group from the PP known as the Association for Equality and Justice. The new government represented a tactical success for Hermannsson as well as for PA leader Olafur Ragnar Grimsson, who negotiated three cabinet positions for members of the PA: the Finance Ministry, the Ministry of Education and Culture, and the Ministry of Agriculture and Communications. The Ministry of Foreign Affairs is occupied by SPD member Jon Baldvin Hannibalsson.

As the year ended the fortunes of the PA appeared significantly improved, but the PA was also in the position of having to accept responsibility for the new government's austere economic policies. Since the new cabinet enjoyed only a one-vote parliamentary majority, it was not in a position to survive divisive political differences within its coalition parties. In view of the individualism of Iceland's political figures, the PA entered 1989 facing the two challenges of ensuring the survival of the coalition government and of maintaining party unity.

The Norwegian Communist Party (NKP) has an estimated membership of 1,500 to 2,000, and competes with several other small parties of the left for popular support, especially the Socialist Left Party (SV), established in the mid-1970s by former members of the NKP. Strongly pro-Soviet in orientation, the NKP is also one of the weakest communist parties of Western Europe. It has not held a seat in the Norwegian parliament since 1973 and exerts virtually no influence on Norwegian political affairs (the SV holds 6 of 157 seats). The future of the NKP was decisively influenced by a split in the party in 1975, when moderate elements within it formed the SV. While the gulf between the two parties has remained wide since 1975, the NKP began a reassessment of its approach to Norwegian politics at its Nineteenth Congress in April 1987. The NKP sought "an alliance of the working-class parties that is able to unite all those who are objective opponents of monopoly capital and imperialism," a position that sharply contrasted with its conclusion that the "Social Democrats are our most important alliance partners on all the major political issues today. We must accomplish the task of developing a constructive and comradely cooperation with the Social Democrats, while at the same time maintaining our fundamental criticism of their policies" (*Friheten*, 30 April 1987).

These two positions were irreconcilable. In 1988, however, the NKP appeared to be moving slowly in the direction of greater flexibility. The election in 1987 of a new party chairman, Kare Andre Nilsen (42 years of age), suggested a decision to infuse the party with new energy. And the declaration in 1988 by former party chairman Hans Kleven that the NKP would support a "red-green" alliance of the left for the national election scheduled for September 1989 was intended to send a clear message to the members of the NKP as well as to the parties of the left generally. How the Norwegian electorate would respond to this effort remained uncertain as the year drew to a close.

The Left Party Communists (VPK) in Sweden have been represented in the Swedish parliament throughout the 1980s, and its membership has remained relatively stable at 17,000 to 18,000. While it has not played a major role in Swedish politics, it has consistently supported the country's Social Democratic governments in the Swedish parliament. In national elections held in September, the VPK received a popular vote of 5.8 percent and won 21 of 349 seats, an increase of 2 seats from the election of 1985. Thus, while 1987 saw "a divided and paralyzed VPK . . . [with] little chance of reversing a falling membership trend, of winning support among today's young, or even of running an effective election campaign" (*Dagens Nyheter*, 27 May 1987), developments in 1988 boded well for the party's future. The Social Democrats and the VPK won a total of 177 parliamentary seats, as compared to 152 seats for the "bourgeois parties"

and 20 seats for the environmentalist "Green" party, which won representation for the first time. Speculation was widespread in Sweden that some Social Democrats deliberately voted for the VPK to assure its representation in parliament. Whether or not this was the case was in some respects moot, for as the VPK entered 1989 it was assured of new political challenges.

Since 1969 the internal affairs of the Finnish Communist Party (SKP) have been dominated by factional strife, which led to a major party split in 1985 with debate on the merits of a new party program, "Socialism with a Finnish Face."

In 1986 and 1987, the SKP, under the leadership of chairman Arvo Aalto, developed a program to expand "international activity, not Eurocommunism . . . the West European communist parties that operate in similar social circumstances [must be] seen as natural and intimate collaborators with the SKP" (*Kansan Uutiset*, 24 January 1986). The Stalinist wing of the party (SKP-Y) elected a "shadow" party leadership in April 1986 with Taisto Sinisalo as chairman. The SKP claims a membership of 20,000, and the SKP-Y claims approximately 15,000 members.

In 1987 the split adversely affected popular support, and this was reflected in Finland's national elections held in March. The SKP received only 9.4 percent of the vote and 16 of 200 parliamentary seats (in 1983 it obtained 14 percent of the vote and 27 of 200 seats), and the SKP-Y received 4.3 percent and 4 seats. In June the SKP-Y held its first congress (organizers claimed it was the SKP's Twenty-first Congress), and called upon the SKP to cancel its party program as a prelude to reunification of both wings of the party, and to form an electoral coalition for the 1988 presidential campaign in Finland. The SKP held its congress one week later and adopted a program that was regarded as Eurocommunist both in its description of Finnish socialism and in its disassociation of the party from the CPSU.

As 1988 began, both wings of the party remained outside the mainstream of the country's political life, and the results of the presidential campaign confirmed this position with the re-election in February of incumbent Mauno Koivisto for a second six-year term. Severely shaken by an internal financial crisis, SKP chairman Aalto resigned in May and was replaced by Jarmo Wahlström (50 years old), a member of the Finnish parliament, a protégé of Aalto, and generally seen as supportive of the efforts to reconcile the differences among the factions of the Finnish communist movement. During the remainder of the year, Wahlström reiterated his support for a broadly-based leftist front, as "an ideological alternative to bourgeois hegemony" (*Hufvudstadsbladet*, 4 July).

Similarly Sinisalo, of the SKP-Y, supported the effort to reconcile party differences. Citing ill health, however, he resigned as chairman after 45 years as a communist activist, and was replaced by Jouko Kajanoja (46 years old). Kajanoja also endorsed efforts to reunify the party, but declared that the minority would only negotiate with the majority as an equal partner. A "forum of the left" was announced for April 1989, but its purpose was unclear, as was the identity of the groups on the left that would participate in it. Thus, in 1988 a new generation of leaders emerged in the Finnish communist movement, and immediately moved publicly to support efforts to overcome the party's division and heal its attendant wounds. They also left the impression, however, that the road to reunification of the communist movement in Finland would be long.

The Communist Party of Austria (KPÖ) and the Swiss Labor Party (PdAS) play minimal roles in the political arenas of their respective countries. The KPÖ has an estimated membership of 15,000 in a country with a population of approximately 7.5 million. In the most recent national election, that of 1986, the party received less than one percent of the vote, and remains pro-Soviet in its views and positions. Throughout 1987 the party systematically endorsed Gorbachev's advocacy of *glasnost'* and condemned the Austrian coalition government formed by the conservative People's Party and the Socialists as a government in opposition to the interests of the working classes. In 1988 the latter theme was not discarded, but it was overshadowed by emphasis throughout the year on the 50th anniversary of the *Anschluss* to Hitler's Third Reich of German-speaking Austria in 1938. This emphasis served as a useful vehicle that allowed the KPÖ to condemn the Austrian government's efforts to join the European Community; it did not, however, improve the popularity of the party among the Austrian electorate to a significant degree.

In Switzerland, the PdAS, pro-Soviet in allegiance, has not played a major role in the political process for many years. In 1987 the party received less than one percent of the vote in the Swiss national elections. As a consequence, the PdAS undertook a major effort in 1987 to rejuvenate the party's leadership, and began this initiative by electing Jean Spielmann, aged 43, as the new general secretary in 1987. Replacement of members of the party's Central Committee has altered the age distribution there as well: 39 percent are under 40 years of age, and 26 percent are between 40 and 50. During 1988, the PdAS stressed issues of disarmament and environmental protection that were designed to appeal to a broader spectrum of the Swiss population than has traditionally been the case. At the end of the year, however, there were no signs that the party was likely to play more than a marginal role in Swiss politics in 1989.

The Socialist Unity Party of West Berlin (SEW) has, according to its own estimate, 7,000 members out of a population of approximately 1.9 million. The party has not been represented in the city's parliament since its formation in 1969. In the last election to the Berlin government, held in 1985, the party received 0.6 percent of the vote. Such poor electoral performances are likely to continue as long as the SEW retains its character of an unswervingly pro-Soviet party and remains financially dependent upon East Berlin. In a city divided by the Berlin Wall and surrounded by mine fields, the party does not appeal to the citizens of West Berlin, who have defended their freedom successfully since 1945. Indeed, the party slogan: "With the SEW for Peace, Work, Democracy, and Social Progress," which served as the motto for the SEW's Eighth Congress held in May 1987, had a hollow ring for the city's electorate.

In the Federal Republic of Germany (FRG) the German Communist Party (DKP) is not represented in the Bundestag and received only 0.5 percent of the vote in national elections in January 1987. In 1988 the DKP faced the most serious crisis in its two decades of existence. For the first time in fifteen years, its membership dropped to 38,000. One half of those who left the party cited political and ideological reasons for leaving, and many who remained are questioning the party's "tendency toward dogmatism" and its opposition to change. In the past the loyalty of the DKP to its East German counterpart, the Socialist Unity Party (SED), and to the CPSU has provided stability and discipline for the party, as has the DKP's support for the Soviet Union as the model of "real socialism." Thus, the DKP's motto has been "To learn from the Soviet Union means to learn to be victorious." The foreign and defense policy objectives of the Soviet Union have also received consistent endorsement from the DKP. Both the East German leader Erich Honecker and DKP chairman Herbert Mies are recipients of the Lenin Peace Prize. The emergence in the Soviet Union of a party leader, Mikhail Gorbachev, whose approach to politics represents a radical departure from that of his predecessors has created a serious dilemma for the DKP.

Gorbachev's support for more democracy has been enthusiastically embraced by some DKP members who have criticized the "lack of possibilities for intraparty influence and participation," in the words of party member Erasmus Schöfer. In 1987, Schöfer acknowledged that embarking on a new path is not without risk, but "communists in the FRG have nothing to lose but their lack of success!" (*Der Spiegel*, 7 September 1987). In May 1987, party chairman Mies pointed to the crux of the problem: ". . . there is hardly another topic on which so many party functions and with such a large number of participants have been held over the past several years . . . The sympathy for the changes in the Soviet Union is unanimous." He recognized that "the attractive power" of Gorbachev's approach has been growing. (*Unsere Zeit*, 20 May 1987.) In 1988, polls indicated the Soviet leader enjoyed greater popularity in West Germany than did any West German or American political leader; indeed, 83 percent of West German respondents considered him to be a "man who can be trusted."

According to Mies, Gorbachev's disarmament proposals presented the DKP with "fresh opportunities in . . . our united action and alliance policy." It has "made it easier for communists to act as respected and equal partners in the peace movement and other democratic movements. Not least important among the fresh opportunities is the possibility of using the growing sympathy for Soviet policy to spread the influence of the DKP as the party of socialism." (Ibid.) Gorbachev's dramatic announcement at the United Nations on 7 December 1988 that the Soviet Union would unilaterally reduce its manpower and weapons in the USSR and in Eastern Europe, and the declaration in Paris on 7 January 1989 that the USSR would begin unilaterally to destroy its stocks of chemical weapons, were the kind of initiatives on which the DKP sought to capitalize. But the apparent changes in the direction of Soviet foreign and domestic policy also contained an implicit threat for the DKP, if it remained unswervingly loyal to the direction given in Moscow. Thus Mies also warned in 1987 that in a capitalist country like West Germany "there can be no imitation of the Soviet approach," and that the party must be careful "not to throw the baby out with the bathwater." Mies endorsed the need for

"invigoration of intraparty life, encouragement of intraparty discussions, and broader involvement of the party membership in the decisionmaking process." But he also cautioned that "intraparty democracy for us is not a game, not an end in itself. It is designed to mobilize the party's collective knowledge and strength, and to unite it for the purposeful and centralized actions in the fight against the highly-organized class enemy facing us. We need to have a further development of intraparty democracy, while keeping our communist principles intact." (Ibid.)

These themes were echoed by Mies during 1988, but he also publicly acknowledged for the first time that differences of opinion within the party were proving extremely difficult to reconcile. Thus party news media have reported disagreements, while the DKP leadership has also emphasized that diversity of opinion must "not lead to political confrontation or to splintering of forces" (*Die Welt*, 23 June). As the year ended and the party prepared for its Ninth Congress early in 1989, it was clear that this dilemma was far from resolved, and that the new year would continue to see serious debate concerning the future direction of the DKP.

Dennis L. Bark
Hoover Institution

Austria

Population. 7,577,072
Party. Communist Party of Austria (Kommunistische Partei Österreichs; KPÖ)
Founded. 3 November 1918
Membership. 15,000 (1986 estimate)
Party Chairman. Franz Muhri (b. 1924)
Politburo. 13 members: Walter Baier, Willi Gaisch, Michael Graber, Franz Hager, Anton Hofer, Hans Kalt (secretary of Central Committee), Franz Muhri, Otto Podolsky (Vienna party secretary), Irma Schwager, Walter Silbermayr (secretary of Central Committee), Rudolf Slavik, Susanne Sohn, Ernst Wimmer

Secretariat. 2 members: Hans Kalt and Walter Silbermayr
Central Committee. 72 members
Status. Legal
Last Congress. Twenty-sixth, 25–28 March 1987, in Vienna
Last Election. Federal, 23 November 1986, 0.72 percent, no representation
Publications. *Volksstimme* (People's voice; Michael Graber, editor), KPÖ daily organ, Vienna; *Weg und Ziel* (Path and Goal; Erwin Scharf, editor), KPÖ theoretical monthly, Vienna

1988 saw a continuation of the KPÖ's efforts to exploit the recession in Austria's nationalized industrial sector. The year also brought forth the party's vehement opposition to Austria's possible joining of the European Common Market. *Perestroika* clearly showed the KPÖ's continuing dependence on the Kremlin; throughout the year, positions awaited events and statements made in Moscow. The year was also the 50th anniversary of the *Anschluss* to Hitler's Germany, coinciding with the publication of an international historian's report on the wartime activities of Federal President Kurt Waldheim. Because the Soviet bloc, unlike the United States, continues to ignore Waldheim's activities in the *Wehrmacht*, the coincidence of the two events kept the KPÖ from fully exploiting its 1938 stand, when it was one of the main supporters of Austria's independence. Further, the KPÖ made every effort to liken Austria's joining of the European Community to the *Anschluss*.

In the year's only provincial election, that of Lower Austria (16 October), the KPÖ held its vote share of 0.8 percent (*Wiener Zeitung*, 18 October). Regionally, the party's vote hardly changed. It showed gains in the industrial Wiener Neustadt and the mixed-economy city of Krems (share in both above 2 percent) and losses in the province's future capital, St. Pölten. The KPÖ polled 9 percent in the town of Traisen, where some workers have supported it since the Soviet occupation; 5 percent in the declining coal-mining town of Grünbach and in Zwentendorf, site of the aborted nuclear plant; and 4 percent in the steel town of Ternitz (*Volksstimme*, 18 October).

Earlier in the year (24 January), the KPÖ was successful in the municipal elections in Graz, Austria's second largest city. The party's vote share rose from 1.8 percent in 1983 to 3.1 percent and was three times that in the last federal election (*Volksstimme*, 26 January). In October, with 7.6 percent

of the vote, the KPÖ's union wing came out second in the shop steward election of Austria's main steel plant in Linz (*Volksstimme*, 14 October).

On 23 January, *Volksstimme* published "1988 like 1938: KPÖ Always for Austria," the party manifesto for the 50th anniversary of the *Anschluss*. Embedded in a Marxist interpretation of the interwar period, this document asserts the undeniable fact that the KPÖ stood for an independent Austria from 1938 to 1945. The rest of the manifesto deals with the allegation that finance capital has been increasingly dominating Austria since 1945 and ends with ringing opposition to Austria's entry into the European Community. Earlier (19, 20, and 21 January), *Volksstimme* reported critically, and in part derisively, about discussions of the 50th anniversary held by the Socialist, People's Freedom, and Green parties. The 29 January *Volksstimme* ridicules the $200–$400 figure the Austrian government proposes to give to every resistance fighter. On 19 February, Franz Muhri and Herbert Mies, the chairman of the DKP, used a meeting in Munich as an opportunity to make a joint memorial visit to the Dachau concentration camp.

For the KPÖ, 11 March, the anniversary of the *Anschluss*, began with the prohibition of a memorial exhibit on the pedestrian mall in Krems, a Lower Austrian city (*Volksstimme*, 11 March). The party held its memorial meeting in Vienna's Austria Center. Muhri's speech had little to do with the *Anschluss* or with communist resistance to Hitler, but consisted mostly of general antifascist slogans and a discussion of Austria and the Common Market. It did, however, contain a demand for Waldheim's resignation. (*Volksstimme*, 13 March.)

The KPÖ's schizoid position on Waldheim is shown in the comment on the report of the international commission of historians published in *Volksstimme* (9 February), which is principally an attack on the World Jewish Congress, NATO, and the European Community. On 10 February, however, *Volksstimme* reported that Muhri was asking for Waldheim's resignation, and the next day's comment (*Volksstimme*, 11 February) blames the Austrian government for not demanding it.

Leadership and Organization. On 14 September, the Central Committee elected Rudolf Slavik, the Lower Austrian party chairman, to membership in the Politburo. *Volksstimme* (16 September) mentions no resignation, and it appears that he is the Politburo's thirteenth member.

The KPÖ celebrated its 70th birthday on 3 November. A memorial session in Moscow was attended by Ernst Wimmer and Friedrich Hexmann (*Volksstimme*, 4 November). The special issue of *Volksstimme* (4 November) contained articles by five current (Muhri, Silbermayr, Wimmer, Graber, and Schwager) and one former (Scharf) member of the Politburo. Among sister parties extending greetings were the Romanian CP (*FBIS*, 8 November), the CPSU (*FBIS*, 9 November), and the SED (*FBIS*, 18 November).

Volksstimme (12 February) reported that the Austrian Federal Youth Ring had refused the application of the KJÖ (Austrian Communist Youth) despite strong majority approval. *Volksstimme* reported that only two "blackballs" were necessary to prevent the admission of a group.

The KPÖ's May Day celebrations were held with the motto "For Austria, Against EC *Anschluss*" (*Volksstimme*, 1 May). On September 3 and 4, *Volksstimme* held its annual festival in Vienna's large amusement park, the Prater (*Volksstimme*, 4 and 6 September). The annual meeting of party secretaries came out for a further opening of intraparty discussions (*Volksstimme*, 4 October). An earlier KPÖ organizational initiative held a symposium entitled "New Social Movements" (*Volksstimme*, 23 February). The conference came out against reductions of social programs and unemployment, and for environmental concerns and alternative lifestyles.

Domestic Affairs. In a September 1987 report to the KPÖ Central Committee (*IB*, January), Muhri suggests an alternative budget and tax policy based on a heavy source tax on big financial holdings and a reduction in defense spending. In his *World Marxist Review* article (June), Wimmer reaffirms the KPÖ's commitment both to the struggle for peace and to resistance against the offensive by capital.

Volksstimme lost no opportunity to protest against further layoffs and plant closings in the nationalized steel industry, or the threatening of steel workers' pension rights (27 January, 25 February, 12 March, 5 May, 25, 29, and 30 June, 16 July, 5 August, 2 September, 7 and 21 October). Efforts—apparently not futile—were made to prevent the canceling of some local railroad trains in Lower Austria (*Volksstimme*, 26 April, 14 and 31 May). There were several attacks on actual or rumored privatization, especially where it involved soft stands by the Socialists (*Volksstimme*, 2 March, 10 June, 19 July, 28 September). Also attacked were

the Socialist finance minister's efforts at tax reform, for affecting negatively low-income earners and municipalities (*Volksstimme*, 29 January, 19 March).

In June, Muhri pointed out that the tax policy of the coalition government of the Socialists and the People's Party would lead to a redirection of pensions and a deterioration of health services (*Volksstimme*, 14 June). Soon thereafter, the KPÖ and the GLB (communist trade unions) issued a joint declaration demanding a lowering of profits rather than pensions (*Volksstimme*, 1 and 2 July).

It is of some interest that the KPÖ focused its environmental concerns on preparations for the World's Fair of 1995, which Vienna plans to stage jointly with Budapest (*Volksstimme*, 17 September, 9 October).

Austria's educational system, which still has essentially an upper-class track leading to elite education, was roundly attacked in a *World Marxist Review* article (February) by Julius Mende, member of the CC of the KPÖ. The KPÖ demanded the integration of the education of handicapped children (*Volksstimme*, 23 April) and the establishment of afternoon (i.e., daylong) instruction in all schools, to equalize children's life-chances and to free working families from the necessity of providing after-school care for their children (*Volksstimme*, 11 May).

One of the major policy concerns of the KPÖ was to support the population of Styria in its losing struggle to have Austria purchase Swedish fighter planes, which were to be stationed in Styria (*Volksstimme*, 22 March, 17 and 21 April, 7, 8, 10, 12, and 14 June, 3 July).

When it became obvious that Chancellor Franz Vranitzky, with his occupational background of banker, would become chairman of the Socialist Party (SPÖ), Muhri began to speak of the "bourgeoisification" of the SPÖ (*Volksstimme*, 20 March). After Vranitzky became party chairman, the KPÖ called the SPO "the second People's Party," an allusion to the name of Austria's Conservatives (*Volksstimme*, 17 May).

International Views. Muhri used his annual *World Marxist Review* article (September) to praise Gorbachev's foreign policy, including the INF treaty, to promote the domestic and international environment, and to voice guarded optimism about Austria's international position.

The major international issue for the KPÖ in 1988 was the Austrian government's serious consideration of joining the European Community before the solidification of the Common Market in 1992. As was mentioned already, the 50th anniversary of the *Anschluss* of Austria to Hitler Germany was used, time and time again, to fight Austria's "EC-*Anschluss*." The campaign was started by Walter Silbermayr on 20 January (*Volksstimme*, 21 January): "Just as the Communists, in 1938, were the only ones who took a stand against the *Anschluss*, so we call today most decisively for resistance to the anti-Austrian forces that prepare the *Anschluss* to the European Community." On March 31, Muhri gave three reasons for fighting the EC-*Anschluss* (*Volksstimme*, 1 April): (1) Austria has fewer unemployed than the European Community; (2) Joining the community would violate Austria's neutrality; and (3) The community splits Europe. At the same time, the KPÖ issued a memorandum "EC-*Anschluss, no*–KPÖ for Austria," illustrated with a cute picture of a big fish about to swallow a little one (*Volksstimme*, 2 April). The Upper Austrian KPÖ coined the slogan "Bitter almonds for Austria, honey for the EC-multinationals" (*Volksstimme*, 4 May).

The *Volksstimme* of 25 June printed a *Pravda* article by Muhri, in which he points to the incompatibility of Austria's EC-*Anschluss* with Austrian neutrality, unless Austria were invited to become a partial member. He also points to the incompatibility of free movement of capital within the EC with the prohibition, established in the Austrian State Treaty of 1955, against former German property falling once again into German hands. *Volksstimme* devoted much space to the issue of joining the community, with musings over just what Vranitzky was told at his Moscow visit with regard to Austria's neutrality (*Volksstimme*, 13 October) and a report of former chancellor Kreisky's continued doubts about the compatibility Austria's membership in the EC and its neutrality (*Volksstimme*, 16 October). Much was made of the possible incompatibility of the EC with Austrian federalism (*Volksstimme*, 15 October, 5 November), a topic not always of interest to the KPÖ.

Meanwhile, Ernst Wimmer made several statements that achievements in nuclear disarmament are not a reason for relaxing vigilance (*Volksstimme*, 19 May; *IB*, June). The KPÖ welcomed Warsaw pact disarmament proposals (*Volksstimme*, 17 and 19 July).

In regard to *perestroika*, *Volksstimme* (6 April) proudly reported that Gorbachev's remarks to Muhri, Silbermayr, and Hans Steiner about the CPSU's responsibility to all communists became the principal item of Moscow's *Vremia* newscast. Werner Pirker, Moscow correspondent of *Volksstimme*, sent a number of articles about *perestroika* discussions (14, 16 April).

On the eve of the 19th CPSU Congress, Muhri made positive remarks on *perestroika* on the *Vremia* newscast (*Volksstimme*, 28 June). In his first report (*Volksstimme*, 3 July) on the congress after his return to Vienna, Muhri said:

> Of particular importance is the decision on a comprehensive concept for the reform of the political system, for the unfolding of socialist democracy with the aim of a still considerably greater participation of the masses in the decisions and the rearrangement of tasks that have been set, as well as a further better realization of social, political, and personal human rights.

In a concluding column on the congress (*Volksstimme*, 19 July), Pirker wrote: "In the long run, there is no room for socialism without openness. For nothing is more demoralizing than the steady chasm between word and deed." On 28 August, Ulrich Perzinger dismissed as superficial comparisons between *perestroika* and Dubcek's "Prague Spring" of 1968.

The KPÖ Politburo included the following in its declaration on *perestroika* (*Volksstimme*, 22 September; translated in *FBIS*, 23 September):

> We have to become aware that perestroika and its effects are opening up new opportunities for us. In this respect, we have to overcome any narrow-mindedness. However, in order to make use of these opportunities we also have to face new and great demands.
>
> It is probably true that in one case or the other we do not yet live up to these demands. It is, however, decisive to adhere to and apply in life the basic line that has been developed: in the newspapers and in discussions in and outside the party. Then we will certainly also be able to make our party benefit from the new, more open and favorable climate established by perestroika.

In line with *glasnost'*, *Volksstimme* (6 October) reported triumphantly that "news from the Central Committee of the CPSU" will be published henceforth. In an interview on *perestroika* (*Volksstimme*, 8 October), Muhri told Graber that the KPÖ stands strongly behind *perestroika*, that it does not lead to capitalism, that the KPÖ began its own *perestroika* as early as 1982 (!), and that it was about time for Austrian Socialists to revise their view that communism equals fascism. In the *Volksstimme* of 28 October, Pirker reported from Moscow about the initial experiences there with competitive elections.

Volksstimme showed itself most appreciative of the closer relations between Austria and the German Democratic Republic. This appreciation even included the visit of the GDR's foreign minister Oskar Fischer to President Waldheim (19 May).

International Activities. On 4 March, Muhri, Silbermayr, and Steiner were received by Gorbachev for a two and one-half hour talk (*Volksstimme*, 5 and 6 March; *Pravda*, 5 March). Gorbachev impressed on the Austrians the functions of, and need for, *perestroika*. On 29 March, Carinthian and Triestine Communists met in Trieste (*Volksstimme*, 31 March), and two weeks later, Hans Kalt visited Belgrade (*FBIS*, 15 April).

During the Reagan-Gorbachev summit in Moscow, on 27 May, Vasil Bil'ák, secretary of the CC of the CSSR CP, and Muhri met in Bratislava. They gave strong support to the summit and discussed interparty relations (*FBIS*, 27 May, 2 and 3 June; *Volksstimme*, 29 and 31 May). On 18 October, Miloš Jakeš, the new general secretary of the CPCA, and Bil'ák, received Muhri and Otto Podolsky in Prague (*FBIS*, 19 October; *Volksstimme*, 19 October).

On 18 November, Günter Mittag, secretary of the CP of the SED, visited Muhri in Vienna and informed him of the economic agreement concluded with Chancellor Vranitzky (*Volksstimme*, 22 October; *Neues Deutschland*, 22/23 October). On the same day, Mittag met Styrian governor Josef Krainer in Graz to discuss economic relations. Two weeks earlier, on 5 November, Károly Grósz, the new chairman of the Hungarian Communist party, met Muhri in Vienna (*Volksstimme*, 6 November; *FBIS*, 7 November). Finally, on 26 November, Polish prime minister Mieczyslaw Rakowski and Muhri met in Vienna (*FBIS*, 28 November).

Trade with the East. In January, VOEST-Alpine received orders for steel pipes from the USSR, and for slag-processing apparatus from Poland (*Volksstimme*, 27 January). On 22 July, *Kurier* (Vienna) reported a marked increase in Austrian-Soviet trade (*FBIS*, 25 July). In October, Friedrich Draszcyk, the trade counselor of the Austrian embassy in Moscow, told *Volksstimme* (9 October) that there had been a brisk increase in Austrian-Soviet

trade, and that 75 leading persons of Austria's economy would accompany Chancellor Vranitzky on his visit to Moscow.

Frederick C. Engelmann
University of Alberta

Belgium

Population. 9,880,522
Party. Belgian Communist Party (Parti communiste de Belgique; Kommunistische Partij van Belgie; PCB/KPB)
Founded. 1921
Membership. Under 5,000
Leadership. National president: Louis Van Geyt; vice president: Claude Renard; Flemish-section president: Ludo Loose; Francophone-section president: Robert Dussart; Brussels-section president: Anne Herscovici
Politburo. 14 members: Louis Van Geyt; Pierre Beauvois, Robert Dussart, Marcel Levaux, Jacques Moins, Jacques Nagels, Claude Renard, Jules Vercaigne (Francophone); Jan Debrouwere, Jos De Geyter, Miel Dullaert, Roel Jacobs, Ludo Loose, Jef Turf (Flemish)
National Secretariat. Marcel Couteau, Robert Dussart, Daniel Fedrigo (Francophone); Miel Dullaert, Roel Jacobs, Ludo Loose (Flemish)
Francophone Bureau. Didier Bajura, Pierre Beauvois, Marcel Bergen, Marcel Couteau, Robert Dussart, Daniel Fedrigo, Michel Godard, Marcel Levaux, Rosine Lewin, Maurice Magis (son), Jacques Moins, Jacques Nagels, Susa Nudelhole, Claude Renard, Jean-Marie Simon (Liège), Jules Vercaigne, Josiane Vrand
Flemish Bureau. Jos De Geyter, Filip Delmotte, Miel Dullaert, Roel Jacobs, Ludo Loose, Dirk Vonckx, Georges De Clercq, Claude De Smet, Hugo De Witte, Bernard Claeys, Tejo Cockx, Willy Minnebo
Brussels Bureau. Michel Godard, Roel Jacobs, Paul Marcus, Patrick Vanderhoeven, and Jacques Moins
Central Committee. 72 members
Status. Legal

Last Congress. Twenty-fifth National, 18–20 April 1986. Extraordinary Congress, 18 June 1988
Last Election. Parliamentary, 13 December 1987, negligible percentage of votes, no representation
Publications. *Drapeau Rouge*, daily party organ in French, André Gerardin, editor; *Rode Vaan*, Dutch-language weekly, Jef Turf, editor

Of the many factors that led to the decline of the Belgian Communist Party, none was more significant than its failure to respond effectively to either the increasing importance of language and region, or the declining importance of social class in postwar Belgium. During the last twenty years, the ethnoterritorial differences separating the Flemish north from the French-speaking Walloons to the south and the francophone majority in the capital have become the central axis of Belgian politics, leading to the regionalization of other Belgian parties and the revision of the Belgian constitution in federalist directions. Yet the PCB/KPB did not free its Flemish and francophone wings from central tutelage until 1986. Nor did it adequately respond to the declining appeal outside of Walloon Belgium of class-based platforms in a country where postwar prosperity has made postindustrial issues concerned with the quality of life increasingly more salient, and in which a vigorous socialist party has provided an attractive alternative on the left to an increasingly isolated communist party in economically declining Wallonia.

Because of its failure to adapt, the PCB/KPB has steadily faded even in its Walloon political base, where it received nearly one vote in ten in 1965 but less than three percent of the vote in the 1987 parliamentary election and the 1988 municipal elections. Its share of the national vote has similarly dropped in the past decade, from 2.3 percent in 1981 to 1.2 percent in 1985, to 0.8 percent (51,074 votes nationwide) in 1987 (*Le Soir*, 2 April 1986; *Drapeau Rouge*, 15 December 1987). Its last parliamentary seat was lost in 1985, reducing the party, in the words of its president, Louis Van Geyt, to "a nonparliamentary role" in Belgian politics (*DR*, 15 December 1987). Even worse from Van Geyt's perspective, the party's refusal to collaborate with noncommunist political forces has meant that "the emergent social movements which championed peace, environmental protection, the cause of the dispossessed strata of the population and solidarity with the oppressed and exploited Third World Peoples, arose outside or next to the working class movements and historical left organizations rather than on their basis" (*WMR*, February).

Party Organization and Structure. During 1988, the party accelerated its already-begun efforts to address the causes of its decline. Party organs highlighted a variety of stories and issues outside of traditional class politics (violence against women; the importance of the environment; the need for an energy policy; the impact of science and technology on society), as well as articles stressing class issues (solidarity with the foreign workers battling racism in Belgium; solidarity with oppressed Belgian workers). Inside the party, self-criticism intended to reduce the generation gap between the traditional leadership and the party's youth corps was also continued. Efforts to achieve the latter had begun in earnest with the decision at the 1986 congress to include more of the party's younger members in its national and regional bureaus, and were stepped up following the party's electoral setbacks in 1987. Thus, the new year began with the publication in the *World Marxist Review* of a dialogue on the generation gap between two members of the party's Central Committee: Jean Blume, 73 years of age; and Eric Remacle, the 26-year-old chair of the Communist Youth of Belgium (*WMR*, March). Still, the party's principal responses to its situation were the 1988 changes in its internal structure and electoral tactics.

At an Extraordinary Congress in June, approval was given to the proposal of a CC special commission to reorganize the party into three regional components. The action was justified on the grounds that the federalist trends in the state and its ethnoterritorial communities required a more flexible party structure. Thus, although the central institutions were left intact in order to maintain unity on such policy matters as foreign affairs and European integration and to facilitate international contacts, the intermediate, regional level between the party's grass-roots organizations and its national leadership was reconstituted. To its Flemish and francophone divisions was added a bilingual Brussels section under the presidency of Anne Herscovici, a 38-year-old party worker previously little known outside of Brussels. (*Pravda*, 19 June; *FBIS*, 22 June; *WMR*, September; *Le Soir*, 22 June.) Attempts to obtain details of Herscovici's background and status in the party's central institutions, and of the effect of the party's reorganization on the composition of its Flemish and francophone bureaus, were unsuccessful at the time of this article's deadline.

This 1988 reorganization was presaged in 1982, when the party adopted a federal structure permitting regional congresses to be held by its Flemish and francophone sections, and was brought a step nearer in 1986, when the party's congress recognized the right of the party's wings to adapt to regional issues (*YICA*, 1987). In a similar fashion, the 1988 changes in the party's approach to electoral politics also may be seen as the culmination of previous developments, rather than a radical shift in party policy. Flemish members were already on record as favoring tactical alliances with other leftist groups and had occasionally pursued this tactic in local elections. Nevertheless, the official decision by party leaders in 1988 to court electoral allies and the pursuit of this strategy by the party's Brussels and Walloon wings in the 1988 communal elections did represent important departures from prior party policy and practice, albeit departures toward which the party moved with some last-minute ambivalence.

Although Van Geyt had long been critical of the former policy of rejecting those who were not communist, his immediate response to the party's 1987 setbacks was to reject both the idea of creating a bloc composed of the PCB and smaller Belgian parties, and any strategy of fusion with other leftists (*WMR*, February; *DR*, 14 December 1987). What thus evolved in 1988 was an open-door approach to short-term electoral alliances, encouraged by a January CC resolution that called upon local organizations to advance their efforts to unite with left-wing forces, including the Ecologists and Socialists. It was also encouraged by example; specifically, Van Geyt's invitation in May to all communist parties representing foreign workers in Belgium to meet with him to discuss the policy implications of the formation of a Socialist-Catholic government. (*WMR*, March; *DR*, 2 May.)

Abetted by the party's reorganization in June, the approach was hastily embraced by local organizations campaigning in the 1988 communal elections—most conspicuously in the pursuit by the newly-formed Brussels bureau of an "Axe rouge-vert" with willing ecological parties (*DR*, 2 May, 19 June). Elsewhere in francophone Belgium the PCB joined with a variety of small and large parties on the left, including the Socialist Party, in offering common lists. It also closely monitored the formation of the extensively Socialist, but officially nonpartisan movement, Wallonia, Region of Europe,

led by Jose Happart, the French-speaking mayor in the Fourons whose unwillingness to learn Flemish began the series of crises that eventually led to Belgium's 1987 elections. (*DR*, 6 and 18 April, 6 July; *Le Soir*, 20 June.)

By the year's end, however, none of these steps had either eased the PCB's strained relations with the Socialist Party or improved its electoral fortunes. The Socialists' decision to join the Catholics in forming a government was viewed by many PCB officials as an error that could be exploited by the PCB, given the unpopularity in Brussels of the proposed constitutional reforms that the new government was pledged to enact. Hence, cooperation between the Socialist and Communist parties in the communal elections was not very uncommon. Moreover, in the elections themselves, with or without allies the Belgian Communist Party's vote continued to slip. Typical were the returns in the key province of Liège, where the PCB did slightly better than it had in the 1987 national elections (3.03 percent of the vote, versus 2.73 percent), but much worse than in the previous communal elections. (*DR*, 11 October, 29–30 October.)

Domestic Politics. The small size and electoral weakness of the PCB/KPB relegated the party to an on-looker/commentator role with respect to the country's principal political events in 1988: (1) the search for a new government following the indecisive 1987 vote; (2) the further regionalization of the Belgian state; (3) the efforts of a foreign investor to gain control of Belgium's largest company, the Société Générale de Belgique (SGB); and (4) the national effort to cope with a 13 percent unemployment rate.

The lengthy search for a new government and the subsequent passage of the constitutional package upon whose terms the government was eventually formulated, provided targets for party criticism for more than half of the year (e.g., *DR*, 13 July). They may have provided as well the catalyst for the party's decision to create a separate bureau for Brussels, which was to receive its own regional executive under the proposed constitutional revision. However, in both instances the PCB/KPB could do little more than react editorially, given its lack of any parliamentary representation. Similarly, although the country's high unemployment rate encouraged the party to adopt the pressure-group tactic of lobbying the governing parties to fulfill their election pledge to reduce unemployment, there is no evidence to indicate that concern with unemployment produced more; for example, that it led to improved relations with either Belgium's socialist parties or Socialist Trade Union Federation.

Of the major developments confronting Belgium, it was the efforts of an Italian financier to gain a controlling, 25-percent share of SGB that most stirred opinion, and that provided party newspapers with their best opportunity to apply doctrine to domestic politics (*DR*, 27 February–2 March, 25–26 April, 24–26 June; *CSM*, 29 January, 21 April; *WSJ*, 25 February). From the party's perspective, this takeover attempt, eventually fought off by a Franco-Belgium consortium, and the Swiss acquisition of Côte d'Or, a major European chocolate manufacturer located outside Brussels, provided vivid illustration of the dangers of—and need for control over—transnational capital (*DR*, 11 and 27 March, 13, 22 and 27 September, 4 October).

Foreign Policy. The Belgian Communist party was more in control of its agenda in its relations with communist states and other communist parties. In April, Van Geyt visited Bulgaria to discuss the implications of the ratification of the INF treaty for communist party policies, stressing the need for all weapons systems to be reduced to the lowest possible level to guarantee peace in Europe (*FBIS-EEU*, 4 and 5 April). The following month, Van Geyt endorsed a Czech proposal to create a zone of cooperation and good neighborly relations along the boundary between NATO and Warsaw Pact states, and later met in Brussels with a candidate of the Czech Central Committee who was visiting Belgium (*Rudé Právo*, 10 May; *Pravda*, in Slovak, 27 May; *FBIS-EEU*, 13 May, 2 June). Finally, the fall witnessed Van Geyt journeying to Madrid to discuss Eurocommunism's recent electoral setbacks with Julio Anguita, general secretary of the Communist Party of Spain, and meeting in Brussels with East German party delegates visiting Belgium (*DR*, 16 September; *Neues Deutschland*, 26 and 31 October).

In part, Van Geyt was able to piggyback on Belgium's active diplomatic relations with communist states in 1988, which included not only the visits of delegations from East Germany and other Warsaw bloc states, communist parties, and youth organizations to Brussels, but also the execution of Sino-Belgian agreements on cooperation in the natural sciences and mutual judicial assistance in civilian cases (*FBIS-EEU*, 25 January, 2 September; *Neues Deutschland*, 24 February, 4 March, 18 and 19 May). However, the Belgian Communist Party's diplomatic advances also reflect a pursuit of its goals of heightening its visibility and increasing its ties with other communist parties.

Throughout the year, the party's foreign-policy activities continued themes of previous years, especially in its emphasis on the need for disarmament and its support for Mikhail Gorbachev's internal and external policies (*YICA*, 1987 and 1986). In stressing the need for peace and arms reductions, extended in 1988 to include conventional as well as nuclear forces and the development of a nuclear-free zone in Europe, the party was continuing its emphasis on the link between arms reductions and the financing of its domestic, "peace economy" program (*WMR*, February). The party's emphasis on peace and disarmament also provided a basis for its applause for Gorbachev's foreign policy in general, and its denunciation of SDI and its support of Gorbachev's Moscow Summit, Poland visit, and United Nations initiative, in particular (*DR*, 31 May–2 June, 12 July, 2–3 October). Other familiar policy themes, such as support for *perestroika* in the Soviet Union and condemnation of imperialism in South Africa, were not abandoned, but they were given much less attention in the party's organs in 1988 than in the previous year.

Joseph R. Rudolph, Jr.
Towson State University

Cyprus

Population. 691,966 (80 percent Greek; 18 percent Turkish)

Party. Progressive Party of the Working People (Anorthotikon Komma Ergazomenou Laou; AKEL)

Date Founded. 1926 (AKEL, 1941)

Membership. 15,000 (Source: Official AKEL statement, 1988)

Composition. Sex: 24 percent women; nationality: all from Greek Cypriot community; age: 30 percent under 30 years old; occupation: 67 percent industrial workers and employees; 20 percent peasants and middle class

General Secretary. Dimitris Christofias

Politburo. 13 members: Dimitris Christofias, Dinos Constantinou, Andreas Fantis, George Christodoulides, Michalis Poumpouris, Donis Christofinis, Loucas Aletras, Andreas Ziartides, Christos Petas, Kyriacos Christou, Andreas Michaelides, Lakis Theodoulou, Antonis Christodoulou

Secretariat. Dimitris Christofias, Dinos Constantinou, Andreas Fantis, George Christodoulides, Michalis Poumpouris, Donis Christofinis, Loucas Aletras

Central Control Committee. Michalis Olympios, chairman

Status. Legal

Last Congress. Sixteenth, 26–30 November 1986; extraordinary, 20 December 1987, to endorse George Vassiliou as presidential candidate

Last Election. 1985, 27.4 percent, 15 of 56 seats in Parliament

Auxiliary Organizations. Pan-Cyprian Workers' Federation (PEO), 75,000 members, Andreas Ziartidis, President, Pavlos Digglis, general secretary; United Democratic Youth Organization (EDON), 14,000 members; Confederation of Women's Organizations (POGO); Pan-Cyprian Peace Council; Pan-Cyprian Federation of Students and Young Professionals; Union of Greek Cypriots in England, 1,200 members (considered London branch of AKEL); Pan-Cypriot National Organization of Secondary Students; Cypriot Farmers' Union

Publications. *Kharavyi* (Dawn), AKEL daily newspaper; *AKEL News Letter* (in English), periodically; *Neos Democratis*, AKEL monthly theoretical magazine; *Ergatiko Vima* (Workers' stride), PEO weekly; *Neolaia* (Youth) EDON weekly; *Kyria* (Mrs.), POGO bimonthly; *Yeni Duzen* (New order), Turkish Cypriot pro-AKEL daily newspaper; *Parikiaki* (Ethnic community), AKEL weekly (London)

Background. Cyprus has been effectively partitioned since 1974 when Turkey landed troops on the northern part of the island. The Turkish Cypriots called Ankara's long-awaited action their "liberation," after having been surrounded in enclaves since the outbreak of ethnic violence eleven years earlier. On the other hand, the Greek Cypriots insist that it was an illegal invasion that brought about the seizure and occupation of over one-third of the island. Removal of the Turkish troops, as well as of thousands of subsequent settlers from mainland Turkey, are issues that confound the ongoing inter-communal talks between the Turkish Cypriot leader, Rauf Denktash, and the newly elected president of the Republic of Cyprus, George Vassiliou. In 1983 President Denktash unilaterally declared the independent Turkish Republic of Northern Cyprus (TRNC), which is recognized only by Turkey. The mainland and island Greeks refuse to recognize the existence of a legitimate state north of the "green line" buffer zone, which has been patrolled by a United Nations peacekeeping force for the past 24 years. The Republic of Cyprus has maintained an economic boycott against the occupied northern part of Cyprus, but the Turkish Cypriots are determined to make the best of what they have.

The AKEL party operates only among the Greek Cypriots in the south, and it has consistently proven to be the island's best organized grass-roots political party, capable of delivering about a third of the electorate in any election. With the backing of the AKEL, Vassiliou was able to win the presidential election in February with 52 percent of the popular vote. For a first-time office seeker, this was truly an outstanding performance, since he also ran as an independent without any formal party backing. While the AKEL maintained that Vassiliou was the best of the four candidates, the communists did not lose sight of the fact that the president's mother and father were life-long revolutionaries and founding members of the AKEL party as well. Even though Vassiliou received university training in Budapest, he has since become a millionaire in the economic research business on the booming island of Cyprus. His family background and his effective support of the AKEL have prompted editorial insinuations about Vassiliou's future course during his five-year presidency. To this criticism, Vassiliou has responded in a matter-of-fact way by saying: "To some extent it was only to be expected that the right-wing press in the West would react guardedly to AKEL's supporting me, because the West does not know the political and social reality in Cyprus." (*WMR*, June.)

While the AKEL is not officially banned in the TRNC, it does not have a formal organization within the Turkish Cypriot community. Communist sentiment in the TRNC flourishes under the umbrella of the Republican Turkish Party (CTP). Founded in 1970, the CTP is the oldest political party in the Turkish community and polled 22 percent of the vote in the 1976 elections in the north. Ozker Ozgur, the CTP chairman, describes his party as "progressive," but it consistently echoes the AKEL line against "American imperialism." In fact, the CTP was the only political party in all of Cyprus that sent a message of condolence to AKEL upon the death of AKEL's general secretary in April. Supposedly the Soviet Union supports the CTP via Bulgaria, where CTP's Revolutionary Youth Organization (DGD) regularly attends conferences. If the north and south of Cyprus were reunited in a future "federated republic," the combined electoral strength of the Greek and Turkish Cypriot communists could produce a majority of the votes in any presidential election under such a novel government.

Leadership and Organization. The AKEL is reputed to be a tightly controlled apparatus, structured on the principle of democratic centralism. The highest body is the congress, which is convened every four years. The Sixteenth Congress, held in 1986, coincided with the 60th anniversary of the first party congress of the founding Communist Party of Cyprus (KKK). All the officials of the governing hierarchy are elected at the party congress, as was the general secretary, Ezekias Papaioannou, who had led the party since 1949. On 10 April that 79-year-old careerist finally succumbed to a chronic lung and heart malady, for which he had been treated over the years in Moscow. A month before he died, he had expressed his desire to resign because of his failing health and to "hand over the party tiller to a younger comrade." (Nicosia Domestic Service, 22 March). Before he expired, Papaioannou finished his memoirs, which were published posthumously later in the year in a 217-page Greek language edition.

At its plenary meeting on 22 April, the AKEL Central Committee elected Dimitris Christofias as its general secretary (*WMR*, July). At age 42, Christofias became the youngest general secretary of a communist party in Europe and simultaneously became the inspiration for the "new look" in the communist party of Cyprus. In his first address to the party's Central Committee plenum as general secretary, Christofias promised to "support President Vassiliou in the implementation of his platform . . . and [to] struggle for a rapprochement between Greek and Turkish Cypriots" (Nicosia Domestic Service, 23 April). After the election of Christofias, the AKEL—reflecting the *glasnost'* in the Soviet Union—revealed its official party membership as 15,000 card-carrying members, which is some 3,000 more than previously estimated by outsiders (Personal communication to author from AKEL headquarters, Nicosia, September 26).

The four dissident journalists who seceded from the AKEL party's official newspaper *Kharavyi* in 1987 have started a new daily publication called *Embros* (Forward). While the editor in chief of *Embros*, Andreas Kannaouros, declared that his newspaper and his three colleagues still belonged to the "communist trunk," the AKEL leadership saw things differently. In September, the AKEL Central Committee decided to expel the four "indefinitely" from the party (*Cyprus Mail*, 11 September). The publishers of *Embros* were accused by the AKEL leaders of "violating the bylaws of the party whereby the members are obliged to respect the decisions of the Central Committee and other guiding bodies" (ibid.). *Embros* was viewed as a "second guiding center which undermines the unity of the party" and its "adherence to the principles of Marxism and Leninism" (ibid.). The editor, Mr. Kannaouros, called this AKEL decision "a live example of Stalinism at a time that this phenomenon of the terrible distortion of socialist ideas is dying" (ibid.).

Domestic Party Affairs. The AKEL support of the successful campaign of George Vassiliou in the February presidential elections was the salient event on the domestic front in the early part of the year. The new president acknowledged his communist support by stating in an interview published in the *World Marxist Review* that "AKEL's role in the socio-political affairs of Cyprus is quite considerable." Particularly at the time of Britain's colonial rule, when it was the only organized political force in the country, the AKEL "made a great contribution to the social and political progress of our country." He went on to say that to understand the current Cypriot political scene, one must know AKEL's policy "which does not at present call for the transformation of society, and therefore has no problem of cooperating politically with parties or persons of different ideologies." He concluded by saying that "what is of paramount importance for AKEL is to solve the Cyprus problem," i.e., to achieve the reunification and demilitarization of the island (*WMR*, June). The AKEL agrees with the new president that the internal aspects, viz. the constitutional and territorial issues, should be the object of intercommunal negotiations between the Greek and Turkish Cypriots.

In addition, the external aspects of the Cyprus problem must also be settled before there can be a solution of its internal aspects. According to both the AKEL leadership and President Vassiliou, these issues include: "the withdrawal of all Turkish troops and settlers, safeguarding the right of all refugees to return to their homes and securing international guarantees for the country's sovereignty." The president and AKEL are in agreement that, since "these issues concern international law, they should be settled by an international conference" (ibid.). If the international conference ploy is successfully carried out, the Cyprus issue would be moved out of the NATO orbit to a forum where the Soviet Union would have an important voice in the ensuing deliberations.

A major breakthrough in the resumption of the stalled intercommunal talks between the Cypriot Greeks and the Cypriot Turks came in August when Denktash and Vassiliou met in Geneva with the U.N. Secretary General Perez de Cuellar. The two leaders agreed to resume the intercommunal dialogue with a target date of June 1989 for arriving at a resolution. This decision fulfilled a campaign promise of President Vassiliou and one of the prerequisites for a solution declared by the AKEL (Nicosia Domestic Service, 24 August). The first round of the talks took place in Nicosia between 16 September and 7 November, but these only served to tell the world that the two sides remain far apart on the major issues. After a fruitless meeting in New York in late November, the two leaders agreed to open a second round of talks on 19 December in Nicosia, which would seek to develop a "wide range of options" for dealing with all the issues between them. (*NYT*, 25 November.)

International Views, Positions, and Activities. During his first visit to the Soviet Union as the AKEL general secretary, Christofias met in May with Anatolii Dobrynin, secretary of the Central Committee of the CPSU. During the meeting, the two sides discussed issues related to "disarmament, the elimination of nuclear weapons, and efforts to ensure international security" (TASS, 21 May). The joint communiqué lauded the signing of the treaty to eliminate intermediate and short-range missiles and saw it as "an achievement of the new political thinking and peace initiatives of the Soviet Union." Also, the signing of the Geneva accords on Afghanistan "was an important contribution to a political settlement of an existing regional conflict." The communiqué continued: "Making the Mediterranean a zone of security and cooperation would promote the common cause of peace and international détente." Furthermore, the communiqué stressed "that the convening of a representative international conference within the U.N. framework could constitute

a significant factor for a settlement of the Cyprus issue." It noted finally that "both parties will continue to struggle for the further development of multifaceted cooperation between Cyprus and the Soviet Union." (ibid.). The AKEL delegation spoke highly of the policy of *perestroika* and noted that "the destinies of peace and civilization and the national liberation and social emancipation of peoples depended on the success of the changes in the Soviet Union" (*WMR*, September).

The funeral of Ezekias Papaioannou in April was an appropriate occasion for fraternal parties to meet on the island of Cyprus. Delegations from seventeen communist parties attended the event, the highlight of which was a funeral address by President Vassiliou. The delegation of the CPSU was personally received by President Vassiliou at his residence before the funeral (Nicosia Domestic Service, 13 April). Two weeks later, Vassiliou was invited to make a future state visit to the Soviet Union and the president "accepted the invitation and expressed his warm thanks" (ibid., 5 May).

In June, an AKEL delegation visited Czechoslovakia, and later that same month another AKEL delegation, led by General Secretary Christofias, went to Bulgaria, where they were received by General Secretary Todor Zhivkov (BTA, 29 June). A parliamentary delegation, which included the AKEL members, made an official visit to Nicaragua in October and was received by President Daniel Ortega (Nicosia Domestic Service, 19 October). A similar parliamentary delegation went to Syria in November and were met by President Hafiz al-Asad (ibid., 2 November). General Secretary Christofias led a delegation to Romania in November and conveyed to President Ceauşescu "warm greetings from President Vassiliou" (*Kharavyi*, 12 November).

Biography. *Dimitris Christofias.* Born into a working-class family on 29 August 1946, Christofias became active in politics at the age of 14. In 1964, after graduating from a Nicosia high school, he joined the AKEL, the Pancyprian Federation of Labour (PEO) and the United Democratic Youth Organisation (EDON), becoming a member of the EDON Central Council in 1969. Christofias majored in philosophy and history and holds a doctors' degree. Elected general secretary of EDON in 1977, he remained in that office until 1987, simultaneously serving in several responsible posts within the party and becoming an alternate and then a full member of the AKEL Central Committee. In

July 1986 he was elected an alternate member of the CC Political Bureau, a full member after the 16th Congress of the AKEL, and an AKEL Central Committee secretary a year later. In April 1988 Christofias served as acting general secretary of the AKEL Central Committee. (*WMR*, July.)

T. W. Adams
Washington, D.C.

Denmark

Population. 5,125,676 (July 1988)
Party. Communist Party of Denmark (Danmarks Kommunistiske Parti; DKP)
Founded. 1919
Membership. Under 10,000 (estimated, including youth and student fronts)
Chairman. Ole Sohn
General Secretary. Poul Emanuel
Executive Committee. 16 members: Ole Sohn, Ib Nørlund, Poul Emanuel, Bernard Jeune, Kurt Kristensen, Dan Lundrup, Freddy Madsen, Anette Nielsen, Bo Rosschou, Frank Aaen (editor *Land og Folk*), Anker Schjerning, Rita Sørensen, Inger Rasmussen, Sten Parker Sørensen, Harry Osborn (last 6 are new in 1987). 1 vacancy
Secretariat. 6 members: Ole Sohn, Poul Emanuel, Frank Aaen, and Bo Rosschou. 1 vacancy
Central Committee. 50 members, 17 candidate members
Status. Legal
Last Congress. Twenty-eighth, April 1987
Last Election. 10 May 1988, 0.8 percent, no representation
Auxiliary Organizations. Communist Youth of Denmark (Danmarks Kommunistiske Ungdom; DKU), Niklas Gudmundsson, chair; Communist Students of Denmark (Danmarks Kommunistiske Studenter; KOMM.S.), Lars K. Christensen, chair
Publications. *Land og Folk* (Nation and people), daily circulation 6,500 weekdays and 13,000 weekends; *Tiden-Verden Rund* (Times around the world), theoretical monthly; *Fremad* (Forward), DKU monthly

1988 was another year of political surprises in Denmark, including a snap general election on 10 May, only eight months after the last parliamentary election. The DKP benefitted little from the excitement, and its voter support declined further. The new DKP chair, Ole Sohn, has sought to guide the party through two general elections during his first year in office, but without any signs of success. To his credit Sohn realizes that the old formulas no longer serve communist interests, and he has cautiously sought new allies on the left. The DKP cooperated electorally with the Left Socialists (Venstresocialisterne; VS), who also continued their slide into oblivion, as well as with the miniscule Trotskyite Socialist Workers Party (Socialistisk Arbejderparti; SAP) and the idiosyncratic leftist Humanists (Det humanistisk Parti; Hum). By the end of the year, little had come of this new tactical alliance intended to surmount the 2 percent threshold required for a party to be proportionally represented in the unicameral Danish Parliament (Folketing).

The May elections ended for the time being the brief, if colorful, parliamentary debut of the Common Course Party (Arbejderpartiet Fælles Kurs; CCP), Denmark's latest Marxist sect. Under the flamboyant leadership of Seamen's Union chief (and former DKP member) Preben Møller Hansen, the CCP had just exceeded the threshold in September 1987. In May the CCP received only 1.9 percent and lost its four seats. The sudden election caught some of the other sectarian Marxist parties uncertified for a ballot position, but none of the radical sectarian parties gained. The VS, torn by continuing internal strife, saw its vote fall back to 0.6 percent, a decline of more than 50 percent from September 1987.

The independent Marxist Socialist People's Party (Socialistiske Folkeparti; SF) broke its record of continuing gains with a loss of 1.6 percent, which dropped it to 13 percent. The decline cost it three seats, but the SF remains the third-largest parliamentary party, having 24 seats. The setback postponed serious consideration of the much-discussed possibility of a coalition between the SF and the reformist Social Democratic Party (Socialdemokraterne; SDP). The latter gained a seat and 0.6 percent of the vote, and with its 55 seats and 29.9 percent of the vote, it remains Denmark's largest party. It governed with the support of the SF in 1966–1967 and 1971–1973, but now would require additional support from a nonsocialist party to repeat the experiment. Altogether, the socialist bloc (SF and SDP) lost two seats; six seats if the CCP is added to the bloc.

Following the 1987 election, conservative prime minister Poul Schlüter's minority coalition government continued in office, supported by uncertain votes from two alternative nonsocialist parties: the centrist Radical Liberals (Det radikale venstre) and the ultraconservative Progress Party (Fremskridtsparti). The new SDP leader continued to harass the government, especially on security matters. This violation of a 40-year-old security-policy consensus, which extends to NATO membership (with special Danish peacetime reservations on nuclear weapons and foreign bases) and encompassed all parties but the Marxist ones, became an increasingly emotional issue after the Schlüter government was formed in September 1982. SDP challenges in security and foreign policies were in part stimulated by a desire to hold on to an increasingly pacifist SDP left-wing and in part intended to increase the possibility of an alternative socialist governing coalition. Although the SDP leadership has never challenged NATO membership *per se*, it may believe a passive role in the alliance would encourage the growing foreign-policy pragmatism of the SF.

In April, the DP (supported by the SF) proposed that NATO ships visiting Denmark be required to be free of nuclear weapons. Although such a restriction is not so rigid as its New Zealand precedent, both the Americans and the British declared that it would render them unable to support Denmark in case of war. After a 48-hour period of complex parliamentary maneuvers, the SF managed to force a vote on the SDP resolution before a milder governmental measure could be considered. The measure passed (in part because of Radical Liberal support), and for the 23rd time the Schlüter government found parliament dictating security-policy restrictions. Schlüter quickly took up the challenge and called for new parliamentary elections. Some leftists looked forward to the elections because, although Danes continue to favor NATO membership, there is little support for any strategy calling for the use of nuclear weapons.

Economic issues were also a major part of the election campaign. 1988 saw continuing economic uncertainty and austerity. Rapid growth and falling unemployment in 1985–1986 had weakened Denmark's precarious balance of payments. The government had been forced to enact austerity (the so-called potato cure), which ended economic growth. In 1988 the GNP remained stagnant; unemploy-

ment rose to about 8.6 percent; and the balance-of-payments deficit improved slightly to seventeen billion kroner (about $2.5 billion). Austerity is expected to continue into 1989.

The May elections produced no gains for the socialist parties or the Schlüter coalition. Although the Conservatives lost three seats (dropping their number to 35), their Liberal (Venstre) partners picked up an equal number (raising their number to 22), and the other coalition parties retained the number of seats they had had before. The Progress Party was the main winner and more than doubled its votes, receiving 9 percent of the ballots and 16 seats. The postelection governmental maneuvers were complex, with the SDP anxious to have a shot at forming an alternative left-center government. It remained far from a parliamentary majority, however, and Schlüter restructured his government to include the Radical Liberals but without the centrist Christian People's and Center Democratic parties. The outcome of this turmoil was that the radical socialists were weakened both electorally and politically; the SDP policy of confrontation failed to dislodge Schlüter; and all of the major parties recognized that rigid foreign- and economic-policy positions led to few political gains. For the radical socialists (including the CCP, the SF, the VS, and the DKP), a second assault on the Schlüter government even over the security-policy issue produced no gains; despite a collective total of one-sixth of the vote, the radical socialists ended 1988 weaker in national politics than at any time during the past decade.

Leadership and Organization. After the death in 1987 of two leading DKP leaders and Ole Sohn's elevation to chair, 1988 was a year of typical DKP stability. Ole Sohn, who is 34 years old, rose quickly through the youth movement (DKU) into union politics (the Semi-Skilled Workers Union; SID) in the Jutland town of Horsens. In 1980 he was elected to the party's Central Committee and three years later to the Executive Committee. In 1982–1984 he sat in the Horsens Town Council. The Twenty-eighth Congress intended Sohn to share the chairmanship with 47-year-old Jan Andersen, a long-time Copenhagen labor activist. Andersen's sudden death in July 1987 ended what might have been an interesting experiment in pluralism at the top of the DKP.

The party's highest authority is the triennial congress. The Central Committee is elected at the congress, and it, in turn, elects the party's Executive

Committee (its politburo), chairman, secretary, and other officers. Despite the attendance of some 460 delegates at the 1987 congress, which showed greater openness, the DKP functions fully on the Leninist model of a self-perpetuating elite. In recent years the Central Committee has met from four to six times annually. In the years when the congress does not meet, the party holds a meeting. Such meetings, typically held in the early autumn, reaffirm the general party goals as set at the congress and are occasions for the party to use the media to make known the party's views on domestic and foreign affairs. Despite the party's weakness, media coverage of its meetings and congresses is surprisingly good.

The 28th Congress was more interesting because of intraparty changes than because of new political positions. The national press wondered whether Gorbachev's *glasnost'* would be felt across the Baltic. The congress was preceded by general discussion of "openness" in the party's press (*Land og Folk*), but the selection of new leaders and the formulation of the party's program seemed very much in the Leninist tradition. The creation of the new post of deputy chair insured that there would be room for both Sohn and Andersen at the top. For years, chief ideologue Ib Nørlund was recognized as the number-two man in the party. Not surprisingly, he and his "old guard" colleagues were not pleased by changes in the DKP (*Information*, 15 April 1987). It is true that several changes were made at the congress in the composition of the 50-member Central Committee and in the party's by-laws, but they were trivial and did not change the practice of "democratic centralism." Although Ole Sohn recently admitted that the party's image of being closed and rigid was a real problem in attracting new activists, he urged greater self-criticism rather than structural or other internal party reforms (*WMR*, April).

Two other young members of the Executive Committee are likely to challenge Sohn's leadership if the party's position does not improve soon. Frank Aaen, political editor of *Land og Folk* and former communist student leader, is a vigorous activist and a new member of the Executive Committee. Jens Bonde Nielsen, a leader of the Popular Movement, which is opposed to the European Community, and a member of the European Parliament, is another prominent member of the younger generation. It is interesting that he was not elected to the new Executive Committee, as his name had been mentioned the year before as a possible candidate for chair. He

has been renominated as first on the list of candidates put forward by the Popular Movement Against the European Community (PM) for the 1989 elections to the European Parliament. His "European" activities might be difficult to combine with a prominent party post.

The DKP has never had difficulty in attracting energetic and talented activists. The challenge has been to hold them inside a rigid, hierarchical, and Stalinist apparatus, when so many more promising opportunities can be found in the Danish left. The party is aware of the problem and increasingly discusses it in both its domestic and international forums. Inertia appears still to command a majority on the DKP's Executive Committee; even Soviet writers about Danish and West European leftist politics seem more open and insightful than the DKP establishment. (*WMR*, April and August.)

Domestic Affairs. With no parliamentary seats and greatly reduced representation in local government, the DKP has become an increasingly irrelevant peripheral observer and critic of Danish domestic affairs. Three areas of action remain on the DKP agenda: electoral campaigns, labor union activism, and general propaganda within the leftist fringe. Elections are important because posts give the party important platforms and resources. Moreover, the Danish election laws are exceptionally generous with regard to radio and television time (all without expense to the parties) for parties appearing on the ballot. Given the frequency of Danish parliamentary campaigns (seven since 1973), the DKP considers it essential to secure a place on the ballot. The autumn 1988 issues of the party daily *Land og Folk* repeatedly pressed efforts to secure the required 25,000 signatures required for electoral participation (*Land og Folk*, 13 October).

Another recent DKP tactic to improve its electoral prospects has been to seek electoral alliances with other radical socialist and Marxist parties. The VS in particular has been attractive to it. None of its leaders are ex-communists (as is the case with CCP leader Hansen), and the VS has had several attractive national and local political leaders, even as the party's electoral fortunes have faded. In March, the DKP CC voted 27 to 12 to pursue such an alliance under the name "Forum for Democratic Renewal." Sohn saw the front as a rallying point for both partisan and nonpartisan radicals, much in the mold of the anti-EC movement (*Ritzau's Bureau*, 21 March). The VS quickly scuttled the idea, however, and the VS's poor performance in the May election (0.6 percent) reduced its attractiveness. Even together, the two parties were still far short of the required minimum. The DKP leadership continues to stress the goal of broad leftist coalitions on the popular-front model (*WMR*, August).

Labor activism continues to absorb much communist attention, even though industrial labor relations have been peaceful in the wake of the 1987 general agreement. Public-sector and unskilled workers continued to lose economic ground relatively, and unemployment especially threatens these groups. Hospital doctors, in whose union DKP elements and other radicals have become increasingly militant, undertook periodic action for improved pay and, especially, reduced duty hours. The DKP courts public employees assiduously, but so do the other radical socialist parties, with considerably more success.

The possibility of a socialist alternative government was backed in principle by all of the leftist parties. Only for the SF was the issue entirely germane. The DKP supported the alternative, but its program, reaffirmed at the April congress, showed little new thinking. There is mainly criticism of the nonsocialists for their various austerity programs and skepticism about various proposals regarding wage-earner funds ("economic democracy") currently being advanced by several Nordic social-democratic parties. True to its history, the DKP calls for "nationalization" of large industrial and financial concerns. Also alive are DKP proposals for shorter working hours (without reductions in wage demands), increased taxation of the private sector, restoration of automatic cost-of-living raises, and restrictions on the movement of capital in and out of Denmark. Meanwhile, public spending on defense is to be cut sharply, while social spending will leap ahead. (*WMR*, August.) Sohn did surprise some with his support for conservative Finance Minister Palle Simonsen's idea of decentralizing public-employment programs so that local governments could experiment with innovative measures (*Ritzau's Bureau*, 22 August). On the whole, however, while DKP tactics change, its program shows little evolution. Although several West European communist parties claim to be a radicalizing force in relation to the larger reformist social-democratic parties, the DKP is of no interest to the Danish SDP except indirectly through struggles in certain labor unions. Just as *glasnost'* is still suspect among DKP stalwarts, "new thinking" about long-term goals is nearly absent (ibid.).

Foreign Affairs. Because they precipitated the sudden elections in May, issues connected with foreign and security policies were especially prominent in Danish politics during 1988. Since the DKP and other socialist parties give foreign and security affairs much attention, 1988 should have been a banner year for them. The DKP's strength has traditionally been closely tied to the cycles of East-West relations. Since the current period of relaxation of tensions began in 1985, however, the DKP, and indeed other leftist parties, have failed to gain support. The DKP cannot project a distinctive foreign policy profile, except for its uncritical support of the Soviet Union. All of the leftist parties (including a minority in even the SDP) are opposed to Danish membership and participation in NATO, the EC, and other forms of Western cooperation. Only the DKP, though, fails to find fault with any aspect of Soviet foreign policy. Although the communist paper *Land og Folk* has been more open in its reporting of the changes in Soviet foreign policy, the DKP has not specifically commented on changes, debates, and setbacks in the Soviet Union, except in terms of Hans Christen Andersen's tale "What Father Does is Always Correct."

The DKP's foreign-policy strategy is strongly oriented toward cooperation with like-minded activists in the peace, anti-NATO, and anti-EC movements. The DKP was an early supporter of the Nordic Nuclear Weapons–Free Zone proposals, but that idea is now widely supported by both socialist and nonsocialist peace activists. About two-thirds of the Danish public strongly supports NATO membership, but when the Danes are forced to choose between membership in NATO and a role for nuclear weapons in the defense of Western Europe, equally strong anti-nuclear feelings surface. There is, however, little support for greater commitment to conventional defense measures (*Jyllands-Posten*, 18 April; *Nordisk Kontakt*, no. 6). Besides the May elections, the peace movement's most visible activity in 1988 was participation in a large international "peace and security" congress in East Berlin. Sohn was one of about twenty prominent Danish peace activists, who included SF chair Gert Petersen and former SDP chair and prime minister Anker Jørgensen. The congress pressed for a variety of nuclear weapons-free zones and for a disarmed corridor in central Europe (*Politiken*, 20 June).

The anti-EC PM remains an area of high priority for the DKP. Executive Committee member Jens Peter Bonde is a PM member in the European

Parliament, where the PM delegation of four (of Denmark's sixteen seats) sits with the communist and Allied Groups bloc. The PM has nominated Bonde to head its list in the European parliamentary elections expected in 1989. The EC remains a favorite target of leftist criticism, as plans for policy harmonization and weighted voting progress toward the 1992 goals.

International Party Contacts. The DKP's internationalism distinguishes it from other Marxist parties. It identifies closely with the "proletarian internationalism" of the CPSU. As the latter has become more ecumenical, so too has the DKP. In late February, Chairman Sohn led a delegation, which included Ib Nørlund and Ingemar Wagner (both members of the old "Stalinist" guard), and Anker Schjerning and Rita Sørensen (new and more liberal members of the DKP's politburo) to Moscow. Their host was Anatolii Dobrynin, the new pro-Gorbachev international secretary of the CPSU CC. Both sides emphasized their complete agreement on foreign policy, especially with regard to efforts to ban nuclear weapons from the Baltic Sea area. They also cited Gorbachev's October 1987 speech in Murmansk, in which he promised Soviet participation in weapons reductions in the Baltic and Nordic area, and said that it should stimulate renewed activity toward a regional agreement (TASS, 29 February).

More innovative was the visit by a DKP delegation, again headed by Sohn, and including Frank Aaen and Kirsten Nissen, to the People's Republic of China in April. The DKP delegation planned discussion with top party and governmental leaders there (*Land og Folk*, 8 April). During the summer, Ib Nørlund went to North Korea and not surprisingly was impressed by everything he saw. Purely Stalinist bastions are increasingly in short supply.

Another typical DKP international activity was the October meeting in Dublin, Ireland, of nine West European communist parties. The main themes of the meeting were opposition to implementation of the EC's single-Europe act and renewed emphasis of national sovereignty. Further, East-West cooperation was cheered. This led to the ironic contradiction that the traditional communist parties are internationalist on almost every issue except those that really matter for their countries: cooperation in the Western and European spheres (ibid, 15–16 October).

Other Marxist/Leftist Groups. The DKP is only one of several left-wing parties currently active in Danish politics. The May elections left only the SF, by far the most powerful of these groups, in Parliament. Originally a splinter from the DKP (in 1958), the SF has steadily gained ground despite a decade of internal splits and electoral setbacks between 1968 and 1977. Ever since it first gained parliamentary representation in 1960, the SF has sought to push the SDP leftward. In 1966–1967 and 1971–1973, SF votes kept the Social Democrats in power. The first experiment in formal SF-SDP collaboration (the so-called Red Cabinet) ended when the SF's left wing split off to form the VS party. Such collaboration with the Marxist left has worried SDP moderates, and in 1973 several right-wing Social Democrats abandoned their party to form the Center Democrats. Until its electoral setback in May, the SF's steady advances through the 1980s made another attempt at SF-SDP collaboration increasingly attractive to left-wing Social Democrats and SF pragmatists (including SF chair Petersen). In the 1987 parliamentary and electoral debates, both the SF and the SDP sought to delineate their differences without excluding political collaboration.

The SDP's traditional centrist ally, the Radical Liberal Party, joined the Schlüter government after the May elections, despite its sympathies with the SDP (and occasionally the SF) on foreign- and security-policy issues. SDP chair Auken's decision to work out budget compromises with the government in both 1987 and 1988 (despite the bitterness caused by the snap election) is evidence that he does not consider a formal or informal coalition with the SF an immediate alternative. The votes are simply not there.

The SF program is at least part of the problem. It is decidely socialist, pacifist, and Marxian, even as it emphasizes Danish values and rejects foreign socialist models. The SF's bargaining starts with five main conditions: (1) adjustment of unemployment insurance and other social-benefit payments to make up for inflation and cuts since 1982; (2) a reduction of the standard working day to seven hours (without wage cuts); (3) compulsory employee profit-sharing and codetermination ("economic democracy"); (4) fiscal and monetary policies that are free from EC interference; and (5) declaration of Denmark to be an unconditionally nuclear weapons–free zone. Its annual congress in May re-elected Gert Petersen as chair, reaffirmed the party's long-term goals, and held forth an olive branch to the Radical Liberals. Its new economic program, announced in November, promised increased public spending (with an immediate increase of some one and a half to two billion dollars) directed to environmental and social programs. Although adamantly opposed to Danish membership in NATO, it has promised a more flexible line toward the EC. It will now seek to work within the EC to protect Danish interests (*Nordisk Kontakt*, no. 8; *Ritzau's Bureau*, 18 November).

The SF is explicitly non-Leninist in both its internal governance and its attitudes toward Danish parliamentary democracy. Its earlier feuds and schism (which occurred especially when it assumed indirect governmental responsibility) have faded under the experienced leadership of its veteran chairman, Gert Petersen. It has captured nearly a sixth of the parliamentary vote, exhibited substantial strength in local and regional government, and even displayed growing strength in the labor movement (especially among public-sector and academic employees). With more than 10,000 members (its membership has more than doubled in the past decade), the SF is an attractive alternative to dissatisfied members of the SDP and other leftists. It offers a "soft" and democratic form of Danish Marxism and democratic-socialist alternatives without reference to, or apologies for unsuccessful experiences elsewhere. It was perhaps the first "Eurocommunist" party (although its rejection of the Leninist model makes it more radical than the more orthodox national-communist parties), but in 1988 the SF declared its desire to have direct contacts with the Communist Party of the Soviet Union. In September, Gert Petersen led an SF delegation to the Soviet Union where it met with Soviet party, government, and labor officials and academics (*Ritzau's Bureau*, 27 September). The SF has become increasingly attentive to feminist concerns, and in 1988 became the first Danish party to have sexual quotas in its parliamentary nominations: women and men will alternate on list positions (*Nordisk Kontakt*, no. 8).

The VS continued its sharp decline in 1988, with its meager parliamentary vote being cut nearly in half. It had rejected electoral cooperation with the DKP and in November 1987 rejected similar cooperation with the SF. Cooperation with other leftist parties was a recurring topic among leftist parties during 1988. The VS party has lost a number of its more pragmatic leaders, and its current spokesman, Keld Albrechtsen, represents the "Leninist" majority in the party's Executive Committee.

Former Copenhagen alderman Villo Sigurdsson has opted for EC parliamentary politics as a candidate on the PM list. The PM's program still calls for a radically decentralized (anarchistic) political and economic collectivism run by "Green councils" of employees, citizens, and consumers (*Berlingske Tidende*, 26 April, 10 June).

Preben Møller Hansen's Common Course Party disappeared from the Parliament after the May election. Its 1.9 percent of the vote was just shy of the threshold for representation. Its program combines many of the same themes of nationalization and confiscation that characterize the programs of the other leftist parties, especially the DKP, on whose Executive Committee Møller sat until his feud with the party's old guard. Unique to the CCP are its anti-immigrant proposals and those regarding refugees. Both immigrants and refugees entered Denmark in significant numbers in the 1980s. These proposals would restrict their entry. Danish laws have already been tightened (over the protests of the other leftist parties), but the CCP believes in harping on populist issues. Its antics provided some entertainment in the normally staid Danish parliament, but reduced the party's political credibility. Whether it will attract a sufficient number of leftist protest votes to stage a political recovery is uncertain. The party intended participation in the European parliamentary election in June 1989, but failed to make the PM list (*Ritzau's Bureau*, 17 October).

The three small sects failed to gather sufficient signatures in time to appear on the May parliamentary ballot. The Communist Workers' Party (Kommunistisk Arbejderparti) is apparently defunct. The International Socialist Workers' Party (SAP) is the Danish branch of the Trotskyist Fourth International; its weekly paper *Klassekampen* (Class struggle) is well informed on Danish leftist politics and the international Trotskyist movement. There is finally the Marxist-Leninist Party (Marxistisk-Leninistisk Parti; MLP), whose pro-Albanian line may seem even more anachronistic in the post-Hoxha world (Hoxha is the late Albanian leader).

Another recently established party, the Greens (De Grønne), again appeared on the ballot and attracted 1.4 percent of the vote. It is not formally a Marxist party, but apparently appeals to similar voters. Its future is more promising than that of the other small excluded parties.

Neither the DKP nor other Danish leftist parties have direct ties to parties in the autonomous territories: Greenland and the Faeroe Islands. The Greenlandic coalition between the socialists of Forward (Siumut) and the Inuit (Eskimo) radicals (Inuit

Atassut; IA) collapsed in 1988. The IA program calls for closing all U.S. and NATO installations in Greenland. Moreover, IA leader Araqaluk Lynge has established close ties with the Soviet Communist party in order to promote his agenda of greater cooperation among the Inuits of Greenland, Canada, Alaska, and the Soviet Union. In August a meeting was held in the Soviet Union with Inuits from the four pertinent countries (*Ritzau's Bureau*, 15 August).

November's local council elections in the Faeroes produced a modest swing to the right. The only significant radical party—the Republicans—ran on a program of full independence, and failed to make headway. All other Faeroese parties support Danish leadership in foreign and security affairs, except for economic issues. With respect to the latter, the Faeroese do what they feel is in the islands' interest (*Berlingske Tidende*, 10 November).

Eric S. Einhorn
University of Massachusetts at Amherst

Finland

Population. 4,949,716 (1988)
Parties. Finnish Communist Party (Suomen Kommunistinen Puolue; SKP), contests elections as part of the Finnish People's Democratic League (Suomen Kansan Demokraattinen Liitto; SKDL); Finnish Communist Party–Unity (Suomen Kommunistinen Puolue-Yhtenäisyys; SKP-Y), claims to be legitimate representative of communist movement and runs candidates through an electoral front group, the Democratic Alternative (Demokraattinen Vaihtoehto; DEVA); Communist Worker's Party (Kommunistinen Tyoekansan Puolue; KTP), "revolutionary" splinter from SKP-Y
Founded. SKP: 1918; SKP-Y: 1986
Membership. SKP: 20,000; SKDL: 45,000; SKP-Y: 15,000; KTP: est. 200
Chairmen. SKP: Jarmo Wahlström (50, teacher); SKDL: Reijo Käkelä (46, theologian); SKP-Y: Jouko Kajanoja (46, civil servant); DEVA: Kris-

tiina Halkola (actress); KTP: Timo Lahdenmaeki (computer technician)
General Secretaries. SKP: Helja Tammisola (42, computer technician); SKDL: Salme Kandolin (40, civil servant); SKP-Y: Yrjö Häkanen; KTP: Heikki Mannikko
Politburo. SKP: includes Aarno Aitamurto, vice-chair (52, lawyer, union official), Tapanie Elgland (journalist), Timo Laaksonen (politician), Tanja Lehmuskoski (party worker), Erkki Kauppila (journalist), Heikki Kiviaho (shipyard worker, union official); SKP-Y: includes Marya-Liisa Löyttyjärvi, vice-chair, Esko-Juhani Tennilä, vice-chair (politician), Taisto Sinisalo (party official), Ensio Laine (politician); KTP: includes Juhani Eero, vice-chair (businessman, editor), Hannu Tukominen, vice-chair (toolfitter, party official), Markus Kainulainen (party official)
Central Committee. Both SKP and SKP-Y: 50 full and 15 alternate members
Status. Legal; SKP, SKDL, and DEVA registered as political parties and eligible for public subsidies
Last Congress. SKP: Twenty-first Congress (12–15 June 1987), Helsinki, legitimacy contested, court decision pending; SKP-Y: First Congress (5–7 June 1987), Espoo; SKDL: Fifteenth Congress (23–25 May 1988), Helsinki; KTP: First Congress (23–24 May 1988), Vantaa
Last Election. General election for 200-seat Eduskunta, 15–16 March 1987; SKDL: 9.4 percent of vote, 16 seats (including 11 SKP); DEVA: 4.3 percent of vote, 4 seats; next scheduled general election March 1991; Presidential election, 31 January–1 February 1988 (popular election), 15 February 1988 (electoral college); Kalevi Kivistö ("Action 88," candidacy endorsed by SKP/SKDL), 10.5 percent of popular vote, 26 (of 301) seats in electoral college; Jouko Kajanoja (DEVA), 1.4 percent of popular vote, no electoral college seats. Local elections, October 1988; SKDL: 10.3 percent of overall vote; DEVA: 2.5 percent
Auxiliary Organizations. SKP: Finnish Democratic Youth League (SDNL), Finnish Women's Democratic League (SNDL); SKP-Y sponsors parallel organizations
Publications. SKP: *Kansan Uutiset* (daily); *Ny Tid* (Swedish-language weekly); SKP-Y: *Tiedonantaja* (daily); (all published in Helsinki)

The Finnish Communist Party (SKP) was founded in exile in 1918 and remained based in Moscow until the party was legalized in 1944, following the armistice with the Soviet Union that ended the Continuation War. Communist candidates in local and parliamentary elections stand for office on slates offered by the Finnish People's Democratic League (SKDL), an electoral coalition that includes the SKP as well as socialists and other "progressive" groups committed to a leftist agenda. The SKDL is regarded as a front organization for the SKP, although noncommunists constitute the large majority of the league's members and voters.

Relations between the SKP and the SKDL are complex, and a different political logic operates in each group. Political rivals within the SKP cooperate in parliament and on local councils as representatives of the SKDL, but prominence in the SKDL does not necessarily guarantee a communist member corresponding influence in the SKP. Communists outnumber noncommunists in the SKDL's parliamentary delegation, within which SKP and socialist factions meet in separate caucuses. The SKDL's executive committee is dominated by communists, although until 1988 the party chairmanship was reserved for a noncommunist. Socialists regularly complain that communist officers of the SKDL and members of the communist parliamentary faction take instructions from the SKP. In response, the SKP expresses concern at perceived anticommunist sentiment in the socialist faction of the SKDL.

Before the SKP was legalized in 1944, the party functioned on two levels, one as a party in exile headquartered in Moscow and the other as an unauthorized interior party that operated in Finland through front groups and was active in the labor movement. This contributed to an early and persistent split in the SKP between a dogmatically pro-Soviet wing and a pragmatic nationalist wing. Although it provides convenient labels for actors in the SKP's internal conflicts, this cleavage obscures the fact that factionalism within the party has stemmed essentially from personal rivalries and disagreement over tactics, rather than ideological differences.

In 1969, the party congress formally adopted a reformist line that was introduced by the "majority," generally representative of the SKP's nationalist wing, in the face of opposition from a significant "minority" faction. Under the leadership of then-party chairman Aarne Saarinen, the SKP majority became outspokenly "Eurocommunist." The SKP no longer describes itself as "revolutionary," but as a party that "adapts and develops Marxist theory" according to unique Finnish circumstances. It acknowledges a commitment to Finland's constitutional system and accepts the market economy, although arguing that its direction should be transferred to the state. The SKP cooperates with "fraternal communist parties" but rejects the suggestion that it is dependent on the CPSU.

The minority faction (sometimes referred to as "Stalinists" or as "Taistoists" after their leader, Taisto Sinisalo) walked out of the 1969 party congress to protest Saarinen's "revisionism," established its own press, and formed separate auxiliary organizations. The majority was excluded from eight district organizations controlled by the minority. (In turn, the minority was excluded from the nine majority-controlled district organizations.)

In 1985, a special party congress called by the new chairman, Arvo Aalto, authorized the SKP central committee to expel minority-controlled organizations for disloyalty. The SKP subsequently purged members identified with the minority by ignoring them when new party cards were issued. The minority refused to recognize their expulsion by the SKP's leadership, and in 1986 Sinisalo's faction and allies set up a new party apparatus exactly mirroring that of the majority-dominated SKP. Calling the dissident group the Finnish Communist Party–Unity (SKP-Y), minority leaders deny that it is a separate party and stress their devotion to the principle of "unity" of the communist movement. They claim that the new organization constitutes the "true" SKP because the majority faction is "revisionist" and has fallen away from Marxist orthodoxy. Both the SKP and the SKP-Y have established parallel organizations in districts where the party was controlled by the other faction.

Consistent with its position that the minority organization is an alternative or "shadow" SKP, the SKP-Y is not registered as a political party. Minority candidates contest elections through a front organization, the Democratic Alternative (DEVA), which is a registered political party and qualifies for public funding of its activities. Unlike the SKDL, in which the SKP is one of several member groups, DEVA is completely the creature of the SKP-Y.

In 1988, a leftist faction of the SKP-Y, opposed to discussion of reconciliation with the SKP and the reunification of the party, met to form the so-called Communist Workers Party (KTP), which its leaders describe as Finland's only remaining "revolutionary" party.

Today communists of all stripes find themselves outside the mainstream of Finnish politics, bypassed by the profound economic and demographic changes that have taken place in Finland since the early 1960s. Traditionally, the SKDL has found its strongest support in the small cities and towns and in the rural working class of eastern and northern Finland and in the large industrial centers of Helsinki, Turku, and Tampere. In its heyday in the late 1950s, the SKDL attracted the votes of nearly a quarter of the electorate and held 50 seats in Finland's 200-member parliament, the Eduskunta. By contrast, the combined vote for the SKDL and DEVA in the 1987 general election accounted for less than 14 percent of the total vote. The nosedive of support for communist-backed fronts has been attributed to the shift in the work force from smokestack to high-technology industries and also to these fronts' lack of appeal to young voters. Blue-collar workers, for example, now make up less than half of the SKP's membership. Fully one-third of its members are pensioners, while only about 5 percent are under the age of 30. (*Hufvudstadsbladet* [*Hb*], 31 May 1987; *Uusi Suomi*, 26 July 1987.) Other important factors in the communist decline are the bitter personal rivalries within the leadership that contributed to the fracturing of the SKP and, more recently, the state of near paralysis in the leadership brought on by the SKP's financial crisis. The SKDL leadership has been at odds with trade union leaders in the party. Rank-and-file communists—in keeping with the spirit of *glasnost'* embraced by both the SKP and SKP-Y—have become more openly critical of the leadership and made demands for a greater voice in the party's affairs. During 1988, a new generation of leaders was appointed in the SKP, SKDL, and SKP-Y. Although new chairmen and general secretaries gave vent to a great deal of self-criticism, they left the impression of being more concerned about quashing internal opposition than about taking positive steps toward reunifying the communist movement in Finland.

That movement continued to lose credibility in 1988. The year opened in the midst of a presidential campaign in which incumbent president Mauno Koivisto was heavily favored to win a second six-year term in office against a field of candidates that included Prime Minister Harri Holkeri and opposition leader Paavo Väyrynen. Koivisto ran as an independent candidate with the endorsement of the Social Democratic Party (SDP); Holkeri was standard-bearer for the conservative National Coalition Party (KOK); Väyrynen for the Center (KESH). The SKDL did not formally nominate a candidate but endorsed Kalevi Kivistö, whose campaign was promoted by "Action 88." This group had

been organized in November 1987 with SKP backing to provide a "broader democratic front" than the SKDL offered. Action 88 sought support for Kivistö from left-wing Greens and dissident Social Democrats, but also made a pitch to minority communists. The campaign committee was headed by Esko Haaht, a prominent figure in the environmentalist movement, and included Esko Helle, SKDL chairman. Kivistö, a socialist who is provincial governor of Keski-Suomi and himself former SKDL chairman, was clearly understood, however, to be representing the SKP/SKDL in the presidential race. DEVA nominated Jouko Kajanoja, one-time government minister and former SKP chairman, as its candidate. Kajanoja also appealed for support from Greens and other "progressive" voters.

Polls indicated that neither communist-backed candidate had much chance of affecting the outcome of the election, but analysts did see the presidential vote as a test of how broad an appeal Kivistö could make outside the SKDL's customary constituency and also how deeply DEVA could make inroads into it (*Hb*, 25 January; *Aftenposten*, Oslo, 26 January). Kivistö adhered closely to the SKP/SKDL line, which was critical of proposed civil service and tax reforms. Calling for greater income equality, he also criticized the trade union leadership for acquiescing to government wage guidelines and demanded compensatory raises for lower-paid workers. Kajanoja picked up on the same domestic issues but stressed a more activist approach in foreign policy, arguing, for example, that Finland should be engaged in preventing West German participation in NATO maneuvers in Norway. Kivistö agreed that this was a concern worth discussing, but counseled that Finland should keep a low profile. Both candidates urged greater efforts for disarmament, condemned arms exports by Finnish companies, supported reductions in defense expenditures, and endorsed proposals for a Nordic nuclear weapons–free zone. Both also advocated closer ties to the Soviet Union.

When votes were counted at the conclusion of the two days of voting (31 January–1 February), Kivistö had run three points ahead of the figure most pre-election polls had predicted. With 10.5 percent of the popular vote in his column, he was left far behind by second-runner Paavo Väyrynen but finished ahead of Prime Minister Holkeri. He also improved on the SKDL's share of the vote in the 1987 general election by a full percentage point. Under Finland's system of indirect presidential election, Kivistö was entitled to 26 seats in the 301-member Electoral College that met on 15 February to determine the election's winner. His campaign had attracted enough Social Democrat defectors to deprive President Koivisto of a first-round victory. (Koivisto was re-elected in the second round.)

The presidential election was an unmitigated disaster for DEVA. Kajanoja won only 1.4 percent of the popular vote, less than a third of DEVA's share in the general election, insufficient for him to claim a single seat in the Electoral College. In the postmortems that followed the election, Arvo Aalto was quoted as saying that DEVA had scarcely any political position left to stand on and repeated his invitation to minority candidates to join SKDL slates in the local elections in October (*Hb*, 21 and 22 February).

At least one fresh initiative for reunifying the SKP came in the fallout from the presidential election. Two communist deputies in the Eduskunta, Esko Seppänen (SKDL) and Esko-Juhani Tennilä (DEVA), jointly issued 40 proposals for healing the schism; these included the unconditional acceptance of expelled party organizations back into the fold and the creation of a new "Left Alliance," which presumably would absorb both the SKDL and DEVA, and which would be composed of individual members rather than member groups (*Hb*, 22 February). Seppänen and Tennilä also proposed that an extraordinary party congress be called to reconcile differences between the factions, while marking the 70th anniversary of the founding of the SKP. Arvo Kemppainen, SKP deputy vice-chairman and regarded by the minority as the majority's most unrelenting revisionist, seconded their call for a special congress; but he, like Tennilä, who was an SKP-Y politburo member, spoke only for himself, and neither had the support of others among the leaders of their groups. Sinisalo discounted any talk of reunification, but saw the possibility of the two leftist fronts collaborating as equals in local elections. The SKDL rejected this suggestion (although the SKDL and DEVA do co-operate on some local councils), and SKP leaders reiterated that minority dissidents would be accepted back into the party only individually, and then as "penitents." In the meantime, the rival central committees announced separate celebrations of the 70th anniversary of the founding of the SKP, that of the majority SKP to take place in July at Tampere, and that of the SKP-Y in August at Turku.

The Fifteenth Congress of the SKDL convened in Helsinki on 23 May to elect new officers and to approve a platform that the party would carry into the local elections. Also on the agenda was the discussion of proposals to broaden the SKDL's membership base, perhaps on the model of Action 88. For the first time in many years, divisions between communists and socialists were not obvious from the outset because the minority faction of the SKP was notably absent from the proceedings.

In a sharp break with custom, the selection committee nominated a communist, Reijo Käkelä, from a list of 21 candidates. Its nominee was given unanimous approval by the congress as the SKDL's next chairman. Käkelä, a member of the SKP Politburo, was favored by the SKDL youth movement and had the support of many socialists. The selection committee, chaired by Jarmo Wahlström, communist leader of the SKDL parliamentary delegation, completely bypassed incumbent chairman Esko Helle in making its choice. Helle, a socialist, had made it known that he wanted to remain as chairman, but his name was conspicuously absent from the list considered by the committee. Käkelä's nomination was challenged in a last-minute move by Claes Andersson, whose surprise candidacy for the chairmanship was backed by trade union delegates to the congress as well as by some communists, including SKP chairman Aalto who had been dropped from the SKDL executive committee. The Trade Union Confederation (SAK) had been outraged by Käkelä's charges that union leaders had not sufficient solidarity with lower-paid workers and the unemployed; Aalto's behind-the-scene efforts to sandbag the election of a fellow communist reflect an intraparty power struggle that was coming to a head as the SKDL congress met. Andersson, a socialist who is better known as a writer and jazz musician than as politician, was one of the rare Swedish-speaking Finns active in the SKDL. Despite the commotion caused by a face-off between two candidates, their brief campaign for the chairmanship was lackluster. Andersson spoke out for a more open SKDL that was "courageous enough to engage in differences of opinion, even in disputes"; but he and Käkelä had no differences over issues to debate, and both agreed on the need to broaden the front's appeal. What separated them were the bases of their support (*Helsingen Sanomat* [*HS*], 23 May; *Hb*, 23 and 24 May; *Kansan Uutiset*, 23 May).

Käkelä won 60 percent of the vote from congress delegates against Andersson's late challenge, but this was a relatively narrow margin of victory coming from an electoral body used to giving unanimous approval to candidates dictated by the selection committee. The 40 percent of the votes cast against Käkelä was regarded as a protest against the selection process rather than a groundswell of support for a noncommunist alternative candidate.

Another communist, Salme Kandolin, was chosen unanimously as general secretary, following her nomination by the selection committee. The SKDL women's organization had difficulty agreeing on a candidate to endorse for the position, customarily held by a woman from the SKP. To avoid a potentially divisive vote, Politburo member Mirya Ylitalo withdrew her name from consideration in favor of Kandolin, who was Käkelä's preference for second-in-command. Hilkka Aalto was elected and Timo Laaksonen re-elected as deputy chairmen. Laaksonen is also a member of the SKP Politburo. (*HS*, 24 May.)

The congress approved a lengthy platform that corresponded in most respects to the SKP's program. The proposal that attracted the greatest attention was the so-called citizen's wage, which would guarantee a minimum income to all adult Finns, unemployed as well as employed and including students, retired persons, and full-time homemakers. More immediately, the SKDL called for a reduction of taxes on lower-income brackets and for compensatory raises for workers in the lowest wage categories. The league remained on record as supporting public control of financial institutions and advocating the introduction of economic "self-management" on the Yugoslavian model. The platform contained a strong environmentalist plank that included opposition to construction in Finland of a planned fifth nuclear power plant. The SKDL's energy policy relies on increased use of Finland's hydroelectric assets and natural gas, which Finland imports from the Soviet Union. The platform called for liberalization of laws governing the acceptance of refugees, a heated issue in 1988, and urged greater attention to the problem of world hunger. The SKDL paid tribute to Gorbachev's peace initiatives, endorsed efforts leading to nuclear disarmament, including establishment of a Nordic nuclear weapons–free zone, and also supported reduction in conventional arms, beginning with those of the Finnish defense force. The platform favored increased trade with the Soviet Union and cautioned against a political and economic tilt toward Western Europe. The congress was also presented with a one-page "Resolution for Determining the Development of the SKDL" for approval. The resolution outlined Käkelä's plan for a "leftist alliance" capable of attracting Greens and disen-

chanted Social Democrats, as well as minority communists. Käkelä repeatedly used the term "movement," rather than "league" or "party," to describe the proposed realignment, leaving some delegates in doubt whether he intended to build on the existing SKDL base or envisioned an entirely new organization. (*HS*, 24 May; *Hb*, 23 and 24 May.)

Working groups at the congress endorsed the proposal for a more broadly based "leftist alliance" that would encompass groups outside the SKDL "family," but delegates opposed changing the league's name and resisted the idea of a "movement open to all." Not all Greens, it was argued, qualify as "leftists." Noncommunists were also cautious about the effect returning minority communists might have on the SKDL. Delegates complained about the way in which the resolution itself had been presented to the congress, served up, like Käkelä's nomination, by a committee, and some insisted that the membership must be consulted before any binding decisions were made on proposals contained in it. Debate was stopped without bringing the "resolution" to a vote; instead, the proposals were approved as a "guideline" for the new chairman.

Käkelä reminded the congress that his most important task as chairman was to unite the "multitude of voices" found in the SKDL, and he admitted that bad feelings existed between the "Helsinki intellectuals" and the trade unionists, who are the largest single group in the league. The challenge to his nomination and argument from the floor on the resolution indicated that it would be an uphill fight for Käkelä to unify the SKDL and consolidate the Finnish left. Analysts suggested that Käkelä's reference to *glasnost'* as it might be applied to the Finnish situation was a shrewd tactical maneuver but lacked ideological conviction. Whatever else might have come out of the SKDL's Fifteenth Congress, it did provide the setting for an open and democratic vote and a forum for the free debate of issues, both unprecedented events.

Although the "movement" proposed by Käkelä would continue to have affiliated groups, such as the SKP, members would join as individuals. According to Käkelä, positions in the SKDL would no longer be allotted on the basis of gender or party affiliation. This was interpreted as indicating that the SKP would also be deprived of its "leading role" in the SKDL. By separating the overlapping political functions of the SKDL and SKP, Käkelä argued, the latter could concentrate its efforts on promoting the interests of the working class. Käkelä, in the meantime, resigned from the SKP Politburo.

Commentators remarked on the irony of the SKDL's first communist chairman attempting to put some distance between the league and the SKP. Some saw the proposed "leftist alliance" as an assertion of the SKDL's independence from SKP control. Others, however, were suspicious of Käkelä's intentions or pessimistic about the prospects for broadening the SKDL. Esko Helle characterized Käkelä's proposed resolution as a scheme for reunifying the SKP and another example of the SKP's using the SKDL as if the latter were its appendage. Helle revived the idea of a formal merger between the SKDL and SKP to form a new "socialist people's party" that would include communists but not be dominated by them. (It was at this point that Aalto accused the socialist faction of "anticommunism," although the "Eurosocialist" solution to relations between the SKDL and SKP had been proposed first by Aarne Saarinen.) Helle found the division between communist and socialist factions in the SKDL artificial, since all "progressive" groups agreed on important issues. He worried that attempting to broaden the SKDL beyond its current base would invite defections to both the left and the right. He was also critical of opening a dialogue with the Social Democratic Party (SDP), which, in his opinion, was compromised as a socialist-bloc party by its contradictory participation in a coalition government with the conservative National Coalition Party (KOK). (*HS*, 23 and 24 May; *Hb*, 23 and 24 May.)

Käkelä renewed Aalto's invitation to DEVA to join an open slate with SKDL candidates in the October local elections. The suggestion provoked protest from noncommunists. The Helsinki branch of the SKDL complained, for example, that it would be necessary to drop socialist candidates from the SKDL ticket in order to carry sitting DEVA city councillors on an open slate. While noncommunists, like Helle, expressed grave concern over continued SKP domination of the SKDL, minority communists saw Käkelä using his SKDL chairmanship to win control of the communist movement. The SKP-Y and the official Green organization both rejected the proposal of an open slate, calling instead for a joint conference with the SKDL and separate organizations to discuss the possibility of electoral cooperation among separate and equal organizations.

Questions regarding the interrelation between the SKP and SKDL and the split in the SKP paled beside the party's financial crisis and the scandal surrounding it as matters of concern for the SKP leadership (*HS*, 12 and 20 May; *Suomen Kuvalehti*, 20 May). The SKP had traditionally followed a conservative investment policy with party funds. By various estimates, the party had a FMk 50–70 million portfolio held in bonds and invested in party-owned development companies. Its main assets were in real estate. But when Jorma Sorvari took over as party financial secretary in the mid-1980s, he initiated a dynamic investment policy designed to take advantage of quick yields on the stock market made possible by a liberalization of investment practices that the SKP opposed. As an investor, the party sustained staggering losses when share prices tumbled in October 1987. Party leaders—and the public—also became aware that Sorvari had sold and taken out loans secured by party-owned property to finance other speculative ventures that included a racing stable and a failing clothing store that he had purchased at a grossly inflated sale price. It is estimated that the party fund lost upwards of FMk 40 million, putting the party budget in deficit by an estimated FMk 10 million. The minister of justice pointed out that the deficit equaled the value of two-years' worth of subsidies paid to the party and thus merited a formal inquiry into the use of public money by the SKP and SKDL. (*HS*, 13 May.) The police subsequently undertook an investigation into Sorvari's financial activities. The case became part of the ideological conflict between the majority and minority when the SKP-Y Politburo condemned the SKP leadership for practicing "casino capitalism" and called for a joint committee to investigate the uses to which party funds had been put. The press blamed the situation on inexperience and "bad luck," but also commented on the SKP's "apparent intellectual unpreparedness" to deal with its financial crisis (*HS*, 12 and 21 May). Ultimately, however, responsibility came to rest on Arvo Aalto's shoulders.

On 11 May, the entire SKP Politburo offered to submit its resignation in advance of the meeting of the Central Committee scheduled for the end of the month. Politburo members explained that they wanted to give the Central Committee an open field from which to choose new leaders who could deal with the party's financial crisis. The "revolt of Aalto's lieutenants" was clearly directed against the party chairman and General Secretary Esko Vainionpää, whom Politburo members held responsible for the scandal. The incident was interpreted, however, as part and parcel of the internal power struggle that had been simmering within the party for years. (*HS*, 12 May.) District chairmen refused to accept the resignations and urged the Politburo to remain on the job. (Reijo Käkelä resigned definitively two weeks later, after he had been elected SKDL chairman.)

Arvo Aalto resigned as SKP chairman on 23 May. Aalto said that he had made up his mind to step down when the Politburo resigned, but the announcement of his departure a few days before the Central Committee's meeting coincided with Käkelä's nomination and virtually assured election as SKDL chairman and Aalto's omission from the front's executive committee. He denied that the financial crisis had anything to do with his resignation, blaming instead "dirty tricks" by the Politburo and a lack of trust that made it impossible for him to continue his tasks as chairman (*HS*, 24 May; *Uusi Suomi*, 24 May).

The SKP Central Committee met at Tampere on 28–29 May to choose new party leadership and to plan the 70th anniversary of Finnish communism scheduled for July. As expected, Jarmo Wahlström was named to succeed Aalto as party chairman. Wahlström, the SKDL parliamentary leader, was one of Aalto's protégés. Aalto had used Wahlström in the past as his hatchetman in party quarrels. His reputation in the party, however, was that of a middle-of-the-roader who favored working out a reconciliation with the minority. He was a government minister in the early 1980s and has demonstrated a particular interest in environmental issues.

Wahlström's election was a forgone conclusion, but it did not go unchallenged. Arvo Kemppainen and Esko Seppanen nominated each other for the chairmanship, both repeating demands for a special party congress. Kemppainen sought to rally SKP "hard-liners" (a term that in the Finnish context refers to strong opponents of the minority "Stalinists") to counter SKDL plans for an open-slate policy toward the minority that Wahlström had welcomed. He won backing from some trade unionists, but was not able to hold the support of his own Lapland district. Kemppainen had not expected to upset Wahlström, but had hoped to make a point. His rejection by the Central Committee and subsequent downgrading was a personal defeat that did not reflect on either the "trade union party" within the SKP or on other "hard-liners." (*HS*, 30 May.)

Helja Tammisola, incumbent deputy vice chair, was elected general secretary, replacing Vainionpää. She was Wahlström's personal choice for the post. Ideologically, Tammisola was identified as a "hard-liner." As deputy vice-chair, however, she had managed to keep above the fray in internal disputes involving the Politburo. Tammisola maintains close ties with SKP trade unionists.

Aarno Aitamurto, a high-ranking SAK official and Politburo member, was named to replace Tammisola as vice-chair. The deputy vice-chairmanship was eliminated to prevent the reappointment of Kemppainen, who was also dropped from the Politburo. Aitamurto, like Kemppainen, had been an instigator of the maneuver to purge the minority from the SKP. At one time, Aalto had favored Aitamurto to succeed him as chairman; he was Wahlström's personal choice for vice-chairman. New appointments to the Politburo included: Tapanie Elgland and Erkki Kauppila, both journalists; Heikki Kiviaho, a union shop steward; Timo Laaksonen, an SKDL member of parliament; and Tanja Lehmuskoski, first secretary of the SKP's women's organization.

The appointments of Tammisola and Aitamurto strengthen the trade union wing of the party. The latter had joined Aalto in supporting Andersson's candidacy for the SKDL chaimanship, and Tammisola had been mentioned by trade unionists as a possible candidate for SKDL general secretary. Käkelä, in turn, backed other candidates for the SKP posts to which they were elected. Tammisola dismissed Kemppainen's proposal for a special party congress, but said that her first tasks in office were to deal with the financial crisis and to promote contacts with the members of the minority.

On 21 May, a group of about 200 dissident minority communists met at the "founding congress" of the Communist Worker's Party (KTP), held at a vocational school in Vantaa, a Helsinki suburb. Most were "Kainuslaiset," the followers of Markus Kainulainen, who as minority district party boss for Uusimaa (the province surrounding Helsinki) had refused to cooperate with either the SKP-Y leadership or the SKP. Most were from Helsinki and Uusimaa, joined by a few delegates who came for the weekend from Lapland; most were old enough to remember the war years. Kainulainen explained that the congress adhered to the same orthodox Marxist-Leninist line that minority communists had followed for twenty years, and that delegates had come together because the SKP-Y leadership could not decide to form a new and independent communist party, even when it was clear that the majority SKP was revisionist and had sold out to the SDP. He characterized the SKP-Y party workers as "students and cultural personalities" who had no experience of working-class life.

Delegates to the congress provided barely

enough manpower to fill party positions, including a 24-member central committee, an 11-member politburo, and those of district organizations. Timo Lahdenmaeki, recently named as DEVA's Uusimaa district chairman, was confirmed as party chairman, Heikki Mannikko as general secretary. Hannu Tuominen and Juhani Eero were selected vice-chairmen. Tuominen had been a member of the SKP-Y Central Committee; Eero, a Helsinki businessman, is also editor of the party's newspaper. Kainulainen took a place in the Politburo.

A party platform condemned the "pluralism" attributed to the Gorbachev regime, as well as "revisionist" heresies in the Finnish communist movement. Predicting that the minority would eventually slip back into the majority-controlled SKP, Kainulainen described the KTP as Finland's only surviving "revolutionary" party. Responding to observations in the press that his followers were the "minority of a minority," Kainulainen told the congress that "we are a majority in our own party again." Delegates pledged unreserved support for the leadership of the new party and agreed not to give statements to the press about congressional proceedings.

Despite the smallness and apparent isolation of the Uusimaa and Helsinki dissidents, the "First Congress" of the KTP received lengthy press coverage (HS, 23 May; Hb, 23 May). There was speculation that Kainulainen's defection and Kemppainen's downgrading removed obstacles to reunification on the left and the right of the communist movement and left the door open for the minority to return to the SKP. The KTP determined not to put up separate lists of candidates in the local elections, but rather to get its supporters onto DEVA lists in Uusimaa and Helsinki. Funds were available to the KTP through a temperance society to which Kainulainen had transferred party assets of the Uusimaa district. The biggest problem facing the KTP was collecting the 5000 signatures required to register as a political party.

Esko Helle was chosen chairman of the SKDL parliamentary group on 2 June to replace Jarmo Wahlström. His appointment was viewed as a consolation prize after he had been turned out as chairman of the front. Heli Astala, a communist, became deputy group leader. (HS, 3 June.)

The SKP celebrated the 70th anniversary of its founding at a conference that convened at Tampere on 2 July. In the opening address, Wahlström reiterated his support for a more broadly based leftist front, hailing the notion as "an ideological alternative to bourgeois hegemony," but he assured his audience that the SKP would retain its "leading role" in any new political alignment; nor, he promised the assembly, would the SKP "abandon [its] most fundamental principles, even though many patterns of thinking and action need to be corrected." The SKP, he continued, remained the party of "unappeasable class struggle." He stressed, however, that the party must come to terms with structural changes in the Finnish economy and society. The present government, he said, had abandoned its responsibility for monitoring those changes. The SKP would work, therefore, for the institution of the "citizen's wage." Speaking later, Aarne Saarinen challenged the minority, who, along with the majority, had embraced glasnost', to deal honestly with the party's "Stalinist past" and become more democratic. (Hb, 4 July.) The liberal press commented that as soon as the CPSU began to investigate its "Stalinist past," the SKP felt obliged to do the same, and suggested that the Finnish party should take the parrot as its symbol (Iltalehti, 4 July).

During the period of soul searching that followed the presidential election, Taisto Sinisalo observed that leftist voters associated DEVA with the conflicts and divisions in the communist movement. He criticized Kajanoja's presidential campaign for putting too much emphasis on foreign policy and leaving the field open to Kivistö to confront domestic issues. He diagnosed DEVA's main problem as a lack of self-confidence, however, noting that a prominent SKP-Y figure like Esko-Juhani Tennilä had chosen not to put his name on DEVA's slate of presidential electors. There was no agreement in the SKP-Y whether DEVA should contest local elections in October with separate slates, or whether minority candidates should join SKDL slates or collaborate with the Greens independently on a case-by-case basis. Sinisalo predicted another electoral disaster if DEVA stood by itself (Hb, 21 and 22 February).

On the eve of the party's 70th anniversary, which was to be celebrated by the majority in Tampere on its actual date, the SKP-Y proposed that the 22nd SKP Congress, scheduled for 1990, be held as a "reparatory" assembly. The proposal was contained in a draft resolution prepared for the SKP-Y's delayed anniversary gathering at Turku in August. The resolution recommended that the two wings of the party cooperate on local councils and district committees in anticipation of the congress. It condemned the merging of the SKP into a "left alliance" as proposed at the SKDL convention in May, but recommended instead that the SKDL and DEVA form a common front in local and trade union elections. The resolution emphasized the importance of a unified communist party. (*HS*, 2 July.)

Four days later, on 5 July, the Supreme Court handed down a decision upholding a 1987 ruling of the Helsinki Court of Appeals on a suit by the SKP-Y. The court found that, although the SKP's special congress in 1985 had been lawfully convened, amendments to the party's bylaws were invalid because insufficient time had been allowed to summon party members. The high court went beyond the lower court in finding that conditions set by the Central Committee under the amended bylaws were likewise invalid. (It was by issuing new party cards that the SKP had sought to expel minority members.) The Central Committee had also used bylaws amended by the special congress to expel the eight minority-controlled party district organizations in 1987. The SKP had attempted to patch up admitted procedural errors at the party's 21st Congress. In a separate suit, still pending in the Helsinki Municipal Court, the SKP-Y has also challenged the legitimacy of the 21st Congress at which the expulsions were confirmed. (*HS*, 5 July.)

Commenting on the Supreme Court's ruling, Wahlström said that the party had given notice equally to all members, and that therefore the 21st Congress had been legally convened and had rectified earlier procedural errors. According to him, the court decision put no obligation on the SKP to readmit expelled members or district organizations. SKP-Y deputy vice-chairman Yrjö Häkanen thought otherwise, however, arguing that the majority leadership had to admit the illegality of the expulsions and take steps to reunify the party. He cited the SKP-Y resolution on the 22nd Congress as providing a basis for taking those steps. Wahlström reminded Häkanen that the minority had been purged because they were "Stalinists," and that a change of heart was required before they could be readmitted to the SKP individually. He saw no basis for cooperation on the district level and no reason for holding a "reparatory" congress in 1990. (*HS*, 5 July.)

Citing poor health, Sinisalo had announced on 6 June that he would step down as chairman of the SKP-Y after 45 years as a communist activist. The minority marked the jubilee of the communist party, of which they claimed to be the legitimate representatives, with a conference in Turku on 27–29 August. The first order of business was to elect Sinisalo's successor. Kajanoja, the favored candidate,

was challenged by Esko-Juhani Tennilä. Kajanoja won the votes of fourteen party districts in the Central Committee; three districts went for Tennilä.

As a nominee, Tennilä had repeated his demand for a special congress to discuss terms for reunifying the party, a proposition that the new SKP leadership had already rejected. Kajanoja took the position that the minority would negotiate with the majority on reunification only as equals. (*HS*, 13 and 15 August.) Wahlström commented that Kajanoja's election did not rule out the possibility of talks on reunification.

Yrjö Häkanen was selected to replace Kajanoja as general secretary. Tennilä succeeded Häkanen as deputy vice-chairman; Marja-Liisa Löyttyjärvi, the incumbent second vice-chair, continued in that post. Ensio Laine, DEVA's parliamentary group leader, was added to the Politburo, in which Sinisalo retained a place. Kristiina Halkola, a "deep green" noncommunist, remained as chairman of DEVA.

Addressing the convention, Kajanoja suggested the "West German model" as a guide for cooperation between the Finnish left and Greens, but he cautioned Wahlström not to expect the minority to come hat in hand, seeking forgiveness. He stressed the differences between the minority and the majority brands of communism. Despite its inherent contradictions, he recognized that capitalism had been a success in providing economic goods and possessed a "reserve of strength" that communists had overlooked in the past. Noting that a re-evaluation of tactics and goals was going on in both the capitalist and socialist camps, he argued that it was necessary for communism to put the class struggle on a more scientific basis, but admitted that there was no predetermined way by which this might be accomplished. Finnish communists would therefore proceed by trial and error, he said. Kajanoja called for closer ties between Finland and the Soviet Union and recommended a free-trade area in eastern Finland as a means of promoting trade between the two countries. (*Tiedonantaja*, 30 August.)

Polls taken in July showed the SKDL picking up support from both DEVA and SDP voters. DEVA was reported likely to lose 30,000 voters to the Greens and the SKDL in the local elections. (*Uusi Suomi*, 24 July.)

The SKDL offered an open slate in the October local elections to attract a list of candidates that was as comprehensive as possible, including crossovers from the minority. The SKP Central Committee supported the tactic, which left it to individual minority candidates to decide for themselves where their political futures lay. Kajanoja agreed to permit local collaboration between DEVA and the SKDL on this basis. In fact, however, relatively few minority candidates accepted the invitation to run on SKDL slates. A continuing role for Action 88 on the local level, anticipated after the presidential election and expected to serve as a model for the future "leftist alliance," never materialized. The local election campaign focused largely on national issues. Communist candidates criticized national government policy, particularly tax reforms that benefited those in higher-income brackets. Overall, SKDL slates won 10.3 percent of the vote, DEVA only 2.5 percent. This represented a nearly one percent increase for the SKDL over the 1987 general election results, while DEVA's share declined by almost 2 percent. The combined support for the SKDL and DEVA (12.8 percent) represented only a marginal drop from the 13.2 percent that SKDL won in the 1984 local elections. (*HS*, 18 and 20 October.)

A poll conducted in October by *Helsingin Sanomat* showed that Finns hardly knew the new communist leadership. Half of all those questioned could not name one "influential" communist leader. More surprisingly, however, one-third of those who identified themselves as communists or SKDL voters were unsure of who the party leaders were. Older communist leaders, such as Saarinen and Aalto, were much better known to the public. Both communists and noncommunists regarded Kajanoja as being more "influential" than either Wahlström or Käkelä, but even the SKP-Y chairman and former presidential candidate had only a 20 percent recognition rate in the general public and among communists. Käkelä was recognized as being "influential" by 16 percent of communists and 5 percent of noncommunists; Tennilä by 13 percent of communists, but by 8 percent of noncommunists. Wahlström was named by only 4 percent of communists and according to the poll, was virtually unknown as an "influential" communist leader among noncommunists. (*HS*, 30 October.) Commenting later on the decline of leftist political activism, Saarinen explained that "socialism no longer has the same ideological attraction as before" because of the sense of social and economic well-being felt by most Finns. He blamed the trade unions for not promoting class consciousness among workers. (*Hb*, 4 December.)

Finnish governments are usually broadly based. President Koivisto is known to favor bringing the SKDL into the coalition government with the KOK and SDP to make it more balanced. The debate within the SDP on cooperation with the SKDL is a perennial one. SDP government ministers were not eager to give it serious consideration, however, when the subject was raised by party chairman Pertti Paasio in 1988, but KOK spokesmen stated that their conservative party was open to all proposals. Tammisola and Kandolin discussed the subject unofficially with the KOK and SDP. The chairmen of these parties remain hostile to the idea in public, though. Käkelä responded that the SKDL would never be interested in joining a government that included the KOK, which he and other communists regard as a "class enemy." Speaking at a meeting of the SKP Central Committee in November, Wahlström and Tammisola also sought to put to rest speculation that the SKDL might be open to an invitation from Koivisto; they remarked that the SKDL stood to lose electoral support if it cooperated with the conservatives. (*HS*, 14 November; *Kansan Uutiset*, 14 November.)

At the same meeting, the Central Committee emphasized its support for a broader union of the left that would reclaim inert and fallen-away communists. Seeming to pull back from Wahlström's earlier pledge that the SKP must continue to play the leading role, the committee agreed that a new and broader front could operate independently of the SKP, and that members should take part in policy- and decisionmaking.

Tennilä and Seppanen continued to campaign for party reunification, speaking together to small audiences in various parts of the country. Tennilä, who is a member of DEVA's parliamentary group, remarked that it was his personal wish to sit again in the Eduskunta as an SKDL member. He predicted that a reunified party would be more responsive to its membership. He and Seppanen want to keep open a dialogue between majority and minority communists and proposed a joint committee to plan the 1990 party congress. After their own meetings, however, Kajanoja and Wahlström concluded that talks alone would not lead to reunification. Wahlström repeated that, while the door to the party was open, the SKP would welcome only "ex-members" of the SKP-Y, which he now refers to as the "Kajanoja faction." Meanwhile, the SKP-Y Central Committee rejected once again the SKDL proposal for a "leftist alliance" based on open membership that would include minority communists, on the grounds that open membership would dilute the front and weaken communist influence in it. Kajanoja restated his position that any leftist movement had to be based on the equality of member groups, including both the majority and the minority SKP. Yrjö Häkanen complained that the SKP had missed an opportunity for bringing reunification closer when it began preparations for the 22nd Congress without the minority. The SKDL announced plans for a "forum of the left" scheduled for April 1989, but uncertainty reigned as to its purpose, or whether the minority would be encouraged to participate. (*HS*, 21 November, 5 December; *Hb*, 22 November, 2 December.)

Throughout the year, a steady stream of minority communists returned to the SKP, applying for new party membership cards; these included a number of local council members. In December, five of the seven DEVA municipal council members in Karkkila, known as Finland's "reddest city," switched to the SKDL. One of them was quoted as saying that there were no ideological differences among communists in Karkkila, and that divisions had been imposed on the party there by people in Helsinki. (*HS*, 3 December.)

In May, the SKP Central Committee set up its own investigating committee, staffed by SAK and private auditors, to clarify the party's financial situation and to propose reforms. Ossi Viijakainen was named financial manager to replace Jorma Sorvari. Viijakainen undertook a review of the SKP's portfolio and property holdings. Immediate measures taken to reduce the party's budget deficit included dismissing a number of central committee employees and making other staff cuts. Two SKP-owned firms, including the party's former investment firm, declared bankruptcy. Property was put up for sale, and the party took out another mortgage on its headquarters, Kulttuuritalo (House of culture). In November, the SKDL leased its headquarters on Kotkankatu and moved into offices on the fourth floor of Kulttuuriatalo that had been left vacant by the personnel cutbacks in the SKP. The national headquarters of both the SKP and SKDL now share the same building. (*HS*, 12 May, 29 June, 4 and 16 November.)

Indictments were requested on 3 November in the Helsinki Municipal Court of two businessmen implicated in the SKP financial scandal, as well as of the former SKP financial manager. Paul Aura and Risto Reijonen, members of the board of Osaomistus Oy, were accused of bribery for purposes of personal profit; Sorvari was charged with accepting bribes. It was alleged that, with Sorvari's collusion, Aura and Reijonen had sold a business worth about FMk 700,000 to the SKP for FMk 11 million. (*HS*, 4 November.)

Trade unionists constitute the largest element in the SKDL, and the internal "trade union party" has always been influential in the leadership of the SKP. Unions are a major source of funding for party activities. Parallel SKDL and DEVA union organizations compete with each other and the SDP in union elections. Communist influence is particularly strong in the 160,000-member Metalworkers Union (ML) and the 100,000-member Construction Workers Union (RL), which is considered the flag-bearer for communist union activity. Prominent communist union officials include SKP vice-chairman Aarno Aitamurto, who was president of the RL before becoming vice-chairman of the SAK, and Pekka Hynonen, current president of the RL. Communist trade unionists give vocal support to SKP and SKDL positions, such as the improvement of bilateral trade with the Soviet Union, through the platform provided for them by the SAK.

The overlapping relationships of the SKP and SKDL to the trade union movement are complex and are not always complementary. Reijo Käkelä was vocal in his criticism of the SAK leadership, including the communists, prior to his nomination to the SKDL chairmanship. Union delegates supported Claes Andersson for the post at the party congress in May. The confrontation appeared to continue when Pekke Ahmauaara was dropped from the SKDL executive committee, where he had been the ranking representative of the SAK. Käkelä later held talks with union leaders in the SKDL and reached an understanding with them, but a degree of distrust probably remains between the chairman and the unions. By contrast, the position of the trade unions in the SKP was reinforced by the elections of Tammisola and Aitamurto to leadership posts in the party.

Responding to criticism that the SAK had not done enough for lower-income workers in contract talks, Hynonen made it clear that his union was not directed from Kulttuuritalo. Although he recognized that the SKP supported centralized contracts, the communist union leader broke ranks by agreeing to union-specific contracts for the RL, noting the special conditions that existed in the construction industry. (*Kansan Uutiset*, 4 March.) Hynonen's demonstration of trade-union independence provoked Käkelä's charge that the SAK lacked solidarity with the workers.

Johannes Pakaslahti, the Finnish general secretary of the World Peace Council, an international communist-front organization based in Helsinki, challenged the leadership of its chairman, Romesh Chandra, an Indian who he said had continued to follow the "Brezhnev line." Pakaslaht, an SKP member, urged in an October statement that the council must move into the "Gorbachev era." The Finnish Peace Defenders, the national organization that represents Finland on the World Peace Council, is led by communists together with members of the Finnish Center (KESH).

The factional struggle between majority and minority communists complicated the appointment of a general secretary of the Finland-USSR Society and, according to observers, has compromised its reputation. All Finnish parties are formally represented in the society, which promotes good relations between the two countries and is a respected fixture in the foreign-policy establishment. The SKP and SKDL have been particularly influential in the selection of officers. When Erkki Kivimaki of the SKP announced his retirement as general secretary during the summer, the SKDL recommended another majority communist, Oiva Bjorkbacka, to succeed him. The society's chairman, Ahti Pekkala, who represents KESH, and the minority communists opposed Bjorkbacka's nomination, however, and Pekkala urged Kivimaki, who is 65, to stay on the job. To prevent a confrontation, Kivimaki withdrew his resignation on 7 December, and the society's executive committee agreed with Pekkala to postpone the election of a new general secretary until 1989. Kalevi Kivistö, representing the SKDL on the committee, denounced KESH and the SDP for yielding to the minority and breaking an agreement with the SKDL on the distribution of offices. The episode was seen by the liberal press as further evidence of Finnish communism's dwindling credibility. (*HS*, 6, 8, 9, and 12 December.)

Finnish communists continued to redefine their relationship with the CPSU in 1988 and also began to reassess historical interpretations of Finnish-Soviet relations. At a time when the SKP's financial crisis was making headlines daily, Arne Saarinen revealed that the Finnish party had been financially dependent on "international support," that is, the CPSU, until the 1960s, but that funding from Moscow dried up after the SKP began to take a more independent line (*Kansan Uutiset*, 12 May; *HS*, 13 and 20 May). Assuming the mantle of an elder statesman, he took the party's 70th anniversary celebration as the occasion for admitting that the Soviet Union was the aggressor in the Winter War, the first time that a Finnish communist had

made such an admission in public (*Hb*, 4 July). Saarinen continued his reminiscences in December, shedding more light on relations between the Soviets and the SKP. He blamed Soviet encouragement of the minority for the split in the SKP (*Hb*, 4 December). Saarinen stressed, however, that the "SKP is [now] more independent than before," and that developments in the Soviet Union were having a positive effect in Finland (*Uusi Suomi*, 22 March). He believed that Gorbachev's efforts to reform the Soviet economy and to democratize the political process in the USSR would, if successful, greatly strengthen the positions of communist parties in other countries (*Hb*, 4 December). None of Saarinen's revelations were news to most Finns, but the fact that they were made was regarded as a significant departure by the SKP from its past practice and indicated for some that the party had indeed become independent of its one-time mentors.

Arvo Aalto also pointed out that the CPSU had acknowledged at its 27th Congress that it was no longer involved in the internal affairs of other communist parties (*HS*, 17 April). In May, however, Käkelä accepted a Soviet invitation to visit Moscow for two days to explain the the SKP's financial difficulties to representatives of the CPSU. He denied suggestions that the invitation was a demonstration of CPSU support for his nomination as SKDL chairman. "The SKDL is an independent organization," he said, "[and the] Soviet comrades do not interfere in our internal affairs." (*HS*, 18 May.)

Finland was host to several officials of the CPSU in 1988. Politburo member Lev Zaykov represented the CPSU at ceremonies in April marking the 40th anniversary of the Soviet-Finnish Treaty of Friendship, Cooperation, and Mutual Assistance (FCMA). Zaykov met with leaders of both the SKP and SKP-Y while in Helsinki. He later visited Turku, where he laid a wreath on a memorial to Lenin. A. N. Gerasimov, first secretary of the Leningrad District and a Central Committee member, headed the Soviet delegation attending the SKP's 70th-anniversary celebration at Tampere in July. (*FBIS-SOV-88-068*, 8 April.) Gerasimov conveyed the greetings of the Central Committee to the SKP-Y as well as to his SKP hosts, but the CPSU departed from its practice of equal treatment of both factions of the Finnish party by sending a lower-ranking official to the SKP-Y anniversary conference at Turku in August. This was interpreted as giving symbolic preference to the majority SKP. Petr Slezko, a candidate member of the Central Committee and deputy chief of its propaganda department, stressed the need for unity in the communist movement during remarks at the minority's conference. (*Hb*, 29 August.)

Arvo Aalto paid a week-long visit to the German Democratic Republic in late February and early March at the invitation of the SED's Central Committee. He concentrated on arms-control topics in talks with General Secretary Erich Honecker, with whom Aalto issued a joint statement supporting Gorbachev's 1987 "Murmansk proposals" and calling for establishment of a comprehensive system of international security that would include a Nordic nuclear weapons–free zone. (*Neues Deutschland*, 29 February, 1 and 3 March.)

Finnish communists were particularly sensitive to developments in Estonia. This was in large measure an acceptance of the implications of *glasnost'*, but it also reflects on the cultural affinity that exists between Finns and Estonians. On the whole, the SKDL was more outspokenly sympathetic to the Estonians' positions than the SKP. The SKDL issued statements in October and November backing the Estonian Peoples' Front in its demand for self-determination and supporting its initiatives for preserving the Estonian national identity. The SKDL also expressed its special interest in the progress of reforms in Soviet Karelia, Leningrad, and Kola. Käkelä proposed opening a Finnish consulate in Tallinn as the best way to establish direct and official ties to Estonia "without interfering in the internal affairs of other countries." (*Hb*, 3 October; *HS*, 21 November.) President Koivisto had responded earlier to a similar suggestion that there were no plans for a Tallinn consulate (*Dagens Nyheter*, Stockholm, 20 November). Among Finnish communists, only Timo Lahdenmaeki of the KTP repeated the old party line that Estonia had joined the Soviet Union at the demand of a majority of its people. Esko Seppanen raised the question in the Eduskunta of when the Finnish government would act to open direct flights between Helsinki and Tallinn. Foreign Minister Kalevi Sorsa replied that the idea was "becoming interesting," but that the government would have to await a move by Moscow. (*HS*, 2 December.)

In July, *Kansan Uutiset* published an interview with Géza Kotal, member of the Central Committee of the Hungarian Socialist Workers Party (MSM), in which he condemned the Romanian government's treatment of the Hungarian minority in Transylvania (5 July). Helja Tammisola admitted that the Romanian actions and the resulting tension between Hungary and Romania created an "awkward situation" for the SKP. In discussions, some members demanded that relations with the Romanian party be severed, but the SKP determined to distance itself from the RCP without breaking formal ties. The SKP postponed all official trips to Romania for an indefinite period and announced that group vacations there, sponsored by the SKP, had been canceled. The SKP stated that it no longer considered the situation an internal Romanian concern. (*HS*, 12 July; *Hb*, 19 August.)

The SKP urged in November that a special parliamentary committee be empaneled to study the development of Western European integration and its impact on Finland. This proposal coincided with the SKP's criticism of the government for moving to harmonize Finnish economic structures with those of the European Economic Community without consulting the Eduskunta. In a statement, the SKP contended that the government had treated Finland's response to Western European integration as if it were a bureaucratic matter only. It charged that the government was moving along lines that favored large export-oriented businesses and neglected the interests of workers. The SKP warned again about a tilt toward Western Europe that would prejudice Finland's relations with the Soviet Union. (*HS*, 14 November.) The SKDL had earlier used a similar argument in opposing Finland's application to join the Council of Europe during debates on the subject in the Eduskunta (*HS*, 5 May).

Robert Rinehart
Washington, D.C.

France

Population. 55,798,282
Party. French Communist Party (Parti communiste français; PCF)
Founded. 1920
Membership. 604,282 (*l'Humanité*, 3 December 1987)
General Secretary. Georges Marchais
Politburo. 22 members: Georges Marchais, Charles Fiterman (propaganda and communication), Jean-Claude Gayssot (party organization),

Maxime Gremetz (foreign affairs), André Lajoinie (president of the communist group in the National Assembly), Paul Laurent (liaison with party federations), Gisèle Moreau (women's activities and family politics), Gaston Plissonnier (coordination of the work of the Politburo and Secretariat), Gustave Ansart (president of the Central Commission of Political Control), François Duteil (urbanism, environment, and consumption associations), Claude Billard (party activity in business and immigration), Pierre Blotin (education of communists), Philippe Herzog (economy), Francette Lazard (director of the Marxist Research Institute), René Le Guen (science, research, and technology), Roland Leroy (director of *l'Humanité*), René Piquet (president of the French communist group in the European Parliament), Madelaine Vincent (local communities, elections), Henri Krasucki (secretary of the CGT), Louis Viannet (Mail Workers' Federation), Antoine Casanova (intellectual, cultural, educational, and university affairs; also director of the review *La Pensée*), Jackie Hoffmann (women's issues)

Secretariat. 7 members: Maxime Gremetz, Jean-Claude Gayssot, André Lajoinie, Paul Laurent, Gisèle Moreau, Gaston Plissonnier, Charles Fiterman

Central Committee. 145 members

Status. Legal

Last Congress. Twenty-sixth, 2–6 December 1987; next congress planned for 1990

Last Election. 1988, 11.3 percent, 25 of 577 seats (plus 1 in December by-election and 2 from overseas departments)

Auxiliary Organizations. General Confederation of Labor (CGT); World Peace Council; Movement of Communist Youth of France (MCJF); Committee for the Defense of Freedom in France and the World; Association of Communist and Republican Representatives

Publications. *L'Humanité* (Paris: Roland Leroy, director; daily national organ); *L'Echo du centre* (Limoges, daily); *Liberté* (Lille, daily); *La Marseillaise* (Marseille, daily); *L'Humanité-Dimanche* (Paris, weekly); *La Révolution* (Guy Hermier, director; weekly publication of the Central Committee); *La Terre* (weekly); *Cahiers du communisme* (monthly theoretical journal); *Europe* (literary journal); *Economie et politique* (economic journal); 5 journals published by the Marxist Research Institute; 4 monthly magazines; other periodicals on sports, children's themes, and the

like, and books on political, economic, and social topics published by Editions sociales, the PCF publishing house in Paris

France's strife-ridden Communist Party appeared stranded in factionalism and electoral decline in 1988, giving fresh evidence that the once touted party of Guesde and Jaurès had become a "sect" of French politics. Party leaders and candidates fought presidential, legislative, and cantonal elections, while continuing efforts—sanctioned by the 26th Congress—to marginalize reformist voices within the party leadership and regional organizations. The elections yielded contradictory results about whether or not the PCF's long slide toward oblivion was finally arrested, but party spokesmen could take heart from the apparent return of prodigal voters from the extreme-right National Front. On the international front, party initiatives continued to lack energy and direction. Feuding with Italian communists subsided in comparison with the previous year, and PCF leaders showed well-publicized solidarity with other European parties at the Dublin meeting called to oppose the social consequences of the European Community's planned market integration by 1992. Relations with Moscow languished further, however, largely due to the PCF's continued loyalty to Stalinist policies and themes. Nonetheless, some party spokesmen continued to embrace Gorbachev's *glasnost'* and *perestroika* initiatives, but at arm's length. At year's end, PCF leaders and their trade-union retainers of the General Confederation of Labor were locked in a test of nerves with the minority Socialist government of Michel Rocard over wage rates for public-sector workers. As relations between the Socialists and communists worsened, pundits across the French political spectrum began to foresee substantially increased difficulties in forging sufficient leftist unity to safeguard PCF officeholders in the municipal elections set for spring 1989.

Leadership and Internal Activities. The period after the 26th Congress of 2–6 December 1987 was dominated by continued ferment over the rival presidential candidacies of André Lajoinie, the official PCF candidate, and Pierre Juquin, recently expelled Central Committee member and founder of the "renovator" (reformist) faction within the party. Polls persistently showed the Communist rivals running neck and neck—with a slight edge to Lajoinie—and this, more than anything else, probably energized the continued efforts of Politburo hardliners to further marginalize the renovators and their sympathizers who still remained in the party central and departmental leaderships. In an internal report that remained secret until leaked to the press shortly before the 26th Congress, dissident and Politburo oldtimer Gaston Plissonnier denounced "the enterprise of liquidation" against the renovators. Nonetheless, among conservatives who still have the whip hand, the principle that "the party reinforces itself by purifying itself" continued to hold sway. Meanwhile, renovator sympathizers and fellow travelers who reportedly "feared for their skins" included Politburo member Mireille Bertrand—reportedly very close to dismissed Politburo member and newly self-declared renovator Claude Poperen, and to Guy Hermier—leader of the powerful Bouche-du-Rhône federation. Hermier retained his post as director of the Central Committee's theoretical organ La Révolution, but he was removed in mid-January from his control of the "intellectual sectors" portfolio in the leadership, reportedly because General Secretary Georges Marchais found his work "insufficient," and because almost everyone in the leadership suspected him of "weakness concerning the renovators." Moreover, "suspected" softs like former minister Charles Fiterman and the increasingly ineffectual CGT boss Henri Krasucki were widely reported to be isolated in the leadership. (Le Point, 16 November 1987, 25 January 1988.)

At the same time, party bosses continued to struggle with still more instances of regional revolt against the national leadership and 26th Congress line. Two episodes drew national attention and embarrassed leaders to the extent that Pierre Blotin, Politburo enforcer (well-known organizer of the PCF's anti-immigrant raid on Vitry in December 1980) was reportedly dispatched by Marchais "to normalize" the widespread dissidence in the Nord and Haute-Vienne departmental federations. There long-smoldering factionalism eventually (December 1987–January 1988) broke into open rejection of the Politburo leadership and especially the party's presidential candidate. In the Nord, the rupture was total, as five of six communist municipal councillors of Lille openly formed a group of elected renovators who called on militants to support Juquin. At Limoges, in the southwest, former minister Marcel Rigout and like-minded reformers who had been dismissed from the leadership of the Haute-Vienne federation reportedly continued to fight a "guerrilla" campaign in support of Juquin. (Le Point, 16 November 1987; NYT, 17 April.) All

of this, in the view of historian and former communist intellectual Philippe Robrieux, reinforced the "image of [the PCF] as a party that is sinking" (NYT, 17 April).

Marchais and Blotin countered reports of disturbances with claims that party membership remained high and was even increasing. They also attributed the open hostility to formidable anti-Soviet and anticommunist forces arrayed against the workers' movement and Lajoinie's candidacy. In the wake of the 26th Congress, Marchais had downplayed media questions about expulsions and censorship of dissent, claiming that "there have been about five or six expulsions among the 605,000 PCF members," and that "the four or five communist mayors who were [expelled] ought not to have forced us to expel them. If they had been honest, they would have left the party themselves." In reference to grass-roots leadership support for Juquin's presidential hopes, Marchais maintained that Juquin had been supported by only seventeen communist mayors out of a total of 1,495. (L'Humanité, 14 December 1987.)

While the leadership argued uniformly that the party was well poised for recovery from its recent electoral doldrums, Lajoinie admitted in the campaign that it had been "a mistake" for the PCF to join the Socialist-led government in 1981 (Le Point, 11 January)—a decision for which Marchais and others escaped responsibility by continuing to argue that Mitterrand had treacherously reneged on the joint leftist policy. As L'Humanité editorialist Gerard le Puill explained succinctly amidst the faltering Lajoinie campaign, "We lost our credibility as defenders of the underdog by joining a government that didn't carry out our policies" (CSM, 18 April).

Distinguishing between the PS leadership and its militants, Marchais charged that not only had Mitterrand led the party to the right, but Socialists were also behind Juquin's renegade candidacy and were in essence trying to cripple the PCF's comeback by a two-pronged tactic—a theme repeated often by PCF campaigners, who usually added that the media were in cahoots with the Socialist strategy and were actually promoting the Juquin candidacy as a way of further smearing the communists. Blotin announced the party's official opening analysis of the election campaign in his report to the Central Committee plenum of early January. He elaborated further the leadership line that Socialists and rightists had converged recently to an even greater extent than in the past, in both domestic and foreign policies. Hewing closely to the line already trumpeted by Lajoinie in the campaign that Mitterrand's seven years in office had represented a "regression of liberties," Blotin made it clear that the PCF's economic agenda for the remainder of the election would dramatize rising unemployment, falling output, and steady deterioration of living standards. (*L'Humanité*, 14 December 1987; *NYT*, 17 April; TASS, 6 January; *Pravda*, 8 January.)

Clearly rebutting reports that party membership was still off, and that the hemorrhage was especially acute among the young and intellectuals (two groups that traditionally represented fertile ground for PCF recruiting), both Blotin and Marchais argued throughout the campaign and year that rising PCF membership was accounted for by "mainly young people." According to Blotin's January report, the party's membership had increased by "tens of thousands" to over 600,000 militants and 27,000 primary organizations. In March, Marchais signaled that officials had issued 25,000 new cards since the start of the year. Marchais maintained further that most federations were in good shape, and that his own Val-de-Marne federation's membership had risen to over 24,000 loyal activists. By the opening of the PCF's September Fête de l'Humanité—the leadership's ritual self-congratulation (this year replete with an Yves St. Laurent fashion show)—Marchais claimed that party ranks had swelled by 50,000 new members. (*Pravda*, 8 January; *Pravda*, 13 September; *L'Humanité*, 21 March.)

The centerpiece of the Central Committee's claims of increasing membership was its simultaneous campaign to win greater support among the young. Led by Ginette Despretz, the Central Committee's youth-section coordinator, the party decided to put out 750,000 copies of the paper *l'Huma de 15 à 25* five times per year. Meanwhile, party publicists maintained that of the 45,000 members who joined the party in 1987 (an unsubstantiated claim), "over one half are under 25." ("Who Are They Going to Follow?" *WMR*, February; "Liberty, Justice, Peace," *WMR*, March.)

The campaigning prior to the first round of presidential balloting on 24 April saw official and dissident communist candidates locked in mortal combat for what pollsters and pundits agreed would total only about 8 percent of the vote, well below the psychologically important mark of 10 percent. Marchais characterized the party's mobilization as "very good," and parroted the well-practiced Politburo theme that communists had emerged from their "negative experience." (*L'Humanité*, 21 March.)

Dissidents, meanwhile, kept a maximum of electoral pressure on the PCF leadership. Juquin, who made a large number of campaign appearances and garnered a disproportionate share of media coverage, billed his organization as a "rainbow coalition," combining recently expelled renovators, disaffected Socialists, long-exiled PCF intellectuals, antiracists, and a few ecologists. Active as Juquin's campaign was, and despite opinion surveys showing he could gather in about 4 percent of the vote, it was nonetheless clear that his candidacy had not become a rallying point for all or even most renovators. High-level defectors like Poperen and Rigout remained aloof from both candidates, demonstrating that while dissidents were similarly determined to change the PCF, they were not allied in a single organization and did not as yet have a single strategy for accomplishing their goal. This became even clearer in the wake of Juquin's poorer-than-expected performance in the first round of the presidential voting, when Poperen and other dissidents appeared to chart a separate course from Juquin. One problem, as an official of France's International Relations Institute put it, was that Juquin projected the image of a "defrocked priest" and as such suffered the consequences of the question, "Who trusts a defrocked person?" The main problem for renovators who distanced themselves from Juquin, however, was clearly the issue of factionalism. In the wake of the elections, Juquin casually announced his intention of joining the Ecologist candidate, Antoine Waechter (who had garnered almost 4 percent of the presidential vote), to form a new movement of "Reds and Greens" that would stand apart from "all existing parties." Before the quickly called parliamentary elections in June, candidates of the new coalition published a manifesto on "Solidarity, Ecology, Democracy," that set out four priorities that were all familiar Ecologist themes. (*Le Monde*, 1 June.) PCF dissidents, however, refused to follow Juquin into alliance with Waechter. In late May, a self-styled "group of 54," apparently headed by Claude Poperen, drafted a document making it clear that the reformers still considered themselves within the PCF. The group's Initiative for Communist Reconstruction (hence, the media's later habit of referring to them as "reconstructors") called on all communists to fight the coming parliamentary elections with determination because, according to them, "a good result by our candidates in those elections will create better conditions for the reconstruction of the great PCF that we want." *Le Monde* reported the initiative had received "almost 1,000 signatures," and that these included important figures in the party. *L'Humanité* originally viewed the initiative as factionalism, but the reconstructor movement eventually met with only mild criticism when the Central Committee convened on 18 May to consider the results of the elections. According to press reports, some signatories were even chosen as PCF candidates in the parliamentary contests. (*Le Monde*, 28 May, 1 June.)

Explaining the election disaster—the worst Communist defeat in its 68-year history—as the work of the allied communist renegades and "rightist" Socialists, party bosses immediately launched a new subscription (equal to the eight billion "old francs" that Marchais claimed was raised for the presidential campaign) to cover the remaining expenses of a long presidential election, which was now almost certain to be followed by legislative elections. (*L'Humanité*, 19 May). They also seemed to foresee further disappointment of the militants in the legislative balloting, claiming at some length that former interior minister Pasqua had gerrymandered districts against communists. They also accused Pasqua of undercutting communist strength by reintroducing the old single member–districts voting system in place of the "more democratic" proportional representation that Mitterrand had enacted in 1984, and that had almost certainly cushioned the PCF's fall to 35 seats in the 1986 legislative elections. (*L'Humanité*, 19 May.) But party candidates won an increased share of the votes in the legislative elections, and therefore the Central Committee meeting of 27–28 June permitted the leadership to trumpet the apparent reversal of the PCF's slide toward ever lower percentages of the vote. Although Marchais and others stopped short of predicting that the party's electoral fortunes had bottomed out, they pointed justifiably to a substantial increase in votes that exceeded any pre-election forecasts. (*L'Humanité*, 28 June.)

Clearly buoyed by their success in the legislative elections, communist spokesmen followed up by playing variations on the theme that Mitterrand's strategy of "opening to the center" had pushed disillusioned Socialist voters into the PCF column. Such predictions appeared borne out by the cantonal elections in early September, so the fall Fête de l'Humanité was staged as a celebration of the party's recovery. (*Le Quotidien de Paris*, 10–11 September; *Pravda*, 13 September.)

Preparations for the party's National Conference, set for 12–13 November, were marred, however, by a revival of renovator protests, this time in the form of an appeal for pluralism. On 4 October *L'Humanité* published a memorandum to the federations to "help them prepare for the conference"—a tract entitled "Let Us Make Each Cell and Each Communist a Decisive Architect of a Union for Self-Defense and Change." The same day, renovators—led by Poperen, Rigout, and Felix Damette—launched a countermemorandum, "Aimed at Opening a Debate Among Members" [of the party]. Rejecting in advance the accusations of factionalism, the advocates of "reconstruction" charged that if the leadership held on to power by any means possible, factions would "inevitably result." Arguing that the parliamentary elections "were in no way a recovery," the group openly allied itself with the "Gorbachevian revolution," which, they argued, was tackling the issues that PCF leaders feared to face. Demanding "the return of Eurocommunism," they labeled Stalinism "a cancer that almost killed Communism and that has not yet been rooted out." The reconstructors were almost certainly emboldened by their own recent gains in cantonal elections. (*Le Monde*, 5 October.)

In the last months of the year, the attention of PCF leaders and reformers was increasingly fixed on the forthcoming municipal elections, in which the party's claims of revival would be tested. For Marchais and other hard-liners the stakes were especially high, since the local officers are the bedrock of communist influence and patronage—the institutional groundwork on which the party's remaining claim to national strength and prestige rested. If city halls fell in large numbers, either to noncommunists or renovators, the leadership would surely face a more virulent outbreak of dissent and even open rebellion among the party's militants.

Domestic Affairs. Although factionalism played a role in all three elections the PCF fought in 1988, it was most significant in the presidential balloting, which took place on 24 April and 8 May (Paris Domestic Service, 3 February). While fending off claims of legitimacy by Juquin, Lajoinie and other PCF spokesmen attempted to focus their campaign on the Socialist incumbent, François Mitterrand, by charging that his policies were not different from those of the beleaguered Chirac government ("continuing to govern the country with the Right," *L'Humanité*, 7 April), and that only the PCF offered a real alternative to disgruntled leftist voters (Paris

Domestic Service, 10 February; reporting the Central Committee meeting of early February). Ultimately, however, the PCF campaign boiled down to a close race between Lajoinie and Juquin for what most polls showed would be a shrunken communist share of the vote. Simulations throughout much of the winter gave Lajoinie about 6 percent, and Juquin routinely followed with between 3 and 4 percent. (Although polls just before the balloting predicted Juquin would carry 2–2.5 percent and Lajoinie 5–7 percent [*Financial Times*, 22 April].) Despite indications that Juquin's candidacy enjoyed significant support on the leftist fringe, Marchais labelled him a crypto-Socialist candidate and charged in mid-February that Juquin could not even muster the 500 signatures of elected officials necessary to run for president without substantial Socialist help (*L'Humanité*, 11 February).

By all accounts, the two campaigns differed dramatically (one weekly newspaper likened them to a Unitarian service and a Catholic mass), with Lajoinie fighting a lackluster and drab series of skirmishes, mostly in the communist hinterland, and Juquin rousing enthusiastic support in speeches to a smaller but colorful assortment of political groups. Juquin early on predicted that he would best Lajoinie and could get 5 percent of the vote; Lajoinie set his goal to improve on the 9.7 percent achieved by PCF candidates in the 1986 parliamentary voting (*The Economist*, 5 March; AFP, 28 March). Juquin's stump themes mirrored the diverse interests of his constituents. He stressed independence from Moscow, ideological compromise, unilateral disarmament, votes for immigrants, mandating equal numbers of both sexes in elected offices, a freeze on wages while cutting the work week, and total independence for the French territory of New Caledonia (*CSM*, 18 April).

Despite relentless attacks on Mitterrand and the PS, PCF spokesmen would not rule out eventual revival of leftist-unity tactics, nor disavow intending to instruct communist voters to support Mitterrand on the second round (something most polls showed communist voters would do anyway), nor rule out local alliances with the PS in the legislative and cantonal elections to follow (*Le Monde*, 22 April). All that Lajoinie would disavow was any temptation to actually join the Mitterrand government as junior partner, as the PCF had done in 1981 (AFP, 28 March; Paris Domestic Service, 13 April). Lajoinie left open a crack in the door of cooperation by nuancing attacks on Mitterrand, declaring that at least the PCF did not put the Socialist

leader on the same level as Chirac (Paris Domestic Service, 13 April).

First-round balloting, which saw a larger than usual voter turnout, dealt a crushing blow to both PCF and renovator hopes. Lajoinie polled only 6.8 percent of the vote, an "historic" low and far short of the 15.5 percent Marchais had received in 1981. Juquin's 2.1 percent was widely regarded as insufficient to bolster reformist strength within the party, and even a leading supporter called it a "botched" job. In contrast, the PCF's archvillain and National Front firebrand Jean-Marie Le Pen garnered a stunning 14.4 percent of the ballots, many of them in former PCF strongholds of the south and southwest. (Paris Domestic Service, reporting Interior Ministry results, 24 April.) Lajoinie polled over 1.5 million votes, while Juquin gathered in another 466,000 (Paris Domestic Service, 24 April).

When Marchais reported the results to the Central Committee on 27 April, two questions were uppermost in observers' minds: what had gone wrong with the communist vote, and what would party bosses decide to do in the second round. The Politburo's analysis of the election emphasized inordinately high rates of abstentions in key PCF bastions, such as the Paris "red belt" precincts of Aubervilliers (25.4 percent), Fontenay (26 percent), Montreuil (26.3 percent), Bagneux (27.2 percent), and Romainville (28.5 percent). This was an unsatisfactory reckoning of the PCF electoral disaster, since it begged the question of the leadership's responsibility for the alienation of so many militants in traditional strongholds. Marchais consoled the party with figures—drawn from unknown polls—showing that only a small portion of usual PCF voters turned out for Le Pen's romp, and that those who defected to other candidates generally chose Mitterrand rather than Juquin. (*L'Humanité*, 28 April.)

While the federations and Central Committee dithered over whether to order militants to vote Socialist in the second round, Juquin quickly instructed his supporters to defeat the "Chirac-Le Pen tandem" by voting for Mitterrand (*Financial Times*, 26 April). Amid increasing indications that Mitterrand planned to emphasize his "opening to the center" theme after the election, the Central Committee reluctantly told communists to vote Socialist. (Paris Domestic Service, 28 April). The rationale was predictable; Marchais declared—as he would in subsequent attempts to put the PCF decision in a positive light—that the tactic would "block the road to power" of the neo-Gaullists and National Front.

(AFP, 28 April; *Izvestiia*, 10 May; *Le Monde*, 10 May; *L'Humanité*, 9 May; Paris Domestic Service, 8 May). *L'Humanité*'s morning-after explanation of the party's historic catastrophe emphasized that the PCF could best bring its locally-based strength to bear in subnational elections. Anyway, as *L'Humanité* editorialist and Central Committee member Claude Cabanes explained, the anticommunist media had carried out a "systematic operation of obstruction" to "block the renewed growth of Communist power." (*L'Humanité*, 25 April; "French Communist Party's Worst Election Result in Its History," Radio Free Europe, RAD Background Report/73, 28 April.)

In a postelection drumbeat of rhetoric that would distract the militants from the recent defeat, party bosses blasted Socialist support for the proposed 1992 European Community market integration, the military budget, and Mitterrand's policies on the festering "neocolonial" status of New Caledonia. Continuing familiar themes from the Lajoinie campaign, PCF journalists and spokesmen flailed Mitterrand's advocacy of closer economic cooperation with other EC countries as a formula for increased unemployment, more poverty, and added pressure on living standards. (*L'Humanité*, 9 May.) Moreover, PCF leaders were able to lambaste both the Chirac government and Mitterrand, when their "cohabitation" government launched a commando-style raid to rescue French policemen taken hostage by Melanasian separatists on New Caledonia. The deaths of 21 people in the attack brought 3,000 leftists into the streets of Paris, led by Pierre Juquin and PCF leaders. (AFP, 6 May.)

Events in New Caledonia and National Front gains in the first round of the recent balloting also prompted a postelection PCF campaign against racism. Marchais and other party leaders had earlier mourned the murders of two Arab immigrants in southern France, and later nominated South African ANC leader Nelson Mandela for the Nobel Peace Prize. Nonetheless, at least one knowledgeable journalist pointed out that during the campaign Lajoinie's set speech had contained "no ringing denunciations of racism in France," though it had plenty of harsh words for apartheid in South Africa. (*L'Humanité*, 13 January; *NYT*, 17 April; *Le Monde*, 10 May.)

The devastating loss in the presidential election raised the stakes for PCF bosses in the parliamentary elections, which Mitterrand called for early June. This was particularly so, because Marchais had earlier claimed on national television that the communists would improve their performances in legislative and cantonal elections (Paris Domestic Service, 14 May). The Politburo's call to arms made no predictions of success, and in its allusions to the presidential results even seemed to have a note of resignation. Nonetheless, party spokesmen and candidates quickly took up the refrain that the 6.7 percent of the votes amassed by Lajoinie in the party's last electoral outing did not reflect the PCF's real influence. Said Marchais, unbelievably, "The election of the President by universal suffrage is the most undemocratic of elections. We condemned it from the start." (*L'Humanité*, 28 April.)

PCF office seekers focused on Mitterrand's now obvious "opening to the center" as a sellout. Candidates also attacked the "Europe-1992" theme of the Socialist campaign as a cruel conspiracy against the rights of labor and a surrender of French sovereignty to the interests of employers and big capital. Marchais was, however, on the defensive personally in the campaign, forced to deny on national television that he was concerned that voters in his own Villejuif (Paris) constituency, who had voted overwhelmingly for Mitterrand in the presidential election, would turn him out of the office he had held for 15 years. (*Pravda*, 23 May; *Izvestiia*, 31 May; *Le Monde*, 28 May; Paris Domestic Service, 5 June; TASS, 4 June; *L'Humanité*, 19 May.)

The results of the elections appeared to show a surprising communist recovery of electoral strength. First-round statistics showed that PCF candidates had piled up 11 percent of the vote, significantly better than in the party's presidential outing and even a slight increase over its performances in the previous legislative elections. After a little chestbeating to ridicule the press predictions of the party's disappearance as a parliamentary entity—some pre-election estimates had the PCF falling to twelve or even nine seats—communist leaders confidently announced a deal with the PS whereby some communist candidates would stand down in some constituencies during the second round on 12 June (Reuters, 2 and 6 June; *NYT* News Service, 8 June), a deal that was apparently not supported by many federations (*Le Monde*, 28 April). This undoubtedly prevented an even worse PS "setback" than occurred. The Central Committee's postelection analysis claimed that Mitterrand's "alliance of the Right" tactics had suffered a major rebuke by voters, who wanted "left-wing forces to rally together for a left-wing policy." (*Le Monde*, 8 and 14 June; *L'Humanité*, 6 June; *Financial Times*, 6 June; Paris Domestic Service, 5 and 6 June).

French voters returned 27 communist deputies—25 from the PCF, 2 independent communists from overseas territories—with a total of 3.4 percent of the popular vote after two rounds (Paris Domestic Service, 12 June; *NYT*, 14 June; Reuter, 14 June). Marchais blamed the actual reduction of communist seats (they had 35 in the old National Assembly) on the return to single-member districts under the Chirac government; claiming that by right the number should have been 65 or 70. Nonetheless, PCF spokesmen touted the dramatic upturn in party percentages of the total vote, and commentaries in the noncommunist French and much of the European press noted the party's "recovery." (*Le Monde*, 14 June; *Pravda*, 16 June; *Financial Times*, 6 June.)

Actual results in some areas were especially gratifying to the leadership. In the Nord, where dissidence and clear voter preference for Mitterrand in the presidential contest had reportedly caused concern that traditional constituencies would fall to Socialists, hard-line communists held their seats. Stalwarts like Alain Bocquet—highpriest of "normalization" and first secretary of the fractious Nord federation—retained his seat, as did the other three antireform communists who had been returned with him from the district in 1986. Bocquet's victory was a special blow to renovators, as was the defeat in the Limousin region of leading renovator Marcel Rigout, who stood down in the second round in favor of the Socialists who swept the southwest. (*Le Monde*, 13 June; "Les cartes du parti," *Le Point*, 13 June.) Meanwhile, PCF leaders relished the National Front's reduction from 32 seats to a single deputy (even though PCF and FN candidates had obtained a comparable number of votes in the first round) (*Le Monde*, 14 June).

Most election analyses, however, emphasize that low voter turnout was the key to the PCF's "victory." The whopping 34 percent abstention—much of it among Socialist voters—enabled communists to claim a relatively larger share of the total vote, even though they still lost seats. Many commentators recalled pre-legislative election talk of "voter fatigue" and "election torpor" owing to the intense campaigning of the presidential contest. Still others maintained that Socialist voters were disillusioned by evidence of their party's drift toward the center, and that these disaffected Socialists abandoned the field to the more disciplined communists. France's leading opinion-research firm concluded that "voters of both the left and right had stayed away from the polls, but the net affect was to boost the

Communists at the expense of the Socialists." (Reuters, 3 and 6 June; *NYT* News Service, 8 June.)

Although communist leaders disparaged the notion of revived leftist unity and fiercely declared themselves outside the presidential majority, they quickly sought a legislative *modus vivendi* with the Socialists, who clearly intended to form a minority government under Rocard. A deal was cut whereby Socialists would change National Assembly rules, reducing from 30 to 20 the minimum seats needed to be an official parliamentary group—a status that brings floor time, television access, office space, and other privileges. In return, PCF deputies voted with the PS to install former Socialist prime minister Laurent Fabius as president of the National Assembly. (*NYT*, 25 June 1988; AFP, 1 July.)

Despite alliances of convenience, PCF leaders soon showed that they considered their election rebound the basis for more strident "oppositionist" tactics against the Rocard government—all the more since it was clear that Mitterrand and Rocard were determined to follow through on a "centrist-oriented" program that included support for "Europe-1992," increased military spending, budgetary "rigor," restrained wage increases for public-sector employees, more workforce flexibility for employers, and a settlement in New Caledonia based on local consensus. Despite some strained parliamentary cooperation, therefore, the summer was marked by generally deepening animosity between the Socialist government and the PCF. The Politburo's statement on the election predicted that the PS would foster "increased unemployment, new austerity measures and additional advantages for financial groups" (*L'Humanité*, 17 June)—themes that were elaborated further in Marchais's eventual report to the Central Committee plenum of 27–28 June (*L'Humanité*, 28 June). As evidence mounted throughout the summer that Mitterrand's "opening" was meeting with little success, communists clearly intensified their attacks on PS government policies. Party leaders labeled Rocard's promised tax on wealth as "insufficient" and condemned the new budget as "regressive" because it emphasized "austerity." Defense policies were branded "militaristic" and "submissive" to U.S. hegemonic interests. In general, press and PS analysts saw the escalation of such tactics as intended to exacerbate the results of Mitterrand's flagging appeal to the center and to reorienting Socialist attention to the need to cooperate in the coming cantonal and even more important municipal elections. (*L'Express*, 9 September; Radio Free Europe, RAD Background Report/73, 28

April; *Le Quotidien de Paris*, 10–11 September; *NYT* News Service, 8 June.)

Despite Prime Minister Rocard's rising popularity—largely on the basis of his personally-brokered settlement on New Caledonia—French voters abstained in near record numbers (50 percent) in the fall cantonal (district) elections. Billed by political observers as a dress rehearsal for the municipal elections in spring 1989, the cantonal abstentions permitted PCF candidates to collect 13.4 percent of the first-round vote—a clear improvement over the party's 12.1 percent in similar balloting in 1985 and adding credibility to Politburo claims of a trend toward recovery. As in the legislative elections, PS and PCF leaders agreed to stand down in districts where one or the other had achieved a larger share of the vote in the first round. (*Pravda*, 27 September; UPI, 25 September; Reuters, 25 September.) But, as in the legislative elections, PCF gains were more apparent than real. In fact, as the noncommunist press quickly pointed out, the party actually sustained a net loss of thirteen seats—all in traditional PCF bastions like the Correze and the Haute-de-Seine—and in some conspicuous cases communist voters returned "renovators" (*Libération*, 4 October). Partly on the basis of their gains, renovators announced formation of a Marseilles-based Communist Reform Party (MRC), headed by well-known PCF dissident Claude Liabres and apparently devoted to arranging joint Communist-Socialist lists in the forthcoming municipal elections (Paris Domestic Service, 23 October). Dissidents also challenged publicly the leadership's analyses of the recent PCF election successes, noting especially the gains made by renovators (*Le Monde*, 5 October). Meanwhile, Socialist spokesmen—notably Interior Minister Joxe and PS functionary Jean Poperen (brother of the PCF "reconstructor")—assailed communists for having reneged on second-round promises of cooperation in some areas and even accused the PCF of helping conservatives in some districts (*Le Monde*, 5 October). The predictable PS offer to "unite the left" for the coming municipal elections—announced by former prime minister Pierre Mauroy on 13 October—infuriated Marchais because it suggested that the arrangement would incorporate the communists into the "presidential majority" (*L'Humanité*, 13 October).

Although the upshot of the cantonal elections was to open a dialogue between the PS and PCF on joint strategy for the municipal elections, the continuation of what communist leaders viewed as the Rocard government's centrist policies led to a running series of confrontations, especially in the fall. PCF leaders were angered most by the government's introduction of an "austerity budget" that held the line on the government's offer of 2.2 percent increases in public-sector wages. Beginning in late summer, France was hit by a series of strikes by nurses, Air France mechanics, social-security office workers, and postal and telegraph employees. Ultimately, even the PS-oriented and white-collar unions joined the communist-dominated CGT on the picket lines. In late November, hostilities culminated in a showdown over government determination to restrain wage increases for public-transport workers, the vast majority of whom belong to the CGT. Workers froze the Paris area transit system and Mitterrand responded by calling in the army to keep the commuter trains running. By mid-December, however, the government had offered sufficient concessions, and moderate unions were willing to settle, but CGT officials—apparently encouraged by the PCF leadership—refused and threatened a nationwide rail strike for the week of 11 December. Although most observers emphasized that economic issues were the crux of the dispute, most also maintained that the PCF's role was calculated to pressure the PS government to abandon its centrist overtures and reforge "leftist unity" for the forthcoming municipal elections on terms acceptable to communists. (AFP, 10 September, 20 October, 15 November; *Financial Times*, 29 November, 6 December; *Le Monde*, 30 November; *Dow Jones* (Paris), 5 December.) According to various press reports, PCF propagandists targeted the PS government's ministers of labor and public works, presumably hoping to force their resignations and thereby embarrass the Rocard government (*Le Monde*, 30 November; *Le Point*, 7 November). Communist claims of recovery and pressure on the Rocard government increased even further in mid-December, when a PCF candidate nosed out a Socialist in a crucial by-election, thereby raising to 28 the number of communists in the National Assembly (*Financial Times*, 13 December).

Foreign Affairs and Security Issues. The PCF's foreign-policy interests were dominated by two issues during the year: the planned EC market integration by 1992 and the party's lingering hostility to the *glasnost'* and *perestroika* initiatives of Soviet president Gorbachev. The 1992 issue boiled down to anxieties about the social costs of lowering or removing economic barriers between members of the EC. Moved initially by its longstanding and strident anti-EC tradition, the PCF's leadership joined other European leftist parties and labor unions in sending up an increasingly shrill cry about the absence of a "social dimension" to the proposed integration. The specter of cross-border corporate mergers that would complicate labor agreements and, more important, fears that integration would permit North European companies to shift operations to the relatively cheap labor pools of the south, prompted French communists to denounce the scheme as a plot by employers and Socialists to further wreck the living standards of working people. Mitterrand, who made "Europe-1992" one of the twin themes of his re-election campaign, took the brunt of the PCF's attacks, which portrayed 1992 as cementing the developing bond between Socialists and the right. (*L'Humanité*, 19 May, 17 and 28 June.) In October, French communists met in Dublin with delegations from most other West European CPs, reportedly to forge a common position on the pernicious social and economic consequences expected from the EC integration (Reuters, 30 October).

Relations with Moscow remained frigid throughout the year. Pouring salt into wounds newly opened by the PCF's devastating presidential defeat, *Izvestiia* editorialist Alexander Bovine drew an angry rejoinder from PCF hard-liners when he characterized their election experience as a "great defeat." Bovine further assailed French communists for having "neither program nor slogans" capable of attracting a large popular vote (*Izvestiia*, 3 May; *Le Point*, 9 May), for wallowing in the "negative forces" that "long characterized" the Soviet Union (i.e., unregenerate Stalinism), and for adopting "strategy and tactics [that] are lagging with respect to the new conditions created by *perestroika*." (*Izvestiia*, 3 May.) As France's noncommunist press hooted both its approval of Bovine's diatribe and its derision of the PCF (*Libération*, 3 May; *Le Monde*, 3 May), *L'Humanité* chief editor Claude Cabanes struck back with invective that both distorted Bovine's words (to downplay criticism of the PCF) and accused the Soviet journalist of ignorance of the conditions under which French communists were operating (*L'Humanité*, 4 May). The rebuke—reminiscent of the 1956 exchanges between Maurice Thorez and Soviet leader Khrushchev over de-Stalinization—was reported in the Soviet media (*Izvestiia*, 6 May). But, as the French press noted, the difference between this altercation and 1956 was

that the PCF no longer commanded 20 percent of the vote and therefore was not able to rebut Soviet charges from a position of strength ("Après la gifle, la claque," *Le Point*, 9 May).

Despite such hissing, PCF and Soviet officials managed to keep most disagreements out of the national limelight. In July, *L'Humanité* published a work of fiction by Soviet writer Alexander Bek that criticized the Stalin era (*Le Quotidien de Paris*, 10–11 September). Arguable PCF successes in the legislative and cantonal elections probably prevented the contretemps with Moscow from touching off a public spat within the PCF leadership, between "conservatives" and those Politburo and Central Committee members—Charles Fiterman, Guy Hermier, Lucien Sève, and Anicet le Pors—thought to represent a "Gorbachevian tendency" (*Le Quotidien de Paris*, 10–11 September). Further, there was no hint of strained relations when Soviet foreign minister Shevardnadze met with Marchais during an October visit to France (TASS, 11 October; Moscow Television Service, 12 October).

Throughout the year, PCF spokesmen and officials also continued to support Moscow's foreign-policy themes, in particular Soviet calls for a negotiated settlement in Afghanistan in parallel with their withdrawal (Marchais cited in TASS, 10 February). French communists also repeated familiar Soviet demands for an international conference on the Middle East that would assure Palestinian statehood on the basis of self-determination (*L'Humanité*, 1 July). Meanwhile, PCF writer Alain Guerin previewed and publicized his intention to write an "objective" account of the Soviet intelligence service. Bearing the folksy title *The People from the KGB*, Guerin's book will be published by *L'Humanité* (*New Times*, no. 36, 1988; Radio Liberty 373/88, RL 411/88, 7 September).

Opposition to U.S. policies and interests focused to a surprising degree during 1988 on charges of U.S. economic domination of Western Europe, in particular of France. Citing expert predictions of slowed economic growth in the coming year, PCF editorialists blamed the expected downturn on G-7 (especially French) "capitulation" at the Toronto economic summit to U.S. demands that they support the dollar (*L'Humanité*, 12 August).

In other foreign-policy initiatives, the PCF blasted French politicians who opposed PLO leader Arafat's visit to France, rejected international terrorism, and reluctantly supported the Rocard government's campaign to secure a "yes" vote on the referendum concerning New Caledonia's future.

Pursuing its customary invective against the Atlantic Alliance, the PCF media also often lambasted Mitterrand and the French Socialists for promoting U.S. hegemony in Europe and highlighted the role of the U.S. military press in cementing the subjecting of Europe by NATO (*L'Humanité*, 14 September, 7 October; *Le Quotidien de Paris*, 10–11 September; Paris Domestic Service, 22 February).

In yet another major security initiative, the PCF also launched a public relations and legislative drive to establish an official committee to oversee the activities of France's intelligence services, which Lajoinie claimed were too secretive (*Valeurs Actuelles*, 22 August).

Peace and disarmament activities focused on the sinister role of the United States and NATO, contrasting the alliance's insistence on nuclear deterrence and maintenance of conventional military strength in Europe with the more benign image of the Soviet Union produced by Gorbachev's initiatives in Geneva and at the Vienna-based Conference on Security and Cooperation in Europe (*IB*, April 1988; *L'Humanité*, 22 January).

Marchais and General Secretary Honecker of the GDR's Socialist Unity Party (SED) embraced the INF agreement and the goal of a 50 percent reduction in strategic nuclear forces, called for the elimination of the imbalance in conventional forces in Europe, and seconded Gorbachev's "Common European Home" theme as the basis for further progress on arms control. Their joint statements were made during the East German leader's visit to France. (ADN International Service, 9 January; AFP, 7 January; *L'Humanité*, 11 January.) In contrast to their description of the relations between the French and GDR communists as peace-oriented, PCF publicists characterized the improving defense cooperation and security dialogue between Paris and Bonn as moves toward "rearmament" and blockage of "denuclearization" in Europe (*IB*, April; *WMR*, April). PCF officials seconded Soviet charges that the bellicose nature of Socialist policy was also evident in Mitterrand's renewed commitment to increased military spending, which was consistent with NATO pledges and embodied in the Rocard government's new Military Programs Law (*Pravda*, 8 January; *L'Express*, 9 September).

International Activities. PCF international activity slackened in 1988, in large part because of the party's strong focus on four national elections and the renewal of "oppositionist" tactics in the fall. In addition to high-level meetings with GDR party

boss Honecker, French communists entertained notable visits from the Soviet human rights group headed by Fedor Burlatskiy, Cuban Politburo and Central Committee members (led by Jorge Risquet), GDR Politburo member and SED Central Committee secretary Guenter Schabowski, and Hungarian party leader Károly Grósz. Meetings with Honecker and Grósz, however, were clearly on the margins of their official visits to Paris, where contacts with Mitterrand and Rocard were the dominant interest. (MTI, 17 November; ADN International Service, 23 and 26 November; *L'Humanité*, 11 and 19 May.) Minor delegations from Third World communist parties also visited their PCF counterparts, most notably a delegation of provincial party officials from the People's Republic of China (*L'Humanité*, 6 September). Third World themes were once again prominent at the Fête de l'Humanité, and the annual gathering attracted a number of foreign delegations. The Soviet group was headed by *Pravda* chief editor and CPSU Central Committee member V. G. Afanasyev (*Pravda*, 13 September).

Maxime Grametz, in charge of the Politburo's Foreign Affairs Department, headed several delegations to East European parties and governments. He visited Yugoslavia in July, apparently to hype PCF gains in the recent legislative elections and to lend support to the embattled Yugoslav government in its dealings with ethnic disturbances (*L'Humanité*, 16 July). Grametz also touted PCF election victories during similar visits to Prague (ČTK, 19 August; Prague Domestic Service, 24 August; MTI, 22 August), while it fell to Lajoinie to explain the PCF's presidential election debacle during a spring visit to the Czech capital (*Rudé Právo*, 17 May). Minor PCF delegations also visited their counterparts in Third World countries. Notable was a reciprocal visit paid by French provincial communist leaders to the PRC (Jinan Shandong Province Service, 12 July).

Various PCF groups visited the USSR during the year. Most important, French communist mayors traveled to Moscow during the summer, with a side trip to Tallinn and Tartu, to meet with Soviet mayors and local officials. Meanwhile, a French communist cultural delegation journeyed to Moscow in August to further contacts with Soviet broadcasters, writers, and film makers. *L'Humanité* director and Politburo hard-liner Roland Leroy also visited Moscow in the fall, reportedly to discuss ways to "better associate" the PCF with "the new image of the USSR" and to pave the way for a visit by Georges

Marchais. (*Le Point*, 7 November; *Pravda*, 13 July, 1 August.)

Edward A. Allen
Washington, D.C.

Germany
Federal Republic of Germany

Population. 60,980,200, excl. West Berlin (July 1988)
Party. German Communist Party (Deutsche Kommunistische Partei; DKP)
Founded. 1968
Membership. 50,000 (claimed, 1988); 38,000 DKP alone or 62,000 including youth and student movements (Federal Office for the Protection of the Constitution [BfV])
Chairman. Herbert Mies (since 1973)
Presidium. 19 members: Herbert Mies, Ellen Weber (deputy chair), Jupp Angenfort, Kurt Bachmann, Irmgard Bobrzik, Martha Buschmann, Werner Cieslak, Heinz Czymek, Gerd Deumlich, Kurt Fritsch, Hermann Gautier, Wolfgang Gehrcke, Willi Gerns, Dieter Keller, Georg Polikeit, Rolf Priemer, Birgit Radow (youth organization chair), Karl-Heinz Schröder, Wilhelm Spengler, Werner Sturmann
Secretariat. 14 members: Herbert Mies, Ellen Weber, Vera Aschenbach, Werner Cieslak, Gerd Deumlich, Kurt Fritsch, Willi Gerns, Marianne Konze, Jofel Mayer, Fritz Noll, Rolf Priemer, Karl-Heinz Schröder, Wilhelm Spengler, Werner Sturmann
Executive. 94 members
Status. Legal
Last Congress. Ninth, January 1989, in Frankfurt am Main
Last Election. 1987, about .5 percent for "Peace List," in which DKP participated; no representation in federal parliament or any land (state) parliament

Auxiliary Organizations. Socialist German Workers' Youth (Sozialistische Deutsche Arbeiterjugend; SDAJ), about 15,000 members, Birgit Radow, chair; Marxist Student Union–Spartacus (Marxistischer Studentenbund–Spartakus; MSB-Spartakus), about 6,000 members; Young Pioneers (Junge Pioniere; JP), about 4,000 members, Gerhard Hertel, chair

Publications. *Unsere Zeit* (Our time), Düsseldorf, DKP organ (editor: Georg Polikeit), daily circulation 23,000, weekend edition about 44,000, Monday edition discontinued. Many issues are distributed to socialist states through East Berlin. *Elan–Das Jugendmagazin*, SDAJ monthly organ, circulation about 19,000; *Rote Blätter* (Red pages), MSB-Spartakus monthly organ, circulation about 11,500; *Pionier* (Pioneer), JP monthly organ, circulation 5,000

History. The DKP, which is unswervingly loyal to Moscow and East Berlin, grew out of the Communist Party of Germany (Kommunistische Partei Deutschlands; KPD). The KPD had been officially founded on 31 December 1918, by left-wing Spartakists who had broken away from the Social Democratic Party of Germany (SPD) following the Bolshevik revolution in Russia a year earlier. The KPD opposed the "bourgeois" Weimar Republic, while growing to be Germany's third largest party. It operated under the mistaken belief that the downfall of that democracy would be the prelude to a communist revolution. Nevertheless, German communists, looking back, believe that their party was the only one correctly to foresee what was coming. The KPD was shattered during the Third Reich. It was outlawed and went underground. Some communists perished in concentration camps and exile. Some engaged in largely ineffective resistance efforts within Germany, opposing Nazism whenever the Soviet Union's state interests were threatened by Hitler's Germany and refraining from such opposition whenever Soviet interests so required, as in the two years following the signing of the German-Soviet nonaggression pact.

After the war, the KPD was the first party to be legalized on 11 June 1945. It sought to merge with the SPD, but this happened only in the Soviet zone of occupation when the Socialist Unity Party (SED) was formed on 22 April 1946. In the Federal Republic of Germany (FRG), the KPD opposed the Basic Law (constitution), which went into effect in 1949. After 1949 communists never again won seats in the Federal Parliament. Its dependence upon a foreign patron, notably the SED in the German Democratic Republic (GDR), contributed to the Constitutional Court's outlawing of the KPD in August 1956 because of its "permanent attitude of hostility toward the basic democratic and liberal order."

After it had been legalized in 1945, the KPD toned down its revolutionary rhetoric and advocated the creation of an "anti-fascist democratic order" and a popular front. It sought to merge with the SPD as a unified German workers' party, something which actually happened in the Soviet zone of occupation on 22 April 1946, when the Socialist Unity Party of Germany (Sozialistische Einheitspartei Deutschlands; SED) was formed. Because of bitter opposition to such merger by leading Social Democrats in the Western zones, especially Kurt Schumacher, no unification took place in the West. The KPD had two representatives (out of a total of 65) on the Parliamentary Council, which existed from September 1948 to May 1949 to produce a Basic Law (constitution) for the FRG; in the end, the KPD decided to oppose the Basic Law, which came into effect in 1949.

In the first federal elections in 1949, the KPD won 5.7 percent of the votes and gained fifteen members in the Bundestag (lower house of the parliament). In the next election in 1953 its vote plummeted to 2.2 percent, far short of the minimum 5 percent required for seats in the Bundestag. Communists never again won seats, and the party's percentage of votes declined steadily. The weakening popular support for the KPD merely increased its dependence upon the SED. Such dependence contributed to Constitutional Court's outlawing of the KPD.

By the time the party was renamed the DKP and, as a concession by Chancellor Willy Brandt to the Kremlin, again legalized in 1968 (with new statutes and statements of purpose carefully crafted to be compatible with the Basic Law), two important developments had occurred. First, the party's membership had shrunk to about 7,000. Second, the tumultuous 1960s had produced in the FRG scores of radical and independent communist or radical leftist groups that compete with the traditional orthodox party. The DKP does not regard itself as having supplanted the KPD, which in theory continues to exist underground. Indeed, the DKP continues to demand that the decision to ban the KPD be rescinded. The year 1988 was the twentieth anniversary of the DKP's founding. This was celebrated by a party rally in Düsseldorf, a visit by party

chairman Herbert Mies to East German party chief Erich Honecker, renewed calls for legalizing the KPD, and assurances from the West German government that this would not be done. Most of the DKP's present leaders and about half its members once belonged to the KPD.

Leadership and Organization. The DKP's ninth party congress took place in Frankfurt am Main in the first week of 1989. The congress was attended by approximately 700 DKP delegates, along with numerous guests from affiliated and communist-influenced organizations, fraternal communist and workers' parties, "anti-imperialist liberation movements," and embassies of socialist countries. It elected the 94-member party executive, the 19-member Presidium and the 14-member Secretariat. According the the DKP's own information, almost all of the delegates were trade-union members, and close to half were women.

The 1986 party congress in Hamburg had supplemented the 1978 party program by adopting certain "theses," which, along with the Executive's report, provide political-ideological orientation for every member of the DKP. They prescribe Marxism-Leninist principles as the guide for the party's actions, which are aimed at the establishment of a socialist state in the FRG. They authorize communists to support movements and citizens' action groups with the aim of attempting to lead them toward seeking basic changes of the social system.

Mies admitted in 1988 that "profound changes had taken place since the eighth congress of the DKP," including changes "in the internal development of the party." Therefore the party leadership drew up for approval by the ninth congress a report called "Bundesrepublik 2000" (Federal Republic 2000), which contained suggestions for a "peace-oriented and democratic reform alternative for the 1990s." The chairman declared that socialism remains the party's goal, but that urgent questions cannot wait until a fundamental restructuring of society has occurred. His party should be able to draw conclusions useful to itself from the process of *perestroika* in the Soviet Union, for which the report contained restrained praise, and free itself from all that is obsolete. In advance of its approval by the ninth congress, this report, which addressed the question of how the party should proceed in the future, was widely discussed within the DKP. Although Mies criticized the attempts being made by some party members to turn the DKP into a pluralist party, he noted that the report is presented as an "offer for discussion to all forces of the working-class movement, all leftist forces, the peace movement, and social and solidarity movements." (*Neues Deutschland* [*ND*], 1 July; *FBIS*, 7 September.)

Reliance upon the SED. Essential to paying the high costs of maintaining party headquarters in Düsseldorf, an office in Bonn, and more than 200 local offices, the production and distribution of propaganda materials, mass rallies and election campaigns, and subsidies to DKP-affiliated or -influenced organizations are a variety of financial sources: membership dues; income from the sale of party publications; the keeping of DKP functionaries on the payrolls of communist firms and travel agencies directed by the SED; and direct subsidies of more than 65 million marks from the SED. This sum is about three times higher than the DKP's revenues from within the FRG. In fact, no other Western communist party is so reliant upon a foreign party as is the DKP on the SED. The DKP is controlled by the Department of International Politics and Economics (which until 1984 was known as the "West Department") of the SED's Central Committee. Leaders of both the SED and DKP must agree on an annual plan for West German communists, and the DKP leadership regularly reports to the SED. Even the DKP personnel files are kept in East Berlin.

Until recently, the DKP's total loyalty to both East Berlin and Moscow created few problems for the party, except that it reduces the DKP's electoral strength in the FRG to practically zero. Just like the SED, it has consistently pointed to the Soviet Union as the exalted model of "real socialism" that is to be emulated. The Communist Party of the Soviet Union (CPSU) was seen as an almost unerring party, and the DKP's motto was: "To learn from the Soviet Union means to learn to be victorious." Both the DKP and SED have always lined up behind the objectives of the Soviet Union's foreign and defense policies and have lent their full weight to their accomplishment. Both Honecker and Mies are recipients of the Lenin-Peace Prize. However, the emergence in the Soviet Union of a leader from the CPSU's new generation, Mikhail Gorbachev, who is attacking corruption and self-serving privilege within the party, and who advocates intraparty democracy, openness (*glasnost'*), and general restructuring (*perestroika*), has for several years created a serious dilemma for the DKP.

On the one hand, Gorbachev's calls for more democracy have been avidly embraced by the DKP's rank and file, who have long been restless because of the "lack of possibilities for intraparty influence and participation," to use the words of party author Erasmus Schöfer. The possibility of embarking upon a new path has its risks, Schöfer admits, but "communists in the FRG have nothing to lose but their lack of success!" (*Spiegel*, 7 September 1987.) Thomas Riecke, a top functionary of the MSB-Spartakus, declared in regard to *glasnost'* that "we must know everything and be able to decide about everything" (*Die Zeit*, 16 October 1987). There are calls for free election of cadres, who are now appointed by the party leadership.

Mies had to admit in a May 1987 interview in *Unsere Zeit* [*UZ*] that "there is hardly another topic on which so many party functions, and with such a large number of participants, have been held over the past several years... The sympathy for the changes in the Soviet Union is unanimous." He recognized that "the attractive power of existing socialism has been growing" under Gorbachev, who, polls indicated again in 1988, enjoys greater popularity in the FRG than does *any* West German or American politician; also 83 percent of West German respondents consider him to be a "man who can be trusted." Only 11 percent (down from 71% in 1980!) believed in 1988 that the Soviet Union threatens world peace, while the United States does not. Gorbachev's welcome disarmament proposals present the DKP with "fresh opportunities in, among other things, our united action and alliance policy." It has "made it easier for communists to act as respected and equal partners in the peace movement and other democratic movements. Not least important among the fresh opportunities is the possibility of using the growing sympathy for Soviet policy to spread the influence of the DKP as the party of socialism." (*UZ*, 20 May 1987.)

Gorbachev's dramatic announcement at the U.N. on 7 December 1988 that the Soviet Union would unilaterally reduce its manpower and weapons in the USSR and Eastern Europe, and the Soviets' declaration in Paris on 7 January 1989 that the USSR would begin unilaterally to destroy its stocks of chemical weapons, are the kind of dramatic initiatives on which the DKP would like to capitalize. Throughout 1988 and at the ninth party congress, DKP leaders repeatedly praised the Soviet Union's arms-reduction proposals and called for nuclear- and chemical-free zones, a "zone of trust and security in Central Europe," reductions of conventional forces from the Atlantic to the Urals, a Western response to unilateral Soviet withdrawal of some short-range missiles from the GDR and Czechoslovakia, and a rejection of NATO plans to modernize its nuclear forces in Western Europe.

On the other hand, the SED remains cool toward the Gorbachev reforms. In August 1987, Max Schmidt, director of the International Institute for Economics and Politics in East Berlin, told a DKP delegation that "much has yet to reach fruition" and "much will perhaps be undone." The SED prevented *Unsere Zeit* from publishing a January 1987 speech in which Gorbachev asserted that "we need democracy as air to breathe." It also threatened not to distribute any copies via East Berlin to other socialist countries. (*Spiegel*, 7 September 1987.) The SED's message is: "Go slowly, and wait and see!" It apparently does not want to be exposed to the bacillus of *glasnost'* coming from both West and East.

The DKP cannot ignore these warnings from East Berlin. Confronted with what the relatively liberal Hamburg DKP organization calls "a crisis in the party," the DKP leadership must try to dampen the enthusiasm caused by the "strong impulses" coming from Moscow. In *Unsere Zeit*, a cautious Mies warned that in a capitalist country like the FRG "there can be no imitation of the Soviet approach," and that the party must be careful "not to throw the baby out with the bathwater." One must not "reduce the splendid history of the Soviet Union . . . to economic and moral problems." DKP members should inform themselves through reports by "fraternal parties," not by "reading tea leaves or using the slanders cooked up by the bourgeois mass media." While there is much need for

> invigoration of intraparty life, encouragement of intraparty discussions, and broader involvement of the party membership in the decisionmaking process, . . . it is not a matter of weakening the principles of democratic centralism in the CPSU . . . Intraparty democracy for us is not a game, not an end in itself. It is designed to mobilize the party's collective knowledge and strength, and to unit it for purposeful and centralized actions in the fight against the highly organized class enemy facing us. We need to have a further development of intraparty democracy, while keeping our communist principles intact. (*UZ*, 20 May 1987.)

Thus the party resorted to censorship to try to silence the enthusiasm for the reform impulses emanating from Moscow. When the party poet and member of the 94-member party executive, Peter Schütt, wrote a poem in 1987 with the lines: "After

decades of radio silence, the red star is again sending signals," and "there are comrades who have held their hands in front of their faces for so long that they have unlearned how to understand the new radio code," he was encouraged by the chief party idealogue, Willi Gerns, not to publish the poem. To Schütt's surprise, the poem was published by the moderately conservative *Frankfurter Allgemeine Zeitung* (*FAZ*). The DKP leadership was reportedly embarrassed by this and especially by the fact that the editors of the Moscow publication *New Time* thanked Schütt for supporting *perestroika* (*Spiegel*, 7 September 1987).

In 1988 the DKP faced the most serious crisis of its two decades of existence. For the first time in fifteen years, its membership dropped to 38,000, and its members' average age is rising. Half of those who left the party gave political and ideological reasons for leaving. Many comrades who remain are disillusioned or unmotivated, owing to the attitudes of the party leaders who are increasingly reproached for having "a tendency toward dogmatism," and for encouraging "conformist behavior and closed, inflexible, and authority-minded thinking." (*FBIS*, 15 September.)

Pronouncements such as that made by Mies in November 1987 go unheeded by many members. He asserted then: "It would be irresponsible, precisely in times of radical change, to eliminate something of the Marxist, revolutionary character of our organizational principles. Precisely in such times, . . . not less, but more Marxism, not less, but more Leninism is required." (*Infodienst* [*ID*], 30 August.) The party leadershp was always proud of having resisted "Eurocommunism," on the grounds that communist parties that had tolerated some pluralism within their ranks had been weakened or split. Deputy chairperson Ellen Weber tried in 1988 to argue that all the talk of *glasnost'* and *perestroika* was merely "the effort of the bourgeois media and politicians to drive wedges and organize dissension." But Hamburg party chief Wolfgang Gehrcke stated forthrightly that "there are fissures that have to be worked on. Everyone is looking toward Moscow." (*Stern*, July 1988.)

But by early 1988 Mies had to admit that, for the first time in the party's history, there are, in fact, differences of opinion within the party that are extremely difficult to reconcile. In his speech before the meeting of the Presidium in Düsseldorf 3–4 September, he acknowledged "two directions or lines within the party." A minority (consisting of *Erneuer* — renewers) is calling certain party principles into question; "a break with essential principles of democratic centralism is appearing in outlines." (*FBIS*, 15 September.)

The DKP has tried to cope with this challenge in two ways. First, it has departed from its customary practice by indeed permitting open discussion within the party and has permitted the party's news organs to report the disagreements discussed. Never before was there so much frankness in the party's publications and in the discussions at party gatherings. At the Presidium's meeting in September, two discussion papers presenting contradictory positions were allowed for the first time; 18 out of the Executive's 94 members had not been able to agree with the top party leadership, and therefore no agreement could be reached on a common text.

At the same time, the DKP tried to place limits on discussions, declaring that they may show a diversity of opinion, but "not lead to political confrontation or to splintering of forces." They must always serve "the conscious unity and strengthening of the fighting power of the party." (*Die Welt*, 23 June.) That is, criticism has to remain subordinate to the principle and goals of the party. In Mies's words, it is important to "withstand a trend that would lead not to a renewed, but to a ruined DKP."

The second way of trying to dam the flood of demands for more "democratization" and a more public party is to discipline those "renewers" who cross the vague line that the party's top leaders have tried to draw between permissible and impermissible criticism. In March the DKP issued a warning to Andreas Müller-Goldenstedt, a Hamburg district leader, who had demanded that the DKP must primarily operate "for our own country," and that the comrades in the GDR must be told once and for all that "we don't want this and that here" [in the FRG]. Disciplinary action was also taken against Helmut Krebs, former member of the Karlsruhe leadership, for writing a discussion paper entitled "How Should the DKP Proceed," in which he faulted the DKP for underestimating the economic strength of the FRG. The deficiencies of socialism can no longer be denied, he wrote, and the West German working class would tolerate a socialist order only if it did not bring a reduction in their living standard or a diminution of their freedom and human rights. Therefore the party should renounce all unconstitutional means of struggle. (*ID*, 27 May.)

Ideological training and propaganda. The GDR and the Soviet Union provide vital educational support for the DKP. Over a third of its members have attended courses in the GDR and USSR. The DKP also maintains long-established institutions for this purpose. Founded in 1968, the Institute for Marxist Studies and Research (IMSF) in Frankfurt am Main cooperates closely with the institutes for Marxism-Leninism of the central committees of both the SED and CPSU. Its director, Heinz Jung, is in the party's presidium, and most of the sixteen members of the "scholarly advisory council," including Presidium members Josef Schleifstein and Robert Steigerwald, are DKP members. Party official Richard Kumpf directs the Marx-Engels Foundation in the Wuppertal, which serves as a site for seminars and conferences. DKP Presidium member Hans Schneider directs the Marxist Workers' Education (MAB), founded in Frankfurt in 1969 to organize all over the FRG courses and lectures, featuring instructors from both Germanies, for politically active Germans who are not members of the DKP. The DKP annually organizes approximately 8,000 educational lectures, seminars, and courses on such subjects as security in the atomic age, communists' roles in economic policies, global affairs, and culture, and electoral alliances and strategy.

It also lays great stress on contacts with fraternal parties. Sometimes communist leaders come to the FRG. In September 1987, Honecker met Mies in Bonn in the presence of Chancellor Helmut Kohl, at which time photographers had the extremely rare opportunity of recording a handshake between a West German chancellor and a DKP chief. In January 1988, Soviet Foreign Minister Eduard Shevardnadze met in Bonn with Mies, who reportedly showed great interest in the reforms taking place in the USSR and expressed total support for Soviet peace initiatives. In August a Soviet delegation led by E. Z. Razumov, the Central Committee's deputy chief of party organization, met with DKP leaders in Bonn.

DKP delegations also travel to the East. In May 1988, a DKP environmental group visited the Soviet Union and toured the Chernobyl site. In July a delegation of DKP ideologists, led by Presidium member Willi Gerns met with Anatolii Dobrynin in Moscow, at the Central Committee's invitation. In June, the DKP was invited to send a delegation to an international meeting in East Berlin on nuclear weapons–free zones, a gathering to which the SPD and the Free Democratic (FDP) parties also sent delegations.

Presidium member Martha Buschmann asserted in 1988 that "the DKP can claim to have utilized its contacts with fraternal parties from other lands, based on proletarian internationalism, to contribute to the continuation of the policy of dialogue." (*ND*, 1 February.) There can be no doubt that communist leaders in the East want to know what the miniscule DKP is doing and want to use it for whatever support it might muster for Soviet policies, especially those regarding security matters. However, there is absolutely no doubt that Soviet and East European leaders place far more value on their contacts with influential noncommunist parties in the West and give them far more coverage in their press.

For instance, 1988 saw numerous visits of leading West German politicians. Top SPD politicians, led by Egon Bahr, met many times with their SED counterparts, led by Hermann Axen, to work out a joint paper entitled "Conflict of Ideologies and Common Security." The DKP cheered these talks, but watched them from the sidelines. Experts from the SED and the Bavarian SPD met in October to discuss environmental problems. SPD minister president of North Rhine-Westphalia, Johannes Rau, travelled to Leipzig in March; SPD party chairman Hans-Jochen Vogel met with the SED chief in April, and Saar minister president and possible future candidate for the office of chancellor, Oskar Lafontaine, journeyed to East Berlin in August. From the ruling parties in Bonn went a steady stream of emissaries to the GDR in 1988: Mayor Eberhard Diepgen of West Berlin; Minister President Bernhard Vogel of Rhineland-Palatinate; the deputy chairman of the CDU parliamentary party, Volker Rühe; the chief of the Federal Chancellory, Wolfgang Schäuble; Foreign Minister Hans-Dietrich Genscher, and the federal ministers for health and the environment. Finally, Chancellor Kohl paid a much publicized visit to Moscow in October. To repeat, these kinds of contacts are much more important for the GDR and USSR than are fraternal contacts with the DKP.

Party publications. The DKP is so insignificant in the FRG that it receives very little attention in the noncommunist press. East German publications, such as the SED party organ *Neues Deutschland*, give it much broader coverage, but they do not report on disagreements or problems within the DKP or with the SED; nor do they normally report precisely how little electoral support the DKP receives within the FRG.

The DKP produces many publications of its own. They include the daily party organ *Unsere Zeit* (*UZ*), founded in April 1969 as a weekly, but ap-

pearing five times a week since October 1973; the eight-page daily now has a circulation of 23,000. Its sixteen-page weekend edition, published Fridays, has a circulation of 44,000. It sometimes publishes special editions with up to 300,000 copies called *Extra Blätter*. The editor claims that the FRG's "professional/occupational proscription" (which places legal restrictions on members of anti-democratic parties serving in the public service) discourages some potential subscribers; in some cases, this is probably true. *Unsere Zeit* is guided by party decisions and operates in close contact with the party leadership, who appoint the editor-in-chief and editorial board. It strives to uphold the German communist press tradition begun by *Rote Fahne* (Red banner), founded by Rosa Luxemburg and Karl Liebknecht, and continued by *Freies Volk* (A free people). In the words of its editor-in-chief, Georg Polikeit, it wages "an uphill struggle against the anti-communist inventions spewed by the mass media the big bourgeoisie controls" (*WRM*, September 1987). In response to the present turmoil within the DKP, the party leadership permits more open discussions in the party press than ever before. Nevertheless, an internal survey revealed that 94 percent of DKP members do not regularly read *Unsere Zeit* (*Spiegel*, 7 September 1987). Half of all new readers cancel their subscriptions within one year, and overall circulation is declining (*ID*, 27 May).

There are other party publications: The *Volkszeitung* (earlier the *Deutsche Volkszeitung/Die Tat*—German people's newspaper/The deed) has a circulation of about 30,000. The *Illustrierte Volkszeitung* (Illustrated poeple's newspaper) appears quarterly. The *DKP Pressedienst* (DKP Press service), *Infodienst* (Info service), which provides print for the party's factory, residential area, and student newspapers, and the *DKP-Landreview* (DKP Rural review) all appear at irregular intervals. On a bimonthly basis, the DKP presidium produces *Praxis—Erfahrungen aus dem Leben und der Arbeit der Partei* (Praxis—Knowledge gained from the life and work of the party), with a circulation of 7,500. *Marxistische Blätter*, published eleven times per year and having a circulation of 7,300, is the party's theoretical organ. The party also publishes approximately 340 factory and 450 local newspapers, some of which annually have a dozen editions with as many as 120,000 copies.

Providing these publications with news are two principal news agencies. The Progressive Press Agency (PPA), with headquarters in Düsseldorf and offices in Bonn, Mannheim, Munich, and Kiel, has approximately fifteen editors and correspondents and publishes five times weekly the *PPA Daily Service*, which features party activities and selected articles from the noncommunist press. About one-third of the material in DKP publications comes from the Allgemeiner Deutscher Nachrichtendienst (ADN), the news agency of the GDR.

Youth organizations. The largest group is the SDAJ, which has approximately 15,000 members in more than 900 local groups. Its self-image is that of a "revolutionary young workers' organization" devoted to "the teachings of Marx, Engels, and Lenin" and fighting for a "socialist Federal Republic," with a planned, socialist economy and power being exercised by the workers. Birgit Radow is not only SDAJ chairperson, but a member of the DKP Presidium and Executive as well. Hans-Georg Eberhard, deputy chairman, belongs to the DKP, and most of the land-chairmen are members of the DKP's land-presidia.

The last SDAJ federal congress on 2–3 May 1987 in Frankfurt am Main was attended by 750 delegates who had an average age of 21 years; 14 percent represented school groups; and 34 percent had functions in labor unions or youth councils in factories. DKP chairman Mies spoke of "a common struggle" with the DKP, and the first secretary of the central council of East German Free German Youth (FDJ), Eberhard Aurich, spoke of an "indestructible alliance" between the two youth organizations and asserted: "We have the same ideals and goals. We have the same friends, and we hate the same enemies." Radow assured the Soviet Komsomol representative, Nikolai Palzew, that the SDAJ was "enthused" about the "revolutionary restructuring" in the Soviet Union, and that its effect in the FRG was to strengthen "the appeal of socialism." To both the Russian and East German visitors, Radow said: "We are proud of our friendship with the GDR and with the young revolutionaries in the FDJ, who make socialism strong in our neighboring country. . . . We are spreading far and wide in the FRG the example of the Soviet Union, the GDR, and the other socialist countries. There the new social order is being built for which we want to fight in our own country." (*ID*, 24 July 1987.)

The group's activities support those of the parent party and are aimed particularly at students, apprentices, and soldiers. It seeks contacts with the Young Socialists (Jusos), the Greens, and various groups within the peace movement. To be appealing to those groups, the SDAJ calls for peace and disarmament and for a shutting-down of all nuclear-energy plants in capitalist countries (but not in socialist countries for the time being, because nuclear energy is "indispensable" there). (*ID*, 24 July 1987.) It maintains ties with communist youth groups in the GDR and other countries. Contacts between the FDJ and SDAJ involve regular planning councils, training sessions, exchanges of delegations, and invitations to "friendship camps" in the GDR. SDAJ members participate in such organizations as the Solidarity Brigade in Nicaragua and the Soviet-controlled World Federation of Democratic Youth. It sponsors evening courses, group-leader schools on the land level, and courses lasting a week at the Youth Education Center at Burg Wahrburg. It also publishes a variety of materials: *Elan—Das Jugendmagazin* is a monthly with a circulation of about 19,000. Every month it puts out an *Artikeldienst für Betriebs-, Lehrlings-, Stadtteil- und Schülerzeitungen* (Article service for plant, apprentice, neighborhood, and pupils' newspapers). The SDAJ also publishes *Jugendpolitische Blätter* (Pages on youth politics), which appears in approximately 2,500 copies.

The Young Pioneers (JP) is for children and counts 4,000 members. Its functionaries are trained at the Youth Education Center at Burg Wahrburg, and many, including its chairman, Gerd Hertel, belong to the SDAJ and/or DKP. Its executive publishes a monthly, *Pionierleiter Info* (Pioneer leader info), a child's newspaper, *Pionier* (circulation 5,000), as well as *Diskussionsmaterial für Pionierleiter* (Discussion material for pioneer leaders). It has ties with children's groups in the GDR and other socialist countries and with the International Commission of Children's and Adolescents' Movements (CIMEA), an auxiliary of the World Federation of Democratic Youth. The FDJ supervises a JP vacation program in the GDR.

Represented at more than 100 postsecondary institutions is the MSB-Spartakus, which has about 6,000 members and publishes monthly *Rote Blätter* (Red pages), with a circulation of 11,500, as well as a newspaper, *avanti*. It is the largest and most powerful left-extremist organization at the university level, and it cooperates with all left-wing groups, including the Liberal Students' League (affiliated with, but to the left of the Free Democratic Party; FDP) and the Jusos. MSB-Spartakus and its permanent alliance partner, the Socialist University League (SHB), occupy about a fifth of the seats in student parliaments and have representation in about half of such assemblies. All leftist extremist groups and groups influenced by them occupied a third of such seats in 1987. (*Verfassungsschutzbericht 1987*, published in 1988 and hereafter referred to as *VSB 87.*) The MSB-Spartakus represents the United German Students' Association (Vereinigte Deutsche Studentenschaft; VDS) in diverse coordinating committees of protest and peace movements. Most top MSB-Spartakus leaders are DKP members. It regards "the struggle for peace" as one aspect of the class struggle and as a revolutionary objective. It works feverishly to undercut NATO and SDI and to gain support for nuclear-free zones and other objectives that have a high priority for Kremlin leaders. Unlike the DKP, however, many MSB activists and leaders unreservedly support the Soviet Union's present reform course. The DKP considers its well-organized students to be the essential contact point between the intelligentsia and the working class.

The DKP regards the intelligentsia in the FRG as a lucrative reservoir of influence. Presidium and Secretariat member Gerd Deumlich wrote that "past and present experience shows that the intelligentsia in the FRG is largely in opposition to the ruling circles" because of the "ignominy of fascism and the guilt of German capital in starting World War II," even though "the views of many intellectuals can hardly be regarded as consistently progressive, and while their thinking is under the influence of bourgeois illusions and anti-communism." He continued: "The FRG is a visual example of the crisis of capitalism permeating and interweaving every aspect of life in the society: economics, politics, ideology, morality and culture." (*WMR*, September 1987.)

Cover groups and citizens' action groups. For decades the DKP and other communist groups have faced mistrust and rejection by the FRG's general population. For this reason, it has operated through a wide variety of cover groups and has sought to cooperate with protest groups enjoying greater respectability. It is supported by approximately 50 organizations and action groups that it heavily influences, but that outwardly appear to be independent; the majority of their members and leaders does not belong to the DKP. Party members are indeed appointed to certain high positions, but the key to these groups' effectiveness is that the DKP's role be downplayed as much as possible. Many of the larger of these cover groups are also affiliated with Moscow-directed front groups, such as the World Peace Council (WPC).

Among the more important DKP front groups is the Association of Victims of the Nazi Regime/League of Antifascists (VVN/BdA), with about 14,000 members and a monthly publication, *antifaschistische Rundschau* (Anti-fascist review), with a circulation of 12,000. The German Peace Union (DFU), with about 1,000 members and a monthly publication *Abrüstungs-Info* (Disarmament-info; circulation 4,000), tries to break down anticommunist sentiments and gain support for the DKP's objectives within bourgeois and Christian circles. It was able to mobilize 85,000 protesters in April 1988 (225,000 according to DFU claims) for its annual "Easter Marches." As usual, the central manifestos and accounts for contributions were traceable almost exclusively to functionaries of the DKP and DFU. The number of demonstrators in the 1988 marches was lower than in earlier years because of the Intermediate-Range Nuclear Forces (INF) Treaty of December 1987, which robbed the peace movement of its most important point of focus.

The DKP did use the opportunity to appear on public platforms with noncommunist organizations and parties, especially the SPD. Such "unity of action" is an important goal of the DKP, designed to establish its acceptance by and equality with other parties. The DKP put on a good face and declared the 1988 marches to have been a success because they again allegedly demonstrated the party's ability to mobilize the masses. The DKP is apparently correct in its assessment of its own importance in the Easter Marches, as recorded in a 1987 internal party paper: "Without the work of the DKP, without its sacrifices especially in small communities . . . there naturally would not be such Easter Marches" (*ID*, 30 August).

The German Peace Society/United War Resisters (DFG/VK), with about 11,000 members, is the largest DKP front group and has the greatest number of noncommunists, but it is plagued by declining membership and revenues and has had to reduce spending for its quarterly publication *Civil Courage* (circulation: 10,000). Communist influence within the DFG/VK is uneven; some groups and individuals have repeatedly criticized the DKP's power at the highest level without being able to do anything about it. Other groups are the Union of Democratic Doctors; the Committee for Peace, Disarmament, and Cooperation (KFAZ), which publishes *Friedensjournal* and *Friedensschnell-*

dienst (Peace journal, and Peace express service); the Democratic Women's Initiative (DFI), which publishes *Wir Frauen* (We women) and focuses on women's issues on which the DKP has a firm position, such as opposition to military service for women; the Association of Democratic Jurists (VDJ), which has about 1,000 members and a publication, *VDJ-Forum*, and is a section of the Soviet-controlled International Union of Democratic Jurists (IVDJ). The Anti-Imperialistic Solidarity Committee for Africa, Asia, and Latin America (ASK) serves as the framework for joint efforts on behalf of "liberation movements" and in opposition to such American objectives as SDI. The ASK publishes about 5,000 copies of a monthly *Anti-imperialist Information Bulletin*. The Patron Circle of the *Darmstädter Signal* was founded by the DKP, the SPD, the Greens, and Protestant and Catholic clergymen in 1983 to dissuade Federal Army (Bundeswehr) soldiers from taking part in nuclear warfare.

Domestic Attitudes and Activities. A party that has never received more than .3 percent of the votes in federal elections has an obvious problem. Mies openly acknowledges this. As he explained in an interview published in the Polish newspaper *Trybuna ludu* on 20 July 1987, "the DKP has not been able to win a suitable place among representative bodies; its influence on the working class as a whole does not suit today's needs. The party realizes this... and right now it is at a stage of productive unrest, involving the seeking of ways generally to increase our influence on the working class."

How can the DKP try to break out of its isolation? It forms electoral alliances, trying thereby to contribute in some way to parliamentary life, and jumps on the bandwagon of extraparliamentary movements, whose momentum stems from dealing with issues of broad concern in the FRG. Looking back over land (state) elections in 1986, the party saw nothing but dismal failures: .1 percent in Lower Saxony in June and .2 percent in Hamburg in November; it did not even enter the Bavarian election in October. Thus, facing the January 1987 Bundestag elections, it decided to form an electoral alliance in order that its demands "be represented in an alliance more effectively," and "in that way to establish contact with more people, with people whom we communists do not yet reach" (*UZ*, September). Its "Peace List" invited the Greens to join in a common front, an invitation which the ambitious Greens rejected (*FAZ*, 12 March 1986).

Nevertheless, the DKP decided to ask its supporters to cast their first vote for the direct candidates of the Peace List and their second vote for either the Greens or the SPD, in an attempt to create a "majority left of the CDU" (*ID*, 3 April 1987). (Every voter has two votes: the first is for a candidate in an electoral constituency the representative of which is elected by plurality; the second is for a specific party, and the number obtained by a party determines the percentage and number of seats the party will receive in the lower house of the Federal Parliament. To win any seats at all, though, the party must win at least 5 percent of second votes in the entire FRG. This is a hurdle that the communists have not come close to clearing since 1949; thus it was no genuine sacrifice to recommend that the communists cast their second ballots for other parties.) This electoral-alliance approach is not new for the DKP. It formed a "Peace List" for the 1969 elections, as it did in the 1984 elections for the European Parliament, when it won 1.3 percent of the votes. In the North Rhine-Westphalia land-election in 1985 a "Peace List NRW" won .7 percent.

More than 40 percent of the Peace List candidates in 1987 were DKP members or functionaries, and a further 30 percent were in the DFU. Two-thirds of the Federal Governing Board are members either of the DKP or of the organizations that the DKP influences. The DKP and its affiliated organizations, the MSB-Spartakus, the SDAJ, and the DFU, bore the brunt of the work and expense for the campaign. However, knowing the average voter's antipathy toward the DKP, the campaign went to great lengths to blur the role of the DKP and DFU in the Peace List. The three top candidates were not communists, and in party publications, only selections of candidates' pictures were published in which communists were a small minority (*ID*, 3 April 1987).

Peace List candidates received 188,602 or .5 percent of the first votes. Its best land results were in the city-states of Bremen (1.3 percent) and Hamburg (.8 percent). In various university towns it topped its countrywide average: Tübingen, 3.8 percent; Freiburg, 1.8 percent; Marburg, 1.7 percent; and Münster, 1.6 percent. The DKP found these meager results to be "relatively satisfactory." In the party leadership's view, the DKP had helped to "debilitate the right-wing parties," particularly the "Steel Helmet faction of arch-conservatives," and to reverse the slide to the right that the FRG had experienced since 1985. It claimed to have "made the issue of peace and détente the focus and touchstone of its electoral effort," and to have "forced each party to speak up on it too," and to "reject the policy of subjecting West Germany to the interests of the Washington administration" (*WMR*, vol. 17, no. 2, 1987). In the words of Presidium member Rolf Priemer, the DKP's electoral strategy had given

> an uplift to the forces to the left of the CDU/CSU, stimulated positive changes in the SPD, reinforced the position of the Greens in the Bundestag, and raised our party's own prestige in the nation at large and particularly among the Social Democrats, the Greens, and activists of the peace movement and of the working class movement. All this provided an immense incentive for future joint or parallel actions in the common front and in the democratic alliances. (*WMR*, May 1987.)

In actual fact, there is very little evidence that the DKP made significant contributions to, or progress toward any of these goals. Both the SPD and the Greens are aware that their electoral performance would be harmed, not helped, by collaboration with the communists, and that the DKP's minuscule vote-getting potential would be irrelevant to any electoral outcome. There are indeed discussions within the SPD and the Green Party concerning possible alliances, but these discussions revolve around alliances with each other, not with the DKP. While the SPD is conducting party-to-party talks with the SED to discuss such goals as nuclear-free zones and more visible defensive military postures, talks which the DKP praises as positive steps, it is not conducting such talks with the DKP. Nor is the SPD or the Greens dealing with defense issues because it has been prodded by the DKP. Defense and arms-control questions are very much on the political agenda in the FRG, an exposed country in the middle of Europe located on the border with the Warsaw Pact nations, and in which there are a million troops from six different countries and thousands of nuclear warheads; all parties therefore pay close attention to defense issues.

The DKP will continue, as its Presidium announced after the 1987 Bundestag elections, to follow "its line, adopted by its eighth congress, to broaden extra-parliamentary action, its policy of alliances and unity of action, and to enhance on this basis its own political role as a mobilizing and motive force, and increase its membership" (*IB*, May 1987). Its membership has declined in recent years, which is a matter of great concern for the leadership. In a paper published by the party's executive, the party sets a target of 7–10 percent of its current membership in the annual recruitment of new members. But the paper also warns about the potential risks of bringing in new members from extraparliamentary alliances. The danger is that

> the allies' ideological and organizational attitudes also have an influence on the communists . . . When working in the alliances, they [communists] use the tactics of compromise, but often also carry them over to relations within their own party, so ignoring the fundamental distinction between a patchwork association and the Marxist-Leninist vanguard of the working class.

The report notes that "there is a change in the social make-up of the DKP." The DKP is also recruiting from social strata other than the working class. Indeed, only 20 percent of communists now work in "material large production." For instance, the biggest DKP plant group in North Rhine-Westphalia, the FRG's most populous land, is not to be found in the coal and steel industry, but in the city hospitals (*Spiegel*, 7 September 1987). Thus, concludes the DKP report, "it is not right to forget that most of the new members lack what the workers acquire in fighting for their rights at enterprises and in the trade unions, namely, the conscious need for organized and collective action" (*WMR*, January 1987).

The DKP tries to appeal to workers, a steadily declining class in the FRG's modern economy, by demanding such measures as a 35-hour work week without pay cuts, job-creation programs, job security, higher real wages, saving the declining steel and shipbuilding industries, protecting the right of participation in the management of mining and steel-producing facilities, and an end to mass lay offs and social welfare cuts (*WMR*, May 1987). But it faces an unmistakable problem in recruiting workers at a time of high unemployment in the FRG. In a well-publicized case in 1987, a postal worker was fired when the Federal Administrative Court in West Berlin ruled that his activities with the DKP were not compatible with his "obligation to loyalty" to the state. This is not the first instance of such firings, and a dismissed DKP member has great difficulty getting another job. As one such person remarked bitterly, "the alleged black mark of DKP membership is an insurmountable hurdle" (*Spiegel*, 19 October 1987). Thus a new recruit must be prepared to sacrifice his livelihood. It is no wonder that the DKP calls for an end to "professional/occupational proscription" (*Berufsverbot*, the term used by those who oppose this law; the official title is *Radikalenerlass*—Radicals Decree) against those deemed to be risks to the state (*ND*, 29 January 1987).

The party orders its members to take an active role in trade unions, with the goal of persuading trade unionists that workers' interests are only served by class struggle. It places great value on its "educational work," particularly with regard to the unions' youth organizations; many union instructors are products of the student movement and advocate orthodox Marxism. Even though few DKP members have risen to leading positions in the unions, three-fourths of them belong to unions, and they exercise influence in some, particularly those of printers, journalists, and the mass media. (*VSB 87*.) In 1985 a Mass Media Trade Union was set up to include the Union of Printworkers, the Union of Journalists, the Union of Writers, the Union of Radio and Television Workers, and the main unions in music, drama, and the figurative arts. According to Gerd Deumlich, DKP Presidium and Secretariat member, this new union "wants to put an end to the power of the monopolies" in the media and is "a strong response to those who have been conducting a reactionary policy in the mass media and who want to limit the sphere of union political activity." (*WMR*, September 1987.) According to a 1987 BfV report, the number of communist workers' groups has risen to about 400, about one-third of which are active in the metal industry and about a fourth in the pulbic-service sector, principally in communal and land administrations. Some have only a few members and engage in action only irregularly. The number of DKP factory newspapers has declined to 340, each with a circulation of several hundred to several thousand and most appearing irregularly. (*Handelsblatt*, 22–23 May 1987.)

Despite any possible dangers, the party does work toward the formation of broad alliances. These can be the "working class unity of actions" namely DKP cooperation with trade unionists, workers not affiliated with any party, Christian workers and Social Democrats. They can also be with intellectuals and the bourgeoisie. Such "coalitions of reason" can seek broader objectives, such as foiling SDI. DKP members need not occupy the leading offices, and they can use "political flexibility" while maintaining "ideological conviction." That is, cooperation should be based on common interests and should not be brought about through compromises with reformist positions. (*ID*, 12 May 1986.)

The DKP leadership believes it sees the wall breaking down between Social Democrats and communists, a wall which has existed since the foundation of the KPD in 1918, and which was strengthened by the effort of the KPD to absorb the SPD after the Second World War. Serious disagreement continues to exist between the two parties on "the system question": what kind of regime and economic order is best for the FRG. It has long sought to eliminate or lessen the "fears of contact" (*Berührungsängste*) that have made most groups in the FRG disinclined to deal with the DKP. While there are no high-level party-to-party contacts and absolutely no talk within the national SPD of any form of alliance or formal cooperation with the DKP, some Social Democrats serve on governing boards of DKP-influenced organizations, as well as in "citizens' action groups" and friendship societies with certain socialist countries. Speakers from both parties sometimes appear at the same discussions or meetings. Also, some interviews with Social Democrats are printed in *Unsere Zeit*. Such speeches and interviews seldom involve prominent Social Democrats, though.

In 1988 the DKP adopted the slogan: "Continue on this path: toward Social Democrats—for unity of action!" (*VSB 87*) Erhard Eppler, SPD Presidium member, proposed in 1988 that one should not exclude the DKP from "internal dialogue." He argues that the SPD can hardly call on the SED not to exclude ecological and church groups in the GDR and take seriously the August 1987 joint paper with the SED, "Conflict of Ideologies and Common Security," when it ignores the DKP. At the same time Eppler noted that the SPD should not fraternize or embark on joint actions with the DKP, which he described as "a much shaken and pretty confused bunch." (*FBIS*, 14 September.) At the university level, the predominantly leftist Social Democratic SHB has for years joined in "unity of actions" with the MSB-Spartakus and, unlike the larger SPD, favors an SPD-DKP alliance (*ID*, 12 May 1987).

The DKP also joins broad-based protest efforts that bring it into contact with a wide spectrum of noncommunist groups and, it hopes, widens its appeal. It now opposes nuclear power or reprocessing plants and is present at the often bloody protests against such installations as the Wackersdorf nuclear reprocessing plant. The DKP claims to have helped expose the true purpose of Wackersdorf: "to be a center for the manufacture of West Germany's own nuclear weapons" (*WMR*, September 1987). In fact, no responsible West German leader advocates the FRG's acquisition of such weapons. In 1988 the DKP demanded that all atomic plants be completely nationalized and placed under strict democratic control (*ND*, 1 February). The DKP advocates protection of the environment and cleaning up the polluted Rhine River. It joined in the movement against the taking of a census. It reasoned that the information thereby gained would strengthen the FRG's character as an "authoritarian surveillance state," as well as support the FRG's "antidemocratic security laws," and thereby serve ultimately "the preparation for war." (*ID*, 15 May 1987.)

Perhaps most important in the party's efforts to reach out to other groups has been its participation in the peace movement. Kurt Schacht, a member of the DKP executive, maintained that "the participation of DKP members in the peace forums has unquestionably given the party valuable experience and . . . has had a positive effect on the peace movement itself. Cooperation between the Communists, Social Democrats, and Greens has been fostered by the considerable concurrence of their views on questions of war and peace" (*WMR*, March 1987). Operating within the peace movement is particularly comfortable for the DKP because it is thereby able to devote its energies to supporting Soviet and GDR security objectives. As the SED organ *Neues Deutschland* wrote on 26 May 1987, "the GDR places extraordinary value on the contribution that the Communists in the FRG make in the struggle for peace and disarmament . . . That is why it [the DKP] energetically set about, with no ands-ifs-or-buts-about-it, having the proposal of the Soviet Union for a zero-option for medium-range missiles realized." In the aftermath of the INF Treaty, the DKP demanded in 1988 that all trials of participants in peace pickets at U.S. missile bases be stopped, and that all convicted peace activists be given an amnesty, on the grounds that the legitimacy of their efforts had been confirmed by the treaty (*FBIS*, 18 February).

Neither the DKP nor the many communist splinter parties (called K-groups) are the initiators or string-pullers of the peace movement, within which they remain a small minority. For a while, their active role was willingly accepted by the noncommunist majority, which in the early 1980s rallied behind such proclamations as the largely communist-inspired "Krefeld Appeal" in 1980. However, by spring of 1982 tensions between communists and noncommunists within the movement became obvious. Robert Steigerwald, a DKP leader, scorned ecological and religious elements as "upper-level salaried employees and intellectuals" because they demanded, in the words of Petra Kelly, a "peace movement which thinks and acts in a bloc-free manner." Heinrich Böll commented that "inasmuch as the Communists are controlled from Moscow, their orders are to destroy what is meaningful in these movements by taking part in them and indeed by forcing their way into them." The noncommunist elements within the peace movement did not reject all forms of logistical support from the communists, which is probably the latter's greatest contribution to the movement; the DKP and its affiliated organizations had a disproportionately large representation in many of the movement's operational coordinating committees. For example, DKP delegates regularly attended meetings of the Coordinating Committee of the Peace Movement (KA), despite the fact that the party did not formally belong. Nevertheless, the Greens and other noncommunist activists in the peace movement intensified efforts to distance themselves from communists. Clearly, the peace movement has in the 1980s been far too large and heterogeneous to be controlled by outside powers or the DKP. (*Armed Forces and Society*, Spring 1984; *VSB 87*.)

Communists have no reason to be happy about their attempts to work together with the badly divided Greens. They were able to recommend to DKP members to give their second vote in the 1987 elections to the Greens (or Social Democrats) on the grounds that the Greens are a consistent radical-democratic force that supports the extra-parliamentary struggle. Although there are former communists within the Greens, including Thomas Ebermann, who in 1987 won the speakership of the Green Party's caucus in the Bundestag, these former communists are from the militant communist splinter parties that tend to be hostile to, or uncooperative with the DKP.

The "fundamentalists" (*Fundis*) had a majority within the Greens' leadership and were fiercely independent, rejecting arguments made by the "realists" (*Realos*) that coalitions with the SPD should be formed. But at the Greens' Karlsruhe congress in December 1988 the pragmatic wing toppled the fundamentalist party executive and thereby took the reins of decisionmaking power into their own hands (*Die Zeit*, North American edition, 16 December). The Greens have never discussed coalitions with the communists. It is true that when cases of East German spies have surfaced in recent years, Greens have ridiculed the need for classified information, and they refuse to sign a security pledge (*CSM*, 9 February 1987). The DKP also agrees with the Fundis' position on violence in demonstrations: that there should be an end to the state's "monopoly on the use of force" (*CSM*, 24 November 1987). Responding to a government statement by Chancellor Kohl, the DKP Presidium declared that "Kohl's stinging attack on those who allegedly resort to 'violence' during demonstrations disguises the intention to curtail still more the right to meetings and demonstrations" (*IB*, June 1987). It should be said, though, that few, if any, of the several hundred militant demonstrators who travel throughout the FRG to turn every demonstration possible into a violent conflict with the police are following orders from the DKP. Such "chaotists" (*Chaoten*) are not suited for the kind of disciplined party that the DKP is.

An obviously exasperated Robert Steigerwald noted that the DKP is "working hard to secure a political alliance with its [the Green Party's] representatives while criticizing the erroneous and sometimes reactionary views of the latter.... Most of the Greens keep aloof from the working class, asserting that it is unable to bring about a revolutionary transformation of society. Marxism is dismissed as a nineteenth-century political theory; political economy is replaced with ecology. Marxists and those who worship economic development are equally presented as prisoners of an obsession with economic growth and consumption." (*WMR*, November 1986.)

The DKP's hope to gain advantages by riding the extraparliamentary-protest wave and participating in the peace movement are bound to be disappointed in virtue of the fact that the momentum and drive of the movement had largely vanished by 1988. There are several reasons for this. The most important is the INF agreement signed in December 1987 by the Soviet and American leaders, calling for the removal from Europe of all American and Soviet medium- and short-range missiles, and the prospect of further steps to reduce strategic arsenals by half. This agreement was made possible by party chief Gorbachev's implicit admission that Soviet missiles are not purely defensive in nature and are part of the problem. This admission undercuts the DKP's persistent efforts to show that the United States and its president were the sole obstacles to disarmament. Also, in contrast with the early 1980s, the peace movement's demands are now incorporated into the SPD and Greens' manifestos. Thus the former ex-

traparliamentary opposition against the arms race has been brought directly into parliament. This has eliminated much of the *raison d'être* of the extraparliamentary peace movement. (*FAZ*, 27 May 1987.) Finally, Gorbachev's dramatic announcement of unilateral conventional-arms cuts at the U.N. on 7 December 1988 was seen by NATO foreign ministers, who were meeting in Brussels, as "among the most promising developments" and a basis for further negotiations aiming at a military balance at a much lower level of armament. Thus arms reductions are in the air, with or without the peace movement's encouragement.

International Views and Party Contacts. The DKP's statements on foreign policy are in perfect harmony with those made by the GDR and the USSR. It follows Moscow's and East Berlin's lead in supporting whatever groups they define as liberation movements. This includes the Sandinista government in Nicaragua. It invariably supports all aspects of the Soviet Union's peace propaganda, including demands for ending SDI and for removal of American atomic weapons from Europe. It applauds the SPD's party contacts with ruling parties in Eastern Europe and the SPD-SED security-policy talks that have resulted in calls for a "security partnership" between both Germanies and the Soviet Union and for the creation in Europe of corridors or zones free of nuclear and chemical weapons. It demands a cut of 10 percent in the FRG's defense budget and an ultimate end to arms exports. The DKP roundly criticizes the Bonn government's making "a big issue of the mythical 'military threat' from the East" and its position "that there is no alternative to the deterrence doctrine in the foreseeable future and that a continued peace will still require 'armed forces with well-balanced conventional and nuclear weapons.'" Finally, the DKP supports unflaggingly the SED's interpretations of the GDR's legal status. It criticizes Bonn's "resurgent fiction of a 'single German nation' and hackneyed contentions that the German question 'remains open in the legal, political and historical sense' and that it is still necessary to maintain the concept of single citizenship." It calls for "a definitive renunciation of great Germany dreams." (*IB*, June 1987.)

The DKP maintains close contacts with all ruling parties in Eastern Europe, especially with the Soviet Union and the GDR. It sends high-level delegations to their party congresses and receives such delegations sent to its own. West German communists were not among the important discussion partners for SED leader Erich Honecker during the latter's historic visit to the FRG in September 1987. No doubt the most important visit with a DKP member he made during his stay was with his sister, Gertrud Hoppstädter, at his home town in the Saarland. DKP leaders of course attended the 70th anniversary of the Bolshevik Revolution in Moscow in November 1987.

Other Leftist Groups. In addition to the DKP, there are many left-extremist small groups and parties, initiatives and New Left revolutionary organizations that are active. All renounce the DKP's pro-Soviet/SED policies and are ideologically deeply divided internally, even though most of them are willing to cooperate in action alliances. Total membership in these organizations, after allowing for multiple affiliations, declined in 1987 to approximately 62,000, with an additional 49,000 in organizations influenced by leftist-extremists. They produce about 200 publications with a total circulation of more than four million. They also operate a few pirate radio stations. (*VSB 87*; *FAZ*, 27 May.) By far the favored cause for cooperation is to protest against atomic power. About one-third of all terrorist acts were attributed to the struggle against the peaceful use of nuclear energy. NATO also provided important targets. (*ID*, 24 July 1987.)

The New Left, composed of Marxist-Leninists, Trotskyites, anarchists, autonomists, and antidogmatic revolutionaries, preaches class struggle. It identifies the proletariat as the essential revolutionary force leading the fight to tarnish the image of the FRG's political order in the eyes of its citizens and to overthrow the bourgeois state and capitalist system. Most advocate establishing a dictatorship of the proletariat culminating in a socialist and ultimately communist order. They are confident that the bureaucratic failures in communist-ruled regimes can be prevented. The autonomous anarchist groups advocate the eradication of the state, to be superseded by a "free" society. Most New Leftists unabashedly advocate using violence to achieve their aims.

Dogmatic New Left. There are a variety of Marxist-Leninist groups, loosely called "K-groups." The strongest of these groups is the Marxist-Leninist Party of Germany (Marxistisch-Leninistische Partei Deutschland; MLPD), which has about 1,300 members organized in twelve districts and approximately 100 local units. It regards itself as the only Marxist-Leninist party in the FRG. Its chairman is Stefan Engel, and its official organ is *Rote Fahne* (Red banner), whose weekly circulation is about 10,000. It participated in the 1987 Bundestag election, winning 13,821 second votes. This 0.0 percent of the total vote indicates how little electoral hope there is for the K-groups. Nevertheless, party spokesman Klaus Vowe called this result "satisfactory," considering that the party had expected to receive only 10,000. Vowe noted that the party would have gotten more votes were it not for the "falsification" of the party's arguments by the bourgeois media. (*ID*, 3 April 1987.)

The MLPD has three ineffective allied organizations with about 300 members. They are the Marxist-Leninist Workers' Youth Association (AJV/ML) with a press organ, *Rebell*, and a children's group, *Rotfüchse* (Red foxes); the Marxist-Leninist Pupils' and Students' Association, whose organ is *Roter Pfeil* (Red arrow), and an active Marxist-Lenist League of Intellectuals.

The United Socialist Party (Vereinigte Sozialistische Partei; VSP) was born from the 1986 merger of the Communist Party of Germany-Marxist Leninist (KPD, earlier known as KPD-ML) and the Trotskyist Group International Marxists (GIM). The VSP, with about 500 members, is led by Horst-Dieter Koch and has its headquarters in Cologne. Its biweekly publication *Sozialistische Zeitung* (Socialist newspaper, circulation 2,400) replaced in 1986 the KPD's earlier *Roter Morgen* (Red morning) and the GIM's *Was Tun* (What to do). Its youth group is the Autonomous Socialist Youth Group (ASJG).

Members of the KPD who opposed the merger that resulted in the VSP reconfirmed their adherence to the old party statutes and program. Calling themselves the "correct KPD," they maintain headquarters in West Berlin. A separate Workers' League for the Reconstruction of the KPD claims about 300 members, maintains a Communist University League in Bavaria, and published two editions of the *Kommunistische Arbeiterzeitung* (Communist workers' newspaper; KAZ).

The League of West German Communists (Bund Westdeutscher Kommunisten; BWK), which emerged in 1980 from a split in the now defunct Communist League of West Germany (KBW), counts approximately 300 members, organized in groups in seven lands. It publishes the biweekly *Politische Berichte* (Political reports), with a circulation of about 1,300 copies, and the *Nachrichtenhefte* (News booklets), with a circulation of about 1,000. The BWK is the dominant member of the People's Front, whose business office is in the BWK's main office in Cologne. The People's Front, with about 700 members and a biweekly *Antifaschistische Nachrichten* (Antifascist news, circulation 700), is an instrument for an alliance of left-extremists, and the BWK is willing to cooperate with the DKP and organizations affiliated with it or influenced by it.

The Communist League (Kommunistischer Bund; KB) has its headquarters in Hamburg, where about half of its approximately 400 followers live. Demanding "confrontation with the state" and abolition of the "capitalist republic," it has considerable influence within the Green-Alternative List (GAL), which won over 10 percent in the November 1986 Hamburg elections with an all-female slate. The KB publishes a monthly *Arbeiterkampf* (Workers' struggle), which has a circulation of about 4,800. The "Group Z" split from the KB in 1979 and joined the Greens; many of its members have risen to top positions in the Greens' federal and land organizations.

About a dozen Trotskyist groups, some existing only in certain regions, have a total of about 500 members. Advocating "permanent revolution" and the "dictatorship of the proletariat," they decry "actually existing socialism" in communist-ruled countries as "bureaucratic" or "revisionist decadence." The League of Socialist Workers is the German section of the International Committee of the Fourth International in London. Together with its Socialist Youth League, it counts fewer than 100 members, and its weekly organ *Neue Arbeiterpresse* (New workers' press) has advocated a general strike to overthrow the government. The small Trotskyist groups, such as the Trotskyist League of Germany, the International Socialist Workers' Organization, the International Communist Movement, the Socialist Workers' Group, and the Posadistic Communist Party, protest against animosity directed toward foreign workers in the FRG and demonstrate in support of revolutionary struggles in the Third World.

The Marxist Group (MG) is a Marxist-Leninist cadre party with a rigidly hierarchical structure, rigorous discipline, intensive indoctrination, and strict secrecy. Its 1,800 members and several thousand sympathizers are mainly students and academics, and the focus of its efforts is Bavaria. It is convinced that trained agitators must spark a class-conscious proletariat to engage in class struggle. It advocates "thoroughly destructive criticism of all existing conditions." (*VSB 87.*) It communicates

through its monthly *MSZ-Marxistische Streit und Zeitschrift-Gegen die Kosten der Freiheit* (Marxist controversy and magazine-Against the costs of freedom, 12,000 copies), the *Marxistische Arbeiterzeitung* (Marxist workers' newspaper, which appears irregularly) and the *Marxistische Schulzeitung* (Marxist school newspaper).

Autonomous anarchist groups of the undogmatic left. These groups renounce strict organizational structures and are extremely divided over aims and whether to utilize violent or nonviolent action in order to change society.

The Free Workers' Union (FAU), which has 200 members in 22 local groups, is a member of the anarchosyndicalist International Workers' Association (IAA) and publishes bimonthly *Direkt Aktion* in Dieburg. It founded Schwarze Hilfe (Black help) to assist imprisoned anarchosyndicalists, anarchists, and autonomists. It also maintains contact with the international coordinating office of the anarchist Black Cross in London. The principles espoused by anarchosyndicalists can be summarized as opposition to the state, to parliament, and to the military. FAU adherents oppose both Western capitalism and the "state capitalism" practiced in communist countries. They see as their supreme task revolutionary work in factories to create collective resistance against capitalism. They dream of a society characterized by decentralization and self-administration. There are some independent opposition FAU organizations that wish to work also outside the factories.

A Violence-Free Action Groups–Grass-Roots counts about 800 followers in about 70 groups and collectives. The contact and coordinating body for them is the Grass-Roots Revolution–Federation of Violence-Free Action Groups, which advocates a nonviolent revolution and creation of a decentralized society based on anarchy and self-administration to replace present state power. Their aims, as indicated by their actions and monthly publication *Grasswürzelrevolution* (Grass-roots revolution), which has a circulation of about 4,000, are primarily antimilitarism, peace and "social defense." Environmental protection, especially through opposition to nuclear power and reprocessing plants, is also important.

The diverse autonomous anarchist groupings within the undogmatic New Left tend to be tiny, loosely organized, short-lived, and prone to violence. They attract several thousand predominantly young people, who engage in "solidarity actions" to support Third World liberation movements. But their contacts with like-minded left-extremist groups outside the FRG were sporadic and generally limited to specific actions.

Unfortunately, many foreign extremist organizations operate within the FRG. Their numbers grow as that country becomes a haven for more and more refugees from the Third World. The presence of so many visibly alien people creates domestic political tensions and provides a convenient scapegoat and target for right-wing West German extremist circles. The BfV estimates that about 81,600 foreigners belong to leftist-extremist organizations (more than twice as many as belong to corresponding right-wing extremist groups). The most active and violence-oriented is the orthodox-communist Workers' Party of Kurdistan (PKK). The Liberation Tigers of Tamil Ealam (LTTE) makes its presence felt, as do violent Palestinian, Iranian, Turkish, and Yugoslavian groups. (*VSB 87*.)

Hard-core terrorist groups. Deadly and destructive terrorist actions continue, although their numbers declined from 1,902 in 1986 to 1,497 in 1987. (*ID*, 30 August.) The hard-core command level (Kommandobereich) of the Red Army Faction (Rote Armee Faction; RAF) is still composed of about twenty underground killers, approximately the same number as in the mid-1970s. They engage in political assassinations and dramatic bombings and claimed responsibility for the attempted assassination of Hans Tietmeyer in September (*FBIS*, 22 September). Closely supporting the RAF terrorists is the organization's second echelon, known as "RAF militants," who number approximately 250. Recruited from the anti-imperialist resistance circles, they handle logistics for the command level, providing documents, vehicles, weapons, explosives, and secret housing. These militants reportedly do engage in violent actions against material targets, but not against human beings. A further echelon is composed of "RAF sympathizers," who number around 2,000. They engage in propaganda and public relations for the terrorists and assist those who are in prison. (*ID*, 24 July 1987; *VSB 87*.) As was proven in 1987, when French police captured four leaders of Action Directe on a farm near Orleans, the RAF maintains close political collaboration with like-minded foreign terrorist groups, such as Action Directe in France, the Fighting Communist Cells in Belgium, the Red Brigades in Italy, and GRAPO in Spain, despite serious setbacks in 1987.

The Red Cells (*Rote Zellen; RZ*), their female affiliate Rote Zora, and various "autonomist groups" also launch terrorist attacks. The RZ find themselves in basic ideological agreement with the RAF's "socialist revolutionary and anti-imperialist" aims. The various other groupings and individuals lumped together as "autonomists" also choose their victims in the same basic way as the RAF and RZ, and apply the same rationales for their attacks as are expressed in the "letters taking responsibility" sent by the RAF and RZ. The common characteristics of all these groups are hatred of the political, social, and economic systems of the FRG and a rigorous readiness to use violence, no matter what it may cost in life and limb.

Die Tageszeitung (The daily newspaper; *TAZ*) is a daily publication close to the alternative milieu and has a circulation of up to 33,000. Its slant is revealed by letters to the editor praising terrorist actions, as when the nuclear engineer Karl-Heinz Beckurts and his driver were gunned down in 1986: "Bravo RAF!"; "This was a spy!"; "Now there is one imperialist swine fewer!"; and "I have no pity with the liquidated manager of the nuclear industry of death!" (*Deutschland-Union Dienst*, 16 July 1986). *De Knipselkrant*, which is published periodically in the Netherlands, also serves as a forum of discussion for the "armed struggle" (*VSB 87*).

The Greens and the SPD's youth, student, and women's organizations are not left-radical groups. Some of their members do share some of the views of the extreme left in an abstract way, and some have been willing to take part in "unity of actions" with leftists and communists. Common ground can often be found in support of the Soviet Union's disarmament campaigns, nuclear- or chemical-free zones in Central Europe, or efforts to reduce the power of the U.S. military, the Bundeswehr, or NATO.

Wayne C. Thompson
Virginia Military Institute

WEST BERLIN

Population. 1,869,000 (1988)
Party. Socialist Unity Party of West Berlin (Sozialistische Einheitspartei Westberlins; SEW)
Founded. 1949
Membership. 7,000 (SEW's figures; the Federal Office for the Protection of the Constitution [BfV] estimates 4,500). 70 percent joined after 1966
Chairman. Horst Schmitt
Politburo. Horst Schmitt, Dietmar Ahrens (deputy

chairman), Inge Kopp (deputy chair), Ralf Derwenskus, Uwe Doering, Helga Dolinski, Detlef Fendt, Klaus Feske, Harry Flichtbeil, Margot Granowski, Heinz Grünberg, Klaus-Dieter Heiser, Volker June, Jörg Kuhle, Hans Mahle, Margot Mrozinski, Monika Sieveking, Eberhard Speckmann, Erich Ziegler

Secretariat. Horst Schmitt, Dietmar Ahrens, Klaus Feske, Harry Flichtbeil, Margot Granowski, Inge Kopp, Jörg Kuhle

Executive. 65 members

Status. Legal

Last Congress. Eighth, 15–17 May 1987

Last Election. 1985, 0.6 percent, no representation

Auxiliary Organizations. Socialist Youth League Karl Liebknecht (Sozialistischer Jugendverband Karl Liebknecht; SJ Karl Liebknecht), about 600 members; Young Pioneers (Junge Pioniere; JP), about 200 members; SEW-University Groups, about 400 members

Publications. *Die Wahrheit* (Truth), SEW daily organ, circulation about 13,000. The party also publishes a quarterly magazine *Konsequent* (Consistent, circulation 2,500) for its propaganda work, and its university groups publish *Rote Wochen* (Red weeks) for their agitation activities.

West Berlin remains under Allied occupation by the armed forces of the United States, the United Kingdom, and France, which maintain about 10,000 troops there. West Berlin is under the NATO defense umbrella. The 1971 Quadripartite Agreement, signed by the three powers above and the Soviet Union, confirms Berlin's special status. It states that West Berlin is not a part of the Federal Republic of Germany (FRG), but that it has links with the FRG. Despite the fact that this agreement was intended to cover the entire area of greater Berlin, the Soviet-occupied eastern sector of the city has been declared the capital of the German Democratic Republic (GDR), which refers to the eastern part of the city simply as "Berlin."

West Berlin is, for all practical purposes, ruled by its own elected Senate (parliament), but the three allied powers can, and sometimes do, veto a law or action of the Senate. Both West Berlin and the FRG seek to maintain close ties with each other; these ties are a diplomatic and economic necessity for West Berlin and a political imperative for Bonn. West Berlin is represented in the federal parliament in Bonn by nonvoting deputies. Residents of West Berlin are not required to serve in the Federal Army (Bundeswehr), a fact which, as is often cited,

prompts many young German dissidents to resettle there and thereby greatly enlivens the alternative scene in the city, where many New Left, left-extremist and terrorist groups are active. Berlin's special status enabled the ruling party in the GDR, the Socialist Unity Party of Germany (SED), which was created in the Soviet-occupied zone of Germany by a forced merger with the Social Democratic Party of Germany (SPD) in 1946, to create a subsidiary party in West Berlin. In 1959 a nominally independent organizational structure was created for the West Berlin section of the SED. The party was renamed the Socialist Unity Party of Germany-West Berlin (SED-WB) in 1962 and renamed again in 1969, when the present appellation was adopted to give it the appearance of an indigenous, independent West Berlin party. Unlike the Communist Party of Germany (KPD) in the FRG, the SEW has never been outlawed or forced to go underground because of possible objectives that are incompatible with the FRG's Basic Law (constitution). Berlin's special status is a major reason for this.

The SEW has, according to its own sources, about 7,000 members, which is about how many votes it received in the last Senate elections in March 1985 (7,713). Its 0.6 percent of the total vote was far short of the minimum required for seats in the city's parliament. Under the banner of the rights to work and to live in peace and democracy, the SEW entered the elections of 29 January 1989 with equally dismal prospects. Such poor electoral performances are likely to continue as long as the SEW retains its character as unswervingly pro-SED and pro-Moscow, tightly organized along standard Marxist-Leninist lines, financially dependent upon East Berlin, and internally divided over *glasnost'* and *perestroika*. West Berlin voters are keenly aware of the truth expressed by SED Politburo member Alfred Neumann when he brought greetings from the SED to the SEW's party congress in May 1987: "The SED and the SEW are linked not only by common roots, traditions, and the same goals and class interests but also by the socialist world view and the communists' confidence in victory." (ADN, 16 May 1987.)

The SEW is broken down into twelve sub-organizations (Kreisparteiorganisationen) and has a number of affiliated organizations. Communist youth are organized in the SJ Karl Liebknecht, which has about 600 members and publishes a monthly journal, *Signal*, with a circulation of 1,000. The Young Pioneers (JP) have about 200 members. Its university organizations consist of around 400 students. The SEW-influenced Action Group of Democrats and Socialists (ADS-Westberlin) embraces approximately 300 persons and publishes the biweekly *ads-info*. Most of its members belong also to the SEW university groups and agitate against government plans to reform the universities. Its Democratic Women's League Berlin (DFB) has about 600 members and publishes about 600 copies of the monthly *Im Blickpunkt der Berlinerin* (From the perspective of the Berlin woman). The Society for German-Soviet Friendship has about 500 members. The West Berlin organization of the Victims of the Nazi Regime/League of Antifascists (VVN/BdA) also has about 500 members and publishes a quarterly antifascist magazine, *Der Mahnruf* (The warning). The SEW exercises considerable influence over the Berliner Mietergemeinschaft e.V. (Berlin Renters' Community), whose 8,000 members oppose the elimination of rent controls. It publishes a bimonthly *Mieterecho* (Renters' echo), with a circulation of 8,000. (*VSB 87*.)

The Eighth Party Congress took place from 15 to 17 May 1987, under the slogan: "With the SEW for peace, work, democracy, and social progress." There were 587 delegates and guests from 37 foreign parties and organizations, including delegations from the Communist Party of Germany (DKP), the Communist Party of the Soviet Union (CPSU), led by Central Committee Secretary Vadim Medvedev, and the SED, led by Neumann. SED chairman, Erich Honecker, sent a telegram to re-elected SEW leader Horst Schmitt, wishing him "success, creativity, and health in implementing the decisions of the Eighth SEW Congress." (ADN 15 May 1987.) The only major newspaper to provide extensive coverage of this congress was the SED's official organ *Neues Deutschland* (New Germany). Perhaps the only thing unusual that occurred at the congress was that Chairman Horst Schmitt was re-elected with fewer than 94 percent of the delegates' votes, a very low percentage for an orthodox communist party (*VSB 87*).

The demands and resolutions produced by the congress provide an accurate picture of the SEW's overall policies and positions. In defense, it totally backs Soviet and GDR demands, something about which party chairman Schmitt makes no bones: "We—the Communists of West Berlin—support with all our strength the peace policy of the Soviet Union, the GDR and the other socialist states." It favors all disarmament proposals made by the So-

viet Union, asserting that "this is ever more necessary because the most aggressive quarters in the U.S. and Western Europe bound up with the military-industrial complex are concocting ever more pretexts to frustrate disarmament moves." The SEW calls for a replacement of deterrence by "a security partnership with the socialist states." Nuclear- and chemical-free zones in Central Europe should be created, nuclear tests stopped, SDI terminated, and no SDI research permitted in West Berlin, and the city should not be "illegally" involved in NATO strategy or "as a NATO policy tool." (*ND*, 17 May 1987; *IB*, September 1987.)

In foreign affairs the SEW is an unfailing spokesman for the SED's policies, especially with regard to the status of West Berlin. It states that it is time to end the backward-looking "myth of a metropolis"—that is, of one Berlin. "West Berlin is not 'part' of a whole city; it is a large city developed in nearly 40 years under the special conditions of an occupied territory." Schmitt asked rhetorically "if it is not time for the governing mayor [of West Berlin] to state publicly that his competence is confined to West Berlin and nothing else." West Berlin's need for broad contacts with the GDR requires that its government recognize the GDR and "stop interfering in the internal affairs of the GDR. Indeed, it corresponds to the spirit of the present for the Senate to recognize the GDR borders as state borders. It is time for all West Berlin authorities at least to respect the GDR citizenship." In 1988 the SEW again called for "strict implementation of the four-power agreement on West Berlin," ignoring the fact that that agreement applies to *all* of Berlin. It also proposed a reduction of U.S., British, and French occupations forces in West Berlin "to symbolic dimensions." (*FBIS*, 13 October.)

Schmitt specifically criticized speeches made on 30 April 1987 by Chancellor Helmut Kohl and Mayor Diepgen on the occasion of the 750th anniversary of Berlin, which, in Schmitt's words, were "slanderous attacks against the GDR." It should be noted that Erich Honecker, after some deliberation, decided not to accept the Senate's invitation to attend these ceremonies, on the grounds that his taking part in a ceremony with representatives of the Bonn government would imply his approval of the ties between Bonn and West Berlin. Honecker would indeed have been embarrassed to hear Kohl and Diepgen criticize the Berlin Wall and state again publicly that the "German question" (i.e., the question of German reunification) remains open. The GDR officially denies that reunification is a future possibility or that Berlin is "in a waiting mode to become the German capital." The SEW agrees entirely with the SED's rationale for the Berlin Wall, which it calls "the secured state border of the GDR vis-à-vis West Berlin: it has led to stability in the area and will remain in place until the reasons for which it was erected in the first place disappear" (i.e., Western meddling). (*ND*, 16–17 May 1987; *IB*, September 1987; ADN, 25 May 1987.)

Like the DKP in West Germany, the SEW is open to "unity of action" with Social Democrats, the Alternative List (in which the West Berlin Greens participate), and trade unions, especially in the "fight for peace." It joined in the opposition to the census, invoking the "right of resistance" on the grounds that the census violates "basic constitutional rights." It also struggles against unemployment, "poverty caused by social dismantling," "hopelessness," denial of renters' rights, capitalist application of education and technology that harms workers, destruction of the environment, especially the "continuing liquidation of small gardens, fields, and forests for the profit-oriented housing development policy," relegation of thousands of artists to a minimal standard of living, and discrimination against women and foreigners. "Our party takes the view that we have a common enemy: monopoly capital." (*ND*, 16–17 May 1987; *ID*, 15 May 1987.)

The objective of the joint struggle is to develop alternatives to the policies of the ruling Christian Democratic Union (CDU), without the SEW having to "renounce our basic principles." It joined many other groups in a demonstration protesting against "police terror and for democratic rights" on the occasion of President Ronald Reagan's visit to West Berlin on 12 June 1987, when he demanded that the wall be torn down. (*ND*, 29 and 30 June 1987.)

The SEW shares in the "spirit of proletarian internationalism" and sends delegations to fraternal party congresses, especially in the GDR and Soviet Union. For the first time, it sent a representative to a congress of the Communist Party of the USA. Schmitt concluded his address at the SEW's Eighth Party Congress with the words: "Our future lies in our Marxist-Leninist firmness in principle, in our undeviating orientation to the interests of the working people, and in our indestructible alliance with the CPSU, with the SED, and with the entire world communist movement." (*ND*, 16–17 May 1987.)

Wayne C. Thompson
Virginia Military Institute

Great Britain

Population. 56,935,845
Party. Communist Party of Great Britain (CPGB)
Founded. 1920
Membership. 9,700 (*Morning Star*, 6 January 1988)
General Secretary. Gordon McLennan
Political Committee. 9 members: Ron Halvarson (chairman), Gordon McLennan (general secretary), Ian McKay, Gary Pocock, Martin Jacques, Jack Ashton, Kerin Halpin, Vishnu Sharma, Nina Temple (*Morning Star*, 21 May 1985)
Executive Committee. 45 members
Status. Legal
Last Congress. Fortieth, 14–15 November 1987 (extraordinary, 24 April 1988, of CPGB dissidents [*Insight*, 30 May; *FBIS-WEU*, 27 April])
Last Election. June 1987, 0.1 percent, no representation
Auxiliary Organizations. Young Communist League (YCL); Liaison Committee for the Defense of Trade Unions (LCDTU)
Publications. *Morning Star*, *Marxism Today*, *Communist Focus*, *Challenge Spark*, *Our History Journal*, *Economic Bulletin*, *Medicine in Society*, *Education Today and Tomorrow*, *New Worker*, *Seven Days*

The CPGB is a recognized political party and contests both local and national elections. It does not, however, operate in Northern Ireland, which it does not recognize as British territory. The party has had no members in the House of Commons since 1950 but has one member, Lord Milford, in the non-elected House of Lords.

Leadership and Organization. The CPGB is divided into four divisions: the National Congress, the Executive Committee and its departments, districts, and local and factory branches. Constitutionally, the biennial National Congress is the party's supreme authority, and except in unusual periods, such as the present, it rubber-stamps the decisions of the Political Committee. Responsibility for overseeing the party's activities rests with the 45-member Executive Committee, which is elected by the National Congress and meets every two months. The Executive Committee comprises members of special committees, full-time departmental heads, and the sixteen members of the Political Committee, the party's innermost controlling conclave.

Party leaders remain deeply preoccupied with the continuing decline in support for the party. Electorally, the party is so battered that it no longer contests as many seats as it once did. Membership, at fewer than 10,000 (only some 50% of whom have actually paid their fees), is at its lowest point since World War II. The decline in electoral support was most graphically illustrated in Britain's last general elections (1987) when the party's nineteen candidates polled a mere 6,078 votes.

However, the poor showing of the CPGB at the polls belies the party's strength in the trade union movement and in influencing opinion. Although it does not directly control any individual trade union, the party is represented on most union executive committees and has played a major role in most government-union confrontations of recent years. The CPGB's success is partly attributable to low turnouts in most union elections, to the fact that it is the only party seeking to control the outcome of these elections, and to its close interest in industrial affairs, which ensures support from workers who might not support other aspects of the party's program.

Domestic Affairs. The long-standing conflict between the party's Eurocommunist leadership and its Stalinist hard-left minority continued in 1988. The party remained in an obvious crisis that has been building for some years. It centers on the dispute between the party's Executive Committee, on the one hand, and the *Morning Star* on the other. The *Morning Star*, once recognized as the party's daily newspaper, is technically owned by the communist, but separate, People's Press Printing Society (PPPS). Throughout 1988, the PPPS continued to be in the hands of Stalinist opponents of the Executive Committee's Eurocommunist policies. The *Morning Star* group has historically been bitterly opposed to the leadership's criticisms (muted though they were) of the Soviet Union and to the transformation of the party's theoretical journal, *Marxism Today*, into a popular, broad-based magazine.

The course of intraparty conflict in 1988 occurred in the context of, and in reaction to, several consecutive years of stinging defeats for the political left in Britain. Most important of these have been the miners' strike of 1984–1985, the left's debacle in controlling the Liverpool city government during 1985–1986, together with the years of unsuccessful struggle with the Thatcher Government on a wide range of issues. As a result, the already fractured communist movement drifted into an even sharper debate within itself: Who was to blame for these defeats? How should the movement proceed to bolster the party's position, along with the position of the left? Should the party adopt a more cooperative relationship with the Labour Party and even parties to the right? How should it deal with the British union movement?

The Eurocommunist majority in control of the CPGB has tended to answer these questions by advocating broad alliances with less ideological left parties and groups. This has infuriated the harder left, which has reacted angrily through the *Morning Star* and its political group, the Communist Campaign Group, as well as the breakaway New Communist Party. To be sure, there have been fractious problems within this opposition, but there is vocal agreement in charging that the Eurocommunist leadership is guilty of soft-headed thinking that has caused the movement to lose its leadership of the working class.

A pattern of vicious attacks from each side against the other, together with actions by the Eurocommunists to expel rebels from the CPGB have almost completely dominated the time of all the participants, which has further hurt the appeal of the party, and the 1987 election results graphically showed how extensive the damage has become. Whereas the party fielded 35 candidates and won more than 11,000 votes in 1983, it offered only nineteen candidates and won less than 7,000 votes in 1987. Moreover, its membership has fallen to less than 10,000, and its full time staff now numbers fewer than twenty.

The election results did nothing to soften the intraparty struggle. The executive was quick to restate the Eurocommunist views by noting that there is widespread acceptance in Britain of "Thatcherite concepts and arguments, even among those who vote Labour." The way forward, they argued, was just the opposite of what the hard left was advocating: the party must "develop a strategy that can challenge the hold of Thatcherite thinking and lead to a level of mass movement higher than ever before, uniting broad sections of the population."

In the wake of postelection recriminations and continued purges, the CPGB held its Fortieth Party Congress in late 1987. The long intraparty conflict came to a head, as the congress, by a vote of four to one, broke the party's ties with the *Morning Star* and upheld the Executive Committee's numerous expulsions of prominent rebels.

The split seemed to become permanent during 1988 when the *Morning Star* and its political group held their own congress in late April. About 150 delegates representing 1,600 dissident communists met in London and agreed to "re-establish" the communist party. They took the name "Communist Party of Britain," in contrast to the name "Communist Party of Great Britain," which is used by the Eurocommunists. Predictably, they claimed that they had finally recreated the true communist party and that socialism would be "firmly" on its agenda.

The CPGB continued to support campaigns, including demonstrations, against most aspects of government policy. During 1988, the main CPGB efforts were directed toward the nurses' pay dispute, funding and administration of the National Health Service, which had become a major national political issue during the 1987 election campaign, and the government's efforts to pass legislation adopting a new individual poll tax in place of property taxes and major educational reforms. The CPGB also began what it promised would be year-long discussions about the rewriting of its party program, *The British Road to Socialism*.

The CPGB also continued to support unilateral nuclear disarmament by the United Kingdom, a position it presses on the Labour Party and Neil Kinnock at every opportunity. In 1988, this issue was coupled with continued strong opposition to U.S. eagerness to encourage Star Wars, which was just as vigorously opposed by the Soviet Union.

Auxiliary Organizations. In industry, CPGB activity centers on its approximately 200 workplace branches. Its umbrella organization is the LCDTU. Although the CPGB is riven by internal disputes, its trade union structure can still command considerable support from prominent trade union leaders.

The YCL, the youth wing of the party, has less than 500 members.

The party retains a number of financial interests, including Central Books, Lawrence and Wishart Publisher, Farleigh Press, London Caledonian Printers, Rodell Properties, the Labour Research Department, and the Marx Memorial Library.

International Views and Activities. Although the CPGB leadership is regarded as revisionist by the breakaway dissident hard-liners who formed the rival Communist Party of Britain in 1988, there are, in fact, few areas in which the CPGB stints in its support of the Soviet Union. The party has been, and is still critical, of the Soviet invasion of Afghanistan and, before that, of Czechoslovakia. It reaffirmed this opposition in 1988 during the twentieth anniversary of the Czech events of 1968. Otherwise, the CPGB agrees with the Soviet Union in favoring arms reductions and opposes the deployment of missiles in Europe and the development of U.S. space weapons. It is critical of Israel and seeks to promote the recognition of the Palestine Liberation Organization.

The Gorbachev reforms in the Soviet Union have naturally attracted the CPGB's intense interest. Although cautious and mildly skeptical, the CPGB seems to be very hopeful that Soviet domestic and international policies are beginning to coincide with its own. Conversely, the *Morning Star* and its supporters in the new Communist Party of Britain seem to be edgy, apparently caught between their traditional unwavering support for the Soviet Union and distrust of the new Soviet policies, which appear to them to be revisionist.

Other Marxist Groups. Besides the CPGB, several small, mainly Trotskyist groups are also active in Great Britain. Although some of these groups grew swiftly in the 1970s, their memberships are now waning.

The most important of the Trotskyist groups is Militant Tendency, which derives its name from its paper of the same name. Militant Tendency claims to be merely a loose tendency of opinion within the Labour Party, but there is no doubt that it possesses its own distinctive organization and for some years has been pursuing a policy of "entryism" (the tactic of penetrating the larger, more moderate Labour Party). Militant Tendency controls about 50 Labour Party constituencies.

The other significant Trotskyist organizations are the Socialist Workers' Party (SWP) and the Workers' Revolutionary Party (WRP). The SWP has been particularly active in single-issue campaigns, notably the antiunemployment campaign. It gave active support to striking miners' families but, in fact, enjoys little support in the coal-mining industry. The WRP's activities are more secretive but are known to center in the engineering, mining, theater, and auto industries. It focuses its attention on the young and has set up six Youth Training

Centres, which are primarily concerned with recruitment.

Gerald Dorfman
Hoover Institution

Greece

Population. 10,015,041
Party. Communist Party of Greece (Kommunistikon Komma Ellados; KKE)
Founded. 1921
Membership. 50,000 (estimated)
General Secretary. Kharilaos Florakis
Politburo. 9 full members: Kharilaos Florakis (75), Grigoris Farakos (64), Nikos Kaloudis (70), Loula Logara (60), Kostas Tsolakis (60), Orestis Kolozof (55), Dimitrios Gondikas (47), Aleka Papariga (42), Takis Mamatsis (62); 4 candidate members: Dimitris Karagoules (36), Dimitris Androulakis (36), Dimitris Kostopoulos (48), Spyros Khalvatzis (42)
Secretariat. Giannis Mavrakis (35), Kostas Voulgaropoulos (48), Thanasis Karteros (43)
Status. Legal
Last Congress. Twelfth, 12–16 May 1987, in Athens
Last Election. 2 June 1985, 9.9 percent, 13 of 300 seats
Auxiliary Organization. Communist Youth of Greece (KNE)
Publications. *Rizospastis*, daily; *Kommunistiki Epitheorisi* (KOMEP) monthly theoretical review

The major development in 1988 was the gradual rapprochement between the KKE and the other leftist parties, primarily E.AR (Greek Left) under Leonidas Kyrkos. E.AR is the new name of the old KKE-Interior that split from the KKE during the military dictatorship (1967–1974). KKE-Interior had adopted more moderate positions and identified itself with Eurocommunism during the 1970s and early 1980s. In its April 1987 congress, KKE-Interior split into two factions; one representing a majority of the delegates and led by Leonidas Kyrkos adopted the title "Elliniki Aristera" (Greek left; E.AR) and removed all familiar trappings of a communist party, including adherence to Marxism-Leninism. A smaller faction under Giannis Banias retained the title KKE-Interior, but added the two words "Ananeotiki Aristera" (Renovating left; A.A.).

Early in the year, Kharilaos Florakis, the KKE general secretary, intensified his efforts to promote a wide alliance (*symparataxis*) of the "forces of the Left," and especially to improve relations with E.AR. In an article published in the *World Marxist Review* (January), Florakis stated that in his view the Panhellenic Socialist Movement (PASOK) "cannot solve the nation's problems . . . nor can the solution be furthered by the return to power of New Democracy, a right-wing party with a 'liberal,' in fact, anti-popular programme." Florakis declared that for the KKE "the solution lies only in a firm alliance of the left forces relying on a common programme with a socialist outlook."

Although E.AR leader Leonidas Kyrkos remained cool to the idea until the middle of summer, a shift began sometime in August—not unrelated to the serious illness of premier and PASOK leader Andreas Papandreou. In an interview (*To Vima*, 22 May) after a meeting with Florakis, Kyrkos had stated that "an alliance is meaningless unless it is preceded by confluence of views, a programmatic agreement on the major problems." Florakis continued the effort and showed willingness to make concessions in order to bring about a broad alliance. By the end of the year, negotiations had progressed to the point that a formal agreement is expected very early in January 1989. A broad coalition of the left will include, in addition to the E.AR, the Socialist Party formed by former PASOK leading personality Gerasimos Arsenis, and several prominent persons with leftist leanings. Apostolos Lazaris, a former cabinet minister in the first PASOK government who broke relations with Papandreou and PASOK in December 1988 over the economic scandals, may assume the titular leadership of the alliance.

The advocates of the alliance are encouraged by the serious decline of PASOK's appeal and the real possibility that many PASOK followers with leftist leanings will leave PASOK in the next parliamentary election (to take place not later than June 1989) and vote for the candidates of this left coalition. The ultimate expectation is that neither PASOK nor New Democracy—which is anti-Marxist and pro-West—will win a clear majority in the Legislature. In this case, the deputies of the wider left alliance will either support a coalition government with PASOK or simply support with their votes a PASOK government in exchange for policies favored by the left. To improve the chances for such an outcome, the KKE and the other parties of the left are pressing for a new electoral law that will provide for a "purer" form of proportional representation. Under such a system, the wider left alliance expects to win between 26 and 30 seats in the 300-seat Legislature, thus playing the role of the king-maker. The New Democracy Party and the smaller Party of Democratic Renewal (DI.ANA)—which split from N.D. in October 1985—have also come out in favor of pure proportional representation. New Democracy prefers the current electoral system of reinforced proportional that provides for a bonus of parliamentary seats to the party with the relatively largest portion of popular votes. However, for political reasons it has declared that it will not object to either system because it is confident of victory regardless of the electoral system. The leaders of both of these two parties seem to expect that many PASOK followers with a centrist orientation will vote for the candidates of either N.D. or DI.ANA. If the purely proportional system is enacted—possibly in February 1989—nothing will rule out the appearance of a separate centrist party under the leadership of individuals with legitimate centrist credentials; such a party would serve to siphon off centrist votes from PASOK. In such a case, a coalition government under N.D. leader C. Mistotakis is possible.

Why does the KKE want a wide alliance of the forces of the left? Florakis correctly expects many leftist voters to leave PASOK in the next election. He also correctly realizes that many of those voters are not prepared to vote for the Communist Party with its Marxist-Leninist ideology and Stalinist mentality. For this reason, he wants a broad alliance in which the image of the Communist Party will become more palatable to the broad masses of left voters.

Leadership and Organization. The KKE has been legal since 1974, yet its organizational structure has not changed substantially from the days when it was illegal. The party members are organized in cells (*pyrines*) in factories, workplaces, schools, or neighborhoods for those who are not working, such as women or retired persons (*aktivs*). Party factions (*fraxies*) are organized by party members within trade unions, professional organizations, and cooperatives in the countryside. Smaller towns and villages have local party organizations headed by a party secretary. Major cities, such as Athens, Piraeus, and Salonika, have city organizations and city committees headed by powerful secretaries. Each *nomos* (prefecture) has its own *nomos* committee, headed by a secretary. In addition, the country has been divided into major regions such as Crete, Pelloponesus, Thessaly, Epiros, Central Macedonia, and Thrace, each headed by party secretaries.

The most powerful organ of the party is the Politburo, which is appointed by the Central Committee. The CC is elected by the Congress, which statutorially meets every four years. The Central Committee has approximately 100 members, regular and alternate. A full list is not available. Although the current general secretary Kharilaos Florakis is very influential within the Politburo, decisions in this organ are reached by consensus. Florakis, who is currently 75 years old, is likely to step down after the next parliamentary election. There is already speculation about his possible successors. At this time, it appears that Grigoris Farakos, a Politburo member and an old-line communist, may be selected as a transition figure before the torch is passed on to one of the leaders from the new generation, such as Dimitris Androulakis or Dimitris Gondikas. Both rose to leadership positions through the KNE.

E.AR has a 101-member Central Committee and an Executive Buro with Leonidas Kyrkos as the first secretary and Gr. Giannaros, D. Giatzoglou, Petros Kounalakis, K. Kourkoutis, Sp. Likoudhis, Ar. Manolakos, Mikh. Papagiannakis, Stergios Pitsiorlas, Giannis Toundas, M. Tsandalidis, D. Khatzisocratis, and D. Psikhoyios as members. The mainstay of E.AR are leftist intellectuals and professionals.

Views and Positions. During the year, the KKE intensified its criticism and opposition to PASOK. Since 1974, the KKE has taken a supportive stand toward PASOK because PASOK has advocated many of the anti-Western and anticapitalist views espoused by the KKE. The KKE cooperated with the PASOK government during its first term of office (1981–1985) and supported some critical PASOK moves, such as the election of a new president of the republic and a revision of the constitution in March/April 1985. The KKE reportedly diverted some communist votes toward PASOK in the parliamentary election of 2 June 1985 in order to assure PASOK's absolute majority of seats in the Legislature. The reasons were clear. PASOK had coopted into its leading echelons many leftists, in fact, many of those who had been in the war-time EAM/ELAS (the communist-led resistance movement) or in the "Democratic Army" (the communist-led guerrilla campaign from 1946 to 1949), and their younger relatives. In its early years in power, PASOK pursued anti-West policies, at least verbally, was very critical of the EEC and NATO, encouraged anti-American propaganda, favored the public sector at the expense of private enterprise, and facilitated the broadcasting of leftist views and programs by the government-controlled radio and television stations.

After 1985, PASOK, facing adverse economic conditions, shifted to a less left-oriented economic policy, which included efforts to encourage private enterprise and a virtual freeze on salary and wage increases and other austerity measures in the face of a 17 to 20 percent inflation rate. The KKE regarded this economic policy as a flagrant departure from the socialist path (*Allaghi*: change) that PASOK had previously advocated. A gradual estrangement between the two parties began, but because of the propaganda advantages still enjoyed by the left in the government-controlled electronic media, the KKE kept its opposition within limits, at least until the end of 1987. At the beginning of 1988, the intensity of KKE opposition rose. A major reason was the unquestioned decline of PASOK's popularity. Polls conducted throughout the year indicated that PASOK, which had received 46 percent of the total vote in the 2 June 1985 election, was down to 26, and in some polls to 22 percent. (ENA, 7 January; *To Vima*, 6 March; *To Vima*, 13 March; *Ethnos*, 14 March; *Ethnos*, 16–18 May.) However, the very large percentage of "undecided" voters, ranging from 15 to 20 percent, indicated that many PASOK voters, dissatisfied with the party's policies and with the economic scandals attributed to government officials, were searching for a new political home. Since a relatively small percentage of the undecided appeared to lean toward the N.D., the KKE concluded that its chances of "capturing" many of those voters were very good, and would improve considerably if it were in a broad alliance of the leftist forces. If such an alliance were formed, even those who might have been reluctant to vote for KKE candidates would feel more comfortable voting for the candidates of a wider left alliance.

To promote this alliance, the KKE has toned down its strident attacks on the European Economic Community and has moved, reluctantly, closer to the position held by E.AR, namely, the acceptance of Greek membership in the EEC as an irreversible fact, and the focusing of the efforts of the leftist forces on obtaining better terms for Greece and on closer cooperation with leftist forces within the other members of the EEC.

The KKE, like the E.AR, opposes the presence of American military bases in Greece—the E.AR does so with less vehemence—but even the KKE is now less strident in its opposition to them.

The KKE now appears to have accepted the E.AR view that the private sector has a role to play in the economy, under proper safeguards against corrupt practices or exploitation. The KKE and, to a lesser extent, the E.AR continue to speak out against the "multinationals," "foreign monopolies," and the like. The KKE also stresses the need for "national independence from foreign power centers," meaning primarily the United States.

The KKE blames PASOK for "betraying" the cause of *Allaghi*, namely, PASOK's promise to promote Greece's "socialist transformation." In this regard, the KKE focuses its electoral appeal on the promise that the broad alliance of the left will bring about the "real change" that PASOK was presumably unable or unwilling to pursue.

The KKE, a devout Stalinist party virtually all of its political life, finds it somewhat difficult to digest the basic tenets of *perestroika*, but it has not come out openly against the Gorbachev policies. At this juncture, the more "humane" image presented by the Soviet Union favors the KKE and improves its image among the voters. Indicative of the public leanings are the results of a recent poll regarding the most admired foreign leaders. Gorbachev was at the top of the list, with President Reagan at the bottom, below such leaders as Arafat and Quaddafi. Accordingly, the KKE treats *perestroika* with political flexibility and tries to benefit by it as much as possible domestically.

One must also note that in its public pronouncements and political actions, the KKE behaves as a fully legitimate party, within the constitutional and political framework. Lately, it has taken positions parallel with those of N.D. in its criticism of PASOK and in its call for a national election to resolve the crisis caused by the economic scandals. Its revolutionary image has been deliberately toned down to the point of invisibility. On occasion, the party has publicly denounced terrorist acts by local leftist groups such as the "17th of November," "First of May," and the like.

Finally, the KKE has expressed its support for a Greek-Turkish rapprochement, but it has also expressed reservations over the manner in which Premier Papandreou has handled this issue.

Domestic Activities. During 1988, the KKE spent a great deal of time and effort in promoting a broad alliance of the leftist forces. Its efforts appeared very close to success by the end of the year. Success, however, was made possible only because the KKE leadership was willing to make significant concessions by toning down its own basic positions. However, the KKE is bound to dominate any alliance of the left because it would be by far the strongest party within such an alliance. In the Legislature and in its public pronouncements, the KKE has sought change of the electoral system to secure a purer form of proportional representation. The KKE supported many strikes, but without the rancor familiar from past years. On the occasion of the party's seventieth anniversary, a memorial volume was published containing the biographies of several thousand party members through the years. Technically, the Communist Party was not established until 1921, but apparently the party has chosen to trace its origins to the founding of the Socialist Workers Party founded in November 1918. Other activities included the preparation of the annual youth festival organized by the KNE in September, the party's massive demonstration on 17 November commemorating the student takeover of the Polytechnic School in Athens in 1973, which led to the resignation of the dictator G. Papadopoulos and the assumption of dictatorial power by his former colleague, Brig. Gen. Dimitrios Ioannides, an outcome not foreseen or wanted by the rebelling students.

Greek terrorist organizations were active again this year. In June Capt. William Nordeen, naval attaché at the U.S. embassy in Athens, was killed in a bomb explosion set by the "17th of November." In July, two explosions in government buildings caused some damage, but no human casualties. In March, a new organization identifying itself as the "People's Revolutionary Solidarity" claimed responsibility for setting off a bomb that destroyed a suburban restaurant. Bombs were placed under the cars of N.D. deputies, but they were detected before they exploded and no damage was caused. The KKE publicly condemned the killing of Naval Attaché William Nordeen.

International Contacts. The KKE was very active during the year in its contacts with other communist parties. On 7 February, East German ambassador to Athens Horst Brie visited Florakis and conveyed the "heartfelt greetings" of Erich Honecker, general secretary of the CC of the SED. On February 10, Orestis Kolozof, Politburo member, visited Belgrade for talks with Bosko Krunič, president of the CC Presidium of the League of Communists of Yugoslavia. The visit is significant because in the past the KKE had no contacts with the LCY. On March 5, a delegation headed by Kolozof visited Israel for talks with the Israeli Communist Party (MAKI). The two parties voiced support for the complete withdrawal of Israel from the territories occupied since 1967. On 24 March, Orestis Kolozof met with Werner Jarowinsky, Politburo member of the CC of the SED. On 28 March, Kh. Florakis visited Budapest at the invitation of the Hungarian Socialist Workers Party and had talks with János Kádár. On 4 April, Grigoris Farakos, Politburo member and editor of *Rizospastis*, visited Sofia at the invitation of the Bulgarian Communist Party. He had talks with Todor Zhivkov. On 15 April, Horst Sindermann, Politburo member of the CC of the SED visited Florakis in Athens. On 25 April, Florakis visited Prague and held talks with Miloš Jakeš, general secretary of the Communist Party of Czechoslovakia. On 30 April, a "working group" of the CC of the KKE headed by CC candidate member Kharalambos Angourakis met a working party from the CC of the Bulgarian CP under the leadership of Vasil Tsanov, a secretary of the BCP/CC. On 23 June, Florakis had talks in Athens with Siegfried Lorenz, member of the SED's Politburo. On 23 July, Oskar Fischer, foreign minister of the German Democratic Republic, paid a visit to Kh. Florakis while on an official visit to Athens. On 16 August, Todor Zhivkov, general secretary of the Bulgarian Communist Party, had talks with Florakis in Varna.

Other Marxist-Leninist Organizations. With the exception of the KKE-Interior AA, under Banias, all other Marxist-Leninist organizations are small, peripheral groups with insignificant influence. Their followers are mostly young, university students, and unemployed university graduates. Such organizations include the Greek International Union-Trotskyites, the Revolutionary Communist Party of Greece (EKKE), and the Communist Party of Marxist-Leninists. Seventeenth of November, First of May, ELA, and People's Revolutionary Solidarity are basically terrorist organizations, although occasionally they issue profound diatribes against capitalism, the monopolies, American imperialism, and the Greek ruling class. At least the 17th of November must have in its leadership well-educated individuals with a good knowledge of Greek political and economic affairs and, of course, of Marxist ideology.

D. G. Kousoulas, Professor Emeritus
Howard University

Iceland

Population. 246,526 (July 1988)
Party. People's Alliance (Althydubandalagid; PA)
Founded. 1968
Membership. 3,000 (estimated)
Chairman. Olafur Ragnar Grimsson
Executive Committee. 10 members: Olafur Ragnar Grimsson, Svanfridur Jonasdottir (deputy chair), Svavar Gestsson, Steingrimur Sigfusson, Gudrun Helgadottir, and five others
Party Secretary. Bjoern G. Sveinsson
Central Committee. 70 members, 20 deputies
Status. Legal
Last Congress. November 1987
Last Election. 1987, 13.4 percent, 8 of 63 seats
Auxiliary Organizations. Organization of Base Opponents (OPO; organizer of peace demonstrations against U.S.-NATO bases)
Publications. *Thjodviljinn* (daily), Reykjavik; *Verkamadhurinn* (weekly), Akureyri; *Mjolnir* (weekly), Siglufjordhur

Icelandic politics and the Icelandic economy are as turbulent as the island's weather. Despite Iceland's remarkable prosperity, its economy is still highly dependent upon marine products for three-fourths of its exports. Swings in fish catches and the currency level can quickly reverse economic trends. After a short but remarkable boom from mid-1985 to mid-1987 (real growth of the gross domestic product was over 6 percent in 1986 and 1987), falling catches and the falling U.S. dollar weakened the economy sharply. This in turn reignited inflation and presented the center-left government of Thorstein Palsson with a severe fiscal crisis. The coalition among the Independence Party (moderate conservative; IP), the Progressive Party (agrarian liberal; PP), and the reformist Social Democrats (SDP) collapsed in September. After extended negotiations Progressive Foreign Minister Steingrimur Hermannsson presented the country with a precariously balanced four-party coalition consisting of his party, the Social Democrats, the People's Alliance, and the one-man splinter group from the Progressives known as the Association for Equality and Justice. Thus, despite the harsh squalls, the People's Alliance had come in from the cold.

The P.A. occupies the left flank of Icelandic politics. It is the successor to a line of leftist parties dating back to 1930, when the Icelandic Communist Party (Kommunistaflokkur Islands) was established by a left-wing splinter from the Labor Party. In 1938, the Social Democratic Party (SDP) also broke from Labor and joined with the communists to create a new party, the United Peoples' Party–Socialist Party (Sameingingar flokkur althydu–Sosialista flokkurinn; UPP-SP). Interestingly, this new amalgamation broke with the Comintern and established the precedent of independent radical socialism without foreign ties. A series of additional splits and mergers produced the current PA in 1968. The PA has participated in governing coalitions most recently (before September) by joining the PP in a coalition headed by the late maverick Gunnar Thoroddsen, formerly of the IP. That government lasted until the April 1983 parliamentary elections, which were a setback for all the constituent parties of the coalition.

The PA suffered another 4 percent setback in April 1987, when it polled 13.4 percent and received eight seats in the 63-seat Althing (Parliament). For the first time since 1942, the reformist SDP, which received 15.2 percent of the vote and ten seats (a gain of two), outpolled the PA. Clearly the PA had been outflanked by the pragmatic SDP under Jon Baldvin Hannibalsson's effective, if somewhat idiosyncratic leadership, and by the unconventional radical feminism of the Women's Alliance (Samtok um kvinnalista; WA), which continues to move ahead in elections and polls.

The new government announced on 28 September was a tactical coup for Steingrimur Hermannsson, but also for the new PA leader Olafur Ragnar Grimsson. The PA holds three portfolios, with Grimsson (who failed to win a parliamentary seat in 1987) at the strategic Finance Ministry, PA deputy chair Svavar Gestsson serving as minister of education and culture, and Steingrimur Sigfusson serving as minister of agriculture and communications. Former finance minister Hannibalsson is now in charge of foreign affairs, which includes national security and NATO issues.

The new cabinet has but a one-vote parliamentary majority and cannot afford dissent within its constituent parties. Given the individualism of Icelandic politics, the government's position is especially precarious.

Leadership and Organization. The PA is run no less democratically than other Icelandic parties. It also suffers from recurring factionalism, which in 1987 caused a bitter leadership fight in the wake of the disastrous parliamentary elections. The victory by the more pragmatic faction led by Olafur Ragnar Grimsson, a professor of political science, was followed by an effort to reconcile the more dogmatic faction of former chair Svavar Gestsson. Internal party tensions flared again when the PA participated in the negotiations leading to the new center-left Hermansson government.

Women PA activists protested that no woman was among the three ministers allotted to the PA. The party's new rules call for at least 40 percent of all posts to go to women. This was especially disappointing to Grimsson's major supporter Gudrun Helgadottir, who has been a leader of the reform faction. She noted that Grimsson's ministerial colleagues from the PA, Gestsson and Steingrimur Sigfusson, were his rivals within the PA. The snub was also likely to weaken the PA's response to the political challenge of the Woman's Alliance, which is a major competitor for leftist women's votes. Gudrun Helgadottir's disgruntlement was at least partially assuaged when she was elected speaker of the parliament in October. Although the position is politically neutral, it is an honor for Helgadottir to be the first woman to hold that post (*Nordisk Kontakt*, no. 14–15).

There were also protests from more radical members of the PA parliamentary group. Geir Gunnarsson was opposed to the PA's participation in the coalition, but promised finally to support the group's decision in parliament. Skuli Alexandersson was more adamant in his opposition and threatened to abstain in crucial votes of confidence. His abstention would undermine the government's razor-thin majority. PA tacticians worked out a complex solution of dubious legality. If a vote of confidence comes up, Alexandersson will absent himself and be replaced (as is the custom for all absent M.P.s) by a substitute, who will support the government. Then Alexandersson will instantly recover

from his "political flu" (ibid., no. 13). Clearly pragmatism still has the upper hand in the PA.

Grimsson's assumption of responsibility for the Finance Ministry will erase the embarrassment of his nonparliamentary status. Given the country's economic crisis, however, the PA will be forced to accept full responsibility for the government's austerity policies. This could trigger additional tension between the party's academic and labor wings. The former dominates the party leadership, while the latter represents most of the PA's voters. AFI (Icelandic Trade Union Federation) leader Gudmundur J. Gudmundsson, who resigned his parliamentary seat in protest over the PA's orientation to academic and service employees, openly proposed a labor-oriented splinter party from the PA. While nearly every Icelandic party has fissioned in recent years, the PA must retain its labor group if it is to continue to be a serious political force (ibid., no. 16 1987).

Domestic Affairs. Economic affairs continue to dominate Icelandic politics and were responsible for the collapse of the center-right Palsson government in September. The Icelandic krona was devalued in February, May, and September for a total reduction of the krona's value amounting to 21.85 percent. A major tax reform sought to replace a variety of excise taxes with a general value-added tax. Disagreements on tax policy and the August wage-price freeze (applied also to agreed-upon increases in wages and agricultural subsidies) finally exploded the coalition.

The PA consistently opposed all aspects of the former government's economic policies. Objections were raised especially to the continuing overvaluation of the krona, the high real-interest rates, and insufficient increases in minimum wages. These matters were raised by Steingrimur Sigfusson in debating the opposition's parliamentary motion of nonconfidence that was defeated 41 to 22 in April (ibid., no. 7).

The new government will test the PA under fire. A revised austerity package was announced almost immediately. It includes a general price and wage freeze from 15 August through 15 February 1989, a period of time somewhat shorter than that of the original plans for the freeze, which extended through 10 April. The earlier termination date was a concession to the PA, as it is also the date for renewed general wage negotiations between Icelandic unions and employers. The new government devalued the krona. The measure also seeks a significant reduction in interest rates as inflation declines, and modified subsidies for fisheries, exports, and industrial electricity rates. Finally, general governmental spending is constrained, despite modest increases for old-age and disability pensions and a rise in the tax-free allowances for low incomes (Central Bank of Iceland, *Economic Statistics Quarterly*, November).

Acceptance of these firm measures suggests that the PA is willing to put its new pragmatism into practice. Inflation had soared to an annual rate of more than 35 percent in the summer before the first freeze was imposed. By the end of the year it was under 5 percent, but whether it will stabilize after the freeze ends remains to be seen. The economic situation is mitigated by typically low unemployment rates (less than 1 percent), and the slowdown is accompanied by widespread labor shortages. Iceland is unique.

Foreign Affairs. The persisting emotional issue of Icelandic foreign policy and a central issue for the PA is membership in NATO, the NATO bases at Keflavik and elsewhere on the island, and overall East-West relations. Icelanders have become more pragmatic in the 1980s, as their government has taken a more active role in NATO matters and followed up on the U.S.-Soviet 1986 summit with personal diplomacy. A month before his government fell, Prime Minister Palsson paid a visit to Washington, the first such visit by an incumbent Icelandic leader. PA chair Grimsson is a seasoned traveler who has paid personal visits to Gorbachev's Moscow. U.S.-Icelandic relations are good despite the sensitivity of the issue of the bases and the unsettled matter of Icelandic hunting of whales for "scientific" purposes.

The new government declared that Iceland's foreign and security policies would remain unchanged, but the PA did secure a pledge for no new military installations. The Keflavik base was not specifically mentioned, although Prime Minister Hermannsson noted that there were no new projects underway at the moment. Two long-range radar stations built with NATO funds became operational, but both have civil as well as military functions and will be manned by Icelandic civilians. (*News from Iceland*, November). NATO discussions about building a reserve air field to supplement Keflavik were shelved at the direction of PA communications minister Sigusson (*Nordisk Kontakt*, no. 14–15).

In government, the PA has generally been less vehement in opposing the bases and Icelandic NATO membership. At the beginning of 1988, PA representatives called for reduction of spending on the bases, but no such plans were launched by the new government. PA chair Grimsson has called for a more nuanced party position on foreign and security affairs, with less emphasis of the traditional xenophobic and isolationist positions. Still, the PA is opposed in principle to the bases and worries about Iceland's economic dependence upon the employment and purchases that the bases provide. The PA also supports various plans for Northern European nuclear weapons–free zones. Improvement in East-West security relations, the INF agreement, and the various European negotiations are likely to keep such issues from becoming a source of controversy for the new government.

Soviet relations with Iceland have mainly been economic. The USSR is a major, but hardly dominant market for Icelandic seafood (usually bartered for oil) and more recently woolens. Iceland is one of the few Western countries that imports more from than it sells to the USSR. Icelanders are insisting that the USSR fulfill its trade treaty obligations (*News from Iceland*, October). In March, a delegation from the Supreme Soviet headed by Presidium deputy chair V. Shevchenko visited the island, but they were guests of the Icelandic government and parliament (TASS, 19 March).

International Party Contacts. The PA and its predecessors have always remained aloof from international communist movements. Indeed, the party was the first to remove itself from any association with Stalin's Comintern and vigorously denounced Soviet interventions in Eastern Europe. Its ties are mainly with other Nordic social-democratic and radical-socialist parties (especially the Norwegian Left Socialist and Danish Socialist People's parties), but even these are not especially intense.

Other Marxist and Leftist Groups. The PA's internal pluralism has discouraged the formation of independent leftist groups, even though the PA itself has often resembled an organized argument more than a political party. Although there were brief flurries of interest in them in the 1970s, Maoism and Trotskyism are not represented in Iceland by organizational structures. As noted, the tumultuous November 1987 PA Congress has brought threats of an alternative socialist party, but thus far there has been no real action toward that end. The PA remains a divided party, but its ability to join the new governing coalition, albeit with some complex internal maneuvers, shows that it is a party with more interest in influence and revival than ideological excess.

The Women's Alliance (Samtok um kvennalista) is an interesting Icelandic phenomenon. Women continue to be more prominent in Icelandic public life, their participation symbolized, of course, by the republic's president, Vigdis Finnbogadottir (whose powers are largely ceremonial, but not irrelevant during cabinet crises). Finnbogadottir won re-election in June by an overwhelming majority. The alliance itself is a radical feminist group, very loosely organized but with a pragmatic domestic program that attracts wide support in this highly egalitarian society. As noted, its large electoral gains made it a logical candidate for participation in the new government. The WA was courted by Hermannsson during the protracted cabinet negotiations in September, but it appears that the WA was not a serious candidate for inclusion in the new government (ibid.).

All of the other parties accord the WA's parliamentary leaders considerable respect. Nevertheless, given the requirements for economic austerity that faced the new government, the WA's demands for massive wage increases for low-paid employees (overwhelmingly women) would have made it a problematic coalition partner. The party's general line tends to be less interest in economic growth and investment and more interest in redistributional questions involving wages, public services, and social policy. On foreign-affairs issues its position is strongly pacifistic and opposed to Icelandic commitments to NATO. The party's internal organization is very loose, with annual rotation of top positions. The WA has clearly attracted many voters who might otherwise have been inclined to support the PA (*Mannlif*, June; *JPRS*, 4 October).

Eric S. Einhorn
University of Massachusetts at Amherst

Ireland

Population. 3,531,502 (July 1988)
Party. Communist Party of Ireland (CPI)
Founded. 1933 (date of record)
Membership. Under 500
General Secretary. James Stewart
National Political Committee. Includes Michael

O'Riordan (chairman), Andrew Barr, Sean Nolan, Tom Redmond, Edwina Stewart, Eddie Glackin
Status. Legal
Last Congress. Nineteenth, 31 January–2 February 1986, in Dublin
Last Election. February, 1987, no representation
Auxiliary Organizations. Connelly Youth Movement
Publications. *Irish Socialist, Irish Workers' Voice, Unity, Irish Bulletin*

The CPI was founded in 1921, when the Socialist Party of Ireland expelled moderates and decided to join the Comintern. During the Civil War, the party became largely irrelevant and virtually disappeared, although very small communist cells remained intact. The CPI was refounded in June 1933, the date the communists now adopt as the founding date of their party.

The party organization was badly disrupted during World War II because of the neutrality of the South and the belligerent status of the North. In 1948, the communists in the South founded the Irish Workers' Party, and those in the North, the Communist Party of Northern Ireland. At a specially convened "unity congress" held in Belfast on 15 March 1970, the two groups reunited.

The CPI is a recognized political party on both sides of the border and contests both local and national elections. It has, however, no significant support and no elected representatives.

Leadership and Organization. The CPI is divided into two geographical branches, north and south, corresponding to the political division of the country. In theory, the Congress is the supreme constitutional authority of the party, but in practice it tends to serve as a rubber stamp for the national executive. The innermost controlling conclave is the National Political Committee. Such little support as the CPI enjoys tends to be based in Dublin and Belfast.

Domestic Affairs. The continuing political division of the country and Ireland's economic problems remained the main issues in 1988. The CPI views the United Kingdom as an imperialist power that gains economically from holding Ireland in a subordinate position. Although continuing to advocate the creation of a single, united socialist Ireland, the party remains opposed to the use of violence and denounces the use of force by armed gangs on either side of the communal divide. For example, it was particularly vehement in its denunciation of the Provisional Irish Republican Army's bombing of the Grand Hotel in Brighton in 1984, which nearly killed several members of the British Cabinet, including Prime Minister Margaret Thatcher.

The party believes Irish unification can be achieved only by promoting working-class solidarity and thus overcoming the communal divide between Protestants and Catholics. Executive Committee member Morrissey put the CPI view succinctly: "As long as the working class is divided along religions or other lines, the exploiting classes will dominate the political stage and Ireland will remain subordinate to imperialism."

The Nineteenth Congress of the CPI met during late January and early February 1986. The delegates devoted the majority of their time to the problems of the North. They strongly denounced the Anglo-Irish agreement, demanding that Britain immediately declare a fixed date by which it would withdraw its political, administrative, and military presence. Additionally, they declared their support for establishment of a devolved Assembly for the North during the transition to a united socialist Ireland. This assembly should have broad political and social powers, sufficient to radically restructure the state, and these powers should be accompanied by a strong Bill of Rights. Interestingly, the delegates also urged that, as a united socialist Ireland is established, it adopt the more liberal North Irish laws on divorce and abortion to replace what it described as the backward prohibitions existing in the South.

International Views and Activities. The CPI is quite untouched by the phenomenon of Eurocommunism and remains staunchly pro-Soviet. Indeed, in a country where there are several larger Marxist groups in operation, the distinctive feature of CPI attitudes is perhaps simple pro-Sovietism. The party is strongly anti-American and denounces U.S. policy in Central America, the Middle East, and elsewhere. It favors arms-reduction talks in Europe and opposes the deployment of missiles and former President Reagan's Strategic Defense Initiative.

The party also remains hostile to the European Economic Community, which it regards as a device for drawing Ireland into NATO planning.

Gerald Dorfman
Hoover Institution

Italy

Population. 57,455,362
Party. Italian Communist Party (Partito Comunista Italiano; PCI)
Founded. 1921
Membership. 1,462,302 (18th congress in March 1989)
General Secretary. Achille Occhetto (52)
Secretariat. Achille Occhetto, Piero Fassino (38; organization), Livia Turco (32; women's commission), Fabio Mussi (40), Gianni Pellicani (56), Claudio Petruccioli (47)
Directorate. 38 members
Central Committee. About 210 members
Central Control Commission. 60 members; Gian Carlo Pajetta (77), president
Status. Legal
Last Congress. Seventeenth, 9–13 April 1986, in Florence
Last Election. 1987, 26.6 percent, 177 of 630 seats in the Chamber of Deputies, and 28.3 percent, 100 of 315 seats in the Senate (1983, 29.9 percent, for 198 seats in the Chamber of Deputies, and 30.8 percent, for 107 seats in the Senate)
Auxiliary Organizations. Italian Communist Youth Federation (FGCI), Italian General Confederation of Labor (CGIL), National League of Cooperatives
Publications. *L'Unità*, official daily, Massimo D'Alema (39), editor, Renzo Foa, coeditor; *Rinascita*, Franco Ottolenghi, editor; *Critica Marxista*, bimonthly theoretical journal, Aldo Zanardo, editor; *Politica ed Economia*; *Riforma della Scuola*; *Democrazia e Diritto*; *Donna e Politica*; *Studi Storici*; *Nuova Rivista Internazionale*. The party also runs a publishing house, Editori Riuniti.

The PCI was founded in 1921, when a radical faction of the Italian Socialist Party (PSI) led by Amadeo Bordiga, Antonio Gramsci, and Palmiro Togliatti seceded from the PSI and joined the Comintern. Declared illegal in 1926 by Mussolini's regime, the PCI went underground; its party headquarters were moved to France; and its membership dropped to a few thousand during the 1930s. The

PCI leaders regrouped in Italy in 1943–1944, and the party participated in broad-coalition governments from the spring of 1944 until the spring of 1947. Meanwhile, membership grew from some five thousand in mid-1943 to about one and a half million by late 1945. The party won 18.9 percent of the votes in the first postwar election in 1946, while the PSI won 20.7 percent and the Christian Democrats 35.2 percent.

After the Comintern's purge of Bordiga, and the Fascists' imprisonment of Gramsci in 1926, the PCI was led by Togliatti until his death in 1964, and then by Luigi Longo (who headed the Communist Youth Federation in the mid-1920s) until his 1972 retirement to make way for Enrico Berlinguer.

In the 1960s, the Togliatti-Longo leadership began to take autonomous positions within the Moscow-centered international communist movement. By then, the emergence of a younger generation of Italian militants who were not imbued with the wartime image of Soviet heroism, coupled with the Sino-Soviet split and the challenge posed by successive center-left coalition governments in Italy, favored such an initiative. The Soviet-led invasion of Czechoslovakia, along with the repressiveness and foreign adventurism of the Brezhnev regime fueled the process, as did the transfer of authority from Longo to Berlinguer in 1972. The Polish Solidarity crisis of 1980–1981 and the declaration of martial law in Poland finally prompted Berlinguer to declare that the October Revolution had "exhausted its propulsive force" and to reject the very idea of an international communist movement separate and distinct from other left-wing forces. The result was the brief but intense polemical *strappo* (breach) in Soviet-PCI relations in 1982.

All the while, the postwar communist party observed the democratic rules of the game within Italy, and its share of votes in national elections gradually grew from 18.9 percent in 1946 to 27.2 percent in 1972, and then jumped to 34.4 percent in 1976. This seven-point electoral leap forward was not, however, followed by a political breakthrough into the national government, despite the PCI's talk of a "historic compromise." Although the communists participated widely in municipal, provincial, and regional governing councils and took part briefly in a parliamentary majority in the late 1970s, they were not offered cabinet posts in a coalition government at the national level.

Thereafter the PCI's electoral strength began to decline. It dropped to about 30 percent in the parlia-

mentary elections of 1979 and 1983, while registering losses in regional and local contests as well. In the 1984 elections to the European Parliament this trend was temporarily reversed when the PCI won 33.3 percent of the vote, slightly surpassing the Christian Democrats for the first time. But this turned out to be a sympathy vote for Berlinguer, who had died of a stroke just days earlier. In the June 1987 parliamentary elections, the communists won only 26.6 percent of the vote for the Chamber of Deputies, a decline from 29.9 percent in 1983. It was the party's worst showing since the 1960s.

Domestic Politics and the PCI. In municipal elections on 29–30 May, the communists fared much worse than they did in the 1987 parliamentary contest, winning only 21.9 percent of the votes cast. Indeed, the respective showings of the PCI, the PSI, and the front-running Christian Democratic Party (DC) bore a certain resemblance to their relative standing in the first postwar election of 1946. While the DC won over one-third of the votes cast (36.8 percent), the PCI and PSI won about one-fifth each. The PSI, with 18.3 percent of the total, gained four percentage points, up from 14.3 percent in the 1987 national election, and came within 3.6 percentage points of the PCI. (*La Repubblica*, 1 June.) In elections in two northern regions on 21 June, the communists also registered losses, even running behind the Socialists in Friuli-Venezia Giulia. There the PSI won 17.7 percent of the ballots, up from 11.3 percent in the previous regional election of 1983, while the PCI declined from the 21.7 percent it won in 1983 to 17.5 percent. The DC won 37.2 percent, a gain of three percentage points over 1983. (Kevin Devlin, *RFE Research*, 29 June.)

The communists' electoral losses at the local level intensified their political isolation at the national level. Already in the early spring they had stood on the sidelines as Italy went through one of its periodic cabinet crises. Largely because of internal bickering within the DC, the five-party coalition government (DC, PSI, Republicans, Social Democrats, and Liberals) formed after the 1987 parliamentary elections collapsed in February (*NYT*, 11 February). In April, it was succeeded by Italy's 48th postwar government, a five-party coalition of similar composition. The only noteworthy change was that the powerful secretary of the DC, Ciriaco De Mita, became premier in place of his fellow Christian Democrat, Giovanni Goria, who had held the post for just six months (*WP*, 14 April). In July, following the PCI's electoral setbacks, the five-party cabinet decided to press forward with a move to abolish the secret ballot in parliament, despite the PCI's declared opposition to this type of piece-meal institutional reform (*La Repubblica*, 21 July). That same month a schism developed between the PCI-dominated Italian General Confederation of Labor (CGIL), on the one hand, and the DC-oriented Italian Confederation of Workers' Unions (CISL) and the center-left Italian Union of Labor (UIL), on the other, when the CISL and UIL affiliates of Fiat signed a separate wage contract with the management of the giant conglomerate (*L'Unità*, 17 and 19 July).

The political isolation of the PCI was accompanied by a PSI-led challenge to the communists to engage in what one might call historical *glasnost'* Italian-style. Triggered by the Soviet Union's rehabilitation of Nikolai Bukharin, spokesmen of parties belonging to the De Mita government repeatedly raised the question of Togliatti's complicity in Stalin's purges. PCI historians and leaders alike readily conceded that Togliatti, by virtue of his position in the Third International, was jointly responsible for Stalin's terror. At the same time, they insisted not only that they had long ago acknowledged this reality, but also that it did not alter the fact that Togliatti was responsible for building a postwar communist party susceptible to democratic evolution. Nonetheless, the polemics continued. (Kevin Devlin, *RFE Research*, 24 February; *L'Unità*, 11, 12, and 17 July.)

Party Leadership, Organization, and Debates. The PCI's losses in the 1987 parliamentary elections sparked a debate that ended in a reaffirmation of the opening to the noncommunist European left proclaimed at the 1986 congress in Florence. In contrast, the party's further decline in the 1988 local elections prompted a change in the general-secretaryship and widespread talk of the need to chart a "new course" and to redefine the very identity of the Italian communist party.

In a letter to the Central Committee and Central Control Commission (CC-CCC) dated 10 June, Alessandro Natta, who had been recuperating from a heart attack since late April, resigned his position as general secretary. As he put it, "Even if I weren't in a condition of physical impairment, I would still ask you . . . to take up the problem of a change in the secretary of the party." He made no bones about the reason. "Recent political events, with the harsh and worrisome result of the administrative elections . . . , have led me to conclude that it is right and

opportune to proceed immediately to a change in . . . leadership." He went on to thank his comrades for their support and to request that they allow him to observe "the rule of the Franciscans among whom the prior who has completed his term returns to being a simple brother!" (*L'Unità*, 14 June.)

The letter was made public on 13 June, following a meeting of the Directorate, or executive body, of the Central Committee. It was also accompanied by a personal note to Vice Secretary Achille Occhetto in which Natta urged him to convene a CC-CCC meeting as soon as possible to effect the leadership transition. According to a senior member of the Directorate, Aldo Tortorella, Natta also expressed concern in the note over the sharp tone of the debate in the upper echelons of the party following the electoral setback in May. (*L'Unità*, 16 June.)

The unprecedented resignation of the general secretary, as well as the internal party recriminations over the PCI's electoral decline, gave rise to speculation in noncommunist quarters that Natta had been forced to resign. In yet another letter to the entire party, Natta angrily denied this, calling the reports "of maneuvers and plots" against him "a grotesque campaign," as well as an "offense to common sense." "I am not in exile and I haven't lost my tongue. So, I can say that it is time to put an end to it." (*L'Unità*, 17 June.)

Just a few days later, on 20–21 June, the CC-CCC met to accept Natta's resignation and to elect Occhetto to succeed him as general secretary. In his address to the plenum, Occhetto spoke about the need for the party to analyze its electoral losses from the vantagepoint of the question of what precisely the PCI's programmatic profile should be. He deplored the "instances of self-torment and outright ungenerosity" in the post-election debate and warmly praised Natta. At the same time, he called for the formulation by the entire party of a "new course" through which the PCI might achieve "the conquest of the center" in Italian politics. And he urged that this be done with more "openness" (*trasparenza*). Specifically, the party should make public the proceedings of the Directorate meetings, should elect "in the most open and direct way possible" all leaders at all levels of the party structure, and should adopt new rules that would permit the clear expression of majority and minority positions on policy issues. (*L'Unità*, 21 June.)

On June 21 the Directorate presented Occhetto to the CC-CCC plenum as its unopposed choice for general secretary. He was thereupon elected by an overwhelming majority, with only three votes cast against him and five abstentions (*L'Unità*, 22 June). (Presumably, most of the 270-odd members of the CC-CCC were present.) This was in striking contrast to Occhetto's election as Natta's deputy in June 1987. On that occasion 11 members of the Directorate had opposed him, while in the CC-CCC 41 had voted against him, and 22 had abstained. (*L'Unità*, 26 and 28 June 1987.)

The near unanimous vote in favor of Occhetto did not mean, however, that harmony reigned within the PCI's upper ranks. For all three negative votes came from the party's liberal wing (in contrast to the centrists, represented by Occhetto, or the left). Edoardo Perna declared that he had opposed Occhetto in 1987 and saw no reason to change his mind now (*L'Unità*, 22 June). Guido Fanti insisted that the political debate must precede the formation of the leadership group, as he had urged in 1987 as well (*L'Unità*, 21 June). And Napoleone Colajanni not only voted against Occhetto but also submitted a letter of resignation from the Central Committee. In it he explained that he (like Fanti) opposed the procedure according to which "the choice of men comes before the debate on the political line." Yet another liberal, Carlo Castellano, did not attend the plenum but submitted his resignation from the Central Committee on the ground that the PCI was not moving in the direction of a necessary "break with the continuity of the past." Of the five abstentions, three were likewise voiced by liberals (Arrigo Boldrini, Luigi Corbani, and Giuliano Procacci), while two came from Armando Cossutta and Luigi Pestalozza of the orthodox pro-Soviet left. (*L'Unità*, 22 June.) Others voted in favor of Occhetto only after expressing reservations. For example, the most prominent liberal, Giorgio Napolitano, was also uneasy over the disjunction between the election of the general secretary and the political debate still ahead, suggesting that Occhetto's management of the party in the coming months would be the ultimate test of his qualifications (*L'Unità*, 21 June). In the same vein, Natta's former personal secretary, Renato Sandri, explicitly criticized recent statements by two younger centrist members of the Secretariat closely associated with Occhetto (Massimo D'Alema and Piero Fassino), as well as the editorial policy of *L'Unità*. He took issue in particular with the daily's recent claim that the communists of today were "another culture, another tradition, another PCI," in comparison to those of Togliatti's time. (*L'Unità*, 21 June.)

The following month the CC-CCC held another plenum (19–21 July) to launch the process of clarification of the PCI's political strategy and identity that was expected to reach its culmination at the party's eighteenth congress, to be convened in early 1989. The crux of the debate over strategy had to do with potential alliance partners and, in particular, the party's policy toward the PSI, while the debate over identity focused on whether the PCI must repudiate its Soviet-oriented past in order to create a viable political profile in the present.

In his opening speech, Occhetto presented his own views on these questions while relegating their final resolution to the forthcoming congress. With regard to potential allies, he sought to "conquer the center" by moving beyond the PCI's rivalry with the PSI to the attainment of "a new hegemony of all forces of renewal, lay and Catholic," in which the autonomy of each would be respected. He called specifically for a reassessment of the Catholic question in order "to define the watershed between democratic Catholics and conservative Catholics." With regard to the PCI's identity, he proposed an "historical reassessment" of the October Revolution and a redefinition of the very meaning of socialism: "It is not a matter of leaving one system in order to enter another already known and well defined. Socialism ought to be seen as a movement capable of furnishing an answer to old and to new contradictions." (*L'Unità*, 20 July.)

Whereas the party's liberal wing remained for the most part silent during the subsequent discussion, the nonaligned and orthodox leftists rose to the attack. Lucio Magri deplored the absence of any criticism of "postindustrial capitalism" in Occhetto's report, and his fellow ex-*Manifesto* radical, Lucian Castellina, bemoaned Napolitano's reference to a "bipartisan consensus" on Italian foreign policy, citing the need to combat the transfer of 72 American F-16 fighter-bombers from Spain to Italy as evidence to the contrary. (*La Repubblica*, 21 July.) The independent-minded Pietro Ingrao urged the PCI to build its new identity on an alliance with the grassroots movements of pacifism, feminism, and environmentalism, while the orthodox Cossutta found Occhetto's new course "vague and unconvincing" (*La Repubblica*, 22 July). The leftists also looked favorably upon the vision opened up by Gorbachev's reforms in the USSR rather than the idea raised by the liberals of a possible convergence between the PCI and what the leftists dubbed "Mediterranean socialism." Even the centrist Alfredo Reichlin spurned any affinity with "Mediterranean socialism," calling upon the PCI to challenge the PSI for "hegemony on the left." (*La Repubblica*, 21 July.)

The July plenum concluded with a series of personnel changes and organizational innovations (the latter pertaining to the preparations for the Eighteenth Congress). With regard to personnel, the 64-year-old liberal Gerardo Chiaromonte retired from the editorship of *l'Unità*, reportedly because of a divergence in political orientation between the communist daily and a sizable portion of the party membership. Chiaromonte was succeeded by the 39-year-old centrist Massimo D'Alema. D'Alema's position as Secretariat member in charge of organization was, in turn, taken over by the 38-year-old centrist Piero Fassino. Both these appointments met with the almost unanimous consent of the CC-CCC. There was, however, some dissension over the promotion to the Secretariat of Chiaromonte's former deputy at *L'Unità*, Fabio Mussi. Opposed by the liberals, apparently because of his predilection for "movement" mobilization, Mussi received nineteen negative votes and thirteen abstentions at the plenum and was also opposed by about one-quarter of the Directorate. (*La Repubblica*, 22 July.) Finally, the CC-CCC reluctantly accepted the letters of resignation submitted at the June plenum by Colajanni and Castellano, despite the urging of the historians Giuseppe Boffa and Giuliano Procacci that the resignations be rejected (*L'Unità*, 22 July).

The procedure for organizing the party congress scheduled for early 1989 also underwent substantial modification. First, instead of presenting a set of theses to the various governing bodies of the party (CC-CCC, local congresses, national congress) for individual debate and amendment, the July plenum agreed to Occhetto's proposal that a single political resolution be drawn up as a unitary, internally coherent policy statement (*L'Unita*, 20 July). Second, in contrast to the situation in 1986 when a 77-member commission had drafted the "theses" submitted for discussion prior to the Seventeenth Congress, a committee of ten was elected to draft a political resolution that would then be revised by the full CC-CCC before being presented to the party as a whole for debate before and during the congress. The membership of this editorial committee was carefully structured to reflect the various tendencies in the party: Magri represented the left; Occhetto, Mussi, and Claudio Petruccioli the center; Gianfranco Borghini and Lanfranco Turci the liberals. There were, in addition, two scholars, Boffa and the philosopher Biagio De Giovanni, and two women, Tiziana Arista and Claudia Mancina. A committee of seven was also elected to draw up the procedural rules of the congress. (*La Repubblica*, 22 July;

L'Unità, 15 October.) In effect, the committee of ten replaced the Program Office established a year earlier.

The actual formulation of what became known as the "congress document" went through several stages. The committee of ten prepared a preliminary version for consideration by the Directorate in mid-October, after which it revised and developed that version into a first draft for discussion by the CC-CCC from 26 to 28 October (*L'Unità*, 15 October). The committee then reworked the first draft on the basis of the debate at the late October plenum (*L'Unità*, 26 November).

A second draft was presented to the CC-CCC plenum that met from 24 to 25 November. The first order of business at the November plenum was procedural. Tortorella proposed a choice between two approaches to handling the second draft: the traditional one of voting on amendments to specific chapters; or a new approach whereby the members of the CC-CCC would express their criticisms on given points, but would then vote on the draft as it stood. The document would then be submitted to the congresses of the local sections and federations of the PCI, and the views expressed at all levels of the party would contribute to the document's final revision at the Eighteenth Congress (now set for the second half of March 1989). After some discussion, the new procedure was approved by a large majority of centrists and liberals, with just twelve negative votes and ten abstentions. (*L'Unità*, 25 November.) The next day, after a "long and heated debate" on the text of the document, a motion to approve its "general orientation" (*indirizzo generale*) was endorsed overwhelmingly, with fourteen abstentions and two nays. It was opposed by only Cossutta (who presented an opposition resolution that was promptly voted down) and his customary supporter, Pestalozza. (*L'Unità*, 26 November.)

The congress document opened with a discussion of the place of the PCI in the West European left. Calling for "a new chapter in the struggle for socialism" that was necessary owing to "the crisis and exhaustion of past historical experiences," it affirmed that "democracy is not a path to socialism but is the path of socialism." It also declared that the PCI, as a "fundamental force of the European left," sought "the construction, in Europe, of a left... united above and beyond its historical lacerations." With regard to the related question of the PCI's identity, the document spoke of "an original identity, socialist and democratic, formed during the course of a complex history, different from that of other parties of the Third as well as of the Second International," and declared that "the ideas, the tradition, the struggles of the Italian communists . . . have made an important and in some cases determining contribution to the renewal of thought and action of the workers' movement in many parts of the world."

As for the "harsh political battle for democracy" going on in the USSR, the document hailed the Gorbachev leadership for being its "tenacious standard-bearer," and asserted that the Italian communists were not "neutral spectators." On the contrary, the PCI "anticipated and championed" that struggle: "More than ten years ago Berlinguer solemnly affirmed in Moscow the universal value of democracy." On the broader issue of East-West contention, moreover, the document expressed what might be termed a "no-fault" assessment of it: "The opposition between the two blocs . . . is burdened with structural elements, political-cultural motives, ideological superstructures," which in fact correspond very little to the multiplication in various countries of "mixed economies." Indeed, the real problems threatening mankind had scant chance of being solved "through the old opposition of two systems in a struggle for predominance."

The second part of the congress document dealt with domestic strategy. After reiterating the PCI's position that "the strategy of the historical compromise is definitely behind us," it discussed the need to build new alignments in order to achieve a "political and programmatic alternative" to the present five-party government. On the one hand, this required that the PSI change *its* policies of "competitive collaboration" with the DC and isolation of the PCI. On the other hand, the PCI should reach out to the progressive associations and movements "of Catholic inspiration," as well as to the reformist currents within the DC itself: "The DC of De Mita," the document pointedly stated, "is substantially cut off from the inspiration and political orientation personified by Aldo Moro in the 1970s."

To broaden the PCI's base of support, the congress document also called in its third section for a "strong reformism" (*riformismo forte*) that would, *inter alia*, give women "full social citizenship without their having to adopt masculine models," undertake the "ecological restructuring of the economy," and recognize the "centrality of labor and laborers" (*lavoratori*) as well as workers' need for an increased say in the workplace and for more flexible and shortened working hours. In this context the document made its only reference to Marx, saying that his prediction of an unprecedented increase in

free time relative to "alienated work" was now "a historically mature possibility even if not inevitable." (*L'Unità*, 25 November.)

International Views and Contacts. The PCI's primary international contacts during the year included a meeting of Natta and Gorbachev in Moscow in late March and the party's warm reception of Alexander Dubček in Italy in November on the occasion of the latter's receipt of an honorary degree from the University of Bologna. While it was Natta's last trip abroad before his heart attack and resignation from the general secretaryship, it was Dubček's first trip abroad since his purge from the leadership of the Czechoslovak communist party in early 1969.

Natta, accompanied by Napolitano, Sandri, and Antonio Rubbi (head of the PCI's international office), flew to Moscow on March 28. Upon their arrival, Natta explained to reporters that this was to be a "working meeting," in contrast to his January 1986 meeting with the Soviet leadership, which had provided the opportunity for "redefining on a basis of autonomy and independence the relations between the two parties." Anatolii Dobrynin and Vadim Zagladin, head and first deputy head, respectively, of the CPSU's International Department, met the Italians at the airport and entertained them at dinner. (*L'Unità*, 29 March.)

The next day Natta and his Italian companions met with Gorbachev for over six hours. Gorbachev was accompanied by Politburo member Alexander Yakovlev, Dobrynin, Zagladin, and Anatoly Cherniaev, a foreign policy adviser. (TASS, 29 March; *FBIS*, 30 March.) Speaking to reporters afterward, the PCI leader remarked, "It was the most lively, interesting and positive meeting I have had—speaking, naturally, for myself." Napolitano nodded in agreement. Natta went on to say that Gorbachev struck him as "even more remarkable" than he had previously thought: "He has a great capacity for looking far ahead, great realism, great inspiration." As for the substance of their talks, they had had a "free-wheeling discussion" about the role of Europe in détente and disarmament, the "political aspects" of democratization in the Soviet Union, the Armenian crisis, and European economic and political integration. With regard to the latter, said Natta, "Gorbachev displayed great realism and interest in the policy the PCI is pursuing" in support of such integration. (*L'Unità*, 30 March.)

In response to this positive assessment, Natta was asked what remained of the PCI's verdict in

1982 that "the propulsive thrust" of the October Revolution was exhausted. He gave the Italian party's by-now-standard reply that the judgment was valid at the time it was made. This was evidenced by the current CPSU leadership's commitment to the formula, "more socialism, more democracy," as well as its reappraisal of the development of the Soviet system "since the 1930s, and even much earlier." In reply to a final question of whether there could be another meeting of global left-wing forces such as the one organized by the Soviets in November 1987, on the occasion of the 70th anniversary of the Bolshevik Revolution, Napolitano replied in the negative. He went on to say that the PCI was now seeking opportunities for a "dialogue among the parties of the European left and the parties of the East." But while the Soviets were interested in this, "it cannot be at their initiative." (*L'Unità*, 30 March.)

Natta's visit to Moscow received extensive coverage over Soviet radio and TV, as well as in *Pravda*. Further, on March 30 President Andrei Gromyko presented Natta with the Order of the October Revolution at a ceremony in the Kremlin (Moscow Television Service, 30 March; *FBIS*, 31 March). Divergences in the two parties' respective views could nonetheless be detected. According to the initial report of the Natta-Gorbachev talks by the TASS International Service, "mutual satisfaction was expressed with the nature of relations between the CPSU and the PCI—*comradely*, equal, open, respectful." TASS also reported that both Gorbachev and Natta advocated more active cooperation "*in setting out the common tasks which can be resolved in the 'common European home' by joint efforts*." (TASS, 29 March; *FBIS*, 30 March—italics added.) Later that day TASS carried a "corrected retransmission" of this same broadcast in which the word "friendly" replaced "comradely" and the entire phrase about common tasks being resolved in a "common European home" was deleted (TASS, 29 March; *FBIS*, 30 March). Natta also gave a news conference on 30 March in which he described PCI-CPSU relations as "friendly, equal, open, and respectful" (TASS, 30 March; *FBIS*, 30 March).

The Italian communists apparently felt that the term "comradely" denoted a return to the kind of formal international communist movement that they had repudiated in 1982, while the reference to a "common European home" ran counter to the PCI's aim of being accepted as an equal partner in the West European left. Uneasiness over these differences was reflected in Napolitano's answer to a Chinese Xinhua correspondent's question about the prospects of the "international communist movement." Napolitano replied that in Western Europe the progressive forces included two components, the communists and the socialists, whose absolute autonomy must be recognized even as their views on certain issues drew closer together. (*Pravda*, 31 March.)

With an eye to domestic Italian reactions to Natta's Moscow trip, *L'Unità* published its version of the press conference of 30 March as well as the gist of the Soviet media's coverage of the two-day visit. The article was most notable for the distinction it drew between the Soviet and Italian communists' definition of democracy, a point that had not appeared in TASS summaries. In Natta's words, "We are for a pluralist political system, we believe in the creative value of democracy; as I have said, ours are the choices of a party that functions in a Western reality." Napolitano added that the PCI's differences with the CPSU in the interpretation of democracy are very clear. *L'Unità* also quoted Napolitano on his differentiation between the notion of an international communist movement and the PCI's conception of the workers' movement as consisting of two components, one communist, the other socialist/social democratic. The dispatch reported, finally, on the "decision to institute a PCI-CPSU working research group on the whole complex of European themes," similar to a group created by the West German Social Democrats (SPD) and the East German communists (SED) to discuss the two Germanies. In this context a noncommittal reference was made to *Pravda*'s mention of a very different kind of project, namely, a "pan-European round table" to discuss themes relating to Gorbachev's idea of a "common house." (*L'Unità*, 31 March.)

In response to a rash of Italian news reports that Natta's visit to the Soviet Union signaled a healing of the 1982 *strappo*, or breach, between Moscow and the PCI, Napolitano gave a long interview to *La Repubblica* upon his return home. He first carefully recapitulated the pertinent facts regarding the *strappo*, beginning with the PCI's celebrated assertion that the October Revolution had exhausted its propulsive force and continuing to Occhetto's recent statement that "a radical historical reappraisal of the October Revolution" was needed to "put its meaning in perspective." He then reiterated the PCI's argument that its criticisms had been vindicated by the struggle on the part of the Gorbachev leadership itself to correct the Soviet Union's systemic flaws. Indeed, the reform process in the USSR was being influenced by the Western idea of "an unbreakable nexus between democracy and socialism." In the course of the interview, Napolitano also expressed irritation over the Italian public's negative reaction to the Natta-Gorbachev meeting and outright anger at the sensation caused by Natta's reference to Gorbachev as "comrade" in their personal encounters. To this Napolitano retorted heatedly that Gorbachev was also addressed as "comrade" by the PSI delegation that took part in the November 1987 Moscow meeting of communist and noncommunist parties on the 70th anniversary of the Bolshevik Revolution. (*La Repubblica*, 5 April; *JPRS*, 21 June.)

The PCI's other major international contact for the year was Alexander Dubček's visit to Italy for a two-week stay beginning 11 November. Prior to Dubček's arrival, the Italian communists, unrelenting critics of the Warsaw Pact's armed suppression of the Czechoslovak reform movement, participated in a campaign to pressure the Gorbachev leadership into acknowledging that the invasion of Czechoslovakia in 1968 had been an unjustifiable violation of national sovereignty and independence. To this end, in July the PCI's Gramsci Foundation and the PSI's Nenni Foundation cosponsored an anniversary conference on the Prague Spring attended by prominent Czechoslovak reformers in exile. On the eve of the twentieth anniversary of the Warsaw Pact invasion, moreover, Napolitano published a lead article in *L'Unità* entitled "Rehabilitate Dubček." In it he argued that the current Soviet reform process demonstrated "the validity and vitality of the ideas that flourished in Prague in 1968." Two days later an editorial in *L'Unità* deplored a recent Soviet TASS dispatch defending the military intervention in 1968 and asked, pointedly: "What is the credibility of a Soviet renewal that does not come to terms...with Czechoslovakia 1968?" (Kevin Devlin, *RFE Research*, 5 September.)

The PCI daily devoted extensive coverage to Dubček's visit to Italy, starting with his receipt of a Czechoslovak exit visa (*L'Unità*, 6 September) and including a report on the University of Bologna's ninth centennial celebration on 12 November, to which Dubček delivered a formal address after being awarded an honorary degree in political science (*L'Unità*, 13 November). *L'Unità*'s account of everything from the technicalities of Dubček's journey to the full text of his speech in Bologna was in itself a political statement. The PCI's support for the hero of the Prague Spring was, however, conveyed in numerous other ways, too. On 13 November Natta invited him to a dinner party during which they exchanged recollections of their reactions to key events during August 1968 (*L'Unità*, 14 November). From Bologna Dubček went to Rome as the guest of the PCI, staying at the party school in Frattocchie. There he had a meeting with Occhetto that was announced on the front page of *L'Unità* with the headline "Occhetto to Gorbachev 'Rehabilitate Dubček.'" During their talk, Occhetto dismissed the idea that one shouldn't interefere in the internal affairs of Czechoslovakia, bluntly stating that "the suffocation of the Spring was in fact imposed from outside." He then insisted that "the success of *perestroika* is tied to a positive evaluation, on the part of *all*, of the Czechoslovak experience." By *"all"* Occhetto meant "the Soviets," as the journalist describing the encounter explained editorially. (*L'Unità*, 18 November.) The next day the communist daily carried a full page of photos of Dubček touring Rome (*L'Unità*, 19 November).

PCI's internal problems of leadership change and political reassessment militated against much other international involvement. Aside from a three-day working visit to Rome in September by Stefan Korosec, secretary of the League of Communists of Yugoslavia (TANJUG, 26 September; *FBIS*, 29 September), and a brief exchange of views in Rome on 1 October between Occhetto and the head of the Spanish Communist Party (Madrid radio, 1 October; *FBIS*, 4 October), the only other contacts of significance were with PLO leader Yasser Arafat. In January, Natta met briefly with the Palestinian leader in Tunis (*L'Unità*, 28 January); and in November, Occhetto did likewise, taking his first trip abroad since becoming party secretary. The purpose of the Occhetto-Arafat meeting was to explore "political-diplomatic" steps that the PCI might take to promote international recognition of the PLO as the government of a new Palestinian state. (*L'Unità*, 19 November.) The talks with Arafat provided, in turn, the occasion for Occhetto to hold his first meeting as PCI head with PSI leader Bettino Craxi, with whom "notable convergences" existed on the Palestinian question (*L'Unità*, 24 November).

The PCI daily's foreign-news coverage paralleled the party's international contacts. On the one hand, it was outspoken in its support for Gorbachev, even as it closely monitored the erratic course of political developments in the Soviet Union. On the other hand, it castigated conservatives and encouraged reformers in Eastern Europe. All the while, it enthusiastically supported East-West détente, the Reagan-Gorbachev summit, and European integration.

L'Unità called the nineteenth CPSU conference that convened at the end of June "the Gorbachev Revolution," reporting upon its proceedings in great detail. It hailed the projected recasting of the Soviet system on the basis of the "rule of law" and praised the Soviet leader's "courageous" opening speech for its acknowledgement that "after seventy years this model of socialism doesn't have a future." The PCI paper also editorialized that an "extraordinary and, until three years ago, unexpected transformation of Soviet politics" would ultimately produce a "new vitality" alongside "the vitality that capitalism has proven to have." (*L'Unità*, 29 June.) Napolitano, when interviewed after the conference, suggested that the point of reference for Gorbachev's reformism was not so much a return to Lenin, but an appreciation of "the positions of the Western left and, more generally, the historical experiences of Western democratic societies." He argued, moreover, that the reason for the reformist impulse was "not only economic stagnation but also a social and cultural maturation that has found expression at the apex of the CPSU." (*La Repubblica*, 2 July.)

While the PCI media were unstinting in their praise of Gorbachev's reform policies, they also repeatedly warned of the dangers posed by conservatives within the CPSU and by escalating ferment among non-Russian ethnic groups. For example, *L'Unità*'s chief Moscow correspondent, Giulietto Chiesa, ascertained in late May that the signed original of the now famous anti-reform letter written by Leningrad college teacher Nina Andreeva was in fact far more blatantly anti-Semitic and pro-Stalinist than the version published in *Sovetskaia Rossia* on 13 March and widely disseminated by Gorbachev's opponents (*L'Unità*, 23 May; Kevin Devlin, *RFE Research*, 26 May). Chiesa likewise obtained a copy of an Armenian memorandum to the Soviet leadership from late 1987 that presented an historical account of the Nagorno-Karabakh question and warned of its explosive potential, and that went unheeded at the time. Extensive excerpts from the document were published in the PCI daily on March 7. (Kevin Devlin, *RFE Research*, 11 March.) By November, sympathetic daily reports began appearing in *L'Unità* detailing the mounting ethnic demands and demonstrations sweeping the USSR from the Baltic to the Black Sea.

Meanwhile, support for reform in Eastern Europe was highlighted not only by the PCI's warm reception of Dubček in November, but also by the publication of a lengthy interview with prominent Solidarity adviser Professor Bronislaw Geremek

(*L'Unità*, 31 May) and by the attendance of Piero Fassino at the dedication in Paris of a symbolic tomb for Imre Nagy. Fassino, welcomed as the representative of "the only communist party that has critically revised its positions of 1956," called Nagy "a communist, a fighter for liberty, democracy, and national independence." (*L'Unità*, 17 June.)

Joan Barth Urban
The Catholic University of America

Luxembourg

Population. 366,232 (July 1988)
Party. Communist Party of Luxembourg (Parti communiste luxembourgeois; CPL)
Founded. 1921
Membership. More than 600
Chairman. René Urbany (re-elected)
Executive Committee. 10 members: Aloyse Bisdorff, François Hoffmann, Fernand Hübsch, André Moes, Marianne Passeri, Marcel Putz, Babette Ruckert, René Urbany, Serge Urbany
Secretariat. 1 member: René Urbany
Central Committee. 33 full and 6 candidate members
Status. Legal
Last Congress. Twenty-fifth, 23–24 April 1988; held in Differdange
Last Election. 1984, 4.9 percent, 2 of 64 seats
Auxiliary Organizations. Jeunesse communiste luxembourgeoise; Union des femmes luxembourgeoises
Publications. *Zeitung vum Letzeburger Vollek* (Newspaper of the Luxembourgian people), daily, 1,500–2,000 copies (CPL claims up to 20,000)

Because of the country's size, which barely equals the area of Rhode Island, and partly because its government is a constitutional monarchy (Luxembourg is a Grand Duchy), the orthodox pro-Soviet CPL plays no significant role in the European communist movement and only a minor domestic political role. In the last federal election to the Chamber of Deputies (July 1984), the communist voting strength gained two seats for the party.

Leadership and Organization. The CPL almost seems to be a family operation, as the political as well as the theoretical leadership of this active party is dominated by the Urbany family. The chairman's father, Dominique Urbany, was one of the party's founders, and led it until 1977. He remained in the CPL as honorary chairman until his death in October 1986 (*Neues Deutschland*, 27 October 1986). Many key positions within the party and its auxiliaries are occupied by members of this family. Jaqueline, René, and Serge Urbany are members of the new Central Committee, and René and Serge Urbany are also in the Executive Committee. Jaqueline Urbany is a member of the important Finance and Control Commission. In addition, René Urbany is director of the party press, which is heavily subsidized by the Society for the Development of the Press and Printing Industry, an organization founded by the SED (the East German communist party). The CPL's publishing company COPE not only prints and distributes the French edition of *World Marxist Review*, but also serves other communist parties abroad. Since 1976 René Urbany has held a seat in the Luxembourg parliament. Although the party's positions have been somewhat strengthened in the capital and in some municipalities of the industrialized south, its political influence has seemed to continue to decline since 1968.

Domestic Affairs. The major event of 1988 for the CPL certainly was the 25th Congress of the party, which was held on 23–24 April in Differdange, a center of the steel industry. Although the CPL is comparatively insignificant, many comradely messages were sent by fraternal party organizations from all over the world. Even M. Gorbachev cordially congratulated "comrade" René Urbany on his (quite predictable) re-election as chairman. One of the senior guests was Jaroslav Kvacek of the Central Committee of the Communist Party of Czechoslovakia, who headed the delegation from Czechoslovakia. He politely conveyed the Czechoslovak communists' high esteem of the CPL's determined struggle for the rights of the Luxembourgian working class, social progress, and peace in the world. The Central Committee of the Communist Party of the Soviet Union (CPSU) in a message to the congress stated that it values highly the "PCL's solidarity with our work in reconstructing Soviet society and with our foreign policy based on the new thinking" (*FBIS*, 26 April 1988). The congress was held under the vague motto "Let's get

going," and the main points discussed were the rapid deindustrialization of Luxembourg, the major shifts in the social structure, and the appeal for world peace and nuclear-free zones. In his opening report, René Urbany lamented that the mining industries' collapse and the complete disappearance of the miners' trade in Luxembourg caused disappointment among many potential followers and apparently dissuaded them from joining the party. Furthermore, according to René Urbany, the number of workers in Luxembourg's steel industry has diminished by 50 percent over the past fifteen years. "In 1970, the steel industry accounted for over 28 per cent of the Gross Domestic Product, and for 12 per cent of all jobs: today the figures are 11 and 9 per cent, respectively" (*WMR*, July). These profound changes have had a tremendous impact on the structure of the industrial proletariat, which has heretofore constituted the backbone of the party.

The CPL congress warned that the party will not tolerate Luxembourg's being converted into a second Switzerland. The personnel employed in banks already exceeds the number of steel workers (*Neues Deutschland*, 25 April). Furthermore, the congress demanded that Luxembourg play an active role in the European peace movement.

According to *World Marxist Review* (July), the CPL recently formed a coalition of left-wing forces, with the participation of the POSL (Socialist Workers Party of Luxembourg) in three regions. Last year the CPL denied reports that it intended to form such a coalition.

In view of the fact that the majority of the citizens receive their information mainly through TV, the party tried to give its newspaper a more attractive format. The *Zeitung vum Letzeburger Vollek* is now placing more emphasis on commentaries, ideology, and interpretation to offset the allegedly bourgeois information given via TV.

International Affairs. Internationally, the party's activities in 1988 were dominated by its support for the fifth Easter March in Duedelingen, where many participants demonstrated against the NATO compensation policy. In March, the relatively small but active Society Luxembourg-GDR celebrated its first twenty years of existence. In the city of Luxembourg, Ernst Walkowski, East Berlin's ambassador to Luxembourg, awarded the organization the order of the Golden Star for Friendship Among Nations. On 24 September, a CPL delegation led by François Hoffmann, a member of the new Executive Committee of the CPL, traveled to Beijing. Song Ping, member of the Politburo of the Chinese CP, received the visitors and briefed them on China's policy of reform and opening to the outside world. This mission was preceded by an official visit of the president of the Luxembourg Chamber of Deputies, Leon Bollendorf, and some businessmen in August (*FBIS*, 23 August).

Besides these modest international activities of the CPL, there were several indications of intensified contacts between the CPL and the SED.

Kurt R. Leube
California State University, Hayward

Malta

Population. 346,890 (June 1988; Malta Central Office of Statistics)

Party. Communist Party of Malta (Partit Demokratiku Malti; CPM)

Founded. 1969

Membership. 300 (estimated)

General Secretary. Anthony Vassallo (69, on full-time party work)

Central Committee. 13 members. C. Zammit (president), A. Vassallo (general secretary), V. Degiovanni (international secretary), R. J. Mifsud (propaganda secretary), L. Borda (economic affairs and finance secretary), D. Mallia (central committee and organizational secretary), J. Attard, L. Attard-Bezzina, J. M. Cachia, A. Caruana, A. Cordina, K. Gerada, M. Mifsud

Status. Legal

Last Congress. Fourth Congress, 15–17 July 1988

Last Elections. 9 May 1987

Auxiliary Organizations. Malta-USSR Friendship and Cultural Society, Malta-Czechoslovakia Friendship Society, Malta-Cuba Friendship and Cultural Society, Malta-Poland Friendship Society, Malta-Korean Friendship and Cultural Society, Communist Youth League (*Ghaqda Zghazagh Komunisti*), Peace and Solidarity Council of Malta, Women for Peace, Association of Progressive Journalists

Publications. *Zminijietna* (Our times), tabloid issued every second month, partly in English and partly in Maltese, Anthony Vassallo, editor; *International Political Review*, monthly, Malta edition of *World Marxist Review*; *Bandiera Hamra* (Red Flag), issued by Communist Youth League; *Bridge of Friendship and Culture*, quarterly journal of Maltese-USSR Friendship and Cultural Society

After its debacle in the 1987 elections, the Communist Party of Malta kept a very low profile throughout 1988 and maintained its visibility mainly through a succession of press releases. On the other hand, there was a steady stream of Soviet visitors and sustained activity by the Soviet embassy, as well as by the embassies of the USSR's satellite countries. In this way, there was hardly a single day throughout the year when the media in the Maltese islands were not giving some form of exposure to one communist activity or another.

The Fourth Congress was a remarkably low-key affair with no press coverage, except in the party tabloid published in late August. No fraternal delegates from abroad attended the congress. The congressional delegates "assessed their increasing involvement in the political, social and economic life of Malta and the need of responding to the challenge of our times in order to gain renewed vitality in the interests of the Maltese working class" (*Zminijietna*, July-August).

The delegates also sought to understand better the changes that are going on in the international communist movement, which is about to enter into a new stage of development. As a result of the congress, the CPM will seek to develop new tactics in cooperation with other left-wing forces "in resisting the current offensive of right-wing conservative forces" (ibid.).

The general secretary was a little more specific in a paper presented to congress and published in the same issue of *Zminijietna*. He said that the CPM "must work for a radical and fundamental change, to take the form of an alliance among all progressive social forces."

A new personality to emerge from the obscurity of the congress was Charles Zammit, who was elected President of the CPM. He is a 43-year-old administrative officer from the parastatal telecommunications corporation of Malta. He has no public political record and is hardly known outside the circles of the CPM.

It is interesting that two representatives of the Central Committee of the CPSU, Igor Shvetz, of the Department of Organization, and Edward

Kovalev, from the Southern European Department of the Central Committee, visited Malta in the first week of March as guests of the CPM.

The declared purpose of the visit was "to explain to the representatives of wide circles of the Maltese people the internal and external policies of the CPSU and to familiarize the delegates with the political and economic situation obtaining in Malta" (*Zminijietna*, March). Observers interpreted this to mean an on-the-spot analysis of the performance of the CPM at the last elections.

The men from the Kremlin seem to have given a clean bill of health to the reconstituted Central Committee. They signed a protocol of cooperation between the CPSU and the CPM for 1988. This provided for the extension of bilateral contacts and the regular exchange of views and informational materials. The CPM is to send delegations to the USSR to familiarize itself with the experience of the CPSU in organizational activity and to gain experience in the communications media. (Ibid.).

The CPM issued a number of pro-forma press releases during the year in support of the workers of Malta's drydocks and on matters of routine controversy, such as broadcasting and budget policy. At the same time, it joined the mainstream of international communist initiatives in the cause of "world peace." Among these initiatives was one in support of "neutrality, nonalignment, and lasting peace" and requesting the withdrawal of U.S. and Soviet fleets from the Mediterranean. This was the main feature of a joint communiqué signed by a visiting Komsomol delegation and a number of left-wing Maltese youth delegations. Another was a CPM declaration welcoming the Reagan-Gorbachev agreement on the elimination of intermediate and shorter-range nuclear missiles; this was linked with "CPM initiatives in support of the creation of Nuclear Free Zones and Disarmament" (*Zminijietna*, January).

The CPM's general secretary attended an international conference in East Berlin on nuclear weapons–free zones (*The Times*, Malta, 4 July).

A major CPM initiative took the form of an elaborate study-paper opposing the policy of the Maltese government that it would apply for membership in the European Economic Community, given the right conditions. This memorandum, dated 25 October, claimed that Maltese membership in the EEC would violate Malta's neutrality and nonalignment, enshrined in the island's constitution. It said that Malta would revert to the status of a "fortress-colony" and to a form of slavery to Brussels-based capitalism, with Malta becoming "an appendix of the West."

Soviet initiatives on the island, via the Kremlin and the USSR's embassy on Malta, were intense and amply made up for the slowdown in CPM activities.

Apart from the CPSU delegation referred to above, there were four other high-level visits by emissaries of the Kremlin. The first was a strong delegation from the Supreme Soviet that returned an earlier visit by members of the Maltese parliament to Moscow. This delegation was headed by the secretary of the Presidium, Tengiz N. Menteshashvili, and included Kondrat Z. Terekh, minister of trade; Elena D. Avrorova, member of the Plan-Budget Commission; Nikolai A. Ponomarev, member of the Commission for Women's Labour Security, Maternity, and Child Protection; Vsevolod Sukhov, deputy head of the First European Department of the Ministry of Foreign Affairs; Grigori I. Denisov, assistant to the secretary of the Presidium; and Serguei V. Sereda, attaché. (*Zminijietna*, April.) The delegation called on the topmost Island personages from the prime minister downwards and visited such places as the university, the government-owned foundry, Malta Drydocks, and Malta's sister island Gozo. The head of the delegation would not be drawn to reply directly to questions put to him by Maltese pressmen about resuscitating mutual trade. At an airport conference before returning to Moscow, he declared that there had been no change in Soviet policy and stressed that "mutually beneficial contacts were developing in the spheres of health, tourism, exchange of information between trade unions, youth and other organizations." He expressed satisfaction that a substantial part of Malta-USSR relations were in the field of education, culture, and sports. (*The Times*, Malta, 24 April.)

Yet another important visit was that of Gendrikh Smirnov, head of the Mediterranean Section of the International Department of the Central Committee of the CPSU. He came as a guest of the Malta Labour Party and had no reported contact either with the government or the CPM. Apart from meeting MLP leaders, he also had talks with senior officials of the General Workers Union. The nature of his talks was not disclosed, but the Maltese-language daily paper of the General Workers Union reported that Smirnov praised the Maltese drydock workers who had blocked the entrance of Malta's Grand Harbor in an effort to prevent the entry on a courtesy visit of the nuclear-capable British aircraft carrier H.M.S. Ark Royal. (*Orizzont*, 31 August.)

The Soviet vice-president G. Tarazevich paid a brief visit on 19 August and discussed with the Maltese foreign minister Vincent Tabone Malta's policy on such topics as the situation in the Persian Gulf, the withdrawal of Soviet troops from Afghanistan, and the meeting of the foreign ministers of nonaligned countries in Nicosia (*The Times*, Malta, 24 August).

The last visit in the series was paid by Yevgeny Denisov, of the African desk of the International Department of the CPSU Central Committee. This visit was described as a "holiday," but Denisov had a meeting with the leader of the Malta Labor Party and discussed the need to reduce tension in the Mediterranean region, among other matters. (*Orizzont*, 14 September.)

In August, the former Labor prime minister Dom Mintoff and Alexander Sceberras Trigona, former Socialist minister of foreign affairs, paid a visit to Moscow for "talks with government officials," the nature of which were not disclosed (*It-Torca*, 11 September).

Meanwhile, the Soviet ambassador and his senior assistants maintained their contacts with the General Workers Union and the Confederation of Malta Trade Unions. GWU representatives were invited to attend the May Day celebrations in Moscow. The Confederation of Trade Unions in the Soviet Union (AUCCTU) has an ongoing relationship with the GWU and sent a delegation to visit the union. (*The Times*, 29 November.) A continuous stream of "experts" and "specialists" were brought to Malta by the Soviet embassy and their activities were given prominent publicity in the news media. Perhaps the most important were Professor S. Shein of the Moscow State Institute of International Relations, who was a guest of the University of Malta, and Georgi Kuznetsov, deputy editor-in-chief of the Soviet weekly *Za Rubejhom*, who was a guest of the Association of Progressive Journalists.

Both delivered public speeches in which they elaborated on disarmament issues and on Mikhail Gorbachev's proposal for the withdrawal of the superpower fleets from the Mediterranean.

Other Soviet "exhibits" included a group of ophthalmologists, a professor of physical culture, a football coach, and a delegation from the Russian Orthodox Church, headed by Metropolitan Pitirim of Volokolamsk and Yuryev. This delegation came at the invitation of the Maltese ministry of education and culture. During its five-day stay, it was given high visibility in Maltese religious circles. The met-ropolitan lost no opportunity to sing the praises of *perestroika*.

The Soviet embassy in Malta has embarrassed the Maltese ministry of education and culture with its largesse. In the course of the year, it presented a quantity of equipment to help start a Maltese school of ballet (*Nazzjon Taghna*, 9 March). It made a number of book presentations, and a donation of computer equipment was made to St. Luke's Hospital, which is the island's general hospital.

During the course of the year, the Soviet embassy held photographic exhibitions, brought over dancing and musical groups, invited several Maltese to visit the Soviet Union, and gave a considerable amount of film and other propaganda material to the media.

The Ministry of Education introduced the teaching of Russian (and Spanish) for the first time in four state secondary schools.

On the commercial and trade fronts, the Soviets were far less forthcoming. In fact, they had been falling short of their commitments as stipulated in the trade protocol they had signed with the preceding Maltese Labor government in 1986. This agreement, which was supposed to run from 1987 to 1990, had been treated as a state secret, and the text had never been published. The present Nationalist government released the text, which was published for the first time in July (*The Times*, 6 July). According to the agreement, the USSR undertook to buy up to 140 million U.S. dollars worth of visible exports and was to spend a further 140 million U.S. dollars to purchase eight timber carriers that would be built in Malta. During 1987, the total value of Maltese visible exports to the USSR amounted to a mere 14.4 million U.S. dollars (*Malta Trade Statistics*, 1987). The Malta Chamber of Commerce held that neither side approximated the "targets" set by the current agreement and asked why such an ambitious agreement had been entered into when it was clear that neither side could generate enough business activity to sustain the preceding 1984 trade protocol (*Commercial Courier*, July).

Maltese ministers made declarations that they expected the Soviets to live up to their commitments. The parliamentary secretary for industry, John Dalli, stated after visiting Moscow, that the Maltese government "was waiting for the Soviet Union to come up with a set of proposals to make up for the sharp drop in Soviet orders for Maltese goods over the past two years," and also that "Malta expected the Soviet side to honor the trade protocol valid up to 1990 through which there was a commitment to buy 40 million U.S. dollars worth of goods each year" (*The Times*, Malta, 12 May).

At a press conference, the Soviet commercial counsellor Nicolai Alexeev, explained that the USSR was experiencing foreign-currency difficulties due to the low price of oil on world markets and the devaluation of the dollar (*Nazzjon Taghna*, 2 February). The Soviet ambassador, speaking at a working lunch with officials of the Federation of Malta Industries, referred to the upheavals and changes arising from *perestroika* in his country (*Orizzont*, 12 February).

The lack of orders led to unemployment in certain factories, and the Federation of Industries publicly expressed its concern through its president J. Grioli.

At about the same time, the leader of the Labor Party opposition, Dr. Carmelo Mifsud Bonnici, publicly urged the Soviets to consider the interests of the Maltese workers and to bear in mind that orders awarded to Maltese factories were a help to the workers (*The Times*, Malta, 8 February).

It has to be pointed out in this context that the Maltese were equally unable to live up to expectations and had not made full use of the trade protocol. This much was admitted by Prime Minister Fenech Adami when he received the Soviet parliamentary delegation in April. (*The Times*, Malta, 23 April.)

The Marsa Shipbuilding Yard had orders to deliver eight timber carriers to the USSR. The first of these ships was due to be handed over at the end of March 1987. The Soviets were responsible for part of the delay because they requested alterations, and because the Polish designs stipulated in the contract needed modifications. The manager of the Maltese shipyard warned the workers that unless the first ship was delivered by June 1988, there was a danger of the yard's losing further Soviet orders (*The Times*, Malta, 7 February). The same general manager declared at a subsequent press conference that his enterprise "was keeping its fingers crossed hoping that at the end of December it would deliver the first ship" (*The Times*, Malta, 10 September). By the end of September, a delegation led by the vice-minister of the merchant marine Boris Alexeevich Junicin insisted on the December deadline (*The Times*, Malta, 29 September).

The end to this cliff-hanger was not foreseeable when this report was written in the first week of December. The first ship on order was still having its sea trials.

The activities of the Soviets were supported and supplemented by other East European communist states.

Czechoslovakia, which operates two joint ventures with the Maltese government, has developed viable cooperation arrangements with the General Workers Union during recent years.

A delegation from the Central Council of Trade Unions of Czechoslovakia (CCCTU), led by the secretary of the Central Committee Hana Lagova, visited the island to extend the agreement of cooperation with the GWU (*Orizzont*, 2 March).

A second delegation from the CCCTU, led this time by a member of the Presidium, Peter Stern, arrived in Malta for more talks with the GWU (*Orizzont*, 11 October). The exact nature of these talks was not disclosed. During the course of the year, Maltese shop stewards went to Prague for purposes of trade union "education." This visit was returned by a group of Czech trade unionists.

The Bulgarians held a number of exhibitions, mostly of a cultural nature, invited a number of Maltese nationals to Sofia, sent over a couple of singers, and announced plans to expand their small electric-motor assembly plant, which they run in a joint venture with the Maltese government. They also held up the prospect of setting up another joint venture to produce jams. Neither of these two projects had materialized by the year's end.

The first deputy chairman of the Bulgarian state council, Peter Tanchev, paid a brief visit to the island and discussed commercial and cultural bilateral relations (*The Times*, Malta, 11 March).

The deputy foreign minister of the German Democratic Republic, Kurt Nier, visited the island and had a round of high-level talks. At an airport press conference before his departure, he declared that his delegation had found common ground with the Maltese government and described his four-day visit as "fruitful and useful." He invited the Maltese foreign minister to visit his country at a later date. (*Sunday Times*, Malta, 7 August.)

Hungary invited a Maltese selling mission to visit Budapest. The Malta Chamber of Commerce signed a cooperation agreement with its Hungarian counterpart during that visit. (*Nazzjon Taghna*, 17 March.)

Not to be outdone, Albania signed a trade protocol with the Maltese government in May. Both sides identified products they wished to exchange between themselves. (*The Times*, Malta, 4 May.)

The Italian Communist Party sent its international secretary Antonio Rubbi to Malta for talks with the leader of the Malta Labor Party Dr. Carmelo Mifsud Bonnici. They discussed "matters of bilateral interest," among which were the latest developments in the Mediterranean region. (*Orizzont*, 5 March.)

North Korea invited senior MLP officials for an official visit to Pyongyang and extended invitations to left-wing youth organizations to attend the Thirteenth Festival of Youth, to be held in the North Korean capital.

Sixty foreign specialists, mainly from Czechoslovakia and Poland, continue to serve in Maltese state hospitals.

Auxiliary Organizations. As in former years, the Malta-USSR Cultural and Friendship Society was the spearhead among the CPM's auxiliary organizations.

The society has developed an ongoing three-pronged program. It offers Russian-language classes and scholarships to the USSR and organizes group or individual visits to the Soviet Union. Every year it offers scholarships to Maltese students "in over 60 different subjects," tenable at Russian universities. In 1988 seven more Maltese students were studying at various Soviet universities under the sponsorship of the society (*Torca*, 28 August).

Its second most important activity is to attract fellow-travelers and sympathizers through the society's functions, where abundant literature is available for the taking.

The other role played by the society is to host Soviet visitors, distinguished and otherwise, including cultural groups, at its Valletta premises. Maltese officials and selected citizens are invited to these occasions. Apart from exposing the Maltese guests to the Soviet visitors, each occasion is regarded as an opportunity for media coverage, thereby giving the impression that the society is socially and officially held in esteem. The society organized public lectures that dealt with such subjects as Soviet foreign policy as it affects the Mediterranean region, the Reagan-Gorbachev summit meeting, *perestroika* and its effect, and the Nineteenth All-Union Conference of the CPSU.

The society's general secretary John Genovese visited Moscow in May and signed another two-year agreement with the Union of Soviet Societies for Culture and Friendship Relations with Foreign Countries (*The Times*, Malta, 19 May).

The CPM's other auxiliary organizations were subdued in their public activities. The Malta-Czechoslovakia Cultural and Friendship Society sent its president Lawrence Attard-Bezzina to Prague, where he took part in a seminar on the Czechoslovak state 70 years after its foundation attended by 75 participants from 50 countries (*Orizzont*, 21 September). The other friendship societies contented themselves with occasional press releases and commemorative functions.

The Communist Youth League took the initiative in coordinating a front organization composed of progressive youth movements and set up a preparatory national committee to organize Malta's representation at the Thirteenth World Youth Festival. The Youth League has been very active in establishing and maintaining contact with other, kindred organizations in Malta and abroad and has given scant publicity to its activities. It has also opened a commercial bureau. (*Zminijietna*, February.)

The Peace and Solidarity Council and Women for Peace sent a delegation to Moscow in September. There they had discussions with various Soviet organizations, including the Soviet Peace Council and the Committee of Soviet Women. (*Zminijietna*, September.)

The general secretary of the CPM Anthony Vassallo attended the meeting of the editorial council of the *World Marxist Review*, two editions of which are published in Malta.

WMR is celebrating its 30th anniversary this year. The September issue of *Zminijietna* observed this anniversary with some remarkable critical comments. It admitted that the *WMR* has not always been abreast of objective changes on the eve of the 21st century and of the endeavors of individual communist parties to take the measure of these changes theoretically and strategically.

It held that *WMR* has "sometimes relied on the simplistic perception of the movement's unity as being synonymous with uniformity. The fact that the forms of interaction of the fraternal parties have begun to lag behind the diverse realities of today's world has been addressed by the journal belatedly."

It was also held that "although party representation on the journal has grown along with the number of national editions, the reach of the journal, its authority, prestige and circulation have not risen accordingly but have even declined somewhat. The *WMR* press runs have slumped in many socialist and industrialized countries." Moreover, "the growing representation of parties on the editorial board of the journal, important as it is, should not obscure the fact that some of the influential parties that were active in our collective periodical before the 1960s have become less active, if at all, over the past few years." As a result, *WMR* has "for years" been short of new problems in theory and unable to inform its readers of the development of quite a few socialist countries, such as Albania, China, Romania, and Yugoslavia, or to discuss in detail the problems and experiences of the communist parties of Italy, France, Japan, and some other countries.

The Maltese editions of *WMR* are hardly to be seen in Malta.

Policies of the Maltese Government. As the Soviets exerted greater pressure, the Maltese government under Prime Minister Eddie Fenech Adami diverged perceptibly from the policies of the preceding Labor government.

Malta is bound by its constitution to maintain a neutral and nonaligned status. The essential import of this is the renunciation of a military role other than in self-defense. On the other hand, the government of Malta is in duty bound to provide security and defend its territorial integrity. When Fenech Adami visited the United States and addressed the American Enterprise Institute in July, he declared openly that Malta needs the cooperation of other countries in providing for its defense and security. He added, "My government would not even consider any defence agreement applicable to Maltese territory except with countries that are free and democratic and that have both the interest and the strength to join in our defence" (*The Times*, Malta, 13 July).

This puts the neutrality agreement signed by Dom Mintoff with the USSR in 1981 into a new perspective.

On the same occasion, Fenech Adami was specific on another point. He said that "it is to make our Western European role obvious, as well as because of our Christian Democratic tradition, that we will seek to become full members of the European Community."

Equally significant has been Malta's lack of interest in Mikhail Gorbachev's proposal for the withdrawal of the USSR and U.S. fleets from the Mediterranean. Malta's foreign minister Dr. Vincent Tabone has stated flatly that Malta is against such a withdrawal "because this would tilt the balance of forces which is so important for peace in the region" (*The Democrat*, 22 October).

On the international plane, the new Maltese government has repeatedly expressed its reluctance to take sides in regional disputes by associating itself with sterile condemnatory statements, since these tend to become stereotypical and discriminatory in nature. This policy is being transferred to Malta's

representative to the Nonaligned Movement, whose Ministerial Committee decided in Cyprus in September to examine the "forms and methods of action" of the movement. Malta's foreign minister will form part of this committee. The committee will be charged with the task of assessing and making recommendations on "the effectiveness of the instrumentality" of the Nonaligned Movement.

While Malta's foreign policy has hardened with regard to Soviet policies, the Maltese government has tried to maintain the flow of commercial relationships with all communist countries, particularly with the USSR, Bulgaria, and Czechoslovakia. If anything, visible trade returns from each of these countries indicated a decline in performance. Attempts to activate trade with Hungary, Poland, East Germany, and Albania proved fruitless.

Perhaps because of this, the CPSU and the Czech communist party developed direct party-to-party links with the Malta Labor Party. Apart from the CPSU-MLP links, Leo Brincat paid a visit to Prague in late November for talks with the Central Committee of the Communist Party of Czechoslovakia (*Orizzont*, 26 November). The Czechoslovak communist party is to return the visit.

J. G. E. Hugh
Valletta, Malta

The Netherlands

Population. 14,716,100
Party. Communist Party of the Netherlands (Communistische Partij van Nederland; CPN)
Founded. 1909
Membership. CPN: 6,000 (estimated). Social composition of delegates to 1984 congress: 10 percent manual workers, 10 percent teachers, 22 percent civil servants (including academics), 10 percent social workers, 20 percent unemployed, 5 percent nurses (Fennema, "The End of Dutch Bolshevism?" in Waller and Fennema, eds., *Communist Parties in Western Europe*, Oxford: Blackwell, 1988)
Chairman. Elli Izeboud
Executive Committee (Partijbestuur). 55 mem-

bers, including Elli Izeboud, Ina Brouwer, Marius Ernsting, Nico Scouten, Jan Berghuis, Leo Molenaar, Jan de Boo, Ton van Hoek, Geert Lameris
Central Committee. 46 members, including Henk Hoekstra, secretary; Ton van Hoek, international secretary; Joop Morriën, John Geelen, Wemke Ketting-Jager, Edward Koen
Status. Legal
Last Congress. Thirtieth, 29 November–2 December 1986, in Amsterdam
Last Election. 1986, 0.6 percent, no seats in Second Chamber (lower house); 1987, 1 of 75 seats in First Chamber (senate)
Auxiliary Organizations. CPN Women, General Netherlands Youth Organization (ANJV), Stop the Bomb/Stop the Nuclear Arms Race, CPN Youth Platform, Scholing en Onderwijs, Women Against Nuclear Weapons
Publications. *De Waarheid* (Truth), official CPN daily, circulation about 10,000; *CPN-leden krant* (Bulletin for party members), appears ten times annually; *Politiek en cultuur*, theoretical journal published ten times annually; *Komma*, quarterly published by the CPN's Institute for Political and Social Research; CPN owns Pegasus Publishers.

In 1909, radical Marxists from the revolutionary left wing of the labor movement and the Labor Party (PvdA) founded the Social Democratic Party (Sociaal-Democratische Partij). In 1919, as the Communist Party of Holland, it affiliated with the Comintern, and in 1935 it took its present name. It won representation in the Staaten Generaal (parliament) in 1918 and remained there until 1986. In 1940, Nazi Germany occupied the Netherlands, but the party remained legal as long as Germany was allied with the Soviet Union. It was suppressed, and lost its parliamentary membership, from 1941 to 1945.

In its ideological and social composition, the CPN resembles other northern European communist parties. Like them, it is a small party that has never captured more than a few percent of the vote, with the partial exception of the immediate postwar years. In 1946, 11 percent of Dutch voters supported the CPN, a figure that fell to 6 in 1951 and 2.4 in 1959. In 1945, likewise, the party newspaper *De Waarheid* briefly enjoyed a circulation of 300,000—more than any other paper in the Netherlands. This temporary upswing reflected popular respect for the CPN's role in the Resistance and sympathy for Stalin and the Soviet Union, rather than any penetration of communist ideology into Dutch political culture or society.

When Nikita Khrushchev gave his Secret Speech in 1956 denouncing Stalin, the CPN did not undertake any process of de-Stalinization in its own ranks or methods. Nevertheless, starting in 1960, the CPN gradually distanced itself from Moscow on a variety of issues, while retaining a Stalinist internal structure and remaining loyal to Marxism-Leninism and the Moscow-led international communist movement. From the early 1960s on, CPN leaders considered revisionism in various forms as the best strategy to widen their base of support. In 1963, the CPN declared a policy of "autonomy" vis-à-vis Moscow and gave some support to China in the Sino-Soviet dispute. In 1968, it denounced the invasion of Czechoslovakia by Warsaw Pact troops. Simultaneously, the CPN pursued "autonomy" at home by opening a dialogue with the rapidly growing forces of the noncommunist intellectual left and with progressive Catholic and Protestant thinkers. This campaign encouraged some 5,000 members of the fast-growing student generation to join the party from 1968 to 1975 and gave it 4.5 percent of the vote in the 1972 elections. As part of this change, the social composition of party congresses and, presumably, of the membership as a whole changed radically. By 1977, students, social workers, and academics—the classic core groups of the "1968 generation"—formed a third of the delegates and outnumbered manual workers, the traditional core of the party. Despite these changes, the CPN remained rigidly Stalinist in its internal organization (Marcel van der Linden and Joost Wormer, "The End of a Tradition: Structural Developments and Trends in Dutch Communism," *Journal of Communist Studies* 4 [1988]:78–87; Meindert Fennema, "The End of Dutch Bolshevism?" in Michael Waller and Meindert Fennema, eds., *Communist Parties in Western Europe: Decline or Adaptation?* Oxford: Blackwell, 1988, pp. 158–78).

Emboldened by the prospect of success in recruiting members of the 1968 generation, younger CPN leaders began arguing in the early 1970s that if the party would develop a broad left strategy using the new themes of pacificism, feminism, and environmentalism, it would be even better placed to attract elements of the progressive middle class and thus turn itself into a serious rival of the PvdA. It was important to make this effort because if the CPN missed that chance it would be seized by other radical parties that were springing up at the time— The Pacific Socialist Party (PSP) and the Radical

Political Party (RPP). These arguments failed to convince the powerful CPN chairman, Paul de Groot, an old-style Bolshevik of the purest type. In the 1977 elections, the PvdA recaptured most of the votes previously lost to the extreme left, including the CPN, which won only 1.7 percent and two seats. De Groot maintained that the CPN had lost because it was no longer Bolshevik enough, had become disloyal to the Soviet Union, and had lost contact with the manual workers. His opponents, naturally enough, argued the opposite position, namely that the CPN was doomed to disappear unless it pursued a New Left strategy far more vigorously.

The result of this internal struggle was a compromise. The CPN rejected Eurocommunism and returned, temporarily, to full loyalty to the Soviet Union, which it had not displayed so completely since 1960. On the other hand, the Central Committee refused to accept that the party's future lay with the class of manual workers, fast disappearing in the Netherlands. Followers and opponents of the pro-Soviet line continued to fight each other as CPN support in the country declined, until the anti-Stalinist feminists, pacifists, and environmentalists won in 1982.

Two currents in Dutch society contributed to the change in the CPN in the 1980s, both growing out of the progressive cultural revolution of the 1960s, feminism and antinuclearism. The feminists accused the party of being male-dominated and obsessed with ideology and demanded equal representation in party organs. Unlike all earlier oppositional movements, the feminists did not represent a coherent ideological position that the Stalinists could easily attack; moreover, the cultural climate made it difficult for them to resist the feminist agenda as such, as they could then be accused of male chauvinism.

Antinuclearism began in earnest in 1978 and accelerated from 1979 to 1983, when the Netherlands was party to the NATO decision to modernize nuclear weapons in Europe. Both currents affected large parts of Dutch society, including the center-right parties. The CPN theoretically stood to benefit from adopting the new progressive agenda, as it did when it adopted a new program in 1984, the first since 1952, which replaced Marxism-Leninism by Marxism-feminism. In 1984, the party officially abolished democratic centralism in its own ranks and announced that it now fully accepted parliamentary democracy. Unfortunately for the party, its reorientation availed it very little, if at all. Some

pro-Soviet Bolsheviks, mostly in Amsterdam, left the party in 1982 and formed a splinter group, the Union of Communists in the Netherlands (VCN). On the other side, many feminists and pacifists, who had supported the CPN in the hope that it was about to adopt their agenda completely, left again in 1985 because change was not coming quickly enough. Membership, which had risen from some 11,000 during most of the 1960s to 15,500 in 1980, plummeted again to 6,000 in 1986, a smaller number than at any time since the 1930s.

These developments on both flanks weakened the CPN as the 1986 elections drew near. Despite attempts to build electoral alliances with the PSP and the RPP, the CPN competed on its own in these elections, which were a disaster for the party. In the municipal elections in March, it lost a third of its seats on municipal councils. In the parliamentary elections in May, it won only a third of the vote of 1982, namely 0.6 percent. As a result there were no communists in the Second Chamber of parliament for the first time since 1918. As in 1977, the PvdA took votes and seats from all three of the small radical parties. It nevertheless failed to oust the center-right coalition of Prime Minister Ruud Lubbers, which continued in office with 81 out of 150 seats.

Apart from internal divisions, another reason for the electoral failure of the CPN was that its new agenda was indistinguishable not only from that of the PSP or the RPP, but even from that of the dominant left wing of the PvdA. The CPN could offer no fresh solutions to the questions raised by radicals inside or outside the working class. Dutch voters sympathetic to antinuclearism or feminism might well ask why they should vote for the CPN or another small party if the PvdA, one of the three major parties in the country, was open to their views. In short, the turn to feminism and pacificism in the 1980s served only to make the CPN irrelevant.

Internal Party Affairs. The CPN held its 1988 annual meeting in Amsterdam in March, which resulted in a conventional declaration in support of nuclear weapons–free zones and the abolition of all nuclear weapons in Europe (*Neues Deutschland*, 28 March). The main problems facing the party continued to be, first, the apparently irreversible decline into insignificance and, second, the split between the feminist and pacifist majority in the CPN and the old-style Stalinists who dominated the party until after 1977.

By far the most important public activity of the CPN in the late 1980s was its intense involvement in the peace movement against NATO's nuclear modernization. Communists dominated large parts of the movement's organizational framework, including its most important element, the Interdenominational Peace Council (IKV). In 1983, a Soviet diplomat reportedly bragged to a Western journalist that the Soviet Union could put 50,000 Dutchmen on the street against NATO missiles within 24 hours. The transmission belt for such an order must presumably have been the CPN. When U.S.-Soviet negotiations ended in the INF Treaty of December 1987 that removed the new NATO missiles, however, the CPN's active role came to an end. From that point on, its proclamations of support for peace and disarmament were no different from those of any other Dutch political party. In April 1988, none other than the Christian Democratic prime minister Lubbers gave the East German party chief Erich Honecker high praise for his "diligent work on behalf of détente, security, and peace" (*Neues Deutschland*, 28 April). No CPN spokesman could have put it differently.

The conservative Dutch government was indeed following its own strategy of maintaining power, a strategy that made it frustratingly difficult not only for the CPN, but for the other radical left parties, to present themselves as the apostles of peace and opponents of NATO war plans. This strategy consisted in adopting the peace rhetoric of the left and welcoming Mikhail Gorbachev's "new thinking" as a sign of a new era in East-West relations, while pursuing a distinctly nonsocialist domestic fiscal and economic policy.

If the CPN still hoped to lead or shape a coalition of social, cultural, and political currents to the left of the PvdA on the issue of feminism and peace, the party faced an analogous challenge in the activities of the PvdA itself. The Dutch Labor Party had since the late 1970s engaged in discussions and negotiations with the CPSU and with Eastern European communist parties on disarmament and peace. In the early 1980s, the PvdA, along with the Belgian, Danish, Norwegian, and Luxembourgeois socialists formed the Scandilux discussion group, the purpose of which was to rally the forces of the northwest European left against NATO's nuclear modernization plans. After the INF treaty, Scandilux continued in a broader European form, with the agenda widened to include the environment and further disarmament. In February, the Scandilux parties plus the West German SPD and the ruling Hungarian communist party met in Copenhagen to praise the INF treaty and to call for further progress toward a chemical weapons–free zone in Europe, conventional disarmament, and a rapid increase in East-West trade and contacts on all levels (*IB*, May). With the PvdA adopting the Gorbachev line, what could be the place for a separate communist party in the Netherlands?

Until 1985, the Stalinists could argue that the CPN was off course in that it was becoming reformist and anti-Soviet. After Gorbachev took power in the Soviet Union and launched *glasnost'* (openness) and *perestroika* (restructuring), the Dutch Bolsheviks could no longer use that argument. Rather, they were now in the position of arguing that reformism, openness, and an honest attitude to history were marks of loyalty to the Soviet Union rather than anti-Soviet deviations. As a Dutch journalist wrote in a somewhat sarcastic article on the split in Dutch communism, "5 years ago . . . the socialism of the Soviet Union and its allies . . . was no stimulus but the source of discord. Once so united, Netherlands Communism actually split over it" (*NRC Handelsblad*, 23 July; *JPRS*, 29 September).

The feminist leadership under Elli Izeboud and Ina Brouwer was the chief obstacle to healing the split with the dissenters from the Marxist-feminist line. These were found within the CPN in the Groningen party group, which continued to uphold a highly conservative form of syndicalism, and in the breakaway VCN. Support for the international policies of a more liberal Soviet Union under Gorbachev provided a possible platform of reunification. In early 1988, the Groningen section resumed friendly contacts with Izeboud and her deputy, Marius Ernsting. Another member of the executive committee, Leo Molenaar, proposed a compromise strategy that would put some distance between the CPN and the social-democratic left of the PvdA. Fre Meis, a party figure of the older generation who sympathized with the Groningen group, while remaining loyal to Izeboud, declared in July that the task for the future was "to lead the masses' struggle against the Lubbers government's budget-cutting policies." To make that struggle more effective in winning new adherents, Meis thought it might be necessary to replace the radical feminist Brouwer at the head of the CPN ballot. This failed to appease the VCN, which demanded that the party leadership repudiate the 1984 feminist and revisionist program and "give way to those willing to take charge on the basis of Marxism-Leninism" (ibid.). This response indicated that there was little chance of bringing the diehard Bolsheviks of the VCN back into the fold, even though the VCN, in the six years of its existence, had moved from rigid Stalinism to Gorbachevism, all in the name of total loyalty to the USSR.

In October, the CPN celebrated its 70th anniversary with a celebration in Amsterdam. Chairman Izeboud announced that the anniversary was occurring "at a time of profound change in the world. The arms race, scientific and technological progress, and exploitation of nature were facing mankind with fundamental problems" (*Neues Deutschland*, 31 October). This statement was evidence that the CPN was groping toward the environmental issue as a rallying cry for the broad left coalition it was hoping to lead, or at least to shape. Again, however, it found itself playing catch up with the major bourgeois parties in Western countries, all of which had environmentalim at the top of their programs by early 1989.

International Contacts. In May, a delegation of the CPN led by Izeboud visited East Germany for talks with Erich Honecker and other German communist leaders. Alluding to the INF Treaty, Izeboud and Honecker stated their "satisfaction that a turn for the better has taken place in international developments. This is due in the first instance to the imaginative and constructive peace policy of the Soviet Union and other socialist states, and to the struggle of the worldwide peace movement... Extreme vigilance and committed effort on the part of all the forces of reason and realism remain necessary, however, if this historical step forward is not to be undermined by increased armament in other areas, as planned by certain circles within NATO" (*Neues Deutschland*, 27 May).

A month earlier, a GDR delegation led by the minister for foreign trade, Gerhard Beil, visited the Netherlands to launch a demonstration of products of East German technology. This was the occasion when Prime Minister Lubbers issued his "personal thanks" to Honecker for the latter's efforts on behalf of peace. Clearly, the GDR was hoping for increased exports to the Netherlands, and in the political sphere for sympathy and cooperation in its attempt to present itself to Western Europeans as a necessary guarantor of European stability. In this effort, the CPN plays at best a marginal role. The PvdA and the governing center-right parties are far more important interlocutors for the East European regimes.

The strategy of Gorbachev and his East European satellites remained in 1988 what it had been for some years previously, namely to seek broad areas of agreement with governments of Western Europe and to ignore local communist parties as transmission belts of Soviet policies. According to observers, Moscow no longer seeks subversion or disruption in the West; rather it, and its allies, seek respect and collaboration in a collective effort to demilitarize and neutralize Western Europe.

Conclusion. The CPN did not provide evidence in 1988 that it had reversed the decline in its membership or support. Its official doctrine of Marxism-feminism was little different from the cultural and social preferences of large parts of the progressive white-collar and middle classes, who voted for the PvdA or even for bourgeois parties. Thus the CPN suffered from the progressive depoliticization of hitherto contentious issues, such as peace, disarmament, women's rights, and environmental protection. The Netherlands, like most of the rest of Western Europe, seemed caught in a period of transition from an era of heightened ideological confrontation over fundamental options, an era that began in the late 1960s and culminated in the struggle over security and defense policies in the 1980s. In 1988, the outcome of that transition remained unclear. Gorbachev had seemingly persuaded a large majority of Europeans that he shared their goals and their understanding of peace, disarmament, and stability. No one was yet willing to say whether that was in fact the case, and what Europeans, including the Dutch, would do if it was not.

David Gress
Hoover Institution

Norway

Population. 4,190,758
Parties. Norwegian Communist Party (Norges Kommunistiske Parti; NKP); Socialist Left Party (Sosialistisk Venstreparti; SV); Workers' Communist Party (Marxist-Leninist) [Arbeidernes Kommunistiske Parti (marxist-leninistene); AKP

(M-L)], which runs as Red Electoral Alliance (Rød Valgallianse; RV) in elections

Founded. NKP: 1923; SV: 1975; AKP: 1973

Membership. NKP: 1,500–2,000 (est.); SV: 11,000 dues-paying members (official figure); AKP: 5,000–7,000 (est.)

Chairs. NKP: Kåre André Nilsen (journalist); SV: Erik Solheim; AKP: Siri Jensen (bookbinder)

Central Committees. NKP: 8 full members: Kåre André Nilsen, Ingrid Negård (deputy chair), Trygve Horgen (deputy chair), Paul Midtlyng, Grete Trondsen, Åsmund Langsether, Gunnar Wahl, Ørnulf Godager; 2 alternate members: Knut Vidar Paulsen, Knut Jarle Berg; SV: 4 members: Erik Solheim, Kjellbjørg Lunde (deputy chair), Per Eggum Maurseth (deputy chair), Hilde Vogt (party secretary); AKP: 17 full members: Siri Jensen (40 years old), Aksel Nærstad (deputy chair for political affairs, 36), Arne Lauritzen (deputy chair for organizational affairs, 40), Eli Aaby (leader for women's affairs, 33), Frode Bygdnes (leader for labor affairs, 36), Sigurd Allern (editor in charge, *Klassekampen*, 42), Kjersti Ericsson (44), Pål Steigan (38), Tellef Hansen (40), Vidar Våde (45), Marion Palmer (35), Torild Nustad (35), Torstein Dahle (40), Solveig Aamdal (41), Geir Johnsen (39), Tone Anne Ödegaard (44), Bente Moseng (38)

Status. Legal

Last Congress. NKP: Nineteenth, 23–26 April 1987, in Oslo; SV: 2–5 April 1987, in Trondheim; AKP: December 1988, "somewhere in Norway" (*Klassekampen*, December 13, 1988)

Last Election. 1985: NKP: 0.16 percent, no representation; SV: 5.46 percent, 6 out of 157 representatives; RV: 0.57 percent, no representation

Auxiliary Organizations. NKP: Norwegian Communist Youth League (NKU); SV: Socialist Youth League; Socialist Information League; AKP: Norwegian Communist Student League (NKS)

Publications. NKP: *Friheten* (Freedom), semiweekly, Arne Jørgensen, editor; SV: *Ny Tid* (New times), weekly; AKP: *Klassekampen* (Class struggle), daily, Sigurd Allern, editor

The Norwegian Labor Party (Det Norske Arbeiderparti; DNA)—a moderate generally pro-Western social democratic reform movement—controlled the Norwegian government continuously from 1935 to 1963. Through most of this period the Labor Party could count on parliamentary majorities. However, in 1961 the Labor Party lost its parliamentary majority, which it has never managed to

regain. In 1963 the Labor government was defeated by a coalition of nonsocialist parties and the Socialist People's Party, and since then the Norwegian government has alternated between Labor Party minority governments and various coalitions of nonsocialist parties. None of the parties to the left of the Labor Party has ever been in government.

In the 1981 election the Labor Party was ousted from power by a center-right coalition led by Conservative Party leader Kåre Willoch. Willoch served as prime minister throughout the 1981–1985 parliamentary term, during which Norway experienced strong economic growth. In the general election of 9 September 1985, Willoch's three-party coalition lost its parliamentary majority, but retained power based on the tacit support of the two representatives of the right-wing Progress Party, a party committed to drastic cuts in the large Norwegian public sector. In May 1986, Willoch resigned after losing a vote to increase gasoline taxes in order to cope with the fiscal crisis caused by declining oil revenues. Willoch's defeat on this bill was a result of the defection of the two members of the Progress Party from his legislative coalition.

The leader of the DNA, Gro Harlem Brundtland, became the new prime minister. Brundtland, the first Norwegian woman to hold this office, had previously served as prime minister for eight months in 1981. Her Labor government held only 71 parliamentary seats. Even including the support of the SV, her government was two seats short of a parliamentary majority. However, Brundtland has been able to survive parliamentary no-confidence motions thanks to the unwillingness of the agrarian Center Party to defeat her government. The Brundtland government has introduced a variety of austerity measures to reduce inflation and the current account deficit. Legislative support for these policies has come mainly from the SV, the Center Party, and the Christian People's Party. Local and regional elections in September 1987 provided a setback for the Labor Party as well as for the Conservatives, whereas the Progress Party registered stunning gains. Opinion polls through 1988 showed continued strength for the Progress Party and weakness for Labor and the Conservatives. The next general election will take place in September 1989.

The Norwegian Communist Party. The NKP began as the minority faction of the DNA, when the majority of the latter party decided in 1923 to sever its ties with Moscow. The NKP gained 6.1 percent of the vote and six representatives in the general election of 1924, but later fell into continual decline and could not elect a single member of Parliament during the 1930s. During World War II, NKP support for the war effort against Nazi Germany and the Soviet liberation of northern Norway boosted the party's popularity, giving it eleven seats (out of 150) in the first postwar Parliament. However, the party's fortunes fell quickly with the onset of the Cold War. In fact, since 1945 the NKP's share of the votes has declined in every single general election. In 1985 the party received no more than 4,245 votes, a drop-off of more than one-third from the previous election. Thus the NKP remains one of the weakest communist parties in Western Europe. It has elected no member of Parliament since 1973, when it ran as part of the Socialist Electoral Alliance and elected its chairman, Reidar Larsen, to the national assembly. Due to its extremism and electoral weakness, the NKP has virtually no impact on Norwegian political debate.

The weakness of the NKP was exacerbated in 1975 when the party split in two over whether to participate in the formation of the Socialist Left Party (SV). Under the leadership of Martin Gunnar Knudsen, the majority faction decided to withdraw from the SV and remain a staunchly pro-Soviet, Stalinist party. However, chairman Larsen and several other party leaders abandoned the NKP and joined the SV. The gulf between the NKP and the SV has remained wide, although both parties have in recent years called for a broad united front of Norwegian left-wing parties, including the DNA, the SV, and the NKP. Former NKP chairman Hans I. Kleven has supported cooperation both in the union movement and in the form of joint electoral lists. A national conference of the NKP in April 1988 advocated a "red-green" alliance for the general election of September 1989. Such an alliance would consist of "forces in the union movement, the peace movement, the environmental movement, the women's movement, the solidarity movement, and the progressive women's movement" (*Friheten*, 13 April 1988). The party congress also decided to appoint a committee of three to examine the events surrounding the party agreement of 1949 and 1950 that led to the expulsion of party leader Peder Furubotn. The committee will consist of Arne Pettersen, Arne Jørgensen, and Hans I. Kleven.

At its Nineteenth Congress in 1987, the NKP adopted a new party program ("program of principle"), replacing its previous program from 1973. In its new program, the NKP reaffirms its commitment to Marxism-Leninism, scientific socialism, and class struggle. However, the new program puts greater emphasis on international peace, "the most important issue of all." The NKP sees the threat of war as a consequence of imperialism and the boundless greed for profit and power in monopoly capitalism. The deterioration of the international situation since the mid-1970s has its primary cause in the United States and its military-industrial complex. In the main resolution adopted at the congress, the NKP advocated forcing the United States to accept a nuclear test–ban treaty, preventing the implementation of the Strategic Defense Initiative, and the creation of a Nordic nuclear-free zone. The communists also rejected Norwegian membership in the European Community. Domestically, the NKP favors greater restrictions on finance capital and expansion of public credit institutions. The party also supports greater subsidies for moderate-income housing. The 1987 party congress also elected Kåre André Nilsen the new party chair. Nilsen, a veteran journalist for *Friheten* and a former manual worker, has been associated with the Knudsen/Jørgensen faction (and against Kleven) in the recent factional struggle in the NKP. However, Nilsen seems most concerned to unite the party. His main political interests are in international and security affairs.

The NKP maintains international contacts primarily with the communist parties of the Soviet Union and Eastern Europe. However, the party also has ties to orthodox communist parties in Western Europe. In March 1988 a working group of the NKP, led by Ørnulf Godager, visited Bulgaria. The group had meetings with the Economic, Scientific, and Technical Department and the Foreign Policy and International Relations Department of the BCP Central Committee, and also visited various other installations and sites (*FBIS*-Eastern Europe, 6 April). In November, NKP chairman Nilsen had talks with Horst Sindermann, president of the DDR's People's Chamber and member of the SED's Politburo, during the latter's visit to Norway (*Neues Deutschland*, 16 November).

The Socialist Left Party. The SV is the strongest party to the left of the Labor Party. Although the party includes Marxist elements, it does not define itself as a communist party, and the current program of principle is more moderate and pragmatic than the previous version. The SV is the result of a merger of the previous Socialist People's Party (Sosialistisk Folkeparti; SF), the Democratic Socialists (Demokratiske Sosialister; DS-AIK), an anti-EEC splinter group of former members of the DNA, and segments of the NKP. These three parties had previously run jointly in the 1973 general election. The electoral support of the SV has increased slowly in the 1980s. In the September 1985 general election the party added two members of Parliament to reach a total of six, and in the regional elections of September 1987 the party slightly increased its vote share from that of the parliamentary election, gaining 5.7 percent of the national vote or approximately 120,000 votes. Opinion polls in 1988 tended to show the party as the fourth or fifth largest Norwegian party, trailing Labor, the Conservatives, and the Progress Party, and about even with the Christian People's Party.

In Parliament the SV has tended to support the Labor minority government led by Gro Harlem Brundtland. Although the SV frequently criticizes the government, it has made no attempt to oust the Labor Party, presumably because the only alternative would be a more conservative government.

A leadership struggle in the SV became apparent when party chairman Erik Solheim challenged parliamentary leader and former chair Theo Koritzinsky for the party's nomination as candidate for its safe Oslo seat in the 1989 general election. Solheim was eventually persuaded to withdraw his candidacy and let himself be nominated elsewhere. According to party reports, the SV currently has a membership of about 11,000 dues-payers, whereas the official rolls stand at approximately 14,000 members. The party has particular strengths among people 35 to 40 years old, women, the well-educated, and urban voters. More than half of all SV supporters work in the public sector, while one-third are industrial workers.

The SV platform for the 1989-1993 parliamentary term will be determined at its party congress in Skien in April 1989. The preliminary (draft) program stresses environmental issues, such as large additional taxes on fossil fuels, restrictions on the use of automobiles in urban areas, and expansion of public transportation. The party wants to combat unemployment through expansion of the public sector (especially in the area of health care and welfare), increased taxation of high incomes and property, and public funds for industrial development. Further, the SV favors better care for children and the elderly and extension of the national maternity leave. Internationally, the SV anticipates renewed discussion of Norwegian membership in the European Community, which it opposes. The SV is also the only Norwegian parliamentary party opposed to NATO membership. The party has in the past criticized the United States's naval strategy in the North Atlantic and called for disarmament and the creation of a nuclear-free zone in the Nordic area. The party wants no foreign bases or arms depots on Norwegian soil and favors banning the entry into Norwegian ports of any ship not certifiably free of nuclear weapons.

The SV maintains international contacts with a variety of socialist and Marxist parties, but has particularly close ties to such Nordic parties as the Swedish Communists (VPK) and the Danish Socialist People's Party (SF).

The Workers' Communist Party. The AKP was born in the late 1960s as a splinter group from the Socialist People's Party (SF), comprising parts of the youth movement of the latter party. The founders were generally Maoist and revolutionary in orientation and dissatisfied with the moderate course of the SF. The AKP emerged as a formal organization in 1973 but has always contested elections as the RV (see below). The RV has not fared well in elections, never reaching one percent of the national vote in general elections or electing a single member of Parliament. However, the party has had greater success in local elections in some of the larger cities and has representation on several city councils.

The AKP has recruited its members mainly among students and other youth and is not a genuine working-class party. However, the party has adopted a policy of proletarianization of its cadres. The party draws a disproportionate share of votes from individuals between the ages of 35 and 45, mainly former student radicals. The party has until recently been highly secretive and sectarian. While the AKP has maintained an estimated 5,000 to 7,000 voters, its support among Norwegian students and intellectuals has declined precipitously since its heyday in the 1970s. The AKP currently stresses its opposition to the austerity policies of the Labor government and especially to wage controls. The party also opposes Norwegian membership in the European Community and favors an open immigration policy and efforts to improve the condition of women.

The Fifth Congress of the AKP took place somewhere in Norway in the first half of December 1988. Contrary to previous practice, the party subsequently held simultaneous press conferences in Oslo, Tromsø, and Bodø, in which the names of all members of the newly elected Central Committee were released. Out of seventeen members, nine are women, eight are workers, and three are from northern Norway. With one exception, all were between the ages of 35 and 45. The congress decided that congresses should henceforth take place every two years, as opposed to every four years in the past. During the press conferences, party leaders stressed the economic crisis in northern Norway, a national plan for public-sector employment, higher corporate taxes, women's issues, and support for refugees and immigrants. Party leaders declined to take a more critical position on Stalin than in the past. There was considerable discussion of the proper evaluation of Stalin during the party congress, which narrowly decided to retain him among the "classics of socialism" (*Klassekampen*, 13 December 1988).

The Red Electoral Alliance. The RV is mainly an offshoot of the AKP, but also contains independent socialists. For electoral results, see above under AKP.

Kaare Strom
University of Minnesota at Minneapolis

Portugal

Population. 10,388,421 (July 1988) (*World Fact Book*, 1988)
Party. Portuguese Communist Party (Partido Comunista Português; PCP)
Founded. 1921
Membership. 199,275 (claimed) (*Avante!*, 3 November; *FBIS*, 19 December)
General Secretary. Álvaro Cunhal (since 1961)
Secretariat. 7 full members: Álvaro Cunhal (75), Carlos Costa, Domingos Abrantes, Fernando Blanqui Teixeira, Jorge Araújo, Luísa Araújo, Octávio Pato; 3 alternate members: Albano Nunes, Artur Vidal Pinto, Francisco Lopes (*Avante!*, 5 December)
Political Secretariat. 8 members: Álvaro Cunhal, Agostinho Lopes, Ângelo Veloso, Carlos Brito, Domingos Abrantes, José Casanova, José Soeiro, Luís Sá (ibid.)

Political Commission. 12 full members: Álvaro Cunhal, Ângelo Veloso, António Gervásio, António Lopes, Carlos Brito, Domingos Abrantes, Edgar Maciel Correia, Jorge Araújo, José Casanova, José Soeiro, Luís Sá, Raimundo Cabral; 10 alternate members: Agostinho Ferreira Lopes, António Orcinha, António Casmarrinha, Bernardina Sebastião, Carlos Carvalhas, Carlos Fraião, Carlos Luís Figueira, Decq Mota, Manuel Sobral, Sérgio Teixeira (ibid.)
Central Committee. 175 members (Lisbon Domestic Service, 4 December; *FBIS*, 9 December)
Status. Legal
Last Congress. Twelfth, 1–4 December 1988, in Oporto
Last Election. 1987, United Democratic Coalition (CDU, communist coalition), 11 percent, 30 of 250 seats
Auxiliary Organizations. General Confederation of Portuguese Workers (Confederação Geral de Trabalhadores Portugueses–Intersindical Nacional; CGTP), which, with 1.6 million members (*WMR*, April), represents more than half of Portugal's 2.5 million unionized labor force, out of a work force of 4.58 million (*World Fact Book*, 1988)
Publications. *Avante!*, weekly newspaper, António Dias Lorenço, editor; *O Militante*, theoretical journal; and *O Diário*, semiofficial daily newspaper (all published in Lisbon)

The only active communist party in Portugal is the PCP, which dominates most of the unionized labor force and what remains of the southern farm collectives. Its political influence has declined since it won 19 percent of the national vote in 1979. The PCP remains the most Stalinist party in Western Europe; even though professing complete solidarity with current Soviet policy, it has chosen not to follow the example of recent Soviet reforms. Other groups to the left of the communists, such as the Popular Forces of April 25, are now defunct or inactive; they appeared following the revolution of April 1974.

Organization and Leadership. In 1988 Álvaro Cunhal successfully rebuffed the most serious challenge up to now to his authoritarian style of leadership. Proposals for party reform launched publicly by rebel "renewalists" were harshly rejected by the Central Committee as "divisive" (Lisbon, *Diário de Notícias*, 16 January; *FBIS*, 2 February). Cunhal was initially reported to be a "centrist" consensus-builder but ended up siding with the party "dinosaurs" against the "tendentious" reformers (Lisbon, *O Diabo*, 29 December 1987; *Diário de Notícias*, 30 June; *JPRS*, 18 February, 25 August). Still, he denied, on being re-elected general secretary at the Twelfth Congress in early December, that there had been any breach in party unity. Others concluded that the congress may have marked a new era for the PCP, since, for the first time, differences of opinion had been openly aired. (Lisbon Domestic Service, 4 December; *FBIS*, 5 December.)

The "renewalist" line was said to be taken by a growing number of young communists frustrated by the PCP's declining size and influence. To revitalize the party, they sought more "openness" and "internal democracy," as well as a broadening of the party's social base among the young, the intelligentsia, and service workers. The aim was to move beyond the "fossilized" old guard's preoccupation with the blue-collar worker. A so-called "Group of Six" leaked to the press documents it had submitted to the Central Committee proposing the secret ballot, free and open discussion, a rejuvenation of the party leadership, and other reforms for the upcoming party congress. (*O Diabo*, 29 December 1987; Lisbon, *O Jornal*, 15–21 January; *Diário de Notícias*, 8 November 1987, 16 January; Lisbon, *Expresso*, 14 May; *FBIS*, 23 November 1987, 2 February, 10 June; *JPRS*, 18 February, 9 March, 30 June.) The rebels went so far as to establish an "Openness" Information and Propaganda Service to publicize facts suppressed by official channels that act behind "iron curtains" rather than the "glass walls" claimed by Cunhal (*Expresso*, 6 February; *FBIS*, 17 February).

A furious Central Committee denounced such "factional activity" as playing into the hands of the right by fueling news-media campaigns serving to discredit the PCP (*Diário de Notícias*, 16 January, 7 May; *FBIS*, 2 February, 3 June). Cunhal described as clearly undemocratic the conduct of comrades acting not according to existing rules, but to a proposal for change not yet accepted by the party (*Avante!*, 5 March; *FBIS*, 24 March). A cautious leadership resisted hard-liners' demands that the "enemy group" be disciplined, since its expulsion could have a negative public impact; rather, the Central Committee is said to have opted for the "internal social assassination" of the six members, while publicly reaffirming the PCP's "broad freedom of discussion" (*Expresso*, 27 February, 2 July; *FBIS*, 16 March; *JPRS*, 25 August).

Top officials reportedly grew increasingly alarmed as criticism from still other groups in the party appeared in print. There were complaints about a lack of collective dialogue and the unexplained dismissal of some local party officials (*Expresso*, 1 April; *JPRS*, 31 May). There were over 100 signatures to a document that criticized the PCP's "coolness" to *perestroika* (*Diário de Notícias*, 30 June; *JPRS*, 25 August). The Central Committee did decide to take action against an outspoken member of the Political Commission, Zita Seabra, by expelling her from that body and later from the Central Committee itself. She was denounced for her "insulting slanders" against the leadership and party line and for frequenting circles—including comrades of the "Group of Six"—that were hostile to the party. The sanction was described by some not as retaliation against her alone, but as a warning to others—a declaration of open warfare against a growing movement. (*O Diabo*, 10 May; *JPRS*, 23 June; *Diário de Notícias*, 7 May, 18 November; *FBIS*, 9 December). It also represented an attempt to prevent Seabra, said to be an effective orator, from upsetting the December congress with her inflammatory views (*RFE Research*, 23 November).

The program submitted to the congress made only a token response to rebel demands. For example, it accepted the "possibility" of secret balloting—a procedure that would make sense, according to Cunhal, "only if a democratic atmosphere did not exist in the party" (*Diário de Notícias*, 7 May; *O Jornal*, 26 August; *FBIS*, 3 June, 20 October). An overwhelming majority of delegates than decided, when the congress opened in Oporto, to vote for officials by the traditional show of hands. They approved the official slate of Central Committee members, which presented 54 new faces, dropped 44, and included none of the outright critics. (Lisbon Domestic Service, 4 December; *FBIS*, 5, 9 December.) This was presumably evidence of a "continuing renewal" promised earlier by Cunhal (*Diário de Notícias*, 7 May; *FBIS*, 3 June; *O Militante*, no. 2; *IB*, June). It was not exactly the type of "rejuvenation" urged by the "Group of Six," which decided to boycott the congress it considered to have been "stripped of even a minimum of democratic legitimacy" (*O Jornal*, 30 September; *Diário de Notícias*, 8 November; *FBIS*, 23, 29 November). This was the same gathering that Cunhal hailed as a symbol of *perestroika* (*FBIS*, 5 December), a concept "misinterpreted" by his critics, he asserted (*Diário de Notícias*, 14 October; *FBIS*, 19 December).

The PCP announced that 57 percent of its members are skilled workers, 20 percent laborers, 2 percent farmers, 5 percent intellectuals, and the remainder in various other categories. Men make up 77 percent and women 23 percent. Slightly over half are between 30 and 50 years of age, with 33 percent older than 50 and 15 percent younger than 30. (*Avante!*, 3 November; *FBIS*, 19 December.)

Domestic Affairs. The PCP was cheered by a reported waning of public support for the ruling Social Democratic Party (Partido Social Democrático; PSD). This weakening was attributed by Cunhal to the "incompetency" of Aníbal Cavaco Silva, a "stubborn and arrogant prime minister. . .at the beck and call of big capital." A call by Cunhal to the Socialist Party (Partido Socialista; PS) to join the communists in fighting the constitutional revision proposed by the government was ignored; a subsequent PSD-PS accord on reform "once more confirmed" Socialist "collaboration" with the right against Portuguese democracy. (Lisbon Domestic Service, 11 September; *FBIS*, 13 September, 5 December.)

The PCP rejoiced that the "anti-communist and conservative prejudice" of the Spanish clergy did not prevent many Catholics from being active alongside the communists in the social and political struggle. In fact, the party claimed, "many thousands" of Catholics are communist militants. (*WMR*, March.)

Auxiliary Organizations. A 24-hour general strike called in March by the socialist labor confederation, the General Workers Union (União Geral de Trabalhadores; UGT) was backed for the first time by the communist-dominated CGTP. Protested was a government bill that would give employers "too much power" to dismiss workers. (*NYT*, 29 March.) The PCP cited the success of the strike as a serious blow to the "myth" of the PSD government's strength (Lisbon Domestic Service, 29 March; *FBIS*, 1 April). The communists seemed surprised that the UGT actually carried out its call for a strike; Cunhal had earlier dubbed the confederation a "company union" that served the interests of big capital and of right-wing governments (Lisbon Domestic Service, 6 March; *FBIS*, 7 March; *WMR*, April).

A later decision by the UGT to support a joint socialist-communist slate in elections of the Bank Workers Trade Union was seen as a socialist attempt to win over communists to the PS so as eventually to reduce the PCP's share of the electorate to 4 percent (*Tempo*, Lisbon, 19 May; *JPRS*, 27 June). The CGTP remains far stronger than the UGT, which is said to have only 200,000 to 300,000 members; even so, the PCP lamented that the membership and number of communist factory cells has diminished because of hundreds of plant closures, layoffs of thousands of workers, union bashing, and the political persecution of workers—sometimes with goons (*WMR*, April; *O Militante*, no. 2; *IB*, June). The CGTP is said to consist primarily of blue-collar workers, while the UGT has mainly white-collar employees (*NYT*, 29 March).

International Views and Activities. Though Cunhal continued publicly to profess a "revolutionary enthusiasm" for the Soviet policy of *perestroika*, he did admit that he did not agree with all aspects. In fact, he was said to have expressed privately some major reservations. (*Expresso*, 27 February, 16 April; *JPRS*, 16 March, 31 May; *Diário de Notícias*, 25 July; *FBIS*, 2 August.) Also apparently concerned about the dangers of *glasnost'* (openness), the PCP leader warned that the influence of various communist parties in Western Europe had ebbed when they began to tolerate party factions and the "horizontal circulation of ideas" (*Expresso*, 9 July; *JPRS*, 22 August).

A former PCP member who lived in Moscow for many years was quoted as saying that Cunhal was far from being as close to Chairman Mikhail Gorbachev as he had been to Leonid Brezhnev and Yury Andropov (*O Diabo*, 10 May; *JPRS*, 23 June). Cunhal insisted that Portuguese communists were unaware of Joseph Stalin's "grave errors and extremely grave conduct" (Lisbon Domestic Service, 19 January; *FBIS*, 26 January). On the other hand, he was thought to be the "foreign friend"—referred to in a Soviet magazine—who was squeamish about an "excessive yearning to reveal the wounds of the past" (*Expresso*, 10 October; *FBIS*, 21 November). A talk given in Lisbon in July by a Soviet economist was attended by some "reformist" militants, but was snubbed by the party hierarchy and was not reported by the PCP's *Avante!* (*Expresso*, 9 July; *JPRS*, 22 August). "Thorough and frank" consultations continued between Soviet and PCP officials in Moscow and in Lisbon; in November, Cunhal was awarded the Order of Lenin on his 75th birthday (*Pravda*, 10 November; *FBIS*, 16 November).

Also reported during 1988 were PCP contacts abroad with East Germany and Poland. The Communist Party of China attended the PCP's congress for the first time ever; Cunhal said this confirmed the complete normalization of relations between the two parties after a 20-year lapse. (*FBIS*, 5 December.) An Italian communist delegation visited Lisbon and stressed that good relations between the two parties were not affected by differences of opinion, such as over membership in the European Economic Community. Integration was regarded by the Italian communists as a "valid horizon," but by the PCP as a threat to Portugal's economy and possibly its independence. (*L'Unità*, Milan, 9 October.)

The PCP demanded the withdrawal of U.S. forces and military bases from South Korea and expressed support for Korean independence and peaceful reunification (KCNA, Phyongyang, 12 October; *FBIS*, 13 October). Cunhal also said that there should be in his own country no foreign bases—which "undermine our independence"—even if the U.S. Congress were to reverse the cut in aid to Portugal voted early in 1988. The aid is a *quid pro quo* for the use of the bases. (Lisbon Domestic Service, 17 March; *FBIS*, 21 March.)

Left-Wing Terrorist Groups. Twenty-five leftists found guilty of terrorist acts between 1980 and 1984 were sentenced to 10- to 15-year jail terms. They were members of the Popular Forces of April 25 movement. (*FBIS*, 2 February.)

H. Leslie Robinson, Professor Emeritus
University of the Pacific

San Marino

Population. 22,986
Party. Communist Party of San Marino (PCS)
Founded. 1921
Membership. 1,200 claimed (*WMR*, July 1987)
General Secretary. Gilberto Ghiotti
Honorary Chairman. Gildo Gasperoni
Last Congress. Eleventh, 27 January 1986
Last Election. 29 May 1988, 28.71 percent, 18 of 60 seats
Publication. *La Scintilla* (The Spark), published every other week, editor unknown (according to *Handbuch der Weltpresse*, 1970)

It has been a busy year for the small republic. On the domestic scene, the regular parliamentary election at five-year intervals and the subsequent continuation of a coalition government formed by the Communist Party of San Marino (PCS) and the Christian Democratic Party (PDCS) took place. In addition, the party's publication *La Scintilla* staged a festival that has been credited with the consolidation and renewal of the party and its spirit (*WMR*, October). In foreign affairs, there were visits from the Soviet Union and the German Democratic Republic, and an exchange of visits with China.

In sharp contrast to the declining support for its parent Italian Communist Party (PCI), the Communist Party of San Marino demonstrated its vigor by gaining an additional 4 percent of the vote (for a total of 28.71 percent) and three more seats in the unicameral legislature (for a total of 18 out of 60) in the elections of 29 May. This show of confidence by the electorate gives the party nearly one-third of the votes in the legislature (*Neues Deutschland*, 31 May).

The recently forged first coalition between the PDCS and PCS (see *YICA*, 1988) seems to be holding. Between them, the two parties have 45 seats and 72.82 percent of the votes, since the PDCS also gained one more seat and nearly 3 additional percent of the votes cast in the parliamentary election. (ibid.) *Neues Deutschland*, in an interesting slip of the facts, mentions a Communist Unity Party (Partei der kommunistischen Einheit) that garnered 8 seats with 13.63 percent of the votes (ibid.). This party is, in fact, the Socialist Unity Party, listed as such in the *World Fact Book* and *Europa Handbook*. In either case, it is a fairly heavily left-leaning parliamentary representation; presumably the Christian Democrats will temper it since the Social Democratic Party (PDS) and the right-wing Republican Party (PRS) are no longer represented in the legislature, each having lost its single seat.

In 1988, one PCS deputy, Umberto Barulli, served his elective six-month term (March to September) as one of the two captains regent, who function as San Marino's heads of state. Erich Honecker, general secretary of the German Democratic Republic's Socialist Unity Party, sent his heartiest congratulations to the captains regent (ibid., 2/3 April).

San Marino continued to foster relationships with the communist superpowers. On 23 February, captains regent Gianfranco Terenzi and Rossano Zafferani, their wives, and Alvaro Selva, secretary of internal affairs of the republic and Central Committee member of the PCS, began a week-long visit to China. No less a personage than President Li Xiannian hosted a banquet in their honor and in his dinner address enumerated the objectives on which the two countries agree: prohibition of chemical weapons, peace, and reduction of nuclear weapons. He also expressed delight at the two countries' mutual trust and cooperation in striving for these ends and praised San Marino's "positive neutral foreign policy" in its work to safeguard world peace. (Xinhua, 24 February; *FBIS-CHI*, 25 February).

Alvaro Selva and Zhu Liang, head of the international liaison department of the Chinese Communist Party's (CPC) Central Committee, met for a discussion. The San Marinese delegation then had vice-foreign minister Zhou Nan as its tour guide for visits to Xian, Shanghai (Xinhua, 26 February; *FBIS-CHI*, 29 February), Nanjing (Shanghai City Service, 28 February; *FBIS-CHI*, 1 March), and Guangzhou (Xinhua, 1 March; *FBIS-CHI*, 2 March), where they visited clothing and appliance factories, a brewery and museums, and were fêted by local dignitaries.

In addition to the official government visit, on 10 October a delegation of the PCS, headed by Central Committee secretariat member Alberto Mino, was received by Hu Qili, member of the standing committee of the CPC Central Committee (Xinhua, 10 October; *FBIS-CHI*, 14 October). At almost the same time, on 11 October, a delegation of CPC officials left Beijing for a visit to Italy and San Marino at the invitation of these countries' communist parties (Xinhua, 11 October; *FBIS-CHI*, 17 October).

On 18 March, on the heels of the government delegation's visit to China, San Marino's Great and General Council welcomed a delegation from the Supreme Soviet, led by Lev Tolkunov, one of the two chairmen of the Supreme Soviet. This was the first official visit by Soviet parliamentarians to this country, reciprocating one by a San Marinese parliamentary delegation to the USSR in 1987, when they were greeted by Tolkunov in Moscow. Captains regent Terenzi and Zafferani praised the excellent relations between their country and the USSR, in which exchanges of parliamentary delegations are of great importance. They expressed admiration of the Soviet Union's "dynamic foreign policy," which seems to have borne results (TASS, 18 March; *FBIS-SOV*, 21 March). Lev Tolkunov, in reply, stated that it is "our sacred duty, the duty of every man to turn Europe," a continent of many nations and the origin of two world wars, into a continent of peace and "fruitful cooperation" (ibid.).

Gabriele Gatti, secretary of state for foreign and political affairs, also expressed satisfaction with the countries' relations, and was pleased that the USSR should be interested in so small a republic. He further promised to use San Marino's neutrality to contribute to the achievement of peace and the successful conclusion of the talks in Vienna (ibid.).

The Soviet parliamentary delegation met with the host legislature, the Great and General Council. They shared parliamentary experiences with its members and discussed East-West relations, especially the importance of the Soviet-American INF treaty. PCS member Umberto Barulli, then still a council member and not yet a captain regent, praised the Soviets' diplomatic activities in quest for peace, a concern of all peoples. He also noted that the PCS has been part of the government of San Marino in coalitions with various parties for more than a decade, and has as its aim the protection of the "interests of the working people of the Republic" (ibid.).

A less dramatic, but nevertheless important gesture toward the communist countries was the two-day discussion on disarmament and prospects of, and cooperation for mutual trust and stability in Europe held in San Marino on 9 and 10 August between Kurt Nier, a representative of the foreign ministry of the GDR, and Secretary of State for Foreign and Political Affairs Dr. Gabriele Gatti. Nier also met with the leaders of the PCS, as well as with Pier Marino Menicucci, general secretary of the PCS's coalition partner, the PCDS. (*Neues Deutschland*, 10 August.)

Margit N. Grigory
Hoover Institution

Spain

Population. 39,209,765 (July 1988) (*World Fact Book, 1988*)
Parties.

- Spanish Communist Party (Partido Comunista de España; PCE)
Founded. 1920

Membership. 62,000–70,000 (claimed) (*WMR*, February, May)

General Secretary. Julio Anguita (47)

President. Dolores Ibárruri (92, legendary La Pasionaria of Civil War days)

Secretariat. 9 members: Julio Anguita, Juan José Azcona, Juan Berga, José María Coronas, Francisco Frutos, Lucía García, Salvador Jové, Josep Palau, Francisco Palero (*Mundo Obrero*, 10–16 March)

Political Commission. 28 members (ibid.)

Central Committee. 101 members (ibid., 25 February–2 March)

Status. Legal

Last Congress. Twelfth, 19–21 February, in Madrid

Last Election. 1986, United Left (coalition of 7 parties, dominated by the PCE), 4.6 percent, 7 of 350 seats

Auxiliary Organization. Workers' Commissions (Comisiones Obreras; CCOO), claimed membership of about 1 million, almost a third of Spain's approximately 3.4 million unionized workers, Antonio Gutiérrez, chairman. (The CC OO is considered an auxiliary organization of the PCE, but all three Spanish communist parties have direct influence in it.)

Publications. *Mundo Obrero* (Labor world), weekly, José Sandoval Moris, editor; *Nuestra Bandera* (Our flag), bimonthly ideological journal, Eulalia Vintro, editor (both published in Madrid)

• Communist Party of the Peoples of Spain (Partido Comunista de los Pueblos de España; PCPE)

Founded. 1984

Membership. 25,000–26,000

General Secretary. Juan Ramos

Chairman. Ignacio Gallego

Status. Legal

Last Congress. Second, April 1987

Last Election. 1986, United Left (coalition of 7 parties including PCPE), 4.6 percent, 7 of 350 seats

Publication. *Nuevo Rumbo* (New direction), biweekly, Armando López Salinas, editor

• Spanish Workers' Party–Communist Unity (Partido de los Trabajadores de España–Unidad Comunista; PTE-UC)

Founded. 1987

Membership. 14,000

General Secretary. Adolfo Pinedo

Chairman. Santiago Carrillo (73)

Status. Legal

Last Congress. First, 8 February 1987

Last Election. 1986, campaigned as Board for Communist Unity, 1.12 percent, no seats

Publication. *Ahora* (Now), weekly, Santiago Carrillo, editor

A continuing concern of a fragmented communist movement in Spain is for the elusive goal of reunification. The mainstream PCE, which lost some 63 percent of its members after 1977, took the initiative in 1986 to begin courting dissidents who had seceded. It forged an electoral coalition with the pro-Soviet PCPE, the members of which had bolted from the PCE in 1983 in protest over the party's Eurocommunist stance. The electoral alliance did not include the PTE-UC. This party was founded by former PCE General Secretary Carrillo, who left the party in 1986, disgruntled at being displaced and ignored.

There are occasional terrorist acts by Marxist guerrillas of Basque Homeland and Liberty (Euzkadi ta Askatasuna; ETA), which demand Basque independence, and by Iraultza (Revolution), created in 1981 to support the Basque labor movement (Madrid Domestic Service, 3 May; *FBIS*, 4 May). During 1988, there was no reported activity by the Catalan separatist groups called Free Land (Terra Lliure) and the Catalan Red Army of Liberation.

Organization and Leadership. Growing anxiety over a "lack of leadership" in a demoralized PCE prompted the Twelfth Congress in February to replace Gerardo Iglesias as general secretary with a younger, more charismatic Andalusian, Julio Anguita. The congress was held in the Madrid premises of the CC OO because the heavily indebted party could not afford to hire a hall. (Madrid, *Epoca*, 4 January; *RFE Research*, 24 February; *JPRS*, 7 March.) The 619 delegates were told that a "very real threat of disintegration" had been averted since the previous congress (*WMR*, May). The PCE must now be invigorated through better organization and an "ideological renewal," communists must be reunited, and the United Left (Izquierda Unida; IU) coalition strengthened (*Rudé Právo*, Prague, 21 March; *FBIS*, 30 March).

Reportedly, Anguita had been more eager to head the IU than the PCE, but Nicolás Sartorius—a deputy general secretary under Iglesias—also coveted the IU leadership. The PCE Central Committee had ruled that both positions could no longer be held by one person, as Iglesias had done. Apparently after much jockeying, Anguita finally accepted the PCE post subject to "certain conditions" not made public. (*RFE Research*, 24 February.) The new general secretary emphasized the importance of the IU as a "catalyst" for rallying communists for swift and effective action. He said the fear of some that they might be "absorbed and dissolved" in the IU traced back to Santiago Carrillo's concept of the party as a "closed entity" resembling a church and operating on the "principle of faith and excommunication." The "submission to the leader" complex of some communists should be discarded in favor of open debate "without any taboo subjects." Rejecting Carrillo's obsession with winning elections at any cost, Anguita said he wanted to revive the classical concept of the party—to develop programs with which to tackle society's problems. (*WMR*, May.)

Though Anguita asserted that there should now be nothing to stand in the way of communist unity, a dialogue that began shortly before the PCE congress failed to break down all PCPE resistance (Madrid, *El País*, 15 January; *RFE Research*, 24 February; *Mundo Obrero*, 12–18 October; *FBIS*, 31 October). The PCE also made contacts with the PTE-UC that Anguita said might lead to negotiations, provided there was acceptance of a one-month time limit, a PCE referendum on whether to approve unity, and an agreement not to discuss the IU (*Ya*, Madrid, 18 May; *FBIS*, 10 June).

Meanwhile, optimism was on the rise within the PCE. Shortly after the February congress, Anguita exulted over an upsurge of hope among members and over a rush by 150 applicants to rejoin the party. By October it was claimed that membership had increased by almost 5,000. At the PCE autumn festival, Anguita attracted the largest audience seen at such a gathering since the late 1970s when the party's influence was at a peak. (*Diario 16*, Madrid, 28 February; *Népszabadság*, Budapest, 31 October; *FBIS*, 10 March, 21 November.)

Domestic Affairs. The PCE charged that it was the target of new types of informational aggression in the Spanish media. The notion is spread that the communists are socially bankrupt; their proposals are hushed up, and their inner-party life is subject to the "most subtle speculation." The party's Twelfth Congress declared that structural changes in the communications map of Spain, along with media control by a few powerful centers, had reduced the facilities and readership of the left-wing press.

(*WMR*, August.) A Spanish public opinion poll in June rated the new PCE general secretary nearly a point higher than his predecessor (*Diario 16*, 27 June; *JPRS*, 12 August).

Anguita admonished the government for having reneged on a campaign promise to provide 800,000 new jobs. Instead, "right-wing" policies had produced three million unemployed, a million more than when the socialists took over, and had made the rich richer. The obvious prescription, he indicated, was a programmed economy to provide at least the minimum wage to all the jobless within two or three years. This could be financed by eliminating the "considerable" tax fraud and by cutting military expenditures. (*Rabotnichesko delo*, Sofia, 3 May; *Mundo Obrero*, 12–18 October; *FBIS*, 10 May, 31 October.)

Auxiliary Organization. The communist and socialist trade union federations reached an unprecedented agreement in February to make a joint frontal attack on the government's labor and economic policies (*RFE Research*, 24 February). Charging that Spain's economic boom was wrought on the backs of the working people, they demanded "progressive social policies" and greater public employment. A series of nationwide protest demonstrations precipitated in midyear a cabinet reshuffle that brought two former socialist union leaders and two former communists into the government. Union leaders dismissed the changes as cosmetic and insignificant. (*NYT*, 19 July; *WP*, 9 July.)

Frustrated at the government's continued resistance to wage, benefit, and pension increases, both unions staged in December a 24-hour general strike—Spain's largest since 1934—that kept almost eight out of ten million workers off the job. Euphoric CC OO leaders said the stoppage was successful "beyond our greatest expectations" (*NYT*, 14 and 15 December; *AP*, 15 December). Government officials warned that the socialist General Workers Union (Unión General de Trabajadores; UGT) had "followed the communist strategy" and was "slipping toward the red end of the spectrum" (*CSM*, 14 and 15 December). Prime Minister Felipe González made some qualified concessions to the unions but stressed that his monetarist, free-market policies would continue. His response was called "positive" by the UGT leader, but "ambiguous" by Antonio Gutiérrez, who replaced Marcelino Camacho as CC OO chairman in early 1988. (*FBIS*, 7 March; *CSM*, 23 December.) Communists were now expected to make gains through the labor movement by exploiting discontent with the government (*RFE Research*, 24 February).

International Views and Activities. The PCE's new general secretary said there was a need for some kind of international communist organization to facilitate concerted action by communist parties. It should be "polycentric" and free from negative historical stereotypes. Anguita also praised Chairman Mikhail Gorbachev's candid discussion of the problems of bureaucracy and corruption, as well as his attempt to demythologize some historical figures. This was testimony, he said, to the strength of socialism, since "only the strong can criticize themselves." (*WMR*, May.) PCE officials, including Anguita, visited the Soviet Union for consultations and to study the Soviet experience in restructuring (*FBIS*, 15 June, 4 August, 29 November). Soviet foreign minister Eduard Shevardnadze made an official visit to Madrid in January, but apparently no mention was made in the Soviet press of any meeting with Spanish communists (*Pravda*, 21 January; *World Affairs Review*, vol. 18, no. 2).

Anguita indicated in June that rather neglected relations with some foreign communist parties had been renewed, with emphasis on ties with Mediterranean and Latin American countries (*Mundo Obrero*, 29 June; *FBIS*, 19 July). Reported during 1988 were meetings with communist officials of Greece, Albania, Italy, Portugal, France, East Germany, Czechoslovakia, Romania, and Hungary.

The PCE denounced Spain's entry into the Western European Union (TASS, 15 May; *FBIS*, 16 May); it also demanded Spain's withdrawal from NATO as well as the elimination of all United States bases from Spain (*Pravda*, 18 January; *World Affairs Review*, vol. 18, no. 2). The party decried "an avalanche of U.S. military offensive actions in the Persian Gulf (TASS, 20 April; *FBIS*, 20 April) and urged Prime Minister González to commit himself to the defense of the Nicaraguan people (Madrid Domestic Service, 18 March; *FBIS*, 21 March).

Rival Communist Parties. There was considerable ambivalence within the PCPE on the subject of unity with the PCE. Half the leadership wavered along with General Secretary Juan Ramos, while the other half sided with Chairman Ignacio Gallego in actively supporting unity. In June the vacillators even ousted seven members who wanted to accelerate the process, and they accused the PCE of "continuing interference" in the PCPE's internal affairs.

They feared that Anguita's group was trying to impose "integration"—i.e., PCE control—instead of "unity," and they even threatened to withdraw from the IU if the PCE continued its "high-handed" dominance of that coalition. (*Diario 16*, 7 June; Madrid Domestic Service, 28 September; *FBIS*, 1 July, 29 September.)

The PCPE chairman maneuvered a decision by his party in November, without the presence of General Secretary Ramos, to agree to the convening of a congress of unity with the PCE (Madrid Domestic Service, 12 November; *FBIS*, 14 November). Gallego rejected the notion that more time was needed to think things over, and he supported Anguita's call for a congress on equal terms between comrades. He insisted there had been considerable progress toward ideological rapprochement, despite Ramos's claim that the PCE had refused to discuss the issues that had caused the party split. (*Ya*, Madrid, 13 November; *FBIS*, 5 December.) At the end of November, Ramos had his revenge: it was reported that the PCPE Secretariat had removed Gallego from his post (Madrid Domestic Service, 30 November; *FBIS*, 30 November).

PTE-UC Chairman Santiago Carrillo was not invited by the PCE to take part in the unity congress, though Gallego thought he should be (Madrid Domestic Service, 12 November; *FBIS*, 14 November). Carrillo continued to reject unification except on two conditions—that the IU alliance should be abandoned, and that the communist groups should be joined in a party federation (*Népszabadság*, Budapest, 31 October; *FBIS*, 21 November).

Left-Wing Terrorist Groups. ETA offered to suspend terrorist attacks for two months if the Madrid authorities would agree to a dialogue. The offer was withdrawn shortly afterward because the government had "failed to respond in good time." Officials countered that there could be talks only if ETA's members first renounced all violence. (*FBIS*, 16 February.) There were occasional reports of renewed terrorism later in the year (*FBIS*, 16 June, 25 August, 28 November).

The group called Iraultza made a terrorist attack on Bilbao's mayor to protest labor policies. It bombed municipal and industrial installations in support of labor disputes. (Madrid Domestic Service, 3 May; *FBIS*, 4 May.)

Biography. *Julio Anguita*, the PCE's new general secretary, was conspicuously successful during the years of the party's political decline in winning a following in his native province of Andalusia. Twice elected mayor of Córdoba, he was known nationally as the "Red Caliph"—the only communist mayor of a major Spanish city. Anguita became chairman of the IU coalition in Andalusia, and in 1986 was elected to that region's parliament as a deputy. The coalition won 18 percent of the provincial votes, while in national elections only 4.6 percent of Spaniards voted for IU candidates.

Born in 1941 in Fuengirola, Málaga Province, Anguita became a secondary-school history teacher. He joined the PCE in 1972 and became an officer in 1983. (*Neues Deutschland*, 22 February; *RFE Research*, 24 February; Moscow Television Service, 23 February; *FBIS*, 26 February; *WMR*, May.)

H. Leslie Robinson, Professor Emeritus
University of the Pacific

Sweden

Population. 8,393,071 (July, 1988), average annual growth rate 0.10 percent
Party. Left Party Communists (Vansterpartiet Kommunisterna; VPK)
Founded. 1921 (VPK, 1967)
Membership. Ca. 17,800, principally in the far north, Stockholm, and Goteborg
Chairman. Lars Werner
Executive Committee. 9 members: Lars Werner, Bertil Mabrink (vice chairman), Gudrun Schyman (vice chairman), Kenneth Kvist (party secretary), Bo Leinderdahl, Bitte Engsell, Birgit Hansson, Gerd Mabrink, Jorn Svensson
Party Board. 35 members
Status. Legal
Last Congress. Twenty-eighth, 23–25 May 1987
Last Election. September 1988, 314,031 votes, 5.8 percent, 21 out of 349 seats
Auxiliary Organization. Communist Youth (KU)
Publications. *Ny Dag* (New day), semiweekly; *Socialistisk Debatt* (Socialist debate), monthly; both published in Stockholm

The ancestor of the VPK, Sweden's Communist Party (Sveriges Kommunistiska Partiet), was established in 1921. Its greatest moment came right after World War II, when it obtained 11.2 percent of the vote in local elections, largely due to the popularity of the Soviet Union at the end of the war. Since that time the communist party (later the VPK) has usually won around 4 or 5 percent of the vote. The party, which has never made a truly major contribution to communist history, has had marginal influence in Swedish politics. Its most important role has been to allow the Social Democrats to govern during much of Sweden's recent history. During the last half-century, the Swedish Social Democrats have been Europe's most dominant social democratic party, and during many of their years in power, they have relied on a combined majority with the communists in the Riksdag (parliament). The communists, however, have never been part of the government. In Sweden, a party has to clear 4 percent in order to be represented in the Riksdag, and after the bitter reaction to the Soviet invasion of Czechoslovakia in 1968, the VPK fell beneath 4 percent and was not represented. In the 1970 and 1976 elections, it received 4.8 percent; and in 1979 and 1982, 5.6 percent of the vote. The VPK dropped to 5.4 percent of the vote in 1985.

The communists changed both the name and the direction of the party during the party congress in 1967. Blue-collar workers had constituted the majority of the communist electorate in previous years, but during the 1970s the VPK increasingly attracted white-collar and younger voters. In the 1979 elections, 56 percent of the voters were under the age of 30, and 36 percent of the voters were in the white-collar class. In the 1982 elections, those under 30 slipped to 45 percent, but those in the white-collar class rose from 36 to 41 percent. Over the years, the VPK has projected a Marxist image, even though it has been regarded as one of the more moderate West European communist parties.

The history of the VPK has been characterized by stormy internal fighting, and the internecine battling in 1987 was worse than usual. The arguments focused on policy and personnel decisions that were to be made by the Twenty-eighth Party Congress in late May. Much of the dispute centered around the chairman, Lars Werner, who had served twelve years as party leader, longer than any other leader in the history of the VPK. (His predecessor, C. H. Hermansson, served eleven years.) Werner came under increasing criticism from members of the party inner circle, because they felt he should take a tougher line against the Social Democrats in the parliament. Some wanted to oust Werner at the Twenty-eighth Party Congress, but it voted to retain him and to remove three of Werner's opponents from the Executive Committee. Some opponents of Werner, however, remained on the Executive Committee.

The 1988 Elections. The dominant political event in Sweden in 1988 was the September election. Based on polls taken in early 1988, there were predictions that the VPK might not surmount the 4 percent barrier and so not be represented in the parliament. A February poll by the Swedish Institute for Public Opinion (SIFO) indicated that only 2.8 percent of the voters said that they would vote for the VPK. An IMU poll taken around the same time found the VPK with support from 3.5 percent of the voters. (*Dagens Nyheter*, 1 March.) These figures were of considerable interest to the Social Democrats, because they were relying on a majority in parliament attained through combination with the VPK to stay in office. Another factor that added uncertainty to the 1988 election was the emergence of the Greens (an environmentalist party). For the first time, it appeared that the Greens might crack the 4 percent barrier. A SIFO poll in January 1987 showed the Greens with 3 percent of the vote. A year later, they registered 4.9 percent. (Arvid Lagercrantz, "Election Year '88: The Political Scene in Sweden Prior to the Autumn Parliamentary Elections," Swedish Information Service, no. 25, August 1988.) Environmental issues have been dominant in Sweden ever since Chernobyl. During 1988, the Swedish media devoted a lot of attention to environmental tragedies such as an infestation of red algae on the west coast and the death of a large number of cub seals in the Baltic. What was not clear was whether the Greens would draw more votes from the Social Democrats and the VPK or from the so-called bourgeois parties.

A wide-ranging editorial in *Dagens Nyheter* (1 March) suggested some other reasons why the VPK (and therefore the Social Democrats, who needed representation of the VPK in parliament) should be concerned about the upcoming September election. One was that although Werner seemed to have a somewhat favorable image in the population at large (and was therefore a political asset to his party), he seemed to be highly controversial within the leadership group of the VPK. Thus he was "incapable of leading and holding the party together." The editorial further pointed out

that in contrast to the 1960s and 1970s, in 1988 the younger voters did not seem attracted to the VPK. Also, the party seems to have lost considerable influence with union members. The editorial stated that, on the other hand, the VPK's greatest advantage was precisely that it had to reach the 4 percent barrier. That is, many Social Democrats vote VPK just to ensure that the Social Democrats stay in office. Electoral research in 1982 found that "35 percent of those who voted with the VPK at the time regarded the Social Democrats as the best party."

One can speculate that, indeed, many Social Democrats did vote for the VPK, as the communists won 5.8 percent of the vote, an increase of .4 percent over the last election in 1985. The VPK increased its number of seats from 19 to 21. The Social Democrats' percentage of the votes dropped from 44.7 to 43.2. Nevertheless, the Social Democrats retained control of the Riksdag, as the Social Democrats and communists combined won 177 seats, compared to 152 for the "bourgeois parties" and 20 seats for the Greens. The percentage of the ballots cast for the Greens jumped from 1.5 in the 1985 election to 5.5 in the 1988 election. This was the first time in three attempts that the Greens won seats in parliament. A fascinating aspect of the last election is that approximately two-thirds of the Greens' support came not from the political left, but from voters who had previously supported right-of-center parties. (Steven Koblik, "Predicting the Great One," *Political Life in Sweden*, no. 26, December.)

All three "bourgeois" parties lost seats. The Moderates, the major party farthest to the right, won 66 seats (18.3 percent), a loss of ten seats; the Liberals, 44 seats (12.2 percent), a loss of 7; and the Center Party, 42 seats (11.3 percent), a loss of two. The major problem that the nonsocialist parties faced was to convince the voters that the three main parties could form a coherent governing coalition. They tended to be fractious partners when they won the elections of 1976 and 1979. Thus the Social Democrat-VPK combination remained relatively stable—losing a total of one seat, whereas the nonsocialist parties lost a total of nineteen seats, while the Greens won twenty seats.

Commenting on the outcome of the election, Werner said, "Certain conclusions should be drawn from the election results. The parties which have gained are the VPK, the Environment Party and the Center Party. These parties have strongly stressed environmental matters... A wider discussion should be held to solve the great environmental problems. Discussions should also be held on how to conduct the policy of the redistribution of wealth." (Stockholm Domestic Service, 18 September.)

Party Internal Affairs. Vila Claesson, a frequent foe of Lars Werner, decided not to seek re-election to the party executive committee, which, in effect, meant that she was stepping down as vice chairman of the party. She gave no reason for doing so. She had recently been involved in internal party disputes about environmental fees, which she opposed. Claesson did not, however, give up her seat in the parliament. Gerd Mabrink was elected to replace Claesson on the executive committee. (*Ny Dag*, 13–19 October.)

The VPK dismissed Editor-in-Chief Ingemar Andersson of *Ny Dag*, the weekly party newspaper, in early January. The firing was but another manifestation of internal party conflict that had been brewing in recent years. According to *Dagens Nyheter*, the dismissal was due to "a lack of political confidence" in Andersson and "at bottom lies a conflict about the role of the newspaper—whether it should be a mouthpiece for the party leadership or an independent organ" (*Dagens Nyheter*, 9 January).

The question of *Ny Dag's* future dominated the meetings of the party's executive committee in February. Finally, an editorial staff of four was appointed to write the editorials and commentaries. The former longtime party chairman, C. H. Hermansson, was brought in, at least temporarily, to be the new editor. Strangely enough, Andersson, the fired chief editor, returned as one of the editorial writers, a highly controversial action. (*Ny Dag*, 18–24 February.)

Foreign Affairs. The Swedes directed considerable attention toward the USSR in 1988. *Svenska Dagbladet* published a long article early in January that summarized the views of many Swedish diplomats about their government's policy toward the Soviet Union and Eastern Europe. According to the newspaper, numerous Swedish foreign-service officers who were experienced in East European affairs felt that "the government should tighten up its security and neutrality policy, formulate a coherent policy towards the East, and properly strengthen its armed forces."

Svenska Dagbladet said that the views of these diplomats had been expressed to the leadership of the Foreign Ministry numerous times verbally and in internal memos. The criticism was made in the context of normalization of relations between the Soviet Union and Sweden. The article quoted at length a memo from a prominent Swedish diplomat who wrote: "What is needed overall is a more self-confident attitude than normally seems natural for us placid Swedes...The Soviet Union, Poland, and the GDR—all...carry on intensive peace-time intelligence and penetration activity, well-coordinated within the Warsaw Pact, against Sweden. Therefore we simply cannot afford not to have our own coherent security policy toward the East, and one that is fairly well coordinated internally." (*Svenska Dagbladet*, 8 January.)

Amid continuing reports that Soviet submarines were penetrating Swedish waters (*Marin Nytt*, no. 4)—as they have for the last several years—Oswald Soderguist, the VPK's spokesman on defense issues, made a strong statement that submarines intruding in Swedish waters should be sunk. The Swedish military, he declared, should take the measures necessary to sink intruding vessels. (*Dagens Nyheter*, 28 December 1987.) Chairman Werner echoed the same general line in October when he said, "We want a strong border defense that will maintain the Swedish policy of neutrality" (*Dagens Nyheter*, 25 October). At the end of the year, a high-level delegation of the Supreme Soviet (the Soviet parliament) visited Sweden for a week at the invitation of the Swedish parliament. The Soviet delegation met with representatives of all the parties represented in the Swedish parliament, including the VPK. (*Dagens Nyheter*, 5 December.)

Virtually nothing was written in 1988 about international party contacts or about rival communist groups. The Communist Workers' Party (APK), founded in 1977, has played a miniscule role in Swedish politics.

Peter Grothe
Monterey Institute of International Studies

Switzerland

Population. 6,592,558 (July 1988)
Party. Swiss Labor Party (Partei der Arbeit der Schweiz/Parti suisse du travail/Partito Svizzero del Lavoro; PdAS)
Founded. 1921; outlawed 1940; re-established 15 October 1944

Membership. 4,500 (estimated)
General Secretary. Jean Spielmann
Honorary President. Jean Vincent
Politburo. 14 members
Secretariat. 5 members
Central Committee. 50 members
Status. Legal
Last Congress. Thirteenth, 27 February–1 March 1987
Last Election. 18 October 1987, about 0.8 percent, one seat in the National Council, the lower chamber of the national parliament; 8.72 percent of the vote in Geneva canton
Auxiliary Organizations. Communist Youth League of Switzerland (KVJS), Marxist Student League, Swiss Women's Organization for Peace and Progress, Swiss Peace Movement, Swiss-Soviet Union Society, Swiss-Cuban Society, Central Sanitaire Suisse
Publications. *VO Réalités* (Geneva), weekly, circulation about 8,000 copies; *Vorwärts* (Basel), weekly, circulation about 6,000 copies; *Il Lavatore*, Italian-language weekly; *Zunder*, KVJS organ

Although Switzerland has three organizations of some significance that can be labeled communist parties, the last election on the federal level on 18 October 1987 showed a further decline of the political influence of the still-Moscow-line communist movement. The largest and oldest of these three groups is the Partei der Arbeit der Schweiz (Swiss Labor Party; PdAS), which is the only communist organization officially recognized by other communist fraternal parties. The other two are the Progressive Organizations of Switzerland (POCH), which has Georg Degen as its secretary, and the Sozialistische Arbeiterpartei (Socialist Workers' Party; SAP), of which Werner Carrobio is secretary.

Although the Social Democratic Party of Switzerland (SPS), which has some radical wings, suffered its worst defeat since 1919 (*NYT*, 20 October 1987), Helmut Hubacher, the party's chairman, apparently developed some closer links to the Hungarian CP (*FBIS*, 31 August). It is of some importance that some left-extremist SPS members gained greater influence within this party's leadership.

POCH was founded in 1972 in Basel by students disappointed with the sterile politics of the PdAS. Under Georg Degen, the now-Zürich-based organization replaced old-fashioned, doctrinaire Marxism with the more attractive ideological concepts of the Greens movement. There are two Greens parties in Switzerland. The first, the Swiss Ecologist Party is known as a "cucumber" because it is (supposedly) all-Green; the second organization, the Green Socialist Alternative is called a "watermelon," because its green peel covers a red, or Marxist, core (*NYT*, 18 October 1987). POCH's new policies along the latter party's lines proved quite successful in the November election, in which the "watermelons" gained nine seats. The Political Bureau of the PdAS therefore recently proposed to POCH, SAP, and the Green alliance the forming of a single left opposition in parliament.

A POCH subsidiary, the Organization for Women's Affairs, is the most important women's group in Switzerland and is quite active among students.

POCH publishes the weekly *POCH-Zeitung*, with an estimated circulation of 6,000 copies. The membership of the organization is reported to be somewhat lower than 6,000, with 65 percent women. This organization was more active than the SPS.

The SAP was founded in 1969 by a group of young Trotskyists who left the PdAS; it was renamed in 1980, and operates mainly in larger cities. Because it is a cadre party, its membership seems to remain constant at about 2,000, but it is supported by at least 3,000 sympathizers. Its leading theoretician continues to be Fritz Osterwalder. In recent years SAP members have attained some important positions, especially in the educational system and the trade unions. It thus exercises a far greater influence than its small membership would indicate. The SAP still advocates the revolutionary class struggle in centers of production and believes in central planning and the nationalization of the means of production. It is active among students under the name Revolutionary Socialist Youth (RSJ) and from time to time in the antinuclear power movement. It is amazing that its main weekly publication appears in all four languages of Switzerland under the titles: *Bresche, La Breche, Rosso,* and *Roia.*

In addition there are several other radical-socialist splinter organizations, such as the Autonomous Socialist Party (PSA), under the leadership of Werner Carrobio, which operates exclusively in the Italian part of Switzerland. The PSA's estimated membership is about 1,000. This fairly agile party is the result of a split within the SPS in 1960. Again there were some indications of a forthcoming merger with the SPS.

Two other very small groups also must be mentioned: the Communist Party of Switzerland/Marxist-Leninist (KPS/ML), and the SAP-connected Gruppe Schweiz ohne Armee/Group for a Switzerland Without Military (GSoA). The two major Swiss peace groups: the Schweizerische Friedensbewegung/Swiss Section of the World Peace Council (SFB) and the International Women's League for Peace and Freedom (IFFF), are controlled by the PdAS. They all seem to be somewhat dormant, though they cooperate on several special occasions.

According to Anjuska Weil, a member of the Politburo of the PdAS who heads the party's youth commission, the Young Communist League "is fairly active in the German-speaking part of the country, Geneva and the Vaud canton" (*WMR*, June).

Leadership and Organization. While the center of Swiss political and economic power lies in the German-speaking part of the country, the PdAS's strongholds are located in the French-speaking areas. The old socialist ideas are more attractive in the country's western part and Basel, whereas the more modern, environmentally oriented approaches have more followers among intellectuals in the German-speaking urban areas.

Despite all its efforts, the party has no cantonal groups in small rural and conservative cantons. Its organization is a territorial one and is structured in accordance with the historically developed regions of Switzerland.

The main organizational change and one of the most notable aspects of last year's congress continues to be the strong effort to rejuvenate the party's leading bodies. The age factor was reflected then in the replacement of eleven members of the Central Committee with younger delegates. By now 39 percent of the delegates are under 40, and 26 percent are aged between 40 and 50 (*IB*, June 1987). Although the *World Marxist Review* claims that "the age problem is no longer a headache for the party organization" (June), the PdAS apparently struggles with its establishment and their old-fashioned class-conscious ideology, vocabulary, and slogans. Last year's defeat in the federal election reflects the party's failure to adjust more quickly to sociological changes.

Domestic Affairs. The Thirteenth Congress passed one major program of domestic action, its chief idea being the "peace economy" and winning over allies needed to pass it. In order to gain a new appeal, the action program emphasized radical options, such as completely banning arms exports (which would hurt the Swiss economy badly), the reduction of military spending, the lifting of banking secrecy, or even calling for a work week of 35 hours with full pay. According to the *WMR*, the document underlined the party's continuing efforts to fight "resolutely in the traditional spheres of class battles—for improving the position of the working people and for defending their gains against the offensive from the Right" (July 1987). Surprisingly, these hollow slogans proved to be somewhat successful among a few students, but failed to attract the disoriented working-class movement. Nevertheless, since 1987 the PdAS has had ten members sitting on Geneva's municipal council.

In April, *Vorwärts*, the party's German-language newspaper held its traditional annual press festival in Zürich. The festival serves as an important fundraiser. Several antiwar organizations and delegates from fraternal parties attended. In November, Jean Spielmann, the agitating 44-year-old general secretary, opened the festival for the party's weekly *Réalités* with an address in which he underscored the PdAS's unshakable solidarity with Third World countries and with those progressives concerned with environmental issues. Several fraternal party newspapers, including *Neues Deutschland* sent their delegations (*Neues Deutschland*, 14 November). It remains a mystery how this small and penurious party can finance its multilanguage publications and its various other activities. The old rumor persists that the PdAS is aided financially by Kremlin sources.

International Affairs. The PdAS used its party congress last year to establish several international contacts. The most intense relationship with foreign party organizations still seems to be the one maintained with those of East Germany. The main international resolution of the congress upgraded the party policies as outlined in the 1971 theses, the 1979 Regensdorf program, and the 1982 decisions and promoted the idea of a "peace-advancing economy." This approach aims at five goals: the repudiation of the arms race; orienting and controlling the economy to solve important problems; balancing scientific and technological progress and protection of the environment; massive support of the Third

World and radical changes in the political ties with lesser developed countries; and peaceful coexistence.

During 1988, the general secretary traveled to a remarkable extent. In April, he conferred with Miloš Jakeš, the general secretary of the Communist Party of Czechoslovakia, in Prague, where they stressed their identical views on current international topics (*FBIS*, 19 April). In May, a delegation of the PdAS under Spielmann's leadership arrived in East Berlin and was warmly welcomed by Günther Sieber, a member of the SED's Central Committee and of the Department of International Affairs (*FBIS*, 16 May). The visit gave the guests, including Rüdi Bantle, a member of the PdAS's Central Committee, ample opportunities to see firsthand the results of applied socialist principles. At the end of this five-day mission, Erich Honecker, general secretary of the SED's Central Committee, received Spielmann and his entourage for a cordial and constructive dialogue (*Neues Deutschland*, 20 May). In August, Jean Spielmann conferred with Milko Balev, Politburo member and secretary of the CC of the Bulgarian Communist Party (*FBIS*, 30 August). During his stay in Bulgaria, Spielmann emphasized on several occasions the importance of *perestroika* and *glasnost'* for the international communist movement (*FBIS*, 26 August).

General Activities. Jean Spielmann seems to understand that the Swiss left nowadays is more focused on problems of disarmament, environmental protection, or the Third World than on old-fashioned class-struggle. Swiss society traditionally is not too tolerant of radical politics. During 1988, there was some occasional cooperation between more or less autonomous leftist student groups on environmental issues. Following international patterns, several antiapartheid actions and organized demonstrations for divestment of holdings in firms in South Africa took place in the major urban centers and universities. The most active universities now seem to be those of Zürich and Basel. Besides some minor actions organized by the SFB and IFFF among Swiss students, there were no signs of significant political activity.

Kurt R. Leube
California State University at Hayward

Turkey

Population. 54,167,857
Parties. Communist Party of Turkey (TCP); Workers' Party of Turkey (TWP); United Communist Party of Turkey (UCPT), established through merger of TCP and TWP
Founded. TCP: 1920; TWP: 1961; UCPT: 1988
Membership. Negligible
General Secretary. TCP/UCPT: Nabi Yagci (aka Haydar Kutlu); other officers of UCPT: Nihat Sargin, president; Mehmet Karaca, deputy general secretary; Osman Sakalsiz, deputy president
Leading Bodies. No data
Status. Illegal
Last Congress. TCP: November 1983; UCPT: October 1988
Last Election. N/a
Auxiliary Organizations. N/a
Publications. The following publications were listed in the indictment of the TCP/UCPT general secretary and attributed to Kutlu's own testimony in the periodical *Atilim*—domestic: *Alinteri* (Toil; literally, sweat of the brow); *Cagdas* (Contemporary); *Gorus* (Viewpoint); foreign: *Atilim* (Progress); *Sol Birlik* (Left union); *Turkiye Postasi* (Turkish mail); *Yol ve Amac* (Means and goals); *Yeni Cag* (New age); *Gercegin Sesi* (The voice of truth); *Proleter Istanbul* (Proletarian Istanbul); *Ileri* (Forward)

On 7 October 1987, Haydar Kutlu, general secretary of the Communist Party of Turkey (TCP), and Behice Boran, chairman of the Workers' Party of Turkey (TWP), issued a statement announcing their intention to merge their parties in a new United Communist Party of Turkey (UCPT) (*IB*, January). Three days later the venerable Mrs. Boran (aged 77) passed away, and her body was returned to Turkey for burial with the permission of the government. On 16 November 1987, Kutlu and Dr. Nihat Sargin, general secretary of the TWP, returned to Turkey together, ostensibly to formally establish the new UCPT. This move preceded the Turkish parliamentary elections of 29 November by less than two weeks and followed public statements by Prime Minister Turgut Ozal to the effect that repeal of two penal code articles outlawing Marxist parties was not outside the realm of possibility. (*YICA*, 1988.) It was speculated that Ozal's statements were motivated by the desire to enhance Turkey's chances for admission to full membership in the European Community, and that Kutlu and Sargin wanted to test the limits of the newly relaxed political atmosphere at a time when repressive action by the Turkish government would be especially embarrassing (*Keesing's Contemporary Archives*, June 1988).

Despite the fact that they were accompanied by a delegation of European lawyers, journalists and politicians, Kutlu and Sargin were detained on arrival and held incommunicado for several weeks. On 5 December, the Ankara State Security Court remanded them to prison, charging them with such crimes as leading an illegal organization, spreading communist propaganda, and "insulting the state authorities." (*Keesing's Contemporary Archives*, June 1988.) Both men claimed they had been tortured. They were formally indicted on 14 March 1988, along with two of their lawyers. Protests against the detentions and reports of the use of torture during the interrogation of Kutlu were published by a variety of communist sources, particularly in the Soviet bloc (e.g., *Neues Deutschland*, various dates). It was also reported in January that Kutlu had suffered a "heart spasm," and that he had been returned to prison after brief treatment at a leading Ankara hospital (Our Radio [clandestine communist-party radio], 21 January; quoted in *FBIS*, 21 January).

The formal indictments of Kutlu and Sargin were filed on 14 March (Ankara Radio, 14 March; *FBIS*, 15 March). The trial opened on 8 June and continued in intermittent sessions thereafter. Reportedly, the cases of Kutlu and Sargin were merged with those of nineteen other accused. Prospective sentences ranged from death for the two principal defendants to five to fifteen years for the others. Requests for removal to a larger courtroom to allow more observers to attend the trial were rejected; this prompted Kutlu's and Sargin's lawyers to withdraw from the court (Ankara Radio, 8 June; *FBIS*, 9 June).

In short, what appeared to be an elaborate attempt to shame the Turkish government into repealing its 60-year-old ban on communist political organizations was failing. Paradoxically, President Kenan Evren, who has frequently excoriated communism and warned of its great dangers for Turkey, unexpectedly announced in October that he was not opposed to the formation of a communist party in Turkey (Ankara Radio, 1 November; *FBIS*, 8 November). In response, the UCPT issued a statement pledging to strive to attain legality, denying that "Communists have . . . [ever] favored the use of terror," and calling for the release of Kutlu and Sargin and the dropping of all charges against them, as well as repeal of the relevant articles of the Penal Code (Our Radio, 29 October; *FBIS*, 2 November). On the previous day, the same source reported that Kutlu and Sargin had "agreed to the idea of holding a public referendum on legalizing the communist party," and had praised former prime minister Bulent Ecevit for making this suggestion (Our Radio, 28 October; *FBIS*, 28 October).

Also in October, on the anniversary of the death of Mrs. Boran, it was announced that the unification of the TCP and TWP had been accomplished, and that Kutlu and Sargin had been elected general secretary and president, respectively (*Morning Star; Neues Deutschland*, 10 October). The new party emphasized peace, democracy, "a political solution to the Kurdish question," and the renunciation of violence (ibid.).

On other leftist fronts, several more trials of defendants arrested since the military coup of 1980 were brought to a conclusion with sentences of death and imprisonment. There were also some violent incidents, particularly a raid on a military depot east of Istanbul in January. The perpetrators were either apprehended or killed in the days that followed; one policeman was also killed and several wounded (*Keesing's Contemporary Archives*, June). There was also a serious altercation when hundreds of labor-union members, under the leadership of seven Social Democratic Populist Party (SDPP) members of the parliament, tried to stage a march on May Day in Istanbul. A large number of students also attempted to protest against a ban that had been imposed against all May Day demostrations. About 1,000 of them became involved with the police after they attempted to occupy the offices of Bosporus University in Istanbul. In Ankara, there were arrests for distribution of reportedly leftwing leaflets and placards, as well as a report that members of the illegal extremist group Dev Sol (Revolutionary left) had put up booby-trapped banners in several cities. Two alleged members of this group were killed in a police raid in Istanbul on 1 May. (*Keesing's Contemporary Archives*, June.) In the midst of these incidents, President Evren warned that if the political parties again allowed law and order to be undermined, as they had in the late

1970s, the military might again find it necessary to intervene (ibid.).

In the southeast, a low-key guerrilla campaign continued throughout 1988, led by such Kurdish separatist groups as the Kurdish Workers' Party (KWP). That organization was apparently based in Syria, prompting discussion of border security on the occasion of a visit to Damascus by Prime Minister Ozal in July. (Ibid.)

Frank Tachau
University of Illinois at Chicago

Select Bibliography, 1987–1988

GENERAL

Arvidsson, Claes, and Lars Erik Blomqvist, eds. *Symbols of Power: The Esthetics of Political Legitimation in the Soviet Union and Eastern Europe*. Stockholm: Almqvist & Wiksell, 1987. 185 pp.

Bergson, Abram. *Planning and Performance in Socialist Economies: The USSR and Eastern Europe*. Winchester, Mass.: Unwin Hyman, 1988. 320 pp.

Bertsch, Gary K. *Controlling East-West Trade and Technology Transfer*. Durham, N.C.: Duke University Press, 1988. 506 pp.

Binnendijk, Hans. *Authoritarian Regimes in Transition*. Washington, D.C.: Center for the Study of Foreign Affairs, Foreign Service Institute, 1987. 336 pp.

Brada, Josef C., and Karl-Eugen Wädekin. *Socialist Agriculture in Transition: Organizational Response to Failing Performance*. Boulder, Colo.: Westview Press, 1988. 445 pp.

Brucan, Silviu. *World Socialism at the Crossroads: An Insider's View*. New York: Praeger, 1987. 208 pp.

Cook, Chris. *The European Left*. Vol. 1. New York: Facts on File, 1987. 237 pp.

Courtois, Stéphane, and Marc Lazar. *Le Communisme*. Paris: M.A. Editions, 1987. 271 pp.

Eberstadt, Nicholas N. *The Poverty of Communism*. New Brunswick, N.J.: Transaction Books, 1988. 317 pp.

Gilberg, Trond, ed. *Coalition Strategies of Marxist Parties*. Durham, N.C.: Duke University Press, 1988. 376 pp.

Hollander, Paul. *The Many Faces of Socialism*. New Brunswick, N.J.: Transaction Books, 1988. 362 pp.

Kanet, Roger E., ed. *The Soviet Union, Eastern Europe and the Third World*. New York: Cambridge University Press, 1988. 249 pp.

Lefever, Ernest W. *Nairobi to Vancouver: The World Council of Churches and the World*. Washington, D.C.: Ethics and Public Policy Center, 1988. 166 pp.

Malik, Hafeez. *Soviet-American Relations with Pakistan, Iran and Afghanistan*. New York: St. Martin's Press, 1987. 431 pp.

Marable, Manning. *African and Caribbean Politics*. London: Verso, 1987. 314 pp.

Moore, Barrington, Jr. *Authority and Inequality under Capitalism and Socialism*. Oxford: Clarendon Press, 1987. 125 pp.

Oded, Arye. *Africa and the Middle East Conflict*. Boulder, Colo.: Lynne Rienner, 1987. 244 pp.

Oquendo, L., and V. Kokorev. *Afrika-Latinskaia Amerika: ot rabotorgovli k sotrudnichestvu*. Moscow: Nauka, 1988. 108 pp.

Perry, Charles M., and Robert L. Pfaltzgraff, Jr., eds. *Selling the Rope to Hang Capitalism?* Washington, D.C.: Pergamon-Brassy, 1987. 248 pp.

Peters, I. A., and I. Iu. Sushinskaia. *Mir sotsializma i mirovoi revoliutsionnyi protsess*. Kiev: Naukova dumka, 1987. 126 pp.

Pirogov, G. G. *What is the World Socialist System?* Moscow: Progress Publishers, 1987. 159 pp.

Popov, B. S., chief ed. *Internatsionalizatsiia opyta stran sotsialisticheskogo sodruzhestva*. Moscow: Mysl', 1987. 319 pp.

Schreiber, Thomas, and Françoise Barry, eds. *L'U.R.S.S. et L'Europe de L'Est: notes et études documentaires*. Nancy: Secrétariat Général du Gouvernement–Direction de la Documentation Française, 1988. 284 pp.

Spanger, Hans-Joachim, and Lothar Brock. *Die beiden deutschen Staaten in der Dritten Welt*. Opladen: Westdeutscher Verlag, 1987. 428 pp.

Staar, Richard F., ed. *1988 Yearbook on International Communist Affairs*. Stanford, Calif.: Hoover Institution Press, 1988. 598 pp.

Toporning, B. N., chief ed. *Sotsialisticheskie konstitutsii: stanovlenie i razvitie*. Moscow: Nauka, 1987. 286 pp.

Tsukanov, S. V., gen. ed., and Yu. S. Oganisyan, comp. *Marxism-Leninism and Our Time: The Communist Response to the Challenge of Our Time*. Prague: Peace and Socialism International Publishers, 1987. 359 pp.

Winiecki, Jan. *The Distorted World of Soviet-type*

Economies. Pittsburgh, Pa.: University of Pittsburgh Press, 1988. 223 pp.

AFRICA

African National Congress. *Documents of the ANC Conference 'Peoples of the World United Against Apartheid for a Democratic South Africa.'* Lusaka, Zambia: ANC, 1988. 60 pp.

Arnold, Millard. *Steve Biko: No Fears Expressed.* Johannesburg: Skotaville Publishers, 1987. 175 pp.

Bark, Dennis L., ed. *The Red Orchestra: The Case of Africa.* Stanford, Calif.: Hoover Institution Press, 1988. 231 pp.

Barnett, Tony, and Abbas Abdelkarim, eds. *Sudan: State, Capital and Transformation.* London: Croom Helm, 1988. 213 pp.

Bindman, Geoffrey, ed. *South Africa: Human Rights and the Rule of the Law.* London: Pinter, 1988. 159 pp.

Campbell, Kurt M. *Southern Africa in Soviet Foreign Policy.* London: International Institute for Strategic Studies, 1987–1988. 77 pp.

Clay, Jason W., and Bonnie K. Holcomb. *Politics and the Ethiopian Famine, 1984–85.* Cambridge, Mass.: Cultural Survival, 1987. 237 pp.

Davies, Robert H. *The Struggle for South Africa: A Reference Guide To Movements, Organizations, and Institutions.* London: Zed Books, 1988. 65 pp.

Derrida, Jacques, and Mustapha Tlili, eds. *For Nelson Mandela.* New York: Seaver Books, 1987. 410 pp.

Essack, Karrim. *The Struggle For People's Power in South Africa.* Dar es Saalam: Thakers, 1986 or 1987. 110 pp. (both years listed in catalog)

Foy, Colm. *Cape Verde.* London: Pinter, 1988. 299 pp.

Feller, Bernard. *Les Etats d'Afrique noire de l'indépendance à 1980: essai de typologie.* Bern: Peter Lang, 1987. 311 pp.

Fleuhr-Lobban. *Islamic Law and Society in the Sudan.* London: Frank Cass, 1987. 282 pp.

Frankel, Philip, et al., eds. *State, Resistance, and Change in South Africa.* London: Croom Helm, 1988. 325 pp.

FRELIMO. *Proceedings of the Fourth Congress of the FRELIMO Party.* 4 vols. N.p., n.d. (Congress held in Maputo, Mozambique, 1983; proceedings published between 1983 and 1987)

Freund, Bill. *The African Worker.* New York: Cambridge University Press, 1988. 200 pp.

Gboyega, Alex. *Political Values and Local Government in Nigeria.* Lagos: Malthouse Press, 1987. 200 pp.

Glickman, Harvey. *The Crisis and Challenge of African Development.* New York: Greenwood Press, 1988. 257 pp.

Gorbunov, Iu. I., comp. *Namibia: A Struggle for Independence.* Moscow: Progress Publishers, 1988. 183 pp.

Hadjor, Kofi Buenor. *On Transforming Africa: A Discourse with Africa's Leaders.* Trenton, N.J.: Africa World Press, 1987. 164 pp.

Harbeson, John. *The Ethiopian Transformation: The Quest for the Post-Imperial State.* Boulder, Colo.: Westview Press, 1988. 239 pp.

Hope, Christopher. *White Boy Running.* London: Secker & Warburg, 1988. 273 pp.

Iliffe, John. *The African Poor: A History.* New York: Cambridge University Press, 1987. 387 pp.

Iyegha, David A. *Agricultural Crisis in Africa: The Nigerian Experience.* Lanham, Md.: University Press of America, 1988. 246 pp.

Jarmon, Charles. *Nigeria: Reorganization and Development since the Mid-Twentieth Century.* Leiden/New York: E. J. Brill, 1988. 169 pp.

Kalu, Viktor Eke. *The Nigerian Condition.* Enugu, Nigeria: The Fourth Dimension, 1987. 248 pp.

Kaplan, Robert D. *Surrender or Starve: The Wars Behind the Famine.* Boulder, Colo.: Westview Press, 1988. 188 pp.

Keller, Edmond J. *Revolutionary Ethiopia.* Bloomington, Ind.: Indiana University Press, 1988. 259 pp.

Kennedy, Paul M. *African Capitalism: The Struggle for Ascendancy.* New York: Cambridge University Press, 1988. 233 pp.

Kim, G. F., chief ed. *Natsional'no-osvoboditel'noe dvizhenie i ideologicheskaia bor'ba.* Moscow: Mysl', 1987. 357 pp.

Kitchen, Helen. *Angola, Mozambique and the West.* New York: Praeger, 1987. 168 pp.

———. *South Africa: In Transition to What?* New York: Praeger, 1988. 201 pp.

Kodjo, Edem. *Africa Tomorrow.* Translated by E. B. Khan. New York: Continuum, 1987. 301 pp.

Koval, B. I., and S. L. Agaev, eds. *Revoliutsionnye dvizheniia i imperialisticheskaia kontrrevoliutsiia.* Moscow: Nauka, 1987. 278 pp.

Legum, Colin. *The Battlefronts of Southern Africa*. New York: Africana, 1988. 451 pp.

Lewis, I. M. *A Modern History of Somalia*. Rev. ed. Boulder, Colo.: Westview Press, 1988. 297 pp.

Lobachenko, Vadim. *Byli efiopskoi revoliutsii*. Moscow: Sovetskaia Rossia, 1987. 260 pp.

Lonsdale, John. *South Africa in Question*. Portsmouth, N.H.: Heinemann, 1988. 244 pp.

Makinwa, P. Kofo, and A. O. Ozo, eds. *The Urban Poor in Nigeria*. Ibadan: Evans Brothers (Nigeria Publishers), 1987. 413 pp.

Markakis, John. *National and Class Conflict in the Horn of Africa*. New York: Cambridge University Press, 1987. 314 pp.

Miles, William F. S. *Elections in Nigeria: A Grassroots Perspective*. Boulder, Colo.: Lynne Rienner, 1988. 168 pp.

Murray, Martin J. *South Africa: Time of Agony, Time of Destiny—The Upsurge in Popular Protest*. London: Verso, 1987. 496 pp.

Nafziger, E. Wayne. *Inequality in Africa: Political Elites, Proletariat, Peasants, and the Poor*. New York: Cambridge University Press, 1988. 204 pp.

Nwankwo, Arthur Agwuncha. *The Military Option to Democracy: Class, Power, and Violence in Nigerian Politics*. Enugu, Nigeria: Fourth Dimension, 1987. 202 pp.

Nyong'o, Peter Anyang, ed. *Popular Struggles for Democracy in Africa*. London: Zed Books, 1987. 288 pp.

Nzongola-Ntalaja. *Revolution and Counter-revolution in Africa: Essays in Contemporary Politics*. London: Institute for African Alternatives–Zed Books, 1987. 130 pp.

Obot, J. U. *Nigeria: The People and Their Heritage*. Calabar: Wusen, 1987. 339 pp.

Olugbemi, Stephen O., ed. *Alternative Political Futures for Nigeria*. [Port Harcourt?]: Nigerian Political Science Association, 1987. 563 pp.

Phimister, I. R. *An Economic and Social History of Zimbabwe, 1890–1948*. New York: Longman, 1988. 336 pp.

Reddy, E. S., ed. *Oliver Tambo and the Struggle Against Apartheid*. New Delhi: Sterling, 1987. 172 pp.

Rimmer, Douglas. *Rural Transformation in Tropical Africa*. London: Belhaven, 1988. 177 pp.

Stadler, Alfred W. *The Political Economy of Modern South Africa*. London: Croom Helm, 1987. 197 pp.

Stoneman, Colin, and Lionel Cliffe. *Zimbabwe*. New York: CUSA, 1988. 220 pp.

Tambo, Oliver. *Preparing for Power: Oliver Tambo Speaks*. New York: George Braziller, 1987. 284 pp.

van Vuuren, D. J., et al., eds. *South African Election 1987*. Pinetown, South Africa: Owen Burgess, 1987. 459 pp.

Wubneh, Mulatu, and Yohannis Abate. *Ethiopia: Transition and Development in the Horn of Africa*. Boulder, Colo.: Westview Press, 1988. 224 pp.

AMERICAS

Amnesty International. *Guatemala: The Human Rights Record*. London: AI Publications, 1987. 234 pp.

Anderson, James. *Sendero Luminoso: A New Revolutionary Model?* London: Institute for the Study of Terrorism, 1987. 87 pp.

Azicri, Max. *Cuba: Politics, Economics and Society*. New York: Pinter, 1988. 299 pp.

Barraclough, Solon, et al. *Aid that Counts: The Western Contribution to Development and Survival in Nicaragua*. Birmingham: Transnational Institute, 1988. 157 pp.

Barros-Lémez, Alvaro. *Arismendi: forjar el viento*. Montevideo: Monte Sexto, 1987. 232 pp.

Blasier, Cole. *The Giant's Rival: The USSR and Latin America*. Rev. ed. Pittsburgh, Pa.: The University of Pittsburgh Press, 1988. 240 pp.

Brenner, Philip. *From Confrontation to Negotiation: U.S. Relations with Cuba*. Boulder, Colo.: Westview Press, 1988. 118 pp.

Burrowes, Reynold A. *Revolution and Rescue in Grenada*. Westport, Conn.: Greenwood Press, 1988. 180 pp.

Bushuev, V. G. *Latinskaia America—SShA: revoliutsiia i kontr-revoliutsiia*. Moscow: Mezhdunarodnye otnosheniia, 1987. 276 pp.

Caceres, Jorge, et al. eds. *El Salvador: una historia sin lecciones*. San José, Costa Rica: Ediciones FLASCO, 1988. 300 pp.

Chin, Henk E., and Hans Buddingh. *Surinam: Politics, Economics and Society*. London: Pinter, 1987. 192 pp.

Clay, Jason W., and Bonnie K. Holcomb. *Politics and the Ethiopian Famine, 1984-85*. Cambridge, Mass.: Cultural Survival, 1987. 237 pp.

Close, David. *Nicaragua, Politics, Economics and Society*. London: Pinter, 1988. 239 pp.

Cruz, Arturo J. *Nicaragua's Continuing Struggle*. New York: Freedom House, 1988. 58 pp.

Ellner, Steve. *Venezuela's Movimiento al Socialismo: From Guerilla Defeat to Innovative Politics*. Durham, N.C.: Duke University Press, 1988. 262 pp.

Falcoff, Mark, Arturo Valenzuela, and Susan Kaufman Purcell. *Chile: Prospects for Democracy*. New York: Council on Foreign Relations, 1988. 80 pp.

Fermoselle, Rafael. *The Evolution of the Cuban Military: 1942–1986*. Miami, Fla.: Ediciones Universal, 1987. 585 pp.

Garthoff, Raymond L. *Reflections on the Cuban Missile Crisis*. Washington, D.C.: Brookings Institution, 1988. 159 pp.

Girardi, Giulio. *Sandinismo, Marxismo, Cristianismo: La confluencia*. Managua, Nicaragua: Ediciones Nuevomar, 1987. 457 pp.

Hamilton, Nora, et al. *Crisis in Central America: Regional Dynamics and U.S. Policy in the 1980s*. Boulder, Colo.: Westview Press, 1988. 272 pp.

Harnecker, Marta. *Fidel Castro's Political Strategy: From Moncada to Victory*. New York: Pathfinder, 1987. 187 pp.

Hartlyn, Jonathan. *The Politics of Coalition Rule in Colombia*. New York: Cambridge University Press, 1988. 332 pp.

Herman, Donald L., ed. *Democracy in Latin America: Colombia and Venezuela*. New York: Praeger, 1988. 344 pp.

Isserman, Maurice. *If I Had a Hammer: The Death of the Old Left and the Birth of the New*. New York: Basic Books, 1987. 250 pp.

Izquierda Unida. Comision de Educacion. *Plan de educacion de Izquierda Unida*. Lima, Peru: Comision de la educacio, I.U., 1987. 201 pp.

Kaufman, Edy. *Crisis in Allende's Chile: New Perspectives*. New York: Praeger, 1988. 416 pp.

Kryzanek, Michael J., and Howard J. Wiarda. *The Politics of External Influence in the Dominican Republic*. New York: Praeger, 1988. 183 pp.

Lagos Escobar, Ricardo. *Hacia la democracia: Los socialistas en el Chile de hoy*. Santiago de Chile: Ediciones Documentas, 1987. 77 pp.

Lewis, Gordon K. *Grenada: The Jewel Despoiled*. Baltimore, Md.: The Johns Hopkins University Press, 1987. 492 pp.

Llovio-Mendez, José Luis. *My Hidden Life as a Revolutionary in Cuba*. New York: Bantam Books, 1988. 466 pp.

Lozza, Arturo Marcos. *Atentad a Pinochet: El FPMR Fija Posicion: Chile Sublevado II*. Buenos Aires: Editorial Antarca, 1987. 81 pp.

Mercado, Rogger. *Algo mas sobre Sendero: Teoria y tactica, violencia, represion y desparecidos: Documentos*. 2 vols. Lima, Peru: Ediciones de Cultura, 1987.

Oseguera de Ochoa, Margarita. *Honduras hoy: Sociedad y crisis politica*. Tegucigalpa: Centro de Documentacion de Honduras, Coordinadora Regional de Investigaciones Economicas y Sociales, 1987. 221 pp.

Painter, James. *Guatemala: False Hope, False Freedom: The Rich, the Poor and the Christian Democrats*. London: Catholic Institute for International Relations, Latin America Bureau, 1987. 134 pp.

Perez, Louis A. *Cuba: Between Reform and Revolution*. New York: Oxford University Press, 1988. 504 pp.

Purcell, Susan Kaufman. *Mexico in Transition: Implications for U.S. Policy*. New York: Council on Foreign Relations, 1988. 157 pp.

Radu, Michael, ed. *Violence and the Latin American Revolutionaries*. New Brunswick, N.J.: USA Transaction Books, 1988. 156 pp.

Reimann, Elisabeth. *Yo fui un contra: Historia de un "Paladin de la Libertad."* Managua, Nicaragua: Editorial Vanguardia, 1987. 349 pp.

Roca, Sergio G., ed. *Socialist Cuba: Past Interpretations and Future Challenges*. Boulder, Colo.: Westview press, 1988. 253 pp.

Rudolph, James D. *Cuba: Country Study*. 3d ed. Washington, D.C.: American University, Foreign Area Studies, 1987. 368 pp.

Skidmore, Thomas E. *The Politics of Military Rule in Brazil*. New York: Oxford University Press, 1988. 420 pp.

United States. Central Intelligence Agency. *Directory of the Republic of Nicaragua* (LDA 88-13399). Washington, D.C.: National Technical Information Service, September 1988. 71 pp.

United States. Department of State. *Nicaraguan Biographies: A Resource Book* (Special Report no. 174). Washington, D.C.: Dept. of State, January 1988. 98 pp.

Wooton, Leland M. *A Revolution in Arrears: The Development Crisis in Latin America*. New York: Praeger, 1988. 207 pp.

ASIA AND THE PACIFIC

Ablin, David A., and Marlowe Hood, eds. *The Cambodian Agony.* Armonk, N.Y.: M. E. Sharpe, 1987. 418 pp.

American Enterprise Institute. *China in the Year 2000: Economic and Security Implications.* Seoul, Korea: Ilhae Institute/AEI, 1987. 198 pp.

Beresford, Melanie. *Vietnam: Politics, Economics and Society.* London: Pinter, 1988. 242 pp.

Bidet, Jacques, and Jacques Texier. *Le Marxisme au Japon.* Paris: L'Harmattan, 1987. 211 pp.

Bouton, Marshall M. *India Briefing, 1987.* Boulder, Colo.: Westview Press, 1987. 222 pp.

Chen, King C. *China's War with Vietnam, 1979.* Stanford, Calif.: Hoover Institution Press, 1987. 234 pp.

Christnacht, Alain. *La Nouvelle-Calédonie.* Paris: La Documentation Française, 1987. 143 pp.

Communist Party of Vietnam. *Sixth National Congress: Documents.* Hanoi: Foreign Languages Publishing House, 1987. 207 pp.

Davidson, Phillip. *Vietnam at War: The History 1946–75.* Novato, Calif.: Presidio Press, 1988. 838 pp.

Derbyshire, Ian. *Politics in China.* New York: Cambridge University Press, 1988. 138 pp.

Fairbanks, John King. *China Watch.* Cambridge and London: Harvard University Press, 1987. 227 pp.

Harding, Harry. *China and Northeast Asia.* Lanham, Md.: University Press of America/New York: The Asia Society, 1988. 81 pp.

———. *China's Second Revolution: Reform after Mao.* Washington, D.C.: Brookings Institution, 1987. 369 pp.

Joffe, Ellis. *The Chinese Army After Mao.* Cambridge, Mass.: Harvard University Press, 1987. 210 pp.

Kane, Anthony J., ed. *China Briefing.* Boulder, Colo.: Westview Press, 1988. 179 pp.

Kim, G. F., chief ed. *Istoriia sotsialisticheskoi ekonomiki MNR.* Moscow: Nauka, 1987. 374 pp.

Kim Ir Sen [Kim Il-Sung]. *Izbrannye proizvedeniia.* Moscow: Politizdat, 1987. 184 pp.

Ladány, László. *The Communist Party of China and Marxism, 1925–1985.* Stanford, Calif.: Hoover Institution Press, 1988. 588 pp.

Lampton, David M., and Catherine H. Keyser, eds. *China's Global Presence.* Washington, D.C.: American Enterprise Institute, 1988. 256 pp.

Lin, Chong-Pin. *China's Nuclear Weapons Strategy.* Lexington, Mass.: Lexington Books/D.C. Heath, 1988. 272 pp.

Manning, Robert, et al., eds. *The Vietnam Experience.* Vol. 25, *War in the Shadows.* Boston: Boston Publishing, 1988.

Matveeva, G. S. *Mongol'skaia Narodnaia Respublika. v sisteme sotsialisticheskoi ekonomicheskoi integratsii.* Moscow: Nauka, 1987. 245 pp.

Merrill, John, and Robert Carlin. *D.P.R. Korea.* New York: CUSA, 1988. 220 pp.

Nikol'skii, A. V., chief ed. *XIX s'ezd Mongol'skoi Narodno-revoliutsionnoi partii.* Moscow: Politizdat, 1987. 168 pp.

Nossiter, T. J. *Marxist State Government in India.* New York: CUSA, 1988. 212 pp.

Pike, Douglas, ed. *Inventory of Vietnamese Documents.* 2 vols. Berkeley, Calif.: Indochina Archive, 1988.

Pye, Lucien W. *The Mandarin and the Cadre: China's Political Cultures.* Ann Arbor, Mich.: Center for Chinese Studies, University of Michigan, 1988. 204 pp.

Rabushka, Alvin. *The New China: Comparative Economic Development in Mainland China, Taiwan and Hong Kong.* Boulder, Colo.: Westview Press, 1987. 254 pp.

Robertson, Myles. *Soviet Policy Towards Japan.* New York: Cambridge University Press, 1988. 240 pp.

Ross, Robert S. *The Indochina Tangle: China's Vietnam Policy.* New York: Columbia University Press, 1988. 361 pp.

Rozman, Gilbert. *The Chinese Debate About Soviet Socialism, 1978–1985.* Princeton, N.J.: Princeton University Press, 1987. 407 pp.

Sanders, Alan J. K. *Mongolia.* Boulder, Colo.: Lynne Rienner, 1987. 179 pp.

Schell, Orville. *Discos and Democracy: China in the Throes of Reform.* New York: Pantheon, 1988. 384 pp.

Shaw, Yu-Ming, ed. *Changes and Continuities in Chinese Communism.* 2 vols. Boulder, Colo.: Westview Press, 1988.

Snow, Philip. *The Star Raft: China's Encounter with Africa.* London: Weidenfeld & Nicholson, 1988. 250 pp.

Somsakdi Xuto, ed. *Government and Politics of Thailand.* New York: Oxford University Press, 1987. 243 pp.

Stavis, Benedict. *China's Political Reforms: An Interim Report.* New York: Praeger, 1988. 158 pp.

Uhalley, Stephen, Jr. *A History of the Chinese Communist Party.* Stanford, Calif.: Hoover Institution Press, 1988. 340 pp.

United States. Central Intelligence Agency. Director-ate of Intelligence. *Directory of Officials of the Democratic People's Republic of Korea* (LDA 88-10201). Washington, D.C.: NTIS, April 1988. 113 pp.

————. *Directory of Chinese Officials and Organiza-tions.* (LDA 88-12114). Washington, D.C.: NTIS, May 1988. 160 pp.

Yathay, Pin, and John Man. *Stay Alive my Son.* New York: The Free Press (Macmillan), 1987. 240 pp.

Young, John Robert. *The Dragon's Teeth: Inside the PLA.* New York: Orion Books, 1987. 224 pp.

Vent Sauvage de Eng Hoa. Paris: Editions Ramsay, 1988. 207 pp.

Willenson, Kim. *The Bad War: An Oral History of the Vietnam War.* New York: New American Library, 1987. 451 pp.

Wu, Yuan-li, et al., eds. *Human Rights in the People's Republic of China.* Boulder, Colo.: Westview Press, 1988. 332 pp.

Zasloff, Joseph J., ed. *Postwar Indochina: Old En-emies and New Allies.* Washington, D.C.: Center for the Study of Foreign Affairs, Foreign Service Institute, 1988. 290 pp.

EASTERN EUROPE

Bogomolov, O. T., chief ed. *Sotsialisticheskoe sodru-zhestvo i problemy otnoshenii vostok-zapad v 80-e gody.* Moscow: Politizdat, 1987. 295 pp.

Borsody, Stephen, ed. *The Hungarians: A Divided Nation.* Columbus, Ohio: Slavica, 1988. 404 pp.

Borsányi, György, and János Kende. *The History of the Working Class Movement in Hungary.* Buda-pest: Corvina, 1988. 225 pp.

Brown, J. F. *Eastern Europe and the Communist Rule.* Durham, N.C.: Duke University Press, 1988. 562 pp.

Búza, Márton. *Trade Unions in Hungary.* Budapest: Népszava, 1988. 271 pp.

Cada, Václav. *The Birth of Czechoslovakia.* Prague: Orbis Press Agency, 1987. 70 pp.

Childs, David. *The GDR: Moscow's German Ally.* 2d ed. Winchester, Mass.: Unwin Hyman, 1988. 384 pp.

Connor, Walter D. *Socialism's Dilemmas: State and Society in the Soviet Bloc.* New York: Columbia University Press, 1988. 322 pp.

Crampton, R. J. *A Short History of Modern Bulgaria.* Cambridge, Engl.: Cambridge University Press, 1987. 221 pp.

Crowther, William E. *The Political Economy of Roma-nian Socialism.* New York: Praeger, 1988. 216 pp.

Czechoslovak Socialist Republic. *The Constitution of the Czechoslovak Socialist Republic.* Prague: Orbis Press Agency, 1987. 128 pp.

Czechoslovakia and Human Rights. Prague: Orbis Press Agency, 1988. 109 pp.

Dawisha, Karen. *Eastern Europe, Gorbachev and Re-form: The Great Challenge.* New York: Cambridge University Press, 1988. 268 pp.

Dennis, Mike. *The German Democratic Republic.* New York: Pinter, 1988. 412 pp.

Fitzpatrick, Catherine, and Jane Fleischman. *From Below: Independent Peace and Environment Move-ments in Eastern Europe and the Soviet Union.* New York: A Helsinki Watch Report, 1987. 263 pp.

Gella, Aleksander. *Development of Class Structure in Eastern Europe.* Buffalo, N.Y.: SUNY Press, 1988. 352 pp.

Gross, Jan T. *Revolution from Abroad: The Soviet Conquest of Poland's Western Ukraine and Western Belorussia.* Princeton, N.J.: Princeton University Press, 1988. 334 pp.

Hahn, Werner G. *Democracy in a Communist Party: The Polish Experience since 1980.* New York: Co-lumbia University Press, 1987. 368 pp.

Haraszti, Miklós. *The Velvet Prison: Artists under State Socialism.* New York: Basic Books/New Re-public Books, 1987. 162 pp.

Havel, Václav. *Letters to Olga, June 1979–September 1982.* Translated by Paul Wilson. New York: Alfred E. Knopf, 1988. 397 pp.

Heitzer, H., ed. *DDR Geschichte der Übergangs-periode, 1945–1961.* East Berlin: Akademie Ver-lag, 1987. 322 pp.

Hodos, George H. *Show Trials: Stalinist Purges in Eastern Europe.* New York: Praeger, 1987. 193 pp.

Holzweissig, Günter. *Sport und Politik in der DDR.* West Berlin: Verlag G. Holzapfel, 1988. 148 pp.

Hoxha, Enver. *Selected Works, July 1980–December 1984.* Vol. 7. Tirana: 8 Nëntori Publishing House, 1987. 865 pp.

Huemmler, Hans. *Sozialismus in der DDR: Gesell-schaftsstrategie mit dem Blick auf das Jahr 2000.* East Berlin: Dietz, 1987. 320 pp.

Jaenicke, Sieglinde. *Hab ich auch was zu sagen? Nachdenken über Demokratie.* East Berlin: Dietz, 1988. 108 pp.

Jeffries, Ian, and Manfred Melzer, eds. *The East Ger-

man Economy. London: Croom Helm, 1987. 328 pp.

Kittrie, Nicholas N., and Ivan Völgyes, eds. *The Uncertain Future: Gorbachev's Eastern Bloc*. New York: Paragon House, 1988. 281 pp.

Kolankiewicz, George, and Paul Lewis. *Poland: Politics, Economics and Society*. London: Pinter, 1988. 210 pp.

Lapp, Peter Joachim. *Die "befreundeten Parteien" der SED*. Cologne: Verlag Wissenschaft und Politik, 1988. 224 pp.

Lawyers Committee for Human Rights. *Repression Disguised as Law: Human Rights in Poland*. New York: LCHR, 1987. 110 pp.

Lepak, Keith John. *Prelude to Solidarity: Poland and the Politics of the Gierek Regime*. New York: Columbia University Press, 1988. 288 pp.

Maier, Harry. *Innovation oder Stagnation*. Cologne: Deutscher Instituts-Verlag, 1987. 248 pp.

Marer, Paul, and Wlodzimierz Siwinski, eds. *Creditworthiness and Reform in Poland: Western and Polish Perspectives*. Bloomington, Ind.: Indiana University Press, 1988. 348 pp.

Matschke, Werner. *Die industrielle Entwicklung in der sowjetischen Besatzungszone Deutschlands von 1945–1948*. West Berlin: Verlag Arno Spitz, 1988. 389 pp.

McFarlane, Bruce. *Yugoslavia: Politics, Economy and Society*. London: Pinter, 1988. 262 pp.

McIntyre, Robert J. *Bulgaria: Politics, Economy and Society*. London: Pinter, 1988. 201 pp.

Mittag, Günter. *Die Arbeit der Partei zur Verwirklichung der vom XI. Parteitag der SED beschlossenen ökonomischen Strategie*. East Berlin: Vortrag an der Hochschule "Karl Marx" beim ZK der SED, 1987. 96 pp.

Pehe, Jiri, ed. *The Prague Spring: A Mixed Legacy*. New York: Freedom House, 1988. 223 pp.

Rothschild, Joseph. *Return to Diversity: A Political History of Eastern Europe Since World War II*. New York: Oxford University Press, 1988. 257 pp.

Rytlewski, Ralf. *Die Deutsche Demokratische Republik in Zahlen, 1945/49–1980*. Munich: Verlag C. H. Beck, 1987. 178 pp.

Sirc, Ljubo (foreword). *Poland: Stagnation, Collapse or Growth?* London: The Centre for Research into Communist Economies, 1988. 100 pp.

Skalnik Leff, Carol. *National Conflict in Czechoslovakia*. Princeton, N.J.: Princeton University Press, 1988. 304 pp.

Staar, Richard F. *Communist Regimes in Eastern Eu-*

rope. 5th ed. Stanford, Calif.: Hoover Institution Press, 1988. 304 pp.

Stoianov, P. *Sotsial'no-pedagogicheskaia sistema v Narodnoi Respublike Bolgarii*. Sofia: Izdatel'stvo Pedagogika, 1988. 224 pp.

Swidlicki, Andrzej. *The Political Trials in Poland, 1981–86*. London: Croom Helm, 1988. 426 pp.

Szent-Miklósy, István. *With the Hungarian Independence Movement, 1943–1947: An Eyewitness Account*. New York: Praeger, 1988. 280 pp.

Teichova, Alice. *The Czechoslovak Economy, 1918–1980*. London: Routledge, 1988. 178 pp.

Tismaneanu, Vladimir. *The Crisis of Marxist Ideology in Eastern Europe: The Poverty of Utopia*. London: Routledge, 1988. 208 pp.

Toma, Peter A. *Socialist Authority: The Hungarian Experience*. New York: Praeger, 1988. 176 pp.

Toranska, Teresa. *"Them": Stalin's Polish Puppets*. New York: Harper & Row, 1987. 384 pp.

United States. Central Intelligence Agency. Directorate of Intelligence. *Directory of Bulgarian Officials*. (A Reference Aid, LDA 88-12740) Washington, D.C.: NTIS, October 1988. 127 pp.

Vaculik, Ludvik. *A Cup of Coffee with My Interrogator*. New York: Readers International/Persea Press, 1987. 128 pp.

Weber, Herman. *Die DDR, 1945–1986*. Munich: Oldenbourg Verlag, 1988. 253 pp.

Zloch-Christy, Iliana. *Debt Problems of Eastern Europe*. New York: Cambridge University Press, 1987. 220 pp.

USSR

Abraham, Richard. *Alexander Kerensky: The First Love of the Revolution*. New York: Columbia University Press, 1987. 503 pp.

Aganbegyan, Abel. *The Economic Challenge of Perestroika*. Bloomington, Ind.: Indiana University Press, 1988. 248 pp.

Babakov, A. A. *Vooruzhennye sily SSSR posle voiny, 1945–1986*. Moscow: Voenizdat, 1987. 287 pp.

Bahry, Donna. *Outside Moscow: Power, Politics and Budgetary Policy in the Soviet Republics*. New York: Columbia University Press, 1987. 236 pp.

Berliner, Joseph S. *Soviet Industry from Stalin to Gorbachev*. Ithaca, N.Y.: Cornell University Press, 1988. 306 pp.

Bialer, Seweryn, ed. *Politics, Society and Nationality*

Inside Gorbachev's Russia. Boulder, Colo.: Westview Press, 1988. 180 pp.

—— and Michael Mandelbaum, eds. *Gorbachev's Russian and American Foreign Policy*. Boulder, Colo.: Westview Press, 1988. 510 pp.

Biloczerkowycz, Jaroslaw. *Soviet Ukrainian Dissent: A Study of Political Alienation*. Boulder, Colo.: Westview Press, 1988. 242 pp.

Bobylev, P. N., chief ed. *Sovetskie vooruzhennye sily*. Moscow: Politizdat, 1987. 415 pp.

Brunner, Georg, and Allan Kagedan, eds. *Minderheiten in der Sowjetunion und das Völkerrecht*. Cologne: Markus Verlag, 1988. 219 pp.

Burov, A. S. *Ekonomicheskoe sotrudnichestvo SSSR so stranami sotsializma*. Moscow: Mezhdunarodnye otnosheniia, 1987. 302 pp.

Carrère d'Encausse, Hélène. *Big Brother: the Soviet Union and Eastern Europe*. New York: Holmes & Meier, 1988. 336 pp.

Chimitdorzhiev, Sh. B. *Rossiia i Mongoliia*. Moscow: Nauka, 1987. 235 pp.

Churchward, L. G. *Soviet Socialism: Social and Political Essays*. New York: Routledge & Kegan Paul/Methuen, 1988. 216 pp.

Daniloff, Nicholas. *Two Lives, One Russia*. Boston: Houghton Mifflin, 1988. 307 pp.

Derbyshire, Ian. *Politics in the Soviet Union: From Brezhnev to Gorbachev*. New York: Cambridge University Press, 1988. 138 pp.

Dziak, John J. *Chekisty*. Lexington, Mass.: Lexington Books, 1987. 234 pp.

Eklof, Ben. *Soviet Briefing: Gorbachev and the Reform Period*. Boulder, Colo.: Westview Press, 1988. 128 pp.

Fedotov, M. A. *Sovety i pressa*. Moscow: Iurizdat, 1987. 171 pp.

Frankland, Mark. *The Sixth Continent: Mikhail Gorbachev and the Soviet Union*. New York: Harper & Row, 1987. 292 pp.

Fröhlich, Sergej. *General Wlassow: Russen und Deutsche zwischen Hitler und Stalin*. Cologne: Markus Verlag, 1987. 402 pp.

Ginsburgs, George. *A Calendar of Soviet Treaties, 1974–1980*. Boston: Martinus Nijhoff, 1987. 666 pp.

Glazov, Yuri. *To Be Or Not To Be In The Party*. Boston: Kluwer Academic Publishers, 1988. 230 pp.

Golan, Galia. *The Soviet Union and National Liberation Movements in the Third World*. Winchester, Mass.: Unwin Hyman, 1988. 368 pp.

Gorbachev, M. S. *Speeches and Writings*. Vol. 2. New York: Pergamon Press, 1987. 230 pp.

Gorokhov, V. M., chief ed. *Partiinoe rukovodstvo sredstvami massovoi informatsii i propagandy*. Moscow: Mysl', 1987. 174 pp.

Gromyko, Anatoly A. *Pamiatnoe*. 2 vols. Moscow: Politizdat, 1988.

—— and Martin Hellman. *Breakthrough: Emerging New Thinking*. New York: Walker, 1988. 281 pp.

Hayit, Baymirza. *Islam and Turkestan under Russian Rule*. Istanbul: Can Matbaa, 1987. 549 pp.

Heller, Mikhail. *Cogs in the Wheel: The Formation of Soviet Man*. New York: Knopf, 1988. 282 pp.

Hewett, Edward A. *Reforming the Soviet Economy*. Washington, D.C.: Brookings Institution, 1988. 404 pp.

Horak, Stephen. *Russia, the USSR and Eastern Europe: A Bibliographic Guide to English Language Publications*. Littleton, Colo.: Libraries Unlimited, 1987. 273 pp.

Kanet, Roger A., ed. *The Soviet Union, Eastern Europe and the Third World*. New York: Cambridge University Press, 1988. 233 pp.

Knight, Amy W. *The KGB: Police and the Politics of the Soviet Union*. Boston: Unwin Hyman, 1988. 348 pp.

Laidi, Zaki. *The Third World and The Soviet Union*. London: Zed Books, 1988. 125 pp.

Laird, Robbin F., ed. *Soviet Foreign Policy*. New York: The Academy of Political Science, 1987. 276 pp.

Laird, Roy D., and Betty A. Laird. *A Soviet Lexicon: Important Concepts, Terms, and Phrases*. Lexington, Mass.: Lexington Books, 1988. 201 pp.

Levchenko, Stanislav. *On the Wrong Side: My Life in the KGB*. Washington, D.C.: Pergamon-Brassey's, 1988. 244 pp.

Lewin, Moshe. *The Gorbachev Phenomenon: A Historical Interpretation*. Berkeley, Calif.: University of California Press, 1988. 192 pp.

Liska, George. *Rethinking US-Soviet Relations*. New York: Basil Blackwell, 1987. 231 pp.

Liubskii, M. S. *Mezhdunarodnye kreditnye otnosheniia stran SEV*. Moscow: Mezhdunarodnye otnosheniia, 1988. 260 pp.

Marantz, Paul. *From Lenin to Gorbachev: Changing Soviet Perspectives on East-West Relations*. Ottawa: The Institute for Peace and Security, 1988. 91 pp.

Medvedev, Zhores, A. *Soviet Agriculture*. New York: Norton, 1987. 464 pp.

Meissner, Boris. *Aussenpolitik und Völkerrecht der Sowjetunion.* Cologne: Wissenschaft und Politik, 1987. 358 pp.

———. *Die Sowjetunion im Umbruch: Historische Hintergründe, Ziele und Grenzen der Reformpolitik Gorbatschows.* Stuttgart: Deutsche Verlags-Anstalt, 1988. 392 pp.

Millar, James R., ed. *Politics, Work, and Daily Life in the USSR: A Survey of Former Soviet Citizens.* New York: Cambridge University Press, 1987. 423 pp.

Miller, R. F., J. H. Miller, and T. H. Rigby, eds. *Gorbachev at the Helm: A New Era of Soviet Politics?* London: Croom Helm/New York: Methuen, 1987. 251 pp.

Naylor, Thomas H. *Gorbachev's Strategy: Opening a Closed Society.* Lexington, Mass.: Lexington Books, 1988. 253 pp.

Negmatov, N. N., and A. I. Vishnevskii, eds. *Istoricheskii progress sotsialisticheskikh natsii.* Moscow: Mysl', 1987. 335 pp.

Oberg, James F. *Uncovering Soviet Disasters: Exploring the Limits of Glasnost.* New York: Random House, 1988. 317 pp.

Pfeiler, Wolfgang. *Deutsche und politische Optionen der Sowjetunion.* Melle: Verlag Ernst Knoth, 1987. 185 pp.

Pinkus, Benjamin, and Ingeborg Fleischhauer. *Die Deutschen in der Sowjetunion.* Baden-Baden: Nomos, 1987. 599 pp.

Poljanski, Nikolai. *Rote Diplomatie: Gespräche mit Urs Graf.* Zurich: Presdok, 1988. 168 pp.

Ponomarev, L. N. *Partiinaia rabotka i ekonomika.* Moscow: Sovetskaia Rossiia, 1987. 303 pp.

Potichnyj, Peter J., ed. *The Soviet Union: Party and Society.* New York: Cambridge University Press, 1988, 272 pp.

Roeder, Philip G. *Soviet Political Dynamics.* New York: Harper & Row, 1988. 456 pp.

Ross, Cameron. *Local Government in the Soviet Union: Problems of Implementation and Control.* London: Croom Helm, 1987. 229 pp.

Rowen, Henry S., and Charles Wolf, Jr., eds. *The Future of The Soviet Empire.* New York: St. Martin's Press, 1988. 346 pp.

Sacks, Michael Paul, and Jerry G. Pankhurst, eds. *Understanding Soviet Society.* Boston: Unwin Hyman, 1988. 268 pp.

Shearman, Peter. *The Soviet Union and Cuba.* London: Routledge & Kegan Paul, 1987. 103 pp.

Shtromas, Alexander, and Morton Kaplan, eds. *The Soviet Union and the Challenge of the Future.* New York: Paragon, 1988. 553 pp.

Simon, Gerhard, ed. *Weltmacht Sowjetunion: Umbrüche–Kontinuitäten–Perspektiven.* Cologne: Verlag Wissenschaft und Politik, 1987. 257 pp.

Smirnov, G. L., and F. Grobart, eds. *Internatsional'noe sotrudnichestvo KPSS i KP Kuby.* Moscow: Politizdat, 1988. 350 pp.

Staar, Richard F., ed. *The Future Information Revolution in the USSR.* New York: Crane Russak, 1988. 217 pp.

Slusser, Robert M. *Stalin in October: The Man Who Missed the Revolution.* Baltimore, Md.: Johns Hopkins University Press, 1987. 281 pp.

Sussman, Leonard R., moderator. *Glasnost: How Open?* New York: Freedom House, 1988. 142 pp.

Tatu, Michel. *Gorbatchev: L'USSR, va-t-elle changer?* Paris: Centurion, 1987. 269 pp.

Tucker, Robert C. *Political Culture and Leadership in Soviet Russia: From Lenin to Gorbachev.* New York: Norton, 1987. 214 pp.

Union of Soviet Socialist Republics. *Dokumenty i materialy XX s'ezda Vsesoiuznogo Leninskogo Kommunisticheskogo Soiuza Molodezhi.* Moscow: Molodaia Gvardiia, 1988. 191 pp.

Vlasov, A. V., ed. *Sovetskaia militsiia: istoriia i sovremennost', 1917–1987.* Moscow: Iurizdat, 1987. 334 pp.

Volkogonov, Dmitrii A. *The Army and Social Progress.* Moscow: Progress Publishers, 1987. 159 pp.

Voronitsyn, Sergei, comp. *A Directory of Prominent Soviet Economists, Sociologists, and Demographers by Institutional Affiliation.* Munich: Radio Liberty, 1987. 118 pp.

Weichhardt, Reiner, ed. *The Soviet Economy: A New Course?* Brussels: NATO, 1987. 352 pp.

Wiles, Peter, ed. *The Soviet Economy on the Brink of Reform.* Winchester, Mass.: Unwin Hyman, 1988. 352 pp.

THE MIDDLE EAST AND NORTH AFRICA

Anwar, Raja. *The Tragedy of Afghanistan: A First Hand Account.* London: Verso Books, 1988. 286 pp.

Aronson, Geoffrey. *Creating Facts: Israel, Palestinians and The West Bank.* Washington, D.C.: Institute for Palestine Studies, 1987. 334 pp.

Barakat, Halim. *Toward a Viable Lebanon.* Washington, D.C.: Center for Contemporary Arab Studies and Croom Helm, 1988. 387 pp.

Bonner, Arthur. *Among the Afghans*. Durham, N.C.: Duke University Press, 1987. 366 pp.

Botman, Selma. *The Rise of Egyptian Communism*. Syracuse, N.Y.: Syracuse University Press, 1988. 212 pp.

Braun, Dieter, and Karlernst Ziem. *Afghanistan: Sowjetische Machtpolitik–Islamische Selbstbestimmung*. Baden-Baden: Nomos Verlag, 1988. 308 pp.

Burrowes, Robert D. *The Yemen Arab Republic: The Politics of Development, 1962–1970*. Boulder, Colo.: Westview Press, 1987. 159 pp.

Cate, Curtis, ed. *Afghanistan: The Terrible Decade, 1978–1988*. New York: American Foundation for Resistance International, 1988. 84 pp.

Chatterji, Nikshoy C. *A History of the Modern Middle East*. New York: Envoy Press, 1987. 638 pp.

Collelo, Thomas, ed. *Syria: A Country Study*. Washington, D.C.: U.S. Department of the Army, 1988. 334 pp.

Farouk-Sluglett, Marion, and Peter Sluglett. *Iraq since 1958: From Revolution to Dictatorship*. London: KPI, 1987. 332 pp.

Ghaus, Abdul Samat. *The Fall of Afghanistan*. Washington, D.C.: Pergamon-Brassey, 1988. 219 pp.

Khalaf, Samir. *Lebanon's Predicament*. New York: Columbia University Press, 1987. 328 pp.

Klass, Rosanne. *Afghanistan: The Great Game Revisited*. New York: Freedom House, 1987. 519 pp.

Menteshashvili, Z. A. *Sotsial'noe razvitie nezavisimogo Marokko: traditsii i sovremennost'*. Moskva: Nauka, 1988. 263 pp.

Rubin, Barnett R. *A Nation Is Dying: Afghanistan under the Soviets, 1979–1987*. Chicago: Northwestern University Press, 1988. 179 pp.

Spiegel, Steven L., Mark Heller, and Jacob Goldberg, eds. *The Soviet-American Competition in the Middle East*. Lexington, Mass.: Lexington Press, 1988. 392 pp.

Urban, Mark. *War in Afghanistan*. London: Macmillan, 1988. 248 pp.

WESTERN EUROPE

Alba, Victor. *Spanish Marxism versus Soviet Communism: A History of the POUM*. New Brunswick, N.J.: Transaction Books, 1988. 323 pp.

Alles, Wolfgang. *Zur Politik und Geschichte der deutschen Trotzkyisten ab 1930*. Frankfurt: ISP-Verlag, 1987. 295 pp.

Becker, Jean-Jacques, and Serge Berstein. *Histoire de l'anticommunisme en France, 1917–1940*. Vol. 1. Paris: Orban, 1987. 398 pp.

Bredow, Wilfried von, and Rudolph H. Brocke. *Krise und Protest: Ursprünge und Elemente der Friedensbewegung in Westeuropa*. Opladen: Westdeutscher Verlag, 1987. 247 pp.

Callaghan, John. *The Far Left in British Politics*. Oxford: Basil Blackwell, 1987. 249 pp.

Caserta, Ernesto G. *Croce and Marxism: From the Years of Revisionism to the Last Postwar Period*. Naples: Morano, 1987. 219 pp.

Colajanni, Napoleone. *Comunisti al Bibio: cambiare fino in fondo o rassegnarsi al declino*. Milan: Arnoldo Mondadori, 1987. 200 pp.

Conraud, Jean-Marie. *Militants au travail: CFTC et CFDT dans le mouvement ouvrier lorrain, 1890–1965*. Nancy: Presses Universitaires de Nancy, 1988. 365 pp.

Cruz, Rafael. *El Partido Comunista de España en la Republica*. Madrid: Alianza Editoria, 1987. 314 pp.

Cunhal, Alvaro. *Desenvolver Portugal, ano 2000*. Lisbon: JCP, 1987. 100 pp.

Dallidet, Raymond. *RAPH—Vive le parti communiste français*. Chatillon-sous-Bagneux: Société d'études générales, 1987. 351 pp.

Donaghy, Peter J., and Michael T. Newton. *Spain: A Guide to Political and Economic Institutions*. Cambridge, Engl.: Cambridge University Press, 1987. 242 pp.

Dorfman, Gerald, and Peter J. Duignan, eds. *Politics in Western Europe*. Stanford, Calif.: Hoover Institution Press, 1988. 330 pp.

Elejabeitia, Carmen. *Liberalismo, marxismo y feminismo*. Barcelona: Anthropos, 1987. 262 pp.

Errigo, Giuseppe. *Dalle tensioni sociali alla fuga del proletario in Calabria: la sezione del PCI di Siderno dal 1954 al 1963*. Rome: Gangemi Editore, 1987. 369 pp.

Fritsch-Bournazel, Renata. *Confronting the German Question: Germans on the East-West Divide*. Oxford: Berg, 1988. 150 pp.

Horchem, Hans Joseph. *Die verlorene Revolution: Terrorismus in Deutschland*. Herford: Verlag Busse & Seewald, 1988. 237 pp.

Janning, Josef, Hans-Joseph Legrand, and Helmut Zander, eds. *Friedensbewegungen—Entwicklung und Folgen in der Bundesrepublik Deutschland,*

Europa und den USA. Cologne: Verlag Wissenschaft und Politik, 1987. 294 pp.

Juillard, Jacques. *Anatomie ouvrière.* Paris: Gallimard/Le Seuil, 1988. 298 pp.

Kellmann, Klaus. *Die kommunistische Parteien in Westeuropa: Entwicklung zur Sozialdemokratie oder Sekte?* Stuttgart: Verlag Klett-Cotta, 1988. 284 pp.

Krebs, Mario. *Ulrike Meinhof: Ein Leben im Widerspruch.* Bonn: Roro Verlag, 1988. 286 pp.

Lagorio, Lelio, and Giancarlo Lehner. *Turati e Gramsci per il socialismo: "due dentro ad un fuoco."* Milan: Sugarco, 1987. 239 pp.

Laguiller, Arlette. *Il faut changer le monde.* Paris: Lutte Ouvrière, 1988. 193 pp.

Lajoinie, André. *A Coeur ouvert.* Paris: Messidor, 1987. 215 pp.

Ledeen, Michael A. *West European Communism and American Foreign Policy.* New York: Transaction Books, 1987. 197 pp.

Mabille, Xavier. *Histoire politique de la Belgique: facteurs et acteurs de changement.* Brussels: CRISP, 1987. 215 pp.

Mandolfo, Santo. *Antonio Gramsci.* Catania: CUEM, 1987. 86 pp.

Meyer, Carolyn. *Voices of Northern Ireland: Growing up in a Troubled Land.* San Diego, Calif.: Harcourt Brace Jovanovich, 1987. 212 pp.

Montalbano, Giuseppe. *Critica al comunismo.* Caltanissetta: Krinon, 1987. 108 pp.

Naneth, R. Y., R. Leonardi, and P. Corbetta, eds. *Italian Politics: A Review.* London: Pinter, 1988. 185 pp.

O'Halloran, Clare. *Partition and the Limits of Irish Nationalism.* Dublin: Gill & Macmillan, 1987. 215 pp.

Parti Communiste Français. *Deuxième congrès national du PCF.* Paris: Cahiers du Communisme, Dec. 1987–Jan. 1988. 511 pp.

Partito Comunista Italiano. *Documenti politici dal 16. al 17. congresso, Firenze, 9–13.* Florence: PCI, 1987. n.p.

Pisano, Vittorfranco S. *The Dynamics of Subversion and Violence in Contemporary Italy.* Stanford, Calif.: Hoover Institution Press, 1988. 210 pp.

Pridham, Geoffrey. *Political Parties and Coalitional Behavior in Italy.* New York: Routledge, 1988. 443 pp.

Raby, D. L. *Fascism and Resistance in Portugal.* Manchester: Manchester University Press, 1988. 288 pp.

Rioux, Jean-Pierre, Antoine Prost, and Jean Pierre Azéma, eds. *Les communistes français de Munich à Chateaubriant, 1938–1941.* Paris: Presses de la Fondation Nationale des Sciences Politiques, 1987. 43 pp.

Rolke, Lothar. *Protestbewegungen in der Bundesrepublik Deutschland: Eine analytische Sozialgeschichte des politischen Widerspruchs.* Opladen: Westdeutscher Verlag, 1987. 636 pp.

Roth, Roland, and Dieter Rucht, eds. *Neue soziale–Bewegungen in der Bundesrepublik Deutschland.* Frankfurt am Main: Campus Verlag, 1987. 405 pp.

Salvaresi, Elizabeth. *Mai en héritage.* Paris: Syros, 1988. 226 pp.

Schnapp, Alain, and Pierre Vidal-Naquet. *Journal de la commune étudiante.* Paris: Seuil, 1988. 890 pp.

Shemenkova, K. A., chief translator. *XII s'ezd kommunisticheskoi partii Gretsii.* Moscow: Politizdat, 1988. 158 pp.

Stavrou, Nikolaos A., ed. *Greece under Socialism: A NATO Ally Adrift.* New Rochelle, N.Y.: Orpheus Publishing Inc., 1988. 428 pp.

Steiner, Anne. *La Fraction Armée Rouge: guerrilla urbaine en Europe occidentale.* Paris: Meridiens-Klincksieck, 1987. 267 pp.

Teague, Paul, ed. *Beyond the Rhetoric: Politics, Economy and Social Policy in Northern Ireland.* London: Lawrence & Wishart, 1987. 243 pp.

Unterwedde, Henrik. *Die Wirtschaftspolitik der Linken in Frankreich: Programme und Praxis, 1974–1986.* Frankfurt am Main, Campus Verlag, 1988. 320 pp.

Valenti, Chiara. *Berlinguer il segretario.* Milan: Mondadori, 1987. 318 pp.

Wagenlehner, Günther, ed. *Die deutsche Frage und internationale Sicherheit.* Koblenz: Bernard & Graefe, 1988. 227 pp.

Waller, Michael, and Meindert Fennema, eds. *Communist Parties in Western Europe.* Oxford: Basil Blackwell, 1988. 282 pp.

Weinberg, Leonard. *The Rise and Fall of Italian Terrorism.* Boulder, Colo.: Westview Press, 1987. 155 pp.

Winkler, Heinrich August. *Der Weg in die Katastrophe: Arbeiter und Arbeiterbewegung in der Weimarer Republic, 1930–33.* East Berlin: Dietz Verlag, 1987. 1024 pp.

Zaenker, Christian. *Die Abkehr der italienischen Kommunisten von Moskau (1964–1983).* Frankfurt am Main: Peter Lang, 1987. 154 pp.

Cumulative Index of Biographies

Index of Names

Index of Subjects